Ellis British Railway Engineering Encyclopædia
Third Edition

Being a compendious reference of specialist engineering terms in common use upon the Railways, Light Railways, Tramways and other guided transport systems of the United Kingdom, its Crown Dependencies and the Republic of Ireland.

Compiled by
Mr Iain Ellis
FPWI

First published September 2006
Second edition 2010
Third edition 2014
Revised third edition 2015

Text, layout and illustrations © 2015 Iain W. Ellis

Front cover design © 2014 Ann Ellis (visit www.annellis.co.uk)
Back cover design © 2014 Iain W. Ellis
Back cover image: Allerton Junction, looking south © Iain W. Ellis

Iain W. Ellis asserts his moral right to be identified as the author of this book.

This book is sold subject to the condition that it may not be reproduced stored in a retrieval system in any form or transmitted by any means electronic mechanical photocopying recording or otherwise without the author's prior consent except that whole single entries may be quoted subject to this author and this work being clearly identified as the author and the source.

ISBN 978-1-326-01063-8

Published through lulu.com

Author's Foreword

Welcome to the third edition of the renowned British Railway Engineering Encyclopædia.

It is more nearly complete than it was, but still not completed, purely because there will forever remain a vast amount of untapped knowledge. As time passes, more and more of this knowledge retires. I hope that the publication of this revised tome will prompt a few more howls and, perhaps more helpfully, even more comments and suggestions for additional entries.

If you do find an error, omission, contradiction or oversight, then please contact me and I will correct, include, remove or clarify as appropriate. To contact me, email **iain@iainellis.com**

Acknowledgements

The author wishes to thank the following for their continued help, support and encouragement:

Ann, my wife, without whose support and continuing patience it would never have come to a first edition, never mind a second or third.

Tony Segust, Quantity Surveyor, without whose questions the first edition would never have been started.

John Ellis, without whose foundations and continuous contributions this would have been a much poorer book all round.

Contributors

All those whose brains have been picked at some point over the eight years that compilation of the first edition took:
Derek Adgo, Paul Batty, Annelise Bishopp, Dennis Bowlby, Hugh Brocklebank, Dave Brooks, Graham Brown, Richard Buckley, Rocky d'Cat, Alun Clarke, Dr. David Cope, Paul Costello, Mick Crabtree, Richard Cradock, Alan Dimaline, Brian Duguid, John English, Paul Frost, Tom Gillard, Alex Graham, Phil Hinchcliffe, Lawrie Kent, David Kitchen, Tony Kornas, Ray Langley, Andy Lund, John Lund, Dave Mason, Andy Morton, Malcolm Pope, Craig Purcell, Dave Pyatt, John Shawcross, Lee Sloan, Paul Steventon, Ron Sumner and Richard Wedge.

To those who came forward with more entries and explanation for the second edition:
Steve Beever, Mark Burge, Mike Christelow, Dr. David Cope, Alan Cudlipp, Paul Davey, Chris Harding, David Hartland, Martin Hinley, Edward Janard, Christian Weirich, Neil Worthington.

Third edition thanks go to:
Dave Alderson, Mark Bailey, Dave Beechey, Rob Camy, Vanessa Conway, Rob Daffern, Ryan Duff, Mike Froud, Chris Goodwin, Peter Hanslip, Chris Harding, David Howes, Tanya Jackson, Michael and Toby Lockyer, Matt Lupton, Phil Mann, Scott McKavett, Dave Mercer, David Munn, Steve Odams, John Payne, Amy Pownall, Roger Reed, Dave Teasdel, Ian Towler, Jeremy Turner, Matt Whittaker, Clive Williams, Robert Williamson, Dave Woods, the Inspectors of the Rail Accident Investigation Branch (RAIB), contributors from District Dave's London Underground Forum (aslefshrugged, Dstock7080, tut) and the RailUK Forum (HSTEd, Hydro)

Dedications

I must pay my continuing respects to all the career railway(wo)men whose dedication, knowledge, and skill continue to keep the railways running: one and all, I salute you.

This third edition is dedicated to the memories of John "Agent" English and Andy Lund, now gone to the greatest position of safety.

Iain Ellis, November 2014.

Preface to Third Edition

By Martin Jurkowski, Network Rail

In my career in the railways, it has been a notable feature that understanding between different parties is hampered by a lack of knowledge of the terminology or language used. What appears straightforward to one party can seem difficult by another just by how it is described or because they do not appreciate its nature.

Although most will not admit it, engineers are notoriously bad at communicating and love to surround themselves in jargon and terminology to mystify their work and exclude outsiders. The railway industry is no different. Given that the rail industry has existed in one form or another for almost two centuries in Britain, there has been plenty of time to develop jargon, acronyms, expressions and other terminology.

As a consequence of the increasing complexity of the railways and the need to express concepts in straightforward or shorthand terms, the rail industry has developed its own specialised vocabulary and jargon, elements of which date from years ago whilst other elements are more recent. Understanding this language can be challenging for those within the industry, more so for those outside of it. Terminology that can be a useful shorthand for one can be a barrier to understanding for another, particularly in the specialised and diverse nature found in today's railway.

Some of the terms or acronyms used often have a historical basis or have been developed because they captured the essence of the subject and became commonly used through familiarity. They can have a history all to themselves and contain fragments of past practices long superseded but still be of use today. For example, that old telegraph terms, developed over 150 years ago as a shorthand to suit the limitations of a long gone system, are still in use is a testament to their enduring power. Others exist to accurately describe features that are peculiar to the industry for which no other terms will do but can be unfathomable if you are not a specialist.

Understanding the terminology used in the railways can help better communication between the different engineering disciplines within the industry and to the wider world outside. Sometimes, when trying to explain an issue, over simplifying it can cause much amusement as was the case with the 'wrong kind of snow' explanation used back in the 1980s regarding the winter performance of new electric trains.

What this book contains is a huge compendium of collected knowledge, painstaking researched by Iain and organised in an accessible way, either for direct reference to address an immediate query or for more casual perusal in quieter moments. It is illustrated with handy diagrams and light hearted elements to bring out the human side of engineering and the railways - after all they are a human enterprise full of human expressions.

This is now the third edition of the book, which is in itself a tribute to its usefulness and the regard in which it is held, and in these times of easily searchable information, it remains an essential reference work for anyone wanting to understand and be understood in the railway today.

Martin Jurkowski

ELLIS' BRITISH RAILWAY ENGINEERING ENCYCLOPÆDIA

Introduction

This work is intended to guide and assist the bewildered newcomer to the British Railway Industry, allowing them to sort their SPICOP from their PICONMP and otherwise their TRC from their TRU. It is therefore illustrative rather than exacting in its presentation. Those wishing to find the weight of an EF27-AWS or the opposite handed equivalent of a PR427 should not be disappointed; this book will only go so far as to explain that the first is a concrete sleeper and the second a type of rail fastening. Readers in search of the details are directed to the many technical publications available, particularly those published by the Permanent Way Institution (www.thepwi.org).

Scope and Clarifications

Certain items have been deliberately omitted; for example there is no information on the uses of standard Railway keys, as this information would be valuable to those of the miscreant tendency.

The views expressed in this work are not necessarily those of Her Majesty's Railway Inspectorate (HMRI), the national Rail Authorities of the United Kingdom, The Republic of Ireland and The Isle of Man, and their subsidiaries, successors, any other operator of Railways or Rail Authority in any country, or any professional, regulatory or voluntary body. Any errors are the author's own, and corrections are gratefully received.

Notes on the regulatory structure of the UK Railway Industry and the internal structure of Network Rail were correct at the time of proof-reading.

Certain terms have specific meanings and procedural significance as defined by certain Rail Authorities and this work does not seek to replace those. The reader should refer to the Rail Authority concerned for their specific requirements. An explanation, definition or description in this work is given for information only and in good faith. It is not intended by the Author that this work should be used in contract or arbitration. No claims for damage, consequential loss, liquidated damages or injury relating to any information in or omission from this work will be accepted and the reader is advised to seek professional guidance before relying on any such information in any way.

Where a limit, quantity or practice is given, this will normally be that which applies on the national, public Railway system of mainland Great Britain unless otherwise noted. Where dimensions are given, the most widely-used or most relevant unit is used first, followed by its nearest equivalent (if any) in other common units. A table of common dimensions and their metric equivalents is given at the rear of the book.

The appearance of a company name or trademarked product is not an endorsement of that company or product; company and product names are included where they are relevant to Railway engineering. Any omission of a relevant name, company detail or product is an oversight on the part of the Author and recommendations for inclusions in future editions are welcome.

Notes on Layout

Term	Denotes an entry in the Encyclopædia. Where a listed Term appears in another definition, then this is shown in **Bold** on the first occasion in each explanation. The symbol ◻ is used to divide phrases into sections, each one of which is defined separately. The common abbreviation (if applicable) is shown following the Term.
TLA	Denotes an entry in the Encyclopædia that is an acronym. Underlined letters in the definition refer to the expansion of the letters in the main entry, where available.
x	Where an italic lower case x appears in a Term, this can denote the place where a numerical digit appears. Multiple appearances of x denote multiple digits.
(*text*)	An occurrence at the start of a definition indicates a phonetic pronunciation where a particular pronunciation is widely used. Note that acronyms are normally pronounced letter by letter, such as A-B-C, and a pronunciation will not be shown. Where an acronym is generally pronounced as a word, such as GEOGIS, a pronunciation will be shown in the text.
[REF]	Indicates that the definition which follows is has a limited usage as indicated. See the table overleaf for the references used. If no specific usage is shown, then the usage is general.
[REF REF]	Multiple uses not separated by commas indicate that the definition which follows is has a limited usage within the second reference, in turn within the first reference. For example, [NR Sig.] means the term is only used in this sense by Signalling Engineers within Network Rail.
[REF, REF, REF]	Multiple uses separated by commas indicate usage in all areas given. For example, [NIR, IÉ] means the term is only used in this sense by Northern Ireland Railways and Iarnród Éireann.
(Tradename)	The Term is a company name, registered trademark or copyrighted name.
See	Indicates that the Term is not the preferred one for the concept and the reader is referred to the more common Term.
Also	Indicates that the following terms are sometimes used in place of the main term.
See also	Indicates that the reader's attention is drawn to related terms and concepts.

ELLIS' BRITISH RAILWAY ENGINEERING ENCYCLOPÆDIA

Table of Usage References

[...]	Usage limited to:
Arch.	Archaic usage, rarely found in modern discussion
BR	The former **British Railways**
Civ.	Civil Engineering
CT	**Channel Tunnel**
CTRL	Channel Tunnel Rail Link (now called **High Speed One**)
Col.	Colloquial, slang, unofficial, not officially approved of and often officially disapproved of.
DLR	Docklands **Light Railway**
EP	Electrical and Plant
ER	The former Eastern **Region** of British Rail (BR) and its predecessor **Railway Companies**
Elec.	**Electrification**
Hist.	Historic, examples exist but not used in new work
HR	**Heavy Rail**
IÉ	Iarnród Éireann
LM	The former London Midland Region of BR, and its predecessor Railway Companies
LR	Light Rail, **Light Rapid Transit**, **Trams**
LUAS	The Dublin **Light Rail** system
LUL	**London Underground Limited**
Mid.	The Midlands of England
MOD	Ministry of Defence
NIR	Northern Ireland Railways
NR	**Network Rail** / **National Rail Network**
NPT	Officially a non-preferred term, usage discouraged.
Nth.	The north of England
Obs.	Obsolescent, no longer used as new
Ops.	**Operations** and **Timetabling**
Pres.	**Preserved Railways**
Prob. Obs.	Probably obsolescent.
PW	**Permanent Way**, **Track**.
RB	**Rule Book** (**Railway Group Standard** GK/RT8000) and precursor documents.
RT	The former **Railtrack** Plc.
Scot.	Scotland and the former Scottish Region of BR.
Sig.	**Signalling**
Sth.	The south of England, the former Southern Region of BR and its predecessor companies
Tel.	**Telecommunications**
TRS	**Traction** and **Rolling Stock** (**Rail Vehicles**)
UK	United Kingdom
Unk.	Status unknown
US	United States
WR	The former Western Region of BR, and its predecessor Railway Companies

ELLIS' BRITISH RAILWAY ENGINEERING ENCYCLOPÆDIA

Symbols

Miscellaneous
- † See **Cut**.
- ‡ See **Dagger**
- ‰ See **Permillage**

Permanent Way Drawings

─⊕─⊕─⊕─ See **Insulated Rail Joint** (IRJ).

●─●─● See **Dumbbell**.
○─○

Sectional Appendix - Features

| Buffer Stop   ∥SD Sand Drag

⟲|(⟳ Swing Bridge or Lift Bridge   ⊥ Weighbridge

/c   Catch Points:
      C: Unworked
      CW: Worked   \|/ Tunnel
      D: Derailer   /|\

|⊞| Overhead Line Neutral Section (OHNS)   ⊳◁ Gates

|1| Passenger □ Platform   Parcels Platform

◀─ Hot Axle Box Detector (HABD)
     Wheel Impact Load Detector (WILD)
     Wheel check device (**Wheelchex**)

Sectional Appendix - Level Crossings

--|-|-- Level Crossing

X40| Level Crossing with **Wrong**
   |X30 **Direction** PS

    |A30
A40| Level Crossings with **PS**
          restriction over crossing only

▲40| |30▼

    |A
 ___|STOP
A |
STOP | Level Crossings where **Trains**
             must come to a stand before
 ___|STOP▼   proceeding over crossing.
▲STOP|

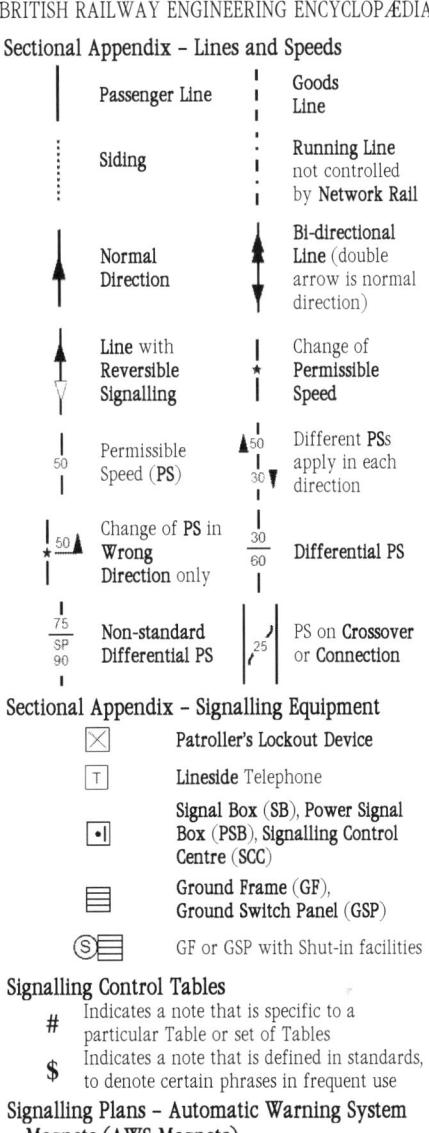

Sectional Appendix - Lines and Speeds

| Passenger Line   ¦ Goods Line

⋮ Siding   ¦ Running Line not controlled by **Network Rail**

▲ Normal   ▲ Bi-directional
| Direction | Line (double
▼   ▼ arrow is normal direction)

▲ Line with | Change of
| Reversible   ★ Permissible
▽ Signalling | Speed

| Permissible   ▲50 Different **PS**s
50   Speed (**PS**)   30▼ apply in each direction

| Change of PS in | 30
★50▲ **Wrong**   60 Differential PS
| **Direction** only |

 75
 SP   Non-standard   )   PS on **Crossover**
 90   Differential PS |25 or **Connection**

Sectional Appendix - Signalling Equipment

⊠   Patroller's Lockout Device

|T| **Lineside** Telephone

|•| Signal Box (SB), Power Signal Box (PSB), Signalling Control Centre (SCC)

☰   Ground Frame (GF), Ground Switch Panel (GSP)

Ⓢ☰ GF or GSP with Shut-in facilities

Signalling Control Tables

\# Indicates a note that is specific to a particular Table or set of Tables

$ Indicates a note that is defined in standards, to denote certain phrases in frequent use

Signalling Plans - Automatic Warning System Magnets (AWS Magnets)

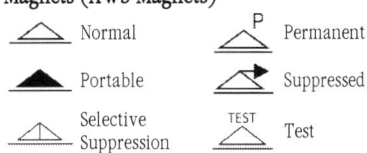

△ Normal   △ᴾ Permanent

▲ Portable   △ Suppressed

△ Selective   △ᵀᴱˢᵀ Test
   Suppression

1

ELLIS' BRITISH RAILWAY ENGINEERING ENCYCLOPÆDIA

Signalling Plans - Colour Light Signals

- Red (R), Red Aspect, Stop Aspect
- Double Yellow Aspect (YY), Preliminary Caution
- Caution Aspect, Yellow (Y), Yellow Aspect
- Green (G), Green Aspect, Proceed Aspect
- Normal Aspect is Green
- Normal Aspect is Red
- Normal Aspect is Yellow
- Optic Diode Signal
- Two Aspect Signals
- Three Aspect Signal
- Four Aspect Signal
- Flashing Single Yellow Aspect (FY)
- Flashing Double Yellow Aspect (FYY)
- Flashing Green Aspect (FG)
- Position Light Signal normally On (shown elevated)
- Position Light Signal associated with Main Signal (shown with Alphanumeric Route Indicator)
- Route Indicator (RI)
- Junction Indicator (JI)
- Approach Lighting

Signalling Plans - Miscellaneous

Point Zone Telephone (PZT), Signal Post Telephone (SPT) direct to Signaller

Signalling Plans - Other Signals

- Banner Repeater

Signalling Plans - Semaphore Signals

- Distant Signal
- Stop Signal

Signalling Plans - Signal Boxes

- Signal Box (SB) with Lever Frame
- Power Signal Box (PSB)
- Power Signal Box (PSB) with separate Indication Panel
- Integrated Electronic Control Centre (IECC)

Signalling Plans - Speed Signs

Warning Indicator (WI)
Speed Indicator (SI)

- Permissible Speed (PS) only
- Standard Differential Permissible Speed
- Non-standard Differential Permissible Speed
- Enhanced Permissible Speed (EPS)
- Miniature (450mm)
- Directional sign

Signalling Plans - Train Detection

- Axle Counter

1-9

% g
% of g
An expression of the rate of acceleration or deceleration a **Train** can achieve based on its measured performance and normally stated as a percentage of the normal acceleration due to gravity of 9.80665 m/s/s. For example, a Train capable of decelerating at 0.98m/s/s would be described as having 10% g Braking.

00
[PW] An obsolescent type of **Bull Head Rail** (**BH**) weighing 97½ **Pounds per Yard**. It was introduced by the **Great Western Railway** (**GWR**) in 1900, hence the name.

$^2/_3$ / $^1/_3$ Rule
a) [PW] A rule of thumb used when applying **Cant** (**C, E**) to **Curves**, where two thirds of the calculated Cant is applied, and one third is left as **Cant Deficiency** (**D**). See also **Equilibrium Speed** (V_e)
b) [Sig.] A requirement that the ratio of **Braking Distances** (**BD**) from **Preliminary Caution Aspect** (**Double Yellow, YY**) to **Caution Aspect** (**Single Yellow, Y**) and Caution Aspect to **Stop Aspect** (**Red, R**) should never exceed the ratio of 2:1 or vice versa, i.e. the two distances should be the same if possible.

1 in 20
[PW] The normal angle of **Inclination** of the **Running Rails** relative to the **Plane of the Rails**, intended to assist the centring action of the **Wheelsets**. See **Inclined**. See also **Coning**.

1 in *x*
a) See **1 in *x* Resleepering**
b) A means of expressing the angle to horizontal of a **Gradient**. The *x* denotes how many units must be travelled horizontally in order to rise or fall one unit vertically
c) See **N Value**.

1 in *x* Resleepering
[PW] (where *x* is a number, generally in the range 2 to 10) Replacing every x[th] **Sleeper**, sometimes on a cyclic pattern, but typically as required by their condition.

1.25
[PW] The approximate mass in tons of a cubic yard of **Ballast**. Equal to 1.33 tonnes per cubic metre.

1.61
[PW] In the days of feet, inches and steam, the multiplier used to determine the **Chord Length** from the **Permanent Speed Restriction** (**PSR**), up to the maximum of 96' - 6".

10 Foot
See **Ten Foot**.

100
100 Pound
a) [PW Obs.] A **Bullhead** (**BH**) pattern **Rail Section** weighing 100 **Pounds per Yard**. See also **BS Rail**
b) [PW Obs.] A **Flat Bottom** (**FB**) pattern Rail Section weighing 100 Pounds per Yard. See also BS Rail.

105
105 Pound
[PW Obs.] A **Flat Bottom** (**FB**) pattern **Rail Section** weighing 105 **Pounds per Yard**, used specifically for **Conductor Rails**.

106
106 Pound
[PW Obs.] A **Flat Bottom** (**FB**) pattern **Rail Section** weighing 106 **Pounds per Yard**, used specifically for **Conductor Rails**.

109
109 Pound
[PW Obs.] An obsolescent **Flat Bottom** (**FB**) pattern **Rail Section** weighing 109 **Pounds per Yard**.

11.82
[PW] The **Cant Constant** for a **Standard Gauge** □ **Railway**.

110
110 Pound
[PW Obs.] An obsolescent **Flat Bottom** (**FB**) pattern **BS Rail Section** weighing 110 **Pounds per Yard**.

110A
[PW Obs.] 110 Amended, a **Flat Bottom** (**FB**) pattern **Rail Section** weighing 110 **Pounds per Yard**, but having a **Rail Head** with **Inclined** side faces.

110kg Chrome Rail
[PW] A **Rail** made from steel containing Chromium as an alloying element. The alloy has a tensile strength of 110kg per square millimetre, hence the name.

113
113 Pound
[PW Obs.] An obsolescent **Flat Bottom** (**FB**) pattern **Rail Section** weighing 113 **Pounds per Yard**, designed for use in high corrosion risk areas, such as in **Tunnels** and adjacent to sea defences.

113A
113A Rail
[PW] A **Flat Bottom** (**FB**) pattern **Rail Section** weighing 113 **Pounds per Yard** but having a thicker **Rail Web** than its predecessor **110A**. From its introduction in 1968 for **Plain Line** (**PL**) and 1969 in **Switch and Crossing** (**S&C**), this Rail Section was the heaviest in use in **Running Lines** in Britain until the introduction of **CEN60E1**. It has been re-titled **CEN56E1**, Also **UIC 54**. See also **Hither Green Accident**.

113A Full Depth Switches
[PW] **Switches** in which the **Stock Rail** and **Switch Rail** are both made from **113A Rail**. Such **Switches** are **Vertical Switches**. See also **Full Depth Switches**.

113A Shallow Depth Switches
[PW] **Switches** in which the **Stock Rail** is made from **113A Rail** and the **Switch Rail** is made from UIC54B Rail, now CEN54E1A1. Such Switches are **Vertical Switches**. See also **Thick Web Switches**.

113A Vertical

113A Vertical S&C
[PW] **Switch and Crossing** Units (**S&C Units**) composed of **113A Rail** arranged vertically.

150 Pound
[Elec.] A **Flat Bottom** (FB) pattern **Rail Section** weighing 150 **Pounds per Yard**, used specifically for **Conductor Rails**.

1958 Letter, The
The letter issued by the **Railway Inspectorate** (**RI**) to **British Rail** (**BR**) clarifying a previous letter of 1933, which in turn attempted to clarify the requirements of section 5 of the **Regulation of Railways Act 1871**. This section deals with which schemes had to be submitted for approval to the RI.

1969
[BR PW] In 1969, **British Rail** (**BR**) had 48 **Track Buckles** on **Continuously Welded Rail** (**CWR**) □ **Track**, a rate of 10.42 per 1000 **Track Miles** (compared with seven the year before). After **Derailments** at Lichfield, Somerton and Sandy, an inquiry concluded that installation and **Maintenance** standards were slipping, and that the suspension systems of **Container Flats** were aggravating the problem. By 1972 the annual rate of Track Buckles had dropped to 4, or 0.62 per 1000 Track Miles. For comparison, the average annual rate for **Network Rail** (**NR**) is 44.5 (for 2000 to 2009) or 0.002 per 1000 CWR Track Miles.

2+1
[TRS] Describing a seating arrangement in an **Open Coach** where the central passageway has two seats on one side and one on the other. Found in **Coaches** intended for long distance travel and **First Class**.

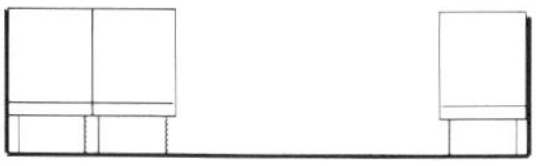

2+2
[TRS] Describing a seating arrangement in an **Open Coach** where the central passageway has two seats on each side. Found in **Coaches** intended for medium distance travel.

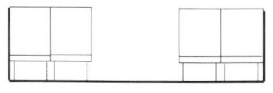

2009 Tube Stock
[LUL] The type of **Train** used on the Victoria **Line** of LUL, built by Bombardier Transportation. The Trains entered service in July 2009 and finally replaced the previous trains of 1967 **Tube Stock** on the Victoria Line in June 2011.

3+2
[TRS] Describing a seating arrangement in an **Open Coach** where the central passageway has three seats on one side and two on the other. Found in **Coaches** intended for short distance **Commuting**.

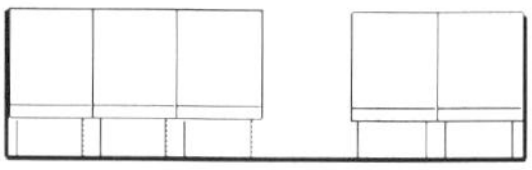

33 Kilo
[PW] More correctly CEN33C1 and formerly UIC33, a 33 Kilograms per Metre □ **Rail Section** used for **Check Rails**.

3-link Coupling
See **Three Link Coupling**.

3MG
Mersey Multi-Modal Gateway.

4 Foot
See **Four Foot**, **Fourfoot**.

4QC
Four Quadrant Converter.

5 Foot
[IÉ, NIR] See **Five foot**.

50 Pound
[PW] A **Flat Bottom** (FB) pattern BS **Rail Section** weighing 50 **Pounds per Yard**, often used on mine and **Tramway** systems. Also **500**.

56 Kilo
[PW] More correctly CEN56E1, the new name for 113A □ **Flat Bottom**.

5th Percentile
The value of a characteristic (e.g. the height of a human being) the magnitude of which is lower in 5 % of a given statistical population. See also **95th Percentile**.

6 Foot
See **Sixfoot**. See also *x*-**foot**.

6 Foot Drain
[PW] A **Track Drain** laid in the **Sixfoot**. Also **Sixfoot Drain**.

60 Kilo
[PW] More correctly CEN60E1, a 60 **Kilograms per Metre** □ **Flat Bottom** (FB) □ **Rail Section** used for **Running Rails** on **Lines** where the **Maximum Axle Load** exceeds 25 tonnes. Also **RT60**, **UIC60**.

60B

60B Rail
[PW] More correctly CEN60E1A1 (formerly UIC60B), a 60 **Kilograms per Metre** □ **Flat Bottom** (FB) □ **Rail Section** used for **Thick Web Switches**.

650
[NR]
a) [Sig.] The nominal standard AC voltage of a **Signalling Power Supply**
b) [Col.] Common shorthand for the Signalling Power Supply.

7DR
[NR] See **Seven Day Railway**.

80 Pound
[PW] A **Flat Bottom** (FB) pattern BS **Rail Section** weighing 80 **Pounds per Yard**, used frequently for **Ballasted Track** on **Tramways**. Also **80A**, **80R**.

85 Pound

85 Pound Bull Head
[PW Obs.] A **Bull Head** (BH) pattern **Rail Section** weighing 85 **Pounds per Yard**.

9 Foot
9 Foot Rule
[NR] See **Nine Foot Rule**.
90kg Chrome Rail
[PW] A **Rail** made from steel containing Chromium as an alloying element. The alloy has a tensile strength of 90kg per square millimetre, hence the name.
95 Pound
95 Pound Bull Head
[PW] A **Bull Head** (**BH**) pattern **Rail Section** weighing 95 **Pounds per Yard**, still commonly found in use in many **Secondary Lines** and **Sidings**. Little used outside the UK. Also **95O**, **95RBS**.
95 Tube Stock
[LUL] The type of **Train** used on the Northern **Line** from June 1998, built by the then GEC Alstom Metro-Cammell.
95th Percentile
The value of a characteristic (e.g. the height of a human being) the magnitude of which is lower in 95% of a given statistical population. See also **5th Percentile**.
97½ Pound
See **00**.
98 Pound
[PW Obs.] An obsolescent **Flat Bottom** (**FB**) pattern **Rail Section** weighing 98 **Pounds per Yard**, designed for use on secondary routes carrying lower densities of low **Axle Weight** traffic than primary routes

A

A
a) [NR] As the last letter in a **Wagon** □ **CARKND**, this denotes that the Wagon has **A**ir **B**rakes only
b) [Ops.] In an abbreviated **T**rack **N**ame, it often denotes **A**voiding
c) [PW] As a prefix it denotes the shortest and tightest Radius **B**ull **H**ead (BH) and **I**nclined □ **F**lat **B**ottom (FB) □ **Switches**. See **Switch Letters**.
d) [Sig.] On a **Signalling Circuit Diagram**:
• As one of the leading letters of an **Equipment Code**, it means **a**pproach, **a**utomatic or **A**rm for a **Relay**
• As the last letter of an Equipment Code, it means **A**xle **C**ounter
e) The letter represented by **Alpha** in the **Phonetic Alphabet**
f) [TRS] Denoting one **D**riven **A**xle, See **Diesel and Electric Locomotive Notation**.

A Leg
[Sig.] The first data or signal route in a **Diversely Routed System**. See also **B Leg**.

A Stock
[LUL] The original A Stock (A60 and A62) built for the District Railway in 1903 as the test for the **Electrification** of the line and used on the Ealing and South Harrow line. The present A Stock is the standard type used on the Metropolitan Line. The "A" designation relates to the intended route – in this case Amersham.

A&NR
[Hist.] The **Pre-Grouping** **A**shby and **N**uneaton Joint **R**ailway, a London & North Western and Midland joint enterprise.

A/C
See **A**utomatic **C**oupler.

A1
[PW] A type of **Elastic Spike** □ **Rail Fastening**.

A4A
See **A**ccess **for** **A**ll (AFA).

AA
See **A**ccredited **A**gent.

AAA
[LUL] **A**ccompanied **A**nimals and **A**rticles.

AAAC
[Elec.] **A**ll **A**luminium **A**lloy **C**onductor, a material used for **Overhead Line Equipment** (OLE) □ **Conductors** offering reduced **Creep** properties and increased strength

AAC
[Elec.] **A**ll **A**luminium **C**onductor, a material commonly used for **Return Conductors**, earth wires and **Auto-transformer Feeder** (ATF) wires in **Overhead Line Equipment** (OLE) systems.

AADT
Annual **A**verage **D**aily **T**raffic.

AAM
[NR] **A**rea **A**sset **M**anager.

AAR
a) [Civ.] **A**lkali / **A**ggregate **R**eaction, see **Alkali Silica Reaction** (ASR).
b) **A**ssociation of **A**merican **R**ailroads.

AARKND
(*arr-kind*) [NR] A single suffix letter used by **TOPS** to differentiate between variants and **Rail Vehicles** having the same **CARKND**. This letter is not displayed on the vehicle itself.

AAS
[Sig.] **A**uxiliary **A**spects **S**ets.

AAT
[LUL] **A**ccept **A**ll **T**ickets

AATC
[Sig.] **A**dvanced **A**utomated **T**rain **C**ontrol.

AB
See **A**bsolute **B**lock.

Abandonment
The giving up and removal of a facility such as a **Branch Line** or **Siding**. This may include the removal of **Signalling**, **Track** and **Switch & Crossing Layouts** (S&C Layouts).

ABB Transportation
(Tradename) **A**sea **B**rown **B**overi Transportation, a manufacturer of **Rolling Stock**, particularly **Multiple Unit Trains**.

Abbots Ripon Accident
Early **Semaphore Signals** were arranged in such a way that when the **Arm** was in the **Off** position (with the **Signal** showing **Proceed**) it disappeared into a slot in the post. On 21st January 1876 a **Slotted Semaphore Signal** like this became seized in the Off position by frozen **Snow**, preventing the Arm returning to **Danger**. Two **Trains** ran past this apparently **Clear** Signal and collided with a stationary coal Train, killing 14. The **GNR** introduced the **Somersault Signal** after this accident.

ABC
[PW] **A**utomatic **B**allast **C**leaner, see **Ballast Cleaner**.

ABC1
Socio-demographic classification based on the National Readership Survey (NRS) social grading system and including the UK's upper middle classes (A) to lower middle classes (C1).

ABCB
See **A**ir **B**last **C**ircuit **B**reaker.

ABCL
See **A**utomatic **B**arrier **C**rossing **L**ocally Monitored, a variety of **Level Crossing** (LC, LX).

ABD
As-**b**uilt **D**rawing.

Abellio
(Tradename) the international arm of the Dutch state-owned **Railway Company** Nederlandse Spoorwegen (NS). Previously NedRailways.

Abermule Accident
The **Station** on the Cambrian **Railway** nearest to the scene of a major collision on 26th January 1921. One of the **Train** drivers was mistakenly given the **Token** for the previous **Section**, and met a correctly signalled **Train** head-on on the **Single Line**. Two drivers and 15 **Passengers** were killed. The working arrangements at Abermule were highly irregular and this, combined with a misplaced trust from a driver who did not examine the Token he had been given, conspired to defeat the otherwise foolproof **Electric Token Block** (ETB) system.

Abnormal Heavy Road Load (AHRL)
Any road load which falls outside the scope of the Construction and Use Regulations because of its weight or weight distribution.

Abnormal Rail Head Conditions
[Ops.] Describing a situation where the normal level of **Adhesion** between the **Rail** and wheel has been reduced by contamination such as fallen leaves or grease. See also **Handite**, **Leaf Fall Season**, **Maximu**, **Sand Pram**, **Sand Rover**, **Sand Stick**, **Sanders**, **Sandite**, **Sandite Train**, **Sandite Unit**.

Abnormal Road Load Indemnity (ARLI)
A form of indemnity submitted to **Network Rail** (NR) by a road haulier as prescribed in the Motor Vehicles (Authorisation of Special Types) General Order 1979 (as amended).

Abnormal Road Load Notification (ARLN)
A notice submitted to **Network Rail** (NR) by a haulier which gives loading details of a proposed abnormal road load movement, its date and time of travel, and its proposed route.

Above Rail Level (ARL)
a) A dimension vertically above the level of the **Rail Head** of a particular **Rail**
b) A dimension above and normal to the **Plane of the Rails**. The opposite is **Below Rail Level**; see also **Below Sleeper Bottom** (BSB).

ABP
[TRS] Air Brake Pipe.

ABS
a) [TRS] Anti-lock Brake System
b) [Ops., Sig.] Absolute Block System, see **Absolute Block** (AB).
c) See **Automatic Ballast Sampler**
d) As Built Sketch.

Absence Switch
[Sig.] An electrical switch provided in a **Signal Box** (SB), operation of which allows the **Signaller** to leave the **Operating Floor** temporarily (as even Signallers must, on occasion; see PNB) but still have telephone calls to the Signal Box registered.

ABSI
[NR] Assistant Buried Services Investigator.

Absolute Block (AB)
Absolute Block Principles
[Ops., Sig.] A system of **Signalling** that is built around the principle that only one **Train** is permitted to enter a **Block Section** at any time. Trains are offered and **Accepted** between **Signal Boxes** (SB) and **Block Posts**, the **Acceptance** only being given when the correct conditions are met. This communication is by means of **Block Bells** using a set of standard **Bell Codes** and **Block Instruments**. Since the **Signaller** is required to observe passing **Tail Lamps**, all Signal Boxes using Absolute Block are two storey, allowing the Signaller to see Trains on all **Lines** even when other Trains are passing.

Absolute Gauging
[PW] The full assessment of clearances between a **Rail Vehicle** and the **Infrastructure** on a **Section** of **Track**, and between the Vehicle and other Vehicles on adjacent Tracks. See **Relative Gauging**.

Absolute Possession
A **Possession** that is given up when the **Engineer** decides, and not before. See also **Engineer's Possession**, T3.

Absolute Track Geometry
[PW] **Geometry** that has a current approved design, normally based on co-ordinate geometry.

ABT
[NR] Under the **Bridge Condition Marking Index** (BCMI) handbook, shorthand for **Abutment**.

Abt Rack System
A **Rack Railway** where the rack consists of two or more vertical toothed **Rails** bolted together with the teeth offset from each other. With this system the toothed wheel is in full engagement for a greater proportion of the time and is prevented from sliding off. Patented by Roman Abt in 1882 and used on the Snowdon Mountain Railway.

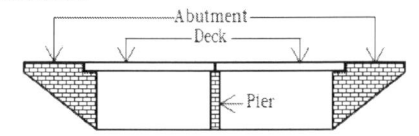

Abutment
[Civ.] The structure that supports the **Deck** at the extreme ends of a **Bridge**. Intermediate supports (with a Deck on both sides) are called **Piers**. See also **Bank Seat**.

Abutting Sections
[Elec.] The additional **Electrical Sections** of **Conductor Rail** that are switched off to minimise the risk of re-energisation of an Electrical Section **Isolated** in an emergency. See also **Hook Switch**.

ABX
[Col.] Shorthand for an **Automatic Barrier Crossing**.

AC
a) [Elec.] Alternating Current. See also **Overhead Line Equipment (OLE)**
b) Air Conditioning.

AC Capacitor-fed Single Rail Track Circuit
[LUL] A common type of **Track Circuit (TC)** on the London Underground Limited system.

AC Electrification System
[Elec.] A means of supplying AC **Traction Current** which typically consists of bare conductors suspended from **Insulators** over the **Track**; the **Traction Units** employ a **Pantograph** to collect the Current. See also **Autotransformer (AT) Balance Weights, Booster Transformer (BT), Catenary, Contact Wire (CW), Dropper, Feeder Station, Headspan, Insulated Overlap, Mid-point Anchor (MPA), Neutral Section (NS), Overhead Line Equipment (OLE), Overlap Span, Portal, Registration Arm, Section Insulator (SI), Single Track Cantilever (STC), Twin Track Cantilever (TTC), Un-insulated Overlap.**

AC Electrified Line
[Elec.] A **Line** equipped with an **Overhead Line Electrification (OLE)** system supplying Alternating Current (AC) to **Electric Trains**.

AC Immune
[Sig.] A description of a **Track Circuit (TC)** or other piece of **Signalling Equipment** that has been designed to be immune from effects of Alternating Current **Overhead Line Equipment (OLE)**. See also **DC Immune**.

AC Track Circuit
[Sig.] A type of **Jointed Track Circuit** that utilises Alternating Current (AC) for its operation. Alternatives include **Audio Frequency Track Circuits** and **DC Track Circuits**.

ACA
[LUL] Asset Condition Assessment.

ACAC
[LUL] Asset Condition Assessment and Certification

ACB
Air Circuit Breaker.

ACC
[Sig.]
a) (Tradename) Apparato Centrale con Calcolatore, the **Computer Based Interlocking (CBI)** system manufactured by **Ansaldo**
b) Area Control Computer, part of the **SIMIS-W** system manufactured by **Siemens**.

ACCA
Advanced Cause Consequence Analysis.

ACCAT
[LUL] **Adhesion** Controller's Condition Assessment Tool, a system operated by Metronet BCV to identify where **Automatic Train Operation (ATO)** can be used safely on the Central Line **Surface Lines** during **Leaf Fall Season**.

Accelerated GRIP
[NR] A formal attempt to streamline the early stages of the **Governance for Railway Investment Projects (GRIP)** process for schemes with low complexity, small scope or large amounts of previous work. Also **Fast Track GRIP**.

Accept
Acceptance
Accepted
[Ops., Sig.] The action of giving permission for a **Train** to proceed into a **Block Section** in an area controlled by **Absolute Block**. This cannot happen until the **Signaller** is certain that the Train in front is safely **Clear**, i.e. is more than 440 **Yards** □ **Beyond** their **Home Signal**, and the Signaller observed the **Tail Lamp** on the rear of the Train as it passed, proving that it was complete. See also **Offered**.

Accepting
Accepting the Route
[LUL] **Signals** indicate to a **Train Operator** the **Route** over which the **Train** is to be directed. When a Train Operator observes the indication and drives the Train over that route it is termed 'Accepting the Route'.

Access
a) A common contraction of **Access Point**
b) [NR] The use of **Track, Stations** and **Depots** by a **Train Operating Company (TOC)** or **Freight Operating Company (FOC)**.

Access Agreement
[NR] An agreement made under the **Railways Act 1993** that sets out the terms and conditions under which **Train Operating Companies (TOC)** and **Freight Operating Companies (FOC)** can obtain access to run **Trains** and use **Stations** and certain types of **Depots**.

Access Charge
[NR] The fee paid by **Train Operating Companies (TOC)** and **Freight Operating Companies (FOC)** for the use of **Track, Traction Supplies, Stations** and **Depots**.

Access For All (AFA)
[NR] A project funded directly by the **Department for Transport (DfT)** as part of the Railways for All Strategy, launched in 2006 to address the provision of an obstacle-free, **Accessible Route** to and between **Platforms** at priority **Stations**. This generally includes the provision of lifts or **Level Access**, as well as associated works and refurbishment along the defined route. Also **A4A**.

Access Permit
[Obs.] A document allowing the holder access to **Network Rail (NR)** □ **Infrastructure**, generally under restrictive conditions. Now called a **Track Visitor Permit (TVP)**.

ELLIS' BRITISH RAILWAY ENGINEERING ENCYCLOPÆDIA

Access Point
A designated point along a **Railway** at which entry to Railway property may be made safely. Most are pedestrian only, often with steps to **Track** level. The remainder are vehicular and range between those that are just simple gates to large levelled areas with level crossing surfaces permitting easy access for **Road Rail** machines (see **Road Rail Access Point (RRAP)**). The presence of an Access Point does not guarantee that access to the Track itself is necessarily safe at that location.

Accessible Route
A route to and between **Platforms** that can be used by all customers, un-aided. This includes provision of alternatives to stairs, conspicuous signage, handrails, wider corridors, etc. See also **A4A**, **Access for All (AfA)**.

Accident
An unexpected and unplanned event which results in injury or death to staff or public, collateral damage, an unsafe condition, a financial loss or a combination of these outcomes. All Accidents are preventable, but sometimes the cost in time and money of the prevention measures is far in excess of the "value" of the outcome avoided. Most **Railway** practice is based on experience and the lessons learned from Accidents. See **ALARP**, **Derailment**, **VOPF**. The reader should remember that the following list of entries covers some 180 years of operation and have been chosen to explain rather than to shock:

- Abbots Ripon, 1876; **Signalling** failure in Snow
- Abermule, 1921; Irregular working on **Single Line**
- Agecroft, 1872, **Signaller** error
- Ais Gill, 1913; **Signal Passed at Danger (SPAD)**
- Armagh, 1889; **Irregular Working**, no Automatic Brake
- Battersea Park, 1937; Signaller error
- Bellgrove, 1989; SASSPAD
- Bricklayer's Arms Junction, 1975; Phantom Aspect, SPAD
- Bushey, 1980; defective **Rail Weld**
- Cannon Street; 1991, driver error
- Castlecary, 1937; SPAD and Signaller error
- Caterham, 1945; driver error, SASSPAD
- Chancery Lane, 2003; mechanical failure on Train
- Cheadle Junction, 1971; **Cyclic Top**
- Clapham, 1988; **Stageworks**, fatigue, wiring error in Signalling System
- Clayton Tunnel, 1861; inadequate Signalling, Signaller error
- Colwich, 1986; driver error
- Cowden, 1994; SPAD
- Doncaster, 1947; Stageworks, Signaller error
- Elliot Junction, 1906; Irregular Working, SPAD
- Elsenham, 2005; failure to heed warning system
- Eltham (Well Hall), 1972; excessive speed
- Eschede, 1998; broken **Wheelset**
- Gidea Park, 1947; multiple SPADs, driver error
- Glanrhyd Bridge, 1987; **Bridge Scour**
- Glasgow St. Enoch, 1903; driver error
- Guildford, 1952; electrical failure on Train
- Harrow and Wealdstone, 1952; multiple SPADs in Fog
- Hatfield, 2000; **Broken Rail** due to inadequate management of **Rolling Contact Fatigue (RCF)**
- Hawes Junction, 1910; Signaller error compounded by **Traincrew** inattention
- Heck, 2001; road vehicle on **Track**
- Hillhouse, 1868, poor communication, inadequate Signalling
- Hither Green, 1967; **Broken Rail**, Reballasting
- Hixon, 1968; collision with abnormal load on **Automatic Half Barrier Level Crossing (AHB)**
- Holton Heath, 1989; poor communication, inadequate Signalling
- Huddersfield, 1919; Signaller error
- Huddersfield, 1989; Irregular Working
- Hyde, 1990; SPAD
- Kentish Town, 1861; inadequate Signalling, driver error, Signaller error
- Kildwick, 1875; inadequate Signalling
- King's Cross, 1987; **Station** fire
- Ladbrooke Grove, 1999; SPAD
- Lambrigg, 2007; defective **Points**
- Lewisham, 1957; driver error, **Bridge** collapse
- Lichfield Trent Valley, 1946; Signalling system failure in Snow
- Lockington, 1986; collision with van on **Automatic Open Crossing Remotely Monitored (AOCR)**
- Lunan Bay, 1975; Irregular Working, excessive speed
- Modane, 1917; inadequate brakes, **Derailment**
- Moorgate, 1975; cause unknown
- Morpeth, 1969 and 1984; excessive speed
- Nairn's, 1982, collision with tractor and trailer on Accommodation Level Crossing
- Newton, 1991; SASSPAD
- Norton Fitzwarren, 1940; driver error
- Nuneaton, 1975; unlit **Commencement Board** resulting in excessive speed
- Paddington, see **Ladbrooke Grove**
- Polmont, 1984; collision with Cow
- Potter's Bar, 2002; defective **Points**
- Purley, 1989; SPAD
- Quintinshill, 1915; Signaller error, fire
- Raynes Park, 1933; Track work
- Salisbury, 1906; excessive speed
- Selby, See Heck
- Sheerness-on-Sea, 1971; driver incapacitated
- Shields Junction, 1973; driver incapacitated
- Shrewsbury, 1907; excessive speed, cause unknown
- Sonning Cutting, 1841; **Earthwork** failure
- Southall, 1997; SPAD, fire
- Staplehurst, 1865; Irregular Working, Track work
- Stewarton, 2009; Bridge collapse
- Stoat's Nest, 1910, mechanical failure on Train
- Tattenhall Junction, 1971; **Track Buckle**
- Tay Bridge, 1879; Bridge collapse in high winds
- Thirsk, 1967, Poor **Wagon** suspension, collision
- Tottenham North Junction, 1929; SPAD
- Urmston, 1958; collision with toppled crane
- Walton Junction, 1867; inadequate Signalling,

Signaller error
- **Watford**, 1996; inadequate Signalling, SPAD
- **West Ealing**, 1973; object hanging from Train
- **Witham**, 1905; Track work

ACCOLC
[TRS] Access Overload Control.

Accommodation Bridge
[Civ.] A **Bridge** provided solely for use by a landowner whose property was divided when the **Railway** was constructed. Many such Bridges were provided merely to appease adjoining landowners, their subsequent use being infrequent. An alternative term for some of the smaller examples is **Cattle Creep**.

Accommodation Crossing
A common contraction of **Accommodation Level Crossing** (ALC).

Accommodation Level Crossing (ALC)
A **Level Crossing** (LC, LX) provided for the sole use of a landowner whose property was divided when the **Railway** was built. Sometimes shortened to **Accommodation Crossing**. Such Level Crossings are generally only provided with a telephone to the **Signaller**.

Accredited Agent
A member of **Railway** staff trained and appointed by the **Rail Accident Investigation Branch** (RAIB) to identify and record perishable evidence pending the arrival of RAIB inspectors.

ACCT
[BR, RT, NR] Automatic Control Centre TOPS/TRUST.

ACE
a) [BR Hist.] See **Area Civil Engineer**. Under **British Rail** (BR), the post responsible for the day-to-day maintenance and renewal of **Track**, **Bridges**, earthworks and fences in a geographical area. The post reported to the **Regional Civil Engineer** (RCE)
b) [Sig.] See **Axle Counter Evaluator**.

ACEIC
[TRS] Auto Coupler Emergency Isolating Cock.

ACFM
[PW] See **Alternating Current Field Measurement**.

ACG
[Elec.] Anti-Climb Guard.

Achievable Reading Distance
[Sig.] The maximum practical distance at which a **Lineside Sign** or **Signal** can be correctly **Read**.

Achilles
[NR] Achilles Group Limited is a specialist consultancy for registration of suppliers and **Contractors**, supplier appraisal and audit services. Appraises and audits **Link-Up** suppliers and NCCA (**Sentinel**) competency training establishments.

ACI
[Sig.] See **Automatic Code Insertion**.

ACIO
Assistant Chief Inspecting Officer (of **Railways**). See Her Majesty's Railway Inspectorate (HMRI).

Ack
A **Railway** □ **Telegraph Code** meaning "Acknowledge Receipt"

ACM
a) [Sig.] **Axle Counter** Module
b) **Area** Contract Manager
c) Area Consents Manager
d) [TRS] Auxiliary Converter Module
e) Asbestos Containing Materials.

ACMR
Asbestos Containing Materials Register.

ACOP
Approved Code of Practice. A non-mandatory document providing guidance on complying with a related mandatory document.

AcoRP
Association of Community **Rail** Partnerships.

ACR
a) [NR] Access Charge Review, See **CPx**
b) Asset Condition Reporting.

ACS
a) [Sig.] **Approach Controlled** □ **Signalling**
b) **Access Charge** Supplement
c) Approved **Contractor** Scheme
d) Access Control System.

ACSC
[Elec.] Automatically Compensated Spatial-Rhombic **Catenary**.

Active Tilt
[TRS] A system that actively predicts the amount by which a **Tilting Train** must **Tilt** in order to maintain a comfortable ride. Typical systems use a combination of geographical databases, **Balises** and inclinometer measurements to determine the required action. See also **Passive Tilt**.

Active Traction Current Section
[LUL] A **Traction Current Section** where the **Traction Current** remains on to allow an **Engineer's Train** to work as required within an **Engineer's Current Area**.

Active Warning
[Sig.] A device which warns users of the imminent arrival of a **Train**. Either visible or audible, they are sometimes found at **Occupation Crossings** (OC).

ACTO
Association of **Charter Train** Operators.

ACTRAFF
[NR] Actual **Traffic**, a system which stores historic details of **Railway** □ **Traffic**.

Actual Extension
[PW] The actual amount of **Rail** stretching achieved during **Stressing** operations. See also **Calculated Extension**.

Acute Crossing
[PW] Alternative term for a **Common Crossing**, describing a **Crossing** in which the two **Running Rails** cross each other at an acute angle.

ELLIS' BRITISH RAILWAY ENGINEERING ENCYCLOPÆDIA

AD Fastening
[PW Obs.] A type of **Rail Fastening** consisting a flat bar secured by means of a screw into an insert in the **Sleeper**. Used on the **F14 Concrete Sleeper**, the initials being those of its champion, Arthur Dean.

AD&R
[NR] **Asset** Development and **Renewal**.

Adams, William Bridges
(1797-1872) the author, inventor and **Locomotive** engineer who, in collaboration with Robert Richardson, patented the **Fishplate** in 1847 and the radial axle in 1865.

Adaptor Vehicle
[TRS] See **Translator Vehicle**.

ADAS System
[NR] Developed by ADAS UK Ltd, a system used by **Network Rail** (**NR**) to classify the risk from fallen leaves on each day during **Leaf Fall Season** for different geographical areas of the **National Railway Network** (**NRN**).

ADB
Approved Document B; part B of the Building Regulations, concerned with fire safety.

ADD
a) See **Automatic Dropping Device**
b) Asset Data Dictionary.

ADE
[IÉ] Assistant Divisional Engineer.

Adelante
(Tradename) The brandname of the **Class** 180 **Diesel Mechanical Multiple Units** (**DMMU**).

ADEPT
Association of Directors of Environment, Economy, Planning and Transport, formerly the County Surveyor's Society (**CSS**).

Adequate Distance
A phrase referring to a sufficient distance to ensure safety under the circumstances, such as a safe **Braking Distance** for the speed of a **Tram** or **On Track Machine** (**OTM**).

ADG
[NR] **Area** Delivery Group.

Adhesion
[Ops., TRS] Describing the friction produced between a **Rail** and a **Rail Wheel**. Therefore, loss of Adhesion is the absence of this friction and the inability to make any forward progress. See also **Abnormal Rail Head Conditions, Handite, Leaf Fall Season, Maximu, Sand Pram, Sand Rover, Sand Stick, Sanders, Sandite, Sandite Train, Sandite Unit, Tribometer**.

Adhesion Worked
Describing a **Railway** that relies on the friction between the **Rails** and wheels to move **Trains**, i.e. most Railways. Non-adhesion systems include **Atmospheric Railways, Funicular Railways** and **Rack Railways**.

ADIP
[NR] **Asset** Data Improvement Programme.

Adjacent Line
[RB] A **Line** or **Siding** next to the Line you are on.

Adjacent Line Open (ALO)
[NR] Generic term describing the situation where engineering work is being carried out whilst **Trains** are still running on one or more **Lines** next to (and close to) the **Worksite**.

Adjustable Dropper
[Elec.] A **Dropper** which can be lengthened and shortened as required. Also **Rat Trap**.

Adjustment Switch

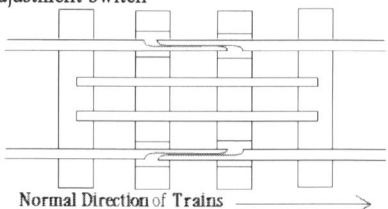

Normal Direction of Trains ⟶

[PW] A scarf joint installed in the **Rails** at the junction of **Continuous Welded Rail** (**CWR**) and **Jointed Track**, and between CWR and some **Switch and Crossing Units** (**S&C Units**) to isolate the adjacent **Track** from longitudinal movement caused by temperature changes in the CWR. They are also located at the ends of long **Underbridges** (**UB**) to accommodate the thermal movement of the **Bridge Deck**. Also **Breather, Breather Switch**. See also **Composite Adjustment Switch**.

Adjustment Time
[Ops.] An allowance made in a **Timetable** (**TT**) to cater for differences in **Permissible Speeds** (**PS**) through the **Routes** of a **Diverging Junction** and the possible presence of **Approach Controls**.

Adlake
Adlake Lamp
(Tradename) An electric lamp originally intended as a replacement for paraffin "**Planlite**" lamps for **Semaphore Signals**.

ADM
a) **Asset** Data **Maintenance**
b) **Asset** Data **Management**.

Admiralty Tray
[Sig., Tel.] A shallow perforated steel or plastic channel used to support cables. On the **Railway** they are used in locations where **Concrete Cable Troughs** would be impossible to install, such as in areas of restricted clearance or on cable bridges and **Over Track Crossings** (**OTX**).

ADP
Automatic Data Preparation.

ADR
Accord Européen Relatif au Transport International des Marchandises Dangereuses par Route; Agreement concerning the International Carriage of Dangerous Goods by Road.

ADRC
[NR] Access Dispute Resolution Committee.

ADU
a) See **Air Distribution Unit**
b) [NR] **Area** Delivery Unit.

Advance
See **In Advance Of**. Also **Beyond**.

Advance Lookout
See **Distant Lookout**.

Advance Warning Board (AWB)
[NR, Sig.] A sign showing a cross of St. George, placed **On the Approach to** some **Open Level Crossings** (**OC**) to provide advance warning of the **Special Speed Restriction Board** (**SSRB**).

Advance Warning Indicator (AWI)
[Sig. NPT] Term now replaced by **Warning Indicator** (**WI**).

Advanced Passenger Train (APT)
[BR TRS Obs.] The ill-fated attempt by **British Railways** (**BR**) to bring **Tilting Trains** to Britain. Sarcastically re-named All Pushed Together, it was an idea slightly ahead of the available technology and not well managed. Advanced Passenger Train Experimental (**APT-E**) was the gas turbine **Train** tested in 1972 which achieved 152.5mph (245.1kph). Advanced Passenger Train Prototype (**APT-P**) was powered by the **Overhead Line Equipment** (**OLE**); Three such Trains were built but the combination of novelty and outstanding technical issues meant that they never reached satisfactory levels of service reliability and were withdrawn. Advanced Passenger Train Squadron (**APT-S**) was the intended third phase – this was never built The concept was later re-born in Italy as **Pendolino**. One example of APT-P survives in **The Railway Age** at Crewe.

Advanced Passenger Train Transponder
[BR TRS Obs.] A fixed passive marker fixed to the **Track** to provide speed information to the **Advanced Passenger Train** (**APT**).

Advanced Starting Signal
[Sig.] The **Starting Signal** furthest **Beyond** a **Signal Box** (**SB**) where multiple Starting Signals are provided within a given set of **Station Limits** on a given **Line**. Also **Section Signal**.

Adze
(adds) [PW] A variety of axe where the head is at right angles to the handle. It was used to dress and modify **Wood Sleepers** and **Bearers** prior to installation. Its use is now a rare thing.

AE
a) [IÉ] Assistant Engineer
b) [NR] Account Executive.

AEA Technology Plc. (AEAT)
(Tradename) A **Railway** technology consultancy which includes the former **British Rail Research** (**BRR**) organisation, specialising in measurement and simulation systems. It produces the **Vision**, **Trackmaster** and **Wheelchex** systems. Now called **Delta Rail**.

AEAT
(Tradename) See **AEA Technology Plc**.

AEDTF
Association Européenne pour le Dévelopement du Transport Ferroviaire (European Association for the Development of **Railway** Transport).

AEEU
Amalgamated Electrical Engineering Union.

AEI
[Hist.] Associated Electrical Industries, a manufacturer of **Signalling Equipment**. Formed by Westinghouse, Metropolitan **Carriage** □, **Wagon** & Finance Company and Vickers in 1926, taken over by **GEC** and now part of Alstom.

AEIF
See **Association Europeenne pour l'Interoperabilite Ferroviaire**.

AEJF
Association Européenne des Journalistes Ferroviaires, the European Association of **Railway** Journalists.

AEM
a) **Area** Environmental Manager
b) Area Engineering Manager
c) [BR] Area **Electrification** Manager.

Aerial Earth
[Elec.] A **Conductor** strung between and connected to multiple **Overhead Line Equipment** (**OLE**) **Structures** (and ultimately to an **Earth** connection point) to provide an Earth. This is an alternative to **Structure to Rail Bonds**.

Aerial Feeder
[Elec.] In an **Overhead Line Electrification** (**OLE**) system, a **Conductor** strung at height between **Structures**, carrying **Traction Current** between a **Feeder Station** and the **Catenary**. An **Aerial Feeder** is therefore not intended to be in contact with **Pantographs**.

AET
[LUL] Automatic Equipment Technician.

AF
a) See **Auxiliary Feeder**
b) See **Autotransformer Feeder**
c) [Sig.] Audio Frequency, see **Audio Frequency Track Circuit**
d) Across Flats.

AF Track Circuit
[Sig.] See **Audio Frequency Track Circuit**.

AFA
See **Access for All**.

AFAIRP
As Fast as is Reasonably Practicable.

Afaria
(Tradename) Software used to manage the Windows™ mobile devices used by **Network Rail's** (**NR**) **Maintenance** organisation. Produced by iAnywhere Solutions, a subsidiary Sybase Inc. of Dublin, California.

AFC
a) Approved for Construction
b) Anticipated Final Cost
c) Automatic Fare Collection
d) Area **Freight** Centre.

AFD
Automatic Fire Detection.

Affect the Normal Passage of Trains
[RB] Any activity or event that allows **Train** □ **Working** to continue but causes diversion, inability to call at a planned destination or introduction of **Degraded-Mode** operations such as **Passing a Signal at Danger**, use of **Handsignallers**, **Manual Route Setting** or **Single Line Working** (**SLW**) arrangements.

Affect the Safety of the Line
[RB] Any activity or event that may, during its course, render the **Track**, the **Formation** or a **Structure** unsafe for the passage of **Trains**, or unsafe for the passage of Trains at normal speed.

Affect the Safety of Train Working
[RB] Any activity or event that may, during its course, render a **Movement** control or **Interlocking** system unusable for the **Signalling** of **Trains**.

AFFF
Aqueous Film Forming Foam, used in fire extinguishers.

AFI
[TRS Obs.] Accelerated Freight AD Inshot, a type of valve fitted to improve the performance of **Vacuum Brakes**. A belated attempt to bring Vacuum Brakes up to the standard of control found with **Air Brakes**, this valve permitted better control of emergency brake applications. The system used two pipes, a reservoir supply and the other operating the brake system. This in itself was an unusual system and is now obsolescent. See **F, G, H**.

AFIGP
[Sig.] Agreed Final Installation Ground Plan. See also **Level Crossing Ground Plan**.

AFILS
[LUL] Audio Frequency Indication Loop Systems.

AFM
a) [PW] Automatische Fahrweg-Kontrollmaschine, or Automatic Finishing Machine. A **Plasser and Theurer** □ **On Track Machine** (**OTM**) which combines a **Ballast Regulator** and a **Dynamic Track Stabiliser** (**DTS**) in one
b) [LUL] Advanced Fare Machine.

AFR
Accident Frequency Rate.

A-frame
A-frame Structure
[Elec.] A type of **Overhead Line Structure** (**OLE Structure**) where the normal upright **Legs** are replaced by an A-frame. This design is generally found in areas equipped with **Mark 1** □ **Overhead Line Equipment**, particularly on **Four Track Railways**, the A-frame structures being used as supports for **Balance Weight Anchors** (**BWA**).

AFSS
[Elec.] Autotransformer □ Feeder Sectioning Site.

AFT
Assistance to Failed **Trains**.

AGC
a) See **At Grade Crossing**.
b) Accord Européenne sur les Grandes Lignes Internationales de Chemin de Fer, a European agreement on international **Main Line** □ **Railways**.

Age of Road Diagram (AOR Diagram)
[PW] A strip map showing a **Track** to scale along the top and details of the ages and specifications of the materials used in its construction arranged beneath. Typical details would normally include **Rail** age, **Rail Section**, **Sleeper** type, **Sleeper Spacing**, the age of the **Ballast** and when the track was lasted visited by a **Tamper**.

Agecroft Accident
In the late morning of 3rd August 1872 the **Signaller** at Agecroft allowed a **Coal Train** out of **Sidings** into the path of an **Express Passenger Train**. The Signaller had correctly **Protected** the movement by **Replacing** his **Distant Signal** and **Home Signal**, but did not wait to check that no **Train** was approaching. The **Line** was not operated on **Block Principles**. Four **Passengers** were killed and ten seriously injured.

Agent de Feu
[CT] A member of **Eurotunnel** or **ICTS** staff observing the departure of an **HGV Shuttle** as a final security check.

AGRRI
Advisory Group for Rail Research & Innovation.

AGT
a) Automatic **Guideway** Transit
b) Automatic Gate.

AHB
See **Automatic Half Barrier Crossing** (**AHBC**).

AHBC
See **Automatic Half Barrier Crossing**. A variety of **Level Crossing** (**LC, LX**).

AHBLC
See **AHBC**.

Ahead
Ahead Of
[NPT] See **Beyond**. Other non-preferred alternatives are **In Advance, In Advance of**. The non-preferred opposite terms are **Behind, In Rear of**, see **On the Approach to**.

AHRL
See **Abnormal Heavy Road Load**.

AI
a) **Asset** Inspector
b) **Asset** Information.

AIM
a) [NR] **Asset** Information Manager
b) All in Metric
c) Accord Concernant le Transport International des Marchandises par Chemin de Fer, an agreement concerning the international carriage of **Goods** by **Rail**.

AIOAMV
Automated Intrusive Observation and Measurement Vehicle.

AIP
a) See **Approval in Principle, Form A**
b) **Asset Improvement Plan**.

AIR
a) See **Approval and Issues Record**
b) See **Association of Independent Railways**.

Air Blast Circuit Breaker (ABCB)
[Elec.] A type of **Circuit Breaker** where a blast of air is used to extinguish the arc which occurs as the two contacts of the Circuit Breaker are moved apart.

Air Blow
[TRS Col.] An alternative term for **Air Piped**.

Air Brake

Air Braked
[TRS] Describes a **Rail Vehicle** equipped with an **Automatic Brake**, operated by air pressure.

Air Brakes
There are two varieties used on **Rail Vehicles**:
a) See **Single Pipe Air Brake**
b) See **Two Pipe Air Brake**
See also **A, B, H** and **X**.

Air Distribution Unit (ADU)
[CT] Equipment which passes air from the **Service Tunnel** to a **Running Tunnel**.

Air Gap
[PW] A break provided in a **Check Rail** to allow the fitting of an **Insulated Rail Joint (IRJ)** in the **Running Rail**.

Air Piped
[TRS] Describes a **Rail Vehicle** equipped with pipes carrying **Air Brake** through the vehicle, but not operating the vehicle brakes (if any). See **G, Q, R** and **W**.

Air Rights Development
Property constructed by an **Outside Party (OP)** above **Operational Land** and often above the **Operational Railway**.

Airlock
a) A system of doors enabling people to pass between two chambers maintained at different air pressures
b) An air bubble preventing correct operation of a hydraulic system.

AIRPS
See **Association of Independent Railways and Preservation Societies**.

Airtrack
A scheme to provide a link between Staines and the existing Heathrow Express (**HEX**) **Route** via Heathrow Terminal Five.

AIS
a) **Air Insulated Switchgear**.
b) **Asset Information Strategy**.
c) **Audio Information System**.

Ais Gill Accident
On 2nd September 1913 at 03:04 an **Express Passenger Train** passed two **Signals** at **Danger** at Mallerstang **Signal Box (SB)** on the Settle and Carlisle (**S&C**) □ **Route** and collided at speed with the rear of another Express Passenger **Train** which had stalled near the top of the Bank at Ais Gill. The **Guard** of the stalled Train had not carried out his duties in placing **Protection**. Sixteen died and 38 were injured. The dead were all in the **Trailing Vehicle** of the stalled Train, where a fire also broke out.

AIT
Asset Inspection Train.

AiTL
See **Assessment in The Line**.

AIV
Accord Concernant le Transport International des Voyageurs par Chemin de Fer, an agreement concerning the international carriage of **Passengers** and baggage by **Rail**.

AIWP
Annual **Integrated Works Plan**.

Ajax
A **Railway** □ **Telegraph Code** meaning "No **Train** signalled by **Bell Code** 2-6-2 or 2-6-3 must be allowed on the **Running Lines** or **Sidings** on both sides of load. To be signalled by the special **Is Line Clear** Bell Code 2-6-2" and applied to **Out of Gauge Loads**.

AJR
[Hist.] The **Pre-Grouping** Axholme Joint **Railway**, a Lancashire & Yorkshire and North Eastern joint enterprise.

AK
[NR] **Asset Knowledge**.

AKM
[NR] **Asset Knowledge Management**.

AKPM
[NR] **Asset Knowledge Project Manager**.

AKSRG
[NR] **Asset Knowledge System Review Group**.

AL
a) See **Avoiding Line**
b) **Analogue Loop**.

ALARA
As Low As Reasonably Achievable. See also **As Low as Reasonably Possible, As Low as Reasonably Practicable (ALARP)**.

ALARM
(*a-larm*) (Tradename) Amey's system for managing **Structures Examinations**.

ALARP
(*a-larp*) See **As Low as Reasonably Possible, As Low as Reasonably Practicable**. Also **AFAIRP, As Low As Reasonably Achievable (ALARA), GAMAB**.

ALC
a) [PW] Automatischer Leitcomputer, see **Automatic Lining Control**
b) See **Accommodation Level Crossing**
c) **Asset Life Cycle**.

ALCF
See **Alternative Line Control Function**.

ALCRM
[NR, Sig.] (*al-cram*) See **All Level Crossing Risk Model**.

Alert Limit
[NR PW] Measurement limit defined in **Network Rail Company Standard** (NRCS) NR/L2/TRK/001 beyond which the local management team needs to start planning actions to address the concern within routine **Maintenance**.

Alias Plate
[NR Sig.] A plate fitted to a **Signal** that gives the radio identification of that Signal, where it differs from the **Signal Number**.

0123

Alight
a) To disembark from a **Train**, e.g. "**Passengers** must not Alight here". See also **Board**
b) [Sig.] Describing a **Signal Lamp** that is giving off light. Also **Lit**.

Aligning
a) [PW] The process of moving the **Track** laterally to be in accordance with a **Design Alignment**
b) [Sig.] The process of re-directing the centre-line of the beam of light emitted by a **Signal** to pass through the **Alignment Point**
c) [Sig.] The process of re-directing a line normal to the display face of a **Lineside Sign** to pass through the Alignment Point.

Alignment
a) The right of way of a **Railway** or **Tramway**
b) [PW] The longitudinal direction, vertically or laterally, of a section of **Track**. Also **Horizontal Alignment**, **Through Alignment**, **Track Alignment**, **Track Geometry**. See also **Longitudinal Section**, **Long Section**
c) [Sig.] Of a **Signal**, the direction in three-dimensional space of the centre-line of the light beam emitted by the **Signal**
d) [Sig.] Of a **Lineside Sign**, the direction in three-dimensional space of a line normal to the display face.

Alignment Point
[Sig.] A spatial reference point, through which the centre-line of the light beam emitted by a **Signal** or the line normal to the display face of a **Lineside Sign** should be directed, so as to achieve satisfactory **Visibility**. The Alignment Point is specified in terms of its height **Above Rail Level** (**ARL**) and its offset relative to the **Left-Hand Rail**, at a particular distance from the **Signal** or **Sign**

Alignment Target
[Sig.] A physical object used during the **Aligning** process to mark the **Alignment Point**.

Alignment Variations
[PW] The divergences from the original horizontal design of a **Track**, generally resulting from poor **Maintenance** and the actions of passing **Trains**. Examples of particular variations include **Flats**, **Overshot Transitions**, **Track Buckles**, **Undershot Transitions**.

Alive
Formal description of a piece of equipment that is charged with electricity. The informal is **Live**.

All Level Crossing Risk Model (ALCRM)
[NR Sig.] A computer model used to calculate the risk at **Level Crossings** (**LC**, **LX**) and to evaluate reasonably practicable improvements to reduce the risk. The process produces a risk rating of A to M ("A" being the highest risk) for users of the Crossing related to the probability of a fatality per year for an average user traversing the crossing 500 times in one year, and a collective risk rating of 1 to 13 (with "1" being the highest collective risk) expressed in terms of **Fatalities and Weighted Injuries** (**FWI**) per annum. For instance, a Crossing rated C4 is a high risk in both senses, whereas M13 is not.

All Night Running
[LUL] The operation of a **Train** service throughout an entire period of **Engineering Hours**

All Orange
[NR] The requirement to wear an approved orange jacket (with retro reflective stripes) and orange trousers (with retro reflective stripes) at all times when **On or Near the Line**. This is on top of the requirement to wear approved reinforced toe cap boots, a hardhat (with chinstrap deployed) and gloves, plus other approved **Personal Protective Equipment** (**PPE**) as required.

All Signals On
All Signals On Switch
[Sig.] A **Signaller's Control Device** that places or maintains all suitable **Signals** in a designated area to or to a **Stop Aspect**. An alternative term is **Group Replacement Switch**.

All Stations
[Ops.] Describing a **Passenger Train** which has a **Booked Call** at every **Station** it passes. Also **Local Passenger Train**, **Stopping Train**.

Allcard, William
(1809-61). British **Locomotive** engineer and contractor on the Lancaster & Preston Junction **Railway**. A former pupil of George **Stephenson** and contemporary of Robert Stephenson, he later went on to work on French Railways.

Alliance
An arrangement where **Client**, consultant(s) and **Contractor(s)** work as a single team and consult on joint project issues.

Allied Traction Current Section
[LUL Elec.] An electrical section which has been **Isolated** to safeguard An **Engineer's Current Area**.

Allocation Diagram
[Elec.] A drawing produced for each new or modified **Structure** by the **Overhead Line Equipment** (**OLE**) designer, showing which components are required and in what arrangement.

ALO
See **Adjacent Line Open**.

Alongside Conductor Rails
[LUL] Describing a walkway that is less than 2m from the nearest **Conductor Rail** with no barrier between them.

ALOSPOSS
[NR] <u>A</u>djacent <u>L</u>ine <u>O</u>pen <u>S</u>elf-powered <u>O</u>verspeed <u>S</u>ensor <u>S</u>ystem. This stops a **Train** that is likely to pass through an **Adjacent Line Open (ALO) Worksite** at excessive speed by activating the **Train Protection Warning System (TPWS)**.

Alpha
The **Phonetic Alphabet** word representing **A**.

Alphanumeric Route Indicator (ARI)
[Sig.] A **Route Indicator** that displays letters and numbers to describe the **Route** ahead to the driver. They are used particularly in **Station** areas where there are many possible **Routes** and **Tracks**. See **Standard Alphanumeric Route Indicators (SARI)**, **Miniature Alphanumeric Route Indicators (MARI)**. See also **Fibre Optic Route Indicator (FORI)**, **Miniature Route Indicator (MRI)**, **Standard Route Indicator (SRI)**. Previously called **Multi-lamp Route Indicators (MLRI)** and **Theatre Route Indicators**, these terms are now obsolete.

ALR
[Sig.] <u>A</u>pproach <u>L</u>ocking □ <u>R</u>elease.

ALRMS
[NR Sig.] <u>A</u>ccess <u>L</u>evel <u>C</u>rossing <u>R</u>isk <u>M</u>anagement <u>S</u>ystem.

ALRV
[LR] <u>A</u>rticulated <u>L</u>ight <u>R</u>ail <u>V</u>ehicle.

ALSF
<u>A</u>ggregates <u>L</u>evy <u>S</u>ustainability <u>F</u>und.

Alstom
(Tradename) A manufacturer of **Signalling Equipment** and **Trains**.

Alternating Current Field Measurement (ACFM)
[PW] A process used to detect surface cracks in metal structures by detecting changes in the strength of an induced magnetic field. The system does not require physical contact and can detail the crack size to within 20%.

Alternative Feed
[Elec.] A route or source of **Traction Current** which is different from that normally used.

Alternative Feed Switch
[Elec.] An electrical switch mounted on an **Overhead Line Structure** that allows an **Electrical Sub Section** to be fed from either of two **Electrical Sections**.

Alternative Line Control Function (ALCF)
[LUL] A term describing the transfer of Jubilee **Line** control functions between Neasden Service Control Centre and the **Control Tower** at Stratford Market Depot.

Aluminium-Stainless Steel Conductor Rail (ASC Rail)
[Elec.] A type of **Conductor Rail** with improved wear and electrical conductivity characteristics compared with traditional **Rail Steel**. An aluminium core (a good conductor of electricity) supports a stainless steel shell (with good wear resistance) on its upper surface. Despite conductivity nearly double that of normal Conductor Rail, ASC Rail weighs only 16.5 **Kilograms per Metre**.

Alumino-thermic
Alumino-thermic Reaction
Pioneered by Hans Goldschmidt in 1895, an exothermic reaction involving the oxidisation of aluminium by iron oxide:

$$2Al(s) + Fe_2O_3(s) \rightarrow Al_2O_3(g) + 2Fe(s)$$

During this reaction temperatures can reach 2400°C, well in excess of that required to melt the iron produced. By the addition of other constituents, it is possible to produce strong "welded" joints between metal components without requiring furnaces or large power sources. See **Alumino-thermic Weld**.

Alumino-thermic Weld
[PW] A **Rail Weld** between abutting **Rails** made by the **Alumino-thermic** □ **Welding** process. The process would be more accurately described as a cast joint between prepared **Rail Ends**, since it employs a tapped crucible and sand moulds. Also (Tradenames) **Amotherm Weld, Delachaux Weld, Thermit Weld**, (Types) **PLA, Railtech Weld, SkV, SkV-F, SkV-L50, SkV-L80, SmW, SoWoS**.

AM
As the two leading letters of a professional membership it means <u>a</u>ssociate <u>m</u>ember.

AM&EE
[Hist.] See **Area Mechanical and Electrical Engineer**.

Amber
a) A **Railway** □ **Telegraph Code** meaning "Cancel my communication regarding ..."
b) [NPT] The incorrect name for **Yellow** on a **Colour Light Signal** (traffic lights on the highway are Amber)
c) (Tradename) Manually propelled trolley with electronic equipment to measure **Track Geometry** parameters. Produced by **Geismar**.

AMBR
AMBR Pantograph
[Elec.] A type of **Pantograph** fitted to older **EMUs** and **Locomotives** and suitable for service at speeds up to 100mph (160kph). Manufactured by **Stone Faiveley** and now largely superseded on **Heavy Rail [HR]** by the **Brecknell Willis High Speed Pantograph**.

AMC
[TRS] See **Amenity Coach**.

AMCL
<u>A</u>sset <u>M</u>anagement <u>C</u>onsulting <u>L</u>imited.

AMEM
<u>A</u>sset <u>M</u>anagement <u>E</u>xcellence <u>M</u>odel.

ELLIS' BRITISH RAILWAY ENGINEERING ENCYCLOPÆDIA

Amenity Coach (AMC)
[CT] A **Passenger Coach** in which lorry drivers are carried on an **HGV Shuttle**.

American Railway Engineering and Maintenance of Way Association (AREMA)
[US] An organisation whose mission is: "The development and advancement of both technical and practical knowledge and recommended practices pertaining to the design, construction and **Maintenance** of **Railway** □ **Infrastructure**". It was formed by the merger of The American Railway Engineering Association (**AREA**) and three other similar organisations in October 1997.

AMI
[BR, Obs.] **A**rea □ **M**ovements **I**nspector.

AMIP
Asset **M**anagement **I**mprovement **P**rogramme

AML
[Ops.] **A**verage **M**inutes **L**ateness.

AMOS
Area **M**anager's **O**perating **S**ystem.

Amotherm Weld
[PW, Obs.] A proprietary type of **Alumino-thermic Welding** process.

AMP
a) See **Asset Maintenance Plan**
b) **A**sset □ **M**aintenance **P**rogramme
c) **A**sset **M**anagement **P**lan
d) **A**sbestos **M**anagement **P**lan.

AMPP
[NR] See **Asset Maintenance Plan Provision**.

AMPS
a) **A**rea **M**aterials **P**rocessing **S**ystem
b) **A**rea **M**anagement **P**rocurement **S**ystem.

AMR
Automatic **M**eter **R**eading.

AMS
a) See **Austenite**, **Austenitic Manganese Steel**
b) [TRS] **A**dhesion **M**anagement **S**ystem
c) [NR] **A**sset **M**anagement **S**ervices.

AMU
Access **M**anagement **U**nit.

AMULET
Asset **M**anagement **U**niversal **L**inked **E**valuation **T**ool.

AMW
[NR] **A**sset **M**anagement **W**orkstream. The team leading a detailed review of **Network Rail's** (**NR**) approach to asset management with the key objective of optimising **Maintenance** and **Renewal** costs.

Anchor
a) See **Anchor Length**
b) See **Rail Anchor**
c) See **Anchor Structure**, **Self-supporting Anchor**
d) [Elec.] A concrete base used to secure a **Back Tie** for an Anchor Structure, see **Tied Anchor**.

Anchor Length
[PW] The length of **Track** required at each end of a length of **Continuous Welded Rail** (**CWR**), during **Stressing** operations, to resist the forces applied by Rail Tensors. See also **Overlap** (**OL**).

Anchor Structure
[Elec.] An **Overhead Line Structure** used to provide an anchorage for one end of one or more **Tension Lengths**. See also **Balance Weight Anchor** (**BWA**), **Fixed Anchor** (**FA**), **Self-supporting Anchor** (**SSA**), **Tied Anchor**.

Anchor Struts
[LUL Elec., PW] Wooden blocks fitted between the **Sleeper Ends** at **Conductor Rail Anchor** locations and intended to reduce the relative movement of the **Sleepers** due to the forces imposed by the Conductor Rail Anchors on the Sleepers.

Ancillary Movement
[Ops.] A movement of **Locomotives** or **Rolling Stock** directly in association with normal timetabled **Train** services.

Ancillary Structures
[LUL] **Structures** which span over or pass under the **Railway**, such as highway **Bridges**, **Footbridges**, pipes, etc. and which are not London Underground **Assets**.

Ancillary Wires
[Elec.] Any conductor running parallel to the **Track** and forming part of the **Overhead Line Equipment** (**OLE**) but not actually over the **Track**, e.g. **Feeders**, earth wires, etc.

Anderton Concrete
(Tradename) A supplier of pre-cast concrete (**PCC**) products, such as Cable Trough, based in Northwich, Cheshire.

Andrew
[Obs.] The obsolescent **Phonetic Alphabet** word representing A. Replaced by **Alpha**.

Angel

Angel Train Contracts (ATC)

Angel Train Group
(Tradename) One of the three **Rolling Stock** Leasing Companies (**ROSCOs**) formed at **Privatisation**. See also **Eversholt, Porterbrook**.

Angerstein Release
[Sig.] A special **Signalling Control** which frees the **Locking** when a long **Train** is using Angerstein Wharf in South **London**.

Angle of Attack (AOA)
[PW TRS] The angle between the **Running Edge** of the **Rail** and the plane of the **Wheel Flange**.

Angle of Depression
[Sig.] The angle between the centre-line of the light beam emitted by a **Signal** and the horizontal plane, in a situation where the beam is inclined downwards away from the **Signal**. See also **Angle of Elevation**.

Angle of Elevation
[Sig.] The angle between the centre-line of the light beam emitted by a **Signal** and the horizontal plane, in a situation where the beam is inclined upwards away from the **Signal**. See also **Angle of Depression**.

18

Angles
[PW Col.] Alternative term for **Common Crossing** and **Obtuse Crossing**.

Anglia Railways (AR)
A **Train Operating Company** (**TOC**).

Anglia Region (AR)
[Hist.] A **Region** of **British Rail** (**BR**) established in November 1987 from that part of the **Eastern Region** (**ER**) which covered the area served by the **Train** services from Liverpool Street and Fenchurch Street stations in **London**, e.g. the **Lines** to Norwich, Cambridge, King's Lynn, Ely, Peterborough, Shoeburyness and **Branches**.

Angus System
[Obs.] An early form of **Track Circuit**-based **Automatic Train Control** (**ATC**) devised in the 1900s by A. R. Angus and first trialled on the former West Somerset **Railway**.

Ankle
[PW] The part of the **Rail Foot** of a **Flat Bottom Rail** (**FB**) directly below the **Rail Web**.

Annett's Key
Annett's Lock
[Sig.] A key system used for remote and / or little-used **Sidings** and other **Connections**. The key can only be released for used by placing the appropriate **Signals** to show a **Stop Aspect**. These Signals cannot then be released until the key is replaced in the **Frame**. They key itself is then used to unlock the remote **Ground Frame** (**GF**), and cannot be removed until the **Levers** are relocked.

Annual Renewal Plan (ARP)
[NR] Plan identifying those assets to be renewed by **Network Rail** (**NR**) in the forthcoming year.

Annunciation Point
[Sig.] The point at which an approaching **Train** is detected and announced to waiting **Passengers** by an **Automatic Train Announcement System** (**ATAS**).

Annunciator
An audible indicator, such as a bell in a **Signal Box** or the noisy end of the driver / **Guard** communication system.

Anomalies
[TRS] Term given to **Train** fault and other event conditions which are monitored and recorded by a **Train Management System** (**TMS**).

Anorak
[Col.]
a) A derogatory term used to describe **Train Spotters**, based on their outer garment of choice. See also **Gricer**, **Stoat**.
b) Describing one who has an encyclopaedic knowledge of a single (often obscure) subject.

Another Train Coming Sign (ATC Sign)
[Sig.] An illuminated sign provided at **Automatic Open Crossing Locally Monitored** (**AOCL**) □ **Level Crossings** on **Two Track Lines** which is **Lit** to warn **Level Crossing** users of a the approach of a second or subsequent **Train**.

ANS
Ambient Noise Sensor.

Ansaldo
(Tradename) A manufacturer of **Signalling Equipment**.

ANSI
American National Standards Institute.

Anteater
[Col.] A nickname given to the **Class** 89 **Electric Locomotive**, due to its appearance.

Anti-attrition Pad
[PW] A 5mm thick **Rubber Bonded Cork** (**RBC**) □ **Pad**, which is fitted between a **Conductor Rail Safety Block** and a **Concrete Sleeper** to prevent abrasion.

Anticipation
[Sig.] A situation where the driver of a **Train** approaches a **Signal** showing a **Stop Aspect**, expecting it to **Clear**, but at too high a speed to stop. This is a frequent cause of **SPADs**. See **Expectation**.

Anti-climb Board
[Sig.] A fabricated metal board locked to the lower end of ladders on **Signals** and **Signal Gantries**. Its purpose is to prevent unauthorised persons using the ladder.

Anti-climber
[TRS] Devices fitted to the ends of a **Passenger Vehicle** to help interlock it with the adjacent vehicles in a collision and prevent the vehicles overriding each other. They consist of a plate with a serrated front face. A pair of these devices are fitted, one each side of the **Coupling**, where **Side Buffers** would normally be located.

Anti-fall Mechanism
[Elec.] A mechanism fitted to **Overhead Line Equipment** (**OLE**) □ **Balance Weights** to prevent the weights hitting the ground in the event of parting of any of the wires. This improves safety and reduces repair time

Anti-preselection
[Sig.] A **Signalling Function** which prevents the **Preselection** of a **Route** when this may reduce the protection provided by the **Signalling System**.

Anti-separation Pin
[TRS] A pin placed through suspension saddle, primary, secondary and **Cup Springs** and frame of a PHA **Wagon** to retain the alignment of the damping component.

AOA
See **Angle of Attack**.

AOCL
See **Automatic Open Crossing Locally Monitored**; A variety of **Level Crossing** (**LC**, **LX**).

AOCL+B
See **Automatic Open Crossing Locally Monitored plus Barriers**; A variety of **Level Crossing** (**LC**, **LX**).

AOCR
See **A**utomatic **O**pen **C**rossing **R**emotely Monitored; A variety of **Level Crossing** (**LC**, **LX**).

AOD
a) **A**bove **O**rdnance **D**atum, referring to a vertical level related to the mean sea level at Newlyn, Cornwall
b) [NR] **A**uxiliary **O**perating **D**uties, a **Safety Critical** qualification.

AOD: HS
[NR] **A**uxiliary **O**perating **D**uties: **H**and**s**ignaller, a **Safety Critical** qualification.

AOD: LXA
[NR] **A**uxiliary **O**perating **D**uties: **L**evel **C**rossing **A**ttendant, a **Safety Critical** qualification.

AOD: PO
[NR] **A**uxiliary **O**perating **D**uties: **P**oints **O**perator, a **Safety Critical** qualification.

AOM
[BR Obs.] **A**rea □ **O**perations **M**anager.

Aonad Imscrúdaithe Timpistí Iarnróid
See **Railway Accident Investigation Unit** (**RAIU**).

AONB
Area of **O**utstanding **N**atural **B**eauty.

AOOU
Asset **O**ut **O**f **U**se. See also **C&P**, **LOOU**, **NIRU**, **OOO**, **OOU**.

AOR Diagram
See **Age of Road Diagram**.

AOSF
[LUL] **A**ll **O**ther **S**tations **F**aulty.

AP
[NR Elec.] See **Authorised Person**.

APA
[NR] **A**sset **P**rotection **A**greement. Also **Basic Asset Protection Agreement** (**BAPA**).

APC
See **Automatic Power Control**.

APC Magnet
See **Automatic Power Control Magnet**.

API
a) **A**pplications **I**nterface
b) **A**pplication **P**rogramming **I**nterface.

Aplan
[NR] **Track Access Planning** system. A system for the planning of Track Access for both permanent and short term **Train** schedules, which replaced **PROTIM**. See **Bplan**.

APM
a) [NR] **A**rea **P**roduction **M**anager
b) **A**ssistant **P**roject **M**anager.

APOLS
APTIS / **PORTIS** **o**n **L**ine **S**ystem.

APOT
After **P**assage **o**f **T**rain.

APP
[NR] **A**nnual **P**ossession **P**lan.

Apparatus Case
Apparatus Housing
Apparatus Housing
[Sig., Tel.] Generic terms encompassing small enclosures containing **Signalling Equipment**, such as **Location Cases** (**Locs**.). See also **Relocatable Equipment Buildings** (**REB**).

Appendix A Braking
[NR Sig.] A reference to Appendix A of **Railway Group Standard** (**RGS**) GK/RT0034 (**Lineside** □ **Signal Spacing**) which covers **Signal Spacings** for all **Trains** other than those on former **Southern Region** □ **Passenger Lines**. See also **Braking Curve**.

Appendix B Braking
[NR Sig.] A reference to Appendix B of **Railway Group Standard** (**RGS**) GK/RT0034 (**Lineside** □ **Signal Spacing**) which covers **Signal Spacings** for **Passenger Trains** other than those on former **Southern Region Passenger** □ **Lines**. See also **Braking Curve**.

Appendix C Braking
[NR Sig.] A reference to Appendix C of **Railway Group Standard** (**RGS**) GK/RT0034 (**Lineside** □ **Signal Spacing**) which covers **Signal Spacings** for **Trains** with **Enhanced Braking**, e.g. 9% of g. See also **Braking Curve**.

Appendix D Braking
[NR Sig.] A reference to Appendix D of **Railway Group Standard** (**RGS**) GK/RT0034 (**Lineside** □ **Signal Spacing**) which covers **Signal Spacings** for **Trains** on former **Southern Region** □ **Passenger Lines**. See also **Braking Curve**.

Application Logic
A technology-based system that provides site-specific command and control instructions within a product. This includes mechanical, electro-mechanical, electronic and software-based logic.

Applied Cant
See **Cant**.

Approach Control
[Sig.] A **Control** built into a **Signalling System** that only allows a **Signal** to be **Released** when either the approaching **Train** has been proved to have stopped at the **Signal**, or to have reduced speed sufficiently to observe the correct speed over a **Junction** or other **Route** with a restricted speed.

Approach Lighting
[Sig.] A **Signal** so fitted only displays a light when a **Train** is approaching, thus saving wear and tear or possible confusion with other **Signals**.

Approach Locking
[Sig.] **Locking** a **Route** from a **Signal** to prevent its **Release** where the driver of an approaching **Train** may have seen a **Proceed Aspect** at the Signal, or may have seen other **Aspects** which may have led the driver to assume that the Signal is showing a **Proceed Aspect**. Should the **Signal** be subsequently **Replaced** to a **Stop Aspect**, the Approach Locking prevents the Route being Released as the driver may be unable to stop their Train at the Signal. See also **Reading Through**.

Approach Release
Approach Released
See **Approach Control**.

Approach Speed
[Sig.] The maximum speed at which a **Train** can legally approach an **Indicator** or **Signal**, therefore the higher of the **Permissible Speed** (**PS**) or **Enhanced Permissible Speed** (**EPS**) □ **On the Approach**, as appropriate.

Approach to
See **On the Approach to**.

Approaching Train
A **Train** that is coming towards you.

Approval and Issues Record (AIR)
[NR] A document used to record modifications, versions and approvals during the **Signalling** design process.

Approval Certificate
[NIR] Certificate confirming that a **Rail Vehicle** imported for use on the **Northern Ireland Railways** (**NIR**) network has been assessed as suitable for safe operation.

Approval in Principle (AIP)
[NR] A document produced early in the design phase, detailing the proposed form of the design, the standards to be used in its design and any departures from standards required to achieve that design. This document is approved by the client's engineer before the detailed design phase is begun. This procedure is intended to remove any possibility that the designer may not design what the client requires. The **Network Rail** (**NR**) standard documents are known as **Form 1**, **Form A**. The equivalent for **Signalling** design is the **Outline Project Specification** (**OPS**).

Apron
a) [PW] The horizontal portion of a **Cast Crossing** which connects together the **Leg Ends**
b) [Civ.] A concrete hard standing located:
• Under a **Track** to catch spilt fuel and effluent and other chemicals where such liquids are regularly transferred to and from **Rail Vehicles**. See also **CET Apron**, **Fuelling Apron**
• At each end of a **Carriage Washer** to catch stray water
• Across one end of a **Shed**, see **Shed Apron**

APRS
The Assisted **Passengers'** Reservations Service, which enables disabled **Passengers** to book assistance at **Stations** and on **Trains** when they travel on the **Railway Network**.

APS
[TRS] Automatic Performance Switching.

APT
See **Advanced Passenger Train**.

APT Transponder
See **Advanced Passenger Train Transponder**.

APTDM
AP Electronics' Time Division Multiplex.

APT-E
[BR, Hist.] **Advanced Passenger Train** – Experimental.

APTIS
Accountancy and **Passenger** □ **Ticket** Issuing System, the computerised system for issuing Passenger Tickets introduced in October 1986. Its introduction also saw a shift from **Edmondson Tickets** (made from pasteboard) to credit-card sized card Tickets printed on stiff paper. The prototype was called the All Purpose Ticket Issuing System. See also **PORTIS**, **SPORTIS**.

APT-P
[BR, Obs.] **Advanced Passenger Train** – Prototype.

APT-S
[BR, Obs.] **Advanced Passenger Train** – Squadron.

APU
[TRS] Auxiliary Power Unit.

APWSS
[BR Obs.] Assistant Permanent Way □ Section Supervisor.

AQL
Acceptable Quality Level.

AQMA
Air Quality Management Area.

AR
a) See **Arm Repeater**
b) Anglia Railways, a **Train Operating Company** (**TOC**).
c) See **Anglia Region**.

ARAFOAL
[Sig.] At Red and Free of **Approach Locking**.

ARAMIS
(Tradename) Advanced Railway Automation, Management and Information System.

Arbour Lights
[LUL Sig.] An arrangement of white lights above a **Colour Light Signal** that displays the **Diverging Route** through a **Junction** to the **Train** driver. See **Junction Indicator** (**JI**).

ARC
[Sig.] Automatic Route Calling.

Arc Chute
Shield made of fire-resistant material designed to contain the products of arcs generated in electrical switchgear and prevent damage to other equipment.

Arc Eye
An eye condition (*actinic keratitis*) with symptoms similar to having sand in one's eyes. It is caused by exposure to the intense ultraviolet light in an electric arc (such as that produced by arc welding or **Trains** using **Conductor Rails**). This condition can be avoided by **Turning Your Back on Passing Trains** (and welders).

Arc Protection
Arc Splash Protection
Materials used to protect vehicles or other equipment from damage due to heavy current arcing or from incandescent particles produced during arcing.

Arch
[Civ.] A curved structure normally composed of brick, concrete or masonry used to create **Bridges** and **Viaducts**. Cast iron and steel are also used to create roofs. The form works on the basis that all components are in compression, allowing relatively low grade materials to be used.

Arch Back
See **Extrados**.

Arch Bridge
[Civ.] A **Bridge** constructed using the **Arch** principle.

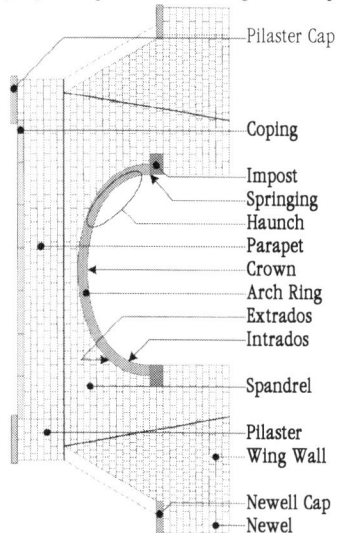

Pilaster Cap
Coping
Impost
Springing
Haunch
Parapet
Crown
Arch Ring
Extrados
Intrados
Spandrel
Pilaster
Wing Wall
Newell Cap
Newel

Arch Cladding
[Civ.] A layer of some impermeable material such as aluminium or glass fibre used to cover the underside of an **Arch**. It is used to deflect water that may leak through the masonry, and therefore makes the space beneath more usable. Also **Arch Lining**.

Arch Crown
[Civ.] The highest part of the **Arch Ring**. Often contracted to **Crown**.

Arch Face
See **Intrados**, **Voussoir**.

Arch Lining
See **Arch Cladding**.

Arch Ring
[Civ.] The curved layer of brick, concrete or stone that is the main supporting element in an **Arch Bridge**.

Arcing
The flow of electricity through the air from one conductor to another. Arcing can produce visible flashes and flames.

ARD
[Sig.] Available Reading Distance.

ARDV
Access Rights Database and Validator.

AREA
[Hist.] American Railway Engineering Association, now called The **American Railway Engineering and Maintenance of Way Association** (**AREMA**).

Area
a) [BR Hist.] The local organisation responsible for maintenance of **Bridges**, **Earthworks**, **Electrification Equipment**, **Signalling** and **Track**, typically in an area covering two or three counties. See **Area Civil Engineer** (**ACE**), Area Mechanical and Electrical Engineer (AM&EE), Area **Signalling and Telecommunications** Engineer (AS&TE)
b) [NR Hist.] A section of the **West Coast Main Line** (**WCML**) project that is responsible for long-term project delivery to the **Network Rail** □ **Territories**, namely West Coast Midlands, Major Works, North West and Scotland.

Area Civil Engineer (ACE)
[BR, Hist.] The post responsible for the day-to-day maintenance and renewal of **Track**, **Bridges**, **Earthworks** and fences in a geographical area. The post reported to the **Regional Civil Engineer** (**RCE**). This post was re-titled on many occasions, and is analogous to **Divisional Civil Engineer** (**DCE**) and **Civil Engineer** (**CE**).

Area Mechanical and Electrical Engineer (AM&EE)
[BR Hist.] The post responsible for the day-to-day **Maintenance** and renewal of the **Electrification Equipment** and plant in an **Area**.

Area of Conflict
[Sig.] A section of **Track** □ **Beyond** a **Signal** showing a **Stop Aspect**, on which a head-on or other collision with another legitimately-positioned **Train** could occur, in the event of a **Signal Passed at Danger** (**SPAD**).

Area Signalling and Telecommunications Engineer (AS&TE)
[BR Hist.] The post responsible for the day-to-day **Maintenance** and renewal of **Signalling Equipment** and **Telecommunications** systems in an **Area**.

AREMA
See **American Railway Engineering and Maintenance of Way Association**.

ARI
See **Alphanumeric Route Indicator**.

ARISE
Automatic Railway Inquiry Systems in Europe, a prototype system providing Passenger □ Timetable information.

ARL
See Above Rail Level.

ARLI
See Abnormal Road Load Indemnity.

ARLN
See Abnormal Road Load Notification.

Arm
a) [Sig.] The pivoted movable part of a Semaphore Signal. Its position relative to horizontal conveys meaning to a driver
b) See Arming Loop. See also Train Protection Warning System (TPWS).
c) See Registration Arm.

ARM
a) Asset Recovery Manager
b) [NR] Active Risk Manager, Network Rail's risk management database.

Arm Repeater (AR)
[Sig.]
a) An electromagnetic mimic of the position of a Semaphore Signal □ Arm, provided when the Signaller cannot actually see the Signal concerned
b) A mechanically linked miniature Arm located near the ground near a Semaphore Signal, allowing a Fogsignalman to correctly observe the Signal □ Aspect when the fog is particularly thick and obscures the top of the Signal. Since the widespread introduction of Colour Light Signals, such provisions are now rare, as are Fogsignalmen.

Armagh Accident
On the 12th of June 1889 an overloaded Excursion Train carrying schoolchildren stalled near the top of a steep Gradient. In an attempt to continue the driver Divided the Train, using the Handbrake on the Guards Van and some stones to prevent the rear portion moving. In moving off the driver collided with this rear portion, overcoming the Handbrake and Scotches, pushing it down the Gradient where it collided with a following Train. 80 Passengers, many of them children, lost their lives, second only in loss of life to the Quintinshill Accident. Automatic Brakes would have prevented this accident, and they were made law that year, see the Railway Regulation Act 1889.

Armbands
Those undertaking key site roles are identified by the wearing of Armbands.
[NR]

COSS — See Controller of Site Safety

CRANE CONTROLLER — See Crane Controller

DP — See Designated Person

ENGINEERING SUPERVISOR — See Engineering Supervisor

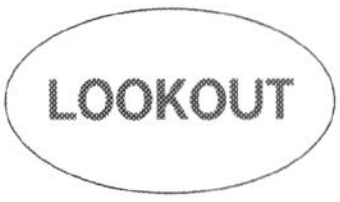

LOOKOUT — See Lookout

MACHINE MC CONTROLLER — See Machine Controller

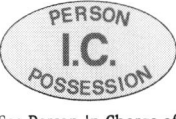

PERSON I.C. POSSESSION — See Person in Charge of Possession (PICOP)

PILOTMAN — See Pilotman

PC — See Protection Controller (PC) 
[LUL]

SITE WARDEN — See Site Warden

SITE PERSON IN CHARGE — See Site Person in Charge (SPIC)

ARME
[NR] Area □ Rail Management Engineer.

Arming Loop
[Sig.] The first Track mounted transmitter a Train encounters as part of a Train Protection and Warning System (TPWS) installation. This Loop starts the timer fitted to the Train. See Overspeed Sensor System (OSS), Train Stop Sensor (TSS), Trigger Loop.

ARMS
a) Automatic Remote Monitoring System
b) Asbestos Risk Management System.

Arneke
(*arr-nee-key*) (Tradename) [BR Obs.] A variety of small crane arranged in pairs or threes on a Salmon □ Wagon, used to load and unload Rails over the side of the Wagon. The generic term is Side Rail Loader. Also Stumec, Elk.

ELLIS' BRITISH RAILWAY ENGINEERING ENCYCLOPÆDIA

Arno
A **Railway** □ **Telegraph Code** meaning "Undermentioned notice received".

ARP
a) See **Annual Renewal Plan**
b) [Hist.] Air Raid Precautions, a programme of strengthening key buildings against attack from the air, carried out during World War Two. Many **Signal Boxes** were fitted with very strong reinforced concrete roofs, some up to 500mm thick.

ARPS
See **Association of Railway Preservation Societies**.

ARRC
Advanced **Railway** Research Centre.

Arriva Trains Northern (ATN)
A former **Train Operating Company (TOC)**.

Arriva Trains Wales (ATW)
A **Train Operating Company (TOC)** which operates a mix of long-distance, regional and local services in Wales, including the Valley Lines network of services around Cardiff, and also in the English border counties and to Manchester, Liverpool and Birmingham. **ATOC** code **AW**.

Arrival
Arrival Line
[Ops.] A **Track** on which **Trains** enter a **Marshalling Yard** and stop to await attention. Typical use also generally includes the direction of travel of arriving vehicles, e.g. **Down** Arrival Line.

Arrol, Sir William
(1839-1913). Civil Engineer who built the second Tay Bridge (see **Tay Bridge Accident**), the Forth Bridge and the Queen Alexandra Bridge in Sunderland.

Arrow
A **Railway** □ **Telegraph Code** meaning "Reply on following subject".

ARS
[Sig.] See **Automatic Route Setting**. Also **Automatic Route-setting Subsystem**.

ART
Alarms, Recording and Telecontrol.

Articulated
Articulated Vehicle

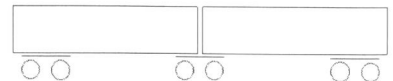

[TRS] A **Rail Vehicle** arranged so that two or more adjacent **Cars** share a common **Bogie** or axle. Although this arrangement is common in modern **Light Rail Vehicles (LRV)**, the **Eurostar** is such a **Train**, as are **Autics** and **Cartics**.

Articulation Module
[LR] A flexible part of a modern **Tram** which allows relative rotational movement between two coupled vehicles.

ARTP
Association of **Rail** Training Providers.

ARU
[TRS] Automatic Regeneration Unit.

AS Chairscrew
[PW] The normal length ($6\,^3/_8$") **Chairscrew** (or **Baseplate Screw**) used to secure **Chairs** and **Baseplates** to **Wood Sleepers** and **Timbers**. See also **LS Chairscrew, LX Chairscrew, M Chairscrew**.

As Low as Reasonably Possible
As Low as Reasonably Practicable (ALARP)
A description of the residual risk that is acceptable, acknowledging that there will always be some small risk remaining irrespective of the funds expended to try to eliminate it. The level of acceptable risk is determined by reference to the Value of Preventing a Fatality (**VPF, VOPF**) aggregated using the **Equivalent Fatalities** principle. Also As Far as is Reasonably Practicable (**AFAIRP**), As Low as Reasonably Achievable (**ALARA**),

AS&TE
See **Area Signalling and Telecommunications Engineer**.

AS(HT) Chairscrew
[PW] A version of the **AS Chairscrew** manufactured from high tensile steel, for use in high lateral stress locations.

AS1
AS1 Chair
[PW] Originally titled the **S1** and for 95 Pound □ **Bullhead (BH)**, see **Common Chair**.

AS2
AS2 Chair
[PW] Narrow version of the **AS1 Chair**, see **Common Chair**.

ASB
a) As Built
b) [Sig.] Adjacent **Signal Box**.

AsBo
Assessment Body. See **Common Safety Method**.

ASBPC
[Sig.] Adjacent **Signal Box** Protocol Converter.

ASC
a) Auxiliary Supplies Cabin
b) Auxiliary Supply Cabinet
c) [Sig.] Automatic Stop Control
d) See **Aluminium-Stainless Steel Conductor Rail**
e) [Sig.] **Area** □ **Signalling Centre**.

ASC Rail
See **Aluminium-Stainless Steel Conductor Rail**.

A-SDO
[TRS] Automatic Selective Door Opening.

Ash
[Hist.] A material sometimes used instead of stone for **Ballast** in **Sidings**, and for making **Cess Paths**. When used as under the track it was usually recovered **Locomotive** Ash.

ASID
[LUL] Additional Stop Information Details.

Ask the Road
[Col., Sig.] To offer on a **Train** to the next **Signal Box** in an **Absolute Block (AB)** area. Also **Be Ready**.

Asking Lever
[Sig.] A **Lever** in a **Ground Frame** (**GF**) operating a sounder (such as a **Gong**) in a **Signal Box** (**SB**), requesting the **Signaller** to **Release** the Ground Frame. Such Levers are rare and normally painted green.

ASL
[Sig.] Adjacent **Signal Box** Link.

ASLEF
(*az-lef*) (Tradename) Associated Society of Locomotive Engineers and Firemen, a Trades Union mainly representing **Traincrew**, particularly drivers.

ASM
a) Assistant Site Manager
b) Asset Strategy Meeting.

ASP
a) See **Auxiliary Supply Point**
b) **Axle Load** □ **Speed Profile**.

ASP Baseplate
[PW] A **Baseplate** for direct fixing to concrete **Bridge Decks**, **Slab Track** etc., fitted with eccentric bushes to permit fine lateral adjustment to be made to the position of the Baseplate. Also **VASP Baseplate**.

Aspect
a) [RB] The indication of a **Colour Light Signals** that the driver sees.
b) [Sig.] A valid indication displayed by a **Signal**. This may be conveyed by the physical position of an **Arm** (**Semaphore Signals**), the positions of lights relative to each other (**Position Light Signals**) or combinations of coloured lights (**Colour Light Signals**). Example descriptions include **Caution Aspect**, **Off Aspect**, **On Aspect**, **Preliminary Caution Aspect**, **Proceed Aspect**, **Stop Aspect**.

Aspect Level
[Sig.] The level of **Interlocking** which must be met before a **Signal** can display a **Proceed Aspect**.

Aspect Sequence
[Sig.] The successive **Signal** □ **Aspects** seen by a driver. These make immediate sense and allow the driver sufficient distance in which to bring their **Train** safely to a stand if required. They are normally presented graphically in the form of an **Aspect Sequence Chart**, which allows the Sequences to be checked.

Aspect Sequence Chart
[Sig.] A network style diagram showing the relationships between aspects on adjacent **Signals**, and therefore the **Aspect Sequence** seen by drivers on all possible **Routes**.

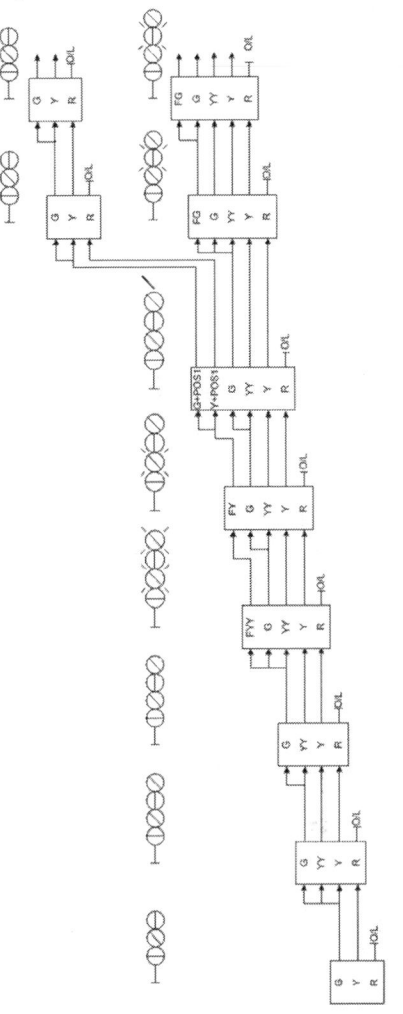

ASPER
Asset Performance Database.

Aspinall, Sir John
(1851-1937). Chief Mechanical Engineer and latterly General Manager of the Lancashire & Yorkshire **Railway** (**L&YR**). Supervised the **Electrification** of the Liverpool to Southport and Manchester to Bury **Lines**.

AsPro
[NR] Asset Protection.

ASR
a) [Sig.] **Arm** and **Slot** □ **Repeater**, an indication in the **Signal Box** (**SB**) of the status of a **Semaphore Signal** and its associated Slot. See also **Arm Repeater** (**AR**)
b) **A**utomatic **S**peed **R**egulation
c) [Civ.] **A**lkali **S**ilica **R**eaction, a malaise affecting concrete structures.

ASRC
[Unk.] **A**utomated **S**ystem of **R**ailway **C**ontrol.

ASS
Auxiliary **S**upply **S**ite.

Assessed Minimum Reading Time
[Sig.] The sum of the times assessed to be essential for a driver approaching a **Signal** to:
- Detect the presence of the Signal,
- Identify the Signal as being applicable to them,
- Observe the information presented by the Signal,
- Interpret the information to determine what action, if any, is required.

Therefore also the time the **Train** should take to cover the **Minimum Reading Distance** (**MRD**) at the **Approach Speed**. Also **Minimum Reading Time** (**MRT**)

Assessment
a) See **Bridge Assessment**
b) See **Earthworks Assessment**
c) See **Structure Assessment**
d) See **Signalling Infrastructure Condition Assessment** (**SICA**)
e) See **Assessment in The Line** (**AiTL**)

Assessment in The Line (AiTL)
[NR] Part of **Network Rail's** competence management system, involving an assessment of competence carried out under the supervision of an employee's line management.

Asset
Collective term for the components such as **Trains**, **Track**, **Signals**, **Bridges**, **Earthworks**, **Drains**, **Stations**, etc. that are owned by a particular company. See also **Infrastructure**.

Asset Condition Speed Restriction
[LUL] The **London Underground** Limited equivalent of a **Condition of Track Speed** (**COT Speed**).

Asset Maintenance Plan (AMP)
[RT Obs.] A plan of remedial and **Maintenance** work outstanding from the previous **British Railways** (**BR**) stewardship, at the creation of **Railtrack** (**RT**). See also **Asset Maintenance Plan Provision** (**AMPP**).

Asset Maintenance Plan Provision (AMPP)
[RT Obs.] The funding provision provided to **Railtrack** (**RT**) on its formation, to complete the works identified in the **Asset Maintenance Plan** (**AMP**).

Asset Steward
[NR] The post with ultimate authority over decisions regarding their particular field.

Assistant Track Section Manager (ATSM)
[NR] An assistant to the manager responsible for the **Maintenance** of a section of **Track**, typically about twenty **Route Miles**.

Assisting in Rear
[Ops.] Describing a **Locomotive**, **Multiple Unit** or **Train** that is providing additional **Tractive Effort** at the rear of another Multiple Unit or Train. Normally only used when the front Multiple Unit or Train is partially disabled by failure, and then only to a location where the front Train can be moved **Clear** of other traffic.

Associated Renewals
Renewal work carried in conjunction with other work because it is cost effective to do so at the time and not necessarily because the Associated work is due. See also **Passive Provision**.

Association Européenne pour l'Interopérabilité Ferroviaire (AEIF)
The organisation mandated by the European Commission to write the **Conventional Interoperability** □ **Technical Standards for Interoperability** (**TSI**).

Association of Community Rail Partnerships (AcoRP)
An organisation which supports approximately fifty **Community Rail Partnerships** (**CRP**) in the United Kingdom. It also offers assistance to voluntary **Friends of Stations** groups that support their local **Stations** through the **Station Adoption Scheme**.

Association of Independent Railways (AIR)
[Hist.] Now merged with the **Association of Railway Preservation Societies** (**ARPS**) to form the **Heritage Railway Association** (**HRA**).

Association of Independent Railways and Preservation Societies (AIRPS)
[Hist.] The former name of the **Heritage Railway Association** (**HRA**).

Association of Railway Preservation Societies (ARPS)
[Hist.] Now merged with the **Association of Independent Railways** (**AIR**) to form the **Heritage Railway Association** (**HRA**).

Association of Train Operating Companies (ATOC)
(Tradename) The umbrella organisation representing **Train Operating Companies** (**TOC**) to the government, regulatory bodies, the media and other opinion-formers on transport policy issues, providing its members with a range of services that enable them to comply with conditions laid on them in their franchise agreements and operating licences.

Aster
[Sig.] A variety of **Jointless Track Circuit** (**JTC**) utilising audio frequency **Alternating Current** (**AC**). See **Audio Frequency Track Circuit**.

ASTR
Advanced **St**arter Control **R**elay.

Astragal
[TRS] A vertical strip of pliable material mounted on the leading edge of a door panel.

ASW
Amended **S**tation **W**orking.

Asymmetric Trapped Conventional Rail (ATC)
[Unk.] A **Flat Bottom Rail** having an asymmetric **Rail Head** and used in coal mines.

Asynchronous Motor
A modern type of **Traction Motor** type using a three phase **AC** electrical supply and now the favoured design for modern **Train** □ **Traction** systems. See also **Synchronous Motor**.

At
In a description of a **Possession** (such as "Nowhere to Somewhere and At Somewhere") it indicates that the Possession includes the named location or **Junction**. Also **Inc.**, **Inclusive**. See also **Exc.**, **Exclusive**.

AT
AT Equipment
a) See **Auto Transformer**
b) See **Automatically Tensioned System (ATS)**.

At Grade
At Grade Crossing
A location at which two transport **Routes** cross at the same vertical level and therefore conflict with each other. The opposite is **Grade Separated**. See also **Flat Junction, Level Crossing, Swing Bridge**.

At Grade Junction
A location where two **Railway** □ **Routes** cross and / or join at the same vertical level, and therefore conflict with each other. The opposite is **Grade Separated Junction**. See also **Burrowing Junction, Flying Junction**.

At Risk Earthwork
[NR Civ.] An **Earthwork** considered at risk of failure during adverse weather conditions.

At Risk Earthworks Register
[NR Civ.] A listing of **Earthworks** considered 'at risk'.

AT System
a) See **Auto Transformer**
b) See **Automatically Tensioned System (ATS)**.

ATA
See **Automatic Track Alignment**.

ATAS
See **Automatic Train Announcement System**.

ATB
a) Automatic **Ticket Barrier**
b) Automated **Ticket** and **Boarding**.

ATC
a) [LUL] Accidental **Train Collision**.
b) See **Automatic Train Control**
c) See **Angel Train Contracts**
d) An acronym representing an Auxiliary Equipment **Trailer** □ **Composite Coach**
e) See **Another Train Coming Sign**
f) See **Asymmetric Trapped Conventional Rail**.

ATC Sign
See **Another Train Coming Sign**.

ATCO
Association of **T**ransport **C**o-ordinating **O**ffices.

ATD
[PW] Automatic **Track Design**, See **Automatic Track Alignment (ATA)**.

ATE
[NR] **A**rea **T**rack **E**ngineer.

ATF
[Elec.] **Aut**otransformer □ **F**eeder. The wires which replace the **Return Conductor (RC)** in an Autotransformer **(AT)** system. Also **AF**.

ATFS
[Elec.] **Aut**otransformer □ **F**eeder **S**tation.

ATG
a) [PW] **A**bsolute **T**rack **G**eometry, See **Fixed Geometry Railway, Track Machine Guidance (TMG)**
b) **A**utomatic **T**icket **G**ates.

ATH
[PW] A BS11 113A □ **Rail Profile** modified to provide additional relief at the **Gauge Corner** and **Gauge Shoulder** on the **High Rail** of **Curves**.

Atk.
[Hist.] Common shorthand for F A Atkinson, a former manufacturer of **Signalling Equipment**.

ATL
[PW] The standard BS11 113A □ **Rail Profile** used on the **Low Rail** of **Curves** and on **Straight Track**.

ATLAS
Automatic **T**unnel **L**aser **A**nalysis **S**ystem.

ATM
a) **A**mended **T**imetable **M**anager
b) **A**utomated **T**eller **M**achine
c) **A**synchronous **T**ransfer **M**ode.

ATME
[NR] **A**ssistant **T**rack **M**aintenance **E**ngineer.

ATMF
Admission **T**echnique du **M**atériel **F**erroviaire, technical acceptance of **Railway** vehicles.

Atmospheric Railway
[Hist.] A **Railway** on which the **Motive Power** is provided by a piston located in a pipe running longitudinally between the **Rails**. The air is evacuated from the pipe **Beyond** the piston, resulting in the piston (and attached **Train**) being drawn forward. The fundamental problem with the system is that there must be a longitudinal slot in the pipe, in order to permit the passage of the connection between piston and Train. It is the difficulties encountered when trying to seal the slot that has rendered all previous attempts uneconomical.

ATMS
See **Automated Track Monitoring System**.

ATN
See **Arriva Trains Northern**.

ATO
See **Automatic Train Operation**.

ATOC
(*ay-tock*) See **Association of Train Operating Companies**.

ATOC Standards
(*ay-tock stan-dards*) Standards documents produced by the **Association of Train Operating Companies**, typically covering areas where standardisation between **Train Operating Companies** (**TOC**) is in the best interests of all, such as **Tickets**.

ATOMIC
(*a-tom-ik*) **A**utomatic **T**rain **O**peration by **M**ini **C**omputer.

ATOR
[LUL] **A**nnual **T**est **o**f **R**ules.

ATP
See **Automatic Train Protection**.

ATPM
Automatic **T**rain **P**rotection **M**anual

ATR
a) See **Automatic Train Reporting**
b) See **Automatic Train Regulation**
c) [Sig.] **A**utomatic **T**rain **R**outing

ATRE
[Sig.] **A**utomatic **T**rain **R**eporting (**ATR**) by **E**xception.

ATS
a) See **Automatically Tensioned System**
b) See **Autotransformer System**
c) [Elec.] **A**uto**t**ransformer **S**ite
d) See **Automatic Train Supervision**
e) [TRS] An acronym representing an Auxiliary Equipment **T**railer ▫ **S**tandard Class ▫ **C**oach
f) [Sig.] **A**utomatic **T**rain **S**top
g) [Ops.] **A**pplicable **T**imetable **S**ervice
h) [LR] **A**utomatic **T**ram **S**top.

ATSM
See **Assistant Track Section Manager**.

ATT
[TRS]
a) **A**ctive **T**ilting **T**rain. See also **Passive Tilt**
b) **A**dvanced **T**ilting **T**rain
See also **Railtrack Advanced Tilting Train** (**RATT**), **Virgin Advanced Tilting Train** (**VATT**).

ATTA
See **Automatic Track and Top Alignment**.

Attainable Speed
The maximum speed a particular **Train** or any **Train** can achieve, given adjacent restrictions of **Enhanced Permissible Speed** (**EPS**), **Permissible Speeds** (**PS**), **Gradient**, and acceleration and braking rates. Using these values as the basis of a design introduces the risk that future, better performing, Trains may be able to exceed them.

ATW
See **Arriva Trains Wales**.

ATWS
See **Automatic Track Warning System**.

A-Type Bridge
[NR] A variety of standard **Half Through** ▫ **Ballasted Deck** ▫ **Bridge** consisting of two I-shaped main girders and a **Composite Deck**. Used for short **Spans** up to 12 metres. See also **B-Type Bridge**, **Z-Type Bridge**.

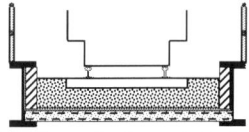

Audible Warning
[Sig.] The warning which sounds when a **Level Crossing Protection System** is activated. See also **Yodalarm**.

Audigage
[PW Obs.] A system of **Rail Flaw** detection utilising variable audio tones rather than the current method of a trace displayed on an oscilloscope.

Audio Frequency Track Circuit
[Sig.] A type of **Jointless Track Circuit** (**JTC**) that utilises high frequency (around 1kHz) Alternating Current (**AC**) for its operation. Alternatives include **AC Track Circuits** and **DC Track Circuits**. See **Aster**, **TI21**.

AUDRI
[LUL] **A**udit of **D**ouble-**R**oyal **I**nstructions.

AUI
Attachment **U**nit **I**nterface.

Austenitic

Austenitic Manganese Steel (AMS)
A name for a type of steel with a smooth grain structure consisting of a solid solution of Iron and Carbon. **Manganese Rail** steels are usually composed of Austenitic steel.

Austroroll
(Tradename) A type of friction reducing roller device for **Switches** manufactured by Enzesfeld Caro Metallwerke AG of Austria. See **Switch Rollers**.

Authorised Movement
A **Train** movement that is being correctly made in accordance with an appropriate **Movement Authority**.

Authorised Person (AP)
[NR] A person certificated as competent to carry out the **Safety Critical Work** (**SCW**) of switching and Isolating **Overhead Line Equipment** (**OLE**).

Authorised User
A person or body registered with the **Infrastructure Controller** as a legitimate user of a specific **Accommodation Level Crossing** (**ALC**) or **Occupation Level Crossing** (**OLC**). Also those visiting, trading with or servicing an Authorised User.

Authorised Walking Route
A designated and safe pedestrian route provided for **Railway** employees going to and from their place of work. Such a route may be via the public highway, or along specially constructed paths alongside and across the **Track**.

Authority to Work
A document issued to staff by their line manager authorising them to work, following a review of their competence each year.
Autic
Autic Six
(*or-tik, or-tik six*) A type of car transporter consisting of two twin deck **Wagons** □ **Articulated** on three axles. See also **Cartic**.
Auto
[Sig.]
a) See **Automatic Signal**
b) See **Automatic Lower**
c) See **Self-restored Points**
d) See **Automatic Raise**.
Auto Ballaster (HQA, JJA)
A large 54 ton capacity **Ballast Hopper** with remotely controlled power-operated doors, used to unload new **Ballast** onto the **Track**.
Auto Coupler
[TRS] A device which simultaneously couples two **Rail Vehicles** together mechanically, often electrically and sometimes pneumatically. Also **Automatic Coupling**, **Buck Eye**, **Scharfenberg**, **Ward Coupler**, **Wedgelock**.
Auto Coupler Contact Block
[TRS] An arrangement of spring-loaded connections within an **Autocoupler** assembly which provide an electrical link between the **Rail Vehicles**.
Auto LCRM
Automatic Level Crossing Risk Model, see **All Level Crossing Risk Model (ALCRM)**.
Auto Lower
See **Automatic Lower**.
Auto Raise
See **Automatic Raise**.
Auto Signal
See **Automatic Signal**.
Auto Telephone
[LUL] The internal network-wide telephone system linking **London Underground Limited (LUL)** locations.
Auto Working
a) [Sig.] Describing a **Controlled Signal** working as an **Automatic Signal**
b) [Ops.] Describing the use of a **Steam Locomotive** in an **Auto Train**.
Autocoach
[TRS, WR] Term used by the Great Western Railway (**GWR**) to describe a **Passenger Coach** with a **Driving Cab** at one end, designed to be coupled to a specially equipped **Steam Locomotive**, allowing the driver to control the **Train** without needing to be located in the Cab of the **Locomotive**. This eliminated the need to run the Locomotive round to the other end of the **Coach** at the end of each journey.

Auto-lower
[Sig.] A function fitted to the **Barriers** and **Half-barriers** of **Level Crossings (LC, LX)** that are **Monitored** (such as **CCTV** types) that starts the lowering sequence as soon as the **Train** has passed the **Strike-in Point (SIP)**. The **Protecting Signal** is not **Cleared** until the **Signaller** presses the **Crossing Clear** button.
Automated Finishing Machine (AFM)
[PW]
a) Alternative term for a **Ballast Regulator**
b) An **On-track Machine (OTM)** that combines a number of processes, including the redistribution of **Top Ballast (Ballast Regulating)**, the removal, storage and unloading of small quantities of **Ballast**, stabilisation of the **Track** and in some models the control of **Track Geometry**.
Automated Track Monitoring System (ATMS)
[PW] an unattended **Track Measurement** system mounted on in-service **Passenger Trains** that measures, processes and transmits **Track Geometry** data to those responsible for the day-to-day **Maintenance** of the **Track**.
Automated Voice Announcer (AVA)
A system that automatically delivers pre-recorded audio messages so that customers receive relevant information at the appropriate time and place.
Automatic Air Brake
[TRS] A type of **Continuous Brake**. See **Air Brake**, **Automatic Brake**.
Automatic Ballast Cleaner (ABC)
[PW] The full title for an **On Track Machine (OTM)** built to excavate, clean and replace the **Ballast** from beneath the same **Track**. For a full description see the more commonly used contraction **Ballast Cleaner**. See also **High Output Ballast Cleaner (HOBC)**, **Matisa Automatic Ballast Cleaner (MABC)**, **Medium Output Ballast Cleaner (MOBC)**, **Plasser Automatic Ballast Cleaner (PABC)**.
Automatic Ballast Sampler (ABS)
(Tradename) A device for rapidly obtaining samples of the **Ballast** and underlying **Formation** without the need for significant excavation. The equipment consists of a hollow steel tube driven into the **Track Bed** by means of a petrol powered reciprocating hammer. At the appropriate depth a flap closes off the end of the tube, allowing the sample to be withdrawn. Sample rates of up to 20 per shift are possible by this means.
Automatic Barrier
[Sig.] A lifting barrier or two **Half Barriers** used to block the highway at a **Level Crossing (LC, LX)** when a **Train** is approaching.
Automatic Barrier Crossing (ABX)
Automatic Barrier Crossing Locally Monitored (ABCL)
An **Automatic Level Crossing** fitted with pairs of **Half Barriers** and traffic lights on the highway, at which the correct operation of the Crossing is monitored by the **Train** driver.

Automatic Brake
[TRS]
a) See **Air Brake**
b) See **Vacuum Brake**
c) The requirement for continuous Automatic Brakes was made compulsory by Act of Parliament in 1889, after many serious accidents. See also **AFI**, **Armagh Accident**.

Automatic Brake Application
A brake application made without the intervention of the driver, either through the parting of the **Brake Pipe** or by the action of a safety system such as the **Automatic Warning System** (**AWS**), **Driver's Vigilance System** (**DVS**), **Tilt and Speed Supervision** (**TASS**), Train **Protection and Warning System** (**TPWS**) or a **Trainstop**.

Automatic Code Insertion (ACI)
[Sig.] A feature of **Integrated Electronic Control Centre** (**IECC**) □ **Signalling Systems** whereby the next working of a **Terminating Train** is automatically identified by the Signalling System.

Automatic Coupling
[TRS] A device for connecting together adjacent **Rail Vehicles** with a minimum of operator input. Electrical and **Automatic Brake** connections are also often made simultaneously, and the assembly acts as the **Buffers** for both vehicles. Types include **Buck Eye**, **Scharfenberg** and **Wedgelock**. Also Autocoupler.

Automatic Dropping Device (ADD)
[TRS] A system fitted to **Pantographs** that lowers the Pantograph if its minimum or maximum height limits are exceeded or if the contact strip becomes damaged. This reduces the damage caused to the **Overhead Line Equipment** (**OLE**) by rogue Pantographs. See also **Dewirement**.

Automatic Function
[Sig.] A **Signalling Function** which is normally operated automatically by the passage of **Trains** and is not **Interlocked** with any other Signalling Function. The function is generally associated with and supervised by a particular **Signal Box**, unless local monitoring is provided.

Automatic Half Barrier Crossing (AHBC)
An **Automatic Level Crossing** fitted with **Half Barriers**, traffic lights on the highway and a telephone to the relevant **Signal Box** (**SB**). The correct operation of the Crossing is monitored by the **Signaller**.

Automatic Level Crossing
Any **Level Crossing** where the warning to highway users and pedestrians is given automatically, triggered by the approach of a **Train** and the Crossing is not Interlocked with any **Protecting Signals**. This includes **Automatic Half Barrier Crossing** (**AHB**, **AHBC**), **Automatic Barrier Crossing Locally Monitored** (**ABCL**), **Automatic Open Crossing Locally Monitored** (**AOCL**), **Automatic Open Crossing Remotely Monitored** (**AOCR**), Crossing with red and green warning lights (**R/G**) and **Miniature Stop Light** (**MSL**) Crossings.

Automatic Lining Control (ALC)
[PW] A system fitted to some **Tamping and Lining Machines** (**Tampers**) that makes adjustments to the **Lining** system according to a **Design Alignment**. Abbreviated from the German term A̲utomatischer L̲eitcomputer.

Automatic Lower
See **Auto Lower**.

Automatic Mode
[LUL] The normal driving mode when the **2009 Tube Stock** is in **Passenger Service**. The **Train** accelerates and brakes automatically once the **Train Operator** has pressed the start buttons after the Train's doors have been closed.

Automatic Open Crossing Locally Monitored (AOCL)
A **Level Crossing** (**LC**, **LX**) with road traffic lights but without **Barriers**, that is equipped with a flashing white light which is observed by the **Train** driver to confirm that the traffic lights are functioning before the Train proceeds over the Crossing.

Automatic Open Crossing Locally Monitored plus Barriers (AOCL+B)
A development of a **Automatic Open Crossing Locally Monitored** (**AOCL**) **Level Crossing** (**LC**, **LX**) in which Half Barriers are added.

Automatic Open Crossing Remotely Monitored (AOCR)
A **Level Crossing** (**LC**, **LX**) without **Barriers** but equipped with road traffic lights on the highway and a telephone to the relevant **Signal Box** (**SB**), from which the correct functioning of the crossing system is monitored.

Automatic Power Control (APC)
[Elec.] On **AC Electrified Lines**, a system that disconnects the **Traction Power** systems of a **Train** as it passes through a **Neutral Section** (**NS**) to prevent arcing. From a **Permanent Way** (**PW**) point of view, the system consists of two pairs of large permanent magnets fitted to the **Sleeper Ends**, one pair each side of the **Insulated Section**. The first pair disconnects the traction system, the second pair re-activating these systems.

Automatic Power Control Magnet
Automatic Power Control Track Inductor
[Elec.] The full title for the large permanent magnets fitted to the **Sleeper Ends** that activate the **Automatic Power Control** (**APC**) system on passing **Electric Locomotives** and **Electric Multiple Units** (**EMU**).

Automatic Raise
[Sig.] A function fitted to **Level Crossings** (**LC**, **LX**) that are **Monitored** (such as **CCTV** types) and have **Full Barriers**, which starts the raising sequence as soon as the **Train** has passed. The system can be suppressed if two or more Trains are expected in rapid succession. Commonly contracted to **Auto Raise**. See also **Another Train Coming**.

ELLIS' BRITISH RAILWAY ENGINEERING ENCYCLOPÆDIA

Automatic Resetting and Restoration to Service
[Sig.] A self-checking process which, with no action by the **Signaller** or engineer, ensures **Correspondence** between the **Signalling System** and the actual state of the **Railway**.

Automatic Route Setting
Automatic Route Setting Subsystem (ARS)
[Sig.] A computer system capable of setting **Routes** for **Trains** based on **Train Reporting Number**, **Timetable** (**TT**) information and **Traffic Regulating Rules** such as priorities of different **Classes** of **Train**. The system can operate without the intervention of the **Signaller**, or it can be used to suggest Routes which the Signaller then authorises.

Automatic SDO
Automatic Selective Door Opening
[TRS] A type of **Selective Door Opening** (**SDO**) fitted to some **Trains** which prevents some **Power Operated Doors** at one or both ends of the Train from opening at **Stations** where the **Platforms** are too short for the Train. Generally utilising **Global Positioning System** (**GPS**) data to identify which Platform is which, the system is not in widespread use. See also **Manual SDO**, **Manual Selective Door Opening**.

Automatic Signal (Auto, Auto Signal)
a) [RB] A **Signal** operated by the passage of **Trains**. The **Signaller** or a person operating a **Signal Post Replacement Switch** can place some Automatic Signals to **Danger**.
b) [Sig.] A **Colour Light Signal** that changes its **Aspect** automatically based on occupation and clearance of certain **Track Circuits** (**TC**) □ **Beyond** it, without intervention by a **Signaller**. The Signaller or a person operating a Signal Post Replacement Switch can place some Automatic Signals to **Danger**. See **Automatic Working**. See also **Controlled Signal**, **Passable Signal**, **Semi-automatic Signal**
c) [LUL] On a **Line** equipped to support **Automatic Train Operation** (**ATO**) a Colour Light Signal which shows a **Red Aspect** following the passage of a **Train**. It can revert to either a Green Aspect when the Line Beyond is **Clear**, or a **Lunar White** Aspect when it is safe for Trains with ATO to pass.

Automatic Speed Control
[TRS] A system which can be engaged by the driver once a certain speed is reached and which will maintain that speed automatically by varying the **Traction Power** applied. Analogous to 'cruise control' in a car.

Automatic Tamping and Lining Machine
[PW] The full title for what is almost universally called a **Tamper**.

Automatic Track Alignment (ATA)
[BR PW] A computer system used to measure, design, implement and audit alignment schemes on **Tampers**. Developed by **British Rail Research** (**BRR**) as an add-on to the existing Tamper fleet, the system uses the **Lining** system to record **Versines** during a measurement run, designs these against known parameters (including **Tied Points**) and automatically adjusts the **Lining Wire** during implementation. As the system is not limited to the length of the Lining Wire, it is better at removing long wavelength **Alignment** errors than the averaging system or **Four Point Lining** normally used. Used in conjunction with regular fixed references (such as **Overhead Line Structures**, see **Running Edge Face of Steel** (**REFOS**)) the system can return the **Track** to its designed Alignment. See also **ATTA**. Also known as **Automatic Track Design** (**ATD**).

Automatic Track and Top Alignment (ATTA)
[BR, PW] A development of **Automatic Track Alignment** (**ATA**), a computer system used to measure, design, implement and audit horizontal and vertical **Maintenance** schemes on **Tampers**.

Automatic Track Design (ATD)
See **Automatic Track Alignment** (**ATA**)

Automatic Track Warning System (ATWS)
A type of **Lineside** warning system that can be installed at a site of work to detect an approaching **Train** and alert personnel who are **On or Near the Line**. Such systems operate independently of the **Signalling System**. They may be installed temporarily for the period of work or it may be installed permanently at a location. See also **Lookout Operated Warning System** (**LOWS**), **Train Operated Warning System** (**TOWS**).

Automatic Train Announcement System (ATAS)
A system that is capable of detecting **Approaching Trains** based on **Track Circuit** (**TC**) information, identifying them based on **Train Describer** (**TD**) data, determining destinations and stopping points from **Timetable** (**TT**) data and making relevant announcements to waiting **Passengers** using pre-recorded messages.

Automatic Train Control (ATC)
a) [Sig. Obs.] Alternative name for the now obsolete contact-based system used on the former Great Western Railway (**GWR**), bearing some similarities of operation to the non-contact **Automatic Warning System** (**AWS**), which was developed from it. See also **Hudd Inductive Automatic Warning System**
b) A generic description of automated systems that support or replace the driver's control of the **Train**
c) A combination of **Automatic Train Operation** (**ATO**) and **Automatic Train Protection** (**ATP**).

Automatic Train Operation (ATO)
[DLR, LUL] A system of **Train** control that dispenses with need for the driver and controls the Train via **Lineside** equipment such **Balises** or data encoded into **Track Circuits** (**TC**). The Docklands **Light Railway** (**DLR**) and the **London Underground Limited** (**LUL**) Victoria and Jubilee Lines are operated on this system. See also **Driverless Train Operation** (**DTO**).

31

ELLIS' BRITISH RAILWAY ENGINEERING ENCYCLOPÆDIA

Automatic Train Protection (ATP)
[Sig.] A communication and control system which utilises **Lineside** equipment (such as **Balises**) to transmit **Permissible Speed** (PS) and **Signal** □ **Aspect** information to **Trains**. Since the **Signalling System** tells the Train how fast it may proceed at any given point, the system is capable of taking control from the driver and applying the brakes automatically should the driver attempt to exceed the **Safe Speed**. See **Automatic Train Control** (ATC).

Automatic Train Regulation (ATR)
[LUL] The automatic intervention through the **Train** Service control system to vary the speed or departure time of Trains so as to optimise the **Headway** between Trains according to a predetermined strategy;

Automatic Train Reporting (ATR)
[Sig.] An electronic system for reporting **Train** movements based on the passage of **Train Reporting Numbers** through a **Train Describer** (TD).

Automatic Train Supervision (ATS)
[Sig.] A system within an **Automatic Train Control** (ATC) system which monitors the system and provides the appropriate controls to direct the operation of **Trains**, to maintain intended traffic patterns and minimize **Train Delays**

Automatic Vehicle Identification (AVI)
a) A system which identifies **Rail Vehicles** by reading data automatically transmitted from the Train to a trackside receiving point.
b) [BR Obs.] A system fitted to **Merry-Go Round** (MGR) **Wagons** that allowed their movements to be traced.

Automatic Warning System (AWS)
[Sig.] A system that provides audible and visual warnings to the driver **on the Approach To** □ **Signals**, certain **Level Crossings** and **Emergency Speed Restrictions** (ESR), **Temporary Speed Restrictions** (TSR) and **Warning Indicators** (WI).
Signalling Symbols:

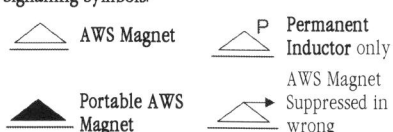

△ AWS Magnet

△P Permanent Inductor only

▲ Portable AWS Magnet

△→ AWS Magnet Suppressed in wrong direction

△ Selective Suppression

△TEST Shed Test Magnet

The system consists of a fail-safe arrangement of a **Permanent Magnet** and an electro-magnet placed in the **Fourfoot**. The Permanent Magnet on its own sets the **Sunflower** to all black. If an active electromagnet is presented within a second (indicating a Signal showing a **Proceed Aspect**), the Sunflower will remain black and a bell (or similar chime) will sound. If an active electromagnet is not presented within the second, (Indicating a **Caution Aspect**, **Stop Aspect** or Warning Indicator) a horn or klaxon will sound and the Sunflower will rotate to show yellow spokes. Failure to acknowledge this horn or klaxon will apply the **Train Brake**. The system suffers from two serious flaws; since all **Main Signals** are fitted with AWS, a driver can become oblivious to the actual actions required, and the other that there is no differentiation between **Caution Aspects** and **Stop Aspects**. Developed in the late 1940s from the **Great Western Railway's** (GWR) □ **Automatic Train Control** (ATC) system and the **Hudd Inductive Automatic Warning System**. See also **Train Protection and Warning System** (TPWS).

Automatic Warning System Cancelling Indicator
[Sig.] A **Lineside Sign** that advises the driver to disregard the **Automatic Warning System** (AWS) indication they have just received, as it applies only to **Movements** made in the other direction.

Automatic Warning System Gap (AWS Gap)
[Sig.] A length of **Track** not equipped with **Automatic Warning System** (AWS) in an otherwise equipped **Route**. This is often found in complex **Station** areas. The start of such a Gap is marked by round white sign with the letters AWS crossed diagonally in red.
The end of the Gap is denoted by a square white sign bearing the letters AWS.

Automatic Warning System Magnet

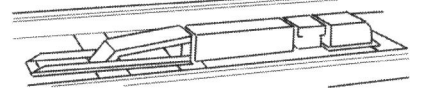

[Sig.] The **Automatic Warning System** (AWS) equipment fixed to the **Track** in the centre of the **Fourfoot**, normally 180 metres on the approach to a **Signal**, which activates the vehicle mounted equipment of passing **Trains**. The system consists of two parts:
• A **Permanent Magnet**. This produces a **Danger** indication in the **Driving Cab**, sounding a horn and turning the Sunflower to show yellow. The driver has five seconds to acknowledge this warning or the brakes will automatically be applied. Installations of a Permanent Magnet only are used with **Emergency Indicators** (EI) and certain **Warning Indicators** (WI)
• An electro-magnet which is energised only when the associated Signal is showing a **Proceed Aspect**. This electro-magnet cancels the Permanent Magnet out and gives a warning indication to the driver. This arrangement is **Fail Safe**, as a power failure leads to a Danger indication being given. Often shortened to **AWS Magnet**.

Automatic Working
[Sig.]
a) Describing **Colour Light Signals** set to operate based on occupation and clearance of certain **Track Circuits** (**TC**) □ **Beyond** without intervention by a **Signaller**. The diagrams below illustrate the passage of a **Train** through a series of **Three Aspect Colour Light Signals**, all of them Automatic:

⊢○○⊖	⊢○○⊖	⊢○○⊖
⊢⊕○○	⊢○○⊖	⊢○○⊖
⊢⊕○○	⊢○○⊖	⊢○○⊖
⊢⊕○○	⊢⊕○○	⊢○○⊖
⊢○⊘○	⊢⊕○○	⊢○○⊖
⊢○⊘○	⊢⊕○○	⊢⊕○○
⊢○○⊖	⊢○⊘○	⊢⊕○○

See also **Automatic Signal, Semi, Semi-automatic Signal**.
b) A **Control Function** that enables a **Controlled Signal** to operate as an Automatic Signal.

Automatically Tensioned System (ATS)
[Elec.] An arrangement of **Overhead Line Equipment** (**OLE**) where the tension in the **Catenary** is maintained automatically by **Balance Weights** or springs. Also referred to as **Auto-tensioned**, **AT Equipment**. See also **Balance Weight Anchor** (**BWA**).

Autonormalisation
Autonormalisation of Points
[Sig.] A **Signalling Control** that returns the **Points** (**Switches**) on a **Route** to their **Normal** lie once the Route over them is **Cleared**. Commonly contracted to **Auto-normalise**. Also **Self-restored Points**, **Self-normalising Points**.

Auto-normalise
See **Autonormalisation**, **Autonormalisation of Points**.

Auto-tensioned (AT)
See **A**utomatically **T**ensioned System.

Auto-tensioner
[Elec.] A device which maintains the **Catenary** and **Contact Wire** (**CW**) of the **Overhead Line Equipment** (**OLE**) at a constant tension by compensating for thermal expansion and contraction over a specified range of temperatures. See also **Balance Weight**.

Auto-train
[TRS WR Hist.] The Great Western Railway (**GWR**) name for a **Train**, powered by a **Steam Locomotive**, which may be driven with the **Locomotive** either hauling or **Propelling** one or more **Coaches**. When Propelling, the Train is driven from a compartment at the front of the leading Coach, where the major driving controls are duplicated. Known on other **Railways** as a **Push-Pull Train**. See also **Driving Van Trailer** (**DVT**).

Autotransformer (AT)
[Elec.] A type of **Transformer** with a single winding and multiple output **Taps**, and is capable of producing an output voltage higher or lower than the input. Used as part of the **Autotransformer System** (**AT, AT System**).

Autotransformer System (AT, AT System)

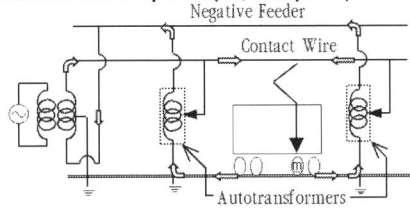

[Elec.] Suffering the lowest voltage drop compared with the **Booster Transformer System** (**BT**) and **Simple Feeding System**, this arrangement uses **Autotransformers** and an additional **Negative Feeder** to maintain the correct **Contact Wire** (**CW**) voltage. As the **Train** draws current, the voltage of the Contact Wire drops and this is automatically compensated for by the Autotransformers as they use the Negative Feeder to source additional current.

Auxiliary
[Sig.] A duplicate lamp or filament on hot or cold standby.

Auxiliary Catenary
Auxiliary Catenary Wire
[Elec.] In a three wire **Catenary** system, this is the middle bare stranded conductor, between the **Catenary Wire** and **Contact Wire** (**CW**). See **Intermediate Catenary Wire**.

Auxiliary Feeder (AF)
[Elec.] An additional conductor connecting a **Feeder Station** (**FS**) to an **Overhead Line Electrification** (**OLE**) system, provided to bypass a location where **Catenary** would impose a current constraint.

Auxiliary Power Circuit
[TRS] An electrical circuit at **Traction Supply** potential used to power electrical equipment other than the **Traction** system.

Auxiliary Reservoir
[TRS] A pressure vessel fitted to an **Air Braked** vehicle, which stores compressed air to supply the brake cylinders when required. See also **Distributor**, **Triple Valve**.

Auxiliary Supply
A low voltage electrical supply provided for control purposes or for the maintenance of essential services in the event of main supply failure.

Auxiliary Supply Point (ASP)
[EP] A location from which a **Signalling Power Supply** can be supplied in the event of the failure of the **Principal Supply Point** (**PSP**).

Auxiliary Token Instrument
[Sig.] An additional **Token Instrument** located at the end of a **Token Section** but away from the **Signal Box**, its purpose being to allow prompt issue and return of **Tokens**.

33

AVA
See Automated Voice Announcer.
AVACS
Aire Valley Control System.
Availability
The percentage of the total time an Asset or system is functional and ready to be used.
AVB
Automatic Vacuum Brake.
AVC
Automatic Vehicle Classification.
AVCS
Advanced Vehicle Control Systems.
Average Gradient
[Sig.] The average calculated Gradient between two Indicators or Signals, used to determine Braking Distances (BD).
Average Size Wheel
[TRS] A Rail Wheel with a diameter half way between that of a new Wheel and a scrap Wheel.
Averaging Out
[PW] Correcting Alignment Variations over a short length of Track by a process of averaging the errors. See also Regulating Versines.
AVI
See Automatic Vehicle Identification.
AVL
Automatic Vehicle Location.
AVM
Automatic Vehicle Monitoring.
Avoiding
Avoiding Line
A Line or Track provided to allow traffic to pass around a Station or other bottleneck. Also Independent Line.
AvON
(Tradename) Aerial View of the Network, an Atkins product.
AVS
AVS Survey
AVS Validation Survey
Alignment Validation Survey.
AvS
[NR PW] Denotes 113A □ Flat Bottom (FB) □ Shallow Depth Switches, length A.
AW
The ATOC code for Arriva Trains Wales (ATW).
AWAC
(ay-wack) Alumaweld Aluminium Conductor, a type of Catenary Wire (CW) manufactured from a central stainless steel core surrounded by aluminium strands. The stainless steel provides the strength, and the aluminium gives good electrical conductivity.
AWB
a) See Advance Warning Board
b) [Hist.] Apply Wagon Brakes.

AWG
a) Adhesion Working Group
b) American Wire Gauge.
AWI
[Sig.] Advance Warning Indicator, see Warning Indicator (WI).
AWIC
Audible Warning Isolating Cock.
AWS
a) See Automatic Warning System
b) Auxiliary Wayside System.
AWS Gap
See Automatic Warning System Gap.
AWS Magnet
See Automatic Warning System Magnet.
AXC
Shorthand for Arriva Cross Country, A Train Operating Company (TOC).
AXIAT
[NR] Assessment of Crossing Alternatives Tool, used to facilitate the closure process for public road Level Crossings.
Axiom Rail
(Tradename) Part of the DB Schenker (DBS) group of companies, including acquisitions such as Marcroft Engineering and Probotec.
Axle Brush
[TRS] The device that provides a path for the Traction Return Current from the Traction Motors to the axles of an Electric Locomotive or Electric Multiple Unit (EMU).
Axle Counter
[Sig.] A Track-mounted device that accurately counts passing axles. By using an Axle Counter Evaluator (ACE) to compare the number of axles entering and leaving an Axle Counter Section, the Signalling System can determine whether the section is Clear or Occupied. In this respect it is analogous to a Track Circuit (TC). Installation of Axle Counters is less involved than that for Track Circuits, and they function irrespective of Rail Head Conditions, type of Train, etc. making them ideal for areas such as lightly trafficked Branch Lines.

Signalling Plan Symbol
Axle Counter Evaluator (ACE)
[Sig.] An electronic processor that receives data from several Axle Counters and decides whether an Axle Counter Section is Clear (or Blocked) on the basis of the number of Axles counted into the Section equalling (or not equalling) the number of Axles counted out of the Section. The output of this device is used as the input to the Interlocking, which, together with routing and Point Detection data, is used as the basis for the Signal Aspects displayed to the driver.
Axle Counter Head
[Sig.] See Counting Head.

ELLIS' BRITISH RAILWAY ENGINEERING ENCYCLOPÆDIA

Axle Counter Section
[Sig.] A section of **Track** between adjacent **Axle Counters** which can normally only be occupied by one **Train** at a time.

Axle End Cap
[TRS] A cover fitted to the end of an axle with screws and which holds the axle bearing in place.

Axle Guard
[TRS] The part of a **Rail Vehicle** □ **Frame** in which the **Axle Box** slides up and down.

Axle Hung
[TRS] Describing a **Traction Motor** whose whole weight is carried on the axle it drives. Mechanically simple, such an arrangement has a high **Un-sprung Mass** and imposes massive impact forces on the **Track** at high speed. See also **Nose Hung**.

Axle Weight
[TRS] The loading imposed on the **Track** by a given axle on a **Train**. See also **Maximum Axle Load**.

Axlebox
[TRS] The axle bearing housing which connects the **Wheelset** to a **Rail Vehicle** via the **Primary Suspension**. There is one Axlebox at each end of a Wheelset.

Axlebox Horn
[TRS] The vertical guide placed either side of an **Axlebox** to restrain it laterally but permit vertical movement of the axle.

Axon, John, GC
(1900 -1957) driver from Stockport who died while trying to stop a **Runaway** □ **Freight Train** on a 1 in 58 **Gradient** near Buxton in Derbyshire after a brake failure. The crew of the **Banking Engine** at the rear of his **Train** were unaware of the problems and kept pushing Driver Axon's Train towards Dove Holes summit. Driver Axon told his **Fireman**, Scanlon, to jump off and try to apply the **Wagon** brakes, but he only managed to apply a few before the train passed the summit and began accelerating down the Gradient towards Chapel-en-le-Frith. Aware of the danger that his train posed he stayed on the footplate. Warned by the **Signaller** at Dove Holes, **Station** staff were able to evacuate a two **Car DMU**, but did not have time to warn the crew of a Freight Train. Axon's Train smashed into it killing both the **Guard** and Axon himself. Axon was posthumously awarded the George Cross.

AZ
[RT Hist.] Anglia **Zone**, see **Railtrack** (**RT**).

B

B
a) [NR] As the last letter in a **Wagon** □ **CARKND**, this denotes that the Wagon has **Air Brakes** and **Through Piping** for **Vacuum Braking** that does not operate the vehicle brakes. Also known as Air Brake, Vacuum Piped. See **Engineering Vehicles**
b) [NR] As the first letter in a Wagon CARKND, it indicates that the vehicle is a steel carrier with **Bogies**
c) See **Switch Letters**
d) [Sig.] On a **Signalling Circuit Diagram**:
- A connection to the positive **DC** busbar
- As one of the leading letters of an **Equipment Code**, it means **b**lock, **b**olt or **B**ack Contact for a **Relay**
- As the last letter of an Equipment Code, it means **B**lock Instrument
e) The letter represented by **Bravo** in the **Phonetic Alphabet**
f) [TRS] Denoting two **Driven Axles**, See **Diesel and Electric Locomotive Notation**
g) [Sig.] The **Normal** □ **Checklock** position, see NBDR
h) **Common Interface File Operating Characteristics Code** for **Vacuum Braked**
i) [LUL] The **B**akerloo **Line**.
j) [NR] Under the **Bridge Condition Marking Index** (**BCMI**) handbook, shorthand for brickwork, masonry, unreinforced concrete and concrete linings.

B Contact
[Sig.] See **Back Contact**.

B Leg
[Sig.] The second data or signal route in a **Diversely Routed System**. See also **A Leg**.

B Stock
[LUL] The original wooden stock introduced on the District Railway for its **Main Line** □ **Electrification** in 1905. It was developed from the trial A Stock and originally comprised 420 cars formed into seven-**Car** trains. Some lasted into the 1940s.

B&C
[NR] **B**uildings and **C**ivils.

B&F
[IÉ] **B**uildings and **F**acilities.

B&MR
[Hist.] The Pre-**Grouping B**recon & **M**erthyr **Railway**.

B&R
Breakdown & **R**ecovery.

B1

B1 Bogie
[BR TRS] The first **British Rail** standard **Bogie** which used a fabricated steel frame and leaf spring **Primary Suspension**.

B2BC
See **B**ack **to B**ack **C**antilevers.

B4

B4 Bogie
[BR TRS] Introduced in 1963 this standard **British Rail** □ **Bogie** reverted to the fabricated steel frame of the B1 Bogie, but had improved coil spring **Primary Suspension**. Fitted as standard to the then new **Mark II Coach**.

BA
a) An abbreviation of **B**essemer **A**cid, a smelting process for **Rail Steel**
b) **B**ritish **A**ssociation Standard thread. A thread form used on small (< 6mm) diameter screws, studs and nuts usually associated with electrical connections. Based upon the Swiss or Thury thread.

BA&CLR
[Hist.] The **Pre-Grouping B**ere **A**lston & **C**alstock **Light Railway**, owned by the Plymouth, Devonport & South Western Junction **Railway**.

BAA
An acronym representing a **Container** □ **Van** British **A**irports **A**uthority.

BABT
British **A**pproved **B**oard for **T**elecommunications.

Back
[PW] An alternative for **Crossing Heel**.

Back 'un
[Col.] A **Distant Signal**

Back Blinder
See **Blinder**. Also **Blinker**.

Back Board
[Sig.]
a) A white board placed behind a **Semaphore Signal** □ **Arm** to improve its visibility. The term is also applied to the black board placed behind a **Colour Light Signal** for the same purpose. See also **Sighting Board**.
b) A term for a **Distant Signal**, found on the areas once controlled by the Great Northern **Railway** (**GNR**) and **Great Western Railway** (**GWR**).

Back Contact
[Sig.] The contact at the rear of a **Signalling** □ **Relay** that is made when the Relay is **Released** and broken when the Relay is **Operated**. The opposite is **Front Contact**.

Back Crossing
[PW] The **Common Crossing** in the **Diamond Crossing** of a **Double Junction** that is furthest from the **Junction** □ **Switches**.

Back Drive
[PW, Sig. Col.] See **Supplementary Drive**. Also **Backdrive**.

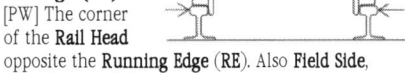

Back Edge (BE)
[PW] The corner of the **Rail Head** opposite the **Running Edge (RE)**. Also **Field Side**, **Outside Edge (OE)**.

Back Edge Corner
[PW] The curved profile of the **Rail Head** between **Running Surface** and **Back Edge (BE)** or **Outside Edge (OE)**.

Back Face
[PW] The vertical surface of the **Rail Head** directly below the **Back Edge** (BE) and the opposite of side of the Rail Head from the **Running Face**.

Back Feed
[Sig.] An unintentional current running through a circuit as a result of an uncontrolled operation of equipment.

Back Fishbolt Hole
[PW] The **Fishbolt Hole** furthest from the **Rail End**. Also **Back Hole**.

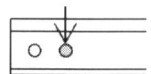

Back Hole
See **Back Fishbolt Hole**.

Back Hole Drilling
[PW] A **Rail End** where only the **Back Fishbolt Hole** has been drilled. This is common practice for Rail Ends that will be temporarily **Fishplated** but will then be permanently joined using an **Alumino-thermic Weld** later. By only drilling the **Back Holes**, no **Cropping** of the Rail End is required prior to welding. See also **Back Hole Fishing**.

Back Hole Fishing
[PW] The action of only fitting **Fishbolts** to the holes furthest from the **Rail End**, generally as a temporary measure. See also **Back Hole Drilling**.

Back Light
See **Backlight**.

Back of Head
[PW] An alternative term for the **Back Face** of a Rail, the opposite to the **Running Face**.

Back of Platform Fence
Back of Platform Wall
A fence or wall constructed to mark the rear of a **Side Platform**, generally because there is a either another **Track**, a large drop or a public thoroughfare behind the **Platform** itself.

Back Platform
[Col.] An outermost **Platform** of a **Station** that has many Platforms.

Back Rails
[PW]
a) Additional lengths of **Rail** in a **Switch Diamond** (SD) used to permit the transfer of stresses between **Wing Rail** and **Switch Rails**
b) The machined **Rails** attached to very **Flat □ Common Crossings**
c) [Col.] Alternative term for **Stock Rails**.

Back Road
[Col.]
a) A **Diversionary Route**
b) The **Siding** furthest from a **Main Line**.

Back Shift
[Col.] A late (afternoon and evening) shift, or the last shift in a **Possession**.

Back Slotting
[Sig.] An arrangement in **Semaphore Signalling** where the **Outer Distant Signal** is **Slotted** by the **Stop Signal** on the same post as the **Inner Distant Signal** that is **Beyond** and by the Stop Signal immediately above. This prevents the Outer Distant Signal from clearing when the Stop Signal above is cleared for a **Move** up to the **Section Signal**.

Back Spectacle
See **Backlight**.

Back Tie
The rod connecting an **Anchor** to an Anchor Structure. See also **Tied Anchor**.

Back to Back Cantilevers (B2BC)
[Elec.] Two **Cantilevers** mounted on opposite sides of one **Overhead Line Mast** (OLE Mast).

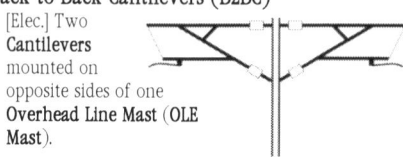

Back to Back Crossovers

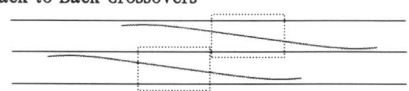

[PW] Two **Crossovers** where the **Through Bearers** (or **Long Timbers**) of one are adjacent to the Through Bearers of the next. See also **Follow-on Crossovers**, **Toe to Toe Crossovers**.

Back to Back Dimension
a) The distance between the backs of the **Flanges** on a railway vehicle **Wheelset**
b) The distance between adjacent **Rails** of adjacent **Tracks**, measured from **Outside Edge** (OE) to Outside Edge. From **Back Edge** (BE), the alternative term for the Outside Edge.

Back to Back Leads

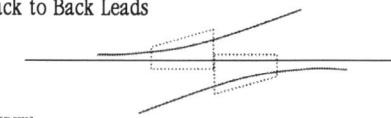

[PW]
a) An arrangement of two **Leads** or **Turnouts** such that the **Through Bearers** or **Long Timbers** of one are adjacent to the Through Bearers or Long Timbers of the next. For this to be the case, one Lead must be a **Trailing Lead** and the other a **Facing Lead**
b) [NPT] An erroneous description of **Switches** placed **Toe to Toe**.

Back to Back Radio
A handheld local radio communication system intended to be used between two people.

Back to Back TTC
Back to Back Twin Track Cantilever

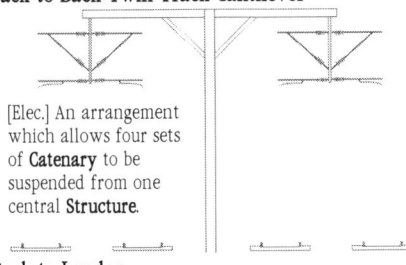

[Elec.] An arrangement which allows four sets of **Catenary** to be suspended from one central **Structure**.

Back to London
Back to Low Mileage

Descriptions of an observer's position in relation to the geography of a **Railway**, i.e. facing away from London or away from the zero **Mile Post**. Also used when describing the **Hands** of **Curves**, London is sometimes replaced with a different city when more relevant, and the reader should remember that the zero Mile Post is not always at the "London" end of the Railway.

Backdrive

[PW, Sig. Col.] See **Supplementary Drive**. Also **Back Drive**.

Backfill

[Civ.] Material placed:
a) To fill a gap between a wall and the adjacent rock face
b) Between a **Structure** and the side of an excavation
c) Or replaced in an excavation.

Backing Up

[PW] The action of butting a new **Rail** up end to end with an existing **Rail** already in-situ.

Backlight

[Sig.] A small lens on the rear of a **Semaphore Signal** that allows the **Signaller** to see that the lamp is **Alight** and the **Signal** is **On**. Also **Back Light, Blinder**.

Backlock

[Sig.] A **Locking** function in a **Mechanical Interlocking** which locks the **Lever** in the **Reverse** position. See **Backlocking**.

Backlocked

[Sig.] Describing a **Lever** that is locked in the **Reverse** position by the **Interlocking**. See **Backlocking**.

Backlocking

[Sig.] The action by the **Interlocking** which prevents the completion of a **Lever** stroke to the **Full Normal** position until the conditions required by the Interlocking are satisfied. See also **Checklocking** and **Indication Locking**.

Backscar

[Civ.] The surface within an **Earthwork** that is left exposed following a **Slip**.

Back-to-back Routes

[LUL] **Routes** which originate from a common **Track** position involving moving forwards to take one Route and in the reverse direction to take the other.

Back-tripped

[LUL] The (generally) unwanted condition created when the rear **Trip Cock** on a **Train** activates the brakes.

BAFE

British Approvals for Fire Equipment.

BAFO

Best and Final Offer.

Bag

[Col.]
a) Term for the flexible hoses used to connect the brake pipes between **Rail Vehicles**
b) In **Steam Locomotive** parlance the leather extension to the discharge pipe of a water tower or water crane, hence "Putting The Bag In"

Baggin

[Col. Arch.] Ones' sandwiches.

Bailey Bridge

Designed by (later Sir) Donald Bailey, a rapidly erected **Temporary** □ **Bridge** structure composed of a kit of standard and interchangeable parts. Originally developed for use in World War Two, but now used to replace collapsed Bridges and provide temporary access. Each element requires no more than eight people to lift and can be connected to form Bridges spanning up to 60m. See also **Military Trestle**.

Baines

[Hist.] Common shorthand for William Baines & Co., a former manufacturer of **Signalling Equipment**.

Bainite
Bainitic

A name for a steel with an intermediate grain structure produced by less rapid cooling of austenitic steel, **Austenite**, than that which produces **Martensite**.

Bainitic Rail

[PW] A **Rail** manufactured to the dimensions of British Standard Specification 11: 1985 but made from Bainitic steel. Bainitic Rails were used in **Switch and Crossing Units (S&C Units)**.

Baker, Sir Benjamin

(1840-1907). Designer of the Forth Bridge and pioneer of **Deep Tube** □ **Underground Railways**.

Balance Plate

See **Equalising Plate**.

Balance Weight

[Elec.] The large weights used to tension the **Catenary** in an **Automatically Tensioned (AT)** □ **Overhead Line Equipment (OLE)** system. Also **Cheese Weights**. See also **Balance Weight Anchor (BWA)**. Also **Auto-tensioner**.

Balance Weight Anchor (BWA)

[Elec.] An **Overhead Line Structure** placed at the ends of a **Tension Length** and provided with **Balance Weights** to tension the **Catenary**.

Balanced Incline
[Hist.] An incline on a **Rope-worked Railway** on which the number of vehicles descending the incline was matched by a similar number of vehicles ascending, both **Sets** being attached to a single rope.

Balanced Maintenance (BM)
[TRS] An additional **Maintenance** examination for **Rail Vehicles** that takes place after a defined mileage or time (e.g. 90,000 miles or two years) which identifies components that require attention or returning to normal condition, eliminating the need for major overhaul during the vehicle's life.

Balanced Semaphore Arm
[Sig.] Alternative for a **Somersault Signal**.

Balanced Stock
[TRS] **Rolling Stock**, especially those with **Bogies**, for which the **Centre Throw** and **End Throw** are equal for a given Radius (**R**) or **Curve**. This configuration is used on LUL □ **Tube Lines**.

Balancing Cant
[PW] An alternative term for **Equilibrium Cant**.

Balancing Speed
[TRS] The speed at which the torque produced by a **DC** □ **Traction Motor** (limited by the supply voltage) equals the rolling resistance of the **Train**. At this speed the Train ceases to accelerate.

Bale
[PW] A short beam with special clamps at each end that allow a **Track Relaying Machine** (**TRM**) to lift a **Track Panel** without the use of chains or straps. The Bale is attached to and is locked onto the **Rail Head** of both **Rails**, and the lifting rope is fixed directly to the Bale. Two Bales are required for one Track Panel, and Track Relaying Machines are normally fitted with such devices. **TRM Beams** for lifting **Sleepers** and some other items of plant and machinery often have suitable short lengths of Rail welded on so that the Bale can be attached and detached quickly.

Balise
[Sig.] A data transmitter located close to the **Track** or in the **Fourfoot** that provides information to passing **Trains**. This information may include **Permissible Speed** (**PS**), **Enhanced Permissible Speed** (**EPS**), **Tilt Authority** and location information. They generally form part of a **Train Control System** (**TCS**), such as **Tilt Authorisation and Speed Supervision System** (**TASS**) and the **European Traffic Control System** (**ETCS**). Also **Eurobalise**.

Balise Encoder Programming and Test Tool (BEPT)
[Sig.] A tool for use with the **Tilt Authorisation and Speed Supervision System** (**TASS**) □ **Track** equipment.

Ball and Claw
[PW] A **Creep Monitor** consisting pair of interlocking castings fitted to an RT60, NR60 or NR56 □ **Switch Half Set** in the **Switch Heel** area to allow accurate longitudinal alignment and retention of the alignment of the **Switch Rail** in relation to the **Stock Rail**. This arrangement is necessary as these Switches do not have **Heel Blocks** or **Stress Transfer Blocks**.

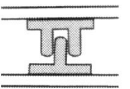

Ballast
a) See **Track Ballast**.
b) Ungraded crushed stone, also known as **Quarry Bottoms**.
c) Large metal or concrete weights used to counterbalance cranes and provide stability to ships.

Ballast Attrition
[PW] The term describing the loss of grading and angularity of **Ballast** caused by **Tampers** and **Trains**. See also **Wet Attrition Value** (**WAV**).

Ballast Bags
[PW] Hessian sacks filled with **Ballast**, used to temporarily support the **Track** or to shore up excavations.

Ballast Basket
[PW Hist.] A large wicker basket carried between two workers and used to transport small quantities of **Ballast**. Now rarely used, they have been rendered largely obsolete by **Ballast Regulators**.

Ballast Bed
See **Bed**.

Ballast Board
a) A board fitted to a **Bridge Deck** to prevent **Ballast** falling through gaps in the structure. Also **Ballast Plate**
b) A pre-cast concrete plank used in many applications where the retention of small quantities of Ballast or other fill material is required.

Ballast Cleaner

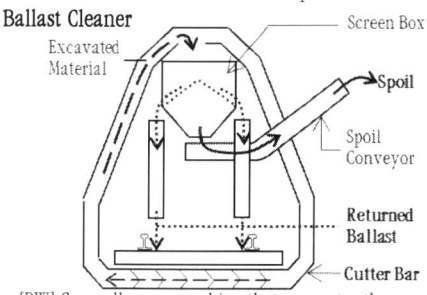

[PW] Generally, any machine that excavates the **Ballast** from under the **Track**, discards the dirt, undersize and oversize pieces, and then returns the good ballast to the Track. Commonly, such devices are self-propelled diesel/hydraulic items fitted with automated depth control. Typical cleaning rates are of the order of 90m (100 **Yards**) per hour for older machines and >180m (200 Yards) per hour for newer types such as the **Medium Output Ballast Cleaner** (**MOBC**) and **High Output Ballast Cleaner** (**HOBC**). Most types can selectively discard all excavated material as spoil, and split the return between under the **Sleepers** and on top of them. Also **Automatic Ballast Cleaner** (**ABC**), **High Output Ballast Cleaning System** (**HOBCS**), Matisa Automatic Ballast Cleaner (**MABC**), Matisa, Plasser Automatic Ballast Cleaner (**PABC**), **Riddler**. A related machine is the **Trac Gopher**.

Ballast Cleaner Ramping

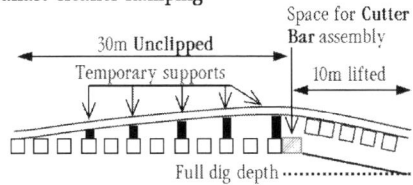

[Diagram: 30m Unclipped, Temporary supports, Space for Cutter Bar assembly, 10m lifted, Full dig depth]

[PW] A method of eliminating steps in the **Formation** at the ends of **Automatic Ballast Cleaner** (**ABC**) sites. The depth of the **Cutter Bar** on a typical ABC is fixed at around 225mm, so the normal method of starting off involves excavating a 300mm deep pit between two **Sleepers** in which the Cutter Bar is assembled. This results in one Sleeper standing on undisturbed and therefore compacted **Ballast**, and the next standing on largely un-compacted new Ballast. Differential settlement **results in a poor Track Quality** (**TQ**) and long-term **Maintenance** issues. Ramping avoids this by starting the Cutter Bar at **Sleeper Bottom** (**SB**) and increasing the **Depth Of Cut** over a length of 10 metres. This is achieved by **Unclipping** the **Rails** for a distance of 30 metres **on the Approach to** the start of work and lifting them onto purpose made supports. This allows the Ballast Cleaner to be driven on and assembled. The other end of the excavation is handled in exactly the same way, but in reverse.

Ballast Cleaner Return

[PW] That part of the material excavated by a **Ballast Cleaner** that is deemed fit to be placed back under the **Track**. This is a grading of material larger than 28mm but no bigger than the original **Ballast**. The remainder is called **Spoil**. Also **Ballast Cleaner Screenings**, Ballast Cleaner Spoil, Returned Ballast. See also **BRAT**.

Ballast Cleaner Screenings
Ballast Cleaner Spoil

[PW] That part of the material excavated by a **Ballast Cleaner** that is deemed unfit to be placed back under the **Track**, and is discarded to waiting **Spoil Wagons** or onto the **Lineside**. Also Spent Ballast.

Ballast Cleaning

[PW] The action of excavating the **Ballast** from under the **Track**, discarding the dirt, undersize and oversize pieces and returning the good Ballast to the Track. This operation used to be performed manually using **Ballast Forks**, but has now largely been mechanised using **Ballast Cleaners**.

Ballast Cleaning System (BCS)

See **High Output Ballast Cleaning System** (**HOBCS**).

Ballast Condition

[PW] A description of the particle size distribution and degree of cleanliness of **Ballast**. New Ballast is almost completely clean and of one nominal particle size. The action of **Trains** and **Tampers** and the ingress of soil and leaves reduce the effectiveness of the Ballast until it becomes a slurry containing small rounded pebbles. A qualitative score can be applied, ranging from one (new) to five (requiring **Renewal**).

Ballast Consolidation

[PW] The process or outcome of compacting the **Ballast** to reduce future settlement and increase the **Lateral Stability** of the **Track**. This consolidation is achieved using vibrating plates (See **Wacker Pack**, **Wacker Plate**) prior to laying the **Track** or using a **Dynamic Track Stabiliser** (**DTS**) afterwards. The passage of **Trains** achieves this result over months.

Ballast Depth

[PW] The depth of the **Ballast**, measured from the **Soffit** (underside) of the **Sleeper**, **Timber** or **Bearer** to the top of the **Formation**. See also **Below Sleeper Bottom** (**BSB**).

Ballast Distribution System (BDS)

[PW] A **Rake** of Octopus (**YDA**) □ **Ballast Hopper** □ **Wagons**, equipped with conveyors allowing them to feed **Ballast** to one end and discharge it. Used to supply additional Ballast to the **High Output Ballast Cleaner** (**HOBC**).

Ballast Drag

[PW Obs.] A large steel frame measuring approximately 10' wide by 14' long (3m by 4.25m) fitted with tines on its lower surface. It was placed under the **Track** and pulled along by a **Locomotive**, the intention being to re-distribute the clean **Ballast** from the **Cribs**. Its passage **Lifted** the Track by some 3" (75mm), and clean Ballast was then unloaded to fill the empty Cribs and to form a **Ballast Shoulder**.

Ballast Fines

[PW] Small particles of **Ballast** broken off by the action of traffic, **Tampers** or other packing activities, or adhering to the ballast following the production process.

Ballast Fork

[PW] A many-tined fork used to extract good re-usable **Ballast** from a mass of excavated material. See also **Ballast Cleaning**.

Ballast Gluing

[PW] Literally, the use of an epoxy resin sprayed over the **Ballast** to improve the **Track's** lateral stability, generally in areas where **Clearances** are critical. See also **Xitrack**.

Ballast Hopper

a) [PW] The **Ballast** storage space on a **Ballast Regulator**
b) [TRS] A **Hopper Wagon** specifically designed to discharge **Ballast** onto the **Track** in a controlled manner. See Autoballaster, Catfish, Dogfish, Octopus, Seacow, Sealion, Stingray, Walrus, Whale.

Ballast Hump

See **Ballast Shoulder Surcharge**.

41

Ballast Memory
[PW] A term used to describe the behaviour of **Track** when the **Top** returns to a previous state following Track works. The underlying mechanism is in fact differential settlement of the disturbed **Ballast**, an effect which may only be avoided by careful attention to excavation depths and **Ballast** thicknesses. Most common is the roller coaster effect produced by laying new **Continuous Welded Rail** (**CWR**) on a **Formation** recently occupied by **Jointed Track**, without adequate **Scarification** or Reballasting. See Also **Cutter Bar Hole**.

Ballast Packing
[PW] The action of placing **Ballast** under **Sleepers** or **Bearers** and consolidating it, either to eliminate **Voids** or to **Lift** the **Track**. The addition of Ballast is done by **Measured Shovel Packing** (**MSP**) or Stoneblowing (**PBI**), the consolidation generally by **Kango Hammer**. The process has also been mechanised, taking the form of a **Tamper**.

Ballast Plate
See **Ballast Board** clause a).

Ballast Plough
[PW, TRS] A device fitted to a **Rail Vehicle** to allow it to redistribute the ballast unloaded from **Hopper Vehicles**. (Vehicles with **Ballast** Ploughs should not be confused with those fitted with **Miniature Snow Ploughs**). See also **Shark** (**ZUV**).

Ballast Profile
[PW] The shape and distribution of **Ballast** across the cross section of the **Railway**. See also **Ballast Shoulder**.

Ballast Pyramid
[PW] An alternative term for a **Ballast Stool**.

Ballast Ramp
[PW] A method of eliminating steps in the **Formation** at the ends of **Reballasting** sites by tapering the depth of excavation from zero to full depth over a distance, usually in excess of 5m. **Network Rail** (**NR**) specifies that the Ramp should be of length equal to the highest of the **Permissible Speed** (**PS**) or **Enhanced Permissible Speed** (**EPS**), in miles per hour, divided by six.

Ballast Regulation
[PW] The action of distributing **Ballast** evenly along the **Track**, and to the correct profile across it. Whilst still a manual activity when required, the process has been mechanised, taking the form of a **Ballast Regulator**.

Ballast Regulator
[PW] An **On Track Machine** (**OTM**) used for **Ballast Regulation** (the action of distributing **Ballast** evenly along the **Track**, and to the correct profile across it), using an arrangement of **Ballast Ploughs** and **Brushes**. Some are equipped with a hopper to allow them to remove and relocate excess **Ballast**.

Ballast Resistance
[Sig.] The resistance between the two **Rails** of a **Track Circuit** (**TC**) and comprises leakage between the **Rail Fastenings**, **Sleepers** and **Earth**. The value of this resistance is dependent upon the condition of any **Insulators**, cleanliness of the **Ballast** and the prevailing weather conditions. The ballast resistance is inversely proportional to the length of the Track Circuit and is expressed as ohm kilometres, typical values being in the range 2 to 10Ωkm.

Ballast Retaining Wall
A wall used to retain the **Ballast Profile** at locations where the **Ballast** is subject to erosion or may otherwise be unstable, e.g. where two adjacent **Tracks** are at very different levels and on **Bridges**.

Ballast Return
[PW] A colloquial contraction of **Ballast Cleaner Return**.

Ballast Riddling
[PW, Col., Nth.] See **Riddling**, clause b).

Ballast Shoulder
[PW] The **Ballast** placed at the ends of the **Sleepers**, **Timbers** or **Bearers** to give lateral stability to the **Track**.

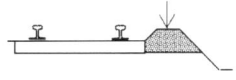

Ballast Shoulder Surcharge
[PW] An oversized **Ballast Shoulder** intended to improve **Lateral Stability**. Also Ballast Hump, Shoulder Hump.

Ballast Sidings
Sidings whose main use is for the loading of **Hoppers** or **Opens** with new **Ballast**.

Ballast Stool
[PW]
a) The **Ballast** that provides support to the **Sleepers**, **Timbers** or **Bearers** of a **Track**. Also **Ballast Pyramid**
b) The small heap of Ballast used to temporarily support a **Track** after excavation of the old Ballast, to allow a **Ballast Hopper** □ **Wagon** to be used to replace the rest of the Ballast. The Track is thus described as being **Up on Stools**. See also **Ballast Bags**

Ballast Tip
[PW] An area adjacent to **Sidings** where **Spoil Wagons** containing spoil and **Spent Ballast** can be unloaded quickly and the **Wagons** returned to use.

Ballast Track
[Obs.] One **Track** of a pair of **Tracks** on a rope or chain worked worked incline used by a set of vehicles ballasted to balance the returning empty vehicles traversing an incline, a practice commonly used in North Wales.

Ballast Train
[Ops.] Strictly speaking an **Engineer's Train** conveying **Ballast** or **Ballast Wagons**, but also commonly used to include all Engineer's Trains.

Ballast Tray
[PW] A shaped metal tray fitted between the **Timbers** or **Bearers** in the **Switch Toe** □ **Bcd** to prevent **Ballast** interfering with the **Switch Operating Mechanism**.

Ballast Wagons
Rail Vehicles built or generally used for carrying Ballast.

Ballast Wall
[Civ.] A wall built on top of the Abutment or Pier of a Bridge to prevent Ballast falling off the structure.

Ballasted Area
[NR] For the purposes of a Lineside vegetation inspection, this is defined as the area between the outside edges of the Ballast Shoulders.

Ballasted Deck
[Civ.] A Bridge Deck that is designed to support and has a layer of Ballast laid on it, onto which the Track is placed. The alternatives are a Direct Fastened Deck, Non-ballasted Deck or Longitudinal Timber Bridge, on which a Ballast layer is not provided.

Ballasted Track
[PW] Track in which the Sleepers are supported by and the inter-Sleeper spaces filled with Ballast. Alternative arrangements are Ballastless Track, Direct Fastened Track, Embedded Track, Grass Track, Longitudinal Timbers, Non-ballasted Track, Paved Track, Slab Track and Street Running Track.

Ballasting
a) [PW] The activity of unloading and / or placing new Ballast onto the Track as part of Track Maintenance activity or following the laying of new Track
b) [PW] The laying of new Ballast into the excavation during Reballasting works
c) The adding of additional mass to a crane counterweight or a ship.

Ballastless Track (BLT)
[PW] Track in which the Sleepers are supported by and the inter-Sleeper spaces filled with something other than Ballast, e.g. in-situ concrete. Also Non-ballasted Track.

Bance Trolley
(Tradename) A Trolley (either motorised or not) manufactured by R Bance & Co Ltd. See also Electric Track Trolley.

Bance Wrench
(Tradename) A variety of Impact Wrench manufactured by R Bance & Co Ltd. This term is also widely used as the generic term for all Impact Wrenches.

Band III
[BR Hist.] The collective name for the VHF frequencies allocated to British Railways (BR), around 200kHz, as part of the National Radio Network (NRN) project. See also BRUNEL.

Banding
[PW]
a) The fitting of tensioned stainless steel straps to Sleeper Ends to delay or arrest their splitting
b) The fitting of tensioned stainless steel straps around piles of Sleepers and Rails placed in the Cess, to prevent their unauthorised movement by vandals
c) The grouping together of certain requirements, often in terms of speed; e.g. one Track Quality Band may cover a range of speed values.

Bang Road
[Col.] Term describing a Movement made in the opposite direction to the normal Signalled Direction. An alternative term for a Wrong Direction Movement.

Bangers
[Col.] A name for Detonators or Railway Fog Signals. Also Crackers, Dets, Foggies, Shots.

Banjo
[Col.]
a) [Sig.] Nickname for a Ground Disc Signal
b) Driver's nickname for certain types of Vacuum Brake valve handle in the Driving Cab, from their shape
c) [PW] A shovel.

Bank
a) A steep Gradient, as in Ais Gill Bank, Camden Bank
b) A contraction of Embankment
c) To assist a Train up a steep Gradient using an extra Locomotive, normally at the rear. See Banker, Banking
d) [Col.] A Cutting □ Slope.

Bank Foot
[Hist.] The lower end of a section of a Rope-Worked Railway operated by a stationary engine.

Bank Head
[Hist.] The upper end of a on a Rope-Worked Railway. Also known as the Bank Top.

Bank Head Man
[Hist.] A person appointed to release Sets of vehicles from the haulage rope of a Rope-Worked Railway following a re-design of the Coupling which allowed the Quoit to be released without the need for a person, a Bank Rider, to ride on the Set.

Bank Seat
[Civ.] A variety of Bridge □ Abutment. Used in cases of low loading, it consists of a mass concrete base that does not extend the whole height of the Bridge.

Bank Slip
[Civ.] The sudden downward movement of an unstable mass of aggregate, rock or soil from the side of an Embankment. This is often triggered by a combination of poor drainage and overloading of the top of the slope with Spoil. See also Cutting Slip, Slip, Slip Circle, Slip Plane.

Bank Top
[Hist.] On a Rope-Worked Railway an alternative for Bank Head.

Bank Trim
An activity which removes surplus material from (generally) a **Cutting** □ **Slope**, either because it has moved, or because additional space is required for the **Track**. See also **Regraded**.

Banker
[Col.] See **Banking Locomotive**.

Banking
Describing a **Locomotive** assisting another **Train** up a steep **Gradient** by **Propelling** it from the rear. Common practice in the days of **Steam Locomotives**, economic pressures and improved Locomotive performance have now rendered Banking virtually obsolete except in times of failure. See also **Assisting in Rear**.

Banking Locomotive
A **Locomotive** engaged in or normally used for **Banking**. Commonly contracted to **Banker**.

Banksman
On a construction site, a person appointed to assist the driver in safely moving or operating an excavator or other large vehicle. This is carried out by observing the rear and sides of the vehicle, any loads on it and persons in the area and communicating as necessary.

Banner
a) [Obs.] A rectangular red cloth hung between two poles across a **Track** during daylight to indicate one end of a **Possession**, see **Possession Limit Board** (PLB)
b) [Sig. Col.] A common contraction of **Banner Repeating Signal** (BR).

Banner Repeater (BR)
See **Banner Repeating Signal** (BR).

Banner Repeating Signal (BR)
[Sig.] A **Signal** provided **On the Approach** to a **Main Signal** to provide an advance warning of the **Aspect** being displayed by the Main Signal. Usually provided where the **Reading Time** of the Main Signal is sub-standard.

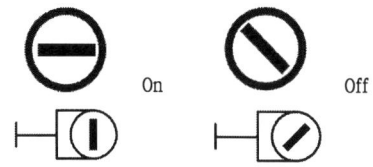

They originally consisted of a backlit circular casing containing a centrally pivoted black bar, but modern types use fibre optics, see **Fibre Optic Banner Repeating Signal**. Historically both **Red** and **Yellow** arms were also used, but black was standardised in 1929. See also **Three State Banner Repeating Signal**.

BAP
Biodiversity Action Plan.

BAPA
(*bappa*) [NR] Basic Access Protection Agreement. Also **Asset Protection Agreement** (APA).

BAR
a) [NR] Under the **Bridge Condition Marking Index** (**BCMI**) handbook, shorthand for **Barrel Arch**
b) Brake Actuate Relay.

Bar
[PW] A steel bar approximately 5 feet (1.5m) long with a straight point on one end and a slightly cranked flattened part at the other. Used widely by **Permanent Way** (**Pway**) staff for a multitude of purposes, it is one of the core tools; see also **Duff Jack**, **Keying Hammer**, **Shovel**. Also **Pinch Bar**, **Point Bar**.

Bar Coupler
Bar Coupling
A bolted, rigid connector between two vehicles of a **Multiple Unit** or **Rake** of certain **Wagons**, fitted instead of a **Coupling**.

Barbel (ZKV)
[NR] A type of **Wagon** used for **Engineering Work**. See **Wagon Names**.

Barbie
[Col.] Nickname for the livery of First Group's bus and rail companies up until Feb 2006, from the purple and pink packaging of Barbie™ dolls.

Bardic Lamp
a) (Tradename) A type of hand signal lamp originally manufactured by Chloride Bardic Ltd., equipped with a rotating filter allowing it to show a white, **Green**, **Yellow** or **Red** light. Used for displaying **Handsignals**.
b) [Col.] Any hand lamp used to display Handsignals.

Bare Feeder (BF)
[Elec.] An un-insulated **Conductor** suspended at height between **Overhead Line Structures** connecting a **Feeder Station** (FS) to a section of **Overhead Line Equipment** (OLE).

Barlow Rail
[PW Hist.] A **Rail Section** designed for **Direct Fastening** to **Longitudinal Timbers**, or directly onto the **Ballast** as originally intended. Developed by **William Henry Barlow** who patented the **Rail** in 1849. Also known as a saddleback Rail.

Barlow, William Henry
(1812-1902). Engineered the Midland Railway (**MR**) from St. Pancras to Bedford, St. Pancras **Station** itself and later he completed the Clifton Suspension **Bridge** in Bristol. Developed the **Barlow Rail** in 1849.

Barrel Arch
An **Arch** whose length is large compared to its **Span**.

Barrier
A gate-like device at a **Level Crossing** (LC, LX) which pivots down about a point at the side of the carriageway in order to close the highway to traffic across its full width when a **Train** is due to pass. See also **Half Barrier**, **Gate**.

Barrier Control Pedestal
[Sig.] A small operating console located in a **Signal Box** (SB), with a view of the **Level Crossing** (LC, LX) it controls.

Barrier Pedestal
[Sig.] The structure supporting a **Barrier** in a **Level Crossing** (**LC**, **LX**) installation and containing the hydraulic equipment used to lift and lower the Barriers. Also **Barrier Unit**. See also **Penguin**, **Western Region Barrier Unit**.

Barrier Skirt
[Sig.] The metal or plastic lattice attached to a **Barrier** at some **Full Barrier** □ **Level Crossings** and designed to reach the ground when the Barriers are in the lowered position. It enables the **Railway** to be effectively fenced off during the passage of **Trains**.

Barrier Unit
[Sig.] An alternative for **Barrier Pedestal**.

Barrier Vehicle
[Ops.] Any vehicle used as a barrier, such as the **Hoppers** of sand placed between **Locomotive** and **Wagons** conveying flasks of nuclear waste. See also **Match Vehicle**.

Barriers Up Indicator
[Sig.] An **Indicator** provided **Beyond** a **Traincrew Operated** (**TMO**) crossing to indicate that the **Barriers** have risen after the passage of the **Train**.

Barrow Crossing
A **Level Crossing** (**LC**, **LX**) provided (often between **Platforms** at **Stations**) for the passage of **Railway** staff, but not the public. Such Crossings are sometimes protected by **White Lights**.

BARS
See **British American Railway Services**.

Bartlett, Charles H
American engineer who further developed the method of **Versines** for realigning **Curves**. See **Hallade**.

Bascule Bridge
An **Underbridge** (**UB**) with a main span generally split into one or two counterweighted sections, each pivoted horizontally at their outer end. When required, the section(s) are rotated upwards to allow the unobstructed passage of (generally) ships. See also **Lift Bridge**, **Swing Bridge**.

Base Rail
[PW]
a) A **Rail** to which a **Fixed Buffer Stop** is attached
b) A **Rail** which carries a **Sliding Buffer Stop**.

Base Station
In a radio system, a local transmitting and receiving station located by the **Lineside**. It is connected to a control point by copper cables or **Fibre Optic Cables** (**FOC**).

Baseband Data Highway
[Sig.] A bidirectional communications link between the **Central Interlocking Processor** of a **Solid State Interlocking** (**SSI**) and the **Trackside Functional Modules** (**TFM**). The Data Highway is operated at the rate of 20kilobits per second and uses a screened twisted-pair cable, duplicated for fault tolerance. See also **Fixed Telecomms Network** (**FTN**), **FTNx**.

Baseplate (BP)
[PW] A generally cast (from lenticular graphite cast iron or spheroidal graphite cast iron), exceptionally rolled or very rarely (in the UK) fabricated steel support for **Flat Bottom Rails** (**FB**). See also **ASP Baseplate**, **BR1 Baseplate**, **Check Baseplate**, **Half Baseplate**, **Mills Baseplate**, **PAN x Baseplate**, **Pandrol Baseplate**, **RCV Baseplate**, **SG Baseplate**, **Slide Baseplate**, **Thick Based Baseplate**, **Two Level Baseplate**, **Universal Baseplate**, **VASP Baseplate**.

Baseplate Gall
[PW] See **Rail Gall**, **Rail Gall** of **Baseplates**.

Baseplate Pad
[PW] A resilient layer fitted between a **Baseplate** (**BP**) and a **Bearer**, typically in **Switch and Crossing Layouts** (**S&C Layouts**) with **Concrete Bearers**.

Baseplate Screw
[PW] See **Chairscrew**.

Baseplate Shims
[PW] Shaped and drilled metal plates (typically available in 1mm increments of thickness up to 25mm) used to correct the **Top** on **Longitudinal Timbers**, etc.

Baseplate Shuffle
[PW] The tendency of inadequately maintained **Baseplates** (**BP**) and **Chairs** on **Long Timbers**, **Switch and Crossing Timbers** and **Wood Sleepers** to move laterally under traffic, so wearing the wood away from under them. Eventually the Baseplate or Chair disappears into the **Sleeper** altogether. See also **Chair Shuffle**.

Basic Visual Track Inspection
[PW] A visual inspection of the **Track**, carried out on foot, which aims to identify any immediate or short term actions that are required. Often referred to as a **Track Patrol**. See also **Patroller**, **Patrolling**.

BASICS
See **British Association for Immediate Care**.

Basil Brush
[Sig. Col.] Nickname for a **Ballast Regulator**.

BASREC
Bridges and **S**tructures **Rec**ord system.

BASS
[BR] **B**ogie **a**nd **S**uspension **S**ection, part of **British Rail's** □ **Derby Research** organisation.

Bass (ZDA)
[NR] A 31.5 ton capacity **Wagon** used for the carriage of general materials. See **Wagon Names**.

Bathymetric Survey
A measured survey of lake, river or ocean floors, usually using depth sounding.

BATNEEC
(*battneek*) [Col.] **B**est **A**vailable **T**echnology **N**ot **E**ntailing **E**xcessive **C**ost.

BATS
Business **A**nalysis of **T**rain **S**ervices.

ELLIS' BRITISH RAILWAY ENGINEERING ENCYCLOPÆDIA

Batter
a) See **Rail End Batter**
b) The sloping face of a **Retaining Wall**
c) [Col.] The slope of a **Cutting** or **Embankment**.

Battered
[Col.] Of a **Passenger Train**, heavily loaded.

Battering
See **Rail End Batter**.

Battersea Park Accident
On the second of April 1937 a busy **Signaller** at Battersea Park **Signal Box** became confused and used the **Emergency Release Key** to override the **Sykes** equipment on the very busy **Four Track Railway** between Clapham Junction and London Victoria. The system was working correctly and his actions allowed the collision of two **Electric Multiple Units** (**EMUs**), killing 10 and injuring 80. This should be a demonstration that *any* safety system in existence can be got round and defeated by human ingenuity.

Battery
[TRS] In a description of a **Passenger Coach** or **Multiple Unit Train** vehicle, it denotes that the vehicle has large batteries slung underneath it to supply electrical power to the **Train**.

Battery Electric Multiple Unit (BEMU)
[TRS] An **Electric Multiple Unit** (**EMU**) powered by a **Battery**. See **Gemini**.

Battery Locomotive
[TRS] A variety of **Electric Locomotive** that runs on rechargeable batteries. Such **Locomotives** are typically used on **Engineering** work on the **Tube Lines** of London Underground Limited (**LUL**).

Battle Deck
[Civ.] A type of **Bridge Deck** consisting of a flat steel plate reinforced with vertical ribs running transversely (and in some cases also longitudinally) beneath.

Battleship Splice

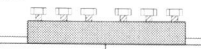

[Elec. Col.] A cast splice used to connect two sections of **Overhead Line Equipment** (**OLE**) **Contact Wire** (**CW**) together end-to-end. The clamp fits into the grove of the contact wire and is secured by bolts tightened down from above. The resulting shape resembles a battleship from the children's game, hence the name.

Baulk Road
[PW Hist.] A form of **Track** construction in which the **Rails** are laid on large **Longitudinal Timbers**, themselves sometimes supported on piles.

Bay
a) [PW] Another term for **Bed**
b) A common contraction of **Bay Line**.

Bay Line
A **Track**, which is not a **Through Line**, at a **Station**, which typically has a **Platform** provided at one or both sides and a **Buffer Stop** at the end.

Bay Platform

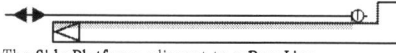

The **Side Platform** adjacent to a **Bay Line**.

BB
a) [PW] An abbreviation of Bessemer Basic, a smelting process used for **Rail Steel**.
b) See **Bearer Bottom**
c) Balfour Beatty.

BB14072
(Tradename) [PW] A 74 **Kilograms per Metre** □ **Rail Section** designed for use with Balfour Beatty's (**BB**) □ **Embedded Slab Track** (**EST**) system. It has a **Rail Profile** at the **Rail Head** compatible with CEN60E1. Also Bbest Rail.

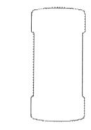

BBASIS
(Tradename) Balfour Beatty Accreditation and Supplier Information System.

Bbest Rail
(Tradename) See BB14072.

BBMS
[LUL] Breakdown Broadcast Messaging System

BBR
(Tradename) Balfour Beatty **Rail**.

BBRM
(Tradename) Balfour Beatty **Rail** □ **Maintenance** Limited.

BBRP
BBRPL
a) (Tradename) Balfour Beatty **Rail** Plant.
b) (Tradename) Balfour Beatty **Rail** Projects Limited.

BBRR
(Tradename) Balfour Beatty **Rail** □ **Renewals**.

BC
Barrow Crossing.

BCAM
[NR] Buildings and **Civils** □ **Asset** Management.

BCF
Bearing Capacity Failure.

Bch.
Common contraction of **Branch Line**.

BCI
[TRS] Brake Control Interlock.

BCK
[TRS] An acronym representing a **Corridor** □ **Brake** □ Composite Coach.

BCL
[TRS] An acronym representing a **Brake** □ Composite **Coach** with Lavatory.

BCMI
See **Bridge Condition Marking Index**.

BCO
[TRS] An acronym representing a **Brake** □ Composite □ **Open Coach**.

BCR
[Hist.] The **Pre-Grouping** Bishop's Castle **Railway**.

46

BCS
See Ballast Cleaning System.

BCT
Buried Concrete Troughing, a type of Cable Route. See Concrete Cable Trough. See also Surface Cable Troughing (SCT).

BCU
[TRS] Brake Control Unit.

BCV
[LUL Hist.] Bakerloo, Central and Victoria, see Metronet Rail.

BD
a) [Sig.] See Braking Distance
b) Buried Direct, a type of Cable Route.

BDB
[TRS] An acronym representing a Battery □ Driving □ Brake □ Coach.

BDBSO
[TRS] An acronym representing a Battery □ Driving Trailer □ Brake □ Standard Class □ Open Coach.

BDM
[RT Hist.] Business Development Manager, a function within Railtrack.

BDMS
[TRS] An acronym representing a Battery □ Driving □ Motor □ Standard Class □ Coach.

BDMSO
[TRS] An acronym representing a Battery □ Driving □ Motor □ Standard Class □ Open Coach.

BDP
Best Demonstrated Practice.

BDS
See Ballast Distribution System.

BDT
[TRS] An acronym representing a Battery □ Driving Trailer □ Coach.

BDTBSO
[TRS] An acronym representing a Battery □ Driving Trailer □ Brake □ Standard Class □ Open Coach.

BDTC
[TRS] An acronym representing a Battery □ Driving Trailer □ Composite Coach.

BDTLV
[TRS] An acronym representing a Battery □ Driving Trailer Luggage Van.

BDTS
[TRS] An acronym representing a Battery □ Driving Trailer □ Standard Class □ Coach.

BDTSO
[TRS] An acronym representing a Battery □ Driving Trailer □ Standard Class □ Open Coach.

BE
[PW] See Back Edge.

Be Ready
[Sig.] The offering of a Train to the Signal Box □ Beyond using the Block Bell. This term probably dates back to some older systems of Block Working, in which the Signaller □ On the Approach stated a Train was coming rather than asking nicely. See Is Line Clear? Also Ask the Road.

Beam
a) See Buffer Beam
b) See Rail Beam
c) See Sleeper Beam
d) [Sig.] Of the light emitted from a Signal, the envelope of space within which the light Intensity is at least 50% of the Intensity on the centre-line at the same distance from the Signal.

Bearer
[PW] A term used to describe a wooden or concrete beam used to support the Track. The term generally applies to long Switch and Crossing (S&C) □ Timbers, Longitudinal Timbers and Waybeams, but can be used to describe any Sleeper used in a Switch and Crossing Layout (S&C Layout).

Bearer Bottom (BB)
[PW] Describing the Soffit (underside) of a Bearer used in Switch and Crossing Units (S&C Units). See also Sleeper Bottom (SB).

Bearer Rake
[PW] The inclination of a Switch and Crossing (S&C) □ Bearer to the horizontal, normally expressed in terms of millimetres over Gauge (analogous to Cant (C,E)). Where all Tracks associated with the Switch and Crossing Unit (S&C Unit) have the same Cant value applied, the Bearer Rake will generally be the same. Where there are different Cant values involved, for instance where Thick Basing is present, Bearer Rake will be some intermediate value, the Cant on the Tracks being achieved using Thick Based Chairs or Thick Based Baseplates. Also known as Timber Rake.

Bearer Wind
[PW] The rate of change of Bearer Rake in a Switch and Crossing Unit (S&C Unit) (analogous to Rate of Change of Cant (RgE)). It is not possible to change the Bearer Rake in an area occupied by Switches or Crossings. Also known as Timber Wind.

Bearing Shelf
[Civ.] Typically a cast concrete unit at the top of an Abutment or Pier which in turn supports the bearings of a Bridge Deck. It is effectively a long Bedstone. See also Cill Beam.

Beater Packing
[PW Obs.] A method of compacting the Ballast beneath the Sleepers by beating it into place by means of a Beater Pick. See also Kango Packing, Measured Shovel Packing (MSP).

Beater Pick
[PW Obs.] A tool similar in appearance to a small pickaxe, having one tine modified to a flattened end, used for packing Ballast under Sleepers, see Beater Packing.

BEA-TT
See **B**ureau d'**E**nquêtes sur les **A**ccidents de **T**ransport **T**errestre.

Bed
[PW]
a) The surface the **Track** sits on (normally used when no **Track** is present) Also **Ballast Bed**.
b) The space between adjacent **Sleepers**, **Timbers** or **Bearers** normally filled with **Ballast**. Also **Bay**, **Crib**.

Bedpan
[Col.] Nickname for the **Midland Main Line** (**MML**) between Bedford and London St. Pancras and associated **Passenger Services**.

Beds
[Col.] Nickname given to **Sleeper** services.

Bedstead
[PW Col.] Name for a type of power wrench, mounted on a wheeled frame which inspired the name. Used for driving and extracting **Chairscrews**.

Bedstone
[Civ.] The masonry block placed at the top of an **Abutment** or **Pier**, which in turn supports one end of a single **Bridge** girder.

Beeching, Dr. Richard
(Later Lord) (1913-1985) the chairman of **British Railways** (**BR**) responsible for the drastic closure of facilities (the "Beeching axe") between 1961 and 1965. The "Beeching Report" is more correctly titled "The Reshaping of British Railways", published in 1963. Whilst it can be argued that he was only carrying out his orders, to most people he is a subject of derision. The second part of his vision (for the strengthening of the remaining **Routes**) never saw the required funding and so never happened. See also **Serpell**.

Behind
[NPT] See **On the Approach to**. The non-preferred opposite is **Ahead of**, see **Beyond**.

Bell Codes
Bell Signals
[Sig.] A means of communication between adjacent **Signal Boxes** (**SB**), in **Absolute Block** (**AB**) areas, using a Morse **Tapper Key** and single stroke **Block Bell**:

1	Call attention
1-1	Answer telephone
1-1-6	Police assistance urgently required
1-2-1	**Train** approaching
1-3-1	Is **Line Clear**? (for a **Class** 3 Train)
1-4	Is Line **Clear**? (for a Class 9 Train)
2	**Train Entering Section**
2-1	Train out of **Section**
2-2-1	Is Line Clear? (for a Class 5 Train)
2-3	Is Line Clear? (for a Class 0 Train)
2-4	**Blocking Back** inside **Home Signal**
2-5-5	Train or vehicles **Running Away** in **Wrong Direction**
3-1	Is Line Clear? (for a Class 2 Train)
3-1-1	Is Line Clear? (for a Class 4 Train)
3-2	Is Line Clear? (for a Class 8 Train)
3-3	Blocking Back outside Home Signal
3-5	Cancel last description sent
4	Is Line Clear? (for a Class 1 Train)
4-1	Is Line Clear? (for a Class 7 Train)
4-5	Train passed without **Tail Lamp** (to Signal Box **On the Approach Side**)
4-5-5	Train or vehicles Running Away in **Right Direction**
5	Is Line Clear? (for a Class 6 Train)
5-2	Train Clear of Section (Release **Token** in **Electric Token Block** (**ETB**))
5-5-5	Opening of **Signal Box**
5-5-7	Closing of Signal Box where **Section Signal** is **Locked** by the **Block**
6	**Obstruction Danger** ("**Six Bells**") Emergency alarm
6-2	Train an unusually long time in **Section**
7	Stop and examine Train
7-5-5	Closing of Signal Box
9	Train passed without **Tail Lamp** (to Signal Box **Beyond**)
16	Testing equipment

(This is not a complete list of all the Codes).

Bell Tapper
[Sig.] See **Tapper Key**.

Bellgrove Accident
At 12:47 on 6th march 1989 a driver made a **Signal at Stop Signal Passed at Danger** (**SASSPAD**) at Bellgrove **Station** and his **Passenger Train** collided with another Passenger Train making a legitimate **Movement** in the opposite direction over the **Single Line** portion of a **Single Lead Junction**. One driver and a **Passenger** died, and 54 were injured. A system such as **the Train Protection and Warning System** (**TPWS**) would have prevented this **Accident**. See also **Hyde Accident**, **Newton Accident**.

Bellows
[TRS] A flexible "tunnel" providing a walkway between adjacent **Passenger Coaches**. It seals the **Coaches** from the environment whilst allowing them to move relative to each other. See also **Floor Plate**, **Gangway**.

Belly Rail
[PW Col.] Name for a **Closure Rail** between **Switch Rail** and **Crossing**. Also **Gut Rail**.

Below Rail Level (BRL)
[PW] The opposite of **Above Rail Level** (**ARL**). See also **Below Sleeper Bottom** (**BSB**).

Below Sleeper Bottom (BSB)
[PW] A term used to describe the depth of **Ballast** as measured from the **Soffit** of a **Sleeper** laid to designed levels. Typical values for new works range between 150 and 300mm.

BEMU
[TRS] **Battery □ Electric Multiple Unit**. An experimental vehicle which was re-cycled as **Lab 16**, **Gemini**.

Benching
[Civ.] Concrete applied to the lower part of the walls of certain types of pipes and **Tunnels**.

Bender Unit
(Tradename) [EP] A unit manufactured by Bender, which continuously monitors the state of **Lineside** power cables and can be set to send an alarm when it detects any signs of insulation breakdown. It is used to provide advance warning of power failure in **Signalling Systems**.

Bendy Dildo
[Col.] Nickname for **Class** 390 **Pendolino □ Electric Multiple Unit** (**EMU**) due to their length, **Tilt** capability and the shape of the nose.

Benjamin
The obsolescent **Phonetic Alphabet** word representing B. Replaced by **Bravo**.

Benkler
(Tradename) A manufacturer of **Railway** equipment, now part of the Sersa Group. Production of Benkler's range of **Insulated Rail Joints** (**IRJ**) was taken over by Tenconi SA of Switzerland. See **Benkler Joint**.

Benkler Joint
[PW Col.] Name for a type of **Dry Insulated Joint** previously manufactured by **Benkler**, and now made by Tenconi SA.

Bent Rail Buffer Stop
[PW] A **Buffer Stop** constructed using lengths of **Bull Head Rail** (**BH**) bent into shape and bolted or riveted together. This pattern of **Fixed Buffer Stop** is now normally only found at the ends of **Sidings**. See also **Friction Retarder Buffer Stop**, **Hydraulic Buffer Stop**, **Sliding Buffer Stop**.

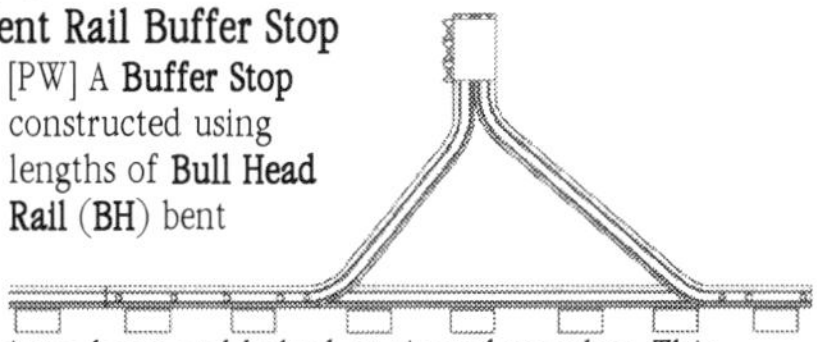

BEPT
See **Balise Encoder Programming and Test Tool**.

Berm
[Civ.]
a) A level area built into the length of a **Cutting Slope** or **Embankment Slope**
b) A long narrow raised mound, a bank of earth.

Berne Gauge
A **Structure Gauge** agreed, for all mainland European **Railways**, to come into force in 1914. It is correctly the Gabarit Passe-Partout International, (**PPI**, as it translates literally as 'pass everywhere international **Gauge**'). The only British **Main Line** built to this Structure Gauge was the **Great Central Railway** (**GCR**). It has latterly been superseded by the **UIC GA** standard, see **W18**, **W18 Gauge**.

Berth
[Sig.]
a) A section of **Railway** that may be occupied by a **Train**. It may consist of one or more **Track Circuits** (**TC**), see **Train Describer Berth** (**TD Berth**)
b) See **Berth Track Circuit**.

Berth Offset
[Sig.] The time lag between a **Train** occupying a **Track Circuit** (**TC**) and it being registered on TRUST.

Berth Track

Berth Track Circuit
[Sig.] The **Track Circuit** (**TC**) that is immediately **On the Approach to** a **Signal**.

Berthed
[LUL] A **Train** is berthed when it is placed in a condition where it is safe to leave it unattended.

Berthing
[Ops.] The placing of a **Locomotive** or **Rolling Stock** in a **Platform** or **Siding**, unattended and not ready for immediate use. Also **Stabling**.

Betts, Edward Ladds
(1815-1872). One of the great early **Railway □ Contractors**, his company built numerous **Lines** and **Structures** in the UK, including the Grand Junction Railway's Dutton **Viaduct**.

Between Trains (BT)
An arrangement where work is carried out in the interval between passing **Trains**. Colloquially called a **Margin**, formally enshrined as a **Line Blockage**.

Beyond
Preferred term describing a position or object which appears after another, from the **Train** driver's point of view.

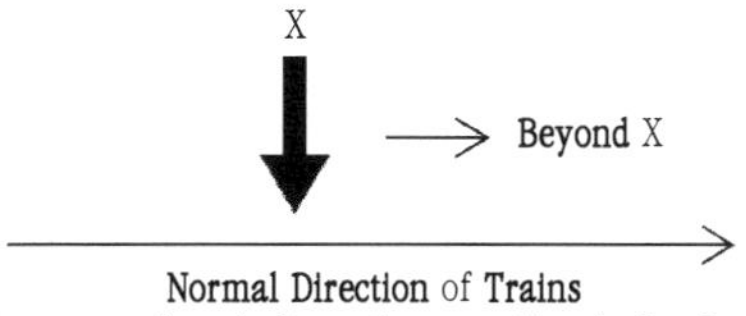

X
↓ → Beyond X
———————————→
Normal Direction of Trains

The non-preferred alternatives are **Ahead of** or **In Advance of**. The opposite is **On the Approach to**.

ELLIS' BRITISH RAILWAY ENGINEERING ENCYCLOPÆDIA

BF
a) See **Bare Feeder**
b) [TRS] An acronym representing a **Brake □ First Class □ Coach**.

BFK
[TRS] An acronym representing a **Corridor □ Brake □ First Class □ Coach**.

BFO
[TRS] An acronym representing a **Brake □ First Class □ Open Coach**.

BG
[TRS] An acronym representing a **Gangwayed □ Bogie □ Brake Van**.

BGB
[Col.] **B**ig **G**rey **B**ox, see **Relocatable Equipment Building (REB)**, **Signal Supply Point (SSP)** or **Track Sectioning Cabin (TSC)**.

BGL
[NR Civ.] Under the **Bridge Condition Marking Index** (**BCMI**) handbook, shorthand for bearing.

BGV
[TRS] **B**rake **G**ateway **V**alve.

BH
[PW] See **Bull Head Rail**.

BHCC
[BR Hist.] **B**landford **H**ouse **C**omputer **C**entre, the first home of **TOPS**.

BHX
a) [PW] **Bull Head □ Crossing**
b) **Bank Holidays Excepted**, meaning not on bank holidays.

Biased Relay
[Sig.] A **Relay** with a coil which only operates when a Direct Current (**DC**) supply of the correct polarity and voltage is applied.

Bible
[Col.]
a) The **Rule Book**
b) The **Great Britain Passenger Railway Timetable** (**GBPRT**)
c) A **Train Spotter's □ Stock Book**.

BIC
[TRS] **B**rake **I**solating **C**ock.

Bi-di
A contraction of Bi-directional as in **Bi-directional Signalling**. See also **Reversible Line**, **SIMBIDS**.

Bi-directional Line
A **Line** on which the **Signalling** allows **Trains** to run in both directions. See also **Reversible Line**.

Bi-directional Signalling
[Sig.] An arrangement of **Signals** and **Interlocking** that allow **Trains** to be run in either direction on a **Reversible Line**. **SIMBIDS** is a reduced provision. Sometimes shortened to **Bi-di**.

BIFA
See **British International Freight Association**.

BIFS
[NR]
a) **B**asic **I**nfrastructure **F**acilities **S**ystem
b) **B**illing **I**nfrastructure **F**reight **S**ystem.

BIFT
Birmingham **I**ntermodal **F**reight **T**erminal.

Big Bang
[Col.] The delivery of a large item of work, such as **Relaying**, **Remodelling** or **Resignalling** schemes in one large stage. See also **Blockade**.

Big Box
[NR Col.] The nickname for a type of specially constructed high capacity MBA / **MDA □ Spoil Wagons** in current use.

Big Ed
[Col.] Nickname for a **Class** 74 **Locomotive**.

Big Four, The
[Hist.] The four **Railway** companies formed under the Transport Act 1921, an occasion called **Grouping**. Officially active from January 1923, they were the **London Midland & Scottish Railway** (**LMSR**), London & North Eastern Railway (**LNER**), Great Western Railway (**GWR**) and Southern Railway (**SR**).

Billet Deck
[Civ.] A type of **Bridge Deck** where the **Bridge Deck Floor** comprises a single solid slab of steel 125mm thick.

BIM
Building **I**nformation **M**odelling. A series of domain-specific models (e.g. architectural, structural, services etc.) with the provision of a single environment to store shared data and information. At the time of writing the application of BIM to **Railways** is relatively embryonic.

BINAT
[CT] See **Channel Tunnel Bi-National Emergency Plan**.

BINAT GO
[CT] The implementation of **the Channel Tunnel Bi-National Emergency Plan** (**BINAT**) procedure.

Binliner
[Col.] Name for a **Train** conveying household waste **Containers**, derived from the name **Freightliner** (**FL**).

Bins
[Col.] Colloquial name for the pre-formed plastic **Catchpits** and drawpit used in **Track Drains** and **Under Track Crossings** (**UTX**).

Bi-parting Doors
[TRS] alternative term for **Centre Opening Doors**. See also **Plug Doors**.

BIR
[TRS] **B**rake **I**ncrease **R**elay.

Bird Mat
[Elec.] A piece of non-conductive material placed between the **Overhead Line Equipment** (**OLE**) and metal structures in close proximity to it (such as steel **Bridge Decks** and certain **Overhead Line Structures**). The intention is to reduce the incidence of birds un-intentionally shorting the system out.

ELLIS' BRITISH RAILWAY ENGINEERING ENCYCLOPÆDIA

Birdcage
[Col.]
a) A **Signal Box** built on a **Gantry** or legs
b) A **Cutting** which has structural steelwork over it, as at Roade Cutting on the **West Coast Main Line** (**WCML**).

BIS
Battery Isolating Switch.

Biscuit
[PW Col.] Alternative term for the **Rail Foot Insulator** used with **Rail Fastenings**.

Bitumen Spray
See **Cationic Spray**.

BJB
a) (Tradename) Bayliss Jones & Bayliss
b) [PW Obs.] An obsolescent type of **Rail Fastening** for **Flat Bottom Rail** (**FB**). The same company also manufactured some **Spring Hook Clip** (**SHC**)
□ **Clips** which also bear their initials.

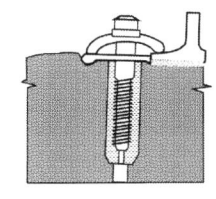

BJR
[Hist.] The **Pre-Grouping** Birkenhead Joint **Railway**, a Great Western and London & North Western joint enterprise.

BK
[Sig.] On a **Signalling Circuit Diagram**, denotes a wire coloured black.

BKF
[TRS] An acronym representing a **Brake** □ **First** □ **Corridor** □ **Coach**.

BKS
[Col.] Shorthand for brackets, see **Admiralty Tray**, **Cable Route**.

BL
See **Branch Line**.

Black
On a **General Arrangement** (**GA**), Layout Plan or **Signalling Scheme Plan** (**SSP**) showing recoveries in **Green** and new work in **Red**, the colour used to represent features that are not altered. See **Colouring Convention**.

Black Diamonds
[Col.] A term for coal, dating from the days when the transportation of coal was very big business. The Black Diamond motif was latterly used in the logo of **Trainload Coal**, a **British Railways** (**BR**) business unit.

Black Gates
[Col.] Traditional term for **Gates** provided at an **Occupation Crossing** or **Accommodation Crossing**, i.e. at a **Level Crossing** not on a public highway. See also **White Gates**.

Black Holes
[PW] A type defect found in **Alumino-thermic Welds** consisting of deep surface holes in the vent area of the **Weld**. A Weld with such a hole is a **Defective Weld**. See also **SkV-E**.

Black Rail
[Col.] Term for a **Rail Head** contaminated with fallen leaves. See **Leaf Fall Season**.

Blacks Lock
[Sig.] A mechanical lock, operated by a Lever, which secures a Level Crossing Gate in position across the Highway.

Blade
See **Switch Blade**. See also **Switch Rail**.

Blade Angle
The angle at which the blades of a ventilation fan or wind turbine are set.

Blank Ended
[PW] Describing a **Rail End** that has not been drilled with **Fishbolt Holes**. Also **Undrilled** (**UD**).

Blanket
[PW] A layer of non-cohesive material placed over the **Formation** to assist in the prevention of contamination of the **Ballast** by clay or silt from the Formation. Also **Blanketing**, **Clay Dig**, **Formation Renewal**, **Sand Blanket**.

Blanket Speed
Blanket Speed Restriction
[Ops.] An **Emergency Speed Restriction** (**ESR**) imposed by **Control** on a whole **Route**, area or occasionally on a national basis in times of crisis such as high winds. Drivers are given written or verbal instructions, but no signs are provided.

Blanketing
See **Blanket**. See also **Sand Blanket**.

Blast Furnace Slag
[PW Hist.] A waste material used in place of **Ballast** in **Sidings** (and on **Main Lines**) in times gone by.

Blastpipe
[TRS] In a **Steam Locomotive**, a pipe within the **Smokebox** used to direct **Exhaust Steam** into the **Chimney** in a way that draws the hot combustion gasses out of the **Firebox**, through the **Boiler Tubes** and into the **Chimney**.

Bleed Resistor Pair
[LUL] Two resistors connected in series between the positive and negative **Traction Power** □ **Conductors**, connection tappings being provided between the two resistors for connection to **Earth**.

Blemished Rail
[PW] **Rail** produced to a reduced standard of quality than that normally required, but otherwise suitable for use in undemanding applications, such as low-category **Running Lines**, as **Check Rails**, **Guard Rails** and in **Sidings**.

Blending
[PW] Making a new **Rail Section** meet a worn one without a step by using a **Rail Grinder**. Often seen where new **Rail** is **Welded** to old and particularly where new Rail is welded to Rail with **Sidewear**.

51

Blenkinsop Rail
[PW, Obs.] A form of combined **Rack Rail** and **Running Rail**, devised by **John Blenkinsop** in the early years of the 19th century. Made of cast iron, it has rounded projections at regular intervals along the outside of the rail with which a powered, toothed wheel on the **Locomotive** would engage to provide improved traction.

Blenkinsop, John
(1783-1831) An early **Steam Locomotive** pioneer. In 1812 produced 'Salamanca', which ran on a **Rack Railway**.

Blind Siding
[Hist.] Alternative name for **Catch Points**.

Blinder
[Sig.] A plate that obscures the **Backlight** on a **Semaphore Signal** when the **Signal** is **Off**, and allows the **Signaller** to observe the correct operation of the **Signal** at night. Also **Back Blinder**, **Blinker**.

Blinker
See **Blinder**. Also **Back Blinder**.

BLK
[LUL] Shorthand for **Blo**cked.

Block
a) See **Protection of the Line**.
b) [Col.] Alternative term for a **Possession**.
c) [Sig.] Describing a section of **Track** divided by the **Signalling System** in which only one **Train** is normally permitted at a time. See **Block Section**.
d) A metal block used **in Switch and Crossing Layouts** (**S&C Layouts**) and **Check Rail** assemblies. See **Check Block, Distance Block, Stress Transfer Block**.
e) [Col.] Term for a **Buffer Stop**, as in **Stop Block**.

Block Bell
[Sig.] A single stroke electromechanical bell used for communication between **Control Points**. A standard series of **Bell Codes** is employed.

Block Code
See **Bell Codes**.

Block Controls
[Sig.] Controls added to the basic **Block Instruments** in an **Absolute Block** (**AB**) area to improve the safety level of the system. See **Home Normal Control, Interlinking, Line Clear Release, Normal Control**.

Block Dropper
[Elec.] A **Dropper** used in older **Overhead Line Equipment** (**OLE**) systems at locations where there are two parallel **Contact Wires** (**CW**). See also **Twin Contact**.

Block End
[Col.]
a) A **Buffer Stop**
b) A **Terminal Platform**.

Block Indicator
[Sig.] The electromechanical **Indicator** within a **Block Instrument** that shows the status of the **Block Section** between adjacent **Block Posts** or **Signal Boxes** (**SB**) in **Absolute Block** (**AB**) areas.

Block Instrument
[Sig.] An item of **Signal Box** equipment used for controlling entry to, and indicating the state of, a **Block Section**. It often consists of a wooden case containing a **Block Indicator**, switches and the bell key for a **Block Section**.

Block Joint
a) [Sig.] The **Insulated Rail Joint** (**IRJ**) forming one end of a **Block Section**. See also **Insulated Block Joint** (**IBJ**)
b) [Col.] Alternative name for an Insulated Rail Joint, widely used as the colloquial term for such items, irrespective of the actual function of the item

Block Marker
[NR] A **Sign** at the side of the **Track** and on the **Signaller's** display on **Lines** equipped with the **European Train Management System** (**ERTMS**) which shows the extent of each **Section** of Track. The system only allows one **Train** at a time into each section.

Block Marker Board
[LUL] See **Headway Post**.

Block Out
[Sig.] To give the 2-1 **Bell Code** to the **Signal Box** (**SB**) □ **On the Approach** to indicate that the **Train** has arrived complete and passed clear.

Block Override
[Sig.] A feature of an **Absolute Block** installation which enables a **Line Clear** (**LC**) to be normalised without requiring a **Train** to pass through the **Block Section**.

Block Post
[Sig.] A **Signal Box** (**SB**) at one end of a **Block Section**.

Block Regulations
[Sig.] Common contraction for The Regulations For **Train** □ **Signalling** By The **Absolute Block System**.

Block Section
[Sig.] The section of **Track** between the **Section Signal** of the first **Signal Box** (**SB**) and the **Home Signal** of a second Signal Box □ **Beyond** in **Absolute Block** (**AB**) areas.

Block Section Circuit
[Sig.] The electrical circuit connecting the system of **Block Bells** and **Block Instruments** between **Signal Boxes** (**SB**) in the **Absolute Block** (**AB**) system.

Block Shelf
[Sig.] The shelf fitted above a **Lever Frame** in a **Signal Box** (**SB**) using **Absolute Block** (**AB**). It is used to support **Block Instruments**, telephone equipment, **Indicators**, etc.

Block Signal
[Sig.] A **Stop Signal** that controls the entrance to, or signifies the termination of, a **Block Section** or **Signal Section**.

Block Signalling
[Sig.] A method of managing the safe passage of **Trains** along a **Railway** by dividing a **Line** up into **Block Sections** and only allowing one Train to enter any Block Section at once. See **Absolute Block (AB), Electric Token Block (ETB), One Train Working (OTW), Pilot Working, Radio Electronic Token Block (RETB), Single Line Working (SLW), Ticket Working, Track Circuit Block (TCB)**. The first Railway to be operated wholly on this principle was the Norwich & Yarmouth Railway in 1844. For methods which do not support the Block principle, see also **Line of Sight Working, Permissive Working (PF, PP), Time Interval Working**.

Block Switch
[Sig.] An electrical switch located in an **Intermediate Signal Box** that switches that **Signal Box (SB)** out of circuit and connects the neighbouring Signal Boxes together, allowing the switched-out Signal Box to be temporarily closed. See also **King Lever**.

Block To Block
[Sig.] Describing situation where a **Route** operated by **Absolute Block (AB)** is running at capacity; as soon as one **Train** □ **Clears** a **Section** another is waiting to enter.

Block Train
[Ops.] A **Train** timetabled to run between two points on a regular basis with the same **Consist** every time. An alternative term is **Unit Train**.

Blockade
Generally a **Possession** of many days duration, used to accomplish large quantities of **Infrastructure** work that would otherwise take a great many **Rules of the Route (ROTR)** □ **Possessions**. The Blockade approach has cost benefits, as a result of the increased amount of useable working time available. This is offset by the greater disruption caused to the **Railway** system during the Blockade. For these reasons Blockades are often planned during the holiday season when **Passenger** demand is supposedly lower.

Blocked
a) [Ops.] A portion of a **Railway** removed from the use of revenue **Traffic** and given to the Engineer to permit work to be carried out **On or Near the Line**
b) [Ops.] A portion of **Line** closed to **Trains** because it has become unsafe or because of mishap.
See also **Possession**
c) Describing a **Crane, Road Rail Excavator** or other piece of lifting plant that is being stabilised by its outriggers. See also **Free on Rail (FOR), Free on Wheels (FOW)**.

Blocked Line
[Ops.] A portion of a **Line** temporarily closed to the passage of **Trains**.

Blocked Road Man (BRM)
[Col.] Term for a person who lifts and replaces the **Protection** at the limit of a **Possession**, on the instructions of the **PICOP** or **Signaller** as appropriate. These duties are performed by a person holding the **Handsignaller (HS)** competency. Also **Blockman**.

Blocked to Electric Trains
Blocked to Electric Traction (BTET)
[Ops.] A **Line** or lines on an **Electric Railway** that has had the electricity terminated, normally as a temporary measure to permit work to be carried out on nearby **Track** or the **Traction Supply System**.

Blocking Back
a) [Sig.] The action of a **Signaller** in an **Absolute Block (AB)** or **Electric Token Block (ETB)** area of blocking the **Section** □ **On the Approach to** their **Signal Box (SB)** in order to protect a **Shunting** □ **Movement** within the **Clearing Point** or On the Approach to the **Home Signal**
b) The outcome of a queue of highway traffic extending across a **Level Crossing (LC, LX)** following some upset on the highway.

Blockman
[Col.] Alternative term for a **Blocked Road Man (BRM)**.

Blocsid
A **Railway** □ **Telegraph Code** meaning "The adjoining **Lines** to be **Blocked** when working from **Running Line** to **Siding** and vice versa" and applied to **Out of Gauge Loads**.

Blondel Formula
[PW] A means of calculating the lateral resistance of a **Track**:

$$H \leq 0.4P + 2$$

Where:
- H is the maximum permissible lateral force
- P is the **Axle Load**

See also **Prudhomme Formula**.

Blood & Custard
[Col.] Nickname for the carmine (red) and cream livery applied to **British Rail (BR)** □ **Coaches** in the 1950 and 1960s.

Bloss
Bloss Spiral
[PW] A type of **Transition Curve** used in NR60 and RT60 pattern **Switch and Crossing Units (S&C Units)**. See also **Clothoid Spiral, Cubic Parabola, Sinusoidal Transition**.

Blow
[Col.]
a) Term for the warning given by a **Lookout (LO)** by means of a horn or whistle
b) Term for the warning given by a **Train** driver using the horn
c) Alternative for **Piped** and **Through Piped**, as in **Air Blow** meaning **Air Piped**. Also **Blow Through, Dual Piped, Vacuum Piped**.

Blow Off
[TRS] The action of a **Steam Locomotive** releasing excess pressure from the boiler by venting it through the safety valves.

Blow Through
See **Through Piped**.

ELLIS' BRITISH RAILWAY ENGINEERING ENCYCLOPÆDIA

Blow Up
[Col.]
a) Term used when requesting the driver to create vacuum or air pressure in order to release the **Train Brakes**
b) Term for the sounding of a warning of an **Approaching Train** by a **Lookout** (**LO**). Also **Blow**
c) To use a **Train's** horn to sound a warning.

Blower Feed Pipes
[TRS] In a **Steam Locomotive**, pipes carrying steam to the **Blower Rings**.

Blower Rings
[TRS] In a **Steam Locomotive**, perforated rings located around the **Blastpipe** which are used to draw hot combustion gasses out of the **Firebox** through the **Boiler Tubes** and out through the **Chimney** when no **Exhaust Steam** is available.

Blow-off
[Elec.] The lateral movement of a **Contact Wire** (**CW**) at **Mid-span** under the action of wind. See also **Blow Off Mast**.

Blow-off Dewirement
[Elec.] A situation where the **Pantograph** of a **Train** loses contact with the **Contact Wire** (**CW**) because the latter is displaced laterally by high winds. It usually results in damage to both the Contact Wire and the Pantograph. See also **Dewirement**.

Blow-off Mast
[Elec.] An additional **Overhead Line Structure** provided at **Mid-span** in areas of high peak wind speed to combat **Blow Off**. Generally, only a lateral **Registration Point** is provided.

Blox
A **Railway** □ **Telegraph Code** meaning "All adjoining **Lines** to be **Blocked** when using **Crossovers**, **Junctions** and **Running Connections**" and applied to **Out of Gauge Loads**.

BLQ
[Tel.] Bad Line Quality.

BLR
[Hist.] The Pre-**Grouping** Brackenhill Light Railway

BLT
See **Ballastless Track**.

Blue Book, The
[Col.] The common name for the **Railway Safety Principles and Guidance** (**RSPG**) issued by Her Majesty's Railway Inspectorate (**HMRI**). Previously issued as a single book with a blue cover, the RSPG is now a multi-volume work, each volume dealing with a different area of the infrastructure, e.g. **Stations**, **Level Crossings** (**LC**, **LX**).

Blue Circle
[NR] A symbol applied to a **Sentinel Card** indicating that the holder does not have normal colour vision and cannot hold certain competencies, such as **Handsignaller** (**HS**) and **Lookout** (**LO**). See also **Green Square**, **Red Triangle**.

Blue Item
[PW Col.] A length of **Continuous Welded Rail** (**CWR**) that has a **Stress Free Temperature** (**SFT**) less than 24°C (75°F). This situation must be corrected by **Stressing** before the start of hot weather if a **Track Buckle** is to be avoided. Blue Items are created when Stressing is not carried out during work on the **Rails** in cold weather. The opposite is a **Red Item**.

Blue Sidings
[BR] **Sidings** generally owned and maintained by a shipper and located on their premises. The term applies to **Private Sidings** transferred from British Rail (**BR**) under the **Network Rail Transfer Scheme**. Analogous to **Purple Sidings** in Network Rail □ **Connection Agreements** (**CA**).

Blue Square
[TRS]
a) A symbol applied to **Traction Units**, in this case most **First Generation Diesel Multiple Units** (**DMU**) with mechanical transmission, denoting which **Multiple Working** control system with which they are fitted. Only Traction Units bearing the same symbol can be connected safely. See **Blue Square**, **Blue Star**, **Green Circle**, **Orange Star**, **Red Circle**, **Red Diamond**, **Red Triangle**, **White Circle**, **White Diamond**, **Yellow Diamond**, **Yellow Triangle**.
b) [Col.] A First Generation Diesel Multiple Unit (**DMU**).

Blue Star
[TRS] A symbol applied to **Traction Units**, in this case **Class** 15, 17, 20, 21, 24, 25, 26, 27, some 31, 33, 37, 40, 44, 45, 46 and 73 **Locomotives**, denoting which **Multiple Working** control system they are fitted with. Only Traction Units bearing the same symbol can be connected safely. S See **Blue Square**, **Blue Star**, **Green Circle**, **Orange Star**, **Red Circle**, **Red Diamond**, **Red Triangle**, **White Circle**, **White Diamond**, **Yellow Diamond**, **Yellow Triangle**.

Blunt Nose
See **Crossing Nose**.

BM
See **Balanced Maintenance**.

BMIS
(*bee-miss*) [NR] Business Management Information System. A system for processing and recording financial and procurement transactions. Formerly known as **FBMIS** or **FBIS**, it replaced Scala-based systems in January 1999.

BMS
[Sig.] Basic Mechanical Signalling.

BN
[Sig.] On a **Signalling Circuit Diagram**:
• A connection to a **DC** busbar of intermediate electrical potential. See also **B** and **N**
• Denotes a wire coloured brown.

Bn NTkm
Billion Net Tonne Kilometres.

Bo
(*boe*) [TRS] Denoting two linked but independently Driven Axles. See **Diesel and Electric Locomotive Notation**.

Board
a) [Col.] A term for a **Speed Indicator** (SI), a **Cross Level Gauge** or a **Marker Board**
b) [Col.] A term for a **Main Signal**, from the days when **Signals** were wooden boards, rotated to display the different aspects. See also **Peg**
c) To get onto a **Train**. See also **Alight**.

Board and Bubble
See **Stick and Bubble**.

Board of Trade
The Board of Trade was the first government department to assume responsibility for **Railways**, in 1840. Their work transferred to the new Ministry of Transport in 1919. See **Her Majesty's Railway Inspectorate** (HMRI) **Railway Inspectorate** (RI).

Boat
[Col.] An alternative to **Cutwater**, after its shape.

Boat Crossing
See **Saddle Crossing**.

Boat Sampling
[PW] A method of removing a boat-shaped portion of the upper surface of a **Rail Head** for subsequent analysis in a laboratory.

Boat Train
[Hist.] A **Train** whose departure and arrival times depended on connections with sea ferries. The effect of this was that these Trains ran at apparently random times of the day, changing with the tides. Sometimes referred to as "the Tidal".

Bobby
[Col.] The nickname given to all **Signallers**. It has its roots in the days when the passage of **Trains** was controlled by **Railway** policemen.

Body Bolster
[TRS] The lateral structural underframe member to which the **King Pin** is attached.

Bodysnatcher
[Col.] Nickname for the **Class** 57 **Diesel Locomotive** as they have the bodies from the **Class** 47. Also **Thunderbird**.

BOEF
Beam on Elastic Foundation, a simple model of **Track** behaviour.

Bogie
a) [TRS] A metal frame equipped with two or three **Wheelsets** and able to rotate freely in plan, used in pairs under **Rail Vehicles** to improve ride quality and better distribute forces to the **Track**. Also **Truck**. See also **Bolsterless Bogie**, **Swing Motion Bogie**, **Three Piece Bogie**, Y*xx*.
b) A colloquial term for a **Hand Trolley**.

Bogie Bolster
a) [TRS] A **Bogie** component that passes the **Carbody** load from the **King Pin** to the Bogie via the **Secondary Suspension**
b) [TRS] A **Freight Vehicle** with Bogies also fitted with a number of transverse **Bolsters** on its loading surface, each Bolster being provided with two or more stanchions for the lateral retention of the load.

Bogie Centre Pivot
[TRS] The vertical pin about which a **Bogie** rotates.

Bogie Centre Pivot Liner
[TRS] The replaceable material that forms the load bearing face within the **Bogie Centre Pivot** casting.

Bogie Centres

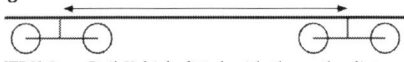

[TRS] On a **Rail Vehicle** fitted with them, the distance between the centres of rotation of the two **Bogies**. This dimension is used in calculating the **Centre Throw** and **End Throw** of the vehicle.

Bogie Frame Twist
[TRS] Distortion of the structural frame on a **Bogie** that results in the one of the primary suspension connection points being out of plane with the others.

Bogie Rotational Resistance
[TRS] The force required to rotate a **Bogie** in plan when loaded.

Bogie Stock
[TRS] Refers to a **Wagon** or **Coach** that is carried on (usually) two **Bogies**.

Bogie Wheelbase

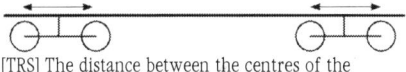

[TRS] The distance between the centres of the outermost axles of a **Bogie**. See **Inner Wheelbase**, **Outer Wheelbase**, **Wheelbase**.

Boiler
[TRS] In a **Steam Locomotive**, the large water-filled tank which is heated to produce steam. See also **Boiler Ticket**, **Boiler Tubes**, **Firebox**, **Firehole Door**, **Fusible Plug**, **Injectors**, **Superheater**, **Tubeplate**, **Washout**.

Boiler Ticket
[TRS Col.] A term for the certificate issued following a successful **Statutory Hydraulic Boiler Test**, conducted at intervals not exceeding 10 years.

Boiler Tubes
[TRS] In a **Steam Locomotive**, typically horizontal metal tubes which carry hot combustion gasses from the **Firebox** to the **Smokebox**, providing additional heating surfaces and improving boiler efficiency.

Boiling Frogs
[Col.] Legend has it that a frog will allow itself to be boiled to death if heated up slowly enough. The expression "Boiling Frog Syndrome" therefore describes failing to act as things get progressively worse. Most recently it has been used by **Railway** journalists to describe ever increasing costs for many Railway **Infrastructure** projects, and the reluctance by the **Railway Industry** to do or say anything about the situation.

Bolster
[TRS]
a) Any narrow lateral structural member that provides support:
- As part of a **Rail Vehicle**, see **Body Bolster**
- As part of a **Bogie**, see **Bogie Bolster**
- A heavy timber section bolted laterally to the floor of a flat **Wagon** to simplify the loading and unloading of the Wagon using a crane
b) A Wagon fitted with Bolsters.

Bolsterless Bogie
[TRS] A type of **Bogie** where the load from the **Carbody** is transferred to the Bogie via springs rather than via a **Bogie Bolster**. Longitudinal movement of the Bogie relative to the Carbody is controlled via links.

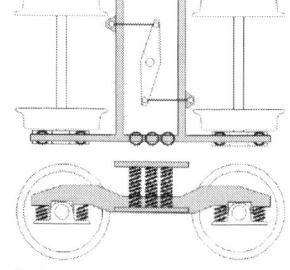

Bolt
[Sig.] In **Mechanical Signalling** a device, controlled by the **Signaller** by means of **Lever**, which secures a moving object in a known position. See **Bridge Bolt**, **Turntable Bolt**, **Underbolt**.

Bolt Hole
[PW] A hole drilled or **Trepanned** in a **Rail** to allow a bolt to be passed through it, to fix a **Distance Block** or **Fishplate**. Such holes are normally cut in the middle of the **Rail Web**, on the neutral axis.

Bolt Retaining Plate
[PW] A plate located under the head of a bolt and shaped to fit the **Rail Web** which prevents the bolt rotating when being tightened.

Bolted-base Mast
[Elec.] An **Overhead Line Structure** fixed to its foundation using holding down bolts cast into the foundation. See also **Planted Mast**.

Bombardier
Bombardier Transportation
(*bom-bar-dee-ay*) (Tradename) An international company, whose Transportation division, head office Berlin, designs and manufactures **Signalling Systems**, **Trams**, **Traction Units**, **Rolling Stock** and vehicle management systems.

Bombtailed
[Sig.] Describing a wire that is left in situ, with a plastic sheath over the end to stop any contact with parts of other electrical circuits.

Bond
a) [Sig.] The generic term for electrical connections and cabling related to **Track Circuit (TC)** □ **Feed End** and **Relay End** connections
b) [Sig.] A contraction of **Bond Wire**
c) [Elec.] Any electrical connection in the **Traction Return Circuit**. See also **Continuity Bond**, **Cross Bond**, **Impedance Bond**, **Red Bond**, **Structure Bond**, **Transposition Bond**, **Yellow Bond**.

Bond Wire
[Sig.] A single strand galvanised steel wire used to ensure electrical continuity between adjacent **Rails** for **Signalling** purposes. They are fitted into specially drilled **Bond Wire Holes** and secured with hammered-in wedges. They are always fitted in pairs. Bond Wire has a multitude of unofficial uses, ranging from securing **Wagon** doors shut to securing **Fishplates**, all of which it does very badly.

Bond Wire Hole
A hole in the **Rail Web** used for attaching **Bond Wires**, generally for **Signalling** purposes. Also Bondhole.

Bonded Joint
a) [Sig.] A **Rail Joint** that has a **Bond** fitted across it. See also **Bond Wire**, **Bonded Out**, **Fishplate Bond**.
b) [Civ.] Brickwork where the vertical joints in adjacent courses do not align (i.e. each layer of bricks overlaps the layers above and below).

Bondhole
See **Bond Wire Hole**.

Bonding
[Elec., Sig.] The making of electrically conductive connections between metal objects in a logical manner to produce a common potential or as part of a circuit. See **Bond**, **Bonding Plan**.

Bonding Plan
[Elec., Sig.] A detailed scale plan showing the **Rails**, positions of **Insulated Rail Joints (IRJ)**, **Track Circuit (TC)** connections with their respective polarities, **Cross Bonds**, **Structure Bonds**, **Impedance Bonds** and similar.

Bone
[Col.] Nickname given to **Class** 58 **Diesel Locomotive** due to their shape.

Boning
Boning Rods
A method of measuring and aligning drainage pipes by sighting along the tops of three or more poles of the same length, the bottoms of which are placed on the **Crown** of the pipe in question.

Bonker
[PW Col.] A nickname for the **Sleeper Integrity Tester (SIT)**.

Booked Call
[Ops.] Describing a **Timetabled** stop at a **Station** made by a **Passenger Train**. See also **Pick up Only**, **Set Down Only**, **Station Stop**.

Booked Speed
[Ops.] The maximum speed at which a **Train** needs to travel in order to maintain the **Timetable** schedule. This will be the speed assumed by the **Sectional Running Time** (SRT)

Booking Hall
The area of a **Station** used by **Passengers** when buying **Tickets**. More modern Stations combine this function with the **Concourse** into one large open area.

Booking on Point (BOP)
See **Signing on Point** (SOP).

Boom
a) [Sig.] An alternative for **Level Crossing** (LC, LX) □ **Barrier**
b) [Elec.] The horizontal part of a **Gantry**.

Boom Lights
[Sig.] The small red marker lights fitted along a **Level Crossing** (LC, LX) □ **Barrier** to improve their visibility in the dark and to try and warn road users of the Barrier's presence when lowered.

Booster
See **Booster Transformer** (BT)

Booster Overlap
[Elec.] In an **Overhead Line Equipment** (OLE) system, an **Insulated Overlap** that is fitted with a **Booster Transformer** (BT)

Booster Transformer (BT)
[Elec.] A transformer which induces the full **Traction Return Current** into the **Return Conductor** (RC) to minimise interference effects and increase efficiency in the system. See also **Auto Transformer** (AT).

Booster Transformer System (BT, BT System)

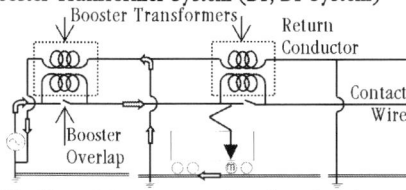

[Elec.] Intended to overcome the voltage drop issue of a **Simple Feeding System**, This arrangement has **Transformers**, called **Booster Transformers** (BT), and a **Return Conductor**. The path to the Earthed side of the **Traction Supply** via the Return Conductor and Booster Transformers has a lower resistance than that via **Earth**, so the **Traction Return Current** takes this route, boosting the voltage in the Contact Wire as it does so. Some voltage is still lost in this system and the Contact Wire has to have Insulated Overlaps introduced at each Booster Transformer location. These disadvantages are eliminated in an **Autotransformer System**.

BOOT
Build Own Operate Transfer.

BOP
a) Booking on Point, see **Signing on Point** (SOP)
b) [Tel.] Box on Post

BoQ
Bill of Quantities. See also **CESMM**.

BoQSoR
(*bok-sor*) Bill of Quantities and Schedule of Rates.

BOR
See Bottom of Ramp.

Borate Rods
[PW] Small rods composed of Borax (sodium octoborate) which are introduced into a wood **Sleeper** to arrest the decay process.

Bore
Describing a main passageway in a **Tunnel**. See **Single Bore Tunnel**, **Twin Bore Tunnel**.

Bored Tunnel
A **Tunnel** excavated using a purpose designed **Tunnel Boring Machine** (TBM).

Bos Primigenius
See **Cow**.

Boschung Plate
(Tradename) A large (tractor mounted) vibrating plate compactor. See also **Wacker Plate**.

Bostwick Gates
(Tradename) Originally invented by Jabez Abel Bostwick (1830 - 1892) in around 1880 but now the common name for the expanding lattice gates used to close off entrances to lifts, **Platforms**, etc.

Bothways Lock
[Sig.] An **Interlocking** arrangement where both positions of one **Lever** locks other Levers.

Bottleneck
[Ops.] A location on the **Network** where the number of **Train Movements** is close to, or projected to exceed the capacity of, that location. See also **Pinch Point**.

Bottom Ballast
[PW] **Ballast** below the level of the **Soffit** (underside) of the **Sleepers**, **Bearers** or **Timbers**. See also **Sleeper Bottom** (SB).

Bottom Chord
[Civ.] The bottom longitudinal structural member of a **Truss**.

Bottom Contact
Bottom Contact Conductor Rail
[Elec.] An uncommon (in the UK) arrangement of **Conductor Rail** where the **Current Collection Shoe** (**Shoe**) bears upwards on the bottom of the **Conductor Rail**. Used on the **Docklands Light Railway** (DLR), Other arrangements are **Side Contact** and **Top Contact** (the most common).

Bottom Endless Haulage
[Hist.] A development of the **Ginney Line** which utilises an endless rope running over the tops of the vehicles which are secured to the rope by a clamping device. Also known as **Under-rope Haulage**. See also **Star Clip**; **Smallman Clip**.

Bottom of Ramp (BOR)
[Civ.] Describing the location along a **Platform** at which the **Platform Ramp** meets the ground. The related term is **Top of Ramp** (**TOR**).

Bottom Roller
[PW] A horizontal roller fitted between a **Free Rail** and a **Sleeper** to support the **Rail** and allow it to move longitudinally during **Stressing**.

BOTTOMS
[Col.] **B**ack **o**n **t**o the **O**ld **M**anual **S**ystem, a nickname for the emergency paper back-up system for **TOPS**.

Bouch, Thomas
(1822-1890) (Later Sir) designer of the ill-fated first Tay **Bridge**, which collapsed in high winds killing 75. See **Tay Bridge Accident**.

Bouncy Castle
[Col.] Nickname given to **Pacers** (**Class** 142, 143 & 144 Diesel Multiple Unit (DMU)) due to their ride characteristics on **Jointed Track**. Also **Nodding Dogs**, **Nodding Donkeys**.

Boundary Hopping
[Sig.] An extreme case of **Joint Hopping** where it occurs on a **Control Area** boundary.

Bounds, Arthur F.
A pioneer of modern **Colour Light Signalling**, he began his career with the Great Central Railway (**GCR**), was appointed **Signal** & Telegraph Engineer of the southern Area of the **London & North Eastern Railway** (**LNER**) at **Grouping** in 1923, and left to join the **London Midland and Scottish Railway** (**LMSR**) as Chief Signal & Telegraph Engineer in 1929. He presented a paper to the **Institution of Railway Signal Engineers** (**IRSE**) in 1915 advocating the use of **Track Circuit Block** (**TCB**) with **Automatic Signals**. He introduced revolutionary speed-control **Signalling** near Mirfield but the installation was not expanded.

BOW
Back **o**f **W**all, often used to describe the location of drainage.

Bow Wire
[Elec.] An **Anchor** for **Overhead Line Equipment** (**OLE**) consisting of a V-shaped arrangement with the **Catenary** attached to point of the V and the legs to buildings, columns, etc. This arrangement is used when a large **Anchor Structure** would be unacceptable, such as within a listed **Station**.

Bowling Green
[Col.] Nickname for the **Fast Lines**.

Bowmac
(*boe-mac*) (Tradename) A manufacturer of modular **Crossing Surface** systems, and adopted as a colloquial name for all such systems.

Box
[Col.] Nickname for both **Class** 08 and 09 **Shunting Locomotives** due to their shape.

Box Chart
See **Box Plan**.

Box of Eggs
See **Conductor Rail Test Lamp Set**.

Box Plan
A chart used for planning works in **Possessions**. Time is represented along the top and location down the side. Each Possession is represented by a box drawn in the appropriate place. Typically some form of colour coding of **Track Names** is included. This presentation is used as it can be manipulated whilst allowing easy assessment of resource levels against each week or Possession. Also **Box Chart**, **Magic Carpet**.

Box Section
[PW] The central hollow portion of a **Cast Crossing**, in the **Crossing Nose** area, between the **Changes of Section**.

Box Sleeper
[PW] A type of **Sleeper** constructed from a hollow steel box, allowing many cables to cross the **Track** in safety. Also **Hollow Sleeper**. See also **Ducted Sleeper**.

Box Spanner
[PW] A device consisting of a socket that fits over the head of a **Chairscrew**, with a long handle and a cross bar on top. It is operated by two people and used to screw in and remove Chairscrews. Its use has largely been replaced by the **Impact Wrench**. Also called a **Dolly**, **Screw Dolly** or **T Spanner**.

Box Time
[Ops.] An alternative term for **Engineering Allowance** as this Allowance is shown in the **Working Timetable** (**WTT**) enclosed in a box or square brackets

Boxing Off
[PW] An alternative term for **Boxing In**.

Boxing-in
[PW] The operation of neatly distributing **Ballast** between the **Sleepers**. See also **Opening Out**.

Boxing-in Ballast
[PW] **Ballast** between the **Sleepers**, **Timbers** or **Bearers**. Also **Top Ballast**.

BP
a) See **Brake Pipe**
b) [PW] Shorthand for **Baseplate**.

BP&GVR
[Hist.] The **Pre-Grouping** **B**urry **P**ort & **G**wendraeth **V**alley **Railway**.

BPA
Brake **P**assenger **A**larm.

BPCA
British **P**est **C**ontrol **A**ssociation.

BPIC
[TRS] **B**rake **P**ipe **I**solating **C**ock.

Bplan
[Ops.] A replacement to the **Aplan**, Bplan is now the "master source" of operational geography including network links, **Sectional Running Times** (**SRTs**) and reference data (e.g. operator, branding, **Train** category codes) used by various **Network Rail** (**NR**) and external systems such as **Train Operating Company** (**TOC**) and **Freight Operating Company** (**FOC**) planning systems. Bplan is a tactical solution which will ultimately be replaced by the **Integrated Train Planning System** (**ITPS**) sometime in the future.

BPM
[TRS] Brake Passenger Master.

BPOT
[TRS] An acronym representing a **Brake** Post Office Stowage **Van**.

BPSIC
[TRS] Brake Pipe Supply Isolating Cock.

BR
a) See **British Railways**, The former national **Rail Authority** in Great Britain
b) [Sig.] Banner Repeater, See **Banner Repeating Signal**.

BR Rail
BR Rail Section
[PW] British Rail **Rail Section**. In the 1950s British Rail (**BR**) decided to plough its own furrow and developed two **Flatbottom** (**FB**) Rail Sections:

Nominal Pounds Per Yard	Height	Rail Foot width	Rail Head width
98	5⅝"	5⅛"	2¾"
109	6¼"	5½"	2¾"

BR1
[PW] Common contraction of **BR1 Baseplate**.

BR1 Baseplate
[PW] A type of **Baseplate** for **Flat Bottom Rail** (**FB**) and **Elastic Spikes**. They are recognisable by the row of three square holes along each side of the **Rail**.

BR1 Bogie
[TRS] Alternative term for the **B1 Bogie**

BR2 Baseplate
[PW] A Baseplate designed to accept **Macbeth Spikes**.

BR930 Series
[Sig.] A range of miniature plug-in **Relays** used in **Signalling**. The range includes numbers BR930 – BR947, BR949, BR960 – BR964, BR966 and BR968.

Bracket Arm
[LR] A form of **Overhead Line Equipment** (**OLE**) support where a horizontal arm (known as the **Cantilever**) attaches at one end to an **OLE Pole** at side of the **Tramway** and is supported vertically by tie ropes. The **Contact Wire** (**CW**) is suspended directly from the **Cantilever**.

Bracket Signal
[Sig.] A Semaphore **Signal** post topped by a horizontal platform that in turn supports two or more subsidiary posts above it. These are often found **On** the Approach to ▫ Diverging Junctions, where each subsidiary post or **Dolly** applies to each **Diverging Route**. In the illustration, there is a **Main Route** and two possible Diverging Routes to the left. The **Signal** is **Off** for the Main Route (with the **Distant Signal** beneath **On**, warning of a possible **Stop Aspect** ▫ **Beyond**). The position and height of the posts indicates which Signals apply to the more divergent Routes ahead.

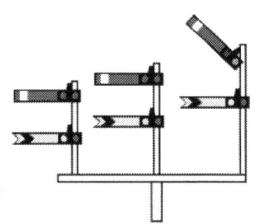

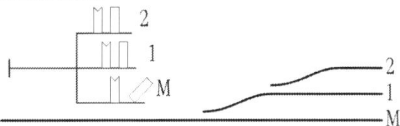

Brains
[Col.] Nickname for those working in **Control**.

Brains Line
[Col.] Nickname for the **Route** connecting Oxford and Cambridge, currently only extant Oxford to Claydon and Bletchley to Bedford. See **East West Rail**.

Brake
[TRS] In a description of a **Passenger Coach**, it describes a vehicle fitted with controls for the **Automatic Brake** and a **Handbrake**. These are often placed in a separate compartment.

Brake Application Time
[TRS] The time that the brake cylinder pressure takes to reach the pressure required to operate the brakes.

Brake Cock
[TRS] A valve fitted in the brake pipe at each end of a **Rail Vehicle** which can be closed to prevent the compressed air or vacuum from leaking away when the Rail Vehicle is marshalled at the end of a **Train**.

Brake Compartment
[TRS] An enclosed area within a **Rail Vehicle** provided with controls for the **Automatic Brake** and **Handbrake**.

Brake Continuity
See **Brake Pipe Continuity**.

Brake Continuity Test
[TRS] A test to confirm the application and release of brakes on all the **Rail Vehicles** in a **Train** when demanded by the driver. For **Locomotive Hauled** ▫ **Trains** using the **Automatic Air Brake** system, the test indicates that the flow of air in the **Brake Pipe** is continuous to the end Rail Vehicle.

Brake Control Unit (BCU)
[TRS] The device forming the interface between the driver's **Brake Controller** and the train brakes, **Wheel Slide Prevention** (**WSP**) equipment and **Sanders**. The unit converts brake demands from the driver into brake cylinder pressures, manages the **Brake Blending** process and logs any faults that have occur within the braking, WSP and sanding systems.

Brake Cooling Switch
See **Cooling Switch**.

Brake Cylinder
[TRS] A pneumatic cylinder used to convert pneumatic pressure into braking forces.

Brake Demand
[TRS] A request made for the application of the brakes by the driver, the **Automatic Warning System** (**AWS**), the **Driver's Vigilance Device** (**DVD**), the **Train Protection and Warning System** (**TPWS**) or a **Trip Cock**.

Brake Force
[TRS]
a) A measure of the stopping power of a **Locomotive**, a vital value in the days of **Unfitted □ Trains**, as the Locomotive was required to stop the whole **Train**. Measured in Tonnes
b) The braking effort required to stop a particular **Rail Vehicle**. Measured in Tonnes
c) A small number of **Rail Vehicles** equipped with an appropriate **Automatic Brake** attached to the rear of a Train. They are used to compensate for any **Piped** vehicles present, thus ensuring that the Train has adequate stopping power, and to ensure that those vehicles will stop automatically should the Train become **Divided**.

Brake Hanger
[TRS] A lever forming part of the **Brake Rigging**, to which the brake block is secured.

Brake Leakage Test
[TRS] A test undertaken to ensure that the brakes on a **Train** are fully operational, in that there is no air leakage which would affect the brake performance.

Brake Pipe
[TRS] In an **Air Brake** system, this pipe is pressurised to release the brakes of the vehicles in the **Train**. The actual air pressure required to operate the brake cylinders is provided by the **Train Pipe**, which is kept permanently pressurised to supply reservoirs on each vehicle. See also **Vacuum Brake**.

Brake Pipe Continuity
[TRS] The state where the **Train Brake** pipe system is intact and functional. Loss of Continuity causes the **Train Brakes** to apply. See **Automatic Brakes**.

Brake Raft
[TRS] Collection of brake gear mounted on a single frame underneath a **Rail Vehicle**.

Brake Retarding Force
[TRS] The decelerating force applied to a vehicle by its brakes.

Brake Rigging
[TRS] The arrangement of mechanical links, cranks and levers connecting the brake cylinders to the **Brake Blocks** or brake pads.

Brake Safety Circuit
[LUL] Electrical circuit forming part of the system which controls the application and release of the **Emergency Brake** on a **Train**.

Brake Supply Reservoir
[TRS] A pressure vessel fitted to all vehicles with **Air Brakes** to store compressed air for use during braking.

Brake Timings
[TRS] The brake application and release timings on **Freight Vehicles** and **On Track Machines** (**OTM**) can usually be set to either '**Passenger**' or '**Goods**' Brake Timings, the former giving a fast change of **Brake Force** and the latter being slower in response, giving time for the rearmost Vehicles of long **Freight Trains** to respond.

Brake Types
[NR] All **Rail Vehicles** have a three letter code uniquely identifying that type of vehicle (the **CARKND** on **TOPS**). The last letter of this code describes which variety or combination of brakes the vehicle has:
A Air Brakes only
B Air brakes, **Vacuum Piped**
E Electro-pneumatic (**EP**)
F AFI brakes only
G AFI brake, **Air Piped**
H **Dual Braked**, AFI and air
O **Unfitted**, no **Automatic Brakes**
P **Unbraked**, Vacuum Piped
Q Unbraked, Air Piped
R Unbraked, **Dual Piped**
V **Vacuum Brake** only
W Vacuum Brake, Air Piped
X Dual Braked, Vacuum and Air
Z Other Automatic Brake system
Since any **Train** that runs on the **National Railway Network** (**NRN**) must now have an Automatic Brake system working throughout the Train, it can be seen that certain combinations of the above are not permissible. This must be borne in mind when making arrangements for **Engineer's Trains**. See also **Brake Force**, **Swinger**, **Unfitted Tail**.

Brake Van
[TRS] Any vehicle with a **Brake Compartment**. When marshalled as part of a **Passenger Train**, such vehicles are often also fitted out for the carriage of mail and are also referred to as **Guard's □ Vans**.

Brake Wire
[TRS] On a **Multiple Unit Train**, a wire which runs the length of the **Train** and powers the **Brake Controller**. If the Train becomes **Divided**, this circuit is broken and each vehicle will automatically apply its own brakes, bringing the Train to rest safely.

Braked
Braked Vehicle
[TRS] A vehicle fitted with a device or system other than a **Handbrake** capable of bringing it to and holding it at rest. The opposite is **Unbraked**.
Braking Curve
[Sig.] The graphical representation of the Braking Distance (BD) of a particular **Train** in relation to **Gradient** and initial speed. See also **Appendix A Braking**, **Appendix B Braking**, **Appendix C Braking**, **Appendix D Braking**.
Braking Distance (BD)
[Sig.] The distance required for a **Train** to come rest from a given speed, or decelerate from higher speed to a lower speed. The actual distance required depends on the reduction in speed, the braking characteristics of the **Train** and the **Gradient**(s) over which the braking is to be performed. See also Deceleration Distance (DD), Emergency Braking Distance, Service Braking Distance.
Braking Steps
[TRS] The different positions on the driver's **Brake Controller** representing progressively greater brake demands, e.g.:
- brake **Step 1** is typically equivalent to a retardation rate of $0.3 ms^{-2}$
- brake **Step 2** to a rate of $0.6 ms^{-2}$ and
- brake **Step 3** to a rate of $0.9 ms^{-2}$.

See also **% of g**, **Emergency Braking**, **Service Braking**.
Branch
Branch Line
A **Route** that serves as a feeder to a **Main Line** or **Secondary Line**.
Brand Mark
See **Branding**.
Brander-shaped Rail
[PW Hist.] A description, based on the shape of a furnace bar (fire bar) used in a report dated 1847, to describe a **Fish-bellied Rail**.
Branding
[PW] The manufacturing information embossed onto a **Rail Web**. It generally gives manufacturer, mill, year, grade of steel, **Rail Section**, mass, alloy and post treatment applied. An example might be:

98 B A WORKINGTON 1957

This example translates as 98 □ **Pound** □ **Flat Bottom Rail** (**FB**) made in Workington in 1957 by the Acid Bessemer (**BA**) process. Also **Rail Branding**.

Brassey, Thomas
(1805-1870) born in Chester. He was arguably the most famous **Railway** □ **Contractor** of all time, starting his career with Bromborough **Viaduct** (a job he won with a little help from **George Stephenson**). He went on to build the Grand Junction, Lancaster & Carlisle, Caledonian, Great Northern, Tilbury & Southend and Shrewsbury & Hereford Railways, amongst others. In total he built around one sixth of the **National Railway Network** (**NRN**), as well as lines in Canada and at Balaclava in the Crimea. He had a long association with **Joseph Locke**.
BRAT
BRAT Test
(brat, brat test) [PW] **B**allast **R**eturn **A**ssessment **T**est, a means of estimating the likely value of a **Ballast Cleaner Return** using a sieving process.
BR-ATP
[Sig.] **B**ritish **R**ailways □ **A**utomatic **T**rain **P**rotection, a collective term for the **Automatic Train Protection** (**ATP**) systems in use in the UK. See also **SELCAB** and **TBL**.
Braunhaus
[BR Col.] Nickname for the headquarters of the former **British Rail** (**BR**). See also **Dark Tower, The**.
Bravo
The **Phonetic Alphabet** word representing B.
BRB
See **B**ritish **R**ailways **B**oard.
BRBS
[BR Hist.] **B**ritish **R**ailways **B**usiness **S**ystems, now part of the SEMA Group.
BRC&W
(Tradename) The Birmingham **Railway Carriage & Wagon**, builders of **Locomotives** such as the **Class** 26, 27 and 33 **Diesel Locomotives**.
BRCATS
[BR Obs.] **B**ritish **R**ail **C**omputer **A**llocation of **T**ickets to **S**ervices.
BREAD
[BR Obs.] **B**ritish **R**ail **E**lectronically **A**rchived **D**ocuments.
Break
[Arch.] Obsolete spelling of brake.
Break its Back
See **Broken its Back**.
Break of Gauge
[Hist.] A point on the **Railway** where the **Track Gauge** changed from **Narrow Gauge** to **Standard Gauge** or **Standard Gauge** to **Broad Gauge**, requiring the **Transhipping** of **Goods** and / or transfer of **Passengers** between **Trains** to continue their journeys. This was most prevalent prior to 1892, when the **Great Western Railway's** (**GWR**) Broad Gauge still existed. Also called a **Change of Gauge**.

ELLIS' BRITISH RAILWAY ENGINEERING ENCYCLOPÆDIA

Break the Timbering
[PW] The maximum practical length for a **Bearer** in **Switch and Crossing Layouts** (**S&C Layouts**) is around 6m (20'). This means that in congested **Junctions** many Bearers laid end to end may be required. The gap between the ends of these Bearers is a break in the **Timbering**. Also **Split Timbered**.

Breaker
[Col.] See **Circuit Breaker**.

Bream (ZEA, ZEB, ZEX)
[NR] A **Runner Wagon**. See **Wagon Names**.

Breast
[Hist.] A wood **Brake Block** fitted to a **Convoy**.

Breather
[Col.] Alternative term for an **Adjustment Switch**.

Breather Length
[Col.] Term for a **Stress Transition Length**, the section of **Continuous Welded Rail** (**CWR**) immediately adjacent to an **Adjustment Switch** that is subject to movement caused by temperature changes in the **Rail**.

Breather Switch
[Col.] Alternative term for an **Adjustment Switch**.

Brecknell Willis
(Tradename) A manufacturer of **Electrification** equipment based in Chard, Somerset. Part of the Fandstan Electric Group.

Brecknell Willis High Speed Pantograph
[TRS, Elec.] Designed during the early 1980s by **Brecknell Willis** and **British Rail Research** (**BRR**) as a replacement for the Stone Faiveley **AMBR Pantograph**, which was limited to 100mph (160kmh).

BREEAM
Buildings Research Establishment Environmental Assessment Method.

BREL
(brell) [BR Hist] **British Rail** Engineering Ltd., now part of Bombardier.

BRENDA
(brenda) [BR, Obs.] **Bridge** Engineer's Data, a **British Railways** (**BR**) computer system recording **Bridge** information for the **Civil Engineer** (**CE**).

BREV
See **Broken Rail Emergency Vehicle**.

Brew
See **Tea**.

BRG
[NR Civ.] Under the **Bridge Condition Marking Index** (**BCMI**) handbook, shorthand for Bracing.

BRI
[BR Hist.] **British Rail** International. The trading arm of the former **British Railways** (**BR**) responsible for running overseas offices and selling tickets to continental destinations. Now trading under **SNCF** ownership as Rail Europe.

Brick
[Col.] Nickname given to the **Class** 153 **Diesel Multiple Unit** (**DMU**) due to their appearance.

Bricked Bricking
[Col.] An act of vandalism in which a brick or concrete block is suspended over a bridge **Parapet** in such a way that it strikes the **Driving Cab** windscreen. Metal bars are also objects of choice for the mindless vandal, and the term is also used to describe the breaking of **Passenger Coach** windows by the hurling of bricks, stones and other objects.

Bricklayer's Arms Junction Accident
At 09:43 on 11th September 1975 an **Electric Multiple Unit** (**EMU**) collided with an **Empty Coaching Stock** (**ECS**) **Train** at Bricklayer's Arms **Junction**, near London Bridge **Station**. The cause was determined to be the driver of the ECS Train passing a **Signal** at **Danger** because a **Phantom Aspect** in a **Position Light Signal** (**PLS**) led him (and his **Second Man**) to believe the **Movement** had been authorised. The collision occurred at 20mph and only nine were injured.

Bridge
a) Generally, a structure designed to allow one route (such as a canal, footpath, highway, **Railway** or watercourse) to cross over or under another without interference to the operations of either. **Bridges** generally consist of two **Abutments** supporting a **Deck** or **Span**, sometimes with intermediate Piers.
b) Particularly in Railway usage, a Bridge carrying other modes of transport beneath the Railway is an **Underbridge** (**UB**), and a Bridge carrying other modes of transport over the Railway is an **Overbridge** (**OB**). A Bridge carrying one Railway over another is an **Intersection Bridge** (**IB**). See also **Overline Bridge** (OB), **Underline Bridge** (UB)
c) [NR] An Underbridge with a **Span** of less than 2 metres is classified as a **Culvert**, and one with five or more Spans is a **Viaduct**. An Overbridge that is larger than 50 metres (55 **Yards**) when measured along the **Track** is considered to be a **Tunnel**
d) An alternative term for a **Signal Gantry**, as in Signal Bridge.

Bridge Arm

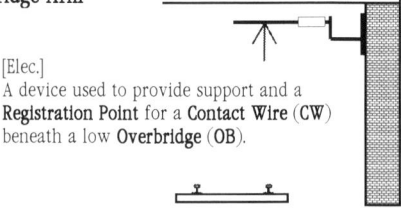

[Elec.]
A device used to provide support and a **Registration Point** for a **Contact Wire** (**CW**) beneath a low **Overbridge** (**OB**).

Bridge Assessment
See **Structure Assessment**.

Bridge Assessment File
[Civ.] The file containing or referring to all relevant records resulting from assessments carried out on a **Bridge**.

Bridge Bash
See **Bridge Strike**.

Bridge Bolt
[Sig.] A **Bolt** which prevents a **Movable Bridge** from moving.

Bridge Chair
[PW] A **Chair**, of smaller base area than a **Common Chair**, used to support **Bull Head** (**BH**) **Rails** on **Longitudinal Timbers**, and in **Switch and Crossing Layouts** (**S&C Layouts**) where space is restricted.

Bridge Condition Marking Index (BCMI)
[NR Civ.] Replaced the **Structures Condition Marking Index** (**SCMI**).

Bridge Deck
[Civ.] The nominally flat and typically largely horizontal part of a **Bridge** which carries the upper corridor over the lower corridor.

Bridge Deck Floor
[Civ.] The horizontal part of a **Bridge Deck** that supports the **Track**.

Bridge Examiner
[Civ.] A person whose role is to inspect and assess **Bridges**, **Culverts** and **Viaducts**.

Bridge Guard
BridgeGuard
(Tradename) [NR] A sensor-based system designed to detect and assess **Bridge Strikes**. Developed by Ferranti in association with **Network Rail** (**NR**).

Bridge Number
[Civ.] An identifying number given to and displayed on every **Bridge**. It is normal to have Bridge 1 located at the lowest **Mileage** end, but not always. **Viaducts** are often numbered as one Bridge, with each **Span** having either a suffix letter or **Span Number**. Intersection Bridges (**IB**) will normally be numbered on both **Routes**, with different numbers on each. On Network Rail (**NR**) lines, Bridge Numbers are only unique on a particular **Engineer's Line Reference** (**ELR**).

Bridge Pier
[Civ.] A vertical supporting structure that has a **Bridge** deck on both sides of it. Frequently contracted to **Pier**. See also **Abutment**.

Bridge Plate
[Civ.] A metal plate affixed to a **Bridge** giving, as a minimum, the **Bridge Number**. Other information may include the **Mileage** and **Chainage** of the Bridge and the **Engineer's Line Reference** (**ELR**) of the **Railway**.

Bridge Rail
a) [PW] A **Rail Section** designed for **Direct Fastening** to **Longitudinal Timbers**, named after its shape. The section was devised by IK Brunel for use on the Great Western Railway (**GWR**) in 1838. See also Barlow Rail
b) [TRS] A **Rail** used to span between adjacent **Rail Vehicles** in special applications such as the **Skip Train** and **CWR Train**.

Bridge Strike
[Civ.] The official term for a road vehicle or ship being driven into part of an **Underbridge** (**UB**), generally the **Deck**. Despite clear signage, flashing warning lights and many other mitigation measures, drivers of tall vehicles still attempt to drive under Bridge Decks with half the vertical clearance required for their vehicle. Also known as a **Bridge Bash**. See also **BSN**.

Bridge Strike Nominee level 1 (BSN1)
[NR] A person passed as competent to inspect **Bridge** and **Track** following a **Bridge Strike** and if circumstances permit re-open the line at 5mph to reduce disruption.

Bridge Strike Nominee level 2 (BSN2)
[NR] A person passed as competent to inspect **Bridge** and **Track** following a **Bridge Strike** and if circumstances permit re-open the line without the imposition of a speed restriction.

Bridging Pieces
[PW] Special steel components that can be fitted to the **Rail Head** to span a **Broken Rail**, allowing **Trains** to run, albeit at 5mph.

Bridle
[Elec.] A short length of additional wire used to support the **Contact Wire** (**CW**) in **Light Rail** (**LR**) systems.

Brill (YAA)
[NR] A **Wagon** used for the transport of **Rails** and **Sleepers**. See **Wagon Names**.

BRIMS
(*brims*) [BR, Obs.] **British Railways** (**BR**) Incident Monitoring System, a database system providing information on accidents and incidents under British Rail, replaced under **Railtrack** (**RT**) by **SMIS**.

Bringing (a Train) Under Control
[Col.] Description for the action of a driver making an immediate and sometimes overly strong brake application at the first sight of an **Indicator** or **Signal** requiring a reduction in speed. The main positive benefits of this action are to prove that the brake system still works and to reduce the speed of the **Train** to a value below the theoretical maximum for the situation.

BRIS
(*briss*) See **British Railways Infrastructure Services**.

British American Railway Services (BARS)
(Tradename) A **Locomotive** and **Rolling Stock** hire company. It is ultimately owned by Iowa Pacific Holdings, head office Chicago USA. Subsidiaries include RMS Locotec, Hanson Traction, Weardale Railway, Dartmoor Railway, and **Devon and Cornwall Railways** (**DCR**).

British Association for Immediate Care (BASICS)
Formed in 1977, BASICS is a registered charity which acts as the national co-ordinating body for both schemes and individuals providing immediate care throughout the United Kingdom. Members throughout the country provide voluntary major incident and event support to the existing emergency services.

ELLIS' BRITISH RAILWAY ENGINEERING ENCYCLOPÆDIA

British International Freight Association (BIFA)
(Tradename) The trade association for UK companies engaged in the international movement of **Freight**.

British Railway Track (BRT)
[PW] The complete guide to **Track** design, **Permanent Way Maintenance** (**PWM**) and **Track Renewal**, published by the **Permanent Way Institution** (**PWI**). The seventh edition will ultimately be published in twelve volumes.

British Railways (BR)
[Hist.] The former national **Rail Authority** in Great Britain. It was formed by the **Nationalisation** of "The Big Four", the four **Railway Companies** of the time, namely the **Great Western Railway (GWR)**, **London Midland & Scottish Railway (LM&SR)** **London North Eastern Railway (LNER)** and **Southern Railway (SR)**. From an engineering point of view it was divided into six **Regions**, these being **Eastern Region (ER)**, **London Midland Region (LMR)**, **North Eastern Region (NER)** (later amalgamated with the **Eastern Region**), **Scottish Region (SR)**, **Southern Region (SR)** and **Western Region (WR)**. **Anglia Region (AR)** was later split from the amalgamated Eastern / North Eastern Region. The headquarters was based in London. Each Region was responsible for operating the **Railway** within its area, with each discipline responding to a director at Headquarters. Directorships included:
- **DoCE** - Director of Civil Engineering
- **DoF** - Director of Finance
- **DoM&EE** - Director of Mechanical and Electrical Engineering
- **DoOps** - Director of **Operations**
- **DoS&TE** - Director of **Signalling & Telecommunications** Engineering

British Railways Board (BRB)
The Board of Directors of **British Railways** (**BR**), and the official title of the headquarters organisation of British Railways.

British Railways Infrastructure Services (BRIS)
[Hist.] An interim **Track Maintenance** and **Track Renewals** subsidiary organisation of **British Railways** (**BR**) that formed a bridge between the old British Railways organisation of **Regions** and **Areas** and the new world of business-led vertically integrated privatised companies, that then failed to appear. It ceased to exist under **Privatisation**, when they were split into **Infrastructure Maintenance Units** (**IMU**) and **Track Renewals Units** (**TRU**).

British Railways Property Board (BRPB)
[BR] The division within the **British Railways** (**BR**) organisation responsible for managing its property assets. Under **Privatisation** responsibility for **Operational Property** transferred to **Railtrack Property**, now **Spacia**, and **Non-operational Property** was vested in **Rail Property Limited**.

British Railways Research (BRR)
[Hist.] The common name for the **British Railways'** Research and Development Division, which was acquired by **AEA Technology** at **Privatisation**. Also referred to as **Derby Research** or simply **Derby**, after the division's main location. **AEA Technology** is now called **DeltaRail**.

British Reference System Plate (BRS Plate)
[LUL] A system of markers used to show the distance from the preceding **Station** The distance is marked (usually every 100 metres) by a BRS Plate. E.g. Walthamstow Central southbound on the Victoria Line is identified as V027 and 200m towards Blackhorse Road a BRS Plate attached to a **Sleeper** will show "V027 200 M". See also **Ongars**.

British Tramways Board (BTB)
(Tradename) An industry body consisting of representatives of the Confederation of Passenger Transport (**CPT**), Passenger Transport Executives Group (**PTEG**), **Light Rapid Transit** Forum (**LRTF**) and **Transport for London** (**TfL**), intended to form a consensus on, and drive development of, common standards for **Tram** systems in the UK.

British Transport Commission (BTC)
[Hist.] The principal body established by the 1947 **Transport Act** to co-ordinate and regulate the activities of the following subordinate Executives:
- The Railway Executive (effectively transferred from wartime Ministry of Transport control)
- London Transport Executive (LTE)
- Docks and Internal Waterways Executive
- Hotels Executive
- Road Transport Executive
- Transport Users Consultative Committee

British Transport Police (BTP)
[NR] The constabulary particularly empowered with policing the **Railways**. They are a fully-fledged force in their own right, possessing offices (with cells) at the larger **Stations**. See also **Q Train**.

Brittle Overload
Component failure where there is little or no deformation of the material prior to its breakage.

BRL
See **Below Rail Level**.

BRM
See **Blocked Road Man**.

Broad Gauge Track
a) **Track** laid to a **Gauge** greater than the **Standard Gauge** of 1435mm
b) [Hist.] The original **Gauge** of the **Track** on the former **Great Western Railway** (**GWR**), namely 7' - 0 $^1/_4$" (2141.4mm), used until 1892.

Broadly Acceptable
A level of individual risk generally regarded as insignificant and adequately controlled. It is the **HSE** view that such risks do not usually require further action to reduce them unless reasonably practicable measures are available.

Brogden Joint
[PW Hist.] A scarfed **Rail Joint** in which the **Rail Ends** are curved like the letter S.

ELLIS' BRITISH RAILWAY ENGINEERING ENCYCLOPÆDIA

Broken its Back
[PW Col.] Describing a **Sleeper**, particularly a **Concrete Sleeper** that is **Centre Bound** and has cracked in the middle of the **Fourfoot** under the weight of passing **Trains**.

Broken Rail
[PW] A **Running Rail** which has either broken completely in two or has a large part of the section broken away. In either case the section of **Rail** will require replacement. Providing the gap is not too large, a **Broken Rail** can be bridged temporarily using a **Bridging Piece**.

Broken Rail Emergency Vehicle (BREV)
[PW Hist.] A small self-propelled vehicle equipped to carry two short lengths of **Rail**, two **Track Welders**, a complete Track Welding kit and a **Lookout**. It was intended that this vehicle would speed up the response to **Broken Rails**, but the idea fell out of favour.

Broken Rail Ramp
[PW] An assembly fitted to the **Sleepers** to carry and guide **Rail Wheels** over a discontinuity in the **Rail Head**. See also **Emergency Bridging Pieces**.

Bronze Command
See **Gold / Silver / Bronze Command**.

Brown's Rail Scale
[PW] A particular type of **Rail Scale**.

BRPB
See **British Railways Property Board**.

BRR
a) See **British Railways Research**
b) [PW] A type of **Rail Anchor** for **Bull Head Rails** (**BH**) developed by British Railways Research (BRR).

BRS
a) British Road Services
b) [Obs.] Business Route Section. A commercially driven sub-division of a geographical Route, allowing costs and revenue to be measured for that section based on expenditure and ticket sales
c) British Reference System.

BRS Plate
[LUL] See **British Reference System Plate**.

BRSA
British Railways (BR) Staff Association.

BRSLOG
British Railways Standard Locomotive Owners Group.

BRT
a) [Hist.] **British Railways ◻ Telecommunications**, the transitional name for the Telecommunications function of British Railways (**BR**). At **Privatisation**, the organisation was bought by Racal, becoming Racal BRT, then Global Crossing, now part of **Thales**
b) Bus Rapid Transit
c) See **British Railway Track**
d) (Tradename) Bentley Rail Track, a computer aided design package.

Bruff
(Tradename) A manufacturer of **Railway** plant, particularly **Road Rail** conversions and other specialist items.

Bruff Grader
(Tradename) [Obs.] A piece of **Railway** plant, manufactured by **Bruff**, designed to be unloaded from a **Wagon** with a **Track Relaying Machine** (**TRM**), and used to level and compact the **Ballast** (using a blade and compacting plate) following removal of the old **Track** on **Complete Renewal** sites. The new **Sleepers** are then laid behind it.

Bruising
[PW] Localised surface damage to a **Rail** caused by impacts from **Rail Wheels** and other heavy metallic objects (such as excavator tracks). Such damage can lead to future **Rail Defects** and **Broken Rails**.

Brunel
(*brew-nell*) [BR] The product name of a custom radiotelephone based on the Motorola Radius GP300. Used with the **Band III ◻ National Radio Network** (**NRN**) system it allowed the worker in the field to dial anywhere on the **Railway** telephone system, **Driving Cab** and other user, as well as having a walkie-talkie function. The design was overtaken by the widespread deployment of cellular mobile telephones. See also **Brunel, Isambard Kingdom, GSM-R**.

Brunel, Isambard Kingdom
(1806-1859) Born in Portsmouth, England. Responsible for the construction of the **Great Western Railway** (**GWR**), as well as (amongst many other things) three innovative trans-Atlantic ships, many dock works and the design of the Clifton Suspension Bridge. One of the greatest all-round engineers of his time, he was renowned for his tenacity, vision and meticulous planning. Also **IKB**.

Brunlees, Sir James
(1816-1892) Civil engineer on many **Railway** projects in the UK and overseas, including the Bolton & Preston Railway and the Mersey Railway, which included a tunnel under the River Mersey. He was also head, with **Hawkshaw**, of the original **Channel Tunnel** project.

Brush
a) See **Ballast Regulator**
b) (Tradename) A manufacturer of electrical equipment and **Locomotives** (**Class** 31 and **Class** 47).

BRUTE
(*brewt*) **British Railways** Utility Transport Equipment, the large wire cages on wheels used for moving newspapers and mail bags around on **Station ◻ Platforms**.

BRV
Brake Release Valve.

BS
British Standard.

ELLIS' BRITISH RAILWAY ENGINEERING ENCYCLOPÆDIA

BS Rail
BS Rail Section
British Standard **Rail Section**. There are three British Standards covering Rail Sections, numbers 9 (for **Bullhead** (**BH**) **Rails**), 11 (for **Flatbottom** (**FB**) **Rails**) and 105 (for **Bridge Rails**):
- BS9 Rails, suffixed BS (pre-1924), **OBS** (post 1924 rail manufactured to the original 1905 standard) **RBS** (post 1924 rail manufactured to the revised 1924 standard)

Nominal

Pounds Per Yard	Height	Rail Foot width	Rail Head width
60	4 $^3/_4$"	2 $^5/_{16}$"	2 $^5/_{16}$"
65	4 $^7/_8$"	2 $^3/_8$"	2 $^3/_8$"
70	5"	2 $^7/_{16}$"	2 $^7/_{16}$"
75	5 $^1/_8$"	2 $^1/_2$"	2 $^1/_2$"
80	5 $^3/_8$"	2 $^9/_{16}$"	2 $^9/_{16}$"
85	5 $^{15}/_{32}$"	2 $^{11}/_{16}$"	2 $^{11}/_{16}$"
90	5 $^{35}/_{64}$"	2 $^3/_4$"	2 $^3/_4$"
95	5 $^{23}/_{32}$"	2 $^3/_4$"	2 $^3/_4$"
100	5 $^{29}/_{32}$"	2 $^3/_4$"	2 $^3/_4$"

BS Rail (*continued*)
- BS11 Rails, prefixed BS. Lighter sections intended for use in mines are suffixed **M**:

Pounds Per Yard	Height	Rail Foot width	Rail Head width
20[1]	2 $^1/_2$"	2 $^1/_2$"	1 $^3/_8$"
25[2]	2 $^7/_8$"	2 $^3/_4$"	1 $^1/_2$"
30[1]	3"	3"	1 $^5/_8$"
30[2]	3 $^1/_8$"	3"	1 $^5/_8$"
35[1]	3 $^1/_4$"	3 $^1/_4$"	1 $^3/_4$"
35[2]	3 $^3/_8$"	3 $^1/_4$"	1 $^3/_4$"
40[1]	3 $^1/_2$"	3 $^1/_2$"	1 $^7/_8$"
40[2]	3 $^5/_8$"	3 $^1/_2$"	1 $^7/_8$"
45[1]	3 $^3/_4$"	3 $^3/_4$"	1 $^{31}/_{32}$"
45[2]	3 $^7/_8$"	3 $^3/_4$"	1 $^{31}/_{32}$"
50[1]	3 $^{15}/_{16}$"	3 $^{15}/_{16}$"	2 $^1/_{16}$"
50[2]	4 $^1/_8$"	3 $^{15}/_{16}$"	2 $^1/_{16}$"
500[3]	100.1mm	100.1mm	52.4mm
55[1]	4 $^1/_8$"	4 $^1/_8$"	2 $^5/_{32}$"
55[2]	4 $^5/_{16}$"	4 $^1/_8$"	2 $^5/_{32}$"
60[1]	4 $^5/_{16}$"	4 $^5/_{16}$"	1 $^{13}/_{32}$"
60A[3]	114.3mm	109.5mm	57.1mm
60R[2]	4 $^1/_2$"	4 $^5/_{16}$"	2 $^1/_4$"
60R[3]	114.3mm	109.5mm	57.1mm
65[1]	4 $^7/_{16}$"	4 $^7/_{16}$"	2 $^5/_{16}$"
65[2]	4 $^{11}/_{16}$"	4 $^7/_{16}$"	2 $^5/_{16}$"
70[1]	4 $^5/_8$"	4 $^5/_8$"	2 $^3/_8$"
70[2]	4 $^7/_8$"	4 $^3/_8$"	2 $^3/_8$"
70A[3]	123.8mm	111.1mm	60.3mm
75[1]	4 $^{13}/_{16}$"	4 $^{13}/_{16}$"	2 $^7/_{16}$"
75[2]	5 $^1/_{16}$"	4 $^1/_2$"	2 $^7/_{16}$"
75A[3]	128.6mm	114.3mm	61.9mm
75R[3]	128.6mm	122.2mm	61.9mm
800[1]	5"	5"	2 $^1/_2$"
80[2]	5 $^1/_4$"	4 $^5/_8$"	2 $^1/_2$"
80A[3]	133.5mm	117.5mm	63.5mm
80R[3]	133.5mm	127mm	66.7mm
85[1]	5 $^{13}/_{16}$"	5 $^3/_{16}$"	2 $^9/_{16}$"
85[2]	5 $^7/_{16}$"	4 $^{13}/_{16}$"	2 $^9/_{16}$"
90[1]	5 $^3/_8$"	5 $^3/_8$"	2 $^5/_8$"
90[2]	5 $^1/_8$"	5"	2 $^5/_8$"
90A[3]	142.9mm	127mm	66.7mm
90R	142.9mm	136.5mm	66.7mm
95[1]	5 $^9/_{16}$"	5 $^9/_{16}$"	2 $^{11}/_{16}$"
95[2]	5 $^{13}/_{16}$"	5 $^1/_8$"	2 $^3/_4$"
95N	147.6mm	139.7mm	69.9mm
95R	147.6mm	141.3mm	68.3mm
100[1]	5 $^3/_4$"	5 $^3/_4$"	2 $^3/_4$"
100[2]	6"	5 $^1/_2$"	2 $^3/_4$"
100A[3]	152.4mm	133.3mm	69.9mm
100R[3]	152.4mm	146.0mm	69.9mm
105[2]	6 $^1/_8$"	5 $^3/_8$"	2 $^3/_4$"
110[2]	6 $^1/_4$"	5 $^1/_2$"	2 $^3/_4$"
110A[3]	158.8mm	139.7mm	69.9mm
113[2]	6 $^1/_4$"	5 $^1/_2$"	2 $^3/_4$"
113A[3]	158.7mm	139.7mm	69.9mm

Notes
[1] To BS11: 1905   [2] To BS11: 1922   [3] To BS11: 1985
Some of the above sections also now have **CEN** designations:

BS60A	Is also	CEN30E2
BS80A		CEN39E1
BS90A		CEN45E1
BS113A		CEN56E1

BS Rail (*further continued*)
- BS105:1919 Rails, prefixed BS or BSC:

Nominal

Pounds Per Yard	Rail Height	Foot width	Rail Head width
14	1 $^3/_8$"	2 $^3/_4$"	1"
16	1 $^7/_{16}$"	2 $^7/_8$"	1 $^1/_{16}$"
18	1 $^1/_2$"	3"	1 $^1/_8$"
20	1 $^9/_{16}$"	3 $^1/_8$"	1 $^3/_{16}$"
24	1 $^{11}/_{16}$"	3 $^3/_8$"	1 $^5/_{16}$"
56	2 $^5/_8$"	6"	2"
70	3"	6 $^1/_4$"	2 $^5/_{16}$"

BS&D
Buildings, **Stations** and **D**epots.

BS&TE
[BR Hist.] **B**usiness **S**ignal & **T**elecommunications **E**ngineer.

BSA
Basic **S**ervices **A**greement.

BSB
See **B**elow **S**leeper **B**ottom.

BSC
Base **S**tation **C**ontroller.

BSE
[NR Civ.] **B**ridge **S**trike **E**xaminer, a **S**afety **C**ritical qualification.

BSI
a) [NR] **B**uried **S**ervices **I**nvestigator
b) (Tradename) Bergische Stahl Industrie, a manufacturer of **Automatic Couplings**
c) **B**ritish **S**tandards **I**nstitute.

BSK
[TRS] An acronym representing a **Corridor** □ **Brake** □ **Standard Class** □ **Coach**.

BSN
See **Bridge Strike Nominee**.

BSN1
[NR Civ.] **Bridge Strike Nominee** Level 1, a **Safety Critical** qualification.

BSN2
[NR Civ.] **Bridge Strike Nominee** Level 2, a **Safety Critical** qualification.

BSO
[TRS] An acronym representing a **Brake** □ **Standard Class** □ **Open Coach**.

BSOT
[TRS] An acronym representing a **Brake** □ **Standard Class** (Trolley/Buffet) **Open Coach**.

BSP
a) See **Bulk Supply Point**
b) British Standard Pipe (a thread form).

BSRIC
[TRS] Brake Supply Reservoir Isolating Cock.

BSS
Base Station Subsystem.

BST
a) [Sig.] Basic Signalling Technology
b) British Summer Time.

BSWMS
Buried Services Work Management System.

BT
a) See **Between Trains**
b) See **Booster Transformer**
c) [TRS] Brake Test.

BT10 Bogie
[TRS] The standard **Bogie** on **Mark** 3 **Coaches**.

BTA
[Hist.] British Transport Advertising. See **BTC**.

BTB
The proposed **British Tramways Board**.

BTC
See **British Transport Commission**. The national organisation that preceded **British Railways** (**BR**). The Commission also had (conflictingly) responsibility for roads and waterways.

BTET
See **Blocked to Electric Trains**.

BTM
a) Shorthand for **Bottom**
b) Balise Transmission Module.

BTOG
(bee-tog) British Transport Officers' Guild, a union for managers and executives.

BTP
See **British Transport Police**.

BTPA
British Transport Police Authority

BTR
a) Buried Tube Route, a **Cable Route** constructed with buried ducts, generally to avoid vandalism. Also **Ducted Cable Route**. See also **Under Road Crossing** (URX), **Under Track Crossing** (UTX).
b) [LUL] **Ballasted Track** Renewal
c) [TRS] Brake Timing Relay
d) British Tyre and Rubber.

BTS
a) Base Transmission Station
b) Blackpool Transport Services
c) Braking to a Target Speed.

B-Type Bridge
[NR] A variety of standard **Half Through** □ **Ballasted Deck** □ **Bridge** consisting of two I shaped main girders and a **Composite Deck** consisting of joists set in concrete. Used for longer **Spans**, up to 18 metres. See also **A-Type Bridge**, **C-type Bridge**.

BU
[Sig.] On a **Signalling Circuit Diagram**, denotes a wire coloured blue or light blue.

Bubble Car
[Col.] Alternative name for a **Single Car** □ **Diesel Multiple Unit** (DMU), particularly the **Class** 101, 121 and 122.

Bubble Stick
See **Offset Stick**, **Stick and Bubble**

Bucholz Relay
[Elec.] A device inserted in the cooling oil circuits of **Electric Locomotive**, **Electric Multiple Unit** (EMU) and other transformers to detect low oil pressure. In this event the **Relay** trips out the power system. These Relays are a source of spurious **Circuit Breaker** (CB) trips if not carefully calibrated.

Buck Eye
Buck Eye Coupling
See **Buckeye**, **Buckeye Coupling**.

Buckeye
Buckeye Coupling
(Tradename) [TRS] A variety of **Automatic Coupling** that consists of a centrally mounted pivoted arm with a horizontal hook at its outer end. All hooks are the same **Hand**, which means that any two vehicles can be coupled together. **Buffers** are not required as the **Coupling** is rigid when made. There are other similar systems, see **Scharfenberg**, **Wedgelock**.

Buckle
[PW] A sudden, severe and short bend in the **Track** caused by a lack of **Lateral Stability**, poor maintenance and (generally) high **Rail Temperatures**. Also **Track Buckle**.

Budget Lock
A simple latch assembly, normally operated with a square key, used to secure access panels and the like.

Buff Pages
[BR] The section of the **Working Manual for Rail Staff** dealing with **On Track Plant** (OTP).

Buffer
[TRS] An impact absorbing device fitted to **Rail Vehicles** to accommodate changes in alignment between adjacent Vehicles and to prevent them from colliding heavily during braking.

Buffer Beam
a) The horizontal timber or metal upper section of a **Buffer Stop** that contacts the **Buffers** of a **Rail Vehicle**
b) [TRS] On older **Rail Vehicles**, the horizontal timber or metal section located at the extreme ends of the **Frame** on which the **Buffers** are mounted. On newer vehicles this component is an integral part of the body of the vehicle, and on those vehicles designed to work solely with **Buck Eye Couplings** no such Buffer Beam is required. Also called a **Headstock**.

Buffer Chock
[Col. Hist.] Term for a **Buffer Stop**, especially on the former North Eastern **Railway** (NER).

Buffer Locking

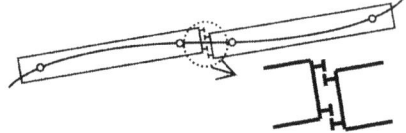

[PW, TRS] An effect produced on a **Direct Reverse Curves** of tight radii, with no intervening **Straight Track**. At the mid-point the **End Throws** of two adjacent vehicles are in opposite directions, which can result in the **Buffers** of the vehicles becoming locked together. When the vehicles later return to the straight a **Derailment** can occur as one vehicle "wrestles" the other off the **Track**.

Buffer Overrun
The formal description of a **Train** colliding with a **Buffer Stop**, almost universally caused by the driver failing to manage the speed of their Train correctly.

Buffer Section
[Elec.] An alternative term for a **Permanently Earthed Section** (PES).

Buffer Stop
A device used to stop **Rail Vehicles** at the end of **Sidings** and other dead-end **Lines**. They come in four main varieties:
- A mass masonry or concrete construction designed to stop any **Train** at all costs. These are found at **Terminal Stations**, particularly those located at the bottoms of significant **Gradients**
- **Fixed Buffer Stops**, where the frame of the Buffer Stop is bolted to the **Rails**. These are used in Sidings where the rate of retardation is not important. They are generally made from **Bull Head Rail** (BH) bent into shape, hence their alternative title of **Bent Rail Buffer Stop**
- Impact absorbing or **Hydraulic Buffer Stops**, which use shock absorbers to accommodate minor impacts. These are often combined with concrete blocks or Sliding Buffer Stops, in the latter case to make a **Dual Mode Buffer Stop**
- **Sliding Buffer Stops**, fixed to the Rails by a clamps. When impacted, this type of Buffer Stop moves, dissipating the energy of the Train. For a fuller description, see **Friction Retarder Buffer Stop**
See also **Interlaced Retarder Trap Points**, **Sand Drag**, **Train Arrestor**.

Buffer Stop Lights
The pair of white or **Red** lights, normally placed vertically one above the other on a **Buffer Stop** or at the start of a **Sand Drag**.

Buffer Zone
[LUL] A **Traction Current Section** that is switched off to protect an adjacent **Traction Current Section** under **Protection** during **Engineering Hours**.

Buffing Area
The part of the **Buffer Beam** of a **Buffer Stop** that is contacted by vehicle **Buffers**, now also used to describe the area of the buffer beam designed to be contacted by **Automatic Couplings**.

Buffing Loads
[TRS] The dynamic loads imposed on a **Rail Vehicle** through buffer contact with adjacent Vehicles.

Built Up and Timbered
[PW] Describing a **Switch and Crossing Layout** (S&C Layout) that is completely assembled at the manufacturer's premises before being dismantled for delivery to site. See also **Laths**, **White Line**.

Built Up Chair
[PW] A metal **Chair** under or adjacent to the **Crossing Nose** of Bull Head Common Crossings which consists of a cast metal plate and cast metal brackets.

Built Up Crossing
See **Fabricated Crossing**.

Bulgarian Wheels
[Col. Hist.] Nickname for **Rail Wheels** displaying a **False Flange**, prompted by the alleged poor geometrical consistency of Rail Wheels produced in that country at the time.

Bulk Freight
A term generally used to describe raw materials, such as aggregates, petrochemicals, etc. that are transported unpackaged in large quantities. Also **Freight**. See also **Goods**.

Bulk Supply Point (BSP)
[LUL] A supply derived from the National Grid at 132kV or above.

Bull
[Hist.] A device to minimise runaway vehicles on a **Rope-Worked Railway** comprising a large hinged wood bar fixed to the ascending side of a **Kip**. The hollowed out end was knocked down by the axles of the vehicles as they passed over it but, should one or more vehicles break away or run back for any reason, the nearest axle on the uphill side of the bar was caught and the **Set** or part Set held. This was a later development of the **Cow** and is also thought to have been called a **Monkey** on some systems.

Bull Head
See Bull Head Rail (BH).

Bull Head Check

Bull Head Check Rail
[PW] A **Check Rail** made from **Bull Head Rail** (BH).

Bull Head Check and Running

Bull Head Check and Running Rails
[PW] **Bull Head Track** fitted with a Bull Head Check Rail.

Bull Head Check, Flat Bottom Running
Bull Head Check, Flat Bottom Running Rails
[PW] **Track** where the **Running Rails** are **Flat Bottom Rail**, but the **Check Rail** is **Bull Head Rail**.

Bull Head Crossing
[PW] A **Crossing** made up from **Bull Head Rail** (BH). They are unusual for having a bolt holding down the **Nose** of the Crossing.

Bull Head Rail (BH)

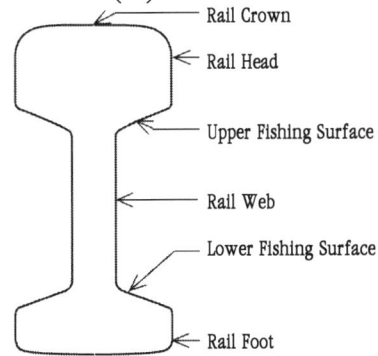

- Rail Crown
- Rail Head
- Upper Fishing Surface
- Rail Web
- Lower Fishing Surface
- Rail Foot

[PW] The former standard **Rail Section** in Britain, developed c. 1858 and not normally laid in as new on **Network Rail** □ **Lines**. However, there are many installations where the reduced resistance to lateral bending (compared with a **Flat Bottom Rail** (FB)) of Bull Head Rails is a positive advantage, particularly in industrial layouts where radii are tight and speeds low. The rail has a **Rail Head** and **Rail Foot** that are similarly shaped. Bull Head is also widely used as a **Check Rail**, where its narrow Rail Foot and lower **Rail Depth** than Flat Bottom allow a simple **Baseplate** arrangement. Typical **Rail Weights** are 85 and 95 □ **Pounds Per Yard**. Also **Bullhead**, BHI.

Bull Head Switch
[PW] A **Switch** fabricated from **Bull Head Rail** (BH). Such Switches are normally **Inclined Switches**.

Bull Head Track
[PW] Track constructed using **Bull Head Rail** (BH) for the **Running Rails**.

Bullhead (BH)
See **Bull Head Rail** (BH).

Bump
[Col.] Term for a **Track Fault** or similar defect as perceived from a moving **Train**. See also **Rough Ride**.

BUO
[TRS] An acronym representing a **Brake** Unclassified **Open Coach** (**Sleeper** Club **Car**).

Bureau d'Enquêtes sur les Accidents de Transport Terrestre (BEA-TT)
The French government agency responsible for the investigation of accidents involving land and inland waterway transport. See also **Rail Accident Investigation Branch** (RAIB).

Burma Road
[Col.]
a) A nickname for a long unmade road access, often one following the **Formation** of a redundant **Line**
b) A nickname for a long single **Siding**.

Burr Lipping
[PW] An even flow of metal over a length of one to metres or more from the **Gauge Corner** and down the **Gauge Face**. See also **Tongue Lipping**.

Burrowing Junction
A **Junction** where a **Diverging Line** is carried under the **Main Line** to avoid conflicting movements. The opposite is a **Flying Junction**. See also **Flyover**, **Grade Separated Junction**.

Bus Section (BS)
[Elec.] Part of a larger Busbar within a switchgear installation which allows the system greater redundancy and operational flexibility.

Bush
[PW] An alternative for **Ferrule**.

Bushey Accident
On 16th February 1980, an **Express Passenger Train** struck a **Defective Weld** in the **Up Fast** (UF) in the Transition between the **Right Hand Curve** and **Straight** at Bushey and became **Derailed**. Upon examination of the remains of the **Alumino-thermic Weld**, it transpired that it was so poorly made (the pre-formed moulds had not even been set vertically) as to render it a positive danger. This accident caused a complete review of **Track Welder** (TW) competency throughout **British Rail** (BR), and a tightening of the relevant standards.

Business Critical Configuration Management
[NR] A process that **Network Rail** (NR) decided to adopt in 2003 with the objective of identifying the functional requirements, safety requirements and potential failure modes for each of the component parts of safety critical assets, prior to analysis that would demonstrate that the functional and safety requirements are met by the design and management arrangements.

Busline
[TRS] An electrical interface which distributes electrical power to separate components of a system, typically within a **Train**.

Bustitution
[Col.] The action of replacing a **Train** or Train service with a bus.

Butler Protocol
[Ops.] A method for generating **Planning Headways** from **Technical Headways** by adding 26 seconds to the Technical Headway and then rounding up to the next 30 second interval.

Button Stick
[PW] A variety of shim, used between the **Jaw** of a **Slide Chair** or **Slide Baseplate** and the **Rail Web** to correct wear in this area.

ELLIS' BRITISH RAILWAY ENGINEERING ENCYCLOPÆDIA

Buttress
[Civ.] A thicker section built into a **Retaining Wall** or other masonry structure to increase its strength or to assist it in resisting earth pressures. See also **Flying Buttress**.

Buzzer Codes
[Ops.] A system of communication between the driver and **Guard** of a **Train**:
1   Stop
1-2   Close doors (on Trains with **Power Operated Doors**)
2   Ready to Start
2-2   Do not open doors (driver and Guard to confer)
3   **Set Back**
3-1   Lock **Central Door Locking** (CDL)
3-2-1   Testing doors
3-3   Guard required by driver, or Guard / driver to attend telephone
3-3-1   Release Central Door Locking
4   Slow down
6   Draw forward
9   Police assistance required
The receiver should acknowledge receipt by repeating the signal, except for 3-2-1.

BV
[PW] **Vertical** ▫ **Flat Bottom** (**FB**) **Full Depth Switches**. The B describes the length and **Switch Radius**.

BVHS
[TRS] An acronym representing a Super **Gangwayed** ▫ **Brake Van**.

BVI
[PW] Basic Visual Inspection.

BVs
[PW] Denotes **113A** ▫ **Flat Bottom** (**FB**) ▫ **Shallow Depth Switches**, length B.

BVS
[PW] Denotes **CEN56E1** ▫ **Flat Bottom** (**FB**) ▫ **Shallow Depth Switches**, length B.

BW
a) Bridleway **Crossing**
b) [Elec.] (Tradename) Brecknell, Willis & Co Ltd., a designer and manufacturer of **Conductor Rail**, **Pantographs**, **Shoegear** and other related items.

BWA
[Elec.] See **Balance Weight Anchor**.

BWH&AR
[Hist.] The **Pre-Grouping** Bideford, Westward Ho! & Appledore **Railway**.

BX
On a **Signalling Circuit Diagram**, a connection to the **Feed** side AC busbar.

BYM
[Col] Big Yellow Machine, an alternative for **On Track Machine** (**OTM**). See also **Yellow Cavalry**.

BZP
Bright Zinc Plated.

C

C

a) An abbreviation of:
- **Chain**
- **Commencement**, the point at which a **Temporary Speed Restriction** (**TSR**) begins. This point is marked by a **Commencement Board**, see **Speed Indicator** (**SI**)
- **Cant**. See also **E**

b) [NR] As the first letter of a **Wagon** □ CARKND, it indicates that the vehicle is a covered bulk carrier

c) See **Switch Letters**

d) [Sig.] On a **Signalling Circuit Diagram**:
- As one of the leading letters of an **Equipment Code**, it means checking, **Proving** or coding.
- As the last letter of an Equipment Code, it means contact

e) The letter represented by **Charlie** in the **Phonetic Alphabet**

f) [TRS] Denoting three **Driven Axles**, See **Diesel and Electric Locomotive Notation**

g) **Common Interface File Operating Characteristics Code** for **Timed at** 100mph

h) [LUL] The **Central Line**

i) [NR] Under the **Bridge Condition Marking Index** (**BCMI**) handbook, shorthand for reinforced concrete

j) [PW] The descriptive letter denoting a **Baseplate** for a **Flat Bottom** □ **Running Rail** and **Check Rail** assembly.

C Board
See **Commencement Board**. Also **Speed Indicator** (**SI**).

C Jumper
[Elec.] An alternative for **Full Current Jumper**.

C Stock
[LUL]

a) The original C Stock was a type of steel bodied stock built for the District Railway in 1910, some of which survived to the late 1950s

b) The later type, built by Metropolitan Cammell between 1969 and 1977, operate the Circle, Hammersmith & City, and Edgware Road to Putney Bridge services. Originally designed for operation by a driver and **Guard** they have since been converted to **One Person Operation** (**OPO**). The two-**Car** □ **Units** have a **Driving Cab** at one end only; they always operate in service as six-Car Trains approximately 92m long. The C designation relates to the intended route – in this case Circle.

C&D
Construction and Demolition.

C&I
Commercial and Industrial.

C&MLR
[Hist.] The **Pre-Grouping** Campbeltown & Machrihanish **Light Railway** Company.

C&OJR
[Hist.] The **Pre-Grouping** Croydon & Oxted Joint **Railway**, a London, Brighton & South Coast and South Eastern & Chatham joint enterprise.

C&P
a) **Clipped and Padlocked**, a variation of **Clipped and Scotched** used to describe a more permanent arrangement for securing **Switches**, **Switch Diamonds** and **Swing Nose Crossings** □ Out of Use (OOU). This term is normally found on **Signalling Plans**. Also **Clipped Out of Use**. See also **Clipped and Scotched**.

b) Contracts and Procurement.

C&W
C&W Inspector
See **Carriage and Wagon**, **Carriage and Wagon Inspector**.

C&WJR
[Hist.] The **Pre-Grouping** Cleator & Workington Junction □ **Railway** Company.

C/1/x
[BR, RT, NR] Standard reference for concrete **Cable Troughs**, the last number referring to the size:

Type	Internal size (WxDxL, mm)
C/1/6	100 x 90 x 1000
C/1/7	130 x 130 x 1000
C/1/8	150 x 200 x 1000
C/1/9	190 x 130 x 1000
C/1/10	250 x 130 x 1000
C/1/29	350 x 130 x 1000
C/1/43	350 x 300 x 1000

The most common size in use is C/1/9. The external width and depth (including lid) is around 50mm larger than those given. Curved, transition and junction sections are available for most sizes.

C/E
See **Country End** (**CE**).

C1
[TRS] A model for **Coaching Stock**, applicable to 20m (65ft) vehicles with conventional metal spring suspensions and 14m nominal **Bogie Centres**. Also C1A, C3, C4

C1 Appendix A
[TRS] A model for **Coaching Stock**. C1 Appendix A describes a basic 20m long **Passenger** vehicle with air suspension and 14m nominal **Bogie Centres**. Also C1, C3, C4

c2c
(Tradename0 A **Train Operating Company** (**TOC**) which operates an intensive, mainly **Commuter**, service into London Fenchurch Street from south east Essex, including the **London** Tilbury and Southend (**LTS**) □ **Line**. ATOC code CC.

C3
[TRS] A model for **Coaching Stock**, applicable to **Mark 3** □ **Coaches** which are 22.15m long, have 16m **Bogie Centres** and air suspension. Also C1, C1A, C4

C3R
[PW Obs.] A variety of **Rail Fastening**, See **Mills Rail Clip** (**MRC**).

C4
[TRS] A model for **Coaching Stock**, in this case **Class 390 Pendolino**. Also C1, C1A, C3.

ELLIS' BRITISH RAILWAY ENGINEERING ENCYCLOPÆDIA

CA
a) See **Connection Agreement**
b) See **Co-acting Signal**
c) **Cable**
d) **Corrective Action**.

Cab
[TRS Col.] A common contraction of **Driving Cab**, the driver's compartment in a **Locomotive**, **Multiple Unit Train**, **On Track Machine** (**OTM**) or **Tram**.

Cab Display Unit (CDU)
[Sig.] The device which displays the electronic token messages to the driver in a **Radio Electronic Token Block** (**RETB**) area.

Cab Pass
[Ops.] A document allowing the holder to travel with the driver in the **Driving Cab**. See **Cab Ride**.

Cab Ride
Travelling in the **Driving Cab** with the driver. Authority for this is in the form of a special **Cab Pass**, as only drivers and **Traction Inspectors** are normally permitted in the **Cab**.

Cab Secure Radio (CSR)
[NR Tel.] A radio system provided to allow **Signaller** and **Train** driver to communicate safety critical information as securely as if they were speaking on a land line, such as a **Signal Post Telephone** (**SPT**). This system is being superseded by **GSM-R**.

Cab Secure Radio Channel Sign (CSR Channel Sign)
[NR] A **Lineside Sign** telling a driver to change the channel on their **Cab Secure Radio** (**CSR**) to the number shown. This system is being superseded by **GSM-R**.

Cab Signal
[Sig.] A **Signal** installed in the **Driving Cab** of the **Train**, either repeating or replacing **Lineside** □ **Signals**.

Cab Signalling
[Sig.] The provision of **Signals** in the **Driving Cab**. This may supplement or replace traditional **Fixed Signals** placed at the **Lineside**. On **High Speed Lines** such a system is mandatory, as adequate observation of Fixed Signals at the necessary distances cannot be relied upon. Also **In-cab Signals**, **In-cab Signalling**.

Cabbage
A **Railway** □ **Telegraph Code** meaning "Do you agree to the following?"

Cable Bridge
A **Bridge** structure expressly provided for the purpose of carrying cables from one side of a **Railway** to the other or to some intermediate area between **Tracks**. The term can also be used as a supplementary description of another structure, such as a **Signal Gantry**. See also **Over Track Crossing** (**OTX**). Not to be confused with a cable-stayed bridge.

Cable Core Plan
A plan showing the functions or systems carried by the individual cores in a cable. See also **Cable Route Plan**.

Cable Post Run
[LUL] A line of posts installed alongside the **Railway** which carry **Signal** and **Traction Power** cables.

Cable Route
The designated cable management system laid alongside a **Railway**. There are six main systems employed, depending on site circumstances:
- Pre-Cast Concrete (**PCC**) □ **Cable Troughs**. These come in a range of sizes ranging from C/1/6 up to C/1/43 and are fitted with pre-cast concrete lids. Manufactured in one metre lengths of straight and various standard radii, this is the most common form of Cable Route construction. See **C/1/x**
- Plastic cable troughs, intended to replace PCC in certain applications
- **Elevated Troughing**. This is a lightweight Cement Asbestos (**CAP**), Glass Reinforced Polymer (**GRP**) or Glass Reinforced Cement (**GRC**) trough section supported at frequent intervals by concrete posts. Used where congestion in the **Cess** does not allow standard concrete Cable Troughs to be used. See **CATOP**.
- **Admiralty Tray**. The last resort, these are pre-punched metal trays fixed to **Retaining Walls** and other structures in **Limited Clearance** areas. The cables are clipped to the tray, which whilst neat is not easy to maintain. Also **BKS**
- **Ducted Cable Route**. This is a group of pipes laid under a surface obstruction such as a road or **Track**. See **BTR**, **Under Road Crossing** (**URX**), **Under Track Crossing** (**UTX**)
- **Buried Direct** (**BD**), where (generally) a single armoured cable is buried to avoid damage by vandalism.

Related items include a **Cable Bridge**, **Over Track Crossing** (**OTX**).

Cable Route Plan
A plan showing the route taken by principal cables between **Signal Boxes** (**SB**), **Interlockings** and **Locations** (**Locs.**). See also **Cable Core Plan**.

Cable Route Survey
A **Survey** undertaken to determine and record one or more of the location, size, contents and remaining capacity of a **Lineside** □ **Cable Route**.

Cable Stile
[LUL] A platform served by ladders or a series of steps used for crossing over a **Cable Post Run**.

Cable Train
A **Rake** of specially adapted **Drum Carriers** used to lay cables along the **Railway**.

Cable Troughs
Pre-Cast Concrete (**PCC**), Glass Reinforced Polymer (**GRP**) or Glass Reinforced Cement (**GRC**) U-section units with matching lids, used to protect and manage **Lineside** cables. See also **C/1/x**, **Cable Route**.

CAC
(*kak*) See **Contractor's Assurance Case**.

Cadweld
(Tradename) A means of attaching studs for electrical **Bonds** to **Rails** and **Overhead Line Structures** by means of a small exothermic chemical reaction similar to an **Alumino-thermic Weld**.

CAF
(Tradename) Construcciones y Auxiliar de Ferrocarriles, a manufacturer of, amongst other things, **Coaches**, **Locomotives**, **Multiple Units**, and **Light Rail Vehicles** (**LRV**). Based in Beasain, in north-eastern Spain.

CAFR
[LUL] Customer Accidental Fatality Rate.

CAGR
Commercial Agreement Guarantee Review.

CAHA
See Claims Allocation and Handling Agreement. See also **Railway Industry Dispute Resolution Rules** (**RIDRR**).

CAI
Central Asset Inventory.

CAIMAN
(Tradename) Customer Announcement and Information Manager, produced by Funkwerk Information Technologies Karlsfeld GmbH of Karlsfeld, Germany.

CAIS
[Elec.] Containerised Air Insulated Switchgear.

CAL
See **Comprehensive Approach Locking**.

Calculated Extension
[PW] The length by which the **Free Rail** must be stretched in order to raise its **Stress Free Temperature** (**SFT**) from the current **Rail Temperature** to the desired Stress Free Temperature, normally 24°-27°C. See also **Actual Extension**.

Call-by
[Sig.] The authority received by a driver from a **Signaller** to proceed past a **Signal** displaying a **Stop Aspect**. This may occur during times of failure of the **Signalling System**, or because the Signaller requires the driver to examine the **Line** □ **Beyond** to discern the problem.

Calling
a) [Ops.] Describing a **Passenger Train** stopping at a **Station** to allow **Passengers** to **Alight** or **Board**, see **Station Stop**
b) [Sig.] Describing the action by an **Interlocking** of requesting that a **Set of Points** be **Normal** or **Reverse** as part of a **Route**, as in 'Calling the **Points** □ **Reverse**'.

Calling-on Light
[LUL Sig.] An **Indicator** situated at the rear of a **Train** which can be activated to indicate to the Train behind that it is safe to approach to give assistance. It is used when a train has stopped due to a defect or failure.

ELLIS' BRITISH RAILWAY ENGINEERING ENCYCLOPÆDIA

Calling-on Route
[NR Sig.] A **Route Class** by which the **Signaller** can permit a **Train** to enter an **Occupied Section**. This situation most commonly occurs at the entrance to a **Terminal Platform**, where part of the **Platform** is already taken up by another **Passenger Train**. See **Permissive Working**.

Calling-on Signal
[NR Sig.] A Subsidiary Signal on a Semaphore Signal that authorises a driver to enter an **Occupied Section**.

Call-on
See **Calling-on Route**.

Camber
[Civ.] The small amount of vertical curvature along the length of an otherwise flat **Bridge Deck** or **Carbody** of a **Rail Vehicle**. This is normally to allow for deflection under **Dead Load** and **Live Load**.

Camlok
(Tradename)
a) A range of lifting clamps manufactured by the Camlok Company.
b) [Col.] Name for any self-clamping **Rail** lifting device.

CAMPS
(*camps*) [BR Obs.] Computer Assisted **Maintenance Planning System**, a system used by **British Railways** (**BR**) to make more effective use of its **Permanent Way Maintenance** (**PWM**) resources.

CAMS
Cable Allocation Management System.

Camshaft
[TRS] A device forming part of the **Resistance Control** system for a **Traction Unit** using **DC** □ **Traction Motors**. The camshaft is actuated by the driver. The cams on the shaft are arranged so that the **Contactors** for each resistor bank open and close in the correct sequence, regulated by the fall in current in the Traction Motor circuit as each bank is cut out. The sound of the camshaft stepping can be heard under many older (pre-solid state) **Trains** as they accelerate. See also **Notching Relay**, **Notching Up**.

CAN
Corrective Action Notice.

Can
[PW] Contraction of **Canister**.

Cancelling Indicator
See **Automatic Warning System Cancelling Indicator**.

Candy
(Tradename) An estimating system developed by Mott MacDonald Ltd. for use on **Railway** projects.

Canister
[PW Hist.] In **Measured Shovel Packing** (**MSP**), the Can (or Canister) is the standard unit of measurement for the **Chippings** used in the operation. One Can of Chippings equates to a **Lift** of $^{1}/_{16}$" (1.5mm) when spread correctly over the **Packing Area**. Also **Can**, **Pot**.

73

ELLIS' BRITISH RAILWAY ENGINEERING ENCYCLOPÆDIA

Cannon Box
[TRS] The sleeve bearing used to mount an **Axle Hung** ◻ **Traction Motor** on its axle under an **Electric Locomotive** or **Electric Multiple Unit** (**EMU**) This device sometimes includes the **Axle Brush**.

Cannon Street Accident
At 08.44 on 8th January 1991 a fully-loaded commuter train ran into the **Hydraulic Buffer Stop** on **Platform** 3 of Cannon Street **Station** at an estimated speed of around 10mph. The collision resulted in the death of two **Passengers**; 542 were injured. Inattentiveness on the part of the driver was cited as the most likely cause, but the driver declined to give evidence at the inquiry.

Cans
See **Canisters**.

Cant (C, E)
[PW] The designed amount by which one **Rail** of a **Curved Track** is raised above the other Rail, measured over the Rail centres. Valid values of Cant currently in force on the **National Railway Network** (**NRN**) are zero to 180mm in increments of 5mm (previously $^1/_4$" (6.35mm)). Cant is applied to negate lateral forces caused by curved Track. Cant is also referred to as **Superelevation**. See **Cant Transition**, **Equilibrium Cant**, **Millican Nail**. See also **Negative Cant**, **Rate of Change of Cant** (**RgE**), **Tilting Trains**. Also abbreviated to **E** (for elevation).

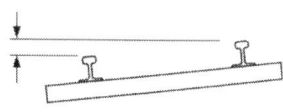

Cant Constant
[PW] The multiplicative value used in the calculation of **Cant** (**C, E**) and **Cant Deficiency** (**D**) for a given Radius (**R**) **Curve** at a given speed. For **Standard Gauge** this value is **11.82**. Assuming gravity remains constant, this value varies as:

$$c = 11.82 \times \frac{(G + Wr)}{1505}$$

Where (in millimetres):
- G is the **Track Gauge** in question and
- Wr is the width of one **Rail Head**.

See also **E+D**, **Equilibrium Speed** (**V_e**) and **Maximum Speed** (**V_m**).

Cant Deficiency (D)
[PW] The theoretical amount by which the **High Rail** must be raised to restore an equilibrium state for a **Train** travelling at a given speed on a **Curve** with a given **Cant**. It is also possible to view Cant Deficiency as the permissible shortfall in Cant (**C, E**) or **Superelevation** of the Track. The maximum **Permissible Speed** (**PS**) for a **Train** on a given section of Track is governed by the value of the **Applied Cant** plus the maximum permissible shortfall, which can be 90, 110 or 150mm depending on **Track Construction**. See also Rate of Change of Cant Deficiency (**RgD**). See also **Equilibrium Speed** (**Ve**).

Cant Deficiency Gradient
[PW] The slope of the **Cant Deficiency** (**D**) change in a **Transition Curve** or **Cant Transition**. See Rate of Change of Cant Deficiency (**RgD**).

Cant Excess
[PW] For a **Train** travelling at a speed lower than the **Equilibrium Speed** (**Ve**) on a **Curve**, this is the value by which the **High Rail** would have to be lowered to restore an equilibrium state.

Cant Gradient (CG)
[PW] The rate at which the **Cant** changes in a **Cant Transition**. Values are given as 1 in *x*, where x is a minimum of 400. It is recommended that x does not exceed 1600, as Cant Gradients this flat are difficult to maintain. See also **Rate of Change of Cant** (**RgE**).

Cant Hook
[LUL] Alternative name for a **Rail Turning Bar**.

Cant Limiting Values
[PW] The minimum and maximum permissible values of **Cant** for a given set of conditions. Minimum values include limits on **Negative Cant**, whilst maximum values apply in **Station** ◻ **Platforms**.

Cant Mark
[PW] A value, generally painted on the **Sleeper** in black on a yellow background, showing the amount of **Cant** required by the design at that point. Cant is marked at five millimetre intervals through **Cant Transitions**.

Cant Nails
See **Millican Nails**.

Cant Plates
[PW] Used as an alternative where it is not practical to mark the **Cant** value on the **Sleepers**, these plates displaying the value are either clipped to the **Rail Web** or affixed to a nearby **Structure**.

Cant Rail
Cantrail
a) [TRS] The point on a **Rail Vehicle** at which the side of the vehicle body meets the roof profile. This longitudinal line (sometimes marked by an orange stripe) is used as a reference point for carriage cleaning and other external **Maintenance** work, above which an **Isolation** must be obtained on **Electrified Lines**
b) [PW] An alternative term for the **High Rail**.

Cant Stick
[PW, Col.] Alternative name for a **Crosslevel Gauge**. Also **Crosslevel**, **Track Gauge**.

74

Cant Transition
[PW] A length of **Track** over which the design **Cant** changes from one value to another. Also sometimes shortened to **Transition**. The **Rate of Change of Cant** is measured in millimetres per second, and denoted by **RgE**.

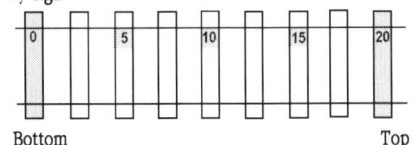

```
 0         5        10       15      20
```

Bottom   Top

A Cant Transition is marked on the Track as shown above. The end with the lowest Cant value is called the Bottom, and that the highest Cant value is the Top. The Cant is marked at five millimetre intervals on the nearest **Sleeper**. The top and bottom Sleepers are coloured yellow for their whole length, whilst intermediate Sleepers have a yellow patch adjacent to the **High Rail**.

Canted Track
[PW] **Track** on which one **Rail** is raised higher than the other, see **Cant**.

Cantilever
a) A horizontal or near horizontal **Structure** supported at one end only. Some **Signal Gantries** are built on this principle. See also **Propped Cantilever**.
b) [Elec.] A structure used to support and position an **Overhead Catenary System** (**OCS**), see **Back to Back Cantilever** (**B2BC**), **Single Track Cantilever** (**STC**), **Twin Track Cantilever** (**TTC**).

CAP
Cement/Asbestos on Post, a type of **Cable Route**.

CAPE
a) (*cayp*) Cancel All Previous Entries:
b) A **Railway** □ **Telegraph Code** meaning "Train Cancelled"
c) Now common shorthand for cancel or cancelled.

Cape Gauge
The **Gauge** most prevalent in the Cape of Africa (e.g. South Africa, Botswana, Namibia and Zimbabwe), measuring 3' - 6" (1067mm), as well as New Zealand and Western Australia.

CAPEX
(*cap-ecks*) Capital Expenditure. See also **OPEX**.

Capital Project
A project resulting in the production or construction of a physical asset.

Capitalstar
(Tradename) Brandname of the **Class** 378 **Electric Multiple Unit** (**EMU**) manufactured by **Bombardier Transportation**.

CAPP
Confirmed Annual Possession Plan.

Capping Stone
[Civ.] A finishing or protective stone that forms the top of an exterior masonry wall. Also **Coping**, **Coping Stone**.

CAPRI
(*cah-pree*) Computer Analysis of Passenger Revenue Information, a fare revenue reporting system replaced by **Latest Earnings Network Nationally Overnight** (**LENNON**).

CAPS
Colchester Area Power Supplies.

C-APT
Control - **Advanced Passenger Train**, the system developed to display in the **Cab** the maximum speed at which the APT could run. It used **APT Transponders** and a very simple computer.

CAR
a) Corrective Action Report
b) Corrective Action Request
c) Control of Asbestos Regulations.

Car
[TRS]
a) An abbreviation of Carriage, a term used when describing the length of **Passenger Trains**, i.e. 12-Car. In this sense a Car is also a **Coach**, **Driving Van Trailer** (**DVT**), **Locomotive** or single vehicle in a **Multiple Unit Train**
b) A **Passenger Coach** with a specific use, such as a dining Car, **Sleeping Car**.

Car Count-Up Markers
[LUL] **Lineside Signs** which carry a white reflective number on a blue background, installed **Beyond** every **Platform** and at some other locations. They give the driver information about the **Train's** position relative to the Platform, following operation of the **Passenger Emergency Alarm Brake** (**PEAB**). They count-up from the end of the Platform (i.e. 1, 2, 3, 4, etc.). Provided the number reached is less than the number of **Cars** in the Train, then escape onto the Platform is still possible.

Car Doors
[TRS] The external entrance doors on a **Train**. See **Bi-parting Doors**, **Centre Opening Doors**, **Central Door Locking** (**CDL**), **Plug Doors**, **Power Operated Doors**, **Slam Doors**.

Car Stop
Car Stop Marker
[NR] Where provided, a **Lineside Sign** indicating to the **Train** driver the correct stopping point for the train. Where Trains of different lengths and from different **Train Operating Companies** (**TOC**) stop at a particular location, several Car Stop Markers may be provided The sign shown applies to a Train with eight vehicles.

```
   8
  CAR
  STOP
```

Carbody
[TRS] The structure of a **Passenger Coach** excluding its **Bogies**, Couplings, etc.

Carbons
[Elec. Col.] Term for the **Contact Strips** on a **Pantograph**.

CARCI
Current Asset Register Catalogue of Information.

75

Card Process, The
[PW Obs.] A method of preserving **Softwood Sleepers** by immersing them in a mixture of zinc chloride, creosote and tar.

Cardan Shaft
[TRS] A shaft with a universal joint at each end, which transmits torque and rotation between two misaligned components of a transmission system.

Carding
[Ops.,TRS] The act of placing a card bearing the words "**Not to be moved**", "**Not to be Reloaded**" or "**Overdue PPM**" on a **Rail Vehicle**, a duty carried out by a **Carriage and Wagon Inspector** (**C&W Inspector**). These cards are different colours, giving rise to the terms **Green Carded, Red Carded**.

CARE
(Tradename) City Airport Rail Enterprises; owns and operates the **DLR** □ **Lines** from Canning Town to King George V.

Care and Maintenance
[MOD] **Track** which has been put **Out of Use** (**OOU**) for **Traffic** purposes but which is to remain in situ, capable of being used at short notice

Cargo Transport Unit (CTU)
[TRS] General term used to describe a freight **Container**, vehicle, **Wagon** or similar unit that is used to transport goods.

CargoSprinter
(Tradename) A variety of **Freight Multiple Unit** (**FMU**) manufactured by Windhoff GmbH of Rheine, Germany.

CARINO
(*car-eye-no*) [NR] The name for the **Wagon Number** displayed on a **Rail Vehicle** and used by the **Total Operations Processing System** (**TOPS**).

CARKND
(*car-kind*) [NR] The name for the three letter codes used by **Total Operations Processing System** (**TOPS**) to identify different types of **Rail Vehicle**. See also **AARKND**.

CARMD
Carriage □ Maintenance □ Depot.

Carnet
Carnet Ticket
a) A small book of pre-printed **Tickets** bought in advance, generally valid for a particular **Route** or area, each of which has to be authorised immediately before use by the **Passenger**
b) A single Ticket bought in advance and authorised by the Passenger immediately prior to use.

Carp (ZBA)
[NR] A 27 ton capacity drop side **Open Wagon** used for the transport of **Ballast** and materials. See **Wagon Names**.

Carriage
An alternative term for a **Coach**. Both terms date from the times when the upper class travelled in their own carriages secured to special flat **Wagons**.

Carriage and Wagon (C&W)
Carriage and Wagon Inspector (C&W Inspector)
[BR] A department and post within **British Railways** (**BR**) whose function was to inspect **Rail Vehicles**, both loaded and unloaded, to ensure that all was in order. See also **Carding, Green Carded, Red Carded**.

Carriage Dock
[Hist.] A **Platform** used to transfer horse drawn carriages to and from **Rail Vehicles**. No longer in use: see **Carriage**.

Carriage Key
[TRS] A simple key used to operate the secondary locks fitted to **Coach** doors and some other access panels on **Locomotives** and **Rolling Stock**. See also Budget Lock.

Carriage Line (CL)
A **Track** mainly used for the transfer of **Passenger Coaches**.

Carriage Maintenance Depot (CMD)
A facility at which **Carriages** (**Coaches**) receive **Maintenance** attention.

Carriage Siding (CS)
A **Siding** used for the storage and/or maintenance of **Passenger** carrying vehicles, i.e. **Coaches**.

Carriage Washer (CW)
Carriage Washing Machine (CWM)
A **Train**-sized heavy-duty vehicle wash, equipped with all the normal brushes and jets, plus acid sprays for removing those particularly stubborn stains. They generally require the driver to pass their Train slowly through the installation, sometimes twice.

Carrier Drain
A **Drain** intended to carry water from one point to another. The pipes are un-perforated, and not intended to collect water along their length. See also Collector Drain.

Carrier Wagon
[CT] A **Wagon** used to carry either lorries or passenger carrying road vehicles.

CARRS
[NR] Civils Asset Register and Electronic Reporting System.

CART
Containerised Automated Rail-highway Transportation.

Cartic
Cartic Four
[TRS] A type of car transporter consisting of four double-deck **Rail Vehicles** □ **Articulated** together on five **Bogies**. See also **Autic**.

Cartridge Heaters
See **Electric Cartridge Heaters**.

CAS
Computer-aided Signalling.

Cascade
a) To use components removed from a superior **Line** in the relaying of a less heavily trafficked one. Normally this includes **Rail** and **Sleepers**. The term is also used to describe a similar re-allocation of **Locomotives**, **Multiple Units** and **Rolling Stock** when new ones are brought into service
b) [Col.] A series of small reductions in **Permissible Speed** (**PS**) in relatively rapid succession, effectively forming a **Staircase of Speeds**
c) [Ops.] An alternative term for **Flighting**.

Cascaded Cut Section
[Sig. Obs.] An arrangement of a **Cut Section** where the **Relay** of one **Track Circuit** is used to control the **Feed** of the next.

CaSL
[NR Ops.] Cancellations and Significant Lateness. "Significant lateness" means more than 30 minutes late.

CASR
[NR] Cardiff Area Signalling Renewal

Cast AMS Crossing

Cast Austenitic Manganese Steel Crossing
[PW] A **Cast Crossing** made from **Austenitic Manganese Steel** (**AMS**). Also **Cast Manganese Crossing**.

Cast Centre Block Common Crossing
See **Cast Centre Block Crossing** (**CCBC**).

Cast Centre Block Crossing (CCBC)
[PW] A **Crossing** in which the major part of the unit is a single casting, to which short lengths of **Rail** are **Flash Butt Welded** (**FBW**) to complete the unit. See also **Cast Centre Block Common Crossing**, **Cast Centre Block Obtuse Crossing**.

Cast Centre Block Obtuse Crossing
[PW] An **Obtuse Crossing** in which part of the **Point Rails** and **Wing Rail**, plus all of the **Check Rail** are a single casting, to which short lengths of **Rail** are **Flash Butt Welded** (**FBW**) to complete the unit. See also **Cast Centre Block Crossing** (**CCBC**).

Cast Conductor Rail Ramp
A **Conductor Rail Ramp** produced by casting. See also **Fabricated Conductor Rail Ramp**.

Cast Crossing
[PW] A **Common Crossing** or **Obtuse Crossing** in which the whole unit is a one-piece casting. See also **Cast AMS Crossing**, **Cast Austenitic Manganese Steel Crossing**.

Cast Manganese Crossing
[PW] See **Cast AMS Crossing**, **Cast Austenitic Manganese Steel Crossing**.

Cast Monoblock Crossing
See **Cast Crossing**.

Cast Vee
[PW] A single casting consisting of the **Crossing Nose** area and the **Vee Front Rails**.

Cast Vee Common Crossing
[PW] A **Common Crossing** in which the **Crossing Vee** is a **Cast Vee**, to which the **Wing Rails** are then bolted or **MGL Pinned**.

Castell Key
(Tradename) A bespoke key that operates the Castell trapped-key interlock in an escalator or lift installation. Widely used on **LUL**.

Castellated Beam
[PW] A steel section secured to the **Bearers** in the **Switch** area of a **Switch And Crossing Layout** (**S&C Layout**). They are generally used to enhance the lateral rigidity of long and high speed **Switches**.

Castellated Nut
A nut with slots cut in one end, which are lined up with a hole in the bolt. A split pin or cotter pin is then passed through both, locking the nut in place.

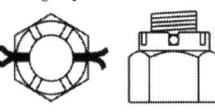

Castlecary Accident
In atrocious **Snow** and wind on 10th December 1937 a **Stopping Train**, approaching a stranded **Goods Train**, overran **Stop Signals** at Castlecary and came to a stand just out of sight of the **Signal Box**. The **Signaller** assumed that it had continued on and Accepted an **Express Train**. This **Train** also overran the **Signals** but collided with the first **Train**, killing 35 and injuring 179.

CAT
a) *(cat)* Cable Avoiding Tool, a specialised radio receiver and metal detector used to locate buried services
b) See Continuous Action Tamper
c) [NR] Capability Analysis Team.

Cat
A small, typically borderline-domesticated, quadruped mammal *Felis silvestris catus* frequently found inhabiting **Mechanical Signal Boxes**. Such animals, being effectively full-time staff, have been subject to formal transfer procedures when their home Boxes are closed. See also **Signal Box Etiquette**.

CAT 1A, 1, 2, 3, 4, 5, 6
See **Track Category**.

Cat's Eyes
[Col.] Term for a **Position Light Signal** (**PLS**).

Catch Handle
[Sig.] The smaller handle attached to the rear of the upper end of a **Lever** that must be operated before the main **Lever** can be pulled or returned to **Normal**. Not fitted to **Levers** manufactured by former **London North Western Railway** (**LNWR**). Also called a **Trigger**.

Catch Handle Locking
[Sig.] An **Interlocking** arrangement in a **Mechanical Signal Box** where it is the operation of the **Catch Handle** that is **Locked**, sometimes in addition to the **Locking** on the main **Lever**. This arrangement reduces the overall wear in the **Interlocking**, as the **Signaller** has a much reduced leverage compared with that available using the **Lever**.

Catch Pit (CP)
A sump fitted in **Track Drains** at regular intervals to allow access to the pipes for cleaning. Formerly composed of brickwork, square Pre-Cast Concrete (**PCC**) rings gained favour for their speed of construction. In modern times circular polythene types have become the material of choice. See also **Bins**.

Catch Point (CP)

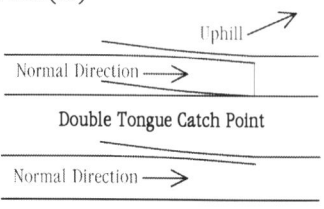

Uphill
Normal Direction ⟶

Double Tongue Catch Point

Normal Direction ⟶

Single Tongue Catch Point

An assembly of one or two **Switch Half Sets** which **Derail** vehicles in the event of their **Running Away** in the **Wrong Direction**. Previously employed at the lower end of gradients steeper than 1 in 260 such arrangements are obsolete on **Network Rail** ▫ **Lines** as Unfitted Vehicles no longer operate. Also **Unworked Catch Points**. See also **Double Tongue Catch Point**, **Single Tongue Catch Points**, **Worked Catch Points**.

Catchment Area
a) The area of land drained by a river or other watercourse
b) The area from within which the users of a transport system begin or end their overall journey.

Catchpit
See **Catch Pit (CP)**.

CATE
(*kate*) [Ops.] Computer Assisted Train Enquiries. An electronic timetabling system using information supplied by **Railtrack (RT)**, now **Network Rail (NR)**.

Category 1A
a) See **Track Category**
b) See **Class of Defect**, **Class of Rail Defect**.

Category A, B, C, D SPAD
See **Signal Passed at Danger**.

Category of Check
[NR] The level of detail and independence of checking that should be carried out, based on the risk of an undiscovered error and the potential outcome of the error:

Category   Type of design
           Maintenance works or component
0 (zero)   replacement with standard items where no design is required
1   Designs for routine renewal with no special features or use of exceptional values
2   Designs involving maximum values; with unusual design features or any design not in Category 0, 1 or 3.
3   Designs involving non-preferred geometries; new or novel designs; complex structures and layouts, anything using exceptional values

Category of Platform
[LUL]
• Category A - A **Platform** where the driver cannot see the full length of the **Train** without assistance when the **One Person Operation** (**OPO**) equipment has failed. If the OPO equipment does fail additional staff will be provided or Trains will be prevented from **Calling**.
• Category B - A **Platform** where the driver can see the full length of the train without assistance when the **One Person Operation** (**OPO**) equipment has failed. If the OPO equipment does fail the Platform can remain open.

Category x
a) For x of 1A, 1, 2, 3, 4, 5 or 6, see **Track Category**
b) For x of 0, 1, 2A, 2B, 3A, 3B or 4, see **Document Review Notice (DRN)**
c) For x of 1 to 5, see **Performance Category**
d) For x of A, B, C, D, E, F1, or F2, see **Station Category**
e) For x of A, B, C or D, see **SPAD Category**
f) For x of 1 to 8, see **SPAD Severity Category**
g) For x of 0, 1, 2 or 3, see **Category of Check**
h) For x of A or B, see **Category of Platform**.

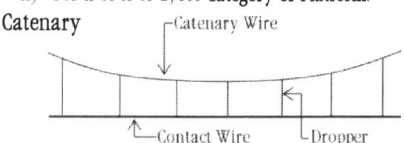

Catenary

Catenary Wire
Contact Wire   Dropper

[Elec.] A description of the complete assembly of tensioned wires that make up the **Overhead Line Electrification** (**OLE**) system. See also **Compound Catenary**, **Contact Wire** (**CW**), **Dropper**, **Intermediate Catenary Wire**, **Simple Catenary**.

Catenary Wire
[Elec.] Particularly, the uppermost wire in an **Overhead Line Electrification** (**OLE**) system. Also **Messenger Wire**. See also **Contact Wire** (**CW**), **Dropper**, **Auxiliary Catenary Wire**.

Caterham Accident
At around 09.35 on 26th June 1945 a **Train** started away from **Platform** 2 at Caterham **Station** as another Train was routed across into Platform 1. In the ensuing head-on collision both drivers died and three **Passengers** were injured. It was determined that the driver of the Platform 2 Train had not complied with the **Stop Signal**. At the time there was no requirement for a **Guard** to check the Signal before giving the driver the **Right Away** signal. See SASSPAD.

Caterham Locking
[Sig.] An arrangement of **Normal** □ **Points** at a **Terminal Station** which directs potential **Runaway** □ **Trains** onto an appropriate **Line** to avoid a **Head On** collision.

Catfish (ZEV)
[NR] A 19 ton capacity **Ballast Hopper** □ **Wagon**. See **Wagon Names**.

Cationic Spray
A bitumen layer placed using a spray, formerly used to stabilise clay **Formations**. Also **Bitumen Spray**.

CATOP
Cement **A**sbestos **T**roughing **O**n **P**osts. See **Cable Route**.

CATT
[PW] **C**omputer **A**ided **T**rack □ **T**amping.

Cattle
[Col.] Derogatory term for **Passengers**, typically **Commuters** and **Standard Class** travellers. See also **Cattle Class**.

Cattle Class
[Col.] Nickname for **Standard Class**. See also **Cattle**, **Third Class**.

Cattle Creep
An **Accommodation Bridge** in the form of a small **Underbridge** (UB), provided for the free passage of livestock from one side of the **Railway** to the other.

Cattle Dock
[Hist.] A **Platform** used to transfer cattle to and from **Rail Vehicles**. Note that livestock is no longer transported by **Rail** in Britain.

Cattle Guard
See **Cattle-cum-Trespass Guard**.

Cattle-cum-Trespass Guard
An arrangement of angled timber sections placed across the **Track** alongside the highway at **Level Crossings** (LC, LX) to deter cattle (and pedestrians) from straying onto the **Track**. Also **Cattle Guard**, **Trespass Guard**.

Causal Factor
Any factor(s) necessary for an occurrence; avoiding or eliminating any one of these factors would have prevented it happening.

Caution
An indication or instruction requiring the driver to be ready to stop. Such an indication or instruction can be given by **Fixed Signals**, **Handsignals**, **Signs** or verbal communication (e.g. from a **Pilotman** or **Signaller**). See also **Caution Aspect**, **First Caution**, **Preliminary Caution**.

Caution Aspect
[Sig.] A **Signal** □ **Aspect** that indicates to the driver that the next **Signal** may be displaying a **Stop Aspect**. Two types exist:
a) A single **Yellow** light on a **Colour Light Signal**
b) A **Semaphore Distant Signal** with its **Arm** horizontal.

CAWS
See **C**ontinuous **A**utomatic **W**arning **S**ystem.

CB
a) See **C**entral **B**attery
b) See **C**ircuit **B**reaker.

CBA
Cost **B**enefit **A**nalysis. Also **CoBA**.

CBCT
[Sig.] **C**ommunications **B**ased **T**rain **C**ontrol.

CBI
See **C**omputer **B**ased **I**nterlocking.

CBL
Closed **B**ranch **L**ine.

CBM
Condition **B**ased **M**aintenance.

CB-OD
See **C**ontrolled **B**arriers – **O**bstacle **D**etectors, A type of **Level Crossing** (LC, LX).

CBR
a) **C**ost **B**enefit **R**atio, see **Benefit Cost Ratio** (BCR)
b) **C**alifornia **B**earing **R**atio.

CBTC
[Sig.] **C**ommunications-**B**ased **T**rain **C**ontrol, see **Transmission Based Train Control** (TBTC).

CC
a) See **C**rossing **C**lear
b) See **C**rane **C**ontroller
c) [PW] The descriptive letter denoting a **Chair** for a **Bull Head** □ **Running Rail** and a Bull Head **Check Rail** assembly
d) **C**apacity **C**harge
e) The **ATOC** code for **c2c**.

CCA
Copper **C**hrome **A**rsenic, See **Tanalisation**.

CCB
a) [PW] **C**ast **C**entre **B**lock, see **Cast Centre Block Crossing** (CCBC)
b) **C**onformance **C**ertification **B**ody.

CCBC
See **C**ast **C**entre **B**lock **C**rossing.

CCE
[NIR, IÉ] [BR Hist] **C**hief **C**ivil **E**ngineer.

CCF
a) See **C**ontrol **C**entre of the **F**uture
b) **C**ontract **C**ontrol **F**orm.

ELLIS' BRITISH RAILWAY ENGINEERING ENCYCLOPÆDIA

C-Change
[RT Hist.] A major business initiative launched in June 1996 to rationalise, clarify and standardise **Railtrack** (**RT**) processes and procedures. The primary focus was to make significant improvements in customer service and control of key activities.

CCI
Confirmation of Client's Instruction.

CCIL
See Control Centre Incident Log.

CCIR
Comité Consultatif International pour la Radio, now the International Telecommunication Union's Radiocommunication Sector (ITU-R).

CCITT
a) Comité Consultatif International Téléphonique et Télégraphique, now the International Telecommunication Union's Telecommunication Standardization Sector (ITU-T)
b) Computer Communications and Information Transfer Technology

CCJP
Contact Centre Journey Planner.

CCLDB
Call Centre Live Departure Boards.

CCQ
[NR PW] Colour Coded Quality. See also **Spotted Dick**.

CCR
[LUAS] Central Control Room. The location from which **Tram** operations are managed and monitored.

CCRM
Cross Country Route Modernisation.

CCRT
Competency, Compliance & Rail Training.

CCS
a) Contract Conditions Safety
b) [CTRL] Control-command **Signalling**.

CCSC
Core Contractor's □ Safety Case. See Contractor's Safety Case (CSC).

CCTV
Closed Circuit Television. A system used to monitor, amongst other things, **Level Crossings** (**LC**, **LX**).

CCTV Level Crossing
A type of **Manually Controlled Barrier** (**MCB**) □ **Level Crossing** (**LC**, **LX**) where the **Signaller** observes the status of the Level Crossing remotely by means of **CCTV**, checking to see if the Crossing is clear before lowering the **Barriers**. See also **Local Control Unit** (**LCU**).

CCU
Core Control Unit.

CCW
Counter Clockwise, meaning anticlockwise. The opposite is clockwise (**CW**).

CCZ
[Elec.] Current Collector Zone.

CD
a) See Cant Deficiency
b) See Clay Dig
c) See Close Doors, Close Doors Indicator (CDI).

CD / RA
CD / RA Indicator
[Sig.] A combined **Close Doors Indicator** and **Right Away Indicator**. These are often found co-located on **Stations** because of their related functions.

CD&D
See Clay Dig and Drain.

CDDS
Condition Data Distribution System.

CDI
a) See Close Doors Indicator
b) Carriage □ Depot □ Indicator.

CDL
See Central Door Locking.

CDM
a) The Construction, Design and Management Regulations, 1994
b) Critical Decision Method.

CDMA
Collision Detection Multiple Access.

CDMS
Condition Data Management System.

CDR
a) See Conditional Double Red
b) Cheap Day Return.

CDRL
Contract Documents Requirements List.

CDS
Conceptual Design Statement.

CDU
a) See Cab Display Unit
b) Change Dispenser Unit.

CE
a) See Civil Engineer
b) See Country End
c) Contract Engineer
d) Conformité Européenne

CE Handbook
See Civil Engineering Handbook.

CEA
See Certificate of Engineering Acceptance.

CEAIS
[LUL] Civil Engineering Asset Information System.

CEAP
[TRS] Cab External Access Panel.

CEB
Comité Euro-International du Béton, the Euro-International Committee for Concrete.

CEBCOS
(seb-koss) [BR Obs.] Civil Engineer's Budget and Control System.

ELLIS' BRITISH RAILWAY ENGINEERING ENCYCLOPÆDIA

CEC
a) [BR] The **C**ivil **E**ngineering **C**ommittee, the overarching committee of the Civil Engineering **Function** within **British Rail**
b) See **C**ivil **E**ngineering **C**onference
c) [LUL] **C**ommunication **E**quipment **C**abinet.

CECA
Civil **E**ngineering **C**ontractors **A**ssociation.

CECASE
Civil **E**ngineering **C**ost **a**nd **S**trategy **E**valuation.

CED
Cab **E**gress **D**evice.

CEDAC
(see-dak) [BR Hist.] **C**ivil **E**ngineering **D**esign **a**nd **C**onstruction, a **Self-accounting Unit** (**SAU**) within **British Railways** (**BR**) that passed into private ownership at **Privatisation**.

CEDG
[BR Hist.] **C**ivil **E**ngineering **D**esign **G**roup, a **Self-accounting Unit** (**SAU**) within **British Railways** (**BR**) that passed into private ownership at **Privatisation**.

CEEQUAL
(see-kwol) **C**ivil **E**ngineering **E**nvironmental **Qua**lity Assessment.

CEFA
[NR Civ.]
a) **C**ivil **E**xamination **F**ramework **A**greement.
b) **C**ivil **E**ngineering **F**ramework **A**greement.

CEGMT
Cumulative **E**quivalent **G**ross **M**illion **T**ons.

CEGS
[LUL] **C**ompany **E**quipotential **G**rid **S**ystem.

CEH
Conférence **E**uropéennes des **H**oraires des Trains de Voyageurs et des Services Directs, a European **Passenger Trains** □ **Timetable** and **Through Carriage** Conference.

CEM
See **C**ontractor's **E**ngineering **M**anager.

CEMM
[LUL] **C**ivil **E**ngineer's **M**anagement **M**eeting.

CEMP
Construction **E**nvironmental **M**anagement **P**lan.

CEN
Comité Européen de Normalisation; European Committee for Co-ordination of Standards.

CEN56 Vertical
CEN 56 Vertical S&C
(sen-56 vurtikal) [PW] The new name for **113A Vertical S&C**, adopted when **113A Rail** was re-designated **CEN56E1**. See also **NR56V**.

CEN56E1
(sen-56-ee-1) [PW] The title for the **Kilograms per Metre** equivalent of **113A** □ **Flat Bottom Rail** (**FB**), though it is not an exact conversion. See also **UIC 56**.

CEN60E1
(sen-60-ee-1) [PW] The full title for the initial type of **UIC 60** □ **Rail Section** in use on **Network Rail** (**NR**) □ **Lines**.

CEN60E1A1
(sen-60-ee-1-ay-1) [PW] An asymmetrical **Rail Section** based on **CEN60E1** (**UIC60**) and used on **Network Rail** (**NR**) □ **Lines** as the basis of the **Switch** Rails in **RT60** □ **Switch and Crossing Layouts** (**S&C Layouts**).

CEN60E2
(sen-60-ee-2) [PW] The full title for the new type of **UIC60** □ **Rail Section** in use on **Network Rail** (**NR**) □ **Lines**. It has a slightly modified **Rail Head Profile** from its predecessor **CEN60E1**.

CEN60E2A1
(sen-60-ee-2-ay-1) [PW] An asymmetrical **Rail Section** based on **CEN60E2** (**UIC60**) and used on **Network Rail** (**NR**) □ **Lines** as the basis of the **Switch Rails** in **NR60** □ **Switch and Crossing Layouts** (**S&C Layouts**). It has a slightly modified **Rail Head Profile** from its predecessor **CEN60E1A1**.

CENELEC
(sen-ee-lek) **C**omité **E**uropéen de **N**ormalisation **E**lectrotechnique, the European committee for electro-technical standardisation.

Central Battery (CB)
[Tel.] A way of powering a number of telephones from a single centrally located battery.

Central Door Locking (CDL)
[TRS] A secondary locking system fitted to some **Slam Door Stock**. Released by the **Guard** from a central point, it was fitted to reduce the number of accidents due to doors becoming open whilst the **Train** was in motion.

Central Emergency Power Supply (CEPS)
[LUL] A supply generated by a source independent of all other supplies which is then distributed to equipment using the normal supply electrical network at a reduced capacity. Provides the basic needs for the evacuation of the **Railway**.

Central Interlocking Processor
[Sig.] Within a **Solid State Interlocking** (**SSI**) system, the **Interlocking** Processor is mainly responsible for the safe operation of the **Railway**. The Central Interlocking Processors operate in (repairable) Triple Modular Redundancy (**TMR**) to achieve high levels of hardware reliability, and to afford fault tolerance. Each sub-module is identical, running identical software and having identical copies of the **Geographic Data**, but independent RAM devices.

Central Trains (CT)
(Tradename) A **Train Operating Company** (**TOC**).

Centre Bound

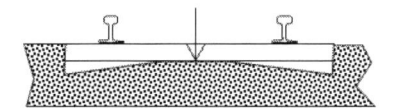

[PW] Describing a **Sleeper** that is supported by **Ballast** only at the centre, with **Voiding** under the **Rail Seats**. This is a fault of incorrect **Packing** of the **Ballast**, and will eventually lead to the Sleeper **Breaking its Back**. See also **End Bound**.

81

ELLIS' BRITISH RAILWAY ENGINEERING ENCYCLOPÆDIA

Centre Line Design
[PW]
a) A method of designing **Track Alignments** that considers only the **Track Centre Line**. The **Running Rails** are added later by means of offsets. See also **Low Rail Design**
b) A little-used method of designing **Switch and Crossing Layouts** (**S&C Layouts**) using only the **Rail Centre Lines** rather than the **Running Edges** (RE).

Centre Line Measurement

[PW] The measurement of the **N Value** of an **Acute Crossing** by means of a line drawn perpendicular to a line bisecting the **Crossing Angle**. The alternative is **Right Angle Measurement**.

Centre Line of Structure Gauge
[PW] A line produced through the **Track Centre Line** normal to the **Plane of the Rails**.

Centre Opening Doors
[TRS] Doors consisting of a pair of (typically) sliding panels, often interconnected so that they open and close simultaneously. Also called **Bi-parting Doors**. See also **Plug Doors**.

Centre Pivot

Centre Pivot Pin
[TRS] The pin about which a **Bogie** rotates.

Centre Pivot Liners
[TRS] The consumable lining which acts as a bearing surface at the **Centre Pivot** point of a **Bogie** allowing rotational movements between **Rail Vehicle** body and Bogie.

Centre Siding
a) A **Siding** located between an **Up** and a **Down Line** with a connection to both, generally provided to allow **Trains** to **Reverse** without standing on the **Running Line**

b) A Siding provided between two **Platform Lines** to allow **Locomotives** to **Run Round**
See also **Middle Road**.

Centre Throw

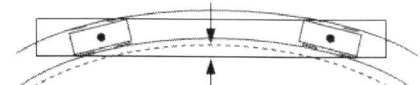

[PW] The lateral offset at the centre of a vehicle when negotiating a **Curve**, relative to its normal position on a straight. See also **Balanced Stock**, **End Throw**.

Centro
(Tradename) Marketing name of West Midlands Passenger Transport Executive (**WMPTE**).

CEPS
See **Central Emergency Power Supply**.

CER
a) Community of European **Railways**
b) [Hist.] The Pre-Grouping Clifton Extension Railway, a Great Western and Midland joint enterprise
c) [Tel.] Communications Equipment Room
d) Change en Route.

CERT
City of Edinburgh Rapid Transport.

Certificate of Conformance for Vehicle Maintenance
[TRS] A certificate issued by a Vehicle Acceptance Body (**VAB**) to confirm that the **Maintenance** regime for a **Rail Vehicle** conforms to the relevant **Railway Industry** and **Railway Group Standards** (RGS).

Certificate of Engineering Acceptance (CEA)
[TRS] A certificate issued by a Vehicle Acceptance Body (**VAB**) to confirm that a **Rail Vehicle** conforms to the relevant **Railway Industry Standards** And Railway Group Standards (RGS).

Certificate of Readiness (CoR)
[Ops.] A document that shows a **Train** has been prepared in accordance with required standards and is verified as safe for travel.

CESM
(*sez-umm*) [BR] Civil Engineering Safety Manual, the British Railways (**BR**) Director of Civil Engineering's (DoCE) safety instructions to staff.

CESMM
(*sez-umm*) Civil Engineering Standard Method of Measurement, used when collating bills of quantities. Section S applies to **Rail □ Track** (sic), but covering only new work.

Cess

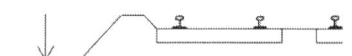

a) [RB] The space alongside the **Line** or Lines. It can provide space for a **Cess Path** but is not always a **Position of Safety**. See also **Safecess**, **Safecess Path**.
b) [PW] From an engineering viewpoint, the part of the **Track Bed** outside the **Ballast Shoulder** that should be maintained lower than the **Sleeper Bottom** (SB) to aid drainage. See also **Cess Drain**, **Cess Heave**.
c) [NR] For the purposes of a **Lineside** vegetation inspection, this is defined as the ground from the outer edge of the **Ballasted Area** to a point three metres from the **Running Rail**.

Cess Drain
A **Track Drain** constructed in the **Cess**.

Cess Heave
The upward movement of the **Cess** that occurs when the **Formation** fails catastrophically under **Traffic**. It is essentially a rotational **Slip** failure.

Cess Path
A path provided in the **Cess** for use by **Maintenance** staff. A Cess Path is *not necessarily* a safe place to walk whilst **Trains** are running, nor a **Place of Safety**. See also **Safecess**, **Safecess Path**.

CET
a) See Controlled Emission Toilet
b) Controlled Emission Tank
c) Central Estimating Team
d) [LUL] Communications Equipment Technician.

CET Apron
A concrete hard standing built under a Track where Controlled Emission Toilets (CET) are emptied in order to intercept spillages.

CFD
[NR] Contracts for Difference.

CFF
Chemins de fer Fédéraux Suisses, see SBB.

CFOR
Carriage Free on Rail.

CG
See Cant Gradient. See also Cant, Cant Transition.

CGIS
[Elec.] Containerised Gas Insulated Switchgear.

CGLR
(Tradename) [DLR] City, Greenwich and Lewisham Rail Ltd., which owns and operates the DLR □ Lines south of Crossharbour.

CH
a) (Tradename) Chiltern Railways, a Train Operating Company (TOC)
b) The ATOC code for Chiltern Railways.

Ch.
An abbreviation of:
a) Chain
b) Chair.

Chain
A unit of length equal to 66 feet or 22 Yards (20.1168m). There are 80 Chains in one standard Mile. Chains are the standard subdivision of Miles used in National Railway Network (NRN) □ Operations. See also Link.

Chainage
a) The location along the Track measured from the previous whole Milepost in Chains (22 Yards, 20.1168 metres)
b) The absolute position along the line of a Route measured from some designated reference point in a standard measurement unit, not necessarily Chains. See also Metreage.

Chaining Out
The action of marking the Track at regular measured intervals (typically 10 metres), to allow a future survey and design to be accurately referenced back to the site.

Chainman
A person employed to carry out the duties of surveyor's assistant. See also Light Duty Men.

CHAIR
Construction Hazard Assessment and Implication Review. A tool that has been developed to help identify and eliminate or reduce the health and safety risks associated with constructing and maintaining an asset in a structured and systematic way

Chair
[PW] A cast or fabricated support for Bull Head Rail (BH). See also Bridge Chair, Common Chair, Check Chair, Crossing Chair, Half Chair, Inside Keyed Chair, Joint Chair, Slide Chair, Thick Based Chair, Two Level Chair.

Chair Gall
[PW] Damage caused to the Rail Foot by a Chair. See Rail Gall.

Chair Liner
[PW]
a) A shim fitted to the Jaw of a Bull Head Chair to compensate for wear in, and ensure the correct fit of, the Key
b) A slotted metal plate fitted in the Rail Web of a Stock Rail between the Jaw Block of a Slide Chair or Slide Baseplate and the Rail. Also Button Stick.

Chair Lock
See Chairlock.

Chair Pad
[PW] A layer of resilient material fitted between a Bull Head (BH) □ Chair and a Concrete Sleeper.

Chair Shuffle
[PW] The tendency of inadequately maintained Chairs and Baseplates on Wood Sleepers to move laterally under traffic, so wearing the wood away from under them. Eventually the Chair or Baseplate disappears into the Sleeper altogether. See also Baseplate Shuffle.

Chairlock
[LUL] A type of Point Machine which locks the Switch Rail to the Slide Chair rather than to the Stock Rail as a Clamplock does.

Chairscrew
[PW] A specialised type of screw used to secure Chairs and Baseplates to Timbers and Bearers. The term Chairscrew is commonly used irrespective of what it is used to secure. Also Baseplate Screw.

Chaldron
a) [Obs.] A coal Wagon constructed largely of wood, in use from about 1730 and capable of holding a Chaldron of coal (see below)
b) [Obs.] A variant spelling of cauldron; a dry English measure of volume, mostly used for coal. It was used from the 13th century until 1963 when it was abolished by the Weights and Measures Act. From 1694 to abolition it was defined as 53 cwt (5936 lb, 2650kg).

CHALET
(*shall-ay*) A mnemonic representing Casualties, Hazards, Access, Location, Emergency services and Time.

Chambers, Austin
(1833 - 1898) Early Signalling pioneer who designed the first fully Interlocked □ Signalling installations at Willesden Junction and Kentish Town Junction, both in 1859.

ELLIS' BRITISH RAILWAY ENGINEERING ENCYCLOPÆDIA

Chamfered Switch
[PW] A **Switch** in which the **Switch Rail** and **Stock Rail** are machined to a matching angled (1 in 4) cut. On **Network Rail** (**NR**) this is the current standard. See also **Straight Cut Switch**, **Undercut Switch**.

Chancery Lane Accident
[LUL] At 13:50 on 25th January 2003 a westbound Central Line **Train** □ **Derailed** near Chancery lane Station. Of the 500 **Passengers** on board, 32 sustained minor injuries. The cause was determined to be a gearbox failure leading to the failure of the fixings of a **Traction Motor**, in turn leading to the Motor falling onto the **Track** and Derailing the last four **Rail Vehicles**. Despite efforts to deal with the issue, previous similar events had not led LUL to disseminate important information to the relevant Line Controllers.

Change of Gauge
[Hist.] See **Break of Gauge**.

Change of Section
Changes of Section
[PW] The points in a **Cast Crossing** where the **Rail** shaped profile of the **Leg** ends merges into the central **Monoblock** profile.

Change Point (CP)
[PW] The point at which the designed level changes from one **Gradient** or **Laser Beacon** to another.

Channel Drain
[PW]
A **Track Drain** constructed from U-shaped pre-cast concrete (**PCC**) units and appropriate extension sections. A lid is added to prevent the ingress of leaves, **Ballast**, **Trackworkers** etc. Such Drains are normally **Cess Drains**, but can be found in the **Sixfoot**.

Channel Rodding
See **Rodding**. Also **Point Rodding**.

Channel Tunnel (CT)
The 50.5km (31.4 mile) rail tunnel linking Folkestone in England and Coquelles in France. Construction of the current tunnel began in 1988 and it opened in 1994 at a cost £4.65 billion. The Channel Tunnel has the longest undersea section in the world at 37.9km (23.5 miles).

Channel Tunnel Bi-National Emergency Plan (BINAT)
[CT] The emergency plan to facilitate the handling of emergencies in the **Channel Tunnel** by permitting emergency response teams from the non-incident side of the Tunnel to cross the boundary between France and the UK to assist the team dealing with the emergency.

Channel Tunnel Rail Link (CTRL)
The specially built line linking London and the north end of the **Channel Tunnel** (**CT**). Now called **High Speed One** (**HS1**).

Channel Tunnel Safety Authority (CTSA)
[CT] A body providing advice on **Channel Tunnel** (**CT**) safety to the Intergovernmental Commission.

CHAPS
(*chaps*) Clearing House Accounts Payable System.

Chargehand
Chargeman
[BR] Title for an employee who had a supervisory role on a **Platform**.

Charlie
The **Phonetic Alphabet** word representing C.

Charter
Charter Train
A **Train** specially hired for a one off event, such as a sporting event or commemoration. There are **Train Operating Companies** (**TOC**) specialising in this market.

Chartered Institute of Logistics and Transport (CILT)
A professional Institute making an active and influential contribution to Government policy by publishing reports, papers and submissions and recommending practical solutions to short-term problems and longer term opportunities with the objective is to promote excellence in logistics and transport.

CHAS
Contractor's Health and Safety Assessment Scheme.

Cheadle Junction Accident
At 21:15 on 21 May 1971 a **Train** of **Merry-go-Round** (**MGR**) □ **Wagons** □ **Derailed** and was struck by another **Freight Train** passing the other way. The cause was determined to be one Wagon having **Hollow Treads**, and **Cyclic Top** on the **Jointed Track**. The driver of the second Train was killed.

Cheap and Cheerful CWR
[PW Col.] See **Lightweight Continuous Welded Rail**, **Lightweight CWR**.

Check Baseplate
[PW]
a) A **Baseplate** that carries both a **Flat Bottom** (**FB**) □ **Running Rail** and a Flat Bottom □ **Check Rail**
b) A **Baseplate** that carries both a Flat Bottom Running Rail and a **Bull Head** (**BH**) Check Rail.

Check Block
[PW] A metal spacing block fitted between **Running Rail** and **Check Rail** □ **Rail Webs** to maintain a fixed dimension between the two. The assembly is then bolted together through these **Blocks** and the Rail Webs. Also **Chogblock**.

Check Chair
[PW] A **Chair** that carries both a **Bull Head** (**BH**) □ **Running Rail** and a Bull Head **Check Rail**.

Check Cover

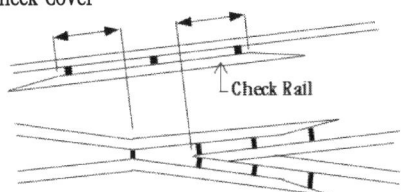

[PW] The distance between the extremities of any discontinuity and the ends of the full section of the **Check Rail** provided to protect it.

Check Locking

[Sig.] An arrangement which prevents the full stroke of a **Lever** until such time as the **Signalling Function** controlled by the **Lever** has completed its movement. See also **Backlocking**, **Indication Locking**.

Check Lump

[PW] An assembly located at the junction of a **Turnout Rail** and a **Check Rail** extended to the point where the **Rubbing Face** of the Check Rail meets the **Outside Edge (OE)** of the **Switch Rail**. Such an assembly would be provided where the **Switch Radius** and **Turnout Radius** require the provision of a Check Rail.

Check Rail

[PW] A **Rail** or other special section provided alongside a **Running Rail** to give guidance to flanged wheels by restricting lateral movement of the wheels. See **Flangeway**, **Raised Check Rail**. On Network Rail (**NR**) □ **Lines**, Check Rails are mandatory on **Curves** with a Radius (**R**) of 200m (220 **Yards**, 10 **Chains**) or less. See also **Gauge Widening**.

Check Rail Gap

[PW]
a) See **Flangeway Gap**
b) A gap in a **Check Rail**, see **Air Gap**
c) [LUL] Term for the **Flangeway** dimension.

Check Rail Gauge

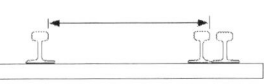

[PW] The dimension measured from the **Rubbing Face** of a **Check Rail** to the **Running Edge (RE)** of the opposite **Running Rail**. On **Standard Gauge Track** this dimension is always 1391mm for 1432mm Gauge Track (1394mm in **NR60** □ **S&C**), irrespective of any **Gauge Widening**.

Check Rail Lubricator

[PW] A **Rail Lubricator** arranged to apply grease to the **Wheel Backs** on sharp **Curves** fitted with **Check Rails**, as a means of reducing noise and wear.

Check Signaller

[Sig. Col.] An additional **Signaller** provided during times of planned disconnection of **Signalling Equipment** to provide an additional check before **Train Movements** are authorised.

Checked

a) A **Train** driver presented with a **Caution Aspect** or **Preliminary Caution Aspect** after a series of **Proceed Aspects** is said to have been Checked
b) [PW] Provided with a **Check Rail**
c) Subjected to a formal review to ascertain compliance with logic, standards, remit specification and/or safety considerations.

Checked Curve

[PW] A length of **Curved Track** fitted with a **Continuous Check Rail**.

Checking

a) [Col.] The action of providing a **Check Rail** or similar arrangement
b) [PW] See **Head Checking**, see also **Gauge Corner Cracking (GCC)**, **Rolling Contact Fatigue (RCF)**
c) Undertaking a formal review to ascertain compliance with logic, standards, remit specification and/or safety considerations.

Cheese Weights

See **Balance Weights**.

Chef de Train

[CT] The member of **Traincrew** in overall charge of a **Channel Tunnel** shuttle who rides in the **Amenity Coach (AMC)** on an HGV shuttle.

Cherries

[LUL Col.] A term for **Current Rail Gap Indicators**. Also **Rail Gap Indicator (RGI)**.

Cherry Picker

[Col.] A type of **Mobile Elevating Work Platform (MEWP)**, generally one equipped with a small platform fitted to a telescopic boom that can be rotated and extended to reach any point within a volume of space. See also **Permaquip**, **Scissor Lift Platform**.

Chicane

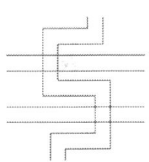

A deviation in the alignment of a walkway which crosses two adjacent **Tracks** to make the position of a **Position of Safety** clear to users.

Chicken Ladder

[PW] See **Step Gauge**, **Stepped Gauge**.

Chief Inspector

[IÉ] A person responsible for ensuring that inspections of **Track** and **Structures** in their area are carried out in accordance with the standards and for carrying out further inspections specified by the Assistant Divisional Engineer (**ADE**) and/or Divisional Engineer (**DE**).

Chief Mechanical Engineer Speed

[LUL] The theoretical speed of **Trains** calculated for a particular location having regard to gradients, location of **Permanent Speed Restrictions**, stopping places, **Train Performance** and **Passenger** loading.

Chik

A **Railway** □ **Telegraph Code** meaning "Following missing, urgently wanted. Have special enquiries made and if with you, forward immediately and reply".

ELLIS' BRITISH RAILWAY ENGINEERING ENCYCLOPÆDIA

Chiltern Railways
(Tradename) A **Train Operating Company** (**TOC**) which operates services throughout the M40 corridor between Birmingham and London.

Chimney
[TRS] In a **Steam Locomotive**, the vertical pipe that allows combustion gases plus **Exhaust Steam** from the **Blastpipe** and **Blower Ring** to escape to atmosphere.

CHIP
(*chip*) Chemical (Hazard Information and Packaging for Supply) Regulations 1994.

Chip Van
[Col.] Nickname for the 12- and 18-seat **Gang Buses** used by **British Rail** (**BR**). Ironically, these were sold at **Privatisation** and are now often used as – chip vans.

Chipping
[PW] A form of **Switch Rail** damage characterised by the breaking away of pieces of metal from the top surface of the Switch Rail within the machined length. It can be in the form of long thin slivers or as irregular 'saw tooth' shape. Likewise, pieces can break out from thin Switch Rails showing signs of **Sidewear**.

Chipping Bin
[PW Obs.] A container placed at regular intervals along the **Track** and used to store **Chippings** for use in packing **Bearers**, **Sleepers** or **Timbers**. Made redundant following the widespread introduction of **Stoneblowers** and **Tampers**.

Chippings
[PW] Crushed stone between 10 and 20mm in size and of angular shape, used to fill voids below **Sleepers** to restore the level of **Rails**, bed pipes in **Drains** and make walkways. Also **Tunnel Ballast**.

Chogblock
[PW Col.] A name for a **Check Block**, **Heel Block** or other spacing block, particularly in **Switch and Crossing Layouts** (**S&C Layouts**).

Choke
[TRS] A restriction in an air pipe that provides a controlled rate of pressure rise within a part of the compressed air system; used within an **Air Brake** system to provide a smooth brake application.

Chopper
[Col.] Nickname for a **Class** 20 **Diesel Locomotive**.

Chopper Control
[TRS] A means of controlling the speed of **Traction Motors** by turning the electrical supply rapidly on and off. More properly called Pulse Width Modulation (**PWM**) the system is normally based around a solid state device such as Gate Turn Off **Thyristors** (**GTO**), Insulated Gate Bipolar Transistor (**IGBT**), Silicon Controlled Rectifier (**SCR**) or Thyristor. The switching process creates electrical noise and can interfere with the **Traction Supply** arrangements, see **Harmonic Filter**.

Chopstick
[Elec. Col.] A term for a **Loop Dropper**.

Chord
a) A line (that is not a diameter of the circle) that intersects the circumference of a circle at two points. A Chord has the property that the distance between the Chord and circle at the midpoint between the intersections is directly related to the Radius (**R**) of the circle. See **Hallade**, **Versine**
b) See **Chord Line**.

Chord Length
[PW]
a) The length of **Chord** used in **Hallade** Surveys
b) Historically, standard Chord Lengths were used based on 1.61 times the **Permissible Speed** (**PS**):

Speed	Chord	Half Chord
30mph	48' - 3"	24' - 1½"
40mph	64' - 4"	32' - 2"
60mph	96' - 6"	48' - 3"

These lengths have the property that the **Versine** equals the **Equilibrium Cant** (**Ve**) at the relevant speed. In modern times the standard Chord/Half Chord lengths have become 30m and 15m, with smaller lengths (such as 20m/10m or 10m/5m) used for more accurate results.

Chord Line
a) A short length of often tightly curved **Track** connecting two **Routes** that cross but have no **Junction**
b) A short length of often tightly curved Track forming the third side of a **Triangle** where two Routes meet.

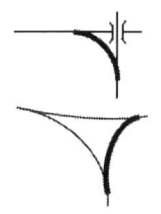

Chromaticity
Of a source of light, the co-ordinates of a colour which may be plotted on a Chromaticity diagram (of hue versus luminance) to graphically represent the colour in question.

Chrome Rail
[PW] **Rail** manufactured with a high Chromium content, making it more resistant to wear. See **110kg Chrome Rail**, **90kg Chrome Rail**.

CHS
Carriage Holding Sidings. See **Carriage Sidings** (**CS**).

CHU
Coin Handling Unit.

Chub (ZCX)
[NR] An **Open Wagon** used for the transport of Ballast and Spoil. See **Wagon Names**.

Chute Wagon
A **Wagon** specially built to allow the end-on unloading of Rail. See **Porpoise** (**YEA**).

CI
Cast Iron.

CIC
[TRS]
a) Control Isolating **Cock**.
b) Coupler Isolating Cock.

CIDS
Customer Information Display System, See **Customer Information System** (**CIS**).

86

CIE
Commission Internationale de l'Éclairage, or the International Commission on Lighting.

CIÉ
See Córas Iompair Éireann.

CIF
See Common Interface File.

Cill Beam
[Civ.] A concrete beam used to support and distribute the loads from **Bridge** bearings onto the **Pier** or **Abutment**. Also **Bearing Shelf**, **Bedstone**.

CILT
See Chartered Institute of Logistics and Transport.

CIM
An international convention concerning the movement of **Goods** by **Rail**.

CIMAH
(*sy-mah*) Control of Industrial Major Accident Hazards Regulations, 1984. Amended by the Control of Major Accident Hazards Regulations (COMAH) in 1999.

CIMU
[Hist.] Central Infrastructure Maintenance Unit (IMU).

Cinderella
[TRS Col.] A vehicle, designed to use **Conductor Rails**, which has lost a **Current Collection Shoe** (**Shoe**).

CIP
a) [NR] Competent Independent Person, see **Independent Competent Person** (**ICP**)
b) (Tradename) Cast Iron Products, formerly Taylor Brothers, based in Sandiacre, Nottingham.

CIPCE
(*sip-see*) Centre d'Information et de Publicité des Chemins de Fer Européennes, the information and Publicity Centre of the European **Railways**.

CIPP
Cured in Place Pipe.

CIPR
Cured in Place Repair

CIRAS
(*sy-rass*) Confidential Incident Reporting and Analysis System. An independent organisation within the **Rail Safety and Standards Board** (**RSSB**), it is available to all **Rail** workers throughout England, Scotland and Wales. All reports to it are confidential
- Freephone: 0800 4 101 101
- Text: 07507 285 887
- Post: Freepost CIRAS

Circle Time
[Ops.] An alternative term for **Pathing Allowance** as this Allowance is shown in the **Working Timetable** (**WTT**) enclosed in a circle or round brackets.

Circuit Breaker (CB)
a) An automatic switch designed to protect an electrical circuit from damage caused by overload or short circuit.
b) [TRS] A device fitted to an **Electric Locomotive** or **Electric Multiple Unit** (**EMU**) to isolate the vehicle power supply when there is a fault, when passing through a **Neutral Section** (**NS**) or for **Maintenance**. On **AC** systems they are usually on the roof near the **Pantograph**
c) [Elec.] A device built into a **Feeder Station** (**FS**) which allows the **Electrical Control Room** (**ECR**) to switch the current to various **Electrical Sections** on and off remotely. There are two types: the **Air Blast Circuit Breaker** (**ABCB**) and the **Vacuum Circuit Breaker** (**VCB**).

Circuit Controller
[Sig.] A multi-pole electrical switch with adjustable contact areas for each pole. The controller is operated by some mechanical device such as a **Point Lever** or **Signal Lever**, and is used to switch in and out other circuits during the cycle of movement. May also be combined with a **Lever Lock**. Also **Lever Band**.

Circular Curve
[PW] A curve of constant Radius (**R**) throughout. See also **Compound Curve**, **Transition Curve**.

Circular Turnout
[PW] A **Turnout** (**Lead**) having a **Circular Curve** from the **Switch Heel** to the **Intersection of Gauge Lines** (**IP**) of the **Common Crossing**. See also **Transitioned Turnout**.

CIRIA
Construction Industry Research and Information Association.

CIS
See Customer Information System. Also Customer Information Display System (CIDS), Passenger Information Display System (PIDS).

CISPR
Comité International Spécial des Perturbations Radioélectriques; ppecial international committee on radio interference.

CIT
Comité International des Transports Ferroviaires, the international **Rail** transport committee.

Citrusol Rail
(Tradename) A solvent based, on d-limonene distilled from orange peel and used to remove leaf contamination from **Rails**. Made by Citrusol.

CIU
Central Interlocking Unit.

Civil Engineer (CE)
a) Those engaged in the design, construction and **Maintenance** of large fixed structures such as **Bridges, Embankments, Tunnels** and buildings
b) [BR] The collective **British Railways (BR)** term for those responsible for **Structures** such as **Bridges** (themselves termed **The Works**) and those responsible for the **Permanent Way (PW)**. See also **Area Civil Engineer (ACE)**, Chief Civil Engineer **(CCE)**, **Divisional Civil Engineer (DCE), Regional Civil Engineer (RCE)**, Director of Civil Engineering **(DoCE)**.

Civil Engineering Committee (CEC)
[Hist.] The over-arching committee of the **Civil Engineering** □ **Function** within **British Rail (BR)**.

Civil Engineering Conference (CEC)
A consortium of **Civil Engineering** □ **Contractors** within the **Railway Industry**, working together to agree good practice.

Civil Engineering Handbook
[Hist.] A suite of Handbooks intended to assist the Engineer in designing and specifying works. A partial list is given below.

No.	Subject
1	Classifying and reporting of **Rail Failures**
1A	Ditto, **Cast Crossings**
2	109lb FB □ **Switches and Crossings (S&C)**
3	**Curving Rules**
4	**Mechanised Maintenance**, latterly: **Structure Gauging**
5	**Track Maintenance**
6	Examination of **Structures**
7,8	*unknown*
9	Mineral working affecting **Railway** property
10	Cleaning and painting of **Bridges**
11	**Continuous Welded Rail (CWR)**
11A	**Lightweight CWR**
12	Oral exams for supervisors and crane drivers
13,14	*unknown*
15	Rules affecting the safety of staff
16	Your personal safety on **Track**
17-21	*unknown*
22	**Lookouts** on **Ballast Cleaners** and **Tampers**
23	**Audigage** Manual
24	Mobile **Mechanised Maintenance** – Guidance
25	**Matisa Track Recording Trolley**
26	Bridge marking system
27	Steelwork specification
28	Inspection of concrete works
29	Inspection of fabricated steelwork
30	Safety precautions, high level Structures, latterly: **DTS** calibration
31	Notes for supervising **Contractors**
32	**Track Welding**
33	Code of practice for scaffolding
34	Code of practice for weed control
35	*unknown*
36	Conditions on work by **Outside Parties**
37	Code of procedure for chemical weed killing
38	**Track Recording Coach (TRC)** user manual
39	Guidance for contract administration
40	Landscaping by **Outside Parties**
41	Concrete repairs
42	Waterproofing Bridge **Decks**
43	Management of **Lineside Vegetation**
44	*unknown*
45	Cleaning masonry and brickwork
46	**Switch and Crossing Maintenance**
47	Assessing **Scour** risk
48	Maintenance system for **Wood Sleepers**
49	Track design manual
50	**Cold Expanding (CX)** of Bolt Holes
51	Selection of **Crossings**
52	Public safety on sites of work

All these documents have now been replaced by **Network Rail Company Standards (NRCS)** and **Railway Group Standards (RGS)**. In many cases the Handbook number has survived the transition (Handbook 49 became NR/L2/TRK/2049, for instance).

Civils, The
[Col.] A modern term describing only those responsible for **Structures** such as **Bridges**.

CJB
Clean Junction Box.

CJC
[Hist.] The **Pre-Grouping** (Carlisle) Citadel Station Joint Committee, a Caledonian and London & North West joint enterprise.

CK
[TRS] An acronym representing a **Corridor** □ **Composite Coach**.

CK&PR
[Hist.] The **Pre-Grouping** Cockermouth, Keswick & Penrith **Railway**.

CL
a) See **Carriage Line**
b) Cross London.

CL:AIRE
Contaminated Land: Applications in Real Environments

Clad Arch
[Civ.] An arch fitted with an **Arch Cladding**. Also **Lined Arch**.

Clag
[Col.] Heavy smoke and exhaust coming from a **Locomotive, On Track Machine (OTM)** or **Multiple Unit**.

Claims Allocation and Handling Agreement (CAHA)
[NR] An agreement between the various companies operating on the **Railway** which empowers Railway Claims Ltd to act on behalf of the **Rail Industry** and its **Contractors** for an accident or incident where a third party claim affects a number of organisations.

Clam (ZCV)
[NR] A 21 ton capacity **Spoil Wagon**. See **Wagon Names**.

Clamp
[PW] The very heavy duty G-shaped device used to secure **Emergency Clamp Fishplates** to the **Rail**. Correct deployment requires four such Clamps.

Clamp Lock
[Sig.] A hydraulic ram arrangement that operates and positively clamps the **Closed Switch** to the **Stock Rail**. It is actuated by a small electrically operated hydraulic pump located adjacent to the **Switch Toe**.

Clamp Lock Heater
[EP] An electrical heater fitted to **Clamp Lock** pump units to ensure that the hydraulic oil does not freeze in cold weather.

Clamp Lock Points
Clamp Lock Switch
Switches operated by means of a **Clamp Lock**.

Clamp Plate
[PW] See **Emergency Clamp Fishplate**.

Clamped Joint
[PW] A joint between **Rail Ends**, fitted with **Emergency Clamp Fishplates** instead of normal bolted ones. Generally a temporary measure, pending **Welding**.

Clamplock
See **Clamp Lock**.

Clapham Accident
The notable disaster that occurred just south-west of Clapham **Junction** at 08:10 on 12th December 1988. The train of events began after an overtired, inadequately trained and ill-supervised **Signalling** Technician failed to correctly remove a redundant wire during a **Re-signalling** project. This led to an **Unprotected Wrong Side Failure** (**UWSF**) and two **Trains** collided. The wreckage was then run into by another Train; 35 died and over 400 were injured, prompting some of the biggest changes in **Railway** engineering culture for many years. One of the outcomes was the **Transport And Works Act** (**TWA**). The enquiry was carried out by Anthony Hidden QC, and so many of the recommendations regarding working times and overtime are known as **Hidden Rules**.

CLARS
[LUL] Changes Locally Amending Routes Serving.

CLASP
(*clasp*) [Hist.] Consortium of Local Authority Special Projects and a common term for a particular type of modular building.

Clasp Brake
[TRS] An arrangement in which the brake blocks bear on the **Tyre** of the **Rail Wheel**, one each side. See also **Disc Brake**, **Tread Brake**.

Class
a) See **Class of Rail Defect**
b) See **Class of Sleeper**
c) See **Class of Supply**
d) See **Class of Tank Wagon**
e) See **Class of Train**
f) See **Dangerous Goods Class**
g) See **Locomotive Class**
h) See **Multiple Unit Class**
i) See **Passenger Class**
j) See **Route Class**

Class of Defect
See **Class of Rail Defect**.

Class of Rail Defect
[PW, NR] A measure of the threat a **Rail Defect** poses to passing **Trains**. The Class has a number (immediate action) and a letter (remedial timescale):

Class	Action
1	20mph **ESR** and fit **Emergency Clamped Fishplates**
2	Fit Emergency Clamped Fishplates
3	No immediate action
A	Remove within 36 hours
B	Remove within 7 days
C	Remove within 13 weeks
C*	Remove < 7 days if clamping impossible
D	**Weld Repair** within 7 days (non-**AMS**), 14 days (AMS), retest within 14 days
E	**Thermit Weld** within 7 days
F	Weld repair within 13 weeks
G	Retest within 13 weeks
H	Remove within 4 weeks
K	Remove within 26 weeks
L	Remove within 52 weeks

These actions are mandated in NR/SP/TRK/001 and a current copy should be consulted for details.

Class of Sleeper
[PW] A description of the **Rail Seat Reaction** (**RSR**) capacity of a **Concrete Sleeper**. The prefix letters (up to F) were originally introduced in British Standard (BS) 986 (now withdrawn).

Class	RSR	*Note*
A	9 tons	Obsolete
B	(possibly) 12 tons	Obsolete
C	15 tons	Obsolete
D	20 tons	Obsolescent
E	22 tonnes	Obsolescent
F (up to F27)	28 tonnes	
F (post-F27)	24 tonnes	
G	28 tonnes	

See also **Efxx**, **Egxx**.

Class of Supply
[LUL] A measure of the reliability of a Low Voltage AC (LVAC) power supply:

Class	Description
A	Derived from a **Bulk Supply Point** with an inherent **Central Emergency Power Supply** (**CEPS**) capability
B	Derived from a Bulk Supply Point without an inherent **Central Emergency Power Supply** (**CEPS**) capability, or where supplies are automatically disconnected in the event of a loss of power. Class B supplies can be derived from a Class A supply that has a CEPS capability but has automatic load shedding in the event of a loss of power.
C	Derived directly from **Distribution Network Operator** (**DNO**) infrastructure also known as 'street supplies'.
G	Derived from standby generation facilities incorporating automatic start/stop facilities.
N	New low voltage technologies not covered by the above. This could include photovoltaic etc.,
O	Derived from an offline battery source.
S	Derived from a self-contained battery source integral to the equipment being supported.
U	Derived from an online battery source.

Class of Tank Wagon
[Ops.]
- Class A - a **Tank Wagon** carrying flammable product(s) with a flashpoint below 23°C
- Class B - a Tank Wagon carrying flammable product(s) with a flashpoint between 23°C and 61°C.

Class of Train
[NR, Ops.]
a) A shorthand system used to group **Trains** into categories for the purpose of **Regulation**:

Class	Description
0	Light Locomotives
1	Express Passenger Trains
2	Stopping Passenger Trains
3	**Mail Trains** and **Freight Trains** authorised to run at more than 75 mph
4	Freight Trains authorised to run at between 60 and 75 mph
5	**Empty Coaching Stock** (**ECS**) Trains
6	Freight Trains running at 50 - 60 mph
7	Freight Trains running at 40 - 45 mph
8	**Engineer's Trains** and Freight Trains authorised to run at up to 35 mph
9	Was: **Unfitted** Freight Trains Now: **European Passenger Service** (**EPS**) Trains

b) A two digit number for **Locomotives** or three digit number for **Multiple Unit Trains** giving the type of vehicle, see **Locomotive Class**, **Multiple Unit Class**.

Classification Society
An organisation that develops and applies technical standards to the design, construction and assessment of ships (and other marine facilities) and which carries out related surveys.

Clawlock
(Tradename) See **Switchlock**.

Clay Balls
[Sig.] Shaped and dried clay spheres used to fill the void beneath a **Location Case**. This type of fill permits easy access for later alterations to the cables.

Clay Dig (CD)
[PW] An alternative term for **Formation Renewal**.

Clay Dig and Drain (CD&D)
[PW] A **Formation Renewal** with **Track Drain** work.

Clayton Tunnel Accident
At the time, Clayton **Tunnel** was "protected" by a variety of **Tail Lamping**, where the first **Train** had to pass through and out before the next was allowed in. In August 1861 three Trains were dispatched towards the Tunnel in rapid succession, the second arriving before the first was **Clear**. The **Signaller** attempted to stop the second one with a **Red** □ **Flag** and the Train pulled up and began to **Set Back**. The Signaller at the exit meanwhile signalled that the first Train was Clear, but the entry-end man assumed this meant both Trains and allowed the third Train in at full speed. 21 died and 176 were injured.

CLC
a) [Hist.] The pre-**Nationalisation** Cheshire **Lines** Committee, a Great Central, Great Northern and Midland joint enterprise. Used as a description of Lines in north west England that came under the control of the CLC, particularly:
b) The name given to the **Railway** connecting Manchester to Liverpool (now) via Warrington Central.

Clean Copy
[Sig.] A **Signalling** □ **Source Record** drawing that does not have any certification or stamps on it.

Clean End
[Sig., Col.] Term for **Signalling Equipment** that is away from the **Track**, e.g. **Relays** and **Signallers' Panels**. See also **Dirty End**.

Clear
a) [Sig.] In terms of an **Axle Counter Section**, **Track Circuit** (**TC**) or **Block Section**, it is the opposite of **Occupied**, meaning there are no **Rail Vehicles** present
b) [Sig.] Describing a **Signal** showing an **Aspect** allowing the driver to proceed
c) [Sig.] To Clear a Route on a **Signaller's Panel** is to remove the intended path for a Train from the **Panel**
d) [Sig.] To Clear a **Signal** is to change its **Aspect** from its **Most Restrictive Aspect** to a less restrictive Aspect. See also **Clear Aspect**.
e) [PW] For a structure adjacent to the **Track**, it is the opposite of **Foul**, meaning that the structure is not in the path of the Trains
f) [PW] To Clear a **Gauge**, a Rail Vehicle or a **Train** on a **Route** is to check a section of **Line** to ensure that a particular Rail Vehicle or set of Rail Vehicles may safely pass without suffering impacts along the way
g) The word used by a **Lookout** to indicate that there are no Trains in sight.

Clear Aspect
[Sig.] A **Colour Light Signal** displaying a **Proceed Aspect**, or a **Semaphore Signal** in the **Off** position.

Clear Back
[Sig. Col.] Term meaning to send **Train** out of **Section** to the **Signal Box** □ **On the Approach** by means of **Bell Code** 2-1. Also **Knock Out**.

Clear Weather Conditions
Daylight visibility of 1000 metres or better, where visibility is measured in accordance with recognised guidelines.

Clearance
[PW]
a) See **Electrical Clearances**
b) See **Passing Clearance**
c) See **Platform Clearance**
d) See **Structure Clearance**

Clearance Bar
[Sig.] A type of **Depression Bar** used to detect the presence of **Rail Vehicles** that are **Foul** of another **Line** or are standing close to or over **Sets of Points**.

Clearance Point (CP)

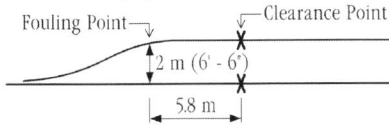

Fouling Point ⟶ ⟵ Clearance Point
2 m (6' - 6")
5.8 m

[Sig.] The point at which two idealised vehicles on **Converging Lines** or **Diverging Lines** would be **Clear** of each other. It is defined, on non-**High Speed Lines** as 5.8 m from the **Fouling Point** (FP), which is in turn the point where the **Running Edges** (RE) are 2 metres (6' - 6") apart.

Cleared
a) [Sig.] Describing a **Block Section** or **Track Circuit** that has been recently vacated by a **Train** or other obstruction
b) [Sig.] Describing a **Signal** that has recently been made to display a less restrictive **Aspect** or a **Proceed Aspect**
c) Describing a section of a **Route** that has been authorised for the passage of certain types of **Train** in certain modes of operation
d) Describing a **Train** that has been authorised to pass along a section of **Route** or to operate in a particular manner.

Clearing Point
[Sig.] In **Absolute Block** (AB) areas, the point to which a **Line** □ **Beyond** must be **Clear** in order to accept a **Train**. This is typically 440 yards (402.6 metres) Beyond the outermost **Home Signal**.

ClearRoute
(Tradename) A software tool, developed by **Laser Rail Technologies**, a division of **Balfour Beatty** Rail Technologies Ltd., used to perform a range of **Gauging** calculations.

Clerestory
Clerestory Roof
In **Railway** usage, a **Carriage** or **Station** roof which has a raised centre section incorporating low windows in the vertical faces.

CLG
Communities and **L**ocal **G**overnment.

Climb the Rail
Climbing the Rail
Describing the action of a **Rail Wheel** being driven up the **Running Face** of a **Rail**. There can be many contributory factors including excess speed, poor **Track Maintenance** and incorrect **Rail Profile** or **Wheel Profile**, but the result will be a **Derailment**. See also **Wheel Unloading**.

Clip
a) [PW] A device fitted to a **Baseplate** or **Housing** to retain a **Rail** in place. See **Rail Fastening**. Also **Rail Clip**
b) See **Insulator Clip**
c) [PW] A device resembling a carpenter's G-clamp, used to render a **Switch** inoperable. Also **Switch Clamp**, **Switch Clip**. See also **Switch Securing Device**
d) [Ops.] To secure a **Set of Points** (**Set of Switches**) in the closed position. See **Clipped and Padlocked** (C&P), **Clipped and Scotched**.

Clip Deflection
[PW] The amount by which certain types of **Rail Fastening** or **Rail Clip** deflect when being installed and/or tightened to produce the designed **Toe Load**.

Clipped and Padlocked (C&P)
[Ops.] A term found on **Signalling Plans**, describing a **Set Of Points** (**Set of Switches**), **Switch Diamond** or **Swing Nose** secured out of use by means of a **Switch Clamp** padlocked in place. See also **Clipped and Scotched**, **Secured Out of Use**.

Clipped and Scotched
[Ops.] A term used to describe a **Set of Switches** (**Set of Points**), **Switch Diamond** or **Swing Nose Crossing** that has been rendered inoperable by use of one or more **Switch Clamps** to secure the Closed side and a **Scotch** to secure the Open side. See also **Clipped and Padlocked** (C&P), **Secured Out of Use**.

Clipped Out of Use
[Ops.] Describes a **Set of Points** (**Set of Switches**), **Switch Diamond** or **Swing Nose Crossing** rendered inoperable by securing the movable parts using a **Switch Clamp** or **Switch Securing Device**. Also **Secured out of Use**.

Clipping Down
[PW] Alternative for **Clipping Up** □ **Rail Fastenings**.

Clipping Up
a) [PW] The process of fitting **Rail Clips** to **Flat Bottom Track**. **Clipping Down** is also used to describe the same operation. More universal terms are **Fastening Down** or **Fastening Up**. A similar activity carried out on **Bull Head Track** is **Keying Up**.
b) [Ops.] A colloquial term for making a **Set of Points**, **Switch Diamond** or **Swing Nose Crossing** □ **Clipped and Scotched**.

Clockface
Clockface Timetable
[Ops.]
a) A **Timetable** arrangement whereby **Trains** to a particular destination all leave a **Station** at the same time past the hour throughout the day
b) A timetable where Trains run at regular intervals (e.g. every 10 minutes).

Clockwork Orange, The
[Col.] Nickname for the Glasgow Underground allegedly due to the **Trains**, at one point, being painted an orange-red colour.

Clogging-on
[PW Hist.] Fixing **Chairs** or **Baseplates** to **Wood Sleepers** on site, in advance of **Relaying Work**.

Clogging-on Gauge
[PW Hist.] A (usually) home-made measuring device used to ensure that the **Chairs** or **Baseplates** are secured at the correct **Track Gauge** during **Clogging-on**.

Close Doors (CD)
Close Doors Indicator (CDI)
[Sig.] An indication to a driver that **Platform Work** is complete and the **Train** doors may safely be shut. Applies to Trains with power operated doors only.

Close Tolerance Fishplate
[PW] A type of **Fishplate** where the clearances included for the **Fishbolts** are reduced to an absolute minimum with maximum accuracy. See also **Tight Joint Fishplate (TJF)**.

Close Viewing Sector (CVS)
[Sig.] Also (and more commonly) known as a **Hot Strip**, an area of a **Signal** lens with a different optical arrangement that allows a driver to observe the **Aspect** of the Signal whilst stopped at it. This is required since the main beam is normally aimed parallel to the **Track**, to a point some 190-250m **On the Approach to** the **Signal**. The position of the Hot Strip is specified in terms of the clock face; the illustration above shows the 5 o'clock position.

On **LED Signals** the Hot Strip is achieved using differently orientated LEDs, often located in the upper left or right corner (10 o'clock or 2 o'clock).

Closed Block
[Sig.] The normal state in **Absolute Block (AB)** in which the **Line** is not **Cleared** for a **Train** to enter a **Block Section** until it is required to do so and the **Signals** controlling the entrance to the Section are normally maintained at **Danger**. See also **Open Block**.

Closed Line
a) [NR] A **Track** over which traffic has permanently ceased to pass, but where the **Permanent Way (PW)** is still in-situ. See also **CBL, Mothballed Line**
b) See **Signed Line**.

Closed Switch
[PW] A **Switch Half Set** where the **Switch Rail** is closed up to the adjacent **Stock Rail**. See also **Left Hand Switch Closed (LHSC), Open Switch, Right Hand Switch Closed (RHSC), Standing Off**.

Closing Up Signal
[Sig.] An additional **Signal** provided to optimise **Headways** or to provide earlier clearance of Junctions □ on the Approach to □ Stations. These Signals may or may not form part of the normal **Aspect Sequence**.

Closing Weld
[PW] The last **Weld** made at a site of **Rail** installation or replacement or **Stressing**, which completes the Welding of the Rails forming one side of the **Track**.

Closure List
[Sig.] The complete and final index of design information issued to the **Tester In Charge (TIC)** during **Testing and Commissioning (T&C)**.

Closure Notice
A formal notice issued to the public detailing the closure of a facility such as **Line**, service or **Station**.

Closure Panel
[PW] A short **Track Panel** used to complete a **Track** assembly, particularly between two **Switch and Crossing Units (S&C Units)**.

Closure Procedure
[NR] The formal method by which the **Infrastructure Controller** (currently **Network Rail**) goes about terminating the operation of a **Line** or **Station**.

Closure Rail
a) [PW] A short length of running **Rail** used to complete a **Track** assembly, particularly between two **Switch and Crossing Units (S&C Units)**
b) [PW] In a **Switch and Crossing Layout (S&C Layout)** the **Rail** between the **Switch Rail** and **Common Crossing** or between the **Obtuse Crossing Point Rail** and **Common Crossing**. Also colloquially **Gut Rail, Belly Rail**.

Clot
[Col. Hist.] Alternative nickname for a **Traffic Apprentice**. Also **Thrombosis**.

Clothoid Spiral
[PW] A type of **Transition Curve**. Also known as Euler's (pronounced *oiler's*) Spiral, it has the following properties:
- A body moving along the locus at a uniform velocity in either direction experiences a uniform rate of rotation
- The reciprocal of the instantaneous radius is proportional to the distance along the curve from its **Tangent Point** with the **Straight**.

This is the most common form of Transition Curve. See also **Bloss**.

CLR
Shorthand for **Clear**.

CLRL
Cross London □ Rail Links.

CLS
See **Colour Light Signal**.

ELLIS' BRITISH RAILWAY ENGINEERING ENCYCLOPÆDIA

Clubman
The brandname of the Class 168 **Diesel Mechanical Multiple Unit** (**DMMU**)

CM&DPR
[Hist.] The **Pre-Grouping** Cleobury Mortimer & Ditton Priors **Light Railway**.

CMD
a) [PW] Central Materials Depot, effectively a warehouse for **Permanent Way** (**PW**) materials. **Track Panels** recovered from **Relaying** sites were dismantled and the serviceable materials stored for re-use.
b) See **Carriage Maintenance Depot**.

CME
Circuit Main Earth.

CMIR
[LUL] Customer Major Injury Rate.

CML
Continental **Main Line**, now **High Speed One** (**HS1**), previously the **Channel Tunnel Rail Link** (**CTRL**).

CMS
a) Competence Management System
b) Capacity Management System
c) Control and Monitoring System
d) Cable Management System.

CNIITEI
Central Scientific Research Institute for Information, Technical and Economical Investigations of **Railway Transport**.

CNM
Corporate Network Model.

Co
(*coe*) [TRS] Denoting three linked but independently **Driven Axles**, See **Diesel and Electric Locomotive Notation**.

CO
[TRS] An acronym representing a **Composite** □ **Open Coach**.

COA
a) Change of Aspect
b) Clear on Arrival.

Coach
[TRS] Generally applied to vehicles specifically built to convey **Passengers** in Locomotive Hauled □ **Trains**. See also **Compartment Coach, Composite Coach, Mark of Coach, Open Coach, Passenger Coach, Tri-Composite Coach**.

Coach Screw
See **Coachscrew**.

Coaching Stock
[TRS] Vehicles designed to be used in **Passenger Trains**, but not always designed to convey **Passengers**.

Coachscrew
[PW] A screw used to secure fittings other than **Baseplates** and chairs to **Timbers**; such as **Insulators** for **Third Rail**, Lateral Resistance End Plates (**LREP**), **Soleplates**, etc.

Co-acting Signal (CA)
[Sig.] An exact duplicate of another **Signal** provided at the same location, but in a different position relative to the **Track**, normally to overcome a problem with **Sighting** the original Signal. Both Signals are generally identical and display the same information at the same time.

Coal Drop
An elevated **Track** designed to allow material to fall freely between the **Rails** onto the ground beneath. Used to quickly unload **Hoppers** containing coal and other similar materials.

Coalfish (MHA)
[NR] A 30 ton capacity **Open Wagon** used for transporting **Ballast** and **Spoil**.

Coaling Line
Coaling Road
A **Track** (generally a **Siding**) on which **Steam Locomotives** stand whilst being re-fuelled. A modern equivalent is a **Fuelling Line**.

Coasting
[Ops.] Removing power from a **Traction Unit** and allowing the **Train** to continue under its own momentum. Used to reduce the power drawn from the **Traction Supply** on **Electrified Railways**.

Coasting Board
A **Lineside Sign** provided to advise the driver to shut off power and coast to the next **Junction** or **Station**. See **Coasting**.

CoBA
Cost Benefit Analysis. Also **CBA**.

Cock
Railway Industry term for a manually operated valve, typically part of a **Rail Vehicle's** braking system.

Cockle
[NR, (Prob. Obs.)] A 12 ton **Brake Van** fitted with **Ballast Ploughs**.

Cockroach
(Tradename) [Elec.] Product name for the 19-strand aluminium cable used as **a Return Screening Conductor** (**RSC**). Manufactured by Eland Cables of London.

CoCoSigTSI
Command, Control & Signalling □ Technical Standard for Interoperability, the TSI covering the European Rail Traffic Management System (**ERTMS**).

CoCP
Code of Construction Practice.

Cod (ZAV)
[NR] A **Wagon** used for the transportation of **Sleepers**. See **Wagon Names**.

Code
[DLR] Data that is transmitted wirelessly and constantly between the **Train** and the control centre (vehicle control computers) via an antenna cable that is laid in the **Four Foot**.

Code of Practice
A statement of best practice, adherence to which is not a legal requirement.

Code Red
[LUL] A call made to **Train Operators** instructing them to stop their **Trains** immediately.

Code Trip Valve
[LUL] A valve which applies the emergency brake on the 1967 **Tube Stock** if the **Automatic Train Protection** (**ATP**) signal is lost.

Coefficient of Adhesion (μ)
The ratio between the actual **Tractive Effort** produced by a **Locomotive** on a given piece of **Track** divided by the theoretical maximum. Denoted by the Greek letter μ (pronounced *mew*), it can range from 0.1 to 0.4. See also **MaxiMu**.

Coefficient of Friction
The ratio of the force required to cause a body to slide along a plane (in the direction of sliding) to the normal force pressing the body and surface together.

COI
Confirmation of Instruction.

Coil
See **Maintenance Coil**, **Vortok Coil**.

Coimisiún Sábháilteachta Iarnróid
See **Railway Safety Commission** (**RSC**).

COL
[NR Civ.] Under the **Bridge Condition Marking Index** (**BCMI**) handbook, shorthand for column.

Cold Expanding of Bolt Holes
Cold Expansion of Bolt Holes (CX)
[PW] A technique which uses a hydraulic apparatus to expand newly drilled undersize holes to their correct dimension, creating a compressed area of metal around the hole This reduces the incidence of **Star Cracks** around **Fishbolt Holes**.

Collar
a) [Sig. Col.] A contraction of **Lever Collar**. See **Reminder Appliance**
b) [PW] A contraction of **Weld Collar**.

Collar Joint
[Civ.] The circumferential mortar bed between **Arch Rings**.

Collaring
[Sig. Col.] Colloquial term for the action of placing a **Reminder Appliance** (**Collar**) over an electrical switch, **Plunger**, push-button or **Lever** to remind the operator that it should not be operated, often due to an **Obstruction**

Collective Risk
The average number of **Fatalities**, or **Fatalities And Weighted Injuries** (**FWI**) per year that would be expected to occur from a hazardous event, or group of hazardous events.

Collector Drain
A **Drain** used to collect water and allow it to run away. Typically consisting of a narrow trench filled with a free draining material such as **Chippings**, a perforated pipe is also normally laid near the bottom, optionally wrapped in a **Geotextile** filter membrane to reduce the ingress of silt. See **Track Drain**. See also **Collector Drain**.

Collector Shoe
[TRS] A device mounted on certain **Electric Trains** that runs along an exposed surface of a **Conductor Rail** and collects the electrical **Traction Current**. Also **Current Collection Shoe**.

Collet Mechanical Ballast Packer
[PW, Obs.] An eight-tool **Ballast** packer which could **Pack** three **Sleepers** per minute.

Colliery Railway
A **Railway**, generally low speed and often **Narrow Gauge**, used to transport coal within and to locations close to coal mines.

Cologne Eggs
[PW] Resilient **Track** fixings, deployed to reduce **Track Noise** and vibration, named after the German city where they were first installed. See also **Delkor Egg**

Colour Light Distant Signal
[Sig.] A **Colour Light Signal** which can only display a **Caution Aspect** or **Proceed Aspect**. In order to improve the visibility of **Semaphore** ▫ **Distant Signals** in **Fog**, the intensity of the **Signal Lamp** was increased over time. Eventually, the Lamp was visible during daylight as well, making the actual **Arm** redundant. Modern versions use two separate lamps rather than one, but the principle is the same. See **Two Aspect Signal**.

Colour Light Signalling
[Sig.] A **Signalling** arrangement which uses **Colour Light Signals** to convey **Movement Authorities** to **Train** drivers. This system is a development of **Semaphore Signalling**.

Colour Light Signals

[Sig.] **Signals** which convey **Movement Authorities** to **Train** drivers by means of coloured lights. These Signals are described as having a number of **Aspects**, e.g. **Four Aspect Signal**, or how many different instructions they can convey. Thus:

Single Aspect Signal, generally a **Caution Aspect** or **Stop Aspect** (**Yellow** or **Red**)

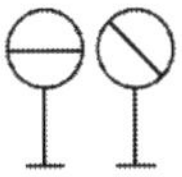

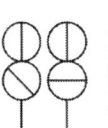

Two Aspect Signal, generally a **Proceed Aspect** and Stop (**Green** and Red), or Proceed and Caution (Green and Yellow)

Three Aspect Signal, generally Proceed, Caution and Stop (Green, Yellow and Red)

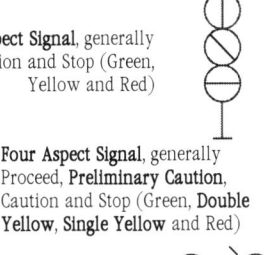

Four Aspect Signal, generally Proceed, **Preliminary Caution**, Caution and Stop (Green, **Double Yellow**, **Single Yellow** and Red)

Flashing Aspect, which as well as the normal four Aspects, is also capable of flashing the Double or Single Yellow aspects to warn of an approaching **Junction**

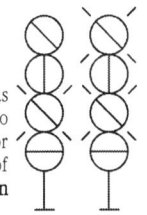

The Red Aspect (if required) is always located nearest the driver's eye level. A variety of Colour Light Signal is the **Position Light Signal (PLS)** or **Ground Position Light Signal (GPLS)**.

Colouring Convention

[Sig.] A set of colours which have specific meaning on **Signalling Scheme Plans (SSP)**:
- **Black** - existing equipment not affected by the works or works carried out under a previous stage
- **Green** - existing equipment decommissioned as part of the works
- **Red** - new equipment commissioned under the works

This convention can also be found on other drawings in other disciplines such as **General Arrangement (GA) Drawings** and **Layout Plans**, as can the use of other colours:
- **Blue** – existing equipment that is relocated or **Slued**
- **Pink** or **Purple** – future **Staging** or observational notes

Colwich Accident

In September 1986 two **Trains** collided virtually head on when the driver of a northbound Train passed a **Signal** showing a **Stop Aspect** and stopped on the **Junction** in front of the other, southbound Train. The first apparently misunderstood the **Aspect Sequence** and assumed that the **Signal** □ **Beyond** would **Clear** from **Red** for him; it was in fact correctly requiring him to stop. This first Train then ran past this Signal, stopping foul of the Junction. 32 **Passengers** were seriously injured and the driver of the second Train died. It was alleged that the **Wheel Slide Prevention (WSP)** system increased the stopping distance of the first Train, but this effect was never satisfactorily recreated.

COMAH

(*coe-ma*) The Control of Major Accident Hazards Regulations 1999, which modified the CIMAH (Control of Industrial Major Accident Hazards) Regulations 1984. The legislation requires the owners and operators of sites where chemicals (and similar hazardous materials) are handled or stored to have robust plans in place to deal with fires, leaks, spills, etc. The local authority is required to have a similar robust plan in place for all such sites within its jurisdiction.

Comb

A complex space-saving arrangement of **Turnouts** found in **Yards** or **Depots**. The **Switch Toe** of the second Turnout lies between the **Switches** and **Crossing** of the first **Turnout**, and so on.

Combination Valve

[TRS] A valve that enables the driver to control both the **Steam Brake** on a **Steam Locomotive** and the vacuum **Train Brake** by moving a single handle.

COMBINE

Enhanced **Control Centre** for a **Moving Block** □ **Signalling System**.

Combined Power-brake Controller

See **Combined Traction and Brake Controller (CTBC)**. Also **Traction Brake Controller (TBC)**

Combined Reading Distance (CRD)

[Sig.] The total Reading Distance available for a **Banner Repeating Signal** and its associated **Signal**.

Combined Traction and Brake Controller (CTBC)

[TRS] A single control which is moved one way to accelerate and the other to apply the brakes.

ELLIS' BRITISH RAILWAY ENGINEERING ENCYCLOPÆDIA

Comeback Possession
Comeback Shift
[Col.] A **Possession** or shift programmed as part of a larger **Track Renewal** Possession, but timed to start some hours after the main Possession finishes. A typical pattern might be 16 hours for the main works, followed by eight hours **Running** under a 20mph **Temporary Speed Restriction** (**TSR**) during Sunday afternoon. The Comeback Possession might then be six or eight hours of **Tamping**, handing the **Track** back at a higher TSR, typically 40 or 50mph.

Command Telegram
[Sig.] Within a **Solid State Interlocking** (**SSI**) system, Command Telegrams convey instructions from the **Central Interlocking Processor** to the **Trackside Functional Modules** (**TFM**).

Commencement
The starting location of a **Temporary Speed Restriction** (TSR). See Speed Indicator (SI).

Commencement Board
[Col.] Term for a marker placed at the start of a **Temporary Speed Restriction** (TSR), giving the maximum permissible speed. Also **C Board**. See **Speed Indicator** (SI).

Commencement Indicator
[Obs.] An obsolete term for a **Speed Indicator** (SI).

Commissioning
[Sig.] The activity during which a new or modified **Signalling System** undergoes final **Testing** and last minute adjustments are made, before **Signing Back In** the whole system into use. See **Closure List**, **Stageworks**, **Tester in Charge** (TIC), **Wheels Free Period**. Also **Testing and Commissioning** (**T&C**).

Common Carrier
[Obs.] A requirement for British **Railways** to carry all and any goods at defined rates and restricting the striking of special deals with particular customers. Designed to regulate a profitable monopoly industry; The **Big Four** lobbied for the removal of the legislation in the 'Square Deal' campaign of 1938, but it was not repealed until the **Transport Act 1962** which abolished the British Transport Commission (**BTC**) and created the **British Railways Board** (**BRB**). The regulations effectively required the Railway to maintain an **Infrastructure** for everyone regardless of its commercial viability, preventing the Railways from investing efficiently. This requirement is no longer in force. Tomorrow

Common Chair
[PW] A **Bull Head** (**BH**) □ **Chair** in general use for the support of a **Running Rail**. Also **AS1, S1, S2**.

Common Crossing

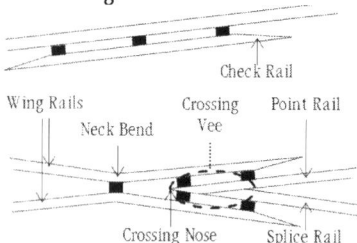

[PW] A **Switch and Crossing Unit** (**S&C Unit**) comprising a **Point Rail** and **Splice Rail** (making a **Crossing Vee**) and two **Wing Rails**. When installed in the track, **Check Rails** are provided adjacent to the opposite **Rail** to ensure wheels do not 'fall into the gap' caused by the discontinuity that exists at the **Crossing Nose**. Also **Acute Crossing**, **Fabricated Common Crossing**.

Common Crossing Point Rail

[PW] One of the two machined rails that form the **Crossing Vee** of a **Fabricated Common Crossing**, this being the one that forms the **Crossing Nose**. The other one is the **Splice Rail**. Also contracted to **Point Rail**.

Common Crossing Splice Rail

[PW] One of the two machined rails that form the **Crossing Vee** of a **Fabricated Common Crossing**, this being the one that is spliced into the **Common Crossing Point Rail**. Also contracted to **Splice Rail**.

Common Crossing Vee

[PW] The assembly formed by fixing together a **Common Crossing Point Rail** and a **Common Crossing Splice Rail**. The term is also used to describe any similar assembly, howsoever made. See also **Cast Vee Common Crossing**, **Electro-slag Welded Crossing Vee**, **Electro-slag Welded Vee**, **Part Welded Crossing**, **Semi-welded Crossing**.

Common Crossing, Parts of

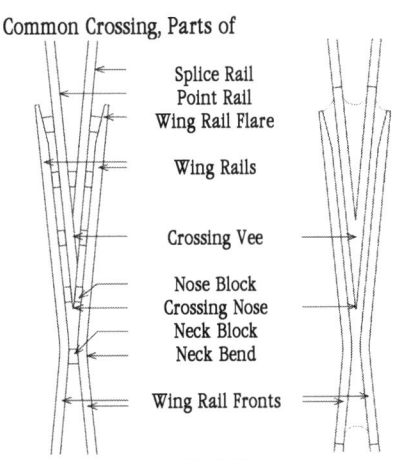

- Splice Rail
- Point Rail
- Wing Rail Flare
- Wing Rails
- Crossing Vee
- Nose Block
- Crossing Nose
- Neck Block
- Neck Bend
- Wing Rail Fronts

Common Interface File (CIF)
An interface system for extracting **Train** schedules from the **Integrated Train Planning System** (**ITPS**). CIF determines the specific data to be distributed to each system requiring Train schedule data.

Common Interface File Operating Characteristics Code
A code item within a **Common Interface File** (**CIF**) that gives further information about a **Train** schedule. See B, C, D, E, G, M, P, Q, R, S, Y, Z.

Common Rail (CR)
[Sig.] The **Rail** in a **Common Rail Track Circuit** that forms part of other **Track Circuits** (**TC**), and the one acting as the **Traction Return Rail** where an isolated Common Rail Track Circuit exists. Also called **Single Rail, Traction Rail**.

Common Rail Bonding
[Sig.] An arrangement of **Track Circuits** (**TC**) where only one **Rail** (the **Insulated Rail**) is divided with **Insulated Rail Joints** (**IRJ**) to separate each Track Circuit. The other (the **Common Rail**) is electrically continuous and is used by all the Track Circuits. Also **Single Rail Bonding**.

Common Rail Track Circuit
[Sig.] A **Track Circuit** (**TC**) where one of the **Rails** also forms part of the circuit of one or more other Track Circuits. Also **Single Rail Track Circuit**.

Common Safety Method (CSM)
A European Union Regulation that came fully into force on 1st July 2012 and is intended to regularise risk evaluation and assessment for the **Main Line** ▫ **Railway Industry** across the EU. The **Railway and Other Guided Transport Systems (Safety) Regulations 2006** (**ROGS**), as amended, require **Railway Undertakings** (**RU**) and **Infrastructure Managers** (**IM**) to develop their Safety Management System (SMS) to manage the risks associated with their activities and to meet specific criteria. One of the criteria for the SMS is that it must apply the relevant parts of CSM. The CSM applies to significant changes to all **Railway** sub-systems, significant changes to the operation of the Railway, and significant organisational changes that could impact on the operating conditions of the railway system.

Common Safety Method Assessment Body (CSM AsBo)
A person or body that is independent from the design, manufacture, construction, marketing, operation or **Maintenance** of the system under assessment and has the professional integrity and competence, experience and resources to check that the **Common Safety Method** (**CSM**) on risk assessment has been followed and also check that the results of the assessment are consistent with process followed

Commonwealth Bogie
[TRS] Successor to the **B1 Bogie** from the late 1950s, this type was cast steel with sealed bearings and coil spring **Primary Suspension**.

Communication Cord
[TRS Hist.] A cord or chain running along a **Passenger Coach** just above the windows and connected to emergency brake valves at each end of the vehicle. When pulled (in an emergency), the cord or chain opens the valve(s) and the brakes are applied. The driver will notice the application and be unable to restart the **Train** until the valves are reset (and the emergency dealt with). Originally the indication that the chord had been pulled was given by a "butterfly" on the brake valve turning from horizontal to vertical and it was reset by turning the "butterfly" back to horizontal. See also **Passenger Emergency Alarm Brake** (**PEAB**).

Communications Based Train Control (CBTC)
[Sig.] An alternative term for **Transmission Based Train Control** (**TBTC**).

Community Rail
a) See **Community Rail Line**
b) See **Community Rail Partnership** (**CRP**)
c) See **Community Rail Service**.
d) See also **Association of Community Rail Partnerships** (**AcoRP**).

Community Rail Line
A **Railway** which is specially supported by local organisations, usually through a **Community Rail Partnership** (**CRP**) comprising a **Train Operating Company** (**TOC**), local councils and other community organisations, or sometimes by a **Rail User Group** (**RUG**). Since 2005 the **Department for Transport** (**DfT**) has formally designated a number of **Lines** as **Community Rail** schemes in order to recognise the need for different, more appropriate standards than are applied to **Main Line** □ **Routes**.

Community Rail Partnership (CRP)
A group formed to support a **Community Rail Line**, typically comprised of a **Train Operating Company** (**TOC**), local councils and other community organisations. See also **Association of Community Rail Partnerships** (**AcoRP**)

Commutator
[Sig.] A rotating shaft with separated electrical contacts upon it. These connect to various fixed contacts as the shaft is turned. Particularly, the knob on the **Block Instrument** that is turned by the **Signaller** to give **Line Clear** (**LC**) or **Train On Line** (**TOL**) to the adjacent **Signal Box** (**SB**) in **Absolute Block** (**AB**) areas.

Commuter
a) [Hist.] Originally, a person who commuted a series of single journey **Tickets** into one Ticket covering a week or month's journeys
b) A person who makes the journey from home to work and back every working day using some form of transportation system.

Commuter Line
A **Route** used virtually exclusively by **Trains** conveying **Commuters**, often **Multiple Unit Trains**.

Company Equipotential Grid System
[LUL] A nominally equipotential grid for all fixed LUL electrical assets and **Rolling Stock**, which has a maximum resistance to earth of 0.7 Ω at any point.

Company Standards
See **Network Rail Company Standards** (**NRCS**).

Comparative Gauging
[PW] The process of comparing the **Swept Envelopes** of a **Rail Vehicle** new to a **Route** with the Swept Envelopes of a Vehicle or Vehicles which have safely used the proposed Route before, the object being to prove that the new Vehicle will or will not be **Clear**.

Compartment
Compartment Coach
Compartment Stock
[TRS] A **Coach** that is divided into separate areas, each seating six or more **Passengers**, with no means of moving between each compartment. A Coach so divided and provided with access between the compartments by means of a door and a corridor running down one side of the vehicle is termed a **Corridor Coach**.

COMPASS
Co̱mbined P̱erformance a̱nd S̱afety S̱ystem.

Compensated Gradient
[PW] A **Curved Track** on a **Gradient** for which the gradient has been lessened or eased to compensate for the increased resistance that would be caused by that **Curve**.

Compensating Bar
[TRS] A part of some **Bogie** suspension systems which comprises a swan-neck shaped steel beam connecting the **Axleboxes** on each side of the Bogie and supporting the suspension springs.

Compensator

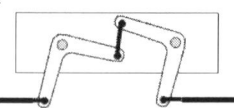

[Sig.] A device composed of two bell cranks and a short link, placed centrally in the length of **Rodding** between **Signal Box** and **Points** to eliminate problems caused by thermal movement.

Competent Independent Person (CIP)
[NR] **Network Rail's** term for an **Independent Competent Person** (**ICP**).

Competent Person
a) [RB] A person who is passed as being qualified and has the required knowledge and skills to carry out a particular rule, regulation, instruction or procedure
b) An individual or body nominated to undertake **Engineering Acceptance** for **Rail Vehicles**. See **Vehicle Acceptance Body** (**VAB**).

Complete Renewal
[PW] The act of renewing all **Rail**, **Sleepers** and **Ballast** and associated components between two **Mileages** as one task. Also described as **Relaying**.

Complete Resleeper
Complete Resleepering
[PW] Changing all the **Sleepers** between two **Mileages** with new or **Serviceable** ones. Also **Continuous Resleepering**. See also **Resleepering** (**RS**).

Complex Points Failure
[NR] A **Points Failure** which needs more **Point Ends** to be **Set** or secured (or both) than a **Simple Points Failure**. It also includes all failures that affect **Switch Diamonds** (**SD**) and **Swing-Nose Crossings** (**SNX**). See **Route Setting Agent** (**RSA**).

Complex Projects Procedure (CPP)
[NR] A formal process by which **Network Rail** (**NR**) attempts to agree and establish the scope of a complex project before the project is fully developed and before issues of timings and compensation are determined. It allows the **Rail Industry** as a whole to provide preliminary input into large projects, and contributes to the efficient progression through the early stages of development. It is an early extension to the normal **Network Change** process, but does not replace the need to issue G1 Network changes.

Composite
Composite Coach
[TRS] A **Passenger Coach** with provision for both **First Class** and **Second Class** (now **Standard Class**) □ Passengers. See also **Tri-composite Coach**.

Composite Adjustment Switch
[PW] An **Adjustment Switch** that has different **Rail Sections** at opposite ends: most commonly these are **CEN60E2** at one end and **CEN56** at the other (**CEN60E1** and **113A** in older examples), allowing the Adjustment Switch to also act as the **Transition Panel**.

Composite Deck
[Civ.] A **Bridge** □ **Deck** that derives its strength from the use of structural steel sections encased in concrete.

Composite Insulator
[PW] A **Rail Foot Insulator** having a metal wear plate fitted to its upper surface.

Composite Weld
[PW]
a) An **Alumino-thermic Weld** (**W**) made between **Rails** of different sections
b) A **Flash Butt Weld** (**FBW**) made between **AMS** and **Normal Grade Rail** steels, which because of their incompatibility utilises an intermediate layer of Stainless Steel between the **Rails**. See also **Tri-metallic Zone** (**TMZ**). Also **Sandwich Weld**.

Composite Wheel
[TRS] A **Rail Wheel** made of two or more dissimilar materials. Typical Rail Wheels consist of a single large casting making up the majority of the wheel, with a thin tyre shrunk onto the rim. A Composite Wheel may consist of the following:
• A wooden centre with a steel tyre shrunk in the manner of a cartwheel, called a Mansell Wheel
• A steel centre part and a steel tyre, separated by a polymer layer, intended to reduce vibration. See Eschede Accident, **SAB Wheel**.

Composite Yards
[PW] A means of measuring a quantity of **Track Renewals** work. The total number of **Yards** of Re-ballasting, Rerailing and Resleepering equals the number of **Composite Yards**.

Compound
a) [PW WR] A **Single Slip Diamond** (**Single Compound**) or **Double Slip Diamond** (**Double Compound**)
b) [TRS] A term used to describe a **Steam Locomotive** having two or more cylinders working at two or more different steam pressures.

Compound Catenary

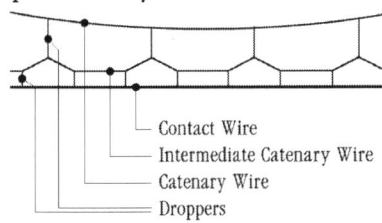

— Contact Wire
— Intermediate Catenary Wire
— Catenary Wire
— Droppers

[Elec.] An arrangement of **Overhead Line Electrification** (**OLE**) equipment where the **Catenary** consists of a **Catenary Wire**, **Intermediate Catenary Wire** and **Contact Wire** (**CW**). See also **Simple Catenary**.

Compound Crossing
See **Saddle Crossing**.

Compound Curve
[PW] A **Curve** of constant **Hand** that has two or more differing radii within it, each pair having a common **Tangent Point** whether separated by **Transition Curves** or not.

Comprehensive Approach Locking (CAL)
[Sig.] An arrangement of **Approach Locking** where the **Locking** is only applied when a **Train** is approaching the **Signal**, in order to provide maximum flexibility.

Compromise Fixed Buffer Stop
A **Fixed Buffer Stop** with several **Buffer Beams** placed at heights compatible with **Rolling Stock** from different systems, e.g. **Network Rail** and **London Underground Limited** (**LUL**).

Compulsory Purchase Order (CPO)
The right to buy property in order to construct new works. See also **Transport and Works Act** (**TWA**).

Computer Based Interlocking (CBI)
[Sig.] A second generation **Interlocking** system that consists of a microcomputer running a specially written program. Developed from the first generation **Solid State Interlocking** (**SSI**) systems, it further integrates the **Signal Box Panel** and **Illuminated Diagram** by using trackballs and VDUs to produce a system that can be altered easily. All its functions, including **Track Layouts**, **Train Describer Berths** etc. are software based.

Con Rail
Conrail
[Col.] A common contraction of **Conductor Rail**. Also **Hot Rail**, **Juice Rail**, **Pozzy Rail**, **Third Rail**.

Conarch
[Civ.] A Pre-cast Concrete (**PCC**) **Arch** section with a squared aperture, used to replace masonry arches and increase headroom over the **Railway**.

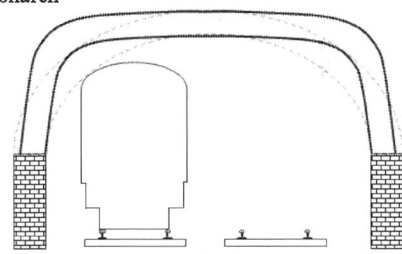

Concast
Concast Rail
[PW] **Rails** produced by the Continuous Casting process, rather than the previous ingot process. Concast production eliminates the slag and impurities present in the head of the Ingot. Rail produced prior to 1975 is most likely to have been rolled from ingots.

Concave Platform
A curved **Platform** where the centre of radius of curvature is on the Platform side of the **Platform Edge**.

ELLIS' BRITISH RAILWAY ENGINEERING ENCYCLOPÆDIA

Concave Vertical Curve

[PW] A **Vertical Curve** (**VC**) provided between two **Gradients** which form a valley. Also **Sag Curve**. The opposite is a **Convex Vertical Curve** or **Hog Curve**.

Concentrator
See **Telephone Concentrator**.

Concession
a) Any agreement which permits one party to operate a service on behalf of another, often in return for favourable trading terms
b) [CT] The premises occupied and operated by **Eurotunnel** plc, including all **Terminal** □ **Tracks** and facilities.

Concession Agreement
[CT] The agreement between **Eurotunnel** and the UK and French Governments specifying the conditions under which Eurotunnel operates the **Channel Tunnel**.

Concession Time
[CT] The time used by **Eurotunnel** for all operating purposes. It corresponds with the time used in France and is usually one hour ahead of that in use in the UK.

Conciliation Grades
Conciliation Staff
[BR Hist.] Under **British Rail** (**BR**), the group of employees that included drivers, **Guards**, **Signallers**, supervisors, etc. See also **Wages Grades**, **P&T Staff**.

Concourse
An open area forming a link between the entrance, **Booking Hall** and **Platforms** of a **Station**, used for ticket purchase, information gathering, retail outlets and passenger waiting space.

Concourse Level
Describing the vertical position occupied by the **Concourse** in a **Station**. This may or may not be different from **Platform Level** and ground level.

Concrete Bearer
[PW] A pre-stressed concrete replacement for the traditional wooden **Bearers** in **Switch and Crossing Layouts** (**S&C Layouts**).

Concrete Cable Trough
Pre-cast concrete (**PCC**) units, U-shaped in section, supplied in 1m lengths. In a range of standard sizes with appropriate lids, they are laid end to end on a level surface and used to protect **Signalling** and **Telecommunications** cables laid along the side of the **Track**. See also **C/1/x**. Also **Troughing**.

Concrete Sleeper
[PW] A pre-stressed concrete replacement for **Wood Sleepers**. They are generally found on the more heavily trafficked lines.

Concrete Switch Bearer
[PW] A **Concrete Bearer** that supports the **Rails** in the **Switch** area of a **Switch and Crossing Layout** (**S&C Layout**).

Concrete Train
A specialist **Train** designed and equipped for mixing and placing concrete, typically used in the construction of **Overhead Line Structure** foundations.

Concreted Track
[PW, LUL] Generic term for **Ballastless Track** designs where in-situ concrete is used to hold the **Sleepers** or **Sleeper Blocks** in position.

Cond.
[Col.] Shorthand for Condemned.

Condition of Track (COT)
[PW] A term used to describe the reason for the imposition of an **Emergency Speed Restriction** (**ESR**) or **Temporary Speed Restriction** (**TSR**). Specific reasons may include poor condition or failure of one or more of **Rails**, **Ballast**, **Sleepers** and **Formation**.

Condition of Track Speed (COT Speed, COTS)
[PW] A **Speed Restriction** imposed due to poor **Condition of Track** (**COT**).

Conditional Double Reds (CDRs)
See **TPWS OS** (**Outer Signal**)

Conditional Locking
[Sig.] An **Interlocking** arrangement that depends on the state of other **Signalling Functions**.

Conditioning
Conditioning the Rail Head
The process by which a contaminated **Rail Head** may be cleaned by the friction caused by passing **Wheelsets**.

Conditions of Carriage
[NR] The rules governing **Tickets**, accommodation, reservations, luggage and lost property on **Trains**. It is worth noting that under these conditions, you are not guaranteed a seat and your luggage may not even be allowed on the Train! See also **NRCOC**, **Railway Byelaws**.

Conductor
a) A common contraction of **Conductor Driver**
b) A metal wire, bundle of wires, rod, strap or tube that carries an electric current
c) The modern title for the person carrying out customer-related management duties on a **Passenger Train**. This role includes the duties of a **Guard**. Also Senior Conductor, **Train Manager**.

Conductor Driver
[Ops.] Where a **Train** driver is unfamiliar with either the **Route** or the controls, a driver who is familiar with such things accompanies the Train to ensure that the Train and Route are both correctly driven. This situation can occur during diversions. See also **Signing a Route**.

Conductor Icing
[Elec.] A build-up of ice on a **Contact Wire** (**CW**) which causes poor electrical contact and rapid electrical erosion of the **Contact Strips**. See also **Conductor Rail Icing**, **Contact Wire Icing**.

Conductor Rail
[Elec.]
a) A **Rail** through which electricity is supplied to **Electric Trains**.

b) [NR, LUL] An additional **Rail**, generally of a unique section such as 150 ▢ **Pounds Per Yard**, used to convey and enable collection of electrical **Traction Current** at **Track Level**. Conductor Rail systems carry voltages of the order of 600 to 1200 Volts, generally **DC**. The Conductor Rails are supported on **Conductor Rail Insulators** (colloquially **Pots**). Also **Current Rail, DC Rail, Juice Rail, Live Rail, Positive Conductor Rail, Positive Rail, Pozzy Rail, Third Rail**. See also **105, 105A, 106, 150, DC Electrified Line, Tunnel Rail**.

Conductor Rail Anchor
[Elec.]
a) A device used to prevent longitudinal movement of a **Conductor Rail**:
b) [NR] A type of **Rail Anchor**
c) [LUL] An insulated bar between the Conductor Rail and **Sleeper** or **Track Slab**. See also **Anchor Struts**.

Conductor Rail Anchor Struts
See **Anchor Struts**.

Conductor Rail Boarding
[Elec.] An alternative for **Guard Boarding**. Also **Kick Boarding, Protection Planking**.

Conductor Rail Equipment (CRE)
[Elec.] The **Conductor Rail** and its ancillary items. See **Conductor Rail Insulator, Hook Switch, Ramp End**.

Conductor Rail Gap
[Elec.] A break in the **Conductor Rail** which provides for:
- **Isolations** and **Junctions** in the **Track**
- Thermal movement of the Conductor Rail.

Conductor Rail Gauge
[Elec.] The position of the centre of the **Crown** of the **Conductor Rails** relative to the nearest **Running Edge** (RE).

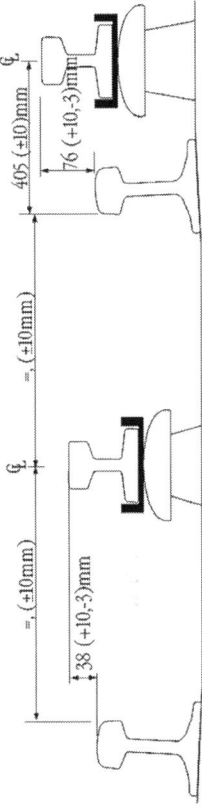

Conductor Rail Icing
[Elec.] A build-up of ice on a **Conductor Rail** which can cause poor electrical contact and rapid electrical erosion of the **Rail** by arcing. See also **Conductor Icing**.

Conductor Rail Insulator
[Elec.] The porcelain item used to support a **Conductor Rail** and insulate it electrically from the **Bearer** or **Sleeper** below. Also **Pot, Third Rail Insulator**.

Conductor Rail Permit (CRP)
a) A form of authority signed and issued by an **Authorised Person** to a person in charge of a group **Working** on, or near to, **Conductor Rail Equipment**. The purpose of the form is to make known to the person in charge exactly which equipment has been made electrically safe (**Isolated**) to allow work to commence.

b) [NR] As a suffix to **COSS** on a **Sentinel** card it means the **COSS** is qualified to receive permits for **Conductor Rail** ▢ **Isolations**.

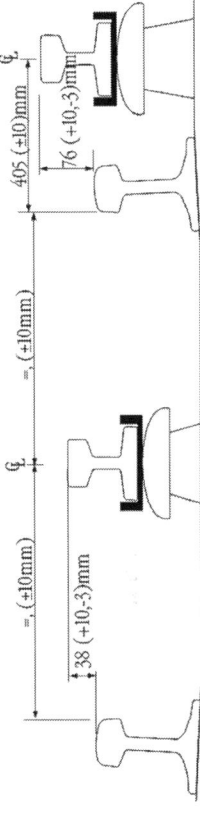

Conductor Rail Ramp
[Elec.] A cast or fabricated ramp section normally welded onto the ends of **Conductor Rails**, its purpose being to guide the **Current Collection Shoes** (**Shoes**) up onto the Rail. Also called a **Contact Ramp**, **Ramp End**.

Conductor Rail Test Lamp Set
[Elec.] A portable device consisting of a wooden enclosure containing six lamps, used to test whether a **Conductor Rail** is **Live** Also **Box of Eggs**, **Nest of Eggs**.

Conductor Rail Tester
[Elec.] Staff responsible for testing if a **Conductor Rail** is **Live** using an authorised **Conductor Rail Testing Device**.

Conductor Rail Testing Device
[Elec.] A device used to test if a **Conductor Rail** is **Live**. See also **Conductor Rail Test Lamp Set**

Cone Packings
[TRS] Discs inserted between the top of an **Axle Box** and bottom of a **Leaf Spring** to adjust the height of a **Rail Vehicle** at that point. See also **Suspension Packings**.

Cone Penetration Test (CPT)
[Civ.] An intrusive test which determines a soil's bearing capacity. The test consists of pushing a cone tip-first into the ground at a slow, controlled rate (typically two centimetres per second) and measuring the force required. Most modern electronic CPT cones now also employ a pressure transducer with a filter to gather pore water pressure data.

Confidence Limits
A statistical concept that sets the limits within which there would be (say) a 90% probability that something would be true.

Configurated Rail Pad
[PW] A pad having dimples, grooves or pimples moulded onto its surface. Also, **Dimpled Pad**, **Grooved Pad**, **Pimple Pad**.

Confined Space
A place which is substantially (though not always entirely) enclosed, and where there will be a reasonably foreseeable risk of serious injury from hazardous substances or conditions within the space or nearby, and which has difficult access.

Confirmed Period Possession Plan (CPPP)
[NR] A planning document created within **Network Rail's** □ **Possession** planning system (**PPS**).

Conflict
A **Railway** □ **Telegraph Code** meaning "No Train conveying **Passengers** or signalled by **Bell Code** 2-6-2 or 2-6-3 must be allowed on the **Running Lines** or **Sidings** mentioned on either side of the load. To be signalled by the special **Is Line Clear** Bell Code 2-6-3" and applied to **Out of Gauge Loads**.

Conflicting Locking
[Sig.] **Interlocking** between two **Routes** that requires one or more **Points** to be **Set** in opposite positions. See also **Direct Opposing Locking**.

Conflicting Move
Conflicting Movement
[Sig.] Any movement of two **Trains** that would force them to occupy the same section of **Track**.

Conflicting Port
See **Foul Notch**.

Conflicting Signal
[Sig.] A **Signal** that is capable of indicating a **Route** that would cause two **Trains** to occupy the same section of **Track**.

Confliction
[Ops.] A point where the movement of a **Train** can be impeded by another **Train** joining from another **Route**.

Conformance Certification Body
[NR] An organisation authorised to issue Certificates of Conformance to verify that **Rail Vehicles** conform to the relevant mandatory requirements of the relevant **Railway** standards.

Conger (YVQ, YXA)
[NR] A **Wagon** originally used for the transportation of girders. See **Wagon Names**.

Coning
[TRS] The application of a coned profile to the **Tyres** of **Rail Wheels** to aid their centering behaviour on **Straight Track**. In order to accommodate this, the **Rail Crown** should be parallel to the Tyre, and thus the whole **Rail** is **Inclined** at 1 in 20 as much as possible. See **Rail Inclination**

Connecting Rod
a) [Sig.] An adjustable metal bar used to connect the **Switch Operating Device** to the **Drive Lug** on the **First Stretcher Bar** of a **Switch**. Also **Drive Rod**, **Pull Rod**.
b) [TRS] Part of the motion of a **Steam Locomotive**, locomotive which links the piston rod to one of the driving wheel cranks via the crosshead, transforming the reciprocating motion into a rotary motion.

Connection Agreement (CA)
[NR] The modern **Network Rail** equivalent of a **Private Siding Agreement** (**PSA**).

Connections
[PW] Generic term for **Crossovers**, **Diamonds**, **Scissors**, **Leads** and **Turnouts** allowing movements to and from a **Line** and between Lines. See **Switches and Crossings** (**S&C**)

Connex
Connex South Eastern
(Tradename) A **Train Operating Company** (**TOC**).

Consist
[Ops.] The list of vehicles making up a **Train**.

Console
[Sig.] That part of a power signal box on which the switches and control buttons are located.

Conspicuity
A subjective term which relates to the ability of an object to capture attention. See also **Signal Sighting**.

Constrained Curving
[PW] An arrangement of **Cant**, **Curvature** and speed that does not allow **Wheelsets** to negotiate a **Curve** without the **Flange** of the outer wheel making contact with the **Rail Head**; guidance is therefore provided solely by the contact between Wheelset and **Running Rail** or **Check Rail**. See also **Free Curving**.

Construction Depth
a) See **System Height**
b) [Civ.] Overall depth of an **Underline Bridge** □ **Deck** from the underside of the deck (the **Soffit**) to **Rail Level**.

Contact Face
[PW] An alternative to **Rubbing Face** for a **Check Rail**.

Contact Gauging
[PW] A very low technology method of assessing the clearances between a **Rail Vehicle** and the **Bridges** and **Structures** on a **Route**; low density polystyrene blocks are fixed to the exterior of the vehicle and it is moved along the Route. Any surviving polystyrene still attached at the end represents the minimum clearance available. See **Gauging**.

Contact Ramp
See **Conductor Rail Ramp**.

Contact Strip
a) [PW] The shiny part of the upper surface of the **Rail Head**, being that part of the **Rail** that is normally run upon by the vehicle wheels. See also **Running Band**
b) [Elec.] The replaceable carbon strips fixed to the upper edges of a **Pantograph**. These strips contact the underside of the **Contact Wire** (**CW**) and thereby provide a path for the **Traction Supply Current**. Also **Carbons**.

Contact System
[Elec.] Generic term for any system used to supply power to **Trains** where part of the train makes contact to draw power e.g. from **Overhead Line Equipment** (**OLE**) via a **Pantograph** or from a **Conductor Rail** via a **Current Collection Shoe**.

Contact Wire (CW)
[Elec.] Normally the lowest wire in an **Overhead Line Electrification** (**OLE**) system, it is this one that the **Pantograph** touches to draw power. Contact Wires are normally an approximately figure-of-eight cross section allowing the suspension clips for **Droppers** to be attached easily.

Contact Wire Icing
[Elec.] A build-up of ice on the **Contact Wire** (**CW**) during cold damp weather. See also **Conductor Icing**.

Contact Wire Splice (CWS)
[Elec.] A joint in the **Contact Wire** (**CW**) that maintains an even surface for the **Pantograph**. Also **Battleship Splice**.

Contactor
A device similar to a **Relay** in that it is a remotely operated switch used to control another (often higher power) local circuit. A contactor is different as it normally latches and has to be released by a separate action. See also **Circuit Breaker** (**CB**).

Container
A large steel box built to a range of standard sizes and securing arrangements, used to convey **Goods** with a reasonable degree of security. Standard dimensions are 2.438m (8'- 0") wide, 2.591m (8' - 6" high) and either 6.096m (20') or 12.192m (40' long). There are also variant 40' Containers called "High Cube" which are 2.896m (9' - 6") tall and there is a standard 13.716m (45') long High Cube Container too. Other forms of construction exist, but all comply with these dimensions. Also known as ISO Containers. See also **Container Vehicles**, **Container Flat**, **Corner Casting**, **FEU**, **TEU**, **Spigot**, **Twistlock**.

Container Carrier
A company that transports freight **Containers**.

Container Flats
Container Vehicles
Container Wagons
[TRS] A long, low ladder chassis fitted with **Bogies** and equipment to secure standard shipping **Containers**.

Containment
a) See **Containment Capacity**
b) The arrangements for protecting cables on and within a structure. See **Admiralty Tray**, **Cable Trough**, **Ducted Cable Route**.

Containment Capacity
[Civ.] On a **Bridge**, the maximum speed that an unreinforced **Masonry** □ **Parapet** may sustain from a saloon car (as defined for low or normal level containment) either to prevent full penetration or to limit damage to the vehicle and occupants to an acceptable level.

Contaminated Ballast
[PW]
a) In the most literal sense, all used **Ballast** is contaminated. It is fouled with human effluent, asbestos, hydrocarbons and whatever else it has carried in its life. However, since the Granite used is non-porous, it is a relatively simple task to remove these impurities
b) A term used to indicate that the Ballast contains **Slurry**.

Contenary
[Elec.] A combined **Catenary** and **Contact Wire** (**CW**) used under low **Overbridges** (**OB**), in **Tunnels** and other locations where the available headroom does not permit a full height Catenary system to be installed. It is a concatenation of Contact and Catenary. See also **Free Running Equipment**.

Continental Notation
[TRS] A method of describing the wheel arrangements of **Steam Locomotives** similar to **Whyte's Notation**, except that only the wheels on one **Rail** are counted and driving wheels are denoted by a letter (A=1, B=2, etc.). Therefore, a 4-6-2 in Whyte's Notation would be a 2C1 in Continental Notation.

Continuity Bond
[Elec.] A **Bond** across a gap in the **Traction Return Rail** in **Switch and Crossing Layouts** (**S&C Layouts**).

Continuity Brake Test
[TRS] A test to confirm that the **Train Brakes** are functional and connected throughout the length of the **Train**.

Continuous Action Tamper (CAT)
[PW] A **Tamper** which moves continuously whilst working, and utilises a **Satellite Tamping Bank** moving rapidly beneath it to implement the **Tamping Cycle**. This arrangement significantly increases output and dramatically reduces operator fatigue, as the machine is no longer subject to rapid acceleration and deceleration between Tamping Cycles.

Continuous Automatic Warning System (CAWS)
[IÉ, NIR] A form of **Cab Signalling** and **Train Protection System** to aid **Train** drivers in observing and obeying **Lineside** □ **Signals**.

Continuous Brake
[TS] A brake system that operates simultaneously throughout a **Train**, and applies itself if vehicles become **Uncoupled**. Also **Automatic Brake**.

Continuous Check
Continuous Checking
Continuous Check Rail
[PW] A **Check Rail** fitted throughout a **Curve** to assist in keeping **Trains** on the **Track**. Such provisions are mandatory on Curves with a Radius (**R**) of 200m or less.

Continuous Place of Safety (CPOS)
[NR] A cleared strip **Clear** of the **Running Line** on which it is safe to stand whilst **Trains** pass. Such provision is generally not wide enough or well specified enough to be described as a **Safecess Path**. See also **Discrete Position of Safety** (**DPOS**).

Continuous Rail
[LUL Sig.] Term for the **Running Rail** that parallels the **Section Rail**.

Continuous Resleepering
[PW] Changing all the **Sleepers** between two **Mileages**. Also **Complete Resleepering**. See also **Resleepering**.

Continuous Route Signing (CRS)
[NR Sig.] The provision on a **Railway** of sufficient highway style signs to allow the route to be safely driven by a driver who has never driven it before. Such signs may include:
- **Commencement** of **Enhanced Permissible Speeds** (**EPS**) and **Permissible Speeds** (**PS**)
- **Warning Indicators** (**WI**) for reductions of speed
- **Reminder Signs** for **Permissible Speeds**
- **Countdown Markers** to **Stations**, **Signals**, etc.
- Radio channel information
- **Junction Names**

Officially, Continuous Route Signage is no longer policy, but there is little difference between current minimum provision and the former requirements of the Continuous Route Signage standards.

Continuous Running Rail (CRR)
[LUL] One **Running Rail** of each **Track** designated and longitudinally bonded to form one continuous **Conductor** for the length of each **Traction Current Section**.

Continuous Welded Rail (CWR)
a) [NR] A **Rail** of length greater than 36.576 metres (120'), or 54.864 metres (180') in certain **Tunnels**, produced by joining **Standard Rails**, either by welding or joining using **Tight Joint** (**TJ**) **Fishplates** or **Track** constructed from such Rails
b) [LUL] Rails welded together to form a single rail with a length greater than 200 metres (217'). See also **Strengthened** and **Stressing**.

Continuous Welded Rail Train (CWR Train)
[TRS, PW] A **Rake** of specially adapted **Rail Vehicles** capable of transporting 36 no. 600' (182.88m) **Strings** of **Rail** to site and unloading them using a gantry mounted grab system and chutes. The term **Long Welded Rail Train** (**LWRT** or **LWR Train**) is also used interchangeably.

Contour Railway
A **Railway** which attempts to avoid large **Cuttings** or **Embankments**, steep **Gradients**, **Tunnels** and **Viaducts** by following a single contour line. Railways built on this principle are generally extremely sinuous.

Contractor
Previously, an organisation only allowed to work on **British Railways** (**BR**) when it could be proved that the skills were not available from within British Railways and after the Unions had been consulted (and thus a swearword of sorts within BR). After **Privatisation,** any organisation supplying another with a service (Thus, nearly every organisation in today's **Railway Industry**).

Contractor's Assurance Case (CAC)
Replacing the **Contractor's Safety Case** (**CSC**), a document that details of the **Contractor's** compliance with the safety requirements laid down by **Network Rail** (**NR**), and the method of compliance with other systems such as quality and environmental.

Contractor's Engineering Manager
[NR] A specific role under **Network Rail Company Standard** (**NRCS**) NR/L2/INI/02009, A competent Engineer nominated by the **Contractor** and appointed by **Network Rail** to be responsible for the engineering coordination of a design or construction project. This role is an equivalent of the **Designated Project Engineer** (**DPE**)

Contractor's Responsible Engineer (Construction) (CRE Construction)
See **Contractor's Responsible Engineer** (**CRE**) clause b).

Contractor's Responsible Engineer (CRE)
[NR]
a) A competent Engineer appointed by the Design **Contractor** to manage and be responsible for the technical aspects of the Contractor's works, known as a **Contractor's Responsible Engineer** (**Design**) (**CRE Design**).
b) A competent Engineer appointed by a **Contractor** to manage and be responsible for the design aspects of the Contractor's works, known as a **Contractor's Responsible Engineer** (**Construction**) (**CRE Construction**).

Contractor's Responsible Engineer (Design) (CRE Design)
See **Contractor's Responsible Engineer** (CRE) clause a).

Contractor's Safety Case (CSC)
[Hist.] The document in which any potential **Contractor** who wished to work on the **Railway** demonstrated their compliance with the mandatory safety requirements. The Contractor's Safety Case has now been replaced by the **Contractor's Assurance Case** (CAC). See also **Railway Safety Case** (RSC)

Contra-flexure
[PW] A **Curve** of opposite **Hand** to another related **Curve**. See also **Contra-flexure Turnout**. The opposite is **Similar Flexure**, see also **Similar Flexure Turnout**.

Contra-flexure Turnout
[PW] A **Turnout** in which the curves of the diverging **Tracks** are of opposite **Hand**. Also **Off the Back**.

Contrast
The difference in colour and brightness that makes an object stand out from other objects or its background. See **Signal Sighting**.

Contra-tilting Pantograph
[TRS] A type of **Pantograph** fitted to **Tilting Trains** that tilts in the opposite direction to the Vehicle, in order to keep the **Electrical Envelope** of the Pantograph central the normal **Track Centreline**. This also minimises the **Swept Path** of the **Train**.

Contributory Factor
Any factor that affected, sustained or exacerbated the outcome of an occurrence. Eliminating one or more of these factors would not have prevented the occurrence but their presence made it more likely, or changed the outcome.

Control
a) [Sig.] Any rule designed into the Interlocking of a Signalling System. See Signalling Control
b) The office within each of the **Network Rail** □ **Routes** that is the nodal point for information and decisions relating to the day-to-day operation of the **Railway**, and the similar arrangements that existed under **British Rail** (BR), **Railtrack** (RT) and elsewhere. See also **Rail Operating Centre** (ROC)
c) See **Survey Control**.

Control Area
[Sig.] The part of the **Railway** controlled by a **Signal Box** (SB). This may consist of one or more **Interlockings** and many **Level Crossings** (LC, LX), **Points** and **Signals**. See also **Signalling Plan**.

Control Centre
[Sig.] A **Signal Box** (SB) covering a large area, usually incorporating other operational functions.

Control Centre Controller
[DLR] A person who monitors and controls the operations of the **Docklands Light Railway** from the Serco Docklands control centre.

Control Centre Incident Log (CCIL)
A common logging system for use by any company in **The Railway Group**. Used in the various control centres it records each incident once but these records can be added to by the stakeholders.

Control Centre of the Future (CCF)
[Sig.] A system used by **Control Centre** staff and others which provides a visual schematic display of **Train** position, both real-time and historic, and presents information on Train **Running**.

Control Device
[Sig.] Any **Lever**, electrical switch, button or VDU monitor target which is operated by a **Signaller** to set **Points** and **Routes**, **Clear** and **Replace** □ **Signals** and operate other **Signalling Functions**.

Control Interpreter
[Sig.] The name given to the generic software running in a **Solid State Interlocking** (SSI), This software interprets the **Geographic Data**. The Control Interpreter has other functions, but all **Interlocking** functions are encoded in the data, except for a few very simple operations `hardwired' into the interpreter for the sake of efficiency. See also **Interlocking Functional Program**.

Control Key
[LUL] A key used to operate the control switch, which in turn enables changes in the operational state of a **Train** to be made.

Control Period (CP)
[NR] A five-year period during which **Access Charges**, **Network** performance and **Network Rail's** (NR) allowances for enhancement works are set:

	From 1st April	To 31st March
CP1	1996	2001
CP2*	2001	2004
CP3	2004	2009
CP4	2009	2014
CP5	2014	2019
CP6	2019	2024
CP7	2024	2029
CP8	2029	2034
CP9	2034	2039
CP10	2039	2044
CP11	2044	2049
CP12	2049	2054
CP13	2054	2059

Note:
*CP2 was shortened by the demise of **Railtrack** (RT) in 2002.

Control Point
[Sig.] Generic term for a location from which a **Signalling System** is controlled, including **Block Posts**, **Gate Boxes**, **Integrated Electronic Control Centres** (IECC), **Power Signal Boxes** (PSB), **Signal Boxes** (SB) and **Signalling Control Centres** (SCC).

Control Speed Area
[LUL] The section of **Track** over which **Control Speed Permission** applies.

Control Speed Permission
[LUL] An arrangement where the **Signalling System** allows the **Train** to proceed only when it is travelling below a specified speed.

Control Table
[Sig.] A specification that details the **Signalling Controls** associated with every **Signalling Function** in an **Interlocking**.

ELLIS' BRITISH RAILWAY ENGINEERING ENCYCLOPÆDIA

Controlled Area
[LUL] An area where the movement of **Trains** is controlled by, or affects, the operation **Of Semi-Automatic Signals**

Controlled Barriers - Obstacle Detectors (CB-OD)
A type of **Level Crossing** (**LC**, **LX**) where the **Level Crossing** is proved clear of road vehicles and pedestrians using a combination of infrared detectors and Light Direction and Ranging (**LiDAR**). They are **Interlocked** with the **Protecting Signals** and are autonomous in operation, i.e. they will **Auto-Lower** and **Auto-Raise** without input from the **Signaller**. See also **Obstacle Detectors**.

Controlled Crossing
See **Controlled Level Crossing**.

Controlled Document
A document issued to a list of named individuals who are responsible for the destruction of the previous revision and compliance with the new document. Such an arrangement is normally used to control the distribution of safety related or other critical information.

Controlled Emission Toilet (CET)
[TRS] A toilet system in which the effluent is stored in tanks under the vehicle until it can be pumped out and disposed to a sewage treatment facility. This type is replacing the **Live Discharge Toilet**, which, as its name suggests, merely empties onto the **Track**.

Controlled Evacuation
[RB] The evacuation of **Passengers** from a **Train** after the **Signaller** has confirmed that all **Lines** have been **Protected**.

Controlled Level Crossing
a) A **Level Crossing** (**LC**, **LX**) with **Gates** or **Full Barriers**, **Interlocked** with **Signals** and often provided with road traffic signals. **Wicket Gates** may also be provided
b) Any of the following types of **Level Crossing**:
- **Manned** crossing with Barriers (**MCB**)
- Manned crossing with Gates (**MG**)
- Remotely controlled crossing with Barriers (**RC**)
- Barrier crossing with closed-circuit television (**CCTV**)
- Barrier crossing with obstacle detection (**OD**)

Controlled Signal
[Sig.] A **Signal** which is made to display a **Proceed Aspect** by **Automatic Route Setting** (**ARS**) or a **Signaller**, as required, during normal operations. Controlled Signals are normally **Non-passable Signals**. Some Controlled Signals have the facility to be set by the Signaller to work as **Automatic Signals**, see **Semi-Automatic Signal**.

Controller
The central point of contact for information and decisions relating to the day-to-day operation of a **Railway**. See also **Control**.

Controller of Site Safety (COSS)
[NR] A person certified as competent and appointed to provide a **Safe System Of Work** (**SsoW**) to enable activities to be carried out by a group of persons on **Network Rail** (**NR**) □ **Infrastructure** in accordance with the requirements of the **Rule Book** (GE/RT8000). On site, a COSS wears a blue **Armband** with COSS in white letters. See also **Protection Controller** (**PC**). This arrangement is to be replaced by **Safe Work Leader** (**SWL**).

Controlling Signal Box
[Sig.] The **Signal Box** (**SB**) that has control over a particular **Signal** or **Points**, or controls the Signal protecting a particular section of **Line**.

Conventional Interoperability
A framework mandating the implementation of common provisions for **Conventional Trains** on non-**High Speed Lines**.

Conventional Rail
[Col.] An umbrella term describing a **Railways** or the operation of a Railway where:
- The **Trains** do not **Tilt**
- Where fixed **Lineside** □ **Signals** are used
- Speeds are generally below 125mph (201kph).

Conventional Route
A Route which is required to meet the **Conventional Interoperability** requirements rather than the those for **High Speed Lines**.

Conventional Signalling
[Sig.] A **Signalling System** based on fixed **Lineside** □ **Signals**, rather than In-**cab Signalling** etc.

Conventional Train
[TRS] A **Train** with no **Tilting** capabilities. See **Conventional Rail**. See also **Permissible Speed** (**PS**).

Converging Lines
Converging Tracks
A pair of **Tracks**, which in the **Normal Direction** ultimately cross or join. The opposite is **Diverging Tracks**.

Converse Locking
[Sig.] The provision of **Interlocking** between two **Signalling Functions** such that if A locks B, then B must lock A. A **Mechanical Interlocking** provides this automatically, but it must be consciously incorporated into other Interlocking systems. Also **Reciprocal Locking**.

Conversion
a) [PW] The action of changing the **Rail Fastening** system used on a **Sleeper** whilst in-situ. Examples include the LC Clip system for **Wood Sleepers** and the installation of **Pandrol** fastenings instead of BJB. Also **Converting**
b) [Ops.] Describing the process of re-training drivers on mass to drive new **Rolling Stock**.

ELLIS' BRITISH RAILWAY ENGINEERING ENCYCLOPÆDIA

Converter
Collective term for any solid state system for converting Alternating Current (**AC**) to Direct Current (**DC**) or vice versa. Where an AC supply is converted to DC it is the specific term is **Rectifier** and where DC is converted to AC it is an **Inverter**.

Converting
See **Conversion**.

Convex platform
A curved **Platform** where the centre of radius of curvature is on the **Track** side of the **Platform Edge**.

Convex Vertical Curve

[PW] A **Vertical Curve** (**VC**) provided between two gradients which form a summit. Also **Summit**, **Hog Curve**. The opposite is a **Concave Vertical Curve** or **Sag Curve**.

Convoy
[Hist.] The name given to a wood brake handle and wood brake blocks fitted to **Wagons**, mainly coal carriers, running on early **Plateways** and **Tramways**.

Convoy Carriage
[Hist.] An early name for a **Locomotive** □ **Tender**.

ConvSig
See **Conventional Signalling**.

Cooling Switch
[TRS] An electrical switch that triggers a reduction in current flowing through the brake coil to prevent overheating on electromagnetic brakes. Also **Brake Cooling Switch**.

COP
[LUL] Correct Operation Protection, a system which checks that a **Train** is performing correctly, and shuts components down on the Train which operate outside a pre-set threshold.

CoPA
Control of Pollution Act 1974.

CoR
See **Certificate of Readiness**.

Coradia
The brandname of the **Class** 175 **Diesel Multiple Unit** (**DMU**).

Córas Iompair Éireann (CIÉ)
[Éire] (Irish Transport System) A statutory corporation answerable to the Government of the Republic of Ireland and responsible for most public transport in the Republic of Ireland. Based at Heuston Station, Dublin, its board are appointed by the Minister for Transport. It provides transport services through three wholly owned subsidiary limited liability companies established under the Companies Acts, as provided for in the Transport (Reorganisation of Córas Iompair Éireann) Act 1986; Bus Éireann (Irish Bus), Bus Átha Cliath (Dublin Bus) and **Iarnród Éireann** (**IÉ**, Irish Rail).

Cordon Cap
[NR] An arrangement that limits the obligation on **Network Rail** (**NR**) to provide only a certain maximum number of **Train Paths** through the cordon (**Route**), even if the **Train Operating Company** (**TOC**) concerned has rights that would exceed this limit. A Cordon Cap is implemented when the total amount of access rights to a **Path**, if used, would exceed the available capacity of the **Railway Network**.

Core Possession
[NR] A **Possession** in which one or more major **Track** items such as **Ballast**, **Rail**, **Sleepers**, **Switch and Crossing** (**S&C**) are replaced. The opposite is a **Non-core Possession**.

CORECT
Continuous Remote Control of **Trains**.

Corf
[Hist.] A small four-wheel **Wagon** having fixed axles and capable of carrying between 5.5 and 6 hundredweight (150kg to 300kg) of 'large coals', Designed by John Curr for use on his type of **Plate Rails**. The wheels did not have flanges and it was intended that they could swap between **Plateway** and conventional road surfaces utilising a specially designed 'run-offs'.

Corner Casting
The hollow steel casting at each corner of a standard freight **Container** with holes on the three exposed walls to accept retaining devices. See also **Spigot**, **Twistlock**.

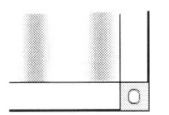

Corporate Memory
Knowledge and information from an organisation's past which can be accessed and used for present and future activities.

CORPUS
[NR] Codes for Operations, Retail & Planning – a Unified Solution. Previously **NALCO**, **CORPUS** is a web-based system that provides the means to link together the codes used in different **Rail Industry** systems to describe the same location and therefore maintain a national set of **Location Codes**. A CORPUS entry contains the following fields:

STANOX	STANOX code
UIC	UIC code
3ALPHA	3-letter location code
TIPLOC	TIPLOC code
NLC	NLC code
NLCDESC	Description of the NLC
NLCDESC16	NLC description (16-character version)

Correct Side Door Enable (CSDE)
[LUL] An electronic signal sent from **Trackside** which allows the **Train** door operation button to be energised for the **Platform** side of the Train only

107

Correlation
[Sig.] The action of comparing the actual configuration of a **Signalling System** with the design records for that system to ensure that they are in agreement. This is particularly important if **Stageworks** are to be undertaken, as all stages are based on making modifications to the existing system. See also **Correlation Waiver**, **Signalling Plan Survey**.

Correlation Waiver
[Sig.] When a recently installed **Signalling System** is to be modified, the likelihood is that the design records are still 100% correct. In this case the designer is excused the time consuming and expensive exercise of carrying out a **Correlation** by obtaining a Correlation Waiver from the **Infrastructure Controller**.

Correspondence
[Sig.] The condition when the **Detected** status of an item of equipment agrees with the **Interlocking**. Also In Correspondence. See also **Out of Correspondence**.

Corridor
a) See **Railway Corridor**.
b) See **Corridor Coach**.

Corridor Coach
[TRS] A **Coach** divided into **Compartments**, each seating six (eight in **Second Class** and **Third Class** on the former Great Western Railway (GWR)) **Passengers**. A **Corridor** is provided down one side of the Coach to allow free movement along the **Train** and between Compartments. A Coach with Compartments but without such a Corridor is a **Compartment Coach**.

Corrosion Trap
[Civ.] A feature of a **Structure** such as a joint, back to back angles or areas of difficult access in which sufficient water and debris may collect to set up a micro-climate which in turn produces a higher corrosion rate than at other parts of the structure.

Corrugation
See **Rail Corrugation**.

COSHH
(*kosh*) Control of Substances Hazardous to Health Regulations 2002.

COSS
(*koss*) See **Controller of Site Safety**.

COSS Brief
COSS Briefing
[NR] A brief given by the **COSS** to all members of a **Work Group** explaining the **Safe System of Work** that protects the group from **Approaching Trains**. On conclusion of the brief all members of the Work Group are required to sign a form confirming that they have been briefed, and understood the brief. See also **RIMINI**.

COSS Handbook
[NR] A book written by the **Rail Safety and Standards Board** (**RSSB**) and issued to each **Controller of Site Safety** (**COSS**) acting as a reference document to assist them in carrying out his duties.

COSS Pack
[NR, Obs.] The documentation formerly supplied to a **Controller of Site Safety** (**COSS**) which includes the form RT9909 and other details as appropriate. This may include the **Task Briefing** (**TB**) for the work, extracts from the **National Hazard Directory** and **Sectional Appendix** (**SA**) and relevant diagrams. See **Safe System of Work Pack** (**SsoW Pack**).

COSS Record of Arrangements and Briefing Form (COSS Form)
[NR] A form completed by the **Controller of Site Safety** (**COSS**) indicating the location of the **Work Site**, the work to be done, the specific hazards of the Work Site, the arrangements in place to mitigate their effect and the **Safe System of Work** (**SSOW**) applied. It is signed by each member of the team whose safety is the responsibility of that COSS.

COSS(P)
(*koss-pea*) [NR] A **Controller of Site Safety**, provisionally qualified.

COT
See **Condition of Track**.

COT Speed
See **Condition of Track Speed** (**COTS**).

COTIF
Convention Relative aux Transports Internationaux Ferroviaires, a convention concerning international carriage by **Rail**.

COTS
a) See **Condition of Track Speed**.
b) Commercial off the Shelf (equipment).

Cotton Bobbin
[Sig., Col., Hist.] Descriptive name given to a type of early rotating board **Signal** as used on the former North Eastern **Railway**, based on its profile.

COU
[TRS] An acronym representing a Courier **Van**.

Countdown Markers

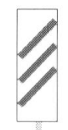

[NR, Sig.] A type of **Lineside Sign** displaying three, two and one diagonal bar(s), giving warning to the driver of the approach of a **Signal** or **Station**.

Counter Conditional Locking
[Sig.] An arrangement of **Interlocking** which prevents a condition from being destroyed, used where other parts of the Interlocking may be dependent on the same condition.

Counterbalanced Incline
[Hist.] Term used in Wales for a self-acting incline.

Counterfort
[Civ.] A support for a **Cutting** or **Embankment** slope.

Counting Head
[Sig.] Wheel presence detection equipment forming part of an **Axle Counter** system. Fixed to the **Rail**, each Counting Head assembly consists of two physical Heads and determines the number and direction of passing **Axles**. Also known as an **Axle Counter Head**.

Country
[Sth.] Normally used to mean the opposite of **London**. See **Country End** (**CE**), **Country Side** (**CS**).

Country End (CE)
Country Side (CS)
[Sth.] Describing the end or side furthest from **London**, opposite of **London End** (**LE**) or **London Side** (**LS**). Commonly used in the south of England.

Coupled
See **Coupled Up**.

Coupled in Multiple
[Ops.] Two or more **Traction Units** □ **Coupled Up** and connected to allow through controls by one driver. Also **Multiple Working**.

Coupled in Tandem
[Ops.] Two or more **Traction Units** □ **Coupled Up** but not otherwise connected; each Traction Unit is separately controlled by its own driver, with through control of the **Automatic Brake** only.

Coupled Up
[Ops.] Attached to another **Locomotive**, **Rail Vehicle** or **Train** by means of a **Coupling**.

Coupler Release Chain
[TRS] A chain used to activate the mechanism for opening the jaws of an **Automatic Coupler** to **Uncouple** two vehicles.

Coupling
a) (noun) [TRS] A device used to connect **Rail Vehicles** together for haulage purposes. See **Automatic Coupling**, **Buck Eye Coupling**, **Instanter Coupling**, **Screw Coupling**, **Three Link Coupling**
b) (verb) See **Coupling Up**.

Coupling Hooks
[TRS] The large heavy-duty hooks placed centrally on a **Buffer Beam** of a **Rail Vehicle**, which are used as the attachment point for connecting the vehicle to another using an **Instanter Coupling**, **Screw Coupling** or **Three Link Coupling**.

Coupling Up
[Ops.] Attaching one **Locomotive**, **Rail Vehicle** or **Train** to another Locomotive, Rail Vehicle or Train by means of a **Coupling**.

Cover
a) An alternative term for **Check Cover**
b) [Civ.] The thickness of concrete measured from the surface to the nearest reinforcing bar.

Cover and Cut
[Civ.] A method of **Tunnel** construction where the walls are built (generally using piles) from the surface, a shallow excavation made and the roof of the Tunnel constructed on top. The excavation is then filled and the Tunnel dug out from underneath. Suitable only for shallow Tunnels, the technique is cost effective compared with other solutions. See also **Bored Tunnel**, **Cut and Cover**.

Cover Check
[PW] A specific term used to describe a **Check Rail** fitted opposite the **Crossing Nose** of a **Common Crossing**. See also **Check Cover**.

Covered Stumec
A **Bogie** □ **Wagon** fitted with **Stumec Cranes** and a mesh roof allowing it to be operated safely under **Live** □ **Overhead Line Equipment** (**OLE**).

Covered Track
[LUL] A **Track** which is fully enclosed in a **Tunnel** for 150m or longer.

Covered Way
a) [Col.] term for a bridge or **Tunnel** constructed using the **Cut and Cover** method but of a length less than that which would classify it as Tunnel
b) [LUL] A structure that covers a gap which is at least twice as wide as its **Span** and was constructed by Cut and Cover.

Cow
a) A large quadruped mammal of the species *Bos primigenius*. See also **Polmont Accident**
b) [Hist.] A device to minimise runaway vehicles on a **Rope-Worked Railway** comprising a pronged implement attached to the drawbar hook of the rear vehicle of an ascending **Set** which, while the haulage rope remained attached to the **Wagons**, trailed over the **Ballast**. However, should one or more of the vehicles break loose the implement dug into the ballast and either stopped them or caused them to **Derail**.

Cowcatcher
See **Obstacle Deflector**

Cowden Accident
At 08:27 on Saturday 15th October 1994 two **Class** 205 **Diesel Electric Multiple Units** (**DEMU**), both dating from the late 1950s, collided head-on in thick fog on the **Single Line** near Cowden in Kent. Five died (including both drivers) and 12 were injured. The cause was determined to be one of the **Trains** passing a **Signal** at **Danger** (a **SPAD**), possibly due to the driver being distracted or by his allowing the **Train** to be driven by the **Guard**.

Cowper, Edward Alfred
(10th Dec 1819 - 9th May 1893) A mechanical engineer who amongst many other things, introduced the **Railway Fog Signal** in 1841, was a founder member of the Institution of Mechanical Engineers (ImechE) in 1847 (later becoming President in 1880), designed the wrought iron and glass roof for Birmingham New Street **Station** in 1854 (the largest span of any roof until St Pancras' in 1868), the Cowper Stove for use in the hot blast steel making process in 1857, the writing telegraph (an embryonic fax machine) in 1879 and could lay claim to the spoked bicycle wheel (if only he had patented it).

CP
a) See **Catch Point**
b) See **Catch Pit**
c) See **Clearance Point**
d) See **Change Point**
e) Compulsory Purchase, see **Compulsory Purchase Order** (CPO)
f) See **Connection Point**
g) See **Cross Passage**
h) See **Control Period**.

CPA
Centralised Public Address.

CPC
Circuit Protective Conductor.

CPD
a) See **Cross Passage Door**
b) [LUL] Capital Programmes Directorate.

CPMT
Central Project Management Team.

CPO
See **Compulsory Purchase Order**.

CPOS
See **Continuous Place of Safety**.

CPP
a) Construction Phase Plan
b) See **Complex Projects Procedure**.

CPPP
See **Confirmed Period Possession Plan**.

CPST
Central Project Sponsor's Team.

CPT
See **Cone Penetration Test**.

CPU
Cable Pressurisation Unit.

CPx
See **Control Period**.

CR
a) [Sig.] On a **Signalling Circuit Diagram**, it denotes a common return **Conductor** for many circuits and insulated from **Earth**
b) Common Rail
c) See **Conventional Rail**
d) Change Request
e) Community Relations
f) **Coasting** □ **Relay**.

CR ENE TSI
Technical Specification for Interoperability (TSI) for Conventional Rail Energy.

CR LOC & PAS TSI
Technical Specification for Interoperability (TSI) for Conventional Rail □ Locomotives and Passenger □ Rolling Stock.

CR WAG TSI
Technical Specification for Interoperability (TSI) for the Conventional Rail □ Freight Wagons.

CRA
a) Call Routing Apparatus
b) Customer Risk Assessment.

Crab (ZBV, ZCV)
a) [NR] A 20 ton capacity **Open Wagon** used for the transport of **Ballast**. Converted from a **Lamprey** (ZBO). See **Wagon Names**
b) [Col.] a variety of 2-6-0 Steam Locomotive intended for **Mixed Traffic** use.

Cracker
[Col.] An alternative for **Detonator**, see **Railway Fog Signal**. Also **Bangers**, **Dets**, **Foggies**, **Shots**.

Crane Beam
[PW] A specially constructed lifting beam that allows a **Rail Crane** to lift transport and place up to 14 **Sleepers** in one lift. See also **Sleeper Beam**, **TRM Beam**.

Crane Controller (CC)
[NR] A person trained and authorised to direct the operation of a crane. See also **Crane Controller Tandem Lift**, **Crane Slinger**, **Machine Controller** (MC).

Crane Controller Tandem Lift
A further level of the **Crane Controller** (CC) competence for persons who are competent to control lifts where two cranes, **Rail Cranes** or **Road Rail Vehicles** (RRV) are used to lift the same object.

Crane Prefixes
[BR,NR] In **British Rail** (BR) days, some **Departmental** cranes had their vehicle numbers prefixed with letters to indicate their allocation, as in ADR:
A   DoM&EE
C   BREL
K   DoS&TE
L   Electrification
T   Operating Department
All cranes have DR main prefixes. See also **Crane Suffixes**.

Crane Rail
A special **Rail Section** used to form the supporting structure for particular types of **Rail** mounted cranes.

Crane Slinger
A person who is trained and authorised to attach and detach loads to and from the hooks of cranes. Sometimes contracted to **Slinger**. See also **Rail Crane**, **Track Relaying Machine** (TRM).

Crane Suffixes
[NR] A letter added to the **DR** part of a **Rail Crane** vehicle number to indicate its original builder, as in DRC:

A	Booth
B	**British Rail (BR)**
C	Cowans Boyd
	Cowans Sheldon
	Clark Chapman
F	Coles
G	Grafton
J	Jones
K	**Kirow**
M	Marshall Fleming
P	**Plasser & Theurer**
R	Ransome and Rapier
S	Smith
T	Taylor & Hubbard
V	Cravens
W	Warwell / Atlas

See also **Crane Prefixes**.

Crank
a) [Sig.] A pivoted L-shaped device used to change the direction of movement of **Rodding**, either through 90° or 180°
b) [TRS] An arm on a shaft or axle for converting reciprocating motion into rotative motion or vice-versa.

Crank Handle
[Sig.] A portable winding handle used to manually operate certain types of **Point Machines** in times of failure or disconnection.

Cranked Fishplate
[PW] Alternative name for a **Lift Fishplate**.

Crankex
[Col.] A **Charter Train** especially for **Railway Enthusiasts**. See also **-ex**.

Crash Pulse
[TRS] The level of deceleration that a vehicle is subjected to in a collision.

Crashworthiness
a) [TRS] The capacity of a vehicle to protect its occupants during an impact
b) [NR] A design method that involves designing the **Train** structure so that it is able to perform to a given standard during a collision. **Railway Group Standard** GM/RT2100 defines the requirements for new vehicles.

Crayfish
[Unk.] A **Mermaid (ZJV)** □ **Wagon** variant, apparently never actually built.

CRD
See **Combined Reading Distance**.

CRE
a) See **Contractor's Responsible Engineer**
b) See **Conductor Rail Equipment**.
c) [Sig.] On a **Signalling Circuit Diagram**, it denotes a common return conductor for many circuits and connected to **Earth**
d) [NR] **C**ustomer **R**elationship **E**xecutive.

CR-E
[NR] **C**ontract **R**equirements, **E**nvironment

Creep
a) See **Rail Creep**
b) [Elec.] The long-term elongation of Contact Wire (**CW**) and Catenary under load; a form of plastic deformation
c) [TRS] A method of improving **Tractive Effort** by arranging for the wheels of a **Locomotive** to rotate slightly faster than that required by the forward speed of the Locomotive. See **Creep Control.**

Creep Control
[TRS]
a) A system fitted to some **Locomotives** which manages the application of **Creep** to the wheels. Utilising input from axle rotation sensors and radar speed measurement, each axle is kept rotating at a rate between 5% and 15% in excess of the speed of the Locomotive, thereby producing maximum **Tractive Effort**
b) A device fitted to some Locomotives to enable them to haul a **Train** at an exactly predetermined (low) speed, used in loading and unloading certain **Freight Trains** such as **Merry-go-Round Trains**.

Creep Monitor
[PW] A device fitted to certain types of **Switches** in place of **Stress Transfer Blocks**. Their purpose is to indicate longitudinal movement due to **Thermal Stress** in the **Closure Rails**. They are not intended to transfer Thermal Stress forces. Also **Ball and Claw**.

Creep Resistance
[PW] A measure of the ability of **Sleepers** and **Rail Fastenings** to resist **Rail Creep**.

Creep Signal
[Sig.] An alternative term for a **Loading / Unloading Indicator**. See also **Toton Signal**.

Cresswell's Compound
[Hist.] A proprietary compound formerly used to plug old **Chairscrew** holes in **Wood Sleepers**.

Crest
[Civ.] The top of a **Cutting** or **Embankment** slope.

Crest Drain
[Civ.] A **Drain** or ditch placed at the top of a **Cutting** slope, its purpose being to intercept groundwater, which would otherwise permeate down the slope, and direct it to an engineered **Outfall**.

CREW
[LUL] **C**o-ordination of **R**ailway □ **E**ngineering **W**ork.

Crew Call System
[TRS] That part of the voice communication system fitted to a **Train** that **Traincrew** use to communicate with one another while dispersed through the Train.

Crewe Heritage Centre
(Tradename) A museum housing **Railway**-related exhibits, located to the north of Crewe **Station**. A notable exhibit includes an **Advanced Passenger Train (APT-P)**. Previously called **The Railway Age**.

Crewling
[Hist.] A term used in North Wales to mean operating a rope-worked incline.

ELLIS' BRITISH RAILWAY ENGINEERING ENCYCLOPÆDIA

CRG
Communications Review Group.

Crib
See Bed.

CRIB
Current Rail Indicator Box. See Current Rail Indicator Device.

CRID
See Current Rail Indicator Device.

Crimp Ended Steel Sleeper
[PW] A type of Steel Sleeper where the end section is formed by crimping the Soffit downwards. The result does not present a large flat area to the Ballast so their Lateral Resistance is limited. Their use has now been superseded by the Spade Ended Steel Sleeper.

Cripple
a) (noun) [Ops.] A defective vehicle not fit to run on the Railway. Also Red Carded, Demic
b) (verb) [PW] To induce a permanent kink into a Rail or Switch.

Cripple Road
Cripple Siding
[Ops.] A Siding used for the storage of defective Rail Vehicles, known as Cripples, awaiting repair or return to a Depot for repair.

Crippled Rail
Crippled Switch
[PW] A Rail or Switch with a short abrupt kink in it, generally in the horizontal plane. This defect is normally caused by bad handling techniques.

Crippling
a) [Ops.] The act of declaring a Rail Vehicle to be a Cripple
b) [PW] The act of mis-handling a Rail or Switch so as to make it a Crippled Rail or Crippled Switch.

Critical Pump Site
[LUL] A pumping site where failure of the pumps would result in restrictions to the operational Railway e.g. by closure of Tracks and or Stations.

Critical Rail Temperature (CRT)
[PW] The calculated (high) temperature at which Continuous Welded Rail (CWR) becomes unsafe and a Speed Restriction must be imposed. Normally the Critical Rail Temperature is around 50°C, higher than the normal maximum Rail Temperature, but this can be reduced by:
• Permanent Way Maintenance (PWM) work which reduces the Lateral Stability of the Track
• Track Construction - lighter Trackforms cannot withstand the higher thermal forces
• Low Stress Free Temperature (SFT) which increases the likely compressive forces present in the Rail at high temperatures.

Critical Rail Temperature (Watchman) (CRT(W))
[PW] The maximum Rail Temperature a section of Track can reach before measures to protect traffic should be taken. The CRT varies with Track Type and condition. The CRT(W) is the temperature at which a Watchman should be appointed to monitor the affected section.

CRN
Calculation of Railway Noise.

CRO
[LUL] Control Room Operator.

Cromptons
[Col.] Nickname for Class 33 Diesel Locomotives, which had Traction Motors made by Crompton Parkinson.

Crop and Weld
[PW] The operation of removing Fishplates, Cropping the Rail Ends just behind the Front Fishbolt Holes and then Alumino-thermic Welding the ends together to form Continuous Welded Rail (CWR) or Long Welded Rail (LWR).

Cropped and Welded
Cropped and Welded Rail
[PW] Continuous Welded Rail (CWR) or Long Welded Rail (LWR) formed from previously Jointed Rail by the Crop and Weld process.

Cropping
[PW] Cutting off the end of a Jointed Rail in order to remove Rail End Batter, Bond Wire Holes and Fish Bolt Holes.

Cross Bond
[Elec.] A Bond between the Traction Return Rails of adjacent Tracks. See also Yellow Bond.

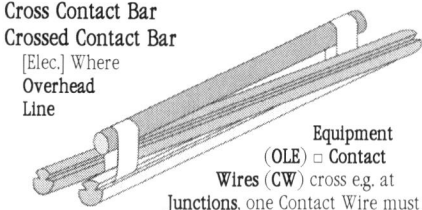

Cross Contact Bar
Crossed Contact Bar
[Elec.] Where Overhead Line Equipment (OLE) Contact Wires (CW) cross e.g. at Junctions, one Contact Wire must pass over the other. A Crossed Contact Bar is used to ensure the two Wires remain at the correct vertical relationship while still permitting along-Track thermal movement. The Bar can be made of straightened contact wire or round section rod.

Cross Dock
The transfer of Freight from one vehicle or mode to another vehicle or mode for onward distribution, with little or no dwell time.

Cross Drain
[PW] A Track Drain laid at an angle under a Track, generally to connect a Sixfoot Drain or Tenfoot Drain to a Cess Drain. Sometimes abbreviated to X Drain.

Cross Girders
See Cross Members.

Cross Level
See **Crosslevel**.

Cross Members
[Civ.] A smaller lateral structural member spanning between the **Main Girders** of a **Bridge**.

Cross Packing
[PW] A method used to remove **Voids** in the **Ballast** under a **Sleeper** by packing the Ballast from diagonally opposite sides of the **Rail Seat** simultaneously. This can be completed using a **Shovel**, **Beater Pick** or hammer.

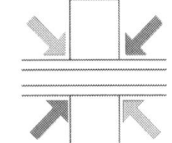

Cross Passage (CP)
[Civ.] A generally smaller access **Tunnel** connecting two larger Tunnels at an angle to both, e.g. connecting a **Running Tunnel** with a **Service Tunnel**, and used for ventilation, pressure relief, staff and emergency access.

Cross Passage Door (CPD)
[Civ.] Doors connecting the **Running Tunnels** to the **Cross Passages**.

Cross Platform
Term for the area immediately the **Buffer Stops** which links the **Platforms** of a **Terminal Station** when a **Platform Screen** is provided between the Platforms and the **Concourse** area.

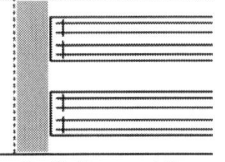

Cross Sleepered Track
[PW] **Track** in which the **Rails** are supported by **Sleepers** laid at right angles to the longitudinal axis of the **Rails**. This is the most common arrangement. See also **Longitudinal Bearers**.

Cross Span Wire
[Elec.] Generally the lowest wire in a **Head Span** assembly, it is this that holds the **Catenary** assemblies in their correct positions relative to the **Tracks** beneath.

CrossCountry
A **Train Operating Company** (**TOC**) which operates a network of long-distance services between Scotland and North East England through to the South West of England, Bournemouth and Brighton. ATOC code XC.

Crossfall
[PW] The transverse (relative to the **Track**) slope applied to the **Formation** to ensure effective drainage. This slope is between 1 in 40 and 1 in 20. Also **Slope of Formation**. See also **Fall**.

Crossing (Xing)
a) [PW] An assembly that permits the passage of **Wheel Flanges** across other **Rails** where **Tracks** intersect. See also **Cast Crossing**. Also **Frog**
b) [Col.] Contraction of **Level Crossing** (**LC, LX**).

Crossing Angle
[PW] The tangent, expressed as a ratio, e.g. 1 in N (**Centre Line Measurement**), of the acute angle (x) of a **Crossing**, where:

$$N = \frac{cot\frac{x}{2}}{2}$$

There are also colloquial descriptions:
- **Flat Angle Crossings** or **Narrow Angle Crossings** that have large values of **N**, e.g. 28, 32
- **Sharp Angle Crossings** or **Wide Angle Crossings** that have small values on N, e.g. 6, 4

See also **N Value**.

Crossing Attendant
See **Level Crossing Attendant** (**LXA**).

Crossing Bearer
[PW] A **Bearer** that supports one or more **Crossings**.

Crossing Box
[Sig.] Alternative term for **Gate Box**.

Crossing Chair
[PW] A **Chair** for a **Common Crossing** or **Obtuse Crossing** built from **Bull Head Rail** (**BH**).

Crossing Clear (CC)
[Sig.] A **Control** built into **Monitored** □ **Level Crossings** (**LC, LX**), which holds the **Protecting Signal** at a Stop **Aspect** following a **Train** passing the **Strike-in Point** (**SIP**) until the **Signaller** confirms that the Crossing is indeed **Clear** by pressing a button.

Crossing Contact Arrangement
[Elec.] See **Cross Contact Bar, Crossed Contact Bar**.

Crossing Control Key
[IÉ] Key stored in a key switch box in the **Signal Box** (**SB**) which facilitates the **Emergency Operator** in the local control of a **Level Crossing** (**LC, LX**) with **Automatic Half Barriers**.

Crossing Heel
[PW] The end of a **Crossing** furthest from the **Crossing Nose** (**XN**). Also **Back**.

Crossing Keeper
a) [Sig.] The person who operates a **Level Crossing** (**LC, LX**) from a **Gate Box**. See also **Crossing Operator**
b) [Col.] See **Level Crossing Attendant** (**LXA**)

Crossing Legs
[PW]
a) All four **Rails** at the extremities of a **Cast Centre Block Crossing** (**CCBC**) or **Fabricated Crossing**
b) [LUL] the **Full Section** □ **Rail Ends** □ **Beyond** the **Crossing Nose** in a **Common Crossing** assembly. Sometimes contracted to **Legs**.

Crossing Nose (XN)
[PW] The blunt machined end of a **Crossing Vee**. Also **Nose, Blunt Nose**.

Crossing Nose to Intersection Point Dimension

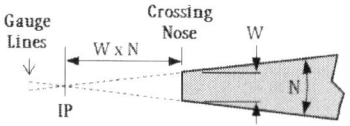

[PW] The distance from the **Crossing Nose** (**XN**) to the **Intersection of Gauge Lines** (**IP**). It is the Crossing Nose width (W) multiplied by the **N Value** of the **Crossing**, as in 1 in N. Thus for **113A Vertical S&C** it is 16 x N, and for a **Bullhead Crossing** it is 19 x N. Also Nose to IP.

Crossing Operator
[Sig.] Generic term for a member of staff employed to manage the safe operation of a **Level Crossing** (**LC**, **LX**) as the majority of their duties. Also **Crossing Keeper**.

Crossing Point Rail
a) See **Common Crossing Point Rail**
b) See **Obtuse Crossing Point Rail**.

Crossing Speed
[Sig.] The maximum **Permissible Speed** (**PS**) applicable to a **Train** approaching and then passing over an **ABCL**, **AOCL** or **AOCR** ▫ **Level Crossing** (**LC**, **LX**). The point from which it applies is at the Train's **Braking Distance** (**BD**) from the crossing at which it can be seen to be clear and the Permissible Speed may be further reduced by the level of road and rail traffic. See also **Stott Criteria**.

Crossing Surface
That part of a **Level Crossing** (**LC, LX**) that is walked on, ridden on or trafficked by pedestrians, cyclists, equestrians or motorists.

Crossing Telephone
[Tel.] Telephones permanently mounted either side of a **Level Crossing** (**LC, LX**) giving a direct line of communication to the **Signaller** controlling the Crossing. See also **Public Emergency Telephone System** (**PETS**).

Crossing Timber
See **Crossing Bearer**.

Crossing Time
[Sig.] The time taken by a user at a **Level Crossing** (**LC, LX**) to cross over the **Railway** from **Decision Point** to a **Position of Safety**, including the time taken to decide to do so in the first place.

Crossing Vee
See **Common Crossing Vee**.

Crosslevel
[PW]
a) The measured difference in level between the two **Running Rails** of a **Track** at particular location. This value should equal the designed value of **Cant** at that location. See also **Crosslevel Error**
b) A device for measuring **Cant** or **Crosslevel** Also **Cant Stick**, **Crosslevel Gauge**.

Cross-level
See **Crosslevel**.

Crosslevel Error
[PW] The difference between the designed **Cant** value and the measured **Crosslevel** value at any given point along the **Track**. See also **Twist**.

Crosslevel Gauge
[PW] A specialised variety of spirit level used to measure the actual level difference between the two **Rails** of the same **Track** at the same point. They are often equipped with some means of setting an offset at one end, allowing a more accurate reading of the **Crosslevel** value to be made. Also, commonly, **Cant Stick**

Crossover (X over)

a) Two **Turnouts** (**TO**) or **Single Leads** connected to permit movements between parallel **Tracks**. Crossovers thus may be **Facing** or **Trailing**
b) [CT] In the **Channel Tunnel**, a section of **Track** where the **Running Tunnels** are combined to enable a **Train** to pass from one Running Tunnel to the other in either direction.

Crossover Speed
[PW] The design maximum speed on the crossover **Route** of a **Crossover**. This speed may be higher than that which is actually permitted.

Crossover Tunnel
[Civ.] A short **Running Tunnel** housing one or more **Crossovers**.

Crossover-based Double Junction
An alternative term for a **Simplified Double Junction**.

Crossrail
A new east-west **Rail** link under **London**, joining Paddington to Stratford and to the Isle of Dogs. See also **CLRL**.

Cross-read
[Sig.] Mistakenly reading another adjacent **Signal** rather than the correct one. See also **Parallel Signals**. See also **Read Through**.

Crow
a) See **Jim Crow**
b) [PW] To bend a **Rail** using a Jim Crow
c) [Ops.] To sound only one tone on a two tone **Train** horn.

Crown
a) See **Rail Crown**
b) See **Arch Crown**
c) [Civ.] The top section of a **Tunnel Lining**.

CROWS
(*croze*) [BR, Obs.] Computerised Renewal of Way System (latterly CROWS 2). An obsolete mainframe database used by **British Railways** to manage **Renewal of Way** (**ROW**) proposals and resources.

Croxley Link
[LUL] The proposed extension to the Croxley **Branch** of the Metropolitan **Line**.

CRP
See Conductor Rail Permit.
CRR
a) Competition & Regulatory Reviews
b) Customer Reasonable Requirement
c) Common Reception Relay
d) See Continuous Running Rail.
CRRD
Congestion-related Reactionary Delay
CRRES
(Tradename) Carnforth Railway Restoration and Engineering Services.
CRS
a) See Continuous Route Signing
b) Computerised Reservation System
c) Current Rail Section, see Conductor Rail, Current Rail
d) [LUL] Central Reporting System
e) [LUL] Change to Rolling Stock
CRT
See Critical Rail Temperature.
CR-T
Contract Requirements – Technical.
CRT(W)
See Critical Rail Temperature (Watchman).
CRUCC
[Hist.] Central Rail User Consultative Committee, now replaced by the Rail Passengers' Council (RPC).
Crucible
[PW] A conical steel vessel with a refractory lining, used to react the Weld Portion in the Alumino-thermic Welding process. See also One Shot Crucible.
Cruciform Pad
[PW] A cross-shaped Rail Pad shaped to fit between the hoops cast into a Concrete Sleeper utilising the SHC Fastening.
Crum.
[Hist.] Common shorthand for Crumlin Viaduct Co., a former manufacturer of Signalling Equipment.
Crumple Zones
[TRS] Areas located at each end of a Rail Vehicle which are designed to deform in a controlled manner and absorb energy during a collision, in order to protect Passengers from a Loss Of Survival Space and excessive accelerations.
Crush Laden
[Ops.] Describing a Passenger Coach that has all its seats occupied and additional Passengers standing in all the available corridors, vestibules and other spaces; to the point where the Boarding of further Passengers is physically impossible. See also Full and Standing, Passengers in Excess of Capacity (PIXC), Pixie.

Crush Load
[Ops.] The absolute maximum number of Passengers that can be fitted into a Passenger Coach, both seated and standing in every available space, to the point where the Boarding of further Passengers is physically impossible. Nominal values equal twice the seated load or 150 in total. This level of loading is used as one of the extreme test conditions in the calculation of a Kinematic Envelope (KE). See also Tare Deflated.,
Crushing
[PW] The deformation of the Rail Head caused by excessive wheel loads. Also Mushrooming.
CS
a) See Carriage Sidings
b) Country Side, see Country End (CE)
c) Control Switch
d) [NR] Denoting a Non-Standard Differential Speed applying to Class 67 Locomotives.
CS&TE
[BR, Hist.] Chief Signal and Telecommunications Engineer.
CS3
[PW] A Rail Fastening developed by British Rail Research (BRR) in the early 1970s and bearing a passing resemblance to the SHC Rail Fastening. Not widely liked or used.
CSA
Cross-Sectional Area.
CSAC
Candidate Special Area of Conservation.
CSC
a) See Contractor's Safety Case
b) Connex South Central, a Train Operating Company (TOC)
c) International Convention for Safe Containers
d) [LUL] Central Supervisory Computer
e) Customer Service Centre.
CSD
a) Circuit Switched Data
b) Carriage Servicing Depot.
CSDE
See Correct Side Door Enable.
CSE
Connex South Eastern, a Train Operating Company (TOC).
CSK
Countersunk.
CSM
See Common Safety Method.
CSM AsBo
See Common Safety Method Assessment Body.
CSMA
(Tradename) The Concrete Sleeper Manufacturers' Association.

CSR
a) See **Cab Secure Radio**
b) See **Customer Service Representative**.

CSR Channel Sign
See **Cab Secure Radio Channel Sign**.

CSRIC
Coal **S**pillage **R**eduction **I**nvestment **C**harge.

CSS
County **S**urveyors' **S**ociety (now renamed **ADEPT**).

CT
a) **C**entral **T**rains, a **Train Operating Company** (**TOC**)
b) See **Channel Tunnel**
c) [LUL] A **C**ontrol **T**railer □ Car with a **Driving Cab**, but no **Traction Motors**.

CTBC
See **Combined Traction and Brake Controller**.

CTC
a) [NIR] **C**entralised **T**raffic **C**ontrol
b) **C**entralised **T**rain **C**ontrol
c) [LUL] **C**ertificate of **T**echnical **C**onformance.

CTCC
Central **T**ransport **C**onsultative **C**ommittee.

CTCSS
Continuous **T**one-**C**ontrolled **S**ignalling **S**ystem.

CTD
[NR] **C**omprehensive **Track Diagram**.

CTDS
[Ops.] **C**omplete **T**raffic **D**ata **S**ystem.

CTI
[Elec.] **C**ontrolled **Track I**solator.

CTNC
Certificate of **T**emporary **N**on-**c**ompliance.

CTP
[LUL] The **C**ooling the **Tube** project.

CTR1
[CTRL] **Channel Tunnel** □ **Route** 1 (via Tonbridge).

CTR2
[CTRL] **Channel Tunnel** □ **Route** 2 (via Maidstone).

CTR3
[CTRL] **Channel Tunnel** □ **Route** 3 (via Redhill).

CTRL
See **Channel Tunnel Rail Link**.

CTRL DS
[CTRL] **Channel Tunnel Rail Link D**omestic **S**ervice.

CTRS
Constant **Traffic** □ **Route** **S**ections

CTRU
[Hist.] **C**entral **Track Renewals Unit** (**TRU**).

CTS
a) **C**ontrolled **Track S**witch
b) **C**entralised **Train** □ **Signalling**
c) **C**ontract **T**echnical **S**pecification.

CTSA
See **Channel Tunnel Safety Authority**.

CTTG
Channel **T**unnel □ **T**rackwork **G**roup.

CTU
See **Cargo Transport Unit**.

C-Type Bridge

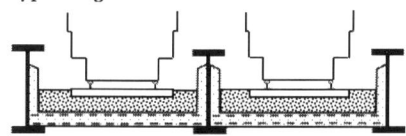

[NR, Civ.] A variety of standard **Half Through** □ **Ballasted Deck** □ **Bridge** consisting of three I-shaped main girders and two **Composite Decks** consisting of joists set in concrete. Each deck supports one **Track**. Used for **Spans** up to 18 metres, the **Deck** joists / centre I-girder connection is a problem, and this type is now replaced by the **E-Type Bridge**.

Cubic Parabola
[PW] A type of **Transition Curve**. See also **Bloss Spiral**.

Cuckoo
a) A **Railway** □ **Telegraph Code** meaning "You will receive the following from ..."
b) [BR, Obs.] A staff paging system installed on the **West Coast Main Line** (**WCML**) at the time of **Electrification**, decommissioned during the 1970s.

CUI
[NR] **C**apacity **U**tilisation **I**ndex. Measures the intensity of usage on the **Rail** network as a percentage of available capacity.

Cullen Report
The report prepared by the Rt. Hon Lord Cullen following the **Ladbrooke Grove Accident**.

Culvert
[Civ.]
a) An enclosed structure with a small span or diameter and whose primary purpose is usually, but not exclusively, to permit water or services to pass under a **Railway** or road
b) [NR] A structure with a span or diameter greater than 450mm but less than 1800mm **Span** specifically designed to carry water under the Railway. Within **Network Rail** standards, the term excludes outside party pipelines.
c) See also **Siphon**, **Siphon Culvert**.

Culverted
Culverted Section
[Civ.] A section of a watercourse that passes through a **Culvert**.

CUP
Capacity **U**tilisation **P**olicy.

Cup and Pin Insulator
[Elec.] An **Insulator** used in **Overhead Line Equipment** (**OLE**), constructed from individual ceramic disks connected together using short metal bars. See also **Polymeric Insulator**.

Cup Spring
[TRS] A small spring that sits within a primary and secondary spring assembly to assist damping on a **Gloucester Floating Axle** suspension unit.

Curr, John
(c. 1756 - 27th January 1823) Manager of the Duke of Norfolk's collieries in Sheffield from 1781 to 1801. An early practitioner of **Railways** utilising metal rails, rather than the then more usual **Newcastle Wagon Way**. Curr has been credited with the development of the earliest form of 'L' shaped **Plate Rail**, see **Curr's Plate Rails**.

Curr's Plate Rail
[PW, Obs.] Cast iron **Plate Rail** to the design of **John Curr** of Sheffield, sometime between 1776 and 1788. Described as being six feet long, having a 3 inch tread, $^1/_2$ inch thick with a 2 inch high flange (1.83m long, 76mm tread, 13mm thick with a 51mm flange). They weighed between 47lb and 50lb (21.3kg and 22.6gg) each and had countersunk nail holes at about an inch (25mm) in from each end.

Currant
A **Railway** □ **Telegraph Code** meaning "Your enquiry respecting following, I agree".

Current Arrangements
[LUL] Schedule of times at which a specified **Current Rail Section** or locally switched section are to be switched on or off.

Current Collection Shoe
[TRS] The flat metal block suspended from an insulated beam on the outside of certain **Bogies**, slightly above **Rail Level** on a **Traction Unit** that utilises **Conductor Rails**. Its purpose is to run on the **Rail Head** of the Conductor Rail and pass **Traction Current** to the **Train**. Normally shortened to **Shoe**. See also **Cinderella**, **Collector Shoe**, **Gapped**, **Shoegear**, **Sparklers**.

Current Equalising Jumper
[Elec.] A bare copper cable connected between two different **Conductors** in an **Overhead Line Electrification** (**OLE**) system to ensure that each part of the connected system carries the same current. They may connect related **Catenary Wire** and **Contact Wire** (**CW**), or they may connect Conductors from different **Wire Runs** at **Diamonds**, **Un-insulated Overlaps**, etc.

Current Rail
[LUL] The preferred term for the **Conductor Rail** or **Positive Conductor Rail**.

Current Rail Gap
[Elec.] A deliberate gap made in a **Current Rail** (**Conductor Rail**) which provides for **Section Isolation** between substations or at **Junctions**.

Current Rail Gap Indicator
[LUL] A **Trackside** □ **Indicator** warning that the **Traction Supply** in the **Electrical Section** □ **Beyond** has been **Isolated** or removed. It shows three red lights when active. Sites with poor visibility are provided with **Current Rail Gap Repeaters**, with three yellow lights. See also **Cherries**.

Current Rail Gap Repeater
[LUL] An additional **Current Rail Gap Indicator** (**RGI**) provided in areas of poor visibility. See also **Current Rail Gap Indicator** (**RGI**).

Current Rail Indicator Box (CRIB)
[LUL, NPT] See **Current Rail Indicator Device** (**CRID**).

Current Rail Indicator Device (CRID)
[LUL] A fixed indicator system that is used to show when the **Traction Supply Current** is on. Previously called a **Current Rail Indicator Box** (**CRIB**).

Current Rail Section
[LUL] An area of DC **Traction Current** network between two positive and negative pairs of **Track Feeder** □ **Circuit Breakers** (**CB**).

Curve

Curved Track
a) [PW] Generally, any piece of **Track** that is not **Straight Track**
b) [PW] Strictly, all **Circular Curves** (Curves of constant Radius (**R**)) but not including **Transition Curves**
See also **Tangent Track**.

Curve Realignment
[PW] The activity of moving a **Track** laterally to suit a **Design Alignment**. Also used as an alternative term for the **Hallade** method.

Curve to Curve Transition
[PW] A curve of uniformly varying Radius (**R**) connecting two **Circular Curves** of the same **Hand** together. See also **Compound Curve**, **Reverse Curve**, **Reverse Transition**, **Transition Curve**.

Curved Planed
Curved Planed Switch

[PW] A **Switch** that contains curved planed **Switch Rails**;, that is the **Running Edge** (**RE**) of the **Switch Rail** is curved, seen in plan. See also **Straight Planed**, **Straight Planed Switch**.

Curving

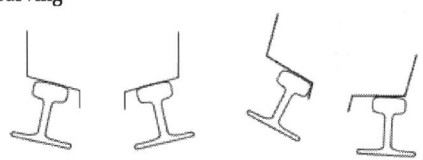

[PW] On a **Curve**, the outer **Rail** is longer than the inner Rail. If the vehicle is travelling at greater than **Equilibrium Speed** (V_e) the **Wheelsets** move laterally as they enter a Curve, with the rolling radius of the outer wheel becoming larger and the other smaller. If the difference in rolling circumference matches the difference in length of the Rails, the Wheelset will steer itself around the Curve.

Curving Rules
[PW] The mandatory limits and relationships between speed, Radius (**R**) and **Cant** (**C,E**) that apply to a **Railway**. The limits are often defined in terms of maximum lateral acceleration on a **Passenger**, tempered by stability and **Maintenance** considerations. On the **National Railway Network** (**NRN**), these were previously contained in **British Railways'** □ **Civil Engineering Handbook** 3. They now appear in **Network Rail Company Standard** (**NRCS**) number NR/L2/TRK/2049.

ELLIS' BRITISH RAILWAY ENGINEERING ENCYCLOPÆDIA

Customer Emergency Plunger
[LUL] A prominent push switch or similar device, located on **Platforms**, which enable the public to stop a **Train** in the event of an emergency;

Customer Host
[Ops.] A member of on-board staff whose principal duties are the serving of refreshments to **Passengers**.

Customer Information System (CIS)
[Tel.] A system of television monitors providing destination, **Platform** and departure time information to passengers.

Customer Service Representative (CSR)
[LR, Ops.] The member of a **Tram's** crew whose primary duty is to provide information to **Passengers** and to collect revenue.

Cut
a) [Civ.] An abbreviation for **Cutting**
b) [PW] An instruction marked up in the **Rail Web** indicating that the **Rail** should be cut there. Often accompanied by a + symbol, indicating the exact place.

Cut and Cover
[Civ.] In this procedure a **Cutting** is dug and the **Tunnel** constructed in it. The space above the Tunnel is then filled using excavated material or by construction of a structural deck. This method is generally only used for Tunnels located close to the surface. See also **Bored Tunnel**, **Cover and Cut**.

Cut and Shut
Cut and Shut Ramp

[PW] A method of making tight radius vertical bends in **Rails**, for use in **Trap Points** and as makeshift **Conductor Rail Ramps**. The **Rail Foot** and **Rail Web** are removed at the point of the required bend, the remaining **Rail Head** bent appropriately and the cut edge welded up.

Cut Down Dozer
[Col.] A **Laser Dozer** that has had the height of the driver's cab reduced to allow **Panels** of **Track** to be lifted over it by a **Tracklaying Machine** (**TRM**).

Cut Section
[Sig.]
a) An alternative for **Repeater Location**
b) A means of dividing a long **Track Circuit** (**TC**) into many smaller individual Track Circuits. These in turn are combined electrically via a repeat **Relay** to operate as one
c) Where a **Track Layout** would require a disproportionate scale in order to accommodate it on a **Signal Box Diagram**, some parts (generally those at one end of the layout that depict simple **Track** arrangements) are severed and placed in vacant areas. These amputated parts are Cut Sections.

Cut Tyre
[PW] An eco-friendly material used for **Rail Pads**, consisting of sections cut from old car tyres. It suffers from generally retaining its curved shape, making it difficult to fit under the **Rail** easily.

Cut-in Insulation
See **In Span Insulation**.

Cut-off
A short **Route** built to correct some defect inherent in the original **Alignment**, such as easing **Gradients**, avoiding troublesome **Structures** or shortening a journey.

Cut-off Contact
[Sig.] An alternative term for an **Economising Contact** in a **Relay**.

Cut-out Speed Indicators
Cut-out Speed Signs
Cut-outs
[Sig.] Until the late 1950s, it was the sole responsibility of the driver to remember to reduce speed appropriately when the curvature or other restriction required it. The introduction of increased high speed running and **Locomotives** with speedometers prompted the introduction of **Lineside Signs** that served as a reminder to the driver of the **Permanent Speed Restriction** (**PSR**) where that speed was lower than the **Linespeed**. Initially, only the starts of such restrictions were marked, but later all changes above 90mph were marked. They are 300mm high metal (latterly Glass Reinforced Polymer (**GRP**)) numerals fixed to a crossbar. The side facing the driver is painted yellow, and the rear is black to reduce confusion. They are being phased out in favour of **Retro-reflective Speed Signs**. See also **Morpeth Accident**, **Morpeth Board**, **Permissible Speed** (**PS**), **Speed Indicator** (**SI**) **Warning Indicator** (**WI**).

Cutter Bar
[PW] The part of an **Automatic Ballast Cleaner** (**ABC**) that excavates the **Ballast** from beneath the **Track** using a continuous toothed chain similar in appearance to an oversized chainsaw.

Cutter Bar Hole
[PW] The excavation made under the **Track** at one end of a **Ballast Cleaning** site, which allows the **Cutter Bar** to be pieced together under the Track. These holes create a sudden step change in the Ballast Depth and degree of consolidation, resulting in poor **Top** forever afterwards. A similar situation can arise at the exit hole. The mitigation is **Ballast Cleaner Ramping**.

Cutting
[Civ.] An area excavated to permit a **Railway** to maintain its level and **Gradient** through high ground without excessive deviation from a straight course. The opposite is **Embankment**.

118

Cutting Slip
[Civ.] The sudden downward movement of an unstable mass of aggregate, rock or soil from the side of a **Cutting**. This is often triggered by a combination of poor drainage and overloading of the top of the slope with **Spoil**. See also **Bank Slip**, **Slip**, **Slip Circle**, and **Slip Plane**.

Cutwater
[Civ.] An additional structure fitted to **Bridge Piers**, intended to guide the passing water or **Trains** around the main structure. Also **Boat**, **Submarine**.

CV
a) [PW] **V**ertical □ Flat Bottom (FB) □ Full Depth Switches. The C describes the length and **S**witch **R**adius
b) [TRS] **C**oupler **V**alve.

CV&HR
[Hist.] The Pre-Grouping **C**olne **V**alley & **H**alstead **R**ailway

CVs
[PW] Denotes **113A** □ Flat Bottom (FB) □ Shallow Depth Switches, length C.

CVS
a) [PW] Denotes **CEN56E1** □ Flat Bottom (FB) □ Shallow Depth Switches, length C
b) See **C**lose **V**iewing **S**ector. See also Hot Strip.

CVT
a) **C**onstant **V**oltage **T**ransformer
b) **C**ontinuously **V**ariable **T**ransmission.

CVWM
The **C**olne **V**alley **W**ater **M**ain.

CW
a) See **C**ontact **W**ire
b) See **C**arriage **W**asher
c) Shorthand for **C**lock**w**ise. The opposite is counter clockwise (**CCW**).

CWDM
a) **C**onventional **W**avelength-**D**ivision **M**ultiplexing.
b) **C**oarse **W**avelength-**D**ivision **M**ultiplexing.

CWM
See **C**arriage **W**ashing **M**achine.

CWR
See **C**ontinuous **W**elded **R**ail.

CWR Train
See **C**ontinuous **W**elded **R**ail **T**rain. Also Long Welded Rail Train (**LWRT** or **LWR Train**), Perch Train.

CWS
See **C**ontact **W**ire **S**plice.

CX
Abbreviation for **C**old **E**xpanding of Bolt Holes.

CX Level Crossing
[IÉ] A manually operated **Level Crossing** (**LC**, **LX**) that is normally closed across the **Railway** and closed across the road by a **Gatekeeper** in order to allow **Trains** pass.

Cybernetix IVOIRE III
(Tradename) A high resolution linescan camera system fitted to the **New Measurement Train** (**NMT**) having cameras looking at the **Rails** in close up and giving both Rails on one picture, as well as a camera on each side looking at a wider view to include the **Rail Fasteners**. Manufactured by Cybernétix SA, France.

Cyclic Maintenance
Regular **Maintenance** work carried out in accordance with a repeating programme. An example is the lubrication of **Fishplates** (**Plate Oiling**), carried out on a two yearly cycle.

Cyclic Sidewear
[PW] **Sidewear** caused by **Horizontal Alignment** errors in **Straight Track**, leading to a medium wavelength **Hunting** motion. Sometimes triggered by poor **Weld** finishing or poorly maintained **Fishplated Rail Joints**, and exacerbated by high-compliance **Bogies** and **Wide Gauge**.

Cyclic Task
An inspection or **Maintenance** task which is performed to a frequency schedule specified in a standard or procedure.

Cyclic Top
[PW] Regular vertical, medium wavelength variations from design level. The main causes include inadequate **Scarification** during **Renewals** works and poor **Maintenance** of **Jointed Track**. Cyclic Top can, at certain speeds, cause the suspensions of **Short Wheelbase** □ Rail Vehicles to resonate. Therefore the imposition of a **Temporary Speed Restriction** (**TSR**) or **Emergency Speed Restriction** (**ESR**) of 40mph may actually worsen the problem.

Cyclic Twist
[PW] A variation of **Cyclic Top**, where only one **Rail** is affected at a time, in turn producing repetitive **Twist Faults**.

Cylinder Drain Cocks
[TRS] Drain valves fitted to a **Steam Locomotive's** cylinders. The Drain Cocks are held open as the Locomotive is started from cold to allow the admitted steam to drive any water from the cylinders. The Cocks can be closed once the Locomotive is moving and the cylinders are warm.

Cyrus
A **Railway** □ Telegraph Code meaning "Have matter put right at once".

D

D
a) See **Cant Deficiency**
b) See **Down**
c) See **Switch Letters**
d) [Sig.] On a **Signalling Circuit Diagram** as one of the leading letters of an **Equipment Code**, it means **Clear** (**Green**), decoding or de-energised for a **Relay** contact
e) The letter represented by **Delta** in the **Phonetic Alphabet**
f) [TRS] Denoting four **Driven Axles**, See **Diesel and Electric Locomotive Notation**
g) [Sig.] The **Reverse** □ **Checklock** position, see **NBDR**
h) [PW] As a suffix to a **Concrete Sleeper** reference (e.g. G44D) it indicates that the **Sleeper** has a duct cast into the top for a single cable.
i) [Ops.] In **Timetable** planning, this refers to the date of a Timetable change, so "D-26" is 26 weeks prior to the date of the relevant Timetable change
j) **Common Interface File Operating Characteristics Code for Driver Only Operation** (**DOO**)
k) [LUL] The **D**istrict **L**ine.

D Stock
[LUL] The original D Stock was a type of steel bodied stock built for the District **Railway** in 1912, some cars of which survived to the late 1950s. It was indistinguishable from the District's C Stock of 1910 (see above). The later type is the D78 stock, now the standard type used on the District. The D designation relates to the intended route – in this case District.

D&A
Drugs and **A**lcohol. See **Drugs and Alcohol Screening**, **Drugs and Alcohol Testing** See also **Safety Critical Staff**. Also DNA.

D&A Screening
D&A Testing
See **Drugs and Alcohol Screening**, **Drugs and Alcohol Testing**.

D&AJR
[Hist.] The **Pre-Grouping** **D**undee and **A**rbroath **J**oint **R**ailway, a Caledonian and North British joint enterprise.

D&B
Design and **B**uild, a form of contract arrangement where the successful **Contractor** is also responsible for the detailed design of the works.

D&BJR
[Hist.] The **Pre-Grouping** **D**umbarton and **B**alloch **J**oint **R**ailway, a Caledonian and North British joint enterprise.

D&C
Design and **C**onstruction.

D&C Engineer
[RT, NR, Hist.] **D**esign and **C**onstruction Engineer. A person appointed within the client's organisation to oversee the technical aspects of design within a project. See **Project Engineer** (**PE**).

D&D
Design and **D**evelopment.

D&DA
Design and **D**evelopment **A**uthority. Also **DDA**.

D&DR
Design and **D**evelopment **R**eport.

D&I
a) [Tel.] **D**rop and **I**nsert
b) **D**esign and **I**mplementation.

D&IA
Design and **I**mplementation **A**uthority. Also **Design Development and Implementation** (**DD&I**).

D2C
Design **2** **C**ost.

DA
[Sig.]
a) See **Dropped Away**
b) See **Signal Assessment Tool / Detailed Assessment**.

DAA
[NR] **D**epot **A**ccess **A**greement.

DAB
a) [Ops.] **D**epartmental **A**dvice (**B**lue), a document used to publish the **Sandite** application programmes proposed for the **Sandite Trains**
b) **D**elay **A**ttribution **B**oard.

Dabbing In
[Col.] **Train Spotter's** jargon for brief trespasses on the **Railway**, generally for the purpose of taking photographs of **Trains**.

DAC
[NR] **D**epot **A**ccess **C**onditions.

Dace (ZCV)
[NR] A 20 ton fixed-sided **Open Wagon** used for the transportation of **Ballast** and **Sleepers**. See **Wagon Names**.

DAG
a) **D**esign **A**ssurance **G**roup
b) **D**elay **A**ttribution **G**uide.

Dagger
Daggered Speed
Daggering
[NR] Where an item of **Track Renewal** is carried out in many small stages, the associated **Temporary Speed Restriction** (**TSR**) is often only applied over a small section, as it is not required on the untouched area and the work carried out some time ago no longer requires such precautions. In these circumstances, the TSR is published normally in **Section A** of the **Weekly Operating Notice** (**WON**) as covering the entire item, but with a Dagger symbol (†) against it, indicating that the actual positions of the **Commencement Indicator** and **Termination Indicator** will move with the works.

Daily Exam
[TRS] A 28-point testing and inspection programme designed to ensure that a **Locomotive** is safe to operate. The exam includes checks for the correct function of suspension, braking, **Drawgear** etc.

121

ELLIS' BRITISH RAILWAY ENGINEERING ENCYCLOPÆDIA

DAISIE
(daisy) [Sig.] Design Aid for **Signal** Engineers.

DAL
Down □ **A**voiding □ **L**ine.

Dalek
[Col.]
a) [Sig.] Term for an **Emergency Indicator**, after their appearance. Also **Metal Mickey**, **Sleeping Policeman**
b) [Sig.] Term for the rubber terminal covers used on some types of **Shelf Relays**
c) The automatic door opening/closing equipment located around the bunker in a power station serviced by **Merry-go-Round (MGR) Wagons**.

Damped Arm
[Sig.] The arm of a **Treadle** that has been mechanically designed such that its return from the depressed position takes place in a controlled timed manner, usually slowly.

Damper
a) [TRS] A variety of shock absorber fitted to **Bogies** to control rotational oscillation of the Bogies at speed. See **Yaw Damper**
b) See **Harmonic Filter**.

Damper Pad
[TRS] A component within a **Gloucester Floating Axle Suspension** that is housed within the **Pedestal** and is pushed against the **Saddle**. The amount of force applied to it determines the amount of friction damping.

Damper Pot
[TRS] A component within a **Gloucester Floating Axle Suspension** that converts the vertical force on the corner of a vehicle into a horizontal force that pushes on the **Damper Pad** to provide the suspension's damping action.

Damping Resistance
A resistance inserted into a circuit to reduce the rate of change of current during switching.

Dandy Cart
[Hist.] A roofless, flat-floored **Rail Vehicle** used on steeply graded **Plateways** and **Tramways** prior to the introduction of steam powered haulage. Attached to the rear (uphill) end of a rake of wagons, the Cart provides a means whereby the horse, normally used to pull the vehicles on either level stretches or on rising gradients, could ride down the inclines.

Danger
[Sig.]
a) A **Signal** indication or **Aspect** meaning that the driver must stop.
b) Universal term for a **Red Aspect** or **Red** □ **Handsignal**. See also **Stop Aspect**.

Dangerous Goods
Materials which are capable of posing a risk to the health and safety of **Passengers**, staff and others, or which have potential to jeopardise the **Safety of the Line**. Such materials may include acids, explosives or biological agents. The instructions for dealing with these materials are contained in the **Pink Pages** of the **Working Manual for Rail Staff**. They include pure chemicals, compounds, manufactured products or articles which can pose a risk to people, animals or the environment if not properly handled in use or in transit. Such materials are categorised:
Class 1 Explosives
Class 2 Gases
  2.1 Flammable gas
  2.2 Non-flammable non-toxic gas
  2.3 Toxic gas
Class 3 Flammable liquids
Class 4 Other flammables
  4.1 Flammable solids
  4.2 Liable to spontaneously combust
  4.3 Emit flammable gases in contact with water
Class 5 5.1 Oxidising agents
  5.2 Organic peroxides
Class 6 6.1 Toxic substances
  6.2 Infectious substances
Class 7 Radioactive materials
Class 8 Corrosives
Class 9 Miscellaneous
  (Materials such as asbestos, car airbags, lithium batteries and environmentally hazardous substances which don't fit into any of the classes 1 – 8)

DAOL
Direct-**a**cting **O**ver**l**oad.

DAP
[Elec.] **D**ouble **A**nchor **P**oint, A type of **Conductor Rail Anchor**.

DAPF
Document **A**mendment **P**roposal **F**orm.

DAPP
[NR] **D**raft **A**nnual **P**ossession **P**lan.

DAR
See **Displacement and Acceleration Recorder**.

Dargan, William
(1799-1867) born near Killeshin, County Laois (now in Éire), Dargan trained under Thomas Telford on the Holyhead Road. In the early 1830s he started his own contracting firm and in 1833 won the contract to build the first **Railway** in Ireland, from Dublin to Dun Laoghaire. He went on to build over 800 miles of Railways in Ireland. His illustrious career was curtailed by a fall from his horse in 1866 and he died a poor man in the following year.

Dark Tower, The
[Col.] Name for the building housing **Network Rail Infrastructure Limited's (NRIL)** head office. It is more properly 40 Melton Street, London, NW1 2EE. See also **Eversholt Street**.

DART
(*dart*)
a) [Éire] Dublin Area Rapid Transit, the Light Rail system in Dublin
b) [Tel.] Digital Advanced Radio for Trains.

Darth Vader
[Col.] Nickname given to Class 460 Electric Multiple Units (EMU) due to the shape of their nose.

Darwin
[NR] Name for the National Real-Time Database (NRTD).

DAS
a) Design Assumption Statement
b) Driver Advisory Systems.

DASS 2
Digital Access Signalling System 2.

DaSTS
Delivering a Sustainable Transport System, a Department for Transport (DfT) strategy.

Data Link Module (DLM)
[Sig.] A device linking a Solid State Interlocking (SSI) with a group of Trackside Functional Modules (TFM) and therefore found in Location Cases and Relocatable Equipment Buildings (REB).

Data Recorder
[TRS] Generically, a device fitted to an On-Track Machine (OTM), Traction Unit or Tram to record and store key parameters, such as speed and driver actions. See also Hasler, On-Train Monitoring Recorder (OTMR), On-Train Data Recorder (OTDR).

Data Telegram
[Sig.] Within a Solid State Interlocking (SSI) system, the reply telegrams from the Trackside Functional Modules (TFM) to the Central Interlocking Processor. Data Telegrams relay the inputs from detection devices in the TFMs (e.g. Lamp Proving, Points Detection and Track Circuit inputs). These inputs are typically copied directly to the Internal State.

Datatrak
[Ops.] A semi-automatic mechanism for reporting Multiple Unit Train movements based on the initial location of Rolling Stock, and subsequent translation to actual Train identities and activities based on the GEMINI system.

Datum Marker
[LUL] Alternative for Datum Plate.

Datum Marks
[PW] Lines marked on the Rail Foot using a pencil or marker and aligned with a suitable reference on the Sleeper beneath (generally the Housing of the Rail Fastening) allowing any longitudinal movement of the Rail to be identified. Such marks are used in the following circumstances:
• Adjacent to the site of an Alumino-thermic Weld during the Weld preparation and cooling, allowing the Track Welder (TW) to assess the integrity of the finished Weld
• At regular intervals along a Free Rail during Stressing to ensure that the Rail is tensioned evenly
• At the end Sleepers within a Stressing site, to permit measurement of the amount by which the Rail moves into (or unusually, out of) the Anchor Length when Unclipped
• At the far end of the Anchor Length to permit an assessment of the effectiveness of the Anchor Length to be made.

Datum Plate
[PW] A small plate attached to a fixed object such as a Bridge, Overhead Line Structure or Platform. They have a movable block that is set to the same height as the nearest Rail. The design Cant (C, E) and measured distance from the plate to the Running Edge (RE) of the noted Rail are recorded on the plate for future reference. The older style is shown above right and the newer type below right. See also Green Block, Red Block.

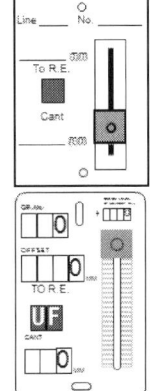

Datum Rail
[PW]
a) The Rail used by a Tamper during the Lining operation. The Lining Chord trolleys are pressed against this Rail by a pneumatic cylinder in order to maintain a consistent reference
b) The Rail that requires least work to bring it back to Design Levels, and is therefore used as the reference during manual Lifting and Packing of the Track.

David
The obsolescent Phonetic Alphabet word representing D. Replaced by Delta.

Days
Alternative term for an early or morning shift.

DB
(Tradename) Deutsche Bahn, the German national Railway Company. Until 1994, Deutsche Bundesbahn, the German federal (state) Railway organisation.

DB Schenker Rail (UK) Ltd.
(Tradename) UK division of Deutsche Bahn Schenker (DBS), the transportation and logistics division of Deutsche Bahn (DB) They now own the former English Welsh and Scottish Railways (EWS). Contracted to DBS.

DBE
[PW] Drilled Both Ends. A description applied to short (generally less than 18.288m (60')) lengths of Rail which have Fishbolt Holes at both ends.

DBF
[PW] Dirty Ballast Failure

DBFO
Design Build Finance Operate.

DBFT
Design, Build, Finance, Transfer, an arrangement whereby Infrastructure projects are funded and implemented by a private sector organisation before being transferred to another body (such as Network Rail) for their operation.

DBHP
[TRS] Drawbar Horse Power.

DBOM
Design, Build, Operate, Maintain. The first DBOM was Phase One of Manchester Metrolink where a consortium of companies built the system and then had a concession to maintain and operate it.

DBS
(Tradename) Deutsche Bahn Schenker. See DB Schenker Rail (UK) Ltd.

DBSO
[TRS] An acronym representing a Driving □ Brake □ Standard Class □ Open Coach.

DBTSO
[TRS] An acronym representing a Driving □ Brake □ Trailer □ Standard Class □ Open Coach.

DBVIC
[TRS] Driver's Brake Valve Isolating Cock.

DC
a) Direct Current
b) [Elec.] Double Channel, a form of construction used for Overhead Line Structures (OLE Structures)
c) The ATOC code for Devon and Cornwall Railway.

DC Electrification System
[Elec.] An Electrification System that supplies Traction Current of the Direct Current (DC) form

DC Electrified Line
[NR] A Line fitted with Conductor Rails supplying Traction Current of the Direct Current (DC) form. See Electrification System.

DC Immune
[Sig.] A description of a Track Circuit (TC) or other piece of Signalling Equipment which has been designed to be immune from effects of Direct Current (DC) □ Traction Supply systems. See also AC Immune.

DC Isolation
A form of Possession in which the Traction Supply Current is disconnected from an Electrical Section of Conductor Rail, and that Conductor Rail is then proved Dead by using a Short Circuiting Bar.

DC Link
[TRS] The connection between the Rectifier and Inverter in a modern Traction Unit using AC Traction Current. Modern Traction Motors use three-phase Alternating Current (AC), whereas the typical Overhead Line Equipment (OLE) supply is single-phase AC. The most efficient arrangement is to convert the single-phase AC from the OLE to the three-phase required for the Motors by Rectifying it to DC and then Inverting the DC to three-phase AC, incorporating the speed control system into the second part of the system. The DC Link is the equipment joining these two parts together.

DC Rail
[Col.] Term for the positive Conductor Rail in a DC Electrification System. Also Hot Rail, Juice Rail, Positive Conductor Rail, Positive Rail, Pozzy Rail, Third Rail.

DC Resistance Control
[TRS, Hist.] A method of Traction Motor control formerly almost universal on Electric Railways using Direct Current (DC), whereby the current to the motors was gradually increased from start up by removing resistances from the power circuit in steps. Originally this step control was done manually but it was later automatic, a Relay in the circuit monitoring the rise and fall of current as the steps were removed. This system has now been superseded by solid state control systems. See also Camshaft.

DC Track Circuit
[Sig.] A type of Jointed Track Circuit that utilises Direct Current (DC) for its operation. Alternatives include AC Track Circuits and Audio Frequency Track Circuits.

DC Train
[TRS]
a) A Train which uses an external DC source Traction Current
b) [Col.] A Train which uses Conductor Rails as a source of Traction Current.

DCA
Data Concentrator Appreciation.

DCD
Driver Competence Development.

DCDS
Direct Current Disconnect Switch.

DCE
[BR]
a) Prior to 1966, District Civil Engineer
b) Post-1966, see Divisional Civil Engineer.

DCI
See Driver's Crossing Indicator.

DCIO
Deputy Chief Inspecting Officer of Railways, a post within Her Majesty's Railway Inspectorate (HMRI).

ELLIS' BRITISH RAILWAY ENGINEERING ENCYCLOPÆDIA

DCK
[NR, Civ.] Under the **Bridge Condition Marking Index** (**BCMI**) handbook, shorthand for deckplates, decking or **Jack Arches**.

DCLDS
Direct **C**urrent **L**oad **D**isconnect **S**witch.

DCM
Design **C**onstruct **M**aintain.

DCO
See **Development Consent Order**.

DCOMD
Design, **C**onstruction, **O**peration, **M**aintenance and **D**ecommissioning.

DCP
a) **D**ocument **C**ontrol **P**oint
b) **D**esignated **C**ompetent **P**erson.

DCR
a) **D**ata **C**ollection **R**ules
b) See **Devon and Cornwall Railways**

DCRDF
Designated **C**ommunity **R**ail **D**evelopment **F**und.

DCS
a) See **Depot Control System**
b) **D**oor **C**lose **S**witch.

DCU
[BR, Hist.] **D**esign / **C**onstruct **U**nit, see **Self-accounting Unit** (**SAU**).

DCVI
See **Doors Closed Visual Indicator**.

DD
See **Deceleration Distance**. See also **Braking Distance** (**BD**).

DD&I
Design **D**evelopment and **I**mplementation, an authority to proceed on a project.

DDA
a) The **D**isability **D**iscrimination **A**ct 1995
b) **D**esign & **D**evelopment **A**uthority. Also **D&DA**.

DDI
a) See **DD&I**
b) [Tel.] **D**irect **D**ial **I**n, a feature fitted to private telephone exchanges that allows outside parties to dial an extension direct. See **ETD**.

DE
[IÉ] **D**ivisional **E**ngineer.

Dead
[Col.]
a) [Elec.] Alternative for **De-energised**
b) [TRS] Describing a non-functional **Locomotive** or **Traction Unit**. See also **DOR**.

Dead Load
[Civ.] The weight of a **Structure** and anything permanently laid on it or fixed to it. In the case of a **Bridge** carrying the **Railway** this includes the **Ballast** and **Track** but not the **Trains**. See also **Live Load**.

Dead Locking
[Sig.] An **Interlocking** arrangement that is not dependent on any other **Control**.

Dead Man's Handle
[TRS, Col.] Common term for the **Driver's Safety Device** (**DSD**). Originally it was a sprung handle that the driver had to hold over in order to proceed. Should they fail to do so the **Traction Power** would be removed and the brakes applied. However, drivers became wont to wedge the handle over using flask or handlamp, rendering it useless. The Driver's Safety Device must be depressed and released in response to an audible cue at irregular intervals, making it impossible to defeat. Also **Deadman**. See also **Drivers Vigilance Device** (**DVD**), **Drivers Vigilance System** (**DVS**), **Vigilance System** (**VS**).

Dead-centre
Position of a mechanism in which the internal components exert no leverage on the mechanism as a whole.

Deadman
[LUL] See **Dead Man's Handle**.

Dead-space Drain Valve
[TRS] Valves fitted to the bottom of a **Traction Unit's** fuel tanks, which allow any accumulation of water to be drained off during maintenance, or to drain the tank to facilitate removal or replacement.

DEBO
Designated **B**ody, an appointment under the **Technical Specifications for Interoperability** (**TSI**).

Debris
A **Railway** □ **Telegraph Code** meaning "I will advise you further".

DECA
Dispositif d'**E**nregistreurs de **C**hocs **A**utomatiques, an automatic impact recording device.

Decapod
[TRS]
a) A **Steam Locomotive** with a 0-10-0 wheel arrangement, see **Whyte's Notation**
b) [BR] The name of **Laboratory** 25, which was a **Bogie Vehicle** with an additional **Wheelset** (giving it 10 wheels) added for testing **Track Forces**.

Decarburised Layer
[PW] A softening of the surface layer caused by the hot rolling of **Rail** during manufacture.

DECC
Department of **E**nergy and **C**limate **C**hange.

Deceleration Distance (**DD**)
[Sig.] The minimum distance that must be provided between a **Warning Indicator** (**WI**) and its associated **Speed Indicator** (**SI**). See also **Braking Distance** (**BD**).

125

ELLIS' BRITISH RAILWAY ENGINEERING ENCYCLOPÆDIA

Decision Point
a) [HR] A point where guidance on crossing safely at a **Level Crossing** (**LC**, **LX**) is visible and at which a decision to cross or wait can be made in safety. For **Footpath Crossings** this is not less than 2 metres from the **Nearest Running Rail** or 3 metres where the **Permissible Speed** (**PS**) is higher than 160kph (100mph). For bridleway crossings and **User Worked Crossings** (**UWC**) this is not be less than 3 metres from the Nearest Running Rail in any case
b) [LUL] Any point in a journey where the customer has a choice between two or more paths (e.g. different network **Lines**, different **Platforms**, different **Routes**, different **Gatelines**, different lifts).

Deck
a) See **Bridge Deck**
b) [Col.] Alternative for the ground, as in **On the Deck**, meaning **Derailed**.

DED
See **District Electric Depot**.

DEDA
Delegated **E**ngineering **D**ecision-making **A**uthority.

Dedication Notices
Legal notices erected at **Foot Crossings**, **Footpath Crossings** (**FPC**) and **Level Crossings** (**LC**, **LX**) stating whether the Crossing has been dedicated as a public right of way or not.

Dedimus
A **Railway** □ **Telegraph Code** meaning "Have you communicated with us in error?"

Deemed Minutes
[NR] A pre-determined value in **Delay Minutes** given to the cancellation of a **Train**.

De-energised
The state of an electrical **Conductor** or system where the electrical supply has been removed, but the conductor or system has not been connected to **Earth** to guarantee its continued de-energised state. Also **Dead**.

Deep Level Tube
[LUL] An alternative for **Deep Tube Line**.

Deep Skirted Fishplate
See **Skirted Fishplate**.

Deep Tube Line
[LUL] Those **Tunnels** comprising the underground sections of the Jubilee **Line**, the Northern Line, the Piccadilly Line, the Bakerloo Line, the Central Line, the Victoria Line and the Waterloo & City Line.

DEF
a) **D**ual **e**nd-**f**ed, an electrical power distribution topology
b) **D**elayed **E**ttringite **F**ormation (or **D**eferred **E**ttringite **F**ormation), an effect where the cycling of curing temperatures, leaching of alkalis from the concrete and voiding leads to the formation of Ettringite ($3CaO \cdot Al_2O_3 \cdot 3CaSO_4 \cdot 32H_2O$) crystals, in turn leading to bursting of the concrete. Known to affect some older batches of **Concrete Sleepers**.

Defect
See **Rail Defect**.

Defective On-train Equipment
[RB] On-train equipment that is:
- not performing its intended safety function, either fully or partly
- isolated
- missing.

Defective Rail
[PW] A **Rail** that has not yet broken but has **Rail Defects** within it that jeopardise the continued **Safety of the Line**. See **Squats**, **Star Cracks**, **Tache Ovale**, **Wheelburns**.

Defective Sleeper
[PW] A **Sleeper** which has ceased to adequately support the **Rails** or maintain the **Track Gauge**. Failure modes include decay, fungal attack, insect attack, weathering and subsequent splitting of **Wood Sleepers**, and cracking of **Concrete Sleepers**. See **Baseplate Shuffle**, **Chair Shuffle**, **DEF**, **Indentation**, **Rail Seat Erosion**, **Sleeper Gall**, **Soffit Erosion**. See also **Banding** (a), **Bonker**, **Borate Rods**, **Sleeper Bonker**, **Sleeper Integrity Tester** (**SIT**).

Defective Weld
[PW] A **Flash Butt Weld** (**FBW**) or **Alumino-thermic Weld** that is improperly made, geometrically sub-standard or one where the **Weld** process was subjected to adverse weather or mechanical stresses that *may* have affected the integrity of the bond. See **Black Holes**, **Hot Tears**, **Pre-tap**, **Wet Weld**.

Defensive Driving
[NPT] See **Professional Driving**.

DEFI
Documentation **E**lectronique **F**erroviaire **I**nternationale, International **Railway** electronic documentation.

Deficiency
See **Cant Deficiency** (**D**).

Defining Structures
[PW] Those individual **Limiting Structures** identified as having the smallest clearances to **Rail Vehicles** which, as a consequence, form the basis for the definition of a **Structure Gauge** for a specific **Route**.

Deflection
a) See **Clip Deflection**
b) The amount by which a **Bridge Deck** will move vertically under a given load. See also **Camber**.

DEFRA
(deff-ra) **D**epartment of **E**nvironment, **F**ood & **R**ural **A**ffairs.

Degraded
Degraded Mode
Describing a system that is not functioning correctly, either not at full power or with certain functions disabled.

Degree of Curvature
The degree of curvature of a circular curve may be determined by:
a) [US] in highway works, the angle subtended at the centre by an arc of the curve 100 feet (30.5 metres) in length
b) [US] in **Railway** work, the angle subtended at the centre by a **Chord** of the curve 100 feet (30.5 metres) in length
c) [UK] In Railway work, the angle subtended at the centre by a Chord of the curve typically 100 metres in length. This method of measurement is not commonly used in the **National Railway Network** (**NRN**).

De-icing Bath
[Elec.] A shallow container of de-icing fluid fitted with rollers and placed at a **Conductor Rail Gap** to assist with removing ice from the **Current Collection Shoes** (**Shoes**) during cold weather.

De-icing Cars
[TRS] **Passenger** □ **Cars** specially equipped to spread de-icing fluid on **Conductor Rails**.

De-icing Train
[LUL] A special **Train** equipped to clear **Snow** and ice from **Conductor Rails**. Also **Sleet Train**.

DEL
a) **Down** □ **Electric** □ **Line**
b) **Down Empty Line**
c) See **Driver's Eye Level**.

Delachaux Weld
[PW, Obs.] A proprietary type of **Alumino-thermic Welding** process. The Delachaux Group owns Railtech International, manufacturer of the **PLA Weld**.

Delay Minute
Delay Minutes
a) [NR] The difference in journey time between that shown in the **Timetable** (**TT**) and the actual time taken between two points in the journey
b) [NR] The total delay to **Trains** caused by Network Rail's (**NR**) failures, in a given period.
c) Also **Train Minute Delay**.

Delayed Yellow
Delayed Yellow Aspect
[Sig.] A means of controlling the approach of a **Train** to a **Colour Light Signal** where the **Signal** does not have a full **Overlap**. The Signal **On the Approach** is held at a **Stop Aspect** until the Train is almost at it, whereupon it is cleared to a **Yellow** □ **Caution Aspect**. This ensures the speed of the Train is reduced appropriately.

Delivery Plan
The programme of work to be undertaken by **Her Majesty's Railway Inspectorate** (**HMRI**) and the timescale for achieving it, relating to a specific **Railway** topic area.

Delivery Unit (DU)
[NR] See **Maintenance Delivery Unit** (**MDU**).

Delkor Egg
[PW] A **Baseplate** designed for use in areas where noise reduction is required. See also **Cologne Egg**.

Dellner Coupling
(Tradename) [TRS] A type of **Automatic Coupling** manufactured by Dellner Couplers of Sweden.

Delta
The **Phonetic Alphabet** word representing D.

Delta Suspension
[Elec., LR] A rope which suspends the **Contact Wire** (**CW**) from a **Cantilever**. Held at its apex either within a clamp or allowed to run freely over a plastic pulley. Both of which connect to a bracket on the Cantilever via shackles and/or quick links. Also known as a **Bridle**.

DeltaRail
(Tradename) The company formerly known as **AEA Technology** plc.

Deltics
[Col.] Common name for **Class** 55 **Diesel Locomotives**. The only surviving examples are privately owned.

DEM
a) See **Departmental Engineering Manager** (**DEM**)
b) See **Designer's Engineering Manager**.

Demand
The number of **Passengers** using a **Station**, **Train** service or specific Train in a given one year period. See also **Passenger Demand**.

Demand Forecast
An estimate of the predicted number of Passengers using a Station, **Train** service or specific Train in a given future year. See also **Passenger Demand Forecast**.

Demand Loop
[LR] A **Track** based receiver that detects the presence of a **Tram** and initiates a timed **Signalling System** sequence, such as the operation of highway traffic lights.

Demic
[Col.] A colloquial term used to describe unserviceable or scrap **Rail Vehicles**. Origin unknown, but it may be a contraction of "academic".

DEMU
See **Diesel Electric Multiple Unit**, see also **Multiple Unit Train**.

DEP
See **Designated Earthing Point**.

Department for Transport (DfT)
Under the **Railways Act 2005** the DfT gained many of the functions formerly carried out by the **Strategic Rail Authority** (**SRA**). The Department also has responsibilities for the overall strategic and financial management of the **National Railway Network** (**NRN**).

Departmental Engineering Manager (DEM)
[NR] A person appointed by **Network Rail** in accordance with **Network Rail Company Standard** (**NRCS**) NR/L2/INI/02009 who has accountability within Network Rail for the overall compliance of projects (in a defined area) with the applicable processes, standards and legislation.

Departmental Vehicles
[BR] A collective term for the **Rail Vehicles** used by the engineering functions of the **Railway**. These include specially built and specially adapted vehicles used for the transport of materials, plant and staff. See also **Drum Carriers**, **Engineering Vehicles**, **Engineering Train**, **Ballast Hopper** □ **Wagons**, **Mess Coaches**, **Opens**, **Side Rail Loaders**, **Tool Vans** and **Wagon Names**.

Departure
See **Departure Line**.

Departure Board
The large electromechanical or electronic information display found in the **Concourses** of larger **Stations**. See also **CIS**, **PIDS**, **Solari**.

Departure Line
A **Track** on which **Trains** leave a **Marshalling Yard**. Colloquial use also generally includes the direction of travel of departing vehicles, e.g. **Down** Departure Line.

Depot
(*depp-oh*) A location at which **Coaches**, **Locomotives** and **Multiple Units** are stabled and maintained. See also **CMD**, **Diesel Maintenance Depot** (**DMD**), **Electric Traction Depot** (**ETD**), **Plant Depot**, **Traction Maintenance Depot** (**TMD**).

Depot Control System
[Sig.] A small-scale **Signalling System** used to control **Train** movements within a **Depot**.

Depot Current Section
[Elec.] A **Current Section** within a **Depot** fed from a substation or switch house.

Depot Facility Operator (DFO)
[NR] The organisation responsible for the day-to-day management and operation of a particular **Depot**. This is typically a **Freight Operating Company** (**FOC**) or **Train Operating Company** (**TOC**).

Depot Protection Master
[LUL] A person certificated to provide protection for I and others when **on or About the Line** within a **Depot**.

Depot Shed Shore Supply
[LUL] A source of **Traction Power** provided by means of a cable plugged into the **Train** and connected to an **Overhead Trolley Supply** or Receptacle Box Supply. This enables the movement or testing of **Trains** in **Depot** sheds where the tracks are not **Electrified**.

Depot Trip Switch
[LUL] A system which allows the **Depot Shed Shore Supply** to be shut off instantly by staff in an emergency..

Depression Bar
[Sig.] A metal bar mounted level with the **Rail Head** in the **Flangeway** area, so that any passing **Rail Wheel** will press down upon it and indicate the presence of the **Rail Vehicle** to the **Signalling System**. Often utilised at the little-used **Buffer Stop** end of a **Bay Line** as an alternative to **Eutectic Strip** and **Track Circuits** (**TC**), as these may be unreliable in the (generally) oily and fouled conditions found at such locations. They were also historically used to lock **Facing Points** when trains were present. Also **Clearance Bar**.

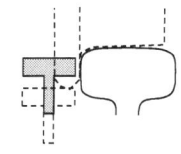

Depth of Cut
[PW] Correctly, the depth to which the **Cutter Bar** of an **Automatic Ballast Cleaner** (**ABC**) digs below **Design Sleeper Bottom** or **Bearer Bottom** (**BB**), but the term can also be applied to any excavation. See also **Below Sleeper Bottom** (**BSB**).

Dequadrification
[Arch.] Removing two **Tracks** from a **Four Track Railway**. See also **Singling**.

Derail
To cause a **Rail Vehicle** to lose the guidance and support provided by the **Rails** by one of the following means:
- By removing the Rail or **Track**, see **Bank Slip**, **Broken Rail**, **Washout**
- By a **Rail Wheel** or **Wheel Set** becoming defective or broken
- Lifting the Wheels so that the **Wheel Flanges** are no longer overlapping the **Rail Head**, see **Twist Fault**
- By causing the Wheel Flange to **Climb** the **Rail**; at some defect, see **Defective Weld**, **Sidewear**, **Track Buckle**; or by unevenly loading the vehicle
- By negotiating too abrupt a **Reverse Curve** for the vehicles, see **Buffer Locking**
- By striking a large object placed on the Track, see **TP&V**
- By deliberately causing the Rail Vehicle to become Derailed at a point particularly designed for the purpose, see **Catch Point**, **Derailer**, **Double Tongue Trap Point**, **Trap Point**, **Trap Road**
- By poor Train handling such as driving too fast or too roughly, see **Overspeed**, **Rough Shunt**
- By means of loose equipment such as doors and **Brake Rigging** hanging from the vehicle

See also **Off the Road**, **On the Deck**, **On the Floor**.

Derailer
a) [RB] A device at an exit from a **Siding** or **Bay Platform** that **Derails** a **Rail Vehicle** making an **Unauthorized Movement**, so protecting the **Adjacent Line**.
b) A **Rail** mounted, ramp-shaped device whose purpose is to Derail a **Train**, particularly one attempting to make an Unauthorised Movement. They are often used in **Depot** areas where speeds are low and space is limited.

Derailment
A gross fault condition where one or all of the wheels of a **Rail Vehicle** have ceased to be guided or supported by the **Rails**. This can be due to many faults, including **Broken Rails**, broken wheels, excessive speed, **Hot Axle Boxes**, **Rough Shunts**, **Twist Faults** and vandalism. See also **Off the Road, On the Deck, On the Floor**.

Derailment Containment
The physical measures put in place to guide a **Derailed** □ **Train** safely along the **Railway** until it comes to rest. Measures include **Guard Rails** and **Robust Kerbs**.

Derailment Quotient
A method of assessing the liability of a **Rail Wheel** to **Derail** by **Flange Climbing** given the value of friction for a given **Wheel Profile** at the contact point with the **Gauge Corner** using the **Nadal Formula**:

$$\frac{L}{V} = \left[\frac{tan\delta - \mu}{1 + \mu \times tan\delta}\right]$$

Where:
- L is the lateral force
- V is the vertical force
- δ is the angle of contact of the Rail Wheel on the **Rail**
- μ is the coefficient of friction

In order for Flange Climb to be avoided:

$$L < V \times \left[\frac{1 - \mu \times cot\delta}{\mu + cot\delta}\right]$$

See also **Prud'homme Equation**.

Derailment Resistance
[TRS] The ability of a **Rail Vehicle** to keep its wheels on the **Rails**, defined by the results of a series of standard tests, such as **Wheel Unloading Tests**.

Derby

Derby Research
[BR, Hist.] The colloquial name for **British Rail Research** (**BRR**), after its home in Derby. Now owned by **DeltaRail**, formerly **AEA Technology**.

Derogation
A formal relaxation of a particular requirement for a particular situation. Derogations are only applicable to the case they were granted for, but are often included in later issues of the relevant standard. Derogations apply forever, unless superseded. See also **Deviation, Temporary Non-compliance** (**TNC**). See also **Railway Group Standard** (**RGS**), Network Rail Company Standard (**NRCS**).

Derwent
A **Railway** □ **Telegraph Code** meaning "Your communication on the following subject received and has attention".

Design Alignment
[PW] The geometrically derived horizontal layout of a **Track**. While this may be developed with the assistance of a computer, the result is normally fully in accordance with standards, whereas some **Maintenance Lining** work is not. See also **Automatic Track Alignment** (**ATA**), **Hallade**.

Design Chainage
The longitudinal distance reference adopted during the survey, design and implementation of a scheme. The **Railway** suffers from not having a single, accurate, universal method for recording distance. Operators use **Miles** and **Chains**, **Permanent Way** (**PW**) uses **Miles** and **Yards**, **Signalling** and **Overhead Line Equipment** (**OLE**) design is normally done in kilometres, but the older records sometimes use Miles and feet. All of these systems are referenced to different features so there is never agreement on where a particular location actually is. To avoid unpleasantness, a single site-wide system based on metres should be established, with a reference point of 1000 metres (to reduce the risk of negative chainages) at a large physical feature that appears in all records and will not be affected by the works; **Bridge Abutments** are recommended for this purpose.

Design Level
a) The vertical level of a design feature referenced to a datum
b) [PW] The geometrically derived vertical layout of a **Track**. While this may be developed with the assistance of a computer, the result is normally fully in accordance with standards, whereas most **Maintenance Tamping** is not. See also **Automatic Track and Top Alignment** (**ATTA**). See **Design Rail Level**.

Design Lifts
[PW] The amounts by which a **Track** must be raised at specified locations in order to put the Track in accordance with the **Design Level** of the **Longitudinal Section** (**Long Section**). Peculiarly, the same term is also used to describe all vertical adjustments, including **Lowerings**.

Design Rail Level
[PW] The vertical position of the **Low Rail** of a **Track** at any given location, according to the design for that **Track**.

Design Sleeper Bottom
[PW] The level of the **Soffit** (underside) of the **Sleepers** of a **Track** when the Track is placed at its design level. The depth of excavation during **Reballasting** is measured from this reference point. See also **Below Sleeper Bottom** (**BSB**).

Design Slues
[PW] The amounts by which a **Track** must be moved laterally at specified locations in order to put the Track in accordance with a **Design Alignment**.

Design Tamping and Lining
[PW] The use of a **Tamper** to implement **Design Lifts** and **Design Slues**, rather than carrying out an averaging exercise. See also **Maintenance Tamping and Lining**.

Designated Earthing Point (DEP)
A nominated point on a **Railway** equipped with an **Overhead Line Electrification** (**OLE**) system. It denotes where the temporary **Earthing** □ **Bonds** may be fitted during **Isolations**. They are designated by a yellow plate lettered DEP.

Designated Person (DP)
[NR] A person nominated to undertake certain duties as detailed in the **Rule Book**. For example, in the **Rule Book Module** □ **T10**, a Designated Person is a person who is responsible for arranging **Protection** as shown in the module and can be defined as a DP in local instructions.

Designated Project Engineer (DPE)
[NR] A specific role under **Network Rail Company Standard** (**NRCS**) NR/L2/INI/02009 a person appointed to be accountable within Network Rail for the co-ordination and integration of technical and engineering aspects of a specific project particularly where the project includes multi-disciplinary activities.. This role is the NR equivalent of the **Contractor's Engineering Manager** (**CEM**)

Designer's Engineering Manager (DEM)
[NR] An unofficial description for someone who is not the **Contractor's Engineering Manager** (**CEM**)but is undertaking a similar role within a design organisation,

Desiro
The brandname of the **Class** 185, 350, 360, 444 and 450 **Multiple Units** (**MU**).

Destress
Destressing
[NPT, PW] An obsolete term for **Stressing**, its usage implying the first time a new **Rail** is **Stressed**.

Detailed Design
a) The design stage which follows the issuing of the **Form A**, **Approval in Principle** (**AIP**) or **Outline Project Specification** (**OPS**) and **Scheme Plan** at the **Outline Design** or **Detailed Feasibility** stage. It is at this stage that every detail and specification is identified, designed and co-ordinated with all other elements of the design. It is this design that is used to construct the works.

b) [NR] In terms of **Network Rail's** □ **Governance for Railway Investment Projects** (**GRIP**) this stage is analogous to GRIP stage 5. Typical products of the Detailed Design phase include:
- Bonding Plans
- Cable Core Plans
- Cable Route Plans
- Conductor Rail layouts
- Control Tables
- **Detailed Design** drawings and **Certificate of Checking** (**Form B**) for **Permanent Way** (**PW**) and Civil Engineering (**CE**) works
- Diversionary Route strategies
- Isolation Diagrams
- Location Area Plans
- Longitudinal Sections (Long Sections)
- Overhead Line Equipment Layout Plans (OLE Layout Plans)
- Overhead Line Structure sections
- Possession plans
- Section C Notices
- Sign □ Sighting Forms
- Signal Sighting Forms (SSF)
- Signaller's Route Lists
- Stageworks Plans
- Staging details
- Stressing Plans
- Switch and Crossing Manufacturers' Drawings
- Temporary Speed Restriction (TSR) schedule
- Temporary Works designs
- Temporary Block Working instructions
- Testing Plan
- Testing Strategy
- Track Drain designs
- Wiring Diagrams
- Yellow Perils

(This list is not exhaustive).

Detailed Examination
Detailed Examination of Structures
[NR, Civ.] As defined in **Network Rail Company Standard** (**NRCS**) RT/CE/S/083, a close examination of all accessible parts of a **Structure**, generally within touching distance, of sufficient quality to produce a record that includes the condition of all parts of the Structure, the uses to which the Structure is being put, recommendations for remedial action and any other relevant facts.

Detailed Feasibility
Detailed Feasibility Study
a) Normally the second stage of scheme development, coming after the initial **Feasibility Study**. At this stage the **Preferred Option** will be developed to a level where it is possible to identify and quantify costs, risks, issues and conflicts. This often requires more detailed survey information and some design. Also called **Outline Design**.
b) [NR] In terms of **Network Rail's** ▫ **Governance for Railway Investment Projects (GRIP)** this stage is analogous to GRIP stage 4, and can involve the production of **Approval in Principle (AIP)** and Form A.

Detailed Planning Meeting (DPM)
[NR] The meeting at which the fine detail of the **Possession Arrangements** for all **Possessions** planned for a particular week are decided, based on submissions made by the various **Contractors** and others.

Detected
[Sig.] Of a **Set of Switches** (**Set of Points**) or other moveable **Rail**, physically proved in the **Normal** or **Reverse** position. See **Detection**.

Detection
a) [Sig.] A **Failsafe** arrangement that proves that a **Set of Switches** (**Set of Points**) are correctly **Set** in the **Normal** or **Reverse** position. Correct detection must be obtained before the **Protecting Signal** can be **Cleared**. See also **Correspondence, Normal, Out of Correspondence, Reverse**.
b) [Sig.] A Failsafe arrangement that proves that any moveable section of **Rail** such as a **Lift Bridge** or **Swing Bridge** is correctly placed to allow **Trains** to run safely.

Detection Contacts
[Sig.] Electrical contacts (sometimes housed inside a **Point Machine**) that close when the operation being monitored is confirmed, **Detection** is achieved and which in turn cause the appropriate **Detection Relay** to be energised.

Detection Equipment
[Sig.] equipment that provides the **Detection** function.

Detection Relay
[Sig.] A **Relay** which becomes energised when a **Set of Points** or a group of related Points correctly occupy the **Normal** or **Reverse** position, closing the appropriate **Detection Contacts**.

Detector Rod
[Sig.] A straight metal bar that connects the **Detection Equipment** to the **Toe** end of the **Switch Rail** so that the position of the Switch Rail can be detected.

Detonator
[Col.] The universal term for a **Railway Fog Signal**, these are a small disc-shaped explosive warning device designed to be placed on the **Rail Head** for **Protection** and emergency purposes. It explodes when a **Train** passes over thus alerting the driver. Despite not fulfilling the definition of an explosive detonator in any way, Detonator is the industry standard term. See also **Bangers, Crackers, Dets, Foggies, Shots**.

Detonator Placer
[Sig.] A device operated from a **Lever Frame** that places **Detonators** (**Railway Fog Signals**) on the **Rail Head** at a point remote from the **Signal Box** (**SB**) in order to warn drivers of danger or obstruction. Such devices are no longer fitted as new.

Detonator Protection
[NR] **Possession** ▫ **Protection** comprising three **Detonators** placed on the **Rail Head** at 20m intervals and a **Possession Limit Board** (**PLB**) opposite the first detonator in the direction of travel.

DETP
[NR] Detailed Engineering Train Plan.

DETR
Department of the Environment, Transport and the Regions, now replaced by **Department for Transport** (**DfT**).

Detrain
Detraining
a) [Ops.] The action of getting **Passengers** off a **Train**, normally used to describe this activity when it takes place away from a **Station** during an emergency
b) A last resort for the Passenger involved in an **Accident**, leaving the **Train** should only be considered if not doing so presents an immediate risk to life; this could include asphyxiation or burns from a fire. This is because, in the immediate aftermath of such an Accident, there is no guarantee that other Trains have stopped or that the **Traction Current** has been removed (on a **Line** so **Fitted**).

Dets
[Col.] A contraction of **Detonator**. See **Railway Fog Signals**, see also **Bangers, Crackers, Foggies, Shots**.

DEV
[Sig.] Double Element Vane. See **Vane Relay**.

De-vegging
(dee vedj-ing) The action of removing all the shrubs, trees and overhanging branches from an area of the **Lineside**, particularly to improve the visibility of **Signals**.

Development Consent Order (DCO)
Under the Planning Act 2008 the single consent which replaces planning permission, conservation area consent, listed building consent, Transport and Works (**TWA**) orders and compulsory purchase orders (**CPO**) for certain Nationally Significant Infrastructure Projects (**NSIPs**). These are issued by the **Infrastructure Planning Commission** (**IPC**).

Development Vehicle (DV)
[NR] Part of the **New Measurement Train** (**NMT**), this vehicle (977993) is used as a test-bed for new measurement technologies such as laser gauging of **Overhead Line Equipment** (**OLE**), automated track component inspection, etc.

ELLIS' BRITISH RAILWAY ENGINEERING ENCYCLOPÆDIA

Deviation
a) [NR] A permission to comply with a specified alternative to a requirement in a **Railway Group Standard** (**RGS**) in circumstances where it is not appropriate to change the RGS requirement. See also **Temporary Non-compliance** (**TNC**)
b) A new **Alignment** introduced to improve the performance or capacity of a **Route**.

Devolution
[NR] A process to devolve Network Rail's central control to ten regional **Routes** by 2012, in a bid to improve efficiency. A Route managing director will run each infrastructure railway business. The Routes and their headquarters locations are:

Anglia	London
East Midlands	Derby
London North East	York
Kent	London
London North West	Birmingham
Scotland	Glasgow
Sussex	Croydon
Wales	Cardiff
Wessex	Woking
Western	Swindon

The resulting structure will bear a passing resemblance to the **British Rail** (**BR**) □ **Regions**.

Devon and Cornwall Railways (DCR)
(Tradename) A **Freight Operating Company** (**FOC**), part of **British American Railway Services** (**BARS**). It has plans to operate **Passenger Trains**. ATOC code DC

Dewirement
[Elec.] A term used to describe a situation where a raised **Pantograph** is no longer beneath the **Contact Wire** (**CW**). In this case the Pantograph would extend to its full height, since it is no longer constrained. An **Automatic Dropping Device** (**ADD**) is fitted to lower the Pantograph should this happen. Possible causes are extremely high winds (where the Contact Wire is blown sideways) or following poorly executed **Tamping and Lining** work (where the **Track** is not correctly located beneath the Contact Wire). See also **Blow Off**.

DF
Down Fast, the most important **Down Line** (**DL**) when there are two. The other is normally called the **Down Slow** (**DS**) though it may have the same **Permissible Speed** (**PS**).

DFF 14
DFF 300
(Tradename) [PW] A **Baseplate** (**BP**) and **Rail Fastening** system intended for use on **Slab Track**. Manufactured by **Vossloh**.

DFL
Down □ Fast □ Line.

DFO
a) See **Depot Facility Operator**
b) [NR] **Depot** Facility Owner.

DFR
The Dean Forest **Railway**.

DfT
See **Department for Transport**.

DFT
[Tel.] Digital Advanced Radio for Trains (**DART**) Fixed Terminal.

DG
a) **Down** □ **Goods**. A **Track** used by **Freight Trains**, and possibly only **Signalled** to **Freight Standards**
b) See **Dangerous Goods**.

DGI
Dangerous Goods Incident.

DGL
Down □ **Goods** □ **Loop**. A **Track** used to recess **Freight Trains** to allow faster **Trains** to pass.

DGN
a) Shorthand for **Derogation**
b) The file extension of Computer Aided Design (**CAD**) drawing files produced using Bentley's Microstation package.

DHMU
See **Diesel Hydraulic Multiple Unit**, see also **Multiple Unit Train**.

DI
a) Door Interface
b) Direction Indicator

DIADS
Diagram Input and Distribution System.

Diagonal
a) [Civ.] In a **Truss** □ **Bridge Deck**, a sloping member connecting the **Top Chord** and **Bottom Chord**
b) [PW] A short **Lath** used on one or both ends of a **Switch and Crossing Layout** (**S&C Layout**) to ensure that the first few **Bearers** are laid **Square**.

Diagram
a) [Sig.] The stylised **Track** schematic provided in a **Signal Box** (**SB**). Such Diagrams can be **Illuminated Diagrams** or Non-Illuminated Diagrams. Also **Signal Box Diagram**
b) [Ops.] The document giving details of which **Rail Vehicles** shall work which services
c) [Ops.] The itinerary of a particular **Traincrew**.

Diamond
Diamond Crossing

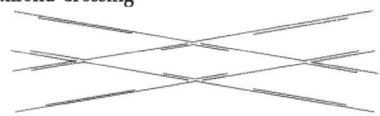

[PW] A **Switch and Crossing Unit** (**S&C Unit**) that consists of two **Common Crossings** and two **Obtuse Crossings**, allowing two **Tracks** to cross each other on the flat. Diamond Crossings come in two varieties: **Fixed Diamond** and **Switch Diamond**, the latter being used for flat angles of intersection, 1 in 7½ or greater. Also **Diamond**.

Diamond Time
[Ops.] An alternative term for **Performance Allowance** as this Allowance is shown in the **Working Timetable** (**WTT**) enclosed in a diamond or angle-brackets.

Diamond with Double Slip
See **Double Slip Diamond**.

Diamond with Single Slip
See **Single Slip Diamond**.

DIBMOF
Dienste **I**ntegrierender **B**ahn **Mo**bilfunk, integrated services **Railway** mobile radio.

DIC
[TRS] **D**oor **I**solating **C**ock.

Didcot Control
See **Foxhall Control**.

Diddy Vest
See **Hi-vis Vest**.

Diesel and Electric Locomotive Notation
See **UIC Classification**.

Diesel Electric
[TRS] A **Traction Unit** that utilises a diesel engine to drive an electrical generator. This current is then used to power **Electric Traction Motors**. This system simplifies the control and transmission systems. See also **DEMU**.

Diesel Electric Locomotive
[TRS] A **Locomotive** whose source of power is a diesel engine and whose transmission is electrical, typically a generator and motor pair. See also **Diesel Electric**, **Diesel Electric Multiple Unit (DEMU)**.

Diesel Electric Multiple Unit (DEMU)
[TRS] A **Multiple Unit Train** whose source of power is an integral diesel engine and whose transmission is electrical, typically a generator and motor pair.

Diesel Electric Traction
[TRS] A **Motive Power Unit** or **Traction Unit** which utlises a Diesel engine as its source of power, and electric **Traction Motors** to turn the **Driven Axles**. This is a more specific description of **Diesel Traction**.

Diesel Hauling
[Ops.] The action of pulling an **Electric Train** □ **Pan Down** with a **Diesel Locomotive**, either because the **Electric Locomotive** has failed, the **Traction Current** is turned off or there is no **Electrification** equipment at all on that **Route**. See also **Diversion**, **Thunderbirding**.

Diesel Hydraulic Multiple Unit (DHMU)
[TRS] A **Multiple Unit Train** whose source of power is a diesel engine and whose transmission is hydraulic.

Diesel Locomotive
[TRS] A **Locomotive** whose power source is a diesel engine. This engine either powers the **Driving Wheels** through either:
* A reduction gearbox
* An hydraulic compressor and hydraulic **Traction Motors**
* An electrical generator and electric **Traction Motors**, see **Diesel Electric Locomotive**.

Diesel Maintenance Depot (DMD)
[TRS] A facility at which **Diesel Traction** is maintained, a more specific description of a **Traction Maintenance Depot (TMD)**.

Diesel Mechanical Multiple Unit (DMMU)
[TRS] A **Multiple Unit Train** whose source of power is a diesel engine and whose transmission is mechanical.

Diesel Multiple Unit (DMU)
[TRS] A **Multiple Unit Train** whose source of power is a diesel engine. The transmission of this power to the driving wheels can be achieved electrically (a **Diesel Electric Multiple Unit (DEMU)**) hydraulically (a **Diesel Hydraulic Multiple Unit (DHMU)**) or mechanically (a **Diesel Mechanical Multiple Unit (DMMU)**).

Diesel Traction
[TRS] A **Motive Power Unit** or **Traction Unit** which utlises a Diesel engine as its source of power.

Differences
[PW] Dimensions marked on an adjacent **Rail** during a **Track Renewal** or **Lifting** scheme to show how much higher (or lower) the nearest Rail of the **Track** being worked on should be than the Rail with the numbers on. This system allows the use of a **Stick and Bubble** to set out the new levels.

Differential Enhanced Permissible Speed Restriction
[NR] A Differential Speed with two different **Enhanced Permissible Speeds (EPS)**, each applying to different types of **Train**. At the time of writing, the upper value normally applies to **Class 221 Super Voyager** Trains and the bottom value to Class 390 **Pendolino** Trains. See **Differential Enhanced Permissible Speed Sign**, **Differential EPS Sign**.. See also **Non-standard Differential Permissible Speed Restriction**.

Differential Enhanced Permissible Speed Sign
Differential EPS Sign
[NR] A **Lineside Sign** displaying two different **Enhanced Permissible Speeds (EPS)**, The Sign's oval shape is necessary to accommodate the large numerals required for readability at 125mph. See also **Non-standard Differential Permissible Speed Restriction**.

ELLIS' BRITISH RAILWAY ENGINEERING ENCYCLOPÆDIA

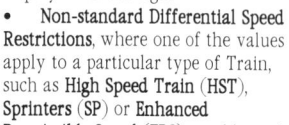

Differential Permissible Speed
Differential Permissible Speed Restriction
Differential Speed
Differential Speed Restriction (DSR)
[NR] A situation where two or more different Permissible Speeds (PS) that apply to different types of Trains are indicated on Lineside □ Signs at the Commencement of where the Differential Speeds apply. There are two main types: 
- Standard Differential Speed Restrictions, where all the values apply to their respective Class of Train. This type of differential is displayed on one sign. 
- Non-standard Differential Speed Restrictions, where one of the values apply to a particular type of Train, such as High Speed Train (HST), Sprinters (SP) or Enhanced Permissible Speed (EPS) capable, such as Pendolino. Each speed has its own sign, the type specific one showing an identifier for the train it applies to (HST, SP, and EPS respectively).
The lowest speed value is always displayed at the top of the group. A maximum of three values can be displayed at one location, and where one value of a Differential Speed Restriction changes, all the values must be re-displayed to avoid confusion. These signs follow the normal convention, having a red border.

Differential Warning Indicator
[NR] A speed Warning Indicator provided to indicate to a driver that a Differential Speed Restriction is ahead. See also Non-standard Differential Warning Indicator, Standard Differential Warning Indicator.
These signs follow the normal convention, with a yellow border.

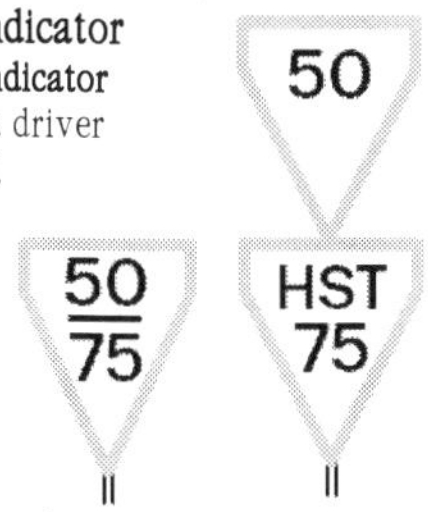

Standard   Non-standard

Dike
[Ops., Col.] A colloquial term meaning to put a Train into a Loop for Regulating purposes.

DIME
[NR] Project codename for the April 2012 reorganisation of Investment Projects (IP).

Dimpled Pad
See Configurated Rail Pad.

Ding Ding and Away
[Col.] A variety of driver error caused by a habitual reaction to receiving the double Right Away (RA) bell from the Guard. The driver subconsciously associates the "ding ding" with moving away, so acknowledges the bell and drives off without checking the Signal in front of the Train. This error was the cause of the Newton Accident. See also Driver's Reminder Appliance (DRA).

Dipped Joint
[PW] Generally a Fishplated Rail Joint that is displaying signs of distress caused by the cyclic transfer of wheel loading from Running-off Rail to Running-on Rail causing compaction of the Ballast, wear in the Fishplates and Fishing Surfaces and plastic deformation of the Rail Ends. It can be used to describe a Weld displaying similar vertical alignment defects.

Direct Drive
Direct Drive RRV 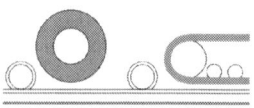
A system whereby a Road Rail Vehicle (RRV) is moved, in Rail Mode, by independently-driven Rail Wheels All Tracked RRVs are Direct Drive. See also High Ride, Low Ride.

Direct Fastened Deck
[Civ.] A Bridge Deck where the Rails are fastened directly to the Deck without Sleepers or Ballast. An alternative and more common alternative is the Ballasted Deck.

Direct Fastened Track
[PW] Rails fastened directly to another structure, such as a Bridge Deck or inspection pit, without Sleepers or Ballast.

Direct Fastening
[PW] A Rail Fastening where the Rail is directly fastened to its support without a Baseplate, Chair or similar.

Direct Lever Locking
[Sig.] An arrangement of Mechanical Locking where the motion of the Lever itself drives the Locking.

Direct Opposing Locking
[Sig.] An arrangement of Interlocking between two Routes, in opposite directions, for which the required lie (i.e. Normal or Reverse) of all Points is the same for both Routes.

Direct Rail Services (DRS)
(Tradename) The Freight Operating Company (FOC) owned by British Nuclear Fuels Limited.

Direct Rail Wheel Brake
On a Road-rail Vehicle (RRV), a braking system that acts directly on the vehicle's Rail Wheels to provide both service and parking brake functions, rather relying on the vehicle's road wheel brakes.

Direct Rail Wheel Brake
A braking system fitted to act directly on the Rail Wheels of a Road Rail Vehicle (RRV) to provide both Service Brake and Parking Brake functions.

Direct Reverse
Direct Reverse Curve

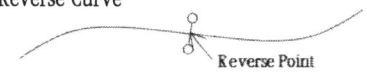

Reverse Point

[PW] A Reverse Curve that has no intervening Straight Track between the two Curves. An Indirect Reverse has a length of Straight Track between the two Curves.

Direct Track Locking
[Sig.] The **Locking** of moveable components such as **Points** when a **Train** is present. This locking is not conditional on the Points being **Set** or otherwise **Locked**. See also **Dead Locking**.

Direction Lever
[Sig.] A means of **Signalling** a **Single Line** without a **Staff** or **Token**. When pulled, the Direction Lever **Locks** all **Conflicting Signals** until the **Train** is proved to have arrived at the far end of the **Section**. It is a form of **Track Circuit Block** (**TCB**).

Directly Operated Railways (DOR)
(Tradename) A company created by the UK Government in 2009 to oversee the management and development of the East Coast **Franchise** until it is re-let to a new private operator.

Director's Saloon
See **Officer's Saloon**.

DIRFT
Daventry International Rail Freight Terminal.

Dirty End
[Sig., Col.] Term for the **Signalling Equipment** located on or close to the **Track**, e.g. **Automatic Warning System Magnets** (**AWS Magnet**) and **Track Circuit Bonds**. Probably adopted because of the atrocious conditions in which such equipment is expected to function. See also **Clean End**.

DIS
[Sig.] A flexible display system, part of the **IECC** replacement for **Signaller's Display Subsystem** (**SDS**).

Dis. Box
(*diss bocks*) A contraction of **Disconnection Box**.

Disab
(Tradename) A manufacturer of vacuum-related plant and machinery, based in Sweden.

DISAC
[Tel.] Double Insulated Super Armoured Cable.

Disastro
[Col.] Nickname for the **Desiro**, **Class** 444 and 450 **Electric Multiple Units** (**EMU**).

Disc Brake
[TRS] An arrangement in which the brake blocks bear on a disc attached to the axle of a **Wheelset**, or a disc built into the wheel itself. See also **Clasp Brake**, **Tread Brake**.

Disc Saw
A type of rotary abrasive saw used for cutting **Rails**, similar in operation to an angle grinder, utilising an abrasive wheel as the cutting edge. Typically these wheels are 18" (450mm) diameter, and the saw is normally used with a hinged support arm to prevent the operator jamming the wheel in the **Cut**.

Disc Signal
[Sig.] A **Shunt Signal** or **Subsidiary Signal** that uses a rotating disc to display its **Aspect**. Also **Ground Disc Signal**.

Discharge of Traction Current
[Elec.] The **Isolation** of the **Conductor Rail** system or **Overhead Line Equipment** (**OHLE**) from the electrical supply.

Discipline
A contraction of **Engineering Discipline**.

Disconnected Signal
[Sig.] A **Signal** that has been adjusted so that it shows only the **Most Restrictive Aspect** for one or more of its **Routes**.

Disconnection
[Sig.] Alternative term for a **Possession** of **Signalling Equipment**; the disconnection or restriction of use of **Signalling Equipment** agreed between **Maintenance** and **Operations** staff to enable work to be carried out on the equipment or to provide protection to other works. See also **Possession**.

Disconnection Box
[Sig., EP] A small **Lineside** enclosure used to terminate **Track Circuit Tails** and **Electric Point Heating** cables. Sometimes contracted to **Dis. Box**.

Disconnection Panel
[LUL] A cubicle housing joints in **Traction Power** cables, normally at joints between lead-sheathed cable and other types.

Discrete Position of Safety (DPOS)
A **Place of Safety** that may only consist of a small area of cleared ground, although typically a prepared surface and some form of marker is provided. See also **Continuous Place of Safety** (**CPOS**), **Refuge**, **Safecess**, **Safecess Path**.

DISCU
[Sig.] DC Interference Signalling Compatibility Unit.

Dish
[Hist.] On a **Rope-Worked Railway** a stretch of **Track** at a **Bank Foot** having a longitudinal section designed with a slight sag onto which a descending **Set** is brought to a stand to permit the rope to be detached.

DISI
[LUL] Defective In Service Instructions.

Dispatch Corridor
[Ops.] A space running the full length of the **Train** or the full length of the **Platform**, whichever is the shorter, including;
- The gap between the Train and the Platform.
- At least 1500mm of the Platform measured from the **Platform Edge**.
- At least the height of the Train doors.

Displaced Asset
An owned **Asset** no longer in use. Also **Redundant Assets**.

Displacement
[Elec.] The lateral distance from the **Contact Wire** (**CW**) to the centre of the **Pantograph** at **Mid-span**. See also **Mid-span Offset** (**MSO**).

Displacement and Acceleration Recorder (DAR)
Portable equipment used for recording **Ride Quality**.

Disproved Wrong Side Failure
[Sig.] A failure which was reported as **Wrong Side Failure** (**WSF**) but where the failure was conclusively shown not to have occurred or to have been a **Right Side Failure** (**RSF**).

Disregard, A
[Ops., Obs.] Former term for one circumstance leading to a **Signal Passed at Danger** (**SPAD**). See **Spad Error Category Group 2**.

Distance Block
[PW] A cast metal block used to maintain the correct separation between two adjacent **Rails**. A specialised variety of this is a **Check Block**, used to hold a **Running Rail** and **Check Rail** in the correct relationship.

Distance Point
[Obs.] A metal post or wall-mounted plate bearing the letters DP positioned on some early **Railways** at the median position of the **Main Line** □ **Platforms** of **Through Stations** or the dead end of a **Terminal Station**. They were also installed to mark the end of a specified **Mileage** at a **Junction**.

Distant Board
[NR] A **Lineside Sign** conveying the same information as a **Fixed Distant Signal**. Also **Reflectorised Distant Board**. Sometimes colloquially termed a **Fixed Distant Board**. See also **Board**.

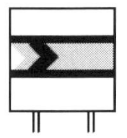

Distant Lookout
A **Lookout** (**LO**) positioned **On the Approach to** the worksite (and **Site Lookout**) in order to give additional **Warning Time** to the working party. The Advance Lookout signals to the Site Lookout by waving a blue and white chequered **Flag** when they sight a **Train** approaching. It is legal to appoint more than one Advance Lookouts to achieve the required Warning Time, but better systems such as **PeeWee** and **Automatic Track Warning Systems** (**ATWS**) exist for this situation. Previously called an **Advanced Lookout**.

Distant Signal
[NR] A **Signal** only capable of displaying a **Proceed Aspect** or **Caution Aspect**. Its purpose is to alert the driver to the fact that, when **On**, the next Signal will be showing a **Stop Aspect**. See also **Semaphore Signal**, **Two Aspect Signal**. A typical identification plate is shown right.

Distantman
Alternative term for a **Distant Lookout**.

Distortion
[PW]
a) A horizontal **Track Fault** caused by **Trains**, often as a result of excess speed on curved **Track**
b) An alternative term for a **Track Buckle**.

Distribution
[NR] The **Engineering Discipline** responsible for the supply of electricity within the **Railway** for purposes other than **Signalling** and **Points Heating**. This typically means **Traction Power**. Also M&E.

Distribution Network Operator (DNO)
Previously known as Regional Electricity Companies (REC), the term for an organisation that owns and operates the network of towers and cables that bring electricity from the national transmission network to homes and businesses. They do not sell electricity to consumers.

Distributor
[TRS] The pneumatic component of an **Air Brake** system which responds to changes in **Brake Pipe** pressure and initiates charging of the **Brake Cylinders**. A more sophisticated version of the **Triple Valve**, a typical modern distributor will have:
- The ability to connect an emergency reservoir to the vehicle brake system, and to recharge it;
- A partial release facility, not usually available with Triple Valves;
- A reapplication feature, to allow the brake to be quickly re-applied following a partial release;
- A graduated release, allowing a partial release followed by a holding of the lower application rate;
- A connection for a **Variable Load Valve** (**VLV**), which matches the brake cylinder pressure to the laden weight of the vehicle;
- Chokes to permit variations in brake application and release times;
- An "inshot" feature to give an initial quick brake application;
- Brake cylinder pressure limiting; and
- **Auxiliary Reservoir** overcharging prevention.

All of these features are achieved mechanically, with no electrical control. Distributors with all these features are normally provided on **Passenger Trains** and high-speed **Freight Vehicles**. See also **Two Pipe Air Brake**.

District Electric Depot (DED)
Forerunner of the **Traction Maintenance Depot** (**TMD**).

Disturbed
a) [PW] Description of **Continuous Welded Rail** (**CWR**) □ **Track** that has work carried out on it which reduces its **Lateral Stability**
b) [Sig.] Of an **Axle Counter**, the result of an interruption having occurred with the Axle Counter systems' ability to record the passage of axles. Although the equipment has returned to working order it cannot determine whether the **Track Section** is **Occupied** or not.

Diverging Junction
a) A **Junction** at which one **Line** branches off from another Line in the **Normal Direction**
b) A Junction at which one **Route** branches off from another Route when viewed with one's **Back to London** or **Back to Low Mileage**.

Diverging Line
A **Line** leaving another Line of greater status, when viewed in the **Normal Direction**.

Diverging Route
[Sig.] A term used to describe any **Route** at a **Junction** that leaves the (generally) fastest or straightest Route.

Diverging Track
See **Diverging Line**.

Diverse Routing

Diversely Routed System
[Sig., Tel.] An arrangement whereby two identical electrical signals or sets of data travel between transmitter and receiver by different routes and / or methods, ensuring that communication is maintained in the event of mishap on one route. Used for all safety related systems, particularly **Signalling** and **Telecommunications**. See also **A Leg, B Leg**.

Diversion
a) [Ops.] A **Route** taken by a **Train** other than that intended in the **Working Timetable** (**WTT**)
b) A short length of **Railway** built to improve the operation of the **Railway**, either by shortening the journey or by avoiding a restrictive **Curve** or **Junction**.

Diversionary Route
[Ops.] The alternative route taken by **Trains** when avoiding a blockage, failure or **Possession**. Some parts of the **National Railway Network** (**NRN**) are retained nearly exclusively for this purpose.

Diversity
See **Diverse Routing, Diversely Routed System**.

Diveunder

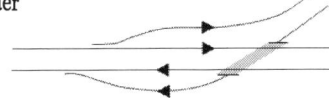

The opposite of a **Flyover**, describing a **Bridge** that carries the **Diverging Line** under the **Main Line** as part of a **Burrowing Junction** or **Grade Separated Junction**. See also **Flying Junction**.

Divided
[Ops.] Describing a **Train** that has become separated into two or more parts during its journey. This is a dangerous situation on an **Unfitted Train** (as neither part will automatically stop), but is safely dealt with by **Automatic Brakes**. See also **Armagh Accident**.

Divisible Train Staff
[Sig.] An alternative arrangement to **Staff and Ticket Working**, in which the tickets are metal and form part of the **Train Staff**. When two or more **Trains** are to pass in the same direction, a ticket is removed from the Train Staff and handed to the driver. All such tickets are retained at the far end of the **Section** and reattached to the Train Staff when it follows.

Division
[Hist.] An alternative title for an **Area**.

Divisional Civil Engineer (DCE)
[BR]
a) Originally, the **British Railways** post responsible for a **Division**
b) Latterly, a transitional **British Railways** (**BR**) organisation responsible for the maintenance of the **Track, Structures** and **Earthworks** in a geographical area, in the run up to **Privatisation**. Previously called **Areas**.

DJR
[Hist.] The **Pre-Grouping** (Carlisle) Dentonholme Joint Committee **Railway**, a Glasgow & South Western, Midland and North British joint enterprise.

DK
[NR] Under the **Bridge Condition Marking Index** (**BCMI**) handbook, shorthand for **Deck**.

DKE
Developed Kinematic Envelope.

DKS
[TRS] Door Key Switch.

DLA
[TRS] Door Lock Assembly.

DLM
See **Data Link Module**.

DLR
See **Docklands Light Railway**.

DLS
[TRS] Door Lock Switch.

DLV
[TRS] An acronym representing a **Driving** Luggage Van.

DM
a) See **Down Main**
b) [TRS] An acronym representing a **Driving** □ **Motor** □ **Coach**.

DMB
[TRS] An acronym representing a **Driving** □ **Motor** □ **Brake** □ **Coach**.

DMBC
[TRS] An acronym representing a **Driving** □ **Motor** □ **Brake** □ **Composite Coach**.

DMBF
[TRS] An acronym representing a **Driving** □ **Motor** □ **Brake** □ **First Class** □ **Coach**.

DMBS
[TRS] An acronym representing a **Driving** □ **Motor** □ **Brake** □ **Standard Class** □ **Coach**.

DMBSO
[TRS] An acronym representing a **Driving** □ **Motor** □ **Brake** □ **Standard Class** □ **Open Coach**.

DMC
[TRS] An acronym representing a **Driving** □ **Motor** □ **Composite Coach**.

DMD
See **Diesel Maintenance Depot**. See also **Traction Maintenance Depot** (**TMD**).

DMDS
[TRS] An acronym representing a **Driving** □ **Motor** □ **Standard Class** □ **Coach** with disabled accommodation.

DMF
[TRS] An acronym representing a **Driving** □ **Motor** □ **First Class** □ **Coach**.

ELLIS' BRITISH RAILWAY ENGINEERING ENCYCLOPÆDIA

DMI
a) [Sig.] **Driver Machine Interface**, a term used to describe the interaction of the driver and **Train**, particularly in terms of **In-cab Signalling** equipment.
b) **Dot Matrix Indicator**.

DML
Down □ **Main** □ **Line**.

DMLV
[TRS] An acronym representing a **Driving** □ **Motor Luggage Van**.

DMM
Depot □ **Maintenance** Manager.

DMMU
[TRS] **Diesel Mechanical Multiple Unit**, See **Multiple Unit Train**.

DMRB
[Civ.] Design Manual for Roads and **Bridges**.

DMRFK
[TRS] An acronym representing a **Driving** □ **Motor** □ **First Class** □ **Coach** with kitchen.

DMS
a) [TRS] An acronym representing a **Driving** □ **Motor** □ **Standard Class** □ **Coach**
b) **Drawing Management System**
c) **Document Management System**.

DMSO
[TRS] An acronym representing a **Driving** □ **Motor** □ **Standard Class** □ **Open Coach**.

DMSS
[Sig.] **Development Manager, Signalling Strategy**.

DMT
[LUL] **Duty Manager Trains**.

DMU
a) Abbreviation of **Diesel Multiple Unit**, See **Multiple Unit Train**.
Also **Diesel Electric Multiple Unit (DEMU)**, **Diesel Hydraulic Multiple Unit (DHMU)**, **Diesel Mechanical Multiple Unit (DMMU)**
b) [NR] On a sign forming part of a **Non-standard Differential Speed Restriction**, it indicates that this value apples only to Diesel Multiple Units (except **Class** 185), where authorised

DMUD
Diesel Multiple Unit □ **Maintenance** □ **Depot**.

DMVIC
Deadman's Valve Isolating Cock.

Dn.
A common contraction of **Down**.

DNA
Drugs and Alcohol, See **Safety Critical Staff**. Also **D&A**.

DNC
Declared Non-compliance.

DNO
See **Distribution Network Operator**.

Do
(*doe*) Denoting four linked but independently **Driven Axles**, See **Diesel and Electric Locomotive Notation**.

DO
a) **Design Office**
b) **Drawing Office**
c) See **Driver Only Operation**

DO Operation (DOO)
See **Driver Only Operation**.

DO Train
See **Driver Only Train**.

Dobbin
[Col.] A **Shunter**.

DoCE
[BR] **Director of Civil Engineering**, See **British Railways (BR)**.

Dock
[Hist.] A short **Platform** specifically intended for the loading and unloading of livestock, goods or vehicles. Also **Carriage Dock, Cattle Dock, Fish Dock, Horse Dock, Parcels Dock**, Restaurant Car Dock, Sleeping Car Dock.

Docklands Light Railway (DLR)
(Tradename) An automated **Metro** system opened on 31st August 1987 to serve the redeveloped Docklands area of **London**. It has since been extended and now reaches to Stratford, Lewisham, Bank, and east to Beckton, London City Airport and Woolwich Arsenal.

Document Review Notice (DRN)
[NR] The standard form used to **record Network Rail's** comments on a submission made by a designer. Individual comments are made (typically) by the Project Engineer (**PE**), **Designated Project Engineer** (**DPE**) and **Route Asset Manager** (**RAM**), depending on the **GRIP** stage the design is submitted at and given a **Category**. The overall DRN then receives a category based on the "worst" comment category:

Comment Category	Meaning	DRN Category
0	Rejected; not compliant to contract; revise and re-submit.	0
1	Accepted	1
2A	Accepted with comments, designer error; resolution recorded by designer in DRN response	2
2B	Accepted with comments, client request; resolution recorded by designer in DRN response	2
3A	Rejected, designer error; resolution recorded by designer in DRN response. design to be re-submitted	3
3B	Rejected, client request; resolution recorded by designer in DRN response. design to be re-submitted	3
4	Comment, designer to note	1

See also **Route to Gold** (**RtG**).

Dodd
[Sig., Col.] Alternative name for a **Ground Signal**. Also **Dummy, Tommy Dodd**.

DOE
See **Drilled One End**.

DoE
Department of the Environment, now the Department of the Environment, Transport and the Regions (DETR).

DoETR
See DETR.

Dog Chart
[Sig.] An alternative term for a Locking Chart.

Dog it In
See Dogging in, Dogging it in.

Dog it Out
See Dogging it out, Dogging out.

Dog Spike
[PW] A steel spike with a shaped top, used to fasten Flat Bottom Rails (FB) directly to Wood Sleepers, though in some applications a Baseplate may be inserted between Rail and Sleeper. Most often used to secure Guard Rails on Viaducts and Flares on Trap Points, they are also common on Heritage Railways, Light Railways, Narrow Gauge Railways and Preserved Railways, where Track Forces are low.

Dog's Dick
[Elec., Col.]
a) That part of a Mark 1 Overhead Line Equipment (OLE) □ Registration Arm assembly which restricts the upward movement of the Arm
b) A Circuit Breaker (CB) contact.

Dogfish (ZFV, ZFW)
[NR] A 21 ton capacity Ballast Hopper □ Wagon. See Wagon Names.

Dogging in
Dogging it in
[Col.] The act of constructing something by placing the materials in a quick and haphazard manner.

Dogging it out
Dogging out
[Col.] The act of removing redundant materials from a site by the quickest means possible, without regard for tidiness or potential re-use of said material.

Dogs
a) [PW] A common contraction of Timber Dogs. Also Nips, Sleeper Dogs, Sleeper Nips, Sleeper Tongs, Timber Nips
b) [Sig.] The metal blocks attached to the Locking Slides in a Mechanical Interlocking and used to perform the Locking function. Also Nibs.
c) The typically pneumatically operated safety catches installed on Tamping Banks, measuring trolleys and similar items fitted to On Track Machines (OTMs) to ensure they stay in the retracted position in transit.

Doll
[Sig.] A small post carrying Semaphore Signal □ Arms on a Bracket Signal or Gantry.

Dolly
a) [Sig., Col.] A Shunt Signal
b) See Box Spanner, also Screw Dolly
c) [PW] A short length of Rail (of the order of 100mm) with a single Fishbolt Hole drilled in it, used to temporarily fill the gap between adjacent Rails where a Train is required to pass through a site when Pulling Back Rails.

Dolphin (YAO)
[NR] A 40 ton capacity flat Wagon used for the transportation of Rails and Sleepers. See Wagon Names.

DOM
See Duty Operations Manager.

DoM&EE
[BR] Director of Mechanical and Electrical Engineering, See British Railways (BR).

Domino Panel
(Tradename) [Sig.] A type of Mimic Diagram manufactured by Henry Williams Ltd., consisting of an array of standard and removable 40mm by 40mm tiles. This system simplifies alterations to the Signalling layout depicted.

Doncaster Accident
At 16:41 on Saturday the 9th of August 1947, an Express Passenger Train collided with the rear of a virtually stationary Express Passenger Train about a Mile south of Doncaster. The area was undergoing Staged □ Resignalling works at the time, and a previously safe and reliable Indication (a bell which announced the Clearing of a Slot) which the Signallers regularly used, had been modified during the works in such a way as to make this misleading and unsafe (the bell now rang irrespective of the presence of a Train in the Section). The Signaller concerned relied on habit rather than correct practice; 18 died and 120 injured.

Donelli
(Tradename) A manufacturer of Railway plant, best known in the UK for a type of Single Line Gantry (SLG).

Donkey
[Hist.] A device comprising a metal bar, forked at each end, hung from the Coupling Hook at the upper end to a vehicle with the lower end of the bar attached to the Tackling Chain. Both connections were achieved by means of a pin and a cotter. On some early curved Inclines the Donkey was used to keep the haulage rope low enough to stay within the sheaves on the incline. To minimise lateral swinging of the Donkey additional chains, known as guide chains, were attached to the lower end of the Donkey and secured to the Wagon □ Buffers. Latter designs of rope-worked curved inclines utilised vertically mounted rollers on the inside of the curve(s) and outside the Rails to restrain the lateral movement of the rope. In these latter installations the haulage rope was attached to the wagons by means of a slip coupling.

ELLIS' BRITISH RAILWAY ENGINEERING ENCYCLOPÆDIA

Donkey Dick
[Sig., Col.] Nickname for a **Train Ready to Start Plunger** located in a **Siding**, allowing a driver to alert the **Signaller** to the driver's readiness to proceed.

DOO
See **Driver Only Operation**

DOO(NP)
Driver **O**nly **O**peration (**N**on-**p**assenger).

DOO(P)
Driver **O**nly **O**peration (□ **P**assenger).

DoOps
[BR] **D**irector **o**f **Op**eration**s**, see **British Railways** (**BR**).

Door Close/Locked Light
[TRS] Lamp indicating that **Train** doors are correctly detected closed and locked.

Door Closed Switch
[TRS] An electrical switch used to detect that the **Door Leaf** is in its closed position relative to the **Door Portal**.

Door Interlock
[TRS] An electrical device used to detect whether an external **Car** door is open or properly closed.

Door Judder
[TRS] The slight movement of **Power Operated Doors** when a **Train** is moving, sufficient to cause the Train's monitoring equipment to detect them as being open.

Door Leaf
[TRS] The moveable element of a door system, i.e. the door itself.

Door Leaf Pin
[TRS] A structural component on the **Door Leaf** which engages with the mechanism on the **Carbody** used to lock the Door Leaf in the closed position.

Door Lock Assembly
[TRS] Sub-assembly that includes the mechanism on the **Carbody** which is used to lock the **Door Leaf** in the closed position.

Door Lock Switch
[TRS] Electrical switch used to detect that the **Falling Latch** on the **Door Lock Assembly** is in the locked position.

Door Motor
[TRS] Electrical motor used to drive the **Door Leaf** on a power operated door open and closed.

Door Portal
[TRS] The fixed element of a door system, i.e. the door frame.

Door Proving Circuit
[TRS] An electrical system that prevents the brakes from being released unless all doors are proved closed; similarly a door opening initiates a brake application.

Door Release
[TRS] A control signal given by the on-board staff granting their permission for door operation.

DOORS
(Tradename) **D**ynamic **O**bject-**O**riented **R**equirements **S**ystem. A project requirements management system produced by IBM of New York, USA and used to manage compliance throughout major projects.

Doors Closed Visual Indicator (DCVI)
[LUL] A light on the **Train Operator's** desk which, when illuminated, indicates that the doors are detected as closed. Commonly known as the "pilot light".

DOP
Driver **O**nly **P**assenger. See **Driver Only Operation**.

DOR
a) See **Directly Operated Railways**.
b) [Ops.] **D**ead **o**n **R**ear, describing an inactive **Locomotive** attached to the **Trailing End** of a **Train**
c) **D**irection **o**f **R**unning.

DoS&TE
[BR] **D**irector **o**f **S**ignalling & **T**elecommunications **E**ngineering, See **British Railways** (**BR**).

DoT
Department **o**f **T**ransport, now the Department of the Environment, Transport and the Regions (**DETR**), the relevant part of which (for Railways at least) is now the **Department for Transport** (**DfT**).

Double Bank
Double Bank Tamper
Double Banker
[PW] An **Automatic Tamping and Lining Machine** (**Tamper**) equipped with two sets of **Tamping Banks**, allowing it to deal with two **Sleepers** simultaneously. These machines are capable of nearly double the output of a **Single Bank Tamper**.

Double Blocking
[Ops.] Operating a **Line** on the basis of long **Trains** occupying two (or more) **Signal Sections**.

Double Compound
a) [PW] An alternative term for a **Double Slip Diamond**
b) See Compound b).

Double Cut
[Sig.] A circuit that has **Relay** contacts in both the positive and negative parts of the circuit to provide greater resilience against fault conditions.

Double Docking
[Col.] A colloquial term for **Permissive Working**, particularly at a **Terminal Station**. See also **Permissive Freight** (**PF**), **Permissive Passenger** (**PP**).

Double Double Junction

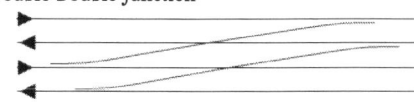

A **Junction** consisting of two **Double Junctions** connecting four **Tracks** in pairs.

140

Double Flange Rail Wheels
A type of Rail Wheel found on specialised plant such as Single Line Gantries (SLG) that has a Flange on both sides to ensure that the wheel stays on the Rail.

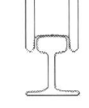

Double Head
Double Headed
a) See Double Heading
b) See Double Headed Rail.

Double Headed Rail
[PW, Obs.] Devised by Joseph Locke c. 1835, An early type of Rail similar in appearance to Bull Head Rail (BH) but which was symmetrical about its neutral axis. This theoretically allowed the Rail to be inverted when the first Rail Head become worn; in practice however the Chair Gall inflicted on the second Rail Head during the first installation cycle rendered it useless as a Running Surface and the practice was discontinued. Sometimes abbreviated to DH.

Double Headed Train
Double Heading
[Ops.] Providing two Locomotives on a Train where one alone would be insufficient to pull the Train. See also Multiple Working, Tandem Working.

Double Junction

A Junction comprising two Turnouts and a Diamond Crossing, where one Two Track Railway connects with another. See also Simplified Double Junction.

Double Line of Way
Alternative description of a Two-track Railway. See also Single Line of Way.

Double Parallel Wing (DPW)
[PW] As a suffix to a description of a Common Crossing, a Common Crossing having a Parallel Wing Rail on both sides of the Crossing Vee.

Double Rail Track Circuit
[Sig.] A Track Circuit (TC) that is either a Jointless Track Circuit (JTC) or is a Jointed Track Circuit defined by Insulated Rail Joints (IRJ) in both Rails at all its extremities. On Electrified Lines, both Rails carry the Traction Return Current.

Double Red Aspects
Double Reds
[Sig.] An arrangement where both the Protecting Signal and the Signal □ On the Approach both display Stop Aspects in order to reduce the likelihood of a Signal Passed at Danger (SPAD) resulting in a collision. This measure forms part of the Robust Train Protection scheme. Under certain circumstances the Signal On the Approach may be Approach Released.

Double Shift
Describing the working of two shifts during one weekend or one Possession.

Double Slip
[PW, Col.] A contraction of Double Slip Diamond and Double Slip Switch Diamond.

Double Slip Diamond

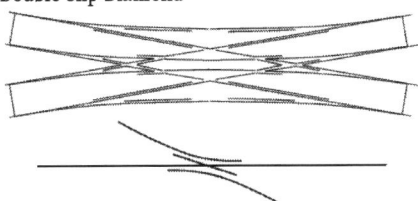

[PW] A Diamond Crossing fitted with four Slip Switches to provide two additional directional facilities. Also Double Slip, Double Compound, Diamond with Double Slip. See also Inside Slip, Outside Slip. The diagram above shows an Outside Slip.

Double Slip Switch Diamond
[PW] A Switch Diamond fitted with four Slip Switches to provide two additional directional facilities.

Double Tamping
[PW] The operation of performing two consecutive Tamping Cycles on the same Sleeper. This is normally done when the Lifts are large, as it allows the Tamper to better consolidate the Ballast beneath the Sleeper.

Double Tandem
[PW, Unk.] An arrangement of three overlapping Turnouts and three additional Common Crossings which allows one Track to split into four, though strictly speaking this is a pair of overlapping Tandem Turnouts. Such layouts are extremely rare and, if found at all, are typically confined to Sidings and Depots.

Double Tongue Catch Point
A rare assembly of two normally Trailing □ Switch Half Sets used to Derail vehicles that are Running Away. See Catch Point (CP).

Double Tongue Trap Point (DTT)
Assembly of two Switch Half Sets used to Derail vehicles making Unauthorized Movements. See Trap Point. See also Single Tongue Trap Point (STT).

Double Track
A route with two Tracks, one Up Line and one Down Line. Also Two Track Railway. The action of converting a Single Line into a Two Track Railway is called Doubling or Twin Tracking.

Double Turnout
[PW] An alternative for Tandem Turnout.

141

ELLIS' BRITISH RAILWAY ENGINEERING ENCYCLOPÆDIA

Double Unit
a) [LRT] Two articulated **Trams** □ **Coupled** together to operate as a single unit
b) [HR] Two **Multiple Units** coupled together (for example, two three-**Car** □ **Units** coupled together)

Double Way
[Hist.] A **Tramway** comprising **Wood Sleepers** and wooden **Rails**, the latter formed from two layers of scantlings, the lower being of fir and the upper (capping) layer being of Beech or Sycamore. Each layer was typically 4" (100mm) to 5" (125mm) deep.

Double Weave Junction

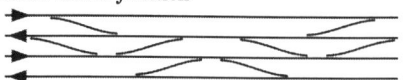

A **Running Junction** provided on a **Four Track Railway** to allow **Trains** on one pair of **Lines** to cross to the other pair of Lines and vice versa. Such **Junctions** are generally arranged to allow high speeds on the **Turnouts** to reduce delays.

Double Yellow (YY)
Double Yellow Aspect
[Sig.] A **Preliminary Caution Aspect** on a **Four Aspect** □ **Colour Light Signal**.

Double-cut
The provision of controls in both **Feed** and return sides of a circuit to reduce the risks posed by **False Feeds** or faults to **Earth**.

Double-end Electrical Section
[Elec.] A length of **Conductor Rail** fed by a supply from both ends.

Double-end Fed
A section of **Conductor**, such as an **Overhead Line Section**, power cable or **Conductor Rail** which is supplied with power from both ends.

Doubling
The operation of converting a **Single Line** into a **Two Track Railway**. The opposite is **Singling**. See also **Double Track**, **Twin Tracking**.

Doughnut
[Col.]
a) [PW] A name for a **Switch Securing Block**, from its shape
b) A nickname for a **Class** 60 **Diesel Locomotives**, so called because you can see straight through the middle of them. Also **Politician**
c) Nickname for a **Class** 92 Locomotive, because of the **Channel Tunnel** ring symbol on side.

Dovetailed Sill
[Hist.] A cast metal **Sleeper**, developed from the **Horned Sill**, in which the horns were superseded by transverse shoulders having a vertical dovetailed profile to both retain **Rails** having appropriately dovetailed vertical profiles at the **Rail Ends** and to provide vertical support. Thought to have been developed as a cast metal equivalent of the **Dovetailed Wood Sleeper** then in use on some **Plateways** during the early years of the 19th century.

Dovetailed Wood Sleeper
[Hist.] A **Wood Sleeper** having dovetailed-sided recesses cut into its upper surface at the specified **Rail Seat** separation to provide **Gauge Retention** and support for **Plate Rails**. Thought to have been developed during the last decade of the 18th century by John Curr of Sheffield.

Down (D, Dn.)
a) In a direction away from **London**, the capital, the original **Railway Company's** headquarters or towards the highest mileage. The choice of which direction is Down is littered with exceptions to convention. **Up** is the opposite direction. See also **Track Names**
b) Describing a **Track Circuit** (TC) where the **Rails** are shorted together, see **Released**. Also **Dropped**.

Down and Up
Traditionally denotes two separate **Lines**, one in the **Down** and one in the **Up** direction. This should be contrasted with **Up and Down**, which denotes a single **Line** that is **Bi-directional** in normal use.

Down Direction
Moving in a direction away from **London**, lowest **Mileage** or the original **Railway Company's** headquarters (See **Down**) but not necessarily on the **Down Line**. Often used when describing **Routes** through complex **Junctions**. The opposite is **Up Direction**.

Down Fast (DF)
The name given to the nominally more important of the two **Down Lines** in a **Four Track Railway**. It may or may not be faster (i.e. have a higher **Permissible Speed** (**PS**)) than the other Down Line, normally called the **Down Relief** or **Down Slow**. See also **Down Main** (DM).

Down Line
A **Track** on which the normal passage of **Trains** is in the **Down Direction**, i.e. away from **London**, the capital, the original **Railway Company's** headquarters or towards the highest mileage.

Down Main (DM)
The name given to the **Down Line** when there is only one Down Line and one **Up Line**.

Down Relief (DR)
[WR] An alternative term for the **Down Slow** (DS), the name generally given to the nominally less important of the two **Down Lines** in a **Four Track Railway**. It may or may not be slower (i.e. have a lower **Permissible Speed** (**PS**)) than the other Down Line, normally called the **Down Fast** (DF).

Down Side
Being located on the same side of the **Railway** as the **Down Line**.

Down Slow (DS)
The name given to the nominally less important of the two **Down Lines** in a **Four Track Railway**. It may or may not be slower (i.e. have a lower **Permissible Speed** (**PS**)) than the other Down Line, normally called the **Down Fast**. Also **Down Relief** (DR).

142

Down Train
[Ops.] Generally, a term applied to **Trains** running in the **Down Direction**, away from **London**, the capital, the former **Railway Company** headquarters or towards the highest mileage.

Downhill
a) Down the local **Gradient**
b) [Ops.] An alternative term for "in the **Down Direction**."

Down-proving
[Sig.] Independently verifying that an electro-mechanical device such as a **Relay** has returned to its un-activated state.

Dowty Retarder
(Tradename) See **Retarder**.

DP
See **Designated Person**.

DPC
a) <u>D</u>ata <u>P</u>rotocol <u>C</u>onverter
b) <u>D</u>evelopment <u>P</u>lanning <u>C</u>entre
c) <u>D</u>amp <u>P</u>roof <u>C</u>ourse.

DPE
See **Designated Project Engineer**.

DPI
See **Dye Penetrant Inspection**.

DPL
a) **Down** □ **Passenger Loop**. A **Loop** of **Track** generally used to **Regulate** the passage of **Trains** by allowing slower ones to "pull in" and allow faster ones past
b) **Down** □ **Platform** □ **Line**.

DPM
a) See **Detailed Planning Meeting**
b) <u>D</u>amp <u>P</u>roof <u>M</u>embrane.

DPNSS
<u>D</u>igital <u>P</u>rivate <u>N</u>etwork <u>S</u>ignalling <u>S</u>ystem.

DPOS
See **Discrete Position of Safety**.

DPPP
a) <u>D</u>isabled <u>P</u>eople's <u>P</u>rotection <u>P</u>olicy
b) [NR] <u>D</u>raft <u>P</u>eriod <u>P</u>ossession <u>P</u>lan.

DPS
[NR] <u>D</u>ifferential <u>P</u>ermissible <u>S</u>peed, see **Differential Speed Restriction** (**DSR**).

DPTAC
(*dip-tak*) <u>D</u>isabled <u>P</u>ersons <u>T</u>ransport <u>A</u>dvisory <u>C</u>ommittee.

DPU
[TRS] <u>D</u>iesel <u>P</u>arcels <u>U</u>nit, a sub-species of **Diesel Multiple Unit** (**DMU**).

DPW
See **Double Parallel Wing**.

DR
a) See **Down Relief**
b) As a prefix to the number of an **On-track Machine** (**OTM**), it means that the Machine is reportable to **TOPS**. See also **DX**.

DRA
a) See **Driver's Reminder Appliance**
b) <u>D</u>esigner's <u>R</u>isk <u>A</u>ssessment

DRACAS
<u>D</u>ata <u>R</u>ecording and <u>C</u>orrective <u>A</u>ction <u>S</u>ystem.

Drag Box
[TRS] the recess in the **Buffer Beam** into which a **Coupling** or **Drawhook** fits.

Drag Length
The length of a **Sand Drag**.

Drain
A pipe, channel or rubble filled ditch intended to collect and or carry water to an **Outfall**. See **Carrier Drain**, **Cess Drain**, **Channel Drain**, **Collector Drain**, **Crest Drain**, **Cross Drain**, **French Drain**, **Sixfoot Drain**, **Track Drain**, **Tenfoot Drain**, **X Drain**.

Drain Train
[NR] A group of **Rail Vehicles** built or adapted to clean **Track Drains**. The original **Train** was a gulley emptying lorry strapped onto a **Well Wagon**, but the current one is a set of bespoke modules fitted onto two **Container Flats** (see **PFA**). See also **Pump Train**.

Drain, The
[Col.] Nickname for the Waterloo and City **Railway**, which passes under the River Thames.

Drainage Survey
a) See **Track Drainage Survey**
b) [Col.] Cover name for a pub crawl.

DRAM
a) [NR] <u>D</u>irector of <u>R</u>oute <u>A</u>sset <u>M</u>anagement
b) <u>D</u>ynamic <u>R</u>andom <u>A</u>ccess <u>M</u>emory.

Draughtsman
[Col.] Nickname for a member of **Technical Staff**, e.g. Technical Officer (**TO**), Senior Technical Officer (**STO**), Principal Technical Officer (**PTO**).

Draw Ahead

Draw Ahead Signal
A **Position Light Signal Subsidiary Signal** that instructs the driver to 'draw ahead', for example to enable a **Set Back** move to take place through a **Trailing Connection**. See also **Calling-on Signal**, **Shunt-Ahead Signal**.

Drawbar
[TRS]
a) A solid bar connecting two **Railway Vehicles** together. The vehicles can only normally be separated by disconnecting the bar using appropriate tools. See also **Emergency Coupling**, **Emergency Drawbar**
b) [Col.] description of the point at which the **Tractive Effort** of a **Locomotive** is measured, normally the **Coupling** at which the **Train** is attached.

Drawbar Pull
[TRS] The longitudinal force produced by a **Traction Unit**. Also **Tractive Effort**.

143

Drawgear
[TRS] The collective term for all the equipment used to connect a **Rail Vehicle** to another Rail Vehicle for haulage purposes. See **Automatic Coupling**, **Buckeye Coupling**, **Coupling Hook**, **Drawhook**, **Instanter Coupling**, **Scharfenberg**, **Three Link Coupling**.

Drawhook
[TRS] The hook on the end of a **Wagon** by which it is coupled to the next **Wagon** in the **Train**.

DRDS
Double Rail Double Series, a **Bonding** layout.

DRE
[NR] Delegated Responsible Engineer.

DRES
Derby Rail Engineering Society.

DRG
[NR] Discipline Review Group.

DRICO
[LUL, Obs.] Driver – Controller, the former **Train Operator** to **Line Controller** telephone system. This is not the same as the **Tunnel Telephone**, although it used the same wires.

Drilled
[PW] Describing a **Rail** that has **Fishbolt Holes** drilled in it. The opposite is therefore **Plain Rail** or **Un-drilled** (UD). It is normal to be a bit more specific; see **Drilled Both Ends** (DBE), **Drilled One End** (DOE)

Drilled Both Ends (DBE)
[PW] Describing a **Rail** having **Fishbolt Holes** drilled in both ends. See also **Drilled One End** (DOE), **Plain Rail**, **Un-Drilled** (UD)

Drilled One End (DOE)
[PW] Describing a **Rail** having **Fishbolt Holes** drilled in one end only. See also **Drilled Both Ends** (DBE), **Plain Rail**, **Un-Drilled** (UD)

Drivability
[Ops.] The ease with which drivers can manage their **Trains** with the information provided to them. This includes the effects of locations of and frequency of changes in **Permissible Speed** (PS), **Signal Sighting** and **Track** layout.

Drive Lug
[PW] An item attached to a **Stretcher Bar** to permit a **Connecting Rod** or **Back Drive** to be connected.

Drive Rod
See **Connecting Rod**.

Driven Axle
[TRS] An axle that has some prime mover attached, making it the means by which a vehicle is moved along the **Track**. Also **Powered Axle**.

Driven Bogie
[TRS] A **Bogie** having mechanically driven wheels. See also **Motor Bogie**.

Driver
The driver in charge, who may be a probationer, driver or supervisor/instructor competent in driving duties.

DRIVER
(Tradename) [Obs.] A **Track Geometry** □ **Maintenance** system developed in Holland and briefly trialled in the UK during the 1980s. The system was fitted to certain **Tamping and Lining Machines** (**Tampers**) and relied on fixed **Lineside** references for both the survey and implementation phases of the work. It was not adopted in the UK.

Driver Assessor
A senior **Train** driver appointed to instruct and assess other drivers.

Driver Machine Interface (DMI)
[Sig.] The display unit **European Rail Traffic Management System** (**ERTMS**) uses to display information to the driver. The UK standard unit displays data in the following areas:
- A speedometer, providing details of current and target speeds
- The brake area, containing a square which grows in size to indicate predicted time to a brake intervention, and a vertical bar which indicates the distance remaining to the brake target (the longer the distance, the larger the bar will be).
- A planning area, which provides the driver with information on upcoming geographic and line features and reduces the driver's reliance on knowledge of the route.
- Areas where radio and additional information, feedback and messages are displayed to the driver via the use of symbols.

Driver Only Operation (DO, DOO)
[Ops.] Operation of (generally) **Multiple Unit Trains** by the Driver, dispensing with the need for a **Guard**. The Driver is assisted in closing the doors by mirrors or **CCTV** equipment on the **Platform** that allow rearward vision down the **Train**. Also **DO Operation**.

Driver Only Run-round Operations
[Ops.] Operation involving **Uncoupling** a **Locomotive** from one end of a **Train** and **Coupling** it to the other without the involvement of any staff other than the driver.

Driver Only Train (DO Train)
[Ops.] A **Train** that is worked only by a driver and does not have a **Guard**.

Driver Vigilance Device (DVD)
Driver Vigilance System (DVS)
[TRS] Alternatives for **Driver's Safety Device** (DSD).

Driver's Assistant
[Ops.] When circumstances require it, a second driver is provided to carry out other duties as required. This may be in addition to the provision of a **Guard**. See also **Second Man**.

Driver's Crossing Indicator
See **Driver's Level Crossing Indicator**.

Driver's Desk
[TRS] Console incorporating the controls and instruments used for driving the **On-track Machine** (**OTM**), **Traction Unit** or **Tram**.

Driver's Eye Level (DEL)
The distance between the average position of the driver's eyes and the **Crown** of the **Left Hand Rail** (**LHR**) in the direction of travel.

Driver's Level Crossing Indicator
[Sig.] A **Signal** provided on the **Approach** to **Automatic Barrier Crossing Locally Monitored** (**ABCL**) and **Automatic Open Crossing Locally Monitored** (**AOCL**) ☐ **Level Crossings** (**LC**, **LX**) to convey the status of the Level Crossing to the driver. See **Driver's Red Light**, **Driver's White Light** (**DWL**).

Driver's Line of Sight
Of a **Signal**, the straight line between the mid-point of the driver's eyes and the **Aspect**.

Driver's Red Light (DRL)
[Sig.] At an **Automatic Barrier Crossing Locally Monitored** (**ABCL**) or **Automatic Open Crossing Locally Monitored** (**AOCL**) ☐ **Level Crossing** (**LC**, **LX**), Part of the **Driver's Level Crossing Indicator**, a **Signal** illuminated when the **Driver's White Light** (**DWL**) is not, i.e. the indicating that the **Level Crossing Protection System** has failed and that it is not safe to proceed.

Driver's Reminder Appliance (DRA)
[TRS] A device in the **Driving Cab** of a **Train** that allows the driver to set a reminder when brought to a stand at a **Signal** showing a **Stop Aspect**. When set, the Driver's Reminder Appliance prevents the driver applying power and moving off.

Driver's Safety Device (DSD)
[TRS] A system that halts the **Locomotive** or **Train** if the driver ceases to respond. Previously commonly known as a **Dead Man's Handle**, most examples are pedals that must be pressed continuously or released and pressed in response to an audible reminder. Also **DVD**.

Driver's White Light (DWL)
[Sig.] At an **Automatic Barrier Crossing Locally Monitored** (**ABCL**) or **Automatic Open Crossing Locally Monitored** (**AOCL**) ☐ **Level Crossing** (**LC**, **LX**), part of the **Driver's Level Crossing Indicator**, a **Signal** illuminated when the **Driver's Red Light** is not, i.e. indicating that the **Level Crossing Protection System** has operated correctly and that it is safe to proceed.

Driverless Train Operation (DTO)
[Sig.] An automated system of **Train** control that eradicates the need for a driver, but employs a Train attendant to supervise door closure, ticket inspection and **Passenger**-to-controller communications. See **Transmission Based Train Control** (**TBTC**). See also **Docklands Light Railway** (**DLR**), which uses this system

Driving
[TRS] In a description of a **Rail Vehicle** normally forming part of a **Multiple Unit Train**, this denotes that the vehicle has at least one **Driving Cab**.

Driving Cab
[TRS] A designated place from which a **Driving Van Trailer** (**DVT**), **Locomotive**, **Multiple Unit Train** or **On Track Machine** (**OTM**) can be controlled by a **Driver**. This is typically a compartment at the **Leading End** of the vehicle, equipped (where applicable) with controls for the **Automatic Brake**, **Automatic Train Protection** (**ATP**) **Automatic Warning System** (**AWS**), **Cab Secure Radio** (**CSR**), doors, **Driver's Safety Device** (**DSD**), **GSM-R** radio, **Horn**, **Handbrake**, lights, **National Radio Network** (**NRN**) radio, **Regulator**, **Sanders**, **Tilt Authorisation and Speed Supervision System** (**TASS**), **Train Protection and Warning System** (**TPWS**) and windscreen wipers. Sometimes contracted to **Cab**.

Driving Cab Etiquette
When **Cab Riding** with a driver, remember that their attention will be focussed on the **Indicators** and **Signals** ahead, and on controlling the **Train** under ever-changing conditions. Therefore:
- Ensure you have the appropriate authority to Cab Ride, generally taking the form of a Cab Pass.
- Never Cab Ride without a sound and valid reason; the driver's life is hard enough without you
- Never assume that you will be able to sit in the Driving Cab, others may be there before you with better reason (and the driver doesn't have to accommodate you anyway)
- Always ask to come aboard, and be prepared to explain exactly why you wish to do so
- Do not speak unless spoken to
- Remember this is the driver's office
- Be prepared to assist the driver should they ask, but never interfere.

Driving Position
[TRS] The location of the driving controls on a **Rail Vehicle**.

Driving Trailer
[TRS] In a description of a **Rail Vehicle** normally forming part of a **Multiple Unit Train**, this denotes that the vehicle has at least one **Driving Cab** but no **Traction Motors**. See also **Driving**, **Trailer**.

Driving Van
Driving Van Trailer (DVT)
[TRS] An un-powered **Rail Vehicle** with a **Driving Cab** at one end, which when attached at the **Trailing End** of a **Train** allows a **Locomotive Hauled** Train to work in both directions without **Running Round**, **Shunting** or **Reversing**. Also **DLV**. See also **Propelling Control Vehicle** (**PCV**).

Driving Wheel
[TRS] A **Rail Wheel** attached to a **Driven Axle**, and the means by which a **Motive Power Unit** is moved along the **Track**.

DRL
See **Driver's Red Light**.

DRN
[NR] Design Review Notice.

ELLIS' BRITISH RAILWAY ENGINEERING ENCYCLOPÆDIA

Drooping
[Sig., Col.] A **Semaphore Signal** which is both not in the correct horizontal **Danger** position and not giving an unambiguous **Clear** indication either. Signals in this condition should be treated as displaying a **Stop Aspect** and reported to the **Signaller**. See also: **Half Cock**.

Drop a Track
Drop a Track Circuit
[Sig., Col.] Term for the activation of a **Track Circuit** (**TC**) by shorting the **Rails** together electrically.

Drop Away
[Sig.] An alternative for **Release** when describing a **Track Relay** (**TR**).

Drop Away Time
[Sig.] The time taken for a **Track Circuit** (**TC**) to register the presence of a **Train**, i.e. the time taken for the **Relay** to **Release**. See also Pick-up Time.

Drop Away Voltage
[Sig.] The voltage at which the last **Front Contact** of a **Relay** breaks.

Drop Down
[Col.] Move towards, as in "Drop down to the **Signal** please, driver."

Drop Head Coupling
Drophead Buckeye Coupler
[TRS] An **Automatic Coupling** (such as a **Buck Eye Coupling**) that can be swung downwards to reveal a standard **Coupling Hook** behind.

Drop Shunt
[Sig.] The highest value of resistance which will cause the **Relay** to **Drop Away** (de-energise) when placed across a **Track Circuit** (**TC**) at the **Relay** end.

Dropped
[Sig.] Describing a **Track Circuit** (**TC**) ▫ **Occupied** by a **Train** or similarly shorted, see **Released**. Also **Down**.

Dropped Away (DA)
[Sig.] Describing a **Relay** that has become **De-energised**, causing the **Front Contacts** to break. The opposite is **Picking-up**.

Dropper
[Elec.] The vertical wire link between **Contact Wire** (**CW**) and **Catenary Wires** in an **Overhead Line Electrification** (**OLE**) system which maintains the Contact Wire at the correct height. Also **Hanger**.

Drott
(Tradename) [Obs.] A type of tracked loading shovel, used for **Reballasting** ▫ **Track**. The word is also used as a verb, describing the operation of **Reballasting**. See also **Trax**, **Traxcavator**.

DRS
a) Down ▫ Refuge Siding
b) See Direct Rail Services.

DRSS
[Sig.] Double Rail Single Series, a Bonding layout.

Drugs and Alcohol Screening
Drugs and Alcohol Testing
The testing of a member of staff for the presence of drugs or alcohol in their body. This is normally carried out for one of the following reasons:
• On a regular 10-year cycle for Sentinel Card holders
• As a result of changing employer
As a result of involvement in an accident or incident, see For Cause Screening, For Cause Testing. See also DNA.

DRUID
[LUL] Double-Royal Unit Information Details.

Drum Carrier
[TRS, Elec.] A **Rail Vehicle** specially modified to carry drums of cable and allow them to be spooled out on the move. See also **Cable Train**.

Drumming
Drumming Schedule
[Elec.] The activity of allocating drums of cable to proposed **Overhead Line Equipment** (**OLE**) works, and the document recording the results.

Drumswitch
[TRS] An electrical switch at the outer ends of a **Multiple Unit Train** which enable the electrical connections to be coupled and uncoupled from another unit.

DRW
Description Received Warning.

Dry
[PW] Describing an **Insulated Rail Joint** (**IRJ**) which does not use epoxy resin in its construction. See **Dry Joint**, **Dry Insulated Joint**.

Dry Insulated Joint
Dry Joint
[PW] A form of **Insulated Rail Joint** (**IRJ**) which is only bolted together; with no adhesive or epoxy resin being used. See also **Glued Insulated Joint** (**GIJ**).

Dryness Fraction
[TRS] A measure to the ratio of dry steam to condensate in saturated steam. Without **Superheating**, this is typically 7%. Superheated steam can have a Dryness Fraction as high as 100%.

DS
See Down Slow. See also Down Relief (DR).

DSA
a) [NR] Development Services Agreement
b) Display Screen Assessment

DSD
See Driver's Safety Device.

DSE
a) See Dynamic Swept Envelope
b) Display Screen Equipment
c) [TRS] Door Sensitive Edge
d) [LUL] Discriminating Sensitive Edge.

DSKY
Display / Keyboard.

ELLIS' BRITISH RAILWAY ENGINEERING ENCYCLOPÆDIA

DSL
a) Down □ Slow □ Line
b) Diesel Shunting □ Locomotive
c) Digital Subscriber Line

DSLF
Distribution System Losses Factor.

DSM
a) Driver Standards Manager
b) Duty Station Manager.

DSR
See Differential Speed Restriction.

DST
a) Data Support Tool
b) Decision Support Tool.

DT
a) Down □ Through Line
b) [TRS] An acronym representing a Driving Trailer □ Coach.

DTAD
(dee-tad) [PW] Detailed Through Alignment Design.
See Through Alignment Design (TAD)

DTB
[TRS] An acronym representing a Driving Trailer □ Brake □ Coach.

DTBS
[TRS] An acronym representing a Driving Trailer □ Brake □ Standard Class □ Coach.

DTBSO
[TRS] An acronym representing a Driving Trailer □ Brake □ Standard Class □ Open Coach.

DTCO
[TRS] An acronym representing a Driving Trailer □ Composite □ Open Coach.

DTE
a) Desk Top Exercise
b) Development and Test Environment

DTF
[TRS] An acronym representing a Driving Trailer □ First Class □ Coach.

DTI
Department for Trade and Industry.

DTLR
Department for Transport, Local Government and Regions, now the Department of the Environment, Transport and the Regions (DETR). See Department for Transport (DfT).

DTM
a) Driver Training Manager
b) Duty Traincrew Manager

DTMF
[Tel.] Dual Tone Multi Frequency.

DTO
See Driverless Train Operation.

DTp
See DoT.

DTS
a) See Dynamic Track Stabiliser
b) [TRS] An acronym representing a Driving □ Trailer □ Standard Class □ Coach.

DTSO
[TRS] An acronym representing a Driving □ Trailer □ Standard Class □ Open Coach.

DTSSo
[TRS] An acronym representing a Driving □ Trailer □ Standard Class □ Semi-open Coach.

DTV
[TRS] An acronym representing a Driving □ Trailer □ Van, see Driving Van Trailer (DVT).

D-Type Bridge
[NR Civ.] A type of standard Half Through □ Ballasted Deck □ Bridge consisting of two I-shaped main girders and a Composite Deck consisting of joists set in concrete. Used for very long Spans, up to 50 metres. See also A-Type Bridge, B-Type Bridge.

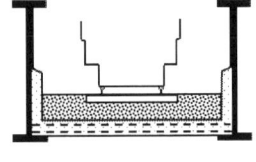

DU
[NR] Delivery Unit, See Maintenance Delivery Unit (MDU).

DU Dry Bearing
[PW] A low friction bearing plate which can be fitted to the Slide Table of a Slide Chair or Slide Baseplate. It does not require lubrication

Dual Aspect
[LUL Sig.] A fault condition on a Two Aspect Signal where both the Green Aspect and Red Aspect are Alight. The Green is showing because the Line □ Beyond is Clear, but the Red is showing because the Train Stop has not lowered (due to a failure) when the Signal □ Cleared.

Dual Blow
[TRS Col.] An alternative term for Dual Piped.

Dual Braked
[TRS]A Rail Vehicle having two Automatic Brake systems, normally Vacuum Brakes and Air Brakes, both of which operate the vehicle brakes. Also Dual Fitted. See H, X.

Dual Electrified Line
[Elec.] A Track fitted with both 650 to 750V DC □ Conductor Rail (Third Rail) and 25kV AC Overhead Line Equipment (OLE) systems, allowing Trains with either Traction system to run under power.

Dual Fitted
[TRS]
a) A Rail Vehicle having two Automatic Brake systems, normally Vacuum Brakes and Air Brakes, both of which operate the vehicle brakes. Also Dual Braked
b) A Train equipped with both Overhead Line Equipment (OLE) and Conductor Rail current collection equipment, more normally called Dual Voltage Stock

147

Dual Gate
[PW] An arrangement which allows the **Ultrasonic Rail Flaw Detector Operator** (**URFDO**) to monitor two different areas of an **Ultrasonic Rail Flaw Detector** (**URFD**) signal simultaneously.

Dual Gauge Track
See **Mixed Gauge Track**.

Dual Heated
[TRS] A **Locomotive** equipped with both **Electric Train Heating** (**ETH**) and **Steam Heating** systems. See also **No Heat**.

Dual Mode Buffer Stop
A **Buffer Stop** which combines (generally) a first stage hydraulic element for minor impacts and a **Friction Buffer Stop** arrangement for heavier ones.

Dual Piped
[TRS] Describing a vehicle with through piping for both **Air Brakes** and **Vacuum Brakes**, neither of which systems operates the vehicle brakes. Also **Dual Blow**. See R.

Dual Signalled Line
[Sig.] A **Line** where **Lineside Signals** are provided for controlling the movement of **Conventional Trains** and a **In-cab Signalling System** controls the movement of **Cab Signalled Trains** in the same geographical area.

Dual Voltage
Dual Voltage Stock
[TRS] Describing a **Traction Unit** that can be supplied by two types of **Electrification** system, typically 25kV AC **Overhead Line Equipment** (**OLE**) and 750V DC □ **Conductor Rails**. Examples include the **Class** 92 **Locomotive** and certain **Multiple Unit Trains**. Also **Dual Fitted** clause b).

Ducklings
[Col.] A nickname for the large trailers with **Rail Wheels** used in conjunction with **Road Rail Excavators**. The name comes from **Rubber Duck**, the colloquial term for a road mobile (rubber tyred) excavator.

Ducted Cable Route
A **Cable Route** comprising a group of polymer pipes (typically four, six, nine, 12 or 16) carrying **Electrification**, **Points Heating**, **Signalling** or **Telecommunications** cables under a surface obstruction such as a road. See also **BTR**, **Under Road Crossing** (**URX**), **Under Track Crossing** (**UTX**).

Ducted Sleeper
[PW] A **Concrete Sleeper** with a shallow (30mm by 30mm) duct cast into the upper surface, allowing a **Bond** or **Track Tail** to be secured without drilling the **Sleeper**. One type is the G44D. See also **Box Sleeper**, **Hollow Sleeper**.

Dud
[Col.] A defective **Rail Vehicle**.

Duff Jack
[PW Col.] The name for any type of **Ratchet Jack** used in **Permanent Way** work. From Duff Norton, the company which produces the commonest type.

Dumb Buffers
[TRS Obs.] A variety of **Buffer** that has no spring element, i.e. it is solid, although some early types used horsehair filling.

Dumbbell
[PW] A symbol used to indicate changes of geometry on **Track** drawings.

STR   R=1000m

Dummy
[Col.] Term for a **Shunt Signal**. Also **Dodd**, **Dolly**, **Tommy Dodd**.

DuPont Report
More formally "Safety Management in the Railway Group", a report commissioned by **Railtrack** (**RT**) on safety culture within Railtrack and the wider **Railway Industry**.

Durlock
(Tradename) A type of fastener which features a serrated surface under the fastener head to ensure good gripping with its mating part. Manufactured by the Unbrako Group.

Dusty Bin
[Col.]
a) Nickname for the **Class** 321 **Electric Multiple Unit** (**EMU**)
b) Term for a waste transfer facility, or a **Train** transferring waste to such a facility. See also **Binliner**.

Dut.
[Hist.] Common shorthand for ST <u>Dut</u>ton & Co., a former manufacturer of **Signalling Equipment**.

Duty Holder
An organisation, or person which has a duty imposed on them by the law intended to protect the health and safety of employees and/or other persons.

Duty Operations Manager (DOM)
On-call manager dealing with operational issues on **Railways**.

DV
a) <u>V</u>ertical □ Flat Bottom (**FB**) Full Depth Switches. The D describes the length and **Switch Radius**
b) Door <u>V</u>alve
c) See **Development Vehicle**.

DVA
a) Driver <u>V</u>isual <u>A</u>cuity
b) Digital <u>V</u>oice <u>A</u>nnouncer.

DVAI
Digital <u>V</u>oice <u>A</u>nnouncer (<u>E</u>mergency).

DVD
[TRS] Driver's <u>V</u>igilance <u>D</u>evice, an alternative for **Driver's Safety Device** (**DSD**).

DVLR
[Hist.] The **Pre-Grouping** Derwent Valley **Light Railway**.

DVR
[Hist.] The **Pre-Grouping** Dearne Valley **Railway**.

DVs
[PW] Denotes 113A □ Flat Bottom (**FB**) □ **Shallow Depth Switches**, length D.

DVS
a) [PW] Denotes **CEN56E1** □ **Flat Bottom** (**FB**) □ **Shallow Depth Switches**, length D
b) See **Driver Vigilance System**
c) [NR] Design **V**alidation **S**urvey.

DVT
See **Driving Van Trailer**.

Dwarf Signal
[Sig, Col.] An alternative for a **Ground Disc Signal**, **Ground Signal** or **Ground Position Light Signal** (**GPLS**).

DWDM
Dense **W**avelength-**D**ivision **M**ultiplexing.

Dwell Time
a) [Ops.] The time additional time a **Passenger Train** uses in stopping at a **Station Stop**
b) [TRS] The length of time that the valves of a **Steam Locomotive** are stationary at the ends of their travel.

DWG
The file extension of Computer Aided Design (CAD) drawings produced using Autodesk's Autocad package.

DWL
a) See **Driver's White Light**
b) **D**ynamic **W**arning **L**ights.

DWWP
[NR] **D**elivering **W**ork **W**ithin **P**ossessions.

DX
a) As a prefix to an **On-track Machine** (**OTM**) number, it means that the Machine is not reportable to **TOPS**.
b) **D**irect **E**xtract, a type of wall mounted air distribution system
c) **D**ocument **E**xchange, also known as Hays DX.

DXF
Drawing **E**xchange **F**ormat, a type of Computer Aided Design (CAD) file, readable by most design packages.

Dye Penetrant Inspection (DPI)
A method of finding cracks in metal by using different colours and viscosities of dye to show them up. Used during the **Weld Repair** of **Rail Defects** to ensure that the whole defect has been found. See also **Magnetic Particle Inspection** (**MPI**).

Dying Pig
[Sig. Col.] A term used to describe an **Annunciator** that sounds on the operation of a **Track Circuit** (**TC**) or **Treadle** □ on the **Approach** to a **Signal Box** (**SB**). The term describes the descending noise produced, as the **Annunciator** is powered by a capacitor, which discharges slowly.

Dynamic
a) [PW] When applied to a measurement such as **Crosslevel**, envelope or **Twist**, Dynamic indicates that the measurement is taken whilst **Trains** are in motion. See **Dynamic Crosslevel**, **Dynamic Level**, **Dynamic Twist**. The opposite is **Static**
b) [Ops.] When describing a facility such as a **Loop**, Dynamic indicates that the facility is normally used without stopping, i.e. a **Dynamic Loop**, see also **Slow Line**.

Dynamic Analysis
[PW] The determination of the operating clearances between a **Rail Vehicle** and a **Structure** based on the **Dynamic Swept Envelope** of the Vehicle including any **Dynamic** vehicle movements determined from the associated **Kinematic Envelope** (**KE**).

Dynamic Braking
[TRS] Collective term for braking systems using the **Traction Motors** of the **Traction Units** to act as generators which provide the braking effort. The power generated during braking is dissipated either as heat through on-board resistors, called **Rheostatic Braking**, or by returning it to the Traction Supply, called **Regenerative Braking**. See also **Grid**.

Dynamic Crosslevel
[PW] The value of the **Track** □ **Crosslevel** whilst it is under load. See also **Dynamic Twist**, **Static Crosslevel**, **Static Twist**.

Dynamic Level
[PW] The level of **Rail** whilst loaded. The opposite is the **Static Level**. See also **Dynamic Crosslevel**, **Dynamic Twist**.

Dynamic Loop
A **Loop** of sufficient length that a **Train** using it need not stop whilst it is overtaken by a following Train. On most **Routes** this **Loop** is of such a length that it requires multiple **Signals** and therefore becomes a **Slow Line**. See also **Passing Loop**, **Relief Line**.

Dynamic Pedestrian Flow Modelling
An analysis of normal throughput rates, congestion and emergency scenarios for pedestrian areas undertaken using a micro simulation software package such as **Legion** or **STEPS**. See also **Static Pedestrian Flow Analysis**.

Dynamic Ratio
[TRS] The difference between the recorded **Axle Load** and the peak Axle Load for a given axle.

Dynamic Swept Envelope (DSE)
[PW] A cross sectional profile, taken at right angles to the **Track**, enclosing all **Dynamic** movement, deflections and offsets due to **End Throw** and **Centre Throw** of all points along the surface of a **Rail Vehicle** that can reasonably occur under the expected range of operating conditions. See also **Kinematic Envelope** (**KE**), **Swept Envelope**.

Dynamic Track Gauge
[PW] The **Gauge** of the **Track**, measured as a **Train** passes over it. It can be estimated by applying a realistic spreading force to the **Gauge Faces** of the **Rails** and measuring the resulting displacement. See also **Static Track Gauge**.

Dynamic Track Stabiliser (DTS)
[PW] An **On Track Machine** (**OTM**) used to accelerate the consolidation of recently **Reballasted** ▫ **Track** by a combination of vertical load and vibration. One pass of this machine is equivalent to a week's worth of **Main Line** traffic. It is used to eliminate **Temporary Speed Restrictions** (**TSR**) by allowing all follow up works to be carried out immediately after **Reballasting** (**RB**), instead of running at a reduced speed for a week to achieve the consolidation.

Dynamic Track Twist
Dynamic Twist
[PW] The value of a **Twist Fault** when the **Track** is under load from a **Train**.

Dynamic Vehicle Gauge
[PW] A **Rail Vehicle** profile defining the maximum **Swept Envelope** allowable to maintain operational clearances to a **Structure Gauge**.

Dynamic Vehicle Profile
An alternative for **Kinematic Envelope** (**KE**).

Dynamometer Car
[TRS] A **Coach** equipped with test and recording equipment used to assess the performance of **Locomotives**. Tests include speed, acceleration and **Drawbar** pull.

E

E
a) [PW] Elevation, See **Cant**
b) In an abbreviated **Track Name**, it may denote east or **Electric**
c) [PW] In the form E*x*, E*xx* or similar it denotes a type of **Shallow Concrete Sleeper**
d) See **Switch Letters**
e) [Sig.] On a **Signalling Circuit Diagram**:
• As one of the leading letters of an **Equipment Code**, it means light, lamp, heat, emergency or **Earth**.
• As the last letter of an Equipment Code, it means light, lamp or Earth
f) The letter represented by **Echo** in the **Phonetic Alphabet**
g) **Common Interface File Operating Characteristics Code** for "Conveys **Mark** 4 Coaches"
h) [LUL] East London Line.

E Board
[NR] On the DC □ **Electrified Lines** in the Liverpool area, when it is necessary to reduce electrical loading on the system, a **Sign** bearing a letter "E" is exhibited at the stopping point of each **Station** within the affected section. The sign indicates to the driver that the 'series' position of the **Power Controller** must be used until a Station is reached where an "E" board is not exhibited.

e Clip
(Tradename) [PW] Collective name for the **e+, e1809** and **e2001** □ **Rail Fastenings** manufactured by Pandrol. See also **Pandrol Rail Clip**.

E Notice
a) See **Emergency Notice**
b) See **Engineering Notice**.

E Stock
[LUL] Type of steel bodied stock built for the District **Railway** in 1914, some **Cars** of which survived to the late 1950s. It was virtually identical to the **C Stock** and **D Stock** of 1910-12 except that it had an elliptical roof in place of the usual **Clerestory** roof of the period.

E&CHR
[Hist.] The **Pre-Grouping** Easton & Church Hope **Railway**, a Great Western and London & South Western joint enterprise.

E&G
Shorthand for the Edinburgh to Glasgow **Route**, part the former North British **Railway** (NBR).

E&M
a) Shorthand for **Earth** and Mark
b) Electrical and Mechanical.

E&OD
Engineering and **Operations** Development.

E&P
a) See **Electrical and Plant**. Also **Electrification and Plant**
b) Engineering and Production.

E&WYR
[Hist.] The **Pre-Grouping** East & West Yorkshire Union **Railway**.

E,L&N
Early, Late and Night shifts. See also **Front Shift, Back Shift**.

E/B
Shorthand for Eastbound.

e+
(Tradename) [PW] A further development of the **e2001** □ **Pandrol Rail Clip**.

E+D
[PW] The combined value of **Cant (C, E)** and **Cant Deficiency (D)** for a given Radius **(R) Curve** at Maximum Speed (V_m). See also **Cant Constant**, Equilibrium Speed (V_e).

e1809
(Tradename) [PW] A **Pandrol Rail Clip**, used everywhere except in **Baseplates** (use PR401 instead).

e2001
(Tradename) [PW] A higher **Toe Load** version of the **e1809** □ **Pandrol Rail Clip**.

EA
a) Environment Agency
b) East Anglia
c) Electronics Appreciation.

EAC
a) [Hist.] Extended Arm **Contractor**
b) [Hist.] Extended Arm Contract
c) [TRS] Engineering Acceptance Certificate, issued by **Vehicle Acceptance Boards** (VAB).

EAD
External Access Device.

EAK
[Sig.] Elektronischen Anschlusskasten or electronic junction-box, part of an **Axle Counter** installation.

EAM
[NR Ops.] **Engineering Access** Manager.

EAMG
[NR Ops.] **Engineering Access** Management Group.

EAP
a) **Earth** Attachment Point
b) Environmental Action Plan

EAPC
Electronic Automatic Phase Controller.

EARJ
European Association of **Railway** Journalists.

EARL
Edinburgh Airport **Rail** Link.

Early Rationalisation of Signalling (EROS)
[NR] An accelerated programme of closures of small **Signal Boxes**, and the consolidation of their control areas under larger Signal Boxes. See also **Integrated Electronic Control Centre** (IECC), Network Management Centre (NMC), Power Signal Box (PSB), Regional Operation Control (ROC)

EARR
Enforcing Authority for **Railways and Other Guided Transport Systems Regulations** (ROGS).
Earth
a) To Earth is to connect an electrified item to the earth or another earthed conductor. See **Earthing**
b) [NR] An Earth is the cable used on an **Overhead Line Electrification** (OLE) system to connect the **Catenary** to a **Designated Earthing Point** (DEP) during an **Isolation**
c) The electrical potential of the ground.
Earth Bar
[LUL] A point at which connections can be made for the purpose of **Earthing** equipment, structures, systems and assets.
Earth Bond
[Col.] Variation of the term **Earth**, meaning a cable used on an **Overhead Line Electrification** (OLE) system to connect a piece of equipment or a **Structure** to Earth.
Earth Distribution Network (EDN)
[LUL] The network of cables and **Earth Bars** that distribute the connection from earth electrodes to the point of connection of individual items of equipment, systems and assets, together with any equipotential bonding.
Earth Farm
In order to achieve a satisfactorily low **Earth** resistance value, it is sometimes necessary to drive many copper rods into the ground and connect them together. This group of buried **Conductors** is an Earth Farm.
Earth Fault
a) A fault condition in which electricity is incorrectly conducted to **Earth**
b) [Col.] A **Derailment**
Earth Fault Detection
[LUL Elec.] A system used to detect earth faults on **Trains** and on the 630V DC network.
Earth Fault Relay (EFR)
See **Ground Relay**.
Earth Flow
[Civ.] A **Slip** resulting from the flow of saturated soil and debris in a semi-viscous, highly plastic state.
Earth Strap
[Elec.] A length of cable used to connect a **Conductor Rail** to earth (e.g. a **Running Rail**) during an **Electrical Isolation**.
Earthing
The act of connecting an apparatus or **Conductor** to the ground or to an **Earth**.
Earthing Switch
[Elec.] An electrical switch mounted on an **Overhead Line Structure** that allows an **Electrical Section** to be connected to **Earth**.
Earthwork Examiner
[Civ.] Person competent to collect information relating to the condition of an **Earthwork**.

Earthworks
[Civ.] Any man-made and earth-related constructions such as **Cuttings** and **Embankments**. And all natural earth slopes
Earthworks Asset Register
[Civ.] The set of records which schedule all of the **Earthworks** within a defined geographical area of the **Railway**.
Earthworks Evaluation
[Civ.] An appraisal of information regarding the stability, condition, use and location of an **Earthwork** to determine the actions required to maintain acceptable levels of safety and performance.
Earthworks Examination
[Civ.] A regular visual examination of an **Earthwork** to identify and record signs of slope instability.
Earwig
A **Railway** □ **Telegraph Code** meaning "Following urgently required".
EAS
a) See **Engineering Access Statement**, formerly known as **Rules of the Route** (ROR)
b) Entrance **Aspect** Sets.
Easement
A right held to make use of another's land for a limited purpose, e.g. laying a pipeline or cable, or building a **Railway**.
Easing
Easing a Curve
[PW] A term describing the activity of flattening (increasing) the Radius (R) of a **Curve**.
East Coast
(Tradename) A **Train Operating Company** (TOC) which operates services along the **East Coast Main Line** (ECML). The Government established a holding company, Directly Operated Railways, to take over the East Coast franchise from 23:59 on 13 November 2009. **ATOC** code **GR**.
East Coast Main Line (ECML)
[NR] The **Route** from **London** (Kings Cross) - Peterborough - York to Edinburgh running up the East side of Britain. The line is **Electrified** on the 25kV AC system throughout.
East Midlands Trains (EMT)
(Tradename) A **Train Operating Company** (TOC) which operates services between London, the East Midlands and Yorkshire (Leicester. Nottingham. Derby. Sheffield and Leeds) and all the central England services linking Nottingham, Derby, Worksop, Lincoln, Cleethorpes, Skegness, Leicester and Cambridge. **ATOC** code **EM**
East West Rail
A project to reinstate Trains on the **Brains Line** from Oxford to Cambridge via Bletchley and Bedford. Major renewal and reinstatement is required between Oxford and Bletchley, and part of the former Bedford to Cambridge **Route** has been sold and built on.

Eastbound (EB)
[LUL] On the District Line the directions of Trains are identified by the terms Eastbound and Westbound (WB) irrespective of the actual orientation of Track at a particular location.

Eastern Region (ER)
[BR] The regional division responsible for the network in the North East of England and the East Coast Main Line (ECML).

Easy Entry Chair
[PW] A Check Chair located in the Flare area of a Bullhead Check Rail.

EAU
Electrification Asset Usage.

EAUC
Electrification Asset Usage Charge

EAWA
Electricity at Work Act (Electricity at Work Regulations 1989).

EAWS
[Sig. Hist.] Enhanced Automatic Warning System. The narrowly-avoided acronym for a system which is now known as Train Protection and Warning System (TPWS).

EAZ
East Anglia Zone. See Railtrack (RT).

EAZIAL
[NR, Hist.] Easy Access Zonal Infrastructure Asset Log.

EB
a) See Emergency Braking
b) See Eastbound.

eB
[NR] Electronic Bookcase, a document management system used by the West Coast Route Modernisation (WCRM) project and latterly Network Rail (NR).

EBB
[Sig.] Emergency Block Bells.

EBD
Emergency Braking Deceleration Curve.

EBIC
Emergency Braking □ Intervention Curve.

EBS
[TRS] Emergency Bypass Switch, found on Rolling Stock.

EBSM
Efficiency Benefit Sharing Mechanism.

EBV
a) Electronic Brake Valve.
b) An acronym representing a Eurostar □ Barrier Vehicle.

EC4T
[Elec.] Electric Current for Traction.

ECA
See Engineer's Current Area.

ECAM
Enhancement Cost Adjustment Mechanism.

ECAP
[Elec.] Electrification Condition Assessment Process.

ECB
a) Earthing □ Circuit Breaker (CB)
b) See Eddy Current Brake.

ECC
English China Clays.

ECD
Electrification Circuit Diagram.

ECE
[BR] Electrification Construction Engineer.

ECEB
See Electric Control of Emergency Braking. See also Electro-pneumatic Brake (EP Brake, EPB).

Echo
The Phonetic Alphabet word representing E.

ECI
Early Contractor Involvement.

ECIC
[TRS] Emergency Coupling Isolating Cock.

ECM
[TRS] Entity in Charge of Maintenance.

ECML
See East Coast Main Line.

ECN
Electronic Consignment Note message.

ECO
See Electrical Control Operator.

Economical Facing Point Lock (EFPL)
[Sig.] A system used in Mechanical Signalling that allows the Facing Point Lock (FPL) bar and the Points themselves to be worked from one Lever, making a saving in Levers and Rodding.

Economiser

Economising Contact
[Sig.] A contact which de-energises the coil of a Lever Lock when the Lever is in the Full Travel Position. See also Cut-off Contact.

ECOS
Electronic Customer Ordering System.

Ecotrack
(Tradename) [PW] A suite of Track Maintenance and Renewal decision support tools developed by ARCADIS which uses the type and age of the Track, and Equivalent Million Gross Tonnes Per Annum (EMGTPA) data to predict remaining economical life.

ECP
[TRS] Electrically Controlled Pneumatic Brake. See also EP, EP Brake.

ECR
See Electrical Control Room.

ECRO
[Elec.] Electrical Control Room Operator, See Electrical Control Operator (ECO).

ECRT
[TRS] Enhanced Crash Resistant Tank, a type of Tank Wagon.

ELLIS' BRITISH RAILWAY ENGINEERING ENCYCLOPÆDIA

ECS
a) See **Empty Coaching Stock**
b) **E**xternal **C**ommunications **S**ubsystem.

ECSAG
[Sig.] **E**uropean Rail Traffic Management System (**ERTMS**) **C**ore System Requirements Specification (**SRS**) **A**ssessment **G**roup.

ECVVR
European **C**entralised **V**irtual **V**ehicle **R**egister.

ECZ
[Hist.] **E**ast **C**oast **Z**one, See **Railtrack** (**RT**).

ED
a) See **E**lectro-**D**iesel
b) [Hist.] **E**ngineering **D**epartment. A historic variety of **Spoil Wagon**, now no longer in service, and a term sometimes colloquially applied to modern 20t capacity Spoil Wagons.

EDC
[NR] **E**ngineering **D**ata **C**entre, Derby.

EDCM
Electronic **D**oor **C**ontrol **M**odule.

EDCOS
See **End Door Cut Out Switch**.

EDCU
See **Electronic Door Control Unit**.

Eddy Current Brake (ECB)
[TRS] A non-contact non-friction braking system which uses a magnet to induce currents in a spinning aluminium disk. These currents in turn create their own magnetic field, which opposes the original one, and the disk is slowed down. This system is used on some **High Speed Trains** (**HST**) as a means of slowing from high speed (the system is useless at low speed as the braking effect is proportional to the rate of rotation). See also **Regenerative Braking**, **Rheostatic Braking**.

Eddy Current Testing
[PW] A means of detecting near-surface flaws in **Cast AMS Crossings** by inducing a steady pattern of eddy currents in the Crossing using a transmitter coil and a second search coil to map variations in these currents (which indicate flaws).

EDGE
Exogenous **D**emand **G**rowth **E**stimation, a method of modelling future **Passenger** demand resulting from non-**Rail Industry** factors but including the effects of changes to fares.

Edge Effect
[LUL] A 500mm wide zone adjacent to the side wall of a **Platform** for equipment, furniture etc.

Edge Rail
[PW] A **Rail** designed and appropriately supported to carry wheels on its upper surface (thus all modern **Rails** are Edge Rails).

EDH
See **Explosive Depth Hardening**.

EDI
Electronic **D**ata **I**nterchange.

EDIFACT
Electronic **D**ata **I**nterchange **f**or **A**dministration, **C**ommerce and **T**ransport (ISO 9753).

EDL
Electro-**D**iesel **L**ocomotive.

Edmondson Tickets
Thomas Edmondson (1792-1851) was employed as a Station Master when he began to devise an improved system of ticketing in 1836, based on pre-printed pasteboard tickets that were dated with a press as they were issued. He licensed the use of his invention to the **Railway Companies**, becoming a very rich man in the process.

EDN
See **Earth Distribution Network**.

EDNE
Emergency - **D**o **N**ot **E**nter.

EDNE Sign
[LUL] A Sign that displays Emergency - **D**o **n**ot enter and a pictogram and emits a specific audible warning. These signs are switched on during emergency evacuation procedures, triggered automatically but they can also be quickly activated, remotely and centrally, by **LUL** staff.

EDP
a) **E**lectrification, □ **D**istribution and **P**lant, see also **Electrification and Plant** (**E&P**)
b) [BR] **E**xtra **D**uty **P**ayment
c) **E**lectronic **D**ata **P**rocessing.

EDR
a) **E**ngineering **D**esign **R**eview
b) **E**mergency **D**oor **R**elease.

EDS
[Sig.] **E**arly **D**eployment **S**cheme, the trial installation of **European Rail Traffic Management System** (**ERTMS**) on the Cambrian **Lines**.

EDTA
A text storage and retrieval system which runs as a utility under **TOPSCICS**.

EDVTCS
[TRS] **E**ngine **D**river **V**igilance **T**elematic **C**ontrol **S**ystem, a Russian **Driver Vigilance Device** (**DVD**).

Edward
The obsolete **Phonetic Alphabet** word representing E. Replaced by **Echo**.

EE
a) **E**ngineering **E**nhancements
b) See **English Electric**
c) **E**lectrification **E**ngineer.

EE&CS
Electrical **E**ngineering & **C**ontrol **S**ystems.

EEA
See **Efficient Engineering Access**.

EEB
[TRS] **E**nhanced **Emergency Braking**.

EEBADS
Earthed **E**quipotential **B**onding and **A**utomatic **D**isconnection of **S**upply.

EECP
Engineering Education Competence Policy.
EECR
Emergency Electrical Control Room.
EED
Earthworks Examination Database.
Eel (YMA)
A flat **Wagon** used for the transportation of **Sleepers**. See **Wagon Names**.
EEN
[NR] Examining Engineer's Nominee, for **Bridge Strikes**. See **Bridge Strike Nominee** (**BSN**).
EF
[PW] In the form Ef.x, Ef.xx or similar it denotes a type of **Concrete Sleeper**. In this case a **Class of Sleeper** F, Shallow Depth Concrete Sleeper.
EFA
Enhancement Facilitation Agreement.
EFE
See **Electrification Fixed Equipment**.
Effective Traffic Moment
An enhancement to the **Traffic Moment** calculation that recognises the non-linear relationship between road traffic volumes and risk. The effective values given in the table are multiplied by the number of Trains to produce the Effective Traffic Moment.

Actual Daily Road Vehicle Users	Effective daily Road vehicle users
250	230
500	425
750	580
1 000	705
1 250	810
1 500	890
1 750	955
2 000	1 010
2 500	1 080
3 000	1 115
3 500	1 115
4 000	1 080
4 500	1 040
5 000	900
6 000	885
7 000	765
8 000	650
9 000	540
10 000	475

At an **Automatic Open Level Crossing Locally Monitored** (**AOCL**) this value is then used to determine the **Maximum Permitted Crossing Speed**:

Effective Traffic Moment	Maximum permitted Crossing speed (mph)
4 000	55
4 600	50
5 400	45
6 500	40
8 200	35
10 130	30
13 100	25
15 000	< 25

ELLIS' BRITISH RAILWAY ENGINEERING ENCYCLOPÆDIA

Efficient Engineering Access (EEA)
[NR] A project to deliver new technology and processes to enable more efficient **Maintenance** and **Renewal** of **Infrastructure**, while minimising major disruption and offering **Train Operating Companies** (**TOC**), **Freight Operating Companies** (**FOC**) and end users improved availability. Some of the initiatives include:
- Access point upgrades;
- New **Fixed Warning Systems**;
- High output **Track Renewal** systems;
- Improved **Junction** lighting;
- Remote conditioning monitoring;
- Faster **Possession** management processes;
- Removal of **Red Zone Prohibition** (**RZP**) areas;
- **Lookout Operated Warning Systems** (**LOWS**);
- Better and integrated planning.

Efficient Infrastructure Delivery (EID)
[NR] An initiative to improve efficiency and reduce cost and possession time by:
- More efficient project management
- Potentially bringing some services in-house
- Generation of standard designs for common items
- Increasing modularity of assemblies
- Introducing "plug & play" connections
- Introducing lightweight equivalents (particularly **Signals**, to take advantage of LED technology)
- Programme resource smoothing

EFPL
See **Economical Facing Point Lock**.
EFR
Earth Fault Relay, see **Ground Relay**.
EFRTC
European Federation of **Railway** □ **Trackwork** Contractors.
EG
a) [BR] Executive Grade, the top range of the **British Railways** grading system
b) [PW] In the form Eg.xx or similar, it denotes a type of **Concrete Sleeper**. In this case a **Class of Sleeper** G, Shallow Depth Concrete Sleeper.
EGF
See **Emergency Ground Frame**.
EGIP
[NR] Edinburgh to Glasgow Improvement Project.
EGL
Existing Ground Level.
Egress Handle
[TRS] Device used to open **Train** doors in order to exit in the event of an emergency.
EGRET
[NR] A performance management information system with downloaded information from **PHIS**. See also **PIPIT**.
Egret (ZCV)
A modified **Grampus** (**ZBO**, **ZBV**) □ **Spoil Wagon**.

155

ELLIS' BRITISH RAILWAY ENGINEERING ENCYCLOPÆDIA

EGTM
Equivalent Gross Tonne Mile. See **Equivalent Million Gross Tonnes Per Annum** (**EMGTPA**).

EH&Co.
[Hist.] Common shorthand for Easterbrook, Hannaford & Co., a former manufacturer of **Signalling Equipment**.

EHD
East Ham Depot.

EHRC
[Ops.] Exceptional Rail Head Conditions.

EI
Electrical Installation.

EIA
See **Environmental Impact Assessment**.

EID
See **Efficient Infrastructure Delivery**.

Eider
A **Railway** □ **Telegraph Code** meaning "Following said handed you by the under-mentioned not reached destination. Trace forward by wire and advise me result, with full particulars. If necessary see senders."

Eight Hole Joint
[PW Unk.] A **Fishplated Rail Joint** using eight bolts and **Fishplates** with eight holes each.

Eighths
Abbreviation of **Eighths of a Mile**.

Eighths of a Mile (Eighths)
An Eighth of a **Mile** is 220 **Yards** (201.168 metres). Often abbreviated to **Eighths**, this unit is widely used in **Track Recording** and analyses of **Track Quality**.

EIM
European Rail □ Infrastructure Managers.

EIMU
[Hist.] Eastern Infrastructure Maintenance Unit (IMU).

EIRENE
European Integrated Railways Radio Enhanced Network for ERTMS. See **European Rail Traffic Management System** (**ERTMS**).

EIS
Entry Into Service.

EIT
See **Enabling Innovation Team**.

Ejector
[TRS] A steam-operated device on a **Steam Locomotive** which uses the Venturi effect to create a vacuum for use with **Trains** equipped with a **Vacuum Brake**. A large Ejector evacuates the **Brake Pipe** and releases the Brake. A small Ejector maintains the Brake Pipe vacuum to overcome minor leakage.

EKR
[Hist.] The **Pre-Grouping** East Kent **Railway**, Rly which remained independent until the **Nationalisation** of the Railways on 1st January 1948

Elapsed Timer
[Sig.] Within a **Solid State Interlocking** (**SSI**), 64 bytes of RAM are reserved for 64 Timers which may be used for any purpose in the **Geographic Data**, but they are normally used for communications with other **Interlockings** and **Swinging Overlaps**. The timers count upwards from zero to the 'sticking' value of 254 in seconds, to an accuracy of ± 2s. Timers are isolated by setting their contents to 255 and are stopped and started from the Geographic Data, but incremented by the **Control Interpreter** at most once per **Major Cycle**.

Elastic Spike

Elastic Spike Fastening
[PW] A form of **Rail Fastening** used on wooden sleepers consisting of an inverted J- shaped spring steel spike which secures a **Flat Bottom Rail** (**FB**) onto a **BR1 Baseplate**, simultaneously holding the Baseplate to the **Sleeper**. See also **Macbeth Spike**.

Elbow
[PW WR] Alternative term for the **Knuckle** (**KN**) in an **Obtuse Crossing**.

ELCB
Earth Leakage Circuit Breaker.

ELCP
Emergency Local Control Panel.

Electra
[Col.] Nickname for a **Class** 91 **Locomotive**, after of their original project name.

Electra Gel
(Tradename) A water-based gel produced by Lawrence Industries in which sand granules and steel shot of a specified size are held in a paste-like suspension. It is used to improve **Adhesion** and **Track Circuit** (**TC**) performance during **Leaf Fall Season**.

Electric
Describing a **Track** equipped with an **Electric Traction Supply**, often used to describe a **DC Electrified Line** in an area generally fitted with **Overhead Line Equipment** (**OLE**).

Electric Arc Weld
[PW]
a) A **Welded** joint between abutting **Rails**, made by the electric arc welding process, normally on the site of Rail installation. This type of **Weld** (**W**) is often used to join **Conductor Rail** together. Also **Phillips Weld**
b) A method of **Weld Repair** for **Rails** and **Crossings**.

Electric Braking
[TRS] The use of the **Traction Motors** as generators during braking, the generated current being returned to the **Traction Supply** (see **Regenerative Braking**) or dissipated as heat from resistors (see **Rheostatic Braking**).

Electric Cartridge Heaters
[EP] An electric heating element fixed into the Jaw Blocks of Slide Chairs and Slide Baseplates, used to heat the Switches and keep them free of Snow and ice. They require many electrical connections and are relatively thermally inefficient, as they do not heat the Switch Rail. They have been superseded, first by Electric Pad Heaters and then by Electric Strip Heaters. See also Point Heaters.

Electric Double-Layer Capacitor (EDLC)
A special variety of electrolytic capacitor which rather than a conventional dielectric consisting of two separate plates separated by an intervening insulator, these capacitors use "virtual" plates that are in fact two layers of the same substrate. The lack of a bulky layer of dielectric, and the porosity of the material used, permits the packing of plates with much larger surface area into a given volume, resulting in high capacitances in small packages. However, the double layer can withstand only a low voltage, which means that electric double-layer capacitors rated for higher voltages must be made of matched EDLCs connected in series. Also called Supercapacitors, these devices are used where short-term storage of large quantities of electrical energy needs to be combined with high rates of charge and discharge.

Electric Locomotive
[TRS] A Locomotive whose motive power is electricity supplied externally from Overhead Line Equipment (OLE) or Conductor Rails. See also Battery Locomotive.

Electric Multiple Unit (EMU)
[TRS] A Multiple Unit that can be driven and controlled as a single Unit from the Driving Cab at the Leading End and whose motive power is electricity supplied externally from Overhead Line Equipment (OLE) or Conductor Rails.

Electric Pad Heaters
[EP] A replacement for Gas Point Heaters and Electric Cartridge Heaters, this system used resistive electric heater elements placed under the Slide Baseplates or Slide Chairs to heat the Switches and keep them free of ice and reduce the build-up of Snow They require many electrical connections and are relatively thermally inefficient. They have been superseded by Electric Strip Heaters. Sometimes shortened to Pad Heaters. See also Points Heating.

Electric Points Heating (EPH)
[EP] Collective term for the electrical systems fitted to Points (Switches) to ensure they remain free of ice and Snow. See Electric Cartridge Heaters, Electric Pad Heaters, Electric Strip Heaters. See also Gas Points Heating, Points Heating.

Electric Railway
A Railway upon which the vehicles are moved by means of Electric Traction, but not one worked by Battery Locomotives.

ELLIS' BRITISH RAILWAY ENGINEERING ENCYCLOPÆDIA

Electric Strip Heaters
[EP] A type of Point Heater, consisting of a thin resistive electric element clipped along the Rail Foot of the Switch Rail and Stock Rail. It heats the Switches to prevent the formation of ice and the build-up of Snow in inclement weather which, in turn, would prevent the correct operation of the Switches. Sometimes contracted to Strip Heater. See also Point Heaters.

Electric Token Block (ETB)
[Sig.] A Signalling System for Single Lines based on the issuing of Tokens to Trains for each Section. Only one Token may be released at a time and Trains may not enter the Section without a valid Token, ensuring that only one Train may occupy each Section at any one time. This system was the one that famously failed as a result of human error at Abermule in 1921.

Electric Token Instrument
[Sig.] The electrical equipment in a Signal Box (SB) used for the issue and return of Tokens in Electric Token Block (ETB).

Electric Track Trolley
A small Trolley fitted with batteries and electric motors, allowing it to be driven along the Track, moving people and / or materials.

Electric Traction (ET)
[Ops.] Collective term for all Motive Power Units and Traction Units that utilise an external supply of electricity as the prime mover.

Electric Traction Depot (ETD)
A facility where Electric Trains are stabled and maintained. See also Traction Maintenance Depot (TMD).

Electric Traction Engineer (ETE)
[Elec., Obs.] The original title of the organisation responsible for the maintenance and operation of the Electrification System.

Electric Traction Supply
Electric Traction System
[Elec.] A general term for the organisation, provision, and equipment required to allow Electric Trains to operate under power. See AC Electrified Line, DC Electrified Line, Electrification System.

Electric Train
[TRS] A Train that requires an external source of electrical power from the Overhead Line Electrification (OLE) or Conductor Rail systems in order to operate.

Electric Train Detector (ETD)
[Sig.] A short length of Conductor Rail provided on the opposite side to the Third Rail and energised by the Current Collection Shoes of passing Electric Trains. This allows the Signalling System to differentiate between Electric Trains and other Trains, such as those being hauled by Steam Locomotives.

157

ELLIS' BRITISH RAILWAY ENGINEERING ENCYCLOPÆDIA

Electric Train Heating (ETH)
[TRS] The high current supply provided by a **Locomotive** to allow the heating systems in **Coaches** to operate. All Locomotives that can provide Electric Train Heating supplies have an **Electric Train Heating Index** (**ETH Index**), and all coaches that use this form of supply also have a similar figure. The total ETH Index of the coaches must not exceed the ETH Index of the supplying Locomotive. Locomotives without Electric Train Heating supply equipment are colloquially referred to as **No Heat**.

Electric Train Heating Index (ETH Index)
[TRS] The amount of **Electric Train Heating** (**ETH**) supply either produced by a **Locomotive** or required by a **Coach**.

Electric Train Staff (ETS)
[Sig.] A **Train Staff** used in conjunction with a system of electrical devices which are **Interlocked** with the **Signals** to prevent **Conflicting Movements**.

Electric Train Supply (ETS)
[TRS] The electrical supply provided by a **Locomotive** to power lighting and other services in **Passenger Coaches**. See also **Hotel Power**.

Electrical and Plant (E&P)
A generic term describing the activities of supplying and distributing electrical power to and on the **Railway**. Also **Electrification and Plant**. See also **Distribution**.

Electrical Bypass Switch
[TRS] An electrical switch on a **Multiple Unit Train** which enables the **Brake Wire**, detecting the complete continuity of the **Train**, to be by-passed to isolate defects and enable the Train to be moved safely.

Electrical Clearances
[Elec.] The separation required between live **Conductors** and adjacent **Bridges**, **Signals** and **Structures** on an **Electrified Railway**. See also **Electrical Envelope**.

Electrical Control of Emergency Brake
[TRS] An arrangement of electrical circuits designed to achieve the requirements of an **Automatic Brake** system without the provision of pressurised hoses between the vehicles. See **Electro-pneumatic Brake** (**EP, EPB, EP Brake**).

Electrical Control Operator (ECO)
[NR Elec.] The person having control over supply to, switching of and **Isolation** of an **Electrification System** in a geographical area. See also **Electrical Control Room** (**ECR**). Previously called an **Electrical Control Room Operator** (**ECRO**).

Electrical Control Room (ECR)
[Elec.] The control centre for an **Electric Traction System** in a geographical area. It is where the **Electrical Control Operator** (**ECO**) or **Electrical Control Room Operator** (**ECRO**) is located, and is similar in function to a **Signal Box** (**SB**). The ECRO has facilities to monitor loads, open and close **Circuit Breakers** (**CB**) and certain other electrical switches remotely, and to impose **Emergency Isolations**.

Electrical Control Room Operator (ECRO)
See **Electrical Control Operator** (**ECO**).

Electrical Envelope
[Elec.] The outline created by adding a clear space around a **Live** object such as a **Conductor** or **Pantograph**. The size of this allowance is dependent on the potential difference between the Live object and the adjacent objects. See also **Electrical Clearances**.

Electrical Release
[Sig.] The removal of **Locking** on a **Function** using an electrical signal, for example, the unlocking of a **Ground Frame** (**GF**).

Electrical Section
[Elec.] A section of **Overhead Line Equipment** (**OLE**) or **Conductor Rail** insulated from all other equipment and fed from a **Feeder Station** (**FS**).

Electrical Sub Section
[Elec.] A small **Electrical Section** that is fed from a larger parent Electrical Section rather than receiving its own independent supply. **Sub-sections** can be arranged to take this supply from more than one Electrical Section, see **Alternative Feed Switch**.

Electrical Supply Tariff Area (ESTA)
A code used to identify the supplier of **Electric Current For Traction** (**EC4T**) to enable the appropriate costs to be calculated.

Electrical Track Equipment (ETE)
[Elec. LUL] All equipment employed to distribute and control electrical energy from the outgoing terminals of 650V DC **Track Feeder** □ **Circuit Breakers** (**CB**) in supply sub-stations, **Track Paralleling Huts** (**TPH**) or track coupler rooms to the **Train**, excluding the **Conductor Rails**. This includes **Shore Supplies** in Depots.

Electrification
a) The act of converting a **Railway** into an **Electric Railway**, e.g. " proposed Electrification"
b) The time at which a particular Railway became an Electric Railway, e.g. "at Electrification".

Electrification and Plant (E&P)
See **Electrical and Plant**.

Electrification Clearances
[Elec.] The dimensions required between **Track** and **Structures** to accommodate **Overhead Line Equipment** (**OLE**). See also **Electrical Clearances**.

Electrification Fixed Equipment (EFE)
[Elec.] That part of an **Electrification System** which is permanently immobile, e.g. **Feeder Stations** (**FS**), Overhead Line Structures, etc., but excluding the Trains.

Electrification Measurement Vehicle (EMV)
[NR, Elec.] a converted **Passenger Coach** (997983) used to survey and measure **Conductor Rail** and **Overhead Line Equipment** (**OLE**).

Electrification System
[Elec.] An assembly of switchgear and electrical conductors provided to supply **Electric Trains** with the current they require. There are two main types:
- **Overhead Line Equipment (OLE)**, which utilises electrical conductors suspended above the **Train** and a **Pantograph** mounted on the roof of the Train to collect current from them
- **Conductor Rail**, which uses an additional **Rail** mounted on **Insulators** on the **Sleeper Ends** and **Current Collection Shoes (Shoes)** to collect the current. See also **Bottom Contact**, **Side Contact**, **Top Contact**.

In both cases the **Traction Return Current** passes back via the **Wheelsets** and **Rails**.
- The **Fourth Rail System** is essentially similar to the **Conductor Rail** system, except that the Train has an **additional Negative Shoe** which makes contact with a **Traction Current Return Rail** mounted on Insulators in the **Fourfoot**. This system allows better management of **Stray Current** issues and is used on London Underground Limited (LUL) □ Lines.

Electrified Line
Electrified Railway
Electrified Track
A **Line**, **Route** or **Track** equipped with an electrical supply for **Traction** purposes. Such **Electrification** is generally by one of two methods, see **Electrification System**.

Electro-diesel (ED)
[TRS] A **Traction Unit** that can operate as an **Electric Train** or under its own diesel engine. Not the same as a **Diesel Electric**.

Electron Beam Weld
[PW, Unk.] A **Welded** joint between abutting **Rails**, made using a beam of high energy electrons.

Electronic Door Control Unit (EDCU)
[TRS] The electronic unit used to control and monitor the operation of an individual door.

Electronic Token
[Sig.] The data message used by a **Radio Electronic Token Block (RETB)** system, analogous to the physical **Token** used in **Electric Token Block (ETB)**.

Electronic Train Recording (ETR)
[Sig.] Computer equipment installed in a **Signal Box (SB)** where **Automatic Train Reporting (ATR)** is not operative, to allow the **Signaller** to record Train □ **Passing Times**. Now replaced by **Simplified Direct Recording (SDR)**.

Electronic Train Register Book (ERTB)
[Sig.] A personal computer based version of the **Train Register** used in **Signal Boxes (SB)**.

Electro-pneumatic Brake (EP Brake, EPB)
[TRS] A variety of **Air Brake** used on **Multiple Unit Trains**, which is controlled by means of electrically operated valves. An electrical ring circuit runs the entire length of the Train, holding the brake valves on each individual **Car** closed when energised. Should the **Train** become divided, the ring circuit will cease to be live and the valves will open, bringing the Train safely to a halt. This system allows any number of separate Multiple Unit Trains to be coupled together as each one generates its own brake pressure, but all act together when required to stop. See E.

Electro-slag Welded Crossing Vee
Electro-slag Welded Vee
[PW] A **Common Crossing** in which the **Crossing Vee** is formed from two **Vee Rails**, Electro-Slag Welded together. The Wing **Rails** are then bolted or **Multi Groove Locking Pinned (MGL Pinned)** onto this. Also **Part Welded Crossing**, **Semi-welded Crossing**.

Electrostar
(Tradename) The brandname of the **Class** 357, 375, 376 and 377 **Electric Multiple Units (EMU)** manufactured by **Bombardier** and used by Southern Railways.

Element
a) [PW] One part of a **Horizontal Alignment** or **Vertical Alignment**, e.g. a Curve, Gradient, Straight, Transition or Vertical Curve
b) [Sig.] One part of a **Signal**. See **Signal Element**.

Element Length
[NR, PW] The length of a **Curve**, **Gradient**, **Straight**, **Transition** or **Vertical Curve** in a **Horizontal Alignment** or **Vertical Alignment**. There is no maximum length, but on **Network Rail [NR]** the following minima apply:
- For any horizontal Element, the minimum length is two seconds at **Permissible Speed (PS)** or **Enhanced Permissible Speed (EPS)**
- For a **Transition**, it is normally 30 metres, with a minimum of 25 metres
- For a **Vertical Curve**, it is normally 20 metres, with a minimum of 30 metres of constant **Gradient** between adjacent **Curves** (unless both radii are greater than 1000 metres.

In any case the number of Elements in a design should be minimised.

Elephant Ears
Elephant Ear Insulated Rail Joint
[PW Col., Obs.] A variety of **Insulated Rail Joint (IRJ)** manufactured by Henry Williams. On each side if the **Rail**, two L-shaped brackets are bolted to the Rails and then to each other using insulated bolts. A layer of insulating material is placed between the rail ends and the "ears" of the brackets.

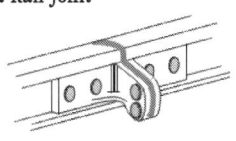

Elevated Troughing
Glass Reinforced Cement (**GRC**) or Glass Reinforced Polymer (**GRP**) U-shaped trough sections supported on posts at frequent intervals and used to protect **Signalling** and **Telecommunications** cables running along the **Lineside**. This system is used where site conditions do not permit the placing of Pre-cast Concrete (**PCC**) **Cable Troughs**. See **CAP**.

Elevation Difference
[Civ.] The difference in height (if any) between the two bearing points of a **Bridge Deck**.

ELGAR
(*el-gar*) The ticket and seat reservation system used by **Eurostar** and others.

ELH
(Tradename) Eisenbahnlaufwerke Halle, a manufacturer of **Bogies** based in Queis near Leipzig.

Elk
[Obs.] A type of **Side Rail Loader**.

ELL
East London □ Line.

Elliot Junction Accident
At 15:30 on 29th December 1906 a **Passenger Train** ran into the back of another at Elliot **Junction**, between Dundee and Arbroath. 22 died and 24 were injured. The primary cause of the accident was excess speed and a **Signal Passed at Danger** (**SPAD**). However, due to one of the most severe snowstorms for 40 years, the **Absolute Block** (**AB**) □ **Signalling** was not working, and an earlier **Derailment** led to the imposition of **Single Line Working** (**SLW**) to further complicate the matter, a situation which was not adequately managed by all concerned.

Ellipse
[NR] A computer based asset management system used by **Network Rail** and others to record and prioritise **Maintenance** work. Formerly known in Network Rail as **MIMS**. See also **WAIF**.

ELLSA
[Elec.] Electrification Supply Systems Analysis.

ELLX
East London □ Line Extension.

ELMTREE
Exceptional Load Management Tool and Routing Enquiry Engine.

Elongation Index
[PW] A measure of the ratios of the perpendicular dimensions of individual pieces of **Ballast**. The ideal shape is a cube, but no piece of real Ballast is actually this shape.

ELP
East London Partnership.

ELPOD
Electrical Load Power Distribution.

ELR
a) See **Engineer's Line Reference**
b) East Lancashire **Railway**, a **Preserved Railway**
c) [Hist.] The **Pre-Grouping** East London Railway, a Great Eastern, London Brighton & South Coast, Metropolitan, Metropolitan District and South Eastern & Chatham joint enterprise
d) [Tel.] Earth Leg Recall.

Elsenham Accident
On the third of December 2005, two teenage girls where attempting to cross the **Line** to catch a **Train** on the far **Platform** at Elsenham **Station**. The two girls did not react to the Red / Green □ **Miniature Warning Lights** and Yodalarm, which indicated that it was not safe to open the **Wicket Gate** and use the Station **Footpath Crossing**. They then stepped out behind a stationary Train and into the path of another, oncoming, Train. Both girls died.

ELSSA
[NR] Electrical System Simulation Analysis.

Eltham (Well Hall) Accident
On 11th June 1972 at 21:36, a **Locomotive Hauled** □ **Excursion Train** attempted to negotiate the 12 **Chain** Radius **Curve** at Well Hall at a speed estimated to be 65mph. The Curve had a **Permanent Speed Restriction** (**PSR**) of 20mph; the gross over-speeding resulted in the Locomotive overturning, the **Derailment** of half the Train and the deaths of the driver and five **Passengers**. 126 Passengers were injured. The driver was found have ingested copious quantities of alcohol immediately prior to and probably during his journey.

ELU
Extra Length Unit. A rarely used unit of measurement equivalent to one tenth of a **Standard Length Unit** (**SLU**), i.e., 2.1 feet (640mm).

ELV
Extra Low Voltage.

EM
The **ATOC** code for **East Midlands Trains**.

Embanking
The action of forming an **Embankment**.

Embankment
A filled area to permit a **Railway** to maintain its level and **Gradient** across low ground without excessive deviation from a straight course. Also Bank, Batter, Embanking.

Embedded Slab Track (EST)
(Tradename) [PW] A type of **Slab Track** pioneered by Balfour Beatty (**BB**) which utilises the BB14072 □ **Rail Section** embedded into the slab, retained by a continuous **Rail Pad** system.

Embedded Track

[PW] form of **Track** construction where the **Rails** are set into a concrete slab with the **Rail Crown** level with the upper surface of the slab. The Rail is often a **Grooved Rail**, sometimes an **Encapsulated Rail** or **Pre-Coated Grooved Rail**. This detail is used for **Tramway** Track built into street surfaces (**Street Running Track**) and recent developments have included the use of figure-of-eight shaped Rails embedded in a concrete upstand on some **High Speed Lines**.

EMC
Electromagnetic Compatibility.

EMCC
[NR] East Midlands Control Centre.

Emergency Alarm
[Sig.] A means of communication provided in **Track Circuit Block** (**TCB**) areas to allow the **Signaller** to alert a **Signaller** in an adjacent **Signal Box** to an emergency. Provided as a substitute for emergency bell communication.

Emergency Brake (EB)
See **Emergency Braking** (EB)

Emergency Brake Plunger
[TRS] A plunger within the **Driving Cab**, similar to an emergency stop switch, which starts a full brake application on a **Train**, also known as **Emergency Braking** (EB).

Emergency Braking (EB)
[TRS] The (abnormal) full application of all available braking effort, sometimes using a more direct and separate part of the control system to signal the requirement for a brake application than that used for the full service application. On certain vehicles, the retardation rate may be specified to be higher than that of the full service braking application; this is described as **Enhanced Emergency Braking**. A more normal occurrence is **Service Braking**.

Emergency Braking Distance
The distance a **Train** requires in order to decelerate from the **Permissible Speed** (PS) or **Enhanced Permissible Speed** (EPS) to a dead stop under **Emergency Braking**.

Emergency Bridging Pieces
[PW] Sections of steel channel used to bridge the gap between the **Rail Ends** at the site of a **Broken Rail**, allowing **Trains** to pass at a severely reduced speed whilst a repair is arranged.

Emergency Call
a) [NR] A direct call, which is given a high priority, that can be made by a **Network Controller** to the driver of a specific **Train** over a dedicated radio network operated and maintained by **Network Rail**
b) [NR] A telephone call to a **Signaller** regarding an emergency. All such calls should begin "This is an Emergency Call." See also **Safety of the Line**.

Emergency Clamp Fishplate
[PW] A **Fishplate** designed to be secured in pairs by **Emergency Clamps** to provide support and registration but not longitudinal restraint to **Undrilled** (UD) □ **Rail Ends**, defective **Welds**, broken rails having a specified gap between the rail ends and suspected **Rail Defects**. Also **Clamp Plates**, **Emergency Plates**, **Emergency Clamp Joggled Fishplates**, **Night Caps**.

Emergency Clamp Joggled Fishplate
See **Emergency Clamp Fishplate**.

Emergency Clamps
[PW] Large, heavy duty devices resembling carpenter's G-clamps, used to secure **Emergency Clamp Fishplates** to the **Rail**.

Emergency Coupling
[TRS] Typically carried by **Multiple Unit Trains**, this is an adaptor which allows a **Locomotive** (fitted with a **Hook Coupling**) to draw a **Train** fitted with an **Automatic Coupler**. These devices are generally lightweight items intended for a limited number of emergency uses. Also **Emergency Drawbar**. See also **Thunderbird**.

Emergency Crossover
A **Crossover**, often **Trailing**, provided to allow **Trains** to cross between **Running Lines** during times of **Degraded Operation** or **Single Line Working** (SLW). See also **Emergency Ground Frame** (EGF).

Emergency Drawbar
[TRS] An alternative term for an **Emergency Coupling**.

Emergency Driving Position
[DLR] See **Lead Emergency Driving Position**.

Emergency Ground Frame (EGF)
[Ops., Sig.] A **Ground Frame** (GF) **Locked** and **Released** by the **Signal Box** or **Signalling Centre**, controlling one or more **Crossovers** used only in times of emergency or **Possession**. See also **Emergency Crossover**.

Emergency Indicator
[NR] A self-contained, battery operated **Lineside** □ **Indicator** designed to draw a driver's attention to the presence of an **Emergency Speed Restriction** (ESR). They are coloured with bold black and yellow chevrons and display two brilliant white flashing lights. Also **Dalek**, **Metal Mickey**, **Sleeping Policeman**. Previously called an **Emergency Warning Indicator** (EWI).

Emergency Isolated Section
[Elec.] The part of an **Electrification System** (**Overhead Line Equipment** (OLE) or **Conductor Rail**) that is de-energized as part of an **Emergency Isolation** imposed by the **Electrical Control Room** (ECR). Without remote access to some of the normal switching arrangements, the extent of the Section may be large, and may on occasion unavoidably contain a **Train**.

161

ELLIS' BRITISH RAILWAY ENGINEERING ENCYCLOPÆDIA

Emergency Isolation
[Elec.] A disconnection of an **Electrification System** (**Overhead Line Equipment** (**OLE**) or **Conductor Rail**) imposed by the **Electrical Control Room** (**ECR**) without prior planning, typically in response to an incident. Once an Emergency **Isolation** has been carried out the OLE becomes safe to approach but not to touch, as it may still contain a small residual potential. See also **Emergency Isolated Section**.

Emergency Loop
[TRS] An electrical wire running through a **Train** that is used to detect the operation of an **Egress Handle** or a **PCA Emergency Brake Handle**.

Emergency Notice (E Notice, EN)
[NR] A document detailing late changes to the **Weekly Operating Notice** (**WON**) typically sent out by fax and Email on the Friday before the WON starts. Whilst not being a good thing, it is not uncommon for multiple Emergency Notices to be issued against a single WON. See also **Wire**.

Emergency Operations Co-ordinator
[CT] A Eurotunnel manager supporting the Emergency On Call Director (**EOCD**), usually the Operations On-Call Duty Manager.

Emergency Operator (EO)
[IÉ] A member of staff trained and certified to operate **Automatic Half Barrier Level Crossings** (**AHB**) manually when necessary.

Emergency Plate
See **Emergency Clamp Fishplate**.

Emergency Protection
Immediate **Protection of the Line** carried out because the **Line** has been obstructed or has become unsafe.

Emergency Protection Equipment
[NR] Items that can be used carry out **Emergency Protection** by **Track Workers**. This includes:
- **Railway Fog Signals** (**Detonators**); now officially called **Signals Railway Track Explosives**
- **Signal Post Replacement Switches**
- **Track Circuit Operating Clips** (**TCOC**)

Emergency Rail Cleaning Unit (ERCU)
A lightweight, single **Rail**, powered brush system for cleaning the **Rail Head** during **Leaf Fall Season**.

Emergency Recovery Adaptor
[TRS] An alternative term for an **Emergency Coupling**.

Emergency Release
[Sig.] A key or other similar device, usually kept in a sealed glass fronted enclosure, the use of which allows some or all of a **Signalling System** to be over-ridden and reset. Intended to allow the **Signaller** to "un-freeze" the system should it become "jammed" by an equipment failure, this facility has been the cause of more than one accident when used without proper reason. See **Battersea Park Accident**.

Emergency Replacement Group
[Sig.] An electrical switch located in the **Signal Box** (**SB**) that allows the **Signaller** to **Replace** a related group of **Signals** to a **Stop Aspect** in an emergency. Typically found at **Junctions**.

Emergency Replacement Switch
[Sig.] An electrical switch located in the **Signal Box** (**SB**) that allows the **Signaller** to **Replace** an **Automatic Signal** to a **Stop Aspect** in an emergency. See also **Replacement Switch** and **Emergency Signals On Control** (**ESOC**).

Emergency Restriction of Speed (ERS, EROS)
An alternative for **Emergency Speed Restriction** (**ESR**).

Emergency Senior On-Call Director
[CT] **Eurotunnel** manager who takes control of incidents within the **Incident Co-ordination Centre** (**ICC**).

Emergency Shunt
[DLR] A manual mode of driving **Trains** on the **Docklands Light Railway** whereby the **Passenger Service Agent** (**PSA**) operates a joystick to drive the Train either forward or backwards. The Train is restricted to a maximum of 20 km/h. during such an operation.

Emergency Signals On Control (ESOC)
A control provided in **Computer Based Interlockings** (**CBI**) to **Replace** all **Signals** in the **Interlocking** to a **Stop Aspect** in an emergency. See also **All Signals On Switch**, **Group Replacement Switch**.

Emergency Speed Restriction (ESR)
[NR] A **Speed Restriction** imposed or extended at short notice and not published in the **Engineering Notice** (**E Notice**) or which is more restrictive than a published restriction. Generally applied for safety reasons, such restrictions are transmitted by **Wire** to those who need to know. Also **Emergency Restriction of Speed** (**ERS, EROS**).

Emergency Switch-off
[NR] A procedure carried out by the **Electrical Control Operator** (**ECO**) when it is essential to switch off the electrical supply immediately,

Emergency Train Lights
[TRS] Lighting on a **Train** that remains illuminated after the **Traction Supply** becomes unavailable. The lights are supplied from batteries on the Train.

Emergency Warning Indicator (EWI)
See **Emergency Indicator**.

Emergency Weather Action Team (EWAT)
[NR] A team of senior managers drawn from the **Operations**, engineering, communications and commercial functions within a **Network Rail** (**RT**) □ **Route** which is activated when extreme weather conditions are forecast.

EMGTPA
See **Equivalent Million Gross Tonnes Per Annum**.

EMI
Electromagnetic Interference.

EML
[NR] Euston to Manchester and Liverpool.

EMMIS
[CTRL] Electrical and Mechanical Management Interface System.

EMMIS Controller
[CTRL]Electrical and Mechanical Management Interface System Controller. The member of staff controlling the power supply to the **Overhead Line Equipment** (**OHLE**) on the **Channel Tunnel Rail Link**. He also monitors and controls **Tunnel** air management, Tunnel water pumping and electricity supply to other services on the **CTRL**.

EMO
Emergency Open.

EMP
a) Engineering Management Plan
b) Environmental Management Plan.

Empties
[Col.]
a) **Spoil Wagons** not carrying spoil or other materials
b) Unloaded **Ballast Hoppers** or **Opens**
c) **Passenger** vehicles not carrying Passengers.

Empty / loaded Changeover Valve
[TRS] Part of a **Wagon's** braking system that can be set to adjust the amount of braking effort applied, dependent on whether the Wagon is empty or loaded. This prevents either the wheels of an empty Wagon locking up, or a loaded Wagon not generating its full braking effort.

Empty Coaching Stock (ECS)
[Ops.] The term for a **Train** consisting of empty **Passenger Coaches** being moved from one place to another (rather than a **Passenger Train** with no **Passengers**). Also **Empty Stock**.

Empty Stock
A common contraction of **Empty Coaching Stock** (**ECS**)

EMS
a) Environmental Management Statement
b) [CT] See **Engineering Management Systems**
c) Engine Management System.

EM-SAT
(*emm-sat*) (Tradename) A **Track Geometry** and position measuring unit, manufactured by **Plasser & Theurer**.

EMT
East Midlands Trains.

EMU
a) See **Electric Multiple Unit**, see also **Multiple Unit Train**
b) [NR] On a **Lineside Sign** forming part of a **Non-standard Differential Speed Restriction**, it indicates that the speed value applies only to Electric Multiple Units, where authorised.

EMUD
Electric Multiple Unit □ Depot.

EMV
See **Electrification Measurement Vehicle**.

EN
a) See **Emergency Notice**
b) See **Engineering Notice**
c) Euro Norm.

Enabling Innovation Team (EIT)
[Hist.] Now absorbed into the **FutureRailway** structure, the EIT formed part of the delivery of activities under the Future Railway umbrella, on behalf of the cross-industry **Technical Strategy Leadership Group** (**TSLG**). It offered support to practical cross-industry demonstrator projects and sought out innovative ideas and proposals from across the industry. The team was hosted by **Railway Safety and Standards Board** (**RSSB**) and was supported by the **Rail Delivery Group** (**RDG**), the RSSB and the **Department for Transport** (**DfT**).

Encapsulated Fishplate
[PW] An electrically insulated **Fishplate** that has the insulating material bonded to the Fishplate. See **Insulated Fishplate**.

Encapsulated Rail
[PW] A **Rail**, normally a **Grooved Rail**, which is factory-fitted with a polymer jacket. Normally used in **Street Running Track**, once the Rail is secured concrete can be poured immediately. The jacket also provides electrical insulation.

Encroachment
Describes an adjoining land owner extending their property over the boundary and onto **Operational Land**. This is frequently found in residential areas, where many back gardens have additional sheds, orchards and occasionally patios built on **Railway** property.

Encumbrance
[Elec.] The vertical dimension measured between the **Catenary Wire** and **Contact Wire** (**CW**) in an **Overhead Line Electrification** (**OLE**) system. Also **System Height**.

End Bound
[PW] Describing a **Sleeper** that is supported by **Ballast** only at its extreme ends. This is caused by incorrect **Packing** of the **Ballast**, and will eventually lead to the Sleeper **Breaking its Back**. See also **Centre Bound**.

End Door Cut Out Switch (EDCOS)
[LUL] A device to disable the opening of the saloon doors adjacent to the end **Cab** (front or rear).

End of Station
[LUL] The top of the **Platform Ramps** in open sections and the **Headwalls** in **Tunnel** sections.

End Post
[PW] Electrically non-conducting preformed spacing piece, shaped to the particular **Rail Section**, inserted between the **Rail Ends** at an **Insulated Rail Joint** (**IRJ**) to prevent the Rail Ends touching and shorting the **Track Circuits** (**TC**). Also **T-piece**.

End Throw

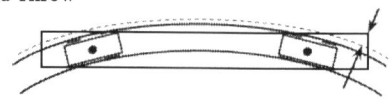

The lateral offset of the end of a vehicle when negotiating a **Curve** relative to its position when on a straight. See also **Centre Throw**.

End-on Junction
In **GEOGIS** terms, a junction between two **Routes** where the **Engineer's Line Reference** (**ELR**) changes. The **Mileage** value and direction may also change, depending in the circumstances.

Energisation Warning Notice
[Elec.] A poster giving notice of a forthcoming energisation of **Electrification Equipment**. Also **Flash Notice**.

Energised
Describing a **Conductor** that has become charged or a **Relay** coil that has a current passing through it. See also **Live**. The opposite is **Isolated** or **De-energised**.

Energy Dissipation Buffer Stop
A collective term for **Buffer Stops** where the kinetic energy of motion is dissipated by friction during the application of a constant force of retardation. This includes **Friction Retarder Buffer Stops**, **Hydraulic Buffer Stops** and **Sliding Buffer Stops**.

Engagement Slot
[TRS] The part of the **Locking Hook** that the **Falling Latch** is designed to enter in order to lock a door so fitted.

Engine
a) See **Locomotive**
b) See also **Engine Line**.

Engine Line
A **Track** used for the passage of **Locomotives**, often to and from their **Stabling Point**. Sometimes shortened to Engine, but preceded by the **Normal Direction**, e.g. Up Engine. See also **Engine Release Line**.

Engine Release Line
A **Track** provided adjacent to a **Terminal Track** solely for the purpose of allowing a **Locomotive** to be detached from the front of the **Train** and moved around it, a facility often found at **Terminal Stations**.

Engine Retention Failure
[TRS Col.] Technobabble term used to describe an engine falling off, out and onto the **Track**.

Engineer, The
Collective term for all the **Engineering Disciplines** on the **Railway**, used in such sentences as "Over-running □ **Engineering Work**".

Engineer's Current Area (ECA)
[LUL Elec.] The defined area within which the **Traction Current** remains on to allow **Engineer's Trains** to work as required. Traction current must be switched off to all of the **Allied Traction Current Sections**. The **Traction Current Sections** which remain live are **Active Current Sections**.

Engineer's Line Reference (ELR)
[NR] A three or four character identification code used to specify a **Route** or section of a Route. Introduced in the 1980s, most ELRs are either three letters or three letters with a single digit suffix. In the latter case this indicates the ELR is a subdivision of a longer Route. For example, CGJ describes the north Cheshire, Lancashire and Cumbria sections of the **West Coast Main Line** (**WCML**), but is subdivided into CGJ1 to CGJ7 for ease. Many ELRs are contractions of the Route name; GOB is Gospel Oak to Barking, for instance.

Engineer's Possession
A formal term for a **Possession**.

Engineer's Saloon
[TRS] A **Passenger Coach** specially equipped with folding steps and large observation windows, used for inspections by engineering staff.

Engineer's Siding
A **Siding** used for the stabling, marshalling, loading and unloading of **Rail Vehicles** used for **Engineering** works. Also **Ballast Sidings**.

Engineer's Train
See **Engineering Train**.

Engineered Safeguard
An engineered system that serves as protection to ensure safety.

Engineering Acceptance
[TRS] The process whereby conformance of **Railway Vehicles** to the mandatory requirements of **Railway Group Standards** (**RGS**) is scrutinised and certificated.

Engineering Acceptance Certificate
[TRS] A certificate issued by a **Vehicle Acceptance Body** (**VAB**) that certifies that the **Rail Vehicle** meets the required standards and gives any necessary operating restrictions.

Engineering Access
The periods of time allocated in the **Timetable** during which **Maintenance** and **Renewal** work can be carried out. See also **No Traffic Period** (**NTP**), **Out of Traffic Hours** (**OOTH**), **White Period**.

Engineering Access Statement (EAS)
[NR Ops.] The document agreed between the **Infrastructure Controller**, **Freight Operating Company** (**FOC**) and **Train Operating Companies** (**TOC**) that records when **Possessions** may be taken and how severe **Temporary Speed Restrictions** (**TSR**) may be. Previously called the **Rules of The Route** (**ROR**, **ROTR**). See also **Outside the Rules of the Route** (**OROR**).

Engineering Allowance
[NR Ops.] Extra time added into a **Train's** □ **Timetable** □ **Path** to to allow for **Temporary Speed Restrictions** (**TSR**) on that **Section** of **Route**. Also **Box Time**.

Engineering Details
[Sig.] The design details from which a **Signalling System** is constructed.

Engineering Discipline
Engineering Function
A relatively modern term used to describe the various specialisations within the **Railway Industry**. The main Disciplines are:
- **Civils**, covering **Bridges**, **Retaining Walls**, etc.
- **Electrical and Plant** (E&P), responsible for the **Signalling Power Supply and Points Heating**
- **Operations** (Ops.), taking care of the planning of the day to day working of the **Railway**
- **Permanent Way** (P Way, PW), specialising in the **Track**
- **Signalling**, covering **Signalling Systems**
- **Telecommunications** (Telecoms), responsible for telephones and data transmission
- **Timetabling**, looking at fitting the various **Train** services together on the **Railway**
- **Traction and Rolling Stock** (T&RS), specialising in **Coaches**, **Locomotives** and **Multiple Unit Trains**
- **Traction Power**, responsible for the **Overhead Line Equipment** (OLE) and **Conductor Rail** systems. Also **Function**.

Engineering Handbooks
[BR] See **Civil Engineering Handbooks**

Engineering Hours
[LUL, DLR] The period of time from when the **Traction Current** is switched off to the time the **Traction Current** is switched back on. This is equivalent to a **White Period** in the **Rules of the Route** (ROR, ROTR).

Engineering Management Systems (EMS)
The management of the ancillary systems such as ventilation and lighting servicing the **Channel Tunnel**.

Engineering Notice (E Notice, EN)
[NR] A document, published weekly and issued as required, giving details of **Possessions**, **Temporary Speed Restrictions** (TSR) and alterations to the operational infrastructure of the **Railway**. See also **Weekly Operating Notice** (WON), **Periodical Operating Notice** (PON).

Engineering Notice Board
A notice board usually within a **Booking-On Point** (BOP) where documents published weekly and issued as required, giving details of **Possessions**, **Temporary Speed Restrictions** (TSR) and alterations to the operational **Infrastructure** of the **Railway** are displayed. Also **New Notice Case**. See also **Weekly Operating Notice** (WON).

ELLIS' BRITISH RAILWAY ENGINEERING ENCYCLOPÆDIA

Engineering Periods
[NR] The nine **Possession** planning **Periods** in a year. They are not equal in length and the precise start and finish dates vary each year. They begin after the **Principal Timetable Change** in mid-December (so approximately Week 38) and run from (generally) Monday to Sunday:

Period	Start Week	Finish Week
A	38	40
B	41	46
C	47	52
D	1	8
E	9	12
F	13	18
G	19	24
H	25	31
J	32	37

Engineering Possession
The closure of a specific section of **Line** to **Railway** **Traffic** to allow **Engineering Work** to take place on the **Infrastructure** in accordance with module T3 of the **Rule Book**.

Engineering Safety Management (ESM)
The activities involved in making sure that the risks associated with changes to the **Railway** are reduced to an acceptable level. This is set out in a document known in the railway industry as the '**Yellow Book**'. The document contains a comprehensive glossary of safety terms.

Engineering Staff
Staff employed upon the **Maintenance** or **Renewal** of the **Infrastructure**, as distinct from those in **Railway Operations**, those driving **Trains** and those selling things.

Engineering Supervisor (ES)
[NR] The person nominated to manage the safe execution of works within an **Engineering Worksite**. This includes arranging the **Marker Boards**, authorising movements of **On-track Plant**, (OTP) **Road-rail Vehicles** (RRV) and **Trains** into and out of the work site and managing access to the site by **Controllers of Site Safety** (COSS). Formerly briefly called **Engineering Supervisor in Charge of Work** (ESICOW). See also **Person in Charge of Possession** (PICOP).

Engineering Supervisor in Charge of Work (ESICOW)
[NR Obs.] The former title given to what is now called an **Engineering Supervisor** (ES).

Engineering Supervisor's Certificate
[NR] A paper form held by the engineering supervisor (ES) authorising a **Controller of Site Safety (COSS)** to start work within an **Engineering Worksite**. The COSS signs this form to acknowledge receipt of the authority before starting work, and after works are complete, to confirm that the authority and any **Conductor Rail Permits** have been returned.

Engineering Token
[Sig.] In **Radio Electronic Token Block** (**RETB**) areas, an electronic **Token** that gives the **Engineer** ◻ **Absolute Possession** of the **Line**.

Engineering Train
A **Train** used in connection with **Engineering** works, including **On Track Machines** (**OTM**).

Engineering Trip Train
A scheduled **Freight** ◻ **Train Path** with a variable **Consist**, used to move **Engineering Vehicles** and **On Track Machines** (**OTM**) between **Depots**, quarries, tips and **Stabling Points** as required.

Engineering Vehicles
[BR, NR] The British **Railway** system employs many dedicated **Rail Vehicles** on its engineering works. The vast majority are used for such mundane tasks as delivering new **Ballast** and carrying **Spoil** away. These vehicles are referred to by **Wagon Names** and **Vehicle Type Codes** (**CARKND**). More properly called **Departmental Vehicles**, they are generally codenamed by species of fish, and although some crustacean, avian, molluscan and mammalian (and fabulous) names creep in, they are generally aquatic in origin. Some are former **Freight Vehicles** retired from revenue service; some rebuilt to suit and the rest (most) are now specially built for the purpose.

Engineering Work
a) Generic term describing the activities of the **Civil Engineer** (**CE**), **Overhead Line Equipment** (**OLE**) engineer, **Permanent Way** (**PW**) engineer, **Signalling** engineer or **Telecommunications** engineer.
b) Catch-all excuse for delays, used in on-board announcements by **Train Operating Company** (**TOC**) staff when the real reason is unclear to them.

Engineering Work Site
[NR] The subdivision of a **Possession** that is delimited by **Marker Boards** and managed by an **Engineering Supervisor** (**ES**).

Engineer's Telephone
[LUL] A telephone that connects to a location that is not always staffed, such as an **Interlocking Machine Room**.

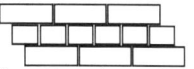

English Bond
[Civ.] A brickwork bond with alternating courses of stretchers (brick laid flat with the long end of the brick exposed) and headers (brick laid flat with the short end of the brick exposed), with the headers centred on the stretchers, and each alternate row aligned vertically. Used to create walls one or one-and-a-half bricks thick.

English Electric (EE)
(Tradename) A manufacturer of electrical equipment and the **Class** 08, Class 20, Class 37, Class 40, Class 50 and Class 55 **Diesel Locomotives**, an experimental **Gas Turbine Locomotive** and some early **Electric Locomotives**. Their factory at Newton-le-Willows was called the Vulcan Foundry.

English Welsh and Scottish Railway (EWS)
A **Freight Operating Company** (**FOC**). On its formation it absorbed the three **Freight** businesses set up under **Privatisation** (**Loadhaul**, **Mainline** and **Transrail**) and the parcels carrier **Rail Express Systems** (**RES**). It is now owned by and called DB Schenker Rail (UK) Ltd.

Enhanced Braking
[TRS] A braking system capable of achieving deceleration rates of 9% of g or better in normal use. All **Trains** in the UK capable of exceeding 100mph must have **Enhanced Braking**.

Enhanced Emergency Braking
A rate of deceleration higher than **Enhanced Braking** (9 % of g). The target value for this for a **Heavy Rail** vehicle is a retardation rate of 12 % of g.

Enhanced Line Clear
[LUL] An operational safety procedure that uses tripping of the **Emergency Traction Current Discharge System** (**ETCDS**, informally the **Tunnel Telephone**), during **Engineering Hours**, to provide additional protection to staff working in **Line Clear** areas.

Enhanced Permissible Speed (EPS)
[NR] The maximum speed, higher than **Permissible Speed** (**PS**), at which a particular **Tilting Train** may operate, when authorised to do so. This is because Tilting Trains can **Tilt** to reduce or negate the effects of increased **Cant Deficiency** (**D**) at this higher speed. Each type of Tilting Train has its own Enhanced Permissible Speed on any given section of **Track**. This currently applies to **Class** 221 and Class 390 **Trains**.

Enhanced Permissible Speed Sign (EPS Sign)

Warning Indicator (WI)   Speed Indicator (SI)
[NR] A suite of special **Lineside Signs** that indicate the **Enhanced Permissible Speed** (**EPS**) to the driver. The Enhanced Permissible Speed is a **Non-standard Differential Speed Restriction** and the signs are used in the same way as **EMU**, **HST MU** or **SP** signs. In order to differentiate them from **Permissible Speed Signs**, signs displaying the EPS have a yellow background. See also **Differential Enhanced Permissible Speed Sign**, **Signs**.

Enhanced Railfreight Intermodal Control (ERIC)
A computer system used to control the movement of **Containers** / **Swap-Bodies** etc. It is linked to **TOPS** to provide information regarding the containers loaded on vehicles.

Enhanced Service Brake
[TRS] A **Train** brake capable of achieving deceleration rates of greater than 9 % of g

ENS
a) European Night Services
b) European Night Stock.

Entrance / Exit Panel (NX, NX Panel)
[Sig.] A **Signal Box Panel** fitted with buttons for all entrances and exits, plus some intermediate points. To **Set a Route**, the **Signaller** depresses the appropriate buttons in front of the **Train** and at its exit point, and a **Panel Processor** sets the **Route**, shown in white lights on the **Illuminated Diagram**. **Trains** are shown as red lights, and the **Train Operated Route Release** (**TORR**) then "unsets" the used part of the **Route** as the **Train** moves along it. Other **Panel** types are **One Control Switch** (**OCS**), **Independent Function Switch** (**IFS**).

Entrance Signal
Entry Signal
[Sig.]
a) The **Signal** at the entrance to a **Route** that has been **Set** by the **Signaller**, particularly on an **Entrance / Exit Panel** (**NX Panel**). See also **Exit Signal**.
b) The **Signal** that controls the entry to a **Depot**, **Loop**, **Platform**, **Siding** or **Yard**.

Entry
[PW] An alternative term for the **Flare** of a **Check Rail** or **Wing Rail**.

Entry Angle
[PW] The angle of the **Planing** of the **Flare** on **Flat Bottom** (**FB**) □ **Wing Rails** and Flat Bottom **Check Rails**.

Environmental Impact Assessment (EIA)
The formal identification and investigation of environmental issues to determine the past, current and potential effects, both positive and negative, of a project's activities on the environment around it.

EO
See **Emergency Operator**.

EOCC
Emergency On Call Co-ordinator.

EOCD
Emergency On Call Director.

EoD
Common shorthand for Evans, O'Donnell & Co., a former manufacturer of **Signalling Equipment**.

EOI
Expression of Interest.

EOL
[Sig.] Extended **Overlap**.

EOLM
End of **Loop** Marker.

EOTD
[Sig.] End of **Train** Device.

EOW
[LUL] Engineering Overhaul Workshop

EP
a) [TRS] Electro-Pneumatic, see **Electro-Pneumatic Brake** (**EP Brake**, **EPB**).
b) Electronic Principles.

EP Brake
See **Electro-pneumatic Brake**.

EPA
Engineering Publications Assistant.

EPB
a) See **Electro-pneumatic Brake**
b) **ERTMS** Programme Board.

EPBIC
[TRS] Electro-pneumatic Brake Isolating **Cock**.

EPDG
[NR] Electrification Plant Development Group.

EPE
[Sig.] Electro – Permanent – Electro, describing an arrangement where two Automatic Warning System Magnets (AWS Magnets) share a common permanent magnet.

EPF
Erosion **Pumping** Failure

EPG
a) Efficient Project Governance
b) Electrical Projects Group.

EPH
See **Electric Points Heating**.

EPR
a) Engineering **Possession** Reminders
b) Ethylene propylene rubber, a material used as the outer cover of electrical cables.

EPROM
(*ee-prom*) Erasable Programmable Read Only Memory.

EPS
a) See **Enhanced Permissible Speed**
b) See **European Passenger Service**. Also **Eurostar**
c) Emergency Power Supply.

EPS Authority
[Sig.] The data message authorising a suitably equipped **Train** such as a **Tilting Train** to exceed the **Permissible Speed** (**PS**) and run at **Enhanced Permissible Speed** (**EPS**).

EPS Sign
See **Enhanced Permissible Speed Sign**.

EPT
ERTMS Programme Team.

EPU
[TRS] Electric Parcels Unit, an **Electric Multiple Unit** (**EMU**) built or converted for the carriage of parcels and mail.

EQAP
Equipment Appreciation.

Equal Split Switch
See **Split Switch**.

Equal Split Turnout
See **Split Turnout**.

ELLIS' BRITISH RAILWAY ENGINEERING ENCYCLOPÆDIA

Equaliser Bar Bogie 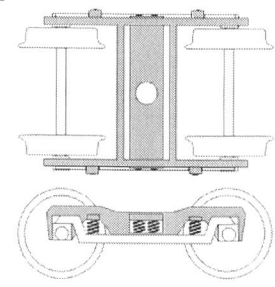
[TRS] A type of Bogie where the Primary Suspension is distributed between the axles using a separate bar. Commonly used on three-axle Bogies.

Equalising Plate 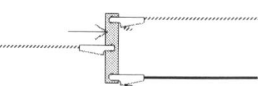
[Elec.] A perforated flat bar which has the Catenary Wire attached to one end, the Contact Wire (CW) attached to the other and a Tail Wire fixed to the middle. Its purpose is to distribute the tension in an Overhead Line Equipment (OLE) □ Catenary evenly. Also Balance Plate.

Equated Track Mileage (ETM)
[BR Obs.] Used between 1985 and 1993, a method of normalising the amount of Track covered by each Permanent Way Maintenance (PWM) organisation. For example, one Mile of heavily-used high speed Main Line might equate to 10 Miles of rural Branch Line. These factors were applied based on a 16-entry grid (4 speed and 4 tonnage bands) named A1 to D4 with a median category of B4. This allowed the unit productivity of each organisation to be compared directly. See also Track Category.

Equilibrium Cant
[PW] The value of Cant (C, E) that creates an equal loading on each Rail at a particular speed of Train. This speed is therefore also called the Equilibrium Speed (Ve).

Equilibrium Speed (V$_e$)
[PW] The particular speed for any given Curve at which a Train negotiating that Curve experiences no lateral forces, e.g. the net resultant force on a Passenger is perpendicular to the plane of the Rails. At this speed there is no Cant Deficiency (D) or Cant Excess. Curves are normally arranged so that the Equilibrium Speed is just higher than the average speed of Trains, to equalise Rail Wear between Low Rail and High Rail. The equation for calculating Equilibrium Speed for Standard Gauge is:

$$Ve = \frac{R \times E}{11.82}$$

Where:
- R is the Radius in metres
- E is the Cant in millimetres
- V$_e$ is the Equilibrium Speed in kilometres per hour

See also Maximum Speed.

EQUIP
[NR] A Telecommunications □ Maintenance database. Allied to FMS.

Equipment Room
Generally, a segregated space within a larger structure, housing specific Signalling Equipment or telecommunications equipment. See also Relay Room.

Equipment Warning
[NR] The new term for a Safe System of Work (SSoW) where staff are protected by receiving a warning from either:
- Automatic Track Warning System (ATWS)
- Train Operated Warning System (TOWS)
- Lookout Operated Warning System (LOWS)

See also Lookout Warning. These terms replace Red Zone, Red Zone Working.

Equivalent Cant
[PW] The combined value of the design Cant and maximum allowable tolerances of that value, used in Gauging calculations.

Equivalent Fatalities
A way of expressing injuries in terms of Fatalities for the purposes of risk assessment. 10 major injuries or 200 minor injuries are equated to one Fatality.

Equivalent Million Gross Tonnes Per Annum (EMGTPA)
[PW] A method of normalising the damage caused to Track by Trains. The number of axles, speed and Axle Load are multiplied by scale factors to produce an annual figure for each type of Train, effectively in terms of "damage tonnes". This figure is used to assess maintenance quality and to mandate forms of Track Construction. Typical values range from 2 (million) for a lightly used Line to over 40 (million) for a busy Main Line. Densely trafficked Light Rail systems experience values around 10 (million).

Equivalent Radius (R$_e$)
[PW] The radius produced when the Radius (R) of a Turnout Curve is adjusted to suit a curved Main Line within a Turnout. The relationship is given by:
For a Contraflexure Turnout;

$$Re = \frac{Rm \times R}{Rm - R}$$

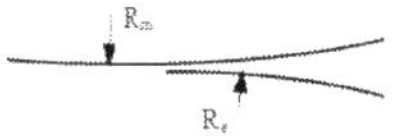

and for a Similar Flexure Turnout;

$$Re = \frac{Rm \times R}{Rm + R}$$

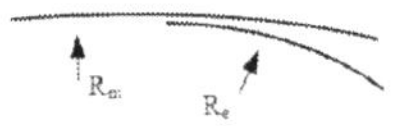

Where:
- R$_e$ is the Equivalent Radius
- R$_m$ is the Main Line Radius
- R is the original Turnout Radius.

ER
a) See Eastern Region
b) [Hist.] The Pre-Grouping Easingwold Railway
c) Employer's Requirements
d) Employer's Representative.

ERA
European Rail Agency.

ERAIL
European Railway Access to Interactive Learning.

ERCU
See **Emergency Rail Cleaning Unit**.
ERDF
European Regional Development Fund.
ERI
Employer's Representative's Instruction.
ERIC
See **Enhanced Railfreight Intermodal Control**.
ERN
Engineering Regulatory Notice.
EROS
(*ear-ross*) [NR]
a) Emergency Restriction of Speed. See **Emergency Speed Restriction** (**ESR**).
b) See **Early Rationalisation of Signalling**
c) Efficiency by means of the Rationalisation of Signal Boxes.
ERPSS
[Elec.] Electrified Railway Power Supply System.
ERRI
European Railway Research Institute.
Errington, John Edward
(1806-62). Civil Engineer who worked with **Locke** on the construction of the Grand Junction (GJR), Caledonian (CR) and Lancaster & Carlisle (**L&CR**) □ **Railways**.
ERS
a) Emergency Restriction of Speed. See **Emergency Speed Restriction** (**ESR**)
b) [PW] Embedded Rail Structure, a generic term describing a **Trackform** where the Rail is restrained in a continuous **Track Slab** by means of an elastomer infill. See **Embedded Track**.
ERTMS
See **European Rail Traffic Management System**, a Europe-wide standard for a form of **Automatic Train Control** (**ATC**). See also **European Train Control System** (**ETCS**).
ERU
[LUL] Emergency Response Unit.
ERWIN
European Railways Wireless In-house Network.
ES
a) See **Engineering Supervisor**
b) Emergency Stop
c) Environmental Statement
d) [NR] Under the **Bridge Condition Marking Index** (**BCMI**) handbook, shorthand for end support (e.g. **Abutment**).
e) The **ATOC** code for **Eurostar**.
ESC
Engineering Support Centre.
Escapement
[Sig.] The collective name given to the end of a **Connecting Rod** assembly together with its sleeve/flanged nuts, sleeves and lock nuts, which enables **Excess Motion** to be introduced between a **Switch Operating Device** and a **Switch**.

Escapement Joint
A joint which reduces the movement of one part relative to the other. Also known as a 'lost motion' joint.
Eschede Accident
On the 3rd of June 1998 an **ICE** □ **High Speed Train** travelling at 200kph (125mph) became **Derailed** after a broken wheel struck **Points** near the village of Eschede in Germany. The cause was discovered to be the design of the wheel, which was isolated from the **Tyre** by a rubber strip. This strip had failed, allowing the Tyre to buckle and fatigue until it broke. 102 died, compounded by the collapse of a road bridge, which was supported by thin **Leaf Piers**, one of which was removed by the derailed **Train**. This type of **Composite Wheel** is no longer used.
ESD
Electrostatic Discharge.
ESG
Engineering Support Group.
ESI
Electricity Supply Industry, collective term for the organisations who are engaged in the business of supplying electricity to users. See **Distribution Network Operator** (**DNO**). See also **Regional Electricity Company** (**REC**).
ESICOW
(*essy-cow*) [BR Obs.] Engineering Supervisor in Charge of Work, replaced by **Engineering Supervisor** (**ES**).
ESM
See **Engineering Safety Management**. See also **Yellow Book**.
ESMS
Engineering Safety Management System.
ESOC
See **Emergency Signals On Control**. See also **Emergency Replacement Switch**.
ESPA
Entities in Charge of **Maintenance** (**ECM**) Service Provision Agreement.
ESPOIR
EDIFACT Solutions for Pan-European Open-Systems Interconnection of **Railways**.
ESR
See **Emergency Speed Restriction**.
ESROG
European Rail Traffic Management System (**ERTMS**) Safety Requirements and Objective Group.
ESRP
Electrical System Review Panel.
ESSD
Electrostatic Sensitive Device.
EST
(Tradename) See **Embedded Slab Track**.
ESTA
a) See **Electrical Supply Tariff Area**
b) Electricity Supply Traction Area.

ELLIS' BRITISH RAILWAY ENGINEERING ENCYCLOPÆDIA

ET
See Electric Traction.
ETA
Expected Time of Arrival.
ETB
a) See Electronic Token Block
b) Early Transmission Berth.
ETCDS
[LUL] Emergency Traction Current Discharge System. See Tunnel Telephone, Tunnel Telephone System (TTS)
ETCDS/TT Plunger
[LUL] Emergency Traction Current Discharge System / Tunnel Telephone Plunger; a manual push-to-operate device provided at Station □ Platform □ Headwalls and used to operate the Tunnel Telephone from the platform in an emergency..
ETCR
European Training Centre for Railways.
ETCS
See European Train Control System.
ETCSOP
[LUL] Emergency Traction Current Switch Off Plunger.
ETD
a) See Electric Traction Depot
b) See Electric Train Detector
c) See Extension Trunk Dialling.
ETE
a) See Electric Traction Engineer
b) See Electric Track Equipment.
ETH
See Electric Train Heating.
ETH Index
See Electric Train Heating Index.
ETHEL
(*eth-el*) [TRS Obs.] Electric Train Heating ex-Locomotive, former Diesel Locomotives adapted to serve as providers of power for Electric Train Heating (ETH) to Stabled □ Locomotive Hauled Sets at locations where the cost of providing Shore Supplies would have been prohibitive.
Ethylene Vinyl Acetate (EVA)
[PW] A polymer material used for Rail Pads.
ETLA
Extended Three Letter Acronym. See also TLA, VETLA.
ETM
a) See Equated Track Mileage
b) [PW] Electric Track Maintenance, i.e. Track Maintenance carried out on Electrified Track
c) Electronic Ticket Machine.
ETML
European Rail Traffic Management Layer.
ETR
See Electronic Train Recording, now replaced by Simplified Direct Reporting (SDR).

ETRB
See Electronic Train Register Book.
ETRM
Engineering Train Routing Map.
ETS
a) See Electric Train Supply
b) Electric Traction Supply
c) See Electric Train Staff.
ETSC
European Transport Safety Council.
E-Type Bridge

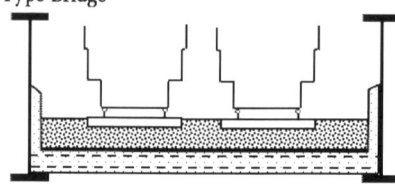

[Civ. NR] A variety of standard Half Through □ Bridge Deck consisting of two I-girder main beams supporting a Composite Deck (joists in concrete) and carrying two Tracks. Used for long Spans of up to 45 metres.
Eucalyptus Diversicolor
See Karri
Eucalyptus Marginata
See Jarra
EUDD
European Union Drivers' Desk.
EUKL
Shorthand for Eurostar (UK) Ltd.
EURATEL
[Tel.] European Railway □ Telecommunications.
Eurobalise
[Sig.] A Balise (a form of data transmitter) forming part of the European Train Control System (ETCS) or European Rail Traffic Management System (ERTMS).
EUROBALT
European Research Project for Optimised Ballasted Track.
EUROFRET
European system for international road Freight transport.
EUROLoop
[Sig.] The group of technical solutions for transmitter Loops in a European Rail Traffic Management System (ERTMS) or European Train Control System (ETCS) installation. See Infill Loop.
European Passenger Service (EPS)
[TRS] From the Infrastructure point of view, the vehicles constructed to run through the Channel Tunnel. These vehicles are of such large dimensions as to necessitate special construction standards for Lineside structures. See also Eurostar.

European Rail Agency (ERA)
The organisation responsible for contributing to the implementation of European Community legislation aimed at supporting a competitive, open market for **Rail** by enhancing the level of interoperability of **Railway** systems; and by developing a common approach to safety on the European Railway system.

European Rail Traffic Management System (ERTMS)
[Sig.] A standardised system of **Rail** traffic control which supplements or replaces the existing conventional fixed **Signalling System**. Drawing together aspects of **Train Protection Warning System** (**TPWS**), **Automatic Train Protection** (**ATP**) and other systems, the physical implementation is called **European Train Control System** (**ETCS**). The system can be implemented in three levels:
- Level One – where the **Train** is detected by normal means (**Axle Counters or Track Circuits** (**TC**)), **Fixed Signals** remain, and the **Signal** data is transmitted to the Train by switched **Balises**, allowing the Train system to safely control Train speed. This level of provision actually reduces the capacity of a typical **Main Line**. System A has no additional data coverage, whereas System B has some
- Level Two – Trains are still detected by normal means, but movement authority data is passed to the Train by **GSM-R** radio. System C retains all Fixed Signals but System D retains few or none. System E is equivalent to **Radio Electronic Token Block** (**RETB**)
- Level Three – where the Train transmits its position to the control centre, and movement authority data is transmitted back, all via GSM-R radio. There are no Fixed Signals. This system is also known as **Moving Block**, and there are no current proposals for such a system in Europe.

European Train Control System (ETCS)
[Sig.] A harmonised system of "signalling" based on **GSM-R** radio and **Balises**, intended to allow full interoperability of all **Trains** on all **Routes** within the European Union. The umbrella project is the **European Rail Traffic Management System** (**ERTMS**). See also **Automatic Train Control** (**ATC**), **Automatic Train Protection** (**ATP**), **Train Protection and Warning System** (**TPWS**).

Euroscan
An installation used to examine the interior of lorries requiring the enclosure of the lorry and the evacuation of the cab.

EuroSPIN
European **S**eamless **P**assenger **I**nformation **N**etwork. An intelligent system which provides up-to-date, multi-modal Passenger transport information to the travelling public.

ELLIS' BRITISH RAILWAY ENGINEERING ENCYCLOPÆDIA

Eurostar
(Tradename)
a) A **Train Operating Company** (**TOC**) which operates **High-Speed** international services between London and Brussels / Paris (centre and Disneyland Paris), the Alps and Rhone Valley. **ATOC** code **ES**
b) The brandname of the **Class** 373 **Triple Voltage** □ **Trains**.

EUROSTIR
A project funded by the European Commission that aims to accelerate the use of **Friction Stir Welding** (**FSW**) in Europe.

Eutectic Strip
See **Track Continuity Welding**. Also **Zigzag Welding**, **Zigzagging**.

EV
[NR PW] **V**ertical □ **F**lat **B**ottom (**FB**) Full Depth Switches. The E describes the length and Switch Radius.

EVA
See **E**thylene **V**inyl **A**cetate.

EVA Bonded Cork
[PW] A material used for **Rail Pads**. See also **Ethylene Vinyl Acetate** (**EVA**).

Evaluation

Evaluation of Earthworks
See **Earthworks Evaluation**.

Evaluation Set
[Sig.] Within a **Solid State Interlocking** (**SSI**), a labelled block of tests on data variables which may be referenced in any context where a test is valid (but reference and label must be in the same data file). See also **Specials**.

Evaluator Equipment
See **Axle Counter Evaluator** (**ACE**).

EVC
European **V**ital **C**omputer.

Eversholt
a) See **Eversholt Leasing**
b) See **Eversholt Street**.

Eversholt Leasing
(Tradename) A **Rolling Stock Leasing Company** (**ROSCO**) which owns and leases **Passenger Stock** and **Freight** □ **Rolling Stock**. The company is owned by Forward Trust. See also **Angel Train Contracts** (**ATC**) and **Porterbrook Leasing**.

Eversholt Street
Number One Eversholt Street was the home of **Network Rail's** (**NR**) □ **West Coast Route Modernisation** (**WCRM**) project. See also **The Dark Tower**.

EVR
a) **E**arly **V**oluntary **R**edundancy
b) **E**arly **V**oluntary **R**etirement.

Evs
[NR PW] Denotes **113A** □ **F**lat **B**ottom (**FB**) □ **Shallow Depth Switches**, length **E**.

171

EVS
[NR PW] Denotes CEN56E1 □ Flat Bottom (FB) □ Shallow Depth Switches, length E.

EW
[Elec.] **Earth** Wire.

EW&S
(Tradename) The former English Welsh and Scottish Railways (**EWS**). See **DB Schenker Rail (UK) Ltd**.

EWA
[Elec.] **E**arth **W**ire **A**nchor.

EWAT
See **E**mergency **W**eather **A**ction **T**eam.

EWD
Every **W**eek **D**ay.

EWI
[NPT] **E**mergency **W**arning **I**ndicator. See **Emergency Indicator**.

EWID&BJR
[Hist.] The gloriously long-winded **E**ast and **W**est **I**ndia **D**ocks & **B**irmingham **J**unction **R**ailway, which became the North London Railway (**NLR**) after three years. It never reached Birmingham on its own.

EWS
(Tradename) The former **English Welsh and Scottish Railways**. See **DB Schenker Rail (UK) Ltd**.

EWSH
(Tradename) **E**nglish **W**elsh and **S**cottish **H**oldings, see **DB Schenker Rail (UK) Ltd**, **English Welsh and Scottish Railways**.

EWSR
(Tradename) The former **English Welsh and Scottish Railways**. See **DB Schenker Rail (UK) Ltd**.

-ex
As a suffix it indicates that the **Train** is an **Excursion Train** or one-off **Special Train**. See also **Footex, Gricex, Nuttex**.

Examination Frequency
The number of times that an inspection takes place during a period of time. See also **Inspection Interval**.

Examination of Earthworks
See **Earthworks Examination**.

Examination of the Line
Formal regulations for the examination of the **Line**, using a **Locomotive** or a service **Train** running at greatly reduced speed through a **Section** to check the Line for damage, obstructions, animals or trespassers on the line.

Examining Engineer
[Civ.]
a) A person who is competent in the examination, assessment and **Maintenance** of **Structures**
b) [NR] The person responsible for managing examinations of a **Structure** or group of Structures.

Exc.
See **Exclusive**.

Excalibur Screw
[PW LUL] A screw used for mounting **Insulators** on **Wood Sleepers**.

Excavating
a) Using earthmoving equipment to remove **Ballast** and **Spoil** from the **Trackbed**
b) [PW] Using a **Ballast Cleaner** to remove Ballast and Spoil from beneath the **Track** and discard all the removed material (rather than **Screening** the useable fraction out and **Returning** it to the Track).

Exceedance
Exceedence
A localised value that is in excess of a pre-described limit. The term is applied to any measurable value, such as **Cant** (C, E), **Cant Deficiency** (D), **Gauge**, **Overhead Line** □ **Stagger**, Top, Twist.

Exceptional Circumstances
[NR] For the purposes of planning and implementing a **Safe System of Work** (**SSoW**), this is defined as any circumstance where there is a need to undertake work to avoid or reduce risks to people, or significant disruption to train services, which could not foreseeably have been planned in advance in the normal timescales.

Exceptional Load
A load that requires special travel arrangements to be authorised. See **Out Of Gauge** (**OOG**).

Excess Motion
The difference in motion between the driving and driven elements of a mechanism due to clearances between the parts. Commonly found in the normal set-up of **Supplementary Drives**. Previously called **Lost Motion**.

Exchange Siding
a) A **Siding** where **Wagons** bound for a **Private Siding**, private terminal or factory are placed to be collected and returned by an industrial **Locomotive** belonging to the facility
b) A **Siding** used to exchange **Rolling Stock** between two different **Railway Networks**, the Siding being connected to both.

Excl.
Exclusive (Exc.)
[Ops.] A term used to denote that a **Possession** excludes the **Junction** at that end of the Possession. Possession descriptions are Exclusive of the end Junctions unless otherwise noted. The opposite is **Inclusive** (**Inc.**). See also **At**.

Excursion Train
A one-off **Passenger Train** typically taking a selected group of people to a single destination, often a considerable distance away. See also **-ex**, **Special Train**.

Execution Set
[Sig.] Within a **Solid State Interlocking** (**SSI**) a labelled block of arbitrary conditional code which may be referenced in any context where a command is valid (but reference and label must be in the same data file). See also **Specials**.

Exhaust Steam
[TRS] In a **Steam Locomotive**, steam which has been used in the cylinders.

Exit Signal
[Sig.]
a) The **Signal** at the end of a **Route** that has been **Set** by the **Signaller**, particularly on an **Entrance / Exit Panel** (**NX Panel**). See also **Entrance Signal**
b) The **Signal** controlling egress from a **Loop** or **Group of Sidings** onto a **Main Line**, see **Loop Exit Signal**.

Exlo
A **Railway** □ **Telegraph Code** meaning "Exceptional load with speed or route restrictions only. To be signalled by the special **Is Line Clear** □ **Bell Code** 2-1-6" and applied to **Out of Gauge Loads**.

Expansion Gap
[PW] The space provided at an **Expansion Joint** between two adjacent **Rails** in **Jointed Track**, in turn related to the current **Rail Temperature**:

From	To	Gap
< 9°C	10°C	10mm
10°C	23°C	6mm
24°C	38°C	3mm
39°C	> 40°C	0mm

Expansion Joint
[PW] A **Fishplated Rail Joint**, provided with an **Expansion Gap** between the **Rail Ends**, which permits the limited longitudinal movement of the Rail Ends due to thermal forces. A **Fishplated Rail Joint** deliberately arranged without an expansion gap is termed a **Tight Joint** (**TJ**).

Expansion Switch
[PW] Alternative for **Adjustment Switch**. Also **Breather**, **Breather Switch**.

Expectation
[Ops Sig.] The driver's pre-disposition towards certain decisions, based on factors such as **Route Knowledge** and previous experience of the way that the **Signalling System** has previously behaved at that location. Expectation can influence a situation prior to the **Train** reaching a point where the **Signal** can be seen, or with a Signal visible, before a **Less Restrictive Aspect** is displayed. Also **Anticipation**.

Explosive Depth Hardening (EDH)
[PW] A method of improving the wear resistance of **Cast Crossings** by detonating an explosive sheet laid over the **Rail Head** areas. This creates a shock wave that work hardens the **Running Surfaces** of the **Crossing**.

Express
Express Passenger Train
[Ops.] A **Passenger** carrying **Train**, normally running long distances at relatively close to **Permissible Speed** (**PS**) or **Enhanced Permissible Speed** (**EPS**) with few intermediate **Station Stops**. This type of Train is a **Class** 1 Train.

Express Sprinter
British Rail (**BR**) brandname of the **Class** 158 **Diesel Multiple Unit** (**DMU**). See also **Sprinter**, **Super Sprinter**.

Express Train
See **Express**, **Express Passenger Train**.

Extendalino
[Col.] An 11-**Car** □ **Pendolino** (which were originally nine-Car).

Extended Bearers
Extended Timbers
[PW] **Bearers** or **Timbers** that are longer on one side of the **Track**, located at the **Toe** of a **Set of Switches**, allowing **Point Machines** to be fitted. See also **Extended Soleplate**, **Switch Toe Bearers**, **Switch Toe Timbers**.

Extended Soleplate
[PW] A **Soleplate** extended out beyond the **Baseplates** or **Chairs**, to accommodate certain types of **Switch Operating Mechanism**.

Extension Trunk Dialling (ETD)
[Tel.] The technical description for ex-**British Railways** (**BR**) national internal telephone system. Some safety critical locations such as **Signal Boxes** (**SB**) are only accessible telephonically via this internal system.

Extrados
[Civ.] The surface of an **Arch** that has the greatest radius. The opposite (and the surface one can normally observe) is the **Intrados**.

EXV
[TRS] An acronym representing an **Exhibition Vehicle**.

Eye
[Civ.] When describing a ventilation **Shaft** in a **Tunnel**, the Eye is the point of intersection of the Shaft and **Tunnel** arch.

Eye Bolts
[TRS] In the suspension system of some **Wagons**, a suspension element consisting of a loop on one end and threads on the other end. They are used to attach the end of a **Leaf Spring** to a **Scroll Iron**.

Eyeing-in
[Col.] The action of aligning components by comparing their position with two points of known accuracy or in relation to undisturbed areas each side. This method is often used when aligning **Sleepers** prior to laying the **Rails**, as it is quick and eases the later installation of the Rail. See also **Pointing On**.

EZP
a) [CTRL] Engineer's Zones of Protection, a **Possession** system
b) Electro-Zinc Plating.

F

F
a) [NR] As the last letter in a **Wagon** □ **CARKND**, this denotes that the Wagon has **AFI** brakes
b) In an abbreviated **Track Name**, it denotes **Fast**
c) [PW] In the form Fx, Fxx or similar it denotes a type of **Concrete Sleeper**, in this case **Class of Sleeper** F, full depth
d) [NR] As the first letter of a Wagon CARKND, it indicates a flat Wagon
e) See **Switch Letters**
f) [Sig.] On a **Signalling Circuit Diagram**:
- As a prefix, it denotes a flashing supply. See also **S**
- As one of the leading letters of an Equipment Code, it means **Feed**, flashing, **Fog** or **Front Contact** for a **Relay**
- As the last letter of an Equipment Code, it means **Detonator Placers**
g) The letter represented by **Foxtrot** in the **Phonetic Alphabet**
h) Friday
i) As the first letter of a professional membership it means Fellow.

f
[Sig.] On a **Signalling Circuit Diagram**:
- As one of the leading letters of an **Equipment Code**, it means frequency
- As the last letter of an Equipment Code, it means fuse.

F Stock
[LUL] 100 cars of all-steel stock built for the District **Railway** in 1920. After the second world war they were transferred to the Metropolitan **Line** and were replaced by the present **A Stock** in the early 1960s.

F/B
a) See **Flat Bottom Rail**
b) See **Footbridge**.
Also **FB**.

F+F
See **Furrer+Frey**.

F2000
[NR] The current version of **Fault Management System** (**FMS**).

F2N
Felixstowe to Nuneaton.

FA
a) See **Fixed Anchor**
b) Fixed Assets.

Fabric
A **Railway** □ **Telegraph Code** meaning "Must not exceed speed of ... mph at or between ..." and applied to **Out of Gauge Loads**.

Fabricated Common Crossing
[PW] A **Common Crossing** made up of individually machined pieces of **Rail** and bolted or **Multi-groove Locking Pinned** (**MGL Pinned**) together. Also **Built Up Crossing**.

Fabricated Conductor Rail Ramp
A **Conductor Rail Ramp** produced by welding together sections of Rail. See also **Cast Conductor Rail Ramp**.

Fabricated Crossing
See **Fabricated Common Crossing**.

Face Ring
[Civ.] The exposed edge of an **Arch**. See also **Voussoir**.

Facer
[Col.] A term used to describe any **Switch and Crossing Unit** (**S&C Unit**) that occupies a **Facing** position. The opposite is **Trailer**.

FACETS
Fully Automated Customer Enquiry and Travel System.

Facing
Aligned towards **Trains** approaching in the **Normal Direction**. The opposite is **Trailing**. See also **Facing Crossing**, **Facing Crossover**, **Facing Junction**, **Facing Points**, **Facing Switch**.

Facing Crossing
A **Crossing** installed such that traffic normally travels from the **Wing Rail Fronts** to the **Crossing Heel**. The opposite is **Trailing Crossing**.

Facing Crossover
A **Crossover** where the **Switches** are installed in the **Facing** direction in the more important **Track**. Also **Facer**. The opposite is **Trailing Crossover**.

Facing Direction
Direction of travel over a **Set of Switches** (**Set of Points**) in which a vehicle can be directed to one of two or more **diverging routes**.

Facing Junction
In **GEOGIS** terms, a **Junction** between two **Routes** where the Routes diverge in the **Down Direction** of the Route approaching the Junction. Alternatives include **Trailing Junction**, **End-on Junction**.

Facing Movement
A **Train Movement** made through a **Crossover** or **Turnout** in the **Facing Direction**, i.e., moving from **Switch Toe** to **Crossing**. The opposite is **Trailing Movement**.

Facing Point Lock (**FPL**)
[Sig.] A device fitted to a set of **Facing Switches** at the **Front Stretcher Bar** position which positively locks the **Switches** in one setting or the other, totally independently of any other **Switch Operating Mechanism**. Such an arrangement is often incorporated into a **Point Machine**. See also **Economical Facing Point Lock** (**EFPL**).

Facing Point Lock Bar
[Sig. Obs.] A **Depression Bar** arrangement provided to **Lock** a **Set** of **Facing Points** when a **Train** is present.

175

ELLIS' BRITISH RAILWAY ENGINEERING ENCYCLOPÆDIA

Facing Point Lock Test
[Sig.] A test to ensure the **Switch Rail** on the closed side is in its correct position and **Locked** in order for the **Signalling System** to obtain detection. With a 3.5mm gauge inserted between Switch Rail and Stock Rail, the lock should not be able to enter the lock slide in the **Point Machine** or **Facing Point Lock** (**FPL**) so preventing the Signalling System obtaining **Detection**, whereas with a 1.5mm gauge inserted, the **Points** should be able to lock and the Signalling System obtain Detection.

Facing Points
Facing Switch

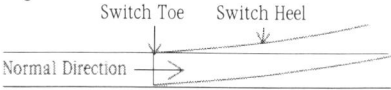

Switch Toe   Switch Heel

Normal Direction →

A **Set of Points** or **Set of Switches** installed so that:
- Two or more **Routes** diverge in the direction of travel
- Traffic travels from **Switch Toe** to **Switch Heel** in the **Normal Direction** of traffic.

Also **Facer**, **Facing**, **Facing Points**. The opposite is **Trailing Switch**.

Factory Acceptance Test (FAT)
[Sig.] The test(s) carried out on the prefabricated control units of a **Signalling System** at the premises of the manufacturer to ensure that the equipment is brought to site functioning correctly. The equivalent in **Permanent Way** (**PW**) is a **Works Inspection**.

Factory Train
[Col.] Description of any **Train** or suite of **On-track Plant** (**OTP**) built to carry out a specific sequence of construction activities.

FADD
[Elec., TRS] Fast-acting **Automatic Dropping Device**.

FADS
Fire Alarm Detection System.

Fag Packet
[Col.] Nickname for the green, white and gold livery used by First Great Western (**FGW**).

Fail Safe
A design principle that requires a failed system to preserve the **Safety of the Line**, particularly applied to **Signalling Systems**. See also **Protected Wrong Side Failure** (**PWSF**), **Right Side Failure** (**RSF**).

Fail to Call (FTC)
[Ops.] Describing a **Train** that has, in error, not made a scheduled stop at a **Station**. See also **Booked Call**.

Failed
[Ops.] Generic description of a broken down **Traction Unit** or **Train**.

Failure to Call (FTC)
See **Fail to Call**.

Fair T
[PW] A variety of **Rail Anchor** for use with **Flat Bottom Rails** (**FB**).

Fair V
[PW] A variety of **Rail Anchor** for use with **Bull Head Rails** (**BH**).

Fairbairn, Sir William
(1789-1874). Scottish **Bridge** and **Locomotive** engineer who invented a revolutionary device for riveting. He worked with **Robert Stephenson** on the Conway and Menai Bridges on the Chester & Holyhead **Railway**, later concentrating on shipbuilding.

Fairmont Tamper
(Tradename) A manufacturer of **On-track Plant** which merged with Pandrol Jackson to become Harsco Track Technologies.

Falcon
a) A **Railway** □ **Telegraph Code** meaning "No trace of receiving the following"
b) A **Telecommunications** Fault Control database
c) [NR] CARKND JNA, a **Bogie** □ **Open Wagon** used primarily to transport new **Ballast** to **Engineering Work Sites** or **Spoil** from Work Sites. They have a 64t capacity and a **Tare Weight** of 26t.

Fall
The gradient of any construction intended to ease the passage of water, such as a channel, ditch, **Formation** surface, roof or **Track Drain**. See **Crossfall**, **Slope of Formation**, **Track Drain**.

Falling Latch
[TRS] Part of a door lock assembly used to secure the **Locking Hook** in order to lock the door.

Falling Snow
See **In Fog and Rain**.

Falling Weight Deflectometer (FWD)
A method for assessing the stiffness of a **Formation** without excavation. A weight is allowed to fall onto the **Sleeper** from a controlled height, and the transient deflection of the Sleeper and **Ballast** under this blow is accurately measured. Since the behaviour of the Ballast layer is relatively consistent, the stiffness of the underlying layer can be deduced. This data is then used to determine the work required to bring the **Formation Stiffness** to the required value.

Fallopia Japonica
Japanese Knotweed. See **Invasive Species**.

False Clear
[Sig.] An incorrect **Track Circuit** (**TC**) indication, when the Track Circuit shows **Clear**, but a **Train** is present on the **Track** at that location.

False Feed
An unintentional connection between two circuits that results in the erroneous operation of one or both. See **Clapham Accident**.

False Flange
[TRS] A situation where a **Rail Wheel** has two **Flanges**, the second caused by excessive wear on the Wheel by the **Rail**. This condition can cause damage to **Crossings** if left untreated. See also **Bulgarian Wheels**.

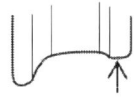

FAMS
Fleet Asset Management System.

Fan
A **Group of Sidings** or the connections to such a Group.
Fang Bolt
Fang Washer
[PW WR] An aid to securing a **Chair** to a **Bearer** or **Sleeper**. The Washer has spikes that grip the wood and projections on the face opposite the spikes A Bolt is passed through the Washer and the wood and is a nut used to secure the item.
FAPB
Fully Automatic Push Button.
FAR
Freight Acceptance Route.
Faregate
Part of an **Automatic Fare Collection** (**AFC**) system, placed at **Station** entrances and exits to regulate access by reading tickets inserted by **Passengers**. See also **Ticket Line**.
Fassetta
(Tradename) A manufacturer of **Railway** plant, including **Emergency Clamp Fishplates** and **Panel Lifting Equipment**.
FAST
(*fast*)
a) Functional Analysis Systems Technique
b) Factory Acceptance System Testing
c) Facility for Accelerated Service Testing
Fast (F)
a) On a **Route** with four or more **Tracks**, the more important pair will often be titled the **Up Fast** (**UF**) and **Down Fast** (**DF**). These may not be any faster than the **Slow Lines**. See also **Main**, **Quick**
b) Describing a **Train** that makes no **Station Stops**, used as an alternative to **Express** when describing **Commuter** services. See also **All Stations**, **Parliamentary**, **Semi-fast**.
Fast Line
Normally describing the **Track** or Tracks with the highest **Permissible Speed** (**PS**) in **Multiple Track Railways**. Sometimes also used to describe the most important Tracks in a layout where all Tracks are the same speed. See **Down Fast**, **Up Fast**. See also **Quick**.
Fast Track GRIP
[NR Obs.] A programme aimed at reducing the length of time spent examining smaller schemes at the early stages of the **Governance for Railway Investment Projects** (**GRIP**), whilst minimising the additional risk introduced. Also **Accelerated GRIP**.
Fastclip
(Tradename) [PW] A **Rail Fastening** system manufactured by **Pandrol**. It is a spring clip system that allows a **Sleeper** to be supplied complete with **Rail Pads**, **Clips** and **Rail Foot Insulators** already installed. It is specifically aimed at fully mechanised **Track Relaying Train** (**TRT**) systems.
Fasten Down
Fasten Up
See **Fastening Down**, **Fastening Up**.

Fastening
See **Rail Fastening**.
Fastening Down
Fastening Up
[PW] The action of fitting **Rail Fastenings** to secure the **Rail** to **Baseplates**, **Bearers** or **Sleepers**.
FAT
(*fat*)
a) See **Factory Acceptance Test**
b) Fully Automatic Train.
Fatalities and Weighted Injuries (FWI)
A concept used by the **Railway Industry** when recording safety performance or comparing risk: one fatality is deemed equivalent to ten major injuries, or to 200 minor injuries.
Fatality
Generic term for a death on **Railway** property. These generally fall into four categories:
- Staff, including **Trackworkers** and **Traincrew**
- Passengers
- Trespassers
- Suicides (though it is arguable that this is often an outcome of the previous category).
FATCOWS
(*fat-cows*) [Obs.] Fixed Automatic Track Circuit Operated Warning System. The former and less polite name for **the Train Operated Warning System** (**TOWS**).
Fatigue
a) Progressive, localised damage that occurs when a material is subjected to frequent, repeated loading. See **Fatigue Crack**
b) Progressive impairment of cognitive functions caused by lack of rest, disruption to sleeping patterns, poor environment and repetition of tasks. See **Fatigue Index** (**FI**).
Fatigue Crack
[PW] A crack in a **Rail** caused by repeated bending or compression / tension cycles. The rate of propagation of such cracks can be accelerated by work hardening of the section, and they are therefore prevalent in the **Rail Head**. See also **Rail Defect**.
Fatigue Failure
The failure of an item by fracture under repeated loads which are of a magnitude which would not normally have caused the item to fail by overloading.

ELLIS' BRITISH RAILWAY ENGINEERING ENCYCLOPÆDIA

Fatigue Index (FI)
The Fatigue Index was developed by the Centre for Human Sciences at the Defence Evaluation and Research Agency (now known as QinetiQ). It was designed to assess the short-term daily **Fatigue** and cumulative Fatigue risks associated with shift work. The FI is based on the five main factors known to have an impact on Fatigue:
- time of day
- shift duration
- rest periods
- breaks within a shift
- cumulative fatigue.

For each component a scoring system operates.

FATWS
Fixed Automatic Train Warning System (ATWS), A permanent installation of ATWS provided at locations where **work on or Near the Line** is carried out regularly.

Fault and Operations Control
[NR] An office from which control is exercised over the operation of the **Railway** in a designated area and to which all **Infrastructure** faults and failures in that area are reported to enable a response to be made.

Fault Control
An office to which all **Railway** ▫ **Infrastructure** faults and failures in an area are reported to enable a response to be made.

Fault Management System (FMS)
[NR] The replacement for **FRAME**, a computer system used to log and manage **Track** and **Signalling** faults. The current version is also known as F2000. FMS Local is the end user application.

FB
a) See Flat Bottom Rail
b) See Footbridge.
Also F/B.

FBAR
See Fixed Block Automatic Routing.

FBI
See Flat Bottom ▫ Inclined.

FBIS

FBMIS
[NR] Finance and Business (Management) Information System.

FBN
Fixed Bearer Network.

FBR Co.
[Hist.] The Pre-Grouping Forth Bridge Railway Company. This Company avoided the 1923 Grouping and remained independent until the Nationalisation of the Railways in 1948.

FBS
[Sig.] Fringe Box Subsystem.

FBW
See Flash Butt Weld.

FC
a) See Flat Crossing
b) The ATOC code for First Capital Connect.

FCAW
Flux-cored Arc Welding.

FCC
See First Capital Connect.

FCDO
[LUL] Front Door Cut Out.

FCFS
See First Come First Served.

FCOV
Flow Cut Off Valve.

FCP
a) Field Communications Processor
b) Forward Capacity Plan.

FCU
Field Control Unit.

FDA
The CARKND representing a **Track Panel** carrier **Wagon**.

FDC
a) See Fire Detection Controller
b) Field Device Controller.

FDCS
Field Data Collection System.

FDDI
Fibre Distributed Data Interface.

FDM
a) See Frequency Division Multiplex
b) Freight Delivery Metric.

FDM-NV
Frequency Division Multiplex - Non-vital.

FDS
Functional Design Specification.

FE
a) See First Engineering
b) Finite Elements
c) Foundation Electronics.

FEA
[NR] The CARKND representing a **Wagon** used to carry plant for the **Track Relaying Train** (TRT).

Feasibility Study
The first stage in scheme development, during which the problem is identified, options evolved and evaluated and budget costs are calculated. It is normal to select one of these options as a **Preferred Option** to go forward to the **Detailed Feasibility** stage. See also **Governance for Railway Investment Projects** (GRIP).

Feather
[Sig. Col.] Term for a **Junction Direction Indicator** (JDI), see Junction Indicator (JI).

FEBIS
Freight European Brake and Information System.

FED
See Fixed Earthing Device.

Feed
[Sig.] The end of a conventional **Track Circuit** (TC) that sources the current to the **Rails**. The opposite end of the circuit is the **Relay** end.

178

Feeder
[Elec. Col.] Contraction of **Feeder Station** (**FS**) A conductor carrying Traction Supply Current from a Feeder Station to the Overhead Line Equipment (**OLE**) or **Conductor Rail**. See also **Aerial Feeder**, **Bare Feeder**.

Feeder Station (FS)
[Elec.] An installation of **Circuit Breakers** (**CB**) and **Transformers**, where the national grid supply is connected to the **Railway** □ **Traction Power** system.

Feeder Switch
[Elec.] An electrical switch mounted on an **Overhead Line Structure** that allows an **Electrical Section** to be connected to its **Feeder**.

Feedwater
[TRS] Clean water that is fed into a **Boiler**. See **Steam Locomotive**.

Felis silvestris catus
See **Cat**.

Fell Centre Rail System

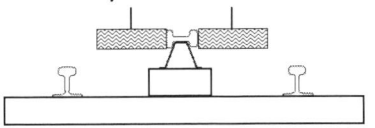

An additional **Rail** mounted horizontally along the longitudinal centre line of the **Track**, normally above the level of the **Running Rails**. Lateral **Driving Wheels** and brake shoes bear on this additional Rail to provide traction and braking. Invented by John Barraclough Fell in 1863 and first tested adjacent to the Cromford and High Peak **Railway**. The only location the system is still used is on the Snaefell Mountain **Railway** on the Isle of Man.

FEMC
Fire & Emergency Management Centre.

Fence
a) See **Back of Platform Fence**
b) See **Fenced**
c) See **Lineside Fencing**
d) See **Post and Wire Fence**
e) See **Railway Boundary**.

Fenced
[NR] The new term replacing **Fenced Green Zone**. It describes an arrangement under which the staff are **Working** separated from **Adjacent Lines** open to **Train Movements** by a rigid barrier, fence, plastic netting or barricade tape. The term **Green Zone** is also obsolete.

Fenced Green Zone
[NR Obs.] See **Fenced**.

Feng
[Col.] Shorthand for First Engineering.

Fennel Report
Fully titled "Investigation into the King's Cross Underground Fire", the report into the disastrous escalator fire at King's Cross London Underground station in 1987. It was written by Desmond Fennell (OBE QC). The report made 157 recommendations. See **King's Cross Accident**.

Ferret and Dartboard
[Col.] Derogatory nickname for the second **British Rail** (**BR**) emblem, introduced in 1956 and featuring a lion rampant holding a wheel. The wheel element has a passing resemblance to a dartboard, from a distance.

Ferrule
(*feh-rul*) [PW] A tapered (formerly hardwood) polypropylene or nylon sleeve fitted into the oversize screw holes in **Chairs** and **Baseplates**, through which the **Chairscrews** pass, so as to accommodate variations in hole and screw dimensions. They are almost universally badly fitted. See **Ferrule Cup**. Also **Bush**.

Ferrule Cup
(*feh-rul kup*) [PW] A device designed to accurately place **Ferrules** in **Chairs** and **Baseplates**. It is sadly rarely used, resulting in damaged, broken and ineffective Ferrules caused by overdriving of the **Chairscrew**.

FETRD
First Engineering Track Renewals Division.

Fettling
[PW Col.] To make small manual adjustments to the **Track**, particularly applied to weekday work following weekend **Relaying** and **Reballasting** operations.

FEU
Forty-foot Equivalent Unit, a size description of shipping **Containers**.

FFCCTV
Forward Facing Closed Circuit Television.

FFF
[Sig.] First Filament Failure. The failure of the first filament of a double filament **Signal Lamp**.

FFFIS
Form Fit and Functional Interface Specification.

FFG
Freight Facilities Grant.

FFM
Few Fare Machine; a **Ticket** vending machine (**TVM**) which can dispense Tickets for up to ten different destinations.

FFS
Ferrovie Federali Svizzere, see **SBB**.

FFT
Functional Fault Tree.

FGE
(Tradename) First Great Eastern, a **Train Operating Company** (**TOC**).

FGL
Finished Ground Level.

FGW
See **First Great Western**, a Train Operating Company (TOC).

FHD
For Home Depot.

FHH
See **Freightliner Heavy Haul**.

FI
See **Fatigue Index**.

Fibre Optic Banner Repeating Signal
[Sig.] A **Banner Repeating Signal** using two **Signal Lamps** and an arrangement of optical fibres to display the **Aspect**, rather than one Signal Lamp and a moveable bar. See also **Tri-state Banner**.

Fibre Optic Route Indicator (FORI)
[Sig.] A **Standard Alphanumeric Route Indicator** (**SARI**) which uses **Fibre Optics**.

Fibre Optic Signal
[Sig.] A type of **Colour Light Signal** which uses fibre optics to combine **Red, Yellow** and **Green** □ **Aspects** in one aperture. The term also applies to **Banner Repeater Signals** and **Position Light Signals** (**PLS**) using this technology.

Fibre-Optic Indicator
[Sig.] An **Indicator** which uses optical fibres to provide the required illuminated indication. Uses include **Standard Alphanumeric Route Indicators** (**SARI**), **Miniature Alphanumeric Route Indicators** (**MARI**), **Close Doors** (**CD**) Indicators, **Right Away** (**RA**) Indicators and **Off Indicators**.

FIBU
Fifty hertz **B**ooster **U**nit.

FIC
Field **I**njection **C**ontactor.

FICE
Fellow of the **I**nstitution of **C**ivil **E**ngineers.

Fiddle Back
a) [LUL] A section of the **Fourth Rail** that has had the **Rail Foot** and part of the **Rail Web** removed over a short length, allowing **Stretcher Bars** to pass freely beneath
b) [PW] A contraction of **Fiddle Back Crossing**, See **Saddle Crossing**.

Fiddle Back Crossing
See **Saddle Crossing**.

Field Corner
[PW Col.] The corner of the **Rail Head** furthest away from the **Fourfoot**. Also **Back Edge Corner**.

Field Engineer
[LUL] An engineer who is designated to act as the **Tube Lines** company representative.

Field Face
[PW Col.] An alternative term for **Back Edge** (BE), **Outside Edge** (OE).

Field Flow
[PW] **Rolling Contact Fatigue** (**RCF**) occurring in the **Rail Head** within 10mm of the **Outside Edge** (OE).

Field Side
(Sth.) Describing the side of a **Line** or **Track** nearest the **Cess**, and so nearest the fields.

Filler Beam Deck
[Civ.] A steel and concrete **Bridge Floor** arrangement comprising transverse spanning steel sections encased within and acting compositely with a concrete slab.

Fillet Radius
[PW] The radius of the **Rail Section** between the **Fishing Surfaces** and the **Rail Web**. See **Lower Fillet Radius, Upper Fillet Radius**.

Filling-in Rail
[PW] A type of **Closure Rail** used in **Switch and Crossing Units** (**S&C Units**) fitted with **Check Lumps**.

Final Decision Point
The final point at which a **Level Crossing** user can safely wait, **Clear** of the **Line**, before deciding to cross.

Final Drive
Final Drive Gearbox
[TRS]
a) The last device or mechanism that transmits torque from and engine or gearbox, through an angle of 90°, to a **Powered Axle**
b) A gearbox mounted on a **Powered Axle** which transmits torque from a **Traction Motor** through to the axle.

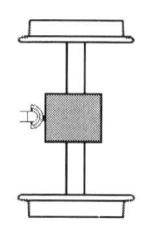

Fine Point (FP)
[PW Hist.] An alternative term for **the Intersection of Gauge Lines** (**IP**) in a **Crossing**. See also **Crossing Nose** (**XN**).

FIO
For **I**nformation **O**nly.

FIP
Field **I**ndications **P**anel.

Fire and Emergency Management Centre
[CT] A control room in the fire and rescue service's facilities within the **Eurotunnel** □ **Concession**.

Fire Detection Controller (FDC)
[CT] The controller in the **Railway Control Centre** (**RCC**) of the **Channel Tunnel**, responsible for monitoring the smoke, fire and ionised gas detection equipment.

Fire Precautions (Sub-surface Railway Stations) Regulations 1989
(Now replaced by the Fire Precautions (Sub-surface Railway Stations) Regulations 2009), the legislation that defines which **Stations** are **Sub-surface Stations** and what special precautions must be taken in those Stations. See also **Kings Cross Accident**.

Firebox
a) [Col.] Term for the metal ducting used to protect cables between a **Cable Trough** and the underside of a **Location Case Platform**
b) [TRS] In a **Steam Locomotive**, a cavity within the **Boiler** in which the fire is lit and maintained.

Firehole
Firehole Door
[TRS] The opening at the rear of a **Boiler** through which fuel is fed into the **Firebox**, the fire is inspected, additional air is introduced into the Firebox, and the door which seals it when required. See also **Steam Locomotive**.

Firelamps
[Hist.] A marker light fitted to a set on a rope-worked **Railway** comprising iron baskets filled with a coal fire and hooked onto the handrail of a **Wagon**.

Fireless Locomotive
[TRS] A variety of **Steam Locomotive** that does not have a boiler. The steam is stored in a pressure vessel on the **Locomotive** until used. Such Locomotives must return to their supplying point at regular intervals to re-charge the steam reservoir. They have particular advantages in explosive atmospheres and other high risk areas.

Fireman
[Ops.] The person responsible for keeping a **Steam Locomotive** supplied with coal and water during a journey, and assisting in the observation of **Signals** when required to do so.

Fireman's call box
[Sig. Obs.] A **Plunger** and indicator provided at ground level close to the place where a **Locomotive** would come to a stand at a **Signal** showing a **Stop Aspect**. At locations where the **Fireman** would normally be required to carry out the provisions of **Rule 55**, the provision of the call box obviated the need for the Fireman either to have to walk a considerable distance to the **Controlling Signal Box** or to cross a complex layout of **Tracks**. Operation of the plunger caused a disc to be released from the appropriate **Block Instrument** in the **Signal Box** to bring the presence of a standing **Locomotive** to the attention of the **Signaller**.

Fire-resistant Blanket
A non-flammable woven material that can protect flammable items from a source of ignition, such as an electrical arc. The material can also be used to smother a burning material.

FIRO
Fellow of the Institute of Railway Operators.

FIRSE
Fellow of the Institute of Railway Signal Engineers.

First Capital Connect (FCC)
A **Train Operating Company** (**TOC**) which operates services on the **Thameslink** □ **Route** between Bedford and Brighton via central London, and the Sutton and Wimbledon Loop.

First Caution
[Sig.] A **Signal** or **Caution Aspect** which gives the driver their first warning of an impending **Stop Aspect**. See also **Preliminary Caution Aspect**.

First Class
The most comfortable **Passenger** accommodation available on **Trains** in Britain. The various **Train Operating Companies** (**TOC**) choose to add variations to this rule, e.g. Club Class. The next level down is **Standard Class**. See **Passenger Class**. See also **Third Class**.

First Come First Served (FCFS)
[LUL] An automatic **Junction Mode** in which the **Signalling Equipment** relies on information received from the **Positive Train Identification** (**PTI**) equipment to direct **Trains**. No account is taken of the **Timetable** and Trains are passed in the order in which they reach a **Junction**.

First Engineering (FE, Feng)
(Tradename) A management buy-out company formed at **Privatisation** from the Scottish **IMU** and **TRU**. Now part of Babcock Rail.

First Generation Diesel Multiple Unit (DMU)
[TRS] The DMUs built by **British Rail** (**BR**) between 1956 and 1963, **Classes** 100 to 131 inclusive. These were typically **Diesel Mechanical Multiple Units** (**DMMU**) though some were **Diesel Hydraulic Multiple Units** (**DHMU**). See also **Second Generation Diesel Multiple Unit** (**DMU**).

First Great Western (FGW)
(Tradename) A **Train Operating Company** (**TOC**) which operates **Fast** services between London Paddington, South Wales, the Cotswolds and the West Country.

First Line of Response (FLOR)
[CT] In the **Channel Tunnel**, a team of fire and rescue staff based at each of the fire stations within the **Concession** at Cheriton or Coquelles. One is on patrol in the **Service Tunnel** at any time.

First Permanent Way Stretcher Bar
[PW] The **Permanent Way** □ **Stretcher Bar** nearest to the **Switch Toe**. The Permanent Way Stretcher Bars form a fixed connection between the **Switch Rails**, transferring the motion of one to the other. If fitted, the other Permanent Way Stretcher Bars are numbered counting up from the Switch Toe, the one located at the Switch Toe being No.1. See also **First Signalling Stretcher Bar**, **Lock Stretcher Bar**.

First Signalling Stretcher Bar
[Sig.] The **Signalling** □ **Stretcher Bar** nearest the **Switch Toe**. The Signalling Stretcher Bars are used only to detect the position of the **Switch Rails**. If fitted, the other Signalling Stretcher Bars are numbered counting up from the Switch Toe, the one located at the Switch Toe being No.1. See also **First Permanent Way Stretcher Bar**, **Lock Stretcher Bar**.

First Stretcher Bar
An alternative for **Front Stretcher Bar**.

First Train Moving Away
[Sig.] A standard **Signalling Control** that can be employed in a number of situations. Essentially, the **Train Detection System** (be it **Track Circuits** (**TC**) or **Axle Counters**) is used to prove that the **Train** ahead of a second **Train** is moving away from the latter. Other applications include the early setting of routes in complex **Junction** areas. Also **Route Away**, **Tunnel Controls**.

First TransPennine Express (TPE)
(Tradename) A **Train Operating Company** (**TOC**) which operates predominantly long-distance inter-urban services linking major centres of population across both North East and North West England.

First Wheel Replacement (FWR)
[Sig.] A **Control** that **Replaces** a **Signal** to the **Most Restrictive Aspect** as soon as the first wheel of the **Train** passes the **Insulated Rail Joint (IRJ)** immediately **Beyond** the Signal (the Replacement Joint). See also **Last Wheel Replacement (LWR)**.

FIS
a) Functional Interface Specification
b) Fault Isolating Switch.

Fish Bellied Rail
Fish Belly Rail

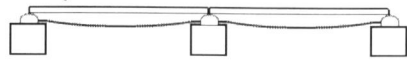

[PW Obs.] An early pattern of short, cast iron **Rails** that had a curved lower edge to give a deeper section in the middle of the Rail.

Fish Dock
[Obs.] A **Platform** used for transferring fish to and from special **Rail Vehicles**. Fish are no longer transported in this manner in Britain.

Fish Plate
See **Fishplate**.

Fishbolt
[PW] A bolt for fixing a **Fishplate**, sometimes made with a pear shaped shank immediately under the head which engages in the appropriately machined or punched hole in the Fishplate, to prevent rotation of the Fishbolt during assembly.

Fishbolt Hole
[PW] A hole drilled in the **Rail Web** at a **Rail End** for a **Fishbolt**.

Fishbolt Insulations
[PW] Electrically non-conducting tubes fitted to **Fishbolts** in some types of **Insulated Rail Joint (IRJ)** to prevent electrical contact between Bolt and **Rail**, and so avoid a conductive path. Also **Sleeves**.

Fishbolt Spanner
[PW] A long handled (around 1.2m or 4 feet long) spanner specifically designed for use on **Fishbolt** nuts, but also finding use on other nuts of the same dimensions. See also **Running-on Spanner**.

Fished End
[PW] A **Rail End** having holes drilled in it to take **Fishbolts**. See also **DBE, DOE, Fishplated Rail Joint**.

Fished Joint
[PW Col.] Common shortening of **Fishplated Rail Joint**. An alternative is **Welded Joint**.

Fishing
[PW]
a) Connecting two **Rails** together using a **Fishplated Rail Joint**
b) A method of **Gauging** a **Structure** over a **Railway** by taking measurements from a number of selected points on the Structure to each **Running Edge (RE)**. See **Pole and Tape**.

Fishing Angle
[PW] The angle of inclination to the horizontal of the **Upper Fishing Surface** and **Lower Fishing Surface** of both **Rail** and **Fishplate**.

Fishing Plane
[PW] An alternative to **Fishing Surface**.

Fishing Surface
[PW] The flat areas on the **Rail Foot** adjacent to the **Ankle** and underside of the **Rail Head** where a correctly installed **Fishplate** contacts. See also **Bull Head Rail (BH), Flat Bottom Rail (FB), Lower Fishing Surface, Upper Fishing Surface**.

Fishkind
[Col.] A term describing the use of the names of fish (as well as many other sea-dwelling creatures, both mythical and real) for **Engineering Vehicles** (**Wagons**). Dating from the use of such code names for Wagons in the days of telegraph, the practice has been continued for simplicity. See **CARKND, Wagon Names**.

Fishplate
[PW] Specially rolled or forged steel plates used in pairs to join two **Rails** at a **Fishplated Rail Joint**. Two, four or six **Fishbolts** are used through the Fishplates and **Rail Ends** to secure the Fishplates to the Rail Ends. There are many possible origins for the name:
• From the Old French "fiche", meaning peg, combined with "plate"; literally a peg-plate,
• From the fish-like shape of early fishplates,
• According to John Wolfe Barry, from the nautical practice of "fishing", meaning to splint a broken mast.
See **Cranked Fishplate, Deep Skirted Fishplate, Emergency Clamp Fishplate, Encapsulated Fishplate, Insulated Fishplate, Jump Fishplate, Junction Lift Fishplate, Junction Fishplate, Lift Fishplate, Skirted Fishplate, Stepped Fishplate, Straight Fishplate, Tight Joint Fishplate**. See also **William Bridges Adams**.

Fishplate Bond
[Sig.] A **Bond** provided at a **Fishplated Rail Joint** to ensure electrical continuity for **Track Circuits (TC)**.

Fishplate Hole
A round hole drilled (or pear shaped hole punched) in a **Fishplate** and designed to take a **Fishbolt**.

Fishplate Insulations
[PW] Electrically non-conducting pre-formed liners used to separate **Fishplate** from **Rail** at an **Insulated Rail Joint (IRJ)**. Also **Shells, Liners**.

Fishplate Limits
[PW] That part of a **Rail End** normally covered by a **Fishplate**. The term has special significance in relation to **Rail Defects**.

Fishplate Shims
[PW] Specially shaped metal sections used between **Fishplate** and **Rail** to remove any vertical play in the joint caused by wear under traffic.

Fishplated Rail Joint

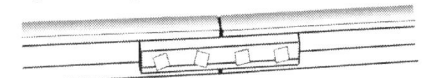

[PW] A mechanical joint between two **Rails** made by means of **Fishplates** and **Fishbolts**. Also **Expansion Joint, Fished Joint, Ordinary Joint, Plated Joint, Tight Joint**.

FIST
[PW Obs.] A type of **Rail Fastening**, designed in Sweden. Used with the **F22 Concrete Sleeper** in the 1960s in the UK and then abandoned.

FIT
Field **I**njection **T**ransformer.

Fit For Traffic
A phrase describing a section of **Line** that is in an acceptable condition for the passage of **Trains**, e.g.:
- The **Sleepers** are present and sufficiently sound, the **Rails** are of adequate **Rail Section** and **Fastened Down** correctly, and there are sufficient correctly fitted and inspected **Fishplates**, **Fishbolts** and **Welds** (if required)
- There is sufficient **Ballast** around and under the Sleepers
- The **Signalling System** is operating normally, or an approved alternative arrangement has been provided
- The **Overhead Line Equipment (OLE)** (if provided) is correctly aligned, functional and energised. See also **Blocked to Electric Traction (BTET)**
- The **Conductor Rail (Third Rail)** and **Negative Rail (Fourth Rail)** (if provided) are correctly aligned, fastened and energised
- There are no **Twist Faults** outside specified limits
- The clearances to adjacent **Structures** are acceptable
- All **Structures** such as **Bridges** and **Viaducts** supporting the **Railway** are in a suitable condition
- There are no **Obstructions** on the Line
- The Track is aligned and consolidated sufficiently to support the **Permissible Speed (PS)**, **Enhanced Permissible Speed (EPS)**, **Emergency Speed Restriction (ESR)** or **Temporary Speed Restriction (TSR)** in force
- All plant and equipment has been moved clear
- All **Protection** measures related to any relevant **Possession** have been correctly removed.

Fitted
a) [TRS] Describing a **Rail Vehicle** that has some kind of **Automatic Brake** facility provided which acts on the wheels. The opposite is **Unfitted**
b) [Sig.] A term used to describe the presence and use of a particular type of **Signalling System** or **Signalling Equipment**, as in "The **Line** is **AWS** Fitted".

Fitter
[Col.] A **Maintenance** technician.

Fittings
[PW Hist.] An alternative for **Switch and Crossing Units (S&C Units)**, irrespective of **Layout**.

FIU
Failure **I**ndication **U**nit.

Five Bar Gate
See **Gate**.

Five Foot
[NIR, IÉ] See **Fivefoot**.

Five Mile Line Diagram
Five Mile Plan
[NR] A type straight-line diagram showing (generally) a five-mile long section of a particular **Engineer's Line Reference (ELR)** on **Network Rail Controlled Infrastructure (NRCI)**. They show the location of **Junctions**, **Stations**, **Level Crossings**, access points, **Signals** and **Bridges**. They may also include details of curve radii, **Permissible Speed (PS)** and **Point Numbers**.

Fivefoot
[NIR, IÉ] The area between **Running Edges (RE)** of a related pair of **Running Rails** and analogous to the **Fourfoot**. Also **5 Foot**.

Fixed Anchor (FA)
[Elec.] A termination of the **Overhead Line Equipment** □ **Catenary** that is fixed rather than being tensioned.

Fixed Balise
[Sig.] A **Balise** that contains data which does not vary according to the **Route** □ **Set** or the **Aspect** displayed by a **Signal**.

Fixed Block
[Sig.] Any system of **Signalling** which uses **Block Sections** that have fixed limits under all circumstances, e.g. between **Fixed Signals**. The alternatives are **Moving Block** (where the limits of the Block Sections move with the **Trains**) and **Permissive Working** (where the conventions of the Block Section are not observed).

Fixed Block Automatic Routing (FBAR)
[LUL] A type of **Automatic Train Control (ATC)** as used on the Jubilee Line Extension (JLE).

Fixed Buffer Stop
A **Buffer Stop** with no moving parts and which is itself firmly fixed. Also **Bent Rail Buffer Stop**. See also **Base Rail**.

Fixed Diamond

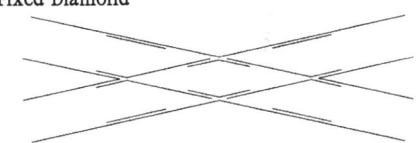

[PW] A **Diamond Crossing** with no movable **Rails**, used where the angle of intersection is greater than 1 in 7½ (e.g. 1 in 6). For smaller angles (e.g. 1 in 9) a **Switch Diamond (SD)** is used.

Fixed Distant
Fixed Distant Signal
[Sig.] A **Distant Signal** only capable of displaying a **Caution Aspect**. See also **Distant Board**.

Fixed Distant Board
See **Distant Board**.

Fixed Earthing Device (FED)
[Elec.] A switch, permanently installed in **a Traction System**, which can be used instead of **Manually Applied Earths** to Earth the system. They can be manual or controlled remotely by the **Electrical Controller**.

Fixed Engine
[Hist.] A power source, either steam or water powered installed at the top of an Inclined Plane to haul (usually) Wagons up the plane; an engine not designed to do anything other than act as a winding engine.

Fixed Equipment
Apparatus used in vital functions within the Railway operation, but excluding movable items such as Locomotives, Rolling Stock, Trains, etc. See also Shore.

Fixed Geometry Railway
A term used to describe a line on which all Tamping work returns the Track to its original design location by reference to fixed survey points. See also Relative Track Geometry.

Fixed Infrastructure
Infrastructure that is not movable, e.g. Bridges, coastal or river defences, Culverts, Cuttings, drainage, Embankments, Platforms, Retaining Walls and Tunnels.

Fixed PeeWee
[BR Obs.] A version of PeeWee where the normally temporary cabling is laid in permanently and installed between fixed sockets placed at 200m (220 Yard) intervals.

Fixed Red
Fixed Red Signal
[Sig.] A Signal which permanently exhibits a Red □ Stop Aspect.

Fixed Short Circuiting Device
A fixed electrical switch or other similar Short Circuiting Device (SCD) used in Conductor Rail systems.

Fixed Signals
[Sig.] Signals which are permanently placed, the alternative being Temporary Signals such as Hand Signals and Flags, or In-cab Signals.

Fixed Tension (FT)
Fixed Tension System (FTS)
Fixed Termination (FT)
Fixed Termination Equipment (FT Equipment)
Fixed Termination System (FTS)
[Elec.] An arrangement of an Overhead Line Electrification (OLE) system where the Conductors are tensioned to a particular force value and then secured. This method has the significant disadvantage over long Wire Runs of producing sagging at higher temperatures, and so the system is only used below 60mph. This restriction is eliminated using an Automatically Tensioned System (AT System, ATS).

Fixed-type Switch
[PW, Arch.] A design of Switch in which both of the Turnout Rails and the Switch Front □ Rail terminate at a cast iron bed plate which supports a cast iron bar which is placed manually according to the direction the Traffic passing over the Switch is required to take. All three Rail ends have a V-shaped notch into which the cast iron bar, each end of which is V-shaped, locates. Designed for use in the Narrow Gauge (578mm) slate quarry lines of North Wales. See also Non-nose Common Crossing..

FJA
The CARKND representing a Super Tench □ Wagon.

FK
[TRS] An acronym representing a Corridor □ First Class □ Coach.

FL
FL95
See Freightliner.

Flag Memory
[Sig.] Within a Solid State Interlocking (SSI), 128 bytes of Random Access Memory (RAM) are allocated to flags (single-bit variables). Flags include Sub-Routes and Sub-Overlaps, whose states may be Locked or Free, and general purpose latches.

Flagging
[Sig.] To operate a section of Line using Handsignallers and Flags. Generally used in times of Signal failure or during Engineering work.

Flagman
Colloquial alternative for a Handsignaller.

Flags
Cloth banners used to convey particular meanings:
- Red - stop.
- Yellow - caution
- Green - proceed
- Blue and white checks - this is used by an Advance Lookout to warn the Site Lookout that a Train is approaching.

Flake
a) To lay a rope or cable in loose coils in order to prevent it tangling
b) To unwind a cable from a drum neatly (see clause a)) in order to pass the cable through an aperture smaller than the drum it came on.

Flakiness Index
[PW] A measure of the liability of Ballast to break up under the effect of normal Traffic loading.

Flaking
a) [PW] A Rail Defect in which the Running Surface breaks away from the rest of the Rail in flakes.
b) To unwind cable from a drum and lay it in loose coils.

Flame Cut
Flame Cut Rail
[PW] A cut made through a **Rail** using a cutting torch, typically oxy-propane, rather than a **Disc Saw** or **Rail Saw**. **Fishbolt Holes**, **Flares** and permanent **Rail Ends** made by Flame Cutting are not permitted in **Running Rails**. Rail Ends cut by this method are permitted provided they are to form part of an **Alumino-thermic Weld** within 24 hours of the cut being made. Also **Gas Cut**. Cutting torches themselves are also known as **Gas Axes**.

Flanch
[Hist.] Alternative spelling of **Flange**, in use in the 19th century.

Flange
a) [TRS] The extended portion of a **Rail Wheel** that provides it with directional guidance. Also **Wheel Flange**, **Wheel Profile**
b) [PW] An alternative for **Rail Foot**.

Flange Angle
[TRS] The designed angle of the face of the **Wheel Flange** nearest the **Rail**, measured from a line normal to the centreline of the axle. For **Rail Wheels** used on **Network Rail** □ **Lines** this is mandated as 68° to 70° or 60° for the P1 Profile. See **Wheel Profile**.

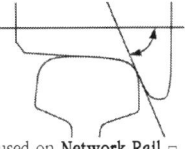

Flange Back
The "inner" face of the **Wheel Flange**, the one furthest from the **Rail**. See **Wheel Profile**.

Flange Back Blend
[TRS] The curved section of the **Wheel Profile** located between the **Flange Back** and **Flange Tip**. It has a minimum Radius of 10mm, 12.7mm for the **P1 Profile**.

Flange Back Clearance
[PW] The dimension between the back of a **Rail Wheel** and the back of an **Open Switch**. This must be positive to allow the wheel to pass without contact. See also **Free Wheel Clearance** (FWC).

Flange Climb
A fault condition in which the lateral force exerted on a **Rail Wheel** is sufficient to force the rotating Wheel up the **Gauge Face** of the **Rail**. Once the **Flange Tip** clears the **Rail Head** (and is no longer constrained laterally) a **Derailment** normally occurs. Flange Climb can be caused by a **Twist**, excessive speed or severe **Sidewear**.

Flange Contact Angle

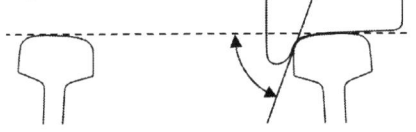

[TRS] The actual angle measured between the **Plane of the Rails** and the plane of contact between the **Wheel Flange** and the **Rail**.

Flange Contact Zone
That part of a **Rail Section** where a **Wheel Flange** can potentially make contact.

Flange Cover
[PW] The area of **Wheel Flange** that lies below the upper surface of a **Check Rail**, **Guard Rail**, **Running Rail** or **Wing Rail**.

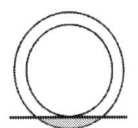

Flange Height
[TRS] The height of the **Wheel Flange** measured from the **Flange Tip** to the **Tread Datum**. This is mandated as 28mm minimum, but 30mm for the **P1 Profile**. See **Wheel Profile**.

Flange Lubricator
[PW] A type of **Grease Distribution Unit** (GDU) arranged to apply grease to the **Wheel Backs**, to reduce wear between the wheels and **Check Rails**. Also **Wheel Flange Lubricator**.

Flange Marks
The marks made in the **Rail Crown** by a **Flange**, normally during a **Derailment**. See also **False Flange**.

Flange Rail
[PW] An alternative name for **Flat Bottom Rail** (FB).

Flange Root
[TRS] The curved section of the **Wheel Profile** located between the face of the **Wheel Flange** nearest the **Rail** and the **Inner Tread**. It has a minimum Radius of 15.9mm for the **P1 Profile**.

Flange Running Crossing
[LR] A **Crossing** in which passing **Rail Wheels** travelling through one or both routes is lifted clear of the **Running Table** by the **Wheel Flange** running on the raised bottom of the **Flangeway**.

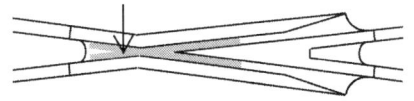

Raised area

This arrangement removes the large space otherwise present at the **Crossing Nose**, and is common in **Embedded Track** on **Street Running** □ **Tramways**.

Flange Thickness
The width of the **Wheel Profile** measured from the **Flange Back** to the outer limit of the **Flange Root**. This dimension is 28mm for the **P1 Profile** and is logically less than 38mm, which is the minimum **Flangeway**.

Flange Tip
The portion of the **Wheel Flange** furthest from the axle. See **Wheel Profile**.

Flange Toe
The curved section of the **Wheel Profile** located between the face of the **Wheel Flange** nearest the **Rail** and the **Flange Tip**. It has a minimum Radius (R) of 10mm, 15.9mm for the **P1 Profile**.

Flanged Rail
An alternative name for **Flat Bottom Rail** (FB).

ELLIS' BRITISH RAILWAY ENGINEERING ENCYCLOPÆDIA

Flangeway
[PW] 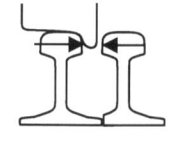
a) The gap between the Running Edge (RE) of a Running Rail and an adjacent Check Rail or Wing Rail. See Flangeway Gap. Also Check Rail Gap, Free Wheel Clearance (FWC)
b) The gap between the inner edge of the Running Rail and the highway or footway surface of a Level Crossing (LC, LX).

Flangeway Clearance
See Flangeway Gap.

Flangeway Dimension
See Flangeway Gap.

Flangeway Gap
[PW] The width of the Flangeway.
a) [NR] This was standardised at 44mm on Standard Gauge Railways, but:
- 41mm in RT60, NR60, 113A Vertical and NR56V ▫ S&C Layouts up to 125mph
- [Obs.] 38mm in 113A Vertical S&C on Curved ▫ Main Lines at speeds greater than 105mph.
b) [LUL]:
- 47mm for Check Rails on Curves in Plain Line
- 44mm for other Check Rails in Plain Line, Flat Bottom S&C on Curves of less than 200m Radius and all those in Bullhead S&C
- 41mm for Check Rails in Flat Bottom S&C on Curves of greater than 200m Radius.

See also Check Rail Gauge.

Flangeway Opening
See Flangeway Gap.

Flangeway Wall
[PW] The vertical sides of the Flangeway between the Wing Rail and Running Rail in a Cast Crossing.

Flank Points
[Sig.] A Set of Facing Points which are used to direct Over-running Trains away from legitimate Train Movements at Junctions. See Flank Protection.

Flank Protection
[Sig.] Arrangements for providing additional protection from Unauthorised Movements on Converging Lines by utilising other Points in the Junction as Trap Points. See also Flank Points.

Flare
[PW]
a) The angled section machined or forged into some Rails to create a smooth entry for Wheel Flanges entering the Flangeway. Also Splay, Entry. See also Check Rail, Wing Rail
b) An alternative for Splay as a suffix to a description of a Common Crossing
c) The Rail provided on the end of the outside Switch Rail in a Trap Point, intended to throw vehicles Clear in the event they use the facility
d) The Rails provided on the Sleeper Ends at the entry ends of Guard Rails, to further guide Derailed vehicles
e) A tapered section formed at the end of a length of Grooved Rail.

Flash Butt Weld (FBW)
[PW] A Welded Joint between abutting Rails, made by a flash (electrical) welding process. Also Flash Weld, Shop Weld.

Flash Notice
[NR, Col.] A poster issued to warn of a forthcoming energisation of new Electrification Equipment. See Energisation Warning Notice.

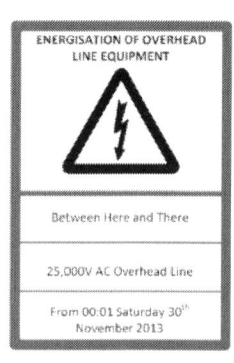

Flash Sign
[NR, Col.] A Lineside Sign indicating the presence of live Overhead Line Equipment (OLE) or Conductor Rails.

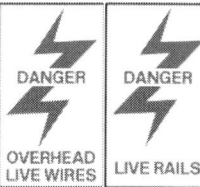

Flash Test
A test to evaluate whether the electrical insulation of electrical equipment or components has sufficient dielectric strength for the working voltage.

Flash Weld
See Flash Butt Weld (FBW).

Flashing Aspect
[Sig.]
a) A normal Caution Aspect or Preliminary Caution Aspect displayed by a Colour Light Signal, which is then made to flash to give prior warning of the Diverging Route through a Junction. It is used where Approach Speeds are high and the speed through the Diverging Route at the Junction is also high. See Flashing Double Yellow Aspect, Flashing Single Yellow Aspect.
b) See Flashing Green Aspect.

Flashing Double Yellow (FYY)
Flashing Double Yellow Aspect
[Sig.] A Preliminary Caution Aspect displayed by a Four Aspect Signal, which indicates to a driver that the next Signal will be displaying a Flashing Single Yellow Aspect and that the Junction ▫ Ahead is Set for its highest speed Diverging Route. See also Aspect Sequence

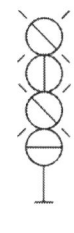

Flashing Green Aspect (FG)
[Sig.] A fifth Aspect provided in certain areas on the East Coast Main Line (ECML) to authorise drivers of Intercity 225 □ Trains to exceed 125mph. A standard Aspect Sequence could therefore be FG → G → YY → Y → R.

Flashing Single Yellow (FY)
Flashing Single Yellow Aspect
[Sig.] An Aspect displayed by a Four Aspect Signal, which indicates to a driver that the next Signal will be displaying a Single Yellow Aspect and have its Junction Indicator set for the highest speed Diverging Route. See also Aspect Sequence.

Flashing Yellow
See Flashing Double Yellow Aspect, Flashing Single Yellow Aspect.

Flash-over
Flashover
An uncontrolled electrical discharge, typically between two bare electrical conductors.

FLAT
[NR Tel.] Fixed Line Assessment Tool.

Flat
a) See Wheel Flat. See also Square Wheel
b) [PW] A short length of increased Radius (R) or straight in a curved section of Line. See Alignment Variations.
c) Alternative for Level, as in no Gradient.

Flat Angle
Flat Angle Crossing
[PW] A Common Crossing having a large N Value, or small angle of intersection between Running Edges (RE). The opposite is a Sharp Angle Crossing or Wide Angle Crossing.

Flat Bottom
Flat Bottom Rail (FB)

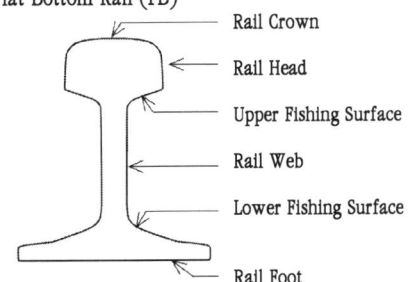

— Rail Crown
— Rail Head
— Upper Fishing Surface
— Rail Web
— Lower Fishing Surface
— Rail Foot

[PW] A Rail Section having a flat based Rail Foot or Flange. See also Vignoles Rail, Flanged Rail, Rail, Stevens Rail.

Flat Bottom Switch
[PW] A Switch fabricated from Flat Bottom Rail (FB). Such Switches can be Vertical Switches or Inclined Switches. See also Shallow Depth Switches, Thick Web Switches.

Flat Bottom Track
[PW] Track constructed using Flat Bottom Rails (FB).

Flat Crossing
[PW]
a) A Switch & Crossing Layout where two Routes intersect at the same level
b) A Crossing with a large N Value or small angle between Running Rails. Also Flat Angle Crossing.

Flat Curve
[PW] A Curve with a large Radius (R). The opposite is a Sharp Curve.

Flat Junction
A Junction that has no Grade Separation, i.e. all Train Movements are made on one level. Also At Grade Junction.

Flatbed Wagons
[TRS] Wagons with flat decks, designed to carry long or bulky items of Freight, e.g. Containers

Flatbottom
See Flat Bottom Rail (FB).

Flatrol
[TRS] Generic term for a low floor Flatbed Wagon intended for the transport of heavy bulky loads and, more recently, excavating plant. Originally the term described a vehicle with Bogies, see also Lowmac.

FLAWS
(flaws) [NR, PW] A computer database of Rail Flaws.

FLC
Full Load Current.

Flecking
[PW] An alternative for Fletching.

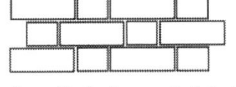

Flemish Bond
[Civ.] A brickwork bond with staggered courses of alternating stretchers (brick laid flat with the long end of the brick exposed) and headers (brick laid flat with the short end of the brick exposed), with the headers centred on the stretchers, and each alternate row aligned vertically. Used to create walls one brick length thick.

Fletcher Fishplates
[PW Obs.] A type of Fishplated Rail Joint where the Fishplate fitted outside the Fourfoot extends up the Rail Head to be flush with the Rail Crown, an arrangement intended to reduce the incidence of Rail End Batter.

Fletching
[PW] Painted marks made by the manufacturer of a new Switch and Crossing Layout (S&C Layout) across the Rail Foot and Baseplate or Bearer, allowing the layout to be subsequently reassembled correctly. See also Flecking, Laths, White Line.

Flexed Layout
Flexed S&C Layout
Flexed Switch and Crossing Layout

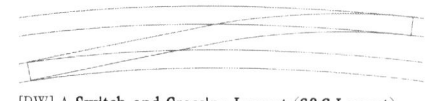

[PW] A **Switch and Crossing Layout** (**S&C Layout**) where the **Main Line** has been made curved. See also **Contraflexure**, **Off the Back**, **Off the Inside**, **Similar Flexure**, **Split Switch**, **Split Turnout**.

Flexible Switch
[PW] A **Switch Rail** that is secured with **Heel Blocks** at the **Switch Heel** and utilises the flexibility of the Switch Rail to achieve the necessary movement at the **Switch Toe**. This is the current design for all installations on **Heavy Rail**. See also **Loose Heel Switch**, **Stub Switch**.

Flexible Train Arrival Point (FTAP)
[NR] An arrangement of temporary **Lineside** signs that allows an **Engineering Train** to be brought close to a **Worksite** without needing to specify exactly where that point is to the driver in advance.

Flexible Wing Crossing
[PW] A **Common Crossing** in which the **Wing Rail** of the least-used route can be moved by vehicle wheels passing in a **Trailing** direction, the Wing Rail otherwise lies up against the **Crossing Vee**. Also **Spring Crossing**, **Spring Wing Crossing**.

FLHH
See **Freightliner Heavy Haul**.

Flight
[Ops.] A group of **Trains** travelling in close succession over the same **Line** in the same direction. See also **Flighting**.

Flighting
[Ops.] Increasing the theoretical capacity of a **Line** by arranging for **Trains** travelling at a similar speed to travel as a group or **Flight**. Typically, a group of faster Trains will precede a group of slower Trains.

Float Rail
[PW] The **Rail** that is not the **Datum Rail** during the operation of a **Tamper**.

Floater
[Col.] A short length of **Conductor Rail**, typically in a **Switch and Crossing Layout** (**S&C Layout**) which remains live during a **Conductor Rail Isolation** because it is connected to a different **Electrical Section**.

Floating Slab Track
[PW] A **Track Construction** in which the **Track Slab** is mounted on rubber pads to reduce the severity of vibration transmitted to adjacent property.

Flood Span
[Civ.] A small low **Span** provided adjacent to the main Span of a **Bridge** over a river, intended to allow flood water to pass more easily. Under normal circumstances the Flood Span has no water beneath it. There may be many such Flood Spans together, giving the structure the appearance of a low **Viaduct**.

Floor Beam
[Civ.] A horizontal member spanning between the main girders of a **Bridge Deck** and therefore forming the floor of the **Bridge**.

Floor Plate
[TRS] Moveable floor panels resting on the underframe and inter-**Coach** □ **Coupling** that create a walking surface between the Coaches whilst allowing the Coaches to move relative to each other. See also **Bellows**, **Gangway**.

FLOR
See **First Line of Response**.

FLT
a) **Freightliner Terminal**.
b) **Fault**.

Fly Move
[Col.] An unauthorised, illegal **Train Movement**.

Fly Rope
[Hist.] A short length of haulage rope, forming part of the equipment of a haulage engine, used for **Shunting** vehicles on a **Rope-hauled Railway**.

Fly Shunting
[Obs.] A **Train** marshalling system where a **Locomotive** hauls **Wagons** towards a **Fan** of **Sidings** at a brisk pace. By deft manipulation of **Point Levers** the Wagons are allowed to overtake the Locomotive and the Wagons then run along the chosen **Route** and onto the target **Siding** or Train being marshalled. This process is no longer common practice. See also **Hump Shunting**, **Loose Shunting**.

Flyer
[IÉ, Ops.] An internal memorandum sent to the **Operations Planning** Office to request a change to the **Possession Arrangements** printed in the **Weekly Circular**.

Fly-fished Joint
[PW] A **Fishplated Rail Joint** in which the **Fishbolts** are fitted through one **Rail** only. An **Emergency Clamp** is often used in lieu of the **Fishbolts** on the other side. Such an arrangement is highly dubious, having severely reduced mechanical security. The passage of any **Train** over such an arrangement is prohibited.

Flying Banana
[Col.]
a) Nickname for the **Great Western Railway** (**GWR**) developed **Railcars** of the 1930s
b) The original nickname for the **Class** 43 based **High Speed Train** (**HST**), after its colour scheme
c) The nickname for the recently introduced **New Measurement Train** (**NMT**), converted from a Class 43 based HST. This **Train** is bright yellow from end to end.

Flying Buttress
[Civ.] A **Buttress** which is not in contact for its full height with the **Structure** it supports; typically lateral loads are transferred via **Arches**.

Flying Ducks
See **Flying Pigs**.

Flying Junction
A Junction where a Diverging Line is carried over the Main Line(s) to avoid conflicting movements. See also Flyover. The opposite is Burrowing Junction.

Flying Pigs
[Col.] A nickname for Section Insulators (SI) used in Mark I ▫ Overhead Line Equipment (OLE). Also Flying Ducks.

Flying Tail

Flying Tail Registration
[Elec.] A type of Registration Arm which is only supported by a single lateral wire, attached to a fixed object at its other end.

Flyover

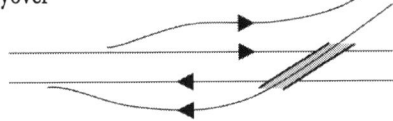

The opposite of a Diveunder, describing an Intersection Bridge (IB) that carries the Diverging Line over the Main Line as part of a Flying Junction or Grade Separated Junction.

FMEA
Failure Mode and Effect Analysis.

FMECA
Failure Modes, Effects and Criticality Analysis.

FMES
Fixed & Mobile Equipment Supply.

FMS
See Fault Management System.

FMU
See Freight Multiple Unit.

FN
Fault Number.

FNW
First North Western, a Train Operating Company (TOC).

FO
[TRS] An acronym representing a First Class ▫ Open Coach.

FOAC
Fibre Optic Adaptor Card.

FOB
Freight Only Branch.

FOC
a) (fock) See Freight Operating Company
b) Fibre Optic Cable
c) Free of Charge.

Fog
See In Fog and Rain...

Fog Hut
[Obs.] The small, typically pre-fabricated wood or concrete, huts used by Fogmen. These can still can still be seen dotted along the Railway.

Fog Machine
[Sig. Obs.] A mechanical device which allowed a Fogsignalman to either remove or apply a Railway Fog Signal (Detonator) from/to the Rail remotely. They were provided where the Fogging Post was some way from a Signal or Signals being covered. Originally capable of holding one Fog Signal, Fog Machines were developed to hold two, four or eight and were adapted for use by Signallers via a designated Lever or Levers within a Signal Box. Also known as: a Detonator Placer.

Fog Object
[Sig. Obs.] The fixed feature (often the Backlight of a Signal) used by a Signaller when deciding whether to call out the Fogman, Fogsignalman.

Fog Signals
See Railway Fog Signals, an alternative for Detonators. Also Bangers, Crackers, Dets, Foggies, Shots.

Foggies
[Col.] See Railway Fog Signals, an alternative for Detonators.

Fogging
[Obs.] The duty carried out by a Fogsignalman in warning Trains of Signals showing Restrictive Aspects when those Signals are obscured by Fog. See also Arm Repeater (AR). The introduction of Colour Light Distant Signals has rendered this activity rare.

Fogging Post
[Sig. Obs.] The designated Signal(s) to which a Fogsignalman was required to attend when called out by the Signaller. See Fogging. See also Fog Hut.

Fogging Repeater
[Sig. Obs.] An additional Signal or Indicator provided inside a Fogging Post or at ground level adjacent to a Signal, allowing the Fogsignalman to actually see the Aspect being displayed by the Signal at which he was undertaking Fogging duties.

Fogman
See Fogsignalman.

Fogsignalman
[Sig. Obs.] Before the introduction of Colour Light Distant Signals, which have superior visibility in foggy conditions, the onset of Fog meant that staff were positioned at critical Semaphore Signals and instructed to place Railway Fog Signals (aka Detonators) on the relevant Line The explosions alerted the drivers to the presence of the Signal and the need for action. Often contracted to Fogman. See also Fog Hut, Fogging Post.

FOL
Freight only Line.

Follow-on Crossover

[PW] Crossovers between multiple Tracks laid Toe to Toe. Also Follow-ons, Back to Back Leads, Back to Back Crossovers, Ladder.

ELLIS' BRITISH RAILWAY ENGINEERING ENCYCLOPÆDIA

Follow-on Lead
[PW Col.] A **Turnout** placed with its **Switch Toe** immediately behind the **Crossing** of the previous **Turnout**. Also **Follow-ons**.

Follow-ons
[PW Col.]
a) **Crossovers** between multiple **Tracks** laid **Toe** to **Toe**, see **Follow-on Crossover**, **Ladder**
b) **Turnouts** placed with their **Switch Toes** immediately behind the **Crossings** of the previous **Turnouts**. See **Follow-on Lead**.

FOOC
Flashing out of correspondence. Describing the indication a **Signaller's Panel** when a **Set of Points** has been commanded to move but have not been detected in the required position.

Foot
a) [PW] The lowest part of a **Rail Section**. Also **Flange**, **Rail Foot**
b) [Civ.] The bottom edge of an **Embankment**, where it meets normal ground level. Also **Toe**.

Foot Crossing
See **Footpath Level Crossing** (FPC)

Foot Relief
[PW] The removal of metal from the **Rail Foot** of a **Switch Rail** near the **Switch Heel**, intended to allow the Switch Rail to flex adequately.

Footbridge (FB)
[Civ.] A pedestrian-only **Bridge** provided to allow persons to cross the **Line** safely.

Footex
[Ops.] A **Special Train** or **Excursion Train** provided solely to convey football supporters to or from a football match. See also **-ex**.

Footfall
The number of **Passengers** ▫ **Alighting** at and departing from a **Platform** or **Station** in a given period, normally 24 hours.

Footpath Level Crossing (FP)
A **Level Crossing** (LC, LX) provided solely for use by pedestrians.

Footplate
a) [TRS] Platform in the **Driving Cab** of a **Steam Locomotive** on which the driver stands to operate the controls
b) [Col.] Term for a Driving Cab.

FOOTPRINT
A pan-European project intending to measure the noise and vibration generated by the interaction of **Rail Vehicles** and **Track** and relate it to the cost of maintaining the **Infrastructure**.

Footstep Light
Light placed at low level and used to illuminate the threshold of a **Train** doorway.

FOP
Flag Operations, see **Minor Cycle**.

FOR
a) See **Fibre Optic Route Indicator**
b) See **Free on Rail**.

For Cause Screening
For Cause Testing
The testing of all those directly involved with an accident or incident to identify whether or not drugs or alcohol are present in those people. See also **D&A Testing**.

Ford Factor
[Col.] A comparison of **Infrastructure** project cost before and after **Privatisation**, coined by the **Railway** journalist Roger Ford. On average, it currently stands at π (3.14) but in some cases is much higher.

FORI
See **Fibre Optic Route Indicator**.

Form 1
[NR Civ.] **Approval in Principle** (AIP).

Form 2
[NR Civ.] Statement of Design Intent.

Form 3
[NR Civ.] Certificate of Design and Check.

Form 4
[NR Civ.] Architectural and Layout Acceptance.

Form 5
[NR Civ.] Certificate Of Fitness To Be Taken Into Use.

Form 6
[NR Civ.] Road/Highway Authority Agreement to Bridgeworks.

Form A
[NR]
a) [Hist.] A document produced by the designer of a **Civil Engineering (CE)** scheme that details the scope of the works, the standards to be used in the design and any departures from those standards. It is agreed by the client before detailed design work commences. See **Form 1**, **Form 2**
b) A document produced by the designer of an **Overhead Line (OLE)** or **Permanent Way (PW)** scheme that details the scope of the works, the standards to be used in the design and any departures from those standards. It is agreed by the client before detailed design work commences. The equivalent document for **Signalling** schemes is the **Outline Project Specification (OPS)**
c) The form used by the **Electrical Room Operator (ERO)** and the **Signaller** to record the details of an **Isolation**.

Form B
[NR]
a) [Hist.] A document produced by the designer of a scheme recording the checking of that design. This document accompanied the final **Detailed Design** of a **Civil Engineering (CE)** scheme, and was signed by the client upon acceptance of the design. See **Form 3**
b) A document produced by the designer of a scheme recording the checking of that design. This document accompanies the final **Detailed Design** of an **Overhead Line (OLE)** or **Permanent Way (PW)** scheme, and is signed by the client upon acceptance of the design
c) The form used by the **Electrical Control Operator (ECO)** and the **Nominated Person (Nommy)** to record the details of an **Isolation**.

Form B2
[NR] The form used to record the switching arrangements associated with an **Isolation** in an area of **DC Electrification**.

Form C
[NR]
a) The document produced by the designer, certifying the correct design of an item of **Temporary Works**
b) The form issued by the **Nominated Person** (**Nommy**) to the **Engineering Supervisor** (**ES**) or **Controller of Site Safety** (**COSS**) recording the details of an **Isolation**
c) The document produced by the **Permanent Way** designer, certifying the checking of an **S&C Manufacturer's Drawing**.

Form D
[NR] Aesthetic Acceptance, a document produced which records acceptance of the architectural elements of a design.

Form E
[NR] Certificate of Fitness to be Taken Into Use, recording that the completed works are ready for use. See **Form 5**.

Form of Signal
[Sig.] An alternative for **Signal Profile**.

Formal Investigation
[NR] A formally-structured investigation of an **Accident** or incident carried out by **Rail Industry** representatives in accordance with **Railway Group Standard** (**RGS**) GO/RT3119.

Formation
a) The prepared surface of the ground, on which any filter or structural materials, the **Ballast** and the **Track** is laid. Other specialists refer to this is the **Sub-formation**. Also **Roadbed**, **Track Bed**. See also **Formation Treatment**
b) A contraction of **Formation Renewal**
c) [Ops.] The order in which the vehicles in a **Train** are marshalled
d) The order in which **On Track Machines** (**OTM**) pass through a site, e.g. **Tamper** - **Regulator** - **Dynamic Track Stabiliser** (**DTS**).

Formation Failure
Describing a **Formation** which has ceased to provide adequate support to the **Track** above. This is typically manifested in the form of poor **Top** and **Wet Beds**. Causes include inadequate **Track Drains**, inappropriate **Formation Treatment** or ingress of water from outside the **Railway** (e.g. run-off). See **Clay Dig** (**CD**), **Formation Renewal**, **Lime Stabilisation**.

Formation Level
The vertical level of the **Formation**, normally specified (if at all) at the point of minimum **Ballast Depth**. See also **Formation Slope**.

Formation Renewal
The operation of **Excavating** down to and removing a failed **Formation** surface and replacing it with suitable fill, reinforcement, filter layer and new **Ballast**.

Formation Slope
a) The **Gradient** of the **Fall** of the **Formation**, from one side of the **Track** to the other. This is typically specified as **1 in** 20 to 1 in 40.
b) The direction of the Fall of the Formation, from one side of the Track to the other. This can vary according to the topography, location of **Track Drains** and curvature of the Track. It is not uncommon to find that the Formation Slope is the opposite way to the **Cant**. See below for typical arrangements of slopes and **Track Drains**. In all cases the arrows indicate the minimum **Ballast Depth**.

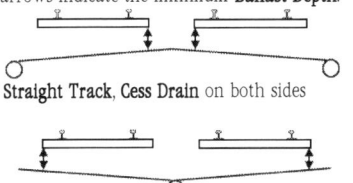

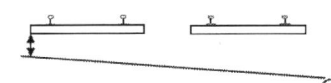

Straight Track, Cess Drain on both sides

Straight Track, **Sixfoot Drain**

Straight Track, **Cess** Drain on one side

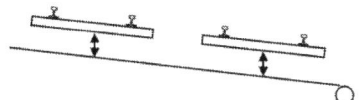

Curved Track, Cess Drain on inside of the Curve

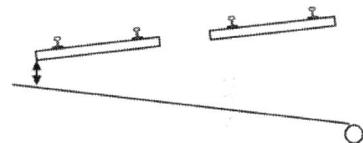

Curved Track, Cess Drain on outside of the Curve

Formation Stiffness
A measure of the degree of deflection of a unit area of **Formation** under a unit load. A **Trackform** utilising **Ballast** and discrete **Sleepers** (called **Ballasted Track**) relies on the overall construction being flexible. Too stiff and a **Hard Road** results, reducing component life dramatically. Too soft and the Formation will be rapidly plasticised, resulting in poor **Ride Quality** and **Track Geometry**. The target stiffness is a minimum of 30kN/mm, ranging up to 100kN/mm for new **Lines** running at over 100mph. See also **Falling Weight Deflectometer** (**FWD**).

Formation Treatment
Collective term for all remedial works carried out to modify the stiffness or re-instate the integrity of a Formation. This includes **Blanketing**, **Cationic Bitumen Spray**, **Clay Dig**, **Formation Renewal**, **Geogrid**, **Geoweb**, **Lime Stabilisation**, **Sand Blanketing**.

Forth Bridge Rail
[PW] A **Rail Section** specially developed for use on the Firth of Forth **Railway** □ **Bridge**. This is different from the **Fourth Rail**, which is a **Conductor Rail**, see also **Negative Rail**.

Forward Route
[Sig.] A **Route** □ **Set** □ **Beyond** a **Signal**.

FOT
[TRS] An acronym representing a **First** □ **Open Coach** with trolley/buffet.

FOU
See **Freight Operating Unit**.

Foul
a) Describing a **Rail Vehicle**, object or **Structure** that is infringing the **Swept Envelope** of Vehicles passing on an adjacent **Line**. See **Gauging Tolerances**
b) [Sig.] Describing a Rail Vehicle occupying a particular **Track Circuit**
The opposite, in both senses, is **Clear**.

Foul Notch
[Sig.] A **Notch** cut into a **Tappet** which causes the **Interlocking** to become **Released** erroneously during the motion of a **Lever**. Also **Conflicting Port**.

Foul Track Circuit
[Sig.] A **Track Circuit** not part of the **Route** from a **Signal**, which has an extremity within the Route and **On the Approach** to the **Clearance Point**.

Fouling Bar
[Sig.] A type of **Depression Bar** used to detect the presence of **Wheel Flanges** at critical locations in **Switch and Crossing Layouts** (**S&C Layouts**).

Fouling Point (FP)
a) [NR] The point at which vehicles on **Converging Tracks** would be in contact with each other. This is deemed to be the point at which the **Running Edges** (**RE**) of the **Tracks** are 6' - 6" (2m) apart. See also **Clearance Point** (**CP**)
b) [LUL] The point at which the clearance between **Static Vehicle Gauges** on two Converging Tracks is 75mm, after allowance for **Cant**, **End Throw** and **Centre Throw**.

Foundation Stone
[Hist.] Alternative name for a **Stone Block Sleeper**.

Four Aspect Colour Light Signal
Four Aspect Signal
[Sig.] A **Colour Light Signal** capable of displaying four **Aspects**:
- Green (**G**) - **Proceed Aspect**, the next Signal may be displaying Green or Double Yellow
- Double Yellow (**YY**) - **First Caution** (**Preliminary Caution**), two Signal intervals to the Stop Signal. The next Signal may be displaying a **Single Yellow**
- Single Yellow (**Y**) - **Caution Aspect**, the next Signal may be displaying a Red □ **Stop Aspect**
- Red (**R**) - Stop Aspect

On **Signalling Plans** the **Normal Aspect** is denoted by having a double line. See also **Fibre Optic Signal**, **Flashing Double Yellow Aspect**, **Flashing Yellow Aspect**, **Optic Diode Signal**, **Searchlight Signal**, **Three Aspect Signal**, **Two Aspect Signal**.

Four Aspect Signalling
A system of **Colour Light Signalling** which provides a **Red Aspect**, **Yellow Aspect**, **Double Yellow Aspect** and a **Green Aspect** in a manner which normally provides a **First Caution** at least two **Signals** before a Signal at **Red**.

Four Bar Gate
See **Gate**.

Four Foot
See **Fourfoot**.

Four Hole
Four Hole Joint
A **Fishplated Rail Joint** with four **Fishbolt Holes**. This is the most common quantity; six holes being used on certain heavy duty **Insulated Rail Joints** (**IRJ**). See also **Eight Hole Joint**, **Six Hole**, **Six Hole Joint**, **Two Hole Joint**, **Three Hole Joint**.

Four Point Lining
A system employed by certain **Tamping and Lining Machines** (**Tampers**) that automatically measures and controls the **Lining** process. It has the effect of averaging errors but not eliminating them, leading to a "bunching" of the errors over time. For this reason it is normal to utilise different Tampers in rotation, and to alternate the direction they work on a particular site.

Four Track Railway

A **Railway** with four **Tracks**, normally two **Fast Lines** (these can also be called **Main Lines**) and two **Slow Lines** (these can also be called **Relief Lines**). There are three common arrangements of **Tracks**:

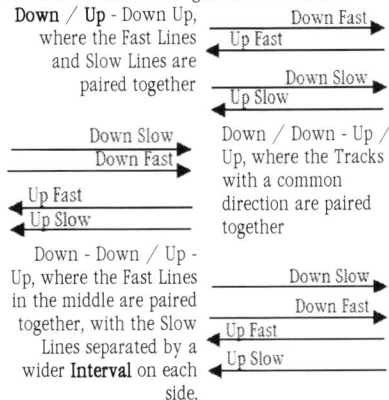

Down / Up - Down Up, where the Fast Lines and Slow Lines are paired together

Down - Down / Up - Up, where the Fast Lines in the middle are paired together, with the Slow Lines separated by a wider **Interval** on each side.

Down / Down - Up / Up, where the Tracks with a common direction are paired together

Convention is normally to draw the Down Line at the top of any diagram, normally with lowest **Mileage** on the left hand end, but there are exceptions in the south of England where this would be confusing. The **Railway Safety Principles and Guidance** (**RSPG**) demand that there should be no more than three Tracks seperated from each other by a **Sixfoot** without a **Tenfoot** being provided as a **Position of Safety**. Other arrangements of Tracks exist, normally as a result of a **Junction** □ **Layout** nearby.

Fourfoot

The area between the two **Running Rails** of a **Standard Gauge Railway**. This is a little odd as the actual dimension of this space is 1435mm (4' - 8¹/₂").

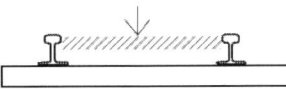

Fourth Rail

See **Negative Rail**.

Four-throw

Three **Turnouts** superimposed with their **Switch** **Toes** in consecutive **Beds**, designed to allow three **Tracks** to connect to a fourth in a very short length. Such are layouts are extremely rare and, if found at all, are typically confined to **Sidings** and **Depots**. See also **Double Tandem**, **Tandem**, **Three-throw**.

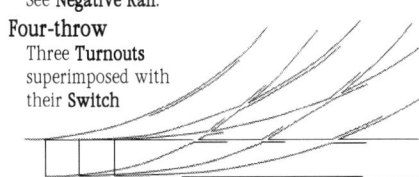

FOW

See **Free on Wheels**.

Fowler, Sir John

(1817-1898) Born in Sheffield. Civil engineer who worked on the Metropolitan **Railway**, forerunner of the **London Underground**, and the Forth bridge (1890) with Benjamin Baker.

Foxhall Accident

On 27th September 1967 an **Express Passenger Train** approached Foxhall **Junction** near Didcot on the **Down** □ **Relief** □ **Line** at over 60mph. It was signalled to cross onto the Down **Main** Line over two 25mph crossovers. The **Train** derailed, killing one and injuring 23. See **Foxhall Control**.

Foxhall Control

[Sig.] This treats the **Signal** at the end of a **Line** which has only one **Route** (e.g. through a **Crossover**) as a **Junction Signal** when a driver may be misled into thinking they are being signalled straight by the **Track Layout**. Also **Didcot Control**.

Foxtrot

The **Phonetic Alphabet** word representing F.

FP

a) See **Fine Point**
b) See **Fouling Point**
c) See **Footpath Level Crossing**
d) **Fuelling Point**
e) **Footpath**.

FPA

Fire Precautions Act 1971.

FPC

See **Footpath Crossing**. Also **Foot Crossing**.

FPI

Facing Point Inspection.

FPIP

Freight Performance Improvement Plan

FPK

Footpath - **Kissing Gates**. See **Footpath Crossing**.

FPL

See **Facing Point Lock**.

FPM

Fire Precautions Manager.

FPO

Footpath - **Open Access**. See **Footpath Crossing**.

FPS

a) [Sig.] **Final Project Specification**. See also **Outline Project Specification** (**OPS**)
b) Footpath - **Stiles**. See **Footpath Crossing**.

FPW

a) Footpath - **Wicket Gates**. See **Footpath Crossing**.
b) **Fire Precautions (Workplace) Regulations** 1971.

FPWI

Fellow of the **Permanent Way Institution**.

FR

a) **Feasibility Report**
b) The former **Furness Railway**.

FR4

[Sig.] A **Network Rail** (**NR**) action plan to develop an integrated company-wide risk framework to inform strategic management decision-making.

FRACAS
a) **F**ailure **R**eporting **A**nalysis and **C**orrective **A**ction **S**ystem
b) **F**lood **R**isk **A**ssessment under Climate **C**hange **S**cenarios.

FRAME
(*frame*) [BR, RT, NR] **F**ault **R**eporting **a**nd **M**onitoring & **E**quipment System. A system that recorded **Signalling** and **Telecommunications** faults. Now replaced by **Fault Management System** (**FMS**).

Frame
a) [Sig.] A contraction of **Lever Frame**
b) [TRS] The chassis of a **Rail Vehicle**
c) [Tel.] An assembly of connector blocks where individual telephone circuits are connected to multicore cables or to other equipment.

Frame Twist
[TRS] Physical deformation of a **Wagon** □ **Frame** which is caused by operational braking techniques, collision with other **Rolling Stock** or poorly managed repair. Compensatory **Shims** or **Packings** are placed in diagonally opposite corners up to a maximum of 15mm to rectify the Twist.

Framework Contractor
An organisation contracted to perform specified tasks on demand, normally to predefined terms.

Frangible Link
Part of the **Current Collector Shoe** system that is designed to break at a pre-set load to minimise damage to the **Shoegear** in a collision between a displaced Shoe and the **Track** or a **Structure**.

FRD
Feasibility **R**equirements **D**efinition.

Fred
[Col.] Nickname given to a **Freightliner** □ **Class** 66 **Diesel Locomotive**, a contraction of "Freightliner Shed"

FREDDY
[BR] **F**lange **R**eading **E**lectronic **D**etector **D**esigned **Y**ork, A non-contact device for detecting **Trains** approaching **Level Crossings** (**LC**, **LX**). The devices are vulnerable to contamination by leaves, and are being replaced by **Treadles**.

Frederick
[Obs.] The obsolescent **Phonetic Alphabet** word representing F. Replaced by **Foxtrot**.

Free
[Sig.]
a) Of a **Lever**, meaning that the Lever is not **Locked**
b) Of a **Set of Points**, meaning the **Points** can be moved.
c) Of a **Sub-Route** or **Sub-Overlap**, meaning that the relevant item is not in use.

Free Curving
[PW] An arrangement of **Cant**, **Curvature** and speed that allows **Wheelsets** to negotiate a **Curve** without the **Flange** of the outer wheel making contact with the **Rail Head**. See also **Constrained Curving**.

Free on Rail (FOR)
Generally describing a **Rail Crane**, **Road Rail Excavator** or other piece of lifting plant that is free to move along the **Track** on **Rail Wheels** with a load. Some Rail Cranes and Road Rail Excavators have outriggers that can be used to increase the safe lifting capacity of the machine, this arrangement is called **Blocked**. See also **Free on Wheels** (**FOW**).

Free on Wheels (FOW)
Generally describing a **Road Rail Excavator** or mobile crane that is free to travel over the ground with a load. See also **Free on Rail**, **Blocked**.

Free Rail
[PW] The length of **Rail** unfastened during the **Stressing** operation. Also **Pull Length**.

Free Running

Free Running Equipment

Free Running OLE
[Elec.] Describing **Overhead Line Equipment** (**OLE**) beneath but not attached to a **Bridge**.

Free Wheel Clearance (FWC)
[PW] The dimension between the **Stock Rail** and the **Switch Rail** on the **Open Switch** side. This must be sufficient to allow a **Rail Wheel** to pass without contact. For CEN60 based layouts this dimension is 60mm, 50mm elsewhere. See also **Flange Back Clearance**.

Free Wired Interlocking
[Sig.] An **Interlocking** that comprises individual **Relays** wired together with single wires. See **Geographical Interlocking**.

Free Yellow
[NR Sig.] An arrangement provided at a **Junction Signal** where the **Main Line** and **Turnout** speeds are very similar, and the risk of an accident due to the driver over-speeding is minimal. The directional indication is given by a **Junction Direction Indicator** (**JDI**) associated with a **Single Yellow Aspect** (**Y**). The driver receives no other prior warning. See also **Approach Release**, **Flashing Aspects**, **Main Route Aspect Release From Yellow** (**MAY**).

Freewheel Time
[TRS] The time elapsed between the command being made for the brakes to apply and the first measurable retardation of speed of the **Train**.

Freight
A collective term describing aggregates, **Containers**, fuels, gases, goods, liquids, manufactured items, produce, raw materials and wastes, as distinct from **Passengers**. Older terms with a similar meaning include **Goods** and **Minerals**. See also **Bulk Freight**, **Unit Loads**.

Freight Differential
[NR Col.] Common term for a reduction in the **Permissible Speed** (**PS**) at certain locations which applies only to **Freight Trains**. See **Differential Speed Restriction** (**DSR**), **Standard Differential Speed Restriction**.

Freight Forwarder
A company or individual that organises the shipment of goods on behalf of a customer.

Freight Grants
Financial aid made available from the **DfT** to support **Railway** ◻ **Freight** projects that reduce road traffic.

Freight Lifted
The tonnage of **Freight** transported.

Freight Line
An alternative term for **Goods Line**, also **Freight Only Line**.

Freight Moved
The tonnage of **Freight** transported, multiplied by the distance that tonnage is transported.

Freight Multiple Unit (FMU)
[TRS] A **Multiple Unit Train** composed of two powered vehicles and a number of intermediate flat vehicles designed to carry **Freight** ◻ **Containers**.

Freight Only Line
A **Track** used solely for the passage of **Freight Vehicles**. See **Freight Standards**.

Freight Operating Company (FOC)
[NR] A company that holds a **Railway Safety Case (RSC)** for and operates **Freight Trains** as its core business. These are currently **DB Schenker Rail (UK) Ltd.** (DBS), **Direct Rail Services** (DRS), **Freightliner** (FL) and **GB Railfreight** (GBRf).

Freight Operating Unit (FOU)
[Hist.] A transitional organisation during **Privatisation**, responsible for operation of a section of **Freight** services. They were named **Freightliner** (FL), **Loadhaul**, **Mainline**, **Rail Express Systems** (RES) and **Transrail**. With the exception of Freightliner, they now all form part of **English Welsh and Scottish Railways** (EWS).

Freight Standards
a) See **Goods Line** (b).
b) The former minimum provisions for **Lines** used only by Freight Trains or **Goods Trains**. Particularly, **Signal Overlaps** were not required, and equivalent protection could be provided by **Trap Points**. **Passenger Trains** are not permitted to use Lines **Fitted** to Freight Standards except by special authority. All new Lines must be built to **Passenger Standards**.

Freight Train
A **Train** composed of **Freight Vehicles**.

Freight Vehicle
A **Rail Vehicle** specially built or adapted for the carriage of aggregates, **Containers**, fuels, gases, goods, liquids, manufactured items, produce, raw materials or wastes.

Freightliner Heavy Haul (FHH, FLHH)
(Tradename) The sub-division of **Freightliner** (FL) which deals with the haulage of non-**Container** ◻ **Trains**.

Freightliner Ltd (FL)
(Tradename) A **Freight Operating Company (FOC)** originally specialising in the transport of **Containers**.

French Drain
A trench filled with broken stone and intended to provide a ready drainage path for surface water.

Frequency
[Ops.] The number of **Trains Per Hour** (TPH). Not the same as **Headway**.

Frequency Division Multiplex (FDM)
[Sig.] A means of transmitting many streams of data over a few wires. Each data stream is allocated to particular frequency or groups of such frequencies. Many frequencies are then transmitted over one cable. Used to connect a **Remote Interlocking** to a **Signal Box** (SB).

Fretting
A wear process which occurs at the interface between two surfaces in loaded contact, which also have small relative movements between them, such as those due to vibration or bending. The process causes mechanical wear at the interface and oxidation of the metallic debris. See also **Snow**.

FRI
Fatigue and Risk Index.

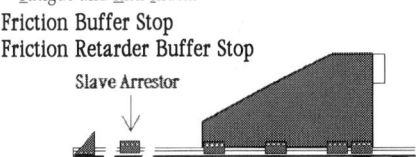

Friction Buffer Stop
Friction Retarder Buffer Stop

Slave Arrestor

A type of **Buffer Stop** designed to arrest a **Train** in a controlled manner by sliding backwards under impact. They are generally used where **Passenger Trains** may use a **Terminal Line**. The structure of the Buffer Stop, carrying the **Buffer Beam**, is clamped to the **Rail Heads** of the **Track** it sits on. Additional brakes (**Slave Arrestors**) are arranged at intervals behind the Buffer Stop. When a Train hits the Buffer Stop, it slides, dissipating the kinetic energy through friction. The greater the energy of the Train, the more Arrestors the arrangement picks up, increasing the available friction accordingly. Additional friction can be produced by providing additional **Rails** in the **Fourfoot**, and fitting these with additional Arrestors.

Friction Stir Welding (FSW)
A welding method particularly suitable for joining aluminium alloys. A cylindrical, shouldered tool is rotated along the joint line between two pieces of sheet or plate material. This generates heat between the tool and the material being welded, causing the material to soften and the plasticised material is transferred around the weld area to form the bond. See also **EUROSTIR**.

Fridera
[PW Obs.] A proprietary compound formerly used to plug redundant **Chairscrew** holes in **Wood Sleepers**.

Friends of Stations
Voluntary community groups that support a local **Station** through the **Station Adoption Scheme**

Frig
Frigging
[Col, NPT] The act of making non-standard and generally temporary modifications to a **Signalling System**, normally in connection with **Reballasting** or **Relaying**. The correct practice is **Stageworks**. Also **Minimum Works Alteration** (**MWA**).
Fringe Box
Fringe Signal Box
[Sig.] The first **Signal Box** (**SB**) located along a **Line** beyond the boundary of the **Control Area** concerned.
Frog
a) [PW] An alternative name for a **Crossing**, based on its shape when seen in plan
b) See **Frog Trolley**
c) [Col.] A **Ticket** that has been illegally reused.
Frog Trolley
[BR Obs.] A rail mounted piece of measuring equipment capable of measuring **Gauge** and **Crosslevel**. The name is derived from the motion of the **Trolley** along the **Track**, as the drive mechanism incorporated a lost motion facility so that the **Trolley** paused at intervals of 1.5m while a measurement was taken, as in a frog moving along in a series of hops.
Front Contact
[Sig.] A contact which is made when the **Relay** is **Operated** and broken when it is **Released**.
Front Fishbolt Hole
[PW] The **Fishbolt Hole** nearest to the **Rail End**. See also **Back Fishbolt Hole**
Front Joint
[PW]
a) The **Rail Joint** at the **Wing Rail Front** of a **Common Crossing**
b) The Rail Joint in the **Stock Rail** in front of a **Switch Toe**.
Front Shift
The first **Shift** in a **Possession**. See also **Back Shift**.
Front Stretcher Bar
The **Stretcher Bar** fitted at the **Switch Toes** of a **Set of Switches**. Also **First Stretcher Bar**. See also **First Permanent Way Stretcher Bar**, **First Signalling Stretcher Bar**, **Lock Stretcher Bar**.
Fronts
[PW] A common alternative for **Switch Fronts**.
Frost Heave
A vertical disturbance of the **Track** caused by the freezing of water in the **Subgrade** or **Formation**. Since ice is of greater volume than water, the resulting expansion takes place upwards, forcing the **Ballast** and / or Formation up with it.
Frozen Joint
[PW] A **Fishplated Rail Joint** in which longitudinal movement of the **Running Rails** is restricted by over-tensioned bolts or inadequate lubrication of the **Fishing Surfaces**. Also **Seized Joint**.

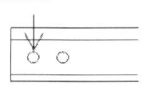

FRP
a) Field Reporting Procedures. The procedures for reporting information to the **Total Operation Processing System** (**TOPS**)
b) Fibre Reinforced Polymer.
FRR
Fault Recovery Report.
FRS
Functional Requirements Specification.
Fruin
Fruin Level of Service
Fruin LOS
A method of describing the acceptable density of occupation of public areas (or Level of Service, LOS) under various conditions. Devised by John. J. Fruin and published in "Planning and Design" in 1971, there are six levels:

	Average pedestrian density m^2/person	Average flow volume people/m/min	Average speed m/min
LOS A - Sufficient walkway area is available to freely select walking speed and manoeuvre to avoid conflicts	>3.26	<=23	>79.2
LOS B - Sufficient walkway area is available to freely select walking speed. Minor conflicts will occur if reverse or crossing movements exist.	2.33- 3.26	22 - 23	75.6 - 79.2
LOS C - Freedom to select walking speed and pass others is restricted. High probability of conflict in crossings and reverse flow requiring frequent adjustment of speed and direction.	1.4- 2.33	33 - 49	68.4 - 75.6
LOS D - Generally, normal walking speed and manoeuvrability restricted. Reverse flow and crossings severely restricted.	0.93- 1.4	49 - 66	67.2 - 68.4
LOS E - Virtually all have their normal walking speed and manoeuvrability restricted. Reverse flow and crossing movements experience extreme difficulty.	0.47- 0.93	66-82	37.8 - 67.2
LOS F - All movement in the major flow direction is extremely restricted, reverse or crossing movements are virtually impossible. Complete breakdown in traffic flow	<0.47	<82	0 - 37.8

Level of Service C is often used to represent a reasonable level of crowding under normal conditions, with D or E used for queuing situations.
FRV
[NR] Under the Bridge Condition Marking Index (BCMI) handbook, shorthand for **Face Ring**, **Voussoir**.

FS
a) See **Feeder Station**.
b) **F**ixed **S**tations, the trackside radio equipment used for **Cab Secure Radio** (**CSR**)
c) See **Full Supervision Mode**.
d) See **Functional Specification**.
e) **F**errovie dello **S**tato Italiane (previously Ferrovie dello Stato), the Italian state **Railway Company**.

FSC
Freight **S**pecific **C**harge.

FSE
Front **S**hovel **E**xcavator.

FSH
See **Full Screen Height**.

FSP
[EP] See **Functional Supply Point**. See also **Auxiliary Supply Point** (**ASP**), **Principal Supply Point** (**PSP**).

FSR
(Tradename) **F**irst **S**cot**R**ail, a **Train Operating Company** (**TOC**).

FSS
Forensic **S**cientific **S**ervices.

FSW
See **Friction Stir Welding**.

FT
See **Fixed Tension**, **Fixed Termination**.

FT Equipment
See **Fixed Termination Equipment**.

FTA
a) **F**reight **T**ransport **A**ssociation
b) **F**ault **T**ree **A**nalysis.

FTABS
Freight **T**rain □ **A**ir **B**rake **S**imulator.

FTAC
Fixed **T**rack **A**ccess **C**harge.

FTAP
See **Flexible Train Arrival Point**.

FTC
See **Fail to Call**.

FTE
Fast **T**ransient **E**arth.

FTL
Fault **T**eam **L**eader.

FTN
a) **F**ixed **T**elephone **N**etwork
b) **F**ixed **T**ransmission **N**etwork.

FTNx
[NR Tel.] The next generation **Telecommunications** and data network being developed by **Network Rail Telecommunications** (**NRT**).

FTP
Friction **T**ransformation **P**rocessing, a method with potential applications in the repairing of **Rails**.

FTPE
(Tradename) **F**irst **T**rans**P**ennine **E**xpress, a **Train Operating Company** (**TOC**).

FTR
[NR] **F**itness **t**o **R**un. All **Locomotives** or **Rolling Stock** that have been in store and need to be moved by **Rail** need to have a Fitness To Run examination before they are moved.

FTS
a) **F**ailed (or **F**ailure) **t**o **S**top. See **Signal Passed at Danger** (**SPAD**)
b) See **Fixed Tension System**, **Fixed Termination System**.

FTT
Forward **T**ime**t**able.

Fuelling Apron
Fuelling Line
Fuelling Road
A **Track** (generally a **Siding**) on which **Diesel Locomotives** and **Diesel Multiple Units** (**DMU**) stand to receive diesel fuel.

FUG
[RT Hist.] **F**reight **U**p**g**rade, the **Freight** equivalent of **Passenger Upgrade** (**PUG**) on the **West Coast Main Line** (**WCML**).

Full and Standing
[Ops.] Describing a **Passenger Train** that has all its seats occupied and further **Passengers** standing in the corridors and vestibules. See also **Crush Laden**, **PIXC**, **Pixie**.

Full Barriers
[Sig.] Vertically hinged booms that close off the full width of the highway carriageway, generally at a **Level Crossing** (**LC**, **LX**). See also **Half Barriers**. See also **Barrier Skirts**.

Full Current Dropper
[Elec.] A **Dropper** capable of ensuring electrically continuity between **Contact Wire** (**CW**) and **Catenary Wire**, obviating the need to use **In Span Jumpers**.

Full Current Jumper
[Elec.] A **Jumper** used in an **Un-insulated Overlap** to provide electrical continuity between the **In Running** (**IR**) and **Out of Running** (**OOR**) □ **Contact Wires** (**CW**). Also **Full Drape**.

Full Depth Switch
[PW] A **Switch** assembly in which the **Switch Rail** and **Stock Rail** are manufactured from the same initial **Rail Section**. See also **Shallow Depth Switch**.

Full Drape
[Elec.] An alternative term for a **Full Current Jumper**.

Full Normal
Full Normal Position
[Sig.] Describing a **Lever** which has been pushed back as far is it is designed to go within the **Frame**. See also **Full Reverse Position**, **Full Travel Position**

Full Overlap
[Sig.]
a) A **Signal Overlap** of at least 200 **Yards** (183 metres) where **Colour Light Signals** are used. On the **West Coast Main Line** (**WCML**) this dimension is typically 225 metres (246 Yards).
b) A **Signal Overlap** of at least 440 Yards (400 metres) where both **Distant Signal** and **Stop Signal** are **Semaphore Signals**.

Full Reverse Position
[Sig.] An alternative term for **Full Travel Position**.

Full Screen Height (FSH)
[PW] A description used in the reporting of **Rail Flaws** discovered by **Ultrasonic Rail Flaw Detector Operators** (**URFDO**) to indicate that the trace on their oscilloscope filled the screen.

Full Section
[PW] Describing the normal cross sectional area of a particular **Rail Section**, measured normal to the vertical and longitudinal axes of the **Rail**.

Full Section Break
[PW] A crack that extends all the way across a **Rail**, splitting it into two or more parts.

Full Service
Full Service Brake
[TRS] A full (non-emergency) brake application.

Full Service Brake Position
[TRS] The maximum **Service Brake** position that can be applied before the driver may select the **Emergency Brake** position.

Full Set of Switches
[PW] A pair of **Stock Rails** and a pair of **Switch Rails** with each Stock Rail and associated Switch Rail assembled with the relevant **Baseplates** or **Chairs**, blocks, bolts, **Switch Anchors** (if BH Rail), **Soleplate**(s) and **Stretcher Bars**. See **Set of Switches**.

Full Supervision Mode (FS)
[Sig.] Under the **European Rail Traffic Management System** (**ERTMS**), the normal **Movement Authority** (**MA**) that gives comprehensive protection. The display of this indication tells the driver that they are permitted to drive their Train at the maximum speed shown on the **Driver Machine Interface** (**DMI**) unit.

Full Travel Position
[Sig.] Describing a **Lever** in a **Lever Frame** that has been pulled as far is it is designed to move. Also **Full Reverse Position**.

Full-Through
[Civ.] A **Bridge Deck** formed on the box principle, with both **Floor Beams** and overhead bracing between the main girders. The Floor Beams are normally hung below the **Bottom Chord**. Also **Through**. See also **Half Through**.

Fully Fitted
[Ops.] Describing a **Train** composed entirely of vehicles having functional **Automatic Brakes**. The opposite is **Unfitted**.

Function
a) A contraction of **Engineering Function**, and alternative for **Engineering Discipline**
b) See **Signalling Function**.

Functional Specification (FS)
A document setting out what the equipment is required to do (including any requirement to interface with other components or equipment), rather than setting out the details of the design, which is then left to the supplier of the equipment to decide upon.

Functional Supply Point (FSP)
[EP] The point at which the power supply distribution system connects with an item of supplied equipment.

Fungus
A **Railway** □ **Telegraph Code** meaning "No trace of forwarding the following".

Funicular Railway
A variety of **Railway** where the **Trains** (more often single vehicles) are hauled by wire ropes. They are often found on steep hills, where an **Adhesion Worked** system would fail.

Furno
A **Railway** □ **Telegraph Code** meaning "Until further notice".

Furrer+Frey (F+F)
(Tradename) [Elec.] A family-owned Swiss company, founded in 1923, head office Berne, Switzerland. Designer of **Overhead Line Equipment** (**OLE**) solutions internationally, including **Conductor Bar** systems and **GEFF** and **Series 1** OLE systems used in the UK.

FUT
Follow Up Tamp.

FutureRailway Programme
Collaboration between **Network Rail** (**NR**) and **RSSB** (formerly the **Railway Safety and Standards Board**), working with the wider **Railway Industry** and the supply chain to deliver the **Rail Technical Strategy** (**RTS**). It manages a cross-industry research, development and innovation programme and incorporates the former **Enabling Innovation Team** (**EIT**).

FV
[NR PW] Vertical □ Flat Bottom (FB) Full Depth Switches. The F describes the length and **Switch Radius**.

FVs
[NR PW] Denotes 113A □ Flat Bottom (FB) □ Shallow Depth Switches, length F.

FVS
[NR PW] Denotes CEN56E1 □ Flat Bottom (FB) □ Shallow Depth Switches, length F.

FWC
See Free Wheel Clearance.

FWD
See Falling Weight Deflectometer.

FWI
See Fatalities and Weighted Injuries.

FWP
Functional Workbank Proposal.
FWR
See **First Wheel Replacement**.
FY&NR
[Hist.] The **Pre-Grouping** Freshwater, Yarmouth & Newport **Railway**.

G

G
a) [NR] As the last letter in a **Wagon** □ CARKND, this denotes that the Wagon has **AFI Brakes** and **Through Piping** for **Air Brakes**. Also known as AFI brake, **Air Piped**
b) In an abbreviated **Track Name**, it denotes **Goods**, as in **Goods Line**
c) [PW] In the form Gxx it denotes a type of **Concrete Sleeper**, **Class of Sleeper** G, intended for use with **CEN60E1** or **CEN60E2** □ **Flat Bottom Rail**, e.g. G44
d) An abbreviation of **Green**
e) See **Switch Letters**
f) [Sig.] On a **Signalling Circuit Diagram**:
 • As one of the leading letters of an **Equipment Code**, it means **Signal**
 • As the last letter of an Equipment Code, it means Signal apparatus.
g) The letter represented by **Golf** in the **Phonetic Alphabet**
h) **Common Interface File Operating Characteristics Code** for **Trainman** (**Guard**) required.

g
a) [Sig.] On a **Signalling Circuit Diagram** as the last letter of an **Equipment Code**, it means lightning arrester
b) The acceleration due to gravity, typically 9.81m/s/s (metres per second per second). See also **% of g**.

G Stock
[TRS LUL] Type of **Clerestory**-roofed stock built for the District **Railway** in 1923 and subsequently absorbed into the **Q Stock**. All **Cars** of this batch were originally **Motor** Cars.

G&PJR
[Hist.] The **Pre-Grouping** Glasgow & Paisley Joint **Railway**, a Caledonian and Glasgow & South Western joint enterprise.

G&SWR
[Hist.] The **Pre-Grouping** Glasgow & South Western **Railway**.

GA
a) See **General Arrangement Drawing**. Also GA Drawing.
b) General Assembly.

GA Drawing
See **General Arrangement Drawing**.

Gabion
(*gay-be-un* or *gabb-ee-on*) [Civ.] A wire mesh basket filled with broken stone or rubble, used as an efficient but plain reinforcing or retaining **Structure** for **Earthworks**.

GADEROS
Galileo Demonstrator for Railway Operation System.

Galaxy Inspection
[RT] The name given to inspections of key assets, such as critical **Junctions**, carried out jointly by **Railtrack** and the relevant **Infrastructure Maintenance Contractor** (**IMC**).

Gall
a) Localised damage and wear between two surfaces caused by friction
b) [PW] A defect caused by a **Chair** or **Baseplate** eroding a **Rail** or vice versa. See **Chair Gall**, **Rail Gall**, **Rail Gall of Baseplates**, **Sleeper Gall**.

Galvanometer
[PW] The large indicators used on older **Tampers** to indicate the direction and magnitude of the required **Lifts** and **Slues**. Also **Galvo**.

Galvo
[PW Col.] A common contraction of **Galvanometer**.

GAMAB
Globalement Au Moins Aussi Bon (globally at least as good); used by the French in preference to **ALARP** (As Low As Reasonably Practical). GAMAB assumes that there is already an 'acceptable' solution and requires that any new solution shall in total be at least as good.

Gane (YLO, YLP)
[NR] A 41 ton capacity flat **Wagon** used for the transportation of **Track Panels** and **Rails**. See **Wagon Names**.

Gang
A group of **Railway** operatives who normally work together. The term is normally used to describe **Permanent Way** (**PW**) groups (as in Permanent Way Gang, Pway Gang, **Relaying Gang**) but can be applied to any discipline (e.g. **S&T** Gang).

Gang Bus
[BR Obs.] The vehicle which a **Gang** uses to travel from job to job. They have drying, **Tea** making and heating facilities, as well as compartments for tools. See also **Chip Van**, **Relaying Bus**.

Ganger
[Obs.] The foreman in charge of a **Permanent Way** (**PW**) □ **Gang**. Latterly termed a **Track Chargeman**.

Gangway
[TRS] The concertina-covered walkway connecting two **Passenger Coaches** or two vehicles in a **Multiple Unit Train**.

Gangwayed
[TRS] Being capable of connection by **Gangways**.

Gannet
[NR, prob. Obs.] A 25 ton capacity **Ballast Hopper**.

Gantry
a) A goalpost-shaped or **Cantilever** construction spanning multiple **Tracks**. There are two common purposes, both employed where simpler arrangements cannot be located between Tracks, namely **Overhead Line Structures** and **Signal Gantries**. The uprights are termed legs, and the horizontal part is the **Boom**
b) [PW] A portal frame machine equipped with **Double Flange Rail Wheels** used in pairs with a **Sleeper Beam** for **Track Relaying**. See **Single Line Gantry** (SLG).

Gantry Relaying
[PW] **Relaying** ▫ **Track** using a pair of **Single Line Gantries** (SLG).

Gantry Signal
[Sig.] A **Signal** located on a **Gantry**. See also **Offset Signal**, **Straight Post Signal**.

Gap Jumper
[Elec.] A heavy duty cable used to temporarily restore the **Traction Supply** to a **Train** via the **Shed Receptacle** in the event of the train becoming **Gapped**.

Gapped
[Elec., Ops.] A state occurring when a **Train** on a **DC Electrified Line** system stops with none of its **Current Collection Shoes** (**Shoes**) in contact with the **Conductor Rail** and therefore without power to restart. Some careful consideration is required during the design stage to prevent this happening.

Garland
[Civ.] A circular channel fixed around the inside of a **Tunnel Shaft** just above the **Eye**, intended to catch water running down the sides of the **Shaft**. Also **Launder**, **Ring Dam**.

Garratt Locomotive
[TRS] A variety of **Steam Locomotive** where the boiler is supported by two large **Bogies**, each of which has a set of pistons and **Driving Wheels**. In general, a large water tank occupied one Bogie and a coal bunker the other. Because of their large number of Driving Wheels and capability to negotiate a relatively tight **Minimum Radius**, they found work hauling heavy **Trains** in mountainous areas.

Gas Axe
[Col.] A colloquial alternative for an oxygen / propane or oxygen / acetylene cutting torch.

Gas Bag Points
See **Train Operated Switch**.

Gas Cut
[PW Col.] Alternative term for **Flame Cut**, i.e. a **Rail** cut with an oxygen / fuel gas cutting torch. See also **Gas Axe**.

Gas Points Heating
[PW Obs.] A **Points Heating** system, fuelled by either a mains gas supply or by stored LPG, which uses a gas flame to warm the **Stock Rail** and keep the **Switches** free of ice and small amounts of **Snow**. The system suffered from interruptions to the gas supply in remote areas (gas from cylinders was used) and an unreliable piezoelectric ignition system. Virtually all such installations have now been replaced by **Electric Pad Heaters**, **Electric Cartridge Heaters** or the newer **Electric Strip Heaters**.

Gas Pressure Weld
[PW] A **Rail Weld** made by heating the **Rail Ends** to be joined to a near molten state, forcing them together and holding them in the correct relationship whilst the **Rail** cools. The result is comparable with a **Flash Butt Weld** (FBW), but the equipment is more portable. The system is not widely used in the UK.

Gas Turbine Locomotive
[TRS] A **Locomotive** utilising burning liquid fuel to produce hot gasses. These in turn power a gas turbine. In early experiments this turbine drove the **Driving Wheels** through a reduction gearbox, but later ones powered an electrical generator, supplying **Electric Traction Motors**.

Gate
a) The side hinged device used to bar the passage of pedestrians and vehicles at some **Level Crossings** (LC, LX)
b) [PW] A device towed behind the **Cutter Bar** of a **Ballast Cleaner** under the **Track**. Its purpose is to level and distribute the **Returned Ballast** during **Ballast Cleaning** operations. Also **Four Bar Gate**.

Gate Box
A **Control Point** provided solely to control the **Gates** or **Barriers** at one or more **Level Crossing** (LC, LX). A Gate Box is not a **Block Post**. Also **Level Crossing Box**.

Gate Stop Lever
[Sig.] At a **Controlled Level Crossing**, a **Lever** which when moved from **Full Reverse** to the **Backlock** (B) position releases the **Rail Gate Stops**, allowing the **Gates** to be moved to close the highway. Moving the Lever to **Full Normal** locks the **Road Gate Stops** in the raised position, holding the Gates closed across the highway. This Lever is **Interlocked** with the **Protecting Signals**.

Gate Wheel
[Sig.] The handwheel provided in a **Gate Box** or **Signal Box**, with which the **Crossing Keeper** or **Signaller** operates the **Gates** of a **Controlled Level Crossing**. See **Gate Stop Lever**, **Rail Gate Stop**, **Road Gate Stop**.

Gatekeeper
[IÉ] A person in charge of the **Gate** or Gates at a **Level Crossing** (LC, LX).

Gateline
An alternative for **Ticket Line**.

ELLIS' BRITISH RAILWAY ENGINEERING ENCYCLOPÆDIA

GATES
(gayts) (Tradename) Graphical and Text Entry System, a Geographical Information System (**GIS**) produced by Parsons Brinkerhoff (**PB**)

GatEx
(gatt-ex) [Col.] Nickname for the **Gatwick Express** services.

Gathering Line
A **Track** at the end of a **Raft** of **Sidings** which is connected to each Siding and which connects the Sidings to an **Arrival Line** or **Departure Line**.

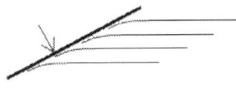

Gathering Rails
[PW] An alternative name for the **Rails** placed outside the **Fourfoot** in the **Flare** of a **Guard Rail** installation.

Gatso Signal
[Sig. Col.] A name for a type of **Colour Light Signal** □ **Signal Head** that can be raised or lowered from its normal operating position. This allows the Head to be cleaned and maintained more easily than the traditional **Gantry Signal** which normally hangs beneath the **Gantry** in a narrow cage.

Gatwick Express
(Tradename) A **Train Operating Company** (**TOC**) operating services between London and Gatwick Airport. **ATOC** code **GX**.

Gauge
a) See **Track Gauge**
b) [PW] A device for measuring **Track Gauge**
c) To measure the profile of a **Railway** □ **Structure** such as a **Bridge**, **Tunnel** or **Platform** using the **Track** as a reference
d) [TRS] The maximum permissible dimensions of **Rail Vehicles** and the minimum permissible dimensions of **Lineside** structures which **Trains** pass. See **Kinematic Envelope** (**KE**), Loading Gauge, Static Vehicle Envelope, Structure Gauge, Swept Envelope.

Gauge Corner
[PW] The curved profile of the **Rail Head** between **Running Surface** and **Running Edge** (**RE**).

Gauge Corner Cracking (GCC)
[PW] A dense pattern of small cracks, local to the **Gauge Corner**, generated under certain cercumstances on **Curves** with high **Cant Deficiency** (**D**) by the rolling action of passing **Wheelsets**. See **Head Checking** (**HC**).

Gauge Face
[PW] The side of the **Rail Head** facing towards the opposite **Running Rail**, e.g. the face to which the **Track Gauge** is measured. See also **Gauge Point**.

Gauge Infringement
The presence of a **Structure** or another **Rail Vehicle** within the **Vehicle Gauge**. See also **Foul**. Also **Infringement**.

Gauge Line
[PW]
a) Seen in plan, a line representing the locus of **Gauge Points** of a particular **Rail**. This depiction is used to simplify drawings, as only one line is required to accurately represent each **Rail**. See also **Intersection of Gauge Lines** (**IP**)
b) An alternative for **Track Centre Line**.

Gauge Management Insulator
[PW] A type of **Rail Foot Insulator** for use with **Pandrol** □ **e+** □ **Rail Fastenings**, allowing adjustment of the **Gauge** during **Maintenance** activity.

Gauge Panel
A **Level Crossing Panel** designed to be fitted between the **Running Rails**.

Gauge Plate
[PW] That part of some **Rail Fastenings** that restricts lateral movement of the **Rail**.

Gauge Point
[PW] The point on the **Running Rail** from which **Track Gauge** is measured. This is 14mm below the **Crown** of the **Rail on Network Rail** (**NR**), 13mm on London Underground Limited (**LUL**).

Gauge Rails
[PW] The two **Running Rails** of a **Track** at a specified **Gauge** (distance) apart.

Gauge Retention
[PW]
a) A physical means of maintaining the **Track Gauge** at its correct value
b) **Maintenance** of the designed Track Gauge between the **Gauge Faces** of the **Rails**, and the ability of a **Sleeper** or **Rail Fastening** system to maintain this dimension.

Gauge Shoulder
See **Gauge Corner**.

Gauge Side
[PW] The side of a **Running Rail** nearest the other related Running Rail. The opposite is **Field Side**.

Gauge Spread
[PW] The tendency of the **Gauge** of inadequately maintained **Track** to become greater, e.g. the **Rails** move away from each other. This is a prime cause of low speed **Derailments** in **Depots** and **Sidings**, which are traditionally places considered low Maintenance priorities. Major causes are **Baseplate Shuffle**, **Chair Shuffle**, rotten **Sleepers** and **Chairscrews** losing their grip in the **Sleepers**. Also Road Spread. See also **Gauge Stop**, **Gauge Tie Bar**, **Tie Bar**, **Vortok Coil**.

Gauge Stop
[PW] A metal plate fixed to the upper surface of a (typically) **Wood Sleeper**, against a **Chair** or **Baseplate** to restrict the outward lateral movement of the **Rail**, see **Gauge Spread**, Road Spread.

Gauge Tie
[PW] Any **Bearer**, **Sleeper** or **Timber** or other device that maintains the two **Rails** of a **Track** at the designed **Track Gauge** between the **Gauge Faces** of the Rails. See also **Gauge Tie Bar**, **Tie Bar**.

203

ELLIS' BRITISH RAILWAY ENGINEERING ENCYCLOPÆDIA

Gauge Tie Bar
[PW] An adjustable metal bar normally constructed with an insulated section in the middle, fixed between **Gauge Rails** to restore and maintain **Track Gauge**. Often shortened to **Tie Bar**.

Gauge Transition
[PW] A short length of **Track** within which the **Track Gauge** changes from one design value to another.

Gauge Variation
[PW] A **Track Fault**. The safe and comfortable **Running** of **Trains** depends on a reliable interface between **Rail** and **Rail Wheel**. Variations in **Gauge** cause **Wheelsets** to wander, and can be an indicator of impending component failure. See also **Gauge Spread**.

Gauge War, The
[Hist.] The intense battle between proponents of **Broad Gauge** (latterly 7' - 0^1/$_4$", (2140mm)) as used on the **Great Western Railway** (**GWR**) and the supporters of **Standard Gauge** (4' - 8^1/$_2$", 1435mm) which raged between 1844, when the GWR reached Gloucester and the Standard Gauge Birmingham & Gloucester Railway, and 1861 when **Mixed-gauge Track** was laid into Paddington Station. See also **Railway Regulation (Gauge) Act 1846**.

Gauge Widening
[PW] Increasing the **Track Gauge** by a small amount to ease the passage of **Wheelsets** around tight curves. Where a **Check Rail** is present, the dimension between the **Rubbing Face** of the Check Rail and the **Running Edge** (**RE**) of the opposite **Rail** is constant at 1391mm, irrespective of the Gauge Widening, See **Check Rail Gauge**.

Gauging
a) [PW] The action of setting the **Running Rails** to the correct **Track Gauge** prior to fixing them in position
b) [PW] The taking of measurements to determine the Track Gauge at a particular point. A related term is **Re-gauging**, which is the act of making the **Gauge** correct, see **Gauging Survey**.
c) [PW] The taking of measurements to record the profile of a structure or many structures relative to the **Track**, to determine whether passing **Trains** will be **Clear** or **Foul**, see **Gauging Survey**
d) The taking of measurements to assess whether a load on a Train is within **Loading Gauge** or **Out of Gauge** (**OOG**).

Gauging Survey
[PW]
a) The measurement of points on a **Bridge**, **Platform**, **Signal** or wall relative to the **Running Rails** at that location to determine what, if any, clearance exists between **Train** and **Structure**. This can be accomplished by means of:
- Laser Sweep™ or similar system
- Point Cloud
- Pole and Tape
- Vehicle mounted scanners, see **Structure Gauging Train** (**SGT**)
- Or, for **Platforms**, a Platform Gauge.

b) The measurement of the **Track Gauge** at specified intervals to determine compliance.

Gauging Tolerances
[PW] The various allowances made during the analysis of **Gauging** data, primarily to ensure that the result is correct under all conditions. Typical additions include:
- An allowance based on the **Track Fixity**; Low Track Fixity will incur a greater allowance
- An allowance based on the method used to collect the data; **Pole and Tape Surveys** and data from the **Structure Gauging Train** (**SGT**) attracts a high allowance, whereas **Laser Sweep Surveys** and **Point Cloud Surveys** have a higher repeat accuracy and attract a lower allowance.

Gauging Train
[NR] A **Train** fitted with profiling and distance measuring equipment, used to carry out rapid **Gauging** of many structures on a **Route**. See also **HSGT**, **OLGA**, **Serco Gauging Train** (**SGT**), **Structure Gauging Train** (**SGT**).

Gauntletted Track
See **Interlaced Track**.

GB&KJR
[Hist.] The **Pre-Grouping** Glasgow, Barrhead & Kilmarnock Joint **Railway**, a Caledonian and Glasgow & South Western joint enterprise.

GBFM
Great Britain **Freight** Model.

GBPRT
See **Great Britain Passenger Railway Timetable**.

GBRf
(Tradename) Great Britain **Rail** □ **Freight** Limited, a Freight Operating Company (FOC).

GBTP
See **Great British Travelling Public**.

GBTT
[Ops.] Great Britain **Timetable**, see **Great Britain Passenger Railway Timetable** (**GBPRT**).

GC
The **ATOC** code for **Grand Central**

GCC
See **Gauge Corner Cracking**.

GCR
See **Great Central Railway**.

GCRN
[Pres.] Great Central **Railway** Nottingham.

GCV
Geismar Concept Vehicle.
GD
[Sig.] On a **Signalling Circuit Diagram**, denotes a wire coloured go<u>ld</u>.
GDI
a) [PW] <u>G</u>rand <u>D</u>amage <u>I</u>ndex, a **Track-Ex** output
b) <u>G</u>raphical <u>D</u>ata <u>I</u>nterface.
GDIP
[NR] <u>G</u>eography Information System (**GEOGIS**) <u>D</u>ata quality <u>I</u>mprovement <u>P</u>roject.
GDO
<u>G</u>eneral <u>D</u>evelopment <u>O</u>rder.
GDU
[PW] <u>G</u>rease <u>D</u>elivery <u>U</u>nit. See **Rail Lubricator**.
GE
a) <u>G</u>reat <u>E</u>astern **Railway** (**GER**)
b) <u>G</u>eneral <u>E</u>lectric Company, not related to the UK based **GEC**.

Gear Pan
[TRS] The casing that encloses the gears linking a **Traction Motor** and its related axle.

GEC
(Tradename) <u>G</u>eneral <u>E</u>lectric <u>C</u>ompany, not related to the US based **GE**.

GEFF
[Elec.] **G**reat **E**astern □ **F**urrer+**F**rey. A **Mark of Overhead Line Equipment** (**OLE**) specifically designed to replace the ex-DC OLE on the Great Eastern route in Anglia from 2009 onward. It used **Autotensioned** □ **Catenary** and **Contact Wire** (**CW**) at 12 and 13.2kN respectively. The design retains the existing structures where possible and uses **Twin-Boom Anchor Portals** for mechanical independence.

Geismar
(Tradename) A company specialising in the manufacture of **Permanent Way** (**PW**) plant and equipment, best known for its **Panel Lifting Equipment** (see **LEM**, **PAL**, **PEM**, **PLUM**, **PUM**).

GEMINI
[Ops., TRS] (*jemi-nee* or *jemi-ny*) A computer system that allows engineers, **Rolling Stock** and performance managers to examine information about their vehicles without the need for access to the feeding systems. GEMINI has two components:
- Web-GEMINI, which stores details of **Multiple Unit** (**MU**) and **Locomotive-Hauled Coaching Stock** (**LHCS**). Data is passed via an open interface (mainly from **GENIUS**).
- GEMINI Mainframe, which provides the only means to communicate this information to, and obtain information from, mainframe systems including **RAVERS** and Network Rail's (**NR**) □ **Passenger** billing systems **PABS**.

Gemini
[Hist.] The codename of **Laboratory** 16, an experimental **Battery Electric Multiple Unit** (**BEMU**).

GEML
[NR] <u>G</u>reat <u>E</u>astern **Main Line**, running from London (Liverpool Street) to Norwich via Romford, Chelmsford and Ipswich. The Line is **Electrified** on the 25kV AC system throughout.

GEN
[TRS] An acronym representing a Generator **Van**.

General Arrangement Drawing (GA, GA Drawing)
A drawing which gives an overview of a project, generally produced at a small scale such as 1:500.

General Engineering Inspection
[IÉ] A systematic visual inspection of a **Structure** that is generally adequate to monitor and assess its condition. Usually undertaken from ground or water level with the assistance of binoculars or ladders where necessary, so that all visible elements are examined.

General Purpose Crane (GPC)
A standard specification 12 tonne Safe Working Load (**SWL**) single telescopic jib hydraulic **Rail Crane** produced for **British Railways** (**BR**) by several manufacturers during the 1970s.

General Purpose Track Repair and Maintenance Machine (GP-TRAMM, TRAMM)
An **On Track Machine** (**OTM**) used for moving material to and from sites of work.

General Repair
[TRS] A **Maintenance** process undertaken prior to 1992 which entailed a full dismantling, refurbishment and rebuild of a **Rail Vehicle**.

Generator
[Col.] Nickname given to the first **Class** 47 **Diesel Locomotives**, which were fitted with an **Electric Train Heating** (**ETH**) generator, causing the engine to run hard whilst standing in **Stations**.

Generator Coach
Generator Van
Generator Wagon
[TRS] A **Coach**, **Van** or **Wagon** equipped with a diesel generating set, used to supply electrical power (and occasionally hydraulic power) to other vehicles. Examples include powering specialist **Engineering Trains** such as the **Track Relaying Train** (**TRT**), High Speed Track Recording Coach (**HSTRC**), Wiring Train or providing **Electric Train Heating** (**ETH**) when the **Locomotive** cannot.

GENIUS
(*gee-nee-uss*) **GEMINI** for <u>N</u>on-<u>i</u>ntegrating <u>U</u>nit □ <u>S</u>tock.

Geoblanket
A synthetic composite material, consisting of an impermeable separating layer with a **Geotextile** filter layer loosely bonded on each side. This is an equivalent construction to a traditional **Sand Blanket**, in that it separates **Formation** from **Ballast** and allows both to drain freely.

ELLIS' BRITISH RAILWAY ENGINEERING ENCYCLOPÆDIA

GEOGIS
(joggis) [NR] (Believed to be a contraction of **Geo**graphic and **I**nfrastructure **S**ystem) A former British Railways (BR) database holding information such as age, construction and responsibility for **Track** nationally. The **Structures** element has been transferred to **CARRS**.

Geographic Data
[Sig.] In a **Solid State Interlocking** (**SSI**) this is the data which specifies the logical relationships between the components of the **Railway**, encoding the **Signalling** □ **Control** functions of the **Interlocking**. The Geographic Data is stored in EPROM.

Geographic Data Language (GDL)
[Sig.] The specialised design notation used to encode the interlocking logic within The **Geographic Data** of a **Solid State Interlocking** (**SSI**). It is a simple language of assignment, sequence and conditional statements, but it is enriched by **Specials** designed to shorten the **Minor Cycle** execution time.

Geographical Interlocking
[Sig.] A type of **Interlocking** in which standard pre-wired assemblies are provided for each **Signalling Function** such as a **Signal**, which are then arranged and electrically interconnected in a geographical manner.

Geographical Junction
A **Switch and Crossing Layout** (**S&C Layout**) at which one **Route** splits into two or more Routes. See also **Running Junction**.

Geogrid
(Tradename) A synthetic mesh used as a strengthening material for soils, manufactured by Tensar Ltd.

Geometry
See **Track Geometry**.

Geometry Marking
[PW] The painting of **Cant** (**C**, **E**), Radius (**R**) and **Transition Length** (**TL**) information on the **Sleepers** for the benefit of **Tamping and Lining Machine** (**Tamper**) operators and others.

Geometry Recording
[PW] The measuring of **Alignment**, Cant (**C**, **E**), Cant Deficiency (**D**) **Crosslevel**, **Gauge**, Radius (**R**), **Top** and **Twist** data, normally for the purpose of assessing **Track Quality**.

George
The obsolescent **Phonetic Alphabet** word representing G. Replaced by **Golf**.

Georgemas Plunger
[Sig.] A device that allows the **Train** driver to operate a **Set of Points** from the **Cab**, as fitted at Georgemas Junction. See also **Plunger**.

Geotextile
A synthetic filter material laid on top of the **Formation** to prevent contamination of the **Ballast** by the underlying soils. See also **Terram**.

Geoweb
(Tradename) A synthetic 'concertina' arrangement that is expanded and laid over the **Formation**, filled with a non-cohesive material to create a semi-rigid layer. It is used to rectify very unstable Formations, e.g. where a **Railway** crosses a marsh. Manufactured by Presto Geosystems of Appleton, Wisconsin.

GER
[Hist.] The **Pre-Grouping** **G**reat **E**astern **Railway**.

GERTRUDE
[Civ.] **G**irder **R**esponse to **T**rain Loading **U**nder **D**ynamic **E**xcitation, a simplified version of **MABEL**.

GETS
(getz) (Tradename) **GE** **T**ransportation **S**ystems.

Getting a Margin
[Col. NPT] A term describing a non-preferred method of arranging a short unofficial **Possession** of the **Line** to carry out some minor task **On or Near the Line**. There is generally no **Protection** or paperwork. The spirit of this arrangement became formalised in **Section T** part 2 of the **Rule Book**. Also called **Between Trains** (**BT**).

GF
See **Ground Frame**.

GFPEBRSS
Guidance for **F**ire **P**recautions on **E**xisting **B**ritish **R**ail □ **S**urface **S**tations.

GFT
[Tel.] **G**round **F**rame **T**elephone, see also **Point Zone Telephone** (**PZT**).

GGI
Grand **G**ap **I**ndex, a **Track-Ex** output.

Ghníomhaireacht um Fháil Iarnród
See **Railway Procurement Agency** (**RPA**).

GI
a) **G**eneral **I**nstruction
b) **G**round **I**nvestigation.

Gib and Cotter
A means of securing a rod to another item, widely used on **Steam Locomotives**.

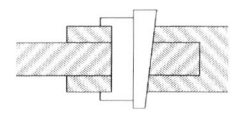

Gibbon
[WR Col.] An alternative term for a **Hand Trolley**. Also **Bogie**, **Trolley**.

Gidea Park Accident
At around 23:17 on 2nd January 1947, a **Passenger Train** collided with the rear of a stationary Passenger Train at 35mph in thick **Fog**. The stationary **Train** was correctly stopped at Gidea Park **Station**, the second over-ran several **Semaphore Stop Signals** showing **Stop Aspects**. The driver's error of excess speed in poor visibility was compounded by the actions of a **Fogman** in failing to correctly place **Detonators** at one of these **Signals**. This Accident was one of a series which prompted the widespread introduction of **Automatic Warning System** (**AWS**). See also **Harrow And Wealdstone Accident**.

GIJ
See **Glued Insulated Joint**. Also **Insulated Rail Joint** (**IRJ**). See also **Block Joint**, **Insulated Block Joint** (**IBJ**) **Insulated Joint** (**IJ**).

Gilchrist Report, The
More fully, "Technical Memorandum: An Investigation into the Causation of **Signals Passed at Danger**" by AO Gilchrist, published in 1989 following a three year study. This was the first formal study of **SPADs** and their causes.

Ginney Line
[Hist.] The name given to a **Narrow Gauge** chain or **Rope-hauled Railway** located in the south Lancashire coalfield. The systems originally utilised plate rails, some until well into the 20th century and chain haulage although the more progressive systems developed into more conventional **Railways** using **Edge Rails** and ropes rather than chains. It was generallly acknowledged that such a system would only work satisfactorily if then **Track** followed a straight horizontal alignment but vertical changes of alignment presented no problems. See also **Bottom Endless Haulage**, **Top Endless Haulage**.

Girdering
[LUL] A structure over a **Sub-Surface Line** with a multiplicity of spanning elements that is not readily defined as a **Bridge** or **Covered Way**.

GIS
a) Gas Insulated Switchgear
b) Geographical Information System.

Give a Warning, to
To alert others to an approaching **Train**, by one of the following means:
- A shouted warning,
- A whistle
- A Horn,
- By touch, in noisy environments
- By the operation of sirens, see **Kango Packing**, **Lookout Operated Warning System** (**LOWS**), **PeeWee**.

Giving On
[Col.] An alternative term for transmitting **Train Entering Section**' to the **Signaller** □ Ahead as a **Train** passes into a **Block Section**.

Giving Out
[Col.] An alternative term for transmitting **Train Out Of Section** to the signaller □ In Rear as a **Train** leaves a **Block Section** and passes beyond the **Clearing Point**.

GJT
Generalised Journey Time.

GKS
Guard's Key Switch.

GL
a) Goods □ Line
b) Ground Level.

Glanrhyd Bridge Accident
At around 07:15 on the 19th of October 1987, a **DMU** ran at reduced speed onto the Glanrhyd **Bridge**, which carries the **Railway** over the river Towy. The **Train** was being used to inspect the **Line** following reports of flooding, and the river was at its highest recorded level thus far. Just prior the **Train**'s arrival several of the **Bridge Piers** collapsed, caused by a combination of high water levels, **Scour** and progressive overloading. Three **Passengers** and the driver died.

GLAP
[LUL] Gate Line Attendant Point.

Glasgow St. Enoch Accident
At about 08:06 on 27th July 1903, the driver of an **Excursion Train** entered Glasgow St. Enoch station at between 12 and 15 mph, underestimated the length of the **Platform** which resulted his **Train** collided with the **Fixed Buffer Stop**. 16 died and 64 were injured. Most of these were in the second **Passenger** vehicle which was **Telescoped** under the leading vehicle.

Glass Signal Box
[Col.] Nickname for the **Integrated Electronic Control Centre** (**IECC**) system.

GLCT
Ground Level Cable Trough. Also C/1/x, GLT, Surface Concrete Trough (SCT).

GLE
Grant Lyon & Eagre.

Global System for Mobile Communications – Railways (GSM-R)
[Tel.] A national radio system which provides secure voice communications between **Trains** and **Signallers**, relaying calls via radio base stations built alongside the **Railway** or on suitable vantage points.

Gloucester Floating Axle
Gloucester Floating Axle Suspension
[TRS] A form of **Wagon** suspension in which increased loading results in increased damping, by means of friction.

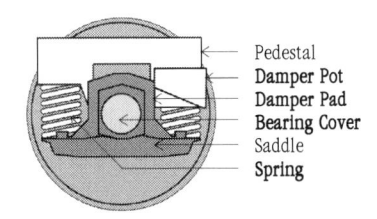

- Pedestal
- Damper Pot
- Damper Pad
- Bearing Cover
- Saddle
- Spring

Gloucester Railway Carriage and Wagon Company (GRC&W)
(Tradename) [TRS Hist.] A **Rolling Stock** manufacturer based in Gloucester, England; from 1860 until 1986, when it was bought by Powell Duffryn Rail. This part of Powell Duffryn, latterly trading as Probotec, was subsequently sold to **Axiom Rail**.

GLT
Ground Level Troughing.

ELLIS' BRITISH RAILWAY ENGINEERING ENCYCLOPÆDIA

Glued Insulated Joint (GIJ)
[PW] An **Insulated Rail Joint** (IRJ) in which the components are resin bonded together as well as being bolted or **MGL Pinned**. Also **Block Joint, Insulated Block Joint** (IBJ), **Insulated Joint** (IJ).

GLV
[TRS] An acronym representing a Gatwick Luggage Van.

GLW
See **Gross Laden Weight**.

GM
(Tradename) General Motors, a manufacturer of **Locomotives**.

GMITA
Greater Manchester Integrated Transport Authority, the new name for Greater Manchester **Passenger Transport Authority (GMPTA)**.

GMPTA
[Hist.] Greater Manchester **Passenger Transport Authority** (PTA), now called Greater Manchester Integrated Transport Authority (**GMITA**).

GMPTE
Greater Manchester **Passenger Transport Executive** (PTE), now called Transport for Greater Manchester (**TfGM**).

GN
a) The **Great Northern Line**, Kings Cross to Cambridge via Royston
b) [Sig.] On a **Signalling Circuit Diagram**, denotes a wire coloured green.

GNER
(*g'nur*) (Tradename) Great North Eastern **Railway**, a **Train Operating Company (TOC)**.

GNR
[Hist.] The **Pre-Grouping** Great Northern **Railway**.

GNRI
[Éire] Great Northern **Railway**, Ireland, a former **Railway Company**, formed in 1876 by a merger of the Irish North Western Railway, Northern Railway of Ireland, and the Ulster Railway.

GNRTS
[Hist.] Greater Nottingham **Rapid Transit** System, now Nottingham Express Transit (**NET**).

GNSR
[Hist.] The **Pre-Grouping** Great North of Scotland **Railway**.

GNSS
Global Navigation Satellite Systems.

GNYE
[Sig.] On a **Signalling Circuit Diagram**, denotes a wire coloured green and yellow.

Go Zone
[CT] In the **Channel Tunnel**, a section of the **Running Tunnel** in which **Trains** making an out of course stop should avoid coming to a stand.

GoA
Grades of Automation, See **Transmission Based Train Control (TBTC)**.

Goal Post
[Col.]
a) [PW] Term for the cast-in steel bars used in the **Spring Hook Clip (SHC)** □ **Rail Fastening** on F19 Concrete Sleepers
b) [Sig. Obs.]Term for the short length of **Bond Wire** used as part of a **Track Circuit** (TC) connection to a **Rail**, a method superseded by the use of a moulded connector bolted to the Rail.

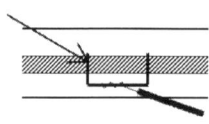

Gobi
A **Railway** □ **Telegraph Code** meaning "The following **Route** must be observed:- ..." and applied to **Out of Gauge Loads**.

GOBLIN
[Col.] Shorthand for the Gospel Oak to Barking **Line**.

Going Round The Corner
[Col.] A term describing a **Train** passing onto a **Branch Line**.

Gold / Silver / Bronze Command
The standard management framework employed at complex or major incidents, mandated by the Civil Contingencies Act (2004). Gold is strategic, Silver is tactical and Bronze is geographical.

Golden Assets
Equipment and facilities situated at locations where any failure of this equipment would have a severe detrimental effect on the operation of the **Railway**.

Goldschmidt Process

Goldschmidt Reaction
See **Alumino-thermic, Alumino-thermic Reaction**.

Golf
The **Phonetic Alphabet** word representing G.

GOMMMS
(*gomz*) Guidance on the Methodology for **Multi-Modal** Studies.

Gong
a) [Sig.] A plate-shaped sounding device used to attract the attention of **Signallers** and **Shunters**. See also **Asking Lever, Shunting Gong**
b) See **Tunnel Gong**.

Gonging-off
[Hist.] Indication from the **Signaller** that the **Route** was **Set** for (especially) a **Steam Locomotive** to depart from a **Locomotive Shed**.

Gooch, Daniel
Later Sir, (1816-1889) born in Bedlington, Northumberland. Beginning his career in the Robert Stephenson & Co. **Locomotive** works in Forth Street, Newcastle, Gooch was appointed Locomotive superintendent of the **Great Western Railway** (**GWR**). He later resigned to follow a new career in telegraphy and politics, returning to the GWR as Chairman in 1865, masterminding the Severn **Tunnel**, which opened in 1886.

Good
[PW NR] A length of **Track** (usually an **Eighth of a Mile**) over which the **Track Quality** (**TQ**) is better than **Satisfactory**, in that the **Standard Deviation** (**SD**) values for **Top** and **Line** are below the 50% values for the **Permissible Speed** (**PS**) or **Enhanced Permissible Speed** (**EPS**).

Goods
The historical term for **Freight**, particularly merchandise, parcels and manufactured items. Aggregates and coal were termed **Minerals**.

Goods Line
a) A **Track** used predominantly for carrying **Freight Trains**. See **Goods**. Also **Freight Line**
b) [NR] A **Running Line** that is not required to be **Signalled** to the standard required for **Passenger Trains**. Particularly, **Signal Overlaps** are not required, and equivalent protection is typically provided by **Trap Points**. Passenger Trains are not permitted to use **Lines** □ **Fitted** to **Freight Standards** except by special authority. All new Lines must be built to **Passenger Standards**.

Goods Loop
A **Loop** or **Siding** connected to a **Main Line** at both ends and intended for use by **Goods Trains** and **Freight Trains**. See **Goods Line** clause (b). Also **Goods Refuge Loop**.

Goods Refuge Loop
An alternative term for a **Goods Loop**.

Goods Station
A **Station** used exclusively for the handling of merchandise, parcels and manufactured items. Such buildings were commonplace in the days when the **Railways** were **Common Carriers**, and were frequently converted from former **Passenger** Stations whose traffic had moved elsewhere.

Goods Train
A **Train** composed of **Rail Vehicles** carrying **Goods**. See **Freight Train**.

GOOSE
Generic Object Orientated Substation Events.

Gooseneck
[Elec.] A type of cantilever tube used to support the **Catenary Wire** and register the **Contact Wire** (**CW**), common in **GEFF** and **Series 1** □ **Overhead Line Equipment** (**OLE**) systems.

GOTCHA
(Tradename) A type of **Wheel Impact Load Detector** (**WILD**) intended as a replacement for **Wheelchex**.

Governance for Railway Investment Projects (GRIP)
(*grip*) [NR] (previously Guide to Railway Investment Projects) A formal procedure through which every investment project on **Network Rail's** (**NR**) □ **Railway** must pass. It consists of the following stages; at the end of each of these a review is carried out, and if the project cannot meet the pass criteria, it is stopped, or held until it does:
- GRIP Stage 1 - **Output Definition**, which lays down the problem to be addressed and identifies key issues
- GRIP Stage 2 - **Pre-feasibility**, which describes the changes to be made to the Railway to meet the Output Definition
- GRIP Stage 3 - **Single Option Selection**, where a small number of possible options are tested. This stage now includes sign-off of the Single Option by the Route Asset Managers (RAM) as **Approval in Principle** (**AIP**). See **GRIP 3 AIP**.
- GRIP Stage 4 - **Single Option Development**, where the single option is developed in detail. At this point the decision to spend real money is made, and the last stages of GRIP cover the delivery of the project:
- GRIP Stage 5 - **Detailed Design**
- GRIP Stage 6 - Construction, Testing and Commissioning
- GRIP Stage 7 - Handback
- GRIP Stage 8 - closing down of the project.

GP
General Purpose (often seen on **Rail Cranes**).

GPC
See **General Purpose Crane**.

GPDO
Town and Country Planning (General Permitted Development) Order 1995.

GPG
Good Practice Guide.

GPL
GPLS
[Sig.] See **Ground Position Light Signal**.

GPR
a) See **Ground Penetrating Radar**
b) General Purpose Relief.

GPRS
General Packet Radio Service.

GPS
Global Positioning System.

GP-TRAMM
(*gee-pea-tram*) See **General Purpose Track Repair and Maintenance Machine**.

GPU
[TRS] Faiveley Grand Plongeur Unique, a type of **Pantograph** fitted to **Class** 373 **Eurostars** for operation at up to 300kph on the **Channel Tunnel Rail Link** (**CTRL**) and up to 177kph on the East Coast Main Line (**ECML**).

GR
a) General Repair
b) The **ATOC** code for **East Coast**

Grade
a) Alternative for **Gradient**
b) To level a surface, such as **Bottom Ballast** or **Cutting** slope, using manual or mechanised methods
c) [PW] A description of the wear resistance properties of certain types of **Rail**, e.g. **Grade A**. See **Wear Resisting Rail**.

ELLIS' BRITISH RAILWAY ENGINEERING ENCYCLOPÆDIA

Grade A
Grade A Rail
[PW] **Rail** steel with a minimum hardness of 260 Brinell used for its improved wear resistance over normal Rail steel. See **Wear Resisting Rail**.

Grade B
Grade B Rail
[PW] **Rail** steel with a minimum hardness of 260 Brinell and a higher manganese content (1.3%-1.7%) used for its improved wear resistance over **Grade A** Rail steel. See **Wear Resisting Rail**.

Grade Crossing Predictor
[Sig.] A device which measures the speed and acceleration of an approaching **Train** and triggers the **Level Crossing Protection System** to give a constant warning time for both slow and fast Trains

Grade of Rail Steel
[PW]
a) See **Grade A**, **Grade A Rail**
b) See **Grade B**, **Grade B Rail**
c) See **Normal Grade**, **Normal Grade Rail**
d) See **Wear Resisting Rail**.

Grade Separated
Grade Separated Crossing
A location at which two transport **Routes** cross at different vertical levels, and therefore do not come into conflict with each other. The opposite is **At Grade, At Grade Crossing**.

Grade Separated Junction
A term describing a **Junction** where **Main Line** and **Diverging Line** are separated vertically to avoid **Conflicting Movements** caused by a **Flat Junction**. The Diverging Line can either pass over the Main Line (A **Flying Junction**) or under it (A **Burrowing Junction**). See also **Flyover**.

Grades of Automation (GoA)
See **Transmission Based Train Control** (TBTC).

Gradient
The rate at which a **Track**, road, path or **Track Drain** rises or falls relative to horizontal. There are two systems for expressing this value:
• 1 in x, where x is the number of units one must move horizontally to gain or lose one unit of height. Thus, small values of x are steeper. Direction is indicated by suffixing the Gradient with the words "rising" or "falling" relative to the direction of movement, as appropriate
• As a percentage rate of gain or loss over distance. Large values of percentage are steeper. A falling Gradient is indicated by a negative value
To convert from 1 in x to a percentage, multiply the fraction by 100. Gradients are normally measured in the **Down Direction** or in the **Normal Direction**.

Gradient Post
A marker post placed at the **Lineside** at changes of **Gradient**, with angled and lettered boards indicating the Gradients in terms of **1 in x**.

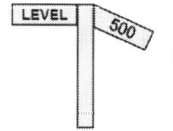

Grampus (ZBO, ZBP, ZBQ, ZBV, ZBW)
[NR] A 20 ton capacity **Open Wagon** used for the transportation of **Spoil**. See **Wagon Names**.

Grand Central
(Tradename) An **Open Access Operator** that provides direct **Fast** services between London King's Cross and Sunderland. **ATOC** Code **GC**.

Grandfather Rights
a) The arrangement by which a product's or process' use is allowed to continue because the product or process existed, was compliant and was used prior to subsequent standards or legislation being brought into force
b) The right to continue using a non-conforming process or piece of equipment or permit a situation to continue where it was regularly used or commonly existed prior to 1st April 1994 (Privatisation).

Grass Track
[PW] **Track** constructed in such a manner as to allow the infilling of the voids of a **Ladder Track** unit or specially cast spaces in a cast **Track Slab** with topsoil and grass seed. Used widely on urban **Light Rail** (**LR**) systems, it allows the Track to blend into its surroundings.

Gravity Shunting
[Obs.] Separating and sorting of **Freight Vehicles** (**Wagons**) using gravity as the prime mover. The **Train** to be sorted was first taken into a **Reception Siding**, the brakes **Pinned Down** and the Train **Uncoupled** into 'cuts' by a **Shunter** to suit the several destinations of the vehicles. The brakes were then released and the **Wagons** allowed to roll down the inline toward the **King Points** of the **Sorting Sidings** and directed into one of the **Fan Of Sidings** which has been selected for a particular departing Train or destination. See also **Fly Shunting**, **Hump Shunting**, **Loose Shunting**.

Gravity-Worked Railway
[Hist.] A **Railway** where **Wagons** are moved using gravity alone. Typically, the greater mass of descending loaded Wagons is used to haul empty Wagons to the top of an Incline by means of a rope passing over a pulley at the **Bank Head**.

GRC
Glass Reinforced Cement. See also **Elevated Troughing**.

GRC&W
See **Gloucester Railway Carriage and Wagon Company**.

Grease Distribution Unit (GDU)
[PW] Generic term for a device used to deliver grease to the relevant part of a **Rail**. See also **Flange Lubricator**, **Rail Lubricator**, **Wheel Flange Lubricator**. Colloquially shortened to **Greaser**.

Greaser
[PW Col.] Contraction of **Grease Distribution Unit** (**GDU**). Also **Rail Lubricator**.

Great Britain Passenger Railway Timetable (GBPRT)
[Ops.] The document issued bi-annually giving Timetable (TT) information for all Passenger Trains on the National Railway Network (NRN). Also GBTT.

Great British Travelling Public, The (GBTP)
[Col.] A somewhat derogatory nickname for the small element among Passengers who appear to have great difficulties with Rail travel; from selecting the correct destination to being unable to read any of the Customer Information Systems (CIS) or destination blinds provided. They are the group who try and get on before you get off, always put their bag on the seat next to them and stand in doorways to make apparently pointless mobile telephone calls.

Great Central Railway (GCR)
a) [Hist.] The Pre-Grouping □ Railway Company and the last Main Line built in Britain, running from London (Marylebone) to Manchester via Rugby, Nottingham and Sheffield (now mostly closed)
b) [Pres.] The Heritage Railway operating over part of the former Great Central, between Loughborough and Leicester.

Great Western Main Line (GWML)
The Route from London (Paddington) to Penzance via Reading and Bristol.

Great Western Railway (GWR)
[Hist.]
a) The Railway Company founded in 1833 with Isambard Kingdom Brunel as Chief Engineer and ran its first trains in 1838 from London Paddington to Maidenhead Bridge Station.
b) One of the Big Four □ Railway Companies created under Grouping, largely consisting of the former Great Western Railway (GWR) and the independent Railway Companies within its territory.

Great Western Renaissance (GWR)
A scheme which would provide additional capacity and possible journey time reductions on the London - Bristol - South Wales Route.

Greater Anglia
(Tradename) A Train Operating Company (TOC) owned by Abellio, operating the Greater Anglia Rail Franchise. It provides local, suburban and express services from London Liverpool Street station to destinations in Essex, Hertfordshire, Cambridgeshire, Suffolk and Norfolk in the East of England. ATOC code LE.

Greathead, James Henry
(1844-1896). Engineer who built on the work of Marc Ismabard Brunel (father of Isambard Kingdom Brunel) and Peter W. Barlow to produce his eponymous circular Tunnelling Shield, used to great effect in the building of London's Tube network.

Greaves' and Douglas Fishjoint Chair and Sleeper
[PW Obs.] A boltless Fishplated Joint for parallel Rails supported in Greaves' □ Pot Sleepers. See also Greave's Surface Packed (Pot) Sleepers.

Greave's Surface Packed (Pot) Sleepers
[PW Obs.] Pot Sleepers designed for use with parallel Rails, incorporating integral jaws into which the Rail was secured by means of a malleable (wrought) iron wedge. The pots were made in three forms:
• with a single pair of jaws but without the facility for the provision of a Tie Bar to maintain pairs of Pots at the required Track Gauge;
• as above but with provision for the fitting of a Tie Bar
• as above but with two pairs of jaws forming supports for a pair of Fishplates which were secured by means of metal wedges. The joint was marketed as Greaves' and Douglas Fishjoint Chair and Sleeper.

Greaves, Hugh
(1810-after 1875) born in Manchester, England. Mechanical engineer who patented many Railway-related ideas, pioneered the use of his Shell Track (British patent number 742), Pot Sleepers and introduced the use of the Ferrule.

Green (G)
a) The colour whose presence indicates a condition of safety, or safe to proceed. See Green Aspect, Proceed Aspect
b) [Sig.] A colour used on Signalling Scheme Plans (SSP) and other drawings to indicate equipment removed or decommissioned, see Colouring Convention.

Green Aspect
[Sig.] The Aspect displayed by a Colour Light Signal to indicate that the Signal may be passed safely. Also Proceed Aspect.

Green Automatic Warning System Magnet
Green AWS Magnet
[Sig.] An extra-strength version of the normal Automatic Warning System Magnet (AWS Magnet), used on DC Electrified Lines to compensate for the different fitment of the AWS equipment on the Rolling Stock (on the Carbody rather than the Bogies).

Green Card
Green Carded
a) See Green Carding
b) [BR] The card listing a Light Duty Man's restrictions.

Green Carding
[Ops.] To place a card coloured green on a Wagon, indicating that it should be taken out of service for repairs at the end of its current journey. See also Not to be Reloaded, Red Carding.

Green Circle
[TRS] A symbol applied to Traction Units, in this case some Class 47 Locomotives, denoting the Multiple Working control system with which they are fitted. Only Traction Units bearing the same symbol can be connected safely. See Blue Square, Blue Star, Green Circle, Orange Star, Red Circle, Red Diamond, Red Triangle, White Circle, White Diamond, Yellow Diamond, Yellow Triangle.

211

Green Pages
Working Manual for Rail staff - Freight Train □ Operations, now a Railway Group Standard (RGS).

Green Square
[TRS] A symbol applied to a Sentinel Card to indicate that the holder has held the Personal Track Safety (PTS) competency for less than six months. See also Blue Circle, Red Triangle.

Green Track
See Grass Track.

Green Zone
[NR Obs.]
a) See Fenced
b) See Safeguarded
c) See Site Warden Warning.

Green Zone Access Co-ordinator (GZAC)
[NR] Correct name for the organisation responsible for processing requests for Line Blockage opportunities. Also called Green Zone Access Manager (GZAM).

Green Zone Access Manager (GZAM)
See Green Zone Access Co-ordinator (GZAC).

Green Zone Working
[NR Obs.] Carrying out Work activities in a Green Zone.

Gregory, Charles Hutton
(1817 - 1898) Early Signalling pioneer who developed the first true Semaphore Signal, the first of which was installed at New Cross in London in 1841. He also installed a basic form of Interlocking (in that Setting □ Conflicting Routes at Junctions were prevented) at Bricklayer Arms Junction in 1843.

Gricer
[Col.] Term describing a Railway Enthusiast or hardened Train Spotter. The verb is "to Grice". One of the many theories regarding the term's origin is that the term derives from Richard Grice, a Train Spotter who became legendary for having travelled the entire British Rail (BR) □ Network. Another is from a Railway Enthusiasts' visit to the Bluebell Railway in the 1970s. They arrived in a van with the name "G. Ricer" on the side. See also Anorak.

Gricex
[Col.] Nickname for a special Train hired and run along unusual Routes and often hauled by rare or little used Locomotives especially for the entertainment of Train enthusiasts (Gricers). See also -ex, Nuttex.

Grid
a) See Gridiron.
b) [TRS] A lattice structure containing high-power resistors mounted on the roofs of some Diesel Electric Locomotives and Diesel Electric Multiple Units (DEMU). They are used to dissipate excess electrical energy during motor or braking power control. See Dynamic Braking, Rheostatic Braking
c) [TRS Col.] Nickname for the Class 56 Diesel Locomotives given because of their large grilles
d) [Sig., Col.] Train Protection and Warning System (TPWS) OSS Loops and TSS Loops.

Gridiron
[Col.]
a) A term describing a large and complex Junction, often the Throat of a major Marshalling Yard. Also Grid.
b) Nickname for a Class 56 Diesel Electric Locomotive.

Grinding
a) See Rail Grinding
b) See Profile Grinding.

GRIP
a) (grip) See Governance for Railway Investment Projects
b) Great Eastern Rapid Improvement Project.

GRIP 3 AIP
[NR] Governance for Railway Investment Projects Stage 3 Approval in Principle; Sign-off of the Single Option proposals by the Route Asset Managers (RAM).

GRN
Glass Reinforced Nylon, a material used for Rail Foot Insulators.

Gronk
[Col.] Nickname for a Class 08 Shunting Locomotive. Also Jockey, Jocko.

Grooved Pad
See Configurated Rail Pad.

Grooved Rail
[PW] A type of Flat Bottom Rail that has an integral Check Rail, giving it a section similar to a wine glass. They are generally used where the Track is to be built as part of a highway, as it simplifies construction. Typical designations are Rixx, where xx is the unit weight in Kilograms per Metre. See also Pre-Coated Grooved Rail, Street Running Track.

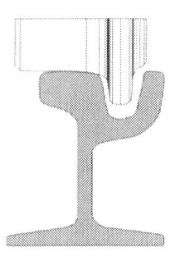

Gross Laden Weight (GLW)
[TRS] The maximum weight of a Rail Vehicle, including its maximum load. See also Tare Weight.

Gross Trailing Weight (GTW)
[Ops.] A measure of Train weight, indicating the maximum possible weight of a Train excluding any Locomotives.

Ground Disc

Ground Disc Signal
[Sig.] A small rotating Semaphore Disc Signal mounted at ground level and used for controlling Shunt Movements. Replaced in Colour Light Signalling with the Ground Position Light Signal (GPLS). Also Dolly, Dummy, Tommy Dodd.

Ground Frame (GF)
[Sig.] A small **Frame** of **Signal** and **Points** □ **Levers** located close to some isolated and infrequently used facility such as a **Trailing Crossover**. These Levers are **Locked** by the **Controlling Signal Box**, and only **Released** when required. Alternatively, the Levers may be Released by means of a key attached to a **Train Staff**, see **Annett's Key**. See also **Emergency Ground Frame** (EGF), **Ground Switch Panel** (GSP).

Ground Frame Operator
[Ops.] A person appointed to operate a **Ground Frame** to permit **Trains Movements**.

Ground Penetrating Radar (GPR)
A microwave based scanning system producing a sectional image of the ground, based on reflections from changes in materials. The results produced allow different areas of **Formation** to be compared and judgements made on construction and condition. The equipment is man-portable and is wheeled along the **Track** concerned.

Ground Plan
See **Level Crossing Ground Plan**.

Ground Position Light (GPL)
[Sig.] See **Position Light Signal** (PLS).

Ground Position Light Signal (GPLS)
[Sig.] A **Position Light Signal** (PLS) located on the ground.

Ground Relay
[TRS] An electrical **Relay** provided in **Diesel Electric Traction** and **Electric Traction** systems to protect the electrical equipment against damage from so-called "grounds". The result of such a Relay operating is usually a shut-down of the electrical drive system. Also called an **Earth Fault Relay** (EFR).

Ground Shunt Signal
[Sig.] A **Shunt Signal** located on the ground.

Ground Signal
[Sig.] A **Signal** mounted at or very near ground level. Generally, **Signals** so arranged are **Position Light Signals** (PLS) for **Shunting**, or **Co-Acting Signals** (CA) in difficult locations.

Ground Staff
[Ops.] Staff employed to check **Trains** and **Wagons** prior to their operational use on the **Rail Network**.

Ground Switch Panel (GSP)
[Sig.] Equivalent to a **Ground Frame** (GF), but using electrical switches or buttons to actuate the **Signalling Functions** rather than **Levers**.

Group
a) See **Group of Sidings**
b) [NR] Two or more persons gathered together (for the purposes of defining a Group in terms of safety rules)
c) See **Railway Group**.

Group of Sidings
The collective description for all the **Sidings** fed from one set of **King Points**. Groups of Sidings are often given letters to identify them, e.g. B **Group**, F Sidings.

Group Replacement Switch
[Sig.] A switch provided on a **Signaller's Panel** that allows a large number of **Signals** to be **Replaced** to **Stop Aspects** in times of emergency.

Group Standard
See **Railway Group Standard** (RGS).

Grouping
[Hist.] The change made to **Railway Company** arrangements under the auspices of the **Railways Act 1921**, whereby the many small companies were consolidated into the **Big Four**, namely the **London Midland & Scottish Railway** (LMSR), **London & North Eastern Railway** (L&NER), **Great Western Railway** (GWR) and **Southern Railway** (SR).

Grout Pads
A pad that sits underneath a **Baseplate** and on top of a concrete slab. The Grout Pad is formed from liquid grout that is poured into formwork and sets. Once the grout pad is 'cured' the Baseplate fixing bolts can be torqued to the specified level.

Growler
[Col.] Nickname given to **Class** 37 **Diesel Locomotive** due to their sound. Also **Syphon**, **Tractor**.

GRP
a) **Gauge** Restoration Project
b) Glass Reinforced Polymer.

GRS
(Tradename) General **Railway** □ **Signal**, a manufacturer of **Signalling Equipment**, based in Rochester, USA.

GSM
a) **Grinding** Supervisory Manager
b) Global System for Mobile Telecommunications. See **GSM-R**.

GSM-R
[Tel.] Global System for Mobile Communications - **Railways**, a Time Division Multiple Access (**TDMA**) radio system using 876MHz — 880MHz: for data transmission from **Trains** and 921MHz — 925MHz: for data reception by Trains. It is used as the basis for the **European Rail Traffic Management System** (**ERTMS**) as detailed under the European Integrated Railways Radio Enhanced Network for ERTMS (**EIRENE**) and Mobile Radio for Railway Networks in Europe (**MORANE**) specifications.

GSP
See **Ground Switch Panel**.

GSPP
General Specification for **Possession Planning**.

GSRP
General Safety Review Panel.

GTC
[Hist.] The **Pre-Grouping** (Carlisle) Goods Traffic Committee, a Caledonian, Glasgow & South Western, London & North Western and Midland joint enterprise.

GTE
(Tradename) Guided Transit Express. A proposed **Guided Busway** system for Oxford.

213

ELLIS' BRITISH RAILWAY ENGINEERING ENCYCLOPÆDIA

GTG
Good Track Geometry.

GTI
a) Ground Transport Interchange
b) [Ops. Col.] Term for Train with a large excess of Tractive Effort, such as three Coaches with an operational Locomotive at both ends.

Gtkm
Gross tonne-kilometres.

Gtm
Gross tonne-miles.

GTO

GTO Thyristor
Gate Turn Off Thyristor, a type of Thyristor which does not require a commutation (reverse flow) circuit to switch it off; see Chopper.

GTRM
(Tradename) [Hist.] The former Central Infrastructure Maintenance Unit (IMU) bought by and renamed GEC Tarmac Railway □ Maintenance, and now part of Carillion Rail.

GTW
See Gross Trailing Weight.

Guaranteed Power Supply
See Secure Power Supply.

Guard
a) A Railway employee who travels on a Train and has duties in connection with the safe running of that Train. A Passenger Train Guard's responsibilities will include ensuring that any Passengers Alight and Board safely, that the Train doors are properly closed before departure and "policing" the Train in transit
b) [Col.] Generic term for a person undertaking the duties of Senior Conductor, Conductor or Trainman.

Guard Boarding
Protective boards placed on one or both sides of a Conductor Rail at certain locations to prevent accidental contact with the Conductor Rail. Also Kick Boarding, Conductor Rail Boarding

Guard Rails

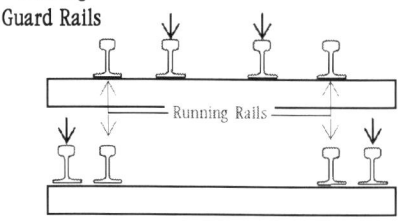

[PW] A Rail or Rails provided either in the Fourfoot between the Running Rails (Inside Guard Rail(s)) or on the Sleeper Ends (Outside Guard Rail(s)) at specific locations, such as Viaducts and Level Crossings for added security in case of Derailment. Guard Rails are not normally in contact with the Wheel Flanges. See also Derailment Kerb, Robust Kerb.

Gudgeon
[NR, prob. Obs.] A 20 ton Ballast □ Wagon.

Guidance and Stabilisation System
[TRS] A mechanism used to support a Door Leaf and guide its sliding motion.

Guide to Railway Investment Projects (GRIP)
Now Governance for Railway Investment Projects (GRIP).

Guided Busway
An arrangement in which otherwise normal buses run along a specially constructed Guideway. The buses are fitted with lateral guidewheels linked to the steering system, allowing the bus to follow the Guideway in a Railway-like manner.

Guideway
The (normally) concrete construction which forms the "track" of a Guided Busway.

Guildford Accident
At 22.24 on 8th November 1952 a two-car Electric Multiple Unit (EMU) □ Ran Away and collided with a Light Engine which had been correctly signalled across its path at Guildford. The cause of the accident was discovered to be a blown fuse on the electrical supply to the Air Brake on the EMU, causing the brakes to fail on a 1 in 100 Gradient. The EMU driver and one Passenger died and 37 were injured. The fitting of control governors (a device which stops the driver taking power if the Brake Reservoir pressure is too low) has made a repeat of this accident largely impossible.

Gut Rail
[PW Col.] Term for a Closure Rail between Switch Rail and Common Crossing Wing Rail. See also Guts.

Guts
[PW Col.] Collective term for all the Closure Rails between the Stock Rails, Switch Rails and Crossings. See Gut Rail.

GUV
An acronym representing a General Utility Van.

Guzunder
[Col.] Nickname for the Viaduct Inspection Unit (VIU).

GV
[PW] Vertical □ Flat Bottom (FB) Full Depth Switches. The G describes the length and Switch Radius.

GVA
(Tradename) Gleiswertverstell-Automatik, a Track Alignment control system fitted to certain Tamping and Lining machines built by Plasser and Theurer.

GVR
[Hist.] The Pre-Grouping Gwendraeth Valley Railway.

GVs
[PW] Denotes 113A □ Flat Bottom (FB) □ Vertical □ Shallow Depth Switches, length G.

GVS
[PW] Denotes CEN56E1 □ Flat Bottom (FB) □ Vertical □ Shallow Depth Switches, length G.

GVT
[Hist.] The Pre-Grouping Glyn Valley Tramway.

GW
a) Great Western
b) The **ATOC** code for **First Great Western.**

GWC
(Tradename) [TRS Col.] Common shorthand for Gloucester Wagon Co., a former manufacturer of **Signalling Equipment** and **Rolling Stock.**

GWESPA
Great Western Earthworks & Structures Partnering Agreement.

GWI
Grand Wear Index, a **Track-Ex** output

GWML
See **Great Western Main Line.**

GWR
a) [Hist.] The **Pre-Grouping** □ **Great Western Railway**
b) See **Great Western Renaissance.**

GWT
(Tradename) Great Western Trains, A **Train Operating Company** (**TOC**).

GWUG
Great Western Upgrade.

GWZ
[Hist.] Great Western Zone.

GX
a) Global Crossing
b) **ATOC** code for **Gatwick Express.**

GY
[Sig.] On a **Signalling Circuit Diagram**, denotes a wire coloured grey or slate.

GZAC
(ga-zak) [NR] See **Green Zone Access Co-ordinator.**

GZAM
(ga-zam) [NR] See **Green Zone Access Manager.**

GZTS
Green Zones: Thinking Strategically.

H

H
a) [NR] As the last letter in a **Wagon** □ CARKND, this denotes that the Wagon has both **AFI** and **Air Brakes**. See also **Dual Braked**
b) [NR] As the first letter of a Wagon CARKND, it indicates that the vehicle is a **Hopper Wagon**
c) [NR] On a card attached to a Wagon, it indicates that the Wagon is overdue for its Vehicle Inspection and Brake Test (**VIBT**)
d) See **Switch Letters**
e) [Sig.] On a **Signalling Circuit Diagram**:
• As one of the leading letters of an **Equipment Code**, it means **Caution** (**Yellow** (**Y**))
• As the last letter of an Equipment Code, it means capacitor.
f) The letter represented by **Hotel** in the **Phonetic Alphabet**
g) [LUL] **H**ammersmith and City **L**ine.

H Carded
[TRS] A **Wagon** with a card attached exhibiting the code 'H' indicating that the Wagon is overdue for a **Vehicle Inspection and Brake Test** (**VIBT**).

H Frame Bogie
[LUL] The type of **Bogie** fitted to D78 surface and 1983 **Tube** stock, with a welded box frame with integral **Bolster** and no **Headstocks**.

H Pad
[PW] A **Rail Pad** shaped to fit around the cast-in **Housings** of Pandrol □ **Rail Fastenings**.

H Rail
[Hist.] Term used to describe **Double-headed Rails**, in use in the mid-19th century

H Stock
[LUL] A batch of former **B Stock** dating from 1905 and rebuilt in the mid-1920s for the District **Railway**.

H&BR
[Hist.] The **Pre-Grouping** **H**ull & **B**arnsley **Railway**.

H&CR
[Hist.] The **Pre-Grouping** **H**ammersmith & **C**ity **Railway**, a Great Western and Metropolitan joint enterprise.

H&K
(Tradename) **H**anning and **K**ahl, A designer and manufacturer of **Point Operating Equipment** (**POE**), communications and **Train Detection** systems, based in Oerlinghausen, north-western Germany.

H&OJR
[Hist.] The **Pre-Grouping** **H**alifax & **O**venden **J**oint **Railway**, a Great Northern and Lancashire & Yorkshire joint enterprise.

H&S
Health and **S**afety.

H&SE
Health and **S**afety **E**xecutive. Also **HSE**.

H/S
See **H**and**s**ignaller (**HS**).

HABD
See **H**ot **A**xle **B**ox **D**etector.

Hackworth, Timothy
(1786-1850), born in Wylam, Northumberland. An early **Steam Locomotive** pioneer and childhood friend of George Stephenson. His entry to the **Rainhill Trials**, 'Sans Pareil', was beaten by the Stephensons' 'Rocket'.

Haddock (ZCO)
[NR] A **Wagon** used for **Engineering** work. See **Wagon Names**.

Hairpin
[PW Col.] Term for a **Lockspike**.

Hake (ZBA)
[NR] An **Open Wagon** used for the transportation of **Ballast**. See **Wagon Names**.

HAL
Heavy **A**xle **L**oad

Half Barrier
[Sig.] A **Barrier** that closes only one half of the carriageway when lowered. See **Automatic Barrier Crossing Locally Monitored** (**ABCL**), **Automatic Half Barrier Crossing** (**AHBC**).

Half Baseplate
[PW] A **Baseplate** for **Flat Bottom Rail** (**FB**) which projects on one side of the **Rail** only. Used with a bolt through the **Rail Web**.

Half Beam Spread
[Sig.] See **Horizontal Half-Beam Angle** and **Vertical Half-Beam Angle**.

Half Chair
[PW] A **Chair** for **Bull Head Rail** (**BH**) that projects on one side of the **Rail** only. Used with a bolt through the **Rail Web**.

Half Chord
[PW] Half the length of the **Chord** used for a realignment scheme, and thus the interval that is marked on the **Track** and at which the **Design Slues** are applied. Typical current Half Chord lengths are 10m and 15m, though historically it was 48' 3" (14.716m). See also **Hallade**, **Versine**.

Half Cock
Half Cocked
[Sig. Col.] description of a **Semaphore Signal** □ **Arm** that is only partially raised (or lowered). Therefore the **Signal** is not showing a clear **On** or **Off** indication. Such a Signal is more properly described as a "**Signal Aspect** imperfectly or improperly shown". A driver observing this state of affairs should report it to the **Signaller** at the earliest opportunity.

Half Diamond
[LUL] The half diamond shaped emergency stop device provided for the use of passengers.

Half Lead
(*harf leed*) [PW] An alternative for **Turnout**.

217

ELLIS' BRITISH RAILWAY ENGINEERING ENCYCLOPÆDIA

Half Loc.
Half Location
[Sig.] A half width **Location Case**, used for small amounts of **Signalling** equipment or **Operator's Cupboards**.

Half Rail
[PW] A standard length of **Rail**, namely 30 feet or 9144mm. See also **Rail Length**.

Half Set
Half Set of Switches
[PW] See **Switch Half Set**.

Half Step
[PW] A **Versine Rise** or **Transition Step** that is exactly half the value of a full Versine Rise (Transition Step). Any other fraction is a **Part Step**. See **Hallade**. See also **Rounding**.

Half Through
[Civ.] A **Bridge Deck** construction where there is no bracing provided between the upper edges of the main girders. Rigidity is provided by utilising the lower lateral members as part of a U-frame. See also **Full Through**, **Through**.

Halibut (YCA)
[NR] A 56 ton capacity **Open Wagon** used for the transportation of **Ballast**. See **Wagon Names**.

Hallade
(*hal-ard*) [PW] After Msr. Emile Hallade, an approximate system for the design and **Maintenance** of **Circular Curves** and **Transition Curves** using a method of overlapping **Chords** and their resulting **Versines**.

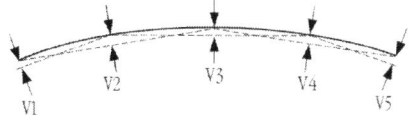

$V_1 \quad V_2 \quad V_3 \quad V_4 \quad V_5$

For any constant Chord length throughout, the following is true:
- A perfect Circular Curve will have a constant non-zero Versine value, $V_1 = V_2 = V_3 = V_4 = V_5 \neq 0$
- A perfect straight will have a constant zero Versine value, $V_1 = V_2 = V_3 = V_4 = V_5 = 0$
- A Transition Curve will have a linearly varying set of Versine values, e.g. $V_1 = n$, $V_2 = 2n$, $V_3 = 3n$, $V_4 = 4n$, etc.

A method of summing of moments allows the **Slues** that are required to achieve any desired alignment to be calculated from survey values. The system is not absolute, but can produce reliable alignment adjustments quickly. The system appears to have built on the work of **Shortt** and **Bartlett**.

Hallade Monument
[PW Obs.] A cast concrete marker with a lead strip set into the top, edge up. They were placed centrally in the **Sixfoot**, and a point three feet (914mm) from each **Outside Edge** (**OE**) being marked in the lead strip with a cold chisel. Other data such as **Cant** (**C**) was also recorded on the monument.

Hallade Recorder
Hallade Track Recorder
[PW Obs.] Developed by Emile **Hallade**, a machine powered by clockwork introduced during the 1930s which recorded the oscillation of a **Passenger Carriage** and therefore measured track quality. It used a system of pendulums attached to a pen to inscribe a line on paper roll.

Hallade Survey
[PW] A survey made of an existing **Track** alignment using a length of **String** and a ruler to measure the **Versines** of a known **Chord** at regular intervals of one half of the length of the Chord. Other information such as **Cant** (**C**), **Track Interval** and lateral offsets to relevant features are recorded for use during the design phase. See also **Hallade**.

Hallade, Emile
Swiss-born Engineer who, whilst working for the Eastern **Railway** of France in the late 1920s as a senior **Track** engineer, developed a non-graphical method of measuring **Versines** or offsets from the curve to mid-**Chord** points on standard Chord lengths at regular intervals. The Great Northern Railway was the first British Railway company to exploit the technique and most others followed. Hallade also invented the **Track Recorder** which bears his name. See **Hallade**. See also **William Hamilton Shortt**.

Halt
A type of **Station** often consisting only of one or two **Platforms** and an access gate. Often **Trains** only stop when requested to do so. Originally pioneered by the **Great Western Railway** (**GWR**) to encourage patronage on rural **Branch Lines**. Alternate spelling [Hist., possibly WR] Halte.

Hambone Clip
[Hist.] A self-tensioning clip used to attach a vehicle to a wire rope over-top haulage rope.

Hammer Blow
[TRS] The inherent dynamic imbalance of the **Driving Wheels** of a **Steam Locomotive** and their linkage rods can cause the **Rails** and hence the Formation and any underlying **Structures** to be subjected to intense and regular pounding, in some cases causing severe damage.

Hand
The direction an item takes relative to a reference:
a) [PW] To the **Permanent Way** (**PW**) Engineer, a **Left Hand Curve** is a **Curve** that turns to the left when viewed with one's back to the lower mileage. A **Right Hand Curve** is the opposite
b) [Elec.] To the **Overhead Line** Engineer, a Left Hand Curve is a Curve that has the left hand **Rail** highest when viewed with one's **Back to Low Mileage**. A Right Hand Curve is the opposite
c) [PW] A **Left Hand Switch** (**LHS**) or **Left Hand Turnout** (**LHTO**) is one that has the laterally set **Stock Rail** on the left when viewed looking from **Switch Toe** to **Switch Heel**, and a **Right Hand Switch** (**RHS**) or **Right Hand Turnout** (**RHTO**) is the opposite
d) [PW] In the former **Great Western Railway** (**GWR**) area, a **Left Hand Common Crossing** is one in

218

which the **Splice Rail** is on the right of the **Point Rail** when viewed from a position in front of the **Nose**. A **Right Hand Common Crossing** is the opposite
e) [PW] In area other than the former **Great Western Railway** (**GWR**) area, a **Left Hand Splice** (**LHS**) □ **Crossing** is one in which the **Splice Rail** is on the left of the **Point Rail** when viewed from a position in front of the **Nose**. A **Right Hand Splice** (**RHS**) □ **Crossing** is the opposite
f) [PW] A **Left Hand Twist Rail** is one in which the **Rail Foot** is rotated to the left when viewed from the **Inclined** portion of the Rail. The opposite is a **Right Hand Twist Rail**
g) [PW] A **Left Hand Transition Rail** is one in which the step in the **Outside Edge** (**OE**) is on the left when viewed from the portion of the Rail with the larger **Rail Section**. The opposite is a **Right Hand Transition Rail**.

Hand Lever
A **Lever** used to manually operate **Hand Points**. Also **Switch Lever**.

Hand Lever Switch
See **Hand Points**.

Hand Points
Points □ (**Switches**) operated by means of a **Hand Lever** fitted on or adjacent to the **Switch Toe Timbers**. Also **Hand Lever Switch**, **Manual Points**. Such Points are not **Interlocked**.

Hand Trolley
A small platform with a **Rail Wheel** at each corner used to transport tools, equipment and materials along the **Railway** for **Maintenance** work. Also called a **Bogie**, **Gibbon** or **Trolley**.

Handback
a) [NR] The return of responsibility for control of the **Infrastructure** of an area formerly subject to an **Engineering Possession** by engineering staff to the **Signaller**.
b) The formal transfer of responsibility for a particular asset back to the owner / maintainer from the **Contractor** following completion of renewal or modification works. See also **Handover**.

Handbook
a) See **Civil Engineering Handbook**
b) See **Rule Book Handbooks**

Handbrake
[TRS] A manually operated brake acting locally on one vehicle. On many older **Rail Vehicles** this is normally operated by a handwheel on the outside of the vehicle or in the **Driving Cab**, but many new **Multiple Unit Trains** and **Locomotives** have electronically operated systems.

Handed
Describing an item which has a **Hand**, and in most cases must therefore be used the right way round.

Handing
[PW] The action of assigning a **Hand** to a **Curve**, **Switch**, **Turnout**, etc.

Handing Back

Handing Back the Road
a) [Col.] Transfer of responsibility for a section of **Railway** back to the **Signaller**
b) [NR] Transfer of responsibility for a section of **Railway** back to the **Signaller**:
• From the responsible person to the relevant person at the end of a **T4** □ **Siding** □ **Possession**
• From a **Controller of Site Safety** (**COSS**) to a **Protection Controller** (**PC**) within a **Line Blockage**
• From a COSS or a PC to the **Signaller** at the end of a **Line Blockage**
• From a COSS to an **Engineering Supervisor** (**ES**) at the end of that element of the work
• From an ES to a **Person in Charge of Possession** (**PICOP**) or **Senior Person in Charge of Possession** (**SPICOP**) at the completion and withdrawal of an **Engineering Worksite**
• From a PICOP or SPICOP to the Signaller at the end of a **T3** Possession.
See also **Signing Back**.

Handite
(Tradename) A hand held **Sandite** applicator.

Handover
The formal transfer of responsibility for a particular asset from the owner / **Maintainer** to the **Contractor** prior to commencement of **Renewal** or modification works. See also **Handback**.

Hands On
[PW Col.] An instruction given to a group of **Track Workers** to indicate that they should grasp the item being moved, in anticipation of lifting or sliding it.

Handsignal
An instruction given to a driver by means of arm movements, coloured **Flags** or coloured hand-held lamps at night.

Handsignaller (HS)
[NR]
a) A competent person authorised to control the passage of **Trains** by means of coloured **Flags** and **Railway Fog Signals** (colloquially called **Detonators**) in the absence of normal **Signalling**
b) A competent person authorised to undertake **Protection of the Line** in emergencies and for planned work.

Handsignalman
[Obs.] The previous name for a **Handsignaller**.

Hanger
[Elec.] Alternative for **Dropper**.

Hanging Sleeper
[PW] A **Sleeper** that is being supported by the **Rails**, rather than the other way round.

Hard Over Tilt Failed (HOTF)
[TRS] Describing a **Tilting Train** whose **Tilt** mechanism has failed with the **Train** tilted to one extreme or the other. See also **Tilt Failed**.

Hard Road
[PW Col.] A length of **Ballasted Track** that does not have the elasticity inherent in this system, i.e. it is too rigid.

Hardboard Packs
[PW Obs.] 610mm by 229mm (24" by 9") rectangles of oil-tempered hardboard available in a range of thicknesses (3.2mm, 4.8mm or 6.4mm; $^1/_8$", $^3/_{16}$" or $^1/_4$") and used in place of **Chippings**.

Hardlock
(Tradename) A type of two-piece lock nut.

Hardwood (HW)
Hardwood Sleeper
[PW] A **Sleeper** normally made from a hardwood such as Jarrah (*Eucalyptus marginata*) or Karri (*Eucalyptus diversicolor*) and related species, and less commonly Oak. The Eucalyptus types require no special treatment as the sap is a natural preservative. The other type of **Wood Sleeper** is a **Softwood Sleeper**.

Harmonic Filter
[Elec.] A device containing resistive and capacitive elements used to remove unwanted interference from the **Traction Supply Current**. Such interference is generated by the switchgear related to the **Traction Motors** on **Electric Trains**. Also colloquially known as **Dampers**.

Harp Brackets
Harp Units
[Civ.] Named for their shape, pre-cast concrete frames commonly used in the 1960s to construct **Platforms**. The fill material is retained by concrete planks fitted into a slot cast into the front vertical of each frame.

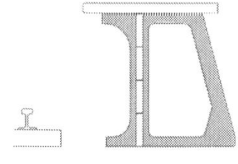

Harrington Hump
[NR] Orignally known as an Easy Access Area. A lightweight **GRP** ramp and deck system that can be fitted to address **Platforms** with a low **Platform Height**. Devised by Network Rail and Cumbria County Council, in conjunction with Pipex Structural Composites and first installed at Harrington in Cumbria in December 2008 after complaints about the large step up and down to **Trains**. The Hump is normally only provided at Train door locations and is not a substitute for compliant Platforms.

Harrow and Wealdstone Accident
The scene of a **Railway** □ **Accident** on 8th October 1952, where a southbound **Express Passenger Train** ran past several **Signals** showing **Stop Aspects** in **Fog** and collided with the rear of a stationary **Local Passenger Train** standing in the **Station**. The resulting wreckage was then hit by another Express Passenger Train. The collisions killed 112 people in total. This accident was one of the catalysts for the introduction of the **Automatic Warning System** (**AWS**). See also Gidea Park Accident.

Harry
[Obs.] The obsolescent **Phonetic Alphabet** word representing H. Replaced by **Hotel**.

Has Been
[Col.]
a) An entry in **Section C** of the **Weekly Operating Notice** (**WON**) which is repeated for information in the weeks after the works have been completed
b) Generally, anything in a design that is assumed to have taken place already, particularly if it is carried out by another scheme. Also **Black**.

HASAW
HASAWA
The **H**ealth and **S**afety **a**t **W**ork Act 1974.

Hasler, The
[Col.] name for a particular type of **On-Train Monitoring and Recording** equipment (**OTMR**). The unit is actually a Teloc unit manufactured by Secheron Hasler, Switzerland.

HAT
Headway **A**nalysis **T**ool.

Hatfield Accident
The site of the **Railway** □ **Accident** on 17th October 2000, caused by various planning failures leading up to a **Broken Rail**. Four died and 70 were injured when a southbound **Express Passenger Train** left the **Track**. The Broken Rail was attributed to **Rolling Contact Flaws** being permitted to develop into vertical fractures, see **Gauge Corner Cracking** (**GCC**), **Head Checking** (**HC**).

Haunch
[Civ.] That part of an **Arch** located between the **Springing** and **Crown**.

Haunching
a) [Civ.] The concrete, masonry or soil infilling behind the **Spandrel Wall** and above the **Haunch** of an **Arch Bridge**
b) The concrete built up around the sides of a **Carrier Drain** or foul water drain to prevent it distorting when the excavation is filled.

Hawes Junction Accident
At about 05:19 on 24th December 1910, a **Double Headed** □ **Express Passenger Train** caught up and collided with a pair of **Light Engines**. 12 died and 17 were injured. Fire broke out. The accident was caused by the **Signaller** becoming distracted and forgetting about the Light Engines standing at his **Starter Signal** and the **Train Crew** of the **Locomotives** not carrying out **Rule 55** and reminding him. The Signaller then incorrectly **Accepted** the Express Train and **Cleared** his Starter Signal for it. The Light Engines moved off but were caught by the Express. The Inquiry recommended the fitting of **Track Circuits** and the replacement of gas lighting with electric lighting in **Coaches**.

Hawk
(Tradename) [Tel.] A brand of **Telephone Concentrator** manufactured by Kestrel Telecom Ltd. of Sturminster Newton, Dorset.

Hawker
[Col.] Nickname for the **Class** 47 **Diesel Locomotive**. So named because **Brush** (their manufacturer) was a subsidiary of Hawker Siddeley at the time.

Hawkshaw, John
Later Sir (9th April 1811 – 2nd June 1891), A civil engineer who initally worked for the Bolivar Mining Association in Venezuela but returned to England in 1834. After working under under Jesse Hartley at the Liverpool docks, he was made engineer in charge of the **Railway** and navigation works of the Manchester, Bolton and Bury Canal Company. In 1845 he became chief engineer to the Manchester and Leeds Railway, and in 1847 to the Lancashire and Yorkshire Railway. In 1850 he moved to London to practise as a consulting engineer. In London he was responsible for the Charing Cross and Cannon Street Railways, the East London railway, and jointly with Sir John Wolfe-Barry he constructed the section of the **Underground Railway** which completed the inner circle between the Aldgate and Mansion House **Stations**. He was also **Engineer** in charge during the building of the Severn **Tunnel**.

HAZ
See **Heat Affected Zone**.

HAZAN
Hazard Analysis.

Hazard
a) A **Railway** ▫ **Telegraph Code** meaning "Running Lines and Sidings mentioned on both sides of the load to be **Clear**. To be signalled by the special **Is Line Clear** ▫ **Bell Code** 2-6-3" and applied to **Out of Gauge Loads**
b) Any circumstance, substance, device, object, or micro-organism that can cause death, harm, injury, damage or loss.

Hazard Brake
[LR] A brake that provides a high rate of retardation for use in emergency situations. The rate is higher than would normally be acceptable to passengers. On a **Tram**, this is often an electro-magnetic device applied to the **Rails**.

Hazard Directory
See **National Hazard Directory** (NHD).

Hazard Lights
Flashing lights on the leading end of a **Train** that may be switched on by the driver to warn the driver of any approaching Train that an **Accident** has occurred.

HAZCHEM
(*hazz-kem*) Hazardous Chemical. See also **Kemler**.

HAZID
Hazard Identification. A structured study to identify all the hazards inherent in a design.

HAZOP
(*hazz-opp*) Hazard and Operability Study. A structured study to identify all deviations from design intent that may have an undesirable effect on safety or operability.

HB
a) See **Civil Engineering Handbook**
b) See **Hand Back**, **Handback**.

HC
a) See **Half Chord**
b) See **Head Checking**
c) The **ATOC** code for **Heathrow Connect**.

HCAMS
See **High Carbon Austenitic Manganese Steel**.

HCD
HCD Curve
See **High Cant Deficiency Curve**.

HDPE
See **High Density Polyethylene**.

HDSL
[Tel.] High-speed Digital Subscriber Line.

HDSL Regenerator
HDSL Repeater
[Tel.] A device which extends the distance over which a High-speed Digital Subscriber Line can be operated.

Head
a) See **Rail Head**
b) See **Head Margin**.

Head Bond
[Elec., Sig.] A **Bond** fitted to the **Outside Edge** (OE) of the **Rail Head** at a **Fishplated Rail Joint**. The Bond is normally a short length of stranded conductor welded to the **Rail** and provides electrical continuity for **Track Circuits** (TC) or **Traction Power**.

Head Checking (HC)
[PW] A more general term for a **Rolling Contact Fatigue** (RCF) defect found in the **Running Band** of the **Rail Head**. Related conditions are **Field Flow** and **Gauge Corner Cracking** (GCC).

Head Code
a) [Col.] Common name for a **Train Reporting Number**
b) [Ops.] A display mounted on the front of a **Train** showing its Train Reporting Number, allowing **Signallers** to identify which Train was which. Their use has been superseded by the advent of **Train Describer** (TD) systems
c) [Hist.] In past times, an arrangement of white lights or white discs on the front of a Train giving a brief guide to the nature (e.g. **Goods** or **Passenger**) and stopping pattern (e.g. **All Stations** or non-stop) of that Train, allowing Signallers to tell successive Trains apart.

Head Margin
[Ops.] A term used to describe the allowance of time a particular point must be **Clear** prior to the arrival of a **Train**. See also **Headway**, **Hind Margin**, **Junction Margin**.

Head On
Describing a collision in which two **Locomotives**, **Trains**, **Rail Vehicles** or combination thereof meet end to end whilst travelling in opposite directions.

Head Planing
[PW] The removal of metal from the **Rail Head** over a sustained length. Examples of this include **Check Rails**, **Stock Rails** and **Switch Rails**.

ELLIS' BRITISH RAILWAY ENGINEERING ENCYCLOPÆDIA

Head Repair Weld (HRW)
(Tradename) [PW] A Thermit process which uses a small Alumino-thermic □ Portion to repair damage to the Rail Head.

Head Rope
[Hist.] On a Rope-worked Railway a rope attached to the leading end of a Set to allow the vehicles to be pulled up the gradient

Head Span

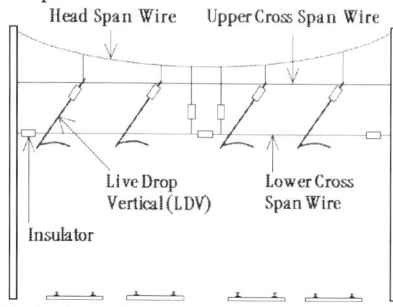

Head Span Wire   Upper Cross Span Wire

Live Drop   Lower Cross
Vertical (LDV)   Span Wire
Insulator

[Elec.] A form of Overhead Line Equipment (OLE) provision where multiple Catenary assemblies are supported by transverse wires strung between Overhead Line Structures. The alternative to this arrangement on Multi-Track layouts is Portals. See also Mechanically Independent Registration (MIR).

Head Span Wire
[Elec.] The uppermost wire in a Headspan assembly that supports all the Overhead Line Equipment (OLE) below.

Headshunt

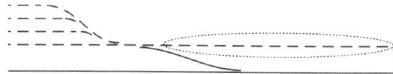

A dead-end length of Track provided to allow Shunting movements to take place in Sidings without those movements fouling the Running Line. Also Shunt Neck.

Headspan
See Head Span.

Headstock
a) [TRS] The horizontal beam forming the end of a Rail Vehicle, used to attach couplings and Buffers
b) The stationary support of a machine or power unit that supports and drives a revolving part.

Headwall
a) [LUL] The flat wall where the Tunnel enclosing a Platform reduces to the narrower diameter Running Tunnel between Stations
b) [Civ.] The wall forming the end of a Bridge Deck.

Headwall Plunger
[LUL] See ETCDS/TT Plunger.

Headwall Tunnel Telephone
[LUL] A telephone in a sealed box located on a platform headwall connected directly to the Tunnel Telephone System, the Service Control Centre or a Line Control Office. It is used to switch off traction current in an emergency. See also ETCDS/TT Plunger.

Headway
a) See Planning Headway
b) See Signalling Headway
c) See Technical Headway.

Headway Chart
[Ops.] A time/distance graph based on standard braking and acceleration curves that is used to determine optimum Signal positions.

Headway Curve
[Ops.] Alternative term for a Headway Chart.

Headway Post
[LUL] An Automatic Signal or Semi-automatic Signal in an Automatic Train Protection (ATP) area. It does not actively display an Aspect, but does transmit a Target Speed to the Train Operator's □ Cab. It is identified by a sign showing its Signal Number.

HEADWAY
POST
999

Headway Speed
See Operating Speed.

Headwear
[PW] The vertical reduction in Rail Depth caused by normal wear on the Rail Head, but not including Rail Gall or Sidewear.

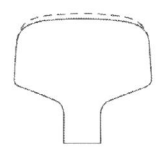

Heat Affected Zone (HAZ)
[PW] The short length of Rail adjacent to a Flame Cut or Weld that has been heated during the cutting or welding process, thus potentially altering its characteristics.

Heat Patrol
[PW] See Hot Weather Patrol.

Heat Treated Rail (HT)
[PW] A Rail manufactured in accordance with Tables 1 and 2 of British Standard Specification 11: 1985 'Normal' but subjected to a closely controlled cooling process during manufacture, to produce additional Rail Head hardness. Also Mill Heat Treated (MHT).

Heater
[TRS Col.] An alternative term for a Hot Axle Box on a Wagon.

Heater Pad
See Electric Pad Heaters.

Heathrow Connect (HC)
(Tradename) A Train Operating Company (TOC) that operates Semi-Fast services between Paddington and Heathrow Airport A joint venture between Heathrow Express (HEX) and First Great Western (FGW). ATOC code HC.

222

Heathrow Express (HEX)
(Tradename) A **Train Operating Company** (**TOC**) that operates dedicated **Fast** services between London Paddington and Heathrow Airport. **ATOC** code **HX**.

Heave
See **Frost Heave**.

Heavy Maintenance (HM)
Collective term for activities such as component replacement, rebuilding and structural repair. See also **Light Maintenance**.

Heavy Rail (HR)
A term used to differentiate between **Light Rail** (**LR**) such as **Tramways** and **Light Rapid Transit** (**LRT**) and the **National Railway Network** (**NRN**).

Heavy Work
[PW Hist.] An alternative term for **Switches and Crossings** (**S&C**)

Heck Accident
In the small hours of 28th February 2001 a Land Rover towing a trailer with another car on it left the M62 motorway near Great Heck in North Yorkshire, travelled across the ground behind the roadside crash barrier and landed on the **East Coast Main Line** (**ECML**). The wreckage was then struck by a southbound **Express Passenger Train** that became **Derailed** into the path of a northbound coal **Train**. Although the closing speed of the two Trains was around 180 mph, the death toll was lighter than this speed would suggest, with 11 dead and 76 injured. The prime cause was discovered to be that the Land Rover driver had fallen asleep at the wheel.

Hedgehog
[BR Obs.] Codename of a **Structure Gauging** vehicle, fitted with a fixed steel framework to permit distance measurements to be made whilst stationary.

Hedgehog Sleeper
[PW] A pre-cast **Concrete Sleeper** that has lengths of reinforcement projecting from it laterally all round. This allows it to be securely cast into other structures, such as a **Track Slab**, see **Slab Track**.

Hedley, William
(1779-1853) born in Newburn, near Newcastle-upon Tyne. Employed as colliery manager at Wylam Colliery, he was asked by the owner to develop a **Steam Locomotive**. In developing the work begun by Richard **Trevithick** with the 'Wylam Dilly' (1813), Hedley was assisted by Timothy **Hackworth**. One of the results was 'Puffing Billy' (1814).

Heel
[PW]
a) See **Crossing Heel**
b) See **Switch Heel**
c) See **Transition Heel**.

Heel Anchor Block
[PW] A cast metal block fitted between **Switch Rail** and **Stock Rail** at the **Switch Heel** for the following purposes:
- Maintain the correct geometry of the **Switch**
- Prevent longitudinal movement of the **Switch Rail** relative to the **Stock Rail**. See also **Stress Transfer Blocks**

See also **Ball and Claw**.

Heel Baseplate
[PW] A fixed **Baseplate** fitted to the **Heel** of a **Flat Bottom Switch**.

Heel Block
[PW] A metal block fitted between the **Switch Rail** and **Stock Rail** at the **Switch Heel** to maintain the correct geometry and prevent longitudinal movement of the Switch Rail. Also **Spacer Block**.

Heel Chair
[PW] A fixed **Chair** fitted to the **Heel** of a **Bull Head Switch**.

Heel Joint
[PW]
a) The **Rail Joint** at the **Heel** end of a **Switch Rail** or **Stock Rail**
b) The Rail Joint at the Heel end of a **Crossing Point Rail** or **Splice Rail**.

Heel of Planing
Heel of the Switch Planing
[PW] The end of the **Switch Planing**, at a specified distance from the **Switch Toe**. At this point the **Planing Radius** tangents with the **Switch Radius**.

Heel of Transition
[PW] The point at which a **Transition Curve** reaches its minimum Radius (**R**).

Heel Setting
[Elec.] The vertical distance from the **Contact Wire** (**CW**) to the pivot point on a **Registration Arm** typically 100mm.

Height
a) See **Wire Height**. See also **Height and Stagger**
b) [Sig.] Of a **Signal** or **Signal Element**, the vertical distance between the centre of the Signal or Element and the **Rail Crown** of the **Left-Hand Rail** in the direction of approach.

Height Adjustment Pad
[PW] A **Baseplate Pad** for an **ASP Baseplate** designed to raise the **Rail** and **Baseplate** assembly by a designed amount.

ELLIS' BRITISH RAILWAY ENGINEERING ENCYCLOPÆDIA

Height and Stagger
[Elec.] Two of the three directly measurable dimensions applicable to the relationship of the **Contact Wire** (**CW**) to the **Track** on an **Electrified Line**:
- Height is the distance between the **Plane of the Rails** and the **Contact Wire** measured at right angles to the Plane of the Rails. This is also known as the **Wire Height**
- Stagger is the lateral offset at a point of **Registration** from the **Track Centre Line** measured parallel to the Plane of the Rails. See also **Negative Stagger**, **Positive Stagger**
- The third dimension is **Mid-span Offset** (**MSO**), which is effectively the Stagger measured at the centre of a **Span**

See also **Wire Gradient**.

Height and Stagger Survey
[Elec.] A Survey undertaken to measure the **Height and Stagger** of the **Overhead Line Equipment** (**OLE**).

Helical Spring Screw
[PW] A resilient **Rail Fastening** having a head similar to a **Jay Flex Spike** but with a screw-threaded shank. Designed and produced by Bayliss Jones and Bayliss (**BJB**).

HEMBOT
High Efficiency **Motor Bogies** for **Trains**.

Henry Williams
(Tradename) A manufacturer of **Permanent Way** (**PW**), **Signalling** and **Points Heating** equipment as well as general metal forgings and highway equipment. Based in Darlington, County Durham. Often abbreviated to **Williams**. See also **Domino Panel**.

HEP
Head End Power, alternative term for **Electric Train Heating** (**ETH**).

Her Majesty's Railway Inspectorate (HMRI)
A body with ultimate responsibility for ensuring that:
- New works are designed and implemented correctly
- The operation of **Railways** of all types is carried out safely
- Accidents are thoroughly investigated.

From 1990 it was a specialist division within the Health and Safety Executive (**HSE**). On 1 April 2006, responsibility for health and safety policy and enforcement on the Railways transferred from HSE to the **Office of Rail Regulation** (**ORR**). This transfer affects the regulation of the operation of Railways and other guided transport systems, including **Heritage Railways**, **Metros** and **Light Rail** systems. However, HSE retains responsibility for **Guided Buses** and trolley vehicle systems. See also **Rail Accident Investigation Branch** (**RAIB**).

Heracleum Mantegazzianum
Giant Hogweed. See **Invasive Species**.

Heritage Railway
A **Railway** operated as a tourist attraction or museum exhibit, and equipped and operated in a manner dating from a previous era. See also **Preserved Railway**.

Heritage Railway Association, The (HRA)
(Tradename) [Pres.] The Heritage Railway Association represents the majority of **Heritage Railways** and **Preserved Railways** in the UK and Ireland.

HERMES
[Tel.] Handling through European **Railways** Messages Electronic System. Begun in 1978 when six railways (**BR**, **DB**, **FS**, **SBB**, **SNCB** and **SNCF**) agreed, under the patronage of the **International Union of Railways** (**UIC**), that there was a need to provide a high quality data communications network across Railway boundaries. Based on the CCITT X.25 network protocol, a common set of HERMES messages was defined and each national system interprets these messages and creates a suitable response. The initial core of the HERMES network was installed in 1981 and from 1983 the first **Freight** and **Passenger** applications run over the network.

HEROE
Harmonisation of European Rules for Operating **ERTMS**.

Heron (YCV)
[NR] A 34 ton capacity **Open Wagon** used for the transportation of **Ballast** based on the **Turbot** (**YCV**). See **Wagon Names**.

Herring (ZLV)
[NR] A **Ballast Hopper** with centre chutes only. See **Wagon Names**.

HET
Hazardous Event (**Train**).

HEX
(*hekks*) An abbreviation for **Heathrow Express**.

Hey-Back
Hey-Back Clip
Hey-Back System
[PW Obs.] A variety of **Rail Fastening** for **Flat Bottom Rail** (**FB**) consisting of a grooved **Baseplate** and a G-shaped rolled spring, used on **Wood Sleepers**. Devised in Norway by Heyerdahl-Larsen and Backe-Hansen and submitted for a patent in 1942.

HF
a) High Frequency
b) Human Factors.

HFDG
Human Factors Development Group.

HGUV
[TRS] An acronym representing a Super General Utility **Van**.

HGV
Heavy Goods Vehicle.

HH
[Sig.] On a **Signalling Circuit Diagram**: as one of the leading letters of an **Equipment Code**, it means **Double Yellow** (**YY**), **Preliminary Caution**.

HHLR
[Hist.] The **Pre-Grouping** H̲alifax H̲igh L̲evel R̲ailway.

Hidden Limits
Hidden Rules
[Col.] A nickname for the recommendations of Sir Anthony Hidden QC's enquiry into the **Clapham Accident** and the modifications to working hours practices that followed. The basic guidelines are:
- Maximum of 12 hours in a rostered shift
- Minimum of 12 hours rest between rostered shifts
- Not more than 72 hours rostered in a seven-day period
- Not more than 13 rostered shifts in any 14-day period.

Hierarchy of Hats
[Col. Hist.] The **Railway** has always contained clear social divisions, largely similar to the distinctions found in the armed forces. In **Civil Engineering**, these divisions were, until quite recently, indicated by types of hat. The lower orders (the workers, equivalent to privates) wore cloth caps; the inspectors (sergeants) wore Bowler hats or Trilbies; the Engineers (officers) wore top hats. This system began to die out from the top down, eventually being wholly extinguished by the mandatory wearing of hard hats on site.

High
[PW] An adjective describing a length of **Track** with a **Rail Level** higher than that which the designer intended. Also **Knob**, **Stiff**. The opposite is **Low**. See also **Slack**, **Swag**.

High Base Chair
[PW] Alternative term for a **Thick Based Chair**. See also **Two-levelled Chair**.

High Cant Deficiency Curve (HCD Curve)
[PW] The normal upper limit for **Cant Deficiency** (**D**) is 150mm; therefore a **Curve** with a value in excess of this is a High Cant Deficiency Curve.

High Carbon Austenitic Manganese Rail (HCAMS)
[PW] A **Rail** manufactured to the dimensions of British Standard Specification 11: 1985 but made from high carbon high manganese steel. See also **Austenitic Manganese Steel** (**AMS**).

High Cube
A 9' - 6" (2.8975m) high **Container**.

High Density Polyethylene (HDPE)
A material used for **Rail Pads** and drainage pipes.

High Leg
[PW, Col.] Term for the **High Rail** (**HR**), particularly in terms of **Stressing** operations.

High Level
A facility elevated relative to another nearby and related facility, for example High Level **Sidings**. See also **Low Level**.

High Level Output Specification (HLOS)
[NR] A document produced under Schedule 4 of the 2005 Railways Act by the Secretary of State for Transport (for England and Wales) and Scottish Ministers (for Scotland). It is supported by a **Statement Of Funds Available** (**SoFA**) to ensure the railway industry has clear and timely information about the strategic outputs that the Governments want the railway to deliver for the public and funds they are prepared to make available to facilitate these requirements.

High Output Ballast Cleaner (HOBC)
[PW] A **Ballast Cleaner** designed for high productivity, e.g. over 270m (300 **Yards**) per hour, and generally self-contained within a **Single Line**. See also **Medium Output Ballast Cleaner** (**MOBC**).

High Output Overhead Plant (HOOP)
High Output Plant System (HOPS)
[Elec.] A purpose built suite of **On-track Plant** (**OTP**) equipped to rapidly install new **Overhead Line Equipment** (**OLE**). See also **Factory Train**.

High Performance Switch System (HPSS)
(Tradename) [Sig.] An **Obstructionless** □ **Switch Operating Mechanism** used on some **RT60** □ **Switch and Crossing Units**. Originally developed by IAD Rail Systems who are now owned by **Network Rail** (**NR**) See also **High Performance Switch Actuator** (**HPSA**).

High Rail (HR)
[PW] The outer running **Rail** of a curved portion of a **Track**, sometimes applied irrespective of the relative heights of the Rails. Also **Outside Rail**, **High Leg**. See **High Ride**.

High Rail Only (HRO)
[PW] A description of an activity applied only to the **High Rail**, e.g. Rerailing. See also **One Rail Only** (**ORO**).

High Rail Wear
[PW] Collective description for the action of **Rail Wheels** on **High Rails**. Symptoms include **Gauge Corner Cracking** (**GCC**), **Sidewear**, **Sidecutting**. See also **Lipping**, **Mushrooming**.

High Ride
High Ride RRV
A system whereby a **Road Rail Vehicle** (**RRV**) is moved, in **Rail Mode**, by its rubber road tyres driving intermediate idler **Rail Wheels**. Also called **High Rail**. See also **Direct Drive**, **Low Ride**.

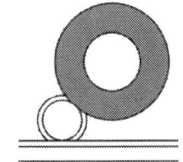

High Risk Failure
[Sig.] A **Wrong Side Failure** (**WSF**) where no other part of the **Signalling System** provides protection. Also known as an **Unprotected Wrong Side Failure** (**UWSF**).

High Speed AC
[CTRL] One of the **Traction Power** systems from which **Eurostar** trains take power. It is used between St Pancras and the **Channel Tunnel**. The system to be used has to be selected before the **Pantographs** of a stationary train are raised.

High Speed Check Rail
[PW] A **Check Rail** fitted at a reduced **Flangeway Gap** dimension of 38mm to increase the control exerted on **Wheelsets** passing at higher speeds. The normal Flangeway Gap in **113A Vertical**, **NR56V**, **NR60** and **RT60** ◻ **S&C Layouts** is 41mm.

High Speed Line (HSL)
a) A business-led term generally denoting a **Route** optimised for **Train** speeds of 125mph (200kph) or higher. The term does however have many other definitions in many other contexts
b) The proposed **Main Line** which would connect London to Scotland using **Trains** ◻ **Running** at over 225kph (140mph). See also **High Speed Two** (**HS2**).

High Speed One (HS1)
[CTRL] The new name for the **Channel Tunnel Rail Link**. See also **High Speed Two** (**HS2**).

High Speed Ramp
A **Ramp End** with a parabolic vertical profile designed for speeds up to 100mph (161kph).

High Speed Track Recording Coach (HSTRC)
See **Track Recording Coach** (**TRC**). See also **New Measurement Train** (**NMT**), **Trackmaster**.

High Speed Train (HST)
[TRS] While this term can be applied to any particularly fast **Passenger Train**, in the UK it has become synonymous with the **Class** 43 **Diesel Locomotive** and attendant **Mark** 3 **Coaches**, the **Intercity** 125 (**IC-125**).

High Speed Two (HS2)
The proposed **High Speed Line** north of **London**, currently announced as:
- London Euston to Armitage, with a **Branch** to Curzon Street in Birmingham and an interchange with **Crossrail** at Old Oak Common (**OOC**) as a first phase, followed by;
- Armitage to Wigan, with a Branch to Manchester Airport and Manchester Piccadilly
- Water Orton to Church Fenton (near York) and Leeds with a Junction at Oulton, running via Toton and Sheffield (Meadowhall)

See also **High Speed One** (**HS1**).

High Speed Two Limited (HS2 Ltd.)
(Tradename) The company set up by the Government to consider and develop the case for a new **High Speed** ◻ **Rail Network** in the UK. See **High Speed Two** (**HS2**)

High Spot
[PW] A localised elevated area in an otherwise constant **Gradient**. See also **Pointing On**.

High Stability Sole Plate
[PW] A metal plate on which a **Point Machine** is mounted that maintains it in the correct spatial relationship with the **Stock Rails**.

High Track Fixity
[NR PW] **Track** whose lateral position is very secure, such as **Slab Track**. See also **Low Track Fixity**, **Medium Track Fixity**, **Track Fixity**. This measure affects some of the **Gauging Tolerances** used in **Structure Gauging**.

High-Floor Tram
[LR] A **Light Rail Vehicle** (**LRV**) that has an internal floor level similar to that found on **Heavy Rail** (**HR**), typically greater than 600mm (24 inches) **Above Rail Level** (**ARL**). See also **Low-floor Tram**.

Highway Authority
An organisation responsible for the maintenance of public roads.

Hillhouse Accident
On 2nd December 1868 two **Trains** collided in thick **Fog** at Hillhouse, near Huddersfield, injuring seven. The **Line** was operated by **Time Interval Working**.

Hind Margin
[Ops.] The allowance of time left behind a **Train** before another is **Timetabled** to cross at a **Junction**. See also **Head Margin**, **Headway**.

Hindwall
[LUL] The opposite end of the **Platform** to the **Headwall**, where the **Running Tunnel** joins the **Station** in the Normal Direction.

His Majesty's Railway Inspectorate (HMRI)
Currently, see **Her Majesty's Railway Inspectorate** (**HMRI**).

Historic TSR
[NR Col.] A **Temporary Speed Restriction** (**TSR**) which was left in place for so long that it had to be made into a **Permanent Speed Restriction** (**PSR**) and has subsequently become a feature in the **Permissible Speed** (**PS**) profile. The original reason for the Restriction may now have gone, but since increases in Permissible Speed require approval from many quarters, it is often hard to remove the anomaly. See **Temporary**.

HIT
Humberside International Terminal.

Hit Area
[Sig.] The area around a particular visual target, which allows commands to be entered into a VDU-based **Signalling Control System** (**SCS**).

Hither Green Accident
On Sunday 5th November 1967, 49 **Passengers** died when a **Train** ◻ **Derailed** on **Jointed Track** at Hither Green in south London. The cause was a **Broken Rail**, which had fractured at a **Fishbolt Hole**. A loose piece of Rail was displaced, elevated and became wedged in such a position as to Derail the remaining vehicles. Normally a robust system, the combination of recent **Reballasting** work under one half of the **Fishplated Rail Joint** and the relatively high speed and **Un-sprung Mass** of the **Electric Multiple Units** (**EMU**) caused a catastrophic fatigue failure. This accident also prompted development of a new, stronger, **Rail Section**; see **113A**, and the acceleration of the introduction of **Continuous Welded Rail** (**CWR**).

Hi-vis. Vest
[Col.] A bright orange tabard with white retro-reflective strips, the wearing of which is mandatory whilst on the **Track** or **On or Near the Line**. See also **Diddy Vest**, **Mini Vest**, **Orange Vest**, **Yellow Vest**.

Hixon Accident
On the 6th January 1968 an **Express Passenger Train** hit an abnormal load (in this case a 120 ton electrical transformer on a low-floor road trailer) on a recently installed **Automatic Half Barrier Level Crossing** (**AHB**) at Hixon near Stafford. The load was passing slowly over the crossing when the automatic cycle began, and was still **Foul** of the **Line** when the **Train** arrived at 75 mph. Neither the driver of the road vehicle and trailer, nor his police escort, were aware of the correct procedures, and as a result the signs adjacent to such crossings now give simple instructions to the user. The resulting collision killed 11 people. See also **Hixon Modifications**.

Hixon Modifications
Hixon Mods
[Sig.] The modifications made to the operating sequence of **Automatic Half Barrier Level Crossings** (**AHB**) as a result of the **Hixon Accident**. These included enhancing the information provided at the **Level Crossing** (**LC**, **LX**) and lengthening the automatic cycle timings.

HJR
[Hist.] The **Pre-Grouping** Halesowen Joint **Railway**, a Great Western and Midland joint enterprise.

HL
a) Shorthand for **High Level**
b) **Home Location**.

HLOS
a) See **High Level Output Specification**
b) Also **High Level Output Statement**.

HM
See **Heavy Maintenance**.

HMFI
Her Majesty's Factory Inspectorate.

HMI
Human / Machine Interface.

HML
Highland **Main Line**.

HMRI
See **Her Majesty's Railway Inspectorate**, **His Majesty's Railway Inspectorate**.

HNC
See **Home Normal Control**, **Home Normal Contact**.

HNRC
(Tradename) Harry Needle Railroad Company, an **Open Access Operator** specialising in **Locomotives**.

HO
a) High Output. See also **High Output Ballast Cleaner** (**HOBC**).
b) See **Hand Over**, **Handover**.

HOBC
See **High Output Ballast Cleaner**.

HOE
Head of Engineering.

Hog Curve
A convex **Vertical Curve** (**VC**) or **Summit**. The opposite is **Sag Curve**.

Hogbacks
[Civ. Col.]
Bridge □ **Main Girders** which have a curved top, seen in elevation.

Hogged Switch
[PW] A **Switch Rail** displaying such severe **Hogging** that the **Switch Rail** is defective. A severely Hogged Switch Rail will not sit evenly on the **Slide Tables** of all the **Slide Baseplates**, accelerating the wear on the one nearest the **Switch Toe**.

Hogging
[PW] The vertical upward curvature of an unfastened **Rail** due to stresses built into the Rail during manufacture. The effect is observed most clearly in **Switch Rails**, see **Hogged Switch**.

HoldFast
(Tradename) Fully titled HoldFast **Level Crossings** Ltd. of Cheltenham, Gloucestershire.

Holding Brake
A brake provided to prevent RRVs rolling away unintentionally during **On-tracking** and **Off-tracking**.

Holding Siding
A **Siding** used for the stabling of **Locomotives**. Also **Lay-by**.

Hollow Axle
[TRS] An axle which purposely has a large void the middle, like a thick-walled tube.

Hollow Bearers
[PW] **Bearers** with a hollow box or channel section used to accommodate **Supplementary Drives**, **Stretcher Bars** and **Switch Operating Mechanisms** in **Switch and Crossing Units** (**S&C Units**). This arrangement leaves the **Bays** or **Beds** clear of obstructions, making **Mechanised Maintenance** such as **Tamping** easier. See also **In Bearer Clamplock**.

Hollow Sleeper
[PW] A type of **Sleeper** constructed from a hollow steel box, allowing many cables to cross the **Track** in safety. Also **Box Sleeper**. See also **Ducted Sleeper**.

Hollow Spandrel
[Civ.] A **Spandrel** where the **Haunching** is replaced by vertical stiffening ribs that in turn carry the load.

Holly
A **Railway** □ **Telegraph Code** meaning "Following now in order".

Holton Heath Accident

At 12:02 on 20th April 1989 a **Light Engine** (**LE**) collided with the rear of a **Freight Train** between Wareham and Hamworthy. The Freight Train had **Shunted** at an intermediate **Siding**, called Holton Heath, the entrance to which was controlled by a **Ground Switch Panel** (**GSP**). The **Line** itself was controlled by **Absolute Block** (**AB**) but with limited **Track Circuit** (**TC**) provision in the Holton Heath area. The Freight Train **Guard** rang the **Controlling Signal Box** on completion of the **Shunting** and said "Frame's □ **Normal** mate" which the Signaller, not having full Track Circuits to advise him, assumed meant the that the Freight Train was in the Siding, when in fact it was on the **Main Line**. The Signaller cancelled the "**Train on Line**" indication to Hamworthy and allowed the Light Engine into the **Section**. The Light Engine driver died. This **Accident** would have been prevented by proper communication and / or fuller provision of Track Circuits (which were later added).

Home No. 1 Signal
[Sig. Obs.] Former term for the **Outer Home Signal**.

Home No. 2 Signal
[Sig. Obs.] Former term for the **Inner Home Signal**.

Home Normal Contact
Home Normal Control (HNC)
[Sig.] A set of electrical contacts that prevent **Line Clear** (**LC**) being given to the **Signal Box** □ **On the Approach** unless the **Lever** controlling the **Home Signal** has been **Replaced** in the **Frame**. This prevents the **Signaller** giving permission for a second **Train** to approach before replacing the Home Signal after the previous Train.

Home Shed
The **Shed** or **Depot** at which a **Traction Unit** is based.

Home Signal

[Sig.] In **Absolute Block** (**AB**) areas, it is the first **Signal** capable of showing a **Stop Aspect** □ **On the Approach** to a **Signal Box**. See also **Inner Home**, **Outer Home**.

Home Station
[Hist.] Under **British Railways** and the companies that preceded it, all staff booked on for duty at their Home Station, unless they were lodging away. Confusingly, Home Stations were not always **Passenger Stations**, or anywhere near where the person lived.

HOOB
[NR] **H**igh **O**utput **O**perational **B**ase.

Hood
[Sig.] A cover (which may be short or long) placed above the individual **Aspects** of a **Colour Light Signal** or **Position Light Signal** (**PLS**) to reduce **Phantom Aspects** caused by sunlight.

Hook Coupling
[TRS] The former standard item of **Drawgear** on all **Rail Vehicles** and **Locomotives**. The hooks were connected together using an **Instanter Coupling**, **Screw Coupling** or **Three Link Coupling** between each vehicle. **Automatic Couplings** are becoming more common on all **Rail Vehicles**, although this has been standard equipment on **Passenger Coaches** for many years.

Hook Switch
[Elec.] An electrical switch attached to a **Conductor Rail** that allows a **Sub-section** to be electrically separated from another Sub-section.

HOOP
See **H**igh **O**utput **O**verhead **P**lant.

Hoops
[PW] The cast-in bars that form part of the **SHC Fastening** and **CS3** systems. Also **Goal Posts**.

Hoover
[Col.] Nickname for a **Class** 50 **Diesel Locomotive**.

Hopper
Hopper Wagon
[TRS]
a) A **Wagon** which discharges its load through doors built into the bottom area of the wagon.
b) A colloquial description of any open-topped chute-equipped Wagon designed for:
- Unloading **Ballast** onto the **Track**, e.g. Auto Ballaster, Catfish, Dogfish, Sealion. See Ballast Hopper
- Transporting **Coal** or **Aggregates** between supplier and consumer.

HOPS
See **H**igh **O**utput **P**lant **S**ystem.

Horizontal Alignment
[PW] Collective term for the straights, **Horizontal Curves** and **Transition Curves** designed into a **Railway**. Sometimes shortened to **Alignment** in common usage. See also **Curve**, **Element Length**, **Reverse Curve**, **Straight**, **Transition**, **Virtual Transition** (**VT**).

Horizontal Curve
A **Curve** whose plane is near horizontal. If not specified, this is the arrangement implied by the term Curve. See also **Vertical Curve** (**VC**).

Horizontal Defect
[PW] A **Rail Defect** aligned along a plane parallel to the **Running Surface** of the **Rail**.

Horizontal Gather
[TRS] The amount of horizontal misalignment an **Automatic Coupling** can be subjected to and still satisfactorily **Couple Up**.

Horizontal Half-beam Angle
[Sig.] The angle between the **Beam** centre-line and the line that represents 50% of the peak Intensity, measured at the surface of a **Signal Element**, in the horizontal plane.

Horizontal Tappet Lever Frame
[Sig.] A **Lever Frame** where the **Locking** is arranged horizontally behind the **Levers** on a **Locking Shelf**. See also **Vertical Tappet Lever Frame**.

Horn
a) The homopneumatic device a **Lookout** may use to warn of **Approaching Trains**
b) [TRS] The two-tone compressed air warning device fitted to **Locomotives** and **Multiple Unit Trains**
c) [Elec.] See **Pantograph Horn**
d) [TRS] See **Axlebox Horn**.

Horn Guide
See **Axlebox Horn**. Also **Pedestal**.

Horned Sill
[PW Hist.] A cast metal **Sleeper** having vertical projections integral to the **Rail Bearing Areas** to both retain **Track Gauge** and to provide vertical support. Thought to have been developed during the latter years of the 18th century for use with **Plate Rails**.

Horse Dock
[Hist.] A **Platform** for transferring horses to and from **Rail Vehicles**. Livestock is no longer transported in this manner in Britain.

HOT
Head of Train, i.e. the front.

Hot Axle Box
Common description of an overheating **Journal** on a **Wheelset**. Modern **Rail Vehicles** have ball bearing Journals, but some older vehicles with oiled plain Journals are still in service and this type overheat if not adequately lubricated, a potential cause of fires. Hot Axle Boxes are detected by **Hot Axle Box Detectors** (HABD). Often contracted to **Hot Box**.

Hot Axle Box Detector (HABD)
A device comprising axle counters, processing equipment and infra-red detectors mounted close to the **Rail** which monitor passing **Trains** and alert the controlling **Signal Box** (SB) if it they sense an overheating or **Hot Axle Box**. If a Train activates a Detector it is brought safely to a stand for examination or remedial action.

Hot Box
A contraction of **Hot Axle Box**.

Hot Rail
[Col.] Term for the positive **Conductor Rail** in a DC **Electrification System**. Also **DC Rail, Juice Rail, Positive Conductor Rail, Positive Rail, Pozzy Rail, Third Rail**.

Hot Strip
See **Close Viewing Sector** (CVS).

Hot Tears
(*hot tares*) [PW] Fissures in an **Alumino-thermic Weld** caused by releasing the **Tensors** around the **Weld** (**W**) site too early, and so subjecting the Weld to high levels of tension whilst still soft. Current practice is to apply additional **Pull Force** whilst the Weld is cooling to remove any possibility of Hot Tears. A new Weld can also be put in tension by sudden cloud cover on a sunny day, so it is important to **Fasten Down** at least 100y (91m) of **Rail** each side of the Weld site before setting up the Weld.

Hot Weather Patrol
[PW] Special **Track Patrols** undertaken during periods of high **Rail Temperatures** (or Rail Temperatures potentially in excess of the **Critical Rail Temperature** (**CRT**) of a section of **Track**) to detect **Track Buckles** or signs of low **Lateral Resistance**.

Hot Weather Site
[PW] A section of **Track** designated by the **Infrastructure Owner** as vulnerable to **Buckling** in hot weather, for which rail temperatures are monitored and **Special Track Patrols** are conducted during the highest risk period of the day. See also **Blue Item**.

Hot Wheel Detector (HWD)
A **Track** mounted sensor which detects the heat produced by skidding **Wheelsets** or dragging brakes.

Hotel
The **Phonetic Alphabet** word representing H.

Hotel Power
[TRS]
a) An alternative term for **Shore Supply**
b) Electrical power for air conditioning, doors, food preparation, public address, reservation displays, etc. on a **Train**.

HOTF
See **Hard Over Tilt Failed**.

HOTR
[PW] High Output Track Relaying.

HOTRT
[PW] High Output Track Relaying Train.

Housetop
[LUL PW] A horizontal metal plate laid above the inside **Switch Rail** in a sharply-curved **Turnout** to provide a **Checking** facility for both **Routes**.

Housing
[PW]
a) Part of a **Rail Fastening** system cast or glued into a concrete **Sleeper** or **Bearer**. Also **Insert**
b) Part of a fastening system that forms an integral part of a **Baseplate**.

HOV
High Occupancy Vehicle. A **Passenger Vehicle** with few seats and many places to stand.

HOWL
[NR] Heart of Wales Line.

HP
Help Point.

HPPE
Higher Performance Polyethylene.

ELLIS' BRITISH RAILWAY ENGINEERING ENCYCLOPÆDIA

HPRail
(Tradename) [PW] A type of hypereutectoid **Rail Steel** produced by Tata Steel (formerly Corus, originally British Steel). It optimises:
- The volume fraction of cementite through an increase in carbon content to a maximum of 0.95%
- The strength of the pearlitic ferrite through solid solution strengthening from silicon additions (0.95% maximum) and precipitation strengthening through vanadium addition (0.14% maximum).
- Precise control of nitrogen and vanadium contents to capitalise on the effect of the vanadium additions and to maximise the magnitude of lower temperature, finer, vanadium carbide precipitates within the pearlitic ferrite.

HPSA
High Performance **Switch Actuator**, the **Point Machine** in a **High Performance Switch System** (**HPSS**) installation.

HPSS
See **High Performance Switch System**.

HQA
The **CARKND** representing an **Auto Ballaster** □ **Wagon**.

HR
a) See **Heavy Rail**
b) See **High Rail**
c) [Hist.] The Highland **Railway**.

HRA
a) See **Heritage Railway Association**, The
b) Hot Rolled Asphalt.

HRC
High Rupture Capacity.

HRO
See **High Rail Only**.

HRW
See **Head Repair Weld**.

HS
See **Handsignaller**.

HS2
See **High Speed Two**.

HS2 Ltd.
See **High Speed Two Limited**.

HSBC

HSBC Rail
(Tradename) Hong Kong and Shanghai Banking Corporation, a major source of funding for new **Rolling Stock**.

HSBV
An acronym representing a **High Speed Train** (HST) □ **Barrier Vehicle**.

HSC
Health & Safety Commission.

HSCB
High Speed **Circuit Breaker**.

HSCC
High Speed Current Collection.

HSCCP
High Speed Current Collection Project.

HSDR
High Speed Data Ring.

HSDT
High Speed Diesel **Train**, which later became the **Intercity 125** (IC125) □ **High Speed Train** (HST).

HSE
Health & Safety Executive. Also **H&SE**.

HSEQ
Health, Safety, Environment and Quality.

HSFV
High Speed **Freight** Vehicle.

HSGT
High Speed **Gauging Train**.

HSISE
How Safe is Safe Enough.

HSL
a) See **High Speed Line**
b) Health and Safety Laboratory.

HSLM
High Speed Load Model.

HSM
Handsignalman, see Handsignaller.

HSR
a) High Speed **Rail**
b) High Speed **Railway**.

HST
a) See **High Speed Train**
b) [NR] On a sign forming part of a **Non-standard Differential Speed Restriction**, it indicates that the speed value shown applies only to **Trains** composed of:
- **Class** 43 Diesel **Locomotives** and **Mark** 3a **Coaches**
- Class 168, 170, 171, 175, 180, 220, 221, 222, 373 and 390 **Trains**
- Class 91 Locomotive, Mark 4 Coaches and a **Driving Van Trailer** (DVT)

c) Generically, any **Conventional Train** with Enhanced Braking.

HST2
The working title of the project to specify and develop the successor to the **Intercity 125** (**Class** 43 **Locomotives** and **Mark** 3 **Coaches**) High Speed Train (HST). See **Intercity Express Programme** (IEP).

HSTR
High Speed **Track Recording**.

HSTRC
See **High Speed Track Recording Coach**. Also **Track Recording Coach** (TRC), **Track Recording Unit** (TRU), generically a **Track Recording Vehicle** (TRV).

HSTRT
See **High Speed Track Relaying Train**. Also **Track Relaying Train** (TRT).

HSWA
Health and Safety at Work Act 1974. Also **HASAWA**.

HT
a) See **Heat Treated Rail**
b) High Tensile
c) High Tension, an alternative for High Voltage (HV)
d) See **Hull Trains**, an **Open Access Operator**
e) The **ATOC** code for **First Hull Trains**.

HTS
High Tensile Steel.

Huck
(Tradename) A manufacturer of fastening devices, most notably a range of **Multi-groove Locking Pins** (**MGL Pins**) and **Multi-groove Locking Studs** (**MGL Stud**). The name has become the colloquial term for all such MGL devices. The company is a subsidiary of Alcoa.

Huck Bolt
Huck Pin
(Tradename) A proprietary type of **Multi-groove Locking Stud** (**MGL Stud**).

Hudd Inductive Automatic Warning System
[Sig. Obs.] Developed in 1930, the forerunner of the **Automatic Warning System** (**AWS**) now employed in the UK. Also Strowger-Hudd.

Huddersfield Accident (1919)
At 17:57 on the 24th December 1919, two **Trains** collided when the **Signallers** □ **Accepted** a second **Train** on a **Route** which took it across the Route already set for the first Train. Four people were injured. See also **Huddersfield Control**.

Huddersfield Accident (1989)
At 21:56 on 6th November 1989, two **Passenger Trains** collided head-on at low speed close to Huddersfield **Station**. 23 people sustained minor injuries. The Station area was being **Remodelled** at the time, with all the normal **Signalling** disconnected. Trains were being **Handsignalled** when poor planning and communication led to one of the **Trains** being misrouted.

Huddersfield Control
[Sig.] A **Signalling Control** provided between a **Platform Starting Signal** and **Call-on Route** reading up to that **Signal**.

Hudson, George
(1800-1871). **Railway** promoter and financier who became known as the Railway King, financing (amongst others) the Midland (**MR**) and York & North Midland Railways by means of insider share dealing, bribes and the sale of non-existent assets.

Hull Trains
(Tradename) A **Train Operating Company** (**TOC**), part of the First Group and which is an **Open Access Operator** and provides a limited number of through services between London Kings Cross and Hull.

Human Factors
a) The science of human behaviour and its influence on the occurrence of human errors.
b) The environmental, organisational and job factors, and human and individual characteristics which influence behaviour at work.

Hump
An artificial summit built in a **Marshalling Yard** to facilitate **Gravity Shunting**. See **Hump Yard**.

Hump Shunting
[Obs.] To use an artificial summit for sorting **Wagons** into **Trains**. The vehicles to be sorted are pushed one at a time over the Hump, and sorted into **Sidings** by changing the **Set** of the **Points** as required. As the lengths of the destination **Trains** increase, **Retarders** are used to slow the descent of the vehicles appropriately. This process was automated before being abandoned when **Freight** working became almost exclusively containerised in the 1970s. See also **Fly Shunting**, **Gravity Shunting**, **Loose Shunting**.

Hump Yard
A **Marshalling Yard** having the facility for the **Gravity Shunting** of vehicles, normally **Wagons**. This is achieved using a **Hump**, over which the vehicles to be sorted are **Propelled**.

Hunting
[TRS] Periodic lateral motion of a **Wheelset**, **Bogie** or whole **Rail Vehicle**. Sometimes violent, it is generally caused by a combination of poorly maintained **Track** and poorly maintained **Wheelsets**. The actual motion is due to the Wheelset wandering from side to side using the small tolerance available between **Wheel Flange** and **Rail** on each side. Normally the conical shape of the **Wheel** and inclined **Rails** act to centre the wheels on **Straight Track** and prevent Hunting.

HUSARE
Human Safe Railway in Europe.

HUSH
HUSH Rail
(hush rale) [PW] A **Flat Bottom** (**FB**) □ **Rail Section** weighing 50 **Kilogrammes per Metre** and having a shallow depth; designed to reduce radiated noise levels.

HV
a) [PW] **Vertical** □ **Flat Bottom** (**FB**) **Full Depth Switches**. The H describes the length and **Switch Radius**
b) High Visibility, as in clothing
c) High Voltage.

HV Vest
High Visibility vest, an orange waistcoat with retro-reflective stripes. Also **Diddy Vest**, **Mini Vest**, **Yellow Vest**.

HVAC
a) Heating, Ventilation and Air Conditioning
b) High Voltage Alternating Current.

HVI
[Sig.] High Voltage Impulse, a type of **Jointed Track Circuit** manufactured by **GEC**.

HVs
[PW] Denotes **113A** □ **Flat Bottom** (**FB**) □ **Shallow Depth Switches**, length H.

HVS
[PW] Denotes **CEN56E1** □ **Flat Bottom** (**FB**) □ **Shallow Depth Switches**, length H.

HW
a) See **Hardwood**, **Hardwood Sleeper**
b) See **HWxxxx**.

HWD
See **Hot Wheel Detector**.

HWxxxx
(Tradename) [Sig.] A range of **Point Machines** manufactured by **Alstom**.

HX
The **ATOC** code for **Heathrow Express**.

Hybrid Box
See **Hybrid Signal Box**.

Hybrid Gauging
A combination of **Comparative Gauging** and **Absolute Gauging**, where Absolute Gauging is used to evaluate only those clearances related to the features of the **Rail Vehicle** which project outside the envelope of the Vehicle being used as a reference.

Hybrid Signal Box
[Sig.]
a) A **Signal Box** (**SB**) equipped with a mix of **Mechanical Signalling** and **Power Signalling** equipment
b) A Signal Box equipped with two different types or ages of Power Signalling equipment.

Hyde Accident
At 09:50 on 22nd August 1990, two **Diesel Multiple Units** (**DMU**) collided head-on at low speed on the **Single Line** section of Hyde North **Junction**, which was a **Single Lead Junction**. The cause was determined to be driver inexperience leading to a **Signal Passed at Danger** (**SPAD**). This is was the second head on collision on a Single Lead Junction in as many years, see **Bellgrove Accident**, see also **Newton Accident**. This Accident would have been prevented by a system such as **Train Protection and Warning System** (**TPWS**).

Hydraulic Buffer Stop
A **Buffer Stop** that utilises the restricted flow of hydraulic fluid to decelerate the **Train**. The hydraulic system may be combined with other systems such as friction elements to provide additional arresting capacity. Relatively large systems can sometimes be found at the terminal ends of **Bay Platforms**, though their age often renders them incompatible with more modern **Stock** with central **Automatic Couplings** and no **Side Buffers**.

Hydrive
[NR] A **Network Rail** (**NR**) developed **Switch Operating Mechanism** which combines the SPX Rail Systems' **In-Bearer Clamplock** (**IBCL**) and the **Alstom** SO hydraulic **Supplementary Drive**.

Hydro-pneumatic Points
Hydro-pneumatic Switch
See **Train Operated Switch**. Also **Gas Bag Points**, **Train Operated Points** (**TOP**).

Hydulignum
(Tradename) [PW] A compressed wood fibre / glue laminate used to manufacture non-conducting **Fishplates** for use in **Insulated Rail Joints** (**IRJ**) With the advent of modern polymers, Hydulignum Fishplates have fallen out of favour. See **Permali**.

Hymek
(Tradename) [Hist.] Brandname of the **English Electric** (**EE**) ▫ **Class** 35 **Diesel Hydraulic Locomotive**.

HyperRoute
(Tradename) [PW] A software tool, developed by **Laser Rail Technologies** (a division of **Balfour Beatty** Rail Technologies Ltd.) used to perform large scale high volume **Gauging** calculations.

I

I
a) In an abbreviated **Track Name**, it generally denotes an **Independent Line**
b) [PW] As a suffix, as in BHI or FBI, it denotes **Inclined**
c) [NR] As the first letter of a **Wagon** □ CARKND, it means the vehicle is an international one of non-UK origin
d) [Sig.] On a **Signalling Circuit Diagram**:
• As one of the leading letters of an **Equipment Code**, it means **Automatic Warning System** (**AWS**).
• As the last letter of an Equipment Code, it means inductor (electromagnet).
e) The letter represented by **India** in the **Phonetic Alphabet**.

I&I
[NR] **Infrastructure** and Investment.

I/L
See **Interlocking**.

IAF
International Austellung Fahrwegtechnik (International Exhibition of **Railway** Construction).

IAL
Identified Asset List.

IAMS
Integrated Asset Management System.

IAP
Industry Access Plan.

IAPI
Industry Access Planning Improvement.

Iarnród Éireann (IE)
A wholly owned subsidiary of **Córas Iompair Éireann** (**CIE**) and the national **Railway Authority** within the Republic of Ireland. See also **Northern Ireland Railways** (**NIR**).

IARO
International Air Rail Organisation.

IATP
a) Intelligent **Automatic Train Protection**
b) [LUL] Intermittent Automatic Train Protection

IB
a) See **Intermediate Block Section**
b) See **Intersection Bridge**.

IB Section (IBS)
See **Intermediate Block Section**.

IBCL
See **In-bearer Clamp Lock**.

Iberian Gauge
A **Track Gauge** of 1668mm (5' - 5$^{21}/_{32}$").

IBH

IBH Signal
See **Intermediate Block Home Signal**.

IBIS
[BR, Obs.] Internal Business Invoicing System, an internal trading system.

IBJ
a) See **Insulated Block Joint**
b) Alternative and often erroneous name for an **Insulated Rail Joint** (**IRJ**).

IBS
[Sig.]
a) See **Intermediate Block Section**
b) See **Intermediate Block Signal**.

IC
See **Intercity**.

IC-125
See **Intercity 125**.

IC-225
See **Intercity 225**.

ICC
a) **Infrastructure** Control Centre
b) See **Integrated Control Centres**
c) [CT] See **Incident Co-ordination Centre**
d) Interim Control Centre.

ICCN
[IE] Intercity and Commuter Network.

ICCS
Integrated Communications Control System.

ICDB
Industry Capacity Database

ICE
a) Inter City Express, the pan-Europe **High Speed Train** network
b) See **Institution of Civil Engineers**.

Ice Mode
[TRS] A control fitted to **Class** 37x that can be switched in to eliminate the risk of the **Train** being shut down by its own **Line Interference Monitor** because of excessive arcing at the **Current Collection Shoes**.

Icelert
(Tradename)
a) Brandname for the Weather Monitoring Control Unit (**WMCU**) systems manufactured by Findlay Irving Ltd. of Penicuik, Scotland
b) Common name for all WMCU systems.

ICIG
Infrastructure Clients Interface Group.

ICM
a) [NR] **Infrastructure** Contracts Manager
b) Infrastructure Cost Model.

ICMU
Interference Current Monitoring Unit, a device fitted to **Class** 373 **Electric Multiple Units** (**EMU**).

ICOM
Inputs, Constraints, Outputs, Mechanisms.

ICONIS
(Tradename) Integrated Control and Information System.

233

ELLIS' BRITISH RAILWAY ENGINEERING ENCYCLOPÆDIA

ICP
a) [RT, NR] Interim Control Points, the proposed step between the current **Power Signal Boxes** (PSB) the future **Network Management Centres** (NMC)
b) See **Independent Competent Person**.

ICPTUR
The International Conference for Promoting Technical Uniformity on **Railways**.

ICR
[PW] Instantaneous Change of Radius (**R**), an alternative description of a **Virtual Transition**.

ICRR
Inter-Capital and Regional **Rail**.

ICRTD
International Cooperation for **Railway** Technical Documentation.

ICS
a) [LUL] Intermediate Communications System
b) An acronym representing an **InterCity** Saloon **Coach**.

ICTS
International Consultants Targeting Security.

ICW
See **In Connection With**.

ID&T
Implementation, Development and Training. Also **IDT**.

IDC
a) See **Interdisciplinary Design Check**
b) Integrated Design Check
c) Insulation Displacement Connector.

IDD

IDDD
Interdisciplinary Development or **Inter**disciplinary Design Development.

IDF
Intermediate Distribution **Frame**.

IDL
See **Internal Data Link**.

IDL Telegram
Telegrams sent over the **Internal Data Link**.

IDLH
Immediately Dangerous to Life or Health.

IDMT
Inverse Definite Minimum Time.

IDP
Integrated Drainage Project

IDR
a) Interim Design Review
b) See **Interdisciplinary** Design Review.

IDT
Implementation, Development and Training. Also **ID&T**.

IÉ
See **Iarnród Éireann**.

IEA
[NR] The **CARKND** representing a 65 ton capacity **Ballast / Spoil Wagon** operated by **Network Rail**.

IEC
International Electro-technical Commission.

IECC
See **Integrated Electronic Control Centre**.

IECC Lite
(Tradename) [Sig.] A PC-based single-workstation **Integrated Electronic Control Centre** developed by **DeltaRail** for use with **Network Rail's** (NR) **Modular Signalling** initiative.

IED
Intelligent Electronic Device.

IEDIM
Identify, Evaluate, Develop a system, Implement, Monitor.

IEE
Institution of Electrical and Engineers. , now part of the **Institution of Engineering and Technology** (IET).

IEI
Initial Environmental Information.

IEP
Intercity Express Programme.

IERS
International Environmental Rating System.

IET
See **Institution of Engineering and Technology**.

IEV
International Electro-technical Vocabulary.

IFA
[NR]
a) [Civ.] Inspection for Assessment
b) The **CARKND** representing a **High Output Ballast Cleaner** (HOBC) support **Wagon**
c) The CARKND representing the **Modular Switch and Crossing** delivery Wagons, manufactured by **Kirow**. See also **Tilting Wagons**.

IFC
See **Infrastructure Fault Control**.

IFE
(Tradename) Innovation for Entrance Systems, a manufacturer of automatic door systems for **Railway Vehicles**. Part of the Knorr-Bremse Group.

IFP
[Sig.] Interface Processor, an obsolete subsystem within the **IECC** system.

IFS
See **Individual Function Switch**.

IGA

IGB
[NR] The **CARKND** representing a **Continuous Welded Rail** carrier **Wagon**.

IGBT
(*igg-bit*) Insulated Gate Bipolar Transistor, see **Chopper**.

IGC
Inter-Governmental Commission, the body responsible for the **Channel Tunnel** and the Safety Authority for works involving the Channel Tunnel.

IGS
[Sig.] Information Generator Subsystem, an obsolete subsystem within the IECC system.
IHA
Interface Hazard Analysis
II
Intelligent Infrastructure.
IIE
a) [NR] Infrastructure Investment, Enhancements
b) Institution of Incorporated Engineers, now part of the **Institution of Engineering and Technology** (IET).
IIF
Interoperability Implementation Forum, a regular meeting of government and industry interests which advises on implementation of **Technical Standards for Interoperability** (TSI) Directives.
IIP
a) [NR] Initial Industry Plan. The plan sets out how the **Railway Industry** can deliver a more efficient and better value **Railway** and how the Railway can play a key role in driving sustainable economic growth. The IIP examines the key choices and options facing funders in specifying the future outputs of the Railway and the level of funding required. These choices will inform the development of the Government's High Level Output Specification (HLOS) and Statement of Funds Available (SoFA).
b) **Infrastructure** Improvement Programme
c) Investors in People.
IJ
Insulated Joint, see **Insulated Rail Joint** (IRJ).
IKB
Isambard Kingdom Brunel, see **Brunel, Isambard Kingdom**.
IKF
[NR] Integrated Kent Franchise.
IL
a) See **Interlocking**
b) Integrity Level
c) Indicator Light
d) The **ATOC** code for **Island Lines**.
ILGGRI
International Liaison Group of Government **Railway** Inspectorates.
Illuminated Diagram
[Sig.] A **Signal Box Diagram** containing lamps displaying the status of the relevant **Track Circuits**.
ILO
International Labour Organization.
ILWS
(*ill-wuss*) See **Inductive Loop Warning System**.
IM
a) Infrastructure □ Maintenance
b) See **Infrastructure Manager**
c) Information Management.
IMACS
(*eye-maks*) [BR Obs.] Inventory Management Accounting and Control System.

IMC
IMCo
[RT Obs.] See **Infrastructure Maintenance Company**, Infrastructure Maintenance Contractor, Infrastructure Maintenance Contract. See also RT1A.
IMC2
[RT Obs.] The second generation **Infrastructure Maintenance Contract**.
IMC2000
[RT Obs.] The third generation **Infrastructure Maintenance Contract** (IMC) which encouraged common goals and openness between **Contractor** and client.
IMDG
International Maritime Dangerous Goods Code.
IMDM
[NR] Infrastructure □ Maintenance Delivery Manager.
IMDU
[NR] Infrastructure □ Maintenance Delivery Unit (MDU).
IME
Infrastructure Maintenance Engineer
IMechE
See **Institution of Mechanical Engineers**.
IMG
[NR] Infrastructure Materials Group.
IMM
a) See **Infrastructure Maintenance Manager**
b) Inspection and Maintenance Model.
Immediate Cause
The situation, event or behaviour that directly results in an occurrence.
Immune
[Sig., Tel.] Describing a **Signalling** or **Telecommunications** system or part thereof that has been **Immunised**. It is normal to include the type of current that the system has been Immunised against, see **AC Immune**, **DC Immune**.
Immunisation
Immunised
Describing the protection of a **Signalling** or **Telecommunications** system or part thereof from interference from **Traction Supply** currents. See **AC Immune**, **DC Immune**, **Immune**.
IMPACT
(*im-pakt*)
a) [NR PW] **Track** assessment system which utilises **Rail Defect**, **Track Geometry**, **Track Quality**, **Train Minute Delay** and component age data to identify sections of **Track** where **Maintenance** or **Renewal** would be most cost effective
b) Improved Manufacturing Performance Through Active Change and Training, a **Westinghouse** partnership initiative.
Impact Coefficient
An enhancement to the normal loading which is designed to simulate the infrequent and exceptional loads to which **Bridges** and the **Track** may be subjected under real service conditions.

ELLIS' BRITISH RAILWAY ENGINEERING ENCYCLOPÆDIA

Impact Wrench
a) A powered hand held rotary device used to drive and remove threaded items. The impact element is a function of the machine's operation, whereby at the limit of the available torque a hammer action is adopted.
b) [PW] A powered hand held rotary device used to drive and remove **Chairscrews**. Also referred to as a **Bance Wrench** (Tradename).

Impact Zone
The 5m wide 20m long (relative to the **Track Centreline**) area behind a **Buffer Stop** in which collapsible structures of any kind are normally prohibited.

Impatiens Glandulifera
Himalayan Balsam. See **Invasive Species**.

Impedance Bond
[Sig.] A **Bond** that permits the **Traction Return Current** to pass but blocks **Track Circuit** (**TC**) signals, thus isolating adjacent Track Circuits from one another. Found on **DC Electrified Lines**. Also known colloquially as a **Spider**.

Impervious Membrane
[PW] A material that does not permit the passage of water, used as a means of minimising the amount of rainwater reaching the **Formation**. The material most commonly used is 1000 gauge polythene sheet, although other composite materials are available. See **Clay Dig**, **Formation Renewal**, **Sand Blanket**.

Implementation
The undertaking of physical works to deliver a **Detailed Design**.

Impost
[Civ.] Alternative name for a **Cill**, the (usually) concrete beam on which the lower part of the **Bridge Bearings** are located.

Improvement Notice
In a **Railway** context, a notice issued by the **Office of Rail Regulation** (**ORR**) that requires the recipient to make improvements to one or more safety-related issues within a defined period of time.

IMPS
Investment Monitoring and Planning System: the British Rail (**BR**) predecessor to **PIPS**.

IMR
a) The Isle of Man (Steam) **Railway**
b) [LUL] **Interlocking** Machine Room.

IMT
Integrated Management Team.

IMU
See **Infrastructure Maintenance Unit**.

In
[Sig.]
a) Of a **Signal Lamp**, lit or alight.
b) Of a **Lever** in a **Lever Frame**, placed in the **Normal** position.
See also **Out**.

In Advance
In Advance of
[NPT] See **Beyond**.

In Connection With (ICW)
[NR] A term used in details of **Possessions** to indicate why the Possession has been taken. Reasons given may include a particular item of work, or another Possession. See **Sympathy Possession**.

In Correspondence
[Sig.]
a) Describing a pair of related **Point Ends** which are lying correctly to each other, e.g. both **Normal** or Both **Reversed** in a **Crossover**
b) Describing a **Set of Switches** (**Set of Points**) which are lying the same way as that required by the **Signalling System**.
c) The opposite of **Out of Correspondence**.

In Fog and Rain...
"*In Fog and Rain and Falling Snow,*
Into the cabin we must go."
[Col.] A rhyme used by many generations of **Railway** staff to remind them of the visibility conditions under which work on the **Track** should not proceed.

In Plane
[PW] Describing two or more adjacent **Tracks** with a common **Plane of the Rails**. See also **Track Stagger**.

In Rear
In Rear of
[NPT] See **On the Approach to**.

In Running (IR)
In Running Wire
[Elec.] At one end of an **Overlap Span**, the **Contact Wire** (**CW**) that is in contact with passing **Pantographs**. The other is the **Out of Running** Wire (**OOR**)

In-running (IR)
In-running Wire
[LR Elec.] The **Tension Length** of **Contact Wire** (**CW**) which is commencing with respect to a particular direction of travel.

In Service
[RB]
a) A **Train** is in service from the time it starts its journey until the time it completes its journey
b) A vehicle is in service when it forms part of a Train which is in service.

In Traffic
[Ops.] Describing **Train Movements** made on a **Railway** that is operating normally, i.e. not in a **Possession** or subject to other special arrangements.

In-bearer Clamp Lock (IBCL)
[Sig.]
a) A **Clamp Lock** actuator mounted within a special metal **Hollow Bearer**
b) [NR] the SPX Rail Systems' product.

Inbound
[LR] Describing **Trams** travelling towards the centre of the conurbation it serves.

Inc.
[Ops.] See **Inclusive**, i.e. including. The opposite is **Exc.**, or **Exclusive**. See also **At**.

In-cab Signalling
In-cab Signals
See **Cab Signalling**.

Incident
a) An unplanned, uncontrolled event which, under different circumstances, could have resulted in an **Accident**
b) [NR] At a **Level Crossing** (**LC**, **LX**), an event that includes: **Near Miss** events in which **Trains** were close to colliding with a road vehicle; and misuse events where incorrect use of a Level Crossing occurs but the Train is still some distance away.

Incident Co-ordination Centre (ICC)
[CT] A control office temporarily established adjacent to the **Railway Control Centre** (**RCC**) in the event of a significant incident, providing facilities for **Eurotunnel** emergency services staff.

Incl.
See **Inclusive**, i.e. including.

Inclination
Inclined
[PW] Describing the longitudinal rotation of the **Running Rails** about their **Running Edges** (**RE**) to improve the interface between Rail and wheel. On **Plain Line** (**PL**) and some designs of **Switch and Crossing** (**S&C**), the Running Rails are normally Inclined towards each other at 1 in 20, to match the **Coning** of the wheels. The Coning and Inclination together assist in centring the **Wheelset** on **Straight Track**.

Inclined Rail
[PW] A **Rail** whose vertical axis is inclined towards the centre line of the **Track**, generally at 1 in 20 on **Railways** in Britain.

Inclined Design S&C
See **Inclined Design Switches and Crossings**.

Inclined Design Switches
[PW] **Switches** in which at least the **Stock Rail** is Inclined. All Flatbottom □ **Switch Rails** are **Vertical** (whether the Stock Rail is or not), and all **Bullhead** Switch Rails are **Inclined**.

Inclined Design Switches and Crossings (Inclined S&C)
[PW] **Switch and Crossing Units** (**S&C Units**) constructed using **Inclined Rails**, typically the 109, 110A and 113A □ **Flat Bottom** (**FB**) designs, which also had **Vertical** versions. **RT60** and **NR60** are also Inclined designs.

Inclusive
[Ops.] A term used to denote that a **Possession** includes the **Junction** at that end of the Possession. Possession descriptions are **Exclusive** of the end Junctions unless otherwise noted. Abbreviated to **Inc.** and **Incl.** See also **At**.

Incoming Feeder (IF)
[Elec.] A supply connection from the National Grid. See also **Outgoing Feeder** (**OF**).

Indentation
[PW] The crushing or erosion of the upper surface of a **Wood Sleeper** or **Bearer**. This is caused by **Baseplate Shuffle** or **Chair Shuffle** or excessive loading on **Sleepers** in poor condition.

Independent Alignment
[PW] A **Track** □ **Alignment** that does not parallel another adjacent Track, typically around a **Bridge Pier**. The term is also sometimes applied to pairs of Tracks (such as **Slow Lines**) not paralleling an adjacent pair.

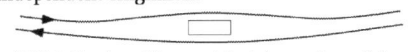

Independent Competent Person (ICP)
Under the **Railways and Other Guided Transport Systems (Safety) Regulations 2006** (**ROGS**), system operators must show that they have procedures in place to introduce new or altered vehicles or infrastructure safely. Where a new or significantly increased risk is involved, they must appoint an Independent Competent Person to help them make sure they go through the right processes. **Network Rail** (**NR**) refers to this role as a **Competent Independent Person** (**CIP**).

Independent Line
A **Track** provided to allow **Trains** to avoid a bottleneck, such as a **Station**. Common usage also generally includes the **Normal Direction** of traffic, e.g. **Down** Independent. Also **Avoiding Line**.

Independent Position Light Signal
[Sig.] A **Position Light Signal** (**PLS**) not associated with a **Main Signal**.

Independently Rotating Wheel (IRW)
[TRS] A **Rail Wheel** either:
- Not attached to an axle, or
- Attached to an axle via a bearing, allowing it to rotate relative to the axle.

India
The **Phonetic Alphabet** word representing I.

Indication Locking
[Sig.] A form of **Locking** whereby the **Full Travel Position** of the **Lever** is inhibited until the operation of the **Function** (such as **Points**) is complete and **Detection** is obtained. See also **Backlocking** and **Checklocking**.

Indicator
[Sig.] Any visual display device:
a) Which is located near the **Line** and gives information to drivers, in which case the Indicator, when located adjacent to a **Signal**, may enhance or qualify the meaning of the Signal. This includes speed and directional information
b) That shows the position, state or condition of part of a **Signalling System**, particularly applied to lamps on a **Signal Box Panel**.

Indirect Fastening
[PW] A **Rail Fastening** where the **Rail** is carried in a **Chair** or **Baseplate** that is in turn directly fastened to the support. See also **Direct Fastening**.

ELLIS' BRITISH RAILWAY ENGINEERING ENCYCLOPÆDIA

Indirect Opposing Locking
[Sig.] A **Control** applied to a **Route** by a Route **Set** in an opposing direction. The two complete Routes are **Conflicting Routes** in that they require at least one **Set of Points** in a different position. However, cancellation of one Route with a **Train** part way through it **Releases** the **Locking** on these Points which, when moved, create the conditions for a **Direct Opposing Route** to be Set. Indirect Opposing Locking is applied to prevent the setting of the Route that has become opposing.

Indirect Reverse

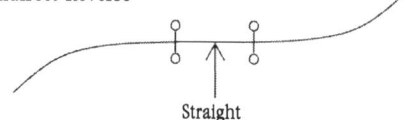

Straight

[PW] A **Reverse Curve** that has a short length of **Straight Track** between the two **Curves**. The opposite is a **Direct Reverse**.

Individual Function Switch (IFS)
[Sig.] A variety of **Signalling** control panel where each controllable **Function** has a separate electrical switch allocated to it.

Individual Point Switch
[Sig.] A switch on a **Signaller's Panel** that can be used to operate **Points** to the **Normal** and **Reverse** positions. The position of the Points is marked by an indication light, Normal or Reverse. A third (flashing) light indicates if the Points are **Out Of Correspondence**.

Individual Risk
The probability of **Fatality** per year to which an individual is exposed from the operation of the **Railway**.

Individual Working Alone (IWA)
[NR] A qualification which permits a person to **Work** □ **On or Near the Line** within certain restrictions. See also **Controller of Site Safety** (**COSS**), **Personal Track Safety** (**PTS**).

Induction loop
A loop of insulated wire located between the **Running Rails** and intended to detect transponders mounted on passing **Trains** and **Trams**.

Inductive Loop Warning System (ILWS)
(*ill-wuss*) [BR Obs.] A staff warning system developed by **British Railways**, based on three important features:
- There were no surface wires, the system being based on contemporary radio pager technology and buried aerial loops
- The system was driven by the **Signalling Equipment** and was thus largely **Fail Safe**
- It could provide warnings for any particular piece of **Track** for any required warning time.

The system was never implemented, due to a lack of funding. It was estimated that it could have contributed to the elimination of all worker **Fatalities** and major injuries due to staff being struck by **Trains**.

Infill Loop
[Sig.] A **European Rail Traffic Management System** (**ERTMS**) or **European Train Control System** (**ETCS**) transmitter **Loop** which is installed at a location, such as **on the Approach to a Signal**, where it is not essential for the safety of **Trains**, but avoids unnecessary delay by transmitting information to the Train as soon as the Signal **Clears**.

Informed Traveller
[RT, NR] An initiative aimed at providing **Outside the Rules of the Route Possession** information to the **Train Operating Companies** (**TOCs**) in sufficient time to allow them to make proper alternative arrangements. This timescale is currently a minimum of 38 weeks prior to the **Possession** date.

Infraco
[LUL] A contraction of **Infrastructure** **C**ompany. Originally formed mainly from the **LU** Engineering Directorate and LU Engineering staff, three Infraco units have been created; **JNP** (Jubilee, Northern and Piccadilly), **BCV** (Bakerloo, Central and Victoria) and **SSL** (Sub-surface lines). These units are now called **Tubelines**, **Metronet BCV** and **Metronet SSL**.

Infrarail
(Tradename) A two-yearly **Railway** □ **Infrastructure** technology trade show, organised by Mack Brooks.

Infrastructure
The fixed equipment and structures on a **Railway**, such as **Bridges**, buildings, **Earthworks**, **Overhead Line Equipment** (**OLE**), Lineside Fencing, **Signalling Equipment**, **Stations**, **Telecommunications** equipment and **Track**.

Infrastructure Asset Management System
[IÉ] A database maintained by **Iarnród Éireann** (**IÉ**) to record details of IÉ's **Track** and **Structure** assets. It also encompasses a condition monitoring module, a fault management system, work order processing and geographical information system. The system was introduced in January 2005.

Infrastructure Controller
The organisation responsible for the control and operation of a **Railway**, or part of a Railway, including the Track, Structures, plant and control equipment. E.g. **Network Rail** (**NR**) is the current Infrastructure Controller for the **Lines** formerly operated by **British Railways** (**BR**), i.e. most of the **Standard Gauge** Lines in Great Britain. See **National Railway Network** (**NRN**).

Infrastructure Fault Control (IFC)
[NR] An organisation that controls the real-time reporting and rectifying of faults on the **Infrastructure**.

Infrastructure Maintenance Company
Infrastructure Maintenance Contractor (IMC)
[Hist.] Formerly, the organisation with responsibility for the **Maintenance** of **Overhead Line Equipment** (**OLE**), **Signalling** and **Track** in a geographical area. See **Infrastructure Maintenance Manager** (**IMM**). These **Functions** have since been brought within **Network Rail's** (**NR**) direct control.

Infrastructure Maintenance Manager (IMM)
[NR] Since 2005, The **Network Rail** organisation responsible for **Maintenance** of the **Infrastructure**.

Infrastructure Maintenance Protection Coordinator (MPC)
[NR] A post responsible for managing all external relationships with **Network Rail's** □ **Maintenance** function within a **Maintenance Delivery Unit** (**MDU**), including other departments of Network Rail, the wider **Railway Industry**, local councils, neighbours and other local community stakeholders. Also involved in delivering local projects to improve the **Railway's** image by engaging local community groups.

Infrastructure Maintenance Unit (IMU)
[Hist.] A transitional trading arrangement during the **Privatisation** process, consisting of the **Track Maintenance**, **Signal Maintenance** and **Electrification Maintenance** functions of the various **British Railways Infrastructure Services** (**BRIS**) units. Most were bought by major construction companies. They were:
- Central (**CIMU**)
- Eastern (**EIMU**)
- Scotland (**SIMU**)
- South Eastern (**SEIMU**)
- South Western (**SWIMU**)
- Northern (**NIMU**)
- Western (**WIMU**)

See also **Track Renewal Unit** (**TRU**).

Infrastructure Manager (IM)
Any person or organisation who is responsible for establishing and maintaining **Infrastructure** or a part thereof, which may also include the management of Infrastructure control and safety systems, but does not include a **Maintainer**.

Infrastructure Planning Commission (IPC)
A new, independent decision-making body whose role is to determine applications for **Nationally Significant Infrastructure Projects** (**NSIP**) and to make or refuse **Development Consent Orders** (**DCO**), subject to the relevant **National Policy Statements** (**NPS**).

Infrastructure Service Unit (ISU)
[Hist.] The transitional **Civil Engineering** organisation between **British Railways** (**BR**) and the **Infrastructure Maintenance Units** (**IMU**) during **Privatisation**.

Infringement
See **Gauge Infringement**.

Injectors
a) The specialised valves which introduce a metered quantity of fuel in the cylinder of a diesel engine
b) A means by which **Feedwater** is forced into a **Boiler**. These use a jet of steam to overcome the pressure inside the Boiler.

Inland Port
A **Rail Freight** interchange used as a destination for trunk flows from a port, reducing port charges and congestion while increasing speed of delivery by locating goods closer to their final destination.

INLORS
Inner London Orbital Route Strategy.

Inner Distant Signal
[Sig.] The **Distant Signal** relating to the **Inner Home Signal**.

Inner Home Signal

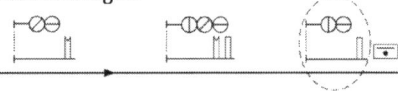

[Sig.] A **Stop Signal**; the **Home Signal** nearest to the **Signal Box** when two such **Signals** are provided on the **Approach**. Latterly the Inner Home Signal was termed the **Home No. 2**. See also **Outer Home**.

Inner Tell Tales (ITT)
[PW] **Tell Tales** placed at the boundary between an **Anchor Length** and a length of **Free Rail** to monitor the effectiveness of the Anchor Length. See also **Outer Tell Tales** (**OTT**).

Inner Tread
[TRS] The **1 in** 20 conical section of the **Wheel Profile**, and the area of a **Rail Wheel** which rests on the **Rail Head**. See also **Tyre**.

Inner Wheelbase (IWB)

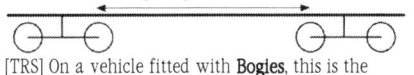

[TRS] On a vehicle fitted with **Bogies**, this is the dimension measured between the axle centres of the two axles nearest the centre of the vehicle. See **Bogie Wheelbase, Inner Wheelbase, Wheelbase**.

INS
[NR] Under the **Bridge Condition Marking Index** (**BCMI**) handbook, shorthand for introduced strengthening, not included in original construction.

Insells Lock
[Sig.] An arrangement whereby a **Signal** □ **Beyond** a **Diverging Junction** is held at a **Stop Aspect** when there is a risk of **Misreading** or **Reading Through** the **Junction Signal**.

Insert
[PW] See **Housing**, clause a).

Inset Switch
[PW Obs.] Experimental **Flat Bottom Switch** in which the **Stock Rail** is machine-planed to accommodate the vertical inside face of the **Switch Rail**. Restricted to use in a **Facing Direction** See also **Planing**.

Inside

Inside a Signal
[Col.] A location **Beyond** a **Signal** and therefore within the area protected by that Signal.

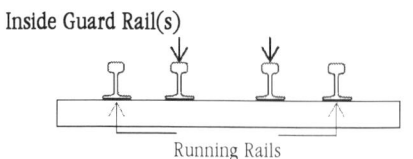

ELLIS' BRITISH RAILWAY ENGINEERING ENCYCLOPÆDIA

Inside Guard Rail(s)

Running Rails
[PW] A **Guard Rail** or Rails provided in the **Fourfoot** between the **Running Rails**.

Inside Keyed Chair
[PW Obs.] A **Chair** in which the **Keys** are fitted on the **Gauge Side** of the **Rail Web**.

Inside Rail
[PW] On a **Curve**, the **Rail** with the smaller Radius (**R**), the one nearest the centre of Curve. The opposite is **Outside Rail**.

Inside Slip

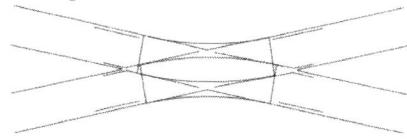

[PW] A **Diamond Crossing** where the **Slip Switch** **Toes** are located between the **Common Crossings**. This is the commonest arrangement. The alternative, where the Slip Switch Toes are outside the Common Crossings, is an **Outside Slip**.

In-span Insulation
[Elec.] A short length of insulating material let into the **Conductors** of a **Catenary**. This arrangement is only used where **Pantographs** do not run in contact with the **Contact Wire** (**CW**). Also called **Cut In Insulation**.

In-span Jumper
[Elec.] A **Jumper** used to distribute the **Traction Current** between **Catenary Wire** and **Contact Wire** (**CW**).

Inspection Interval
The time interval between successive inspections. See also **Examination Frequency**.

Inspection Saloon
[TRS, PW] A specially modified **Passenger Coach** with one or more large observation windows at one or both ends and steps that can be deployed down to ground level. They are used for the rapid inspection of the **Railway** on the move, as well as detailed site inspection should the need arise. Also **Director's Saloon**, **Officer's Saloon**.

Installation Temperature
[PW] The **Rail Temperature** at the time the **Rail** was **Fastened Down**.

Installer
[Sig.] A **Signalling Engineer** specialising in the installation of new **Signalling Equipment**. See also **Tester**.

Instantaneous Change of Bearing (ICOB)
Instantaneous Change of Direction
[PW] Point at which two **Alignment** elements meet at an angle, e.g. the two elements do not share a common tangent. This situation can force a violent lateral "lurch" in the passage of **Trains** and is therefore undesirable.

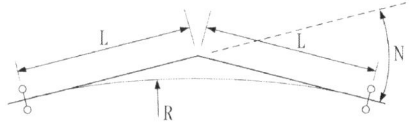

For two **Straights**, it assumed that a **Curve** of Radius R can be used to join them. Using

$$R = 2LN$$

to calculate the Radius of the connecting Curve. Where:
- 2L is the length of a **Virtual Transition** (**VT**), normally 12.2m
- N is the angle between the two straights, see **N Value**.

The **Rate of Change of Cant Deficiency** (**RoCD**) can then be calculated by treating the Straight to Curve **Tangent Point** as a Virtual Transition.

Instantaneous Change of Radius
See **Virtual Transition** (**VT**).

Instanter Coupling

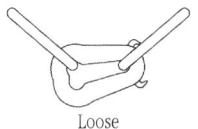

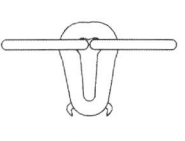

Loose   Tight

A chain-like assembly of two standard oval links connected by a special pear shaped link, used to connect the **Coupling Hooks** of two adjacent **Rail Vehicles**. The special middle link allows the chain to be shortened once it is fitted, so ensuring that the assembly is secure. See also **Screw Coupling**.

Institution of Mechanical Engineers (IMechE)
An independent engineering society based in central London, representing mechanical engineers. It was founded in 1847 in Birmingham by George Stephenson, receiving a Royal Charter in 1930.

Institute of Rail Welding. (IoRW)
(Tradename) [PW] Established in 2002, its mission is to provide focus for individuals and companies involved in Rail Welding. It is currently underwritten by **Network Rail** (**NR**) (formerly **Railtrack** (**RT**)), the UK **Rail Authority**. It is administered by **The Welding Institute** (**TWI**) and contains representatives from a range of organisations involved in Rail Welding. The Institute also has the backing of the **Civil Engineering Conference** (**CEC**), an association of the principal **Contractors**.

Institute of Railway Research (IRR)
(Tradename) The former Manchester Metropolitan University **Rail** Technology Unit (**MMURTU**) which transferred to Huddersfield University in 2012.

Institution of Civil Engineers (ICE)
Founded in 1818, an independent professional association representing civil engineers. It is committed to supporting and promoting professional learning, managing professional ethics and safeguarding the status of engineers, and representing the interests of the profession in dealings with government, etc. It works with industry and academia to progress engineering standards and advises on education and training.

Institution of Engineering and Technology (IET)
The largest multidisciplinary professional engineering institution in the world. The IET was formed in 2006 from two separate institutions: the Institution of Electrical Engineers (IEE), dating back to 1871, and the Institution of Incorporated Engineers (IIE) dating back to 1884.

Institution of Railway Operators (IRO)
[Ops.] The IRO "exists to advance and promote the safe, reliable and efficient operation of the **Railways**, by improving the technical and general skills, knowledge and competence of those engaged in the operation of the Railways."

Institution of Railway Signal Engineers (IRSE)
[Sig.] Founded in 1912, their objective is "... the advancement of the science and practice of **Railway** □ **Signalling**, **Telecommunications** and related matters".

Instruction Board
[Sig.] A **Lineside Sign** conveying instructions to the driver, such as **Stop and Await Instructions (SAI)** or **Stop and Telephone**.

Insulated Block Joint (IBJ)
[Sig.] Specifically, an **Insulated Rail Joint (IRJ)** which forms the end of a **Block Section**.

Insulated Fishplate
[PW] A **Fishplate** fitted with insulating material to isolate it from the **Rails** it joins together. This is either a bonded coating (see **Encapsulated Fishplate**) or loose polymer mouldings (see **Fishplate Insulations**, **Shells**), in pairs at an **Insulated Rail Joint (IRJ)**.

Insulated Joint (IJ)
[PW] Alternative name for an **Insulated Rail Joint (IRJ)**.

Insulated Knuckle
[Elec.] An **Overhead Line Equipment (OLE)** □ **Knuckle** in which the two **Catenaries** cross but are electrically insulated from each other except when a **Pantograph** passes beneath. See also **Un-Insulated Knuckle**.

Insulated Overlap
[Elec.] An **Overlap Span** arranged so that two adjacent **Tension Lengths (TL)** can be electrically separated using an electrical switch.

Insulated Rail
[Sig.] The **Rail** of a **Common Rail Track Circuit** that is separated from adjacent **Track Circuits (TC)** using **Insulated Rail Joints (IRJ)**. The Insulated Rail does not carry the **Traction Return Current**. Also called the **Signal Rail**.

Insulated Rail Joint (IRJ)
[PW] A **Fishplated Rail Joint** in which one **Rail** is electrically insulated from the abutting **Rail** for **Signalling** or **Electrification** purposes, normally utilising **Insulated Fishplates**. Also **Block Joint**, **Dry Insulated Joint**, **Glued Insulated Joint (GIJ)**, **Insulated Joint (IJ)**, **Insulated Block Joint (IBJ)**.
Permanent Way Drawing symbols:

— Four Hole □ Site Fitted Dry Insulated Joint

— Four Hole close tolerance Site Fitted Dry Insulated Joint

— Six Hole close tolerance Site Fitted Dry Insulated Joint

— Four Hole Site Fitted Glued Insulated Joint

— Six Hole Site Fitted Glued Insulated Joint

— Four Hole Shop Fitted Glued Insulated Joint

— Six Hole Shop Fitted Glued Insulated Joint

Insulated Section
[Elec.] A length of **Overhead Line Catenary** that is not electrically connected to any other part of the system, but is also not connected to **Earth**. This is an undesirable situation, as the electrical potential of the section is unknown. A preferred arrangement is a **Permanently Earthed Section (PES)**.

Insulated Soleplate
[PW] A **Soleplate** equipped with insulated sections, for use on **Track Circuited** □ **Lines**.

Insulated Stretcher Bar
[PW] A **Stretcher Bar** with a non-conducting central section, for use on **Track Circuited** □ **Lines**.

Insulating Trough
An insulating cover used to shield the **Conductor Rail** from accidental contact.

Insulator
a) See **Rail Foot Insulator**
b) [Elec.] The porcelain device upon which a **Conductor Rail** is supported. Also **Pot**, **Conductor Rail Insulator**.
c) [Elec.] The porcelain or polymer device used to isolate the live parts of an **Overhead Line Electrification (OLE)** system from its supports.

Insulator Flashover
A failure of an electrical **Insulator** caused by damage or surface contamination, such as soot. Either of these causes the electrical resistance of the Insulator to be degraded, resulting in the **Live** part 'flashing over' to the part connected to **Earth**. This phenomenon is common in damp weather.

Integrated Control Centre (ICC)
[NR] An arrangement where staff from **Network Rail (NR)** □ **Control** and their counterparts in the relevant **Train Operating Company (TOC)** are co-located to improve communication and co-ordination. See also **Rail Operating Centre (ROC)**.

241

ELLIS' BRITISH RAILWAY ENGINEERING ENCYCLOPÆDIA

Integrated Electronic Control Centre (IECC)
[Sig.] A type of **Signal Box** (**SB**) that controls the **Points** and **Signals** for a whole **Route** or a large geographical area by electronic means. The **Signallers'** interface is normally a VDU, keyboard and pointing device. **Automatic Route Setting** (**ARS**) is a feature of such installations. IECCs are gradually replacing **Power Signal Boxes** (**PSB**) on major routes. See also **Network Management Centre** (**NMC**)

Integrated Train Planning System (ITPS)
[Ops.] A planning and publication system which produces **Timetable** information for planned services including **Trains**, buses and ships. Interfaces are available for Common Interface Format (**CIF**) and Local Access to Timetable Information (**LATIN**).

Integrated Transport Authority (ITA)
A body responsible for setting out a local authority's transport policy and expenditure plans to be allocated for public transport.

Integrated Transport Smartcard Organisation (ITSO)
A member-controlled organisation that maintains the ITSO Specification for members and the Crown. The membership of ITSO is broadly based and includes **PTEs**, Local Authorities, Passenger Transport Operators and suppliers of equipment, systems and services. The specification for interoperable contactless smartcards that ITSO has developed covers the entire system; smartcard, point-of-sale/service, back office, data formats, data transfer, and security architecture.

INTER
Integration of Networking Technologies for Harmonising the European **Railways**.

Inter-car Jumper
[TRS] A cable interconnection carrying power or electrical signals between two **Cars**.

Interchange
a) A **Station** that has been specifically arranged to allow simple and rapid transfer between **Trains** and other modes of transport, such as road and air
b) A **Line** used for the movement of **Rail Vehicles** between two different **Railway** systems, e.g. **Network Rail** (**NR**) and **London Underground Limited** (**LUL**).

Intercity (IC)
[Hist.] The brand name used by **British Railways** (**BR**) for its long-haul **Passenger Trains** running between major cities, and now used to describe all such services.

Intercity 125 (IC-125)
[BR] The brand name of the high-speed **Passenger** service operated by **Class** 43 **Diesel Locomotives** and **Mark** 3 **Coaches** running at up to 125mph, also known as **High Speed Trains** (**HST**). The name comes from the maximum speed of these **Trains**.

Intercity 225 (IC-225)
[BR] Brand name for **British Railways** (**BR**) □ **Passenger Services** composed of **Mark** 4 **Coaches** hauled by **Class** 91 **Electric Locomotives**. The name comes from the maximum speed of these **Trains**, but the number is somewhat misleading, as it refers to 225kph (140mph) not 225mph.

Interdisciplinary
A term describing the areas of interface between the various **Disciplines**.

Interdisciplinary Check (IDC)
A check made on any design by a specialist **Engineer** from each of the relevant specialisms, e.g. **Civils**, **Distribution**, Environmental, Geotechnical, Operations, Overhead Line Equipment (**OLE**), Permanent Way (**PW**), Plant, **Signalling** and **Telecommunications** to ensure the design is correct.

Interface Slab

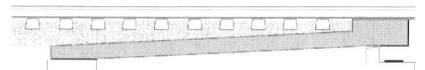

[Civ. PW] A connecting unit between **Ballasted Track** and **Slab Track** or between Ballasted Track and **Direct Fastened Track**. Its function is to provide a smooth and controlled change from full **Ballast Depth** to no **Ballast**. Also **Transition Beam**, **Transition Slab**.

INTERFRIGO
(*inter-freego*) International **Railway**-owned refrigerated transport company.

Interim Voice Radio System (IVRS)
[NR Tel.] Introduced in 2002, a voice-only implementation of the **Global System for Mobile Communications – Railway** (**GSM-R**) used, in designated areas, to contact the **Signaller** in an emergency where protection of the line is required. This was a safety requirement in areas where **Axle Counters** replaced **Track Circuits** as the means of **Train Detection**. From 2009 commissioning of full GSM-R began on some routes, meaning the IVRS system will become redundant by 2013.

Interlaced Bearers
[PW] See **Interlaced Sleepers**, **Interlaced Timbers**.

Interlaced Retarder Trap Points
[PW] An arrangement of **Trap Points** where the **Switches** lead to a length of **Interlaced Track** where the **Gauge** is progressively widened. This widening causes the **Check Rails** to grip the **Wheel Backs**, slowing the **Train**.

242

Interlaced Sleepers
Interlaced Timbers

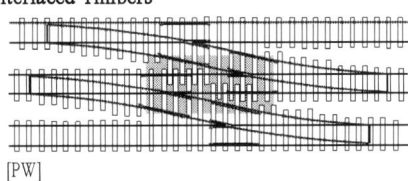

[PW]
a) Additional **Bearers**, **Sleepers** or **Timbers** fitted between the existing Bearers, Sleepers or Timbers
b) An arrangement of Bearers in a complex **Switch and Crossing Layout** where the ends of the Bearers under the **Main Line**, converging and diverging routes are interleaved under common **Rails**, rather than providing single and unmanageable **Long Bearers** (**Through Bearers**) under all **Tracks**.

Interlaced Track

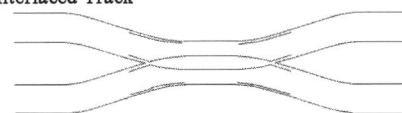

[PW] A length of **Track** over which a second Track is overlapped with one **Rail** in the **Fourfoot** of the other, usually over a short distance, to permit two-way working within a restricted width without the need for **Switches**. Also **Gauntletted Track**.

Interlinking

[Sig.] A link provided between **Signal Boxes** in **Absolute Block** areas to enforce **Sequential Locking**, **Proving** of **Home Signal** and **Distant Signal** □ **On** and **Berth Track Circuit** □ **Clear** before allowing **Line Clear** (**LC**) to be transmitted and the **Acceptance** of the second **Train**.

Interlock

[Sig.] An electrical contact attached to an electrical switch to ensure that certain electrical circuits operate in the correct relationship to the electrical switch.

Interlocking
Interlocked

[Sig.]
a) [RB] A general term applied to equipment that controls the **Setting** and **Releasing** of **Signals**, **Points** and other apparatus to prevent an unsafe condition of the **Signalling System** arising during the passage of **Trains**.
b) **Controls** fitted between **Points** and **Signals** that prevent the **Signaller** from **Setting** conflicting **Routes**. In **Mechanical Signalling** this was achieved by **Locking Slides** on a **Locking Shelf**, which locked conflicting **Levers**. More modern systems use a **Relay** based logic (**Route Relay Interlocking** (**RRI**)), microprocessors (**Solid State Interlocking** (**SSI**)) or computers (**Computer Based Interlocking** (**CBI**)) to perform the same functions
c) [LUL] An electro-pneumatic machine that provides the controls between **Points** (**Switches**) and **Signals** that prevents **Conflicting Routes** from being **Set**.

Interlocking Area

[Sig.] The area of a **Railway** controlled by a particular **Interlocking**.

Interlocking Boundary

[Sig.] The edge of an **Interlocking Area**, where the **Interlocking** function transfers to another **Interlocking**.

Interlocking Frame

[Sig.] An alternative term for a **Lever Frame**.

Interlocking Functional Program

[Sig.] A program within a **Solid State Interlocking** (**SSI**) □ **Central Interlocking Processor** whose main functions are:
- interpreting the **Geographic Data**
- initiating communications with **Trackside Functional Modules** (**TFM**),
- encoding and decoding all **Command Telegrams** and **Data Telegrams**
- performing single fault recovery,
- implementing the **TMR** voting mechanism
- implementing the start-up and shutdown procedure,
- implementing the inter-SSI communications protocol,
- interfacing with the **Panel Processor** and diagnostic processors.

Interlocking of Level Crossings

[Sig.] A system whereby the operation of a **Level Crossing's** □ **Protecting Signals** are dependent upon the state of the **Level Crossing Gates** or **Barriers**.

Intermediate Block

[Sig.] See **Intermediate Block Section** (IB Section, IBS)

Intermediate Block Home

Intermediate Block Home Signal (IBH Signal)

[Sig.] In **Absolute Block** (**AB**) areas, the Stop Signal controlling the exit from an **Intermediate Block Section** (IBS) into the next **Block Section**.

Intermediate Block Section (IB Section, IBS)

[Sig.] In **Absolute Block** (**AB**) areas the Section of Line between the Section Signal and Intermediate Block Home Signal (IBH Signal) controlled by the same **Signal Box** (**SB**). Such sections are equipped with **Track Circuits**.

Intermediate Block Signal (IBS)

[Sig.] See **Intermediate Block Home Signal**.

Intermediate Catenary Wire

[Elec.] The middle wire of a **Compound Catenary** system. Formerly called the **Auxiliary Catenary Wire**.

Intermediate End Vestibule

[TRS] The entrance area in the vicinity of a **Passenger Door** located at the end of one vehicle that is **Coupled** to another.

Intermediate Lookout

A Lookout provided to further extend the **Warning Time** provided; an Intermediate Lookout would be placed between the **Site Lookout** and the **Distant Lookout**.

Intermediate Point
[NR] A location other then the limits at the ends of a Possession where an Engineering Train can enter or leave the Possession from or to an Open Line or a Siding that is not under Possession.

Intermediate Signal Box
[Sig.] A Signal Box (SB) located between two other Signal Boxes.

Intermediate Token Instrument
[Sig.] A Token Instrument provided at a facility part way along a Token Section, permitting a Train to be Shut In and the Release of the Token.

Intermediate Vehicle
[TRS] A Vehicle without a Driving Cab in a Multiple Unit Train.

Intermittent Sidewear
[PW] Sidewear which is only present in random lengths of Rail. Most typically caused by isolated Alignment faults such as poor Alumino-thermic Welds, Fishplated Rail Joints and inconsistent Track Alignment and aggravated by the use of Rolling Stock with poor or limited Bogie yaw damping. See also Cyclic Sidewear.

Intermodal

Intermodal Freight
The movement of Freight by more than one mode of transport (e.g. Train, lorry, ship).

Inter-modal Freight Terminal
A facility where freight Containers are transferred from one mode of surface transport to another (e.g. from road to Rail).

Intermodal Unit
A load carrying unit designed to be carried on more than one mode of transport.

Internal Data Link (IDL)
[Sig.] A component within a Solid State Interlocking (SSI) this is a separate communications channel to provide inter-SSI communications. The IDL is primarily used for setting Routes across SSI boundaries, and for controlling Signals and Points in the Fringe areas.

Internal Rail Flaw
[PW] A Rail Defect or Rail Flaw wholly within the Rail Section, and thus only detectable using Ultrasonic Rail Flaw Detection (URFD) or following a Full Section Break.

Internal State
[Sig.] The Internal State of the Solid State Interlocking (SSI) represents the current status of the Railway. Each SSI holds up to 256 Track Circuit memories, 64 Points and 128 Signals, together with logical control variables for Routes, Timers, Sub-routes, and other binary flags. These data represent 1,216 bytes of "live" memory upon which the Geographic Data and Control Interpreter operate.

International Organization for Standardization (ISO)
A worldwide federation of national standards bodies that develops and publishes international technical standards.

International Rail Research Board (IRRB)
Formed in 2005, an organisation involving UIC members and several scientific and research institutions in joint activities in research and development in the field of Rail transport.

International Union of Railways (UIC)
Union Internationale des Chemins de Fer; an association of international Railway Companies that, among other roles, develops specifications, standards and interfaces for Railways.

Interoperability
The concept that disperate systems can be made to have sufficient common characteristics to allow common operation. In Railway terms, this is, effectively, the operation of one system's Trains on another system and vice versa.

Interoperability Directives
Two European directives requiring harmonisation of systems and standards for high speed and conventional Railways respectively

Interoperable Train
A Train that can be operated on a Railway that complies with the appropriate Interoperability Directive.

Interpose
[Sig.] To enter a Train Reporting Number (e.g. 6L43) in a Train Describer (TD).

Intersecting Switch
[PW] A design of Switch where the projected Running Edge (RE) of the Switch Curve crosses the Running Edge of the Stock Rail. See also Non-intersecting Switch, Tangential Switch.

Intersection Bridge (IB)
[Civ.] A Bridge carrying one or more Lines over other Lines. See also Diveunder, Flyover, Overbridge (OB), Underbridge (UB).

Intersection of Gauge Lines (IP)
[PW] The point at which the lines of the Running Edges (RE) cross at a Crossing. Not to be confused with the Crossing Nose (XN) or Knuckle, where the Rail stops. A Crossing Nose is as far as 450mm (18 inches) away from the actual Intersection Point (IP). Also Fine Point (FP). See also Crossing Nose to Intersection Point Dimension.

Intersection Point (IP)
[PW]
a) The point at which two Gradients meet. See also Vertical Curve.
b) An alternative for Intersection of Gauge Lines.

Inter-tripping
[Elec.] A system designed to open all the Circuit Breakers (CB) feeding a Double-fed Section if the Circuit Breakers at only one end are tripped.

Interval
a) [PW] The space between the **Tracks**, like the **Sixfoot**, **Tenfoot**
b) [Ops.] The actual time or distance between consecutive **Trains** on the same **Track**
c) [CT] A section of one **Running Tunnel** either between a **Portal** and one of the **Crossovers**, or between the Crossovers. They are numbered from the UK to France, odd numbers in the **Running Tunnel South** and even in the **Running Tunnel North**.

Intervention
a) [Sig.] Describing the action of an automated system such as **Automatic Train Protection** (**ATP**), **European Rail Traffic Management System** (**ERTMS**), European **Train Control System** (**ETCS**), Tilt **Authorisation and Speed Supervision System** (**TASS**) or **Train Protection and Warning System** (**TPWS**) when it takes over power and braking controls in the event of the driver failing to adequately control the speed of the **Train**. See also **Safe Speed**
b) A proposal to undertake a project which would enhance the **Infrastructure** and its capabilities over and above normal **Maintenance**.

Intervention Curve
[Sig.] Under **European Rail Traffic Management System** (**ERTMS**) or European **Train Control System** (**ETCS**), a profile representing the maximum safe speed at any given location. If the driver attempts to exceed this value, then an Intervention by the system will occur to reduce the speed of the **Train**.

Intervention Limit
[NR] The value of a measurement at which corrective actions must be implemented within a prescribed timescale.

INTIS
(*in-tiss*) Intermediate **T**icket **I**ssuing **S**ystem.

Intrados
[Civ.] The internal, visible surface of an **Arch**; that is the surface with the smallest radius. Also **Arch Face**. See also **Extrados**.

Intrinsic Roll-over Wind Speed
[TRS] The wind speed that is just sufficient to cause a **Rail Vehicle** to roll over (i.e. just sufficient to cause 100% unloading of the wheels on the windward side) when the vehicle is running within a **Train Formation** at its maximum operating speed on **Straight and Level Track**, and the wind is blowing perpendicular to the direction of travel of the Vehicle.

Invasive Species
Any non-native organism that presents a threat to bio-diversity, typically because of a lack of local predation. Some of the high-profile species in the UK include:
- Japanese Knotweed (*Fallopia japonica*)
- Giant Hogweed (*Heracleum mantegazzianum*)
- Himalayan Balsam (*Impatiens glandulifera*)
- Signal Crayfish (*Pacifastacus leniusculus*)

Invensys Rail
(Tradename) A division of Invensys Plc., based in Chippenham, Wiltshire, specialising in **Signalling Equipment** and design. Previously commonly contracted to **Invensys**, the company is now part of **Siemens** AG.

Invert
a) [Civ.] The inverted brick or masonry **Arch** constructed beneath the **Track** employed to resist lateral forces on **Tunnel** walls
b) The lowest point of any tubular construction, including **Drains** and Tunnels.

Invert Level
The vertical level of the lowest part of a **Drain** or the **Invert** of a **Tunnel**.

Inverted Siphon
An alternative for **Siphon**, **Siphon Culvert**.

Inverter
An electronic device producing Alternating Current (**AC**) from Direct Current (**DC**). These devices are used to drive **AC Traction Motors** and provide other AC supplies from DC sources. See also **Converter**, a term with which Inverter is often confused, and **DC Link**.

IO
a) **I**nvestigating **O**fficer
b) [LUL] **I**nstructor **O**perator.

IOA
[NR] The **CARKND** representing a 75 ton capacity **Open Wagon** used for **Ballast** and **Spoil** by **Network Rail**.

IOPI
Infrastructure **O**utput **P**rice **I**ndex.

IOR
Inspecting **O**fficer of **Railways**.

IORPS
Integrated **O**perational **Railway** **P**lanning **S**ystem.

IoRW
See **Institute of Rail Welding**.

IOS
a) (*eye-oss*) **I**ncremental **O**utput **S**tatement
b) [Elec.] **I**nsulated **O**verlap **S**pan

IP
a) See **Intersection Point**
b) See **Intersection of Gauge Lines**
c) **I**nvestment **P**roposal
d) [NR Hist.] **Infrastructure** **P**rojects
e) [NR] **I**nvestment **P**rojects
f) **I**ntellectual **P**roperty.

IPC
Integrated **P**rotection and **C**ontrol.

IPF
Isolation **P**lanning **F**orm.

IPL
[Sig.] **IECC** **P**C **L**ogger.

IPPR
Industry **P**eriod **P**erformance **R**eport.

IPU
Integrated **P**lanning **U**nit.

IR
See In Running.
IRC
[Elec.] Insulated Return Conductor (RC).
IRCA
International Railway Congress Association.
IRF
Industry Risk Fund.
IRIS
(*eye-riss*) [NR] A Rail Vehicle used to test the strength of radio signals.
IRJ
a) See Insulated Rail Joint
b) International Railway Journal.
IRM
Integrated Risk Management.
IRMS
International Risk Management Services.
IRO
See Institution of Railway Operators.
Iron and Steelwork Only
[PW] Describing a Switch And Crossing Layout (S&C Layout) where the Timbers or Bearers are not supplied. The layout is assembled at the manufacturer's premises before being dismantled for delivery to site. See also Built up and Timbered, Ironwork Only.
Iron Horses
Alternative term for Iron Men.
Iron Lung
[Col.] Nickname for the Class 14 Diesel Locomotives due to their poor Availability.
Iron Men
(Tradename) [PW] Pairs of small gantries fitted with chain hoists and Rail Wheels, used to transport Rails, Crossings and Switch Half Sets to and from sites without using powered plant. Also known as Iron Horses.
Ironwork Only
[PW] Describing the supply of only Baseplates, Blocks, bolts, Chairs, Closure Rails, Crossings and Switches for a Switch and Crossing Unit (S&C Unit), but excluding the Bearers.
IRR
International Rail Regulator.
IRRB
See International Rail Research Board.
IRRRS
Interim Requirements for Road Restraint Systems.
IRRS
Irish Railway Records Society
IRSA
Independent Railway Safety Activity.
IRSE
See Institution of Railway Signal Engineers.
IRTN
[Tel.] International Railway □ Telecommunication Network.

IRW
See Independently Rotating Wheel.
IS
a) [Sig.] Intermediate Signalling
b) Ice Scraper
c) [NR Civ.] Under the Bridge Condition Marking Index (BCMI) handbook, shorthand for intermediate support (e.g. a pier).
Is Line Clear?
[Sig.] A message sent by Block Bell to the Signal Box (SB) □ Beyond requesting permission to send a Train into the Section.
ISA
Independent Safety Advisor.
Isaac
The obsolescent Phonetic Alphabet word representing I. Replaced by India.
ISBP
[NR]
a) Industry Strategic Business Plan, published in January 2013
b) Initial Strategic Business Plan.
ISDN
Integrated Services Digital Network.
ISG
Infrastructure Support Group.
Island Line
Island Line Trains (IL)
(Tradename) Part of Southwest Trains (SWT). It operates services on the Isle of Wight. ATOC code IL.
Island Platform

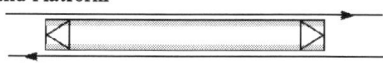

A Platform that has Through Lines on both sides. This type of Platform must be at least 4m wide. Passenger access is normally via a Bridge, Subway or Level Crossing (LC, LX). See also Bay Platform, Side Platform.
ISLG
Infrastructure Safety Liaison Group.
ISM
[Sig.] Integrated Electronic Control Centre (IECC) System Monitor.
ISMS
[Sig.] Implementation of Signalling □ Maintenance Specifications.
ISO
See International Standards Organisation.
ISO Container
See Container.
Isolated
Physically disconnected from the electrical power source, but not necessarily connected to Earth.

Isolation
The formal procedure of:
a) [Elec.] De-energising a section of **Traction Supply** equipment, **Earthing** it, verifying its lack of potential and issuing of a certificate to that effect. See **Conductor Rail Permit (CRP), Form A, Form B, Form C**
b) Disconnecting a piece of equipment from its power source.

Isolation Diagram
[Elec.] A variety of **Single Line Diagram (SLD)** that shows **Point Numbers, Signals, Track Names** and an overlay of the **Electrical Sections** and **Sub-Sections** to assist in the correct **Isolation** of a particular area.

ISP
a) [Sig.] Intelligent **Signalling Plans**
b) Internet Service Provider.

ISPBX
[Tel.] Integrated Services Private Branch Exchange.

ISRS
International Safety Rating System.

I-SSI
[Sig.] Interfaced **Solid State Interlocking**.

ISTP
[Sig.] Intermediate **Signalling** Technology: Principles.

ISU
See **Infrastructure Service Unit**.

IT
Isolée Terre (isolated **Earth**).

ITA
See **Integrated Transport Authority**.

ITCS
[CTRL] **Interlocking** and **Train Control System**.

ITD
[Sig.] Information **Train Describer**.

Item
[PW Col.] A common contraction of **Relaying Item**.

Item of Work
[NR] An activity identified to be undertaken by a **Work Group** under the control of a **Controller of Site Safety (COSS)**.

ITFS
Initial Technical **Feasibility** Study.

ITL
[CTRL] Intermittent Transmission Loop.

ITPS
a) Integrated **Trackside** Power Supplies
b) See **Integrated Train Planning System**.

ITS
a) **Infrastructure** Testing Services
b) (Tradename) Interactive Trackwork Services Ltd.

ITSL
[Elec.] Intermediate **Track** Section Location.

ITSO
See **Integrated Transport Smartcard Organisation**.

ITSS
Indicative **Train** Service Specification.

ITT
a) See **Inner Tell Tale**. See also **Outer Tell Tale, Tell Tale**
b) Invitation to Tender.

ITU
International Telecommunications Union.

IVPS
Intermediate Voltage Power Supply.

IVRS
a) See **Interim Voice Radio System**
b) Interactive Voice Recognition System.

IVS
Infrastructure Video System.

IVV
Independent Validation & Verification.

IWA
(*eye-wah*) See **Individual Working Alone**.

IWB
See **Inner Wheelbase**.

IWCR
[Hist.] The **Pre-Grouping** Isle of Wight Central Railway.

IWR
[Hist.] The **Pre-Grouping** Isle of Wight **Railway**.

IXL
[Sig. Col.] Shorthand for **Interlocking**.

J

J
a) [PW] Shorthand for **Joint**, see **Fishplated Rail Joint**
b) [NR] As the first letter of a **Wagon** □ **CARKND**, it means that the vehicle is an international vehicle with **Bogies**
c) [Sig.] On a **Signalling Circuit Diagram**:
- As one of the leading letters of an **Equipment Code**, it means time or **Timer**, as in delayed action
- As the last letter of an **Equipment Code**, it means diode or rectifier
d) The letter represented by **Juliet** in the **Phonetic Alphabet**
e) [LUL] The Jubilee **Line**.

J Door
[LUL] The door between the **Cab** and saloon.

Jack
[Obs.] The obsolescent **Phonetic Alphabet** word representing J. Replaced by **Juliet**.

Jack Arches

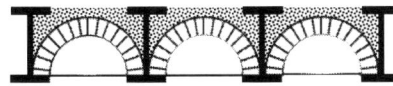

[Civ.] A form of **Bridge Deck** construction where the spaces between the supporting girders are in-filled with small masonry **Arches** founded on the bottom flanges of the girders.

Jack Points
The **Turnout** (**TO**) forming the third division of a **Fan** or **Group** of **Sidings**.

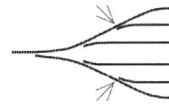

Jacker Packer
[PW prob. Obs.] A lightweight powered trolley fitted with two large hydraulic jacks. It clamps itself to the **Rails** at the chosen point and extends its jacks, lifting itself and the **Track** into the air. The machine can then lightly consolidate the **Ballast** under the Track (fairly ineffectually) using a set of non-vibrating tines. Generally used in conjunction with a **Ballast Cleaner**.

Jacobs
(Tradename) More formally Jacobs Engineering Group Inc., of Pasadena, California, USA, it is an international engineering, architecture, and construction company. In recent years it has absorbed SKM, Alexander Gibb and Partners and Babtie Group.

Jaflex Clip
[PW Obs.] An **Elastic Spike Rail Fastening** for **Flat Bottom Rail** on **Wood Sleepers**.

James, William
(1771-1837). Surveyor; engineer and land agent turned **Railway** promoter, involved in the early promotion of the Liverpool & Manchester Railway and the author of a master plan for nationwide network of **Routes**. Only a small section of this vision was built, near Stratford-upon-Avon.

Janglers
[PW Col.] Nickname for the short lengths of chain and specialised hooks used to lift **Sleepers** in conjunction with a **Sleeper Beam**.

Jarrah
[PW] A type of Eucalyptus hardwood (*Eucalyptus marginata*) used for **Hardwood Sleepers** (**HW**) and **Bearers** for **Switch and Crossing** (**S&C**). See also **Karri**.

Jarvis
(Tradename) A former **Contractor** organisation, which went into administration in March 2010.

Javelin
(Tradename) Brandname of the **Class** 395 **Electric Multiple Unit** (**EMU**) manufactured by Hitachi.

Jaw
[PW]
a) The two vertical parts of a **Bull Head** □ **Chair** that are provided to restrain the **Rail** laterally. The Rail sits between these and is retained with a **Key**
b) The vertical part of a **Slide Baseplate** which supports the **Stock Rail** and to which the Stock Rail is bolted. See also **Jaw Block**.

Jaw Block
[PW] A cast metal distance block that is designed to fit between the **Jaw** of a **Slide Chair** or **Slide Baseplate** and the outside (non-**Gauge**) face of the **Rail Web** of the **Stock Rail** of a **Half Set** of **Full Depth Switches**. Also **Chogblock**.

Jc.

Jcn.
Common contractions of **Junction**, also Jct., Jn., Jnc.

JCMBPS
Joint Committee on Mobility of Blind and Partially Sighted People.

JCN
Job Cost Number.

JCT
See Joint Closure Temperature.

Jct.
Common contraction of **Junction**, also Jc., Jcn., Jn., Jnc., Jt.

JDI
Junction Direction Indicator, see **Junction Indicator** (JI).

Jerk Limit
[TRS] A limit placed on the rate of change of acceleration from rest of a **Train**, intended to improve **Passenger** comfort.

Jessop, William
(1745-1814). Canal and builder of early **Railways**, founder of the Butterley company in Derbyshire, which built numerous iron Railway **Bridges**.

JI
See **Junction Indicator**.

Jig
[Hist.] The name given to a **Self-Acting Incline** in south Derbyshire.

249

ELLIS' BRITISH RAILWAY ENGINEERING ENCYCLOPÆDIA

Jim Crow
[PW] A device used to induce controlled bends into **Rails**. A 1.2 – 1.5m long beam with hooks on each end is placed over the Rail to be bent, and a large screw or hydraulic ram pushes the Rail in the centre, producing the bend. Jim Crows come in various sizes according to their maximum **Rail Weight** capability. Sometimes shortened to **Crow**.

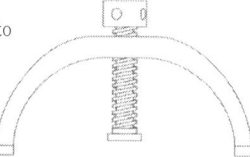

JJA
[NR] The **CARKND** representing an **Auto Ballaster** □ **Wagon**.

JLE
[LUL] Jubilee Line Extension.

JN
Common contraction of **Junction**, also Jc. Jcn., Jct. Jnc. And Jt.

Jn.
Common contraction of **Junction**, also Jc. Jcn., Jct. JN, Jnc. And Jt.

JNA
[NR] The **CARKND** for a **Falcon** □ **Wagon**.

JNAP
Joint Network Availability Plan.

Jnc.
Common contraction of **Junction**, also Jc. Jcn., Jct. JN, Jnc. And Jt.

JNP
[LUL] Jubilee, Northern, Piccadilly

Jockey
Jocko
[Col.] Nickname for a **Class** 08 **Shunting Locomotive**. Also **Gronk, Pilot, Station Pilot**.

Joggle
Joggled Stock Rail
[PW] A small lateral reversed bend in a **Stock Rail** intended to allow the **Switch Toe** to lie clear of passing **Wheel Flanges** when closed up, a **Stock Rail** with such a step in it.

Joggled Switch
[PW] See **Straight Cut Switch**.

John Bull Rail Saw
[PW Hist.] An early type of **Rail Saw**.

Joint
[PW] See **Fishplated Rail Joint**.

Joint Chair
[PW] A **Bull Head** □ **Chair**, with a larger base than a **Common Chair**, used either side of a **Fishplated Rail Joint**.

Joint Closure Temperature (JCT)
[PW NR] The **Rail Temperature** at which it is assessed that two thirds or more of the **Rail Joints** in a section of **Jointed Track** will be fully closed up. Further increases in **Rail Temperature** beyond the JCT increase the risk of a **Track Buckle**.

Joint Hopping
[Sig.] Where a fast-moving **Rail Vehicle** with a **Short Wheelbase** (such as a **Light Locomotive**) passes from one **Track Circuit** to the next, the difference between the **Drop-away Time** of the first and the **Pick-up Time** of the next can cause the vehicle to be momentarily undetected. See also **Boundary Hopping**.

Joint Industry Cost
[NR] Costs incurred by **Network Rail** (**NR**) on behalf of customers and then passed on to them.

Joint Packing
[PW] The activity of restoring the correct **Design Rail Level** at a **Fishplated Rail Joint**. See also **Fishplate Shims, Plate Oiling, Rail Joint Straightening**.

Joint Points Team (JPT)
[NR] A team made up of members of (typically) the **Permanent Way** (**PW**) and **Signalling** □ **Disciplines** within the **Maintenance** □ **Function**, tasked with the **Maintenance** of **Points** (**Switches**) in an area.

Joint Railway
[Hist.] A **Railway** owned and managed by more than one **Railway Company**.

Joint Regulating
[PW] The activity of moving **Jointed Rails** longitudinally in order to ensure that the correct **Expansion Gap** is provided at each **Fishplated Rail Joint**. Also **Pulling Back**.

Joint Sleeper
[PW] A **Sleeper** adjacent to a **Fishplated Rail Joint**. These **Sleepers** are often placed closer together than the normal **Sleeper Spacing** to provide additional support to the Joint.

Jointed Rail
Jointed Track (Jtd.)
[PW NR] A **Rail** shorter than 36.576m (120 feet) drilled with **Fishbolt Holes** and intended to be connected together using **Fishplated Rail Joints** allowing the Rail to freely expand, or **Track** constructed from such Rails.

Jointed Track Circuit
[Sig.] A **Track Circuit** (**TC**) whose limits of detection are defined by the provision of **Insulated Rail Joints** (**IRJ**). See also **Jointless Track Circuit** (**JTC**). Varieties include **AC Track Circuits, DC Track Circuits, HVI**. The opposite is a **Jointless Track Circuit** (**JTC**). See also **Reed**.

Jointless Track Circuit (JTC)
[Sig.] A **Track Circuit** (**TC**) using audio frequency energy that does not require **Insulated Rail Joints** (**IRJ**) at the boundaries of circuits. Types include **Aster, TI21**. Also **Audio Frequency Track Circuit**. See also **Virtual Joint**. The opposite is a **Jointed Track Circuit**. See also **Reed**.

250

ELLIS' BRITISH RAILWAY ENGINEERING ENCYCLOPÆDIA

Journals
[TRS] The bearings supporting a **Rail Vehicle** on its axles. Formerly, these were plain metal on metal bearings running in an oil bath and generally on the ends of the axle. Failure of this lubrication system would result in the bearing overheating, called a **Hot Axle Box**, and the cause of many fires on wooden vehicles. Newer vehicles have roller bearings, fitted outside or inside the wheels. See also **Hot Axle Box Detector** (HABD).

Journey
[RB] The route between the **Depot, Siding, Platform Line** or other authorised place where the **Train** enters **Service** and the Depot, Siding, Platform Line or other authorised place where either the Train reaches its destination, or is required to:
- Reverse before continuing to its destination
- Have vehicles attached or detached
- Terminate short of its destination, as a result of an infrastructure fault, **Line Blockage, Defective On-Train Equipment** or any other operational reason.

This also applies to short-distance **Shunting Movements**.

Journey Time Improvement (JTI)
An **Infrastructure** scheme which proposes to reduce journey times in a cost-effective way by implementing a combination of the following measures:
- Removal of "dips" in the existing speed profile
- Improvements to overall **Permissible Speeds**
- Introduction of **Differential Permissible Speeds**
- Removing **Approach Controls** on **Signals**
- Improving **Turnout Speeds** in **Junctions**
- Reducing **Junction Margins**
- Reducing and removing **Junction Conflicts**
- Removing unnecessary **Engineering Allowances** and **Pathing Allowances** from the timetable.

This kind of scheme should not be confused with a **Linespeed Improvement** (LSI) scheme.

JPIP
(*jay-pip*) [NR] Joint Performance Improvement Plan.

JPT
a) See **Joint Points Team**
b) Joint Project Team.

JRI
[Sig.] Junction Route Indicator, See **Junction Indicator** (JI).

JRU
Juridical Recording Unit.

JS1
[Sig.] Basic **Signalling** cable jointing and testing.

JS2
[Sig.] Advanced **Signalling** cable jointing and testing.

JST
See **Junction Screening Tool**.

Jt.
a) [PW] Shorthand for Joint, See **Fishplated Rail Joint**
b) Shorthand for **Junction**.

JTC
See **Jointless Track Circuit**.

JTD
Jtd.
[PW] Shorthand for **Jointed Track**.

JTI
See **Journey Time Improvement**.

JTS
Journey Time Saving.

JTW
Journeys to Work.

Juice Rail
[Col.] Term for the positive **Conductor Rail** in a DC **Electrification System**. Also DC Rail, Hot Rail, Positive Conductor Rail, Positive Rail, Pozzy Rail, Third Rail.

Juliet
The **Phonetic Alphabet** word representing J.

Jump Fishplate
[PW] Alternative name for a **Lift Fishplate**. Also **Stepped Fishplate**.

Jumper

Jumper Cable
a) [Elec.] In the **Overhead Line Equipment** (OLE), the flexible connections provided to transfer the **Traction Current** between parts of the **Catenary** system. See **C Jumper, Full Current Jumper, Full Drape, In Span Jumper, Potential Equalising Jumper**
b) [TRS] On a **Passenger Coach** the cables which pass the **Electric Train Heating** (ETH), communications and lighting supplies between adjacent vehicles. See also **Inter-car Jumper**
c) [Col.] An alternative term for a person committing suicide, derived from their typical choice of jumping off **Bridges** and **Platforms** in front of **Trains**.

Jumper Pit
[LUL Col.] An alternative to **Platform Safety Pit**. Also **Suicide Pit**.

Junction
[PW]
a) A layout of **Switch and Crossing Units** (S&C Units) at the intersection of **Tracks** and **Routes**
b) A layout of **Switches and Crossings** (S&C) at which it is possible to move between many Tracks Abbreviations for these include Jc., Jcn., Jct., Jnc., Jn.
c) A **Rail Joint** where the two **Rails** are of different Rail Sections. See also **Composite Weld, Junction Fishplate**.

Junction Conflict
[Ops.] A situation where two (or more) **Trains** are **Timetabled** to take conflicting **Paths** through a **Junction**.

Junction Direction Indicator (JDI)
See **Junction Indicator** (JI).

Junction Fishplate
[PW] A **Fishplate** used to join two **different Rail Sections**, and thus **Rail Depths**, together.

Junction Indicator
See **Position Light Junction Indicator** (PLJI).

Junction Layout
- Types of, see **Geographical Junction, Running Junction, Station Throat**
- Arrangements of, see **Double Double Junction, Double Junction, Double Weave Junction, Grade Separated Junction, Ladder, Quadruple Junction, Simplified Double Junction, Single Junction, Single Lead Junction, Square Crossing, Through Connection, Turnout.**

Junction Lift Fishplate
[PW] **Fishplates** that allow **Worn Rails** of different **Rail Sections** to be **Fishplated** together. See also **Junction Fishplate, Lift Fishplate**.

Junction Margin
[Ops.] The amount of time that must be allowed between two **Trains** using the same **Junction** but over **Conflicting Routes**. Different **Junction Margins** may apply to different combinations of **Routes** over the same Junction. See also **Headway, Head Margin, Hind Margin, Junction Occupancy**.

Junction Mode
[LUL] One of four possible modes into which a **Junction** may be set to work. These are:
- Normal Mode
- Programme OnlyMode
- First Come First Served (**FCFS**) Mode
- No Out Of Turn (**NOOT**) Mode

Each mode controls the movement of **Trains** at Junctions according to a set of prescribed rules. A Junction will not necessarily have all three modes available.

Junction Name Board
A **Lineside Sign** displaying the name of a **Junction** to aid drivers and others in locating their position.

Junction Names
The naming of **Junctions** should be carried out in a way which minimises potential confusion as much as possible:
- It is a good aid to poor memories if the Junction Name reflects some local feature (such as a street, public house, village, river or landmark) that is shown on maps
- Words with two or more syllables are best, as they least likely to cause confusion when spoken
- Care should also be taken to avoid overly long names that become longer still when other junctions are built nearby, forcing suffixes e.g.: Junction Road East Junction South **Chord** North Junction (which potentially abbreviates to Jn. Rd. E. Jn. S. Chord N. Jn.)
- Names should as far as possible be unique to avoid potential incidents.

Junction Occupancy
[Ops.] The time required for each **Train** to pass through a particular **Junction**.

Junction Railway
[Hist.] A **Railway** constructed to provide a link between two other Railways, often built as a joint effort.

Junction Route Indicator (JRI)
See **Junction Indicator (JI)**.

Junction Screening Tool (JST)
[Sig.] A simple quantitative assessment of the risk of **Conflicting Movements** within a **Junction Layout**. Normally used at an early stage in the design to reduce the number of options.

Junction Signal
[Sig.]
a) A **Signal** protecting **Facing Points** that have more than one possible **Main Route** □ **Beyond** them
b) In **Colour Light Signalled** areas, a **Signal** protecting **Facing Points** where the only **Main Route** is not the straight-ahead Route.

Junction Vee
The space between the **Main Line** and **Diverging Route** immediately adjacent to a **Diverging Junction**.

Junctionwork
[LUL] Alternative for **Junction**.

Juniper
(Tradename) The brandname of the **Class** 334 **Electric Multiple Unit (EMU)**.

Juridical Recording Unit
[TRS] A recording device fitted to **Trains** as part of the **European Rail Traffic Management System (ERTMS)** equipment which records information relevant to the operation of the ERTMS.

JV
Joint Venture.

K

K
a) [NR] As the first letter of a **Wagon** □ **CARKND**, it means the vehicle is an international vehicle with two axles.
b) [Sig.] On a **Signalling Circuit Diagram**:
- As one of the leading letters of an **Equipment Code**, it means indicating or detecting
- As the last letter of an Equipment Code, it means electromechanical **Indicator**

c) The letter represented by **Kilo** in the **Phonetic Alphabet**.

K Stock
[LUL] Type of **Clerestory**-roofed stock built for the District **Railway** in 1927 and subsequently absorbed into the **Q Stock**. All **Cars** of this type were originally **Motor Cars**.

K&BJR
[Hist.] The **Pre-Grouping** Kilsyth & Bonnybridge **Joint Railway**, a Caledonian and North British joint enterprise.

K&ESR
[Hist.] The **Pre-Grouping** Kent & East Sussex **Railway** This Railway avoided the 1923 **Grouping** and remained independent until **Nationalisation** of the Railways in 1948..

K&WVR
Keighley & Worth Valley **Railway**.

Kango

Kango Hammer
(Tradename) [PW] The colloquial name given to a hand-held electric hammer tool used to consolidate the **Ballast** beneath **Bearers** and **Sleepers**. These are used where **Tamping** is impossible or where the volume of work does not justify mobilising a **Tamper**.

Karri
A variety of hardwood (*Eucalyptus diversicolor*) used for **Hardwood Sleepers**. See also **Jarrah**.

KCA
The **CARKND** representing a former **Mark 1 Passenger Coach** converted to form part of the **Weedkilling Train**.

KDC
Key Distribution Centre.

KDR
Key Diversionary Route.

KE
See **Kinematic Envelope**.

Keay
[Sig. Hist.] Common shorthand for EC&J Keay, a former manufacturer of **Signalling Equipment**.

Keel Board
[PW Obs.] An attachment fitted parallel to the **Rails** between slots made in two adjacent **Sleepers** in the **Fourfoot**, and embedded in the **Ballast** in the manner of a ship's keel to increase the **Lateral Resistance** of the **Track**.

Keel Board Sleeper
[PW Obs.] A **Concrete Sleeper**, type F27P, to which a **Keel Board** can be fitted.

Keep

Keeper Flange
[PW] The part of a **Grooved Rail** which forms the groove, on the opposite side to the **Rail Head** proper.

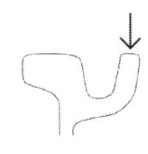

Kemler Panel
[Col.] Nickname for the **HAZCHEM** codes used by the **ADR** system, named after the French delegate in charge of implementing the system.

Kennedy, James S. T.
(1930 – 21st Dec 1973) A security guard for **British Rail Engineering Limited** (**BREL**) in Glasgow. In the early hours of the 21st December 1973, six armed men attacked the security guards who were moving the pay-roll. During the attack two guards were slightly wounded by shots from a sawn-off shotgun. Mr. Kennedy, who was on duty at the main gate, heard the shots and knowing that the criminals were armed stood in the gateway in an attempt to prevent their escape. They attacked Mr. Kennedy and stunned him by hitting him with the barrels of their shotguns. Shortly after, Mr. Kennedy recovered consciousness and undeterred by his injuries, made another attempt to prevent the criminals' escape by running towards the getaway van. He was killed by two shots fired from the vehicle and was posthumously awarded the George Cross.

Kentish Town Accident
Shortly after 19:10 on the 2nd of September 1861, an unscheduled **Excursion Train** collided with a **Ballast Train** near Kentish Town **Station**. The cause was determined to be a combination of ineffective **Signalling** arrangements, the Excursion driver not obeying **Signals** and the failure of the inexperienced **Signaller** to carry out his duties correctly. The inspecting officer recommended the fitting of **Automatic Brakes**. 16 died, 20 were seriously injured and another 301 received minor injuries. See **Lock, Block and Brake**.

KER
[Hist.] The **Pre-Grouping** Knott End **Railway**.

KESS
Kinetic Energy Storage Systems

KETS
(Tradename) Kestrel Emergency Telephone System. See also **Public Emergency Telephone System** (**PETS**).

Kettle
[Col.] Mildly derogatory term for a **Steam Locomotive**.

Key
a) [PW] A shaped wedge of spring steel, oak or teak that secures a **Bull Head Rail** in a **Chair**. Also **Rail Key**
b) The smaller, wedge-shaped segment in a segmental **Tunnel** lining.

Key a Signal to Danger
[Sig.] To use a **Signal Post Replacement Key** in the **Signal Post Replacement Switch** of a **Colour Light Signal** in order to force the **Signal** to show a **Stop Aspect**. This is generally carried out during **Protection of the Line** for a **Possession**.

Key Liner
[PW] A **Shim** fitted to ensure the correct fit of worn **Keys** in **Bull Head** □ **Chairs**.

Key Locking
[Sig.] An arrangement whereby little used and remote facilities such as **Sidings** and **Level Crossings** (**LC**, **LX**) are kept locked out of use by means of a key, rather than any provision of **Signalling Equipment**. Removal of the key from the **Controlling Signal Box** generally requires the **Signals** protecting the facility to be placed to **Stop Aspects** first. See **Annett's Key**, **Annett's Lock**.

Key Strap
[Elec.] A **Short Circuiting Strap** or **Fixed Short Circuiting Device** used adjacent to a **Circuit Breaker** (**CB**) to protect the integrity of an **Isolation** in a **Conductor Rail** system.

Key Token
[Sig.] A variety of miniature **Token**, often in the form of a key-shaped object, used in the **Electric Token Block** (**ETB**) system.

Keyed to Danger
See **Key a Signal to Danger**.

Keying Hammer
[PW] A variety of sledgehammer weighing six or ten pounds and having a narrow elongated head. Originally intended for fitting and removing **Keys** on **Bull Head Track**, this implement is now the hammer of choice for all **Permanent Way** (**PW**) tasks.

Keying up
[PW] The activity of fitting and driving **Keys** to secure a **Bull Head Rail** into **Chairs**.

Keylocks
[Sig.] A method of **Interlocking** assisted by manually operated keys operating locks fitted to **Level Crossing Gates**. This can be linked to either the Interlocking, or directly to the **Signals** in the case of a 'non-standard' Keylock system.

Keywood Scantlings
[PW] Wooden beams with a cross section equivalent to a **Bullhead Key**, manufactured as such to allow for ease of stacking and seasoning.

KGT
(Tradename) A type of **Road Rail Excavator** manufactured by **Geismar**.

Kgtkm
Thousand Gross Tonne Kilometres.

Kick Boarding
An alternative for **Guard Boarding**. Also **Conductor Rail Boarding**.

Kick the Quoit
[Hist.] To disconnect the **Wagon** from the **Haul Rope** on a **Rope Hauled Railway**.

Kicking
[PW] The violent upward movement of a **Switch Rail** caused by the passage of fast traffic; a somewhat dangerous occurrence prevented by **Kicking Straps**.

Kicking Strap
[PW] The extended section of a **Stretcher Bar** that is located under the **Stock Rail** (or **Wing Rail** in a **Switch Diamond** (**SD**)) and thus prevents excessive upward movement (**Kicking**) of the **Switch Rail** under passing **Trains**.

Kildwick Accident
On the 28th August 1875, an **Express Passenger Train** ran into the rear of an **Excursion Train** at Kildwick, between Skipton and Leeds. This **Accident** would have been prevented by the adoption of **Block Working**. Seven died and 40 were injured. See **Lock, Block and Brake**.

Kilo
a) [PW] Shorthand for **Kilograms per Metre**
b) The **Phonetic Alphabet** word representing **K**.

Kilograms per Metre
[PW] The metric equivalent of **Pounds per Yard**, used to describe **Rail Sections**. See **33 Kilo**, **56 Kilo**, **60 Kilo**. Also **Kilo**.

Kilometerage
The metric distance from a reference (typically the 0 (zero) kilometre post). The term is used to avoid confusion with the terms **Chainage** and **Mileage**. See also **Metreage**.

Kilometre Plate
[LUL] A plate fitted to a **Kilometre Post** or **Tunnel** wall, showing the **Kilometerage** at that point, measured from the former terminus of the **Central Line** at Ongar.

Kilometre Post (KP)
[LUL] A **Trackside** post to which a **Kilometre Plate** is fixed.

Kinematic Envelope (KE)
[TRS] The maximum sectional outline that a **Rail Vehicle** occupies under various conditions and combinations of speed, **Tilt**, wheel wear, **Cant Deficiency** (**D**), **Track Tolerances**, loading, load distribution, suspension failure, wind and aerodynamic factors. It excludes the effects of **End Throw** and **Centre Throw**. **Kinematic Envelopes** tend to be somewhat larger than the **Static Envelope** for the same vehicle. Most modern **Vehicle Gauges** are kinematic, the alternative being a **Static Vehicle Gauge**. See also **Contact Gauging**, **Kinematic Gauging**, **Static Gauging**, **Swept Envelope**, **Swept Path**.

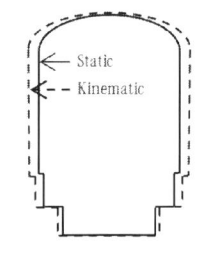

Kinematic Gauging
[PW] The operation of comparing a single **Structure** or many Structures along a **Route** with the **Kinematic Envelope** (**KE**) of one or many types of **Rail Vehicle**. See also **Gauging**.

Kinematic Vehicle Gauge
An alternative for **Kinematic Envelope** (KE).

King
The obsolescent **Phonetic Alphabet** word representing **K**. Replaced by **Kilo**.

King Lever
[Sig.]
a) A **Lever** in a **Signal Box** (SB) the operation of which changes the **Interlocking** within the **Frame**. Such a facility is required when a **Signal Box** is to be **Switched Out** of circuit using a **Block Switch**
b)

King Pin
[TRS] The vertical stub shaft that forms the connection between a **Bogie** and the vehicle above, allowing the Bogie to rotate freely but resists the longitudinal and lateral forces produced by cornering, braking and acceleration.

King Points
The **Turnout** forming the first division of a **Fan** or **Group of Sidings**.

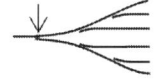

King Post Wall
[Civ.] A wall comprising vertical posts (often large I-section steel beams) that retain horizontal wooden or concrete beams.

King, Railway
See **Hudson, George**.

Kings Cross Accident
On 18th November 1987, a fire started in an escalator at Kings Cross and spread rapidly through the **London Underground Limited** (LUL) □ **Station**, producing large quantities of poisonous smoke and very high temperatures. In the ensuing inferno 30 **Passengers** and a firefighter lost their lives. The inquiry into this tragedy resulted in the **Fire Precautions (Sub-surface Railway Stations) Regulations 1989**, legislation that defines which Stations are **Sub-surface Stations** and the special precautions must be taken in those Stations.

Kip
[Hist.] An artificial **Hump** constructed at **the Bank Head** of a **Rope-Worked Railway** which allowed the ascending rope to slacken off as a **Set** passed over the Kip thereby allowing, initially the **Set Rider** and later a bank head man working from ground level to detach the rope from the vehicles.

Kirow
(*Keer-ov*) (Tradename) A manufacturer of, amongst other things, **Railway** plant, based in Leipzig, Germany. See **IFA**, **Kirow Crane**.

Kirow Crane
(*Keer-ov crayn*) (Tradename) Representing the "next generation" of **Rail Cranes**, these machines have a maximum lifting apacity of 125 tonnes at 9.5m radius **Blocked**, or 36.5 tonnes at 24m **Free on Rail** (FOR). A self-levelling device allows the crane to be used on **Cant** up to 160mm. They can operate at full duty with the boom horizontal, allowing long and heavy loads to be carried under **OHLE Equipment** and **Bridges**.

Kiss and Ride
[Col.] Describing the activity found at a **Railway** □ **Station** frequented by **Commuters**, where potential **Passengers** are dropped off from private cars by their spouses.

Kiss Bend
A location where a highway meets, turns to run parallel with for a short distance and then turns away from a **Railway**.

Kissing Gates
[Civ.] A type of small gate, which swings between two posts forming an enclosure which allows one person at a time to pass. Frequently found at **Footpath Crossings** (FP, in this case FPK), intended to allow pedestrians to pass but to bar livestock. A **Kissing Gate** requires no latch.

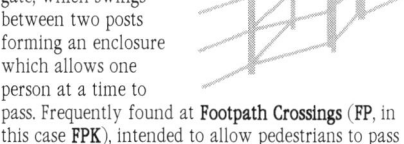

KJA
The **CARKND** representing the discharge conveyor **Wagon** from the Lafarge **Self Discharging Train** (SDT)

KJT
Key **J**ourney **T**imes.

kN

KN
a) See **Knuckle**.
b) Kilo Newton, a measure of force, equal to 1000 Newtons. A Newton is 1kg/m/s and is correctly written kN.

Knee
[Elec.] The junction between the **Boom** and **Leg** of a **Portal** □ **Overhead Line Structure**.

Knee Brace
[Elec.] A diagonal reinforcing member connecting the **Boom** and **Leg** of a **Portal** □ **Overhead Line Structure** at the **Knee**.

Knee Frame
[Sig.] A **Signal Box** □ **Frame** with the base roughly at knee height rather than at the normal position of level with the floor.

Knitting
[Col.] **Nickname** for the **Overhead Line Equipment** (OLE), inspired by its apparent complexity.

Knob
[PW Col.] A localised **High** area in a section of **Track**, and an undesirable feature. Also **Stiff**. The opposite is **Slack**, **Swag**. See also **Low**.

Knock Out

Knocking Out
[Sig. Col.] A term meaning to send "**Train out of Section**" to the **Signal Box** □ **On the Approach** by means of **Bell Code** 2-1. Also **Clear Back**.

ELLIS' BRITISH RAILWAY ENGINEERING ENCYCLOPÆDIA

Knuckle (KN)
a) [PW] In an **Obtuse Crossing**, the central bend in the **Obtuse Wing Rail** about the point formed by the **Intersection of Gauge Lines** (IP) of the **Point Rails**. Also **Elbow**.
b) [Elec.] In the **Overhead Line Equipment** (OLE), an arrangement where two **Catenaries** meet at an angle. There are two types, **Insulated Knuckles** and Un-Insulated Knuckles.

KP
a) Kilometre Post
b) Kilometre Point.

KPI
Key Performance Indicator.

KRA
a) The **CARKND** representing a **Sleeper** carrier **Wagon**, ex. **Jarvis**.
b) Key Risk Area.

KVB
[CTRL] Contrôle de Vitesse par **Balises**, a system of speed control using Balises. See also **Tilt and Speed Supervision System** (TASS).

KWA
[NR] The **CARKND** representing a **Bogie ▫ Well Wagon** used for carrying excavating plant.

L

L
a) In an abbreviated **Track Name**, it denotes **L**ine, **L**ocal or **L**oop
b) [PW] Marked in a **Rail Web**, indicates that the following value is the **Level Difference** between the **Rail** so marked and the nearest Rail the value can be seen from. These figures are used in conjunction with a **Crosslevel** to control depths during excavation and **Reballasting** operations
c) [PW] Marked on a **Sleeper**, it indicates that the following value is the **l**ength of the next **Transition Curve**
d) [PW] In a description of **Switches, Crossings, Check Rails, Chairs** and **Baseplates**, it means **l**eft or left side
e) [TRS] As the last letter in an acronym describing types of **Passenger Coaches**, it indicates the fitting of a **l**avatory
f) [Sig.] On a **Signalling Circuit Diagram**:
• As a bracketed suffix, it denotes a **l**ocal power supply
• As one of the leading letters of an **Equipment Code**, it means **Locking** or left
• As the last letter of an Equipment Code, it means lock
g) The letter represented by **Lima** in the **Phonetic Alphabet**.

L Stock
[LUL] Type of **Clerestory**-roofed stock built for the District **Railway** in 1931 for the Upminster extension and subsequently absorbed into the **Q Stock** fleet.

L&BR
[Hist.] The **Pre-Grouping** Lynton & Barnstaple **Railway**.

L&CR
[Hist.] The **Pre-Grouping** Liskeard & **C**aradon **Railway**, a **Great Western Railway** (**GWR**) enterprise.

L&E
[LUL] **L**ifts and **E**scalators.

L&LR
[Hist.] The **Pre-Grouping** Liskeard &**L**ooe **Railway**, a **Great Western Railway** (**GWR**) enterprise.

L&MR
[Hist.] The **Pre-Grouping** Llanelly & **M**ynydd Mawr **Railway**.

L&NWR
[Hist.] The **Pre-Grouping** London and **N**orth **W**estern **Railway**. Also **LNWR**.

L&SWR
[Hist.] The **Pre-Grouping** London & **S**outh **W**estern **Railway**.

L&Y
[NR] **L**ancashire & **Y**orkshire, an administrative division.

L&YR
[Hist.] The **Pre-Grouping** Lancashire & Yorkshire **Railway**.

L/O
An abbreviation of **Lookout**.

L/S
a) See **Loose Sleeper** (**LS**)
b) **L**ate **S**tart
c) See **London Side** (**LS**).

L/X
LX
See **Level Crossing** (**LC, LX**).

L1
a) See **Level One Exceedence**
b) See **European Rail Traffic Management System** (**ERTMS**)
c) A **Chair** for 95 RBS □ **Bullhead Rail** (**BH**) having a smaller bearing area than an **S1** or **AS1**.

L2
a) See **Level Two Exceedence**
b) See **European Rail Traffic Management System** (**ERTMS**)
c) A chair for 85 Pound □ **Bullhead Rail** (**BH**) having a smaller bearing area than an **S2**.

L3
See **European Rail Traffic Management System** (**ERTMS**).

L50
[PW] Common contraction of **SkV-L50**.

L80
[PW] Common contraction of **SkV-L80**.

257

Lab *x*
Laboratory *x*
[BR] A group of **Coaches** and **Multiple Unit Trains** used for testing, measurement and development by British Rail Research (BRR), some were named. Some of the numbers, names and purposes were:

1	*No name*	Vehicle dynamics
2	Electra	**Rapid Transit** □ **Bogie** Test; TAIM
3	MENTOR	**Overhead Line** testing
4	Hastings	Suspension and **Tilt** test
5	*No name*	TRIM □ Unit
6	Prometheus	Electrical systems testing
7	Phoenix	Fire testing facility
8	Pilot	APT suspension development
9	Hydra	**Traction** system testing
10	*No name*	Match Vehicle
11	*No name*	**Adhesion** testing
12	*No name*	Acoustics testing
13	*No name*	Aerodynamics testing
14	Wren	Acoustics testing
15	Argus	High speed instrumentation
16	Gemini	**Train** control testing
17	Hermes	**Driving Trailer** testing
18	Mercury	C-APT instrumentation
19	**Iris, Iris 2**	Radio testing
20	Elliot	**Track** testing
21	*No name*	Vehicle Dynamics
22	*No name*	**V Laser** □ **Track Maintenance**
23	*No name*	Generator Coach
24	*No name*	**Trestrol** □ APT □ **Bogie** testing
25	Decapod	**Track Force** testing
26	*No name*	**Rail Flaw** probe guidance testing
-	Atlas	Trestrol **Track** measuring vehicle
-	Cyclops	Ditto

Most of the surviving ones have been taken over by Serco, and the relevant vehicles re-titled **Test Cars**.

LABP
[LUL] Level Access Boarding Point.

Lacer
A **Railway** □ **Telegraph Code** meaning "Must not use **Crossovers** between **Platforms**" and applied to **Out of Gauge Loads**.

Ladbrooke Grove Accident
A **Signal Passed at Danger** (**SPAD**) on 5th October 1999 resulted in 31 dead and 227 injured. A **Local Passenger Train** passed SN109 **Signal** which was showing a **Stop Aspect** and collided head-on with a **High Speed Train** (**HST**). Many reasons were cited for the accident, not least poor **Signal Sighting**, the absence of **Automatic Train Protection** (**ATP**) and a lack of driver experience. The Public Inquiry was chaired by The Rt. Hon. Lord Cullen, and the resulting report is known as the **Cullen Report**.

Ladder
See **Ladder Junction**.

Ladder Junction
A series of **Crossovers**, **Diamond Crossings**, **Slips** or **Turnouts** which allow **Trains** to cross many **Tracks** in a ladder-like manner. See also **Through Connection**.

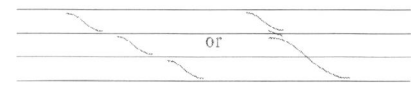

Ladder Track
[PW] A type of track construction in which the **Rails** are laid on longitudinal steel or concrete supports with transverse connectors holding the Rails at the correct **Gauge** distance. Ladder track can be considered a development of the **Baulk Road** in which the rails were supported on **Longitudinal Bearers**.

Laden Spring
[TRS] The stiffer of two **Nested Springs**.

LADS
See **Linear Asset Decision Support**.

Lambeth Paving
Lambeth Deterrent Paving
A form of paving where the upper surface is formed into a number of low-height square pyramids to deter pedestrians and cylists.

Lambrigg Accident
At 20:12 on 23rd February 2007, a nine **Car** □ **Class** 390 **Pendolino** travelling at 95mph **Derailed** on 2B **Points** at Lambrigg **Emergency Ground Frame** (**EGF**), located near Grayrigg in Cumbria. One **Passenger** died and 28 Passengers, the driver and one other member of **Traincrew** suffered serious injuries. The primary cause of the **Derailment** was the failure, by breakage or detachment, of all the **Stretcher Bars**, allowing the **Left Hand Switch Rail** to move of its own accord.

Lamp Proving
[Sig.] An arrangement which monitors the current drawn by a **Signal Lamp** and can be arranged to **Replace** the **Signal** □ **On the Approach** to a **Stop Aspect** should the filament fail.

Lamp Repeater
[Sig.] A single **Needle Indicator** which displays the status of an electrical circuit. The circuit also includes a bimetallic strip held in the flame of the **Signal Lamp**. When the lamp is lit the bimetallic strip completes the circuit and the Indicator shows **In**. The strip opens if the light is out, breaking the circuit and causing the Indicator to show **Out**.

Lamprey (ZBO)
[NR] A 20 ton capacity **Open Wagon** used for the transportation of **Ballast** and materials. See **Wagon Names**.

Land Clearance
[NR] The internal process by which **Network Rail** ascertains if areas of un-used **Operational Land** can be used for buildings, structures or disposed of.

Land Severance
The process by which two parcels of land (both formerly one parcel and under common ownership, and thus subject to **Accommodation Rights** across the **Railway** when the **Railway** was built) are acquired by different owners, removing any Accommodation Rights between the two parcels.

Landing
[Hist.] A level **Twin-track Section** between two **Single Track** □ **Rope-worked Inclines**. Designed to allow the **Sets** to interchange between the inclines.

Landslide
Landslip
[Civ.] A movement of a large mass of earth and rock down a mountainside, cliff, **Cutting Slope** or **Embankment**. See **Bank Slip**. See also **Slip**, **Slip Circle**, **Slip Plane**.

Lap
[Ops.] A setting on the control of an **Air Brake** system that maintains the pressure in the **Brake Pipe** at its current level.

LAPTIS
(*lap-tiss*) [BR] Little All-purpose Ticket Issuing System, see also **APTIS**.

Lardner, Dionysius
(1793 –1859) An Irish scientific writer who popularised science and technology and was also a serial philanderer. He famously engaged **Isambard Kingdom Brunel** in many arguments including **Locomotive** efficiency, the speed of runaway **Trains** in Box Tunnel and the range of the SS Great Western; he lost every single one.

Laser Beacon
A device that emits a circular plane of visible or infra-red Laser light. Standard features include:
- The ability to offset the plane of light to the horizontal by a known angle (generally a percentage) in one or two axes
- An internal power source, such as batteries
- A fitting on the base to affix it to a tripod

Also **Turret Beacon**.

Laser Dozer

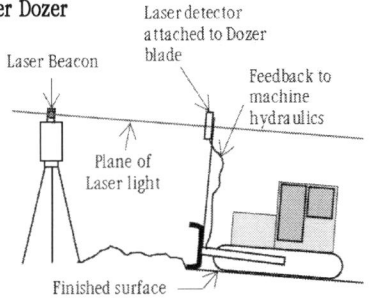

[PW] A bulldozer equipped with laser receivers, adjustable masts, hydraulic servo valves and automated controls, allowing it to accurately follow the plane of Laser light emitted by a **Laser Beacon**. This system allows **Bottom Ballast** and other fill materials to be spread to within 5mm ($c.^1/_4$ inch) of the design level, with similar accuracy in **Crossfall** or **Cant** (**C, E**) over distances of 400m (440 Yards).

Laser Levelling
The surveying and setting out of vertical levels using a **Laser Beacon**. Often also used to describe the laying of **Ballast** using a **Laser Dozer**.

Laser Lining

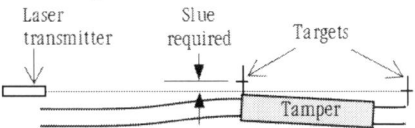

[PW] A method of aligning **Straight Track** using a system of Laser transmitter and two targets to provide a reference for the **Alignment** operation. The transmitter and first target are set up at each end of the desired **Straight**, a known distance away from the **Running Edge** (**RE**). The Laser is then aligned on this target. The **Tamper** has the second target, arranged so that it moves with the **Leading End** of the **Lining Wire** at an appropriate offset. The operator then aligns the machine target with the Laser beam using the **Lining** controls, and the machine produces near perfect **Straight Track**.

Lasersweep
Lasersweep Survey
(Tradename) Developed by Laser Rail Ltd, now a division of Balfour Beatty Rail Technologies Ltd., a survey method used for profiling **Bridges** and **Structures** that utilises a laser distance measurement device referenced to one **Rail** and arranged to rotate in a plane normal to the **Running Edge**. By measuring angle and distance, coordinates can be generated for the inside face of the Structure. These are then used for **Gauging** purposes See also **Fishing**, **Pole and Tape Survey**, **Structure Gauging Train** (**SGT**).

Last Mile Cost
Costs incurred in delivering **Freight** from a **Rail Freight** interchange to a destination point.

Last Wheel Replacement (LWR)
[Sig.] A **Control** which **Replaces** a **Signal** to the **Most Restrictive Aspect** only after the last wheel of the **Train** passes the **Insulated Rail Joint** (**IRJ**) immediately **Beyond** the **Signal** (the **Replacement Joint**) See also **First Wheel Replacement** (**FWR**).

Latch
[Sig.]
a) A memory location that switches between two states, representing a particular **Signalling Function**. The states are commonly known as **Set** and **Unset**.
b) An alternative for **Stick**.
See also **Signal Stick**, **SPAD Latch**.

Late Notice Arrangements
[Ops.] A means of providing **Train** drivers with information of a short-term or emergency nature at the time they commence their driving shift.

Late Surrender Protection
[LUL] Protection arranged for staff who have been working under the **Line Clear** or **Line Safe** procedure and will fail or have failed to pass a **Site Clear** or **Site Safe** message to the track access controller by the call back time

ELLIS' BRITISH RAILWAY ENGINEERING ENCYCLOPÆDIA

Lateral Alignment Datum
[PW] A virtual longitudinal line along the centre of a section of **Track** that is calculated and used as a reference when surveying the **Horizontal Alignment**. Divergences in the actual Horizontal Alignment of the Track are measured and recorded as variations from this virtual line.

Lateral Resistance (LR)
[PW] A measure of the **Track's** resistance to lateral forces. It is composed of the sliding friction between **Sleeper** and **Ballast** (the small component) and the end resistance of the Sleeper acting on the **Ballast Shoulder** (the larger component). It is the **Shoulder Ballast** that is critical to ensuring the stability of Track with **Continuous Welded Rails** (**CWR**). Locally reduced Lateral Resistance generally forms the catalyst for **Track Buckles**, but they can be triggered by poor **Alignment** and poor **Fishplated Rail Joint** maintenance. Lateral Resistance is also reduced by **Track Maintenance** or **Track Renewal** activity involving disturbance to the **Ballast**; see **Critical Rail Temperature** (**CRT**).

Lateral Resistance End Plate (LRE, LREP)

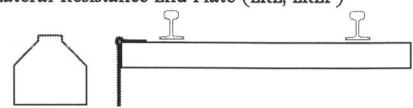

[PW] An inverted L-shaped pressed metal bracket which is screwed to the end of a **Sleeper** to increase the cross sectional area and therefore its **Lateral Resistance**. They were fitted on sharp **Curves** of between 500m and 375m Radius (**R**), to permit the use of **Continuously Welded Rail** (**CWR**). The current approved system on **Network Rail** (**NR**) is the Vossloh SN.

Lateral Ride
The amount of horizontal or lateral movement that a **Rail Vehicle**, load or person would be subjected to during a journey. See also **Vertical Ride**.

Lateral Stability
[PW] An alternative term for **Lateral Resistance** (**LR**).

Laths
[PW] Long, rough sawn pieces of wood, marked with **Timber** or **Bearer** positions and appropriately numbered, used to ease the building up of new **Switch and Crossing Layouts** (**S&C Layouts**) on site. Used in conjunction with the **White Line** system. See also **Fletching**.

LATS
London Area Transport Study.

Lattice Girder

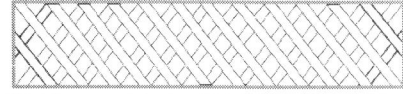

[Civ.] An open girder in which the web consists of diagonal pieces arranged in a latticework.

Laughing Train
[Col.] A **Train** composed of HAA **Coal** ▫ **Hopper Wagons**; Haa, Haa, Haa, ...

Launder
See **Garland**.

LAWS
(*lorrs*) Low **Adhesion** Warning System.

Lay-by
[Col.] Alternative term for a **Through Siding** or **Loop**.

Laying In
[PW] The placing of **Track** or **Switch and Crossing Units** (**S&C Units**) onto a prepared **Ballast** layer or **Track Bed**.

Laying Out
[PW] The act of placing **Track** components, **Switch and Crossing** (**S&C**) components, **Rails** and **Cable Troughs** in either their final position or adjacent to their final position.

Layout
[PW] A descriptive term for a collection of multiple **Switches and Crossings** (**S&C**). See also **Junction Layout**.

Layout Plan
[Elec.] A scale plan view representation of the main features of a section of the **Overhead Line Equipment** (**OLE**), typically showing **Auto-transformer Feeders** (**ATF**), **Balance Weight Anchors** (**BWA**), **Fixed Anchors** (**FA**), **Head Spans**, **In Running** (**IR**) ▫ **Contact Wires**, **Mid-point Anchors** (**MPA**), **Neutral Sections** (**NS**), **Out of Running** (**OOR**) **Contact Wires**, **Overhead Line Structures**, **Overlap Spans**, **Permanently Earthed Sections** (**PES**), **Registration Points**, **Return Conductors** (**RC**), **Section Insulators** (**SI**), **Span Lengths**, **Stagger**, **Wire Heights** and **Wire Runs**.

Layout Risk Assessment (LRA)
[NR Sig.] The exercise of evaluating a new or modified **Junction** or **Track Layout**. This may or may not include the use of a **Layout Risk Model** (**LRM**).

Layout Risk Model (LRM)
[NR Sig.] A numerical model created to analyse the risks arising from **Train Movements** through a particular **Track Layout**. It generally includes factors such as **Conflicting Movements**, outcomes from **SPADs** and **Unauthorised Movements** and degraded operation, where some part of the Layout is disabled.

Lazy
[Col.] A term used to describe a **Supplementary Drive** which is not holding a **Switch Rail** correctly closed to the relevant **Stock Rail**.

LB
See **Line Blocked**.

LB&SCR
[Hist.] The Pre-Grouping London, Brighton & South Coast Railway.

LBR
[Pres.] The Leighton Buzzard Railway.

LBRA
[NR Sig.] Line Blockage Risk Assessment.

LBW
[LUL] Lillie Bridge Workshops.

LC
a) See **Level Crossing**
b) See **Line Clear**
c) See **Locally Controlled Manned Level Crossing**
d) See **Low Cost Clip**
e) Inductor / Capacitor, a type of electrical filter circuit, see also **Damper**, **Harmonic Filter**.

LC Clip
See **Low Cost Clip**.

LCA
See **The Level Crossings Act 1983**.

LCAMS
(*el-kams*) See **Low Carbon Austenitic Manganese Steel**.

LCB
Limited **C**learance □ **B**oard.

LCC
a) See **Low Cost Clip**
b) [LUL] **L**ine **C**ontrol **C**entre. See **Line Controller**.

LCM
Level **C**rossing **M**anager.

LCO
[LUL] **L**ine **C**ontrol **O**ffice. See **Line Controller**.

LCP
[Sig.] **L**ocal **C**ontrol **P**anel.

LCR
See **London and Continental Railways**.

LCS
[LUL] **L**ocation **C**oding **S**ystem.

LCTCS
Low **C**ost **T**rain **C**ontrol **S**ystem.

LCU
See **Local Control Unit**.

LCWS
See **WaveTrain LCWS**.

LD
a) **L**ight **D**iesel, a more precise description of a **Light Locomotive**
b) Shorthand for lo**ad**ed. See also **MT**
c) Liquidated **D**amage(s)
d) [Tel.] **L**oop **D**isconnect.

LDB
Live **D**eparture **B**oard

LDB-SV
Live **D**eparture **B**oard - **S**taff **V**ersion

LDC
a) **L**ocal **D**istribution **C**entre
b) **L**ocal **D**epartmental **C**ommittee.

LDG
[Obs.] **L**ist of **D**angerous **G**oods.

LDO
a) [TRS] **L**ocal **D**oor **O**peration
b) [NR] **L**ead **D**esign **O**rganisation.

LDRP
Long **D**istance **R**ecovery **P**lan.

LDT
[Tel.]
a) **L**ong **D**istance **T**erminal
b) **L**ong **D**istance **T**ermination.

LDTSS
Long **D**istance **T**rain **S**ervice **S**pecification.

LDV
See **Live Drop Vertical**.

LE
a) **L**ight **E**ngine, see **Light Locomotive**
b) **L**ight **E**lectric, a more precise description of a **Light Locomotive**
c) See **London End**.
d) The **ATOC** code for **Greater Anglia**.

Lead
[PW]
a) See **Lead Length**
b) An alternative term for a **Turnout** (**TO**)
c) The amount by which one **Rail Joint** is ahead of the joint in the opposite **Rail**. Also **Stagger**.

Lead Emergency Driving Position
[DLR] The position in which the **Passenger Service Agent** would travel at the front of the **Train**. The Passenger Service Agent would be looking ahead to see if there were any obstructions on the **Track**. They can stop the Train by operating the emergency stop button on the **Driving Console**. Also called the **Emergency Driving Position**

Lead Length
[PW]
a) The dimension from **Switch Toe** to the **Intersection of Gauge Lines** (**IP**) in a **Turnout** (**TO**)
b) The dimension by which the two Intersections of Gauge Lines on adjacent **Tracks** are spaced in a **Crossover**, measured parallel to the centre line of one **Track**. See also **Nose to Nose Dimension**
c) The dimension between the Intersection of Gauge Lines of a **Common Crossing and Obtuse Crossing** in a **Diamond Crossing**
d) An alternative for **Toe to Nose Dimension**
e) The dimension by which two related **Fishplated Rail Joints** on a Track are staggered, generally as a result of either curvature or **Rail Creep**.

Leadaway
[Sig.] The opening at the base of a **Mechanical Signal Box** through which the **Channel Rodding** and **Signal Wires** pass. See also **Leadaway Timber**.

Leadaway Timber
[Sig.] The large wood baulk laid horizontally just outside the **Leadaway**. It is used to provide a base for the **Cranks** for the **Channel Rodding** and pulleys for the **Signal Wires**, required to change the direction of the majority of these Rods and Wires at this location.

Leading Cab
[Ops.] When a **Locomotive**, **On-track Machine** (**OTM**) or **Traction Unit** is being driven, the **Leading Cab** is the **Cab** at the front in the direction of travel. The opposite is **Trailing Cab**.

Leading End
[Ops.] The front end of a **Locomotive**, **Multiple Unit Train**, **Train** or **Traction Unit** in the direction of travel. The opposite is **Trailing End**.

Leading Vehicle
[Ops.] The first **Rail Vehicle** in a **Train**, in the direction of travel.

Leaf Fall Contamination (LFC)
A build-up of a residue of crushed leaves on the **Rail Head** which can cause **Train** wheels to slip, impairing braking and causing failures in the operation of **Track Circuits** (**TC**). See also **Leaf Fall Season**.

Leaf Fall Season
[Ops.] The Autumn period between early September and late December, during which time the **Railway** is most at risk from the **Abnormal Rail Head Conditions** produced by leaf mulch on the **Rail Head**. See also **Defensive Driving**, **LOTL**.

Leaf Fall Timetable
[Ops.] A special **Timetable** (**TT**) put in place during **Leaf Fall Season**, to allow drivers to carry out additional **Defensive Driving** when approaching **Stations** and **Stop Aspects**.

Leaf Pier
[Civ.] A **Bridge** □ **Pier** which is very narrow and elongated when seen in plan. Such **Piers** are generally made of concrete.

Leaf Springs
[TRS] A simple spring, widely used for **Rail Vehicle** suspensions, comprising one or more layers (leaves) bound together. The outer ends are anchored to the **Vehicle** and the load is supported at the centre.

Leaky Feeder
[Sig. Tel.] A combination of a connecting cable and an aerial, used to allow two way radio frequency transmissions in **Tunnels**. Leaky Feeders are laid along the complete length of the Tunnel, allowing these normally dead areas to send and receive radio and data traffic.

Lean-mix Concrete
Low-strength concrete which contains a smaller proportion of cement.

Learning the Road
[Ops.] The process by which a driver becomes familiar with a **Route**, and the features on it, including braking landmarks, **Enhanced Permissible Speeds** (**EPS**), **Junctions**, **Signals**, **Permissible Speed** (**PS**) and **Stations**. All this information becomes the **Route Knowledge**, without which a driver cannot **Sign the Road**, and without that signature he cannot drive the Route unsupervised. See also **Road Learning**.

Least Restrictive Aspect
[Sig.] A generic description of the **Aspect** displayed by a given **Signal** which has least effect on the speed of **Trains**. A typical **Three Aspect Signal** can display a Proceed Aspect (**Green**, highest speed), a Caution Aspect (**Yellow**, reduced speed) and a Stop Aspect (**Red**, no speed). Therefore on this signal the **Proceed Aspect** is the Least Restrictive Aspect. The opposite is **Most Restrictive Aspect**.

LED
a) [Ops.] **Light** □ **Electro Diesel** (**ED**), a more precise description of a **Light Locomotive**
b) Light Emitting Diode, a semiconductor device using the electroluminescent principle to produce light whose wavelength depends on the band-gap energy of the materials used.

LED Signal
[Sig.] A **Colour Light Signal**, **Junction Indicator** (**JI**) or **Position Light Signal** which utilises groups of coloured **Light Emitting Diodes** (**LEDs**) to display the relevant **Aspect** or Aspects.

LEEC
[LUL] **Lifts** and **Escalators** (**L&E**) Extended Closure.

Left Hand Common Crossing
[PW]
a) [WR] In the former **Great Western Railway** (**GWR**) area, A **Common Crossing** with the **Splice Rail** on the right of the **Point Rail** when viewed from the **Wing Rail Fronts**. The opposite is a **Right Hand Common Crossing**.
b) Elsewhere, a **Right Hand Splice** (**RHS**) □ **Crossing**.

Left Hand Curve
a) [PW] The direction in which a **Curve** diverges from the straight when viewed with one's **Back to Low Mileage**. A Curve to the left is thus a Left Hand Curve
b) [Elec.] A Curve in which the **Left Hand Rail** (**LHR**) is highest, viewed with one's **Back to Low Mileage**, therefore generally the opposite view to the Permanent Way Engineer.
The opposite (!) is a **Right Hand Curve**.

Left Hand Parallel Wing (LHPW)
[PW] As a suffix to a description of a **Common Crossing**, a **Common Crossing** having a **Parallel Wing Rail** on the left hand side of the **Crossing Vee**. The opposite is **Right Hand Parallel Wing** (**RHPW**). See also **Double Parallel Wing** (**DPW**).

Left Hand Rail (LHR)
a) [PW] The **Rail** on the left hand side of a **Track**, when viewed with one's **Back to Low Mileage**
b) [Sig.] The Rail on the left hand side of a **Track**, when viewed in the direction of travel.
The opposite is **Right Hand Rail** (**RHR**).

Left Hand Relay
[Sig.] The left hand half of a **Twin Relay**, viewed from the front. The opposite is a **Right Hand Relay**.

Left Hand Running
[Ops.] The normal arrangement of operation on a pair of **Tracks** in mainland Britain, where **Trains** run on the left hand **Track** in the direction of travel. The world's railway systems are relatively evenly split between Left Hand and **Right Hand Running**.

Left Hand Side (LHS)
a) [PW] Being on the left of centre when viewed with one's back to the **Fronts**
b) Being on the left of centre when viewed with one's back to **London** or **Back to Low Mileage**
See also **Right Hand Side** (RHS).

Left Hand Splice (LHS)
[PW] A **Splice Rail** fitted on the **Left Hand Side** (LHS) of the **Point Rail** when viewed from the end of the **Wing Rail Fronts**. This description is also applied to the **Crossing** itself, so a Crossing with a Left Hand Splice is a **Left Hand Common Crossing**. See also **Hand** clause c). The opposite is **Right Hand Splice** (RHS).

Left Hand Switch (LHS)
[PW]
a) A **Set of Switches** in which the **Stock Rail Set** is on the left hand side **Switch Half Set** when viewed from the **Switch Toe** looking towards the **Crossing**
b) The left hand side Switch Half Set when viewed from the Switch Toe looking towards the **Switch Heel**
The opposite is **Right Hand Switch** (RHS).

Left Hand Switch Closed (LHSC)
When viewed from the **Switch Toe** end, this describes which **Switch Half Set** is closed up to its related **Stock Rail** when the **Switches** are Normal. The opposite is **Right Hand Switch Closed** (RHSC).

Left Hand Transition Rail
[PW] A **Transition Rail** in which the step in the **Outside Edge** (OE) is located on the left when viewed from the portion of the **Rail** with the larger **Rail Section**. The opposite is a **Right Hand Transition Rail**.

Left Hand Turnout (LHTO)
[PW] A **Turnout** in which the **Stock Rail Set** is on the **Left Hand Switch** (LHS) when viewed from the **Switch Toe** looking towards the **Crossing**. The opposite is a **Right Hand Turnout** (RHTO).

Left Hand Twist Rail
[PW] A **Twist Rail** in which the **Rail Foot** is rotated to the left when viewed from the **Vertical** portion of the **Twist Rail**. Seen from the Vertical portion, this **Rail** would be located on the left of the **Track**. The opposite is a **Right Hand Twist Rail**.

Leg Ends
[PW] The ends of the four **Running Rails** (**Legs**) of a **Crossing**.

Legging
[PW]
a) Lowering a short length of **Track** using **Bars** and **Shovels**, generally to correct an error made during previous **Track Relaying**
b) An alternative for **Opening Out**
c) Rarely, the shortening of **Crossing Legs**.

Legion
(Tradename) A pedestrian flow modelling and simulation programme produced by Legion International Ltd. See also **STEPS**.

Legs
[PW] See **Crossing Legs**.

LEM
a) (*lemm*) (Tradename) Lorrie, Elevateur de Motorise or Elevating Motorised Trolley, a radio controlled trolley used in conjunction with **PEM**
b) [LUL] Line Engineering Manager.

LEMS
Labour, energy, materials and services cost measure.

Length
[PW]
a) [Col.] A contraction of **Standard Rail Length**, 18.288m or 60 feet
b) [Hist.] The section of **Track** patrolled and maintained by a **Track Maintenance** □ **Gang**.

Length Over All (LOA)

◁─────────────────────▷
⊖──┼─⊖   ⊖─┼──⊖

[TRS] The length of a **Rail Vehicle** measured over its furthest extremities. See also **Length Over Headstocks**.

Length Over Headstocks (LOH)
[TRS] The length of a vehicle excluding its **Automatic Couplings** or **Buffers**.

Lengthman
[PW Hist.] Archaic term for a **Maintenance** employee who worked on a **Length**.

LENNON
(*lenn-on*) [NR] Latest Earnings Network Nationally Overnight. The national fare revenue reporting and allocation software used by the **National Rail Network** (NRN). This replaces the **CAPRI** system.

LEP
Local Emergency Plan.

LEPS
[LUL] See **Local Emergency Power Supply**.

Leptospiral Jaundice
Leptospirosis
A severe viral infection carried in **Rat's** urine. It is therefore vital to be scrupulous regarding personal hygiene and the treatment of cuts when working in areas where the risk of exposure exists, such as the **Cess** of a **Railway**. See **Washing the Hands, Importance of**. Also known as **Weil's Disease**.

LER
[Hist.] The **Pre-Grouping** London Electric **Railway**.

LES
[LUL] Longitudinal Earth System.

Letter of No Objection (LONO)
A letter written by **Her Majesties' Railway Inspectorate** (HMRI) in response to a proposal to it, when it has no objections to the proposal. Whilst not a positive commendation, it serves to reassure the proposer that the proposal does not contain any contentious issues.

LEU
a) **Lineside** Electronic **U**nit
b) **L**ineside **E**ncoding **U**nit.

LEV
(Tradename) [Hist.] **L**eyland **E**xperimental **V**ehicle, a **Diesel Multiple Unit** (**DMU**) and forerunner of the **Class** 14x **Pacer** or **Nodding Dog**.

Level
a) Describing a **Railway** or part of a **Railway** with no measurable **Gradient**
b) [PW] Describing **Track** that has no **Cant**
c) An optical device which permits the collection of vertical measurements to a known horizontal plane, see **Level Survey**.

Level 3
On a **Class** 22x **Voyager**, the name given to the classification of fault or event conditions (anomalies), monitored and recorded by the **Train Management System** (**TMS**), which affect safety or are service critical.

Level Crossing (LC, LX)
a) An arrangement where a road or footpath crosses a **Railway** with the road or footpath surface at the same level as the **Rail Crown**. There are many varieties. The principal groups are:
- **Open Level Crossings**, which have no **Barriers**, **Gates**, warning systems or supervision at all. Abbreviated to **OC**
- **Accommodation Crossings**, **Occupation Crossings** and **Footpath Crossings**, which may have **Gates** and / or some form of warning system.
- **Manned Level Crossings**, which are monitored and operated by **Railway** staff. Types include: Closed Circuit Television (**CCTV**), **Locally Controlled Manned Level Crossing** (**LC, LX**), **Manually Controlled Barriers** (**MCB**), **Manually Controlled Barriers – On Call** (**MCB-OC**), **Manually Controlled Barriers – Obstacle Detection** (**MCB-OD**), **Trainman Operated** (**TMO**), **Remotely Controlled Manned** (**RC**)
- **Automatic Level Crossings**, where the advance warning to traffic and subsequent closure of the highway is triggered by the passage of **Trains**. Types include: **Automatic Half Barrier** (**AHB**), **Automatic Barrier Crossing Locally Monitored** (**ABCL**), **Automatic Open Crossing Locally Monitored** (**AOCL**), **Automatic Open Crossing Remotely Monitored** (**AOCR**)

b) [Hist.] Rarely, an alternative to **Flat Crossing** or **Square Crossing** where two **Railway** □ **Routes** cross.

Level Crossing Attendant (LXA)
[NR] A person appointed to operate a **Level Crossing** (**LC, LX**) during a **Possession** or to supervise a **Temporary Level Crossing**.

Level Crossing Barriers
[Sig.] Booms hinged at their outer ends allowing them to be lowered across the full width of the highway to prevent the passage of road traffic during the passage of **Trains**. See **Full Barriers**, **Half Barriers**. See also **Level Crossing** (**LC, LX**), **Level Crossing Gates**. Sometimes shortened to **Barriers**.

Level Crossing Box
[Sig.] A small **Signal Box** (**SB**) provided for the express purpose of controlling a **Level Crossing** (**LC, LX**) and the associated **Signalling**. Also **Gate Box**.

Level Crossing Gates
[Sig.] Gates hinged at their outer ends allowing them to be swung across the full width of the highway to prevent the passage of road traffic during the passage of **Trains**. See also **Level Crossing** (**LC, LX**).

Level Crossing Ground Plan
[Sig.] A dimensioned scale plan showing the arrangement of all equipment, services and associated features in the area of a **Level Crossing** (**LC, LX**), and the details necessary for engineering, operating and statutory requirements.

Level Crossing Keeper
[Ops.] A person (other than a **Signaller**) who operates a **Level Crossing** (**LC, LX**) from a position near the **Crossing**.

Level Crossing Order
A statutory instrument made under the **Level Crossings Act 1983** (and earlier Acts) describing in detail the arrangement of and method of operation and control to be employed at a particular **Level Crossing** (**LC, LX**).

Level Crossing Panel
A pre-fabricated unit which, with other units, forms a **Level Crossing Surface** suitable to carry road traffic **at Grade** over the **Railway**. See also **Gauge Panel**.

Level Crossing Predictor
[Sig.] A system which uses the position and speed of an approaching **Train** to determine when to activate the **Level Crossing Protection System**.

Level Crossing Protection System
[Sig.] The means by which the method of operation of a **Level Crossing** (**LC, LX**) is activated, either manually or automatically by an approaching **Train**.

Level Crossing Surface
The construction that permits both highway traffic and **Trains** to cross paths in the same plane. Typically this takes the form of heavy duty rubber panels which fit between the **Rails** and between the **Cess Rails** and an edge beam, creating a flat surface with appropriate **Flangeways** at the same level as the **Rail Crown**. See alo **Level Crossing Panel**.

Level Crossing Warning Sign
[Sig.] An alternative for **Advance Warning Board** (**AWB**).

Level Crossings Act 1983 (LCA)
An act which attempted to regularise the various statutes relating to **Level Crossings** (**LC, LX**) and introduced the **Level Crossing Order** as a way of recording the arrangements at each **Level Crossing** so covered. Unless upgraded or modified since 1983, a **Level Crossing** may not have an Order.

Level Difference
[PW] The difference in vertical level between either the **Low Rails** of two adjacent **Tracks** or adjacent **Running Rails** of adjacent **Tracks**. Also **Differences**. See also **Plane of the Rails**, **Track Stagger**.

Level of Service
See Fruin, Fruin Level of Service, Fruin LOS.

Level One Exceedence (L1)
[NR PW] A **Track Geometry** fault requiring attention, but not urgently.

Level Survey
[PW] To carry out a survey of the vertical position of the **Track** at regular intervals. Sometimes shortened to **Levelling**.

Level Three
[NR] Formerly Global Crossing, The organisation that manages the Extension Trunk Dialling (**ETD**) telephone network.

Level Track
a) A section of **Track** that has no **Gradient**
b) Rarely, a section of Track that has no **Cant**.

Level Two Exceedence (L2)
[NR PW] A **Track Geometry** fault requiring urgent attention.

Levelling
A common contraction of **Level Survey**.

Lever
[Sig.] The device used in **Mechanical Signalling** to operate **Points** (**Switches**) and **Signals**. Levers are assembled, together with an **Interlocking** system, to make **Lever Frames**. Levers are painted to assist in differentiation. Standard colours are:

Acceptance	Red upper, brown lower
Asking Lever	Green
Barriers	Brown
Stop Signal	Red
Detonator Placer	White with black chevrons
Direction Lever	Blue upper, brown lower
Distant Signal	Yellow
Facing Point Lock	Blue
King Lever	Brown and white stripes
Lever Worked to Maintain Locking	White upper, appropriate colour lower
Points / Switches	Black
Spare Lever	White

Other local colour schemes exist, normally retained from **Pre-Grouping** times.

Lever Badge
[Sig.] An alternative term for a **Lever Plate**, **Lever Nomenclature Plate**. Also **Lever Tablet**, **Pull Plate**.

Lever Band
[Sig.] The curved copper drum in a **Circuit Controller**, operated by a **Mechanical Signalling** ▫ **Lever**, used to detect the **Lever** position.

Lever Collar
[Sig.] A **Reminder Appliance** specifically intended for use on a **Lever Frame**, normally consisting of a large metal device placed over the top of the **Lever**. In **Signal Boxes** (**SB**) with **Catch Handles**, the **Lever Collar** often prevents operation of the **Catch Handle** as well.

Lever Frame
[Sig.] An assembly of two or more **Levers** and an **Interlocking** system, arranged to control the **Points** and **Signals** in an area. See also **Ground Frame** (**GF**), **Mechanical Signal Box**.

Lever Lead
(*leever leed*) [Sig.] Alternative term for a **Lever Plate** or **Lever Nomenclature Plate**.

Lever Lock
[Sig.] An electrical solenoid which, when de-activated, prevents the **Signaller** moving a **Lever** in a **Lever Frame**. Often used as a supplementary form of **Interlocking** in Mechanical **Signal Boxes**, where alterations to the **Locking Slides**, **Tappets** or **Tumblers** caused by **Remodelling** would be prohibitively expensive.

Lever Nomenclature Plate

Lever Plate
[Sig.] A plate fixed to a **Lever** describing the function of the **Lever**, together with the **Order of Pulling** details. Also **Lever Badge**, **Lever Lead**, **Lever Tablet**, **Pull Plate**. See also **Switch Plate**.

Lever Tablet
[Sig.] An alternative term for a **Lever Plate**, **Lever Nomenclature Plate**. Also **Lever Badge**, **Pull Plate**.

Lever Worked to Maintain Locking
[Sig.] A **Lever** not controlling any **Signalling Function** but remaining connected to the **Mechanical Locking**. It is not a **Spare Lever**.

Lewisham Accident
On the 4th of December 1957 an **Express Train** driver missed both a **Double Yellow Aspect** and **Single Yellow Aspect** in thick **Fog** and collided with a **Commuter Train** which was stopped under an **Intersection Bridge** (**IB**). The collision demolished the **Piers** and brought the huge **Bridge** down on the wreckage. 90 died and 175 were injured.

LFC
See **Leaf Fall Contamination**. See also **Leaf Fall Season**.

LFPR
Lift Failure Powered Recovery.

LGRI1
Ladbroke Grove Rail Inquiry Part 1.

LGRI2
Ladbroke Grove Rail Inquiry Part 2.

LGS
Leaf Guard System.

LGT
See **Longitudinal Timber**.

LGV
a) Laser Gauging Vehicle
b) Ligne Grande Vitesse: a French High Speed Line.

LHCS
See **Locomotive Hauled Coaching Stock**.

LHCV
Locomotive Hauled Coaching Vehicle; see **Locomotive Hauled Coaching Stock** (**LHCS**).

LHPW
See Left Hand Parallel Wing.

LHR
See Left Hand Rail.

LHS
a) See **Left Hand Splice**
b) See **Left Hand Side**
c) **Locomotive Holding Siding**.

LHSC
See **Left Hand Switch Closed**.

LHTO
See **Left Hand Turnout**.

LICB
Lasting **I**nfrastructure **C**ost **B**enchmarking

LICC
Local **I**nformation **C**ontrol **C**entre

Licensed Operator
[NR] A company or organisation granted a licence by the **Office of Rail Regulation** (**ORR**) to operate **Trains** and **Rail Vehicles** on the **Track**, under the terms and conditions defined by the ORR.

Lichfield Trent Valley Accident
On 1st January 1946 at 18:58, a **Train** of fish **Vans** ran at speed into the rear of a stationary **Local Passenger Train**, killing 20 and injuring 30. The **Passenger Train** was standing in the **Station** on the **Up Slow** □ **Line** when the fish Train (which should have continued along the **Up Fast**) was incorrectly diverted onto the Up Slow. This happened because the **Depression Bar** which operated the **Facing Point Lock** was fouled by frozen **Ballast**, leading the **Signaller** to believe that he had returned the **Crossover** to Normal. In fact, the Facing Point Lock had prevented this, and the Crossover was still **Reversed**.

LIDAR
Light **D**irection **a**nd **R**anging (a surveying tool).

LIFE
London **I**nternational **F**reight **E**xchange.

Lifeguards
[TRS] Heavy metal brackets fitted vertically immediately in front of the **Leading End** wheels of a **Rail Vehicle**, one over each **Rail**. Their purpose is to deflect small objects away from the path of the wheels. See also **Obstacle Deflector, Policeman Irons**.

LIFT
London **I**nternational **F**reight **T**erminal.

Lift Bridge
[Civ.] A type of **Movable Bridge**, an **Underbridge** (**UB**) with a centre section that is lifted vertically to increase the headroom under the **Bridge** and allow (generally) ships to pass. See also **Bascule Bridge, Swing Bridge**.

Lift Fishplate
[PW] A **Fishplate** used to join two **Rails** of identical original **Rail Section** but of different Rail **Depths** together. Also **Cranked Fishplate, Stepped Fishplate, Jump Fishplate**.

Lifted Line
A **Track** or **Line** where the **Permanent Way** (**PW**) has been removed.

Lifting
[PW] The activity of making vertical adjustments to the **Track**, either by hand or mechanical means. The manual activity is most commonly called **Lifting and Packing**. The term is also prefixed according to what form of **Lifts** are being made; see **Design Lifts, Maintenance Lifts**.

Lifting and Packing
[PW] The action of raising the **Track** to its designed level and adding **Ballast** beneath the **Sleepers**. The term is normally associated with a manual operation involving Ratchet **Jacks** and **Shovels**, but can include **Tamping**.

Lifting on Top
[PW] The action of **Lifting** the **Track** out of and onto the available **Ballast**. See also **Lifting Through**.

Lifting Scheme
[PW] A local redesign of the vertical **Track** position, generally undertaken to remove an irregularity (see **Slack, Swag**) or to provide more **Ballast** under the Track.

Lifting the Protection
The act of removing **Detonators** and the **Possession Limit Board** (**PLB**) in order for a train to exit or enter an **Engineer's Possession**.

Lifting Through
[PW] The action of **Lifting** □ **Track** that has been flooded with **Ballast**, often up to **Rail Level**, so that it has a more normal **Ballast Profile**.

Lifts
[PW] The vertical adjustments required to bring a **Track** up to a particular **Design Level** or **Longitudinal Section**. Whilst **Lift** is used both in the positive and negative sense, i.e. minus 20mm Lift, the opposite is **Lowerings**.

Ligaments
[PW] The curved part of the **Stretcher Bar Bracket** between the **Switch Rail** and the **Stretcher Bar** assembly.

Light
Describing a **Locomotive** that is not hauling or **Propelling** any other vehicles. See **Light Locomotive**.

Light Diesel (LD)
A **Light Locomotive** that is also a **Diesel Locomotive**.

Light Duty Men
[BR] Collective term for many of the **Chainmen**, van drivers, messengers, timekeepers, **TOPS** clerks and **Nippers**, etc., employed by **British Railways** (**BR**). The relatively high incidence of back injuries, deafness, worsening eyesight and occasional lost fingers led to many men being unfit to continue working on the **Track**. Rather than a costly pensioning-off, they were allocated lighter duties. Also colloquially referred to as **Green Carded**.

Light Electric (LE)
[Ops.] Specifically, a **Light Locomotive** utilising **Electric Traction**.

Light Emitting Diode Signal
See **LED Signal**.

Light Engine (LE)
Alternative to **Light Locomotive**.

Light Loco
Light Locomotive
[Ops.] Any self-contained **Locomotive** not coupled to, hauling or **Propelling** another vehicle.. See **Light Diesel (LD)**, **Light Electric (LE)**, **Light Engine (LE)**, **Light Steam**.

Light Maintenance (LM)
The collective term for such activities as cleaning, superficial repair and adjustment. See also **Heavy Maintenance (HM)**.

Light Maintenance Depot (LMD)
A facility in which **Locomotives**, **Coaches** and **Multiple Unit Trains** receive basic maintenance attention, such as lubrication, topping up of battery electrolyte levels and replacement glazing. See also **Diesel Maintenance Depot (DMD)**, **Electric Maintenance Depot (EMD)**, **Electric Traction Depot (ETD)**, **Traction Maintenance Depot (TMD)**.

Light Rail (LR)
A collective term for **Tramways** and similar, used to distinguish them from **Heavy Rail (HR)**.

Light Railway
A **Railway** operated within the provisions of the **Light Railways Act 1896**, incorporating restrictions on speed and construction of vehicles and relaxations on the requirements for **Signalling**.

Light Railways Act 1896
Legislation enacted to allow the construction of **Railways** that did not meet the standards required for **Main Line Railways**, subject to limits on **Maximum Axle Load** and **Permissible Speed (PS)**. It allowed for reduced **Signalling** provision and lighter vehicle construction, both aimed at improving competitiveness with road vehicles.

Light Rapid Transit (LRT)
A generic term for all **Rail**-based systems optimised for the rapid mass movement of people over relatively short distances. Such systems include **Monorails** and **Tramways**.

Light Steam
[Ops.] A **Steam Locomotive** not drawing or **Propelling** a **Train**. See also **Light Locomotive**.

Lightweight Continuous Welded Rail
Lightweight CWR
[PW] **Continuous Welded Rail (CWR)** produced by:
- Cropping and Welding □ **Flat Bottom Rails (FB)** and supplementing the original **Elastic Spikes** with **Low Cost Clips (LC Clips)**. Also **Cheap and Cheerful CWR**
- Cropping and Welding **Bullhead Rails (BH)** and selectively replacing **Keys**.

Both cases require the **Ballast Shoulders** strengthening to the standard for **Concrete Sleepered** CWR together with the replacement of decayed, split or otherwise **Defective Sleepers**.

Lightweight Track
[PW] **Track** consisting of **Steel Sleepers** or **Wood Sleepers** and / or a **Rail Section** with a low value of **Pounds per Yard**.

Like for Like
Like for Like Renewal
a) [Sig.] The replacement of an item or system for an fundamentally identical one, without changing the function or operation of the item or system in any way
b) [PW] To the **Permanent Way Engineer (PWE)**, the replacement of a **Switch and Crossing Layout (S&C Layout)** with something of similar geometry or **Plain Line** with something of similar construction
c) [PW] Rarely, the replacement of **Plain Line** without alteration to its **Alignment**.

Lima
The **Phonetic Alphabet** word representing L.

LIMBO
Large **I**nvestment **M**ajor **B**usiness **O**pportunities.

Lime Stabilisation
A method of improving the strength and stiffness of clay **Formations** by adding lime. Depending on the initial and target values required, between 1% and 6% by volume of lime is added to the clay using an industrial sized rotavator. Cement can also be added later to reduce the treated layer's sensitivity to frost. Widely used in Highways construction, this method would have many applications on the **Railways** was it not for the many re-visits required over a period of weeks to apply the treatment and the cement.

Lime Street Control

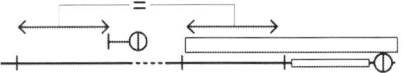

[Sig.] A **Signalling** □ **Control** that ensures that a **Train** approaching an occupied **Bay Platform** will fit. It achieves this by providing a **Measuring Track Circuit** as the **Berth Track Circuit** for the **Signal** controlling access to the **Platform**. If the **Train** fits wholly within this **Track Circuit (TC)**, and the corresponding Track Circuit in the **Platform** is **Clear**, then the **Train** is allowed to proceed.

Limestone
Limestone Ballast
[PW] A form of calcium carbonate, it is a softer and cheaper rock used for **Ballast**. Its chemical composition $CaCO_3$ renders it susceptible to chemical attack from carbon dioxide dissolved in rain (i.e. carbonic acid).

Limit of Shunt
Limit of Shunt Indicator (LOS)
[Sig.] An **Indicator** denoting the physical limit to which a **Shunt Movement** may be made where no other **Signal** exists.

Limited Clearance
[NR] An area where there is insufficient space to stand safely during the passage of **Trains** on the adjacent **Line**. These areas are normally marked by a red and white chequered **Sign**. Also **LCB**.

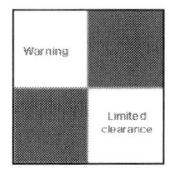

Limits of Deviation (LOD)
The boundary lines within which a proposed **Guided Busway**, **Railway**, road or **Tramway** must stay during construction. This area is determined during the Inquiry process.

Limpet (MKA, ZKA)
[NR] A 32 ton capacity **Open Wagon** used to transport **Ballast** and **Spoil**. See **Wagon Names**.

LIMRV
Linear Induction Motor Research Vehicle.

Line
a) One **Track** of many, e.g. **Down Line**
b) A group term for all the Tracks of a **Railway**, e.g. **On or About the Line**
c) An alternative term for a **Route**, e.g. The **West Coast Main Line** (**WCML**)
d) [PW] The horizontal alignment of a **Track**. See also **Hallade**, **Lining**, **Track Alignment**.

Line Blockage
[NR] The term which replaced sections **T2** and **T12** of the **Rule Book**, covering protection of personnel carrying out activities on the **Line**. Prevention of **Trains** from moving on the Line is managed by placing or maintaining **Signals** at **Danger**.

Line Blocked (LB)
[Sig.] The description of the default status of a **Block Section**, e.g. when no **Train** has been given permission to enter the Section. See also **Line Clear** (**LC**), **Train on Line** (**TOL**).

Line Breaker
A **Circuit Breaker** (**CB**) placed in a **Traction Motor** power circuit between the live **Conductor** and the greater part of the traction control system. It is normally closed to start the **Train** and remains closed all the time power is required. It is opened in response to various fault conditions and to isolate the traction system for repairs.

Line Capacity
[Ops.] The maximum practical number of **Trains per Hour** (**TPH**) that a particular section of **Line** and **Signalling System** can support

Line Clear (LC)
a) [Sig.] In **Absolute Block** (**AB**) areas, the description applied to a **Block Section** when a Train has been **Accepted** into the Section but the **Train** has not yet entered the Section. See also **Line Blocked** (**LB**), **Train on Line** (**TOL**).
b) [LUL] The safety procedure used to ensure that it is safe to work in **Tube** □ **Tunnels** during **Engineering Hours**.

Line Clear Area
[LUL] All **Lines** and the first 600mm back from each **Platform Edge** on the **Subsurface Lines** and **Tube Lines**, except:
- Non-electrified Lines
- Lines within **Depots** or **Sidings** where the **Traction Current** is normally present at all times
- **Platforms** at **Stations** fitted with **Platform Edge Doors** (**PED**) when the doors are fully closed.

Line Clear Message
[LUL] A message passed from the Track Access Controller to the Power Control Room Operator before **Traction Current** can be switched on to a Traction Current Section that is wholly or partly within the **Line Clear Area**.

Line Clear Procedure
[LUL] The safety procedure by which staff are permitted to go into the **Line Clear** area during **Engineering Hours**.

Line Clear Release
[Sig.] A **Signalling Control** in **Absolute Block** (**AB**) which prevents the **Signaller** pulling the **Lever** for the **Section Signal** until the **Line Clear** (**LC**) is received from the **Signal Box** □ **Beyond**. The Lever is released either for **One Pull** or **One Train**, see **One Train Release**.

Line Clear Verification
[NR] An enhanced safety procedure intended to verify that a **Section** of **Line** is **Clear** after **Engineering Work** where Axle Counters are present. It consists of an independent cross-check of the number of vehicles the **Person in Charge of Possession** (**PICOP**) and **Engineering Supervisor** (**ES**) have recorded as entering and leaving a **Worksite**.

Line Controller
[LUL] The post responsible for co-ordinating the day to day working of part of the system.

Line Guard
[Elec.] A short length of protective conductive covering fitted to an **Overhead Line Conductor** (**OLC**) to reduce the damage caused by the fitting and removal of **Local Earths**.

Line Interference Monitor (LIM)
[TRS] A system fitted to some **Classes** of **Electric Train** which monitors the **Train's** connection to the **Traction Power** system and shut the Train down if frequencies which could affect **Signalling Equipment** are detected.

Line Isolating Unit (LIU)
A 1:1 transformer used to provide electricial isolation between two parts of a circuit.

Line Light
[TRS] A lamp placed in the **Driving Cabs** of an **Electric Locomotive** or **Electric Multiple Unit** (**EMU**) that shows the driver that the **Traction Supply Current** is present.

Line Loss
[Elec.] The reduction in voltage (and consequently in power transmitted) over the length of a section of **Overhead Line**, caused by the resistance of the **Conductor**.

Line Name
See **Track Name**.

Line of Sight (LOS)
[Ops.] A method of working **Trains** or **Trams** in which the driver observes the **Line** □ **Beyond** and controls the speed of the Train appropriately. Often employed by **Tramway** systems in **Street Running** areas, where speeds are lower.

Line Safe Area
[LUL] See **Line Clear Area**.

Line Safe Message
[LUL] A message passed from the Track Access Controller to the Power Control Room Operator before **Traction Current** can be switched on to a **Traction Current Section** that is wholly within the **Line Safe Area**.

Line Side
See **Lineside**.

Line Speed
See **Permissible Speed** (PS). See also **Linespeed**.

Line Standard
[RT Obs.] Common contraction of **Railtrack Line Standard** (RLS), documents latterly known as **Railtrack Company Standards** (RCS) and (effectively) now called **Network Rail Company Standards** (NRCS). See also **Civil Engineering Handbooks**.

Linear Asset Decision Support (LADS)
[NR PW] An interactive tool that aids decision making by bringing together **Age of Road** data, Track Geometry and **Track Quality** outputs and intervention histories to provide asset deterioration rates and identify recurring issues.

Lined Arch
See **Clad Arch**.

Linemen's Boards
[Obs.] Small, distinctly shaped and coloured boards bearing either the letter S (for signal technician) or T (for telegraph technician) displayed at the end of a signal box not equipped with speaking telegraph circuits to allow the signaller to indicate the failure of the signal and telegraph equipment. The drivers of passing trains were required to observe these indicators and to pass on to the appropriate department any reported instances of incorrect equipment at their next scheduled calling point. Their use was largely overtaken by the general provision of telephones during the early years of the 20th century.

Line-of-Sight Distance
The straight-line distance from the driver's eyes to a **Signal** or **Element**.

Liners
a) See **Fishplate Insulations**. Also **Shells**
b) [PW] Thin metal shims inserted between the vertical face of a **Chair** and the **Key** securing a **Bullhead Rail** to compensate for wear
c) See **Bogie Centre Pivot Liner**.

Lineside
a) [NR] Defined in the **Rule Book** as 'You are on the Lineside if you are within the **Railway Boundary** but greater than 3m away from the **Nearest Running Rail** and you can be seen by the driver of an **Approaching Train**'
b) [Col.] On **Railway Land** but beyond the **Ballast Shoulder**.

Lineside Fencing
a) [Hist.] The fence the **Railway Administration** is obliged to provide under the provisions of the **Railway Clauses (Consolidation) Act 1845** at or inside the boundary of its property. It is worthwhile to note that the actual fence (or wall) is often up to a **Yard** inside the actual boundary, to allow the fence or wall to be maintained from within **Railway** property. Originally, such a fence was required only to prevent Railway employees straying off the Railway, and cattle from straying onto the Railway.
b) Subsequent legislation, most notably the Health and Safety at Work Act (**HASAW**), has modified this to place the onus for the security of the fence against trespassers onto the Railway Administrations.

Lineside Security
a) The **Maintenance** and integrity of the **Lineside Fencing**, gates, etc.
b) The requirement to ensure that tools, plant and materials left **On the Lineside** are secured to prevent vandals placing them on the **Line**.

Lineside Signs
The various **Indicators** and information **Signs** provided along the **Railway**. These include:
- Cab Secure Radio (CSR) Signs
- Coasting Boards
- Countdown Markers
- Gradient Posts
- Global System for Mobile Communication – Railways (GSMR) Signs
- Junction Name Boards
- Kilometre Posts
- Limited Clearance Signs
- Mileposts
- National Radio Network (NRN) Signs
- Neutral Section (NS) Signs
- No Refuges Signs
- Special Speed Restriction Boards (SSRB)
- Speed Indicators (SI)
- Warning Indicators (WI)
- Whistle Boards.

Lineside Spares
[PW] Large and difficult to transport **Track** components (such as **Crossings**, **Sleepers** and **Switch Half Sets**) stored adjacent to the Track at key locations for use as replacements in an emergency.

Lineside Telephone
[Tel.] A Telephone provided within the boundary of the **Railway**, but that is not a **Signal Post Telephone** (SPT). See also **Operational Telephone**.

Linespeed
a) [NR Obs.] The maximum speed at which **Trains** may run when not subject to any other restriction. Because all limits on speed are published and denoted by signs, this term no longer has a formal usage in this sense; see Permissible **Speed** (PS).
b) [NR Col., IÉ] the maximum speed of Trains at a particular location.
See also **Enhanced Permissible Speed** (EPS).

ELLIS' BRITISH RAILWAY ENGINEERING ENCYCLOPÆDIA

Linespeed Handback
[PW] The giving up of a **Possession** without the imposition of any **Emergency Speed Restrictions** (**ESR**) or **Temporary Speed Restrictions** (**TSR**). Normally used in context with **Track Renewals** work to mean a site that has been **Tamped** and consolidated by a **Dynamic Track Stabiliser** (**DTS**) to achieve a **Track Geometry** fit for the published **Permissible Speed** (**PS**) or **Enhanced Permissible Speed** (**EPS**).

Linespeed Improvement (LSI)
A scheme that proposes to increase the **Permissible Speed** (**PS**), **Differential Permissible Speed**, or both, over a section of **Line**. This kind of scheme should not be confused with a **Journey Time Improvement** (**JTI**) scheme.

Ling (ZCO)
An **Open Wagon** used to transport **Ballast** and **Sleepers**. See **Wagon Names**.

Lining
[PW] The action of moving a **Track** to the correct lateral position relative to fixed datums, or to smooth out **Alignment** irregularities using a **Tamper** or other means. See **Automatic Lining Control** (**ALC**), **Automatic Track Alignment** (**ATA**), **Automatic Track and Top Alignment** (**ATTA**), **Curve Realignment**, **Four Point Lining**, **GVA**, **Hallade**, **Laser Lining**, **Sixfooting**, **Track Machine Guidance** (**TMG**).

Lining Chord

Lining Wire
[PW] The steel **Wire** running from the front to the back of a **Tamping and Lining Machine** (**Tamper**), which is used by the machine to calculate the **Slues** necessary to remove the more severe **Alignment Errors** from the **Track**. The front end of this **Wire** can normally be offset to the left or right by measured amounts, allowing the machine to implement **Design Slews**. See **Four Point Lining**, **Three Point Lining**.

Link
a) [Obs.] Imperial unit of length used on some older drawings. 100 Links is one **Chain**, making one Link approximately equal to 7.92 inches or 201.2mm
b) [Ops.] An alternative for the **Diagram** for a driver.

Link and Pin Suspension
[TRS] A suspension arrangement in which the ends of the springs are attached to short link bars, in turn attached to downward projections on the chassis. The ends of the arms attached to the springs are free to swing, allowing the spring to flex.

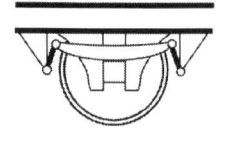

Link-up
a) See **Railway Industry Supplier Qualification Scheme** (**RISQS**)
b) [Col.] The former UK **Rail Industry** supplier qualification scheme, providing a single common registration, qualification and audit process for suppliers, which is then shared by the UK Rail Industry
c) [TRS] To adjust the cut-off or duration of admission of steam to the cylinders of a **Steam Locomotive**, especially when starting from rest or climbing long, steep gradients.

LINX
(Tradename) Layered Information Network Exchange.

LIP
Locomotive Inspection Point.

Lipped Pad
[PW] A **Rail Pad** shaped to provide retaining strips that locate along the transverse edges of the **Bearers** or **Baseplates**, intended to restrict movement of the **Pad** in the direction of the longitudinal axis of the **Rail**.

Lipping 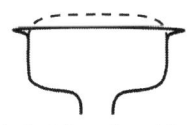
[PW] A description of the effect on a **Running Edge** (**RE**) being subjected to the rolling action by passing **Wheelsets**, causing plastic deformation of the **Rail Head**. The symptom of this is thin strips of metal developing laterally from the Running Edge. Eventually these strips break away. The phenomenon also occurs longitudinally at the **Rail Ends** associated with **Fishplated Rail Joints**. A related problem is **Mushrooming**. See also **Plastic Deformation of the Rail Head**, **Tongue Lipping**.

LISN
[LUL] Line Impedance Stabilisation Network.

Lit
See **Alight**.

Little Red Cable, the
[LUL] the strapline of the campaign to educate **Trackworkers** about the importance of the **Transmission Based Train Control** (**TBTC**) cable loops laid in the **Fourfoot** on the **Jubilee Line**.

Littleboy
[LUL] A (typically wooden) device used to ensure that dimensions are accurately related to the **Running Edge** (**RE**). Also **Rail Clip**. Named after its inventor. See also **Rail Shoe**.

LIU
See **Line Isolating Unit**.

Live
Connected to an electrical supply and being at an electrical potential higher than that of the surroundings. See also **Alive**.

Live Discharge Toilet
[TRS] A toilet system that discharges raw effluent onto the **Track**. This system is being replaced by **Controlled Emission Toilets** (**CET**) on all new **Stock**. However, many older **Passenger** vehicles will still have Live Discharge Toilet systems for some years, so it is vitally important to **Turn Your Back on Passing Trains** and to wash one's hands thoroughly after work.

Live Drop Vertical (LDV)
[Elec.] A component in some arrangements of **Overhead Line Equipment** (**OLE**), consisting of a near-vertical rigid tube with an **Insulator** at its upper end. The tube is suspended by this Insulator, and is restrained laterally by a **Cross Span Wire** at its lower extremity. The **Registration Arm** and **Catenary Wire** are then fixed to the tube itself. See **Head Span**, **Portal Structure**.

Live Load
[Civ.] The load imposed on a **Bridge** or **Structure** by pedestrians, vehicles and other moving objects. See also **Dead Load**.

Live Rail
See **Conductor Rail**.

Lizard
(Tradename) A type of portable electromagnetic array detector used in the detection and measurement of **Rail Defects** such as surface cracking. Manufactured by Newt International Limited.

LJU
[Tel.] Line Jack Unit.

LKT
An abbreviation for **Lookout**. Also LO, L/O.

LL
Low Level, See **Track Names**.

Llantarnum Type Bridge
[NR] A variety of standard **Bridge**. See **Western Region Box Girder Bridge**.

LLAU
Limit of Land to be Acquired or Used. See **Transport and Works Act** (**TWA**). See also **Limits of Deviation** (**LOD**).

LLFA
Lead Local Flood Authority.

LLPA
[Tel.] Long Lead Public Address.

LM
a) See **London Midland Region**
b) See **Light Maintenance**
c) The **ATOC** code for **London Midland**.

LM&SR
[Hist.] An alternative for the **LMSR**.

LMA
[Sig.] Limit of Movement Authority. See also **Limit of Shunt** (**LOS**).

LMC
Lower Machine Chamber.

LMD
See **Light Maintenance Depot**.

LMDSM
Light Maintenance Depot Stewardship Measure.

LMR
a) Lift Machine Room
b) See **London Midland Region**.

LMSR
[Hist.] **London Midland & Scottish Railway**, one of the **Big Four** following **Grouping**. Also **LM&SR**.

LMW
Load Measuring Wheelset.

LN
Leeds Northern.

LNER
[Hist.] **London North Eastern Railway**, one of the **Big Four** following **Grouping**.

LNEZ
London North East Zone. See **Railtrack** (**RT**).

LNSD
See **Low Negative Shoe Detector**.

LNW
London North West.

LNWR
[Hist.] The **Pre-Grouping** London North Western Railway. Also **L&NWR**.

LO
a) An abbreviation of **Lookout**
b) The **ATOC** code for **London Overground**.

LOA
See **Length Over All**.

Load Examination
Load Examined
[Ops.] A certificate that must be present on every **Rail Vehicle** carrying a loose load (such as a load strapped to a flat **Wagon**) before the **Train** can enter **Traffic**.

Load Examiner
[Ops.] A member of staff who has been passed competent to sign **Load Examination** labels and assess **Traffic** as fit to travel.

Load Factor
[Ops.]
a) The fraction of a **Freight Vehicle's** payload capacity taken up by its payload
b) The amount of seats occupied on a **Train** service expressed as a percentage of total seats available. See also **Pixie**, **PIXC**.

Loader Wagon
[CT] In the **Channel Tunnel** system, a **Shuttle Wagon** used to load either lorries or **Passenger** carrying road vehicles. Vehicles are not carried on it during transit.

Loadhaul
[Hist.] A **Freight Operating Unit** (**FOU**) set up under **Privatisation**, and then bought and merged with the others (**Mainline** and **Transrail**) plus the postal carrier **Rail Express Systems** (**RES**) to form the **Freight Operating Company** (**FOC**) □ **English Welsh and Scottish Railways** (**EWS**). See DB Schenker Rail (UK) Ltd.

Loading / Unloading Indicators
[Sig.] A variety of **Position Light Signal** (**PLS**) used to control the movement of **Merry-go-Round** (**MGR**) and other similar **Trains** during loading and unloading operations. The **Signals** are normally operated by the person in charge of the loading or unloading operation. Also called **Creep Signals**, **Toton Signals**.

- ● ● ● Draw ahead
- ● ● ● Slow down
- ● ● ● Reverse
- ● ● ● Stop

Loading Dock
A **Platform** used for the loading and unloading of **Goods** or livestock to and from **Trains**. See also **Carriage Dock**, **Cattle Dock**, Fish Dock, **Horse Dock**, **Parcels Dock**.

Loading Gauge
Strictly, the set of dimensions that a load on a **Rail Vehicle** must be within in order to run in normal **Traffic**. Any load that cannot be made to fit is classed as **Out of Gauge** (**OOG**), and special arrangements for its passage must be made. It is also used incorrectly as an alternative to **Structure Gauge**.

Loading Slip
[Ops.] A document that is given to the driver providing details of what **Train** loading has taken place.

Lobster (ZVV)
[NR] An **Engineer's** support **Van**. See **Wagon Names**.

Loc.

Loc. Case
(*loke*) A common contraction of **Location** and **Location Case**.

Local
a) Pertaining to immediately adjacent equipment or to a single **Rail Vehicle**
b) See **Local Passenger Train**
c) See **Local Line**.

Local Control
[Sig.] The manual operation of an **Automatic Level Crossing**, **CCTV Level Crossing** or **Remotely Controlled Manned Level Crossing** from a point adjacent to the **Level Crossing**. The term is normally applied when this method of operation is unusual.

Local Control Unit (LCU)
[Sig.] The cabinet located adjacent to an **Automatic Level Crossing**, **CCTV Level Crossing** or **Remotely Controlled Manned Level Crossing** that allows the **Level Crossing** (**LC**, **LX**) to be operated manually from a point adjacent to the **Crossing**.

Local Door
[TRS] On a **Multiple Unit Train**, a door that can be opened independently from all the others, allowing the **Guard** or **Train Manager** to **Alight** or **Board** as part of their duties. Generally, any door can be controlled as a **Local Door**.

Local Earth
[Elec.] A heavy duty insulated cable with clamps at each end that is fitted between **Isolated** □ **Overhead Line Equipment** (**OLE**) and a **Designated Earthing Point** (**DEP**) in order to ensure that the conductors remain safe under all conditions. See **Short Earth**, **Long Earth**.

Local Emergency Power Supply (LEPS)
[LUL] A supply derived from a source local to the point of utilisation and feeds equipment provided to guarantee the safety of **Passengers** and staff. LEPS normally uses batteries to Provide the basic needs for the evacuation of **Station** areas.

Local Instructions
Documents issued by the relevant **Infrastructure Controller** mandating the method of operation for a particular location or circumstance. This might include a method of operation that deals with quarry blasting near the **Railway** or how a **Signaller** should deal with a **Train** that is longer than the **Siding** it is supposed to access.

Local Knowledge
Knowledge that is specific to a defined area of the **Railway** that supplements the universal information contained in national and regional publications. Local Knowledge includes an understanding of relevant **Local Instructions** and familiarisation with the position and, where necessary, the operation of equipment in that area.

Local Line
On a **Multiple Track Railway**, the **Local Lines** are normally the ones utilised for **All Stations** □ **Passenger Trains** or **Stopping Passenger Trains**, and therefore have a nominal status lower than a **Relief Line** or **Slow Line**.

Local Panel
[Sig.] A subsidiary control panel (often provided within a **Remote Interlocking**) that allows control of the **Signalling System** in an emergency. In **Solid State Interlocking** (**SSI**) systems, the analogous provision is the **Technician's Terminal**.

Local Passenger Train

Local Train
[Ops.] A **Passenger Train** timetabled to call at **All Stations** or most **Stations** on a **Route**. Also **Stopping Train**. See also **Express Passenger Train**, **Parliamentary Train**, **Parly**, **Semi-fast Passenger Train**.

Local Working Instructions
Instructions issued by the operator of a facility regarding the safe operation of that facility.

Locally Controlled Manned Level Crossing (LC)
The full title for a **Level Crossing** (**LC**, **LX**) operated by a **Signaller** or **Crossing Keeper** from a **Signal Box** (**SB**) or **Crossing Box** adjacent to the **Level Crossing**. Such installations generally have **Full Barriers** or **Gates**.

Location (Loc.)
[Sig.]
a) A site at the **Lineside** where one or more **Location Cases** are placed
b) [Col.] one **Location Case**.

Location Area Plan
Loc. Area Plan
(*loke air-rea plan*) [Sig.] A scale layout drawing, similar to a **Signalling Plan**, showing every **Location**, their identities, sizes and the areas to which the equipment in them relates,

Location Case (Loc. Case)
[Sig.] A small steel cabinet placed at the **Lineside** housing power supplies and other equipment related to **Signals**, **Track Circuits** and **Telecommunications**. See also **Relocatable Equipment Building** (**REB**), **Superlocs** and **WILH**.

Location Case Platform
[Sig.] A prefabricated steel (previously wood and concrete) platform used to provide a level base for **Location Cases** in **Cuttings** and on **Embankments**. A Location Case Platform intended for just one Location Case is a **Single Location Case Platform** (**SLC Platform**). See also **Firebox**.

LOCIP
(*low-sip*) London Overground Capacity Improvement Programme.

Lock
[Sig.]
a) An **Interlocking Function** in a **Mechanical Interlocking** which holds a **Lever** in the **Normal** position when other conflicting **Levers** are **Reverse**. See also **Backlock**, **Conditional Locking**
b) The opposite of **Release**.

Lock and Block
[Sig. Col.] Shorthand for the two cornerstones of safe signalling practice; **Interlocking** and **Block Signalling**.

Lock Slide
[Sig.] That part of a **Clamp Lock** □ **Point** mechanism which carries out the **Locking** and operation of the **Switches**.

Lock Stretcher
Lock Stretcher Bar
[Sig.] The **Stretcher Bar** located at the **Switch Toe** which forms part of the **Facing Point Lock** (**FPL**) mechanism fitted to **Facing Points** in areas with **Mechanical Signalling**. See also **First Permanent Way Stretcher Bar**, **First Signalling Stretcher Bar**.

Lock, Block and Brake
[Hist. Col.] The battle cry of the **Board of Trade** between 1860 and 1889. It refers to the adoption of **Interlocking** of **Points** and **Signals**, **Block Working** and the fitting of **Automatic Brakes**. Despite numerous fatal accidents the Board of Trade were powerless to force the Companies to comply. It took the **Armagh Accident** to prompt the **Regulation of Railways Act 1889**, 79 days later, before such provisions were made mandatory.

Locke, Joseph
(1805-1860), born near Sheffield. Apprenticed to **George Stephenson**, Locke worked on the Stockton & Darlington and Liverpool & Manchester **Railways**. He was appointed joint Chief Engineer with Stephenson on the Grand Junction; however Stephenson later resigned leaving Locke to finish the job. Locke went on to pursue a brilliant civil engineering career all over Europe.

Locked
[Sig.]
a) The term describing a **Signalling Function** that is being prevented from changing state by another part of the **Signalling System**. See also **Lock**, **Release**
b) Of a **Sub-Route** or **Sub-Overlap**, meaning that the relevant item is in use.

Locked Wheel Ramp
[PW] A device fitted to the **Switch Rail** to guard against possible **Derailment** and damage from a **False Flange** on a **Rail Wheel**.

Locking
See **Mechanical Locking**.

Locking Actuator
[TRS] A component within the **Tilt Actuator** system of a **Tilting Train** that physically locks, upon activation, the **Tilt System** out of use with the vehicle **Carbody** in the centre upright position relative to the **Bogies**.

Locking Bar
[Sig.]
a) A type of **Depression Bar** fitted at **Facing Points** which **Locks** the **Facing Point Lock** when a **Train** is present, now generally obsolete
b) An alternative for **Locking Slide**.

Locking Chart
[Sig.] A pictorial representation of the **Interlocking** elements such as **Dogs**, **Locking Slides** and **Tappets** that are required to make a particular **Mechanical Interlocking**. Also **Dog Chart**, **Mechanical Locking Chart**.

Locking Fitter
[Sig.] A technician competent to carry out repairs and alterations to **Mechanical Signalling** equipment, particularly **Interlockings**. See also **Locking Frame**, **Locking Shelf**, **Locking Slides**, **Mechanical Locking**.

Locking Frame
[Sig.] In certain **Mechanical Signal Boxes**, a vertical arrangement of **Locking Slides**, beneath the **Levers** and in the **Locking Room**.

ELLIS' BRITISH RAILWAY ENGINEERING ENCYCLOPÆDIA

Locking Hook
[TRS] Part of a **Door Lock Assembly** used to retain a **Door Leaf Pin** in order to lock the door

Locking Level
[Sig.] The **Interlocking** level; the one at which the **Controls** between various **Signalling Functions** must be met before a **Route** can be **Set**.

Locking Level Release
[Sig.] The level at which the **Interlocking** □ **Releases** a **Route**, either by **Trains** □ **Clearing** □ **Track Circuits** (**TC**) or by Trains being **Timed to a Stand** on a particular **Track Circuit**. See also **Route Locking**.

Locking Room
[Sig.] The space below the **Operating Floor** of certain Mechanical **Signal Boxes** that contains the **Interlocking**. See also **Locking Frame**, **Locking Shelf**, **Locking Slides**, **Mechanical Locking**.

Locking Shelf
[Sig.] The horizontal structure in certain **Mechanical Signal Boxes**, generally located behind the **Levers** that supports the **Locking Tray**. See also **Locking Frame**.

Locking Slides
[Sig.] In **Mechanical Signal Boxes**, the long horizontal bars, located behind the **Levers** on a **Locking Shelf** or below the Levers in a **Locking Frame**, that forms the **Mechanical Locking** between the Levers. The Levers each move one or more Locking Slides, each of which has an arrangement of notches cut in it. Each Lever also has a **Tappet** attached to it, which engages with the Locking Slides. Unless all the appropriate notches are aligned with the Tappet, The Lever cannot be moved. A complex layout may require hundreds of Locking Slides. Also known as **Locking Bars**. See also **Interlocking**.

Locking Tray
[Sig.] In a **Mechanical Interlocking**, a metal construction with lateral channels containing the **Locking Slides**, **Dogs** and **Nibs**, and **Races** containing the **Tappets**. All this is often supported on a **Locking Shelf**.

Lockington Accident
On the 26th of July 1986 a van ignored the flashing stop lights at Lockington **Automatic Open Crossing Remotely Monitored** (**AOCR**) and was struck by a four-**Car** □ **Diesel Multiple Unit** (**DMU**). The van was destroyed and the **Train** □ **Derailed**. Nine died and 59 were injured. This accident prompted the **Stott Report** and the wide-scale conversion of AOCR **Level Crossings**.

Lockout

Lockout System
[Sig.] A system which allows a person requiring access to the **Track** to provide personal protection by placing restrictions on the permissible **Routes** for **Trains**. One example is a **Patroller's Lockout Device** (**PLOD**), typically used to bar Trains running in the **Wrong Direction** on a **Reversible Line**.

Lockspike
[PW] A folded steel pin used to secure **Pan 5** and **Pan 8 Baseplates** to **Wood Sleepers**. Also known as **Hairpins**, after their shape. Devised in the USA in 1950 by Arthur Corbus.

Loco
(*low-ko*) [Col.] A common contraction of **Locomotive**.

LOCO
(Tradename) <u>Lo</u>w <u>Co</u>st Integrated Navigation System for Train Control Applications, a **Train Control** system using GPS and inertial measurement systems.

Loco Shed
See **Locomotive Shed**.

Locomotive
[TRS] A **Rail Vehicle** specifically designed and built to pull other Rail Vehicles and for no other purpose. The source of energy to power the Locomotive may come from:
- An external source (as in an **Electric Locomotive**) or
- From a store carried with the Locomotive (as in a **Battery Locomotive**, **Diesel Locomotive**, **Fireless Locomotive**, **Gas Turbine Locomotive**, **Steam Locomotive** or **Steam Turbine Locomotive**).

All **Locomotives** are **Traction Units**, but not all Traction Units are Locomotives. See also **Diesel and Electric Locomotive Notation**, **Multiple Unit Train**, **Whyte's Notation**. Sometimes referred to colloquially as an **Engine** and shortened to **Loco**.

Locomotive Class
[TRS] All current **Locomotives** on the **National Railway Network** (**NRN**) have a two digit **Class** number, ranging from 04 to 92, although the list is not fully populated. The numbering is banded:
- 01 to 69 covers **Diesel Locomotives**
- 70 to 79 covers DC □ **Electric Locomotives**
- 80 to 99 covers **AC** Electric Locomotives.

Locomotive Engine
[Hist.] A term coined in the early days of steam **Traction** to differentiate between **Fixed Engines** or stationary engines and those able to travel under their own power along a **Railway** (now commonly shortened to **Locomotive** or **Loco**).

Locomotive Hauled
[TRS] **Passenger Coaches** and similar **Departmental Vehicles** that are normally pulled by **Locomotives**. The opposite for **Departmental Vehicles** is **Self-propelled**.

Locomotive Hauled Coaching Stock (**LHCS**)

Locomotive Hauled Set
[TRS] **Passenger Coaches** that are pulled by **Locomotives**, often travelling as a fixed **Formation**.

Locomotive Shed
A building in which **Locomotives** are constructed, stored or maintained. Sometimes shortened to **Loco Shed**.

LOD
a) <u>L</u>oss <u>o</u>f **Detection**
b) See **Limits of Deviation**.

Log Book
[LUL] A bound book in which events and decisions taken by the **Service Controller** are recorded. When a Service Controller starts duty, entries in the log book are discussed as necessary with the Controller going off duty.

LOH
See **L**ength **O**ver **H**eadstocks.

LOLER
(*low-ler*) **L**ifting **O**perations and **L**ifting **E**quipment **R**egulations 1998.

LOM
a) **L**ine **O**pen to **M**ovements. See also **Open Line**. Also **Adjacent Line Open** (**ALO**)
b) [NR] **L**ocal **O**perations **M**anager.

London
Used as geographical locator, it is the opposite of **Country**. See **Country End** (**CE**), **Country Side** (**CS**), **London End** (**LE**), **London Side** (**L/S, LS**).

London & North Eastern Railway (LNER)
[Hist.] One of the **Big Four** □ **Railway Companies** following **Grouping**.

London and Continental Railways (LCR)
[CTRL] The company originally selected by the UK Government to build and operate the **Channel Tunnel Rail Link** (**CTRL**), and own and operate the **Eurostar** train service in the UK.

London and South East Operators
[NR] Collective term for the operators of London **Commuter** and other South East of England **Train** services.

London End (LE)
Describing the end or side nearest **London**. Opposite of **Country End** (**CE**) and **Country Side** (**CS**). Commonly used in the south of England. Also **London Side** (**L/S, LS**).

London Midland
A **Train Operating Company** (**TOC**) that operates express services between London Euston, Milton Keynes and Birmingham New Street (via Northampton). **ATOC** code **LM**.

London Midland & Scottish Railway (LM&SR, LMSR)
[Hist.] One of the **Big Four** □ **Railway Companies** following **Grouping**.

London Midland Region (LMR)
[BR Hist.] One of the regional administrations under **British Railways** (**BR**). Based originally in Euston House, in 1986 it relocated to Birmingham and was responsible for the **Infrastructure** in the Birmingham, Crewe, Liverpool, Manchester, Nottingham, Preston and Watford Areas.

London Overground (LO)
(Tradename) Contraction of **London Overground Rail Operations Ltd.** (**LOROL**) and the brand name for services operated by them on behalf of **Transport for London** (**TfL**).

London Overground Rail Operations Ltd. (LOROL)
(Tradename) A **Train Operating Company** (**TOC**) which operates services between Richmond and Stratford via Willesden Junction, together with the Willesden Junction/Clapham Junction and Gospel Oak/Barking Lines. Its brand name is **London Overground**. **ATOC** code **LO**.

London Side (L/S, LS)
See **London End** (**LE**).

London Transport (LT)
[Hist.] Now **Transport for London** (**TfL**).

London Underground (LU)
See **London Underground Limited** (**LUL**).

London Underground Combined Access System (LUCAS)
[LUL] The smartcard scheme for construction and engineering workers requiring access to work on **London Underground** (**LU**) **Infrastructure**.

London Underground Limited (LUL)
[Hist.] Informally **London Underground** (**LU**), previously a wholly-owned subsidiary of **London Transport**. LUL was formed in 1985, but the system dates back to 1863. London Underground Limited serves three million **Passenger** journeys a day, with 275 **Stations** and over 408 km (253 miles) of **Route**. London Transport is now **Transport for London** (**TfL**). See also **Deep Tube Lines**, **Surface Lines**, **Tube Lines**.

London Underground Line
[LUL] A **Track** or **Line** used mostly by London Underground Limited (**LUL**) □ **Trains**. See also **Tube Line**.

Lone Working
[RB] Work being undertaken by a person **Working** alone. See also **Individual Working Alone** (**IWA**).

Long Base Versine Error
[PW] A lateral misalignment of the **Running Rail** over a length of 5m or more.

Long Bearers
[PW] An alternative term for **Long Timbers**, describing **Bearers** that run under two or more distinct **Tracks** in a **Switch and Crossing Layout** (**S&C Layout**).

Long Distance Operators
Operators of high speed, interurban **Train** services.

Long Earth
[NR] A **Local Earth** longer than 1.5m, for use at locations other than **Designated Earthing Points** (**DEP**). They have a **Pole Applied Clamp** at one end and a manual clamp at the other. They are generally coloured blue. See also **Short Earth**.

Long End
[Col.] Describing the end of a **Rail Crane** where the superstructure is furthest from the **Buffer Beam**. The opposite is **Short End**. See **Over End**.

Long Rail
[LUL PW] Any continuous **Rail** greater than 40m in length.

Long Route
[Sig.] A **Route** that comprises two or more other **Routes**.

Long Section
[PW Col.] A common contraction of **Longitudinal Section**.

Long Section Token
[Sig.] A **Token** covering more than one **Token Section**, normally found in areas using **Radio Electronic Token Block** (**RETB**).

Long Span Underline Bridge
[NR Civ.] An **Underbridge** (**UB**) with one or more **Spans** of greater than 50m.

Long Timbers
a) [Col.] A contraction of **Longitudinal Timbers**
b) [NR PW] Describing **Switch and Crossing** (**S&C**) **Timbers** that run under two or more distinct **Tracks** in a **Switch and Crossing Layout** (**S&C Layout**). Also **Long Bearers**.

Long Tom
[LUL Sig.] An older type of **Trainstop**.

Long Wavelength Corrugations
[PW] **Rail Corrugations** with a wavelength in excess of 500mm. At typical **Permissible Speeds** (**PS**) this represents a frequency of 50Hz and below.

Long Welded Rail (LWR)
[PW]
a) [NR] A **Rail** of between 120' (36.576m) and 600' (182.88m) in length produced by **Welding** together up to ten **Standard Rails**. Rails longer than 600' (182.88m) are classified as **Continuous Welded Rail** (**CWR**), and many Rails Welded together are termed a **String**
b) [LUL] Rails up to 91.4m (300') in length Welded or **Tight Jointed** together to form a single Rail with a length between 200m (655', 218 **Yards**) and 730m (798 Yards).

Long Welded Rail Destressing Key
[LUL PW] A wood **Key**, with an attached softwood block, which retains the **Bullhead Rail** within the **Chair** whilst allowing some lateral and longitudinal movement of the **Rail** during **Destressing**.

Long Welded Rail Train (LWRT, LWR Train)
A **Rake** of specially adapted **Rail Vehicles** capable of transporting up thirty-six 600' (182.88m) **Strings** of **Rail** to site and unloading them using a gantry mounted grab system and chutes. The term **Continuous Welded Rail Train** (**CWR Train**) is used interchangeably.

Long Wheelbase
[NR] Describing a **Rail Vehicle** with a **Wheelbase** of more than 8m (approximately 26' - $2^3/_4$"). See also **Short Wheelbase**.

Longitudinal Change of Section
[PW] The area of a **Cast Crossing** where the cross section changes from a box to an ordinary **Rail** and vice versa.

Longitudinal Levels
[PW] The vertical level of the **Track** measured at (generally regular) intervals along the Track.

Longitudinal Profile
[PW] The vertical profile of a short section of **Rail** measured along the **Rail Head**.

Longitudinal Section
[PW] A formal elevation drawing showing existing and proposed **Rail Levels**, **Gradients**, **Vertical Curves** (**VC**), drainage details, **Track Geometry**, **Platform** and **Structure** details. Such drawings are often drawn to compressed horizontal scales. Also **Long Section**.

Longitudinal Timber (LGT)
[PW] A **Bearer** which runs parallel to the **Rails**, instead of at right angles to them, and supports the **Baseplates** or **Chairs**. Such **Timbers** are often found on **Bridges**. Also **Long Timbers**, **Wheel Timber**.

Longlo
A **Railway** □ Telegraph Code meaning "Long **Welded Rail Train** (**LWRT**) which does not require the imposition of conditions of travel."

LONO
(*low-no*) See **Letter of No Objection**.

Lookout (LO, L/O)
A competent person whose duties are to watch for and to give an appropriate warning of **Approaching Trains** by means of whistle, **Horn** or **Lookout Operated Warning System** (**LOWS**). See also **Advanced Lookout**, **Distant Lookout**, **Intermediate Lookout**, **Site Lookout**.

Lookout Operated Warning System (LOWS)
The generic term for any system that warns staff of the approach of **Trains** that is triggered by a **Lookout**. An example is **PeeWee**. See also **Train Operated Warning System** (**TOWS**).

Lookout Warning
[NR] A **Safe System of Work** (**SSoW**) where staff are protected by receiving a warning from a **Lookout** (**LO**). See also **Equipment Warning**. These terms replace **Red Zone**, **Red Zone Working**.

Lookoutman
[Obs.] An older term for a **Lookout** (**LO, L/O**).

Loop
a) Any short length of **Track** connected to another **Line** at both ends:
• Which allows **Locomotives** to **Run Round**, or slow **Trains** to be passed by faster ones, see **Goods Loop**, **Platform Loop**
• Which allows Trains travelling in opposite directions on an otherwise **Single Line** to pass one another, see **Passing Loop**
• Which allows Trains to return to their origin without **Reversing**; see also **Merry Go Round Loop** (**MGR Loop**)
b) A Track-mounted coil of wire used to transmit data to Trains, see **Arming Loop**, **TPWS Loop**, **Trigger Loop**.

Loop Dropper
[Elec.] A loop shaped **Dropper** used in low Encumbrance areas, such as beneath **Overbridges** (**OB**). Also **Chopstick**.

Loop Exit Signal

[Sig.] A **Signal** located at the egress end of a **Loop** which controls the passage of **Trains** out onto the **Main Line**.

Loop Line
An alternative for **Loop**.

Loose Coupled
a) Describing a **Train** with no **Automatic Brake** of any kind, whose constituent vehicles are connected together using **Instanter Couplings** or **Three Link Couplings**. See also **Unfitted**
b) A Train in which the **Rail Vehicles** are attached to each other by either chains, Three-link Couplings, Instanter Couplings or un-tightened **Screw Couplings** rather than tightened Screw Couplings or **Buckeye Couplings**.

Loose Heel Switch
[PW] A **Switch** in which the **Switch Rails** are not fastened to the **Stock Rails** at the **Switch Heel** and the pivot points of the **Switch Rails** are at the **Switch Heel Joints**. Largely obsolescent on modern lines, they are found on **Heritage Railways**, **Mine Railways**, **Preserved Railways** and **Tramways**. The modern system is the **Flexible Switch**. See also **Stub Switch**.

Loose Shunting
The **Train** marshalling system where a **Locomotive** propels a **Wagon** towards a **Fan of Sidings** at a brisk pace having first uncoupled it from the Train and set the **Points** appropriately. The Wagon then runs along the chosen **Route** and onto the target **Siding** or Train being marshalled. This process subjects the Wagons to numerous impacts and is no longer common practice. Also **Fly Shunting**, **Gravity Shunting**, **Hump Shunting**.

Loose Sleeper Beam
[PW] See **Sleeper Beam**.

Loose Sleeper Relaying (LSR)
[PW] Replacing **Sleepers** by means of a **Sleeper Beam**, rather than using **Plant Rails**, **Service Rails** or **Relaying** in **Panels**. In this method groups of Sleepers are lifted and placed simultaneously, the **Rails** being added later.

LOOU
Locked Out of Use.

LOP
Loss of Power.

LOPI
Low Oil Pressure Indicator, used to identify leaks of oil insulation in pressurised **Trackside** cables.

LOR
a) Line of **Route**
b) [Hist.] The Liverpool Overhead **Railway** which closed in 1956.

Loram
(Tradename) A manufacturer of **Railway** plant, best known in the UK for **Rail Grinding Trains** (RGT).

LOROL
See **London Overground Rail Operations Ltd**.

LOS

LoS
a) See **Limit of Shunt**
b) See **Line of Sight**
c) See **Fruin Level of Service**.

Loss of Survival Space
Loss of the spaces on a **Train** normally occupied by **Passengers** or **Traincrew**, caused by severe structural damage and often resulting in serious or fatal injury if the affected spaces were occupied at the time of an **Accident**.

Lost Motion
See **Excess Motion**.

LOTL
Leaves on the Line, see **Leaf Fall Season**.

Low
[Col.] An adjective describing a section of **Track** with a **Rail Level** lower than that which the designer intended. The opposite is **High** or **Stiff**. See also **Knob**, **Slack**, **Swag**.

Low Carbon Austenitic Manganese Steel Rail (LCAMS)
[PW] A **Rail** manufactured to the dimensions of British Standard 11, but made from Low Carbon High Austenitic Manganese Steel.

Low Cost Clip (LC Clip)
[PW] A flat **Rail Fastening** for **Flat Bottom Rails** (FB) fitted using one of the holes a **Baseplate** intended for an **Elastic Spike Fastenings**. One of the three holes on each side is reamed out, and the **Low Cost Clip** fitted using a **Chairscrew**. They are used in conjunction with **Cropping** and **Welding** to convert **Jointed Track** with **Elastic Spikes** into Cheap and Cheerful Continuous Welded Rail (Cheap and Cheerful CWR).

Low Joint
[PW Col.] Alternative term for a **Dipped Joint**.

Low Leg
[PW Col.] Alternative term for the **Low Rail**.

Low Level
Describing a facility placed at a lower level than another nearby and related facility, for instance **Low Level Sidings**. See also **High Level**.

Low Negative Shoe Detector (LNSD)
[LUL] A device, typically fitted at the entrances and exits to **Depots**, which checks the height of passing **Negative Shoes**. Because the **Negative Conductor Rail** (**Fourth Rail**) is lower than the **Positive Conductor Rail** (**Third Rail**) the height of the Negative Shoe is critical.

Low Rail (LR)
a) [PW] The lower of the two **Running Rails** of the same **Track** (if applicable)
b) [PW] The inner **Running Rail** of a **Curved** portion of a Track, sometimes applied irrespective of the relative heights of the two **Running Rails**. Also **Inside Rail**, **Low Leg**
c) See **Low Ride**.

Low Rail Design
[PW] A design process for **Track** where the **Low Rail** is designed first and the other **Rail** is related to it using the proposed **Cant** (**C**, **E**) value. An alternative method is **Centreline Design**.

Low Rail Wear
[PW] Collective term for the action of **Rail Wheels** on the **Low Rail**. This normally occurs where the average speed of **Trains** is lower than **Equilibrium Speed** (V_e), resulting in a higher vertical load on the Low Rail. Symptoms include **Mushrooming**, **Lipping**.

Low Ride
Low Ride RRV
A system whereby a **Road Rail Vehicle** (**RRV**) is moved, in **Rail Mode**, by its rubber road tyres bearing directly on the **Rails**, with idler **Rail Wheels** just providing guidance. Also called **Low Rail**. See also **Direct Drive**, **High Ride**.

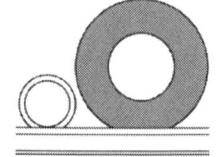

Low Risk Failure
[Sig.] A **Wrong Side Failure** (**WSF**) where another part of the **Signalling System** provides an acceptable level of protection. Also known as a **Protected Wrong Side Failure** (**PWSF**).

Low Ropes
[Hist.] An early method of lighting the more congested areas at least of **Colliery Railways**, **Staithes**, etc, comprising iron baskets filled with a coal fire and suspended from poles.

Low Speed Ramp
A **Conductor Rail Ramp** for use at speeds up to 60km/h.

Low Speed Signal
A control signal indicating that the **Train** speed is lower than a pre-defined threshold

Low Track Fixity
[NR PW] **Track** whose lateral position is insecure, such as **Ballasted Track**. See also **High Track Fixity**, **Medium Track Fixity**, **Track Fixity**. This measure affects some of the tolerances used in **Structure Gauging**.

Low Track Force (LTF)
[TRS] A designation that applies to **Primary Suspension** and **Secondary Suspension** systems that have been designed to minimise the forces exerted on the **Track**.

Lower Fillet
[PW] The curved portion of a **Rail Section** between the **Rail Web** and the **Lower Fishing Surface**.

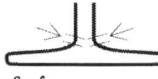

Lower Fishing Surface
[PW] The contact surface between the upper surface of the **Rail Foot** and the lower surface of a **Fishplate**.

Lower Quadrant Signal (LQ)
[Sig.] A **Semaphore Signal** that is in the **Clear** position when the **Arm** is 45° below horizontal. See also **Upper Quadrant Signal** (**UQ**).

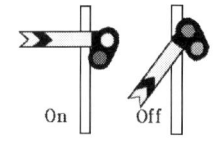

Lowerings
[PW] The opposite of **Lifts**, particularly in terms of the **Track**.

Low-floor Tram
[LR] A **Light Rail Vehicle** (**LRV**) that has an internal floor level as close as possible to **Rail Level**, typically 300 to 350mm (12 to 14 inches) above it. See also **High-floor Tram**.

Lowmac
[NR] A generic term for a low-floor two axle **Wagon** used for the transportation of excavating plant. See also **Flatrol**.

LOWS
(*loze*) See **Lookout Operated Warning System**.

LPT
Liquid Penetrant Testing.

LPTB
[Hist.] London **P**assenger **T**ransport **B**oard, the "nationalised" version of **London Underground** (**LU**) created in 1933, later London Transport Executive (**LTE**) in 1948, and then **London Underground Limited** (**LUL**).

LQ
See **Lower Quadrant Signal**.

LR
a) See **Light Rail**.
b) See **Low Rail**.

LR55
LR55 Rail
(Tradename) [PW] A **Rail Section** promoted by James Harkins of Warrington, UK, for use in **Street Running Track**.

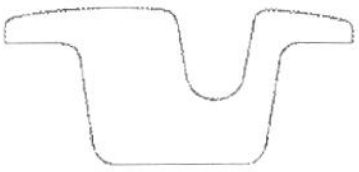

LRA
See **Layout Risk Assessment**.

LRAS
Low Rail Adhesion Site.

LRBG
[Sig.] Last **R**elevant **B**alise **G**roup.

LRCL
[LUL] **L**ong **R**ange **C**olour **L**ight Signal.

LRE

LREP
See **Lateral Resistance End Plate**.

LRM
See **Layout Risk Model**.

LRP
[PW] **L**ongitudinal **R**ail **P**rofilometer.

LRPC
London **R**egional **P**assenger **C**ommittee.

LRT
a) See **Light Rapid Transit**
b) The former London Regional Transport, the parent body of **London Underground Limited** (LUL). See **TfL**.

LRU
Line Replaceable Unit.

LRV
Light Rail Vehicle, often called a **Tram**.

LS
a) Line Standard, see **Network Rail Company Standards** (NRCS)
b) See **Loose Sleeper Relaying** (LSR)
c) See **London Side**.

LS Chairscrew
[PW] A longer (8 $^1/_8$", 206mm) version of the **AS Chairscrew** for use in built-up **Bullhead Crossing** "A" **Chairs**, **Thick Based Baseplates** and **Thick Based Chairs**.

LSE
a) **Linespeed** Enhancement
b) London and South-east
c) [NR] Under the **Bridge Condition Marking Index** (**BCMI**) handbook, shorthand for secondary girder or longitudinal beam, exposed.

LSFOH
Low Smoke and Fume Zero Halogen.

LSI
a) **Linespeed** Improvement
b) [NR] Under the **Bridge Condition Marking Index** (**BCMI**) handbook, shorthand for secondary girder or longitudinal beam, inner

LSL
Long Swing Link **Bogie**.

LSP
Linespeed Profile.

LSR
a) See **Loose Sleeper Relaying**
b) Local Supply **Relay**.

LSS
London Shift Supplement.

LSSE
[NR] Leeds **Station** Southern Entrance.

LSVG
Lower Sector **Vehicle Gauge**.

LSZH
Low Smoke Zero Halogen.

LT
a) Shorthand for Lockout.
b) Shorthand for Light, as in **Light Locomotive**
c) See **London Transport**
d) Low Tension, an alternative for **Low Voltage** (**LV**)
e) The **ATOC** code for the **London Underground** (**LUL**) Bakerloo **Line**, the District Line to Richmond and the District Line to Wimbledon.

LT&SR
[Hist.] The **Pre-Grouping** London Tilbury & Southend **Railway**.

LTA
Lost Time Accident.

LTB
[Hist.] London Transport Board, which became London Transport Executive (**LTE**) in 1970, and is now called **London Underground Limited** (**LUL**).

LTC
Long Term Charge.

LTE
[Hist.] London Transport Executive, which became the London Transport Board (**LTB**) in 1963, then London Regional Transport (**LRT**) in 1984, and is now called **London Underground Limited** (**LUL**).

LTF
See **Low Track Force**, a description of certain types of **Bogie**.

LTF25
[TRS] A type of **Low Track Force** □ **Bogie** developed by **British Rail Research** (**BRR**) and sold to the **Gloucester Railway Carriage and Wagon Company** who were later bought by **Powell Duffryn Rail**, who developed the design into the **TF25**.

LTI
Lost Time Injury.

LTM
a) [BR Hist.] Leading **Trackman**
b) **Loop** □ **Transmission** Module.

LTP
a) Local Transport Plan
b) Long Term Plans.

LTPP
Long Term Planning Process.

LTS
a) The London, Tilbury and Southend **Line**. Also **LT&SR**
b) Local Transport Strategy.

LTT
[PW]
a) Last **Through Timber** (**TT**)
b) Last **Tied Timber** (**TT**).

LTUC
London Transport Users Committee, formerly the London Railway Passenger Committee (**LRPC**).

LU
See **London Underground**.

LUCAS
(*loo-kas*) [LUL] See **London Underground Combined Access System**.

Lucy
[Obs.] The obsolescent **Phonetic Alphabet** word representing L. Replaced by **Lima**.

LUJR
[Hist.] The **Pre-Grouping** Lancashire Union Joint Railway, a London & North Western and Lancashire & Yorkshire joint enterprise.

LUL
London Underground Limited, See London Underground.

ELLIS' BRITISH RAILWAY ENGINEERING ENCYCLOPÆDIA

LUL Group
The main group of duty holders comprising **London Underground Limited** (**LUL**), Metronet SSL, Metronet BCV and **Tubelines**.

LUL Line
See **London Underground Line**.

LUL S3
[LUL] A paste containing sand and stainless steel threads used on **London Underground Limited** (**LUL**) to improve **Adhesion** and the operation of **Track Circuits** (**TC**). See also **Sandite**.

Lumen
The SI unit of luminous flux.

Luminance
The quotient of the **Luminous Intensity** in a given direction, by the projected area on a plane perpendicular to that direction. This quantity most closely describes the brightness of a surface.

Luminous Flux
The total light energy emitted by a light source.

Luminous Intensity
The quotient of the **Luminous Flux** emitted in a given direction by a point light source, in an infinitesimal cone containing that given direction, by the solid angle of that cone.

Lunan Bay Accident
At about 11:24 on 26th October 1975 a **Light Engine** (**LE**) ran into the back of the **Failed** □ **Passenger Train** it was on the way to assist. The **Guard** of the Passenger Train had given the wrong location for his **Train** and the driver of the Light Engine was travelling too fast to stop, despite a **Caution** from the **Signaller**. One Passenger died and 42 people were injured.

LURS
London Underground □ Railway Society.

Luting Sand
[PW] The sand / clay mixture used to fill in gaps between the moulds and **Rail** during preparation for an **Alumino-Thermic Weld**.

LV
Low Voltage.

LVDC
Low Voltage Direct Current.

LVDT
Linear Variable Differential Transformer.

LVT
[PW] Low Vibration **Track**.

LWD
Light-weight Deflectometer, a more portable version of the **Falling Weight Deflectometer** (**FWD**) equipment.

LWR
a) See **Long Welded Rail**
b) See **Last Wheel Replacement**.
c) Load Weight Relay.
d) Locked Wheel Ramp.

LWR Train

LWRT
See **Long Welded Rail Train**. Also **Continuous Welded Rail Train** (**CWR Train**).

LX
Shorthand for **Level Crossing**. Also LC.

LX Chairscrew
[PW] A long (12", 305mm) **Chairscrew** used for fixing Crossing Timbers.

LXA
See **Level Crossing Attendant**.

Lxing
[NPT] Shorthand for **Level Crossing** (LC, LX).

LXRAM
Level Crossing Risk Reduction and Mitigation Group.

LXRMT
Level Crossing Risk Management Toolkit.

LZB
Linienzugbeeinflussung or Linear **Train** Control, a type of **Automatic Train Control** (**ATC**).

M

M
a) In an abbreviated **Track Name**, it denotes **M**ain, as in **Main Line**
b) [TRS] An acronym representing a **Motor** ▫ **Coach**
c) [NR] As the first letter of a **Wagon** ▫ **CARKND** it means that the vehicle is a **Mineral Wagon**
d) [Sig.] On a **Signalling Circuit Diagram**:
• As one of the leading letters of an **Equipment Code**, it means marker or magnetic
• As the last letter of an Equipment Code, it means motor
e) The letter represented by **M**ike in the **Phonetic Alphabet**
f) **M**onday
g) **C**ommon **I**nterface **F**ile **O**perating **C**haracteristics Code for **Timed At** 110mph.
h) As the first letter of a professional membership it means **m**ember
i) [LUL] The **M**etropolitan **Line**
j) [NR] Under the **Bridge Condition Marking Index** (**BCMI**) handbook, shorthand for metal.

M Chairscrew
See **Maintenance Chairscrew**.

M Door
[LUL] The door at the front of a **C**ab used for emergency **Detraining**.

M Stock
[LUL] Type of **Clerestory**-roofed stock, based on District **Railway** ▫ **Rolling Stock** designs, built for the Hammersmith & City **Line** in 1935 and subsequently absorbed into the **Q Stock** fleet.

M&C
See **M**easurement and **C**ompensation.

M&CR
[Hist.] The **Pre-Grouping** **M**aryport & **C**arlisle **R**ailway.

M&E
Mechanical and **E**lectrical.

M&EE
Mechanical & **E**lectrical **E**ngineer or **M**echanical & **E**lectrical **E**ngineering.

M&GNR
[Hist.] The **Pre-Grouping** **M**idland and **G**reat **N**orthern **R**ailway, a Great Northern and Midland joint enterprise.

M&R
Maintenance and **R**epairs.

M&SWR
[Hist.] The **Pre-Grouping** **M**idland & **S**outh **W**estern **J**unction **R**ailway, a London & North Western, Midland and North London joint enterprise.

MA
a) See **Movement Authority**
b) [Sig.] **M**ultiple **A**spect, see **Colour Light Signals**.

MAA
Moving **A**nnual **A**verage.

MABC
See **M**atisa **A**utomatic **B**allast **C**leaner.

MABEL
Multi-modal **A**nalysis of **B**ridges by **E**igen **L**oading. See also **GERTRUDE**.

Macbeth Spike
[PW] A **Rail Fastening** consisting of a roughly W-shaped spike driven through a special **Baseplate** into a **Wood Sleeper** beneath. The middle curve of the W is bent to grip the **Rail Foot**. As with all driven spike type systems, they are only as good as their grip in the supporting **Sleeper**.

Machine Controller (MC)
[NR] A trained person who is authorised to control and supervise an item of **Road Rail Plant** or **On Track Machine** (**OTM**) other than a **Rail Crane** (see **Crane Controller**).

Machine Mounted Short Circuiting Device
A **Short Circuiting Device** (**SCD**) mounted on an **On Track Machine** (**OTM**).

Machine Operator
[NR] A trained person who is authorised to operate an item of **Road Rail Plant** or **On Track Machine** (**OTM**) other than a **Rail Crane**.

Mackenzie, William
(1794-1851). British **Railway** ▫ **Contractor**, builder of the Liverpool Lime Street **Tunnel** (1836), the Grand Junction Railway (**GJR**, 1837) and parts of the **West Coast Main Line** (**WCML**) in England and Scotland.

Mackerel (ZMV)
[NR] A **Ballast Hopper** with centre chutes. See **Wagon Names**.

MADD Box
[TRS] Derived from the French term 'Module Additionale', a module within a door system containing electrical control relays.

MAFA
Multi-**a**sset **F**ramework **A**greement.

MAFEA
[Civ.] **M**asonry **A**rch **F**inite **E**lement **A**nalysis, A computer program used to analyse masonry **Bridge** characteristics, **Safe Working Load** (**SWL**) and structural behaviour.

MAFF
Ministry of **A**griculture, **F**isheries and **F**ood.

Magic Carpet
[Col.] An alternative term for a **Box Chart**.

281

ELLIS' BRITISH RAILWAY ENGINEERING ENCYCLOPÆDIA

Maglev
A contraction of Magnetic Levitation, a system of electromagnets and superconductors designed to support, guide and propel **Railway**-style vehicles along a purpose built "track" at speeds of 560kph (350mph). Whilst not in any real engineering sense a Railway, there are sufficient similarities in operation for the two systems to be considered together. The only commercial UK system was located at Birmingham International and ran (at 26mph) from 1984 until 1995, when it was decommissioned on cost grounds.

Magnet
a) See **Automatic Power Control Magnet** (**APC Magnet**)
b) See **Automatic Warning System Magnet** (**AWS Magnet**)
c) See **Temporary Magnet**.

Magnetic Braking
[LR] A type of **Track Brake** consisting of a friction brake applied electromagnetically directly to the **Rail Head** under **Hazard Braking**.

Magnetic Particle Inspection (MPI)
[PW] A method of detecting the presence of surface cracks that takes advantage of the effect such cracks have on the passage of a magnetic field through a steel **Rail**.

Mail Train
[Ops.] A **Train** conveying letters and parcels, often formed from specially adapted **Rail Vehicles**. See also **Travelling Post Office** (**TPO**).

Main and Tail Haulage
[Hist.] A system of haulage using either two ropes and two stationary engines, one hauling uphill and the other downhill, or one rope and a return wheel both powered by one stationary engine. In the latter case, which was the more economical system, the end of the rope nearest to the engine was the **Main End** and that furthest from the engine was the **Tail End**.

Main Arm
[Sig.] A **Semaphore Signal** □ **Arm** controlling a **Running Movement**.

Main Aspect
[Sig.] That part of a **Signal** which provides **Movement Authorities** for a **Main Route**. This excludes **Position Light Signals** (**PLS**), **Route Indicators** and **Shunt Signals**.

Main Cable
[Sig.] A twin or multicore **Lineside** cable carrying **Signalling Functions** or power supplies between **Location Cases** or **Equipment Rooms**.

Main Girders
[Civ.] In certain **Bridge Decks**, generally the largest structural members and those that run the length of the **Span**. See also **Cross Members**.

Main Line
Main Lines
a) The principal **Track** on a **Railway**. Also **Fast Line**, **Through Line**
b) [NR] The term used to describe those **Routes** seen as being of national importance, e.g. the **West Coast Main Line** (**WCML**), **Midland Main Line** (**MML**), **East Coast Main Line** (**ECML**), **Great Western Main Line** (**GWML**)
c) [PW] The fastest, least **Curved** or most important path through a **Junction**, **Switch and Crossing Layout** (**S&C Layout**) or **Switch and Crossing Unit** (**S&C Unit**)
d) [TRS] An alternative for **Main Reservoir Pipe** in a braking system. Also **Train Line**.

Main Reservoir Cock
[TRS] Manually operated valve at the end of the **Main Reservoir Pipe**. Only some **Wagons** are so fitted and when connected to the **Locomotive** provides a means to directly charge the **Auxiliary Reservoirs**.

Main Reservoir Pipe
[TRS] The pipe provided in a **Two Pipe Air Brake** system to recharge the **Auxiliary Reservoir** on each vehicle as quickly as possible. Also **Main Line**, **Train Line**.

Main Route
[Sig.] A **Route** for a **Running Movement** from one **Main Signal** to the next Main Signal. The setting of this Route will require the **Section** and **Overlap** □ **Beyond** it to be **Clear**. See also **Route Class**.

Main Route Aspect Release From Red (MAR)
[Sig.] A **Control** that holds the **Main Aspect** of a **Junction Signal** at a **Stop Aspect** (**Red**) until the speed of the approaching **Train** has been proved to be sufficiently low as to allow the Train to take the (generally) lower speed **Diverging Route** safely. See also **Main Route Aspect Release From Yellow** (**MAY**)

Main Route Aspect Release From Yellow (MAY)
[Sig.] A **Signalling Control** that holds the **Main Aspect** of a **Junction Signal** at a **Caution Aspect** (**Yellow**) until the speed of the approaching **Train** is deemed sufficiently low as to allow the Train to take the (generally) lower speed **Diverging Route**. See also **Flashing Aspects**, **Free Yellow**, **Main Route Aspect Release From Red** (**MAR**).

Main Signal
[Sig.] Either:
- A **Colour Light Signal**,
- A **Semaphore Distant Signal** or
- A **Semaphore Stop Signal**
which controls **Train** □ **Movement Authorities** on a **Running Line** and is not a **Shunting Signal**.

Mainline
(Tradename) [Hist.] A **Freight Operating Unit** (**FOU**) set up under **Privatisation**, and then bought and merged with the others (**Loadhaul** and **Transrail**) plus the postal carrier **Rail Express Systems** (**RES**) to form **English Welsh and Scottish Railways** (**EWS**). See also **Freight Operating Company** (**FOC**).

Maintained Locking
[Sig.] An alternative term for **Route Locking**.

Maintainer
[RT, NR Col.] Term for the **Contractor** responsible for the day to day upkeep of a particular part of the **Infrastructure**. See also **Infrastructure Maintenance Company**, **Infrastructure Maintenance Contractor** (all abbreviated to **IMC**). This function has now been taken back into **Network Rail** under **TUPE**. See **Infrastructure Maintenance Manager** (**IMM**).

Maintainer's Panel
[Sig.] An additional indication **Panel** which provides a duplicate set of the indications given to the **Signaller**, allowing the **Maintainer** to monitor the **Interlocking**. These Panels often have additional fault indications.

Maintainer's Terminal
[Sig.] A separate **Signaller's Workstation** connected to a **Solid State Interlocking** (**SSI**) or **Integrated Electronic Control Centre** (**IECC**) system that allows diagnostic information to be obtained, and additional restrictive **Controls** to be placed on the system, including **Signing Out a Route**. Also **Technician's Console**, **Technician's Terminal**.

Maintenance
The action of adjusting, cleaning and replacing minor components in order to extend the failure free life of a system.

Maintenance Ballast
[PW] **Ballast** unloaded as part of **Permanent Way Maintenance** (**PWM**) activities to compensate for the natural loss of **Ballast** volume (by wear and distribution). Also called **Maintenance Stone**.

Maintenance Chairscrew
[PW] An **AS Chairscrew** with slightly larger threads used as a replacement for loose and worn **Chairscrews**. Also **M Chairscrew**.

Maintenance Coil
[PW] A helical metal liner used in worn **Chairscrew** holes in **Wood Sleepers**. Also **Coil**, **Vortok Coil**.

Maintenance Delivery Unit (MDU)
[NR] A unit consisting of staff responsible for the **Maintenance** of an area of a **Railway** and reporting to an **Infrastructure Maintenance Manager** (**IMM**).

Maintenance Holidays
[BR Col.] A cost saving exercise based around the concept of doing as little work as possible, apart from the basic activities required to preserve the **Safety of the Line**. This was a common cost-cutting theme of the late 1980s and early 1990s, around **Privatisation**.

Maintenance Lifts
[PW] Vertical adjustments made to the **Track**, intended to remove small anomalies. When applied to the activities of **Tamping and Lining Machines** (**Tampers**) it means an averaging out of errors by applying a small overall **Lift** of around 25mm. It can be seen that repeated **Maintenance Lifting** will raise the Track generally. See also **Design Lifts**, **Maintenance Tamping**, **Measurement and Compensation** (**M&C**).

Maintenance Lining
[PW] The action of making small adjustments to the horizontal position of a **Track**, commonly by using a **Tamper**, to place the Track back into its designed position. It is also used to describe a Tamper using some form of averaging system such as **Three Point Lining** or **Four Point Lining** to average out small errors without reference to the original design. See also **Automatic Lining Control** (**ALC**), **Design Lining**, **GVA**, **Laser Lining**, **Automatic Track Alignment** (**ATA**), **Automatic Track and Top Alignment** (**ATTA**), **Measurement and Compensation** (**M&C**), **Track Machine Guidance** (**TMG**).

Maintenance Scheduled Task (MST)
[NR] A cyclic inspection or **Maintenance** task which has a frequency prescribed in **Network Rail Standards** (**NRS**) and which is scheduled using the **ELLIPSE** system.

Maintenance Screwspike
[LUL] Longer **Screwspike** used as a replacement for loose Screwspikes.

Maintenance speed
[LUL] The speed used for **Inspection** and **Maintenance** purposes, typically a quarter of **Permissible Speed**.

Maintenance Stone
[PW] See **Maintenance Ballast**.

Maintenance Tamping
[PW] The action of using a **Tamper** to apply a small **Lifts** and **Slues** to the **Track**, utilising some form of averaging action to remove small errors and correct the **Crosslevel**. Since the machine cannot lower the Track, the overall trend is upward, causing problems with **Clearances**, **Gauging** and **Overhead Line Equipment** (**OLE**). See **Maintenance Lifts**.

MAIS
Multi-lingual Automatic Inquiry System, a system designed to provide **Passenger** □ **Timetable** information in the local language.

Major Cycle
[Sig.] A complete cycle of communication between a **Solid State Interlocking** (**SSI**) and the maximum of 63 **Trackside Functional Modules** (**TFM**) it can support. Each TFM requires one **Minor Cycle**, the "0th" Minor Cycle being used for diagnostic purposes and updating the SSI with commands from the **Technician's Terminal**. A **Major Cycle** is 64 Minor Cycles in duration irrespective of the actual number of TFMs attached, and has a duration of between 608 milliseconds (ms) and 1000ms.

Major Feeding Diagram (MFD)
[NR Elec.] A schematic showing the arrangement of **Feeders**, **Neutral Sections** and major switchgear for an **Overhead Line Equipment** (**OLE**) system.

ELLIS' BRITISH RAILWAY ENGINEERING ENCYCLOPÆDIA

Major Project Notice (MPN)
[NR] A document issued to the relevant **Train Operating Companies** (**TOCs**) that an **Infrastructure** project will require a **Possession** or series of Possessions of one or more **Sections** of **Track** extending over a period of more than one year, or a period which contains two or more **Passenger Change Dates**. This has now been superseded by the **Possession Strategy Notice** (**PSN**).

Major Station
[NR] A **Station** operated by **Network Rail**. They tend to be large Stations, usually but not necessarily termini. There are currently 18 Major Stations:
- Birmingham New Street
- Cannon Street (**London**)
- Charing Cross (London)
- Edinburgh Waverley
- Euston (London)
- Fenchurch Street (London)
- Gatwick Airport
- Glasgow Central
- King's Cross (London)
- Leeds
- Liverpool Lime Street
- Liverpool Street (London)
- London Bridge (London)
- Manchester Piccadilly
- Paddington (London)
- St Pancras (London)
- Victoria (London)
- Waterloo (London)

Make Up Time
a) (verb) [Ops.] The action of driving as fast possible to regain the time lost during a previous delay.
b) (noun) See **Recovery Time**.

MAMS
[NR Obs.] Modular Asset Management Software i.e. MIMS.

Manhattan Skyline
[NR PW Col.] Nickname for a particular type of report produced by the **High Speed Track Recording Coach** (**HSTRC**) and **New Measurement Train** (**NMT**) recording system, showing a bar graph representation of the **Standard Deviation** (**SD**) recorded in each **Eighth of a Mile** for each of the recorded channels.

Manned Level Crossing (LC)
A **Level Crossing** (**LC, LX**) that is operated or supervised by a **Railway** employee. See **CCTV Level Crossing**, **Locally Controlled Manned Level Crossing** (**LC**), **Manually Controlled Barriers** (**MCB**), **Remotely Controlled Manned Level Crossing** (**RC**), **Trainman Operated** (**TMO**).

MANOP
Maintenance and Operability Study.

Manta (YKA)
[BR Obs.] Converted from a **Passenger Coach**, a **Wagon** forming part of a **Long Welded Rail Train** (**LWRT, LWR Train**), 62 feet long overall. See **Wagon Names**.

Manual Points
A **Set of Points** that are moved from **Normal** to **Reverse** by means of a **Hand Lever**. Also **Handpoints**.

Manual Route Setting
[Sig.] The action of setting each **Set of Points** individually on a **Panel** that normally provides some degree of automation (e.g. an **NX Panel**).

Manual SDO
Manual Selective Door Opening
[TRS] A system fitted to some **Trains** which prevents some **Power Operated Doors** at one or both ends of the Train from opening at **Stations** where the **Platforms** are too short for the Train. Operated by the **Train Manager** or driver, the system is not in widespread use. See also **Automatic SDO**, **Automatic Selective Door Opening**.

Manually Adjust Points
To ensure, if necessary by levering the **Switch Rails** across, that a **Set of Points** are correctly set for the direction in which a **Rail Vehicle** is to proceed.

Manually Applied Earth
[Elec.] An Earth that is attached to the Electrification by a person on site; see also **Fixed Earthing Device** (**FED**).

Manually Controlled Barriers – On Call (MCB-OC)
[Sig.] A type of **Level Crossing** (**LC, LX**) where the **Barriers** are normally closed across the highway and are only opened when requested by the highway user. This reduces delays to **Trains** at little-used Level Crossings.

Manually Controlled Barriers (MCB)
[Sig.] A **Manned Level Crossing** with **Full Barriers** operated locally from a **Signal Box** (**SB**) or **Level Crossing Box**.

Manually Controlled Gated Crossing
See **Manually Controlled Gates** (**MGH**).

Manually Controlled Gates (MGH)
[Sig.] A **Manned Level Crossing** with **Gates** which close across the full width of the road when a **Train** needs to pass and are operated locally from a **Signal Box** or **Level Crossing Box**.

Manufacturers' Drawings
See ·**Switch and Crossing Manufacturers' Drawings**.

Map Search
[Sig.] Within a **Solid State Interlocking** (**SSI**), a Map Search interrogates the **MAP** file to see if the relevant conditions for a **Route Release** are met. A Map Search involves a look back from a feature reference such as a **Signal** or **Track Circuit** (**TC**) for evidence of an **Approaching Train** (i.e., an **Occupied** □ **Track Circuit**).

MAR
a) See **Main Route Aspect Release From Red**
b) [Sig.] **Movement Authority Request**
c) Motor Alternator Rectifier.

MARA
[NR] Master Availability and Reliability Agreement. The contract between **DfT Rail** and the **Train** service provider for the **Intercity Express Programme** (**IEP**).

MARCO
Multilevel **A**dvanced **R**ailways **C**onflict Resolution and **O**peration Control.

Margin
a) [Col.] An interval between successive **Trains**
b) [Obs., NPT] Used to describe an informal arrangement with a **Signaller** to carry out work in the time between **Trains**; see **Getting a Margin**.

Margin Book
A document that defines the data accuracy requirements for every **TRUST** reporting point within a **Region**.

Marginal
[NR] **Slope Condition Rating** for an **Earthwork** such as an **Embankment**, **Cutting** or natural slope; the mid-risk categorisation between **Poor** and **Serviceable**, allowing an intermediate inspection frequency.

MARI
See **M**iniature **A**lphanumeric **R**oute **I**ndicator.

Mark
a) See **Mark 1, 2, 3, 3a, 3b, 4, Mark I, II, III, IIIA, IIIB, IIIC**
b) [Hist.] The point on a on a **Rope-Worked Railway** at which the **Set Rider** detached the haulage rope

Mark 1, 2, 3, 3a, 3b, 4
Mark I, II, III, IIIA, IIIB, IIIC
a) See **Mark of Coaching Stock**
b) See **Mark of Overhead Line Equipment**.

Mark of Coaching Stock
[TRS]
• Mark 1 – The original **British Rail (BR)** □ **Passenger Coach** model design dating from the 1950s, now being withdrawn
• Mark 2 – A refinement of the Mark 1 built towards the end of the 1960s and into the early 1970s. Mainstay of the **Intercity** fleet, but limited to 110mph
• Mark 3 – Coaches used exclusively in **High Speed Train (HST)** formations
• Mark 3a and 3b – **Locomotive Hauled** versions of the Mark 3
• Mark 4 – The 125mph Intercity Coach, as used on **East Coast Main Line (ECML)** services, previously **Intercity 225**.

Mark of OLE
Mark of Overhead Line Equipment
[NR Elec.] There are several different arrangements of **Overhead Line Equipment (OLE)** □ **Catenary**:
• Mark I – The original type of OLE, using corrosion resistant bronze components, typically having a large **System Height**. **Portal Structures** on **Multi-track Railway** and **Cantilever Structures** on **Two Track** sections
• Mark II – A development of Mark I, using cheaper galvanised components
• Mark III – A lower **System Height**, higher tension development of Mark II
• Mark IIIA – Widespread use of **Headspans**, **Cantilever Structures** on **Two Track** sections and **AWAC Catenary**
• Mark IIIB – Similar to Mark IIIA, but using metric components
• Mark IIIC – Similar to Mark IIIB, but with imperial components and copper **Catenary**.
See also **Series One OLE**, **Series Two OLE**, **UK1**.

Marker Board
[NR] A device used to delimit the ends of an **Engineering Worksite**. They are made of yellow plastic and are fitted with two highway-style flashing road lamps. These show **Yellow** on the **Worksite** side and **Red** on the **Possession** side. One is placed on each **Track** at each end of the Worksite, and the area between them is under the jurisdiction of the **Engineering Supervisor (ES)**. Outside this area is controlled by the **Person in Charge of Possession (PICOP)** or **Senior Person in Charge of Possession (SPICOP)**.

Marker Lights
[LUL] Lights that are permanently installed at either end of the **Electric Track Trolleys** and trailers and are lit either white or red depending on direction of travel.

Marker Plate
An alternative for **Datum Plate**.

Marking Up
[PW] The action of providing setting out information for the person on site by writing it on the **Rail Web** of an adjacent **Line**. A typical set of markings is shown below:

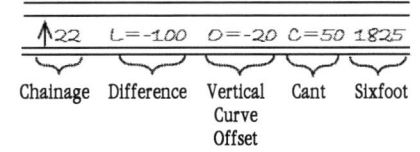

↑22 L=-100 D=-20 C=50 1825

Chainage Difference Vertical Curve Offset Cant Sixfoot

MARLIN
(*mar-lin*) [NR] **M**aps of **R**ailway □ **L**ines; a database system storing boundary plans and other record data.

Marlin (YKA)
[BR Obs.] Converted from a **Passenger Coach**, a **Wagon** forming part of the **Long Welded Rail Train (LWRT, LWR Train)**, 67 feet long overall. See **Wagon Names**.

MARPAS
(*marr-pass*) [BR Obs.] **M**aintenance and **R**enewal **P**lanning **A**id **S**ystem. A program running on a mainframe computer that allowed **Permanent Way Engineers** (**PWE**) to plan their work using analytical and programming tools. See also **Mini MARPAS**.

Marshalling Sidings
See **Sorting Sidings**.

Marshalling Yard
A number of **Sidings** or **Groups of Sidings** at one location used for the marshalling of vehicles into **Trains**. Also **Gridiron**.

Martensite
A name for steel with a coarse grain structure produced by the very rapid cooling of **Austenite**.

Martin, Albinus
(1791-1871) Resident Engineer on the London and South-Western **Railway** (**L&SWR**) and early **Signalling** pioneer

Mary
The obsolescent **Phonetic Alphabet** word representing **M**. Replaced by **Mike**.

MAS
See **M**ultiple **A**spect **S**ignalling.

Mass Detector
[LR] A form of metal detector with its detecting loop mounted between the **Running Rails** and /or buried in the road surface. It consists of a tuned resonant circuit whose natural frequency changes when a large mass passes over.

Mast
[Elec. Col.] Name for the upright part of an **Overhead Line Structure** (**OLE Structure**). Also **Stanchion**.

Master Control Switch (MCS)
See **Master Switch**.

Master Controller
[TRS] Driver's power control device located in the **Driving Cab**. The driver moves the handle of the **Master Controller** to apply or reduce power to the **Locomotive** or **Train**. See also **Regulator**.

Master Record
[Sig.] The version of the **Signalling** design record which carries the certification and from which duplicates are made for issue. See also **Source Record**.

Master Switch
[TRS] An electrical switch operated by the driver to activate the relevant **Driving Cab** and to select the direction of travel. Also **Master Control Switch** (**MCS**)

Match Wagon
a) An **Engineering Vehicle** designed to support the jib of a **Rail Crane** or spoil conveyor of an **Automatic Ballast Cleaner** (**ABC**) where this projects beyond the main vehicle
b) A specially adapted **Rail Vehicle** with different **Drawgear** and / or **Buffers** on each end to allow dissimilar vehicles to be coupled together. Such vehicles do not have facilities for translating between dissimilar braking and electrical systems; this is done using **Translator Vehicles**.

Material Train
A Departmental □ **Train** carrying equipment or materials such as **Ballast** in connection with **Engineering Works**.

Mathematical Switch Toe
Mathematical Toe
[PW] In a **Closed Switch**, the intersection or tangent of the **Running Edges** (**RE**) of the **Stock Rail** and the **Curve** of the **Switch Rail** projected. This may not be the physical end of the **Switch Rails**. See also **Real Toe**, **Switch Toe**.

Matisa
(Tradename) A manufacturer of **Track Maintenance** equipment. Also used as a colloquial description of any **Ballast Cleaner**.

Matisa Automatic Ballast Cleaner (MABC)
(Tradename) [Obs.] The first **Automatic Ballast Cleaner** (**ABC**) used in Britain. The early machines were hauled along the worksite using a wire rope and winch, instead of the newer machines which have hydraulic drive to the axles. Colloquially known as **Matisas**.

Matisa Ballast Cleaner (MBC)
See **Matisa Automatic Ballast Cleaner**.

Maximo
[LUL] **Tube Lines**' □ **Asset** management system.

Maximu
(Tradename) [Obs.] A proprietary product dispensed from **Rail**-mounted **Train**-operated applicators onto the treads of passing **Rail Wheels** to improve **Adhesion**.

Maximum Axle Load
a) For a **Rail Vehicle**, it is the maximum load that any one axle will exert on the **Track** at the **Gross Laden Weight** (**GLW**) of the vehicle
b) For a **Route**, it is the maximum load that any single axle may exert on the Track. In this respect it is directly related to **Route Availability** (**RA**).

Maximum Control Speed
[LUL] The speed below which a **Train** must approach a **Signal** to enable the Signal to show a **Green** or **Yellow** □ **Aspect**.

Maximum Permissible Speed
See **Permissible Speed** (**PS**).

Maximum Permitted Crossing Speed
See **Effective Traffic Moment**.

Maximum Permitted Speed
a) The fastest speed that a particular **Rail Vehicle** or **Traction Unit** can safely attain, irrespective of curvature or **Gradient**
b) [IÉ] The maximum speed at which **Trains** may safely negotiate a section of **Track**.

Maximum Rail Temperature (MRT)
[PW] The highest **Rail Temperature** recorded during **Relaying** or **Rerailing** operations. It is used to calculate the highest safe temperature (the **Critical Rail Temperature** (**CRT**)) that **Continuous Welded Rail** (**CWR**) should be allowed to reach following **Relaying** work, before a **Speed Restriction** is imposed.

Maximum Safe Speed (MSS)
The highest speed a **Train** can achieve without becoming unstable and falling over. At any given point this speed is determined by the **Cant** (**C, E**), **Cant Deficiency** (**D**), loading conditions, peak wind speed, **Rate of Rotation of Carbody** and Tilt ability. Since the **Maximum Speed** (V_m) is based on limits imposed by **Passenger** comfort, the **Maximum Safe Speed** will always be higher.

Maximum Speed (V_m)
[PW]
a) The highest speed at which a non-**Tilting Train** can safely negotiate a **Curve** of a particular Radius (**R**), **Cant** (**C, E**) and **Cant Deficiency** (**D**). For **Standard Gauge**, These are related by the equation:

$$V_m = \sqrt{\frac{R \times (E + D)}{11.82}}$$

The same relationship applies when calculating the Cant required on a given curve at a given speed:

$$E + D = \frac{11.82 \times V_m^2}{R}$$

Where:
- V_m is the Maximum Speed in Kilometres per hour
- R is the Radius in metres
- E is the Cant in millimetres
- D is the Cant Deficiency in millimetres

See also **Equilibrium Speed** (V_e)
b) In **Track Quality** assessment, describes the highest speed that a **Train** may safely attain at that point. This will be the highest of **Permissible Speed** (**PS**), **Enhanced Permissible Speed** (**EPS**), Standard Differential Speed Restriction or Non-standard Differential Speed Restriction. See also **Cant Constant**.

MAY
See **Main Route Aspect Release From Yellow**.

May Peak
[NR Hist.] A small but consistent peak in **Signal Passed at Danger** (**SPAD**) occurences for the **National Rail Network** (**NRN**) during Spring, usually around May, which occurred repeatedly after 2001 but has now been replaced by one at the commencement of **Leaf Fall Season**.

MB
a) A **Level Crossing** (**LC, LX**) with **Manually Controlled Barriers** (**MCB**)
b) [TRS] An acronym representing a Motor ◻ Brake ◻ Coach.

MBC
Matisa **B**allast **C**leaner. See **Matisa Automatic Ballast Cleaner** (**MABC**).

MBJT
Modification **B**usiness **J**ustification **T**ool.

MBLS
[TRS] An acronym representing a Motor ◻ Brake Restaurant/Buffet Luggage Standard Class ◻ Coach.

MBO
Management **B**uy **O**ut.

MBRSM
[TRS] An acronym representing a Motor ◻ Brake Buffet **Standard Class** Modular **Coach**.

MBS
[TRS] An acronym representing a Motor ◻ Brake ◻ Standard Class ◻ Coach.

MBSO
[TRS] An acronym representing a Motor ◻ Brake ◻ Standard Class ◻ Open Coach.

MC
a) See **Machine Controller**
b) [TRS] An acronym representing a Motor ◻ Composite ◻ Coach
c) **M**aintenance ◻ **C**ontractor.

MCB
a) See **Manually Controlled Barriers**
b) **M**iniature **C**ircuit **B**reaker.

MCB-CCTV
MCB With CCTV
[Sig.] **Manually Controlled Barriers** supervised remotely by a **Signaller** via closed circuit television.

MCBF
Mean **C**ycles **B**etween **F**ailures.

MCB-OC
See **Manually Controlled Barriers – On Call**.

MCCB
Moulded **C**ase **C**ircuit **B**reaker.

McK&H
[Col.] Common shorthand for **McK**enzie & **H**olland, a former manufacturer of **Signalling Equipment**.

MCM
[TRS] **M**otor **C**onverter **M**odule.

McNulty Report, The
[NR] Sir Roy McNulty's independent "Rail Value for Money Study" was published in May 2011. The review, jointly sponsored by the **Department for Transport** (**DfT**) and the **Office of Rail Regulation** (**ORR**) recommends ways in which the whole **Rail Industry** can work towards delivering a safe and efficient **Railway** which represents value-for-money for customers and taxpayers. Also **RVfM**.

MCS
a) [Sig.] **M**odular **S**ignal **C**ontrol System
b) See **Master Control Switch**.

MD&HB
[Hist.] The **Pre-Grouping M**ersey **D**ocks & **H**arbour **B**oard **Railway**.

MDA
[NR] The **CARKND** representing a 71 ton capacity **Bogie** ◻ **Open Wagon** which are cut-down Big Box Wagons.

MDBF
[LUL] **M**ean **D**istance **B**etween **F**ailures.

MDBM
Maintain (the existing **Infrastructure**), **D**esign, **B**uild, **M**aintain (the new Infrastructure).

MDF
a) [Tel.] **M**ain **D**istribution **F**rame
b) **M**edium **D**ensity **F**ibreboard.

MDU
See **Maintenance Delivery Unit**.
MDUM
[NR] **Maintenance Delivery Unit Manager**.
ME
a) See **Mining Engineer**
b) The **ATOC** code for **Merseyrail**.
Measure Both Ways
[PW] The standard method of quantifying the extent of **Switch and Crossing Units** (**S&C Units**) and used to calculate amount of **Ballast**, etc. Within each S&C Unit, each possible **Route** is measured from **Switch Toe** to **Metre Opening** or Metre Opening to Metre Opening along the **Track Centre Line**. All the relevant **Switch Front** to **Switch Toe** lengths are then added to give the total length.
Measured Shovel Packing (MSP)
[PW] A manual technique for accurately addressing small vertical errors in the **Track**. The **Lift** required is measured, and an appropriate number of **Cans** of **Chippings** are introduced under the **Sleeper** to achieve this Lift. **Pneumatic Ballast Injection** (**PBI**, commonly **Stone Blowing**) is the mechanised development of this system. Its primary advantage is that the surrounding consolidated Ballast is not disturbed, considerably reducing settlement and improving the finished product.
Measurement and Compensation (M&C)
[PW] A method of **Tamping** whereby the **Tamper** calculates the amount the Track is to be lifted and re-aligned from measurements made on site. See also **Maintenance Lifts**, **Maintenance Lining**, **Plasser** clause b).
Measuring Track Circuit
[Sig.] A **Track Circuit** (**TC**) used to ensure that a **Train** is short enough to proceed. This is done by making the Measuring Track Circuit the requisite length and detecting whether the Train is not **Occupying** any adjacent **Track Circuits**. See also **Lime Street Control**.
Mechanical Cab Signalling
[Hist.] A system devised by staff of the former North Eastern **Railway** □ **Locomotive** department in the 1890s whereby two **Track** mounted trip arms were connected to the **Signal Wire** of an adjacent **Semaphore Signal** and which, when the **Signal** was displaying a **Stop Aspect**, caused an arm on the Locomotive to actuate a valve which in turn admitted boiler steam to a whistle in the **Driving Cab**. When the Signal was indicating **Clear** the track mounted arms were lowered and no contact was made.
Mechanical Interlocking
Mechanical Locking
[Sig.] A collective term for the **Locking Slides**, **Tappets** and **Tumblers** used as the **Interlocking** system in **Mechanical Signalling**. Often contracted to **Locking**.

Mechanical Locking Chart
[Sig.] A plan showing the arrangement of **Locking Slides** and **Tappets** required to meet the requirements of the **Control Tables** for a **Mechanical Signal Box**. Also **Locking Chart**.
Mechanical Points
See **Mechanical Switches**.
Mechanical Signal Box
[Sig.] A **Signal Box** (**SB**) equipped with **Mechanical Signalling**. Other types include **Hybrid Signal Box**, **Integrated Electric Control Centre** (**IECC**), **Network Management Centre** (**NMC**), **Power Signal Box** (**PSB**), **Rail Operating Centre** (**ROC**).
Mechanical Signalling
[Sig.] A **Signalling System** that is operated entirely by human effort, with no external power assistance. See also **Catch Handle**, **Compensator**, **Disc Signal**, **Economical Facing Point Lock** (**EFPL**), **Facing Point Lock** (**FPL**), **Ground Frame**, **Lever**, **Lever Frame**, **Locking Slides**, **Order of Pulling**, **Rodding**, **Semaphore Signal**, **Signal Wire**, **Tappet**.
Mechanical Switches
[Sig.] A **Set of Points** or **Set of Switches** operated by means of **Levers** and **Rodding** from a **Ground Frame** (**GF**) or **Signal Box** (**SB**). Also **Mechanical Points**. See also **Hand Points**, **Power Operated Points**, **Power Operated Switches**.
Mechanically Independent Registration (MIR)
[Elec.] A **Registration Point** in an **Overhead Line Electrification** (**OLE**) system which can be adjusted or removed without influencing the position of any other Registration Point and vice versa. Therefore a Registration Point on a **Headspan** is not Mechanically Independent, but a Registration Point on a **Portal Structure** can be.
Mechanised Maintenance
[PW] The collective term for activities such as **Ballast Cleaning**, **Ballast Regulation** and **Tamping** that have been mechanised. The machines employed include **Automatic Ballast Cleaners** (**ABC**), **Ballast Regulators**, **Dynamic Track Stabilisers** (**DTS**), Stoneblowers and **Tamping and Lining Machines** (**Tampers**). The collective nickname for these machines is the **Yellow Cavalry**, after their colour and propensity for appearing in groups.
Mechanised Maintenance Envelope (MME)

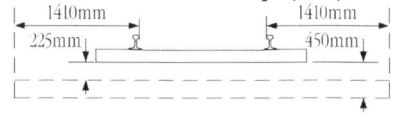

1410mm	1410mm
225mm	450mm

[PW] The clear space required around the **Track** to permit unhindered use of **Automatic Ballast Cleaners** and **Tampers**. This a space 1410mm laterally from each **Running Edge** (**RE**) and a minimum of 225mm **Below Sleeper Bottom** (**BSB**), although 450mm BSB is preferred.

Medium Output Ballast Cleaner (MOBC)
[PW] An **Automatic Ballast Cleaner** (**ABC**) capable of output rates of between 150 and 300 **Yards** (135 and 270m) per hour. Such machines are generally developments of older standard designs, incorporating faster belts and larger **Screening** boxes.

Medium Track Fixity
[PW] **Track** whose lateral position is reasonably secure, such as Track that has been treated by **Ballast Gluing**. See also **High Track Fixity**, **Low Track Fixity**, **Track Fixity**. This measure affects some of the **Gauging Tolerances** used in **Structure Gauging**.

Medscreen
[Col.] To be 'for cause' screened for drugs and alcohol (**D&A**, **DNA**) following a safety-related incident.

Meetings

[Hist.] A **Passing Loop** on an **Inclined Plane** having three **Rails** only, shared between the two **Tracks**, except at the **Passing Loop** where the construction widens to four Rails. Also **Pass-by**.

MEF
[Sig.] Modern Equivalent Form, a specific term used when describing **Resignalling** proposals that update the equipment used but do not significantly change the operation of **Signalling System**.

Megafret
[TRS] An **Intermodal Wagon** with a floor height of 835mm to carry **Swap-body Vehicles** or **Containers**.

MEL
(Tradename) Marcroft Engineering Limited.

Mental Model
An internal mental representation of an external reality. For instance, people develop a mental model of how to use a **Level Crossing** (**LC**, **LX**) from their prior experience of using similar or comparable crossings (or road junctions), from instructions or by observing the behaviour of other users.

MENTOR
(*men-torr*) [NR Elec.] Mobile Electrical Network Tester and Observation Recorder, a test and inspection vehicle used on **AC Electrified Lines**. The equipment from this vehicle is now fitted to the **New Measurement Train** (**NMT**).

Mephisto
(Tradename) A single **Rail** □ **Rail Trolley** with a laser measurement and calculation module mounted on it, capable of measuring the position of any fixed point relative to the **Running Edge** (**RE**). It has a range of 30m over a 300° horizon.

Merdog (ZFV)
[NR prob. Obs.] A 21 ton capacity **Ballast Hopper** used for **Engineering** work. Similar to a **Dogfish**. See **Wagon Names**.

Meridian
(Tradename) The brandname for the **Midland Main Line** (**MML**) (now **East Midlands Trains**) version of the **Class** 222 **Diesel Electric Multiple Unit** (**DEMU**). See also **Pioneer**.

MERIT
Model to Evaluate the Reliability of Infrastructure and Timetables.

MERITS
Multiple European **Railways** Integrated **Timetable** Storage.

Mermaid (ZJV)
[NR prob. Obs.] A 12 ton capacity **Open Wagon** used for transporting **Ballast**. These **Wagons** are capable of tilting their upper deck so as to tip the load out sideways. See **Wagon Names**.

Merry-Go-Round Loop (MGR Loop)
A piece of **Track** used by **Merry-Go-Round Trains** (**MGR Trains**) during the course of loading or unloading

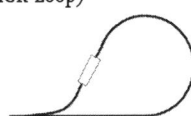

Merry-Go-Round Train (MGR Train)
[Ops.] A (normally coal) **Train** composed of **Hopper Wagons** that can be opened and closed automatically. The Trains are loaded whilst drawing slowly through an overhead loading system, and then run to the delivery point where fixed equipment opens the Hopper doors as the Train draws slowly over a **Coal Drop**. They are named **Merry-Go-Round** because, in the course of a normal shift, they never stop moving around a loop-shaped route.

Merseyrail
(Tradename) A **Train Operating Company** (**TOC**) which provides services on the partially underground **DC Electrified Lines** between Liverpool and Southport, Ormskirk, Kirby, Hunts Cross, New Brighton, West Kirby, Chester and Ellesmere Port. ATOC code ME.

Merseytravel
The trading name of the **Merseyside Passenger Transport Executive** (**MPTE**).

Mess Coach
Mess Van
[TRS] A **Coach** or similar **Rail Vehicle** converted for use by **Engineering** staff, often found attached to **Ballast Cleaners**, **Recovery Trains** and **Wiring Trains**.

Messenger Wire
[Elec.] An alternative term for the **Catenary Wire** in an **Overhead Line Equipment** (**OLE**) system.

MET
Main Earthing Terminal.

Metal Mickey
[Col.] Term for an **Emergency Indicator**. Also **Dalek**, **Sleeping Policeman**.

Metals
[Hist.] Poetic alternative term for the **Rails** or **Track**. Most frequently found when reference is made to **Track** belonging to other **Railway Companies**.

ELLIS' BRITISH RAILWAY ENGINEERING ENCYCLOPÆDIA

Method of Working Document
A document that describes the method of carrying out an operation undertaken at a particular location and the risks associated with that operation. See also **Method Statement**.

Method Statement
A document that details the way a work task or process is to be completed. The Method Statement should outline the hazards involved and include a step by step guide on how to do the job safely. On **Network Rail Controlled Infrastructure** (**NRCI**) this document has been developed into the **Work Package Plan** (**WPP**) and **Task Briefing** (**TB**) system.

Metospir Strip
(Tradename) A V-section metal strip which can be fitted inside a worn **Chairscrew** hole, allowing the Chairscrew to be re-fitted correctly. Not now used, see **Vortok Coil**.

Metre Opening
[PW] The point in a **Switch & Crossing Layout** (**S&C Layout**) where the **Running Edges** (**RE**) of the **Crossing Vee Rails** or the **Closure Rails** attached to them are one metre apart. Beyond this point it is normal to **Break the Timbering**. It is also a reference point for **Measuring Both Ways** in **Switch and Crossing Layouts** (**S&C Layouts**).

Metreage
The metric equivalent of **Chainage**, the distance measured along the **Track** from some predetermined reference point. See also **Kilometreage**.

Metreage Barrier
[LUL] The position of an instantaneous change in **Kilometreage** caused by the convergence at one point of **Track** Kilometreages measured along two different **Routes**.

Metro
a) The trading name of the **Merseyside Passenger Transport Executive** (**MPTE**)
b) A colloquial term for an urban **Light Rapid Transport** (**LRT**) system.

Metro-Cammell
(Tradename) A manufacturer of **Trains**, principally **Multiple Unit Trains** (**MU Trains**), now part of GEC □ Alstom.

Metronet Rail Limited
[LUL Hist.] One of two **Infrastructure** companies (see also **Tube Lines Limited**) in a Public-Private Partnership [PPP] with **London Underground**. Metronet was responsible for the **Maintenance**, renewal, and upgrade of the Infrastructure on nine London Underground **Lines** from 2003 to 2008. It had five shareholders; Atkins, Balfour Beatty, Bombardier, EDF Energy, and Thames Water. It consisted of separate trading companies, Metronet Rail **BCV** Ltd and Metronet Rail **SSL** Ltd, BCV covering the Bakerloo, Central and Victoria lines and SSL the **Sub-surface Lines** (Circle, District, East London, Hammersmith & City and Metropolitan). It was placed in financial administration on 18 July 2007 and was formally liquidated by early 2011.

MEWP
(*mupe*) See **Mobile Elevating Work Platform**.

MF
a) See **MF Anchor**
b) An acronym representing a **Motor** □ **First Class** □ **Coach**.

MF Anchor
A type of **Rail Anchor** for use on **Flat Bottom Rails** (**FB**).

MFA
[NR] The **CARKND** representing a 32 ton capacity **Open Wagon** used for **Spoil**.

MFAS
Modern Facilities at Stations.

MFBV
[TRS] An acronym representing a **Mark 4 Barrier Vehicle**.

MFBW
See **Mobile Flash Butt Welder**.

MFC
a) Multi-functional Contractor
b) Multi-functional Consultant.

MFD
a) See **Major Feeding Diagram**
b) [TRS] An acronym representing a **Motor** □ **First Class** □ **Coach** with disabled accommodation.

MFM
[LUL] **Multi-fare Machine**, A vending machine on which can sell any **Ticket** valid for one day.

MFSDD
Management of **Freight** Services During Disruption.

MG
Motor Generator.

MGE
[NR] Under the **Bridge Condition Marking Index** (**BCMI**) handbook, shorthand for main girder or longitudinal beam, exposed.

MGH
An abbreviation for a **Manned** □ **Level Crossing**, Gated and Hand operated.

MGI
[NR] Under the **Bridge Condition Marking Index** (**BCMI**) handbook, shorthand for main girder or longitudinal beam, inner.

MGL
Multiple Groove Locking. See **Multi-groove Locking Pin** (**MGL Pin**), Multi-groove Locking Stud (**MGL Stud**).

MGL Pin
See **Multi-groove Locking Pin**.

MGL Studs
See **Multi-groove Locking Stud**.

MGR

MGR Train
See **Merry-Go-Round Train**.

MGR Loop
See **Merry-Go-Round Loop**.

MGW
Manned, Gated, Worked Mechanically, Level Crossing.
MHA
[NR] The CARKND representing a Coalfish □ Wagon.
MHH
MHH Rail
(Tradename) [PW] Micro Head-hardened, a low-alloyed pearlitic Heat-treated Rail produced by Tata Steel, mainly for heavy-haul Track with High Axle Loads or in Sharp Curves experiencing heavy wear. It is produced by an off-line process, incorporating rapid and closely controlled induction reheating followed by accelerated air cooling.
MHSAW
MHSW
MHSWR
The Management of Health and Safety at Work Regulations 1992.
MHT
[PW] Mill Heat Treated. See Heat-treated Rail. Also HT.
MI
a) See Miniature Indicator
b) Mechanical Installation Practices.
MICE
Member of the Institution of Civil Engineers.
MICR
a) Magnetic Ink Character Reader
b) Magnetic Ink Character Recognition.
Middle Block
a) [PW] The metal spacing block fitted between the Point and Splice Rails of a Common Crossing
b) See Middle Road Block.
Middle Road
a) A Siding or Through Line located between two Running Lines
b) A Running Line that has other Running Lines on both sides of it.
Middle Road Block
A Possession which occupies the middle two Tracks of a Four Track Railway or two adjacent non-outer Tracks of a Multi-track Railway. Sometimes contracted to Middle Block.
Midland Main Line (MML)
a) The Route from London St Pancras via Bedford to Sheffield
b) A Train Operating Company (TOC).
Midnight
[Obs.] Since 00:00 is ambiguous (is it later today, early tomorrow or was it first thing?) Railway practice avoids it and uses 23:59 or 00:01 instead, as required. For all practical purposes the intervening two minutes do not exist. This can lead to some interesting philosophical debates about overtime payments and a two minute gap in Possessions that run from Friday night into Saturday, but is safer in the long run.

Mid-platform Signal
[Sig.] A Signal provided to allow two Trains to occupy a single Platform whilst satisfying the normal requirements of Block Signalling. Such a Signal may not always form part of the normal Aspect Sequence.
Mid-point Anchor (MPA)
[Elec.] The arrangement provided at the mid-point of a Wire Run in an Automatically Tensioned (AT) □ Overhead Line Electrification (OLE) system to restrain the Catenary longitudinally. Each free end is then tensioned by a Balance Weight Anchor (BWA).
Mid-point Connection (MPC)
See Return Conductor to Rail Bond.
Mid-rail
[PW] That part of a Jointed Rail that is not within Fishplate Limits, i.e. most of it.
Mids.
Shorthand for Midlands.
Mid-span
a) [Elec.] A point half way between adjacent Registration Points on an Overhead Line Electrification (OLE) system
b) [Civ.] A point halfway along a Bridge Deck.
Mid-span Offset (MSO)
[Elec.] The lateral offset of the Contact Wire (CW) from the Track Centre Line half way between adjacent Registration Points on an Overhead Line Electrification (OLE) system.
Midway Lock
Midway Release
[Sig.] A device and method for mechanically releasing a Ground Frame when the Ground Frame is located at a distance from the Controlling Signal Box that is greater than the normally permitted maximum for a single run of Point Rodding. This comprised a Lever in the Signal Box which could only be pulled if no Conflicting Signals had been Cleared. The Lever operated conventional Point Rodding which terminated in a locking box halfway to the Ground Frame. Another set of Point Rodding extended from the locking box to the Ground Frame Release Lever, which could only be pulled if the Signaller had pulled their Release Lever.
Migration
[Sig.]
a) See Silver Migration
b) See Signalling Migration.
Mike
The Phonetic Alphabet word representing M.
Mile
The commonest large distance division in use on the National Railway Network (NRN). Subdivisions and conversions are:

8000 Links	5280 feet
1760 Yards	1609.344m
88 Lengths	80 Chains.

ELLIS' BRITISH RAILWAY ENGINEERING ENCYCLOPÆDIA

Mileage
The distance along a **Railway** from the 0 (zero) **Milepost** (**MP**). There is no fixed rule for which end of a **Line** is the 0 Milepost end, but the following is given as a guide. Note that for every definition there is an exception!
- For **Main Lines**, the 0 Milepost is typically at the capital city end. See also **London**. An exception was the Great Central Railway (**GCR**) which was mileaged from Manchester to London
- For **Secondary Lines**, it is normally nearest the headquarters of the **Railway Company** that built the Line
- For **Branch Lines**, the 0 Milepost is usually at the original Main Line end.

It is possible to have a **Negative Mileage**, as Routes are rarely re-mileaged, ever. Mileages are generally expressed in **Miles** and **Chains** or **Miles** and **Yards**, but Miles and feet are used on some **Signalling Plans**. A few Lines have been metricated, see **Kilometerage**.

Mileage Yard
[Hist.] A **Siding** or **Group of Sidings** provided for handling **Wagon** load **Traffic** charged by the mile, where the customer (rather than **the Railway Company**) was responsible for loading and unloading the **Wagons**.

Milepost (MP)
a) Originally, a requirement of the **Railway Clauses Consolidation Act** 1846; "The company shall cause the length of the railway to be measured, and milestones, posts, or other conspicuous objects to be set up and maintained along the whole line thereof, at the distance of one quarter of a mile from each other, with numbers or marks inscribed thereon denoting such distances."

b) A post placed at one-**Mile** intervals along the **Railway**. Intervening quarter-mile intervals (quarter, half and three quarter) are also similarly marked. Often, the quarter, half and three quarter miles are indicated by one, two or three symbols such as dots, triangles or lines. The posts are coloured, generally yellow, though other colours (such as blue) are used when two different **Routes** run adjacent to one another. Mileposts (and quarter intervals) often "wander" along the **Line** over the years, resulting in long and short miles. The reader should also be alert to missing "0" Mileposts, Routes that have had a longer or shorter diversion added without changing the surrounding posts, and Mileage reversals at **Junctions** that no longer exist. In other words, the system is largely useless for the accurate measurement or expression of distances.
See also **Kilometre Post, Kilometerage**.

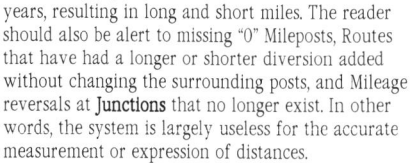

Milepost Sequence Change
[LUL] A **Track Recording** term for the sequence of **Kilometre Posts** across a **Metreage Barrier**.

Military Trestle
[Civ.] A kit of standard heavy steel sections which can be bolted together to make temporary supporting structures for **Bridges**.

Mill Heat Treated (MHT)
Mill Heat Treated Rail (MHT Rail)
[PW] See **Heat Treated Rail**.

Millican Nail
[PW Obs.] Broad-headed nails with raised numerals indicating the **Cant** (**C, E**) at that point in inches. They fell out of use with the widespread introduction of **Concrete Sleepers**. Cant was then painted on the **Sleepers**, in millimetres, in black on a yellow background, but modern practice uses thermally bonded decals. See **Cant Transition**.

Millirad
An angular measurement; being one thousandth of a radian (approximately 0.05729577950560 of a degree).

Mills
See **Mills Rail Clip** (**MRC**).

Mills Baseplate
[PW] A **Baseplate** intended for use with the **Mills Rail Clip** (**MRC**).

Mills Rail Clip (MRC)
[PW Obs.] A C-shaped **Rail Fastening** manufactured by James Mills Ltd and used in some **Switch And Crossing Layouts** (**S&C Layouts**) but mostly in **Plain Line** (**PL**). The current pattern is the **C3R**, but this is not installed new in the UK.

Mimic Diagram
Mimic Panel
[Sig.] A not-to-scale **Signaller's Panel** which contains live indications of the **Points**, **Signals** and **Track Circuits** (**TC**) under their control.

MIMS
(*mimms*) [NR] Mincom Information Management System, a work planning system used by **Network Rail** (**NR**), replaced by **Ellipse**.

Mine Railway
A **Railway** constructed to carry materials and workers in and out of a mine. Typically these are low speed, **Narrow Gauge Railway** systems using **Battery Locomotives**, **Diesel Locomotives**, horses, ponies or, in some instances human muscle.

Mineral
Minerals
a) A term used to describe materials such as ore, aggregate and coal
b) [Obs.] A type of **Spoil Wagon** converted from former ore **Wagons**; **CARKND** □ **ZHV**
c) A term used on Ordnance Survey maps to describe all **Freight Only Lines**.

Mineral Extraction
The removal of a resource such as brine, coal, gypsum or oil from below a **Railway**, often resulting in settlement or later subsidence of the Railway.

Mini MARPAS
(*Minnie mar-pass*) [BR Obs.] The personal computer based version of **MARPAS**.

Mini MIMS
[Obs.] The pilot version of **MIMS** for **Railtrack** (**RT**).

Mini Vest
[Col.] See **Hi-vis. Vest**.

Miniature Alphanumeric Route Indicator (MARI)
[Sig.] A small short range **Alphanumeric Route Indicator** (**ARI**). Also formerly called a **Stencil Indicator**.

Miniature Arm
[Sig.] A smaller **Semaphore Signal** □ **Arm** used to control **Shunt Movements** and other **Non-running Movements**.

Miniature Indicator (MI)
[Sig.] An **Alphanumeric Route Indicator** (**ARI**) meeting the requirements of **Performance Category 3** for **Readability**. See also **Standard Indicator** (**SI**).

Miniature Lever Frame
[Sig.] A **Lever Frame** built with miniature **Levers**, each of which controls a **Signalling Function** by electrical means. This arrangement formed an interim stage between full **Mechanical Signalling** and full **Power Operated Signalling**. In general, it should be noted that Miniature Lever Frames are physically little smaller than Lever Frames with full size Levers.

Miniature Railway
A **Railway** with a **Track Gauge** of between 7 and 15 inches (178mm to 381mm) where everything is of much reduced size, including the **Locomotives** and other **Rolling Stock**, but is functional in that it carries **Passengers**. See also **Model Railway**, **Narrow Gauge Railway**.

Miniature Red / Green Lights
Miniature Red / Green Warning Lights (R/G)
See **Miniature Stop Lights** (**MSL**).

Miniature Route Indicator (MRI)
[Sig.] A small **Route Indicator** (**RI**) which typically accompanies a **Position Light Signal** (**PLS**). Also **Subsidiary Route Indicator** (**SRI**).

Miniature Snow Plough (MSP)
[TRS] A small **Snow Plough** attached to the front of a **Locomotive** or **Multiple Unit** which can clear snow up to 450mm **Above Rail Level** (**ARL**).

Miniature Stop Lights (MSL)
[Sig.] Miniature lights, most often **Red** (**R**) and **Green** (**G**), used as the warning at certain types of **Level Crossing**. Previously **Miniature Warning Lights** (**MWL**).

Miniature Warning Lights (MWL)
See **Miniature Stop Lights** (**MSL**).

Minimum Ballast Depth
[PW] The shallowest permitted layer of clean **Ballast** that must be provided below **Design Sleeper Bottom** at the time of **Renewal**. The depth depends on the **Enhanced Permissible Speed** (**EPS**), **Permissible Speed** (**PS**) and **Equivalent Million Gross Tonnes Per Annum** (**EMGTPA**) values for the **Line** concerned. See also **Below Sleeper Bottom** (**BSB**).

Minimum Flangeway
[PW] A specified minimum distance between the **Gauge Face** of a **Stock Rail** and the **Back Edge** of the **Switch Rail** in an **Open Switch**. See **Free Wheel Clearance** (**FWC**).

Minimum Length
a) [Sig.] Of a **Track Circuit** (**TC**), see **Track Circuit Minimum Length**
b) [PW] Of an **Element** within a **Horizontal Alignment** or **Vertical Alignment**, see **Element Length**.
c) [PW] Of a **Rail**, see **Minimum Rail Length**.

Minimum Radius
[PW]
a) The smallest Radius (**R**) of horizontal **Track** curvature permitted in design: on **Network Rail** (**NR**) this is 125m
The smallest Radius (R) of horizontal Track curvature that a particular **Rail Vehicle** can negotiate. For example, for **Diesel Locomotives** intended for use on **Main Lines**, this value is typically 90m (99 **Yards**, $4\,^{1}/_{2}$ **Chains**).

Minimum Rail Depth
[PW] The lowest value of **Rail Depth** permissible for a **Running Rail**, not including any **Gall**. This value varies according to the original depth of the Rail and the anticipated future traffic over it.

Minimum Rail Length
[PW] The shortest permitted length of **Plain Rail**. This normally varies according to how the **Rail** is connected at each end. For example, on **Network Rail** (**NR**) □ **Lines** 9144mm (30 feet) is the shortest preferred length for **Jointed Rails**, but 4500mm is permitted between adjacent **Welds**.

Minimum Rail Temperature (MRT)
[PW] The lowest **Rail Temperature** recorded during the **Clipping Up** or **Keying Up** of a length of **Unstressed** □ **Continuous Welded Rail** (**CWR**). This figure and certain modifying factors such as **Lateral Resistance** (**LR**) are then used to calculate the **Critical Rail Temperature** (**CRT**).

Minimum Reading Distance (MRD)
[Sig.] The distance a driver requires to read and process the **Indicator** or **Signal** at the **Approach Speed**, and therefore the distance a **Train** covers at the **Approach Speed** during the **Minimum Reading Time** (**MRT**).

Minimum Reading Time (MRT)
[NPT] See **Assessed Minimum Reading Time**.

Minimum Warning Time
The time required by a person or working party to acknowledge the warning, stop work, remove tools, etc. from the **Track** and move to a **Position of Safety**. For a large group with welding equipment or **Duff Jacks** this time can be considerable, of the order of minutes.

Minimum Works Alteration (MWA)
[Col.] A polite euphemism for a temporary and non-standard solution. See also **Frig**.

Mining Engineer (ME)
[NR] The post with responsibility for monitoring **Mineral Extraction** activities likely to affect the **Railway**.

MiniProf
(Tradename) A measuring device used to record **Rail Profiles** and **Wheel Profiles**. Manufactured by Greenwood Engineering A/S of Denmark.

Minnow (ZCO)
[NR prob. Obs.] An **Open Wagon** for transporting **Ballast** and **Sleepers**. See **Wagon Names**.

Minor Cycle
[Sig.] The basic execution cycle during which a **Solid State Interlocking** (**SSI**) will process and issue one command telegram, and receive and process one reply telegram (from the **Trackside Functional Module** (**TFM**) addressed in the previous **Minor Cycle**). It will also process $1/64^{th}$ of the commands in the flag operations (**FOP**) data file, and update $1/64^{th}$ of the **Approach Locking**, **Track Circuit** (**TC**) and elapsed timers in the **Interlocking**. If these actions can be completed in less than 9.5 milliseconds (ms) the SSI will process one **Panel** request, if any are pending. A Minor Cycle has a minimum duration of 9.5ms and should be no longer than 30ms; otherwise the TFMs may interpret the gaps in the communications as failures.

Minor Injuries
Any physical injuries that are not listed in Regulation 2(4) of the **Railways (Accident Investigation and Reporting) Regulations 2005**.

Minor Obstacle Deflector
[TRS] A lighter-weight version of an **Obstacle Deflector**, retrofitted to some second generation **Diesel Multiple Units** (**DMU**) such as **Class** 150 following the findings of the **Polmont Accident**.

MINT
Mincom Intelligent Terminal Emulator.

MIP
a) Mobility Impaired Person
b) **MIMS** Implementation Programme
c) Management Incentive Plan.

MIPS
Mobility Impaired Passenger Services.

MIR
See **Mechanically Independent Registration**.

MIRO
Member of the Institute of Railway Operators.

MIRSE
Member of the Institution of Railway Signal Engineers.

Miscommunication
[Obs.] Former but now colloquial term for the particular circumstances leading to a **SPAD**. See **SPAD Error Category**, Group 1.

Misjudgement
[Obs.] Former but now colloquial term for the particular circumstances leading to a **SPAD**. See **SPAD Error Category**, Group 4.

Misread
[Obs.] Former but now colloquial term the particular circumstances leading to a **SPAD**. See **SPAD Error Category**, Group 3.

Mission
[CT] A cross-Channel journey carried out by a **Shuttle** in the **Channel Tunnel**.

Mitchell, Joseph
(1803-1883) born in Forres, Scotland. Built the Highland **Railway** (later the Inverness & Perth Railway) and later extensions that included many grand **Bridges** and **Viaducts**.

MITTE
(*mitty*) Model Invitation to Tender Enquiry.

MIU
The Department for Transport's (**DfT**) Mobility and Inclusion Unit, responsible for the **Railways for All Strategy** and **Access for All** (**AFA**) funding.

Mixed Gauge Track
[PW] Track fitted with one or more additional **Rails** to provide two or more different **Track Gauges**. Also **Dual Gauge Track**.

Mixed Traffic
A combination of **Freight Trains** and **Passenger Trains**.

Mixed Train
[Ops.] A **Train** carrying both **Passengers** and **Freight**.

MJR
[Hist.] The **Pre-Grouping** Methley Joint **Railway**, a Great Northern, Lancashire & Yorkshire and North Eastern joint enterprise.

MKA
[NR] The **CARKND** representing a **Limpet** □ **Wagon**.

MKS
[TRS] An acronym representing a **Motor** Kitchen Standard Class □ Coach.

ML
a) See **Main Line**
b) [Sig.] Common shorthand for ML Engineering, a manufacturer of **Signalling Equipment**, now part of Bombardier (with Interlogic Control Engineering). See **TI21**.

MLA
[NR] The **CARKND** representing the 65 ton capacity **Bogie** □ **Open Wagons** used by **Network Rail** (**NR**).

MLF
[Ops.] **Main Line** □ Freight.

MLFIC
[TRS] **Main Line** Filtered Isolating Cock.

MLIC
[TRS] **Main Line** Isolating Cock.

MLRI
See Multi-lamp Route Indicator.

MLSO
[TRS] An acronym representing a **Motor** Luggage Standard Class □ Open Coach.

MLV
[TRS] An acronym representing a **Motor** Luggage **Van**.

MLW
[TRS] An acronym representing a **Motorail** Loading Wagon, used where end-on access is not available..

MM
See **Mott Macdonald Ltd**. Also **MML**.

MMA
[PW] **M**anual **M**etal **A**rc, a **Welding** method.

MMA x
[NR PW] A competency grading (1 to 4) awarded by **Network Rail** (**NR**) for the **Manual Metal Arc Weld Repair** processes. **Weld Repairs of Switch Rails** requires **MMA** 5. Welders who do not carry out **Switch Rail** welding for a period of six months or more have their MMA 5 approval suspended until successful completion of refresher training and reassessment.

MME
See **M**echanised **M**aintenance **E**nvelope.

MMI
Man / **M**achine **I**nterface.

MML
a) See **Midland Main Line**
b) See **Mott Macdonald Ltd**. Also **MM**.

MMURTU
(Tradename) [Hist.] **M**anchester **M**etropolitan **U**niversity **R**ail **T**echnology **U**nit. In 2012 this transferred with all staff to the University of Huddersfield to form the **Institute of Railway Research** (**IRR**).

MOA
[NR] The **CARKND** representing a 72 ton **Bogie** ▫ **Open Wagon** used for **Ballast** and **Spoil**; it is an **MBA** with lower sides.

MOABS
Mast **O**perated **A**utomatic **B**allast **S**ampler.

MOBC
(occasionally, *mob-see*) See **M**edium **O**utput **B**allast **C**leaner.

Mobile Elevating Work Platform (MEWP)
The generic name for a self-propelled machine designed to provide a safe working platform for one or more operatives who can adjust the position of the platform. Other names of related machines include **Cherry Picker**, **Permaquip**, **Scissor Lift Platform**. The term can also include specially adapted excavators and **Road Rail Excavators**.

Mobile Flash Butt Welder (MFBW)
[PW] A (generally) **Road Rail**-capable truck which has its own generator and equipment to make **Flash Butt Welds** (**FBW**). One of the first in the UK was christened "**Sparky**".

Mobile Operations Manager (MOM)
(*mom*) [NR Ops.] An **Operations** manager who provides first-line response to incidents.

Mobile Shunter
[Ops.] An employee who undertakes the duties of a **Shunter** at a number of locations, travelling between them as their workload requires.

MOD
Ministry **o**f **D**efence.

Mod.
a) [Sig.] Shorthand for **mod**ification, see **Modifications** (**Mods**)
b) [Hist.] Shorthand for the **Modernisation Plan**.

Mod. Sheet
[Sig.] See **Modification Sheet**.

Mod. State
[Sig.] See **Modification Status**.

Modal Split
The relative shares of transport activity between different modes of transport.

Modane Accident
On 12th December 1917 a **Troop Train** carrying 1000 French soldiers back from Italy ran away on the average 1 in 33 **Gradient** ▫ **Beyond** the Mont Cenis Tunnel. Only four **Vehicles** out of the nineteen had **Automatic Brakes**, and the driver's application of these caused fires under the **Train** but no deceleration. Four **Miles** later, at an estimated speed of 75mph, the Train Derailed. In the ensuing fire, fed by the wooden Coach bodies, 543 troops died. This is the worst loss of life in a single preventable Railway accident in Europe.

Mode A Train Radio
[IÉ] A discrete **Train** radio system which communicates voice and telegram messages between **Signalling Centres** and Trains.

Mode x Startup
[Sig.] Within a **Solid State Interlocking** (**SSI**), the mode chosen by heuristics in the initialisation software, ranging from 1 to 3.
• A Mode 1 start-up is the most severe, necessitating a reset of the entire contents except the **Technician's Controls** and the **Elapsed Timers** whose contents are set to one. The processing of **Panel Requests** is suspended while the system is brought up-to-date by incoming **Data Telegrams**, and while the Technician's Controls are released manually from the **Technician's Terminal**,
• Mode 2 start-up involves a similar reset, but preserves the Technician's Controls, and the system restarts automatically after a four minute suspension in processing Panel Requests,
• Mode 3 start-up preserves the status of **Route Memory**, and allows an immediate restart.

Model Railway
A **Railway** with a **Gauge** of less than 7 inches (178mm), which does not carry **Passengers** and where all the **Locomotives** and **Rolling Stock** are scaled replicas of the originals. See also **Miniature Railway**, **Narrow Gauge Railway**, **Prototype**.

Modernisation Plan
[Hist.] Published on 1st December 1954 by the **British Transport Commission** (BTC), this report was commissioned in an attempt to stem the financial losses being incurred as a result of competition from road and air traffic. Among the recommendations taken up and implemented from 1956 onwards were a (then) massive spending of £1.2bn on:
- The replacement of all **Steam Traction** with **Diesel Traction** and **Electric Traction**
- **Electrification** of the **West Coast Main Line** (**WCML**)
- Construction of vast **Marshalling Yards** using **Automated Shunting**
- Construction of **Grade Separated Junctions** and **Flyovers**.

The failure of the Plan was perhaps that nothing was done to address pre-war working practices, or the **Common Carrier** requirements. The failure of the Plan led directly to the **Beeching Report** and **Line** closures ten years later. See also **Nationalisation**. Abbreviated to **Mod**.

Modification Sheet
[Sig.] The document which records the modifications to be made to a **Signalling** design. This sheet may only show the relevant part of the design.

Modification Status (Mod State)
[Sig.] The current revision of the **Signalling** design, including any **Modification Sheets** issued.

Modifications (Mods)
[Sig.] Changes made to a **Signalling** design during installation, **Testing and Commissioning** (**T&C**).

Mods
See **Modifications**.

Modular S&C
See **Modular Switch and Crossing**.

Modular Signalling
[NR Sig.] A system of standardised **Signalling Equipment** (power supply units, **Signals**, **Train Detection** equipment) which can be assembled to provide cost-effective modern **Signalling** on simple **Routes**, rather than each **Signalling** installation being custom designed and built. The pilot installations are:
- Ely – Norwich awarded to Signalling Solutions Ltd. and will use an **Alstom** □ **Smartlock** system
- Crewe – Shrewsbury Line has been awarded (2009) to **Westinghouse** and will use a **WESTRACE** □ **Interlocking**

See also **IECC Lite**.

Modular Station
[NR] A concept developed by **Network Rail** to simplify and accelerate the design and construction process for new **Stations** by using a suite of modular, prefabricated designs. The first two were at Mitcham Eastfields and Corby. They have been criticised for being uninspiring, and the overall costs have yet to show any major advantage over more traditional designs.

Modular Switch and Crossing
[NR PW] A method of delivering and installing **Switch and Crossing Layouts** (**S&C Layouts**) where each Layout arrives as two or more large **Panels** on specially-built tilt-bed **Wagons** and is assembled using a **Rail Crane**. This approach minimises the need for **Possession** time. See **IFA**.

MOIRA
(*moy-ra*) Model of Inter-regional Activity. A Timetable-based model of the **Rail** market and **Passenger Train** choice. It projects future demand and revenue based on Timetable (**TT**) alterations, including the market elasticity and revenue change using data from the **Passenger Demand Forecasting Handbook** (**PDFH**) and LENNON.

MOLA
[Hist.] Master Operating Lease Agreement. The lease terms which applied to the **British Rail** (**BR**) □ **Traction And Rolling Stock** (**T&RS**) bought by the **Rolling Stock Companies** (**ROSCOs**) at Privatisation and therefore the lease agreement between the ROSCOs and the **Train Operating Companies** (**TOCs**).

Mole, The
(Tradename) A tracked machine capable of continuously excavating one **Track Width** of **Ballast** and discharging it to **Opens** on the adjacent **Line**. More manoeuvrable than an **Automatic Ballast Cleaner** (**ABC**), it is capable of greater production rates than the more normal 360° excavators used for such work. Pioneered by Jarvis Ltd.

MOM
See **Mobile Operations Manager**.

Monitored
[Sig.] Describing the checking of the status of a **Level Crossing** (**LC**, **LX**) by a **Signaller** by means of remote indicators. See also **Supervised**.

Monkey
See **Bull**.

Monobloc
[PW] The part of a **Cast Crossing** between the **Changes of Section** of **Crossings** with an N Value lower than 28. In this area the **Crossing Vee** and **Wing Rails** are produced by shaping the upper surface of the casting as appropriate. The casting itself is hollow beneath.

Monoblock Sleeper
[PW] A **Sleeper** consisting of a single pre-stressed concrete unit, the typical pattern found on **Main Lines** on the **National Railway Network** (**NRN**). See also **Twin Block Sleeper**.

Monoboom Anchor Portal
[Elec.] An **Overhead Line Equipment** (**OLE**) **Structure** used in **Series 1** to anchor the wires directly above the **Track**. It offers the same advantages as a **Twin Boom Anchor Portal** but eliminates the need to **Flake** □ **Wires** through between the **Booms**.

Monorail
A **Railway** constructed with a single **Rail** to provide support and guidance to vehicles. The vehicles are either suspended from or supported by the Rail.

Monte Carlo Simulation
A (generally computerised) mathematical technique used to study the effect of multiple parameters which affect an outcome. Each parameter is randomly sampled between specified limits to form a set of inputs which are used to calculate an outcome. This process is repeated as many times as required to study what might happen within a population and to derive a probability distribution curve for the outcome.

Monument
[PW] See **Hallade Monument**.

Moorgate Accident
On 28th February 1975 a **London Underground Limited** (LUL) □ **Train** overran the end of the **Line** on the Moorgate **Branch** and collided with the end of the **Tunnel**. The Train was still under power just prior to the impact, and no attempt was made to brake. The driver and 42 **Passengers** died. No satisfactory explanation has ever been determined for the driver's actions.

Moorgate Control
a) See **Trains Entering Terminal Stations** (TETS)
b) [NR] An arrangement such as a **Train Stop** or **TPWS Mini** that enforces a low speed approach to a **Terminal Platform**. See **Moorgate Accident**.

MOP
Member of (the) Public.

MORANE
Mobile Radio for Railway Networks in Europe. See also **GSM-R**.

Morpeth Accidents
On 7th May 1969 {and 24th June 1984} a northbound **Express Passenger Train** attempted to negotiate the 40mph {50mph} **Curve** through Morpeth at around 80mph. Five **Passengers** and a **Ticket Inspector** were killed, and 121 Passengers injured {35 injured}. These accidents were responsible for driving the provision of **Warning Indicators** (WI) and **Automatic Warning System Magnets** (AWS Magnets) where the reduction in **Permissible Speed** (PS) is one third or more from a speed of 60mph or above. See also **Morpeth Board**.

Morpeth Board
[BR, RT, NR Col.] Common name for a **Warning Indicator** (WI) giving warning of a reduction in **Permissible Speed** (PS) of one third or more from a speed of 60mph or above. See also **Morpeth Accidents**.

MOS
a) Motor Operated Switch, See **Motorised Switch**
b) Mobile **Operations** Supervisor.

Moselle
A **Railway** □ **Telegraph Code** meaning "Give matter special attention".

Most Restrictive Aspect
[Sig.] A generic description of the **Aspect** displayed by a **Signal** which reduces the speed of **Trains** to the lowest level. A typical **Three Aspect Signal** can display a **Proceed Aspect** (Green, highest speed), a **Caution Aspect** (Yellow, reduced speed) and a **Stop Aspect** (Red, no speed). Therefore on this signal the Stop Aspect is the Most Restrictive Aspect. The opposite is **Least Restrictive Aspect**.

Mothballed Line
A **Route** or **Track** over which **Traffic** has temporarily ceased to pass but is still operable should the need arise. Mothballing a Route normally includes removing **Signallers** from **relevant Signal Boxes** (SB), removing physical access by **Securing Out of Use** the relevant **Points** or **Switches** and extinguishing the **Signals**.

Motive Power
[Ops.]
a) A contraction of **Motive Power Unit** (MPU)
b) An alternative for **Locomotive**.

Motive Power Depot (MPD)
A **Maintenance** facility for **Locomotives** and **Multiple Unit Trains**. Also **District Electric Depot** (DED), **Diesel Maintenance Depot** (DMD), **Traction Maintenance Depot** (TMD).

Motive Power Unit (MPU)
[Ops.] An alternative term to **Traction Unit**, meaning (generally) a **Locomotive** or **Multiple Unit Train**.

Motor
[TRS] A contraction of **Motor Coach**.

Motor Blowers
[TRS] The **Traction Motors** on **Electric Locomotives** and **Electric Multiple Units** (EMU) produce large amounts of waste heat, so to keep their temperature at a reasonable level for long periods of hard work they are often fitted with electric fans called Motor Blowers. See also **Wrong Kind of Snow**.

Motor Coach
[TRS] A vehicle within a **Multiple Unit Train** equipped with **Powered Axles** and providing **Tractive Effort** to the **Train**. An un-powered vehicle is a **Trailer**. See also **Power Car**.

Motor Operated
See **Motor Worked**.

Motor Operated Switch (MOS)
a) See **Motorised Switch**
b) See **Power Operated Points**.

Motor Points
An alternative term for **Power Operated Points**.

Motor Worked
[Sig.] Meaning operated by a motor. This can apply to **Detonator Placers**, **Derailers**, electrical switches, **Points** and **Semaphore Signals**. See also **Motor Operated**, **Motorised Switch**, **Power Operated**.

Motorail
Motorail Train
[Obs.] A **Train** service that conveyed both **Passengers** and their cars, the latter in special **Vans** or cut-down former **Passenger Coaches**. See also **MLW**, **MRV**.

Motorised Switch
[Elec.] An electrical switch mounted on an **Overhead Line Structure** and operated by an electric motor that is in turn controlled remotely, generally from an **Electrical Control Room**. Also **Motor Operated Switch** (**MOS**).

Motorman
[SR Obs.] Former title given to drivers of **Electric Multiple Units** (**EMU**).

Mott MacDonald Ltd. (MM, MML)
A multidisciplinary **Infrastructure** and engineering consultancy whose head office is in Croydon, UK.

MoU
Memorandum of Understanding.

Mouseholes
The small holes which are sometimes designed into an assembly to allow inspection of otherwise hidden welds.

Movable Angles
[PW] An alternative term for **Switch Diamonds**.

Movable Bridge
A **Bridge** where one or more **Spans** can be lifted, rotated or otherwise moved out of line with the **Railway**. See **Bascule Bridge**, **Lift Bridge**, **Swing Bridge**. See also **Bridge Bolt**.

Movable Crossing
See **Swing Nose Crossing** (**SNX**).

Movable Infrastructure
[Sig.] **Points**, controlled **Level Crossings**, Movable **Bridges** and **Derailers**.

Movable Length
[PW] The part of a **Switch Rail** that moves laterally when the **Switches** are moved from **Normal** to **Reverse** or vice versa. This normally consists of the length between the **Switch Toe** and **Switch Heel**.

Move

Movement
[Ops.] The act of relocating a **Locomotive**, **Rail Vehicle**, **Train**, etc. from one place to another, generally with a clearly defined starting point, **Route** and end point.

Movement Authority (MA)
[Sig.] An indication made to a driver giving them permission to make a particular **Movement** (subject to certain conditions imposed on the driver by the nature of the indication). Examples include:
- **Main Signals**, used in the course of normal **Running**, which display **Movement Authorities** valid as far as the next Main Signal
- **Position Light Signals**, used for **Calling-on Routes** and **Shunt Routes** where the **Line** □ **Beyond** may be **Occupied**
- **Handsignals**, made by the waving of arms, coloured lights or **Flags**. These are normally used for ad-hoc **Shunt Movements** or in dire emergencies where no **Fixed Signal** could be used
- Radio, used in conjunction with a **Reassurance Tone** to control regular **Propelling Movements** and **Shunt Movements** in **Marshalling Yards** and **Depots**.

Movements Inspector
[Obs.] A member of the **Operating Department** responsible for policing **Train** □ **Movements** in a given geographical area.

Moving Block
Moving Block Signalling
[Sig.] As opposed to **Fixed Block** where the **Signals** are fixed and only one **Train** is allowed in one **Block Section** at one time, a system of **Signalling** where the appropriate separation between Trains is maintained by a system of detectors, beacons and a computer. The speed of the second Train is managed so that it safely follows the one in front. In other words, the length of Block Section is related to the following Train's speed and ability to stop, and the Block Section's position is related only to the first Train. The system is intended to provide maximum capacity on any given Line. There are no working systems in the UK. See **ERTMS** clause d), **In-cab Signalling**.

MP
See **Milepost**.

MP&I
[RT, Hist.] Major Projects & Investment.

MPA
See **Mid-point Anchor**.

MPATS
[Elec.] Mid-point Autotransformer Site.

MPC
a) [Elec.] Mid-point Connection, See **Return Conductor to Rail Bond**
b) See **Maintenance Protection Coordinator**.

MPD
a) See **Motive Power Depot**
b) [RT NR Hist.] Major Projects Division, an organisation responsible for projects such as Crossrail, Thameslink 2000 and the **West Coast Route Modernisation** (**WCRM**).

MPI
See **Magnetic Particle Inspection**.

MPM
See **Multi-processor Module**.

MPN
See **Major Project Notice**.

MPT
Magnetic Particle Testing.

MPTA
Merseyside Passenger Transport Authority (PTA).

MPTC
Miles Per Technical Casualty, with a 'casualty' defined as a technical or **Maintenance** defect on a **Train** which causes a delay of five or more minutes.

MPTE
Merseyside Passenger Transport Executive (PTE).

MPTSC
[Elec.] Mid-point Track Sectioning Cabin (TSC).

MPTSL
[Elec.] Mid-point Track Sectioning Location (TSL).

MPU
See Motive Power Unit.

MPV
See Multi-purpose Vehicle.

MPWI
[PW] Member of the Permanent Way Institution.

MR
a) [TRS] Main Reservoir, See Air Brake
b) Midland Railway.

MRA
a) Maintenance Requirements Analysis
b) [NR] The CARKND representing a 55 ton (two sections of 27.5 tons each) tipping Wagon used for Ballast.

MRB
The Midland Railway, Butterley.

MRBS
[TRS] An acronym representing a Motor Restaurant Buffet Standard Class □ Coach.

MRC
See Mills Rail Clip.

MRD
See Minimum Reading Distance.

MRE
Marginal Revenue Effect.

MRI
See Miniature Route Indicator. See also Subsidiary Route Indicator.

MRP
[TRS] Main Reservoir Pipe, See Two Pipe Air Brake.

MRR
Maintenance, Repair and Renewal.

MRSP
Most Restrictive Speed Profile.

MRT
a) See Maximum Rail Temperature
b) (Tradename) [PW] A machine for removing and inserting Sleepers. Manufactured by Geismar
c) See Minimum Reading Time.

MRV
[TRS] An acronym representing a Motorail Van/Car Carrier.

MS
a) Management Staff, a grade structure within British Railways (BR)
b) Method Statement
c) An acronym representing a Motor □ Standard Class □ Coach
d) [LUL] A Motor □ Shunting □ Car
e) [LUL] A Motor Shoegear Car.

MSC
a) Mutual Screening Conductor
b) Manchester Ship Canal.

MSD
[TRS] An acronym representing a Motor □ Standard Class □ Coach with disabled accommodation.

MSE.
a) [NR] Maintenance Support Engineer
b) Midland Suburban Electrification
c) Mean Square Errors.

MSIL
Minimum Site Infrastructure Limits.

MSIP
[NR] Management System Improvement Programme.

MSJ&AR
[Hist.] The Pre-Grouping Manchester South Junction & Altrincham Railway, a Great Central and London & North Western joint enterprise.

MSL
a) See Miniature Stop Lights
b) A Level Crossing with Miniature Stop Lights.

MSLR
[Hist.]
a) The Pre-Grouping Mid-Suffolk Light Railway
b) The Manchester Sheffield and Lincolnshire Railway, precursor to the Great Central Railway (GCR).

MSO
a) See Mid-span Offset
b) [TRS] An acronym representing a Motor □ Standard Class □ Open Coach
c) Machine Switch Out.

MSP
a) See Measured Shovel Packing
b) See Miniature Snow Plough.

MSRB
[TRS] An acronym representing a Motor □ Standard Class □ Coach with restaurant/buffet.

MSRP
[NR Sig.]]
a) Major Schemes Review Panel
b) Minor Schemes Review Panel.
In both cases, a committee of senior Signalling Engineers convened to examine Signalling design proposals.

MSRS
Mode Shift Revenue Support grants: payable to shippers on a per unit basis for moving Goods by Rail that would otherwise go by road.

MSS
See Maximum Safe Speed.

MSSCC
Manchester South Signal Control Centre.

MST
Maintenance Scheduled Task

MT
(em-tee) Shorthand for empty.

MT/276 Examination Schedule
[TRS] A standard issued by British Rail (BR) in 1984 detailing the examinations required before a Steam Locomotive was allowed to run on British Rail Infrastructure. This has now been adopted by Network Rail (NR).

ELLIS' BRITISH RAILWAY ENGINEERING ENCYCLOPÆDIA

MTA
[NR] The **CARKND** representing 32 ton capacity **Open Wagons** used for **Ballast** and **Spoil**.

MTB
[TRS] Magnetic Track Brakes.

MTBF
Mean Time Between Failures.

MTBFF
Mean Time Between Functional Failures.

MTBHE
Mean Time Between Hazardous Events.

MTBSF
Mean Time Between Service Failures.

MTBWSF
Mean Time Between Wrong Side Failures.

Mtce.
Shorthand for **Maintenance**.

MTDS
See **WaveTrain MTDS**.

MTL
Mersey Travel Ltd.

MTP
[PW] Managed Track Position.

MTPA
Million Tonnes Per Annum. See **Equivalent Million Gross Tonnes Per Annum (EMGTPA)**.

MTRT
Matisa □ Track Recording Trolley.

MTTF
Mean Time to Failure. See also **MTBF**.

MTTR
Mean Time to Repair.

MTTRS
Mean Time to Restore Service.

MTTS
Mean Time to Service.

MTU
(Tradename) An international manufacturer of diesel engines based (in the UK) in East Grinstead.

MU
[NR] On signs forming part of a **Non-standard Differential Speed Restriction**, it indicates that the speed value applies only to **Multiple Unit Trains** (except **Class** 185).

Mu (μ)
(*mew*) The Greek letter used to represent the coefficient of friction between wheel and **Rail**. See **Adhesion**.

MU Train
See **Multiple Unit Train**.

MUBV
[TRS] An acronym representing a **Multiple Unit □ Barrier Vehicle**.

Muckle Bolt
[PW, Col.] Term for a type of **Stock Rail Bolt** made with a slot-in detachable head, allowing it to be fitted and replaced with the **Switch Rail** in situ.

Mullet (YLA)
[NR] A 50 ton capacity flat **Wagon** used for transporting **Rails**. See **Wagon Names**.

MultiEst
[NR] Network Rail's internal estimating system for projects. It utilises historic out-turn data to predict future cost.

Multifret
An **Intermodal Wagon** with a deck height of 945mm to carry **Swap-bodies** or **Containers**.

Multi-groove Locking (MGL)
A system of fastenings employing a bar with parallel grooves machined into one end, onto which a deformable collar is compressed following tensioning of the system. The patents are held by Huck International Inc., a division of Alcoa. See also **Huck Bolt**, **Huck Pin**, **Multi-groove Locking Pin (MGL Pin)**, **Multi-groove Locking Stud (MGL Stud)**.

Multi-groove Locking Pin (MGL Pin)
A hydraulically tensioned alternative to normal bolts similar to the **Multi-Groove Locking Stud (MGL Stud)** described below, but having the other end shaped into a permanent head. Also **Huck Pin**.

Multi-groove Locking Stud (MGL Stud)
A hydraulically tensioned alternative to normal bolts with a standard threaded portion on the non-grooved end, allowing the use of a nut for coarse adjustments prior to tensioning. Used for securing **Check Blocks**, **Stock Rails** and **Crossings**. Also **Huck Bolt**.

Multi-lamp Route Indicator (MLRI)
[Sig.] An obsolete term for an **Alphanumeric Route Indicator (ARI)**. See also **Theatre Route Indicator**, which is also an obsolete term.

Multiple Aspect Signalling (MAS)
[Sig.] A **Signalling System** employing **Colour Light Signals**, **Track Circuits (TC)** and often some level of **Route** setting automation.

Multiple Track Railway
A **Route** having more than two **Tracks**. Sometimes also described in terms of the actual number of Tracks at a given point, e.g. a six Track section.

Multiple Unit (MU)
See **Multiple Unit Train (MU Train)**

Multiple Unit Class
[TRS] All types of **Multiple Unit** on the **National Railway Network (NRN)** have a three digit identifying number ranging from 101 to 508, though this list is not completely populated. The numbering system is banded:
- 100 to 199 – **Diesel Hydraulic Multiple Units** (**DHMU**) and **Diesel Mechanical Multiple Units** (**DMMU**)
- 200 to 299 – **Diesel Electric Multiple Units** (**DEMU**)
- 300 to 399 – AC □ **Electric Multiple Units (EMU)**
- 400 to 499 – DC □ **Third Rail** Electric Multiple Units on the **Southern Region**
- 500 to 599 – other DC Third Rail Electric Multiple Units

The higher class numbers are yet to be used.

Multiple Unit Train (MU Train)
[TRS] A **Train** consisting of one or two or more vehicles semi-permanently coupled together, that can marshalled with other similar Trains to make a Formation that has a **Driving Cab** at both ends. All the Traction Power and Brakes on all vehicles can be controlled from either Cab. Some or all the vehicles may be equipped with powered axles. There are five main varieties:
- **DEMU** - Diesel Electric Multiple Unit, where electrical power is generated by a diesel engine and transferred to electric **Traction Motors** which propel the vehicle
- **DHMU** - Diesel Hydraulic Multiple Unit, where hydraulic pressure is generated by a diesel engine and transferred to hydraulic Traction Motors which propel the vehicle
- **DMMU** - Diesel Mechanical Multiple Unit, where a diesel engine drives the wheels via a gearbox
- **DMU** - Diesel Multiple Unit, where a diesel engine is the source of power for **Traction** purposes
- **EMU** - Electric Multiple Unit, where an external electrical current from **Overhead Line Equipment** (**OLE**) or a **Conductor Rail** is the source of power for Traction purposes.
- An experimental **Battery Electric Multiple Unit** (**BEMU**) was tried, but was not a success.

See also Parry People Mover.

Multiple Working
[TRS Ops.] The coupling of two **Motive Power Units** together such that all the power and braking controls are managed by a driver in the **Leading End** □ **Driving Cab**.

Multi-processor Module (MPM)
[Sig.] The part of a **Solid State Interlocking** (**SSI**) that performs the **Interlocking** functions. Each module contains many processors, and three modules are required to make up one **Interlocking**, working on a majority voting system to ensure safety and reliability.

Multi-purpose Vehicle (MPV)
A self-propelled diesel powered flat-bed **Rail Vehicle** with a **Driving Cab** at one end, normally coupled in pairs, used for **Maintenance** work, transporting equipment and other duties.

Multi-section
See **Cut Section**.

Multi-SPAD Signal
[Sig.] A **Signal** that has been **Passed At Danger** under **Category A SPAD** conditions more than once in the preceding five year period.

Multi-strike Bridge
[NR] A bridge that has suffered three or more **Bridge Strikes** (**Bridge Bashes**) in any preceding 12 month period.

Multi-track
Multi-track Railway
See **Multiple Track Railway**.

MUR
Maintenance **U**nit **R**ates.

Muscleman
(Tradename) [PW] A small wheeled trolley capable of clamping itself to the **Rails**, to which a heavy duty movable frame is fitted. Once attached to the Rails, the machine can lower the frame onto the **Ballast** and **Slue** itself and the **Track**. Manufactured by Permaquip.

Mushroom
[Col.] A nickname for:
a) An **Electric Points Heating** □ **Transformer**
b) The electronic part of a **SIMIS-W** □ **Axle Counter** installation.

In both cases they are named after their shape and **Cess** location.

Mushrooming
[PW] A description of the effect produced by the rolling action of wheels on the **Low Rail** on **Curved Track**. See **Plastic Deformation** of the **Rail Head**. See also **Burr Lipping**, **Lipping**.

MUTCD
Manual on **U**niform **T**raffic **C**ontrol **D**evices.

MVAIR
(*em-vair* or *ma-vair*) [Hist.] **M**anchester **V**ictoria **A**rea **I**nfrastructure □ **R**enewals.

MVDC
Medium **V**oltage **DC** □ **T**rack **C**ircuit (**TC**).

MVLC
[Elec.] **M**edium **V**oltage **L**ine **C**over, a polymer-based clip-on cover used to reduce the likelihood of **Tripping** or arcing at locations with sub-optimal electrical clearances

MW
[IÉ] **M**aintenance of **W**ay. See **Permanent Way Maintenance**.

MWA
See **Minimum Works Alteration**.

MWD
Mid**w**eek **D**ay (shift)

MWL
a) See **Miniature Warning Lights**
b) A type of **Automatic Level Crossing** equipped with **Miniature Red / Green Warning Lights** to indicate to users whether it is safe to cross.

MWN
Mid**w**eek **N**ight (shift)

MWO
a) **M**inor **W**orks **O**rder
b) **M**ondays and **W**ednesdays **O**nly.

MZ
[Hist.] **M**idlands **Z**one, see **Railtrack** (**RT**).

N

N
a) See **N Value**
b) [Sig.] On a **Signalling Circuit Diagram**:
- A connection to the negative **DC** busbar
- As one of the leading letters of an **Equipment Code**, it means **Normal**. See also **NBDR**
- As the last letter of an Equipment Code, it means hand operated electrical switch, key, push button, **Plunger** or **Release**
- On a **Cable Plan**, a conductor returning to a power supply. Also **NX**
c) The letter represented by **November** in the **Phonetic Alphabet**
d) [LUL] The Northern **Line**.

N Value
[PW] A means of describing the angle of intersection of the **Running Rails** in an **Acute Crossing**. It has the advantage of being verifiable by site measurement. The relationship is:

$$N = \frac{\cot\frac{x}{2}}{2}$$

Where:
- x is the value of the **Crossing Angle** in degrees.

See **Centreline Measurement**. See also **Right Angle Measurement**.

N&BR
[Hist.] The **Pre-Grouping** Neath & Brecon **Railway**.

N&SJR
[Hist.] The **Pre-Grouping** Norfolk & Suffolk **Joint Railway**, a Midland & Great Northern Joint and Great Eastern joint enterprise.

N&SWJR
[Hist.] The **Pre-Grouping** North & South Western Junction **Railway**, a London & North Western, Midland and North London joint enterprise.

N&VMP
Noise and Vibration Management Plan

N/B
Shorthand for Northbound.

Nabla
(Tradename) An early type of **Elastic Rail Fastening** used on early **Concrete Sleepers**.

Nadal Formula
See **Derailment Quotient**.

Nairn's Accident
At 14.45 on 4th May 1982 an **Express Passenger Train** hit an agricultural tractor and trailer which become grounded whilst traversing Nairn's **Accomodation Level Crossing**. 30 **Passengers** were taken to hospital, 13 of whom were detained, one with serious injuries. The driver of the tractor had left his machine to try and warn the **Train** and was therefore uninjured. The inquiry found that the surfacing, gradient and poor signage on the approaches to the Crossing and the Crossing Surface itself had contributed to the tractor and trailer becoming stuck. See **Nairns Programme**.

Nairns Programme
[Hist.] A project dealing with the re-profiling of **Accomodation Crossings** and **Occupation Crossings** (**OC**), particularly those used by farms, to improve the **Gradient** profiles of the roads and address other issues.

NALCO
National Location Codes. See **CORPUS**.

NAPS
[Obs.] National Accounts Payable System, a former British Rail (**BR**) computer system.

Narrow Angle Crossing
[PW] A **Crossing** with a large **N Value**; one with a small angle between the **Running Edges** (**RE**). Also **Sharp Angle Crossing**.

Narrow Gauge Railway
A **Railway** that uses **Track** laid to a **Gauge** of between 15 inches (381mm) and **Standard Gauge** (1435mm, 4 feet 8 $^1/_2$ inches) See also **Miniature Railway**.

Narrow Gauge Track
[PW] **Track** laid to a **Gauge** less than **Standard Gauge** (1435mm, 4 feet 8 $^1/_2$ inches). When the **Great Western Railway** (**GWR**) had Broad Gauge Track, they referred to Standard Gauge as **Narrow Gauge**.

NASR
Newport Area **Signalling** Renewal.

NAT
Not Applicable **Timetable**.

National Bearer Network (NBN)
[NR] The transmission systems and telephone exchanges linked by a fibre optic and copper cable network that is located mainly within **Lineside** ▫ **Troughing** routes.

National Competency Control Agency (NCCA)
The organisation responsible for managing the issue and control of qualifications to **Safety Critical Staff** such as **Controller of Site Safety** (**COSS**) and **Personal Track Safety** (**PTS**). See also **Sentinel**.

National Delivery Service (NDS)
[NR] A centralised **Network Rail** (**NR**) supply system dealing with **Ballast**, **Rail** and **Sleepers** etc.

National Electronic Sectional Appendix (NESA)
[NR] A website that enables **Rail Industry** users to access the NESA system to perform searches of all **Sectional Appendices**.

National Express East Anglia (NXEA)
(Tradename) A **Train Operating Company** (**TOC**) which operates **Main Line** services between London, Colchester, Ipswich and Norwich and local services across Norfolk, Suffolk and parts of Cambridgeshire.

National Hazard Directory (NHD)
[NR] A database maintained by **Network Rail** (**NR**) which contains details of the health, safety and environmental hazards known to exist on **Network Rail Controlled Infrastructure** (**NRCI**).

303

ELLIS' BRITISH RAILWAY ENGINEERING ENCYCLOPÆDIA

National Incident Report (NIR)
A reporting system in the UK to initiate, disseminate and manage urgent safety related defects in **Rail Vehicles**, plant and machinery. It is coordinated by RSSB.

National Location Code (NLC)
[NR] A six-digit code used for physical locations such as **Stations** and **Junctions** as well as codes relating to accounting and other purposes. For instance, Leeds is 848700.

National Network, The
See **National Railway Network** (NRN).

National Radio Network (NRN)
[BR, NR]
a) A scheme developed by **British Railways** (BR) to provide a two way radiotelephone service for the **National Railway Network** (NRN). It was based on Band III VHF technology and following the **Clapham Accident** all **Driving Cabs** were equipped with the radios.
b) A dedicated national radio network operated and maintained by **Network Rail** that allows direct communication between driver and network controller.
See also BRUNEL, GSM R, ORN.

National Railway Museum (NRM)
Based in York, a branch of the Science Museum dealing specifically with the archaeology and history of the **Railway**, as well as the preservation of working examples of **Signalling Equipment**, **Locomotives** and **Rolling Stock** from all eras.

National Railway Network (NRN)
The system of **Railway** □ **Lines**, **Stations**, **Depots** and associated facilities previously run by **British Railways** (BR), formerly under the stewardship of **Railtrack** (RT) and now **Network Rail** (NR). Sometimes colloquially contracted to The National Network or The Network.

National Records Group (NRG)
[NR] The central organisation that maintains and manages the **Signalling** design records (**Source Records**) for the **National Railway Network** (NRN).

National Route Code (NRC)
[BR Obs.] A numeric identification code for sections of a **Route** between **Junctions**. This system has now been largely superseded by the use of **Engineer's Line References** (ELR), which are shorter and simpler.

National Safety Authority (NSA)
[IÉ] The national body entrusted with the tasks regarding **Railway** safety in accordance with European directive 2004/49/EC.

National Seasonal Infrastructure Treatment Plan
[NR] The document recording which parts of the network will receive **Rail Head** treatment during **Leaf Fall Season**, exactly when, and at what frequency.

National SPAD Focus Group (NSFG)
[NR] The industry body leading the driver to reduce the incidence of **Signals Passed At Danger** (SPADs) on the UK **Rail Network**.

Nationalisation
[Hist.] Provided for by the **Transport Act 1947**, Nationalisation of the network saw the merger of the **Big Four** and the creation of **British Railways** (BR) on 1 January 1948. Initially under the control of the Railway Executive of the **British Transport Commission** (BTC), under the **Transport Act 1962** this organisation was abolished and BR became the **British Railways Board** (BRB). See also **Privatisation**.

Nationally Significant Infrastructure Project (NSIP)
A project which comes under the Planning Act 2008. It will meet one of the following three categories of Railway schemes:
• It is on **Main Line** □ **Infrastructure**: this means a project on a Railway network whose operator is licensed by the **Office of Rail Regulation** (ORR) and is designated by an order of the Secretary of State made for the purposes of the Act, unless the project is covered by **Permitted Development** rights. Most of **Network Rail's** (NR) network is expected to be so designated, as is the **Channel Tunnel Rail Link** (CTRL) / High Speed **One** (HS1) and the **Heathrow Express** (HEX).
• It is a **Rail Freight** terminal where, amongst other things, the proposed land area exceeds 60 hectares.
• It is a "cluster" project or associated development. As part of the new regime, the Secretary of State has the power to direct that a series of similar projects (ones that are of the same type) although individually below the appropriate threshold, should be referred to the **Infrastructure Planning Commission** (IPC).

NATM
[Civ.] New Austrian Tunnelling Method.

Natrasolve
(Tradename) A solvent based on d-limonene distilled from orange peel and used to remove leaf contamination from **Rails**. Made by JohnsonDiversey Inc.

Natural
[Col.] A contraction of **Natural Stressing**.

Natural Angle
[PW] The angle of **Intersection of Gauge Lines** (IP) of the **Common Crossing** of a **Turnout** formed by a particular Radius (R) of **Turnout Curve** and a straight **Main Line**.

Natural Crossing
[PW] A **Common Crossing** whose angle, when formed into a **Turnout** (TO) with **Switches** of a specified description, enables the **Turnout Radius** to equal the **Switch Radius** from the **Switch Heel** to the **Intersection of Gauge Lines** (IP) of the **Common Crossing**.

Natural Rubber
[PW] A material used for **Rail Pads**.

Natural Slope
Sloping ground that has been formed by natural processes.

Natural Stressing
[PW] Obtaining a **Stress Free Temperature** (**SFT**) by the simple means of carrying out the **Stressing** when the **Rail** is already at a **Stress Free Temperature**, obviating the need for **Tensors**. Also referred to as a **Natural**. Also Sun Locking.

Natural Turnout
[PW] A **Turnout** (**TO**) or **Lead** in which the tangents to the **Crossing** and **Switch Heel** produce a **Turnout Curve** with the same Radius (**R**) as the **Switch Radius**. Therefore also a **Turnout** or **Lead** containing a **Natural Crossing**.

NAU
[NR] National Access Unit, the organisation which co-ordinates **Possession** planning and publication of **Weekly Operating Notices** (**WON**).

NAWR
The Noise at Work Regulations 1989.

NB
[TRS] No Boiler, referring to a **Locomotive** not equipped with a **Steam Heating** boiler. The term is now obsolete on modern **Rolling Stock**, as all such heating is **Electric Train Heating** (**ETH**). See also **No Heat**.

NBA
[BR, NR] **National Radio Network** (**NRN**) Base station Alignment.

NBDR
[Sig.] The four standard Locking positions provided on a **Lever** of a **Frame** or **Power Frame**:
- N - **Normal**
- B - Normal **Checklock**
- D - **Reverse** Checklock
- R - **Reverse**

NBN
See **National Bearer Network**.

NBR
[Hist.] The **Pre-Grouping** North British **Railway**.

NBS
[Ops.] No Booked Service. See **White Period**.

NC
a) See **Non-compliance**. See also **Temporary Non-compliance** (**TNC**)
b) Of an electrical switch, **Relay** or contact, Normally Closed. The opposite is **Normally Open** (**NO**)

NCAP
[NR] National Core Audit Programme.

NCB
See **Network Certification Body**

NCC
National Control Centre.

NCCA
See **National Competency Control Agency**.

NCL
Northern City **Line**.

NCM
[NR] **Network Change** Manager.

NCN
[NR] **Network Change** Notice.

NCR
Non-conformance Report. Also **Corrective Action Report** (**CAR**).

NCRG
National Route Crime Group.

NCT
[Sig.] Non-communicating **Train**, a Train not equipped with **Train Control System** (**TCS**) facilities, **Running** on a **TCS** □ **Fitted** □ **Line**.

NCU
Node Cabinet Unit.

NDA
a) [Sig.] Not Described Alarm, an indication that a **Train** has been presented to a **Train Describer** (**TD**) from the previous TD with no **Train Reporting Number** entered
b) Nuclear Decommissioning Authority

NDAD
National Digital Archive of Datasets.

NDC
National Distribution Centre.

NDE
Non-destructive Examination.

NDF
No Defect Found. See also **NFF**.

NDM
a) [TRS] **Non-driving** □ **Motor**
b) Network Development Manager.

NDN
National Data Communications Network.

NDS
See **National Delivery Service**.

NDSD
Non-described Special Description.

NDT
a) Non-destructive Testing
b) Nuclear Density Testing.

Near Miss
Better called a near hit, this describes a situation which did not result in an accident, but potentially could have done so under slightly different circumstances. Near Misses normally occur where safety procedures are ignored. A common Near Miss results from **Controllers of Site Safety** (**COSS**) providing inadequate **Safe Systems of Work** (**SSoW**); resulting in staff leaping out from in front of a **Train**.

Nearest Open Line
Describing the closest **Open Line** to a particular point.

Nearside
In the UK, The left hand side of a **Train** in the **Normal Direction** of travel.

NEBOSH
(*nee-bosh*) National Examination Board in Occupational Safety & Health.

Neck
a) [PW] The narrowest area of a **Common Crossing** which contains the **Neck** bend of the **Wing Rails**, immediately ahead of the **Crossing Nose**
b) [PW] The point where the **Check Rail** and **Wing Rail** are closest together in an **Obtuse Crossing**.
c) See **Shunt Neck**.

Neck Block
[PW] Distance block used to maintain the correct spacing between the **Rails** at the **Neck** of a **Common Crossing** or **Obtuse Crossing**.

NED
Non-effective Depth.

Needle Indicator

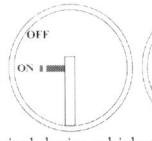

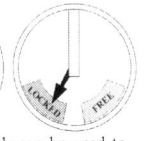

An electromechanical device which can be used to convey a variety of facts to the **Signaller** regarding the status of the **Signalling System** but typically provide to give confirmation of the correct operation of a remote item.

NEG
National Express Group, a **Train Operating Company** (**TOC**).

Negative Cant
[PW] Describing the situation where the **Outside Rail** of a **Curve** is lower than the **Inside Rail**, i.e. **Cant** (**C**, **E**) that increases the value of **Cant Deficiency** (**D**) on that Curve rather than reducing it. This situation can arise in the **Turnout** (**TO**) area of a short **Contraflexure Turnout** located on a Curve.

Negative Cant Deficiency
[PW] A situation which arises when a **Train** is moving slowly relative to the **Equilibrium Speed** (**V_e**) on a **Curve** and experiences a surfeit of **Cant** and therefore a lack of **Cant Deficiency**. Also called **Cant Excess**.

Negative Conductor Rail
See **Negative Rail**.

Negative Conductor Rail Pedestal
[LUL] A vertical pillar supporting the **Negative Conductor Rail** through the **Platform Safety Pits** of **Tube Line** ▫ **Station Grounds**.

Negative Feeder
[Elec.] The additional **Conductor** provided as part of the **Traction Return Circuit** in an **Autotransformer** (**AT**) ▫ **Electrification System**.

Negative Mileage
A situation where a **Railway** has **Track** ▫ **On the Approach** to the **0 Milepost**. This situation can arise in the following situations:
• Where a **Terminal Station** is rebuilt with longer **Platforms** but leaving the **Station Throat** untouched. A notable example is Euston **Station**
• Where a **Junction** with a **Branch Line** is moved as part of **Remodelling** work.
See also **Mileage, Milepost**.

Negative Rail
[LUL] A second **Conductor Rail** at a nominal voltage of -150V used as a **Traction Current Return**, positioned on the centre line of **Gauge** in the **Fourfoot**. Universal on **London Underground Limited** (**LUL**) ▫ **Lines**, this provision is also found on some **Network Rail** (**NR**) Lines where LUL **Trains** operate. Also **Fourth Rail**, **Negative Conductor Rail**, **Neggy Rail**.

Negative Shoe
[LUL] A device similar to a **Current Collection Shoe** mounted centrally under the **Bogies** of **Trains** and used to pass the **Traction Return Current** to the **Fourth Rail**.

Negative Splay
The fabricated junction piece used to guide the **Negative Shoe** of **Trains** running through **Turnouts** (**TO**) on **Lines** fitted with **Negative Rails** (**Fourth Rails**).

Negative Stagger

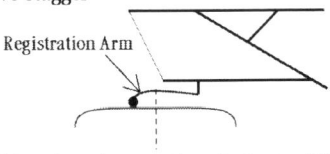

[Elec.] Describing the case where the **Contact Wire** (**CW**) is on the opposite side of the centre line of the **Pantograph** from the fixed point at which the **Wire** is registered. The opposite is **Positive Stagger**. See **Stagger**.

Neggy Rail
[Col.] A term for the **Negative Conductor Rail**.

Negligible Risk Failure
A failure which does not result in the protection provided by the **Signalling System** being reduced. Also known as a **Right Side Failure** (**RSF**). See **Fail Safe**.

Neighbour Notifications
The process for notifying neighbours of any new planning application that may affect them.

Nellie
[Obs.] The former **Phonetic Alphabet** word representing **N**. Replaced by **November**.

NEM
[NR] National Estimating Manager.

NEMA
National Electrical Manufacturers Association, the association of electrical equipment and medical imaging manufacturers in the United States

NEP
[NR]
a) National **European Rail Traffic Management System** (**ERTMS**) Programme, previously the Single National ERTMS Programme (**SNEP**)
b) National **Electrification** Programme.

NEPA
[LUL] See **Nightly Engineering Protection Arrangements**.

NEPTUNE
(*nep-chewn*) [PW Obs.] North Eastern Peak Tracing Unit and Numerical Encoder. An early **Track Recording** system installed in the **Matisa Track Recording Trolleys** and later superseded by the use of the **High Speed Track Recording Coach** (**HSTRC**).

NEQ
Net Explosive Quantity.

NER
a) See **North Eastern Region**.
b) [Hist.] The former North Eastern **Railway**.

NESA
See **National Electronic Sectional Appendix**.

Nest of Eggs
See **Conductor Rail Test Lamp Set**.

Nested Coil Springs
[TRS] Two or three coil springs placed inside each other, typically on a **Wagon**. When the Wagon is lightly loaded only the lower stiffness spring is engaged. As the Wagon load is increased beyond a threshold, the second stiffer spring also comes into play. If the Wagon load is increased further beyond the next threshold, the third stiffer spring comes into play, where fitted.

NET
[LR] Nottingham Express Transit.

NETF
[LUL] New Engineering Train Fleet.

NETRAFF
[BR, NR] A system used for generating **Track** tonnage statistics. It interfaces with the **GEOGIS** database.

Network Certification Body (NCB)
(Tradename) A subsidiary of **Network Rail Infrastructure Ltd**, independent of its parent organization, which provides certification and assessment services in the **Rail Industry**.

Network Change
[NR] The formal procedure by which the **Infrastructure Controller**, previously **Railtrack** (**RT**), now **Network Rail** (**NR**), gains assent from the **Train Operating Companies** (**TOC**) and **Freight Operating Companies** (**FOC**) for alterations to the facilities it provides, e.g. the closure of a **Route** or relocation of a **Loop**. See also **Station Change**.

Network Code
[NR] The Network Code is a set of rules forming part of each access contract between **Network Rail** (**NR**) and a holder of **Access Rights**. It does not create any contractual relationship between operators of trains. The purpose of the Code is:
- To regulate changes to the **Working Timetable** (**WTT**), **Rail Vehicles** specified in an Access contract, the **Network**, computer systems and Network Code itself
- To establish procedures relating to environmental damage
- To establish a performance monitoring system
- To establish procedures in the event of operational disruption.

The Code is divided into twelve sections:
Part A General Provisions
Part B Performance Monitoring
Part C Modifications
Part D **Timetable Change**
Part E Environmental Protection
Part F Vehicle Change
Part G **Network Change**
Part H Operational Disruption
Part J **Changes to Access Rights**
Part K Information
Part L Performance
Part M Appeals

Network Management Centre (NMC)
[RT] The next generation of **Signal Box** (**SB**). Nine were proposed, each one controlling a whole **Route** or geographical region (e.g. Saltley would control the **West Coast Main Line** (**WCML**)). They are the logical progression from **Integrated Electronic Control Centres** (**IECC**) and include **Electrical Control Room** (**ECR**) and **Regional □ Control** in one facility. This concept is now called a **Rail Operations Centre** (**ROC**).

Network Management Statement (NMS)
[RT] The document detailing that company's plans for **Maintenance**, upgrade and enhancement. **Railtrack** was obliged to publish this document by the **Strategic Rail Authority** (**SRA**) to ensure transparency of Railtrack's plans for the **National Railway Network** (**NRN**).

Network Modelling Framework (NMF)
An integrated suite of models that predict demand, revenues, costs, punctuality, and safety performance for different investment strategies.

Network Rail Business Process Documents
[NR Obs.] The title for the re-issued **Network Rail Company Standards** (**NRCS**). The final numbering remained largely unchanged: e.g. RT/CE/S049 (**Track Design Manual** (**TDM**)) became NR/SP/TRK/049 (Track Design Handbook, now NR/L2/TRK/2049).

Network Rail Company Standards (NRCS)
[NR] Previously called **Railtrack Company Standards** (**RCS**) these documents were renamed following the transfer of responsibility from **Railtrack** (**RT**) to **Network Rail**. The Standards provide the Network Rail specific detailed requirements, each Standard corresponding to a higher level **Railway Group Standard** (**RGS**). See also **Network Rail Business Process Documents**.

Network Rail Connecting Network
[NR] Alternative term for the **National Rail Network** (**NRN**) in **Network Rail □ Connection Agreements** (**CA**).

Network Rail Controlled Infrastructure (NRCI)
[NR] The land, buildings and systems owned and managed by **Network Rail** (**NR**).

Network Rail Infrastructure Limited (NRIL)
(Tradename) A wholly owned subsidiary of **Network Rail Ltd.**, NRIL (previously **Railtrack** plc) is the owner and operator of most of the **Rail Infrastructure** in Great Britain. Both have registered addresses at Kings Place, London N1.

ELLIS' BRITISH RAILWAY ENGINEERING ENCYCLOPÆDIA

Network Rail Ltd. (NR)
(Tradename) A not-for-profit company owned by members. These members are drawn from **Rail** organisations, the public and the **Strategic Rail Authority** (**SRA**). The company successfully purchased all **Railtrack's** assets for £500m on the 2nd of October 2002. As of 2014, Network Rail Ltd. owns:
- Network Rail (High Speed) Ltd.
- Network Rail (Projects) Ltd.
- Network Rail (Spacia) Ltd.
- Network Rail (Stations) Ltd.
- Network Rail (VY1) Ltd.
- Network Rail (VY2) Ltd.
- Network Rail Certification Body Ltd.; see **Network Certification Body** (NCB)
- Network Rail Consulting Ltd.
- Network Rail Development Ltd.
- **Network Rail Infrastructure Ltd.**
- Network Rail Property Ltd.
- **Spacia** (2002) Ltd.
- Victoria Place Shopping Centre Ltd.

Network Rail is now directly controlled by the **Department for Transport** (**DfT**).

Network Rail Standard
[NR] The title for the re-issued **Network Rail Business Process Documents**. Divided into three levels, most have now been renumbered again: RT/CE/S049 (**Track Design Manual** (**TDM**)), which became NR/SP/TRK/049 (Track Design Handbook) and is (currently) NR/L2/TRK/2049.

Network Rail Telecommunications (NRT)
[NR] (Tradename) Announced in late 2011, an internal organisation created to deliver a single, unified telecommunications organisation focusing on improving the effectiveness of the deployment and use of telecoms assets. The new organisation is almost identical to **British Railway Telecommunications** (**BRT**) in concept.

Network South East (NSE)
[BR Hist.] The brandname of the trading division of **British Railways** (**BR**) responsible for services in the south east of England between 1988 and 1995.

Network, The
See **National Railway Network** (**NRN**)

Networker
(Tradename) The brandname of the **Class** 365 **Electric Multiple Units** (**EMU**).

Networker Turbo
(Tradename) The brandname of the **Class** 165 and 166 **Diesel Mechanical Multiple Units** (**DMMU**) operated by **Thames Trains** (**TT**) and **Chiltern Railways** (**CH**)

Neutral Relay
[Sig.] A **Relay** which operates with either polarity of **DC** supply to the coil.

Neutral Section (NS)
[Elec.] A short non-conducting section introduced into the **Overhead Line Equipment** (**OLE**) to separate two **Electrical Sections**, so arranged that a passing **Pantograph** does not connect them electrically. See also **Automatic Power Control** (**APC**).

Neutral Section   Neutral Section
Warning Indicator   Indicator

Neutral Temperature
[PW Col.] An alternative for **Stress Free Temperature** (**SFT**).

New
Material that has not previously been installed or carried **Traffic**. See also **Serviceable**, **Scrap**.

New Line
[Col.] A term typically given to a **Diversionary Route** built after the **Main Line**, e.g. the Hertford **Loop**, Northampton Loop, the Old Oak West – High Wycombe – Aynho Junction line, etc. See also **Diversion**, **Old Line**.

New Measurement Train (NMT)
[NR] A geometry and **Track Recording** □ **Train**, largely based on existing **High Speed Train** (**HST**) vehicles, existing **Track Recording Coaches** (**TRC**) and surplus **Sleeper** □ **Coaches**. Nicknamed the **Flying Banana** as a result of its bright yellow colour scheme, this formation can record **Cant**, **Crosslevel**, **Gauge**, **Contact Wire** (**CW**) □ **Height**, **Curvature**, **Cyclic Top**, **Radius** (**R**), **Overhead Line Equipment** (**OLE**) □ **Stagger**, **Rail Corrugation**, **Top** and **Twist** data at speeds of up to 125mph.

New Notice Case
[Ops.] A display case holding only new **Notices** displayed at a driver's **Booking On Point** (**BOP**). See also **Engineering Notice Board**.

New Working Timetable
[Ops.] The revised **Prior Working Timetable** that ultimately becomes the **Working Timetable** (**WTT**) at the next **Timetable Change**.

Newcastle Chaldron
[Hist.] See **Chaldron**.

Newcastle Road

Newcastle Wagon Way
[Obs.] A **Tramway** comprising wood **Rails** supported on transverse **Wood Sleepers** to accommodate flanged-wheel **Wagons**.

Newel
[Civ.] A column marking the lower end of a **Wing Wall**.

Newlands, Alexander
(1870-1938) born in Elgin, Scotland. Appointed Chief Engineer of the Highland **Railway** in 1913 and Chief Engineer of the **London Midland Scottish Railway** (**LMSR**) in 1927. Responsible for improving standardisation of **Track** equipment and introducing **Colour Light Signals** to the Manchester area.

Newton Accident
The fatal accident that occurred at Newton Station on 21st July 1991 where a driver failed to observe the **Signal** □ **Beyond** (which was displaying a **Stop Aspect**) before acknowledging the **Guard's** □ **Right Away** (**RA**) □ **Bell Signal** and moving off. Because of the **Single Lead Junction** present Beyond the Signal, the driver met another **Train** □ **Head On**. Four died and 22 were injured. This failure to correctly react to a Signal at the end of a **Platform** is colloquially known as **Ding Ding and Away**. See also **Starting Against Signal SPAD** (**SASSPAD**). This was the third similar **Accident** in three years, see also **Bellgrove Accident, Hyde Accident**

Nexus
(Tradename) The trading name of Tyne and Wear **Passenger Transport Executive** (**PTE**). ATOC code **TW**.

NFDC
National Federation of Demolition Contractors.

NFF
[Sig.] No Fault Found, used in reports of **Signalling System** defects. See also **NDF**.

NFM
[NR] National Fares Manual.

NFRIP
(*en-frip*) National Fleet Reliability Improvement Programme.

NG
See **Normal Grade Rail**.

NGP
National Gauging Project.

NGT
[Hist.] New Generation Ticketing. See **TRIBUTE**.

NHCT
Nottingham Heritage Transport Centre.

NHD
See **National Hazard Directory**.

NHDMT
[NR] **National Hazard Directory** Maintenance Tool.

NHU
Note Handling Unit.

Nibs
An alternative for the **Dogs** in a **Mechanical Interlocking**.

Nicknames
[Col., NPT] Quite apart from the huge quantity of nicknames for individual items of **On Track Plant** (**OTP**), **On Track Machines** (**OTM**), Rolling Stock, **Wagons, Locomotives** and materials, whole engineering departments rejoice with their own personalised moniker:
- Disco Lights - **Signal Engineers**
- Knitting and Springs - The **Overhead Line Equipment** (**OLE**) **Engineers**
- Sick & Tired - The **Signal and Telecommunications** (**S&T**)
- The Great Unwashed - The **Permanent Way** (**PW, Pway**)
- Wet Bedders - The Permanent Way (again)
- Wick Trimmers - Signal Engineers (again)
- Wood Spoilers - Civil Engineers
- Woodentops - Train drivers.

NICS
See Non-Intrusive Crossing System.

NID
[NR] National Infrastructure Database.

Night Caps
[PW, Col.] A set of **Emergency Clamp Fishplates**, inspired by their frequent use overnight prior to the completion of **Welding**.

Nightly Engineering Protection Arrangements (NEPA)
[LUL] A document detailing the areas in which the **Traction Current** will be **Discharged**, which **Lines** are to be subject to **Possessions** and what activies are taking place during **Engineering Hours**.

Nile
A **Railway** □ **Telegraph Code** meaning "Following not to hand".

NIMBY
(*nim-bee*) Not in my Back Yard, a term coined to describe members of the public who are violently opposed to any scheme which adversely affects their view or property value, but have no view at all on any other proposal.

NIMU
(*nim-yew*) [Hist.] Northern Infrastructure Maintenance Unit (IMU).

Nine Foot Rule
[NR Col.] The requirement for staff, plant and equipment to remain nine feet (2.75m) from the nearest part of the 25kV AC **Overhead Line Equipment** unless it is proved to be **Isolated**.

Nipper
The member of a **Permanent Way** (**PW**) □ **Gang** whose duties are those of tool management, **Tea** making, **Gang Bus** tidying, etc. Not always the most junior member, some Nippers were **Light Duty Men**.

Nips
[PW Col.] A common contraction of **Timber Nips**, See **Timber Dogs**. Also **Dogs, Sleeper Dogs, Sleeper Nips, Sleeper Tongs**.

ELLIS' BRITISH RAILWAY ENGINEERING ENCYCLOPÆDIA

NIR
a) Northern Ireland Railways
b) See National Incident Report
c) National Incident Register
d) National Incident Reporting.

NIRU
See Not In Regular Use.

NIS
a) Not in Service
b) Not in Stock.

NITHC
Northern Ireland Transport Holding Company.

NKL
[NR] North Kent Line.

NLC
See National Location Code.

NLCSG
National Level Crossing Safety Group. Also NLXSG.

NLL
[NR] North London Line.

NLR
[Hist.]
a) The Pre-Grouping North London Railway
b) North London Railways, a Train Operating Company (TOC), part of Silverlink Metro, and now operated by London Overground Rail Operations Limited (LOROL).

NLRIP
[NR] North London □ Route Improvement Project.

NLU
[NR] National Logistics Unit.

NLXSG
National Level Crossing Safety Group. Also NLCSG.

NMC
See Network Management Centre.

NMF
See Network Modelling Framework.

NMP
New Maintenance Programme.

NMS
See Network Management Statement.

NMSI
National Museum of Science and Industry, now the Science Museum Group (SMG).

NMT
See New Measurement Train.

NNS
a) Notified National Standards, See Technical Standards for Interoperability (TSI)
b) No Numeric Standard.

NNTRs
Notified National Technical Rules, National specifications covering items such as UK Vehicle Gauges, where Technical Standards for Interoperability (TSIs) cannot be applied.

NO
Of an electrical switch, Relay or contact, Normally Open. The opposite is Normally Closed (NC).

No Block

No Block Line
[Sig.] A Line on which no monitoring of the Block Section is carried out by a Signaller.

No Heat
[TRS] Describing a Locomotive that has no facilities for Electric Train Heating (ETH).

No Out Of Turn (NOOT) Mode
[LUL] A Junction Mode which enforces the correct order of Trains through the Junction.

No Refuges
[NR] An area where there are no Refuges on that side of the Line, and Refuges are required. The limits of the restriction are denoted by a blue and white chequered Sign as shown.

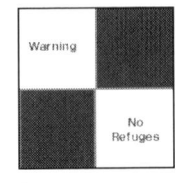

No Signaller Key Token (NSKT)
[Sig.] A variety of Electric Token Block (ETB) where the Token Instrument at one end of the Block Section is operated by the Traincrew using a key.

No Signaller Token (NST)
[Sig.] A variety of Electric Token Block (ETB) where the Signaller gives a Release for each Token issued, but the Token Instruments at one or both ends are operated by the Traincrew.

No Signaller Token Remote

No Signaller Token with Remote Crossing Loops (NSTR)
[Sig.] A variety of Electric Token Block (ETB) where an intermediate Token Instrument at a Passing Loop is operated by the Traincrew.

No Train Period (NTP)
An alternative term for Out of Traffic Hours (OOTH). Also White Period.

No Volts Relay
A Relay that detects a loss of voltage at a set value.

No.x End

No.x End Cab
[TRS] A Locomotive normally has two Driving Cabs, one at each end. To differentiate them, they are known as and marked as No.1 or No. 2 End Cab.

NoBo
(no-bow) See Notified Body.

NOC
a) National Operation Centre.
b) National Operations Council.

Nodding Dogs

Nodding Donkeys
[Col.] A nickname given to the Class 14x Diesel Multiple Unit (DMU), based on its behaviour at speed on Jointed Track.

NoL
North of London, an alternative description of a regional Eurostar □ Set.

310

Nominated Location
[NR] A location named in a **Track Access** contract between **Network Rail** (**NR**) and a **Freight Operating Company** (**FOC**) as a location at which either a **Train** starts, calls for Train **Working** purposes or ends its journey.

Nominated Person (NP)
[Elec] The suitably qualified person responsible for implementing an **Isolation** of the **Overhead Electrification Equipment** (**OLE**).

Nommy
[Col.] Common shortening of **Nominated Person**.

Non-adjustable Stretcher Bar
[PW] A **Permanent Way Stretcher Bar** of a design where the dimension between the two **Switch Rails** cannot be altered after initial installation.

Non-block Signal
[Sig.] A **Signal**, capable of showing a **Stop Aspect** that protects a **Level Crossing** (**LC**, **LX**) or similar, but does not mark the start or end of a **Block Section**.

Non-compliance (NC)
Where a design or installation cannot be made to meet all relevant **Railway Group Standards** (**RGS**) then this situation is a Non-compliance. Where the failure to meet standards only exists for a short time due to reasons other than difficulties with a standard (such as a temporary situation during **Remodelling** works) then this is a **Temporary Non-compliance** (**TNC**). See also **Derogation**.

Non-core Network
[NIR] the **Northern Ireland Railways'** system north of Ballymena, i.e. the **Lines** from Ballymena to Londonderry and Coleraine to Portrush.

Non-core Possession
[NR] A **Possession** in which no major **Track** items are replaced. See also **Stressing**, **Tamping**.

Non-cyclic Task
a) Any task which is not being performed to a frequency schedule specified in standards
b) [NR] For the purposes of planning **Safe Systems of Work** (**SSoW**), this would include any **Cyclic Task** which has not yet been verified by the **Responsible Manager**, in conjunction with **a Controller of Site Safety** (**COSS**) or **Individual Working Alone** (**IWA**) who is familiar with the area.

Non-disruptive Change
[NR] A change to planned **Engineering Work** that will not affect either the running of **Train** services or other planned work.

Non-driver's Side
[TRS] The opposite side of a **Train** from the driving position. Typically in the UK on **Heavy Rail** this is the right hand side of the Train in the direction of travel, as the driver normally sits on the left of the **Driving Cab**. See Also **Second Man**.

Non-driving
[TRS] An end vehicle in a **Multiple Unit** that does not have a **Driving Cab**.

Non-electrified Line
The opposite of an **Electrified Line**, a **Line** not provided with any electrical **Traction Supply** equipment.

Non-franchisable
[CT] A **Sign** indicating that the **Block Section** □ **Ahead** is not **Permissive** (Block Sections in the **Channel Tunnel** are Permissive unless signed otherwise).

Non-illuminated Diagram
[Sig.] A **Signal Box Diagram** that does not have facilities to display **Track Circuit** indications. See also **Illuminated Diagram**.

Non-intersecting Switch
[PW] A design of **Switch** where projected **Running Edge** (**RE**) of the **Switch Curve** does not meet, tangent with or cross the Running Edge of the **Stock Rail**. See also **Intersecting Switch**, **Tangential Switch**.

Non-intrusive Crossing System (NICS)
(Tradename) An arrangement of removable temporary ramps which, when placed over **Plain Line**, allow a **Train** to be diverted off one **Line** and onto another. The system does not require any modification to the existing **Track**, since it is only used within a **Possession**, does not affect the **Signalling System**. Manufactured by Scott-Track Ltd.

Non-multi
[Ops. Col] A **Multiple Unit** (**MU**) with a defective **Coupling** at one end, meaning it cannot be coupled to another Unit.

Non-nose Common Crossing
[PW Obs.] A design of **Common Crossing** in which the two **Crossing Legs** and the two **Wing Rail Fronts** terminate at a cast iron bed plate that supports a cast iron bar which is in turn placed manually to accord with route the **Traffic** passing over the **Switch** is required to take. Each of the rails has a V-shaped notch into which the cast iron bar, each end of which is V-shaped, locates. Designed for use in the **Narrow Gauge** (578mm) slate quarry **Lines** of North Wales. See also **Fixed-type Switch**.

Non-operational Property
[NR] Buildings, land and **Structures** that are no longer used by the **Railway** and now form no part of its requirements. This portfolio is now managed by **British Railways Property Limited**. See also **Operational Property**.

Non-passable

Non-passable Signal
[Sig.] A **Signal** which must not be passed without the express permission of the **Signaller**, because it prevents a significant conflict arising. Non-passable Signals are normally **Controlled Signals**. See also **Passable Signals**

311

ELLIS' BRITISH RAILWAY ENGINEERING ENCYCLOPÆDIA

Non-passenger Stock (NPS)
[TRS] **Coaching Stock** not built or adapted for the carrying of **Passengers**. An alternative for Non-Passenger Carrying Coaching Stock (**NPCCS**).

Non-running Movement
[Ops., Sig.] Any **Movement** of a **Train** or **Locomotive** that is not made from one **Main Aspect** to the next **Main Aspect**. This includes **Shunting** and **Single Line Working** (**SLW**).

Non-running Rail
[PW] A **Rail** on which **Rail Wheels** do not run. Examples of this are **Check Rails** and **Guard Rails**.

Non-safety Related
Those parts of a system, particularly **Signalling Systems**, whose failure does not directly affect the **Safety of the Line** or the integrity of the whole system. Also **Non-vital**.

Non-standard Differential Speed Restriction
[NR] A **Permanent Speed Restriction** (**PSR**) with two values.

The lower figure (normally the highest value) applies to **Trains** of a particular type, and the top figure (normally the lowest value) applies to all other **Trains**. Sometimes referred to as "top over bottom", in this case "75 over HST 100".

The upper value can also be replaced by a **Standard Differential Speed Restriction**, giving three values. This is a **Triple Differential Speed Restriction**. This arrangement is referred to as "top over middle over bottom", which in this example would be "50 over 75 over HST 100".

Current varieties of Train types include:
- CS – Covers **Class** 67 **Locomotives**
- EMU – Meaning all types of **Electric Multiple Unit**
- EPS – Which covers Trains capable of **Enhanced Permissible Speeds**, currently Class 221 and 390
- HST – Which covers **High Speed Trains** and Class 220 **Voyager** Trains
- MU – Which includes most **Multiple Unit Trains**
- SP – Which covers (amongst others) Class 150 to Class 159 **Sprinter**-type **Diesel Multiple Unit** (**DMU**) Trains.

Non-standard Differential Warning Indicator
[NR] A speed **Warning Indicator** (**WI**) provided to indicate to a driver that a **Non-standard Differential Speed Restriction** is Ahead. See also **Differential Warning Indicator**

The upper value can also be replaced by a **Standard Differential Speed Restriction Warning Indicator**, giving three values. This is a **Triple Differential Speed Restriction Warning Indicator**.

Non-standard Four-aspect Sequence
[Sig.] A series of **Signal Aspects** in **Four Aspect Signalling** that does not conform to the normal rules. The two acceptable variations are:
- Two successive **Double Yellow Aspects** (YY), e.g. G – YY – YY – Y – R, which is only permitted to achieve the correct **Braking Distance** (**BD**) from first YY to the Stop Aspect; or
- Two successive **Single Yellow Aspects** (Y), e.g. G – YY – Y – Y – R, which is only permitted to achieve the correct Braking Distance from first Y to the Stop Aspect

Non-track Circuited Line
[Sig.] A piece of **Railway** that is not equipped with functioning **Track Circuits** (**TC**). This may be because:
- There are no Track Circuits fitted, either because they are not required or because **Axle Counters** are fitted instead
- The Track Circuits have been disconnected temporarily.

Non-vital
[Sig. Obs.] Former term for **Non-safety Related**.

NORD-LOCK
(Tradename) A wedge-effect washer used in pairs to provide self-locking nut and bolt assemblies.

Normal (N)
a) [Sig.] For a **Set of Points** or **Set of Switches**, this is the default position, decided generally as being the position which permits the passage of **Trains** on the most used **Route**. This position is depicted on the **Signalling Plan**. The opposite is **Reverse**
b) [Sig.] Describing the default setting of a **Lever**, **Set of Points**, **Signal** or **Relay**
c) Describing a system functioning correctly, free from defect. The opposite is **Degraded**
d) A term used by **Train** enthusiasts to describe a non-enthusiast. See also **Anorak**, **Gricer**, **Prototype**.

Normal Aspect
[Sig.] The **Aspect** normally displayed by a **Signal** when no **Train** is present:
- For a **Controlled Signal**, this will be its **Most Restrictive Aspect**
- For an **Automatic Signal** it will be the Aspect dictated by the **Signal Overlap** of the Signal **Beyond** it

Normally shows **Red** (Stop Aspect)	Normally shows **Double Yellow** (Preliminary Caution Aspect)	Normally shows **Green** (Proceed Aspect)

For a **Colour Light Signal**, the Normal Aspect is indicated on the **Signalling Plan** by a double line rather than a single one. A **Semaphore Signal** will be drawn with the **Arm** in the **Normal Aspect** position.

Normal Control
[Sig.] In **Absolute Block** (AB) an arrangement where the **Home Signal** and **Distant Signal** □ **Arms** or **Levers** are **Proved** to be **On** before the **Signaller** can give **Line Clear** (LC). See Home Normal Control. See also Interlinking.

Normal Direction
[Ops. Sig.] The direction that **Trains** run under normal circumstances. **Lines** are normally named to reflect the Normal Direction, e.g. **Up Slow**, **Down Main**. Lines with no dominant direction (i.e. a roughly equal number of **Trains** in each direction) are normally named to reflect this, e.g. **Up and Down** □ Goods Line, Bi-directional □ Slow Line.

Normal Grade
Normal Grade Rail (NG)
[PW] A **Rail** manufactured in accordance with Tables 1 and 2 of British Standard Specification 11: 1985 'Normal' and having a hardness of 220HB (Brinell) at the **Rail Crown**. Also NQ.

Normal Mode
[LUL] A **Junction Mode** wherein if a **Train** arrives which is not the next **Timetabled** Train through the **Junction** and the Train can be routed through the Junction without delays, the control system will provide a warning to the Operator; without intervention, the system will set the Timetabled **Route** for the Train after a pre-determined time period (typically a minute) has elapsed.

Normal Ventilation System (NVS)
[CT] The air supply system used to ventilate the **Channel Tunnel** during normal operation.

Normalise
[Sig.] To return a **Lever**, **Set of Points**, **Signal** or **Relay** to their default setting.

North Eastern Electrical Cab Signalling
[Sig. Obs.] An early 1900s precursor to the much later **Automatic Train Protection** (ATP) system, this sytem comprised **Track**-mounted ramps and **Locomotive**-mounted contact arms, a bell and a miniature **Semaphore Signal Arm** in the **Driving Cab**, together with additional pointers. As the Locomotive passed the triggering position located 90m **on the Approach** to a **Distant Signal**, the miniature Semaphore Signal Arm indicated Danger and a warning bell started to ring. If the Distant Signal was clear the Arm in the Cab dropped to the **Clear** position and the bell stopped ringing; if the Distant Signal was at **Caution** the bell continued to ring and the Arm continued to indicate Danger.

North Eastern Region (NER)
[BR, Hist.] The North Eastern **Region** was a region of British Railways (BR) from **Nationalisation** in 1948. It was the near-direct descendant of the North Eastern Railway that had merged with some other companies to form the **LNER** in 1923. In 1958, in a major re-drawing of the **Region** boundaries, it gained those former **LMS** lines that lay in the present-day West and North Yorkshire. It was merged into **Eastern Region** (ER) in 1967.

Northern Rail
(Tradename) A **Train Operating Company** (TOC) which operates a range of inter-urban, commuter and rural services throughout the north of England.

Northern Spirit
[Hist.] A former **Train Operating Company** (TOC).

Northern Way
Until 2010 (when its funding was withdrawn) the Northern Way was an initiative, bringing together partners across North of England to work together to improve the economic performance of the North, with the aim to re-balance the UK economy.

Norton Fitzwarren Accident
On the 4th November 1940 a **Passenger Train** called at Norton Fitzwarren Station on the **Great Western Railway** (GWR). The layout at this point is a **Four Track Railway**, with the **Relief Lines** outside the **Fast Lines**. Unusually, the Fast Line **Signals** were located on the right hand side, and the Relief Line Signals on the left. GWR practice also placed the driver on the right hand side of the cab. The **Train** moved off, with the driver mistakenly reading the Fast Line Signals, which were **Clear** for a non-stop **Train**. Beyond Norton Fitzwarren the **Route** becomes a **Two Track Railway**, and the **Trap Points** were **Set Against** the driver. By the time he realised his error it was too late and the Train ran off the end of the **Trap Road**, killing 27 people. See also the **Ladbrooke Grove Accident**.

NOS
a) Network Operations Strategy
b) Network Operating Strategy
c) National Operating Strategy.

Nose
See **Crossing Nose**.

Nose Block
[PW] A **Distance Block** used to maintain the correct spacing between the **Wing Rails** and **Point Rail** at the nose of **Common Crossings**.

Nose Drop
[PW] The reduction in level over time of a **Crossing Nose** relative to the **Wing Rails** due to wear. Also **Nose Wear**.

Nose Hung
[TRS] Describing a **Traction Motor** that is suspended from the **Bogie Frame** or some other similar point, rather than **Axle Hung**. This reduces the **Un-sprung Mass** and thus the forces imposed on the **Track**.

Nose to Intersection Point
Nose to Intersection Point Dimension
Nose to IP
[PW] See **Crossing Nose to Intersection Point Dimension**.

Nose to Knuckle
Nose to Knuckle Dimension
[PW] The dimension between the **Nose** of one of the **Common Crossings** and the centre of the **Knuckle** in a **Diamond Crossing**. It is possible for all four such dimensions to be different in a given layout.

Nose to Nose
Nose to Nose Dimension
[PW] The dimension between the two **Crossing Noses** of a **Crossover**, or adjacent noses elsewhere in a **Switch and Crossing Layout** (**S&C Layout**). It is measured directly, whereas the **Lead** is measured parallel to the **Track Centre Line**.

Nose Wear
[PW] The wear on a **Crossing Nose**. Also **Nose Drop**.

Nosing
[Civ.]
a) The front edge of a **Platform Coping** adjacent to the **Track**
b) The front edge of a stair tread.

Nosing Force
The lateral force generated on the **Track** by a **Train** as it encounters a **Curve**.

Not in Regular Use (NIRU)
A note used on diagrams to indicate that the **Line** or **Connection** concerned is infrequently (if at all) used.

Not to be Moved
[Ops.] The wording found on labels attached to certain **Wagons** after they have been inspected by the **Carriage and Wagon Inspector** (**C&W Inspector**). The Wagon must receive attention for some defect before it can be moved. This may be because it is improperly loaded, has a mechanical fault or has been involved in an incident. The act of attaching such a label (called a **Card**) to a Wagon is called **Carding**. See also **Green Card**, **Red Card**.

Not to be Reloaded
[Ops.] The wording found on labels attached to certain **Wagons** after they have been inspected by the **Carriage and Wagon Inspector** (**C&W Inspector**). The Wagon must receive attention for some defect after it has been unloaded. This may be because it has a mechanical fault or has been involved in an incident. The act of attaching such a label (called a **Card**) to a Wagon is called **Carding**. See also **Green Card**, **Red Card**.

Notch
a) [Sig.] A slot cut in a **Tappet**. Also called a **Port**.
b) [TRS Col.] An increment of **Traction Power**

Notch Down
Notch Up
[TRS Col.]
a) To vary the cut off point of steam admission to the cylinders of a **Steam Locomotive**, derived from the notches cut into the quadrant guides of the reverser lever.
b) To decrease or increase the power on any **Traction Unit**.

Notching Relay
[TRS] A **DC Traction Motor** power circuit **Relay** which detects the rise and fall of current in the circuit and inhibits the operation of the **Contactors** controlling the resistance during the acceleration sequence of automatically controlled motors. The Relay operates a Contactor stepping circuit so that, during acceleration of the motor, when the current falls, the Relay detects the fall and calls for the next step of resistance to be switched out of the circuit. See **DC Resistance Control** and **Camshaft**

Notice, the
Notices
a) See **Weekly Operating Notice** (**WON**)
b) See **Weekly Circular**.

Notified Body (NoBo)
An organisation with the delegated responsibility to audit the correct application of national standards under the **Technical Standards for Interoperability** (**TSI**) regulations for **Railway** schemes. It makes its recommendations to **Her Majesties Railway Inspectorate** (**HMRI**).

November
The **Phonetic Alphabet** word representing **N**.

No-Volt Relay
[TRS] A **Relay** in a **DC Resistance Control** □ **Traction Power** circuit which detects if power is lost for any reason and ensures that the control sequence is returned to the starting point before power can be re-applied.

NP
See **Nominated Person**.

NPCCS
[TRS] Non-Passenger Carrying Coaching Stock. Also **Non-passenger Stock** (**NPS**).

NPM
[NR]
a) Network Planning Manager
b) National Procurement Manager.

NPMEA
[NR] National Planning Manager, Engineering Access.
NPP
[Ops.] No Possessions Possible, an abbreviation used in the Engineering Access Statement (EAS).
NPPR
[NR] Network Period Performance Report.
NPS
a) See Non-passenger Stock
b) Negative Phase Sequence
c) National Passenger Survey
d) National Payroll System
e) National Policy Statements(s).
NPT
Non-productive Time.
NPW
Normal Place of Work.
NQ
[PW] Normal Quality, See Normal Grade Rail.
NR
a) See Network Rail
b) Notching Relay.
NR&EE(T)
[NR] National Renewal and Enhancement Engineer (Track).
NR4
[NR PW] Shorthand for the NR4 Sidewear Gauge.
NR56V
[NR PW] The latest suite of standard Switch and Crossing (S&C) geometries, based on the CEN56 rail section and the previous NR60 designs.
NR60
[NR PW] The suite of standard Switch and Crossing (S&C) designs which replaced the RT60 selection. This suite uses the CEN60E2 and CEN60E1A1 Rail Sections.
NR60I
[NR PW] Term used to differentiate older Inclined ▫ NR60 ▫ Switch and Crossing (S&C) layouts from the newer Vertical ▫ NR60V.
NR60V
[NR PW] The latest suite of CEN60 - based Switch and Crossing (S&C) designs, based on the 113A Vertical designs.
NRA
a) National Rail Academy, now the Railway Skills Council (RSC).
b) National Rivers Authority.
NRAB
[NR] Network Rail Acceptance Board. The new name for the Rolling Stock Acceptance Board (RSAB).
NRB
[NR] Network Rail Board.
NRC
See National Route Code.
NRCC
National Rail Communication Centre.

NRCI
See Network Rail Controlled Infrastructure.
NRCOC
National Rail Conditions Of Carriage.
NRCS
See Network Rail Company Standards.
NRDF
[NR] Network Rail Discretionary Fund. A sum of money set aside to internally fund small enhancements.
NRES
[NR] National Rail Enquiry Service.
NRG
See National Records Group.
NRHS
Network Rail High Speed.
NRI
Network Rail ▫ Infrastructure.
NRIC
National Rail ▫ Infrastructure Controller.
NRIF
Network Rail ▫ Infrastructure Funding.
NRIL
See Network Rail Infrastructure Limited.
NRLS
[NR] Network Rail Line Standards, now Network Rail Company Standard (NRCS).
NRM
a) Nominated Responsible Manager
b) The National Railway Museum, based in York.
NRN
a) See National Radio Network
b) See National Railway Network.
NRNA
National Radio Network (NRN) Appreciation.
NRP
[RT] National Recovery Plan.
NRPS
National Rail ▫ Passenger Survey.
NRS
a) (Tradename) National Railway Supplies, an Infrastructure materials supplier and wholesalers, based in Crewe. Now operated by Unipart Rail
b) National Reservation Service.
NRSC
[NR] Network Rail ▫ Railway Safety Case (RSC).
NRSWA
New Roads and Streets Works Act.
NRT
a) See Network Rail Telecommunications
b) National Rail ▫ Timetable. See also Great Britain Passenger Railway Timetable (GBPRT)
NRTD
National Real-Time Database, Also known as Darwin.
NRTS
Network Rail Technical Strategy

315

ELLIS' BRITISH RAILWAY ENGINEERING ENCYCLOPÆDIA

NRVCG
[NR] **N**etwork **R**ail **V**ehicle **C**onformance **G**roup.

NR*x*
[NR] Where *x* is between 1 and 18, a **Network Rail** standard form of contract for:
1 Purchase of goods
2 Purchase of services, replaces RT10
2S Purchase of Services
3 Professional Services
4 Short Form Works Contract
4MT Measured term version of NR4
5 Sale of used materials and equipment
6 Operation and Maintenance of non-NR plant and equipment
7 Operation and maintenance of On-Track Plant (OTP)
8 ICE Measurement version 7th edition (Jan 2003 incorporating July 2004 amendments) (Re-measurement contract)
9 ICE Design & Construct 2nd Edition (Sept. 2001 incorporating Oct. 2001 and July 2004 amendments) (Lump sum contract)
10 JCT 05 Design & Build (2005 Edition) (Lump sum contract)
11 MF/1 Rev 4 (2000 Edition) (Lump sum contract)
12 ICE Target Cost (February 2006 Edition) incorporating design (Reimbursable contract)
12A ICE Target Cost (Feb. 2006 Edition) (Reimbursable contract)
13A Framework Contract for Goods
13B Framework Contract for Services
13C Framework Contract for Works
14 JCT SBC 2005 with Quantities (Lump sum contract)
15 MF/2 Rev 1 (1999 Edition) (Lump sum contract)
16 Provision of Labour Services
17 *unknown*
18 Design, modification, refurbishment and servicing of Rail Vehicles

This series replaced the **RT*x*** versions.

NS
a) See **Neutral Section**
b) The former **Train Operating Company** (**TOC**) **Northern Spirit**, now effectively part of **Northern Rail**.

NSA
See **National Safety Authority**.

NSAC
National **S**tations **A**ccess **C**onditions.

NSARE
National **S**kills **A**cademy (for) **Rail** **E**ngineering.

NSC
[NR] **N**ational **S**upply **C**ontract.

NSDG
[NR] **N**ational **S**ignalling **D**esign Update **G**roup.

NSE
See **Network South East**.

NSFG
National **S**ignal **P**assed **a**t **D**anger (**SPAD**) **F**ocus **G**roup, See **National SPAD Focus Group**.

NSIP
a) [NR] **N**ational **S**tation **I**mprovement **P**rogramme
b) **N**ationally **S**ignificant **I**nfrastructure **P**roject.

NSIT
National **S**afety **I**mprovement **T**eam.

NSKT
See **No Signaller Key Token**.

NSR
a) **N**ot **S**upported or **R**egistered
b) [Hist.] The **Pre-Grouping** **N**orth **S**taffordshire **Railway**.

NST
See **No Signaller Token**.

NSTR
See **No Signaller Token Remote**.

NSZ
No **S**topping **Z**one. An area where it is undesirable to stop **Trains** (except in an emergency) such as a **Tunnel**.

NT
The **ATOC** code for **Northern Rail**.

NTC
(Tradename) The **N**ew **T**rack **C**onstruction machine, built by Harsco for Balfour Beatty.

NTI
Next **T**rain **I**ndicator.

NTM
National **T**ransport **M**odel, the **Department for Transport** (**DfT**) model of growth in demand for travel across all modes including **Rail**.

NTN
[Tel.]
a) **N**ational **T**elephone **N**etwork
b) [Prob. Obs.] **N**ational **T**eleprinter **N**etwork.

NTP
a) [Tel.] **N**etwork **T**erminating **P**oint
b) See **No Train Period**
c) **N**orth **T**rans-**P**ennine.

NTPD
[NR] **N**ational **T**elecommunications **P**erformance **D**atabase.

NTPO
[NR] **N**ational **T**elecom **P**roject **O**ffice.

NTR
[NR] **N**ational **T**rack **R**enewals.

NTRU
[Hist.] **N**orthern **T**rack **R**enewals **U**nit (**TRU**).

NTS
a) **N**o **T**imetabled **S**ervice
b) **N**ational **T**ravel **S**urvey
c) **N**ot **t**o **S**cale
d) **N**on-technical **S**kills

NU
A common contraction of **NUJR**.

NUCKLE
(*knuckle*) [NR] Nuneaton to Coventry Line Enhancement.

Nucleus
[PW] The origin of a **Rail Defect** produced by fatigue action. This is generally a gas or steam bubble.

NUJR
[Hist.] The **Pre-Grouping** North Union Joint **Railway**, a London & North Western and Lancashire & Yorkshire joint enterprise.

Nuneaton Accident
At 01:54 on 6th June 1975 the driver of a northbound **Sleeping Car** □ **Train** failed to spot the **Warning Board** for a **Temporary Speed Restriction** (**TSR**) of 20mph through Nuneaton **Station**. The Warning Board lights were out (the gas for the mantle lamps had run low) and the driver therefore assumed the Restriction had been **Spated**, and so approached the Restriction at around 80mph; four died and 38 were injured in the ensuing **Derailment**. This accident prompted the use of **Portable Automatic Warning System Magnets** (**Portable AWS Magnets**) with Warning Boards.

NUS
[NR] Network Utilisation Strategy.

NUTS
Nomenclature d'unités Territoriales Statistiques; Nomenclature of Units for Territorial Statistics, is a geocode standard for referencing the subdivisions of EU countries for statistical purposes. For instance inner **London** is UKI1. Suffix numbers (e.g. NUTS1, NUTS2 or NUTS3) indicate which level of the NUTS classification is being referred to.

Nuttex
[Col.] An alternative term for **Gricex**, a **Special Train** for **Railway** enthusiasts. See also **Anorak, -ex, Gricer**.

NVC
[NR] Network and Vehicle Change. See also **Network Change**.

NVR
a) National Vehicle Register
b) The Nene Valley **Railway**, a **Preserved Railway**
c) [Hist.] The **Pre-Grouping** Nidd Valley **Railway**.

NVS
See **Normal Ventilation System**.

NW
North Western.

NWEP
North West **Electrification** Programme.

NWML
[NR] North Wales **Main Line**.

NWNG
[Hist.] The former North Wales **Narrow Gauge Railway**.

NWPTUF
North West Public Transport Users Forum.

NWR
Normal **Working** Resumed.

NWRR
[Hist.] North West Regional **Railways**.

NWT
[Hist.] North Western Trains, a former **Train Operating Company** (**TOC**).

NWZ
[RT] North West Zone, see **Railtrack**. Now part of London North Western **Territory**.

NX
a) See **Entrance / Exit Panel**.
b) On a **Signalling Circuit Diagram**, a connection to the return side AC busbar
c) On a **Cable Plan**, a **Conductor** returning to a power supply. Also **N**.

NX Panel
See **Entrance / Exit Panel**. Also **NX**.

NXEA
National Express East Anglia, a **Train Operating Company** (**TOC**).

NXEC
(Tradename) National Express East Coast, a **Train Operating Company** (**TOC**).

NXMM
National Express Midland Metro.

NXWM
National Express West Midlands.

NY
The **ATOC** code for North Yorkshire Moors Railway.

Nylon
[PW Col.] A common term for the **Rail Foot Insulator** used in **Pandrol** and **SHC** □ **Fastening** assemblies.

NYMR
The North Yorkshire Moors **Railway**.

317

O

O
a) [NR] As the last letter in a **Wagon** □ **CARKND**, this denotes that the Wagon has no **Continuous Brakes** or **Automatic Brakes**. Also known as **Unfitted**
b) Shorthand for **Offset**
c) [NR] As the first letter of a Wagon CARKND, it means that the vehicle is an **Open Wagon**
d) [NR] On a card attached to a Wagon, it indicates overdue for **Planned Preventative Maintenance** (**PPM**)
e) [Sig.] On a **Signalling Circuit Diagram**:
• As one of the leading letters of an **Equipment Code**, it means retarding
• As the last letter of an Equipment Code, it means heater or resistor
f) The letter represented by **Oscar** in the **Phonetic Alphabet**.

O Carded
[NR] A **Wagon** with a card attached exhibiting the code **O**, indicating that the Wagon is overdue for its **Planned Preventative Maintenance** (**PPM**).

O Stock
[LUL] Type of **Train**, now extinct, which was first introduced in 1937 for use on the Hammersmith and Circle **Lines**. It had an unusual flared body profile.

O&AT
[Hist.] The **Pre-Grouping** Oxford & Aylesbury Tramroad, owned by the Metropolitan & Great Central Joint company.

O&IJR
[Hist.] The **Pre-Grouping** Otley & Ilkley Joint **Railway**, a Midland and North Eastern joint enterprise.

O&M
Operation and **Maintenance**.

O/B
See **Overbridge** (**OB**). See also **Overline Bridge** (**OB**).

OA
a) See **Open Access**
b) Open Hearth Acid, a smelting process for **Rail Steel**.

OA&GBR
[Hist.] The **Pre-Grouping** Oldham, Ashton-under-Lyne & Guide Bridge **Railway**, a Great Central and London & North Western joint enterprise.

Oakes, Wallace Arnold GC
(1932-1965) On 5 June 1965 driver Oakes was in charge of a **Passenger Train** when, outside Crewe, the fire blew back from the **Firebox**, filling the **Driving Cab** with smoke and flames. **Fireman** Gwilym Roberts climbed out of the Cab window and extinguished his clothing, but Oakes stayed at his post to close the **Regulator** and apply the brakes. Fireman Roberts found his mate lying on the **Embankment** next to the **Train**, badly burned, but evidently having remained in the Cab until the Train stopped. Oakes suffered 80% burns and died week later. For his gallantry Oakes was awarded the George Cross.

OAO
See **Open Access Operator**.

OB
a) See **Overbridge**. See also **Overline Bridge** (**OB**)
b) An acronym for Open Hearth Basic, a smelting process for **Rail Steel**.

OBS
a) [TRS] An acronym representing an **Observation Coach**
b) On Board Services
c) Organisation Breakdown Structure.

Obscuration
An interruption of the driver's view of a particular **Signal Element**. See also **Partial Obscuration**, **Total Obscuration**.

Observation Coach (**OBS**)
Observation Saloon
[TRS] A **Passenger Coach** fitted with large side windows and a very large rear window. Normally marshalled at the rear of a **Train**, it allows the **Passengers** in it to have a panoramic view of the world.

Obstacle Deflector
[TRS] A stout angled metal plate, similar in appearance to a Snowplough, fitted vertically under the **Leading End** of a **Traction Unit**. Its purpose is to reduce the risk of a **Derailment** in the event of a collision between the **Train** and a large obstacle on the **Track**. They are attached to the body of the Vehicle rather than the **Bogies**, so are generally placed 200mm **Above Rail Level** (**ARL**) to provide for movement of the suspension system. Colloquially called a **Cowcatcher**, their fitting became widespread following the **Polmont Accident**. See also **Lifeguard**.

Obstacle Detection
a) [TRS] A facility to detect the presence of objects in the path of a closing door. See **Sensitive Edge**
b) [Sig.] Equipment employed to detect the presence of significant obstructions on **Level Crossings**. See **MCB-OD**.

Obstructed
Obstruction
[Obs.] Describing a **Line** on which the passage of **Trains** is impeded by a Train, part of a Train, some other object or an **Accident**.

Obstruction Danger
[Sig.] In **Absolute Block** (**AB**), the message sent from one **Signal Box** (**SB**) to the adjacent Signal Boxes by **Block Bell** to stop all **Trains**. Also known as **Six Bells**.

Obstructionless
A tool or piece of equipment that be left in situ on the **Track** whilst:
a) **Trains** are **Running**, see **Obstructionless Stressing Equipment**
b) **Tamping** takes place, see **Obstructionless Rail Lubricator**.

Obstructionless Lever
A **Hand Lever** that lies down flat to the ground when not in use, presenting a reduced hazard to **Shunters**, etc.

Obstructionless Rail Lubricator
[PW] A **Rail Lubricator** that does not require removal before **Tamping** can take place (this is now the standard type).

Obstructionless Stressing Equipment
[PW] **Rail Tensors** that can be left in place and under tension during the passage of **Engineering Trains**, allowing **Ballasting** works to take place before **Welding**.

Obtuse Crossing

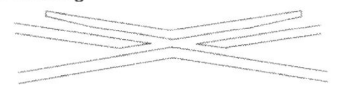

[PW] A **Crossing** which allows two **Running Rails** to cross at an obtuse angle. It is made up of two **Obtuse Point Rails**, a single **Obtuse Wing Rail** with a **Knuckle** (**KN**) in it, a single **Check Rail** and an assortment of **Distance Blocks** and bolts. See **Crossing, Parts of**.

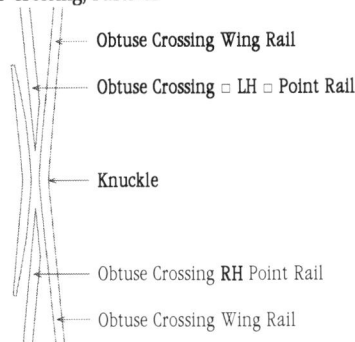

Obtuse Crossing Point Rail
[PW] A short length of **Rail**, forming part of an **Obtuse Crossing**, which has a **Nose** machined into one end. Used in handed pairs, they are secured to the **Obtuse Crossing Wing Rail** and **Check Rail** using **Distance Blocks** and bolts. See **Obtuse Crossing, Parts of**.

Obtuse Crossing Wing Rail
[PW] A **Rail** that has a **Knuckle** (**KN**) bent into it of the appropriate angle for the **Obtuse Crossing**. It is secured to the **Obtuse Crossing Point Rails** and **Check Rail** using **Distance Blocks** and bolts. See **Obtuse Crossing, Parts of**.

Obtuse Crossing, Parts of

- Obtuse Crossing Wing Rail
- Obtuse Crossing □ LH □ Point Rail
- Knuckle
- Obtuse Crossing RH Point Rail
- Obtuse Crossing Wing Rail

OC
See **Open Level Crossing**.

OCAM
Output **C**ost **A**djustment **M**echanism.

OCB
Oil **C**ircuit **B**reaker.

OCC
Occ.
Shorthand for **Occupied**.

Occlusion
See **Obscuration**.

Occupation
a) [NR Col.] A term describing a temporary closure of a **Line**, see **Line Blockage**
b) [Col.] An alternative for **Possession**.

Occupation Bridge
A **Bridge** taking a private road over or under a **Railway**, and therefore not a public right of way. Originally provided for the use of the land owner or their tenants when access to a piece of land or property was severed by the construction of a **Railway**.

Occupation Crossing
A common contraction of **Occupation Level Crossing** (**OLC**).

Occupation Level Crossing (OLC)
a) A **Level Crossing** (**LC**, **LX**) provided solely to allow an adjacent landowner access across the **Railway** where they have property on both sides of the **Track**
b) A **Level Crossing** on a private road leading to several premises or residences, usually provided when the road was severed at the time the Railway was constructed. Other persons, whose lands do not necessarily adjoin the Railway, may have acquired rights to use the occupation road since.
Such Crossings are generally equipped with user operated **Gates** and an emergency telephone, but no traffic control system as such. See also **Accommodation Bridge, Accommodation Crossing, Occupation Bridge, Occupation Crossing**.

Occupied
Occupied Line
Occupied Section
[Sig., Ops.] Describing a **Block Section** or **Track Circuit** (**TC**) with a **Train** on or in it. The opposite is **Clear**.

Occurrence Book
[Sig.] A book used by **Signallers** to record any occurrences (other than **Train Movements**, for instance requests to cross at **User Worked Crossings** (**UWC**)) that may have happened during their shift.

OCL
a) [Elec.] **O**verhead **C**ontact **L**ine. See **Overhead Line Conductor**
b) **O**perational **C**ommunications **L**ink.

OCLZ
[Elec.] **O**verhead **C**ontact **L**ine **Z**one.

OCP
Operator **C**ontrol **P**anel.

OCR
[Elec.] **O**verhead **C**ondition **R**enewals.

OCS
a) See **One Control Switch**
b) **O**n **C**ompany **S**ervice
c) See **Overhead Contact System**, see also **Overhead Line Equipment** (**OLE**).

OCS Panel
See **One Control Switch Panel**.

ELLIS' BRITISH RAILWAY ENGINEERING ENCYCLOPÆDIA

Octopus (YDA)
[NR]
a) An 80 ton self-discharging **Ballast Hopper**, part of the **Plasser and Theurer** □ **Ballast Distribution System** (BDS)
b) An 80 ton self-discharging **Hopper Wagon** for **Spoil**, part of the **Starfer** □ **Single Line Spoil Handling System** (SLSHS).
c) An 80 ton self-discharging Ballast Hopper, part of the **DB Schenker** train manufactured by **Skako**. See **Wagon Names**.

Octopus Train
[BR] A purpose built **Engineer's Train** equipped to carry out eight different **Maintenance** activities.

OCU
See **Operator's Control Unit**.

OD
a) Operating Department, see **Railway Operations**
b) Outside Diameter
c) Origin and Destination
d) See **Ordnance Datum**.

O-D Matrix
Origin – Destination Matrix. A matrix of demand showing origins and destinations of pedestrian movements within a space such as a **Station**.

ODA
Overlapping Design Agreement.

ODIL
See **Outside Door Indicator Lights**.

ODM
[NR] Operations Delivery Manager.

ODN
Ordnance Datum Newlyn.

ODR
[NR] Other Diversionary Route.

ODS
[BR] See **Operating Department Supervisor**.

OE
See **Outside Edge**.

OEE
Overhead **Electrification** Equipment.

OEIS
One Engine in Steam.

OEL
Occupational Exposure Limit.

OES
One Engine in Steam.

OETR
[NR] Outline **Engineering Train** Requirements.

OFAF
Oil Forced Air Forced, a type of **Booster Transformer** (BT).

Off
[Sig.] Describing a **Signal** showing any **Aspect** other than its **Most Restrictive Aspect**. The opposite is **On**. See also **Off Aspect**, **Off Indicator**.

Off Aspect
[Sig.] For a **Signal** capable of displaying two **Aspects**, such as a **Position Light Signal** (PLS), Semaphore Signal or Two Aspect Signal, this is the Least Restrictive Aspect. For a **Three Aspect Signal** or **Four Aspect Signal** the Off Aspects are any Aspect other than the **Most Restrictive Aspect**. The opposite is On Aspect.

Off Indicator
[Sig.] An illuminated Indicator provided on a **Platform** to inform the **Guard** and Platform Staff that the **Signal** □ **Beyond** the **Train** is Clear (**Off**) and that it is safe to give the **Right Away** (**RA**) to the driver. See also **Close Doors** (CD).

Off Side
[NR] The right hand side of a **Train** in the Normal Direction of travel. The opposite is **Near Side**.

Off the Back
[PW] See **Contra-flexure Turnout**.

Off the Inside
[PW] See **Similar Flexure Turnout**.

Off the Rails

Off the Road
[Col.] Alternatives for **Derailed**.

Off the Street
[Col.] Without any **Railway** background.

Offered

Offered On

Offering
[Sig.] The process by which a **Signaller** in an **Absolute Block** (AB) area asks permission from the **Signaller** □ **Beyond** to allow a **Train** into the next **Block Section**. See also **Acceptance**.

Office of Rail Regulation (ORR)
[UK] The safety regulator for the **Railways** in Great Britain. Established on 5th July 2004 under the **Railways and Transport Safety Act 2003**, ORR is an independent statutory body led by a Board. Its key roles are:
a) Ensuring that **Network Rail** (**NR**) manages the network efficiently and responsibly;
b) Encouraging continuous improvement in health and safety performance and to ensure compliance with relevant health and safety law, including taking enforcement action as necessary. This includes the activities of **Her Majesty's Railway Inspectorate** (HMRI)
c) Develop policy and enhance relevant **Railway** health and safety legislation
d) Licensing **Operators** of Railway assets, setting the terms for access by Operators to the **National Railway Network** (NRN) and other Railway facilities, and enforcing competition law in the **Rail** sector.
See also **Rail Safety and Standards Board** (RSSB), **Strategic Rail Authority** (SRA).

321

Office of the Rail Regulator (ORR)
The organisation that was set up under **Railway □ Privatisation** in 1994 to issue licences to **Railway Operators** and protect the interests of **Rail** users. Superseded by the creation of the **Office of Rail Regulation (ORR)** in July 2004.

Officer's Saloon
[TRS] A specially modified **Coach** used for observing and inspecting the **Railway**. They generally have a large observation window at one or both ends and special retractable steps that allow staff to descend to ground level. Also **Director's Saloon**, **Inspection Saloon**. See also **Observation Coach**, **Observation Saloon** (**OBS**).

Officer's Special
[Ops.] A **Train** conveying an **Officer's Saloon**, and therefore a Train that may stop in **Section** to permit personnel to **Alight** and undertake inspections.

Offset (O)
a) See **Vertical Curve Offset**
b) [Sig.] The horizontal distance between the **Running Edge** (**RE**) of the relevant **Left Hand Rail** (**LHR**) and the centre of the **Signal** or **Signal Element**.
c) [Sig.] The horizontal distance between the **Running Edge** of the Left Hand Rail and the centre of the top surface of the driver's seat
d) [PW] The minimum horizontal dimension from the **Track** to an adjacent structure measured normal to the Track.

Offset Signal
[Sig.] A Signal arranged so that the **Signal Head** is closer to the **Track** than the **Signal Post**. See also **Gantry Signal**, **Straight Post Signal**.

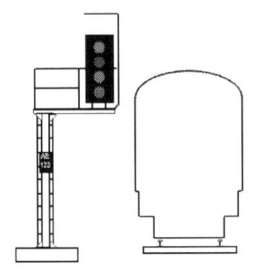

Offset Stick
[PW Col.] An alternative term for a **Stick and Bubble**. Also **Bubble Stick**.

Off-track
Not on or involving the **Track**.

Off-track
a) (noun) Describing a location not on the track, see also **Lineside**
b) (verb) See **Off-tracking**.

Off-track Inspector
[NR] A member of staff responsible for inspecting and recording the condition of **Off-Track** assets.

Off-tracking
a) Moving a **Rail Vehicle** off the **Track** and onto a transporter or **Stillage**
b) Driving a **Road Rail Vehicle** off the Track. The opposite action is **On-tracking**.

OFG
See **Operations Focus Group**.

OG
On a **Signalling Circuit Diagram**, denotes a wire coloured orange.

OGL
Original Ground Level.

Oglo
A **Railway □ Telegraph Code** meaning "Out of Gauge load where **Running Lines** and **Sidings** need not be **Clear** between the points mentioned. To be signalled by the special **Is Line Clear □ Bell Code** 2-6-1".

Ohio
A **Railway □ Telegraph Code** meaning "Send on all speed".

OHL
Over Head Line. See **Overhead Line Equipment** (**OLE**). Also **OHLE**, **OLE**.

OHLE
See **Overhead Line Equipment** (**OLE**).

OHNS
Overhead **Neutral Section** (**NS**).

OJEC
Official Journal of the European Community.

OL
See **Overlap**.

OLB/EFR
Overload Braking / **Earth Fault Relay**.

OLBI
Off-line Battery Inverter.

OLC
See **Occupation Level Crossing**.

Old Hand
[Col.] A person of many years' **Railway** service. Retiring at the age of 65 with 47 years of unbroken service is not unique – as is not actually retiring, ever. To the author's knowledge the oldest, active, **Personal Track Safety** (**PTS**) card holder is just over 80 years old.

Old Line
[Col.] Term applied to the original **Route** when a newer one (often itself called the **New Line**) is built parallel to it.

OLE
See **Overhead Line Equipment**.

OLE Pole
[LR] A slender, vertical, typically cylindrical structure used to support the **Cantilevers**, Brackets and **Span Wires** of the **Overhead Line Equipment** (**OLE**) on a **Tramway** system. See also **Headspan Mast**, **OLE Mast**.

OLEAR
[NR] **Overhead Line Equipment** (**OLE**) **Asset Register**.

OLEC
Overhead Line Equipment Competence.

OLEMI
[NR] **Overhead Line Equipment** (**OLE**) Master Index.

OLGA
(*ol-gah*) On Line Gauging Apparatus, A Rail Vehicle used for Gauging Structures. See also Structure Gauging Train (SGT).

OLIVE
[Elec.] Overhead Line Inspection Vehicle:
a) DB998901, now residing at the Middleton Railway
b) (Tradename) A system developed by AEA Technology (now called DeltaRail) for detecting and reporting faults in the Overhead Line Equipment (OLE).

Oliver
[Obs.] The Phonetic Alphabet word representing O. Replaced by Oscar.

OLM
Overload Monitoring.

OLP
See Overhead Line Permit.

OM
Operations Manager.

OM&R
Operating, Maintenance and Renewals

OMA
Operations, Maintenance and Asset Management.

Omnia
(Tradename) [Elec.] An extruded aluminium cantilever arm manufactured by Bonciani SpA of Ravenna, Italy. See Series I Design Range, Series II Design Range.

Omnibus Telephone
Omnibus Telephone Circuit
[Tel., Arch.] An arrangement where many telephones are permanently connected to one circuit, all of which can speak and listen at the same time to all the other instruments.

Omnicom
(Tradename) Common contraction of the OmniSurveyor3D system and Omnicom Engineering Ltd., the company that owns it.

OmniSurveyor3D
(Tradename) Trademark of Omnicom Engineering Ltd, York, a system which includes seven cameras mounted on a Rail Vehicle to record the view forward, to the sides and down onto the Rails. The system is calibrated so that measurements can be taken from the video. OmniSurveyor3D is a trademark of Omnicom Engineering Ltd.

OMR
Operations, □ Maintenance and Renewal.

On
[Sig.] Describing a Signal showing its Most Restrictive Aspect. The opposite is Off.

On Aspect
[Sig.] For a Signal capable of displaying two or more Aspects, such as a Position Light Signal (PLS), Semaphore Signal, Two Aspect Signal, Three Aspect Signal or Four Aspect Signal, this is the Most Restrictive Aspect. The opposite is Off Aspect.

On Indicator
On/Off Indicator
[Sig. Obs.] An Indicator which displayed On when the Platform Starting Signal was showing a Stop Aspect. See also Off Indicator.

On or Near the Line
[NR] A position on the Track or within 3m (9' - 10") of the Nearest Rail. This excludes areas that are on the other side of a permanent Fence or structure, even if it is less than 3m from the Nearest Rail.

On Sight Mode (OS)
[Sig.] A Movement Authority (MA) given by a European Rail Traffic Management System (ERTMS) that still gives protection but will allow entry into an occupied Section. The display of this indication tells a driver that they are permitted to run at a speed which allows them to stop short of any obstruction such as a Train standing on the Line □ Ahead.

On the Approach
On the Approach Side
On the Approach to
[NR] Describing a position or object which appears before another, from the driver's point of view.

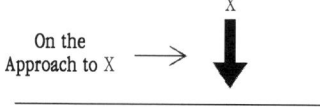

```
                              X
       On the                  ↓
       Approach to X  →       ▼
   ─────────────────────────────────────→
                Normal Direction of Trains
```

The opposite is Beyond. The non-preferred alternatives are In Rear or Behind.

On the Block
[Col.] A Rail Vehicle left near a Buffer Stop

On the DC
[Col.] Describing an activity taking place on a Line fitted with Conductor Rail Equipment (CRE). See also Under the Wires.

On the Deck
On the Floor
[Col.] An alternative for Derailed.

On the Lineside
[NR] Being inside the boundary Fence but not On or Near the Line, i.e. not within 3m (10 feet) of the Outside Edge (OE). Also Lineside.

On the Stops
[Col.] Describing a Rail Vehicle left stationary adjacent to a Buffer Stop.

On Track
a) (noun) On or involving the Track, including the Ballast Shoulders
b) (verb) See On-track.

On Track Machine (OTM)
Any piece of specialist **Railway** plant which moves only on the **Rails** and is normally **Self Propelled**, e.g. **Ballast Cleaners**, **Dynamic Track Stabilisers** (DTS), **Pneumatic Ballast Injection Machines** (PBI, **Stoneblower**), **Rail Cranes**, **Regulators**, **Tamping and Lining Machines** (**Tampers**), **Track Relaying Machines** (TRM) and **TRAMM**. Also **On Track Plant** (OTP).

On Track Plant (OTP)
Engineering plant with **Rail Wheels**, including **On Track Machines** (OTM) and **Road Rail Vehicles**.

On Track Plant Depot (OTPD)
A facility that specialises in the maintenance and repair of engineering plant with **Rail Wheels**, including **On Track Machines** (OTM) and **Road Rail Vehicles**.

On Train Data Recorder (OTDR)
On Train Data Recording
On Train Monitoring Recorder (OTMR)
On Train Monitoring and Recording
[TRS] A data recorder fitted to **Traction Units** collecting information about the performance of the train. Including:
- Speed
- **Regulator** and brake control positions
- Activations of horn, **Driver's Safety Device** (DSD) and **Automatic Warning System** (AWS) cancel button, etc.

This data is recorded to a crash-proof memory and is used to analyse driver performance and train behaviour during normal operations or following an incident or accident.

ONAN
[Elec.] Oil Natural Air Natural, a type of **Booster Transformer** (BT).

One Control Switch (OCS)
One Control Switch Panel (OCS Panel)
[Sig.] A type of **Signal Box Panel** on which each **Route** from each **Signal** has a unique electrical switch.

One Diesel in Derv
One Engine in Steam
[Col.] Alternatives for **One Train Working** (OTW). Also **One Train in Steam**.

One In
[WR Sig. Col.] Term meaning to admit a **Train** to an **Occupied Section** in **Permissive Block** on the former **Western Region** (WR). Refers to that Region's use of a one-beat **Bell Code** to accept a **Train** into an **Occupied Section**.

One On
a) [Col.] The traditional words used by a **Lookout** having given warning of an **Approaching Train**, often including the name of the **Line** on which the **Train** is approaching, e.g. "One On the **Up**"
b) A generic hail giving warning of an Approaching Train when no other means of warning such as a horn or whistle is available.

One Pull
[Sig. Col.] Alternative terms for **One Train Release**. Also **One Shot**.

One Rail Only (ORO)
[PW] Any activity which concerns only one **Rail**. See Also **High Rail Only** (HRO).

One Shot
See **One Pull**.

One Shot Crucible
[PW] A pre-formed **Crucible** for use in making **Alumino-thermic Welds** and which is replaced after use in making one **Weld**.

One Shot Sanders
[TRS] A means of delivering measured quantities of sand onto the **Rail Head** under the **Driving Wheels** to improve **Adhesion**. This particular type can only be used once before having to be reset and re-filled. See also **Sanders**.

One Train in Steam
[Col.] Alternative term for **One Train Working** (OTW).

One Train Release
[Sig.] A control which allows the **Signaller** to operate the **Section Signal** once and only once for each **Line Clear** (LC) given by the **Signal Box** ▫ **Beyond**. Also **One Pull**, **One Shot**.

One Train Staff Instrument
See **Staff Instrument**.

One Train Working (OTW)
[Sig.] A method of **Signalling** a **Single Line**, whereby only one **Train** is allowed onto the **Line** at one time. Colloquially referred to as **One Train In Steam**. See **One Train Working by Train Staff** (OT(S)), **One Train Working Without Train Staff** (OT).

One Train Working by Train Staff (OT(S))
[Sig.] A particular method of operating a **One Train Working** (OTW) ▫ **Single Line**, using a **Train Staff** to ensure only one **Train** is present on the **Single Line** at any one time. See also **One Train Working Without Train Staff** (OT).

One Train Working Without Train Staff (OT)
[Sig.] A method of operating a **One Train Working** (OTW) ▫ **Single Line**, normally by means of **Sequential Track Circuits**. See also **One Train Working by Train Staff** (OT(S)).

One Under
[LUL, Col.] Term for someone being struck by or falling under a **Train**.

One Way Lever
A **Hand Lever** that operates a **Set of Switches** or **Set of Points** in one direction only. The return operation is accomplished by springs in the mechanism or by vehicles **Trailing** the Switch. See also **Two Way Lever**.

One Way Switch
See **Train Operated Switch**.

Ongars
[LUL Col.] Alternative for **Chainage**, coined because Ongar in Essex is the zero point for the LUL system. Ongar is no longer on the LUL network, the **Line** beyond Epping having been closed on 30 September 1994.

On-track
On-tracking
a) Moving a **Rail Vehicle** onto the **Track** from a transporter or **Stillage**.
b) Driving a **Road Rail Vehicle** onto the **Track** and placing it in **Rail Mode**.
The opposite action is **Off-tracking**.

On-track Machine
See **On Track Machine**.

On-track Plant
See **On Track Plant (OTP)**.

OOARL
On or **A**ffecting the **R**unning **L**ine.

OOC
Old **O**ak **C**ommon.

OOCPA
Old **O**ak **C**ommon and **P**addington **A**pproaches (part of **Crossrail**).

OOG
See **O**ut **o**f **G**auge.

OOGLI
Out **O**f **G**auge **L**oads **I**nspector.

OOO
Out **o**f **O**rder.

OOR
See **O**ut **o**f **R**unning, **O**ut **o**f **R**unning Wire.

OOS
Out **O**f **S**ervice.

OOTH
See **O**ut **o**f **T**raffic **H**ours.

OOU
Out **o**f **U**se. An annotation used on diagrams to indicate that a section of **Track** or a **Connection** is temporarily closed, generally pending removal. See also **Not in Regular Use (NIRU)**.

OP
a) See **Outside Party**
b) **O**perator **P**anel.

OPAS
Operational **P**roperty **A**sset **S**ystem.

Open
a) See **Open Coach**
b) See **Open Crossing**, **Open Level Crossing (OC)**
c) See **Open Line**
d) A **Ticket** that has no time limit imposed on its use.

Open Access (OA)
[NR] The policy under which any enterprise wishing to run **Passenger Train** services can do so, provided they satisfy the relevant safety legislation.

Open Access Operator (OAO)
[NR] A **Train Operating Company (TOC)** that operates **Passenger Train** services and is not part of the **Passenger Rail Franchise** system. Examples include **Eurostar**, Grand Central Railway and **Hull Trains**.

Open Block
[Sig. Obs.] The original form of **Absolute Block** in which a **Block Section** was always regarded as being **Clear** for a **Train** to enter whether or not one was due unless there was a **Train** already in the Section. Under this method of operation it was the policy to return **Signals** to Clear as soon as **Train Out of Section (TOS)** had been given.

Open Coach
[TRS] A **Passenger Coach** that does not have **Compartments** or other significant divisions within it.

Open Crossing
Open Level Crossing (OC)
A type of **Level Crossing (LC, LX)** with no **Barriers**, **Gates**, warning system (apart from a **Whistle Board** and / or road signs on the highway) or monitoring. These are generally confined to lightly-used railways and roads.

Open Line
A **Line** or **Track** upon which **Trains** are **Running**, i.e. a Line not subject to a **Possession**.

Open Switch
A **Switch Rail** not closed up to the adjacent **Stock Rail**. The opposite is **Closed Switch**. See also **Left Hand Switch Closed (LHSC)**, **Right Hand Switch Closed (RHSC)**.

Open Wagon
[TRS] Collective term for **Engineering Vehicles** intended for carrying spoil or **Ballast** (but not including **Hopper Vehicles**).

Opening Out
a) [PW] The action of removing all the **Ballast** from around a **Sleeper** down to the **Soffit** of the Sleeper in preparation for its inspection, removal or **Respacing**. See also **Boxing In**, **Legging**
b) [Civ.] The action of converting a **Tunnel** into a **Cutting** by removing the material above and the **Tunnel Lining** down to the **Springing**.

Opens
[PW Col.] See **Open Wagon**.

Operate
Operated
[Sig.]
a) Describing a **Lever**, **Plunger** or **Treadle** that has been pulled, depressed or activated
b) The state of a **Relay** when the coil is **Energised**, the relay is unlatched or the Relay is **Picked Up**, thus closing the **Front Contacts** and opening the **Back Contacts**.
The opposite is **Released**.

Operating Department (OD)
See **Railway Operations**.

Operating Department Supervisor (ODS)
[BR Ops.] A field operative engaged in the duties of **Railway Operations**.

325

Operating Floor
[Sig.] The (generally) horizontal surface in a **Signal Box** (SB) on which the **Signaller** stands to carry out their normal duties.

Operating Irregularity
[Ops.] Any **Train Movement** carried out contrary to the rules and regulations, irrespective of whether it is unsafe or not. See also **Near Miss**, **Possession Irregularity**.

Operating Notice
[NR Ops.] Formal name for what is universally known as a **Yellow Peril**.

Operating Notice Diagram
[NR Ops.] A simplified layout plan for publication in, or with, the **Signalling** alterations section of an **Operating Notice**, such as the **Weekly Operating Notice** (WON) or a **Periodical Operating Notice** (PON).

Operating Publication
[Ops.] A document detailing one of the following:
a) How the **Signaller** should deal with situations, see **Signal Box Instructions**
b) Explanations of new and revised **Operational Layouts** to drivers, see **Operating Notice**, **Yellow Peril**
c) Details of **Possessions**, **Speed Restrictions**, minor alterations to the **Operational Layout** and other general instructions, see **Periodical Operating Notice** (PON), **Weekly Operating Notice** (WON)
d) Providing last minute alterations to Possessions and Speed Restrictions, see **Emergency Notice** (E Notice)
e) Details of the **Lines**, their **Normal Direction**, **Permissible Speed** (PS), **Enhanced Permissible Speed** (EPS), **Route Availability** (RA) data, **Platform Lengths** and other relevant information, see **Sectional Appendix** (SA). See also **National Electronic Sectional Appendix** (SA).
f) Detailing the correct procedures for dealing with **Freight** and **Dangerous Goods**, see **Working Manual for Rail Staff**.

Operating Speed
[LUL] The normal speed of **Trains** in operating conditions. Also **Headway Speed**.

Operation Skyhawk
[NR] An initiative to locate suspected **Trespass and Vandalism** (T&V) offenders using a helicopter.

Operation Time
[Sig.] The interval between the rated voltage being applied to a **Relay** coil and the first **Front Contact** making. The opposite is **Release Time**.

Operational Irregularity
See **Operating Irregularity**.

Operational Layout
Not only the arrangement of **Switches and Crossings** (S&C) and number of **Tracks**, but also the positions of **Clearance Points** (CP), **Platforms**, **Signal Overlaps**, **Signals**, **Section Insulators** (SI) and **Shunt Signals**.

Operational Platform Length
The length of a **Platform** that can be used by **Passenger Trains** for the purposes of allowing **Passengers** to **Board** and **Alight** whilst obeying the restrictions of the **Signalling System**. On the diagram above, S indicates the **Signal Standback Allowance**, typically 15 to 25m.

Operational Property
[NR] Buildings, land and **Structures** in use as part of the **Operational Railway**. This portfolio is managed by Rail Property Limited, now **Spacia**.

Operational Railway
A collective term describing the land contained within the boundaries of the **Railway**.

Operational Telephone
[Tel.] A telephone used directly in the normal operation of the **Railway**. See **Point Zone Telephone** (PZT), **Signal Post Telephone** (SPT).

Operational Use
The utilisation of an asset for the purposes of running **Trains**.

Operationally Equivalent
A replacement item which is functionally identical to the item it replaces, though the replacement may utilise newer materials or technology. See also **Like for Like**, **Modern Equivalent Form** (MEF).

Operations
See **Railway Operations**.

Operations Focus Group (OFG)
[NR] A body which co-ordinates the dissemination of information relevant to **Operations**, and runs the OPSWEB website.

Operations Planning (Ops. Planning)
[NR] The organisation that manages the specification, compilation and agreement of **Timetables** (TT).

Operator
a) [NR] A common contraction of **Freight Operating Company** (FOC) and **Train Operating Company** (TOC). Also **Train Operator**
b) A person engaged in the activities of **Railway Operations**
c) [LUL] See **Train Operator**.

Operator's Control Unit (OCU)
[Sig.] The **Signaller's** interface with a **Train Describer** (TD) system. It normally consists of a keyboard and VDU or other digital display.

Operator's Cupboard
[Ops.] A small cupboard or **Half Loc.** placed adjacent to **Switch and Crossing Layouts** (S&C Layouts) and used to house **Point Clips**, **Scotches** and padlocks for use in **Clipping and Scotching**. They also typically contain a pair of very greasy gloves.

OPEX
(*opp-ecks*) Operating Expenditure. See also **CAPEX**.

OPM
Operational Planning Manager.
OPO
[LUL] One Person Operation, an alternative term for Driver Only Operation (DOO).
OPO(T)
One Person Operation (Tube).
Oppenheim Report
More correctly "Pedestrian Safety at Public Road Level Crossings", produced in April 1983 by a committee chaired by the Rt. Hon Sally Oppenheim MP. It concluded that further safeguards should be applied in the conversion of **Level Crossings** (**LC**, **LX**) to automatic operation. This included uniform signage provision, enhanced audible warnings, segregation of pedestrians from road traffic, enhanced facilities for crossings used by high risk groups such as school children, more detailed reporting of incidents and wider consultation of conversion plans.
Oppos
A Railway □ **Telegraph Code** meaning "**Running Lines** and/or **Sidings** mentioned on the right-hand side of the load looking in the direction of travel must be clear, and no **Train** signalled 2-6-2 or 2-6-3 must be allowed on the Running Lines and/or Sidings on the left-hand side of the load. To be signalled by the special 'Is Line Clear?' signal 2-6-3". See also **Bell Codes**.
Opposing Locking
[Sig.] A **Control** applied to certain **Signals** whereby when a **Route** is **Set** leading up to the **Signal** in the **Wrong Direction**, then that Signal cannot be **Cleared**. This prevents **Head On** collisions.
Opposite Flexure
[PW] A **Curve** of opposite **Hand** to another related Curve, also **Contra-Flexure**, as in Contra-flexure Turnout. The opposite is **Similar Flexure**.

Main Line
Turnout

OPR
[Sig.] Off **Proving** □ **Relay**.
OPRAF
(*oh-praff*) [Hist.] Office of **Passenger** □ **Rail Franchising**, then called the **Strategic Rail Authority** (**SRA**) until 2006 when it became part of the **Office of Rail Regulation** (**ORR**).
OPS
[NR] See **Outline Project Specification**.
Ops Planning
See **Operations Planning**.
Ops.
Shorthand for Operations, See **Railway Operations**.
OPSRAM
[Ops.] **Operations**, Safety, Reliability, Availability and Maintainability.

Optic Diode Signal
[Sig.] A type of **Colour Light Signal** that uses high intensity lamps to produce the two coloured **Aspects** through a single aperture. It is necessary to have two such units to produce a **Double Yellow Aspect**.
Optimism Bias
The demonstrated tendency for appraisers to be over-optimistic about key project parameters such as capital costs, project duration, operating costs and delivery of benefits. This is countered by allowances added at the development stage, which can range up to 40%.
OPU
Operational Planning Unit.
OPUG
Other **Passenger** Upgrades.
OR
Old **Railway**.
ORA
a) Operations Risk Advisor
b) Operational Risk Advisor
ORAM
(*oh-ram*) [NR] See **Overrun Risk Assessment Model**.
Orange Pipe
A polyethylene pipe of around 100mm nominal bore used to protect cables such as **Track Tails** and **Points Heating** cables when they must cross a **Track** immediately under the **Rails**. They are bright orange, a noble but sadly often vain attempt to make them more obvious to the operators of **Tampers** and **Ballast Regulators**. A better solution in the form of a **Hollow Sleeper** is now available.
Orange Sidings
[NR] The part of the **National Railway Network** (**NRN**) which **Network Rail** (**NR**) provides and maintains only to connect a **Private Siding** to the rest of the Network. The term applies only to Network Rail **Connection Agreements** (**CA**) but is analogous to **Red Sidings** in **Private Siding Agreements** (**PSA**).
Orange Sleeve
[Elec.] A **Sleeve** fitted to a normally closed (**NC**) **Hook Switch** that has been opened, to prevent it from being closed accidentally.
Orange Square
[TRS] A symbol applied to **Traction Units**, in this **Class** 50 **Locomotives**, denoting the **Multiple Working** control system with which they are fitted. Only Traction Units bearing the same symbol can be connected safely. See **Blue Square**, **Blue Star**, **Green Circle**, **Orange Star**, **Red Circle**, **Red Diamond**, **Red Triangle**, **White Circle**, **White Diamond**, **Yellow Diamond**, **Yellow Triangle**.

Orange Star
[TRS] A symbol applied to **Traction Units**, in this case most **First Generation Diesel Multiple Units** (**DMU**) with hydraulic transmission, denoting the **Multiple Working** control system with which they are fitted. Only Traction Units bearing the same symbol can be connected safely. See **Blue Square**, **Blue Star**, **Green Circle**, **Orange Star**, **Red Circle**, **Red Diamond**, **Red Triangle**, **White Circle**, **White Diamond**, **Yellow Diamond**, **Yellow Triangle**

Orange Vest
[Col.] An item of high visibility clothing required when **On or Near the Line**. See also **All Orange**, **Diddy Vest**, **Hi-vis Vest**, **Yellow Vest**.

ORBIS
[NR] Offering Rail Better Information Services.

ORBITA
(Tradename) [TRS] A fleet management system produced by **Bombardier** which remotely downloads data from the train's **Train Management System** (**TMS**) for maintenance use.

ORCATS
(*or-katz*) Operational Research Computerised Allocation of Tickets to Services, which allocates Ticket revenue to the appropriate **Train Operating Companies** (**TOC**).

ORCC
Operational Risk Control Coordinator.

Order of Pulling
a) [PW] The sequence in which **Tensors** should be used in and around **Switch and Crossing Units** (**S&C Units**) to maintain their correct geometrical tolerances. See also **Stressing Diagram**, **Stressing Plan**.
b) [Sig.] The order in which the **Levers** in a **Mechanical Signal Box** must be operated in order to **Set** a particular **Route**.

Order to Move
[NR Ops.] A document used to enter details onto the **Total Operations Processing System** (**TOPS**).

Ordinary Acting Relay
[Sig.] A **Relay** without a particular stated specialised operating characteristic.

Ordinary Joint
[PW] Describing a normal **Fishplated Rail Joint** with a standard **Expansion Gap**, but not an **Insulated Rail Joint** (**IRJ**).

Ordnance Datum (OD)
A vertical datum used by the **Ordnance Survey** (**OS**) as the basis for deriving altitudes. This is defined as the mean (average) sea level at Newlyn in Cornwall between 1915 and 1921. Prior to 1921, OD was taken from the mean level of the Victoria Dock, Liverpool. Also **ODN**.

ORE
Office of Research and Experiments, part of the **Union International des Chemins der Fer** (**UIC**).

ORFEUS
Open Railway □ Freight Electronic Data Interchange (EDI) User System.

Orientation of Close Viewing Sector
[Sig.] The angle between the 12:00 (o'clock) position (the direction vertically upward) and a radial line drawn through the centre of the **Close Viewing Sector** (**CVS**) of the **Signal Aspect**. The angle is measured clockwise from the 12:00 position.

ORN
[Tel. Obs.] Overlay Radio Network, see **National Radio Network** (**NRN**).

ORO
See **One Rail Only**.

OROR

OROR Possession

OROTR

OROTR Possession
See **Outside Rules of the Route**.

ORR
a) See **Office of Rail Regulation**
b) See **Office of the Rail Regulator**.

ORS
[NR] Operational Requirements Specification.

Orthotropic Deck
[Civ.] A **Bridge Deck** constructed typically from a flat steel plate with longitudinal and transverse ribs beneath.

OS
a) See **On Sight Mode**
b) Ordnance Survey.

OS3D
(Tradename) OMNISurvey 3D, a Graphical Information System (**GIS**) produced by Omnicom Engineering Ltd.

OSA
Overhead System Allocation.

OSBM
Ordnance Survey Bench Mark.

Oscar
The **Phonetic Alphabet** word representing O.

OSD
[Elec.] Overhead System Design.

OSDIL
See **Outside Door Indicator Lights**.

OSG
Operation(al) Safety Group.

OSGR
Ordnance Survey Grid Reference.

OSI
Open Systems Interconnect.

OSL

OSL Rail
(Tradename) [Sig.] Obcon Solutions Limited Rail. A company which provides **Signalling** design, testing and commissioning services to the UK national **Rail** sector, head office Crewe.

OSLO
(Tradename) [Elec.] Overhead Electrical System Loading, a modelling package for Electrification systems developed by AEA Technology (now called Delta Rail).

OSP
Operational Safety Plan.

OSP&I
Operational Safety Plan & Instructions

Osprey (YKA)
[NR] A modified Salmon (YFA, YMA, YMB, YMO, YSA, YWA, YXA) Wagon, with additional Stanchions.

OSRPA
The Offices Shops and Railway Premises Act, 1963.

OSS
See Overspeed Sensor System. Part of the Train Protection and Warning System (TPWS).

OSS+
[Sig.] Overspeed Sensor System Plus, an additional OSS fitment provided up to 750m On the Approach to a Signal, intended to provide protection at approach speeds higher that the normal 60-75mph.

OSTI
Other Single Till Income.

OT
See One Train Working Without Train Staff.

OT(S)
See One Train Working by Train Staff.

OTDR
a) See On Train Data Recorder. See also On Train Monitoring Recorder (OTMR)
b) Optical Time Domain Reflectometer, a distance measurement system.

OTIF
a) Online Ticket Issuing Facility.
b) Organisation Intergouvernementale pour les Transports Internationaux Ferroviaires, an intergovernmental organisation for international carriage by Rail.

OTM
a) See On Track Machine
b) [Elec.] Overhead Line □ Traction □ Maintenance
c) [Elec.] On-Train Metering (of Traction Supply).

OTMR
a) See On Train Monitoring Recorder
b) On-Train Monitoring and Recording (equipment)
See also On Train Data Recorder (OTDR).

OTP
a) See On Track Plant
b) Optimised Traffic Planning.

OTPD
See On Track Plant Depot.

OTROTR
See Outside the Rules of the Route.

OTT
See Outer Tell Tales.

OTTC
See Over the Top Cantilever.

Otter (YXA)
[NR] A vehicle forming part of a Long Welded Rail Train (LWRT, LWR Train), and providing limited propulsion to the Train on site. See Wagon Names.

OTW
See One Train Working.

OTX
See Over Track Crossing.

Out
[Sig.]
a) Of a Signal Lamp, not lit
b) Of a Lever in a Lever Frame, placed in the Reverse position.
See also In.

Out of Correspondence
a) [Sig.] Describing a pair of related Point Ends which are lying contrarily to each other, e.g. one Normal and one Reversed in a Crossover. This situation is detected and indicated by Split Detection
b) [Sig.] Describing a Set of Switches (Set of Points) which are lying opposite to the way required by the Signalling System.
The opposite is In Correspondence.

Out of Gauge (OOG)
Any load on a Rail Vehicle or Rail Vehicle that is itself larger than the Loading Gauge. Special arrangements must be made for the passage of these vehicles, including stopping other traffic and severely reduced speed.

Out of Gauge Rail
[Elec.] A short length of Conductor Rail supported on Insulators out of reach of the Current Collection Shoes and used to bridge gaps in the Conductor Rail layout, typically at Switch and Crossing Layouts (S&C Layouts).

Out of Running (OOR)

Out of Running Wire
[Elec.] A Contact Wire (CW) that is not in contact with passing Pantographs. The opposite is an In Running Wire (IR)

Out of Square
[PW] Describing two features (such as Switch Toes or Rail Joints) which are (incorrectly) not directly opposite each other.

Out of Synchronisation
[Sig.] When applied an Automatic Level Crossing, a situation in which the electrical signal from operation of the Strike-in Treadle is "stored" by the Signalling System, so that the Crossing Closure Sequence is initiated when the Signaller □ Clears the Signal on the approach to the Crossing. As a consequence, the Crossing is closed for longer than when an Approaching Train operates it automatically.

Out of Traffic Hours (OOTH)
[Ops.]
a) The time between the last timetabled Train of one day and the first Train of the next day
b) A time of day when no Trains are timetabled to run. Also White Period, No Train Period.

329

ELLIS' BRITISH RAILWAY ENGINEERING ENCYCLOPÆDIA

Out of Turn Working
[Ops.] A **Train Movement** or **Working** made with an unusual combination of **Locomotive**, **Rolling Stock** or **Route**.

Outer Distant Signal
[Sig.] The **Distant Signal** relating to the **Outer Home Signal**.

Outer Home Signal
[Sig.] A **Stop Signal**; the first **Home Signal** a **Train** driver encounters when approaching a **Signal Box** (**SB**) in an **Absolute Block** (**AB**) area. The Outer Home Signal was previously called the **Home No.1 Signal**.

Outer Tell Tales (OTT)
[PW] The **Tell Tales** placed at the boundary between **Anchor Length** and surrounding undisturbed **Track** to monitor the effectiveness of the Anchor Length.

Outer Tread
[TRS] The **1 in 10** or **1 in 15** conical section of a **Wheel Profile**, which does not contact the **Rail Head** in normal **Running**.

Outer Wheelbase (OWB)

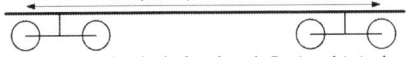

[TRS] On a **Rail Vehicle** fitted with **Bogies**, this is the distance between the axle centres of the outermost axles at each extreme end of the Rail Vehicle. See **Wheelbase**. See also **Inner Wheelbase** (**IWB**).

Outfall
a) The point at which one drainage system discharges into another drainage system or watercourse
b) [NR] The location at which a **Track Drain** leaves **Network Rail** property.

Outgoing Feeder (OF)
[Elec.] A **Feeder** along which power is supplied from a substation to the equipment being supplied. See also **Incoming Feeder** (**IF**).

Outline Design
[NR] The third stage of scheme development, coming after **Detailed Feasibility**. Following the gathering of detailed site data such as topographical survey data, ground information, existing wiring information, asset condition information, existing **Non-compliances** (**NC**) and ownership information, the agreed option from Detailed Feasibility is developed so that all issues and risks are either designed out or clearly identified. The end of this stage is normally marked by the production of **Form A**, **Approval in Principle** (**AIP**) or **Outline Project Specification** (**OPS**) and **Scheme Plan** depending on discipline. It is equivalent to the **Governance for Railway Investment Projects** stage 4 (**GRIP** 4). The next stage of development is normally **Detailed Design**, GRIP 5.

Outline Project Specification (OPS)
[NR] A document detailing the features and functions of a proposed **Signalling Scheme**, including the standards that will be applied and the type of **Signalling System** being proposed. It is analogous to the **Civil Engineer's** ▫ **Form A** document.

Out-of-service Lock
[TRS] Key operated device used to manually lock a door and preventing its use in normal service.

Outside

Outside a Signal
[Col.] A location **In Advance Of** a **Signal** and therefore outside the area protected by that Signal.

Outside Door Indicator Lights (OSDIL)
[LUL] The lights, fitted to the outside of **Trains**, to indicate to waiting **Passengers** that the Train doors are (or could be) open.

Outside Edge (OE)
[PW] The outside face of the **Rail Head**, that which is not contacted by the **Wheel Flanges**. Also **Back Edge** (**BE**), **Back Face**, **Back of Head**, **Field Side**. See also **Running Edge**.

Outside Guard Rail(s)

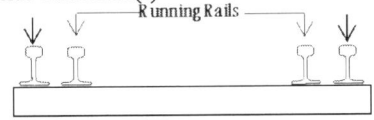

[PW] **Guard Rail**(s) provided on the **Sleeper Ends**. See also **Inside Guard Rails**.

Outside Party (OP)
[NR] A person or organisation which is not part of the **Infrastructure Controller**, so from the point of view of the **National Railway Network** (**NRN**), any person or organisation other than **Network Rail** (**NR**).

Outside Rail
On a **Curve**, the **Rail** with the larger Radius (**R**) and the one furthest from the centre of Curve. The opposite is **Inside Rail**.

Outside Rules
Outside Rules Possession
See **Outside the Rules of the Route** (**OROR**, **OROTR**), **Outside the Rules of the Route Possession**.

Outside Slip

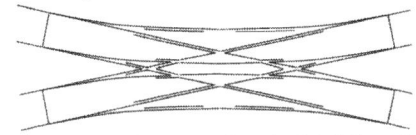

[PW] A **Diamond Crossing** where the **Switch Toes** of the **Slip Switches** are outside the **Common Crossings**. In this case it may be possible to use standard **Switches**. This arrangement is the most unusual. A Diamond Crossing where the Switch Toes of the Slip Switch are inside the Common Crossings is an **Inside Slip**.

Outside the Rules of the Route (OROR, OROTR)
Outside the Rules of the Route Possession
[NR] A **Possession** that has times or limits outside that permitted in the **Rules of the Route** (**ROTR**). Such Possessions are normally negotiated many months in advance.

Over End
Over End Relaying
Over the Short End
[Col.] Lifting, transporting items such as Track Panels using a Rail Crane working with its jib in line and extended, normally so that the minimum amount of chassis is under the jib. This arrangement is known as Over the Short End.

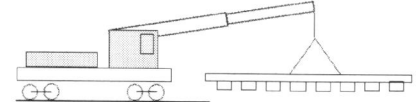

Over the Top Cantilever (OTTC)
[Elec.] A small Cantilever arrangement fitted to Overhead Line (OLE) □ Portal Structure to support the Catenary Wire. These are replacing the original pulley system, where fitted.

Over Track Crossing (OTX)
A cable crossing where the cables pass over the Line. Also Cable Bridge. See also Under Track Crossing (UTX).

Overbolt
See Underbolt.

Overbridge (OB)
A Bridge that allows passage over the Railway. Also Overline Bridge.

Overcharge, To
Overcharge Brakes, To
[TRS] Applying additional pressure through the Air Brake system to facilitate the release of all Brakes.

Over-current
A current which is higher than the continuous rating of an electrical circuit. See also Circuit Breaker (CB).

Overdriving
[Sig.] A term used to describe a Point Machine or Supplementary Drive which is attempting to (incorrectly) move a Switch Rail beyond the point where it contacts the Stock Rail.

Overdue PPM
[TRS] Overdue for Planned Preventative Maintenance (PPM), The wording found on labels attached to certain Wagons indicating that the Wagon is late for regular Maintenance attention. The act of attaching such a label (called a Card) to a Wagon is called Carding. See also Green Card, Red Card.

OVERHEAD
(Tradename) [Elec.] An Overhead Line Equipment (OLE) modelling package produced by DeltaRail.

Overhead Contact System (OCS)
[Elec.] The Contact Wire (CW), Catenary Wires and associated support mechanisms providing the interface between the Traction Power system and the Pantograph mounted on a Traction Unit. See also Overhead Line Equipment (OHLE, OLE).

Overhead Line
See Overhead Line Equipment (OHLE, OLE).

Overhead Line Conductor (OLC)
[Elec.] An electrical Conductor used in an Overhead Line Electification (OLE) system.

Overhead Line Engineer (OLE Engineer)
[Elec.] A specialist working on the specification, design, installation or Maintenance of Overhead Line Electification (OLE) systems.

Overhead Line Equipment (OHLE, OLE)
[Elec.] An assembly of metal Conductor □ Wires, insulating devices and support structures used to bring a Traction Supply Current to suitably equipped Traction Units. The conducting wires are normally strung between masts or poles in some form of Catenary arrangement, but simple systems may have a single Trolley Wire. Other related terms include Contact Wire (CW), Dropper, Head Span, Insulator, Intermediate Catenary Wire, Neutral Section (NS), Overhead Contact System (OCS), Return Conductor (RC), Section Insulator (SI), Tension Length (TL), See also Pantograph.

Overhead Line Gantry
[Elec.] An alternative term for an Overhead Line Structure, often used to mean a Portal Structure spanning many Tracks. Also Stanchion.

Overhead Line Mast (OLE Mast)
[HR Elec.] Common description of an Overhead Line Structure with a single upright, such as a Single Track Cantilever (STC). Also Stanchion.

Overhead Line Permit (OLP)
[NR Elec.] As a suffix to COSS on a Sentinel card it means the COSS is qualified to receive permits for Overhead Line Equipment (OLE) □ Isolations.

Overhead Line Stanchion (OLE Mast)
See Overhead Line Mast (OLE Mast).

Overhead Line Structure
[NR Elec.] Generally any structural steel portal or Cantilever structure supporting the Overhead Line Equipment (OLE) □ Catenary and associated equipment. The term is also used to include the relevant part of any construction fulfilling such a role, see Bridge Arm. Also OLE Mast, OLE Stanchion, Overhead Line Mast, Overhead Line Stanchion, Stanchion.

Overhead Trolley Leads
[Elec.] The Cables and plugs used on Shed Roads in Depots to provide power to DC Trains as part of the Overhead Trolley Supply system.

Overhead Trolley Supply
[Elec.] An arrangement of overhead conductors provided in Sheds to allow DC Trains to be moved without the need to provide Conductor Rails at ground level.

Overheads
[Col.] Common shortening of Overhead Line Equipment (OHLE, OLE).

Overlap (OL)
a) See Signal Overlap
b) [PW Col.] A term for an Anchor Length formed from recently Stressed Rail
c) see Overlap Span.

331

Overlap Joint

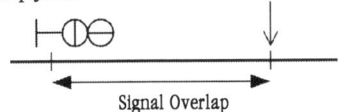

Signal Overlap
[Sig.] The **Insulated Rail Joint** (**IRJ**) at the end of a **Signal Overlap** furthest from the **Signal** itself.

Overlap Span
[Elec.] The **Span** in which two **Tension Lengths** of **Overhead Line Equipment** (**OLE**) □ **Overlap** (**OL**), allowing passing **Pantographs** to smoothly transfer from one to the other. There are two types, **Insulated Overlaps** and **Un-Insulated Overlaps**. The Overhead Line Equipment is divided into Tension Lengths (generally a kilometre or so long) to allow the variations in length caused by thermal effects to be adequately managed. See also **Balance Weight Anchor** (**BWA**).

Overlapping Design
See **Parallel Design**.

Overlay Track Circuit
[Sig.] A **Track Circuit** (**TC**) within another Track Circuit but operating separately from it, used to more accurately determine the position of a **Train**.

Overlift
[PW] The amount of additional **Lift** applied during **Track Maintenance** works over the value required to correct a defect. The Overlift is applied to compensate for subsequent settlement of the **Ballast** disturbed by the lifting works. Approximately half of any Lift will subsequently be lost in settlement.

Overline Bridge (OB)
An alternative term for **Overbridge** (**OB**) used to avoid confusion (Highway Engineers would claim that this type of **Bridge** is an **Underbridge** (**UB**)). The opposite is **Underline Bridge** (**UB**).

Overload
A current which is so high as to be potentially or actually damaging to an electrical circuit.

Overload Relay
[TRS] A **Traction Power** circuit **Relay** which detects excessive current in the circuit and switches off the power to avoid damage to the **Traction Motors**.

Override
[Sig.] An emergency facility provided on some **Remote Interlockings** which allows a limited functionality (**All Signals On**, selected **Signals** on **Auto Working**, limited **Route** selection at **Junctions**, etc.) in times of failure. Also **Through Routes**.

Overriding Switch
[PW] A type of **Switch** where the **Rail Foot** of the **Switch Rail** is arranged to overlap the un-machined Foot of the **Stock Rail** when the Switch is **Closed**.

Overrun
[Ops.]
a) A **Possession** that is not handed back to the **Signaller** by the due time. See **Possession Over-run**
b) A **Train Movement** that takes an **Electric Train** onto a **Track** that is not equipped with **Overhead Line Equipment** (**OLE**), see also **Over-run Wire**
c) A **Train Movement** passing a **Signal** at **Danger**, See **SPAD**
d) A **Propelling Movement** that results in a **Train** demolishing a **Buffer Stop**, See **Buffer Over-run**, **Siding Over-run**.

Overrun Risk Assessment Model (ORAM)
[NR] A model evolved to allow the quantitative analysis of the risk of a **Train** passing a **Signal** at **Danger**, typically used in assessing the risks introduced by new **Junction Layouts**.

Overrun Wire
[Elec.] A short length of **Overhead Line Equipment** (**OLE**) provided on a connecting **Line** to safely guide the **Pantographs** of misdirected **Electric Trains** where a **Non-electrified Line** meets a **Line** equipped with OLE. The additional equipment keeps the Pantograph clear of the **Return Conductor** (**RC**) and any **Head Spans** before the **Contact Wire** (**CW**) runs out. See also **Automatic Dropping Device** (**ADD**).

Oversail Block
[Civ.] A specially produced block designed to sit on a **Platform Wall** and support the **Platform Copings**. See **Platform Section**.

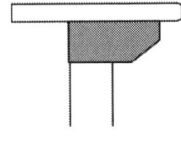

Oversetting
[Sig.] The **Setting** of a **Route** for a second **Train Movement** before the preceding Train Movement has **Cleared** the Route or **Overlap**. Also **Restroking**, **Pumping**.

Overshot Curve
Overshot Transition
[PW] A horizontal Track misalignment resulting in the Track **Reversing** in order to meet the following straight. This is often caused by too much **Maintenance Tamping** and too little **Design Tamping**, compounded by the excessive use of **Tamping and Lining Machines** working in one direction.

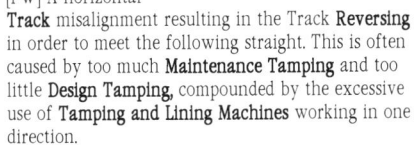

Overspeed
Overspeed Derailment
Describing a **Derailment** caused by a **Train** being made to travel too fast for the **Track Geometry** of the **Line**.

Overspeed Sensor System (OSS)
[NR] Part of the **Train Protection and Warning System** (**TPWS**), this system consists of two transmitter loops in the **Fourfoot** □ on the **Approach** to a reduction in the **Permissible Speed** (**PS**) or a **Stop Signal**. When activated, the first of these, the **Arming Loop**, arms the receiver mounted on the passing **Train**. The second loop is the **Trigger Loop**; if the Train passes over this before 0.974 seconds has elapsed, the brakes are automatically applied. By adjusting the distance between the loops the maximum speed can be set, this is the **Set Speed**. The system is activated in conjunction with **Signals** showing **Stop Aspects** to enforce a controlled approach, and drastically reduces the likelihood of **SPADs** travelling **Beyond** the **Signal Overlap**. See also **Train Stop Sensor** (**TSS**).

Overstressed Rail
[PW] **Continuous Welded Rail** (**CWR**) that has a **Stress Free Temperature** (**SFT**) higher than 27°C (80°F), i.e. it displays a lower than normal compressive stress at high temperatures and a higher than normal tensile stress at low temperatures. See also **Red Item**.

Overturning Block
See **Safety Block**.

Overview

Overview Diagram
[Sig.] A **Signalling Diagram** or display that shows the whole of the area being controlled, usually with reduced detail.

OWB
See **Outer Wheelbase**.

Oyster
a) [NR, prob. Obs.] A **Plough Brake**, CARKND □ ZUP.
b) Smartcard-based prepayment **Ticket** system available to passengers on **TfL** transport (including **London's** buses, **Trams**, **London Underground Limited**, **Docklands Light Railway**, **London Overground**, **National Rail** and boats.)

P

P

a) [NR] As the last letter in a **Wagon** □ **CARKND**, this denotes that the **Wagon** is **Through Piped** for **Vacuum Brakes**, which does not operate the vehicle brakes. This means it has no **Automatic Brake** or **Continuous Brake**. Also known as **Vacuum Piped**. See **Unfitted**

b) In an abbreviated **Track Name**, it denotes **Passenger**, as in **Passenger Loop**

c) [NR] As the first letter of a Wagon CARKND it means that the vehicle is an international **Cartic** □ **Set**

d) [Sig.] On a **Signalling Circuit Diagram**:
- As one of the leading letters of an **Equipment Code**, it means repeating
- As the last letter of an Equipment Code, it means **Lever** latch or **Trigger** contact

e) The letter represented by **Papa** in the **Phonetic Alphabet**

f) An abbreviation of **Platform**. Also **Pfm**.

g) **Common Interface File Operating Characteristics Code** for **Push/Pull** train

h) [LUL] The Piccadilly **Line**.

P and C

P&C

[PW] **Point and Crossing**. An alternative name for **Switch and Crossing (S&C)**.

P Stock

[LUL] Type of **Train**, now extinct, which was first introduced in 1938 for use on the Metropolitan and District **Lines**. It was very similar to the **O Stock** except that it had the **Guard's** controls in the **Passenger** saloon, as on other Underground **Rolling Stock**.

P Way

A contraction of **Permanent Way**. Also **Per Way, PW**.

P&E

Plant and **E**quipment.

P&F

[Sig.] **P**ost and **F**ittings

P&LJR

[Hist.] The **Pre-Grouping P**reston & **L**ongridge **J**oint **Railway**, a London & North Western and Lancashire & Yorkshire joint enterprise.

P&M

Plant & **M**achinery.

P&T

P&T Staff

[BR] **P**rofessional and **T**echnical Staff. Under **British Rail (BR)**, the group of staff that included Technical Officers **(TO)**, Senior Technical Officers **(STO)** and Principal Technical Officers **(PTO)**, See also **Conciliation Grades, Conciliation Staff, Wages Grades**.

P&TS

[NR] **P**rogramme **a**nd **T**echnical **S**ervices.

P&WJR

[Hist.] The **Pre-Grouping P**ortpatrick and **W**igtownshire **J**oint **Railway**, a Caledonian, Glasgow & South Western, London & North Western and Midland joint enterprise.

P&WYR

[Hist.] The **Pre-Grouping P**reston & **W**yre **Railway**, a London & North Western and Lancashire & Yorkshire joint enterprise.

P1

P1 Profile

[TRS] The standard **Wheel Profile** in use on **Rail Vehicles** built prior to 1970, such as **Mark** 1 **Coaches** and **Class** 08 **Shunting Locomotives**. It is based on an LMSR drawing and is a simple 1 in 20 cone intended to place the load from the **Wheel** directly over the centreline of the **Rail**.

P10

P10 Profile

[TRS] A **Wheel Profile** based on the UIC S1002 continental Profile, found on **Freightliner** and continental **Freight Vehicles**. It has optimal performance on **Rails** □ **Inclined** at 1 in 40.

P11

P11 Profile

[TRS] A **Wheel Profile** based on the **P1 Profile** but with material removed from the **Flange Root**. Generally confined to **Mark II Coaches**, it is also found on some Mark I Coaches and **Post Office Vehicles**. It was developed to improve the **Ride Quality** of Mark II Coaches at **High Speed**.

P12

P12 Profile

[TRS] A **Wheel Profile** which has relief (a smaller diameter) near the **Flange Root** when compared to **P8**, designed to reduce **Rolling Contact Fatigue** (**RCF**) with only a small compromise in curving performance

P3

(Tradename) Primavera Project Planning. This is **Network Rail's** preferred programme planning and management system.

P5

P5 Profile

[TRS] A modified continental **Wheel Profile** that has a thicker **Flange**. It is found on heavy **Freight Vehicles**, particularly those with Y-25 **Bogies**.

P6

P6 Profile

[TRS] A **Wheel Profile** based on a partly worn **P1 Profile**, found on older **AC Electric Locomotives** and heavy **Freight Vehicles** not fitted with Y-25 **Bogies**. This profile is an attempt to improve the cornering characteristics of these vehicles.

P8

P8 Profile

[TRS] A **Wheel Profile** based on a worn **P1 Profile**, found on most **Passenger** vehicles built since 1970 and **Class** 91 **Locomotives**.

P9
P9 Profile
[TRS] A **Wheel Profile** based on the **P1 Profile**, but with material removed from the back of the **Flange**. Found on the centre axle **Co-Co Bogies** (see **Diesel and Electric Locomotive Notation**) and some **Steam Locomotives**, it helps reduce jamming of the centre **Wheelset**.

PA
Public Address.

PAB
[NR] Plant Acceptance Body.

PABC
(Tradename) [PW] Plasser **Automatic Ballast Cleaner** (**ABC**). A type of **Ballast Cleaner** produced by **Plasser & Theurer** (A Tradename).

PABS
[NR] **Passenger** □ **Track Access** Billing System.

PABX
[Tel.] Private Automatic Branch Telephone Exchange.

Pacer
The brandname of the **Class 14x Diesel Multiple Unit** (**DMU**) They are also nicknamed **Nodding Dogs** after their sometimes violent passage along poor quality **Jointed Track**. The original prototype **Units** were based on Leyland buses. See **LEV, Nodding Donkey**.

Pacifastacus Leniusculus
Signal Crayfish. See **Invasive Species**.

Packet 44
[Sig.] Packet 44 is a means to transmit data for national applications between **Trains** and **Track** and vice versa, using the data transmission facilities included within the **European Train Control System** (**ETCS**), in turn part of the **European Rail Traffic Management System** (**ERTMS**). Packet 44 data is not processed by ETCS, but is handled by application specific systems. **Tilt Authorisation and Speed Supervision System** (**TASS**) is an example of such an application.

Packing
a) See **Ballast Packing**
b) [TRS] Discs, Shims or other material inserted in a suspension to adjust the height of the **Wagon** at that point.

Packing Area
[PW] The area of a **Sleeper** or **Bearer** within 300mm (12") of the **Running Edge** (**RE**) that should be packed in order to support the **Sleeper** or **Bearer** correctly. See also **End Bound, Centre Bound**.

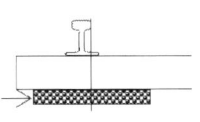

PACT
PACT Track
(*pakt trak*) (Tradename) [PW] Paved Concrete Track. A type of **Slab Track**. Also **Paved Track**.

PACTS
See **Parliamentary Advisory Council for Transport Safety**.

PAD
(*padd*) See Pre-Assembly Depot.

Pad
See **Baseplate Pad, Chair Pad, Rail Pad**.

Pad Heater
See **Electric Pad Heater**.

Paddington Accident
See **Ladbrooke Grove Accident**.

Paddle
a) A paddle shaped wooden device used to lift a **Current Collection Shoe** (**Shoe**) clear of the **Conductor Rail**
b) A paddle shaped wooden device used in conjunction with a **Short Circuiting Bar** when taking **DC Isolations**.

PADS
(*padz*)
a) Poor Adhesion Display Signs, a system of fixed **Lineside** warning signs that can be activated by the **Signaller** to warn the driver of an area of **Abnormal Rail Head Conditions** ahead
b) [NR] Parts and Drawing System
c) Product Approval Database System
d) [LUL] Pumps and Drainage Strategic initiative.

Paid Area
That area of a **Station** accessible only by **Passengers** in possession of a valid **Ticket**. See also **Unpaid Area**.

Paint Drop
[PW Col.] A location marked with coloured dye to indicate a geometry **Exceedence**. This is generally done by a **Track Inspection Vehicle** (**TIV**) during a measurement run. Colloquially known as a **Washdrop**.

PAIP
Portsmouth Area Infrastructure Project.

PAL
a) [NR] Property Action Line. A **Network Rail** Property telephone help desk for customers to report problems and provide feedback.
b) (*pal*) (Tradename) [PW] Portique Aluminium Leger or Lightweight Aluminium Gantry, the reduced functionality version of the **PUM** □ **Panel Lifting Equipment** that can be dismantled into man-portable pieces. No longer in regular use in the UK. Manufactured by **Geismar**.

PALADIN
(*pall-a-din*) [NR] See **Performance and Loading Analysis Database Information**.

PALAS
(*pal-ass*) (Tradename) [PW] Developed in Switzerland by J Mueller AG, a computer-assisted, automatic, continuous, three-dimensional real-time **Track** measurement, **Tamper** guidance and control system produced by **Matisa**. The PALAS hardware consists of two sensor units mounted on a measuring trolley in front of a **Tamper**. The units are a laser scanner and a three-dimensional gyrocompass. Adjustments for the **Tamper** to implement are captured by scanning **Lineside** reflectors and are provided as the machine progress to adjust the **Track**. Swiss **Railways** started to use PALAS in the mid-1990s. See also **Track Machine Guidance** (**TMG**).

PALWIN
PALADIN for Windows™. See **Performance And Loading Analysis Database Information**.

PAM
(*pam*) [NR] **P**ossession **A**ccess **M**anager. See also **Green Zone Access Manager** (**GZAM**).

PAMELA
Pedestrian **A**ccessibility **M**ovement **E**nvironment **L**aboratory.

PAMX
[Tel.] **P**riv**a**te **M**anual Branch Telephone E**x**change.

Pan
[Col.]
a) A common shortening of **Pandrol**
b) A common shortening of **Pantograph**, also **Panto**.

Pan Down
[Col.] Common description for an **Electric Locomotive** or **Electric Multiple Unit** (**EMU**) that normally uses **Overhead Line Equipment** (**OLE**) but is being moved by another form of **Traction**, e.g. a **Diesel Locomotive**. See **Diesel Hauling**, **Thunderbirding**.

PAN *x*
(*pan ~*) [PW] A type of **Baseplate** designed to use **Pandrol Rail Clips**, **Pandrol** □ **Rail Fastenings**. The *x* denotes the particular type; 1, 3, 6, 9, and 11 are common.

Panchex
(Tradename) [Elec.] A **Trackside** □ **Pantograph** monitoring system which determines the up-lift force of the pantograph of each **Locomotive** or **Multiple Unit** that passes. This is achieved by measuring the **Uplift** of the **Contact Wire** (**CW**), the **Train** speed, wind speed and direction, and by identifying the vehicle number, **Pantograph** type and direction.

Pandrol
(Tradename) [PW] From Per Pande-Rolfsen, the inventor.
a) A manufacturer of **Rail Fastening** systems based in Surrey, UK. Pandrol Ltd. was formerly the Elastic Rail Spike Co. Ltd.
b) The colloquial term for **PR***xxx*, **PR***xxx***A**, **e1809**, **e2001** and **e+** □ **Clips** for **Flat Bottom Rails** (**FB**).

Pandrol Baseplate
[PW] A baseplate intended to be fitted with **Pandrol Rail Clips**.

Pandrol Clip
[PW Col.] Common contraction of **Pandrol Rail Clip**. Also **Pandrol** (b).

Pandrol Rail Clip
(Tradename) [PW] A **Rail Clip** for **Flat Bottom Rail** (**FB**) manufactured by the **Pandrol** company. Devised by Pande Rolfson in Norway in 1957.

Panel
a) [Sig.] A section of the control desk of a **Power Signal Box** (**PSB**). See **Signal Box Panel**
b) [PW] An alternative term for a **Track Panel**
c) See **Level Crossing Panel**
d) [Elec.] The length of **Overhead Line Equipment** (**OLE**) between two adjacent **Droppers**

Panel Lifting Equipment
[PW] The generic term for small lifting gantries which, when used in multiple, can lift, transport and position large **Panels** of **Track**, particularly **Switch and Crossing Layouts** (**S&C Layouts**). Types include **Fassetta**, **PAL**, **PEM**, **PLUM** and **PUM**.

Panel Multiplexer
[Sig.] In a **Solid State Interlocking** (**SSI**), the device which converts the individual electrical switch settings on the **Signal Box Panel** into data that is usable by the **Signalling System**, and conversely converts data from the Signalling System into individual indications on the **Illuminated Diagram**.

Panel Processor
[Sig.] Within a **Solid State Interlocking** (**SSI**), the Panel Processor handles non-critical duties such as handling **Panel Requests** issued at the **Signaller's Control Panel** or **Automatic Route Setting** (**ARS**) computer and passing them over to the **Control Interlocking Processor**, and updating the display. Panel Processors are operated in duplex, with a hot standby.

Panel Processor Module (PPM)
[Sig.] A subdivision of a **Panel Processor**, controlling a part of the **Signal Box Panel**.

Panel Request
[Sig.] Within a **Solid State Interlocking** (**SSI**), the **Panel Processor** converts commands issued at the **Signaller's Control Panel** into a stream of inputs to the **Control Interlocking Processor**. Because both Panel Processors are normally operational, the **Control Interlocking Processor** receives and executes two copies of each request. These are stored by the central interlocking in a buffer and processed during **Minor Cycles** which are otherwise completed in under the minimum Minor Cycle time. At most one Panel Request will be served in any Minor Cycle.

Panel Signal Box
[WR Sig.] A term for a **Power Signal Box** (**PSB**).

Panelling Out
[PW] Describing the removal of old **Track** in **Panels**, normally using a **Track Relaying Machine** (**TRM**). Alternative methods include **Loose Sleeper** (**LS**).

Panlock Key
(Tradename) [PW] A spring steel W-shaped replacement for the traditional wooden **Key** manufactured by **Pandrol** Ltd. It is shaped in such a way as to positively lock itself into the **Chair**. Used for securing **Bullhead** (**BH**) □ **Running Rails** and **Check Rails**. See also **Steel Key** (which works in a different way).

Pannier Turnout
[PW] An alternative for **Tandem Turnout**.

Panpuller
(Tradename) [PW] A special bar used to insert and remove **Pandrol Rail Clips**.

Pansetter
(Tradename) [PW] A special bar used to align **Rails** relative to **Housings** to allow the insertion of the **Insulator** and **Pandrol Rail Clip**.

Pansway
(*pan sway*) See **Pantograph Sway**.

Panto
[Col.] A common shortening of **Pantograph**. Also **Pan**.

Pantograph
[TRS]
a) The device fitted to the roof an **Electric Locomotive** or **Electric Multiple Unit** (**EMU**) that contacts the **Contact Wire** (**CW**) of the **Overhead Line Equipment** (**OLE**), allowing the **Traction Unit** to draw current. Colloquially abbreviated to **Panto** or **Pan**
b) In a description of a vehicle in a **Multiple Unit Train**, it indicates that the vehicle in question is equipped with a Pantograph.

Pantograph Hook-over
[Elec.] A fault condition in which the **Pantograph Horn** is above the **Contact Wire** (**CW**).

Pantograph Horn
[TRS] The curved outer section of a **Pantograph**. In normal use this never touches the **Contact Wire** (**CW**), but under conditions such as high winds and poor **Registration** will continue to guide the Pantograph. These are frangible items forming part of a low voltage circuit, and if broken by an obstruction activate the **Automatic Dropping Device** (**ADD**) to prevent further damage to both Pantograph and **Overhead Line Equipment** (**OLE**).

Pantograph Sway
[TRS] The lateral deviation of a **Pantograph** from a central position over the **Track**. This can be caused by a combination of suspension movement, wind loading and the flexibility in the Pantograph itself. This sway increases with increasing **Wire Height** but is independent of vehicle speed. Also referred to as **Pansway**.

Papa
The **Phonetic Alphabet** word representing **P**.

Paper Trap
[LUL] A device provided at the end of **Platform Safety Pits** to trap litter and loose rubbish.

Parallel Bonding
[Sig.] An arrangement of **Bonding** that provides Diverse electrical paths. **Track Circuits** (**TC**) bonded like this are not **Fail Safe**, as failure of a single **Bond** may result in a loss of vehicle detection. See also **Yellow Bond**.

Parallel Design
The practice of allowing multiple designers to work on a single project simultaneously. While this can work well when there is good communication and cooperation between all parties, typically it is a recipe for disaster and spiralling costs. Also **Overlapping Design**.

Parallel Design Agreement (PDA)
[NR] A formalisation of the responsibilities, timescales, formats and communication channels to be observed by all the parties engaged in a project requiring **Parallel Design**.

Parallel Feeders
Parallel Feeder Wires
[Elec.] Additional along-**Track** conductors which run parallel to, but separate from, the **Catenary** and **Contact Wires** (**CW**). These conductors increase the effective cross-sectional area of the system and thus reduce the electrical resistance. Also known as **Aerial Feeders**.

Parallel Movements
[Ops.] **Train Movements** made through a **Junction** in both the **Down Direction** and **Up Direction** simultaneously between a pair of **Tracks** and two other Tracks.

Parallel Signals
[Sig.]
a) **Signals**, applying to parallel **Lines** signalled in the same direction, which have been placed in the same longitudinal position.
b) Where two or more **Lines** on a **Route** are equipped with **Signals** in the same direction, then where there is a **Main Signal** on one Line, there should be a Signal on all Lines **Signalled** in that direction. This is to avoid confusion to drivers, as at each location there are the same number of Signals. This rule is also applied where there are multiple Routes through a large **Junction** between two locations, i.e. the driver should see the same number of Signals irrespective of the **Route** taken through the Junction.

Parallel Wing (PW)
[PW] See **Parallel Wing Rail**.

Parallel Wing Extension Rail
[PW] A length of **Rail** that connects to the **Parallel Wing Rail** of a **Common Crossing**. This Rail has a **Flare** at the non-connecting end, and acts as a **Check Rail** for the **Turnout Route**.

Parallel Wing Left (PWL)
[PW] As a suffix to **Chair** or **Baseplate** description, a Chair or Baseplate designed to support a **Left Hand Parallel Wing** (**LHPW**) □ **Rail**, on the left hand side of a **Common Crossing**, together with the **Crossing Vee Rails**.

Parallel Wing Rail
[PW] A **Wing Rail** without a **Flare** that connects to a **Parallel Wing Extension Rail**. Such Wing Rails can be right or left handed (as seen from the **Switch Toe**) or both. Also **Parallel Wing**. See also **Double Parallel Wing** (**DPW**), **Left Hand Parallel Wing** (**LHPW**), **Right Hand Parallel Wing** (**RHPW**).

Parallel Wing Right (PWR)
[PW] As a suffix to **Chair** or **Baseplate** description, a Chair or Baseplate designed to support a **Right Hand Parallel Wing** (**RHPW**) □ **Rail** on the right hand side of a **Common Crossing**, together with the **Crossing Vee Rails**.

Parallel Working
[Ops.] The ability or practice of having an **Up Direction** □ **Train Movement** at the same time as a complimentary **Down Direction** □ **Train Movement** on a parallel **Line** or **Connection**. Also **Parallel Movements**.

Parapet
Parapet Wall
[Civ.] The low wall or railing built along the edges of a **Bridge Deck** or **Arch** to prevent **Ballast**, pedestrians or vehicles straying over the edge and onto that which lies beneath.

Parapet Coping
[Civ.] The masonry or pre-cast concrete (**PCC**) construction placed on top of a **Parapet Wall**, to enhance its appearance, reduce water ingress into the wall beneath and in some cases to prevent persons climbing over the **Parapet**. See also **Steeple Coping**.

Parcels Dock
A **Platform** used for loading and unloading parcels to or from **Rail Vehicles**.

Park and Ride
Facilities deliberately aimed at the **Commuter**, making it a simple process to park one's car in a secure car park and catch a readily available **Train**. See also **Kiss and Ride**.

Parking Brake
A brake that is intended to prevent a stationary vehicle from moving. See also **Handbrake**.

Parkway
Generally used as a suffix to the name of a **Station** (e.g. Bristol **Parkway**) normally indicating that the Station has enhanced **Park and Ride** facilities.

PARL
Percentage Asset Remaining Life.

Parliamentary
See **Parliamentary Train**.

Parliamentary Advisory Council for Transport Safety (PACTS)
A registered charity and an associate Parliamentary Group. Its charitable objective is "To promote transport safety legislation to protect human life". Its aim is to advise and inform members of both Houses on air, **Rail** and road safety issues. It brings together safety professionals and legislators to identify research-based solutions to transport safety problems having regard to cost, effectiveness, achievability and acceptability.

Parliamentary Train (Parly)
[Hist.] Originally a **Train** that a **Railway Company** was obliged to run once per day each way at a specified average speed of 12mph and stop at **All Stations** on a **Route**, a requirement of the **Regulation of Railways Act 1844**. It latterly became the nickname for any All Stations **Stopping Train**. The original requirement for **Passengers** to be charged no more than one penny per mile has since been dropped. The term is also used to describe a limited Train service retained for the sole purpose of maintaining a **Route**. Sometimes shortened to **Parly**.

Parly
See **Parliamentary Train**.

Parr (YMA, YQA)
[NR] A 49 ton capacity flat **Wagon** used for the transport of **Panels**, **Rails** and **Sleepers**. See **Wagon Names**.

Parry People Mover
(Tradename) [TRS] A **Rail Vehicle** whose normal source of energy for **Traction** is a flywheel. This flywheel can be charged by a remote electrical supply, an internal combustion engine or even solar power. The flywheel is also recharged during braking. Manufactured by Parry People Movers Ltd and is a **Class** 139.

Part Fabricated Crossing
[PW] See **Part Welded Crossing**.

Part Step
[PW] A **Versine Rise** or **Transition Step** between successive **Versines** in a **Transition Curve** that is not a full Versine Rise (Transition Step) or half that value. A Versine Rise (or Transition Step) of exactly half is a **Half Step**. See **Hallade**. See also **Rounding**.

Part Welded Crossing
[PW] A **Common Crossing** comprising an **Electro-Slag Welded Vee** and bolted or **MGL Pinned** on **Wing Rails**. Also Part Fabricated Crossing, Semi-welded Crossing.

Partial Obscuration
[Sig.] An **Obscuration** which only affects part of the **Signal Element**. See also **Total Obscuration**.

Partially Fitted Train
[Ops.] A **Train** composed of a mix of vehicles with and without **Automatic Brakes**. In current times such Trains are very rare, and are most often **Engineer's Trains**. See also **Brake Force**.

Partition Door
[TRS] The door separating the driver's **Cab** from the **Passenger** compartment.

Pass Booked Services (PBS)
[NR Ops.] An instruction found in **Possession Arrangements**, which requires the **Person In Charge of Possession** (**PICOP**) to relinquish and retake the Possession for **Timetabled** ▢ **Trains** to pass.

Passable
Passable Signal
[NR Sig.] A **Signal** which can be passed without specific authority from the **Signaller** provided certain conditions are met. Such Signals are normally **Automatic Signals**, **Semi-automatic Signals** or **Intermediate Block Signals** (**IBS**), where the risk of conflict arising from the passing of the Signal is low. See also **Non-passable Signal**.

Pass-by
[Hist.] Alternative for **Meetings**.

Passcomm
[Col.] Passenger communication apparatus

Passcomm / Door Activated Light
[TRS] Lamp used to alert the driver to the operation of either a **PCA Emergency Brake Handle**, or that a door has become unlocked (for example though operation of the **Egress Handle**).

ELLIS' BRITISH RAILWAY ENGINEERING ENCYCLOPÆDIA

Passed at Danger
[Ops.] Unless specifically authorised by either:
- The **Signaller**,
- By dated, written instructions to do so,
- The **Pilotman**,
- By a **Person in Charge of Possession** (**PICOP**) or **Senior Person in Charge of Possession** (**SPICOP**) within a **Possession**,

a driver may not pass a **Signal** displaying a **Red Aspect**. A driver so doing without permission has Passed at Danger. See **Signal Passed at Danger** (**SPAD**).

Passed out
A driver being certified as possessing the required **Route Knowledge**.

Passenger
A person who has purchased a valid ticket, is at a **Station** and is travelling or anticipating travelling by **Train**. All other persons, excluding those legitimately at work on the **Railway** and those persons using **Level Crossings** (**LC, LX**), are trespassers. See also **Passenger Trespasser**.

Passenger / Freight Changeover
[TRS] A manual valve which allows the response of **Train** brakes to be changed between slow-acting for **Freight Trains** and fast-acting for **Passenger Trains**.

Passenger Carriage
See **Passenger Coach**.

Passenger Change Dates
[NR] The two occasions in a year when the **National Passenger Timetable** (**NPTT**) is re-issued. These are normally mid-May and mid-December and are always Saturdays.

Passenger Class
Since the early days of **Railways**, increased levels of comfort have been available to those willing to pay extra. Originally three levels were available, **First Class**, **Second Class** and **Third Class**. Second class was abolished between 1870 and the early years of the 20th century, with the exception of the Newhaven **Boat Trains** which continued to have First, Second and Third until 1955. The reason that Third remained was due to the requirement under the **Railway Regulation Act 1844** to run **Parliamentary Trains**. This continued until 1956 when Third was re-named Second. Second Class was then re-titled **Standard Class** in 1985. There are other names, including Club Class, but these are not universal.

Passenger Coach
[TRS] A **Rail Vehicle** specially built or adapted to carry **Passengers**. Common usage of this term applies only to Rail Vehicles that are pulled by a **Locomotive**. The Passenger Coaches of a **Multiple Unit Train** are normally referred to as **Cars**.

Passenger Communication Apparatus (**PCA**)
On-train system provided to enable **Passengers** to communicate with the driver in the event on an emergency, and which automatically applies the train's emergency brake. The brake application can be overridden by the driver to prevent the train stopping in an unsuitable location.

Passenger Demand
A measure of the number of **Passengers** using a **Train Service** or **Station** in a given period.

Passenger Door
[TRS] In a **Rail Vehicle**, a door intended to be used by **Passengers**.

Passenger Emergency Alarm (**PEA**)
[LUL] A system provided for **Passengers** to communicate to the driver or **Train Operator** that an emergency situation is present on a **Train**.

Passenger Emergency Alarm Brake (**PEAB**)
[LUL] A system on a **Train** that, when operated by activation of a **Passenger Emergency Alarm** (**PEA**) handle, will alert the driver to a problem and automatically apply the brakes. See also **Communication Cord**.

Passenger Line
A **Line** or **Track** equipped with a **Signalling System** suitable for **Passenger Trains**, e.g. built to **Passenger Standards**. This would normally include full **Signal Overlaps** and no **Trap Points**.

Passenger Loop
A **Track** used to recess **Passenger Trains**, allowing other **Trains** to pass.

Passenger Mile
A measure of patronage, defined as one **Passenger** travelling one **Mile**.

Passenger Operations Information System (**POIS**)
[NR] A major sub-system of the **TOPS** system, this is a mainframe system designed to provide resource control and management facilities for **Locomotive Hauled** ▫ **Passenger Trains** and the corresponding **Rolling Stock**. It consists of two main elements: a database of **Coaching Stock** ▫ **Diagrams** (representing the planned activity for individual **Sets** of **Coaches**) and real-time reporting of actual Sets matched to those Diagrams.

Passenger Rail Franchise
[NR] An agreement between the Department for Transport (**DfT**) and a **Train Operating Company** (**TOC**) whereby the TOC agrees to provide a minimum level of **Train** services on specified **Routes** for a fixed period. These agreements also contain details of grants, subsidies and investment. See also **Open Access**, **Open Access Operator**.

Passenger Service
[Ops.] A **Train** consisting of **Passenger Vehicles** to which the public has access.

Passenger Service Agent
[DLR] A person who travels on every **Dockland Light Railway** ▫ **Train**, normally undertaking ticket and revenue duties. This person can also be requested to drive the Train, when required and also carry out a **Sweep** of the **Track** if necessary.

Passenger Standards
A set of minimum provisions applicable to **Lines** on which **Passenger Trains** are permitted to run. In summary, these require that full **Signal Overlaps** be provided at all **Signals**, and that any **Trapping Arrangements** should consider **Accidents** involving Passenger Trains. The alternative is **Freight Standards**. All new works must conform to Passenger Standards.

Passenger Track Access Agreement
[NR] The binding agreement which sets out the arrangements agreed between **Network Rail** (**NR**) and a **Train Operating Company** (**TOC**), including payment, **Paths**, penalties and mechanisms for communication.

Passenger Train
[Ops.] A **Train** composed of **Rail Vehicles** specifically intended for the conveyance of **Passengers**. See also **Coach**, **Sleeping Car**.

Passenger Transport Authority (PTA)
The bodies established to assess the public transport needs of the metropolitan areas and make policy decisions about public transport provision. They include:
- Greater Manchester PTA (**GMPTA**). Now Greater Manchester Integrated Transport Authority (**GMITA**)
- Merseyside PTA (**MPTA**)
- Strathclyde PTA (**SPTA**)
- Tyne and Wear PTA (**TWPTA**)
- West Midlands PTA (**WMPTA**)
- West Yorkshire PTA (**WYPTA**)

Each of these has a corresponding **Passenger Transport Executive** (**PTE**).

Passenger Transport Executive (PTE)
The bodies established to deliver the public transport policies created by the relevant **Passenger Transport Authority** (**PTA**) in the metropolitan areas Some examples include:
- Greater Manchester Passenger Transport Executive (**GMPTE**, now Transport for Greater Manchester, **TfGM**)
- Merseyside Passenger Transport Executive (**MPTE**), trades as **Merseytravel**.
- South Yorkshire Passenger Transport Executive (**SYPTE**)
- Strathclyde Passenger Transport Executive (**SPTE**)
- Tyne and Wear Passenger Executive (**TWPTE**), trades as **Nexus**
- West Midlands Passenger Transport Executive (**WMPTE**), trades as **Centro**
- West Yorkshire Passenger Transport Executive (**WYPTE**), trades as **Metro**.

Passenger Trespasser
A person who is either travelling legally or intending to travel but is in a place on the **Railway** where they are not permitted to be.

Passenger Upgrade (PUG)
[RT Hist.] The proposed improvement works to be carried out on the **West Coast Main Line** (**WCML**). These works are required to permit the new **Class 390 Pendolino** □ **Tilting Trains** to run at **Enhanced Permissible Speed** (**EPS**). The work was split into two phases, the first achieving 125mph from 110mph and the second 140mph. The first phase was **PUG1** and the second **PUG2**. It is now unlikely that the second phase will ever be implemented on the current **Railway**.

Passenger Vehicle
[TRS] Any **Rail Vehicle** specially built or adapted to carry **Passengers**, whether **Locomotive Hauled** or **Self Propelled**.

Passengers In Excess of Capacity (PIXC)
[Ops.] The measure of by how much the average number of **Passengers** exceeds the design capacity of the **Coach**. Values of 45% for **Trains** approaching some **Terminal Stations** used by **Commuters** during the rush hour are not uncommon. The abbreviation is pronounced **Pixie**. See **Crush Load**.

Passing a Signal at Danger
[Ops.]
a) In error, see **Signal Passed at Danger** (**SPAD**), **Signal Passed at Stop** (**SPAS**)
b) Deliberately, see **Talking Past**.

Passing Clearance
[PW] The closest theoretical approach between the **Kinematic Envelopes** (**KE**) of two **Rail Vehicles** passing each other on adjacent **Tracks**, taking **Cant** (**C, E**), **Cant Deficiency** (**D**) **Centre Throw**, **End Throw**, loading effects, suspension failures and **Track Stagger** into account. See also **Crush Laden**, **Hard Over Tilt Failed**, **Tare Deflated**.

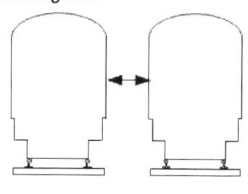

Passing Loop

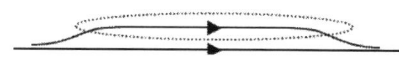

a) A **Track** onto which traffic may be diverted or held to allow other traffic to pass. Also **Loop**, **Lay-by**, **Passenger Loop**, **Freight Loop**, **Goods Loop**. To qualify as a Loop, the **Track** concerned should have no more than one **Signal**, namely the **Loop Exit Signal**. If it has more than one Signal, the Track is a **Slow Line**

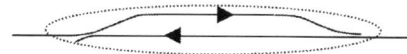

b) A Loop provided between two lengths of **Single Line** to allow **Trains** travelling in opposite directions to pass each other.

Passing Time
[Ops.] The time a **Train** passes a location, the time of its passing being recorded on the **Train** Running System on **TOPS** (**TRUST**) system. See **TIPLOC**.

ELLIS' BRITISH RAILWAY ENGINEERING ENCYCLOPÆDIA

Passive Provision
Allowances made for future enhancements within the current design. For instance, in carrying out works to the **Overhead Line Equipment** (**OLE**), **Signalling** and **Track** to extend a **Platform** to accommodate **Trains** with six **Cars** or **Coaches**, space might be included to extend the Platform to 10 Car capacity in the future. This is cost effective, because the cost of two major schemes is more than the cost of carrying out all the major works in one scheme.

Passive Tilt
[TRS] A mechanism that rotates a suitably equipped **Rail Vehicle** about a longitudinal axis, the degree of this rotation being directly and solely related to the curvature of the **Track** the vehicle is standing on, irrespective of speed. This is normally achieved by forming a linkage between the angle of the vehicle **Bogies** to the longitudinal axis of the vehicle and the suspension system. See also **Active Tilt**, **Self-steering Bogie**.

PAT
a) Performance Action Tracking
b) Portable Appliance Testing.

Patch Resleepering
[PW] Changing only those **Sleepers** in the worst condition in a given mileage. The fraction to be done is expressed as 1 in x, where x is generally between 3 and 10, 3 being the most common number. See also 1 in x Resleepering, Sleeper Integrity Tester (SIT).

Path
a) [Ops.] A clear **Route** between two points built into a **Timetable** (**TT**)
b) See **Cess Path**
c) See **Authorised Walking Route**.

Pathing Allowance
[Ops.] Extra time added into a **Train's** □ **Timetable** □ **Path** to ensure the Path doesn't conflict with others at a **Junction** or to accomodate Trains running at different speeds along a **Route**. Also **Circle Time**.

Patrol Ganger
[IÉ PW] A person who is trained and competent to undertake **Patrolling** duties on a specified length of **Track**.

Patroller
[NR PW] A person who carries out **Patrolling** duties. Previously called a **Patrolman**.

Patroller's Lock Out Device (PLOD)
(*plodd*) [Sig.] A system that allows a **Patroller**, with the permission of the Signaller, to prevent **Train Movements** in one direction (generally the **Wrong Direction**) on a **Bi-directional Line** so that they may safely inspect the **Line**.

Patrolling
[PW] A pedestrian visual inspection of the **Track** (and superficial inspection of other **Lineside** items) carried out by a trained member of staff (**Patroller**) on a regular basis. See **Track Patrol**.

Patrolling Diagram
[NR PW] A document which provides, in both text and visual form, the details of the section of **Line** to be inspected by a **Patroller**. It includes instructions on where the Patroller should walk and the positions from which the various Tracks should be inspected.

Patrolman
[PW Obs.] former name for a **Patroller**.

Patrolman's Lock Out Device
See **Patroller's Lock Out Device** (PLOD)

Pattress Plate
[Civ.] A large, often circular plate used to spread the load of a tie bar passing through brickwork or masonry. Such a bar would be intended to improve the strength of the **Structure** to which it was fitted.

PAVA
Public Announcement and Voice Alarm.

Paved Concrete Track (PACT)
Paved Track
See **Slab Track**.

Pawlock
See **Switchlock**. Also **Clawlock**.

Pax
[Col.] Shorthand for **Passengers**.

PAX
[Tel.] Private Automatic Telephone Exchange.

PB
a) See **Power Box**
b) (Tradename) Parsons Brinkerhoff, an engineering consultancy.

PBDTSO
[TRS] An acronym representing a **Pantograph** □ **Battery** □ **Driving Trailer** □ **Standard Class** □ Open Coach.

PBI
[PW] See **Pneumatic Ballast Injection**. Also **Stoneblowing**.

PBS
See **Pass Booked Services**.

PBX
[Tel.] Private Automatic Branch Telephone Exchange. Also **PABX**.

PC
a) See **Protection Controller**
b) See **Power Car**.

PC&BR
[Hist.] The former Portmadoc, Croesor & Beddgelert Railway.

PCA
Passenger Communication Apparatus.

PCA Emergency Brake Handle
[TRS] **Passenger** Communication Apparatus Emergency Brake Handle. A Device provided to enable **Passengers** to alert the driver during an emergency.

PCB
a) Polychlorinated Biphenol, a poisonous chemical used in electrical equipment
b) Printed Circuit Board.

PCC
Pre-Cast Concrete.

PCD
a) Parcel Concentration Depot
b) Pitch Circle Diameter.

PCE
Principal Civil Engineer.

PCF
[PW] Plastic Coated Fishplate.

PCL
[NR Civ.] Under the Bridge Condition Marking Index (BCMI) handbook, shorthand for padstone, cill or bedstone.

PCM
a) Point Condition Monitoring
b) Pulse Code Modulation
c) Pneumatic Camshaft Mechanism.

PCN
a) [PW] Shorthand for Pads Clips and Nylons. Also Smalls
b) Personnel Certificate in Non-destructive testing.

PCP
Polychloroprene (Neoprene), a material used to insulate electrical wiring.

PCR
Private Crossing Regulations.

PCRO
[LUL] Power Control Room Operator.

PCS
[Obs.] Protocol Converter Subsystem, an obsolete subsystem within the IECC system.

PCS&TE
[BR] Profit Centre Signal & Telecommunications Engineer.

PCSE(M)
[BR] Profit Centre Signal Engineer (Maintenance).

PCSE(W)
[BR] Profit Centre Signal Engineer (Works).

PCT
See Powered Canopy Trolley.

PCTE
[BR] Profit Centre Telecommunications Engineer.

PCV
[TRS] An acronym representing a Propelling Control Vehicle.

PD
a) Parcel Depot
b) Project Delivery
c) Protective Devices
d) [NR] Project Definition
e) See Permitted Development.

PD&SWJR
[Hist.] The Pre-Grouping Plymouth, Devonport & South Western Junction Railway.

PDA
See Parallel Design Agreement.

PDAC
[NR] Performance Data Accuracy Code. A contractual document defining the standards Network Rail (NR) must achieve in collecting Train running data.

PDF
Projects Development Framework.

PDFH
Passenger Demand Forecasting Handbook; a Rail Industry document providing guidance on the preparation of forecasts for:
• Investment appraisal
• Pricing decisions
• Timetabling and operating decisions
• Business planning and budgeting.

PDG
Project Development Group.

PDH
Plesiochronous Digital Hierarchy.

PDI
Pre-detailed Inspection.

PDI-F
[NR] Passenger Disruption Index - Freight

PDI-P
[NR] Passenger Disruption Index - Passenger

PDJR
[Hist.] The Pre-Grouping Princes Dock Joint Railway, a Caledonian, Glasgow & South Western and North British joint enterprise.

PDMX
Programmable Digital Multiplexer.

PDP
[NR] Project Definition Phase.

PDR
[NR]
a) Project Development Requirements
b) Project Design Requirements.

PDS
[NR]
a) Project Design Specification
b) Project Definition Stage.

PDU
Passenger Display Unit.

PE
a) Project Engineer
b) Protective Earth.

PEA
See Passenger Emergency Alarm.

PEAB
See Passenger Emergency Alarm Brake.

Peak Period
[Ops.] The period during the day with the highest level of Passenger Demand. Typically, the AM Peak is 0700-1000 and the the PM Peak is 1600-1900. See also Shoulder Peak

Peaks
[Col.] Nickname for **Class** 44, Class 45 and Class 46 **Diesel Locomotives**.

Pearlitic Rail
[PW] A **Rail Steel** composed of Pearlite, which is composed of alternate plates of Ferrite (a form of pure Iron) and Cementite (a carbide of iron). All Rail steels other than Manganese steels are Pearlitic.

PEARS
[NR] Performance and Loading Analysis Database Information (**PALADIN**) Data Extract and Recording System.

Pease
Common shorthand for JF Pease & Co., a former manufacturer of **Signalling Equipment**.

Pease, Edward
(1767-1858). Supporter of **George Stephenson** and promoter of the Stockton & Darlington **Railway**.

PEAW
[TRS] Passenger Emergency Alarm, Wheelchair.

PEC
a) **Passenger** Event Condition
b) **Public** Electricity Company
c) Project Environmental Co-ordinator.

PED
See **Platform Edge Doors**.

Pedestal
a) [PW Hist.] Original name for a **chair** supporting an **Edge Rail** on a stone block.
b) [TRS] Alternative term used to describe the **Axlebox Horn**.

Pee-Wee
PeeWee
Portable Warning Equipment). A system which uses a remotely controlled siren to allow one **Lookout** (**LO**) to give up to $1^1/_2$ miles' warning of **Approaching Trains**. On heavily **Curved** sites, this can save up to nine intermediate Lookouts. Also **Fixed PeeWee**. This is a form of Lookout Operated Warning System (**LOWS**). See also **Automatic Train Warning System** (**ATWS**), **Inductive Loop Warning System** (**ILWS**), **Train Operated Warning System** (**TOWS**).

Peg
a) [Col.] A **Signal**
b) A 50x50mm section 600mm long (2" by 2" by 2') wooden stake with a point on one end. Used to set out **Curved Track** and other important geometries
c) [Col.] To Peg in **Absolute Block** (**AB**) areas is to set a **Block Instrument** to **Train on Line** (**TOL**) or **Line Clear** (**LC**). See **Pegging Block Instrument**.

Peg Number
a) [Sig. Col.] An alternative for **Signal Number**.
b) [BR PW] The unique number given to each **Track Renewal Item**, the term originating from the practice of driving a coloured wooden **Peg** bearing this number at each end of the **Item**. This procedure is no longer common.

Peg Over
Peg Up
[Sig. Col.] Term meaning to change the **Block Instrument** to **Line Clear** (**LC**) or **Train On Line** (**TOL**). The term refers to the now rare **Pegging Block Instrument**.

Pegging Block Instrument
[Sig. Obs.] A now rare **Block Instrument** where a metal pin or peg is required to hold the handle on the Instrument in the **Line Clear** (**LC**) or **Train On Line** (**TOL**) positions. See **Peg Over**, **Peg Up**

PEM
(*pemm*)
a) (Tradename) [PW] Portique Extensible de Manutention or Extendable Handling Gantry, a radio controlled item of **Panel Lifting Equipment**, used in conjunction with the **LEM** trolley. Produced by Geismar
b) Programme Engineering Manager.

PEME
People, Equipment, Materials, Environment.

Pendolino
(Tradename) The brand name of the **Class** 390 **Tilting Train**. Also Railtrack Advanced **Tilting Train** (**RATT**), **Virgin** Advanced Tilting Train (**VATT**).

Penguins
[Sig. Col.] A nickname for the short grey pedestal units used on **Automatic Half Barrier** (**AHB**) **Level Crossings**.

Penning Layer
[Obs.] An alternative for **Pitching**.

PER
Portable Equipment Room.

Per Way
See **Permanent Way** (**PW**).

Perch (YEA)
[NR] The **Wagon Name** applied to the flat **Wagons** that make up the **Continuous Welded Rail Train** (**CWR Train**).

Perch Train
[NR] An alternative name for the **Continuous Welded Rail Train** (**CWR Train**).

PERCY
Passenger Service Requirement Compliance Yardstick.

PERFORM
[NR] A **British Rail** Business Systems data extraction and analysis system that uses data from **PALADIN**.

Performance
[Ops.] A general term for the punctuality and reliability of the **Railway**.

Performance Allowance
[Ops.] Extra time added into a **Train's** □ **Timetable** □ **Path** to provide a margin or buffer for late running on a day-to-day basis. Also **Diamond Time**.

Performance and Loading Analysis Database Information (PALADIN)
[Ops.] A centralised store of historic **Train Movements** (actual and planned), vehicle formation, loading and delay details for **TRUST**. See also **PALWIN**.

Performance Category
[Sig.] An objective rating of a **Signal** or **Indicator** based on the distance at which the unit is considered readable by a typical driver.

Category	Readable distance (m)	Readable Speed (mph)
1	800	Up to 125
2	250	Up to 60^{1,2}
3	100	Up to 15^2
4	400	Up to 100^2
5	65	Up to 15

Notes:
1. Category 2 **Banner Repeating Signals** and **Preliminary Route Indicators** shall be readable up to 125 mph
2. For **Semaphore Signals**, category 4 applies to the **Arm** and the **Backlight**.
See also **Readability**.

Performance Historic Information System (PHIS)
[Ops.] A database designed to store completed **Train** performance records, including both scheduled and ad-hoc services plus summarised details of any train delays. PHIS is used by performance managers in **Train Operating Companies** (**TOC**) and **Freight Operating Companies** (**FOC**), either directly or indirectly.

Period
a) See **Control Period**, **CP**x
b) [NR] A four-week, 28-day period, used as a basis for financial and operational planning. There are 13 Periods in most years, with **Week One** commencing at 00:01 on the first Saturday on or after April 1st. Every six years there are therefore 53 weeks and 14 Periods
c) See **Engineering Periods**.

Periodic Review (PR)
[NR] The process by which the **Office of the Rail Regulator** (**ORR**) establishes **Network Rail's** (**NR**) revenue requirements for a five year period (see **Control Period**). Reviews so far are:

PR08   The 2008 review (relating to **CP4**)
PR13   The 2013 review (relating to **CP5**)
PR14   The 2014 review of High Speed One (HS1)
PR18   The 2018 review of (relating to **CP6**)

The following Control Period related reviews are thus likely to be in 2023 (for CP7) and 2028 (for CP8).

Periodical Operating Notice (PON)
[NR] Bi-monthly publications, one for each **Territory** of **Network Rail** (**NR**), containing amendments to the **Sectional Appendix** (**SA**), **Rule Book**, Regulations, and other notices concerning **Operations** on the **Railway**. These amendments have appeared previously in the **Weekly Operating Notice** (**WON**).

PERM
Platform Egress Risk Model.

Permali
(Tradename) [PW] A contraction of Permali Gloucester Ltd. and Permali Dehoplast Ltd., manufacturers of composite materials including **Hydulignum Fishplates** and Permali **Insulated Fishplates**.

Permali Joint
[PW] An **Insulated Rail Joint** (**IRJ**) made with **Permali** □ **Insulated Fishplates**.

Permanent AWS Inductor
[Sig.] The large permanent magnet placed in the **Fourfoot** as part of an **Automatic Warning System** (**AWS**) installation relating to a **Signal**, or on its own for a **Warning Indicator** (**WI**).

Permanent AWS Magnet
[Sig.] An alternative term for **Permanent AWS Inductor**.

Permanent Inductor
The large permanent magnets used:
a) [Sig.] In the **Fourfoot** as part of an **Automatic Warning System** (**AWS**) installation relating to a **Signal**.
b) [Sig.] In the **Fourfoot**, in isolation, relating to a **Warning Indicator** (**WI**)
c) See **Permanent AWS Inductor**
d) [Elec.] On the **Sleeper End** as part of the **Automatic Power Control** (**APC**) system relating to a **Neutral Section** (**NS**). See **Automatic Power Control Track Inductor** (**APC Track Inductor**).

Permanent Magnet
[Sig.] An alternative term for **Permanent Inductor**.

Permanent Speed Restriction (PSR)
A speed restriction applied permanently to a length of **Track** because it has a maximum **Permissible Speed** (**PS**) lower than the **Linespeed** for that **Route**. Permanent Speed Restrictions are most commonly due to **Track Geometry** problems, but can also be imposed for **Overhead Line Equipment** (**OLE**) and **Structure Clearance** reasons. Since the advent of speeds in excess of 90mph and the widespread introduction of **Reflectorised Speed Signs** on the **National Railway Network** (**NRN**), the concept of Linespeed has been abandoned. This is because the whole **Railway** is subject to one Permanent Speed Restriction or another, rendering the term redundant. It is still used conversationally to indicate a length of **Line** whose **Track Geometry**, **Gauging** or **Signal Sighting** limits the speed at which **Trains** may pass.

Permanent Way (P way, Per Way, PW, Pway)
a) The **Track**, complete with ancillary installations such as **Rails**, **Sleepers**, **Ballast**, **Formation** and **Track Drains**, as well as **Lineside Fencing** and **Lineside Signs**
b) [Hist.] Formerly used to differentiate between the permanent **Track** under construction, and the **Temporary Way** that was used to aid the construction and removed later
c) A collective term used to describe those persons engaged in the upkeep of the **Track** on the **Railway**.

Permanent Way Drawing
[PW]
a) A plan drawing, normally drawn at a scale of 1:500, 1:200 or 1:100, depicting the **Track Geometry**, **Track Construction**, extent of track works and **Insulated Rail Joints** (**IRJ**), as well as related details of **Electrification** equipment and **Structures**.
b) See **Longitudinal Section**

ELLIS' BRITISH RAILWAY ENGINEERING ENCYCLOPÆDIA

Permanent Way Engineer (PWE)
[PW] An engineer responsible for the design, **Maintenance** or renewal of the **Track** and associated items. See **Permanent Way Maintenance (PWM)**, **Track Renewal**.

Permanent Way Inspector
a) [IÉ PW] A person responsible for the day to day track inspection and maintenance activities for both track and structures. They must ensure that their patrol gangers undertake their inspections to the required frequency and submit defect reports.
b) [NR PW Hist.] A now colloquial term for a **Permanent Way Section Manager (PWSM)**. See also **Hierarchy of Hats**.

Permanent Way Institution, The (PWI)
(Tradename) [PW] An international professional body whose aim is "...advance the knowledge of **Railway** □ **Civil Engineering**, in particular **Track** and **Infrastructure** and to promote, spread and exchange such knowledge amongst those who work in **Railways** and **Rail** systems world-wide." The Institution publishes **British Railway Track**, something of a bible to the **Permanent Way Engineer (PWE)**.

Permanent Way Maintenance (PWM)
[PW] The collective term for the day-to-day activities carried out in order to preserve the **Safety of the Line** and prolong the life of the **Permanent Way (PW)**. Such activities include:
- **Alignment** design
- **Ballast Regulation**
- **Lineside Fencing** repairs
- **Gauging** (all senses)
- **Geometry Marking**
- **Geometry Recording**
- **Insulated Rail Joint (IRJ)** replacement
- **Joint Regulation**
- **Lineside** tidiness
- **Lifting Schemes**
- **Patrolling**
- Pest and rodent control
- **Plate Oiling**
- Public complaints
- **Rail Grinding**
- **Repadding**
- **Stressing** and **Restressing**
- **Tamping** and **Lining**
- **Track Drain** cleaning
- **Ultrasonic Rail Flaw Detection (URFD)**
- Unloading **Ballast** (**Maintenance Ballast, Maintenance Stone**)
- Vegetation management
- Weed spraying

All other activities carried out on the **Track** (such as major component renewal, e.g. **Complete Renewal, Formation Renewal, Rerailing, Resleepering Reballasting**, etc.) are classed as **Track Renewal** (also called **Renewal of Way (ROW)**).

Permanent Way Maintenance Engineer (PWME)
[BR PW] Under **British Railways**, the post responsible for managing **Permanent Way Maintenance (PWM)** in a roughly county-sized area.

Permanent Way Section (PWS)
[BR PW] Under **British Railways** a sub-division of an **Area** or **Division**, under the control of an inspector, supervisor or supervisory manager and responsible for the day-to-day inspection and maintenance of the **Permanent Way (PW)** in that area.

Permanent Way Section Manager (PWSM)
[BR PW] Under **British Railways** the last title of the supervisory post responsible for the day to day maintenance of the **Track** within a **Permanent Way Section (PWS)** of an **Area** or **Division**. See also **Permanent Way Section Supervisor (PWSS)**.

Permanent Way Section Supervisor (PWSS)
[BR PW] Under **British Railways** the penultimate title of the supervisory post responsible for the day to day maintenance of the **Track** within a **Permanent Way Section (PWS)** of an **Area** or **Division**. See also **Permanent Way Section Manager (PWSM)**.

Permanently Coupled
[TRS] Describing two or more **Rail Vehicles** that are permanently connected together, often using a bolted connection.

Permanently Earthed Section (PES)
[Elec.] A **Sub Section** of the **Overhead Line Equipment (OLE)** that is permanently connected to **Earth**. They are sometimes used to guide **Pantographs** under very low **Overbridges (OB)**.

Permaquip
a) (Tradename) A subsidiary of Harsco **Track** Technologies and manufacturer of small to medium sized plant for use on **Railways**
b) See **Permaquip Trolley**.

Permaquip Trolley
(Tradename) A small self-propelled scissor lift platform manufactured by **Permaquip** and used for **Overhead Line Equipment (OLE)** maintenance, See also **Mobile Elevating Work Platform (MEWP)**.

Permillage
A rate or proportion per thousand. Therefore, 10‰ or ten per mille (thousand) is the same as 1%. As a ratio that would be 1 in 100. Continental Railways often express **Gradients** in this way.

Permissible Speed (PS)
[NR] The maximum speed at which **Conventional Trains** may safely negotiate a section of **Track**, as published in the **Sectional Appendix (SA)**. The limiting factor governing this value is often the **Cant Deficiency (D)**, but other factors such as **Structure Clearances** and **Signal Sighting** also apply. See also **Enhanced Permissible Speed (EPS)**.

Permissible Speed Indicator (PSI)
Permissible Speed Sign
[NR] A **Lineside Sign** showing the **Permissible Speed (PS)** for the **Line** □ **Beyond** it, as far as the next **Permissible Speed Sign**.

(75)

346

Permissive

a) As part of a **Track Name** or description, this indicates that **Permissive Working** is permitted for some or all **Trains**

b) [NR] Permissive Working for **Freight Trains** only is denoted by **PF** and for **Passenger Trains** (and therefore all Trains) is denoted by **PP**.

Permissive Block
See **Permissive Working**.

Permissive Freight (PF)
[NR] Denotes a section of **Track** where **Permissive Working** is permitted by **Freight Trains** only.

Permissive Movement
[Ops., Sig.] A legal **Train Movement** made at **Caution** into a **Section** already occupied by another **Train**. See **Permissive Freight** (PF), Permissive Passenger (PP), Permissive Working.

Permissive Passenger (PP)
[NR] Denotes a section of **Track** where **Permissive Working** is permitted by **Passenger Trains**. By implication this allows Permissive Working by **Freight Trains** as well, since **Passenger Standards** are higher. See also **Permissive Freight** (PF).

Permissive Working
[Sig.] An exception to the **Fail Safe** design of **Signalling**, where one **Train** can be permitted to enter a **Section** already **Occupied** by another Train. This is necessary to allow coupling of Trains in **Platforms**. It is inherently dangerous and its provision is being phased out on new works, unless there is no alternative. See **Permissive Freight** (PF), **Permissive Passenger** (PP).

Permit to Work
A document intended to ensure that a potentially hazardous job is undertaken safely, taking into account all the foreseeable circumstances which could arise during the course of the task concerned. Typically such permits are used in connection with hot work and excavations.

Permitted Development (PD)
Rights which allow certain types of development to be carried out without the requirement to apply for planning permission. This covers a wide range of developments which can include those carried out by statutory undertakers. **Network Rail** (**NR**), as a statutory undertaker, has the right to carry out certain development on its **Operational Land** in connection with the movement of **Traffic** by **Rail** without having to make a planning application. These rights are set out in Part 17 of Schedule 2 to the Town and Country Planning (General Permitted Development) Order 1995 (**GPDO**).

Permitted Speed
[NPT] See **Permissible Speed** (PS).

Person In Charge of Nightly Maintenance Possession (PICONMP)
[NR] The competent person nominated to manage the taking and relinquishing of the regular overnight **Possession** during the shutdown on the **Merseyrail** Underground Railway system. Whilst superficially similar to a standard Possession, different **Protection** methods are employed as the system is totally closed overnight and no **Trains** run.

Person in Charge of Possession (PICOP)
[NR] The competent person nominated to manage the following:

- Safe and correct establishment of the **Protection** for the **Possession**, complete with **Detonators**, **Point Clips**, **Possession Limit Boards** (PLB) and **Signals** Keyed to Danger as required
- Managing access to the Possession area by **Engineering Supervisors** (ES)
- Managing the establishment of **Engineering Work Sites** within the Possession
- Liaising with the **Signaller** regarding the passage of the **Train** into and out of the Possession
- Controlling the movement of the Train between the Protection and Work Sites. If there is more than one Train in a Possession, then the PICOP must be qualified to **Senior Person in Charge of Possession** (SPICOP) level
- Ensuring that all the foregoing is correctly removed in reverse sequence, the Possession is relinquished and the **Line** handed back to the Signaller at the due time.

Person In Charge of Work (PICOW)
a) [NR, Obs.] Replaced by **Controller of Site Safety** (**COSS**)

b) [DLR] A certificated member of staff who is responsible for the safety of a working party, analogous to a Controller of Site Safety on **Network Rail**.

Personal Track Safety (PTS)
[NR] The minimum training and certification required before being allowed **On or Near the Line**. The course introduces basic concepts of safety and emergency action. See also **National Competency Control Agency** (**NCCA**), **Personal Track Safety Certification**, **Sentinel**.

Personal Track Safety Certification
[NR] A national system for ensuring that all staff who work on or about the **Railway** are trained and satisfactorily tested in the safety procedures to be followed to achieve their safety. See also **National Competency Control Agency** (**NCCA**), **Personal Track Safety** (PTS), **Sentinel**.

PERTIS
(*pertiss*) Permit to travel Ticket Issuing System.

PES
See **Permanently Earthed Section**.

PESG
Programmable Electronic Systems Group.

Peter
[Obs.] The obsolescent **Phonetic Alphabet** word representing P. Replaced by **Papa**.

Peto, Sir Samuel Morton
(1809-1889). British **Railway** □ **Contractor** and engineer, constructed parts of the **Great Western Railway** (**GWR**) & **Great Northern Railway** (**GNR**), and the Palace of Westminster in London.

PETS
(*petts*) See **P**ublic **E**mergency **T**elephone **S**ystem.

PF
See **P**ermissive **F**reight.

PFA
[NR] The **CARKND** representing a **Container Flat**, found in use carrying the modules of the **Network Rail** □ **Drain Train**

PFB
[TRS] An acronym representing a Pullman **First Class** □ **Brake** □ **Coach**.

PFK
[TRS] An acronym representing a Pullman Parlour **First Class** □ **Coach** with kitchen.

PFL
[TRS] An acronym representing a Pullman **First Class** Lounge Bar **Coach**.

PFM
[Sig.] **P**oints **F**ree to **M**ove.

Pfm.
Abbreviation of **Platform**. Also **P**.

PFMD
[Elec.] **P**antograph **F**orce **M**easuring **D**evice.

PFP
[TRS] An acronym representing a Pullman Parlour **First Class** □ **Coach**.

PFR
Phase **F**ailure **Relay**.

PGI
[PW] **P**re-**g**rind **I**nspection.

PGM
Permanent **G**round **M**arker, used to establish fixed points as references in topographical surveys.

PgRS
[NR] **P**rogramme **R**equirements **S**pecification. See also **PRS**.

PHA
a) **P**reliminary **H**azard **A**nalysis.
b) **P**rocess **H**azard **A**nalysis.

Phantom Aspect
[Sig.] An apparently **Lit** □ **Signal Lamp** caused by (normally) sunlight entering the **Aspect** from the front and being reflected back out again. See also **Hood**.

Phantom Overlap (POL)
[Sig.] A **Signal Overlap** (**OL**) that can be **Proved** □ **Clear** by the **Signalling System**, but which does not correspond to a physical **Track Section** □ **Insulated Rail Joint** (**IRJ**) at the required distance from the **Signal**. It is used where an Overlap distance falls short of a **Set of Points** and those Points are not **Locked**.

Phantom Restricted Overlap (PROL)
[Sig.] A **Signal Overlap** (**OL**) that is both a **Restricted Overlap** (**ROL**) and a **Phantom Overlap** (**POL**).

Phantom Signal
[LUL Sig.] A **Semi-Automatic Signal** in an **Automatic Train Protection** (**ATP**) area on London Underground Limited (**LUL**). It does not display an **Aspect** but a **Target Speed** is displayed in the driver's cab. Its position is marked by a sign giving its **Signal Number**.

PHBT
Person **H**it **B**y **Train**. See also **Fatility**.

PHCC
[EP] **P**oints **H**eating **C**ontrol **C**ubicle.

Phillips Weld
[PW Obs.] A variety of **Electric Arc Weld**, usually site made, used to join together **Rails** to make **Continuous Welded Rail** (**CWR**).

PHIRES
(*fires*) [BR] **P**lant **Hire** **S**ystem

PHIS
(*fiss* or *fizz*) See **P**erformance **H**istoric **I**nformation **S**ystem.

Phonetic Alphabet
A system in which each letter of the alphabet is replaced by a word. The words are chosen to ensure their intelligibility when spoken over a radio:

A	Alpha	N	November
B	Bravo	O	Oscar
C	Charlie	P	Papa
D	Delta	Q	Quebec
E	Echo	R	Romeo
F	Foxtrot	S	Sierra
G	Golf	T	Tango
H	Hotel	U	Uniform
I	India	V	Victor
J	Juliet	W	Whisky
K	Kilo	X	X-ray
L	Lima	Y	Yankee
M	Mike	Z	Zulu

PHoT
[NR PW] **P**rofessional **H**ead **o**f **Track**.

PHP
Passenger **H**elp **P**oint.

PhX Rail
(Tradename) [PW] Bespoke **Gauging** analysis software, owned by DGauge Limited of Pilton, Somerset.

Phylplug
[PW Obs.] A proprietary compound formerly used to fill redundant **Chairscrew** holes in **Wood Sleepers**.

PIC
a) [Col.] **P**erson **I**n **C**harge, generally a shortening of **Person In Charge of Possession** (**PICOP**) but also applied to others with specific responsibilities
b) See **P**roject **I**nterface **C**oordinator.

Pick Up
a) See **Picked Up, Picking Up**
b) [PW] An alternative term for **Lifting**, particularly used in relation to a **Running Rail** which is too low relative to another, related, **Rail**.

Picked Up
Picking Up
a) [Sig.] Describing a **Track Circuit** (**TC**) that is or is becoming re-**Energised** following the exit of a **Train**, or **Relay** that is or is becoming re-energised
b) [TRS Col.] Describing a **Train** whose wheels are sliding, typically during braking.

Pick-up Only
[Ops.] A **Booked Call** or **Station Stop** provided so that **Passengers** may **Board** only. It is used as a means of discouraging overcrowding. The opposite is **Set Down Only**.

Pick-up Time
a) [Sig.] The time taken for a **Track Circuit** (**TC**) to register the absence of a **Train**, i.e. the time taken for the relay to make. See also **Drop-away Time**
b) [Ops.] To run faster than scheduled in order to get back on time.

PICOD
Person in Charge of Dispatch.

PICOM
Person in Charge of Machine.

PICONMP
See **Person in Charge of Nightly Maintenance Possession**.

PICOP
(*pie-cop*) See **Person in Charge of Possession**.

PICOP Briefing
PICOP Meeting
(*pie-cop breefing, pie-cop meeting*) [NR] The final planning meeting which confirms the working arrangements which will apply within an **Engineering Possession**.

PICOS
[NR] Person in Charge of Siding □ Possession.

PICOT
[NR] Person in Charge of Testing.

PICOW
(*pie-cow*) [NR Obs.] **Person in Charge of Work**, a term now effectively replaced by **Controller of Site Safety** (**COSS**).

PICP
Pollution Incident Control Plan.

PIDD
Passenger Information During Disruption.

PIDS
(*pidds*) **Passenger** Information Display System.

Piece Up
[PW Col.] To join or attach parts of such things as **Trains, Switch and Crossing Layouts** (**S&C Layouts**), **Jointed Rails**, etc.

Piecemeal
[PW]
a) Describing a **Switch and Crossing Unit** (**S&C Unit**) where only the **Crossing** and **Switches** are pre-assembled by a manufacturer, the **Closure Rails** being cut to suit on site
b) Describing **Track Relaying** where the components are cut to suit and fitted together on site. See also **Prefab Relaying**.

Pier
See **Bridge Pier**. See also **Abutment**.

Pig's Ear
[SR, LUL Sig.] A small additional lens formerly fitted to some **Signals** on the **Southern Region** (**SR**) and **London Underground Limited** (**LUL**). It served the same purpose as a **Close Viewing Sector** (**CVS**).

Piggy Back Baseplate
[PW] A type of **Baseplate** where the **Rail** is secured to the Baseplate using **Rail Clips** and the Baseplate is then secured to the **Concrete Bearer** or **Track Slab** using more Rail Clips.

Piggyback
A system of **Freight** transport where the trailers of articulated lorries are loaded onto specially constructed low floor **Wagons** for onward transport by **Rail**. The intention is that local collection and distribution is carried out by road, with inter-city and international transfer by **Rail**.

Piggyback Trailer
A road trailer designed to be lifted or driven (whole) onto a specially adapted **Rail Vehicle** for onward movement by **Rail**

Pike (ZAA)
[NR] A 31 ton capacity drop side **Open Wagon** used for the transportation of materials. See **Wagon Names**.

Pilaster
[Civ.] A column forming a termination point of the **Parapet** of a **Bridge**.

Pilchard (YCO)
[NR, prob. Obs.] An **Open Wagon** used for the transportation of materials. See **Wagon Names**.

Pilot
[Col.] An alternative term for a **Shunting Locomotive**, particularly one whose duties are confined to a **Station**. See also **Station Pilot**.

Pilot Working
[Ops. Col.] A method of running **Trains** on a **Temporary Single Line** or **Un-Signalled Line** by means of a **Pilotman**. See also **Single Line Working** (**SLW**).

Pilotman
[Ops.] A member of **Railway** staff whose duty is to ensure that **Trains** are worked safely (one at a time) over a **Single Line Section** during times of **Signal** failure or during emergencies, often by riding on each Train through the Section. See also **Pilot Working, Single Line Working** (**SLW**).

349

ELLIS' BRITISH RAILWAY ENGINEERING ENCYCLOPÆDIA

PIM
Train □ Accident □ Precursor Indicator Model, A system which measures the risk, per million **Train Miles**, of a Train Accident - i.e. collision, **Derailment**, fire or striking a road vehicle on a **Level Crossing** (**LC, LX**). It is managed by the **Rail Safety and Standards Board** (**RSSB**). It was set to 100 in March 2002 and provides a measure of the change in risk relative to this level, lower being better.

Pimple Pad
See **Configurated Rail Pad**.

PIMS
(*pimms*) Project Information Management System.

Pin Code
See **Registration Pin Code**.

Pinch Bar
[PW] A long **Bar** used as a lever between the **Rail** and **Rail Wheel** to move vehicles in **Sidings** and **Depots** when no **Locomotive** is available.

Pinch Point
a) A location where the physical layout and number of **Tracks** is constrained
b) [Ops.] A location where the number of **Train Movements** is constrained by the layout of the **Track** or by a **Junction**
c) [LUL] A location within a **Station** through which all Station users must pass and thus be observed by CCTV.

Pine
A **Railway** □ **Telegraph Code** meaning "**Train**(s) as under terminate(d) short of destination". See also **Cape**.

Pink Copies
[Col.] See **Testing Copies**. Also **Pinks**.

Pink Pages
[NR] The section of the **Working Manual for Rail Staff** dealing with the loading, movement and unloading of **Dangerous Goods**.

Pinks
See **Testing Copies**. Also **Pink Copies**.

Pinning Down
Pinning Down Brakes
[Ops.] The action of depressing and restraining the brake levers of **Freight Vehicles**. Still carried out in **Sidings** where such vehicles are stored (many **Engineering Vehicles** still have levers rather than **Handbrake** wheels), the practice was formerly carried out at the top of steep hills to control the descent of heavy **Unfitted Trains**.

PINS
The **British Transport Police** (**BTP**) crime recording system.

Pioneer
(Tradename) The brandname for the **Hull Trains** version of the **Class** 222 **Diesel Electric Multiple Unit** (**DEMU**). See also **Meridian**.

PIP
Passenger Information Point.

Pipe Bridge
[Civ.] A **Bridge** carrying pipes (typically containing gas or water) over the **Railway**. The pipe itself is often the main structure of the Bridge.

Piped
Piped Vehicle
[TRS] An arrangement where a pipe for a particular braking system is carried through the vehicle but is not connected to the vehicle's brakes. See **Air Piped**, **Dual Piped**, **Vacuum Piped, G, P, Q, R, W**. See also **Air Blow**.

Piping
[PW] A vertical **Rail Defect** caused by gas bubbles originally trapped in the billet being rolled long and thin and becoming included in the **Rail Section**.

PIPIT
[Ops.] Performance system which records the reasons for **Train** delays, compatible with **EGRET**.

PIPS
PIPS 2
(*pips*) Packaging and Investment Planning System and its successor.

PIR
Post Implementation Review.

Piranha (PNA)
[NR Col.] Unofficial name for the 24 ton capacity **Open Wagon** □ **CARKND** □ **PNA**.

PIRU
[Sig.] Panel Interface Relay Unit.

PIS
Passenger Information System. See also **CIS, PID**.

PISG
Passenger Information Strategy Group.

Piston Relief Duct
[Civ.] A duct connecting two **Running Tunnels** allowing air to flow from one to the other, reducing the **Trains'** power consumption and air turbulence. They can be closed remotely as required, for example to prevent the spread of fire.

Pitblocks
[LUL] Vertical pedestals, normally made from concrete, used to support the **Rails** above an inspection pit or the **Platform Safety Pit** in Tube Line □ **Stations**.

Pitching
a) [PW] A layer of large stones laid on top of the **Formation** to improve its general longevity and stability, a popular method during the heyday of **Railway** construction, but now largely superseded by the use polymer **Geogrids** and Geo-composites in modern construction. In most cases the Pitching is preventing the Railway sinking into an area of poor ground, and it should not be removed unless other stabilisation measures are to be put in place
b) [TRS] Rocking motion of a vehicle, back and forth parallel to the direction of travel.

Pivot Light
[Sig.]
a) The light that appears in both the **On Aspect** and **Off Aspect** of a **Position Light Signal** (**PLS**)
b) The common lamp of a **Position Light Junction Indicator** (**PLJI**) where more than one **Diverging Route** exists.

PIXC
Pixie
(*pick-see*) See **Passengers in Excess of Capacity**.

PjRS
[NR] **P**roject **R**equirements **S**pecification. See also **PRS**.

PK
a) [Sig.] On a **Signalling Circuit Diagram**, denotes a wire coloured pink
b) [CT] See **Poste Kilometrique** (**Kilometre Post**).

PKC
[TRS] An acronym representing a Pullman Kitchen Composite Coach.

PL
a) See **Plain Line**
b) See **Pocket Length**
c) [Sig.] **P**osition **L**ight, see **Position Light Signal** (**PLS**).

PLA
(Tradename) [Sig.] A type of **Alumino-thermic Weld** manufactured by Railtech International, part of the Delachaux Group.

PLA 68
(Tradename) [Sig.] A variety of **Alumino-thermic Weld** and **Wide Gap Weld** manufactured by Railtech International, part of the Delachaux Group.

Place of Safety (POS)
A location near to the **Track** in which a person may stand safely when **Trains** are passing. See **Position of Safety** (**POS**). See also **Continuous Place of Safety** (**CPOS**), **Discrete Place of Safety** (**DPOS**), **Refuge**, **Safecess**, **Safecess Path**.

Plaice (ZCV)
[NR] A 22 ton capacity drop side **Open Wagon** used for the transportation of **Ballast** and sand. See **Wagon Names**.

Plain Line (PL)
[PW] Track without **Switches and Crossings** (**S&C**).

Plain Line Pattern Recognition (PLPR)
[NR PW] An automated system being developed by Omnicom Ltd. to identify missing **Track** components using recorded video.

Plain Line Tamper
[PW] A **Tamping and Lining Machine** (**Tamper**) that is only equipped to work on **Plain Line** (**PL**), not **Switch and Crossing Layouts** (**S&C Layouts**). See **Switch and Crossing Tamper** (**S&C Tamper**), **Third Rail Tamper**.

Plain Line Track Renewals (PLTR)
[PW] **Track Renewals** activity carried out on **Plain Line** (**PL**), rather than **Switch and Crossing Units** (**S&C Units**). Such activities can include **Ballast Cleaning**, **Track Drain** replacement, **Formation Renewal**, **Reballasting** (**RB**), **Relaying**, **Rerailing** (**RR**) and **Resleepering** (**RS**). See also **Renewal of Way** (**ROW**).

Plain Lining
[PW] Replacing all or part of a **Switch and Crossing Layout** (**S&C Layout**) with **Plain Line** (**PL**). Also applied when temporarily replacing **Switches** or **Crossings** with **Plain Rails** due to component failure.

Plain Rail
[PW] A **Rail** that has not been drilled or machined, other than being cut to length. See also **Undrilled** (**UD**).

Plane of the Rails
[PW] A flat plane which contains the highest point of the **Rail Crown** of both **Running Rails** of a **Track**. See also **In Plane**.

Planed Rail
[PW] Any **Rail** whose normal **Rail Section** has been reduced by planing. This includes **Switch Rails** and **Adjustment Switch** Rails.

Planing
[PW] The process of reducing the width of the **Rail Head** (and sometimes the **Rail Foot**) by machining. It generally used to produce **Rails** for **Switch and Crossing Units** (**S&C Units**). See **Switch Planing**, **Top Planing**.

Planing Heel
[PW] See **Heel of Planing**.

Planing Length
[PW] The dimension measured along the **Switch Rail**, from the **Switch Toe** to the end of the **Head Planing**. At this location the **Running Edge** (**RE**) to Running Edge offset to the **Stock Rail** is 70mm for **113A** and **Bullhead** (**BH**) **Rail** and 72mm for **CEN60E1A1** with the Switch Rail in the closed position.

Planing Radius
[PW] The Radius (**R**) of the **Rail Head** □ **Planing** over the **Planing Length**.

Planlite
(Tradename) [Hist.] A type of kerosene lamp used as **Backlights** in **Semaphore Signals**, manufactured by the Lamp Manufacturing and Railway Equipment Ltd. under a patent of Welch.

Planned Maintenance
Maintenance performed as a result of assessment, to reduce the likelihood of failure. At first sight this approach seems expensive, but the saving in **Train Minute Delays** avoided easily offsets this. The opposite is **Re-active Maintenance**. See also **Steady State Maintenance**.

ELLIS' BRITISH RAILWAY ENGINEERING ENCYCLOPÆDIA

Planned Preventative Maintenance (PPM)
a) **Maintenance** activity planned to take place on a regular basis to reduce the incidence of failures in service.
b) [TRS] **Maintenance** for **Rail Vehicles** based on a prescriptive schedule of component replacement and carried out on a regular basis

Planning Headway
[Ops.]
a) The Planning **Headway** in **Track Circuit Block** (**TCB**) areas is the minimum time interval between successive **Trains** in the same direction for timetable planning purposes. This is calculated by using the **Technical Headway** and adding a percentage for performance.
b) The Planning Headway in **Absolute Block** (**AB**) areas is calculated as the time taken for the train to run between **Signal Boxes**, plus two minutes for the **Signaller's** duties.
Where this figure varies along a route the largest value is used for the **Route**.

Planning Meeting
[NR] A meeting, chaired by **Network Rail** (**NR**), at which applications for **Possessions** and **Work Sites** are discussed, and overlaps and clashes are resolved. See **T-14** and **T-6**.

Planning Oversight Group (POG)
A forum which involves representatives of **Network Rail** (**NR**), **Train Operating Companies** (**TOC**), **Freight Operating Companies** (**FOC**) and suppliers.

PLANS
(*planz*) (Tradename) [Sig.] An additional software package used with Bentley's Microstation CAD programme to draw **Signalling Plans**. Currently owned by Balfour Beatty Limited.

Plant Operator Licence Holder
[NR] A corporate entity licensed by **Network Rail** as capable to operate **Rail Plant** in **Engineering Possessions**.

Plant Rails
[PW]
a) **Rails** temporarily installed in a **Track** to speed installation or removal of Track during **Relaying** operations. Also **Slave Rails**
b) Rails used to facilitate the use of **Single Line Gantries** (**SLG**). Also **Service Rails**.

Planted Mast
[Elec.] An **Overhead Line Structure** embedded in the concrete of its foundation. See also **Bolted-base Mast**.

Plasser
(Tradename)
a) A contraction of **Plasser & Theurer**
b) (verb) [Col.] To Plasser an **Alignment** is to use the **Four Point Lining System** on a **Tamper** to smooth out irregularities in the **Horizontal Alignment** of the **Track**.

Plasser & Theurer
(Tradename) A manufacturer of **On Track Machines** (**OTMs**) based in Linz, Austria.

Plastic Deformation
The change seen in an object's dimensions when a stress is applied which leaves a permanent deformation once the stress is removed.

Plastic Deformation of the Rail Head
[PW] Formal term for **Lipping**.

Plate
a) [PW] A common contraction of **Fishplate**
b) [Hist.] The short L-shaped beam that forms the running surface of a **Plateway**.

Plate Oiling
[PW] The activity of removing, cleaning, lubricating and replacing **Fishplates** carried out on a regular cycle to ensure the effective operation of the **Fishplated Rail Joint** across the range of **Rail Temperatures**. Modern practice uses grease rather than oil, carried out on a two-year cycle. It is common to find one of the **Fishbolts** fitted the opposite way round from the others on alternate Joints, indicating that these Joints should be greased in odd years, the rest in even years.

Plate Rails
[Hist.] The (typically) short L-section **Rails** used in a **Plateway**.

Plated Joint
[PW] A colloquial contraction of **Fishplated Rail Joint**.

Platelayer
a) [Hist.] A person who laid the **Plates** on a **Plateway**
b) [Col.] A term for a manual worker engaged in the day-to-day **Maintenance** of the **Permanent Way** (**PW**).

Plateway
[Obs.] A **Railway**-like transportation system on which guidance of the vehicles is achieved by using the vertical face of L-shaped flanged **Plates** to guide flangeless wheels.

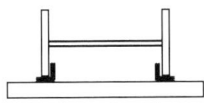

Platform
a) A raised level surface provided alongside a **Railway** to permit **Passengers** to easily **Board** and **Alight** from **Trains**. See also **Platform Construction**. Abbreviated to P, Pfm
b) See **SLC Platform**.

Platform Construction

On **Standard Gauge Railways**, the following requirements apply to **Platforms**:
- They should be long enough to accommodate the longest **Train** booked to call
- They should not be built on **Gradients** steeper than 1 in 500 (0.2%)
- They should be located on **Straight Track** if at all possible, or **Curves** □ **Flatter** than 1000m Radius (**R**) if not
- They must be 915mm +0/-25mm high **Above Rail Level** (**ARL**)
- They must be set 730mm back from the nearest **Running Edge** (**RE**) (measured in the **Plane of the Rails**), unless **Centre Throw**, **End Throw** or other **Kinematic Envelope** (**KE**) issues require this dimension to be increased
- The requirements for **Stepping Distance** must be met
- They must be at least 2.5m wide (4m for **Island Platforms**) of which the 2m nearest to the **Track** must be clear of all obstructions (larger dimensions apply at speeds in excess of 125mph (200kph))
- Sufficient clear area must be available to safely accommodate peak **Passenger** numbers (at a busy **Terminal Station** this area may be considerable)
- Where the **Track** extends beyond the Platform, the Platform may end in a **Platform Ramp** down to ground level at not steeper than 1 in 8 (12%) or can be fitted with steps
- There must be 2.5m clear headroom over the area within 2m of the **Platform Edges**
- The upper surface must **Fall** away from the rear of the **Platform Coping**, see **Platform Crossfall**
- The Platform Edges must be appropriately marked, including provisions for persons with reduced visual acuity
- Suitable access and egress arrangements must be available to cater for likely peak Passenger flows and levels of physical mobility.
See **Platform Section**.

Platform Coping
The Pre-Cast Concrete (**PCC**) or masonry slab, supported by the **Oversails**, that forms the **Platform Edge**.

Platform Crossfall
The degree to which a **Platform Surface** slopes, measured at right angles to the **Platform Edge**. The diagram shows current standard guidance. Older platforms were often built with a positive fall, i.e. they sloped towards the **Track**; this was probably to aid natural drainage but is now a contributory factor in accidents involving runaway prams and wheelchairs.

50 (80 to 40)

Platform Edge
The edge of the **Platform** surface that is nearest to the **Track** generally composed of stone slabs or Pre-Cast Concrete (**PCC**) **Platform Coping** sections.

Platform Edge Doors (PED)
See **Platform Screen Doors**.

Platform Face
The vertical face of the **Platform**, below **Platform** level and nearest to the **Track**.

Platform Furniture
The equipment provided on a **Platform** for use by **Passengers**, including seats, information boards, signs, telephones and lighting.

Platform Gauge
a) The standard set of dimensions (heights and offsets) applied to **Platforms**
b) A device for setting or measuring the dimensions and offsets of a **Platform** relative to the **Plane of the Rails**. See **Gauging Survey**.

Platform Height
The vertical offset of the **Platform Edge** measured perpendicular to the **Plane of the Rails**. This dimension is normally 915mm +0/-25mm.

Platform Length
The useable length of a **Platform**, measured between the tops of the **Platform Ramps** or between Platform Ramp and the face of the **Buffer Stop** on a **Terminal Platform**. See also **Operational Platform Length**.

Platform Level
Collective term describing the vertical position occupied by the **Platforms** in a **Station**. See also **Concourse Level**, **Track Level**.

Platform Line
A **Track**, at a **Station** which has a **Platform** provided at one or both sides.

Platform Loop
A **Loop** provided so calling **Trains** can move clear of the **Main Line** before stopping at the **Station**.

Platform Nosing
The rounded edge of the **Platform Coping** nearest to the **Track**.

Platform Numbering
Platforms at a **Station** are normally numbered sequentially, rising in units of one from (usually) 1.
a) [NR] There is no definitive starting point adopted. Platform one can be on any side, but it has been suggested that platform 1 should be on the **Up Side**.
However, there are exceptions:
- Kings Cross, Cardiff Central and Stockport all have a platform 0 (zero), which in most cases avoided re-numbering the station
- Some small stations on both networks are completely un-numbered
- Letters can be used to differentiate a part of a Station serving a different route from the rest
- Numbers are not always sequential (Northampton) and numbered platforms don't necessarily have numbers displayed on them, or **Track** next to them.
b) [LUL] Platforms are normally numbered in geographical order starting at the lowest number (usually 1) as the extreme westbound (**WB**) or northbound (**NB**) □ **Line** as the case may be. Where there is more than one Line then the upper level is

353

numbered first, the other Lines being numbered in increasing depth (but treating lines at approximately the same depth as a single level). Local exceptions are possible where this would be more logical to **Passengers**.

Platform Offset
The lateral dimension from the nearest **Running Edge** (**RE**) to the **Platform Edge**, measured parallel to the **Plane of the Rails**. This dimension is a minimum of 730mm, but varies with curvature and **Kinematic Envelope** (**KE**) requirements.

Platform Ramp
The ramped end of a **Platform**. This ramp was required by statute and may not be steeper than 1 in 8 (17%).

Platform Roll Space
See **Platform Safety Space**.

Platform Safety Pit
[LUL] The shallow concrete-lined pit provided in the **Fourfoot** at **Stations**, making it less likely that a suicide will actually succeed and easier to remove the remains of any successes. Also called the **Jumper Pit**, **Suicide Pit**.

Platform Safety Space
The 300mm wide clear space located between the **Platform Edge** and the **Platform Wall**, intended to provide an emergency refuge for persons caught out by oncoming **Trains**. Also **Platform Roll Space**, **Roll Space**. See **Platform Section**.

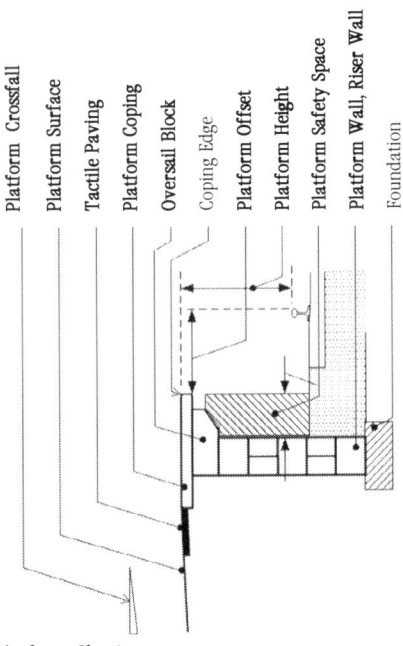

Platform Screen
Particularly found at **Terminal Stations** with single all-over roofs, this is typically a vertical metal and glass structure dividing the **Concourse** from the **Platforms**. See also **Cross Platform**.

Platform Screen Doors
Doors placed along the **Platform Edge** to keep **Passengers** on the Platform. Usually found on **Light Rapid Transit** (**LRT**) systems where doorways appear in predictable locations. They may be used for safety reasons or to reduce energy wastage in extremes of climate. Also known as **Platform Edge Doors** (**PED**).

Platform Section

(diagram labelled: Platform Crossfall, Platform Surface, Tactile Paving, Platform Coping, Oversail Block, Coping Edge, Platform Offset, Platform Height, Platform Safety Space, Platform Wall, Riser Wall, Foundation)

Platform Sharing
[Col.] Term describing the use of **Permissive Working** in a **Station** □ **Platform** other than for the purposes of attaching, detaching or removing vehicles. The current view is that whilst this arrangement may be necessary at **Terminal Stations**, its use at **Through Stations** is no longer allowed. See also **Mid-Platform Signals**.

Platform Starter
Platform Starting Signal
A **Stop Signal** located at the departure end of a **Station** □ **Platform** or within 200 **Yards** or one **Train Length** of it.

Platform Surface
The upper surface of a **Platform**, which should **Fall** away from the **Platform Edge**, see **Platform Crossfall**.

Platform Train Interface (PTI)
A term used when assessing the risks associated with the interface between **Trains** and **Passengers** on **Platforms**.

Platform Wall
The brick or concrete wall forming the face of a **Platform** nearest the **Track**. Also **Riser Wall**.

Platform Work
[Ops.] Collective term for opening and closing the doors of a **Passenger Train**, assisting **Alighting** and **Boarding** □ **Passengers**, ensuring that the doors are closed and giving the driver the **Right Away** (**RA**).

Platform Yellow Line
A single yellow line, 100mm wide, painted the length of the **Platform** implemented to encourage **Passengers** to stand back from the **Platform Edge**, to mitigate the risk from passing **Trains** and turbulence.
a) [LUL] 300mm back from the Platform Edge
b) [NR] 1.2m (4') back from the Platform Edge.

Platform Zone
[Ops.] Introduced in the early 1990s on **Intercity** □ **Routes**, a system of dividing **Platforms** in to coloured zones to aid **Passengers** in locating their **Coaches**. The colours are Gold, Pink, Blue and Orange.

PLATO
(*play-toe*) Peak Loading Analysis of Timetable Operation.

PLB
See Possession Limit Board.

PLBE
[Civ.] Principal Load Bearing Elements.

PLC
Programmable Logic Controller.

PLGS
Position Light Ground Signal, see Ground Position Light Signal (GPLS).

PLH
Prefabricated Lineside Hut.

PLJI
Position Light Junction Indicator. See Junction Indicator (JI).

PLOD
(*plod*) See Patroller's Lock Out Device.

Plough
Plough Brake
See Ballast Plough.

PLPR
See Plain Line Pattern Recognition.

PLRA
[NR] See Private Locomotive Registration Agreement.

PLS
See Position Light Signal.

PLTR
See Plain Line Track Renewals.

Plug
a) See Scotch
b) [Col.] Nickname for the **Class** 170 **Diesel Multiple Unit** (**DMU**) because of their lights.

PLUG
[NR, Obs.] **PRIDE** Local User Group.

Plug Doors
[TRS] Exterior doors which initially open bodily outwards, before either swinging away, which is unusual, or more normally sliding clear. See also **Bi-parting Doors**, **Centre Opening Doors**.

Plugging
[PW] The filling of redundant **Chairscrew** holes in **Wood Sleepers** or **Bearers** using wooden dowels allowing the re-drilling of the holes if required.

PLUM
(*plum*) (Tradename) [PW] Portique Leger Universal Manutention or Lightweight Universal Handling Gantry, the faster lightweight successor to the **PUM** □ **Panel Lifting Equipment**. Produced by **Geismar**.

Plunger
[Sig.] A button that is depressed to activate a **Signalling Function**.

PMA
Preventive Maintenance Analysis.

PMB
[TRS] An acronym representing a **Pantograph** □ **Motor** Buffet **Standard Class** □ **Coach**.

PMBX
[Tel.] Private Manual Branch Exchange.

PMCS
Project Management Control System.

PME
[EP] Protective Multiple Earthing.

PMI
Project Manager's Instruction.

PMMS
Property Maintenance Management System.

PMS
[TRS] An acronym representing a **Pantograph** □ **Motor** □ **Standard Class** □ **Coach**.

PMSE
Principal Maintenance Support Engineer.

PMUX
Pmux
(*pee-muks*) See Panel Multiplexer.

PMV
[TRS] An acronym representing a **Pantograph** □ **Motor** □ **Van**.

PMVT
Primary Means of Vertical Transportation.

PNA
[NR] The **CARKND** representing the 24 ton capacity **Open Wagon**, unofficially nicknamed "**Piranha**".

PNB
Personal Needs Break.

Pneumatic Ballast Injection (PBI)
[PW] The overly long proper term for **Stoneblowing**.

Pneumatic Ballast Injection Machine
[PW] The overly long proper title of a **Stoneblower**.

Pneumatic Door Seal
[TRS] A device fitted to a **Door Leaf** which is inflated by air to seal the gap between the **Door Leaf** and the **Door Portal**.

PO
See Point Operator.

PO/CL
POCL
Private Owner Circulation Letter.

POA
Passenger Open Access.

355

Pocket Length (PL)
Of a crack, the distance measured from material surface to the deepest extremity of the pocket along the plane of the crack. This is not necessarily the vertical measurement.

Pocketed Formation
[PW] A **Formation** that has failed and become depressed under the **Packing Area** of the **Sleepers** or **Bearers**.

POD
a) See **Point of Derailment**
b) **Passenger Oriented Display**.

POE
[Sig.] **Point Operating Equipment**.

POG
See **Planning Oversight Group**.

Point Bar
[PW] Alternative for a **Bar**.

Point Clip
A device similar to a G clamp used to securely clamp the **Closed Switch** in position when required. They can be locked in position using a padlock to discourage unauthorised removal of the Point Clip. A device performing a similar function is the **Switch Securing Block**.

Point Cloud

Point Cloud Survey
A surveying method in which a Laser scans the site, taking angle, time of flight and reflectivity measurements to whatever it 'sees' within a 40° swath (360° on newer machines). The resulting data is a cloud of apparently uncoordinated points, which require specialist software to reconstitute into a three dimensional model. See also **LiDAR**.

Point Controller
[LR] A local electronic controller which responds to inputs from the **Signalling System**, **Track Circuits** (**TC**) and **Mass Detectors**, and outputs commands to a **Point Machine**.

Point Detection

Point Detector
[Sig.] An arrangement of electrical switches that independently detect the position of a **Set of Points** or **Set of Switches**. This information is used within the **Interlocking** to determine whether a **Route** may be safely set over the **Points** or **Switches**. An alternative term is **Switch Detection**.

Point End
A term describing a pair of **Switch Half Sets** assembled to make a **Set of Points** or **Set of Switches**.

Point End Identification Plate
[Sig.] A small plate with raised numerals and letters, normally located adjacent to the **Switch Half Set** that is **Normally Closed**, giving the **Point Number**.

Point Handle
[Sig.] The collective name for any manual actuating device used to operate a **Point Machine**. See **Crank Handle**, **Pump Handle**.

Point Heater
See **Points Heating**. Also **Switch Heater**.

Point Machine
[Sig.] A generic term for any powered device that operates a **Set of Points** (**Set of Switches**). Types include **Clamp Lock**, **HPSA**, **HW**xxx, In-bearer Clamplock (**IBCL**), **M63**. Also **Point Motor**, **Switch Motor**.

Point Motor
See **Point Machine**.

Point Numbers
[Sig., Ops.] All **Sets of Points** (**Sets of Switches**) are given numbers to reduce potential confusion. Generally, all Sets of Points that always act together (like the two ends of a **Crossover** or a **Switch Diamond** (**SD**)) have the same number. Where two or more Sets of Points act together and therefore have the same number, each one is given a suffix (A, B, etc.) to uniquely identify them. There are two common conventions for the adding of suffix letters:

- The "A" end is always nearest **London** or low Mileage (the current preference)
- The "A" end is always nearest the **Controlling Signal Box**

It is conceivable to have suffix letters ranging up to "G" in older more complex **Junction Layouts**, but modern practice avoids such complexities and suffix letters rarely range above "D".

Point of Derailment (POD)
In a **Derailment**, the precise point where the first wheel **Derailed**. The **Sleeper** closest to this point on site is normally designated as **Sleeper Zero**.

Point of Vertical Curve (PVC)
[PW] The "start" of a **Vertical Curve** (**VC**); see also **Point of Vertical Tangency** (**PVT**).

Point of Vertical Intersection (PVI)
[PW] The point at which the two gradients associated with a **Vertical Curve** (**VC**) would intersect if projected.

Point of Vertical Tangency (PVT)
[PW] The "other end" of a **Vertical Curve** (**VC**); see also **Point of Vertical Curve** (**PVC**).

Point Rail
See **Common Crossing Point Rail**, **Obtuse Crossing Point Rail**.

Point Rodding
[Sig.] An alternative term for **Rodding**. Also **Channel Rodding**.

Point Watching
[Col.] An unofficial method of working based on observing the position of **Points** (**Switches**) to determine whether an **Approaching Train** will actually require action by the **Work Group**.

Point Wing Rail
[PW] A combined **Obtuse Point Rail** and **Wing Rail**, used in **Diamond Crossings** with sharp angles (e.g. small values of **N**).

Point Zone Telephone (PZT)
[Tel.] A telephone communicating with a **Signal Box** (**SB**) and located adjacent to a **Junction** or other group of **Points**. Similar in function and operation to a **Signal Post Telephone** (**SPT**), they are used by **Shunters**, **Maintenance** staff and by **Points Operators** (**PO**) in times of failure.

PointCare
[BR] A joint initiative between the former **Signalling** and **Civil Engineering** disciplines aimed at ensuring that the main area of joint responsibility; namely **Sets of Points** (**Sets of Switches**) were correctly inspected and **Maintained**. Small teams of Signalling and **Permanent Way** (**PW**) staff would regularly visit every Set of Points in their **Area** and carry out all relevant **Maintenance** work in co-operation. See **Joint Point Team** (**JPT**).

Pointing On
[PW Col.] The action of moving the end of a tool (often a **Bar**) along the **Running Band** of a **Rail**, allowing a second person located close to the Rail some distance away to observe when the tool coincides with the centre of a **Track Fault** such as a **Swag** or **Alignment** error. This method allows minor faults to be rectified without using surveying equipment and is used during the **Repairing** phase of a **Track Renewals Item**.

Points
a) An assembly of **Switches and Crossings** (**S&C**) designed to divert trains from one **Line** to another
b) Another name for a **Set of Switches**. The term Points is preferred by **Signalling** and **Railway Operations** staff, **Switches** by **Permanent Way** types.
c) Thought possibly to be a contraction of the word "pointers", used to describe the short tapered **Rails** used in early **Switches** to divert vehicle wheels from one track to another. See also **Point End**.

Points and Crossings (P&C)
See **Switches and Crossings** (**S&C**).

Points Data
[Sig.] Within a **Solid State Interlocking** (**SSI**), Points Data specifies the "free to move" conditions under which **Points** may be switched, with one set of data required for each lie of the Points. Points Data may be called from other data files, particularly the **Route Request Data** in deciding the availability of **Routes**.

Points Failure
[Sig.] A fault condition where one or more Sets of Points (**Sets of Switches**) fails to respond correctly, either through malfunction or loss of power. See also **Points Operator** (**PO**), **Route Setting Agent** (**RSA**)

Points Heating
A device fitted to **Points** (**Switches**) to prevent the formation of ice and to reduce the build-up of **Snow** in inclement weather that would otherwise prevent the correct operation of said Switches. Systems are typically rated to maintain the **Stock Rails** (and **Switch Rails** in some systems) at +3°C at an ambient air temperature of -25°C but not to deal with drifting Snow. Basic types are:
- **Electric Points Heating** (EPH): these include **Electric Cartridge Heaters**, **Electric Pad Heaters** and **Electric Strip Heaters**
- **Gas Points Heating**.
Also **Switch Heater**.

Points Indicator

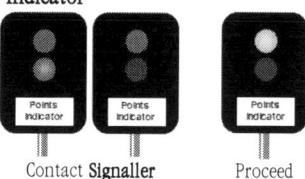

Contact **Signaller**   Proceed

[NR Sig.] An **Indicator** that informs a driver that the **Points** associated with the Indicator are correctly **Set**. Normally used on **Facing Points** (**Facing Switches**). Also **Points Position Indicator** (**PPI**).

Points Memory
[Sig.] Within a **Solid State Interlocking** (**SSI**), 64 bytes of random access memory (RAM) which are used to store the state of **Points**.

Points Operator (PO)
[NR] A responsibility mandated by the **Rule Book**, covering the operating and securing of **Power Operated Points** during times of **Points Failure** or in connection with **Possessions**. Also **AOD:PO**, **Route Setting Agent** (**RSA**).

Points Position Indicator (PPI)

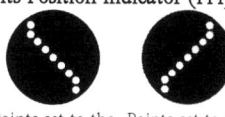

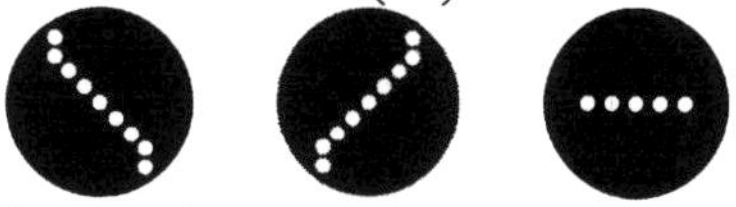

Points set to the left   Points set to the right   No **Detection**

[LR] White position light signals that provide the driver with an indication of how the **Points** are **Set** (as in **Normal** or **Reverse**) as a **Tram** approaches. See also **Points Indicator**.

Points Rodding
[Sig. Col.] An alternative term for **Channel Rodding**, **Rodding**.

Points Run Through
A **Trailing Movement** through a set of **Non-Trailable** ▫ **Trailing Switches** (**Trailing Points**) that are not correctly **Set** for the Movement.

POIS
See **P**assenger **O**perations **I**nformation **S**ystem.

POL
See **Phantom Overlap**.

Pole and Tape
Pole and Tape Survey
[PW] A rapid but somewhat inaccurate method of carrying out a Gauging Survey (**Gauging a Structure**) by means of measurements taken from the two **Running Edges** (**RE**) of one **Track** beneath the Structure. The **Track Gauge** and its **Crosslevel** can be measured directly, so each pair of taped measurements can be plotted and the profile of the Structure drawn. Since the technique involves attaching a tape to the end of a pole, it is also known as **Fishing**.

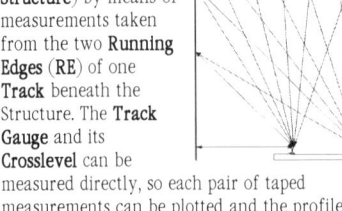

Pole Applied Clamp
[Elec.] A device fitted to one or more ends of a **Local Earth** that allows those ends to be attached to and detached from the **Overhead Line Equipment** (**OLE**) using an insulated pole, thereby removing any danger of electrocution or falling from height during the operation.

POLI
(*polly*) [NR] Provision of **Lineside** □ **Infrastructure**.

Policeman
[Hist.] Term for the person controlling **Train Movements** at **Stations** and **Junctions** from 1830 to about 1860. After the latter date the duties of **Signallers** were separated from those of general security staff, but not before the name stuck. See **Bobby**.

Policeman Irons
[Hist., Col.] Alternative term for **Lifeguards**.

Politician
[Col.] Nickname for the **Class** 60 **Diesel Locomotive** because you can see right through them. Also **Doughnut**.

Pollock (ZCA)
[NR] A 30 ton capacity **Open Wagon** used for the transportation of materials. See **Wagon Names**.

Polmont Accident
On 10th July 1984 a **Train**, travelling at speed, hit a **Cow**, largely stationary, near Polmont causing a **Derailment** in which 13 died and 17 were injured. See **Obstacle Deflector**. See also **Lifeguard**.

Polychloroprene
The longer, chemical name for Neoprene, a material used in wetsuits, electrical insulation and synthetic rubber bushes.

Polymeric Insulator
An **Insulator** used on **Overhead Line Equipment** (**OLE**), constructed in a single casting from a polymer material. See also **Cup and Pin Insulator**.

POM
a) [NR] (*pomm*) **P**ossession **O**ptimisation **M**anager
b) **P**assenger **O**perated **M**achine; any machine used by **Passengers** to purchase **Tickets**;

PON
(*ponn*) See **P**eriodical **O**perating **N**otice.

Pony Truck
Normally found at the front or rear of **Steam Locomotives**, used to reduce the **Axle Load** produced by the **Driving Wheels**. It consists of a frame fitted with one **Wheelset**. It is attached to the main vehicle by a horizontal A-frame and a pin joint. The upper surface of the Pony has a bearing surface on which the frame of the main vehicle rests.

Poor
a) [NR] A length of **Track** (usually an **Eighth of a Mile**) over which the **Track Quality** (**TQ**) is worse than Satisfactory, but better than **Very Poor**, in that the **Standard Deviation** (**SD**) values for **Top** and **Line** are between the 90% and 100% values for the **Permissible Speed** (**PS**) or **Enhanced Permissible Speed** (**EPS**).
b) [NR] **Slope Condition Rating** for an **Earthwork** such as an **Embankment**, **Cutting** or natural slope; the high-risk categorisation, the others being **Marginal** and **Serviceable**.

POPMAR
Policy, **O**rganisation, **P**lanning, **M**easuring, **A**udit and **R**eview.

Porous Weld
An **Alumino-thermic Weld** which has gas bubbles within it, typically of hydrogen or steam. The most common cause is a damp **Welding Portion**. This type of **Weld** will normally rapidly fail by fracturing under tension.

Porpoise (YEA)
[NR] The **Chute Wagon** forming part of the **Continuous Welded Rail Train** (**CWR Train**). See **Wagon Names**.

Port
[Sig.] A slot cut in a **Tappet**. Also called a **Notch**.

Portable Automatic Warning System Magnet
Portable AWS Magnet
A portable permanent magnet used in conjunction with a **Warning Board** to alert drivers to the presence of an **Emergency Speed Restriction** (**ESR**) or **Temporary Speed Restriction** (**TSR**) ahead. It gives the driver the same indication they would receive from a **Signal** showing a **Caution Aspect** or **Stop Aspect**. Colloquially called a **Temporary Magnet**.

Portal
a) [Civ.] The extreme end of a **Tunnel**
b) [Elec.] A goal post shaped structure supporting the **Overhead Line Equipment** (**OLE**), see **Portal Structures**
c) [TRS] The aperture in the **Carbody** into which the door is fitted. See **Door Portal**.

Portal Structures
[Elec.]

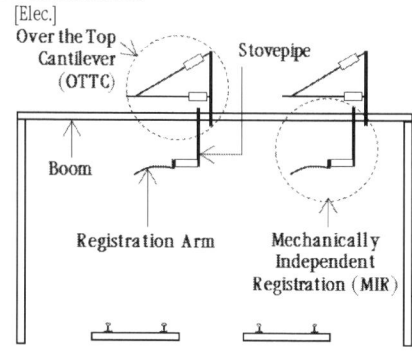

Over the Top Cantilever (OTTC)

Stovepipe

Boom

Registration Arm

Mechanically Independent Registration (MIR)

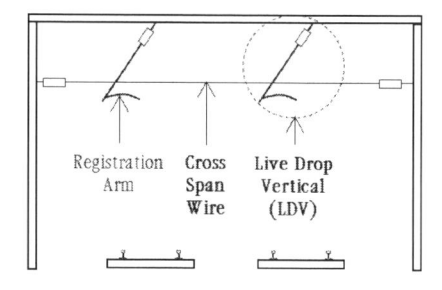

Registration Arm

Cross Span Wire

Live Drop Vertical (LDV)

Portec Rail
(Tradename) [PW] A manufacturer of Track related products, including Fishplated Rail Joints and Rail Lubricator systems.

Porterbrook
Porterbrook Leasing
(Tradename) A Rolling Stock Company (ROSCO). See also Angel, Eversholt.

PORTIS
(*por-tiss*) Portable Ticket Issuing System. A relatively small and lightweight device capable of issuing printed tickets to Passengers. Widely used by Conductors and Guards on Passenger Trains. See also APTIS, SPORTIS.

POS
a) [Sig.] The prefix defining the indicator position (1 to 6) on a Junction Indicator (JI), e.g. POS 4
b) See Place of Safety
c) See Position of Safety
d) [TRS] An acronym representing a Post Office Sorting Van.

Pos.
Abbreviation of Possession.

PoSA
See Proceed on Sight Authority.

Position Light Ground Signal (PLGS)
See Ground Position Light Signal (GPLS), see also Independent Position Light Signal (IPLS).

Position Light Junction Indicator (PLJI)
[Sig.] A type of Junction Indicator (JI) consisting of an arrangement of lines of white lights mounted above a Junction Signal in Colour Light Signalled areas which, when lit, displays the Diverging Route through a Junction to a driver. They are used for high speed Lines. For lower speeds Alphanumeric Route Indicators (ARI) are used. The illustration shows all possible Positions. This is unlikely as current preference is to avoid providing Positions 1 and 6 together, 2 and 5 together or 3 and 4 together, as they could be confused. The areas shaded in grey in the diagram are filled in according to which of the route indications are used.
A simple Junction consisting of one Turnout (TO) to the left would have only Position 1 fitted:

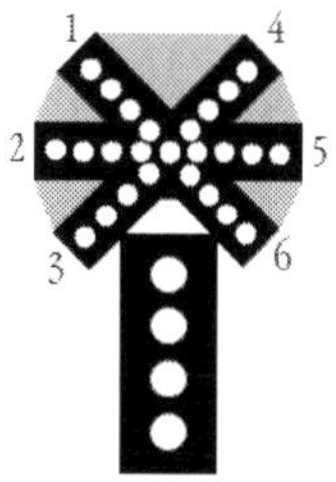

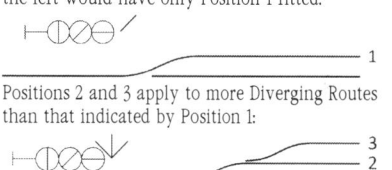

Positions 2 and 3 apply to more Diverging Routes than that indicated by Position 1:

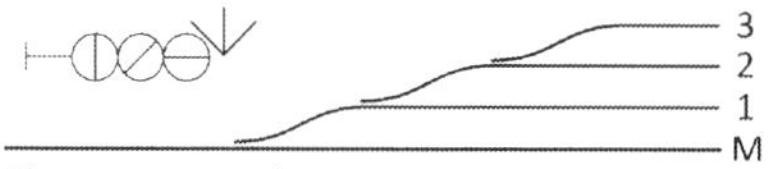

The same is true for routes diverging to the right:

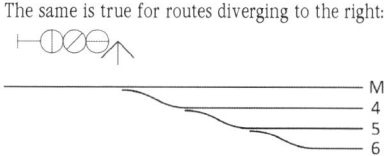

See also Bracket Signal, Miniature Alphanumeric Route Indicator (MARI), Preliminary Route Indicator (PRI) Standard Alphanumeric Route Indicator (SARI).

Position Light Signal (PLS)
[Sig.] A Signal that conveys its instructions by means of light positions, although the colour of those lights also has meaning. Such Signals are generally used to control Shunting and other Non-running Movements. The lamp that remains on at all times is the Pivot Light, and the lower left hand lamp can be either Red or Yellow according to the instructions conveyed by the Signal.

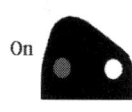

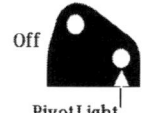

Position Light Subsidiary Signal
[Sig.] A Subsidiary Signal that is a Position Light Signal (PLS).

ELLIS' BRITISH RAILWAY ENGINEERING ENCYCLOPÆDIA

Position of Safety (POS)
A place far enough from the **Track** to allow a person to safely avoid being struck by passing **Trains** or **Trams**. For example, on **Network Rail** (**NR**) ▫ **Infrastructure** this is 1.25m (4 feet) where Trains approach at speeds of up to and including 100mph, 2m (6 feet 6 inches) at speeds of up to 125mph, and 2.75m (9 feet) at speeds of over 125mph. See also **Place of Safety** (POS).

Position *x*
See **Junction Indicator** (JI).

Positive Cant
[PW] The normal situation for a **Curved Track**, where the outer **Rail** is higher than the inner **Rail**. The opposite is **Negative Cant**.

Positive Conductor Rail
[Elec.] The positive supply **Conductor Rail** on a DC **Electrified Line**, generally used to distinguish it from the **Negative Conductor Rail** or **Fourth Rail**. Also DC **Rail**, **Hot Rail**, **Juice Rail**, **Live Rail**, **Pozzy Rail**, **Third Rail**.

Positive Insulator Stool
[LUL] A timber support provided for the **Positive Conductor Rail** and **Insulator** on **Bridges** with **Longitudinal Timbers**.

Positive Rail
See **Positive Conductor Rail**.

Positive Stagger
[Elec.] Describing the case where the **Contact Wire** (**CW**) is on the same side of the centre line of the **Pantograph** as t the fixed point from which the **Wire** is registered. The opposite is **Negative Stagger**. See also **Stagger**.

Positive Train Identification (PTI)
a) [NR] A transponder / receiver system which identifies a **Train** directly by its transponder signal, rather than by means of a **Train Describer** (TD).
b) [LUL] A control system which identifies each **Train** and instructs the **Signalling Equipment** where to route it.

Posn.
Abbreviation of **Possession**.

Poss.
Abbreviation of **Possession**.

Possession
a) A formal temporary closure of a **Line** to **Trains** for safety reasons or to allow **Engineering Work** to take place
b) [NR] A period of time during which one or more **Lines** are **Blocked** to **Trains** to permit work to be safely carried out **On or Near the Line**. Possessions are available in three main varieties:
• A **Line Blockage**, taken between Trains and given up whenever a Train is to be run over the affected section.
• A Possession taken for an agreed period without the facility to run Trains in the area during that period, until such time as the holder of the Possession decides to relinquish it. Currently called a **T3 Possession**
• A Possession taken of **Sidings**. Currently called a **T4 Possession**
• A Possession taken of **Signalling Equipment**, see **Disconnection**.
A T3 Possession is sometimes referred to as an **Absolute Possession**, **Engineer's Possession**. See also **Blockade**. For further details see the **Rule Book** (GE/RT8000).

Possession Arrangements
a) The physical limits, times, **Lines** ▫ **Blocked** and special conditions for a **Possession**.
b) [NR] These are normally published in advance of the work in **Section B** of the **Weekly Operating Notice** (**WON**). See also **Protection Arrangements**.

Possession Book
[NR] Document containing details of the **Work Sites** discussed at the **T-14** planning meetings which have been agreed and linked to a **Possession**.

Possession Change Control Form
[NR] A form completed by **Engineering** planning staff in order to request additional or amended work in a **Possession** at late notice.

Possession Irregularity
An action or occurrence which contravenes the **Rule Book** or other instructions related to the taking, management or giving up of a **Possession**. This would include incorrect or missing **Protection Arrangements**, improper **Train Movements** entering or leaving the Possession and failure to relinquish the Possession area **Fit For Traffic**.

Possession Limit Board (PLB)
[NR] A miniature version of the stop sign used on the roads, denoting the end of a **Possession**.

Possession Manager
a) [NR] The organisation appointed at the T-14 □ Planning Meeting to provide the Person in Charge of Possession (PICOP) and to liaise with the other organisations having Engineering Work Sites within the Possession
b) [NR] In very large and complex Possessions, a person appointed to make strategic decisions about the works carried out within the Possession, for implementation by the PICOP.

Possession Master
[LUL] A person certificated to take and give up a Possession..

Possession Only Vehicle
[NR] A vehicle or item of mobile plant which is only permitted to operate on the Track within an Engineering Possession.

Possession Overrun
A Possession that has exceeded the agreed time at which it should have been handed back to normal Traffic. See also Train Minute Delay.

Possession Planning System (PPS)
[NR] A single system used for the recording of national engineering and access requirements. These requirements are captured in real time as Possessions, Work Sites and Temporary Speed Restrictions (TSRs).

Possession Strategy Notice (PSN)
[NR] A document sent to the Train Operating Companies (TOC) and Freight Operating Companies (FOC) detailing the Possessions planned to undertake the works required by a particular project. In some newer Passenger Track Access Agreements this document replaces the Major Project Notice (MPN).

PossMan
[NR] A work management tool that combines data from Ellipse and the Possession Panning System (PPS) to display Track Access opportunities linked to job bank data.

Post and Wire Fence

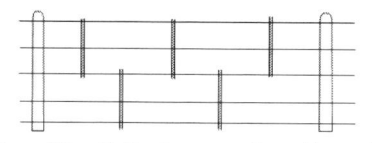

A type of Lineside Fencing commonly used in rural areas. Horizontal wires (typically six to nine in number) are secured to concrete posts with wire ties threaded through the posts. The fence is further strengthened by the addition of intermediate dropper bars.

Post Incident Brake Test
A mandatory test of Train or Rail Vehicle brakes following certain types of incident, to determine the functionality against the relevant standard.

Poste Kilometrique (PK)
[CT] Lineside marker defining the location of a point in the Channel Tunnel.

Pot
a) See Conductor Rail Insulator, Third Rail Insulator
b) [PW] Nickname for the crucible used in Alumino-thermic Welding
c) See Can.

Pot Sleeper
a) [PW Obs.] A concrete or stone block that supports only one Chair, Baseplate or Rail
b) [Col.] Infrequently, a Sleeper that supports a Pot, or Conductor Rail Insulator
c) [Obs.] A type of pseudo-Sleeper where the support to the Rails is provided by a pair of large, inverted, shallow cast iron dishes, one under each Rail. These could be linked by a Gauge Tie-bar to preserve the Track Gauge. See Greave's Surface Packed (Pot) Sleepers

Potential Equalising Jumper
[Elec.] A Jumper used in an Insulated Overlap to ensure that the In Running (IR) and Out of Running (OOR) □ Contact Wires (CW) are at the same electrical potential.

Potential-free Contacts
[Sig.] Alternative term for Volts-free Contacts.

POTIS
(*poe-tiss*) Passenger Operated Ticket Issuing System.

Potter's Bar Accidents
a) On 19th March 1898, the 19:50 from Hatfield to Kings Cross ran past Signals at Danger and crashed onto the Platform. No one was killed or seriouslt injured
b) On 10th February 1946, a Local Passenger Train travelling towards Kings Cross hit a Buffer Stop at Potters Bar and Derailed foul of the Main Line. Two Express Passenger Trains travelling in opposite directions then hit the wreckage. Two Passengers were killed and 17 injured were taken to hospital. The driver of the local Train was eventually held to blame but a Signalman was found to have contributed to the Accident by moving a Set Of Points as the Train passed over them.
c) On 10th May 2002 seven Passengers died and 40 were injured when a Set of Facing Points became incorrectly set under a Commuter Train. The fault was due to loose and missing nuts on the Stretcher Bars, but opinions vary as to how this situation arose. See also Lambrigg Accident.

Pound
[PW] A common contraction of Pounds per Yard, e.g. 113 Pound.

Pounds per Yard
[PW] A description of a Rail Section in terms of the weight in pounds of one Yard of the Rail, rounded to the nearest whole number of Pounds. Typical values include:
- 85, 95, 97$^1/_2$ □ Pound □ Bull Head Rail (BH)
- 50, 80, 98, 109, 110 and 113 Pound Flat Bottom Rail (FB)
- 105, 105A, 106 and 150 Pound Conductor Rail.

See also Kilograms per Metre.

POV
See Possession Only Vehicle.

Powellising
[PW Obs.] A method of preserving **Wood Sleepers** by immersing them in a solution of saccharine and insecticides / fungicides.

Power Box
[Sig. Col.] A common contraction of **Power Signal Box** (**PSB**).

Power Car (PC)
[TRS] Part of a **Multiple Unit Train** or **Permanently Coupled** □ **Train Formation** (such as a **High Speed Train** (**HST**)) that provides **Tractive Effort** for the **Train** but has no seating for **Passengers**. See also **Motor Coach**.

Power Controller
[TRS] The device used by a driver to apply and remove power to the **Traction Unit** allowing the **Train** to accelerate or **Coast**. See also **Combined Traction Brake Controller**.

Power Disable Test (PDT)
[Sig.] A test carried out periodically by the redundancy management software within a **Solid State Interlocking** (**SSI**) system to determine whether a **Signal Module** can control its power disabling relays. A PDT takes place approximately every five hours or on an output change after more than one hour since the previous PDT. The PDT typically takes place when the **Signal** is changing **Aspect** and is not visible to a driver.

Power Frame
[Sig.] A **Lever Frame** controlling power operated **Signalling Equipment**. See also **Miniature Lever Frame**.

Power Operated Doors
[TRS] **Train** doors that are released, opened, closed and locked by the driver or **Guard** from a central location. Universal on newer **Trains**, they are replacing **Slam Doors**.

Power Operated Points
Power Operated Switches
[Sig.] **Switches** (**Points**) operated by means of a **Point Machine**. Also **Motor Points**, **Powered Switch**.

Power Signal Box (PSB)
[Sig.] A large **Signal Box** (**SB**) which controls the **Points** and **Signals** over a large area by electrical means, rather than the former system of small **Signal Boxes** at **Junctions** controlling the **Points** and **Signals** by means of **Rodding** and **Wires**, called **Mechanical Signalling**. Power Signal Boxes are gradually being superseded by **Integrated Electronic Control Centres** (**IECC**). Sometimes shortened to **Power Box**. See also **Network Management Centre** (**NMC**).

Power Signalling
[Sig.] The opposite of **Mechanical Signalling**, this is where the effort of the **Signaller** is supplemented or replaced by power derived from an external source, generally electricity. See also **Power Signal Box** (**PSB**).

Powered Axle
[TRS] An axle that has some prime mover attached, making it the means by which the vehicle is moved along the **Track**. Also **Driven Axle**.

Powered Canopy Trolley (PCT)
[PW prob. Obs.] A small **Self Propelled** trolley with an extendable awning and capable of transporting a small **Track Welding** team plus a **Lookout** to and from site.

Powered Switch
[Sig.] **Switches** (**Points**) operated by means of a **Point Machine**. Also **Motor Points**, **Power Operated Points**.

Pozzy Rail
[Col.] A common contraction of **Positive Conductor Rail**, see **Conductor Rail**. Also **Hot Rail**, **Juice Rail**, **Live Rail**, **Positive Rail**, **Third Rail**.

PP
a) See **Permissive Passenger**
b) [NR] Period available for **Possessions**
c) Peripheral Post.

PPE
Personal Protective Equipment.

PPI
a) Gabarit Passe-Partout International, the formal equivalent of **Berne Gauge**, see **UIC GA Gauge**
b) See **Points Position Indicator**. See also **Points Indicator**.

PPM
a) See **Planned Preventative Maintenance**
b) See **Panel Processor Module**
c) See **Public Performance Measure**
d) See **Parry People Mover**
e) Pence Per Mile.

PPP
a) [NR] Period **Possession** Plan.
b) Public Private Partnership, see **London Underground Limited** (**LUL**)
c) Purchasing Power Parity

PPPC
[BR] Powered Plant Proficiency Certificate

PPS
See **Possession Planning System**.

PPT
[NR] Under the **Bridge Condition Marking Index** (**BCMI**) handbook, shorthand for **Parapet**.

PPTC
Powered Plant Training – Chainsaw.

PPTD
Powered Plant Training - Disc Cutter (**Disc Saw**) and Class 9 Cutting-off Wheels.

PPTE
Pre-Production Testing Environment.

PQS
Plant Quality Supervisor.

PR
a) See PR*xxx*, PR*xxx*A, Pandrol Clip
b) See **Periodic Review**.

PR Series Clip
See PR*xxx*, PR*xxx*A.

PR08
Periodic Review for 2008.
PR2000
Periodic Review for 2000.
PRAMS
Progress Reporting and Management System
Prawn (YNO)
[NR] A flat **Wagon** used for the transportation of **Rails**. See **Wagon Names**.
PRB
[NR] Personalised **Rule Book**
PRD
[Civ.] Piston Relief Duct, a small passage linking two single bore **Railway** □ **Tunnels**, which limits the fluctuations in air pressure caused by passing **Trains**.
PRDC
Princess Royal Distribution Centre, the Royal Mail **Railnet** facility at Willesden.
Pre-Assembly Depot (PAD)
[PW] A facility where new **Track Panels** are built up and surplus Track Panels are taken apart to recover any **Serviceable** components.
Pre-coated Grooved Rail
[PW] A **Grooved Rail** with a Polyurethane elastomer coating applied to the two sides and base of the **Rail**. It is intended that the Rail can then be cast into the highway structure, simplifying construction. Widely used on **Tramway** systems as means of reducing ground-borne vibration and **Stray Current**.
Pre-curved Rail
[PW] A **Rail** that has been evenly bent in one or two dimensions to a pre-determined Radius (**R**) prior to delivery. This is normally done where the Radius of the **Curve** to be installed is small.
Pre-departure Examination
[Ops.] A physical examination of a **Freight Train** undertaken in a **Depot** or **Siding** before it is allowed onto **Running Lines**.
Prefab. Relaying
[PW] **Track Relaying** using pre-assembled **Track Panels**. These are put together in a **Prefab. Assembly Depot (PAD)**. The main alternative method is **Loose Sleeper Relaying (LSR)**.
Preferred Option
The design option which gains most support from the **Stakeholders** during a **Feasibility Study**. In a perfect world this term would be "Correct Option", but is very rare for all Stakeholders to agree unanimously. See also **Single Option Development (SOD)**.
Preferred Route
[Sig.] Where a **Junction** controlled by an **NX Panel** has two or more possible **Routes** which ultimately lead to the same destination, then one of these will normally be chosen over the other by the **Interlocking**, unless the **Signaller** intervenes. This is the Preferred Route.

Pre-Grouping
[Hist.] The period of UK **Railway** history immediately prior to 1923, when the majority of **Railway Companies** then extant were grouped together into the **Big Four** under the **Railways Act 1921**. See also **Grouping**.
Preliminary Caution
Preliminary Caution Aspect
[Sig.] A **Signal Aspect** that indicates to a driver that the next **Signal** may be showing a **Caution Aspect**. It is indicated by a **Double Yellow Aspect**.
Preliminary Hazard Analysis
An analysis performed to identify possible hazards that could be created by the system being designed. This information can then be used to reduce the severity or build-in safeguards against the effects of the identified hazards.
Preliminary Route Indicator (PRI)
[Sig.] An **Indicator** provided on the Approach to a **Junction Signal** fitted with a **Position Light Junction Indicator**. It provides information on which **Route** is Set at the **Junction**.

↑	Junction Signal is **Off** for straight-ahead Route
↖	Off for LH □ **Diverging Route**, Position 1
←	Off for LH Diverging Route, Position 2
↙	Off for LH Diverging Route, Position 3
↗	Off for RH Diverging Route, Position 4
→	Off for RH Diverging Route, Position 5
↘	Off for RH Diverging Route, Position 6
	Junction Signal is **On**

Premature Renewal of Track
[PW] The **Renewal** or **Relaying** of **Track** that is not yet in need of replacement. This is often carried out on economic grounds, either in conjunction with a nearby major scheme or where the introduction of new types of **Traction Units** or **Rolling Stock** necessitate improved or stronger **Track Components** where the cost of a return visit is greater than the value of the premature work. See also **Renewals Avoided**.
Prepare a Locomotive
See **Train Preparation, Train Preparer**.
Prepare a Train
See **Train Preparation, Train Preparer**.

Prepare Loop
[LR] A **Track** based receiver that detects the presence of a **Tram** and arms the **Signalling System** to expect it.

Presco
(Tradename) A manufacturer of **Relocatable Equipment Buildings** (**REBs**), now part of the Elliot Group which is based in Cannock, Staffordshire.

Preselection
[Sig.] The ability to select a **Signalling Function**, group of Signalling Functions or **Route** prior to the correct conditions being available, so that the selection is automatically made when the correct conditions do apply, generally following the passage of a preceding **Train**. See also **Anti-preselection**.

Preserved Railway
A **Railway** that continues to operate in a manner reminiscent of, and using technology from, a time now passed. Typically, but not universally, such **Railways** are owned and staffed by enthusiasts, with the main source of **Traction** being **Steam Locomotives** or early **Diesel Locomotives**.

Pre-set Shunt
[Sig.] An arrangement whereby any **Facing** □ **Shunt Signals** in any other **Route Class** selected will be **Cleared** automatically before the **Main Signal** Clears.

Prestressed Concrete Sleeper
[PW] A **Concrete Sleeper** produced in a pre-formed mould by casting concrete around pre-tensioned wires or, more usually, pre-tensioned strand reinforcement.

Pre-tap
[PW] Describing a situation where an **Aluminothermic Weld** crucible has been tapped (either accidentally or by the tapping pin failing) before the proper time for the reaction of the **Weld Portion** to to be completed. A Pre-tap renders the **Weld** a **Defective Weld**.

Pretendolino
[Col.] Nickname for the **Class** 90 hauled services that run between Birmingham and Euston in the place of **Class** 390 **Pendolinos**.

Prevent Shunt
[Sig.] The highest value of resistance, which when placed across the **Rails** in a **Track Circuit** (**TC**), will cause the **Relay** to just energise, that is just complete **Picking-up**. See also **Drop Shunt**.

PRG
[NR] Project Review Group.

PRHC
Poor Rail Head Conditions.

PRI
See **Preliminary Route Indicator**.

PRIDE
(*pride*)
a) [NR Obs.] Possession Resource Information Database. Replaced by **Possession Planning System** (**PPS**)
b) Passenger □ Rail Information Display Equipment.

PRIMA
(Tradename) Professional **Rail Industry Management** Association.

Primary Function Relay
[Sig.] The **Relay** by which the logic required to control a **Signalling Function** is brought together. It is the first relay in a chain that directly controls all **Safety Critical** Signalling Functions. It is the only function Relay which has **Back Contacts** valid for use in safety critical functions.

Primary Gate
[Sig.] At a **Level Crossing** (**LC**, **LX**) with overlapping **Gates**, the Gates which are hinged to the left of the **Railway** (as seen from an **Approaching Train**) and are the first set of Gates to be closed to the road. See also **Secondary Gates**.

Primary Member Of Service (PRIMOS)
The National Express Midland Metro (**NXMM**) member of staff who takes charge of an incident on behalf of the **Tramway** and liaise with other agencies pending the arrival of an **Incident Officer**.

Primary Suspension
[TRS] Those components of a suspension system connected to the axles. Any components other than these are the **Secondary Suspension**.

Primary Timetable Change
[NR] The **Timetable Change** which occurs in December every year.

Priming
[TRS] In a **Steam Locomotive**, the unwanted inclusion of water with the steam being drawn from the **Boiler**. This can be caused by too high a water level in the Boiler or high levels of solids and other contamination in the **Feedwater**.

PRIMOS
See **Primary Member Of Service**.

PRINCE 2
(Tradename) Projects in Controlled Environments, version 2. A project management methodology.

Principal Direction
An alternative for **Normal Direction**.

Principal Station
[NR] A **Station**:
- That is an interchange or on a **Converging Route**
- Where **Passengers** could practically change from, or to, another **Train Operating Company's** (**TOC**) services
- That has a heavy **Footfall**
- That provides interchange with other modes of transport (e.g. airports).

According to guidance published by the **Association of Train Operators** (**ATOC**), "If a **Train** has not called at a Principal Station, as defined above, for over 20 minutes then the next Station should be regarded as a Principal Station for on-Train announcements. To ensure that Passengers receive a consistent level of information, each TOC should determine which of its Stations are Principal Stations and which are not."

Principal Supply Point (PSP)
[EP] The equipment which takes an electrical supply from a Domestic Network Operator (DNO) and converts into a Signalling Power Supply. The security of this supply is normally protected by Un-interruptible Power Supplies (UPS) and alternative power sources such as Traction-derived Supplies or local generator sets.

Prior Working Timetable
[NR Ops.] The version of the Working Timetable (WTT) used to develop the New Working Timetable

PRISM
a) Network Rail's (NR) supplier performance scoring system
b) Policy Responsive Integrated Strategy Model, a transport model.

Prism Rail
[Hist.] An early Train Operating Company (TOC). Originally awarded the London Tilbury and Southend (LTS), Wales and West (W&W), West Anglia Great Northern (WAGN) and Valley Lines □ Franchises, Prism Rail was acquired by the National Express Group (NEG) in 2000.

Private Locomotive Registration Agreement (PLRA)

Private Operator Circulation Letter
[NR] Letters sent by the Private Wagon Registration Agreement department within Network Rail (NR) to private Wagon and Locomotive owners to brief them on Railway related matters.

Private Owner Wagon
[BR, Obs.] Prior to Privatisation, a Wagon not owned by British Rail (BR) but moved from place to place by BR or its predecessors.

Private Railway
A Railway system operated for the benefit of a single individual, a company or an organisation but not open to the public. Examples include systems serving mines and steelworks and those running around private gardens. These systems are not subject to the same regulations as Public Railways.

Private Siding (PS)
[NR] A Siding, connected the Network, that provides Rail access to private premises such as a factory or warehouse.

Private Siding Agreement (PSA)
[BR] A document that formalised the arrangements for the operation and maintenance of a Private Siding (PS). See Connection Agreement (CA).

Private Wagon
See Private Owner Wagon.

Private Wagon Registration Agreement (PWRA)
a) [BR] Prior to Privatisation, a document detailing the ownership and compliance status of a Wagon not owned by British Rail (BR) but moved from place to place by British Rail
b) [RT] A document detailing the ownership and compliance status of a Wagon not operating on the Network
c) [NR Hist.] A document detailing the ownership and compliance status of a Wagon not owned by Network Rail (NR). This arrangement (where NR acts as the "Professional Head" for vehicle approvals on behalf of the owners of Private Wagons) has now been superseded by Entity in Charge of Maintenance (ECM) Service Provision Agreements (ESPA).

Privatisation
a) The colloquial name for the events of 1994 and 1995 when the Railways Act 1993 came into force, transferring British Railways (BR) into multiple private ownerships. Stewardship of the Infrastructure and daily operation of same was vested in Railtrack (RT) for the sum of £1.8 billion, and all the other subsidiary activities such as Maintenance of Signals, Track and Structures, ownership, Maintenance and operation of Trains, catering and the running of Stations were sold as one of over 100 separate companies or franchises for a further £680 million. See also Freight Operating Companies (FOC), Infrastructure Maintenance Companies (IMC), Nationalisation, Office of Passenger Railway Franchising (OPRAF), Office of Rail Regulation (ORR), Office of the Rail Regulator (ORR), Rolling Stock Companies (ROSCO), Strategic Rail Authority (SRA), Technical Services Companies (TESCO), Track Renewal Companies (TRC), Track Renewal Units (TRU), Train Operating Companies (TOC).
b) A (possibly) complete list of engineering companies, Self-accounting Units (SAU) and other parts of the organisation which changed hands at this time is:

Company	Bought by
BRIS design offices	
BPE	James Scott BPE (**AMEC**)
CEDAC, London	WS Atkins (**WSA**)
CEDG, York	British Steel, then Corus, now Tata
DCU Birmingham	Owen Williams Railways, now Amey
IDG Glasgow	Scott Wilson Kirkpatrick, now **URS**
Mainline Swindon	Scott Wilson Kirkpatrick, now **URS**
Powertrack Engineering	WS Atkins
BRIS Companies	
Central **IMC**	**GTRM** (**GEC** Alsthom / Tarmac **JV**).
Central **TRC**	Tarmac, now Carillion
Eastern IMC	Balfour Beatty
Eastern TRC	Fastline Rail Services
Northern IMC	**Jarvis** (no longer trading)

Northern TRC	Fastline Group, then Jarvis (no longer trading)	Porterbrook Leasing Co.	Consortium, led by management team

Other companies

Scotland IMC	TrackAction, **MBO**, then **First Engineering**	BRT	Racal Electronics, Then Thales, see **NRT**
Scotland TRC	Relayfast, MBO, then First Engineering	OBS Services	European Rail Catering Company, MBO
South East IMC	Broomco (919), (MBO / Balfour Beatty JV)		

PRM
Persons of Reduced Mobility.

South West IMC	Amec
Southern TRC	Balfour Beatty
Western IMC	Amey Railways, MBO
Western TRC	Relayfast, then Jarvis

PRMP
Procurement Risk Management Procedure.

Proceed

BR Maintenance Ltd.

Proceed Aspect

Chart Leacon Rail **Mtce**.	ABB
Doncaster Rail Mtce.	ABB

[Sig.] A **Signal Aspect** which authorises a driver to pass that **Signal**.

Eastleigh Rail Mtce.	Wessex Traincare, MBO
Glasgow Rail Mtce	Railcare (Babcock / Siemens JV)

Proceed at Caution

[Ops.] A formal instruction to a driver that means that they must, in addition to obeying any limits on **Permissible Speed** (**PS**), proceed at such a speed that will allow the Train to be safely stopped within the distance they can see to be clear along the Line ◻ **Ahead**. See also **Stop and Caution**.

Ilford Rail Mtce.	ABB
Swindon Electronics Service Centre	ABB
Wolverton Rail Mtce.	Railcare

BR Central Services

Proceed on Sight Authority (POSA)

Baileyfield **S&C** Works	VAE Baileyfield
BR Projects	Addspice, MBO
Castleton **Rail Welding** Works	British Steel, then Corus, Tata and now closed.
College of Railway Technology	Advicepart, MBO

[Sig.] An **Aspect** used during failures of the **Signalling System**, instructing the driver to pass a **Signal** on the basis of **Line of Sight**, being prepared to stop short of any obstruction.

Production Copies

[NR Sig.] The copies made of a **Signalling Design** which are then used in the wiring fabrication and assembly of the **Signalling System**.

Ditton Timber Treatment Works	PTG Holdings, now closed.
Interfleet Technology	Broomco., MBO
Interlogic Control Engineering	ABB
Meldon Quarry	ECC
Network Train Engineering Services	WS Atkins
Quality and Safety Services	Ingleby (805), MBO
Railways Occupational Health	Occupational Health Care

Production Vehicle (PV)

[NR] Part of the **New Measurement Train** (**NMT**), this converted **Mark III** ◻ **Coach** (977994) replaced the older **Track Recording Coach** (**TRC**). It is equipped to measure, record, analyse or derive:

- Location;
- Speed;
- Top;
- Alignment;
- Cant;
- Twist;
- Gauge;
- Sixfoot;
- Ballast Shoulder height;
- Curvature; and
- High resolution still images.

SCUK	WBS
Special **Trains** Unit	Waterman Railways
The Engineering Link	MBO

BR Freight and Parcels

Freightliner (1995)	MBO, now **Freightliner**
Loadhaul	North & South Railways (consortium), latterly **EWS**, now **DB Schenker UK Rail**
Mainline Freight	Ditto
Rail Express Systems (RES)	Ditto
Red Star Parcels	MBO, latterly EWS, now DB Schenker UK Rail
Transrail Freight	N&SR, latterly EWS, now DB Schenker UK Rail

This vehicle is typically coupled to the **Development Vehicle** (**DV**).

ROSCOs

Angel Train Contracts	GRS Holdings (consortium)
Eversholt Leasing	Eversholt Holdings, (consortium), Then HSBC Rail

Professional Driving
[Ops.] A **Train** driving technique which actively encourages drivers to anticipate and respond appropriately to operating and environmental conditions (e.g. the early control of speed **On the Approach to** □ **Caution** and **Stop Signals**). This method reduces the incidence of **Trains** overshooting **Station Stops** and **Signals Passed At Danger** (**SPAD**) by more effective braking and better judgement of **Rail Head Conditions**. This is one element of the professional **Train** driving initiative recommended by the **National SPAD Focus Group**. See **Professional Driving Policies**. Colloquially and incorrectly called **Defensive Driving**.

Professional Driving Policies
Policies prepared by **Train Operating Companies** (**TOCs**) that describe, amongst other things, **Train** driving practices that the company expects its drivers to adopt in order to ensure safe and efficient **Train** operations. Such practices include:
- Braking at an early stage to avoid **Signals Passed at Danger** (**SPADs**);
- Stopping 20m short of **Signals at Danger**;
- Always assuming that the next **Signal** after a **Caution Aspect** will be at **Danger**;
- Reducing speed to 20mph (32kph) by 200m before a **Signal at Danger**;
- Reducing speed to 10mph (16km/h) by the **Platform Ramp** when approaching a **Bay Platform**.

Profile Board
See **Sighting Board**.

Profile Bucket
[PW] An attachment for a 360° excavator or **Road Rail Excavator**, designed to allow the machine to distribute **Ballast** along the **Track**. They are shaped to fit around the **Rails** and **Fastenings**.

Profile Grinding
[PW] The grinding of the remains of an **Alumino-thermic Weld** riser to the final **Rail Profile**, following initial removal with a **Weld Shear**. See **Rail Grinder**. See also **Blending**.

Programme Level x
[NR] A categorisation of the level of detail of a project programme:
0 Contains no detail, effectively just a start and finish date.
1 Limited detail with few individual activities each of more than 10% of the overall duration.
2 Relatively detailed; number of activites reflects items of work or deliverables, each activity is less than 10% of the overall duration.
3 Detailed; number of activites reflects indvidual items of work or single deliverables, each activity is less than 1% of the overall duration.

Programme Machine
[LUL] An electrically operated machine that controls the setting of **Routes** and **Signals** according to a predetermined sequence, timing or trigger conditions based on the timetable.

Programme Machine Roll
[LUL] The replaceable plastic roll within a **Programme Machine** that contains **Timetable** and **Train** routing information.

Programme Only Mode
[LUL] A **Junction Mode** where the **Programme Machine** will only work to the **Timetable** (**TT**).

Progressive Collapse
[Civ.] The ultimate failure of a complete structure, such as a multi-**Span** □ **Bridge**, as a result of a failure of part of the structure triggering the failure of other parts, and so on.

Progressive Driving
[Ops.] Alternative term for **Defensive Driving**.

Prohibition Notice
A notice issued by the **Office of Rail Regulation** (**ORR**) that prohibits a work activity until remedial action is taken.

Project Ariel
[NR Hist.] The alternative "rescue" plan carried out by the then Secretary of State for Transport, Stephen Byers, involving replacing a bankrupt **Railtrack** (**RT**) with a not-for-profit company (initially RenewCo, later called **Network Rail** (**NR**)). Sadly the shareholders of Railtrack received a derisory sum for their shares.

Project Elephant
[RT] A project whose purpose was to assess feasibility and costs of increasing **Freight Vehicle** payloads and **Maximum Axle Loads**.

Project Engineer (PE)
[NR] A post responsible for the assisting on the development, checking and approval of engineering designs. Analogous to a **Contractor's Responsible Engineer** (**CRE**).

Project Evergreen
[RT, NR] A **Railtrack** project supporting the 20-year Chiltern Railway franchise. Comprising three phases, the project provided **Linespeed** increases, **Headway** improvements and **Bi-directional Signalling**.

Project Interface Coordinator (PIC)
[NR] A single point of contact from the **Maintenance** organisation whose role is to liaise between a project and that Maintenance organisation.

Project Mercury
[BR, RT] A project in which Mercury, a Public **Telecommunications** Operator (**PTO**), laid its Fibre Optic Cables (**FOC**) in **Cable Troughs** on the **Railway**.

Project Rainbow
[RT] The rescue plan proposed by **Railtrack** (**RT**) in 2001, involving Government finance for a restructuring of the company and writing off a considerable debt. This proposal was rejected by the then Secretary of State for Transport, Stephen Byers, in favour of **Project Ariel**.

Project Release
[RT] An initiative started in 1998 to classify, review and rationalise **Railtrack Line Standards** (**RLS**). See **Network Rail Company Standards** (**NRCS**).

Project Resolve
[RT] An initiative aimed at spreading awareness of Railtrack Line Standards (RLS). See Network Rail Company Standards (NRCS).

PROMISE
(*prom-iss*) Planning and Resources Monitoring System.

PROMPT
(*prompt*) [RT] Priority on Managing Performance Trends: a Railtrack (RT) performance improvement initiative.

PROMT
(*promt*) Programme Management Team.

Propel

Propelling
[Ops.] The act of pushing a Train from the rear using a Locomotive, where the driver is not driving from the Leading End. See also Set Back.

Propelling Control Vehicle (PCV)
[TRS] A Rail Vehicle fitted with Automatic Brake control, Horn control and a headlamp, allowing it to be the vehicle at the Leading End of a Train being Propelled. A Guard uses these controls, whilst the driver has control over the Regulator at the rear.

Propelling Move
Propelling Movement
[Ops.]
a) A Movement made with a Train using a Locomotive at the rear
b) A movement where the driver is not driving from the leading Cab of the Leading Vehicle.
c) See Propelling.

Proposal
See Relaying Proposal.

Propped Cantilever
[Civ.] A Cantilever structure which has a pin-jointed prop at its "outer" end.

Protected
[RB] When a Train is involved in an incident or cannot be moved for other reasons when on a Running Line, the Rule Book requires it to be Protected from Movements of other Trains which might otherwise collide with it. This protection involves:
- Placing Signals to Danger;
- Use of Track Circuit Operating Clips;
- Showing a Red □ Flag or light;
- Use of Detonators, if there are no suitable Signals nearby.

Protected Manual
[LUL] The manual mode of driving using the Traction Brake Controller where the Train is protected by the Automatic Train Protection (ATP) system and where the speed is limited to that allowed by the ATP system.

Protected Wrong Side Failure (PWSF)
[Sig.] A situation where the Signalling System fails the wrong side of safety, and where the resulting situation is protected by other measures or other Signals. See also Unprotected Wrong Side Failure (UWSF) Wrong Side Failure (WSF).

Protecting Signal
[Sig.]
a) A Signal that prevents Trains from entering a Section where Conflicting Movements may take place
b) The The last signal on the Approach to a Level Crossing (LC, LX) that the Signaller may place at Danger in the event of an emergency situation
c) The Signal that is used to protect a Possession
d) The Signal preventing Train Movements towards a particular point, such as an Obstruction.

Protection
a) See Protection of the Line
b) See Protection Arrangements.

Protection Arrangements
The specific details of a Possession of the Line:
- Where it begins and ends (the Possession Limits)
- Which Lines are Blocked
- Where the Detonator Protection is to be placed
- Which Signals are to be maintained at Danger
- Which Points are to be Secured and whether Normal or Reverse,

Protection Controller (PC)
[NR] A nominated competent person whose duties are to arrange and manage the Possession arrangements where two or more Controllers of Site Safety (COSS) are working under the same Protection.

Protection Duties
[RB] The duties carried out by the driver and Guard in accordance with the Rule Book (Module M, Train Stopped by Train Accident, Fire, or Accidental Division) to protect Trains from other Traffic in the event of an Accident.

Protection Key Switch
[LUL] A device used to Replace □ Semi-automatic Signals to Danger to provide protection for staff going onto the Track. See also Signal Post Replacement Key.

Protection Master
[LUL] The person responsible for providing protection from operational risks during Traffic Hours or Engineering Hours. The Protection Master's certificate will be endorsed to show Traffic Hours or Engineering Hours or both.

Protection of the Line
a) The marking of the limits of a portion of Line that has been Blocked
b) The emergency action carried to protect a mishap or failed Train
In either case normal measures may include placing Detonators on the Rail, Possession Limit Boards (PLB), Handsignals, Keying a Signal to Danger, using Track Circuit Operating Clips or applying Track Circuit Operating Devices (TCOD).

Protection Planking
An alternative term for **Guard Boarding**.

Protection Wire
A bare **Conductor** connected to the **Overhead Line Structures** whose purpose is to carry any **Insulator Flashover** away to the **Traction Return Circuit**, where the **Return Conductor** (**RC**) is insulated from the **Structures**.

PROTIM
(*pro-tim*) [Ops.] A computer based system for calculating **Train** timings, arranging **Paths** and creating **Timetables** (**TT**).

Prototype, The
[Col.] The term used by **Railway** modellers to describe the system their model is based on, namely the real, full-size Railway.

Proved
Proving
[Sig.] A **Function** fitted to an item of **Signalling Equipment** to verify its correct operation. Should correct operation cease, another part of the **Signalling System** will protect the failed equipment until the problem can be rectified. A particular example would be in a **Colour Light Signal** where a set of **Lamp Proving** □ **Relays** monitor the current drawn by each lamp, and should one fail the **Signal** □ **On the Approach to** it will display a **Stop Aspect**. See also **Detection, Fail Safe**.

PRoW
Public Right of Way.

PRR
[Sig.] Panel □ Route Request.

PRS
[NR]
a) Programme Requirements Specification, also PgRS
b) Project Requirements Specification, also PjRS.

PRT
a) **Possession** Round **Train**, describing the taking of a Possession around an **Engineering Train** or **On Track Machine** (**OTM**). This method removes delays from Possessions in which the only **Engineering Worksite** is an On Track Machine
b) [NR] Under the **Bridge Condition Marking Index** (**BCMI**) handbook, shorthand for **Pier** or trestle
c) Personal Rapid Transit.

Prud'homme Equation
[TRS] A mathematical description of the maximum lateral force a **Wheelset** can be subjected to without **Derailing**:

$$Y = \frac{W}{3} + 10$$

Where:
- Y is the maximum permissible lateral force in kilo Newtons (kN)
- W is the static **Axleload** in kN.

To avoid shifting the **Track**, the average lateral force measured over a 2m length should be less than the value deduced from the equation. Developed by A. Prud'homme in the 1960s. See also **Derailment Quotient**

PR*xxx*
PR*xxx*A
(Tradename) [PW] Types of **Pandrol Rail Clip**.

PS
a) See **Permissible Speed**
b) See **Private Siding**
c) Position Switch.

PSA
See **Private Siding Agreement**

PSB
See **Power Signal Box**

PSC
Project Safety Case.

PSD
Platform □ Stepping Distance.

Pseudotsuga Menziesii
Douglas Fir. See **Softwood Sleeper**.

PSI
See **Permissible Speed Indicator**.

PSICA
(*pea-seeka*) [NR] Primary **Signalling** □ **Infrastructure** Condition Assessment. See also **SICA, SSICA**.

PSK
[TRS] An acronym representing a **Pullman** Kitchen Second Class □ **Coach**.

PSLG
[NR] Project Safety Leadership Group.

PSM
[Sig.] PC **SPAD** Monitor.

PSN
See **Possession Strategy Notice**.

PSO
a) Public Service Obligation. See **Public Service Obligation Grant** (**PSOG**)
b) [LUL] Published Switch Off.

PSOG
(*pea-sog*) See **Public Service Obligation Grant**.

PSP
a) Power Supply Point
b) Principal Supply Point
c) [TRS] An acronym representing a Pullman Parlour **Second Class** □ **Coach**.

PSPP
[NR] Particular Specification for Possession Planning.
PSR
a) See Permanent Speed Restriction
b) Public Service Requirement.
PSSI
[Sig.] Pseudo Solid State Interlocking (SSI).
PSTN
[Tel.] Public Switched Telephone Network.
PSU
a) Power Supply Unit
b) Power Supply Upgrade.
PSUP
[NR] Power Supply Upgrade Project.
PT&R
Promotion Transfer and Redundancy.
PTA
See Passenger Transport Authority.
PTB
[TRS] An acronym representing a Pullman □ Brake □ Third Class □ Coach.
PTBSO
[TRS] An acronym representing a Pantograph □ Trailer □ Brake □ Second Class □ Open Coach.
PTC
Positive Train Control.
PTE
See Passenger Transport Executive.
PTEG
Public Transport Executive Group
PTF
[TRS] An acronym representing a Pantograph □ Trailer □ First Class □ Coach.
PTG
a) [PW] Poor Track Geometry
b) Passenger Transport Grant.
PTI
a) See Platform Train Interface
b) See Positive Train Identification.
PTI Corridor
See Dispatch Corridor.
PTM
Permanent Timetable Manager.
PTO
a) [Hist.] Principal Technical Officer, originally a British Railways (BR) grade
b) [Tel.] Public Telecommunications Operator (e.g. British Telecom, Mercury). See also BRT, Thales.
PTP
[TRS] An acronym representing a Pullman Parlour Third Class □ Coach.
PTQ
[PW] Predicted Track Quality.
PTS
a) See Personal Track Safety
b) Positive Train Separation.

PTSH
Personal Track Safety Handbook.
PTSO
[TRS] An acronym representing a Pantograph □ Trailer □ Standard Class □ Open Coach.
PTSRMB
[TRS] An acronym representing a Pantograph □ Trailer □ Standard Class □ Coach with buffet/shop.
PTT
Perturbed Test Track.
PTW
Permit To Work.
PTZ
Pan Tilt Zoom, a facility fitted to CCTV cameras.
Public / Book Differential
[NR Ops.] An offset introduced between the Working Timetable (WTT) and Public Timetable for a particular Train.
Public Emergency Telephone System (PETS)
[NR Tel.] A special telephone system for use at Level Crossings (LC, LX) that includes circuit integrity and Level Crossing status indication facilities. The speech system takes priority.
Public Performance Measure (PPM)
[NR] The percentage of franchised Passenger Trains arriving at their destination, having made all Booked Calls, and within a specified lateness margin (typically five minutes for local services and ten minutes for long-distance services).
Public Railway
A Railway system that is run for the good of the public in general, a term also used to infer some degree of State control. See Private Railway.
Public Service Obligation Grant (PSOG)
[BR Hist.] The money paid by HM Treasury to finance the continued operation of loss making but necessary Lines. The Grant's value decreased steadily in the latter years of British Railways, due largely to increased efficiency. It stopped at Privatisation.
Public Timetable
[NR ops.] The Timetable (TT) made available to the Passenger. It is different from the Working Timetable (WTT) in that it only shows Trains on which the public may travel, and the times are given to the minute, not the half minute. See also Great Britain Passenger Railway Timetable (GBRPT).
Puffin (ZCV)
[NR] A type of Spoil Wagon, converted from a Catfish (ZEV).
PUG
See Passenger Upgrade.
Pull Force
[PW] The force required to extend a Continuous Welded Rail to a pre-determined length, thus raising its Stress Free Temperature (SFT) above its Rail Temperature. Typical Tensors can generate up to 690kN (equivalent to 70 tonnes) of Pull Force for this operation.

Pull Length
[PW] The amount of **Free Rail** tensioned during a particular single **Stressing** operation. Also **Free Rail**.

Pull Off
a) [Sig.] To Pull Off is to operate the controls for a **Signal** such that it then shows a less restrictive **Aspect** or a **Proceed Aspect**. In **Mechanical Signalling** it is a literal description of the action of the **Signaller** pulling the relevant **Lever**. See also **Put Back**.
b) [Elec.] A **Registration Point** in an **Overhead Line** ▫ **Catenary** which acts in tension, pulling the Catenary laterally. See also **Push Off**.

Pull Plate
[Sig.] An alternative term for a **Lever Plate**, **Lever Nomenclature Plate**. Also **Lever Badge**, **Lever Tablet**.

Pull Rod
See **Connecting Rod**.

Pull Test
[Ops.] A test of brake retarding force, carried out by measuring the force required to pull a **Rail Vehicle** along the **Track** with its brakes applied.

Pulled Off
[Col.] Describing a **Signal** that has been changed from displaying a **Stop Aspect** to a **Caution Aspect** or **Proceed Aspect** by the action of a **Signaller**. See also **Pull Off**.

Pulling Back
Pulling Back Rails
[PW] The activity of moving **Rails** in **Jointed Track** longitudinally as part of **Joint Regulating**.

Pulling Point
[PW] The location at which a length of **Free Rail** is tensioned to the appropriate **Pull Force** during a **Stressing** operation and the **Closing Weld** made.

Pulling the String
[Col.] Operating the manual brake release (which is often a length of string) on an **Air Braked** vehicle.

Pulling Through
[PW] The task of providing a relatively undamaged **Rail Seat** on a **Timber** or **Wood Sleeper** by unfastening the **Baseplates** or **Chairs**, removing the **Ballast** from the end of the Timber or Sleeper for the direction it is to be moved, sliding the Timber or Sleeper longitudinally under the Baseplates or Chairs, refastening them and replacing the Ballast.

PUM
(*pumm*) (Tradename) [PW] Portique Universal Manutention, Produced by **Geismar**, a system of wheeled lifting gantries, elevating wheeled platforms and lightweight sectional **Track** which is used to transport very large **Switch and Crossing Layouts** (**S&C Layouts**) whole, reducing the length of time required to install them. Such systems are generically known as **Panel Lifting Equipment**. See also **Fassetta**, **LEM**, **PAL**, **PEM**, **PLUM**.

Pump Handle
A temporary handle used to operate **Clamp Lock** hydraulic pump units manually during times of failure or disconnection. They are normally stored in a special **Operator's Cupboard** or in the **Controlling Signal Box**. A **Crank Handle** performs a similar function for **Point Machines**.

Pump Train
[LUL] **Train** used to pump out and unblock **Trackside** drainage. See also **Drain Train**.

Pumping
a) [PW] A failure mode of the **Formation**, where fine material is forced up through the **Ballast** by the action of passing **Trains**. See also **Formation Failure**, **Wet Beds**
b) See **Oversetting**.

PUMPS
[NR] A computer system which processes information contained in the **Train** ▫ **Running** System on **TOPS** (**TRUST**) and Fault Reporting and Monitoring & Equipment System (**FRAME**) databases to produce detail on delays caused by **Signalling** failures.

Purley Accident
At 13:39 on 4th March 1989 the driver of a **Passenger Train** failed to respond to two **Caution Aspects** and then passed a third **Signal** at **Danger**. Despite applying **Emergency Braking** the **Train** collided broadside at approximately 55mph with another service which was correctly crossing onto the same **Line**. The over-running Train **Derailed** and ran down an **Embankment**. Five **Passengers** were killed and 88 injured. The driver of the **Over-running** Train later pleaded guilty to manslaughter. This accident would have been prevented by a system such as the **Train Protection and Warning System** (**TPWS**).

Purple Sidings
[NR] The **Sidings** which are the responsibility of the **Private Siding** owner and which are usually located on their property. The term applies only to **Network Rail** ▫ **Connection Agreements** (**CA**) but is analogous to **Blue Sidings** in **Private Siding Agreements** (**PSA**).

Push Button
[LUL] The direct control of the settings of **Points** at a **Junction** by the **Service Operator** without the use of automatic equipment.

Push Off
[Elec.] A **Registration Point** in an **Overhead Line** ▫ **Catenary** where the **Registration Arm** acts in compression, pushing the Catenary laterally. See also **Pull Off** clause b).

Push Out
[LUL] The procedure by which a **Failed** ▫ **Train** is **Coupled** to and **Propelled** to a **Depot** or **Siding** by another Train.

Push Rod
[TRS] A rod that pushes the **Brake Blocks** against the **Wheel Tread**.

371

Push-Pull
Push/Pull
[Ops.] A method of **Train** operation where the **Locomotive** is permanently coupled at one end of the **Train** and a **Driving Cab**, generally in the form of a **Driving Van Trailer** (**DVT**) at the other (see also **Auto-train**). This removes the need to **Run Round** the **Train**. If the second Driving Cab is provided in the form of another Locomotive, then this is called **Top and Tail** working.

Put Away
Put Inside
[Ops. Col.] A term meaning to divert a **Train** into a **Goods Loop** or to **Shunt** it into a **Refuge Siding**.

Put Back
[Sig. Col.] (verb) To operate the controls for a **Signal** such that it then shows a more restrictive **Aspect** or a **Stop Aspect**. In **Mechanical Signalling** it is a literal description of the action of the **Signaller** pushing the relevant **Lever**. See also **Pull Off** clause a).

Putting The Bag In
[Col.] Filling a **Steam Locomotive's** tanks or the **Tender** thereof with water. See **Bag**.

PUWER
(*pue-err*) Provision and Use of Work Equipment Regulations 1998.

PVC
See **Point of Vertical Curve**.

PVG
[TRS] An acronym representing a **Gangwayed Packing Van**.

PVI
See **Point of Vertical Intersection**.

PVT
See **Point of Vertical Tangency**.

PVT Clip
[PW Obs.] A type of **Rail Fastening** used in **Switch And Crossing Layouts** (**S&C Layouts**) with **Shallow Depth Switches**. The Clip is used to secure the **Gauge** side of the **Rail Foot** of the **Stock Rails**.

PW
a) See **Permanent Way**. Also **Per Way**, **PWay**
b) See **Parallel Wing**.

PWay
A contraction of **Permanent Way** (**PW**).

PWHT
Post-weld Heat Treatment.

PWI
a) See **Permanent Way Institution, The**
b) [PW] **Permanent Way** Instruction
c) [IÉ] Permanent Way Inspector.

PWI-brow
(*pee-double-you-eye-brow*) [Col.] The propensity of older **Permanent Way** Engineers to sport bushy eyebrows.

PWL
[PW] Parallel Wing Left, see **Left Hand Parallel Wing** (**LHPW**).

PWM
a) See **Permanent Way Maintenance**
b) Pulse Width Modulation, a method of controlling the speed of **Traction Motors** by the controlled switching of the supply. See also **Chopper**.

PWMA
[PW] Permanent Way Maintenance (PWM) Assistant.

PWME
[PW] Permanent Way Maintenance (PWM) Engineer.

PWR
a) [PW] Parallel Wing Right, see **Right Hand Parallel Wing** (**RHPW**)
b) See **Parallel Wing Rail**
c) Passenger Warning Relay.

PWRA
See **Private Wagon Registration Agreement**.

PWRAMG
Private Wagon Registration Agreement Management Group.

PWS
[PW]
a) See **Permanent Way Section**
b) Permanent Way Supervisor.

PWSF
See **Protected Wrong Side Failure**.

PWSI
[PW] Permanent Way (PW) Special Instruction.

PWSM
[PW] Permanent Way Section (PWS) Manager.

PWSS
[PW] Permanent Way Section (PWS) Supervisor.

PYS
[TRS] Primary Yaw Stiffness, see **Yaw Damper**.

PZT
See **Point Zone Telephone**.

Q

Q

a) [NR] As the last letter in a **Wagon** □ **CARKND**, this denotes that the Wagon is **Through Piped** for **Air Brakes**, which do not operate the vehicle brakes. This means it has no **Automatic Brakes** or **Continuous Brakes**. Also known as **Air Piped**. See also **Unfitted**
b) See **Q Path**
c) [Sig.] On a **Signalling Circuit Diagram**:
- As one of the leading letters of an **Equipment Code**, it means bar or **Treadle**
- As the last letter of an Equipment Code, it means bar, local coil of a **Double Element Relay** or **Treadle**

d) The letter represented by **Quebec** in the **Phonetic Alphabet**
e) In equations, the letter normally used to represent vertical wheel forces. See also **Y**.
f) **Common Interface File Operating Characteristics Code** for Runs as required.

Q Path

[NR Ops.] A **Path** to which no **Train** is actually identified in the **Timetable** (**TT**); such Paths are used when required.

Q Stock

[LUL] Type of older **Rolling Stock** used on the District Line until the early 1970s. It was formed from a mixture of old and some newer vehicles introduced in 1938.

Q Train

[NR] A **Train** conveying **British Transport Police** (**BTP**) officers and surveillance equipment, to catch and charge trespassers and vandals found along the **Line**.

Q/D limit

[NR TRS] The maximum ratio of static **Wheel Load** (Q) to Wheel Tread Diameter (D) or twice the **Rolling Radius**. The current limit of 0.13 is based on representative Q/D ratios in use on the **Rail Network** at the time the relevant standard was developed.

QCRA

Quantitative Cost Risk Assessment.

QDR

Qualitative Design Review.

Qlink

[NR] The database operated by **Linkup** which holds information relating to prequalification of suppliers to the **Railway Industry**.

QRA

a) Quantitative Risk Analysis, a method by which the likely project cost can be estimated by costing the "risk" items, and producing a probability distribution for the various factors
b) Qualitative Risk Assessment, a process by which likely risks are identified and their potential likelihood and impact assessed
c) Quantified Risk Assessment.

QRBSS

Queensland Risk Based Scoring System.

QSRA

Quantitative Schedule Risk Assessment.

QTron

[TRS] A type of **On Train Monitoring Recorder** (**OTMR**) or "Black Box".

Quadrification

Adding a **Track** or Tracks to make a **Four Track Railway**. See also **Doubling**.

Quadruple Junction

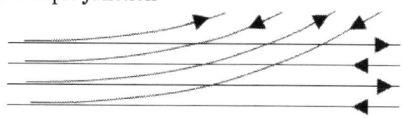

[PW] A **Junction** where one **Four Track** □ **Route** meets another. See also **Double Junction**.

Quadruple Track

A section of **Railway** where there are four parallel **Running Lines**.

Quail Map

(Tradename) [Col.] The name used for a suite of **Track Diagrams**, grouped by **British Railways** (**BR**) □ **Region**, showing **Track** layout, **Junction Names**, **Stations**, **Mileages** and other information. Originally published in the late 1980s by the Quail Map Company (now **Trackmaps**), they contain detailed track-level information and are standard references in the **Railway Industry**.

Quarter Chord

[PW] Additional alignment information calculated at the quarter and three-quarter positions of each **Chord** in a **Transition Curve**. Their aim is to aid the setting out of the Transition, the most difficult type of geometry.

Quebec

The **Phonetic Alphabet** word representing Q.

Queen Points

The **Turnout** forming the second division of a **Fan** of **Sidings**.

Queenie

[Obs.] The obsolescent **Phonetic Alphabet** word representing Q. Replaced by **Quebec**.

QUENSH

Quality, Environment, Safety, Health

Quercus Robur

Oak. See **Key**.

Quick

[Col.] An alternative to **Fast**, as in **Up** Quick.

Quick Swings

[Col.] The practice whereby when the **Level Crossing Gates** of a **Manned Level Crossing** (**MB**) are closed upon a request from the **Signaller**, the **Crossing Keeper** requests that the **Gates** are then opened for a short period to allow road traffic to cross. The Signaller decides whether there is enough time for this to take place before the train reaches the Crossing.

ELLIS' BRITISH RAILWAY ENGINEERING ENCYCLOPÆDIA

Quill Drive
[TRS] A method of separating the heavy **Traction Motors** from the axle to reduce impact forces on the **Track**. The Traction Motor is fixed to the **Bogie** and drives one end of a hollow tube via a flexible coupling. The other end is connected to the axle via a similar coupling and the axle passes through the tube to connect the wheels. This arrangement allows the axle to move freely and independently of the Traction Motor. See also **Axle Hung**, **Nose Hung**.

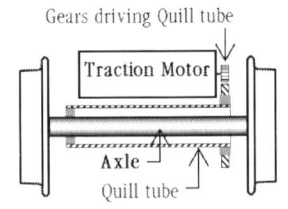

Quintinshill Accident
The disaster which occurred near Quintinshill on the 22nd May 1915 cuased the greatest loss of life in any single UK **Railway** □ **Accident**. Operating irregularities led to the **Signaller** accepting a **Troop Train** and an **Express Passenger Train** from opposite directions into a stretch of **Line** already occupied by two **Freight Trains** and a **Local Passenger Train**. The Signaller was distracted by **Train Crew** in the **Signal Box** (**SB**), and the area was not equipped with **Track Circuits** (**TC**). In the resulting collision and fire (fed by gas cylinders used for lighting the Trains) 227 **Passengers** and troops died and 245 were injured.

Quoit
[Hist.] On a **Rope-hauled Railway** a circular metal ring forming part of the rope coupling which secured the over-centre pivoted steel bar of the coupling until released (kicked off) by the bank rider to detach the set from the haulage rope. See also **Kicking the Quoit**.

QY&MJR
[Hist.] The **Pre-Grouping** Quaker's Yard & Merthyr Joint **Railway**, a Great Western and Rhymney joint enterprise.

374

R

R
a) Abbreviation for Radius
b) [NR] As the last letter in a **Wagon** □ CARKND, this denotes that the Wagon is **Through Piped** for both **Vacuum Brakes** and **Air Brakes**, neither system operating the vehicle brakes. This means it has no **Automatic Brake** or **Continuous Brake**. Also known as **Dual Piped**. See also **Unfitted**
c) [NR] As the first letter of a Wagon CARKND, it means that the vehicle is a **Barrier Vehicle** or similar
d) In an abbreviated **Track Name**, it denotes **Relief**, as in **Relief Line**
e) See **Speed Reminder Sign**
f) [Sig.] On a **Signal**, see **Right Away Indicator** (RAI)
g) [Sig.] On a **Signalling Circuit Diagram**:
• An individual connection to the return side of a power supply
• As one of the leading letters of an **Equipment Code**, it means danger (**Red**), **Reverse** or right. See also **NBDR**
• As the last letter of an Equipment Code, it means **Relay** or **Contactor**
h) The letter represented by **Romeo** in the **Phonetic Alphabet**.
i) **Common Interface File Operating Characteristics Code** for air conditioned with PA system.

R Board
[LUL] A red **Lineside** sign which has a black R and a white cross at a **Station** when there is defective radio equipment ahead.

R Door
[LUL] Hinged connecting doors between **Cars**. Also **S Door**.

R Stock
[LUL] District **Line** □ **Rolling Stock** introduced in batches from 1947 to 1959. The 1949 batch (known as R49 Stock) was the first London Underground stock to be constructed with aluminium bodies and some **Cars** were delivered unpainted; unpainted bodies were universally adopted by LU until the 1992 Tube Stock.

R&CT
[Hist.] The **Pre-Grouping** Rye & Camber **Tramway**.

R&KFR
[Hist.] The **Pre-Grouping** Rowrah & Kelton Fell **Railway**.

R&R
a) [Sig.] Rationalisation and **Resignalling**
b) Rest and Recuperation
c) [Sig.] Common shorthand for Ransome & Rapier, a former manufacturer of **Signalling Equipment** and **Rail Cranes**.

R&SBR
[Hist.] The **Pre-Grouping** Rhondda & Swansea Bay **Railway**.

R&VM
Risk and Value Management.

R(SCW)
See **Railway** (**S**afety **C**ritical **W**ork) Regulations 1994.

R/G
[Sig.] **R**ed / **G**reen □ **Miniature Warning Lights** (**MWL**), used at certain low-traffic **Level Crossings**. See **Miniature Stop Lights** (**MSL**).

R/T
a) See **Railtrack**
b) **R**ight **T**ime.

R2P2
Reducing **R**isks, **P**rotecting **P**eople.

RA
a) See **Route Availability**
b) See **Right Away**. See also **Right Away Indicator** (RAI).

Ra Ra
Rail on - **Ra**il off, describing a sea ferry equipped with Rails and capable of loading and unloading **Rail Vehicles** in the normal **Railway** manner. Also **RoRo**.

RA93
See **Railways Act 1993**.

RAB
Regulatory **A**sset **B**ase.

Rabbit's Ears
[Sig., Col.] A **Junction Indicator** (**JI**), particularly one with position 1 and position 4.

RACI
Responsible, **A**ccountable, **C**onsulted, **I**nformed.

Rack Railway
A **Railway** on which the normal **Adhesion** of wheel on **Rail** has been supplemented by a toothed wheel fitted to the prime mover, meshing with a toothed rack fixed to the **Track**. See also **Abt Rack System**.

RACOP
(*ray-cop* or *rac-op*) [NR] **R**ailway **S**afety **A**pproved **C**ode **o**f **P**ractice, previously **Railtrack** Approved Code of Practice.

RADAR Report
[RT] The **R**oute **A**nalysis and **D**ynamics **A**ssessment **R**esearch Report, commissioned in 2001 by the **Strategic Rail Authority** (**SRA**) to investigate why **Performance** on the **Railway** had not recovered to pre-**Hatfield Accident** levels after the **Renewals** programme was completed, based on analysis of delay attribution data recorded in **TRUST**

Radial Arm
[TRS] Part of a **Wagon's** suspension that houses the end of a **Wheelset** at one end and connects to the **Bogie** at the other.

Radio Block Centre (RBC)
[Sig.] The part of the **European Rail Traffic Management System** (**ERTMS**) that issues **Movement Authorities** (**MA**) to **Trains** via the **Global System for Mobile Communications – Railways** (**GSM-R**).

ELLIS' BRITISH RAILWAY ENGINEERING ENCYCLOPÆDIA

Radio Electronic Token Block (RETB)
[NR Sig.] A **Signalling System** used mainly on **Single Lines**, where an **Electronic Token** is transmitted between the **Controlling Signal Box** and **Train**. It is a modern development of **Electric Token Block (ETB)** □ **Signalling** in which the **Token** takes the form of an encoded data message transmitted to a receiver on the **Train**. The system ensures that only one Train is in possession of any single radio token at one time, and that the preceding Train is **Clear** of the **Section** concerned before re-issuing it to the next Train. It was developed to allow cost effective **Signalling** on sparsely populated **Lines**, particularly the Highlands of Scotland and Welsh coastal areas.

Radio Survey Coach (RSC)
[NR] These converted **Passenger Coaches** (977868 and 977997) are used to survey coverage and reliability of **Global System for Mobile Communications - Railway (GSM-R)**, **National Radio Network (NRN)** and **Cab Secure Radio (CSR)**.

RADSAFE
(*radsafe*) A consortium of organisations that have come together to offer mutual assistance in the event of a transport accident involving radioactive materials. In the event of such an accident, RADSAFE deploys appropriate experts to the site in order to advise emergency services and other organisations.

RAFT
a) (*raft*) [PW] **Rail Force Transducer**, a device which, when fitted to a **Continuous Welded Rail (CWR)**, can deduce the **Stress Condition** of that Rail. See also **Verse Testing**
b) Regulatory Agreement on Fares and Ticketing.

Raft
[Ops.] Two or more **Locomotives**, **Multiple Units** or similar **Wagons** coupled together. See also **String**.

Rafted Station
A **Station** that has a structure of sufficient plan area built over it as to render the Station a **Sub-surface Station** under the **Fire Precautions (Sub-surface Railway Stations) Regulations 1989**. Birmingham New Street is an example of this.

RAG
a) (*rag*) Red, Amber and Green
b) Regulatory Accounting Guidelines.

RAI
[NPT] See **Right Away Indicator**

RAIB
See **Rail Accident Investigation Branch**.

Rail
[PW]
a) A special rolled steel section used to support and guide vehicles on a **Railway**
- Parts of; see **Ankle**, **Back Edge**, **Field Side**, **Flange**, **Gauge Side**, **Lower Fillet**, **Lower Fishing Surface**, **Outside Edge (OE)**, **Rail Crown**, **Rail End**, **Rail Foot**, **Rail Head**, **Rail Web**, **Running Band**, **Running Edge (RE)**, **Running Face**, **Upper Fillet**, **Upper Fishing Surface**
- Descriptions of, see **Rail Depth**, **Rail Section**, **Rail Weight**

- Types of; see **Aluminium Stainless Conductor Rail (ASC Rail)**, **Barlow Rail**, **Bridge Rail**, **Bull Head Rail (BH)**, **Conductor Rail**, **Continuous Welded Rail (CWR)**, **Crane Rail**, **Flat Bottom Rail (FB)** **Forth Bridge Rail**, **Grooved Rail**, **HUSH Rail**, **Jointed Rail**, **Long Welded Rail (LWR)**
- Uses of; see **Check Rail**, **Closure Rail**, **Guard Rail**, **Plant Rail**, **Running Rail**, **Service Rail**, **Slave Rail**, **Strap Rail**
- **Switch and Crossing (S&C)** Rails; see **Belly Rail**, **Foot Relief**, **Gut Rail**, **Joggled Stock Rail**, **Point Rail**, **Splice Rail**, **Stock Rail**, **Switch Rail**, **Wing Rail**
- Alloys, see **Bainitic Rail**, **Chrome Rail**, **Low Carbon Austenitic Manganese Steel (LCAMS)**
- States of; see **Blemished Rail**, **Defective Rail**, **New Rail**, **Scrap Rail**, **Serviceable Rail**
- Faults and defects in; see **Corrugation**, **Crippled Rail**, **Baseplate Gall**, **Chair Gall**, **Gauge Corner Cracking (GCC)**, **Field Flow**, **Head Checking**, **Lipping**, **Mushrooming**, **Piping**, **Rolling Defects**, **Sidecutting**, **Sidewear**, **Star Cracks**, **Squats**, **Tache Ovale**, **Tongue Lipping**, **Wheelburns**, **Wires**
- Prepared Rails; see **Back Hole Drilled**, **Drilled Both Ends (DBE)**, **Drilled One End (DOE)**, **Eutectic Strip**, **Flash Butt Welded (FBW)**, **Pre-curved Rail**, **Ramp End**, **Standard Rail**, **Standard Short Rail**, **Transition Rail**, **Un-drilled (UD)**, **Zigzag Welding**

b) A generic term describing transport by means of a **Railway** (i.e. going by Rail)
c) Common suffix added to the titles of subsidiary companies specialising in Railway works, e.g. Carillion Rail, Balfour Beatty Rail (Tradenames).

Rail / Wheel Interface
Collective term describing the complex interactions present between a **Rail** and a moving **Rail Wheel**.

Rail Accident Investigation Branch (RAIB)
An independent body enacted under the **Railways and Transport Safety Act 2003 (RTSA)**, whose function is to ensure that all accidents on the national **Railways** of Great Britain are thoroughly and independently investigated. It is administratively part of the Department for Transport (**DfT**) See also **Railway Safety and Standards Board (RSSB)**.

Rail Adhesion Train
[LUL] A Train used in the application of LULS3 during the **Leaf Fall Season**.

Rail Adjusting
Rail Adjustment
[PW] The activity of moving **Jointed Rails** longitudinally to obtain the correct **Expansion Gaps** and to **Square** the **Fishplated Rail Joints**. Also **Joint Regulating**, **Pulling Back**.

Rail Alloy
[PW] The metallurgical composition of the **Rail**, see Bainitic **Rail**, **Chrome Rail**, **Low Carbon Austenitic Manganese Steel (LCAMS)**.

Rail Anchor
[PW]
a) A manufactured steel clip fitted to the underside of the **Rail Foot** which bears against the vertical face of a **Sleeper** or **Chair**, fitted to increase the assemblies' resistance to longitudinal **Rail Creep**. See **BRR**, **Fair T**, **Fair V**, **MF Anchor**
b) See **Conductor Rail Anchor**
c) See **Train Anchor**.

Rail Attachment
[LUL] A device placed on the **Conductor Rails** to obtain a **Traction Current** supply for the movement of a **Train**. This device consists of a contact plate with a wood-sided shroud. See also **Gapped**.

Rail Authority
An organisation legally and financially responsible for the operation of a **Railway**. See also **Infrastructure Controller**.

Rail Beam
[PW] A spreader beam that allows a single jib crane to safely lift **Rails** and **Switches** up to 60 feet (18.288m) in length.

Rail Bearer
[Civ.] A component member in a **Bridge Deck** that runs directly beneath each **Rail**, spanning across or between the **Cross Girders**. The Rail Bearer may not be in contact with the **Track**.

Rail Bearing Area
[PW] The area of a **Baseplate** or **Sleeper** on which the **Rail** sits directly.

Rail Bonding
[Sig., Elec.] Electrical interconnection of **Rails** to provide a minimum of resistance for electric current, see **Track Circuit Bonding**, □ **Traction Bonding**.

Rail Branding
[PW] Raised markings on a **Rail Web** that identifies rail type, material grade, date of manufacture and the name or initials of the manufacturer. See **Brand Mark**, **Branding**.

Rail Callipers
[PW] A compass-like device with inward-facing points used to measure the distance between the top and bottom or opposite sides of a **Rail**. The tips of the calliper are adjusted to fit across the points to be measured, the calliper is then removed and the distance read by measuring between the tips with a ruler.

Rail Centre Line
Rail Centres
[PW] A line or point located halfway across the **Rail Head**. The distance between the **Rail Centres** of the **Running Rails** is used when calculating **Cant Deficiency** and **Equilibrium Speed** (V_e).

Rail Circuit
[Sig.] General term for **Train Detection** equipment using the **Rails** in an electric circuit which detects the presence of a **Train** (as opposed to its absence). This arrangement is not **Failsafe**. See **Track Circuit** (**TC**), **Overlay Track Circuit**.

Rail Clip
[PW]
a) A manufactured metal device for fixing **Flat Bottom Rails** (**FB**) either to a **Baseplate** or directly to a **Sleeper**. See also **Rail Fastening**
b) See also **Littleboy**.

Rail Corrugation
[PW] A pattern of alternate high and low areas spread along the **Rail Crown**. They are caused by the normal **Rail** / wheel interaction, and are generally removed by **Rail Grinding**. Colloquially known as **Roaring Rails**, Corrugation comes in two distinct types: **Short Wavelength Corrugation** and **Long Wavelength Corrugation**, which in some instances overlap.

Rail Crane
A crane mounted on **Rail Wheels**, generally capable of travelling along the **Track** under load, called **Free on Rail** (**FOR**).
• Prior to 1976, Rail Cranes of 5t, 8.5t, 10t and 18t capacities were available but were not designed to operate under the **Overhead Line Equipment** (**OLE**)
• In 1976 the General Purpose Crane (GPC) was introduced with a capacity of 12t
• The specialised **Recovery Cranes** are rated to 75 tonnes, but this rating is only achieved **Blocked**
• The largest Rail Cranes currently in use are the 125 tonnes **Kirow Cranes**
• **Road Rail** Excavators working in Rail Crane mode are normally rated in the 3 to 8 tonne range.

Rail Creep
[PW] The longitudinal movement of a **Rail** caused by one or more of a number of factors including traffic loading, thermal effects, **Rail Corrugation**, the effects of track gradient or train handling. In **Jointed Track** Rail Creep causes bunching up of Rails and this reduces the expansion gaps, making the rails more vulnerable to **Buckling**. Sometimes shortened to **Creep**.

Rail Crossing Diversion Order (RCDO)
An order under section 119A of the Highways Act 1980 covering the diversion of footpaths, bridleways and **Footpath Crossings** (**FP**) crossing **Railways**.

Rail Crossing Extinguishment and Diversion Orders Regulations 1993
Legislation defining how applications to close or divert footpaths and **Footpath Crossings** (**FP**) crossing **Railways** (including Bridleway crossings) should be prepared and managed. The Regulations came into force on 31st January 1993.

Rail Crossing Extinguishment Order (RCEO)
An order under section 119A of the Highways Act 1980 covering the stopping up of footpaths, bridleways and **Footpath Crossings** (**FP**) crossing **Railways**.

Rail Crown
[PW] The highest point of the **Running Surface** of a **Rail**.

Rail Datum Mark
[Sig.] As part of **Signal Sighting**, a temporary reference line inscribed across the **Rail Crown** of the **Left Hand Rail** (**LHR**) in exactly the same longitudinal position as the display. Used to assist measurement during positioning or Sighting a **Signal**.

Rail Defect
[PW] Any deformity, metallurgical fault or crack in a **Rail**. See also **Field Flow**, **Gauge Corner Cracking** (**GCC**), **Lipping**, **Mushrooming**, **Piping**, **Rail Corrugation**, **Rail Gall**, **Rolling Contact Fatigue** (**RCF**), **Rolling Defects**, **Sidecutting**, **Sidewear**, **Star Cracks**, **Taches Ovale**, **Tongue Lipping**, **Wheelburns**, **Wires**.

Rail Delivery Group (RDG)
[NR] A committee made up of the Chief Executives of the **Passenger** and **Freight** owning groups and **Network Rail** (**NR**).

Rail Depth
[PW] The minimum overall depth of a **Rail**, i.e. measured from **Rail Crown** to underside of **Rail Foot**.

Rail Dogs
[PW] A scissor-like tool with inward facing hooks at one end and handles at the other. Fitted with the hooks under the **Rail Head** and operated by two staff, the tool makes the task of lifting a **Rail** easier. Typically a member of staff would be assigned to lift one **Yard** of **Rail**, subject to a minimum of four staff per Rail. Also known as **Rail Nips**, **Rail Tongs**.

Rail Drill
[PW] A specially adapted drill for cutting **Fishbolt Holes** in **Rails**. In earlier days these were hand-operated chain drive machines, but these were replaced by devices equipped with small two stroke petrol engines. The most modern versions were electric, fed by a portable generator. All these were relatively slow twist drill based machines, but the **Rotabroach** system of an annular cutter powered by an electric motor is now virtually universal because of its high output rate.

Rail End
[PW] The end of a **Rail** prepared for joining to an adjacent Rail. See also **Drilled**.

Rail End Batter
[PW] A type of **Rail End** deformation found at **Fishplated Rail Joints**, where vertical movement of the two Rail Ends relative to each other has allowed passing **Rail Wheels** to impact the exposed corner of the **Rail Head**. This produces a flattened inclined area at the Rail End. The normal cause is a failure of the **Fishplates** to adequately fix the Rail Ends, in turn a result of loose or broken **Fishbolts** and poor **Ballast** conditions.

Rail Express Systems (RES)
[Hist.] The specialist parcels and **mail Freight Operating Unit** (**FOU**) formed under **Privatisation**, then part of **English, Welsh and Scottish Railways** (**EWS**) and now owned by **DB Schenker** Rail (UK) Ltd.

Rail Fastening
[PW] Any device used to secure **Rails** into **Chairs**, onto **Baseplates** or directly to **Sleepers** or **Bearers**. See **Rail Clip**, **Dogspike**, **Key**.

Rail Flaw
See **Rail Defect**.

Rail Flaw Detector
See **Ultrasonic Rail Flaw Detector** (**URFD**).

Rail Foot
[PW] The lower part of a **Rail Section**. Sometimes shortened to **Foot**.

Rail Foot Insulator
[PW] Preformed polymer (normally nylon) spacers fitted between the **Rail Clips** and cast-in **Rail Fastening** □ **Housings** (lugs on **Steel Sleepers**) to prevent the leakage of electrical current from **Rail** to **Earth** via the Fastenings. Also **Biscuit**, **Nylon**. Commonly contracted to **Insulator**.

Rail Freight
Freight transported by a **Railway**.

Rail Freight Group (RFG)
(Tradename) An organisation which has over 100 member companies, ranging from the world's largest container shipping line to high street retailers, including customers, logistics providers, suppliers, terminal operators, ports and **Freight Operating Companies** (**FOC**). It aims to serve the interests of members by improving the political, legal and planning environment in which the **Rail Freight** industry operates, to attract new investment and to promote the development of the industry through the organisations which use, supply and deliver competitive quality Rail Freight services.

Rail Gall
[PW] The loss of **Rail Section** around the **Rail Foot** caused by wear between a **Rail** and a **Baseplate** or **Chair**. Rail Gall can also be caused by **Concrete Sleepers** if the **Rail Pad** is allowed to deteriorate sufficiently.

Rail Gall of Baseplates
[PW] Wear of the vertical face of a **Baseplate** adjacent to the **Rail Foot**, caused by many faults, including poor alignment, **Rail Creep**, Sleepers being **Out of Square** and vertical **Rail** movement relative to the Baseplate.

Rail Gap
See **Conductor Rail Gap**.

Rail Gap Indicator
See **Current Rail Gap Indicator**.

Rail Gap Repeater
See **Current Rail Gap Repeater**.

Rail Gate Stop
[Sig.] A mechanical locking device, **Released** by a **Lever** in the Gate Box or **Signal Box**, which holds the **Level Crossing** (**LC**, **LX**) □ **Gates** closed across the **Railway**. See **Gate Stop Lever**, **Road Gate Stop**.

Rail Grinder
[PW] A petrol powered single stone grinder used by a **Track Welder** to remove the last part of the **Weld** riser and create a smooth longitudinal **Running Edge** (**RE**) and **Rail Crown**. The device is mounted centrally in a frame, in turn fitted with two **Rail Wheels** that provide the reference for the grinding operation. See also **Blending**, **Rail Grinding Train** (**RGT**).

Rail Grinding
[PW] Normally the grinding of a **Rail Head** to return it to its original profile, to remove minor surface cracks such as **Gauge Corner Cracking** (**GCC**) and **Head Checking** (**HC**) and to provide specific Rail Head profiles on the **High Rails** of **Curves** on higher speed **Routes**. This is typically carried out by a specialised **Rail Grinding Train** (**RGT**) or Rail Grinding Unit (**RGU**) although the term can be applied to grinding carried out using smaller manual **Rail Grinders**.

Rail Grinding Train (RGT)
[PW] An **On Track Machine** (**OTM**) equipped with a large number of grinding wheels. The machines are capable of restoring the correct profile to the **Rail Head** of both **Rails** at a considerable forward speed. Current machines use around 48 wheels per Rail, each one independently controlled for angle and depth of cut by a computer that optimises the treatment to remove the least possible metal. **Speno** is a tradename, and also a colloquial name for such **Trains**. See also **Loram**.

Rail Head
[PW] The bulbous upper part of a **Rail Section**. Related terms: **Running Edge** (**RE**), **Back Edge**, **Outside Edge** (**OE**), **Rail Crown**.

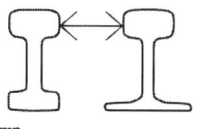

Rail Head Conditions
[Ops.] The state of the **Rail Head** in terms of the amount of adhesion or "grip" available to a **Train**. This can be adversely affected by **Snow** and ice, leaves, grease, etc. See also **Abnormal Rail Head Conditions**, **Defensive Driving**, **Leaf Fall Season**, **Leaf Fall Timetable**, **One Shot Sanders**, **Sanders**, **Sandite**, **Sandite Train**.

Rail Head Profile
[PW] The cross section shape of a **Rail Head**. See also **Rail Profile**.

Rail Head Treatment Train (RHTT)
[NR] An **MPV** or a set of specialist **Rail Vehicles** marshalled with a **Locomotive** both ends used to apply **Sandite** or high pressure water jets to combat **Rail Head Contamination** during **Leaf Fall Season**.

Rail Inclination
[PW] The angle between the vertical axis of a **Rail** and the longitudinal axis of the **Bearer** or **Sleeper**, normally expressed as an **N Value**, e.g. 1 in 20. This angle matches the **Coning** of the **Rail Wheels**, reducing stresses at the **Rail / Wheel Interface**.

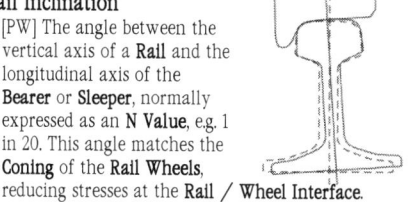

Rail Industry Group (RIG)
[Hist.] Top level forum for stakeholders and industry parties, led by the **SRA**.

Rail Joint
[PW] The fixing together of two **Rails** end-on. See also **Fishplated Rail Joint**, **Insulated Rail Joint**, **Weld**.

Rail Joint Straightener

Rail Joint Straightening (RJS)
[PW] The plant and process used to eliminate **Dipped Joints** at **Fishplated Rail Joints** by locally bending the relevant **Rail Ends** upwards. There are two methods used for this purpose:
- Manual Rail Joint Straighteners, which are man-portable and treat one Rail at a time
- [Unk.] **RASTIC**, a small off-trackable machine produced by **Fairmont Tamper**, now **Harsco**
- [BR Unk.] **STRAIT**, a modified **Tamper** capable of carrying out Rail Joint Straightening on both **Rails** simultaneously and **Tamping** the result to achieve a longer life from the operation.

Rail Key
See **Key**.

Rail Length
[PW] The standard unit of **Rail** is the Rail Length, being 60 feet or 20 **Yards** long (18.288m). See also **Standard Rail**.

Rail Level
[PW] The level of the **Rail Crown** of a specified **Rail**. Practice in certain quarters uses this description for the **Low Rail**.

Rail Lubricator
[PW] A type of **Grease Distribution Unit** (**GDU**), a device for delivering a measured quantity of lubricant (generally grease) onto the **Running Edge** (**RE**) of a **Running Rail** in order to reduce the friction between the **Rail** and **Wheel Flange** on **Curved Track**. Rail Lubricators are used to reduce noise and increase Rail life on such **Curves**. The general principle relies on passing trains operating a small piston pump to move lubricant from a reservoir to an applicator mounted on the **Rail Web**. See also **Obstructionless Rail Lubricator**. Colloquially known as a **Greaser**.

Rail Mode
For a **Road Rail Vehicle** (**RRV**), this describes the Vehicle set up for use on the **Rails**, e.g. **Rail Wheels** deployed, appropriate lighting lit and steering locked. The opposite is **Road Mode**. See also **Travel Mode**.

Rail Mounted Maintenance Machine (RMMM)
[NR] Collective term for any machine equipped with **Rail Wheels** and capable of carrying out **Maintenance** work. This therefore includes **Ballast Cleaners**, **Dynamic Track Stabilisers** (**DTS**), **Pneumatic Ballast Injection Machines** (**PBI**, **Stoneblower**), **Rail Cranes**, **Regulators**, **Road Rail Vehicles** (**RRV**), **Tamping and Lining Machines** (**Tampers**), **Track Relaying Machines** (**TRM**) and **TRAMM**.

Rail Nips
See **Rail Dogs**. Also **Rail Tongs**.

Rail Operating Centre (ROC)
[NR, Sig., Ops.] The current title for the (effectively) regional control centres, into which all **Electrical Control Rooms** (ECR), Gate Boxes, **Integrated Electronic Control Centres** (IECC), **Integrated Control Centres** (ICC), **Network Management Centres** (NMC), **Power Signal Boxes** (PSB), **Signal Boxes** (SB) and **Signalling Control Centres** (SCC) will have migrated by (at the time of writing) 2047. Each of the 12 ROCs will supervise, manage and control a wide area. They are proposed for:
- Basingstoke
- Cardiff
- Derby
- Didcot
- Edinburgh
- Gillingham (Kent)
- Glasgow
- Manchester (Ashburys)
- Romford
- Rugby
- Three Bridges (Sussex)
- York

Ashford and Saltley were dropped from the list of conversions in December 2013. The existing **Control** offices will be relocated into the new Centres and Manchester (AC) and Three Bridges (DC) will become the only **Electrical Control Rooms** (ECR) for the whole country.

Rail Pad
[PW] A resilient layer of rubber or similar material fitted between:
- A **Rail** and **Bearer**
- A **Rail** and **Baseplate**
- A **Rail** and the slab in **Slab Track** construction, see **Strip Pad**.

Rail Passengers' Council (RPC)
The organisation which replaced the **Rail Users' Consultative Committee** (RUCC) and also known as **Passenger** Focus.

Rail Planing
Rail Planing Machine
[PW] An experimental process intended to correct severe problems with the **Rail Head Profile**, such as **Rail Corrugations**. Its implementation on **British Railways** (BR) was in the form of an **On Track Machine** (OTM) equipped with tools for planing away the **Rail Head**. The system was dropped by BR on economic grounds.

Rail Plant Association (RPA)
An organisation representing **Rail Plant** suppliers.

Rail Profile
[PW] The cross section shape of a **Rail**. See also **Rail Head Profile**.

Rail Property Limited
The organisation responsible for the disposal of **Non-operational Property**.

Rail Puller
[PW] Portable hydraulic equipment used for **Rail Adjusting, Joint Regulating**.

Rail Regulator
A common contraction of **Office of the Rail Regulator** (ORR), also applied to its successor the Office of Rail Regulation (ORR).

Rail Research UK Association (RRUKA)
A partnership between the British **Rail Industry** and UK universities. It was set up in 2010 and has the following aims:
- The support and facilitation of **Railway** research in academia.
- The common understanding of research needs to support the Rail Industry and its future development.
- The identification of research, development and application opportunities in Railway science and engineering.
- The provision of solutions to the Rail Industry.

It is jointly funded by the **Rail Safety and Standards Board** (RSSB) and **Network Rail** (NR).

Rail Rolling Over
See **Rail Rotation**.

Rail Rotation
[PW] The effect produced by passing **Trains** on **Curved Track** with some amount of **Cant Deficiency** (D), where the lateral loading on the **Rail Head** causes the **Rail** to rotate, generally about its outer edge. This mechanism is most common with a poorly-supported **Rail**, which rotates within its **Fastenings**, sometimes lifting the supporting **Baseplates** or **Chairs** from the **Bearers** as a **Train** passes over it, resulting in **Gauge Widening**. Also **Rail Rolling Over**.

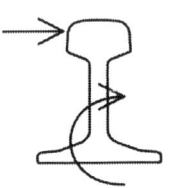

Rail Safety and Standards Board
[Hist.] The former name for **RSSB**.

Rail Safety Case
A document demonstrating a company's capability to discharge its duty as the **Infrastructure Controller**.

Rail Saw
[PW]
a) Generic term for any device intended to cut **Rails** by means of a sawing action, see **Disc Saw**
b) Specifically applied to a petrol powered reciprocating saw used for cutting Rails. This machine has almost universally been superseded by the **Disc Saw**. Also **John Bull Rail Saw**.

Rail Scale
[PW] A special type of ruler that allows the measured height of a worn **Rail** to be converted into its current **Unit Weight**. Some types allow the degree of **Rail Gall** and **Sidewear** to be taken into account. A particular type is **Brown's Rail Scale**.

Rail Seat
The area of a **Chair**, **Baseplate**, **Bearer** or **Sleeper** that is in contact with and supports the **Rail**.

Rail Seat Depth
[PW]
a) The thickness of the section of a **Baseplate** or **Chair** measured vertically below the centre line of the **Rail**
b) The thickness of the section of a **Concrete Bearer** or **Concrete Sleeper** measured vertically from the **Sleeper Soffit** to the centre of the **Rail Seat**.

Rail Seat Erosion
[PW] The wearing away of the **Rail Seat** area of a **Bearer** or **Sleeper** by vertical and / or longitudinal movement of the **Rail**. On **Concrete Sleepers** this effect can be seen when the **Rail Pads** are allowed to deteriorate sufficiently to permit the Rail to sit directly on the concrete.

Rail Section
[PW]
a) A term used to describe the sectional shape of a given **Rail**. Most descriptions utilise the **Unit Weight** ('weight per unit length') approach, e.g. 110 **Pounds per Yard** or 54 **Kilograms per Metre**. Typical types and weights are:
- 85, 95, 97½, 100 Pounds per Yard **Bull Head** (BH) □ **Rail Sections**
- 98, 109, 110, 110A, 113, 113A Pounds per Yard **Flat Bottom** (FB) Rail Sections
- 33, 54A, 54B, 56, 60, 60B Kilogram per Metre UIC Rail Sections
- 100, 105, 105A, 106 and 150 Pounds per Yard **Conductor Rail** sections
- **Tunnel Section Conductor Rail**

(Suffixes generally denote modified versions of the same base section)
b) [Sig.] A length of **Running Rail** with **Fishplated Rail Joints** and **Fishplate Bonds** whose ends are defined **by Insulated Rail Joints** (IRJ).

Rail Settlement Plan (RSP)
[NR]
a) The **Rail Industry** agreement covering the sale of **Tickets** and the apportionment of revenue to individual operators
b) An **Association of Train Operating Companies** (**ATOC**) organisation responsible for co-ordinating **Ticket** sales, fares and allocating the resulting revenue among the relevant **TOCs**.

Rail Shoe
An L-shaped device used by surveyors to ensure that they are accurately measuring the **Running Edge** (**RE**). See also **Littleboy**.

Rail Skate
A small roller-skate device, with two **Double Flanged Wheels**, which is designed to run along the **Rail Head** of one **Rail**, used to assist in the transportation of heavy items of equipment along the **Track**.

Rail Steel
[PW] Alloy from which **Normal Grade Rail** is manufactured.

Rail Technical Strategy (RTS)
The strategy to meet future technical needs on the Railway. It was published on 13 December 2012. See also **Rail Research UK Association** (**RRUKA**).

Rail Temperature
[PW] The measured temperature of a **Rail**. This information is used in calculations for **Stressing** operations, and to see if the **Critical Rail Temperature** (**CRT**) has been exceeded. It can range from -20°C to +52°C (21°F to 152°F) under relatively normal circumstances, reaching a peak at around 1400 hours in east-west **Cuttings**, on still days, during the summer.

Rail Tensors
[PW] An assembly consisting of a pair of hydraulic rams and special **Rail** clamps that between them are capable of producing up to 690kN of tensile force across a gap in the Rail. They are used to achieve the desired **Stress Free Temperature** (**SFT**) in the Rail when the actual **Rail Temperature** is lower. There are two main varieties, hand pumped and motorised.

Rail Thimble
[PW] A small, wheeled grab that is closed around a loose **Rail** and can then be moved longitudinally whilst simultaneously lifting the Rail. This allows a suitable **Rail Crane**, **Road Rail Excavator** or **Track Relaying Machine** (**TRM**) to reposition infinitely long lengths of Rail laterally with a high degree of control.

Rail Threader
[PW] A machine equipped with two sets of wheeled grabs that can be moved inboard and outboard along runners independently of each other. The machine has a lifting device that allows the machine and the **Rails** that it is clamped onto to be raised and the Rails then moved laterally. It is used to reposition long lengths of Rail safely and quickly using a minimum of labour. They find particular use in **Rerailing** work on **Electrified Lines** where their low height means they can work without an **Isolation**.

Rail Tongs
See **Rail Dogs**. Also **Rail Nips**.

Rail Traffic Management Controller
[CT] The controller managing the movement of **Trains** on the **Channel Tunnel** □ **Railway** Network.

Rail Training Audit Service (RTAS)
(Tradename) An organisation whose aim is "... centred on the licensing and subsequent regulation (by audit) of all training and assessment organisations and trainers /assessors who wish to be involved in the delivery of training relating to track safety, signaller and rail incident officer competencies and the conduct of related assessments".

Rail Turning
[PW]
a) Rotating a **Rail** about its longitudinal axis in order to correctly place it in **Baseplates**, **Chairs** or onto **Sleepers**
b) Rotating a **Rail** end-for-end in order to place the former **Outside Edge** (**OE**) as a new **Running Edge** (**RE**). Also **Winging**. See also **Transposing**.

Rail Turning Bar
[PW] A specially shaped tool used to rotate a **Rail** about its longitudinal axis in order to correctly place it in **Baseplates**, **Chairs** or onto **Sleepers**. See also **Cant Hook**.

Rail Vehicle
A vehicle with specially designed wheels intended specifically to run on a **Railway**. See also **Coach**, **Engineering Vehicles**, **Freight Vehicle**, **Locomotive**, **Multiple Unit**, **On Track Machine** (**OTM**), **Road Railer** (**RR**), **Wagon**.

Rail Vehicle (Exemption Applications) Regulations 1998
[TRS] Legislation which sets out how **Operators** should apply for an exemption to the **Rail Vehicle Accessibility Regulations 1998** (**RVAR**) and the information required in support of their application.

Rail Vehicle Accessibility Regulations 1998 (RVAR)
[TRS] Regulations directing how the requirements of the Disability Discrimination Act 1995 (**DDA**) are to be applied to **Rail Vehicles** carrying **Passengers**. See also **Rail Vehicle (Exemption Applications) Regulations 1998**.

Rail Vehicle Records System (RAVERS)
[TRS] A system which records maintenance information for **Locomotives** and **Rolling Stock**. RAVERS has a direct interface with **GEMINI**.

Rail Vehicle Section

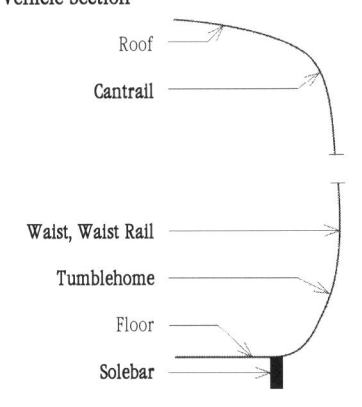

Roof

Cantrail

Waist, Waist Rail

Tumblehome

Floor

Solebar

Rail Warmers
Rail Warming
[PW] Early **Stressing** operations used large propane powered heaters to warm the **Continuous Welded Rail** (**CWR**) to the appropriate temperature before **Fastening Down** commenced. This method has generally been replaced by the use of **Tensors** except in and around very complex **Switch and Crossing Layouts** (**S&C Layouts**).

Rail Wear
[PW] Since the **Rail / Wheel Interface** is a largely un-lubricated metal on metal system, it is inevitable that some wear must occur on both. Rail Wear occurs in three main forms:
- Vertically, from general use and braking, see **Lipping**, **Mushrooming**, **Rail Depth**
- Laterally, as a result of the forces imposed by **Trains** on **Curves**, see **Sidewear**
- **Rail Gall**, caused by the interaction of the **Rail** and its supporting **Baseplate** or **Chair**.

See also **False Flange**.

Rail Web
[PW] The midsection of a **Rail** between **Rail Head** and **Rail Foot**.

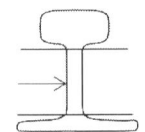

Rail Weight
[PW] The description of a **Rail Section** universally includes its unit weight, in terms of **Pounds per Yard** or unit mass in terms of **Kilograms per Metre**, usually rounded to the nearest whole number. So, 110 **Rail** is 110 Pounds per Yard, and **UIC33** is 33 Kilograms per Metre. Prefixes to the number are generally the initials of the regulating body (see **AREA**, **BS**, **UIC**), and suffixes generally denote variations on the basic sections, although there are exceptions to this. Rail Weights are always for one **Rail** only.

Rail Weld
[PW] A **Weld** made to joint two **Rails** together. See **Alumino-thermic Weld**, **Delachaux Weld**, **Electron Beam Weld**, **Flash Butt Weld** (**FBW**), **Gas Pressure Weld**, **PLA 68**, **Shop Weld**, **SkV-E**, **SkV-F**, **SkV-L50**, **SkV-L80**, **SMW**, **SoWoS**.

Rail Wheel
[TRS] A metal wheel with a radial **Flange** on its inner edge which guides it along a **Rail**. Two such wheels arranged so as to mirror each other mounted an axle are required for full guidance, and this is called a **Wheelset**.

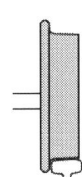

Rail Wheel Brake
In connection with a **Road Rail Vehicle** (**RRV**), a brake that is applied directly to the **Rail Wheels** rather than the road wheels.

Rail-built Buffer Stop
[PW] A **Buffer Stop** constructed using (generally) **Bull Head Rail** (**BH**). Often the **Buffer Beam** is also made from **Rails**, but occasionally a **Wood Sleeper** is employed.

Railcar
[TRS] Describing a single **Car** □ **Diesel Multiple Unit** (**DMU**) normally used on **Rural Lines**

Railcote
(Tradename) A **Rail** treatment, produced by Tata Steel, which provides a high purity zinc coating aimed at improving Rail life in locations such as **Level Crossings** (**LC**, **LX**), coastal lines, wet **Tunnels** and high stray current environments.

RAILDATA
(*rale-day-tah*) [NR PW] The system that records reports of **Broken Rails** and **Defective Rails**.

Railfail
[LUL] Database used to record **Rail Failures**..

Railhead
[Ops.] A description of the nearest **Depot** or **Station** to a given location. Often used to describe unloading or disembarking points for construction works or military activity.

RAILNET
(*rale-net*) The former expansion of the transport of mail by **Train**, which involved contributions by **Railtrack**, Royal Mail and **Rail Express Systems** (**RES**), latterly **English Welsh and Scottish Railways** (**EWS**), now **DB Schenker Rail** (**UK**) **Ltd**. With Royal Mail's withdrawal of support, the project is now dormant.

Railsys
(Tradename) [Ops.] A **Timetable** (**TT**) modelling system produced by Rail Management Consultants of Hanover, Germany.

RAILTEL
Railway Telephone project.

Railtex
(Tradename) A two-yearly **Railway** technology trade show, organised by Mack Brooks.

Railtour
[Ops.] A privately chartered **Train** run specifically for **Railway** enthusiasts, featuring either unusual **Routes** or **Locomotives** or both. See also **Gricer**.

Railtrack (RT)
[Hist.] The successor organisation to **British Railways** (**BR**). Created under the Railways Act 1993 it became solely responsible for operations in 1995 (an event called **Privatisation**). It was responsible for the **Maintenance**, renewal and operation of the public **Railway** □ **Infrastructure** (the **National Railway Network** (**NRN**)) in England, Scotland and Wales. On establishment it was divided into eight **Railtrack Zones**, namely:
- Scotland Zone (**SCZ**),
- North East Zone (**NEZ**),
- East Coast Zone, East Anglia Zone (**EAZ**),
- Southern Zone (**SZ**),
- Great Western Zone (**GWZ**),
- Midlands Zone (**MZ**) and
- North West Zone (**NWZ**).

North East Zone and East Coast Zone latterly combined to make London North Eastern Zone (**LNEZ**). London North East Zone and Anglia Zone then combined to form **Eastern Region** (**ER**). The organisation directly employed the **Signallers**, but contracted out the majority of its other activities. Its income was generated by charging franchisee **Train Operating Companies** (**TOC**) and **Freight Operating Companies** (**FOC**) on a fee per **Train Mile** basis for trains passing over its **Track**. It was taken into **Railway Administration** in October 2001 and replaced by a not-for-profit organisation called **Network Rail** (**NR**) on the 3rd October 2002.

Railtrack Company Standard (RCS)
[RT] Previously called **Railtrack Line Standards** (**RLS**), all these documents have now been migrated to **Network Rail Company Standards** (**NRCS**).

Railtrack Line Standards (RLS)
[RT] Previously **Railtrack Company Standards** (**RCS**), now called **Network Rail Company Standards** (**NRCS**).

Railtrack Zones (RTZ)
[RT] The regional divisions of the former **Railtrack**, being:
- Anglia Zone (**AZ, EAZ**) (latterly merged with London North East Zone to form Eastern Region)
- East Coast Zone
- Great Western Zone (**GWZ**)
- London North East Zone (**LNEZ**)
- Midland Zone (**MZ**)
- North West Zone (**NWZ**)
- Scotland Zone (**SCZ**)
- Southern Zone (**SZ**)

See **Network Rail** (**NR**), **Region**, **Territory**.

Railway
a) Simply, a transport system established for the guided passage of vehicles having flanged wheels running on the upper surface of **Rails**
b) A collective term for the fixed infrastructure, buildings, vehicles, operations and staff of a large scale system based on transportation by **Rail**. See also **Funicular Railway, Heritage Railway, Light Railway, Miniature Railway, Narrow Gauge Railway, Preserved Railway, Private Railway, Public Railway, Rack Railway, Tramway**.

Railway Accident Investigation Unit (RAIU)
[Éire] (**Aonad Imscrúdaithe Timpistí Iarnróid**) A functionally independent investigation unit within the **Railway Safety Commission** (**RSC**), the safety regulator for **Railways** in the Republic of Ireland.

Railway Administration
a) An alternative term for an authority or company whose main business is the operation, **Maintenance** and renewal of a **Railway**. Also **Infrastructure Controller, Railway Company, Railway Authority**. See also **British Railways** (**BR**), **Railtrack** (**RT**), **Network Rail** (**NR**)
b) An arrangement described in the Railway Administration Order Rules, 2001 and used once, which allowed Railtrack to be declared insolvent and taken into administration. Because of the unique situation, a unique version of the Insolvency Act is required.

Railway Age, The
a) See **Crewe Heritage Centre**.
b) See the **Further Reading** section at the rear of this book.

Railway Boundary
The limit of the land in the ownership of a particular **Railway Administration**. This may or may not coincide with the location of a fence or wall, or with the **Limits of Deviation** (**LOD**) and Limits of Land Acquired and Used (**LLAU**).

Railway Byelaws
[NR] Byelaws made under Section 219 of the **Transport Act 2000** and confirmed under Schedule 20 of the **Transport Act 2000** by the Secretary of State for Transport for regulating the use and working of, and travel on or by means of, **Railway** □ **Assets**, the maintenance of order on Railway Assets and the conduct of all persons while on Railway Assets. They cover the following sections:
1. Queuing
2. Potentially dangerous items
3. Smoking
4. Intoxication and possession of intoxicating liquor
5. Unfit to be on the Railway
6. Unacceptable behaviour
7. Music, sound, advertising and carrying on a trade
8. Unauthorised gambling
9. **Stations** and Railway premises
10. **Trains**
11. General safety
12. Safety instructions
13. Unauthorised access and loitering
14. Traffic signs, causing obstructions and parking
15. Pedestrian-only areas
16. Control of animals
17. Compulsory **Ticket** areas
18. Ticketless travel in non-compulsory Ticket areas
19. Classes of accommodation, reserved seats and sleeping berths
20. Altering Tickets and use of altered Tickets
21. Unauthorised buying or selling of Tickets
22. Fares offences committed on behalf of another person
23. (Giving of) name and address
24. Enforcement
25. Interpretation
26. Coming into operation of the Byelaws and revocation of previous byelaws

See also **Conditions of Carriage**, NRCOC.

Railway Clearing Act 1850
[Hist.] The Act granting legal status to the **Railway Clearing House (RCH)**.

Railway Clearing House (RCH)
[Hist.] Established by the **Railway Clearing Act 1850**, the RCH was originally intended to deal with the distribution of ticket revenues from **Through Tickets** and Freight revenues from through Freight services between the various **Railway Companies** involved. In 1895 it facilitated the production of a common set of **Block Regulations** for **Absolute Block (AB)** and in 1904 a standard common **Rule Book** with 281 rules. See also **Rule 55**.

Railway Communication System (RCS)
[NR] The national secure **Cab** to **Signaller** communication system based on the **Global System for Mobile Communications - Railway (GSM-R)** specification.

Railway Company
A company whose core business is the operation of a **Railway**. There have been many variations on this theme, ranging from the early giants such as the **Great Western Railway (GWR)** who, like many others, owned and operated everything including ocean liners, hotels and motor buses, to the modern **Infrastructure Controller** who only manages the **Track**, **Electrification** and **Signalling**, but not the **Trains** themselves. See also **Railway Administration**.

Railway Control Centre (RCC)
[CT] An office controlling the movement of **Trains** and the associated **Infrastructure** services in real time on the **Channel Tunnel** □ **Railway** network.

Railway Corridor
The strip of land occupied by a **Railway**, generally assumed to be that which is between the Railway **Boundary Fences**.

Railway Curves
a) [Hist.] Boxwood or Acrylic drawing curves with very flat radii, generally supplied in sets ranging from around 100mm to 10m Radius (**R**). Many of the examples found in regular use in drawing offices are labelled in inches, typically from 1½ inches up to 400 inches.

b) The correct industry term for bends in a **Railway**:
The smallest Radius (**R**) commonly found in the UK is 100 **Yards** (91.4m, $4^1/_2$ **Chains**)
- Radii less than 200m (200y) on **Running Lines** require a **Check Rail**
- Radii greater than 56.25km (34.95 **Miles**) can be considered to be straight for design purposes.
- Radii greater than 112.5km (69.9 Miles) are always deemed to be straight for all practical purposes.

c) See **Curve**, **Curved Track**.

Railway Engineer's Association (REA)
[Hist.] A forum attended by the Chief Civil Engineers (**CCE**) of the **Pre-Grouping** (pre 1923) **Railway Companies** at which common standards were discussed.

Railway Enthusiast
Descriptive term for one who has an enthusiasm for **Railways**. This term is most often applied to those interested in **Preserved Railways**, but can also be used as an alternative to describe **Anoraks**, **Gricers** and **Train Spotters**. See also **Stoat**.

Railway Facility
[NR] Defined in Section 83(1) of the Rail**ways Act 1993** as "any **Track**, **Station** or **Light Maintenance Depot (LMD)**".

Railway Fires Act 1905
[Hist.] Describes the liability of **Railway Companies** to make good damage to crops caused by their **Locomotives**.

Railway Fog Signal
[Hist., NPT] The formal name for a **Detonator**, now called **Signals Railway Track Explosives**. Developed and introduced into general used by Edward A. Cowper in 1841, they are a biscuit-shaped explosive device applied to the **Rail Head** to warn **Train** drivers of obstructions and to draw their attention, during **Fog**, to **Signals** showing **Restrictive Aspects**. They are now also used to ensure that **Train** drivers are aware of the presence of a **Possession**, and to stop **Trains** in an emergency. Also known as **Bangers, Crackers, Dets, Shots**. See also **Fogman**.

Railway Group
[NR] The organisation consisting of **Railtrack (RT)** (now **Network Rail (NR)**) and all those duty holders of **Railway Safety Cases (RSC)** accepted by Railtrack or Network Rail (e.g. **Freight Operating Companies (FOC)**, **Train Operating Companies (TOC)**, **Train** builders).

Railway Group Member (RGM)
[NR] The collective name for a body, company or organisation that is represented in the **Railway Group**. It is these member organisations who shape Railway Group policy through the production, review and publication of **Railway Group Standards (RGS)**.

Railway Group Standard (RGS)
[NR] A document that mandates technical and operational requirements to members of the **Railway Group**, e.g. **Network Rail (NR)**, **Train Operating Companies (TOC)** etc., to ensure that a system, process or procedure interfaces correctly with other systems, processes and procedures. **Network Rail (NR)** produces **Network Rail Company Standards (NRCS)** that detail how the requirements of the Railway Group Standards are to be achieved on its system and the **Association of Train Operating Companies (ATOC)** does the same for its members.

Railway Heritage Committee
[Hist.] The statutory body which operated under the authority of the Railway Heritage Act 1996 as amended by the **Railways Act 2005**. It had the function of 'designating' records and artefacts still within the ownership of the post-**British Rail (BR)** companies. A new **Railway Heritage Designation Advisory Board**, reporting to the Trustees of the Science Museum Group (**SMG**), took over the statutory powers from 1st April 2013.

Railway Heritage Designation Advisory Board
Part of the Science Museum Group (**SMG**), this organisation took over the statutory powers of the **Railway Heritage Committee (RHC)** from the 1st April 2013.

Railway Industry
Collective description for all the consultants, **Contractors**, **Freight Operating Companies (FOC)**, the **Infrastructure Controller**, manufacturers, suppliers and **Train Operating Companies (TOC)** that are involved in paying work on the **Railway**.

Railway Industry Association (RIA)
(Tradename) A trade body representing suppliers of goods and services to the **Railway Industry**.

Railway Industry Supplier Qualification Scheme (RISQS)
The new name for **Link-Up**.

Railway Infrastructure Network Model (RINM)
[NR] The planned geospatially-referenced replacement for **GEOGIS**. See also **ORBIS**.

Railway Inspectorate (RI)
The common contraction of Her Majesty's Railway Inspectorate (**HMRI**) and the original name for the organisation formed in 1840. It became part of the Health and Safety Executive in 1991.

Railway Legislation (Current)
The following is a current list of the statutory instruments specific to **Railways** in the UK:
- **Railways Act 1993 (RA93)**
- **Railways Act 2005**
- The **Railways and Other Guided Transport Systems (Safety) Regulations 2006 (ROGS)**
- The **Level Crossings Act 1983**
- The **Railways (Interoperability) Regulations 2011**
- The **Health and Safety (Enforcing Authority for Railways and Other Guided Transport Systems) Regulations 2006 (EARR 2006)**
- The **Railways Infrastructure (Access and Management) Regulations 2005**
- The **Railways (Licensing of Railway Undertakings) Regulations 2005**
- The **Railways (Access to Training Services) Regulations 2006**
- The **Railway Safety Levy Regulations 2006**
- The **Railway and Transport Safety Act 2003 (RATS)**
- The **Transport Act 2000**

Railway Level Crossings Act 1839
[Hist.] The first formal legislation on **Level Crossings (LC, LX)**, which required the **Railway Company** to pay for and construct a suitable crossing with **Gates** to protect highway users from **Trains** and employ a competent person to operate the Gates. It also laid down penalties for failing to do so.

Railway Operations (Ops.)
a) Generally, the activities involved in a **Railway** going about its normal day-to-day business
b) The function responsible for managing the safe operation of a **Railway** system, including the preparation and dissemination of relevant information to drivers, management of traffic arrangements during incidents and **Possessions**, input into designs for new facilities and approval of new works in terms of its effect on the day to day running of the Railway. Often shortened to **Operations**, also known as the **Operating Department (OD)**.

Railway Order, The
[Col.] The Railways (Notice of Accidents) Order 1986.

Railway Procurement Agency (RPA)
[Éire] (**An Ghníomhaireacht um Fháil Iarnród**) The RPA is an independent statutory agency responsible for the procurement of **Railway Infrastructure** systems in the Republic of Ireland. It is a State Agency of the Department of Transport charged with the development of light railway and metro infrastructure, established in December 2001 under the Transport (Railway Infrastructure) Act 2001. Many of the staff of the agency moved from the **Light Rail** Project Office of Córas Iompair Éireann (**CIÉ**), which dissolved upon the RPA's inception. The agency operates completely independently of CIÉ. The RPA's main role is overseeing the operation of the **Luas** system in Dublin, along with the planning of new Luas and Metro lines.

Railway Regulation (Gauge) Act 1846
[Hist.] This Act determined that all new **Lines** would be constructed to the **Standard Gauge**, 4' - 8^1/$_2$" (1435mm), heralding the end for the **Great Western Railway's** (**GWR**) □ Broad Gauge.

Railway Safety Case (RSC)
a) A document by which a potential operator of **Trains** demonstrates their compliance with mandatory safety standards. Many **Contractors** have Railway Safety Cases to enable them to operate **On Track Machines** (**OTM**)
b) A **Safety Case** prepared pursuant to Regulations 3, 4 or 5 of the **Railways (Safety Case) Regulations 1994**.
See also Contractor's Assurance Case (CAC), Contractor's Safety Case (CSC).

Railway Safety Commission (RSC)
[Éire] (**An Coimisiún Sábháilteachta Iarnróid**) Established under the Railway Safety Act 2005, it has responsibility for matters of **Railway** and cableway safety on **Passenger** and **Freight** carrying systems where they interface with public roads.

Railway Safety Limited
[Hist.] A wholly owned subsidiary of **Railtrack** (**RT**), now absorbed into the **Railway Safety and Standards Board** (**RSSB**).

Railway Safety Principles and Guidance (RSPG)
[Obs.] The documents produced by **Her Majesty's Railway Inspectorate** (**HMRI**) detailing the rules to be applied to the design and operation of **Light Railways**, **Railways** and **Tramways**. Colloquially known as the **Blue Book**, these documents are now advisory only.

Railway Undertaking
Any private or public undertaking whose principal business is to provide **Rail** transport services for **Goods** and/or **Passengers**, with a requirement that the undertaking must provide **Traction**. See also Freight Operating Company (FOC), Railway Administration, Railway Company, Train Operating Company (TOC).

Railways (Accident Investigation and Reporting) Regulations 2005 (RAIR)
These regulations enabled the Secretary of State to establish the **Rail Accident Investigation Branch** (**RAIB**). These regulations were amended in 2005. See also **Railways and Transport Safety Act 2003**.

Railways (Conveyance of Mails) Act 1838
[Hist.] This Act obliged the **Railways** to carry mail traffic when so required, a requirement now repealed.

Railways (Prevention of Accidents) Act 1900
[Hist.] This act empowered the **Board of Trade** to make rules relating to the safety of workers on the **Track**. One of the outcomes was the mandatory introduction of **Lookouts**. At the time 350 staff died each year from **Train**-related accidents. Compare this with 2 in the year 1993/4!

Railways (Safety Case) Regulations 1994
[Hist.] An Act which came into force on 28th February 1994 and were one of a set of **Railway** health and safety Regulations which were intended to ensure the maintenance and, where necessary, improvement of health and safety standards on the privatised Railways. Other Regulations relevant at the time included:
• The **Railways (Safety Critical Work) Regulations 1994** (**RSCWR**);
• The **Carriage of Dangerous Goods by Rail Regulations 1994**.
The Regulations were made under the **Health and Safety at Work Act 1974** (**HASAWA**) and monitored and enforced by HM Railway Inspectorate (part of the Health & Safety Executive at the time). This legislation has been replaced by the **Railways and Other Guided Transport Systems (Safety) Regulations 2006** (**ROGS**).

Railways (Safety Cases) Regulations 2000 (RSCR)
An amendment of the **Railways (Safety Case) Regulations 1994** and further amended in 2003, these regulations mandate the form and content of a **Railway Safety Case** (**RSC**), and who (generally those operating some form of **Railway** service such as **Trains** and **Stations**) must have one accepted by the Health and Safety Executive (**HSE**). Now replaced by the **Railways and Other Guided Transportation Systems (Safety) Regulations** (**ROGS**).

Railways (Safety Critical Work) Regulations 1994 (RSCWR, R(SCW))
Regulations governing the certification, behaviour and audit of persons carrying out activities classed as critical to the **Safety of the Line**, such as drivers, engineering technicians and **Signallers**. See **Railways and Other Guided Transportation Systems (Safety) Regulations** (**ROGS**).

Railways Act 1921
[Hist.] This Act proposed the amalgamation (**Grouping**) of the 100-plus **Pre-Grouping** □ **Railway Companies** into seven groups. This plan was modified after opposition was encountered and the number of Companies was reduced to four (The **Big Four**). The Act was intended in part to deal with the increasingly difficult problem of fares and tariffs, which were controlled by law and had become out of step with reality. The Act also tidied up most of the Victorian **Railway** legislation, which had become outdated. See also **Transport Act 1962**.

Railways Act 1993 (RA93)
The Act of parliament that established the **Privatisation** of the **National Railway Network** (**NRN**), the creation of **Railtrack** (**RT**) and the effective abolition of **British Railways** (**BR**) in all but name. See also **Transport Act 1962**.

Railways Act 2005
Legislation which introduced the following key changes:
- Allowed the government to take charge of setting the strategy for the **Railway**, and to streamline the structure of the **Railway Industry** at the national level
- Wound up the **Strategic Rail Authority** (**SRA**), passing some of its functions to the Secretary of State and, in some cases, to devolved administrations
- Established the **Office of Rail Regulation** (**ORR**) as a combined safety and economic regulator. Responsibilities for Railway safety regulation (i.e. Her Majesty's Railway Inspectorate (**HMRI**)), transferred to ORR from the **Health and Safety Executive** (**HSE**)
- The **Rail Passengers Council** (**RPC**) established as a single national body reporting to the Secretary of State, replacing the regional committees (such as **Rail User's Consultative Committees** (**RUCC**))
- Set out revised procedures for operators and public sector funders to follow when they wish to discontinue all **Passenger Services** on a **Line**, from a **Station** or to close all or part of a network or Station.

Railways and Other Guided Transport Systems (Safety) Regulations 2006 (ROGS, ROGTS)
(*roggs*) A single piece of legislation which replaces and unifies the following legislation:
- The **Railway and Other Transport Systems (Approval of Works, Plant and Equipment) Regulations 1994** (**ROTS**)
- The **Railway (Safety Critical Work) Regulations 1994** (**RSCWR** and **R(SCW)**)
- The **Railway (Safety Cases) Regulations 2000** (**RSCR**).

Railways and Other Transport Systems (Approval of Works, Plant and Equipment) Regulations 1994 (ROTS)
(*rottz*) Regulations which require approval to be obtained before any new or altered works, plant or equipment (which are capable of affecting the safe operation of a relevant transport system) are first brought in to use. See also **Blue Book**. See **Railways and Other Guided Transportation Systems (Safety) Regulations** (**ROGS**).

Railways and Transport Safety Act 2003 (RTSA)
This legislation established the **Office of Rail Regulation** (**ORR**) as a separate corporate body, taking over the function of the **Rail Regulator**, previously created by the **Railways Act 1993**. It created the **Rail Accident Investigation Branch** (**RAIB**) within the Department for Transport (**DfT**), reformed the **British Transport Police** (**BTP**) and amended the laws relating to alcohol and drug use by shipping and aviation staff. See also **Railways Act 2005**.

Railways Clauses Act 1863
[Hist.] This legislation:
- Allowed works to be altered provided they remained within the **Limits of Deviation** (**LOD**),
- Prohibited **Shunting** over **Level Crossings** (**LC**, **LX**),
- Required the construction of a lodge for highway users at Level Crossings,
- Allowed the **Board of Trade** to insist on a **Bridge** in lieu of a Level Crossing,
- Stated that a **Junction** was the responsibility of the first **Line** at the second Line's cost,
- Required the **Railway** to respect navigable waterways,
- Allowed parties affected by extensions to the time taken for construction to have compensation for additional damage.

Railways Clauses Consolidation Acts 1845
[Hist.] These two Acts (one for England and one for Scotland) forced standardisation of the format of **Railway** Bills in a bid to save Parliamentary time.

Railways for All Strategy
A Department for Transport (**DfT**) strategy aimed at improving the accessibility of all aspects of the **Rail Industry** including:
- Information, ticketing and reservation systems, see **APRS**
- **Station** buildings and **Platforms**, see **Access for All** (**AFA**)
- **Train** □ **Carriages**
- The quality and consistency of staff training.

Railways Infrastructure (Access and Management) Regulations 2005
Legislation which:
• Implements a European Directive concerning the liberalisation of international **Passenger** □ **Rail** services. It extends current European legislation on access rights to **Infrastructure** for international **Rail Freight** services and international groupings to all international **Passenger Rail** services.
• Provides for the transfer of certain regulatory responsibilities in relation to **High Speed 1 (HS1)** facilities from the Secretary of State to the **Office of Rail Regulation (ORR)**.
• Provides for the ORR to pre-approve framework agreements between the **Infrastructure Manager** and **Railway Undertakings** on the HS1 network

Rain
See **In Fog and Rain...**

Rainhill Trials, The
In October 1829 the Liverpool and Manchester **Railway** held a competition to find the most appropriate **Locomotive** to use on new their **Railway**. The prize was £500 (over £75,000 today) and the promise of future commissions to provide Locomotives for the company. Held near Rainhill, the trials lasted a number of weeks, with five Locomotives competing in tests of efficiency, reliability and speed. The five entrants were: Braithwaite and Ericsson with Novelty, **Hackworth** with Sans Pareil, the **Stephensons** with Rocket, Brandreth with Cycloped (which was powered by a horse), and Burstall with Perseverance. The Stephensons' Rocket won.

RAIR
See **Railways (Accident Investigation and Reporting) Regulations 2005.**

Raised Check Rail
[PW] A **Check Rail** supported on special **Baseplates** such that the **Rail Head** of the **Check Rail** is above the level of the **Running Rails**.

RAIT
Railway **A**ccident **I**nvestigation **T**ool.

RAIU
See **Railway Accident Investigation Unit**.

Rake
a) [PW] Describing the inclination of **Switch and Crossing (S&C)** □ **Bearers**, where this is different from the **Cant (C, E)**. This situation can arise where the **Switch and Crossing Unit** has **Thick-based Baseplates** or **Thick-based Chairs**. See also **Timber Wind**
b) [Ops.] Two or more identical **Rail Vehicles** coupled together
c) [Ops.] A series of Rail Vehicles coupled together as part of a semi-permanent formation; normally applied to **Coaches**, **Hoppers** and **Container Flats**.

RAM
a) [NR] **R**oute **A**sset **M**anager
b) **R**eliability, **A**vailability and **M**aintenance.

RAMP
[NR] **R**oute **A**sset **M**anagement **P**lan.

Ramp End
See **Conductor Rail Ramp**.

Ramping
Ramping In
Ramping Out
See **Ballast Cleaner Ramping**.

RAMS
(*rams*) **R**eliability, **A**vailability, **M**aintainability and **S**afety.

Ramsar
An international convention concerning wetland habitats (named after Ramsar in Iran, where the agreement was made in 1971).

RAP
a) [TRS] **R**oll **A**way **P**rotection.
b) **R**emedial **A**ction **P**roject.

Rapper
[Hist.] A mechanically actuated warning device installed on a **Rope-Worked Railway** the sounding of which indicated that a **Set** or **Run** was ready to depart.

RAR
(*raah*) [Obs.]
a) **R**ailtrack **A**sset **R**egister
b) **R**ailway **A**sset **R**egister.

RASTIC
(Tradename) A **Rail Joint Straightener** produced by Fairmont Tamper.

Rat
a) A rodent of the genus *Rattus*, the species most common on the **Railway** is *Rattus norvegicus*, the so-called Brown Rat. See **Leptospiral Jaundice**, **Washing the Hands, Importance of**
b) [LUL Col.] A **Battery Locomotive**
c) An object that it is pulled through a duct to ensure that the duct is clear.

RAT
[NR] **R**isk **A**ssessment **T**emplate.

Rat Hole
[Col.] Nickname for the short **DC Line** □ **Tunnel** at Camden (and no doubt many others), after its primary residents, see **Rat** clause a).

Rat Trap
[Col.] A term for an **Adjustable Dropper**.

Ratchet Jack
A mechanical lifting device which uses a ratchet action to support the load. The load is raised by means of a lever operated by the user, each depression of the lever resulting in around 12mm ($^1/_2$") of vertical lift, the distance between the teeth of the ratchet. Colloquially called **Duff Jacks**, after Duff Norton, the original manufacturer.

Rate of Gain of Cant (RgC, RgE)
[PW] The rate at which the designed **Cant (C, E)** varies, measured as a number of millimetres per second (mm/s) at a given speed. The maximum value in the UK in normal design is 35mm/s (mm/s), 55mm/s maximum and 80mm/s under exceptional circumstances. See also **Cant Gradient**, **Rate of Rotation of Carbody**, **Twist**.

Rate of Gain of Cant Deficiency (RgD)
[PW] The rate at which the designed **Cant Deficiency** varies, measured as a number of millimetres per second (mm/s) at a given speed. The maximum value in the UK in normal design is 35mm per second (mm/s), 55mm/s maximum and 80mm/s under exceptional circumstances.

Rate of Rotation of Carbody
[TRS, PW] The measure of the rate at which a **Tilting Train** can change its **Tilt** attitude relative to the **Track** when negotiating a **Transition Curve**. Measured as a number of millimetres per second (mms[-1]), analogous to the manner in which the **Rate of Change of Cant Deficiency** (RgD) is expressed. The maximum value in normal design is 140mm per second (mm/s)

Rationalisation
The activity of removing un-needed facilities and **Infrastructure** from a **Junction**, **Route** or **Station**.

RATS
[Elec.] Rationalised Autotransformer System.

RATT
[TRS] **Railtrack** Advanced **Tilting Train**, see **Pendolino**. See also **VATT**.

Rattus

Rattus Norvegicus
See **Rat**.

Raven, Vincent, L.
(3rd December 1859 to 14th February 1934) Later Sir Raven; Chief Mechanical Engineer for the North Eastern **Railway** and developer of the Raven **In-Cab Signalling** system.

RAVERS
(*ravers*) See **Rail Vehicle Records System**.

Raw Edges
[PW] Describing the incorrectly formed extremities of the **Rail Foot** in a **Blemished Rail**. It is caused by errors in rolling the **Rail**.

RAWPE
Railways Approval of Works, Plant and Equipment, see **Railway and Other Transport Systems** (**Approval of Works, Plant and Equipment**) **Regulations 1994** (ROTS).

Raynes Park Accident
On 25th May 1933 a serious derailment occurred when **Track** □ **Lifting** was carried out **Under Traffic** without proper precautions being taken. Five died and 34 were injured.

Raynes Park Control
An arrangement which ensures **Approach Control** is effective by **Proving** the Approach Control **Relay** to be not **Operated** to the **Signal Box** □ **On the Approach**.

RB
a) See **Reballasting**
b) [TRS] An acronym representing a Restaurant Buffet **Coach**.

RB(T)
[PW] **Reballasting** by **Traxcavator**. See also **Trax**, **Traxcavate**.

RBC
a) See **Rubber Bonded Cork**
b) See **Radio Block Centre**.

RBH
[PW] Rolled **Bull Head**. See **Bull Head Rail** (BH).

RBR
[Sig.] Run Back Relay.

RBS
[PW] Revised British Standard, as in **95 Pound** RBS.

RBT
a) See **Running Brake Test**
b) [PW] **Reballasting** by **Traxcavator**. See also **Trax**, **Traxcavate**.

RC
a) See **Remotely Controlled Manned Level Crossing**
b) See **Return Conductor**.
c) Reinforced Concrete
d) Remote Control
e) Resistive / Capacitive, a filter circuit composed of resistive and capacitive components used to block certain frequencies of **AC** signal. See also **LC**

RCC
a) [LUL] Rear **Cab** Clear
b) [CT] The Railway Control Centre, part of the **Channel Tunnel** system.

RCCD
Residual Circulating Current Device.

RCD
a) [PW] Rate of Change of Deficiency, see **Rate of Gain of Cant Deficiency** (RgD)
b) Residual Current Device.

RCDO
See **Rail Crossing Diversion Order**.

RCE
a) [PW] Rate of Change of Elevation, see **Rate of Gain of Cant** (RgC, RgE)
b) [NR] Route Communications Engineer
c) See **Regional Civil Engineer**.

RCEA
Railway Civil Engineers Association, an affiliate of the Institution of Civil Engineers (**ICE**).

RCEO
See **Rail Crossing Extinguishment Order**.

RCF
See **Rolling Contact Fatigue**.

RCH
a) See **Railway Clearing House**
b) **Railway** Convalescent Homes
c) Railway Children's Homes.

RCI
[Hist.] **Railtrack** Controlled Infrastructure, see **Network Rail Controlled Infrastructure** (NRCI).

RCM
a) See **Reliability Centred Maintenance**
b) Remote Condition Monitoring.

R-CR
Requirements - Change Request.

ELLIS' BRITISH RAILWAY ENGINEERING ENCYCLOPÆDIA

RCS
a) See **R**ailtrack **C**ompany **S**tandards
b) See **R**ailway **C**ommunications **S**ystem.

RCTIS
Remote **C**ontrol **T**rack **I**solating **S**witch (TIS).

RCV
[PW] **R**aised **C**heck Rail □ **V**ertical, an arrangement of a Raised Check Rail and a Vertical Running Rail.

RCV Baseplate
[PW] A **B**aseplate for a **V**ertical □ Flat Bottom (FB) □ Running Rail and a Raised Check Rail.

RD
a) GEC □ **T**ime **D**ivision **M**ultiplex (TDM), type RD
b) On a **S**ignalling **C**ircuit **D**iagram, denotes a wire coloured **r**e**d**
c) See RD Clip.

RD Clip
[Obs.] Designed by the (then) Research Division of British Railways (BR) at Derby for use with either E10 or F10 Concrete Sleepers. The clip is secured by means of a screw into a beechwood insert in the Sleeper.

RD9
[TRS] A Wheel Profile based on the P8 Profile, with modifications to the Tread and Flange. Applied to High Speed Train (HST) □ Mark III Coaches operating on the East Coast Main Line (ECML).

RDA-RT
Remote **D**ata **A**ccess – **R**outer **T**rain.

RDC
Regional **D**istribution **C**entre, a facility where Goods arrive from various suppliers and are then re-grouped for delivery to customers within a region.

RDE
[NR] **R**esponsible **D**esign **E**ngineer.

RDF
a) **R**ailway **D**evelopment **F**und
b) **R**egional **D**evelopment **F**und.

RDG
See **R**ail **D**elivery **G**roup.

RDL
Rail **D**ynamics **L**aboratory.

RDMS
[PW, NR] **R**ail **D**efect **M**anagement **S**ystem.

RDO
Reserved **D**omestic **O**perator.

RDR
Rest **D**ay **R**elief.

RDS
Railway **D**evelopment **S**ociety.

RDT
a) **R**ail **D**elivery **T**rain. Also CWR Train, LWR Train
b) **R**oute □ **D**rivability **T**ool
c) **R**ail **D**efect **T**racker.

RDW
Regulator's **D**isplay **W**orkstation.

R$_e$
See Equivalent Radius. See also R$_m$.

RE
a) See **R**unning **E**dge
b) **R**esponsible **E**ngineer, see **Contractor's Responsible Engineer (CRE)**
c) **R**esident **E**ngineer.

Re
(Tradename) a type of Rail Fastening produced by Pandrol, where the Rail Foot Insulator is integral to the Rail Fastening and the position of the Rail is restrained laterally by sideposts bonded to the Rail Pad.

RE/PW
RE/PW Drawings
Railway Equipment / Permanent Way Drawings. A range of standard drawings, development of which commenced in 1946, showing Track components such as Chairs, Baseplates, Switch and Crossing Layouts (S&C Layouts), Rails, Sleepers, Stretcher Bars and Track Tools. See also SRE/PW, SRE/PW Drawings.

REA
See **R**ailway **E**ngineers' **A**ssociation.

Reach-stacker
A wheeled machine, similar to a very large fork lift truck, that lifts and transports Containers around a Freight facility.

REACT
(Tradename) A talking sign system that enables blind or partially sighted people to activate real-time information messages as the user approaches speaker units along their route. The system works by using a trigger fob. Using the trigger fob, users can also get more detailed messages.

Reactionary Delay
[Ops.] The delay to a following Train resulting from a delay to a previous Train.

Reactive Maintenance
Maintenance performed as a result of a failure or incident. Whilst the theoretical cost of this approach is attractive, the additional cost due to Train Minute Delays is often very high. The opposite is Planned Maintenance. See also Steady State Maintenance.

Read
[Sig.] Applied to a Lineside Sign or Signal it means the action of observing the Sign or Signal and determining the message being conveyed. See Reading Time.

Read Through
See Reading Through.

Readability
[Sig.] General description of the Performance Category of an Indicator or Signal.

Reading Through
[Sig.] A result of poor Signal Sighting, this is the situation where a driver can mistakenly observe a Signal or Signals Beyond the Signal the driver is approaching. It is most commonly a result of vertical or horizontal curvature and can result in a SPAD.

Reading Time
[Sig.] The time required for a driver to read and process the information being presented by a **Signal**. This must not exceed the **Sighting Time** for the same Signal at the highest **Permissible Speed** (PS) or **Enhanced Permissible Speed** (EPS). See **Minimum Reading Time** (MRT).

Ready To Start Indicator
[Sig. NPT] An alternative term for **Right Away Indicator** (RAI). See also **Train Ready To Start Plunger** (TRTS Plunger).

Ready To Start Plunger
[Sig.] An alternative term for **Train Ready To Start Plunger** (TRTS Plunger).

Reagan System
[Sig. Obs.] An experimental **Track Circuit**-based **Automatic Train Control** (ATC) system trialled on the former Great Eastern **Railway** during the 1920s.

Real Toe
[PW] The actual location of the free end of a **Switch Rail**, to distinguish it from the **Mathematical Switch Toe** if the two locations are different.

Realignment
See **Curve Realignment**, **Hallade**. See also **Slue**.

Reasonably Practicable
A determination of the balance between remaining risk and the sacrifice (money, time or trouble) needed to avert the risk. This is more than comparing the safety benefit of a measure with its cost (a cost benefit analysis) because the risk reduction measure should be implemented unless it requires a sacrifice that is grossly disproportionate. See also **As Low as Reasonably Practicable** (ALARP).

Reassurance Tone
A regular note transmitted between two two-way radios and **Pee-Wee** systems so that the users can be sure that the system is working during periods of silence on the part of the sender.

REAZ
[Hist.] **Railtrack East Anglia Zone**.

REB
See **Relocatable Equipment Building**.

Reballast (RB)
Reballasting
[PW]
The action of renewing the **Ballast** by:
a) Excavating using **Drotts**, **Traxcavators**, **Road Rail Excavators**, **Sidetips**, 360° excavators, JCBs, **Shovels**, etc., see **RBT**, **RB(T)**.
b) Using a **Ballast Cleaner**
c) By lifting the **Track** by the order of 100 to 200mm (4 to 8 inches) to provide a layer of new Ballast under the **Sleepers**.

REBS
Route-Based Efficiency Benefit Sharing.

REC
See **Regional Electricity Company**.

Recast
Recasting
[Ops.] The act of completely revising a **Timetable** (TT). This is a relatively rare occurrence as it is a long and complicated task.

Reception Line
Reception Siding
A **Track**, usually at the entry to a **Marshalling Yard**, where vehicles await transfer to the sorting area. Colloquial use also generally includes the direction of travel of arriving vehicles, e.g. **Up** Reception Line.

Recess Siding
Recessing Siding
A **Siding** intended to allow **Recessing** (temporary parking) of **Freight Trains**, often for protracted periods such as during peak **Passenger** flows. See also **Refuge Siding**.

Recessing
[Ops.] The action of routing a slow moving **Train** onto a **Loop** or into **Recess Siding** whilst faster Trains pass.

Reciprocal Locking
See **Converse Locking**.

Reconnaissance Visit
[NR Civ.] A site visit carried out prior to a **Detailed Examination** of a **Structure**. The visit's purpose is to identify what, if any, special arrangements are required to carry out the Examination itself.

Recording Traces
[PW] Graphical output from the **Track Recording Train** that shows the amplitude **Of Track Geometry** features (such as **Cant**, **Track Gauge**, **Horizontal Alignment**) against distance along the **Track**.

RECOS
[Elec.] **R**unning **E**dge to **C**entre **o**f **S**tructure. See also **Running Edge Face of Steel** (REFOS).

Recovery Crane
A heavy duty **Rail Crane** used to lift damaged and **Derailed** □ **Rail Vehicles** back onto the **Track**. Such Cranes are generally rated at 75 tonnes capacity **Blocked** and are specifically designed and equipped for lifting Rail Vehicles.

Recovery Time
[Ops.] The small quantity of extra time built into a **Timetable** (TT) □ **Path** that allows a late running **Train** to get back on time. Since a small delay is inevitable at some point on a long journey, a few minutes are added at key points and towards the end.

Recovery Train
A specialised **Train** of **Coaches** and **Vans** carrying blocks, cutting equipment, jacks, tools and messing facilities used at crash and **Derailment** sites to support rescue and recovery operations. They are often seen accompanying **Recovery Cranes**.

Rectifier
An electrical device capable of converting Alternating Current (**AC**) into Direct Current (**DC**). Typically found in:
- The **Traction Supply** arrangements for DC **Electrified Lines**, where modern solid state devices have replaced the older mercury arc rectifiers
- An AC **Electric Locomotive**, which will usually have at least two, one for the **Traction Power** circuits and one or more for the **Auxiliary Power** circuits.

Red (R)
a) The colour whose presence indicates **Danger** or stop. See also **Stop Aspect**
b) [Sig.] A colour used on **Signalling Scheme Plans** (**SSP**) to indicate equipment commissioned as part of the works. See also **Colouring Convention**.

Red Aspect
[Sig.] A physical description of the **Stop Aspect** on a **Colour Light Signal**. This Aspect is normally located at the bottom of a signal, nearest to the driver's eye line. For a **Signal** placed at ground level, it would be located at the top for the same reason.

Red Bond
[NR Elec.] A **Bond** that, if disconnected, would lead to it or the equipment it connects rising to a dangerous voltage. They are coloured **red** to warn **Railway** staff of the potential danger. Red Bonds are most common on **Overhead Line Electrification** (**OLE**) systems, located at the middle of an **Electrical Section**. See **Return Conductor To Rail Bond**. See also **Mid-point Connection**.

Red Card
Red Carding
[Ops.] The Red Card (or the action of placing it) on a **Rail Vehicle** to denote that it should not be used and must be returned to the workshops for repairs. See also **Green Card**, **Not to be Moved**.

Red Circle
[TRS] A symbol applied to **Traction Units**, in this case most **Class** 16, 28, 29 **Locomotives** and some Class 21 and 31 Locomotives, denoting which **Multiple Working** control system they are fitted with. Only Traction Units bearing the same symbol can be connected safely See **Blue Square**, **Blue Star**, **Green Circle**, **Orange Star**, **Red Circle**, **Red Diamond**, **Red Triangle**, **White Circle**, **White Diamond**, **Yellow Diamond**, **Yellow Triangle**.

Red Diamond
[TRS Obs.] A symbol applied to **Traction Units**, in this case **Class** 17, 56 and 58 **Locomotives**, denoting which **Multiple Working** control system they are fitted with. Only Traction Units bearing the same symbol can be connected safely. See **Blue Square**, **Blue Star**, **Green Circle**, **Orange Star**, **Red Circle**, **Red Diamond**, **Red Triangle**, **White Circle**, **White Diamond**, **Yellow Diamond**, **Yellow Triangle**.

Red Item
[PW Col.] A length of **Continuous Welded Rail** (**CWR**) that has a **Stress Free Temperature** (**SFT**) higher than 27°C (80°F). This situation must be corrected by **Stressing** before the start of cold weather if **Broken Rails** are to be avoided. Red Items are created during work on the **Rails** in hot weather. The opposite is a **Blue Item**.

Red Siding
[NR] A **Siding** provided solely for access from the **National Railway Network** (**NRN**) to a **Private Siding** covered by a **Private Siding Agreement** (**PSA**). Red Sidings are normally maintained by **Network Rail** (**NR**), at the Siding owner's expense. The term applies only to Private Sidings transferred from **British Rail** (**BR**) under the Network Rail Transfer Scheme. See also **Orange Sidings**.

Red Triangle
a) [TRS Obs.] A symbol applied to **Traction Units**, in this case Derby **Lightweight** □ First Generation Diesel **Multiple Unit** (**DMU**) with hydraulic transmission, denoting which **Multiple Working** control system with which they are fitted. Only Traction Units bearing the same symbol can be connected safely. See **Blue Square**, **Blue Star**, **Green Circle**, **Orange Star**, **Red Circle**, **Red Diamond**, **Red Triangle**, **White Circle**, **White Diamond**, **Yellow Diamond**, **Yellow Triangle**.
b) A symbol applied to a **Sentinel Card** to indicate that the holder must be accompanied by a person holding a Sentinel Card not having a Red Triangle on it, typically but not exclusively because they are under 18 years of age or they have a medical condition that places them at higher risk. Such persons cannot hold certain competencies. See also **Blue Circle**, **Green Square**.

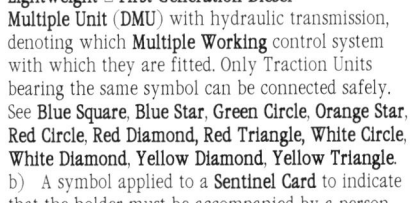

Red Zone
[RT, NR Obs.] A classification of **Safe Systems of Work** (**SSoW**) □ **On or Near the Line** which included work on **Lines** still **Open to Traffic**. This classification has now been replaced by:
- See **Equipment Warning**
- See **Lookout Warning**

Red Zone Prohibition (RZP)
[NR] A length of **Track** on which work cannot be carried out safely if **Trains** are **Running**. This is normally due to a **Place of Safety** not being available in the area. A typical example is the Track located between two **Station** □ **Platforms**.

Red Zone Working
[NR Obs.] Carrying out **Work** activities in a **Red Zone**. See **Equipment Warning**, **Lookout Warning**.

Red/Green Lights (R/G)
Alternative term for **Miniature Stop Lights** (**MSL**)

Rede
(*reed*) A **Railway** □ **Telegraph Code** meaning "Arrange and advise all concerned".

REDG
[NR] **R**ail □ **E**lectrification **D**elivery **G**roup.

ELLIS' BRITISH RAILWAY ENGINEERING ENCYCLOPÆDIA

Redifon MEL (RMEL)
(Tradename) Based in Crawley, Surrey, a company supplying, amongst other things, **Train Protection and Warning System** (TPWS) equipment. Part of the **Thales** Group.

Redlands SDT
See **Self-discharging Train**.

REDP
[NR] **Rail** □ **Electrification** **D**evelopment **P**rogramme.

Reduced Overlap
[Sig.] An **Overlap** that is shorter than the minimum permitted length of a **Full Overlap**, but where the permitted **Approach Speed** is below a specified level allowing an unrestricted approach to a **Signal** at **Danger**. This is not the same as a **Restricted Overlap** (ROL).

Redundant Assets
Items of **Signalling**, **Track** and **Electrification** equipment still in-situ that are no longer required but have some residual value, generally as scrap.

Redundant Track
A **Track** surplus to operational requirements but still in-situ. Such **Tracks** are often physically disconnected from the rest of the **Railway** or have all **Connections** to them **Secured out of Use** or **Plain Lined**.

Reed

Reed Track Circuit
[Sig. Obs.] A variety of (normally) **Jointed Track Circuit**. Using audio frequency **AC**. The system could be installed as a **Jointless Track Circuit** (JTC) under specific conditions.

REF
Rail **E**ngineers' **F**orum.

Reflectorised Distant Board
See **Fixed Distant Board**.

Reflectorised Speed Signs
[Sig.] **Lineside Signs** constructed using reflective sheeting to display **Permissible Speed** (PS) and **Enhanced Permissible Speed** (EPS) information to drivers. There was a requirement to replace all **Cut-out Speed Indicators** on **Network Rail Controlled Infrastructure** (NRCI) with Reflectorised Speed Signs by the end of 2003. See also **Speed Indicator** (SI), **Warning Indicator** (WI).

REFOS
(*re-foss*) See **R**unning **E**dge **F**ace **o**f **S**teel.

Refuge
a) See **Refuge Siding**
b) A recess, platform or handrail provided in areas of **Limited Clearance** such as **Tunnels** to allow staff to stand clear of passing **Trains**.

Refuge Siding
A single ended **Siding** off a **Running Line**, formerly used for **Train** □ **Regulation** purposes but now most likely to be used to **Stable** □ **On Track Machines** or as a **Road Rail Access Point** (RRAP).

Re-gauging
[PW] The action of unfastening **Baseplates** or **Chairs** from **Bearers** or **Sleepers**, **Pulling Through**, plugging the holes, realigning the **Rail** to the correct **Gauge**, re-drilling the holes and refitting the **Chairscrews**.

Regenerative Braking
[TRS] A system of **Train** braking fitted to some **Electric Trains**. When the brakes are applied, the connections to the **Traction Motors** are reversed and the motors used to generate a current. This is in turn fed back into the **Traction Supply**, for use by other **Trains**. It is not widely used in the UK, as the Traction Supply equipment is not capable of dealing with the attendant variations in current and voltage. See also **Rheostatic Braking**.

Region
a) [BR] Under **British Railways**, each Director's organisation (**Civil Engineering** (DoCE), Mechanical and Electrical Engineering (DM&EE), **Signalling** and **Telecommunications** Engineering (DoS&TE), etc.), within **British Railways** (BR) were divided into **Regions**, each of which was responsible for the **Maintenance** and **Renewal** of the equipment within their speciality. The Regions were:
• Eastern Region (ER)
• London Midland Region (LMR)
• North Eastern Region (NER)
• Scottish Region (ScR)
• Southern Region (SR)
• Western Region (WR)
North Eastern Region was later absorbed into Eastern Region, and later again Eastern Region was split into **Anglia Region** (AR) and Eastern Region.
b) [NR] The revised geographical management structure adopted by **Network Rail** (NR). The titles are not wholly dissimilar from those that existed under British Railways, being:
• East Anglia Region
• Western Region
• London North Eastern Region
• Midland Region
• North Western Region
• Southern Region.
These were then superseded by **Territories**, with similar names. See also **Network Rail Routes**.

Regional Civil Engineer (RCE)
[BR] The **Civil Engineering** (**Bridges**, **Track**) functions of **British Railways** (BR) were divided into **Regions**, each of which was responsible for the **Maintenance** and **Renewal** of **Bridges** and **Track** within its control whilst also reporting to the **Director of Civil Engineering** (DoCE) at British Railways Headquarters (BRHQ). Each Region was further divided into **Areas**, or **Area Civil Engineers** (ACE).

Regional Electricity Company (REC)
An organisation engaged in the business of supplying electricity to users. See **Distribution Network Operator** (DNO).

Regional Operators
Operators of interurban, local and rural **Passenger Train** services outside **London** and the South East.

Regional Railways (RR)
[BR] The trading division responsible for provincial **Passenger** services between 1990 and 1994. Other divisions included **InterCity** (**IC**) and **Network South East** (**NSE**).

Register
[Elec.] The lateral position of the **Contact Wire** (**CW**) relative to the **Track Centreline**, and the activity of making it correct.

Register Arm
See **Registration Arm**.

Register Point
See **Registration Point**.

Registration
Common contraction of:
a) Register Arm, Registration Arm
b) Register Point, Registration Point.

Registration Arm
[Elec.] The horizontal rod pivoted in the vertical plane about one end. The other end is attached to the **Contact Wire** (**CW**) of an **Overhead Line Equipment** (**OLE**) □ **Catenary**. Its purpose is to fix the horizontal position of the Contact Wire over the **Track**, whilst allowing the Contact Wire to move upward as **Pantographs** pass beneath.

Registration Pin Code (Pin Code)
[Sig.] An arrangement of metal locating pins on the base of a **Relay**. Not used for electrical purposes, these pins prevent the insertion of an incorrect Relay into an appropriately configured base.

Registration Point
[Sig.] A location at which a **Contact Wire** (**CW**) is restrained horizontally. See also **Pull Off**, **Push Off**, **Registration Arm**, **Stagger**, **Wire Height**.

Regrade
a) [Civ.] To amend the angle of an **Earthwork** slope by removing or redistributing material. See also **Bank Trim**
b) [Elec.] To adjust the longitudinal profile of an **Overhead Line** (**OLE**) □ **Contact Wire** (**CW**)
c) To review the grade classification of a post following a re-organisation.

Regulate
See **Regulation**.

Regulating Versines
[PW] A simple method of calculating **Slues** from the **Versines** of regular overlapping **Chords**. See also **Hallade**.

Regulation
a) [PW] To redistribute **Top Ballast** along a section of **Track** by manual (**Shovels**) or mechanical (**Ballast Regulator**) means
b) [PW] To adjust the longitudinal position(s) of **Jointed Rails** in order to make the **Expansion Gaps** equal, see **Joint Regulation, Pulling Back, Rail Adjusting**
c) [PW] To undertake the survey of and making minor adjustments to alignment **Pegs** to eliminate errors in setting out the Pegs, see **Regulating Versines**
d) [Ops.] To manage the passage of **Trains** on a **Route** using **Junctions** and **Loops**, so that slower Trains do not impede faster ones
e) To attempt to ensure that the **Privatised** □ **Railway** provides best value to its users, see **Office of Rail Regulation** (**ORR**).

Regulation of Railways Act 1840
[Hist.] This act mandated the following:
- No **Railway** to be opened without one month's prior notice to the **Board of Trade**,
- **Traffic** and **Accident** returns to be made by **Railway Companies**
- Appointment of Board of Trade inspectors,
- The right of the Board of Trade to inspect all Railways and Accidents thereon,
- **Railway Byelaws** to be approved by the Board of Trade
- Prohibition of drunkenness by Railway employees
- Prohibition of trespass on Railways

See also **Her Majesty's Railway Inspectorate** (**HMRI**).

Regulation of Railways Act 1842
[Hist.] Building on the 1840 Act, **Railways** were required to erect **Lineside Fences**, maintain **Level Crossings**, and were given rights to enter neighbours property in times of **Accident** or emergency, compulsory purchase and deal summarily with persons impeding the safe operation of the Railway. All these powers have been repealed and re-enacted elsewhere.

Regulation of Railways Act 1844
[Hist.] This legislation introduced the following concepts:
- New **Lines** would be authorised with the condition that they could be purchased by the State after 21 years, opening the door to **Nationalisation**
- State control of all **Railways** in times of national emergency
- State control over fares and tariffs
- The introduction of the **Parliamentary Train**.

Regulation of Railways Act 1871
[Hist.] This Act contained further amplification of previous legislation. See also **1958 Letter, The**.

Regulation of Railways Act 1889
[Hist.] This Act made the following compulsory:
- The adoption of **Block Working** on all **Passenger Lines**,
- The fitting of **Interlocking** between all **Points** and **Signals** on Passenger Lines,
- The fitting of **Continuous Brakes** on **Passenger Trains**.

See also **Lock, Block and Brake**.

Regulator
a) [PW] A common contraction of **Ballast Regulator**
b) [TRS] The control handle by which a driver applies or removes power to and from the **Traction Unit**
c) See **Office of Rail Regulation** (ORR).

Relative Gauging
[PW] An analysis of the clearances between a **Rail Vehicle** and a **Structure** or between two passing Rail Vehicles undertaken by comparing results previously obtained using Rail Vehicles with similar characteristics.

Relative Track Geometry
[PW] **Track Geometry** that is not always verified against fixed references during **Maintenance Tamping**, and therefore is not fixed. See **Fixed Geometry Railway**. See also **Sixfooting**.

Relatives
Relative Differences
Alternatives for **Differences**.

Relay
a) [PW] A common contraction of **Relaying**
b) [Sig.] An electromechanical device that utilises an electromagnet to make and break related sets of electrical contacts. Therefore, one electrical signal can be used to determine the connection or disconnection of many other circuits. Used widely in **Power Signalling**, the standard type has a set of Normally Closed (NC) (when the coil of the electromagnet has no current flowing through it) **Back Contacts** and a set of Normally Open (NO) □ **Front Contacts**. There are many types and varieties. See **Biased Relay, Slow to Operate Relay, Slow to Release Relay, Time Element Relay, Twin Relay**. See also **Contactor**.

Relay Interlocking (RI)
[Sig.] An **Interlocking** constructed using individual electromechanical **Relays**. Also **Free Wired Interlocking**. See also **Geographical Interlocking**.

Relay on Top
[PW] A method of replacing **Track** in which the old is removed, the **Ballast** levelled and the new laid in. The amount by which the new **Track** is higher or lower depends on the type of **Sleepers** and the **Sleeper Spacing** before and after the operation is carried out.

Relay Room
[Sig.] A building housing safety critical electrical and electronic **Signalling Equipment** such as **Relays**, that interface with **Trackside** equipment such as **Points** and **Signals**.

Relayer
[PW] One who is involved in **Relaying** activities.

Relaying
[PW] Any activity involving renewal of one or more of the major components of the **Permanent Way** (PW), e.g. the **Rails**, **Sleepers** or **Ballast**. The term can also be used to mean **Complete Renewal**. See **Renewals, the**.

Relaying Bus
[BR PW] A larger than usual (up to 18 seat) **Gang Bus**, required by the larger than average sizes of **Relaying Gangs**.

Relaying Gang
[BR PW] A **Gang** whose normal work was carrying out **Relaying** and **Renewal** of the **Permanent Way** (PW).

Relaying Item
Relaying Proposal
[BR, PW] A length of **Track** identified by the **Maintainer** that will require **Relaying** in the next three to five years. The exact work required will then be determined closer to the due date, and may include **Ballast Cleaning, Bank Trim, Complete Renewal, Lifting**, laying new **Track Drains, Earthworks, Rerailing, Formation Renewal, Reballasting, Resleepering**, or any combination of these activities. See also **Renewal of Way** (ROW) **Item, Renewal Proposal, Renewals Item**.

Release
[Sig.]
a) The freeing of a **Lever** or similar operating device by the **Interlocking**. It is therefore the opposite of **Lock**
b) The permission given by **Signaller** to a **Ground Frame Operator**, allowing them to operate the **Ground Frame** (GF)
c) See also **Released**.

Release Key
See **Emergency Release**.

Release Speed
[Sig.] The theoretical safe speed at which a **Main Route Aspect Release From Red** (MAR), **Main Route Aspect Release From Yellow** (MAY) or **Delayed Yellow** □ **Signal** is allowed to **Clear** to a less restrictive **Aspect**.

Release Time
[Sig.] The interval between the rated voltage being removed from a **Relay** coil and the last **Front Contact** breaking. The opposite is **Operation Time**. See also **Dropped Away, Picking-up**.

Released
a) [Sig.] The state of a **Relay** when the coil is De-energised, the Relay is unlatched or the relay has **Dropped Away** (DA) thus closing the **Back Contacts** and opening the **Front Contacts**. Also **Dropped, Down**. The opposite is **Operated**
b) [TRS] The state of vehicle brakes when the brakes are not acting to slow or hold the vehicle. See also **Release**.

395

Relevant Earthworks
[NR Civ.] **Earthworks** which meet the definition in RT/CE/P/030 and are to be included in the inspection and evaluation regime.

Reliability Centred Maintenance (RCM)
A policy of planning **Maintenance** work based on achieving the best possible reliability from the asset. This is a type of **Planned Maintenance**, see also **Reactive Maintenance**.

Reliance
A **Railway** □ **Telegraph Code** meaning "Relying on your concurrence, I have agreed".

Relief
Relief Line
[WR] Alternative title for a **Slow Line**.

Relieving Bogie
[TRS] An additional detachable **Bogie** fitted to a **Rail Crane** to reduce the individual **Axle Loads** imposed by the Rail Crane on the **Track**.

Reliostop
[Sig. Obs.] A mechanical/pneumatic arrangement, similar to a Tripcock in operation, developed on the former Great Central **Railway** in the years following the first World War.

Relocatable Equipment Building (REB)
[Sig.] A "Portacabin" style structure used to house **Signalling** or **Telecommunications** equipment. It permits much of the testing phase of the installation to be carried out in the factory. Smaller Relocatable Equipment Buildings are sometimes referred to as **Superlocs** or Walk in Location Housings (**WILH**). They are manufactured in standard lengths, all with a 2.4 metre width:

Size	Length
1	2.4m
2	3.6m
3	4.8m
4	6.0m
5	7.2m
6	8.4m
7	9.6m
8	10.8m
9	12.0m

See also **Loc**, **Location Case**, **Location**, **WILH**.

Reminder Appliance
[Sig.] A device used by a **Signaller** to remind the Signaller that a particular **Lever**, electrical switch or **Plunger** (button) should not be **Operated**, often because that device operates a **Signalling Function** which is protecting a **Possession** or **Obstruction**. Also called **Collars**, **Lever Collars**.

Reminder Sheets
[Sig.] Sheets used by **Signallers** to record and be used as a reminder of when certain **Sidings** or **Lines** are blocked by **Engineering Trains**.

Reminder Sign
[Sig.] A **Lineside Sign** provided to repeat the information given by a previous **Sign**. This may be because the driver joined the **Route** at a **Junction** after the previous sign, or because it is perceived that they may miss the previous sign due to poor **Sighting** or intermittent **Obscuration**. Also **Repeater Sign**.

Remodelling
The altering of a **Junction** or **Station Throat** to provide alternative **Routes**, different facilities or higher speed.

Remote Interlocking
[Sig.] An **Interlocking** that is located some distance from the **Signal Box** that controls it. The two are generally connected using some form of data link such as **Time Division Multiplex** (**TDM**). Also **Satellite Interlocking**.

Remote Route Request
[Sig.] **Routes** that cross **Interlocking Boundaries** require special treatment since two (or more) **Interlockings** must cooperate to set them up safely. When the Interlocking controlling the **Entrance Signal** receives a **Panel Request** for such a Route, it issues a Remote Route Request via the **Internal Data Link** (IDL) to the Interlocking(s) controlling the other part(s) of the Route. Only if an acknowledgement to this remote request is received from the other Interlocking (within a prescribed period) will the first Interlocking go ahead and **Set** the Route.

Remote Securing of Points
[LUL] A system which allows Trains to pass through Junctions during certain failure conditions. The system displays an **Indication** to the **Train Operator** when the **Points** are correctly **Set** and **Locked** in a particular direction. This removes the immediate need to manually secure the points using a **Clip and Scotch**.

Remotely Controlled Level Crossing
Remotely Controlled Manned Level Crossing (RC)
A **Manned Level Crossing** located within normal visual range of its operator and equipped with **Full Barriers**.

Renewal
Renewal of Way (ROW)
The general term for replacing life expired **Track**.

Renewal by Stealth
[Col.] A description of the outcome of a long-standing policy of replacing individual components under **Maintenance**, rather than one of **Complete Renewal**. The upshot is typically a **Switch & Crossing Layout** (**S&C Layout**) where every component is a different age and condition, and the Layout does not, overall, warrant **Renewal**.

Renewal Item
See **Renewal of Way Item** (**ROW Item**).

Renewal of Way Item (ROW Item)
[PW] A length of **Track** or a **Switch and Crossing Unit (S&C Unit)** that has been identified for complete **Reballasting, Rerailing, Resleepering** or any combination of these. See also **Relaying Item, Relaying Proposal**.

Renewals Avoided
The calculated value of all the **Renewal** works that would be rendered unnecessary by a proposed scheme. This value can be offset against the cost of the scheme itself.

Renewals Proposal
See **Renewal of Way Item (ROW Item)**.

Renewals, The
[PW Col.] A collective description of the group of staff whose main work is renewing **Track** or **Relaying**.

Renlog
Infrastructure □ **Renewals log**.

Repadding
[PW] The action of removing life expired **Rail Pads** and replacing them with new items.

Repair
[PW] Generally, the stage in a **Track Renewals Item** following any **Reballasting** work. The work comprises bringing the **Reballasted** □ **Track** up to a standard fit for the passage of **Ballast Hoppers** and **Tampers**. Particularly applied on **Automatic Ballast Cleaning (ABC)** sites.

Repeater
[Sig.]
a) An alternative term for an **Indicator** in a **Signal Box (SB)**. See also **Arm Repeater (AR)**.
b) An abbreviation of **Repeater Signal** (or **Repeater Sign**); a supplementary **Lineside Sign** or **Signal** providing advanced warning of the information or **Aspect** being shown by the main **Sign** or **Signal**.
c) [NPT] See **Banner Repeating Signal**.

Repeater Location
[Sig.] A **Location** provided so that long electrical **Signalling** circuits can be interrupted by **Relays** to reduce the effects of interference voltages.

Repeater Sign
[Sig.] An alternative term for **Reminder Sign**.

Repeater Signal
[Sig.]
a) A **Signal** which is not itself a **Stop Signal**, capable of displaying a **Cautionary Aspect**, that informs the driver about the state of the next Stop Signal **Beyond**.
b) [NPT] See **Distant Signal**.
c) [NPT] See **Banner Repeater Signal**.

Replace

Replacement
[Sig.]
a) To over-ride the normal **Signalling System**, generally to force a **Signal** to show a **Stop Aspect**.
b) To return a **Signal** to its **Most Restrictive Aspect** following the passage of a **Train**.

Replacement Joint
[Sig.] In **Colour Light Signal** areas, the first **Insulated Rail Joint (IRJ) Beyond** a **Signal**. This Joint is located 20 metres Beyond the Signal and marks the start of a **Track Circuit (TC), Occupation** of which triggers **Replacement** of the Signal. See **First Wheel Replacement (FWR), Last Wheel Replacement (LWR)**.

Replacement Switch
[Sig.] An electrical switch (**Plunger**) provided in a **Signal Box**, which allows the **Signaller** to **Replace** an **Automatic Signal** in an emergency. The **Signal** is **Proved** to be showing a **Stop Aspect** and be **Alight**. See also **All Signals on Switch, Emergency Replacement Switch, Group Replacement Switch**.

Reporting Number
See **Train Reporting Number**.

Reprofiling
[PW] The action of **Rail Grinding** or **Rail Planing** to restore the transverse profile of a **Rail**.

REPTA
(*rep-tah*) **R**ailway **E**mployees **P**rivilege **T**icket **A**ssociation.

Request Stop
[Ops.] A **Halt** or **Station** at which **Trains** do not make **Booked Calls**, but only stop if there are **Passengers** wishing to **Alight** or **Board**.

Required Reading Distance
[Sig.] The distance **On The Approach to** a **Signal** that the **Signal Sighting Committee (SSC)** decide is to be provided and maintained for **Sighting** a Signal.

Required Sighting Distance
[Sig.] The distance from a **Work Group** at which **Trains** must be visible in order to provide the **Required Warning Time**.

Required Warning Time
[RB] The time required for the observation of **Trains** (which may require additional allowance for multiple directions and multiple **Lookouts**), everyone in the **Workgroup** to stop work, down tools and reach a **Position of Safety** with ten seconds to spare. The Required Warning Time and the maximum speed of **Approaching Trains** are used to calculate the **Required Sighting Distance**.

Requires
[Sig.] A term used to denote that an operation is dependent on the state of some other **Function** within an **Interlocking**.

Rerailing (RR)
a) [PW] The action of renewing the **Rails**. This can be done either one Rail at a time, called **One Rail Only (ORO)** or **High Rail Only (HRO)**, or both together. When not specified, the term means both Rails
b) The action of lifting or jacking a **Derailed** □ **Train** back onto the **Track**.

RES
See **Rail Express Systems**.

397

Reset and Continue
[NR Sig.] The action by a driver in his **Cab** to reset the **Train Protection and Warning System** (**TPWS**) and continue driving. This may or may not be a legitimate action: see **Reset and Continue Incident**.

Reset and Continue Incident
[Ops.] The failure of a driver to follow the correct procedures (e.g. contacting the **Signaller**) after a **Train Protection and Warning System** (**TPWS**) **Intervention** before resetting the TPWS and restarting.

Resetting
[Sig.] Placing equipment or systems (for example **Axle Counters**) into a state which is suitable for restoration to service.

Residual Lift
[PW] The small amount of **Lift** still being applied by a **Tamper** at the end of a run, caused by its averaging action. The Residual Lift is removed by setting a small negative value of **Design Lift** and working until zero actual Lift is achieved. See **Run Out**.

Residual Slue
[PW] The small amount of **Slue** still being applied by a **Tamper** at the end of a run, caused by its averaging action. The Residual Slue is removed by setting a zero value of **Design Slue** and working until zero actual Slue is achieved. See **Run Out**.

Residual Switch Opening (RSO)
[PW] The remaining distance between the **Stock Rail** and **Switch Rail** on the **Closed Switch** side of a **Set of Switches**.

Resignalling
Resignalling Scheme
[Sig.] A project whose main purpose is to replace an existing life expired or restrictive **Signalling System** with a new one meeting all current and near future needs. Such works as these often require relatively major modifications to the **Track Layout** as well, so a Resignalling Scheme can range from works to two **Signals** up to an entire 200 **Mile** stretch of **Main Line**.

Resilient Wheels
[TRS] Wheels assembled with a rubber layer between the **Tyre** and wheel hub. They are intended to reduce noise, vibration and **Maintenance** costs. See also **Eschede Accident**.

Resleepering (RS)
[PW]
The action of renewing the **Sleepers** by:
a) Replacing all the Sleepers between two **Mileages**, called **Complete Resleepering** or **Continuous Resleepering**
b) Replacing a fraction of the Sleepers between two Mileages, generally the worst ones, called **Spot Resleepering** or **Patch Resleepering**. Also referred to as **1 in x Resleepering**.

Respacing
[PW] The process of sliding the **Sleepers** under a **Track** (generally) closer together and inserting additional new Sleepers in the gaps produced. This is generally carried out to increase the **Track Category** of a **Line**, enabling it to carry increased traffic. Typically Track with Sleepers at 24 per **Length** would be respaced to 28 per Length, and one new Sleeper added every five **Yards**.

Responsible Manager
[NR] The person responsible for the management of staff who are **Working □ On or Near the Line**. This would typically be their line manager or an on call manager

Rest Day
A day within a work roster when an employee is designated as free from duty.

Restoration to Service
Accepting equipment or systems that have been reset back into service.

Restressing (RS)
[PW] Technically referring to the activity of returning **Continuous Welded Rail** (**CWR**) to its previous correctly **Stressed** state, this term is also colloquially applied to all **Stressing** activities. See also **Destressing**, **Stress Restoration**.

Restricted Manual (RM)
[LUL] A manual mode of driving where the maximum speed of the **Train** is automatically limited to 10mph (16kmh). The Train is not protected by the **Automatic Train Protection** (**ATP**) system in this mode.

Restricted Overlap (ROL)
[Sig.] A shorter **Signal Overlap** that allows a **Train** to be authorised to pass the preceding **Signal** under a suitable **Control** such as **Approach Release**. This is not the same as a **Reduced Overlap**.

Restrictive Aspect
[Sig.] An **Aspect** which requires a driver to reduce speed, therefore any **Main Signal** Aspect other than **Green**. See **Most Restrictive Aspect**. See also **Least Restrictive Aspect**.

Restroking
[Sig.] On a **Signal Box Panel**, an alternative term for **Oversetting**.

Retaining Wall
[Civ.] A brick, concrete or masonry wall whose function is to hold back the side of an excavation or filled area. Retaining Walls are the natural step between a **Cutting** and a **Tunnel**.

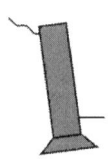

Retarder

A large **Track** mounted device consisting of movable **Check Rails** that grasp the **Flanges** of passing **Rail Vehicles** and reduce the Vehicle's velocity. Generally found in **Hump Shunting** Yards, they are usually power operated, and allow the **Shunting** system to accurately and safely assemble **Trains** without the heavy collisions that would result from the unchecked progress of a **Wagon** over the **Hump**. Also **Dowty Retarder**.

RETB
See **Radio Electronic Token Block**.

Return
a) See **Returned Ballast**
b) The supply neutral, negative or **N** connection to an apparatus. The opposite is **Feed**.

Return Conductor (RC)
[Elec.] A wire generally carried on **Insulators** and strung between **Overhead Line Structures**, which carries the **Traction Return Current** to the **Feeder Station** (**FS**) in an **Overhead Line Electrification** (**OLE**) system.

Return Conductor to Rail Bond
[Elec.] A **Bond** between the **Return Conductor** and **Traction Return Rail** that carries the **Traction Return Current** to the **Feeder Station** (**FS**). These Bonds are universally designated **Red Bonds**. Also called a **Mid-Point Connection** (**MPC**).

Return Rail
[Elec.] The **Rail** used to carry the **Traction Return Current** in an **Electric Traction System**. This Rail may be one of the **Running Rails**, or a Rail specially provided for the purpose, i.e. the **Fourth Rail**.

Return Working
[Ops.] The movement of a **Train** from an intermediate destination back to its point of origin. The term is also applied to **Traincrew** who are working a Train back to their **Signing on Point** (**SOP**).

Returned Ballast
[PW] The **Ballast** that is fit for re-use and is placed back under the **Track** by a **Ballast Cleaner**. Also **Ballast Cleaner Return**.

Returning
[PW] The opposite of **Excavating**, i.e. using a **Ballast Cleaner** to put the re-usable **Ballast** back under the **Sleepers**. Also **Screening**. See also **Total Loading**.

Revenue
A term describing **Trains** or individual **Rail Vehicles** whose operation directly generates money. See also **Departmental Vehicles**, which do not.

Reverse
a) [PW Col.] Contraction of **Reverse Curve**
b) [Sig.] For a **Set of Points** or **Lever** this is the "wrong" position, either permitting the passage of **Trains** on the least used **Route** or pulled fully forward in the **Lever Frame** respectively. The opposite is **Normal**
c) To move the **Switch Rails** of a **Set Of Switches** so as to present the required Route
d) [Ops.] To change direction, normally used in the context of **Timetables** (**TT**) and **Train Arrangements**. Also **Turn Back**.

Reverse Curve

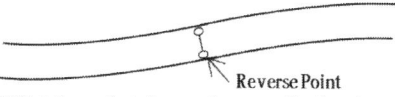

[PW] A **Curve** that changes from one **Hand** to the other part way along its length. See also **Direct Reverse**, **Indirect Reverse**.

Reverse Point
[PW]
a) The part of a **Reverse Curve** where the change of Hand takes place
b) The point at which two abutting **Curves** of opposite **Hand** have a common tangent. See **Direct Reverse**
c) The point at which the common tangent of two Curves of opposite Hand, connected by a **Reverse Transition**, intersect a line connecting the centres of the two Curves. This is also the point at which the connecting **Transition Curve** has infinite Radius (**R**).

Reverse Transition
[PW] A **Transition Curve** with a constant rate of change of Radius (**R**) that connects two **Curves** of opposite **Hand**. The two Curve-to-**Straight** sections of this Transition may be of different lengths if the two Curves being joined are of different Radii, as the **Rate of Change of Cant** (**RgC**, **RgE**) and the **Rate of Change of Cant Deficiency** (**RgD**) are both kept constant through a Reverse Transition. Also **Curve to Curve Transition**.

Reverser
[TRS] On a **Steam Locomotive**, a control which modifies the operation of the valve gear to achieve forward or reverse operation and allows adjustment of the cut-off point of steam entering the cylinders.

Reverser Key
[TRS] A brass key which is inserted in the **Driving Cab** desk by the driver of a **Diesel Locomotive** or **Electric Locomotive** to allow the **Locomotive** to start and run.

Reversible Line
[NPT] See **Bi-directional Line**.

Reversible Signalling
[Sig.] The permanent provision of **Signals** which enable a **Track** to be operated in either direction. Also **Bi-di Signalling**, **SIMBIDS**.

Reversible Working
See **Reversible Line**.

Reversing
[Ops.] Turning a **Train** end for end using a **Reversing Siding**, **Triangle** or similar means.

Reversing Siding
A **Siding** at a non-**Terminal Station** used as the termination point of a service prior to the formation of a **Return Working**. Also **Turn Back**, **Turn Back Siding**.

Reversion
See **Signal Reversion**.

Reverted
[Sig.] The action of a **Signal** returning to its **Most Restrictive Aspect**. See also **Replaced**.

RF
[TRS] An acronym representing a Restaurant **First Class** □ **Coach**.

RFA
[PW] Route Fleet Analysis, A **Track-Ex** output.

RFB
[TRS] An acronym representing a Restaurant Buffet **First Class** □ **Coach**.

RFC
See **Ride Force Count**.

RFD
a) **Rail Flaw Detection**
b) Railfreight Distribution, see **RfD**. See also **English Welsh and Scottish Railways** (**EWS**).

RfD
Railfreight Distribution, which became part of **English Welsh and Scottish Railways** (**EWS**), now DB Schenker Rail UK Ltd. Also written as **RFD**.

RFDV
[PW] **Rail Flaw Detection Vehicle**.

RFF
Reseau Ferre de France, the French equivalent of **Network Rail** (**NR**).

RFG
(Trademark) **Rail** □ **Freight Group**, an organisation representing over 150 organisations involved in the movement of **Freight** by **Rail**. Its aim is to promote the expansion of these activities.

RFI
a) **Rail Freight Interchange**, a facility specialising in the transfer of **Freight** between **Rail** and road.
b) Request For Information.

RFM
[TRS] An acronym representing a Restaurant **First Class** Modular **Coach**.

RFO
[TRS] An acronym representing a Restaurant **First Class** □ **Open Coach** - No Kitchen.

RFOA
Rail Freight Operators' Association.

RFP
Request for Proposal.

RgC
[PW] **Rate of Gain of Cant**, normally **RgE**.

RgD
See **Rate of Gain of Cant Deficiency**.

RgE
[PW] Rate of Gain of **Elevation**, see **Rate of Gain of Cant**.

RGI
[Elec.] **Rail Gap Indicator**, See **Current Rail Gap Indicator**.

RGM
See **Railway Group Member**.

RGS
See **Railway Group Standard**.

RGSP
Railway Group Safety Plan.

RGT
See **Rail Grinding Train**.

RGU
[PW] **Rail Grinding Unit**.

RH&DR
The Romney, Hythe & Dymchurch **Railway**.

RHA
Road Haulage Association.

RHC
See **Railway Heritage Committee**.

Rheostatic Braking
[TRS] A variety of **Regenerative Braking** where the current generated is fed into a suitable resistance to dissipate the energy. This variation is used where the current cannot be fed back into the **Traction Supply**, for instance on a **Diesel Electric Multiple Unit** (**DEMU**). Modern **Traction Units** can generally be switched between "off" and these two modes (where applicable). See **Grid**.

RHM
Rolled High Manganese.

RHPMS
[PW] **Rail Head Profile Measurement System**.

RHPW
See **Right Hand Parallel Wing**.

RHR
See **Right Hand Rail**.

RHS
a) See **Right Hand Side**
b) See **Right Hand Splice**
c) See **Right Hand Switch**
d) Rectangular Hollow Section.

RHSC
See **Right Hand Switch Closed**.

RHT
Railway Heritage Trust.

RHTO
See **Right Hand Turnout**.

RHTT
See **Rail Head Treatment Train**.

RI
a) See **Relay Interlocking**
b) See **Route Indicator**
c) See **Railway Inspectorate**.

RIA
See **Railway Industry Association**.
RIAC
Railway Industry **A**dvisory **C**ommittee.
RIAG
[NR] **R**ail □ **I**nfrastructure **A**ssurance **G**roup, part of the Infrastructure Safety Liaison Group (**ISLG**).
RIC
a) **R**ail **I**ncident **C**ommander
b) **R**egolamento **I**nternazionale **C**arrozze; regulations for the international exchange of **Passenger** □ **Carriages**.
RICA
(Tradename) **R**ail **I**ndustry □ **C**ontractors' **A**ssociation.
RICCL
Rail **I**ndustry **C**ommodity **C**lassification **L**isting.
RICD
Rail **I**ndustry **C**ost **D**atabase.
RICP
Rail **I**ncident **C**ontrol **P**ost.
RID
a) [LUL] **R**oute **I**dentification **C**ode.
b) **R**èglement Concernant le Transport **I**nternational Ferroviaire des Marchandises **D**angereuses, regulations concerning the international carriage of **Dangerous Goods** by **Rail**.
Riddler
[PW Nth. Col.] A nickname for a **Ballast Cleaner**, from its major operation.
Riddling
a) [PW Nth. Col.] An alternative term for **Returning** or **Screening**, describing a **Ballast Cleaner** working normally. The opposite is **Excavating** or **Total Loading**
b) [Hist.] Manual **Ballast Cleaning** using a riddle (sieve) to separate fine material from **Track Ballast** shovelled from the **Beds**, the cleaned stone being returned and any shortfall made good.
RIDDOR
(*ridd-orr*) **R**eporting of **I**njuries, **D**iseases and **D**angerous **O**ccurrences **R**egulations 1995.
RIDE
Rail **I**nternational **D**esign **E**nvironment.
Ride Force Count (RFC)
[TRS] A calculation of Suspension Factors that are used to determine the track access charging regime for a given freight vehicle. It is based on dynamic vertical wheel loads obtained from simulations. Using a pre-defined **Track Geometry** file. Once filtered, these are the vehicle's ride forces. The ride forces are then expressed in terms of **Standard Deviations** (**SD**) over 200m segments and related to the SDs of the vertical Track Geometry over the same 200m segments. Evaluation of the ride forces against the **Vertical Track Geometry** SD population returns a single value which is the Ride Force Count. This measure is related to **Suspension Bands** as follows:
  RFC   Suspension Former

factor	band	Wagon type description
1.098	1	Four-wheel Wagon with Pedestal Suspension
1.058	2	Four-wheel Wagon having leaf springs, friction damped
1.018	3	Bogie Wagon with Three Piece Bogie
0.978	4	Bogie Wagon with Swing Motion Bogie and four-wheel Wagon with parabolic springs
0.938	5	Basic bogie wagon with primary swings, e.g. Y25
0.898	6	Bogie wagon with enhanced primary springs – Low Track Force bogies, TF25, 'axle motion' (like HV primary sprung bogies)
0.858	7	Bogie wagon with enhanced primary springs and steering

Ride Quality
[PW] Collective term for the outcome of a quantitative assessment of the **Track Geometry** data. This data can be interpreted in terms of the comfort of a **Passenger** experiencing it, hence the term. See also **Track Quality** (**TQ**), **Track Quality Band**.
RIDRR
Railway **I**ndustry **D**ispute **R**esolution **R**ules, see also Claims Allocation and Handling Agreement (**CAHA**).
RIFAA
Rail **I**ndustry **F**irst **A**id **A**ssociation.
RIFF
Rail **I**ndustry **F**orecasting **F**ramework.
RIG
See **R**ail **I**ndustry **G**roup.
Right Angle Measurement
[PW] The measurement of a **Crossing Angle** by means of a right angled triangle.

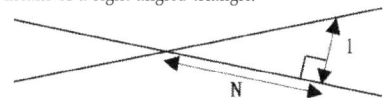

Whilst this measure gives a different value from a **Centre Line Measurement**, it is more directly useful when setting out the **Crossing**.
Right Away (RA)
[Ops.] An indication given to a driver that they may move off from a **Station** if it is safe to do so;
• When given a by a **Guard**, this takes form of two short indications on the buzzer. See **Buzzer Codes**
• When given by a **Right Away Indicator** (**RAI**).
Right Away Indicator (RA)
[Sig.] An illuminated display provided to relay a **Train Ready To Start** (**TRTS**) signal to a driver, so that they may start off from a **Station**. It consists of an illuminated display bearing the letter **R** or letters RA. Also **Right Away** (RA).
Right Away Plunger (RA Plunger)
[Sig.] The **Plunger** or other device used to initiate the operation of a **Right Away Indicator** (**RA**). See **Train Ready To Start Plunger**.

ELLIS' BRITISH RAILWAY ENGINEERING ENCYCLOPÆDIA

Right Direction
Right Direction Move
Right Direction Movement
[Ops.] The opposite of **Wrong Direction** and **Wrong Road**, namely a **Train Movement** made in the **Normal Direction** for that **Line**. Also **Right Road**.

Right Hand Common Crossing
[PW]
a) [WR] In the former **Great Western Railway** (**GWR**) area a **Common Crossing** with the **Splice Rail** on the left of the **Point Rail** when viewed from the **Wing Rail Fronts**. The opposite is a **Left Hand Common Crossing**.
b) Elsewhere, a **Left Hand Splice** (**LHS**) □ **Crossing**.

Right Hand Curve
a) [PW] The direction in which a **Curve** diverges from the **Straight** when viewed with one's **Back to Low Mileage**. A **Curve** to the right is thus a **Right Hand Curve**
b) [Elec.] A **Right Hand Curve** is one in which the **Right Hand Rail** (**RHR**) is highest, viewed with one's **Back to Low Mileage**, therefore generally the opposite way to the **Permanent Way Engineer**
See also **Left Hand Curve**.

Right Hand Parallel Wing (RHPW)
[PW] As a suffix to a description of a **Common Crossing**, it describes a **Common Crossing** having a **Parallel Wing Rail** on the right hand side of the **Crossing Vee**. See also **Double Parallel Wing** (**DPW**).

Right Hand Rail (RHR)
[PW] The **Rail** on the right hand side of a **Track**, when viewed with one's **Back to Low Mileage**. The opposite is **Left Hand Rail** (**LHR**).

Right Hand Relay
[Sig.] The right hand half of a **Twin Relay**, as viewed from the front.

Right Hand Running
[Ops.] An arrangement of operation on a pair of **Tracks** where **Trains** run on the right hand **Track** in the direction of travel. The opposite is **Left Hand Running**.

Right Hand Side (RHS)
a) [PW] Being on the right of centre when viewed with one's back to the **Switch Fronts** in a **Switch and Crossing Layout** (**S&C Layout**)
b) Being on the right of centre when viewed with one's back to **London** or **Back to Low Mileage**
See also **Left Hand Side** (**LHS**).

Right Hand Splice (RHS)
[PW] A **Splice Rail** fitted on the **Right Hand Side** (**RHS**) of the **Point Rail** when viewed from the end of the **Wing Rail Fronts**. This description is also applied to the **Crossing** itself, so a **Crossing** with a **Right Hand Splice** is a **Right Hand Common Crossing**. See also **Left Hand Splice** (**LHS**).

Right Hand Switch (RHS)
[PW]
a) A **Set of Switches** in which the **Stock Rail Set** is on the **Right Hand Side** □ **Switch Half Set** when viewed from the **Switch Toe** looking towards the **Crossing**
b) The Right Hand Side Switch Half Set when viewed from the Switch Toe looking towards the Switch Heel.
See also **Left Hand Switch** (**LHS**).

Right Hand Switch Closed (RHSC)
[PW] When viewed from the **Switch Toe** end, this describes which **Switch Half Set** is closed up when the **Switches** are **Normal**. The opposite is **Left Hand Switch Closed** (**LHSC**).

Right Hand Transition Rail
[PW] A **Transition Rail** in which the step in the **Outside Edge** (**OE**) is located on the right when viewed from the portion of the **Rail** with the larger **Rail Section**. The opposite is a **Left Hand Transition Rail**.

Right Hand Turnout (RHTO)
[PW] A **Turnout** in which the **Stock Rail Set** is on the **Right Hand Side** □ **Switch Half Set** when viewed from the **Switch Toe** looking towards the **Crossing**.

Right Hand Twist Rail
[PW] A **Twist Rail** in which the **Rail Foot** is rotated to the left when viewed from the **Vertical** portion of the **Twist Rail**. Seen from the Vertical portion, this **Rail** would be located on the right of the **Track**. The opposite is a **Left Hand Twist Rail**.

Right Road
Right Road Move
Right Road Movement
Colloquial alternative for Right Direction, Right Direction Move, Right Direction Movement.

Right Side Failure (RSF)
[Sig.] A failure that causes a piece of equipment to cease functioning correctly but without causing danger to the **Safety of the Line**. Also known as a **Negligible Risk Failure**. See also **Fail-Safe**.

Right Time
[Ops.] Term describing the on-time departure, arrival or passing of a **Train**.

Right Time Railway (RTR)
a) An initiative by the UK **Railway Industry** to improve and maintain punctuality
b) [Unk.] A **Railway** on which all **Trains** always arrive and depart at the advertised times.

RII
RIIF
[Sig.] Remote Interlocking Interface.

RiLA
(Tradename) **Rail Infrastructure** Alignment Acquisition System. A system which uses a GPS measurement system combined with inertial measurement and laser scanning to survey the position of the **Track**, **Rail Profile**, and record parameters such as **Track Gauge** and **Cant**. Developed by RailData BV of Utrecht, the Netherlands.

RIM
Radio Interface Module.

RIMINI
(*rim-inn-ee*) [NR] Risk Minimisation, a standardised process for identifying and recording the safest practical Safe system of Work (SSoW) for a particular activity undertaken On or Near the Line.

RIMINI Form
(*rim-inn-ee form*) [NR] The colloquial name for the RT9099 'COSS Record of Arrangements and Briefing Form' that records the arrangements for working on the track. It provides the opportunity for information about the location, hazards, working methods and details of protection to be recorded, including sighting distance and lookout arrangements. It also records the details of who is present and the reference number of their current competency certificate

Ring Dam
See Garland.

RINM
See Railway Infrastructure Network Model.

RIO
Railway Incident Officer.

RIPG
Rail Industry Planning Group.

RIR
Railway Interoperability Regulations.

RIRG
a) Rail Industry Review Group
b) Route Investment Review Group.

RIS
Railway Industry Standards.

RISAS
Railway Industry Supply Approval Scheme. See also Link-up.

RISB
[NR] Rail Industry Safety Body, The organisation that Lord Cullen recommended should replace Railway Safety. See Rail Accident Investigation Branch (RAIB).

Riser Wall
See Platform Wall.

RISF
Rail Industry Skills Forum.

Risk
The product of the severity of a hazard and probability of its occurrence.

Risk Landscaping Tool (RiLa)
A simulation-based risk modelling tool developed by the Swiss Federal Office of Transport (FOT). It has a generic structure for calculating risk estimates from Infrastructure data and Timetable (TT) information, which uses separately developed safety models to input hazards into the simulation at appropriate rates.

Risk-based Maintenance
A policy whereby Maintenance activities are prioritised on the basis of the overall risk introduced by not carrying the Maintenance at all. See also Reactive Maintenance, Steady State Maintenance.

RISQS
The Railway Industry Supplier Qualification Scheme.

RISSC
Railway Industry Standard Strategy Committee.

RITC
Railway Industry Training Council.

RITS
Rail □ Infrastructure Transport System.

RIU
Radio In-fill Unit.

RIV
Regolamento Internazionale Veicoli; regulations governing the international exchange of Freight Vehicles.

RJIS
Rail Journey Information Service.

RJS
See Rail Joint Straightening.

RJWG
Route Joint Working Group.

RK
[TRS] An acronym representing a Restaurant Kitchen Coach.

RKB
[TRS] An acronym representing a Restaurant Kitchen Buffet Coach.

RL
a) See Relief Line. See also Slow Line
b) See RL Loading.

RL Loading
[Civ.] A Bridge loading model for use only on Passenger □ Rapid Transit □ Railway systems on Lines where Main Line □ Locomotives and Rolling Stock do not operate. See also RU, RU loading.

RLB
[TRS] An acronym representing a Restaurant Lounge Buffet Coach.

RLE
Rail Link Engineering.

RLEE
Red Light Enforcement Equipment.

RLS
[NR] Railtrack Line Standard, now called Network Rail Company Standard (NRCS).

R_m
Main Line Radius (R), see Equivalent Radius, R_e.

RM
See Restricted Manual.

RM3
Railway Management Maturity Model.

RMB
[TRS] An acronym representing a Restaurant Miniature Buffet Coach.

RMBF
[TRS] An acronym representing a Restaurant Miniature Buffet **First Class** □ **Coach**.

RMBT
[TRS] An acronym representing a Restaurant Miniature Buffet (Trolley/Buffet) **Coach**.

RMC
[TRS] Rolling Moment Co-efficient.

RMDS
Remote Monitoring and Diagnostics System

RME
Rail Management Engineer.

RMEL
See Redifon MEL.

RMMM
See Rail Mounted Maintenance Machine.

RMP
Reverse Movement Protection

RMT
a) (Tradename) National Union of **Rail**, **Maritime** and **Transport** workers, representing **Traincrew** and blue collar workers on the **Railway**, formerly the National Union of Railwaymen (NUR)
b) Royal Mail Terminal.

RM*xx*
RM*xxx*
[PW] Types of **Plasser Automatic Ballast Cleaner** (**PABC**). (numbers include 62, 74, 90, 95, 900)

RNA
Railway Notification of Accidents Regulations.

RNAS
Route Network Availability Strategy.

RNxx Clip
[PW Obs.] A **Rail Fastening** developed in France 1946. Used with **Flat Bottom Rail** carried on the F16 and F17 **Concrete Sleepers**. The RNB6 was intended for use with **109 Pound** and the RNB7 for **110A**.

RO
Rail Operator.

RoRo
Roll on Roll off, a more general alternative to **Ra-Ra**.

ROA
[Ops.] Right on Arrival.

Roach (ZDA)
[NR] A 23 ton capacity **Open Wagon** used for materials. See **Wagon Names**.

Road
[Col.]
a) A term for a single **Line** of **Railway**, e.g. Up Road, see **Bang Road**, **Hard Road**, **Right Road**, **Wrong Road**
b) A term for a **Route**, particularly in terms of **Route Knowledge**, e.g. **Road Learning**. See also **Learning the Road**.

Road Gate Stop
[Sig.] A mechanical locking device, activated by a **Lever** in the **Gate Box** or **Signal Box**, which holds the **Level Crossing** (LC, LX) □ **Gates** closed across the highway. This Stop normally lies flush with the highway surface. See **Gate Stop Lever**, **Rail Gate Stop**.

Road Learning
[Col.] The shorter name for **Learning the Road**.

Road Mode
Describing a **Road Rail Vehicle** (**RRV**) prepared for travel by road, e.g. **Rail Wheels** retracted, steering unlocked and normal lights activated. See also **Rail Mode**, **Travel Mode**.

Road Rail
Able to move equally well as a road vehicle and as a **Rail Vehicle**. See also **Road Rail Dozer**, **Road Rail Dumper**, **Road Rail Excavator**, **Road Rail Vehicle** (**RRV**), **Road Railer** (**RR**).

Road Rail Access Point (RRAP)
(*rap*) A **Level Crossing** (LC, LX) style installation provided for the sole purpose of allowing Road Rail (**RR**) plant to access the **Track** easily. Such facilities are normally closed off with a barrier when the **Line** is open to **Trains**.

Road Rail Dozer
A bulldozer fitted with auxiliary **Rail Wheels** that allow it to move itself to site along the **Railway** without damaging the **Sleepers**.

Road Rail Dumper
A vehicle, incorporating a large bucket for carrying materials, which can operate both on the road and on the **Rails**.

Road Rail Excavator
A rubber tyred **Road Rail** 360° excavator equipped with auxiliary **Rail Wheels**, and generally fitted with equipment allowing it to function as a crane. These machines have revolutionised the way in which many types of construction, **Track Maintenance** and **Track Renewal** works are carried out, as they are simultaneously a small **Locomotive**, a **Rail Crane**, and an excavator. Sometimes contracted to **Road Railer** (**RR**).

Road Rail Vehicle (RRV)
Any vehicle adapted to operate equally well on road and **Rail**. Base vehicles include Land Rovers, lorries, Unimogs and **Mobile Elevating Work Platforms** (**MEWP**). They are now used in nearly every role including delivering materials, carrying out inspections, **Track Recording**, **Overhead Line Equipment** (**OLE**) □ **Maintenance** and emergency response. Sometimes contracted to **Road Railer** (**RR**). See also **Bruff**, **KGT**, **Permaquip**.

Road Railer (RR)
Generally, a road vehicle or piece of construction plant adapted to operate equally well on road and **Rail**, commonly used to describe the following:
a) A rubber tyred road **Rail** 360° excavator with auxiliary **Rail Wheels** and equipment allowing it to function as a crane, see also **Road Rail Excavator**
b) A **Mobile Elevating Work Platform (MEWP)**, Land Rover or lorry equipped with auxiliary Rail Wheels, see also **Road Rail Vehicle (RRV)**.

Road Spread
[PW] A **Track** failure in which the **Running Rails** move apart from each other. Also called **Gauge Spread**, it is generally caused by rotten **Sleepers**, in turn caused by poor **Track Maintenance**. A common cause of **Derailments** in **Sidings**.

Road Traffic Signal
At a **Level Crossing** (LC, LX), a stop signal mandatory for road traffic, comprising a steady amber then two flashing red lights.

Crossing clear   Warning   Stop
                  (steady amber) (alternating flashing red)

Also **Wig-wags, Wig-wag lights**.

Roadbed
See **Formation**. Also **Solum**.

Roaring Rails
[Col.] A term for **Rails** displaying **Short Wavelength Corrugation**, which produces a roaring noise as **Trains** pass over it.

Robel
(Tradename) A manufacturer of **Track Tools**, **Maintenance** machinery and other **Track**-related products, based in Freilassing, southeastern Bavaria, Germany.

Robert
[Obs.] The obsolescent **Phonetic Alphabet** word representing R. Replaced by **Romeo**.

Robust Kerb
[Civ.] A vertical construction, typically 350mm **Above Rail Level (ARL)**, running the length of a key area of **Railway** such as an **Underbridge (UB)** and intended to guide **Derailed** ▫ **Trains** along the **Railway**. Whilst such a Kerb should be 1.5m from the **Nearest Rail** (so that a Derailed **Wheelset** is guided by that **Rail** first) this is often not practical. See also **Derailment Containment, Guard Rail**.

Robust Train Protection
[Sig.] A suite of measures applied to **Signalling Systems** to reduce the risk of collisions due to **Signals Passed at Danger (SPAD)**. Typically this includes provision of **Double Red Aspects** and better **Flank Protection**.

ROC
a) See **Rail Operating Centre**.
b) See **Route Operations Centre**.

ROCC
[NR] **Regional Operations Control** Centre. See **Railway Operations Control**.

Rock Armour
[Civ.] Large pieces of rock placed at the base of a **Structure** or earthwork to reduce the effects of **Scour** or wave damage.

Rock Combing
[Civ.] A process of identification and removal of loose rock elements from a rock face to prevent such debris falling onto the **Railway**.

Rock Slope Hazard Index (RSHI)
[Civ.] A score reflecting the potential for a rock slope to fail and cause harm.

Rocker Frame
[Sig.] A type of **Lever Frame** which utilises a rocker arrangement to achieve the **Locking** ▫ **Function**; typically a type of **Catch Handle Locking**.

Rodding
The $1^{5}/_{8}$ inch by $1^{1}/_{4}$ inch (41.3mm by 31.8mm) channel section bar weighing around 10 **Pounds per Yard**, used to link mechanical items in the signalling system, such as **Compensators, Cranks, Levers, Switches**, etc. Also **Point Rodding**.

RODS
Rail **O**rigin **D**estination **S**urvey.

ROEP
Rise **o**f **E**arth **P**otential.

ROF
Royal **O**rdnance **F**actory.

ROGS
(*roggs*) See **Railways and Other Guided Transport Systems (Safety) Regulations**.

ROGTS
[NPT] alternative abbreviation for **ROGS**, see **Railways and Other Guided Transport Systems (Safety) Regulations**.

ROL
See **Restricted Overlap**.

Roll Away
An alternative for **Runaway**.

Roll Space
See **Platform Safety Space**.

Roll-by Test
[Ops.] A planned visual check that the **Rail Wheels** of **Wagons** passing an observer at slow speed are all rotating correctly.

Roller Baseplate
[PW] A **Slide Baseplate** equipped with rollers in the **Slide Table** that reduce the effort required to **Throw** the **Switches**; Schwihag and Austroroll are tradenames.

Rolling Contact Fatigue (RCF)
[PW] Collective term for all **Rail Defects** directly attributable to the rolling action of a **Rail Wheel** on the **Rail**. See **Gauge Corner Cracking (GCC)**.

405

Rolling Contact Flaw
[PW] A **Rail Defect** on or very near the **Running Surface** of a **Rail** caused by the interaction of wheels on said Rail. See also **Gauge Corner Cracking** (GCC)

Rolling Radius
The effective wheel radius measured at the point where a **Rail Wheel** contacts the **Rail**.

Rolling Radius Difference

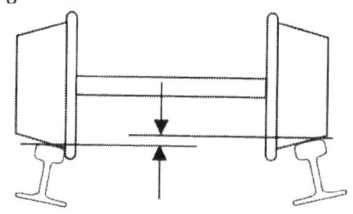

The difference in effective wheel radius caused by the conical **Wheel Profile** when a **Wheelset** negotiates a **Curve** at a speed which causes **Cant Deficiency**. The diagram above is exaggerated for clarity.

Rolling Stock
Collective term for all **Rail Vehicles** excluding **Traction Units** as they move themselves and do not need to be rolled.

Rolling Stock Acceptance Board (RSAB)
[RT] The body established by **Railtrack** (RT) to manage the acceptance process for new or modified **Rail Vehicles** designed to operate over its **Infrastructure**. This body was subsequently replaced by the **Network Rail Acceptance Panel**.

Rolling Stock Library (RSL)
[NR] A system linked to **TOPS** and containing details of all **Rolling Stock** approved by **Network Rail** (NR) for operation on its **Infrastructure**.

ROM
Regional Operating Manager.

Romeo
The **Phonetic Alphabet** word representing R.

Root Ball
A mass consisting of any large or small roots of a tree and the earth attached to them.

ROP
Rules of the Plan, now called **Train Planning Rules** (TPR).

Rope-worked Railway
A **Railway** where the motive power is provided by a stationary engine or motor hauling a rope to which the **Rail Vehicles** are attached.

ROR
[NR, Ops.] Rules of the Route, now called the **Engineering Access Statement** (EAS).

ROS
Restriction of Speed, see **Speed Restriction**. See also **Emergency Speed Restriction** (ESR), **Permanent Speed Restriction** (PSR), **Temporary Speed Restriction** (TSR).

ROSCO
(*ros-ko*) **Rolling Stock** (Leasing) Company. A transitional organisation during **Privatisation** which provided leasing services associated with **Traction and Rolling Stock** (T&RS). The original names were Angel (now **Angel Train Group**), **Porterbrook** (now **Porterbrook Leasing Company**) and **Eversholt** (now HSBC Rail).

RoSE
Reliability Centred Maintenance of **Signalling Equipment**.

ROSIN
Railway Open System Interconnection Network.

ROSS
Rationalisation of **Signalling** Scotland.

ROSY
Route Opportunity System.

Rotabroach
(Tradename) A type of **Rail Drill** which uses an annular cutter to speed up the drilling process. See **Trepanning**.

Rotary Block
[Sig.] A form of **Block Instrument** used on the former **Midland Railway** which combined **Block Controls** and a form of **Lock And Block** to minimise **Signaller's** errors in **Block Signalling**. The Signaller was provided with a handle which could only normally be rotated clockwise through **Line Blocked**, **Line Clear** and **Train on Line** positions, which corresponded with the Indications above it on the Instrument. Various **Treadles** and **Controls** fitted to the system prevented the Signaller from advancing (or reversing) the handle unless all relevant conditions were met:
- After moving the handle from Line Blocked to Line Clear, the needle itself would only turn if the Home Signal was On. This would release the Starting Signal at the Signal Box □ on the Approach to be pulled for one **Train** only
- The handle could not be restored from here to Line Blocked unless both Signallers operated a co-operative Line Clear Cancel button on their instruments which would electrically release the ratchet
- When the Train entered the **Section**, the Signaller would rotate the handle to Train on Line, where it would lock
- When the train passed, it would operate a **Treadle** near the Starting Signal. Provided the Home Signal was **Off**, the lock on the instrument would be **Released**, allowing the Signaller to advance it to Line Blocked. However, if the Signal was not **Replaced** behind the Train, the needle would remain at the Train on Line position
- If it was necessary to release the instrument from Train on Line in any other circumstance, a glass-protected plunger had to be operated.

Also **Midland Rotary Block**.

Rotation Damper
Equipment for inhibiting any rapid rotational motion of a vehicle **Bogie**. See also **Yaw Damper**.

Rotational Failure
[Civ.] A catastrophic failure of a **Cutting Slope** or **Embankment** resulting in a mass of material rotating about a virtual centre point. This type of failure is Slip Circle or Slip Plane. aggravated by poor drainage of the slope and overloading of the top of the slope. Colloquially known as a **Bank Slip** or **Slip**. See also **Slip Circle**, **Slip Plane**.

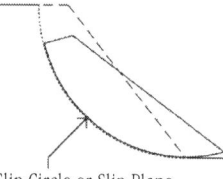

Rotational Stiffness
[TRS] The measurement of the resistance to rotational motion of a vehicle **Bogie**. See also **Yaw**.

ROTE
Risk-based **Maintenance** of **T**elecommunications **E**quipment

ROTP
[NR, Hist.] **R**ules **o**f **t**he **P**lan, now called **Train Planning Rules** (TPR).

ROTR
[NR, Hist.] **R**ules **o**f **t**he **R**oute, now called the **Engineering Access Statement** (EAS).

ROTS
(*rotts*) See **Railway and Other Transport Systems (Approval of Works, Plant and Equipment) Regulations 1994**.

ROTT
[PW] **R**efurbishment **o**f **T**imber **T**rack.

Rough Ride
[Ops.]
a) A term used to describe the experience of travelling over a **Track Fault** or **Track Irregularity**
b) The colloquial term for the report made by a driver as a result of such an occurrence.

Rough Shunt
[Ops.]
a) Describing an improper **Shunting** operation, one in which the **Rail Vehicles** are pushed or stopped violently
b) The colloquial term for a **Derailment** resulting from such improper Shunting operations.

Roundhouse
An archaic term for a circular **Engine Shed** containing a **Turntable** and many radially arranged **Sidings**.

Rounding
[PW] The adjustment applied to the first and last **Versines** in a **Transition Curve** to correct geometrical inaccuracies in the **Hallade** method. If the first or last **Versine Rises** (**Transition Steps**) are equal to or greater than a **Half Step**, then one sixth of the full Versine Rise (Transition Step) is deducted from the appropriate terminal Versine value.

Route
a) A high level description of a **Railway's** alignment or a **Train's** journey, e.g. London to Birmingham via Rugby, Old Line, Chat Moss
b) [Sig.] The **Signalled** path from one **Signal** to the next **Signal**
c) [Sig.] The series of **Normal** and **Reverse** □ **Points** and **Clear** □ **Signals** that make up a **Train's** path through a **Junction** or along a Railway.

Route Acceptance Request
[NR] An application by an operator, owner, etc. to run a new or modified **Rail Vehicle** on **Network Rail's** (NR) □ **Infrastructure**.

Route Availability (RA)
[NR]
a) A number which describes the effective loading a **Rail Vehicle** applies to the **Track**, ranging from 1 (least) to 10 (most)
b) A number which describes the effective loading a particular Track or **Bridge** can withstand, ranging from 1 (least) to 10 (most) at a particular speed (or the **Permissible Speed** (PS) if no other speed is stated).
The Route Availability of a Rail Vehicle must not exceed the relevant Route Availability value(s) of any **Structure** along its journey at its **Permissible Speed**. This leads to **Routes** being given Route Availability values between **Junctions**, based on the lowest value on that part of the Route, or may cause the Permissible Speed to be reduced for Trains conveying Rail Vehicles with higher RA values.

Route Bar
[Sig.] Within a **Solid State Interlocking** (SSI), an additional control added from the **Technician's Console** (**Technician's Terminal**) which prevents the **Signaller's** being able to **Set** certain **Routes**.

Route Card
The card which records the **Routes** a driver is considered competent to drive unaccompanied. It is signed by the driver and counter-signed by their **Driver Manager**.

Route Class
[Sig.] The category of a signalled **Route**, which in turn determines the **Controls** to be applied to that Route and the circumstances under which it may be Set. See **Calling-On Route**, **Main Route**, **Shunt Route**, **Warning Route**, **POSA**.

Route Drivability Tool
[NR, Sig.] An online tool that allows the assessment of the impacts of a proposed or existing **Signalling Scheme** design on a driver's workload, or the **Drivability** of a **Route**.

Route Handed
[PW] Describing a **Turnout** in which the **Main Line** is curved at the same Radius (R) as the normal **Turnout Curve**, making the **Turnout Route** into **Straight Track**.

Route Holding
See **Route Locking**.

407

Route Indication
[Sig.] The information provided to a driver by a Route Indicator (RI) or Junction Indicator (JI).

Route Indicator (RI)
[Sig.] An Indicator associated with a Signal that shows a driver which Route is Set where more than one Route is available. See Position Light Junction Indicator (PLJI), Miniature Alphanumeric Route Indicator (MARI), Standard Alphanumeric Route Indicator (SARI). See also Junction Indicator (JI).

Route Knowledge
Before any driver can drive a Train along a particular Route, they must first learn the locations of Junctions, Stations, Signals, Permissible Speeds (PS), etc. This is Route Knowledge. The process of acquiring it is colloquially called Learning the Road or Road Learning. See also Signing a Route.

Route Lever
[Sig.] A Lever in a Mechanical Signal Box which, when pulled, Sets a complete Route. It was the precursor of the Route Setting capabilities of the Power Signal Box (PSB) □ Panels. See also Automatic Route Setting (ARS).

Route Locking
[Sig.] A variety of Interlocking where the whole Route is maintained as Set by the Signaller until the Train passes the equipment being Locked. Also Maintained Locking, Route Holding. See Train Operated Route Release (TORR).

Route Memory
[Sig.] Within a Solid State Interlocking (SSI), 64 bytes of RAM which are used to record the status of 256 Routes.

Route Miles
The geographical distance between two points on a Railway.

Route Operations Centre (ROC)
See Rail Operating Centre (ROC).

Route Proving
[Sig.] The test applied to ensure that a Signalled Route is ready for the Train to use it, i.e. that all Points are Set correctly and Locked, and there are no other Trains on it. See also Proved, Proving.

Route Relay Interlocking (RRI)
[Sig.] An arrangement of Relays within an Interlocking in a Route based manner, rather than a function based topology. Also Free-wired Interlocking.

Route Release
Route Releasing
[Sig.] The Release of Route Locking: the action of cancelling a Set □ Route before a Train has passed over it. This normally involves a set time elapsing during which all Signals affected are returned to a Stop Aspect, thus ensuring that Trains come to a stand. See also Sectional Route Release.

Route Request Data
[Sig.] Within a Solid State Interlocking (SSI), the data file which contains commands that are executed only on demand, when the SSI serves a Panel Request. Route request data specifies the availability conditions and Locking conditions for each Route defined in the Interlocking.

Route Setting
[Sig.] A high-level Signalling control system in which all the Points, Signals and Indicators for a Route are Set by the operation of a few buttons (Plungers). See also Automatic Route Setting (ARS). See also Route Lever.

Route Setting Agent (RSA)
[NR] A competent person appointed to co-ordinate the operation of Points (Switches) manually during a Complex Points Failure. The Agent may be assisted by a Points Operator (PO).

Route Setting Controls
[Sig.] The buttons on a Route Setting Panel, which allow the operator to Set a Route rather than having to Set each Set of Points and every Signal.

Route Setting Panel
[Sig.] A Signal Box Panel for a specific geographical area equipped with Route Setting capability, and displaying the condition of all Signals within that area.

Route to Gold (RtG)
[NR] An initiative to record the outcomes of Document Review Notices (DRN) with a view to assessing the technical performance of Contractor's Responsible Engineers (CRE) and Network Rail Project Engineers (PE).

Routes
[NR] The Network Rail (NR) devolved management units. They are:
- Anglia
- Kent/HS1
- Merseyrail
- Midland &Continental
- North Eastern
- North Western
- Scotland
- Sussex
- Wessex
- Western
- Wales

By mid-2012 these replaced Territories, which in turn replaced Zones, which in turn were based on the Regions of British Rail (BR). However, the boundaries will be familiar ...

ROW
a) (*roe*) See Renewal of Way, see also ROW Code.
b) Right of Way.

ROW Code
(*roe code*) [PW Obs./Col.] Renewal of Way Code, An index number relating to the type of work proposed within a particular Relaying Item.

ROW Item
(*roe item*) [PW Obs./Col.] See Renewal of Way Item.

Rowlets
[Hist.] A 17th century term for roller-like wheels fitted to **Chaldron** □ **Wagons** on **Wagonways** with wooden **Rails** in the north east.

ROY
[TRS] An acronym representing a Royal **Train** □ **Coach**.

Roy Method
[TRS Hist.] A means of determining the lateral **Rail / Wheel** clearances for **Locomotives** with many coupled **Axles**, e.g. **Steam Locomotives**. The method assumes that the outer wheel of the **Leading Axle** is in contact with the **Outer Rail** and the **Trailing Axle** sits radial to the **Curve**.

RP
a) **Route** Planner
b) [Ops.] Railplan, a London-wide public transport model covering **London Underground** (**LUL**), **London Overground** (**LOROL**), Network Rail (**NR**), Docklands Light Railway (**DLR**), **Trams** and London bus services.

RPA
a) See **Rail Plant Association**
b) Rotary Pneumatic Accelerator
c) [Éire] **Railway** Procurement Agency
d) Regional Planning Assessments.

RPB
Regional Planning Body.

RPC
a) **Rail** Passengers' Council
b) **Railway** Policy and Cullen.

RPCL
Rail Point **Clamp Lock**.

RPF
Rail Performance Fund.

RPG
Regional Planning Guidance.

RPI
Revenue Protection Inspector, the modern name for a **Ticket Collector**.

RPL
[NR] **Rail** Property Limited.

RPOS
[CTRL] Responsible Person on Site, the equivalent within **Channel Tunnel Rail Link** of a **Person in Charge of Possession** (**PICOP**).

RPP
a) **Rail** □ **Passenger** Partnership
b) Reliability Programme Plan.

RPPS
Rail □ **Passenger** Partnership Scheme.

RPR
Rheostatic Proving **Relay**.

RPT
Route Programme Team.

RR
a) See **Road Railer**
b) See **Rerailing**
c) See **Regional Railways**
d) See **Run Round**.

RRAP
(*rap*)See **Road Rail Access Point**.

RRD
a) See **Rolling Radius Difference**
b) Retractable Restraining Device.

RRI
See **Route Relay Interlocking**.

RRIP
[Sig.] **Route Relay Interlocking** Processor.

RRNE
[Hist.] **Regional Railways** North East, latterly Northern Spirit (**NS**), effectively a predecessor of **Northern Rail**.

RRNW
[Hist.] **Regional Railways** North West, latterly First North Western (**FNW**), effectively a predecessor of **Northern Rail**.

RRSC
[Obs.] **Railtrack** (**RT**) □ **Railway Safety Case**. See **Network Rail Safety Case** (**NRSC**).

RRUK
Rail Research UK – Based at Birmingham University.

RRUKA
See **Rail Research UK Association**.

RRV
See **Road Rail Vehicle**.

RRWD
[PW] **Rerail**, □ **Weld**, □ **Destress**. An alternative acronym describing **Rerailing** □ **Continuous Welded Rail** (**CWR**).

RS
a) See **Resleepering**
b) See **Restressing**
c) **Railway** Safety
d) Release Speed.

RSA
a) See **Route Setting Agent**
b) **Railway** Study Association
c) **Rail** Systems Agency.

RSAB
(*arr-sab*) See **Rolling Stock Acceptance Board**.

RSAG
Railway Safety Advisory Group.

RSAP
Rail □ **Station** Accessibility Programme, a **Greater Manchester Integrated Transport Authority** (**GMITA**) initiative.

RSAR
[NR] The Reading **Station** Area Redevelopment project.

RSBS
Railway Standard Building Specification.

RSC
a) See **Railway Safety Case**
b) See **Radio Survey Coach**
c) Railway Skills Council, the skills council for the **Railway Industry** sector
d) Return Screening **Conductor**
e) [Éire] Railway Safety Commission.

RSCo.
Common shorthand for **Railway** □ **Signal** Co., a former manufacturer of **Signalling Equipment**.

RSCWR
Railway (Safety Critical Work) Regulations 1994. Also R(SCW).

RSD
a) **Railway** □ **Signalling** Design
b) Reference Standard Design.

RSDT
Rail / Sleeper Delivery Train.

RSF
See **Right Side Failure**.

RSHI
See **Rock Slope Hazard Index**.

RSIS
Rail □ **Station** Improvement Strategy, a **Transport for Greater Manchester** (TfGM) initiative.

RSL
See **Rolling Stock Library**.

RSMD
Rolling Stock □ Maintenance □ Depot.

RSO
See **Residual Switch Opening**.

RSP
See **Rail Settlement Plan**.

RSPG
a) See **Railway Safety Principles and Guidance**
b) [NR] Route Strategy Planning Group

RSRP
Rail Safety Research Programme.

RSRS
Railtrack Safety Rating System.

RSS
a) [TRS] An acronym representing a Restaurant Self-service **Coach**
b) Regional Spatial Strategy.

RSSB
[NR] Formerly the **Rail Safety and Standards Board**, A body established in April 2003, implementing one of the core sets of recommendations of Lord **Cullen's** inquiry into the **Ladbroke Grove Accident**. The Company's key objectives are:
- To lead and facilitate the **Railway Industry's** work to improve the health and safety performance of the **Railways** in Great Britain
- To manage the **Railway Group Standards** (**RGS**) on behalf of the Industry
- To lead formal inquiries to ensure safety lessons are learned
- To publish annual Railway Strategic Safety Plans
- To measure, report and inform on health and safety performance, safety intelligence, trends, data and risk
- To support cross-industry groups in national initiatives which address major areas of safety concern
- To represent the UK **Rail Industry** in the development of European legislation and standards that impact on the rail system.

RSSB is a not for profit company owned by major industry stakeholders. It is independent of any single **Railway Company** and of their commercial interests.

RST
[LUL] **Route** Setting Tape. See also **Programme Machine**.

RSU
[PW] Roller Search Unit. The Sperry wheel probe fitted to the U15 □ **Walking Sticks** and **Ultrasonic Test Vehicles**.

RSWLCM
Rolling Stock Whole Life Cost Model.

RT
a) See **Railtrack**
b) Radiographic Testing

RT10S
[RT, NR, Hist.] The purchase order conditions for the purchase of services (England and Scotland). This has now been replaced by **NR3**.

RT12
[RT, NR, Hist.] The conditions for a services agreement. This has now been superseded by **NR2**.

RT16
[RT, NR, Hist.]The **Special Conditions** for use in conjunction with the **ICE** Design and Construct Conditions of Contract. This has now been replaced by **NR9**.

RT1A
[RT, Hist.] The former standard **Infrastructure Maintenance Contract** (**IMC**), now replaced by **IMC2000**. See also **Infrastructure Maintenance Manager** (**IMM**). All such activities have now been taken in-house by **Network Rail** (**NR**).

RT1B
[RT, Hist.] The former standard **Track Renewals** contract.

RT21
[RT, NR, Hist.] The **Special Conditions** for use in conjunction with the JCT Measured Term of Contract. This has now been superseded by **NR4**.

RT22
[RT, NR, Hist.] The **Special Conditions** for use in conjunction with the JCT Intermediate Form of Building Contract for works of simple content (1998 edition). This has now been superseded by **NR4**.

RT23
[RT, NR, Hist.] The **Special Conditions** for use in conjunction with the JCT Standard Form of Management Contract (1998 edition). This has now been superseded by **NR4**.

RT24
[RT, NR, Hist.] The **Special Conditions** for use in conjunction with the IChemE Reimbursable Contract. This has now been replaced by **NR12**.

RT27
[RT, NR, Hist.] The contract for rapid response to structure damage and flooding. This has now been superseded by **NR4**.

RT3
[RT, NR, Hist.] The **Special Conditions** for use in conjunction with the **ICE** Conditions of Contract (sixth edition). This has now been superseded by **NR4**.

RT3189
[NR] A form completed by the **Signaller** with the driver of a **Train** that has been involved in a **Signal Passed at Danger** (**SPAD**) incident.

RT60
[RT, NR] The title of a suite of standard **Switch and Crossing** (**S&C**) designs utilising **CEN60E1** and **CEN60E1A1** ▫ **Rails**. The designs use improved **Bloss Transition** forms, allowing RT60 designs to be shorter than other designs at the same **Maximum Speed** (V_m) through the **Turnout Route**. Now being superseded by **NR60**.

RT9
[RT, NR, Hist.] conditions of contract for the purchase of **Goods**. This has now been replaced by **NR1**.

RT9099
[NR] The '**COSS** Record of Arrangements and Briefing Form' that records the arrangements for working **On or Near the Line**. It provides the opportunity for information about the location, hazards, working methods and details of **Protection** to be recorded, including **Sighting Distance** and **Lookout** arrangements. It also records the details of who is present and the reference number of their current competency certificate or **NCCA** card. Also colloquially known as a **RIMINI Form**. See also **SSoW Pack**.

RT9S
[RT, NR, Hist.] Purchase order conditions for the purchase of **Goods**. This has now been replaced by **NR1**.

RTA
Road Traffic Accident.

RTAC
[RT, Hist.] **Railtrack** Access Conditions.

RTAS
See **Rail Training Audit Service**.

RTC
[Hist.] **Railway** Technical Centre. The former **British Rail Research** (**BRR**) facility at **Derby**. Also **Derby Research**.

RTCC
Rail ▫ **Traffic** Control Centre.

RTCIG
[PW] **Rake** to **Cant** in **Gauge**. A requirement in certain areas of some **Thick-based** ▫ **Switch and Crossing Layouts** (**S&C Layouts**) that the Rake of the **Timbers** be equivalent to the design Cant (**C**, **E**) at that location.

RTCS
[RT, Hist.] **Railtrack** (transmission based) **Train Control System**. See **European Train Control System** (**ETCS**).

RTFN
[RT, Hist.] **Railtrack** Fault Number.

RtG
[NR] See **Route to Gold**.

RTG
[RT, Hist.] **Railtrack** Group PLC. See **Network Rail** (**NR**).

RTHQ
[RT, Hist.] The former **Railtrack** Headquarters, at Railtrack House, Euston Square, London NW1.

RTI
Real Time Information.

RTIS
[RT, Hist.] **Railtrack** Information Systems.

RTLS
a) See **Railtrack Line Standard** (**RLS**), once called **Railtrack Company Standards** (**RCS**), now **Network Rail Company Standards** (**NRCS**)
b) Road Traffic Light Signals, see **Wig-wags**.

RTLs
Road Traffic Lights.

RTM
Rail **Traffic** Management.

RTMZ
[RT Hist.] **Railtrack** Midlands Zone.

RTN
[CT] See **Running Tunnel North**.

RTP
Real Time Protocols.

RTPI
Real Time **Passenger** Information.

RTPS
Real Time Positioning System.

RTR
See **Right Time Railway**.

RTS
a) [CT] See Running Tunnel South
b) Rapid Transit System, see Light Rapid Transit (LRT)
c) (Tradename) Rail Tech Solutions
d) Regional Transport Strategy.

RTSA
The Railways and Transport Safety Act 2003, which established the Rail Accident Investigation Branch (RAIB).

RTST
(Tradename) Rail Trackbed Stiffness Tester, operated by URS.

RTTM
Real Time Train □ Movements.

RTU
a) Remote Terminal Unit
b) Rail Technology Unit

RTZ
[RT, Hist.] See Railtrack Zone.

RU
a) See RU Loading
b) Railway Undertaking.

RU Loading
[Civ.] A Bridge loading model that allows for all combinations of vehicles currently running or projected to run on Railways in the Continent of Europe, including the United Kingdom, and is to be adopted for the design of Bridges carrying Main Line railways with a Track Gauge of 1400mm and above. See also RL, RL loading.

Rubber Bonded Cork (RBC)
[PW] A material used for Rail Pads.

Rubber Crumb
[Civ.] A material used for protective mats on Bridge Decks, used to prevent the Ballast from puncturing the waterproofing layer.

Rubber Cushion Chair
[PW, Hist.] A proposal dating from c. 1912 to install a rubber pad between a Bullhead (BH) Rail and the supporting Chair in an endeavour to reduce wear and ultimately breakage of the Chairs to allow higher Train speeds.

Rubber Duck
[Col.] name for a 360° excavator with rubber tyred wheels, also applied to Road Rail Excavators.

Rubbing Face
[PW] The face of a Check Rail which the backs of the Wheel Flanges can contact.

Rubbing Plate
[TRS] A flat, vertical plate at a Rail Vehicle extremity that provides lateral stability and a consistent tension to the Coupler when two such vehicles are Coupled together.

RUCC
Rail Users' Consultative Committee, now replaced by the Rail Passengers' Council (RPC).

Rudd (ZBA)
[NR] A 21 ton capacity Wagon used for the transportation of materials. See Wagon Names.

Rugex
[Col.] A special service for a rugby match. See also – ex, Excursion.

Rule 55
[Hist.] The old title of an instruction to drivers requiring them to remind the Signaller of their presence if detained at a Signal for more than two minutes. When originally formulated in 1883 this was Rule 41A and was only renumbered to Rule 55 with the publication of the 1897 edition of the Railway Clearing House (RCH) □ Rule Book. Although most Lines are now equipped with Track Circuits (TC), rendering the rule obsolete, the practice is still maintained. See Signal Post Telephone (SPT).

Rule Book
a) [NR] Railway Group Standard (RGS) GE/RT8000, which is the publication detailing the general responsibilities of all staff engaged on the Railway system, and the specific duties of certain types of staff such as Train drivers and Signallers. See entries Section A to Section Z and Rule Book Handbooks
b) [IÉ, LUL, NIR] The internal publication specifying the duties of Railway personnel to ensure the safe and efficient operation of the Railway.

Rule Book Handbooks
[NR] A suite of documents generally containing requirements removed from Section T of the Rule Book:
1. General duties and Track safety for Track Workers
2. Instructions for Track Workers who use Emergency Protection Equipment
3. Duties of the Lookout and Site Warden
4. Duties of a Points Operator and Route-Setting Agent - moving and securing Points by hand
5. Handsignalling duties
6. General duties of an Individual Working Alone (IWA)
7. General duties of a Controller Of Site Safety (COSS)
8. IWA, COSS or PC blocking a Line
9. IWA or COSS setting up Safe Systems Of Work within Possessions
10. Duties of the COSS and person in charge when using a Hand Trolley
11. Duties of the Person In Charge Of A Possession (PICOP)
12. Duties of the Engineering Supervisor (ES)
13. Duties of the Person In Charge Of The Siding Possession (PICOS)
14. Duties of the person in charge of loading and unloading Rail Vehicles during Engineering Work
15. Duties of the Machine Controller (MC) and On-Track Plant operator
16. AC □ Electrified Lines
17. DC Electrified Lines
18. Duties of a Level Crossing Attendant (LXA)
19. Work on signalling equipment - duties of the signalling technician

Rules of The Plan (ROP, ROTP)
[NR, Obs.] See Train Planning Rules (TPR).

Rules of The Route (ROR, ROTR)
[NR, Obs.] See Engineering Access Statement (EAS).

Ruling Gradient
The steepest significant (i.e. of the order of a Train length) Gradient on a Route, the one which determines the maximum load that may be hauled along a Route by a given Traction Unit.

Rumble Strip
[Col.] Alternative term for Track Circuit Continuity Welding. Also Eutectic Strip, Zigzag Welding, Zigzagging.

Run
a) The Route taken by a recording vehicle such as MENTOR, the New Measurement Train (NMT) or the Ultrasonic Test Unit (UTU)
b) [Elec.] See Wire Run.
c) [Hist.] A steep down gradient in the 'loaded' direction of a Tramway or Plateway, over which the vehicles could be expected to move under the force of gravity alone.
d) [Hist.] Alternative term for Set of Wagons coupled together to run as a unit on a On a Rope-Worked Railway or Gravity-Worked Railway

Run In
[PW] To "blend" an existing Alignment into a Design Lift or Design Slue by gradually increasing the Lift or Slue from zero over a reasonable distance prior to the start of the designed area.

Run Out
a) [PW] To "blend" a Design Lift or Design Slue into the existing Alignment by gradually reducing the Residual Lift or Residual Slue to zero over a reasonable distance beyond the end of the design
b) [PW] A failure of an Alumino-thermic Weld during the pour phase that results in the molten Portion passing straight through the moulds and onto the Ballast
c) A length of Line onto which Trains will be directed by Trap Points. In some locations the Run-Out may direct the Train into a Sand Drag in order to decelerate it. Also Run-Off
d) The total variation in position (measured parallel to the axis of rotation) of the edge of a wheel.

Run Round (RR)
a) An arrangement of Switch and Crossing Units (S&C Units) and Track that is specifically provided for the purpose of allowing the Running Round of Trains. This is often provided in the form of a separate Run Round Loop
b) The process of detaching a Locomotive from one end of a Train, running it to the opposite end on a different Track and reattaching it to enable the train to travel in the Reverse direction
c) An instruction found in Train Arrangements, meaning that the Locomotive should be detached and replaced on the other end of the Train, as in b).

Run Round Facility
One or more Crossovers provided within a Track Layout that allow a Locomotive to Run Round its Train using other Running Lines.

Run Round Loop
A length of Track specifically provided for the purpose of Running Round a Train.

Run Through
See Points Run Through.

Runaway
[Ops.] A Locomotive, Rail Vehicle or group of Rail Vehicles that is Running Away.

Runner Wagon
[TRS]
a) A Wagon provided to deal with a load (i.e. Rails) or fixed equipment (i.e. a crane jib) that overhangs the end of another Wagon
b) Alternative term for a Match Wagon.

Running
A term denoting the movement of Trains in some form or another. See Running Away, Running Band, Running Edge (RE), Running Face, Running Junction, Running Movement, Running Rail, Running Round, Running Signal, Running Surface.

Running Away
[Ops.] A **Locomotive**, **Rail Vehicle** or group of Rail Vehicles unintentionally moving of their own accord, generally by rolling down a **Gradient**. Common causes include:
- Vandalism
- Failure to correctly secure the vehicle(s) by the **Traincrew** or other responsible persons
- Failure of the **Handbrake** or other measures such as **Scotches**. This can be caused by sudden impacts during **Shunting**, see **Rough Shunt**, or by thermal expansion in the vehicles themselves.
- An **Unfitted** □ **Train** becoming **Divided** (this is now rare, as Unfitted Trains are not permitted)
- Sudden incapacity of the driver, a circumstance which is now unlikely with the widespread introduction of **Driver's Safety Devices** (DSD).

Running Band
[PW] That part of the **Running Surface** upon which the majority of vehicle wheels make contact. It appears as a shiny strip on the **Rail Head**. The location and consistency of location of this strip can tell an observer much about **Cant Deficiency**, **Rail Head Profile** and **Track Gauge**.

Running Brake Test
[Ops.] A brake test performed by the driver whilst the **Train** is in motion.

Running Connection
A **Junction** connecting two **Running Lines**.

Running Edge (RE)
[PW]
a) [NR] A line drawn on the **Gauge Face** of the **Rail Head**, 14mm down from the **Rail Crown**.
b) [LUL] as above but the vertical offset is 12mm.
Also **Running Face**, **Gauge Face**.

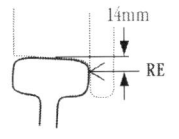

Running Edge Face of Steel (REFOS)
Running Edge Face of Structure (REFOS)
[Elec.] A scheme by which the lateral distance from **Overhead Line Structure** to **Running Edge** (RE) was recorded on the Structure, together with the design **Cant** (C, E) at that point. This allowed the **Track** and **Overhead Line Equipment** (OLE) to be maintained to a common **Alignment**, removing the main source of problems for the OLE **Maintainer**. The system was particularly suited to the use of **Automatic Track Alignment** (ATA) systems on **Tampers**, as the Track could be reliably placed within 25mm of its correct position by the Tamper crew. **Track Machine Guidance** (TMG) is a development of this system.

Running Face
[PW] The vertical face of the **Rail Head** of a **Running Rail** of which the **Running Edge** (RE) forms part, namely the Face nearest the **Fourfoot**.

Running Gear
[TRS] The equipment fitted to a **Rail Vehicle** directly associated with movement and stopping, including axles, **Axleboxes**, **Bogies**, brake linkages, **Wheels**, **Yaw Dampers**, etc.

Running Junction
A **Junction** between pairs of **Tracks** used for **Train** □ **Regulation** purposes. Also **Geographical Junction**.

Running Line
A **Track** other than a **Siding** over which **Running Movements** are made. Also **Road**.

Running Movement
A **Train Movement** made on a **Running Line** under the control of a **Main Aspect**.

Running Pressure
[TRS] The pressure in the **Brake Pipe** that causes the brakes to be **Released** and to be maintained Released.

Running Rail
[PW] A **Rail** that supports and guides the flanged steel **Rail Wheels** of a **Rail Vehicle**. A **Rail** that does not support a wheel is a **Non-Running Rail**.

Running Round
The act of moving a **Locomotive** from one end of a **Train** to the other. See also **Run Round Facility**, **Run Round Loop**.

Running Shunt Signal
[Sig., Col.] A **Signal** provided to permit **Shunting Movements** which is also cleared for normal **Train Movements**.

Running Signal
[Sig., Col.] An alternative term for a **Main Signal**.

Running Surface
[PW] The area of the **Rail Head** contacted by vehicle **Tyres**, extending from the **Gauge Corner** to the **Back Edge Corner**. See also **Running Band**.

Running Tunnel
A **Tunnel** housing one or more **Running Lines**. See also **Crossover Tunnel**.

Running Tunnel North (RTN)
[CT] In the **Channel Tunnel**, the northerly of the two **Running Tunnels**, used by **Trains** travelling from the UK to France during normal operation.

Running Tunnel South (RTS)
[CT] In the **Channel Tunnel**, the southerly of the two **Running Tunnels**, used by **Trains** travelling from France to the UK during normal operation.

Running-off End
[PW] The **Rail End** at which at which traffic in the predominant direction of travel leaves a **Rail**.

Running-off Rail
[PW] At a **Rail Joint**, the **Rail** on which **Trains** travelling in the **Normal Direction** approach the Joint. See also **Running-off End**.

Running-on End
[PW] The **Rail End** at which at which traffic in the predominant direction of travel first contacts a **Rail**.

Running-on Rail
[PW] At a **Rail Joint**, the **Rail** on which **Trains** travelling in the **Normal Direction** leave the Joint. See also **Running-on End**.

Running-on Spanner
[PW] A short handled **Fishbolt Spanner** (around 300 to 450mm, 12 to 18" long) used to quickly run a **Fishbolt** nut on prior to using a full size and rather cumbersome spanner or a torque wrench to correctly tighten it.

Run-off
The space in front of an escalator, staircase or ticket gate where **Passengers** re-orientate themselves and move away from the element. This space should be kept free of obstructions.

Ruping Process
[Obs.] An obsolescent method of preserving **Wood Sleepers** by treating them with zinc meta-arsenate.

RUPP
Road Used as a Public Path.

Rural Barriers
A variety of **Barrier** provided at rural **User Worked Crossings** (**UWC**), designed to be operated by the user. See also **Black Gates**.

Rural Line
Describing a **Line**, often a **Branch Line**, which serves a rural area rather than an industrial or urban one. See also **Suburban Line**.

RUS
Route Utilisation Strategy.

Rutways
[Hist.] Parallel grooves either resulting from wear caused by vehicle wheels or from cutting manually into the bedrock. Whilst they provide a degree of guidance to the wheels of **Wagons** this arrangement is not considered to be **Railways** as such.

RVAR
See Rail Vehicle Accessibility Regulations 1998.

RVfM
The Rail Value for Money (study), led by Sir Roy McNulty and published in May 2011. **Also McNulty Report, The.**

RVL
Shorthand for **Reversible Line**.

RVP
Rendezvous Point.

Rx
[Sig.] On a **Signalling Circuit Diagram**:
- As one of the leading letters of an **Equipment Code**, it means receiving
- As the last letter of an Equipment Code, it means receiver.

RYTOFF
[BR] (*rye-toff*) (Tradename) A computerised system developed by British Rail Research (BRR) in the 1970s and now maintained by **AEA Technology** (now called **DeltaRail**) to examine the **Track Geometry** in the area of a **Derailment** in order to establish whether the **Track** was a contributory factor.

S

S
a) In an abbreviated **Track Name**, it denotes **Slow**, as in **Slow Line**
b) See **Transition Shift**
c) [NR] As the first letter in a **Wagon** □ CARKND it denotes that the vehicle is a two axle steel carrier
d) [Sig.] On a **Signalling Circuit Diagram**:
- As a prefix letter it denotes a steady supply
- As one of the leading letters of an **Equipment Code**, it means **Stick**

e) [Sig.] Abbreviation found on drawings of **Signal Box Diagrams**, denoting **Spare Levers**.
f) The letter represented by **Sierra** in the **Phonetic Alphabet**
g) Common Interface File Operating Characteristics Code for **Steam Heated**.

S and C
a) [PW] Common contraction of **Switch and Crossing**
b) The **S**ettle and **C**arlisle **Line**.

S Door
[LUL] Hinged connecting doors between **Cars**. Also R Door.

S Stock
[LUL] Sub-surface **Trains**, delivered in 2010 by Bombardier Transportation of Derby, replacing 177 Trains on the Metropolitan, District, Hammersmith & City, and Circle **Lines** with a standardised fleet of 191 Trains (1,395 **Cars**). The stock has two sub-types, S7 and S8.

S&C
a) [PW] Common contraction of **Switch and Crossing**
b) The **S**ettle and **C**arlisle Line.

S&C Layout
See **Switch and Crossing Layout**.

S&C Unit
See **Switch and Crossing Unit**.

S&D
S&DJC
S&DJR
[Hist.] The **Pre-Grouping S**omerset & **D**orset **J**oint **C**ommittee / **Railway**, a London & South Western and Midland joint enterprise.

S&EE
[LUL] **S**ignal and **E**lectrical **E**ngineer

S&F
a) **S**witches and **F**ittings, see **Switch and Crossing (S&C)**.
b) [Hist.] Common shorthand for **Saxby & Farmer**, a former manufacturer of **Signalling Equipment**.

S&HJR
[Hist.] The **Pre-Grouping S**hrewsbury & **H**ereford **J**oint **Railway**, a Great Western and London & North Western joint enterprise.

S&I
Scope and **I**ntegration.

S&KR
[Hist.] The **Pre-Grouping S**winton & **K**nottingley **Railway**, a Midland and North Eastern joint enterprise.

S&MJR
[Hist.] The **Pre-Grouping S**tratford-upon-Avon & **M**idland **J**unction **Railway**.

S&MLR
[Hist.] The **Pre-Grouping S**hropshire & **M**ontgomeryshire **L**ight **R**ailway.

S&P
Strategy and **P**lanning.

S&S
a) [Hist.] Common shorthand for **S**tevens & **S**ons, a former manufacturer of **Signalling Equipment**
b) **S**uitability and **S**ufficiency.

S&SD
a) **S**ystems and **S**afety **D**epartment
b) [Hist.] The former **Railtrack S**afety **and S**tandards **D**irectorate
c) [NR] **S**afety **and S**ustainable **D**evelopment.

S&T
[Sig.] **Signal and Telecommunications**. Also used as a collective description for all those employed in the design, installation and maintenance of **Signalling Equipment** and **Telecommunications** systems, as in "The S&T". See also **Sick and Tired**.

S&TE
[BR] **S**ignal and **T**elecommunications **E**ngineer.

S/B
Shorthand for **S**outh**b**ound.

S/W
Shorthand for **S**oft**w**ood, as in **Softwood Sleeper**.

S1

S1 Chair
[PW] A **Common Chair**, predecessor of the **AS1 Chair** for use with **95 Pound** □ **Bull Head** □ **Rail**. See also S2.

S2

S2 Chair
[PW] A **Common Chair** intended for use with **85 Pound** □ **Bull Head** □ **Rail**. See also S2.

Sa
Saturday.

SA
a) See **Sectional Appendix**
b) **S**ponsor's **A**gent
c) **S**afety **A**uthority
d) **Signalling A**ssistant
e) **S**ervice **A**cceptance.

SAA
[NR] **S**tation **A**ccess **A**greement.

SAB
a) **S**afety **A**dvisory **B**oard
b) See **SAB Wheel**.

SAB Wheel
A type of **Composite Wheel** manufactured by the Swedish company <u>S</u>venska <u>A</u>ktie<u>b</u>olaget <u>B</u>romsregulator (now part of SA WABCO) and fitted to the **Class** 86 **Electric Locomotive** when their **Maximum Permitted Speed** was raised to 110mph.

Sabot
A **Rail** mounted friction wheel stop.

SABRE
[LUL] <u>S</u>ite <u>A</u>ccess <u>B</u>ooking for **Railway** Engineering. A system used to control engineering access to **London Underground Limited** □ **Infrastructure**.

SAC
a) See **Site Access Control**
b) **Station** <u>A</u>ccess <u>C</u>onditions
c) **Station** <u>A</u>ccess <u>C</u>ontract
d) **Special** <u>A</u>rea of <u>C</u>onservation.

SACC
[Hist.] <u>S</u>ite <u>A</u>ccess <u>C</u>ontrol <u>C</u>entre, A **West Coast Route Modernisation** (**WCRM**) function.

SACP
Structure **A**sset **C**ost **P**rofile.

Saddle
a) [TRS] The casting on a suspension unit incorporating the **Axle Journal** and spring assembly
b) [PW Obs.] A cast metal **Baseplate** for **Plate Rails** having raised upstands along the narrower (transverse) edges to retain the **Rails** to **Gauge** and to provide vertical support. The Saddle was designed to be secured to the supporting stone block by a single spike driven through a pre-formed hole in the Saddle and into a wood plug located in a hole bored in the block.

Saddle Chair
[PW Obs.] A **Chair**, used with **Bullhead Rail** (**BH**), which has no **Jaw**; it merely supports the **Rail** vertically.

Saddle Crossing
[PW] An **Obtuse Crossing** for a **Scissors Crossover** having additional **Rails** and/or additional **Common Crossings** included as one unit. Also **Boat Crossing**, **Compound Crossing**, **Fiddle Back**, **Triple Intersection**.

Saddle Rail
[PW Obs.] A triangular **Rail Section** devised by Seaton and used on some parts of the **Great Western Railway** (**GWR**) in the 1860s. It was supported on **Longitudinal Timbers** with a triangular cross section, over which the **Rail** was secured.

Saddle Tank
[TRS] A **Steam Locomotive** with the water tank positioned over the boiler.

SAE
[NR] See **Structures Assessment Engineer**.

Safe Overrun Distance (SOD)
[Sig.] The area **Beyond** a **Signal** showing a **Stop Aspect** into which is safe for a **Train** to run without this resulting in a collision. This term is used as an amplification of the requirements of **Signal Overlaps** when considering **Over-run Risk Assessment Models** (**ORAM**).

Safe Speed
[Sig.] The highest instantaneous speed of a **Train** which is compatible with **Signal Aspects** and **Permissible Speeds** (**PS**). This value is generated by the **Automatic Train Protection** (**ATP**) system, which will take over should the driver attempt to exceed it. See also **Intervention**.

Safe System of Work (SSoW)
[NR] An arrangement of precautions which ensure that workers are exposed to least possible risk. This can include **COSS Briefings**, provision of special equipment, **Possessions** and **Isolations**. The latter arrangements are the responsibility of a **Controller of Site Safety** (**COSS**) or **Protection Controller** (**PC**). See also **COSS Brief**, **RIMINI**.

Safe System of Work Pack (SSoW Pack)
[NR] The collection issued to a **Controller of Site Safety** (**COSS**) prior to work commencing. See **COSS Brief**, **Task Briefing** (**TB**).

Safe System of Work Planning System (SSOWPS)
[NR] A software system developed by **Network Rail** to assist the planning of **Safe Systems Of Work** □ **On or Near the Line**.

Safe Work Leader (SWL)
[NR] Replacing the current **Controller of Site Safety** (**COSS**) competency, a Safe Work Leader will be accountable not only for planning and risk assessing tasks but also for the safe delivery of those tasks on site

Safecess
[NR] A set of minimum standards for the state of the **Cess** and the appearance, position and construction of **Safecess Paths**. All Safecess Paths are in a **Position of Safety**. See also **Continuous Position of Safety** (**CPOS**).

Safecess Path
[NR] A **Cess Path** constructed to certain minimum standards, one of which is that the Path must be a **Position of Safety**.

Safegaurded
[NR] Describing a **Safe System of Work** (**SSoW**) where **Train Movements** are stopped on one or more **Lines** to protect staff. This term replaces **Safegaurded Green Zone**. The term **Green Zone** is also obsolete.

Safegaurded Green Zone
[NR Obs.] See **Safegaurded**.

Safelock
[PW Obs.] An early type of **Elastic Rail Fastening** used on early **Concrete Sleepers**.

Safety Block
[LUL] A concrete channel section fitted under the **Conductor Rail** to prevent it becoming unintentionally displaced and falling onto the **Sleepers** or rotating away from the vertical position. Also **Overturning Block**.

Safety by Design (SbD)
A movement that encourages designers to "design out" health and safety risks as far as possible during design development. The concept supports the view that along with quality, programme and cost, safety is determined during the design stage.

Safety Case
a) A document submitted in support of a system or process, providing evidence that the system complies with the relevant safety objectives
b) A document setting out the arrangements which a **Railway Company** has put in place for controlling the risks created by its operations, as required by the **Railways (Safety Case) Regulations 2000**. Following the introduction of the **Railway and Other Guided Transport Systems (Safety) Regulations 2006 (ROGS)** Network Rail's (**NR**) Safety Case has now been replaced by a safety management system which is the subject of authorisation by the safety authority (in this case the **Office of Rail Regulation (ORR)**.
See also **Contractors Safety Case (CSC)**, **Railway Safety Case (RSC)**. See also **Contractors Assurance Case (CAC)**.

Safety Critical
Having direct responsibility for or directly influencing safety. See **Safety Critical Staff**, **Safety Critical Work (SCW)**.

Safety Critical Communications
Any message given or received which may affect the safe operation of the **Railway**.

Safety Critical Staff
Persons whose normal duties include **Safety Critical Work (SCW)**, whether they are actively engaged in those duties or not. Such persons are subject to stringent training and regulation, including random screening for Drugs and Alcohol (**D&A**, **DNA**). See also **AOD:HS**, **AOD:LXA**, **AOD:PO**, **Authorised Person (AP)**, **Conductor Rail Permit (CRP)**, **Controller of Site Safety (COSS)**, **Engineering Supervisor (ES)**, **Handsignaller (HS)**, **Individual Working Alone (IWA)**, **Lookout (LKT, LO)**, **Nominated Person (NP)**, **Overhead Line Permit (OLP)**, **Personal Track Safety (PTS)**, **Person In Charge of Possession (PICOP)**, **Protection Controller (PC)**, **Points Operator (PO)**, **Rail Incident Officer (RIO)**, **Route Setting Agent (RSA)**, **Senior Person In Charge of Possession (SPICOP)**, **Signaller**, **Track Welder (TW)**.

Safety Critical Work (SCW)
a) Work on **Electrification**, **Signalling**, **Structures** and **Track** (including supervision and **Protection** of such work) that directly has the potential to jeopardise the **Safety of the Line** or the health and safety of other people on the **Railway** system
b) The activities of a person as a driver, **Guard**, **Conductor**, **Shunter**, **Signaller**, **Train Examiner** or in any other capacity in which they can control or affect the movement of a **Rail Vehicle**
See also **Safety Critical Staff**.

Safety Factor
An additional multiplicative allowance applied to the initial design assumptions to accommodate unusual events and deterioration of the designed system. For **Structures**, Safety Factors of 2 and higher are not uncommon.

Safety Integrity Level (SIL)
One of four specific measures of safety integrity (SIL 4 having the highest integrity).

Safety Loop
[TRS] An electrical wire passing through a **Train** used to confirm that the doors which appear to be closed and locked are closed and locked.

Safety Management in Railways (SAMRAIL)
A project intended to develop a comprehensive and consistent safety management programme for the European **Railways**.

Safety Management Information System (SMIS)
[NR] A database of incidents and accidents occurring on the **National Railway Network (NRN)**, managed on behalf of the **Railway Industry** by RSSB. Safety related incident data entered, together with associated code tables, is stored on an Oracle database. This database stores all of the information on each safety event in a single record, which can be accessed rapidly by every **Infrastructure Manager** and **Railway Undertaking** organisation involved in the safety event.

Safety of the Line
The condition of freedom from danger to the operators, **Passengers** and **Traffic** of a **Railway**. Safety of the **Line** is the most important aspects of the Railway culture and many courageous acts have been carried out to protect it. See also **ALARP**, **John Axon GC**, **Fail Safe**, **Wallace Arnold Oakes GC**, **Protection of the Line**, **Soham Incident**.

Safety of the Line Incident
An incident caused as a result of a deviation from the normal rules and regulations governing the operation of the **Railway**.

Safety Points
[Arch.] See **Trap Points**.

Safety Related
Those parts of a system, particularly **Signalling Systems**, whose failure directly affects the **Safety of the Line** or the integrity of the whole system. Also **Vital**.

Safety Risk Model (SRM)
A computerised model, managed by the **Rail Safety and Standards Board (RSSB)**, which is a quantitative representation of the potential **Accidents** resulting from the operation and **Maintenance** of the **National Railway Network (NRN)**.

Safety Speed
[NR] A **Temporary Speed Restriction (TSR)** applied for the duration of work to reduce the risk to an adjacent **Worksite**.

Sag
a) See **Sag Curve**
b) See **Sagged Contact**, **Sagged Contact Equipment**.

Sag Curve
A **Concave Vertical Curve**. The opposite is a **Hog Curve**.

Sagged Contact
Sagged Contact Equipment
An **Overhead Line Equipment** (**OLE**) □ **Catenary** in which the **Contact Wire** (**CW**) is given a small sag towards **Mid-span** to counteract the greater tendency for **Uplift** at Mid-span.

SAI
Stop and **A**wait **I**nstructions, words normally found on **Instruction Boards** at the entrances to **Private Sidings** and other areas that are under the control of a **Shunter**.

SAIP
[NR] **S**tafford **A**rea **I**mprovement **P**rogramme.

SAL
An acronym representing a Saloon **Coach**.

Salisbury Accident
At 01:57 On the 1st July 1906 a **Boat Train** from Plymouth to London ran through the sharp **Left Hand Curves** at Salisbury at approximately 65 mph, when the safe and official **Permissible Speed** (**PS**) was 30mph. The **Locomotive** overturned and the Train **Derailed**, killing 28 and severely injuring seven. The driver had not previously driven a non-stop train through Salisbury. Modern arrangements make a repeat of this kind of accident unlikely. See also **Morpeth Accidents**.

Salmon (YFA, YMA, YMB, YMO, YSA, YWA, YXA)
[NR] An 18.3m (60 feet) long 51 ton capacity flat **Wagon**, used to transport **Track Panels** and **Rails**. A special one carried the **Bruff Grader**. See **Wagon Names**.

SAM
a) **S**ite **A**ccess **M**anager, see **Site Access Controller** (**SAC**)
b) **S**witch **A**ctuating **M**echanism, see **Switch Operating Mechanism**. See also **Point Operating Equipment**
c) **S**cheduled **A**ncient **M**onument.

SAMNET
Safety **M**anagement and **I**nteroperability Thematic **Net**work for **Railways** Systems.

SAMP
Signalling □ **A**sset □ **M**aintenance **P**lan.

SAMRAIL
See **Safety Management in Railways**.

SAMS
Strategic **A**sset **M**odel for **S**ignalling.

Sand Blanket
A variety of **Formation Renewal** where (typically) a 100mm layer of sand, one layer of 1000 gauge polythene and a further 100mm sand layer are placed on the **Formation** to act as a separator and filter system. Also **Blanket**, **Clay Dig**.

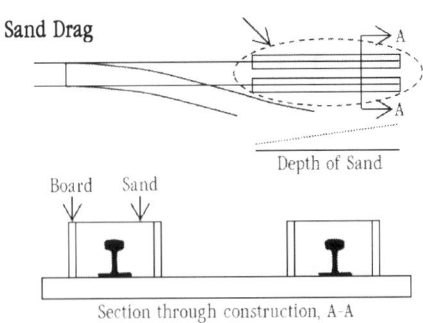

Sand Drag

Depth of Sand

Board   Sand

Section through construction, A-A

A form of **Trap Point** where the **Trap Road** has sand heaped over the **Rails** to arrest and stop a **Train**. They are used at locations where it may be necessary to stop a **Passenger Train** making an **Unauthorised Movement** at speed. Sand Drags can be up to 30m (100 feet) long depending on the likely weight and speed of the approaching Train. Also **Arrestor**.

Sand Pram
(Tradename) A large manual wheeled sand dispenser reminiscent of a child's pram. Made by Lawrence Industries.

Sand Rover
A Land Rover adapted to run on **Rails** and dispense **Traction Gel** onto the **Rail Head**.

Sand Stick
A small manual sand dispenser.

Sandberg Process
(Tradename) Hardening of the **Rail Head** by:
• Spraying the hot **Rail Head** with water and then blowing cold air over it, to develop **Sorbite**, followed by
• Controlled cooling of the whole **Rail**.

Sanders
A means of delivering small amounts of sand onto the **Rail Head** near the **Driving Wheels** of a **Traction Unit** in order to improve **Adhesion** in areas of very poor **Rail Head Conditions**. The system consists of a hopper of sand, a valve, a jet of compressed air and a pipe that delivers the sand as close as possible to the wheel. See also **One-shot Sanders**.

Sandite
A sand and antifreeze mixture applied to the **Rail Head** to improve **Adhesion** during the **Leaf Fall Season** and icy weather. It is applied either by specially modified **Rail Vehicles** running **In Traffic**, or by **Handite** hand-held applicators.

Sandite Train
Sandite Unit
A special **Train**, **Multiple Unit Train** or **Multi-purpose Vehicle** (**MPV**) specially modified to dispense **Sandite** onto the **Rails**.

Sandwich Weld
[PW Col.] Alternative name for the **Tri-metallic Zone** (**TMZ**) where the **Closure Rails** are flash welded to a **Cast Austenitic-manganese Steel Crossing** (**Cast AMS Crossing**). See also **Composite Weld**.

Sap
A **Railway** □ **Telegraph Code** meaning "Keep me well advised"

SAP
a) Safety Assessment Panel
b) Strategic Access Planning
c) Single Anchor Point, a type of **Conductor Rail Anchor**
d) Safety Advisory Panel
e) Systems Assurance Plan
f) Safety Action Plan
g) **Station** Announcement Point
h) Staff Assembly Point.

SAPA
(*sapper*) Stand Alone Pocket Archive, a database drawing management system.

SAPB
Spring Applied Parking Brake.

SARI
a) See **Standard Alphanumeric Route Indicator**
b) [LUL] Seek Assistance Repeater □ Indicator.

SARPA
Shrewsbury to Aberystwyth **Rail** □ **Passenger** Association.

SASSPAD
(*sass-spad*) See **Starting** (or Start) **Against Signal Signal Passed At Danger**. Also called a (Start-Away) Signal Passed at Danger (SA) **SPAD**.

SAT
(*satt*)
a) Site Acceptance Test
b) [NR] Systems Analysis Team
c) See **Signal Assessment Tool / Detailed Assessment**. See also SORAT.

SAT/DA
(*satt dee-ay*) See **Signal Assessment Tool / Detailed Assessment**.

Satellite Interlocking
See **Remote interlocking**.

Satellite Tamping Bank
[PW] On a **Continuous Action Tamper** (**CAT**) the **Tamping Banks** are fixed to a small frame (the Satellite) that moves forward and backward independently of the main machine. This allows the lightweight Satellite to start and stop quickly, whilst the rest of the machine moves at a constant speed, significantly increasing output.

Satisfactory
[NR PW] A length of **Track** (usually an **Eighth of a Mile**) over which the **Track Quality** (**TQ**) is worse than **Good** but better than **Poor**, in that the **Standard Deviation** (**SD**) values for **Top** and **Line** are between the 50% and 100% values for **Permissible Speed** (**PS**) or **Enhanced Permissible Speed** (**EPS**).

SATS
a) Sectioning □ Autotransformer Site
b) [LUL] Station Assistant Train Service.

SATURN
Simulation and Assignment of Traffic to Urban Road Networks, a transport model.

SAU
See **Self-accounting Unit**.

Savo
A **Railway** □ **Telegraph Code** meaning "**Crossovers** at the following places not to be used:-" and applied to **Out of Gauge Loads**.

Saxby and Farmer (S&F)
[Sig. Hist.] (Tradename) Manufacturer of **Signalling Equipment** founded by **John Saxby** in 1856. John Farmer joined as partner in 1860 and in 1920 the Westinghouse Brake Company acquired a controlling share of the company (along with other similar concerns) and changed its name to the Westinghouse Brake and Saxby Signal Company Ltd. In 1935 This became the Westinghouse Brake and Signal Company Ltd., which is now part of the **Invensys Rail** Group as **Westinghouse Rail Systems Ltd.** (**WRSL**).

Saxby, John
(1821-1913) Born in Brighton; after initially working as a carpenter he became interested in the problems of **Railway** □ **Signalling**. He went on to be the inventor of the first successful system of **Interlocking** □ **Points** and **Signals**, patented in 1856 and first used that year on the London Brighton & South Coast Railway (LB&SCR) at Bricklayer's Arms Junction. See also **Saxby and Farmer**.

SB
a) See **Signal Box**. Also **Signalbox**
b) See **Sleeper Bottom**.

SB1

SB1c
Swap Body 1, a standard **Vehicle Gauge** that permits the passage of **Swap Body Vehicles**, now called **W9 Gauge**.

SBB
a) Safety Bus Bar
b) Schweizerische Bundesbahnen, the national **Railway Company** of Switzerland. Normally referred to by its initials in German, the company is also called Chemins de fer Fédéraux Suisses (**CFF**) in French or Ferrovie Federali Svizzere (**FFS**) in Italian.

SBC
a) Station □ Barrow Crossing
b) Safety Bonding Cable.

SbD
See **Safety by Design**.

SBDC
Service Brake Deceleration Curve.

SBI
Service Brake Interface.

SBIC
Service Brake Intervention Curve.

SBP
[NR] Strategic Business Plan.

SBR
Styrene Butadiene Rubber.

ELLIS' BRITISH RAILWAY ENGINEERING ENCYCLOPÆDIA

SC
a) See **Signalling Centre**
b) **S**ignalling **C**ontrol
c) **S**ub-**c**ontract.

SC3 Clip
See **S**pring **H**ook **C**lip (SHC).

SC4
See **Schedule 4**.

SC8
See **Schedule 8**.

SCADA
(*skar-dah*) **S**upervisory **C**ontrol **a**nd **D**ata **A**cquisition, a remote control and measurement system widely used in **Feeder Stations** (FS).

SCAG
[NR] **S**tation **C**apacity **A**ssessment **G**uidance.

SCALA
Society of **C**hief **A**rchitects of **L**ocal **A**uthorities

SCAM
Safety **C**ase **A**ssessment Criteria **M**anual.

Scar
Scar Face
[Civ.] The surface within an **Embankment** or **Cutting** that is left exposed following a **Slip**. See also **Slip Plane**.

Scarifying
Scarification
[PW] The process of removing the compacted **Ballast** ▫ **Beds** left when old **Track** is removed, generally prior to the placement of new **Track**. This is done with a tractor/harrow combination or a bulldozer with a ripper bar attachment. It is vitally important to expunge all traces of the previous hard **Ballast Pyramids**, or a very irregular **Top** is produced.

SCAT
[LUL] See **S**peed **C**ontrol **A**fter **T**ripping, see also **Trip Cock**.

SCC
a) See **Signalling Control Centre**
b) An acronym representing a **Sleeper** Club **Coach**
c) **S**upervisory **C**ontrol **C**entre
d) [LUL] **S**ervice **C**ontrol **C**entre.

SCCFG
Safety **C**ritical **C**ommunications **F**ocus **G**roup.

SCD
See **S**hort **C**ircuiting **D**evice.

SCF
[LUL] **S**tation **C**ontrol **F**acility.

SCG
Self-**c**hanging **G**ears.

Scharfenberg
(Tradename) A variety of **Automatic Coupling**.

Schedule 1
Types of **Accidents** and incidents (other than those occurring in the **Channel Tunnel**) which must be notified to the **Rail Accident Investigation Branch** (**RAIB**) immediately, as defined in the **Railways (Accident Investigation and Reporting) Regulations** 2005. These are generally incidents which have caused deaths, serious injuries, blockages of the **Line**, **Buffer Stop** collisions, the release of **Dangerous Goods** or could under slightly different circumstances have led to such an incident.

Schedule 2
Types of **Accidents** and incidents (other than those occurring in the **Channel Tunnel**) which must be notified to the **Rail Accident Investigation Branch** (**RAIB**) as soon as practicable and within three days, as defined in the **Railways (Accident Investigation and Reporting) Regulations 2005**. These are generally incidents resulting in injuries, derailment, **Trains** becoming **Divided**, **Near Misses** with fixed objects and failures of haulage equipment.

Schedule 3
Types of **Accidents** and incidents (other than those occurring in the **Channel Tunnel**) which must be notified to the **Rail Accident Investigation Branch** (**RAIB**) as soon as practicable and no later than 10 days after the end of the month in which the event occurred, as defined in The **Railways (Accident Investigation and Reporting) Regulations 2005**. These are generally **SPADs**, **Broken Rails**, collisions with road vehicles, failures of **Structures** and failures of **Signalling Systems**.

Schedule 4 (SC4)
a) Types of **Accidents** and incidents occurring in the **Channel Tunnel** which must be notified to the **Rail Accident Investigation Branch** (**RAIB**) immediately, as defined in The **Railways (Accident Investigation and Reporting) Regulations 2005**. These are broadly similar to **Schedule 1**.
b) [NR] The section covering **Possession** planning included in **Passenger** ▫ **Track Access** Contracts.

Schedule 5
Types of **Accidents** and incidents occurring in the **Channel Tunnel** which must be notified to the **Rail Accident Investigation Branch** (**RAIB**) as soon as practicable and within 3 days, as defined in The **Railways (Accident Investigation and Reporting) Regulations 2005**. These are broadly similar to **Schedule 2** and **Schedule 3**.

Schedule 8 (SC8)
[NR] The section covering performance included in **Passenger** ▫ **Track Access** Contracts, detailing the relationship between a **Train Operating Company** (**TOC**) and **Network Rail** (**NR**).

Scheme Plan
See **S**ignalling **S**cheme **P**lan (SSP).

SCHLID
Schedule **Id**entity, the **TOPS** abbreviation for the reference number of a **Train** schedule.

Schweerbau
(*shweer-bow*) (Tradename) A manufacturer of Railway plant, known in the UK for its Rail Grinding Train (RGT).

Schwihag
(*shwee-hagg*) (Tradename) A manufacturer of friction reducing roller devices for Switches. See Switch Rollers and fastenings for Flat Bottom Rail.

Scissor Lift Platform
A type of Mobile Elevating Work Platform (MEWP), generally one equipped with a larger platform that can only be adjusted vertically relative to the machine. See Permaquip. See also Cherry Picker.

Scissors
Scissors Crossing
Scissors Crossover

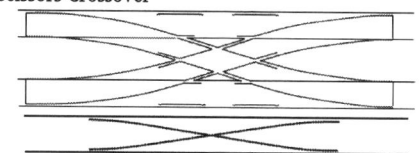

Two intersecting Crossovers of opposite Hand, allowing movements in any direction between two adjacent (and generally parallel) Tracks.

SCM
Station Choice Model.

SCMI
Structures Condition Marking Index; replaced by Bridge Condition Marking Index (BCMI).

SCMMM
Supply Chain Management Maturity Model

SCO
[LUL] Signalling Control Operator.

SCOC
[BR] Stock Control and Ordering Centre.

SCOT
Scot.
Scotland.

Scotch
A wedge shaped piece of timber that is placed as follows:
a) Between Switch Rail and Stock Rail to ensure an Open Switch remains so. Also Plug, Scotch Block
b) Behind a vehicle wheel to ensure the vehicle does not roll away. A more advanced version of this is a Slipper.

Scotch Block
An alternative term for a Scotch.

Scotch Gauge
[Hist.] A Track Gauge of 4' - 6" (1371.6mm) to which the Edinburgh & Dalkeith Railway, opened in part on 4th July 1831, was built. The Railway was worked partly by horses and partly via a Rope-worked Incline.

Scotrail
(Tradename) A Train Operating Company (TOC) which provides 95% of all Passenger services within Scotland and has services to Carlisle and Newcastle.

Scottish Region (ScR)
[BR] Under British Railways (BR), the regional organisation responsible for Scotland. Its headquarters were in Glasgow.

Scottish Region Tokenless Block
[Sig. BR Scot.] A system of signalling Single Lines that was developed for use in the former Scottish Region.

Scour
[Civ.] The removal of material from the bed or bank of a watercourse or material from a beach by current or wave action. This is a particular problem where the removed material was providing support or restraint to a Structure such as Bridge Pier or Retaining Wall, ultimately leading to its collapse.

SCP
a) Status Control Panel
b) Station Control Point
c) Safety Control Point.

SCR
a) Silicon Controlled Rectifier, see Chopper
b) Station Control Room

ScR
See Scottish Region.

Scrap Rail
[PW] Rail which is too worn, damaged, flawed or short as to render it unfit for further use in the Track.

Screen Box
[PW] A large hopper forming part of a Ballast Cleaner. The hopper has a bottom consisting of two or more mesh screens of varying sizes, and the whole is made to vibrate when in use. The excavated Ballast is fed into the top and the Screen Box separates the Returned Ballast from the Spoil.

Screening
[PW Col.] Describing a Ballast Cleaner operating normally, i.e. returning the suitable Ballast to the Track and disposing of the Spoil. The opposite is Excavating or Total Loading.

Screw Coupling

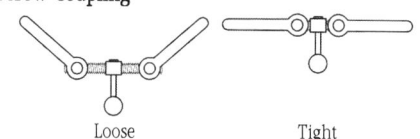

Loose   Tight

[TRS] A variety of Coupling used to connect Rail Vehicles together. It consists of a pair of loops connected by a threaded bar with left and right-hand threads on opposite ends, allowing the coupling to be lengthened and shortened as required when connected between the Coupling Hooks of the vehicles. See also Instanter Coupling, Three Link Coupling.

Screw Dolly
See Box Spanner.

Screw Fastening
[PW]
A type of screw used to:
- Secure **Chairs** and **Baseplates** to **Sleepers**, **Switch and Crossing** □ **Timbers** and concrete **Bearers**
- Secure the extended **Noses** of some designs of **Bull Head Crossings** to the supporting **Timbers**
- Fix **Third Rail Insulators** to the **Sleeper Ends**

Also **Chairscrew**, **Baseplate Screw**, **Coach Screw**, **Screwspike**.

Screwspike
[LUL] Term for a **Chairscrew**.

Scroll Irons
[TRS] A steel bracket fastened to the underside of a **Wagon** □ **Frame** and to which the suspension is attached.

Scrote Controls
[Col.] **Signalling Controls** fitted to prevent the malicious operation of **Treadles** causing incidents at **Level Crossings**.

SCS
See **Signalling Control System**.

SCT
Surface Concrete Troughing, see **Cable Route**.

SCU
a) Signalling Compatibility Unit
b) Station Control Unit.

SCUK
(*skuk*) Signalling Controls UK Ltd, now part of **Westinghouse Rail Systems Ltd**. (**WRSL**).

SCW
a) See Safety Critical Work
b) Shorthand for the **Railway Safety Critical Work Regulations 1994** (R(SCW), RSCW).

SCWID
Safety Critical Work Identification.

SCWO
[Sig.] Shows Clear When Occupied, a type of **Track Circuit** (**TC**) fault. See also **SOWC**, **Wrong Side Failure** (**WSF**).

SCWS
Signal Controlled Warning System.

SCZ
Scotland Zone, See **Railtrack** (**RT**), **Railtrack Zone**.

SD
a) See Standard Deviation
b) Series Diode
c) Smoke Detector
d) Sustainable Development.

SDA
[Sig.] Solid State Interlocking Data Appreciation.

SDD
Standard Design Details.

SDEF
[Sig.] Signalling Data Exchange Format.

SDG
a) Shorthand for **Siding**
b) [NR] Signalling Design Group
c) (Tradename) Steer Davies Gleave
d) [LUL] Stations Delivery Group.

SDH
Synchronous Digital Hierarchy. See also **PSDH**.

SDO
a) See Selective Door Opening
b) Selective Door Operation.

SDP
Safety Decisions Programme.

SDR
See **Simplified Direct Reporting**.

SDRG
System Design Review Group.

SDS
a) See **Signaller's Display Subsystem**, the predecessor of **DIS**
b) Systems Definition Specification.

SDSC
Station Development Safety Case.

SDT
a) See **Self-discharging Train**
b) See **Sleeper Delivery Train**
c) Service Disruption Threshold.

SDV
[TRS] An acronym representing a **Sandite** vehicle.

SE
a) See **Sealing End**
b) See **Swept Envelope**
c) [TRS] An acronym representing a Seated **Coach** – Eurostar
d) Systems Engineering
e) [IÉ] Senior Engineer
f) The **ATOC** code for **Southeastern**.

SE&CR
[Hist.] The **Pre-Grouping** South Eastern & Chatham Railway.

SEA
Strategic Engineering Access, an initiative aimed at improving the efficiency of Engineering Access and the balance between this and **Timetable** (**TT**) demands.

Sea Urchin (ZCA)
[NR] A 26 ton capacity **Spoil Wagon** used for the transportation of **Ballast** and **Sleepers**. See **Wagon Names**.

Seacow (YGA, YGB)
[NR] A 41 ton capacity **Ballast Hopper** used for delivering **Ballast** directly onto the **Track**. Each one holds 40 Tonnes and can discharge to both sides and into the **Fourfoot**. See **Wagon Names**.

Seahare (ZCA)
[NR] A 25 ton capacity **Open Wagon** used for the transportation of **Ballast**. See **Wagon Names**.

Seahorse (ZCA)
[NR] A 25 ton capacity **Open Wagon** used for the transportation of **Ballast** and **Spoil**. See **Wagon Names**.

Seal (ZGA)
[NR] A 21 ton capacity **Open Wagon** used for the transportation of materials. See **Wagon Names**.

Sealed Release
[Sig.] An **Emergency Release** which requires a seal or glass to be broken in order to operate it. See **Battersea Park Accident**.

Sealing End (SE)
The end of an large insulated cable where the insulating sheath and armour are terminated and sealed to prevent water ingress.

Sealion (YGH)
[NR] A 40 ton capacity **Ballast Hopper** used for delivering **Ballast** directly onto the **Track**. It can discharge to both sides and into the **Fourfoot**. See **Wagon Names**.

Searchlight Signal
[Sig.] A variety of **Colour Light Signal** that:
a) [Hist.] uses one lamp and interchangeable coloured filters to display the various **Signal Aspects**
b) Can display **Red**, **Yellow** and **Green** Aspects from a single assembly through a single aperture using fibre optics or light emitting diodes (**LEDs**).

Seated Load
[TRS] The seating capacity of a **Passenger Coach**. See also **PIXC**, **Seated Load Factor**.

Seated Load Factor
[Ops.] The number of **Passengers** on a **Train** expressed as a percentage of the total number of seats available on the Train; see also **Seated Load**.

Second Class
Formerly the middle level of comfort available to the potential **Passenger** (**Third Class** being even worse and **First Class** being the best), until Third Class was done away with. Latterly re-titled **Standard Class** to improve its image.

Second Generation Diesel Multiple Unit (DMU)
[BR, NR TRS] The **Diesel Mechanical Multiple Units** (**DMMU**) built by **British Rail Engineering Limited** (**BREL**) and others between 1978 and 2011. This includes **Classes** 139 to 185 inclusive. See also **First Generation Diesel Multiple Unit (DMU)**.

Second Line of Response (SLOR)
[CT] A team of fire and rescue staff which provide a back-up to the **First Line Of Response** (**FLOR**).

Second Man
[Ops. Obs.] The official title given to **Firemen** following the introduction of **Diesel Locomotives**. Their duties were principally to operate the **Steam Heat** boiler, but this duty has now become obsolete with the introduction of **Electric Train Heating** (**ETH**). When required for other specific duties, a **Driver's Assistant** may be provided.

Secondary Drive
See **Supplementary Drive**. Also **Back Drive**. See also **Torsional Back Drive**.

ELLIS' BRITISH RAILWAY ENGINEERING ENCYCLOPÆDIA

Secondary Gate
At a **Level Crossing** (**LC, LX**) with overlapping **Gates**, the Gates which are hinged to the right of the **Railway** (as seen from an approaching **Train**) and are the second set of Gates to be closed to the road. See also **Primary Gate**.

Secondary Impact
The impact between occupants or between occupants and the vehicle interior, caused in turn by the **Passenger** compartment of a **Train** being subject to severe accelerations arising from a primary impact event, such as collisions with other **Rail Vehicles** or **Infrastructure**, and **Derailments**.

Secondary insulation
[Elec.] A protective device, usually made of a polymer, fitted to the **Catenary** in areas of reduced electrical clearance (for instance under a **Bridge**) to reduce the risk of electrical flashover.

Secondary Line
A **Line** of lower status than a **Main Line**, but higher than a **Siding**. This term is typically used when describing **Branch Lines** and **Commuter Lines**.

Secondary Suspension
[TRS] The part of a suspension system that is not connected to the axles. These first components are the **Primary Suspension**.

Section
a) [NR] A term referring to a local **Permanent Way Maintenance** (**PWM**) organisation
b) [Sig.] A length of **Track** bounded by **Signals** or other similar control arrangements. See **Block Section**
c) [PW] A short length of **Track**. See **Track Panel**
d) [Elec.] A length of **Overhead Line Equipment** (**OLE**) between **Switching Stations**, or between Switching Stations and a **Terminal End**
e) [Elec.] A length of **Conductor Rail** that can be isolated by the operation of **Circuit Breakers** (**CB**). See also **Sub Section**
f) [NR] Part of the **Weekly Operating Notice** (**WON**)
g) [NR] Part of the **Rule Book**.

Section A
a) [NR] The first section of the **Weekly Operating Notice** (**WON**), a section concerned with **Possession Arrangements**
b) [RB] The part of the **Rule Book** concerned with the general responsibilities of staff, security and safety.

Section B
a) [NR] The second section of the **Weekly Operating Notice** (**WON**), a section concerned with **Temporary Speed Restrictions** (**TSR**)
b) [RB] The part of the **Rule Book** concerned with the safety of staff **On or Near the Line** and staff working on **Rail Vehicles**.

Section C
a) [NR] The third section of the **Weekly Operating Notice** (**WON**), a section concerned with alterations to **Track** and **Signalling**. See also **Section C Notice**
b) [RB] The part of the **Rule Book** concerned with **Signals**.

Section C Notice
[NR] A formal announcement in **Section C** of the **Weekly Operating Notice** (**WON**) concerning impending or completed alterations to the **Track Layout** or **Signalling** in a specified area. Where such an entry would render the WON unwieldy (i.e. many alterations as part of a major **Remodelling** scheme) then a separate **Operating Notice** or **Yellow Peril** is issued.

Section D
a) [NR] The fourth section of the **Weekly Operating Notice** (**WON**), a section concerned with alterations and amendments to other publications
b) [RB] The part of the **Rule Book** concerned with **Signals Passed at Danger** (**SPAD**) and **Wrong Direction Movements**.

Section E
[RB] The part of the **Rule Book** concerned with the failure, **Maintenance** and **Renewal** of **Signalling Equipment** and the arrangements for dealing with **Signalling** failures.

Section F
[RB] The part of the **Rule Book** concerned with the duties of **Handsignallers** and the manual operation of **Power Operated Points**.

Section G
[RB] The part of the **Rule Book** concerned with the duties of staff working at **Passenger** □ **Stations**.

Section Gap
[Elec.] In a system of **Conductor Rails**, this is a physical gap left between adjacent **Sections** for electrical purposes.

Section H
[RB] The part of the **Rule Book** concerned with the **Working** of **Trains** and **On Track Machines** (**OTM**) in **Train Formation**.

Section Insulator (SI)
[Elec.] A short **Insulator** placed between two **Electrical Sections** of **Overhead Line Equipment** (**OLE**), separating them electrically except during the passage of a **Pantograph**. They are designed to allow the Pantograph to pass smoothly from one **Section** to the other.

Section J
[RB] The part of the **Rule Book** concerned with **Shunting**.

Section K
[RB] The part of the **Rule Book** concerned with **Trains** or **Rail Vehicles** detained on **Running Lines** or **Sidings**.

Section L
[RB] The part of the **Rule Book** concerned with **Level Crossings**.

Section M
[NR] The part of the **Rule Book** concerned with **Trains** stopped due to **Accidents** (including fire and becoming **Divided**) and the means of providing assistance.

Section N
[RB] The part of the **Rule Book** concerned with **Single Line Working** (**SLW**).

Section P
[RB] The part of the **Rule Book** concerned with the normal working of **Single Lines**.

Section Proving
[Elec.] A testing activity which involves opening **Section Switches** and loading or **Earthing** adjacent **Electrical Sections** whilst Traction Current is applied to the Electrical Section under test.

Section Q
[RB] The part of the **Rule Book** concerned with the operation of **On Track Plant** (**OTP**), **On Track Machines** (**OTM**).

Section R
[RB] The part of the **Rule Book** concerned with the loading and unloading of **Rail Vehicles** during **Engineering** work.

Section Rail
[LUL] The **Running Rail** that is **Track Circuit Rail**, usually arranged to be on opposite side to the **Positive Conductor Rail**.

Section S
[RB] The part of the **Rule Book** concerned with the safe operation of **Hand Trolleys** on the **Line**.

Section Signal
[Sig.] A **Stop Signal** that controls access to the next **Block Section** or first **Intermediate Block Section**. Often referred to as the **Starter**. See also Home Signal, Starting Signal, Platform Starter.

Section SP
[RB] The part of the **Rule Book** concerned with **Permissible Speeds** (**PS**).

Section Supervisor
[BR PW] See **Permanent Way Section Supervisor** (**PWSS**), which later became **Permanent Way Section Manager** (**PWSM**).

Section Switch
[Elec.] An electrical switch mounted on an **Overhead Line Structure** that allows one **Electrical Section** or **Electrical Sub Section** to be connected to another.

Section T
[RB] The part of the **Rule Book** concerned with **Possessions** and **Protection**. It is divided into sub-sections:
- T1A Work on **Signalling Equipment**
- T1B Movement of **Trains** during failure of, or when working on, Signalling Equipment
- T2 Protecting **Engineering Work** or a **Hand Trolley** on a **Line** not under **Possession** (withdrawn Dec 2010)
- T3 Possession of a **Running Line** for Engineering Work
- T4 Possession of a **Siding** for Engineering Work (withdrawn June 2011)
- T5 Operating **Power-Operated Points** by hand (withdrawn June 2010)
- T6 **Walking** as a group and **Working** □ on or **Near the Line** (withdrawn June 2010)
- T7 **Safe Systems of Work** (**SSoW**) when Walking or Working on or Near the Line (withdrawn Dec 2010)
- T8 **Handsignalling** duties (withdrawn June 2010)
- T9 Loading and unloading **Rail Vehicles** during Engineering Work (withdrawn June 2011)
- T10 Protecting personnel when working on Rail Vehicles and in Sidings
- T11 Movement of **Engineering Trains** and **On-track Plant** (**OTP**) during T3 arrangements (withdrawn June 2011)
- T12 Protecting personnel carrying out activities on or Near the Line that do not affect the **Safety of the Line** (withdrawn Dec 2010)

See **Rule Book Handbooks**.

Section Token
[Sig.] The electronic **Token** for one **Section** in a **Radio Electronic Token Block** (**RETB**) area.

Section U
[RB] The part of the **Rule Book** concerned with **Emergency Speed Restrictions** (**ESR**), **Enhanced Permissible Speeds** (**EPS**), **Permissible Speeds** (**PS**) and **Temporary Speed Restrictions** (**TSR**).

Section V
[RB] The part of the **Rule Book** concerned with arrangements for dealing with **Broken Rails** and **Bridge Strikes**.

Section W
[RB] The part of the **Rule Book** concerned with arrangements for dealing with bad weather.

Section Y
[RB] The part of the **Rule Book** concerned with arrangements for dealing with accidents.

Section Z
[RB] The part of the **Rule Book** concerned with instructions for working on **AC Electrified Lines**.

Sectional Appendix (SA)
[NR] The publication, produced by each **Network Rail** (**NR**) □ **Route**, containing layout and location details for **Running Lines**, **Stations**, **Permanent Speed Restrictions** (**PSR**), **Tunnels** etc. The full list of contents is:
- Controlling Signal Boxes
- Cab Secure Radio (**CSR**) area numbers
- Differential Speed Restrictions (**DSR**)
- Electrical Control Room (**ECR**) details
- Enhanced Permissible Speeds (**EPS**)
- Junctions, Junction Names
- Level Crossings (**LC**, **LX**)
- Local Instructions
- Loop lengths
- Signalling arrangements
- National Radio Network (**NRN**) area numbers
- Permissible Speeds (**PS**)
- Permissive Working arrangements
- Platform Lengths
- Route Availability (**RA**)
- Route Clearance for Rolling Stock
- Running Lines, Stations and Tunnels

Location information is given in **Miles** and **Chains**.

Sectional Route Release
[Sig.] An arrangement where a **Route** is **Released** in sections, normally one **Track Circuit** at a time, behind a **Train**. See also **Train Operated Route Release** (**TORR**).

Sectional Running Time (SRT)
[Ops.] The allowance of time given to a particular **Train** between two points, used in the compilation of **Working Timetables** (**WTT**). See also **Technical Running Time** (**TRT**), **Timing Load** (**TL**).

Sectioning
[Elec.] The dividing up of the **Conductor Rail** or **Overhead Line Equipment** (**OLE**) system into sections to reduce the impact of **Isolations** and unplanned outages.

Sector Plate
[Hist.] A rotating deck structure, pivoted at one end and rotating through an arc of around 90°, which allows vehicles arriving on a single **Track** to be directed onto one of many Tracks. Effectively a reduced functionality **Turntable**, Sector Plates were often found in **Traction Maintenance Depots** (**TMD**).

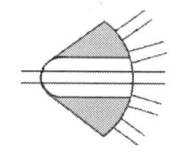

Secure Power Supply
[Sig.] A power supply system arranged to keep those parts of **Signalling System** which are critical to the **Safety of the Line** working when all other forms of electrical supply fail.

Secured Out of Use
Describing a **Set of Switches** (**Set of Points**) which have been rendered temporarily inoperable. Similar in usage to the term **Clipped out of Use**, Secured out of Use is normally used to include more permanent actions such as the use of a **Fishplate** and **Chairscrews** to hold the **Closed Switch** closed and sometimes the additional disconnection of the **Switch Operating Mechanism**. See also **Spiking**.

SED
Staff Egress Device.

See-tru Bolt
A bolt having a rubber sleeve fitted to its lower portion. As the assembly is tightened the sleeve is compressed vertically with a corresponding increase in its diameter. Used to attach **Conductor Rail Insulators** and **Signalling Equipment** such as **AWS Magnets** to **Concrete Sleepers** they are preferred to other forms of 'expanding' bolts as there is virtually no tendency for the Concrete Sleeper to split as the bolt is tightened.

Segregated Track
[LR] A route for **Trams** which is not shared with road vehicles or pedestrians. Such **Track** is normally **Ballasted Track**.

SEI
(Tradename) [Hist.] South East **Infrastructure**, now Balfour Beatty Railway Maintenance (**BBRM**). Also South East **Infrastructure** Maintenance Unit (**SEIMU**).

SEIMU
[Hist.] South East Infrastructure Maintenance Unit (**IMU**).

Seized Joint
See **Frozen Joint**.

SEJ
Structured Engineering Judgement.

Selby Accident
See **Heck Accident**.

SELCAB
(Tradename) An **Automatic Train Protection** (**ATP**) system fitted on the Chiltern **Lines**. It is manufactured by Alcatel. See also **BR-ATP, TBL**.

SELCAT
Safer European Level Crossing Appraisal and Technology.

Selective Door Opening (SDO)
Selective Door Operation
A system fitted to certain **Multiple Unit Trains** that allows the **Guard** or **Train Manager** to open a reduced number of external doors when calling at **Stations** with **Platforms** that are shorter than the **Train**. There are two types, see **Automatic Selective Door Opening** (Automatic SDO) and **Manual Selective Door Opening** (Manual SDO).

Self-accounting Unit (SAU)
An arrangement within **British Railways** (**BR**) where parts of the organisation that could survive in the open market were made into wholly owned subsidiary companies. An example was the Civil Engineer's Design Group (**CEDG**) that was bought by British Steel (Then Corus, now Tata) under **Privatisation**.

Self-acting Incline
Self-acting Inclined Plane
[Hist.] An **Inclined Plane** usually provided with some form of powered haulage device, which has two **Tracks**, one each for ascending (usually unloaded) vehicles and one for descending (loaded) vehicles. By balancing the mass of the descending vehicles more or less with those ascending, the power input required from the haulage device was minimised.

Self-discharging Train (SDT)
(Tradename) Previously pioneered by Redland Aggregates, and now operated by Lafarge Aggregates, a **Train** consisting of a discharge **Wagon** and a number of special **Hopper Wagons** equipped with conveyors to move material to one end of the Train. The Hopper Wagons come in **Sets** of five or ten, giving a minimum capacity of 185 tonnes, and a maximum capacity (in 30 hoppers) of 1100 tonnes. The system can cope with any size of aggregate, from sand up to normal **Ballast**, and can discharge out to a radius of 15m (50 feet).

Self-maintaining Brake System
A brake system which automatically compensates for unintended air leakage from the system.

Self-normalising Points
See also **Autonormalisation**.

Self-propelled
Describing an **On Tack Machine** (**OTM**) or piece of **On Track Plant** (**OTP**) that is capable of moving itself along the **Track** at speed. Most recent machines are capable of this, the term having been introduced when few machines could. See also **Working Drive**.

Self-restored Points
See also **Autonormalisation**.

Self-steering Bogie
[TRS] A **Bogie** which attempts to provide a better path around a **Curve** by angling each axle to keep them radial to the Curve. This is normally achieved passively by mechanical means.

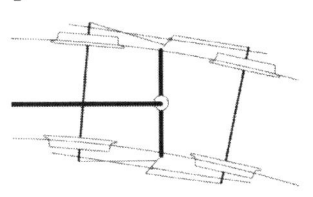

Self-supporting Anchor (SSA)
[Elec.] An **Overhead Line Structure** that acts as an anchorage point for a **Catenary** without any assistance from backstays or **Anchors**.

Self-tapping Thimble
[PW] A ceramic **Thimble** fitted with a fusible plug which melts after the correct amount of heat has been applied for the correct time, releasing the molten **Weld Portion** into the **Moulds**. This type of Thimble does away with the need for the **Welder** to push the **Tapping Pin**.

SELNEC
SELNEC PTE
[Hist.] South East Lancashire North East Cheshire Passenger Transport Executive, predecessor of Greater Manchester Passenger Transport Executive (GMPTE), now Transport for Greater Manchester (TfGM).

SELRAP
Skipton East Lancashire Railway Action Partnership.

SELV
Safety Extra Low Voltage; e.g. not capable of exceeding a voltage of 50V **AC** (RMS) or 120V **DC**.

Semaphore Disc Signal

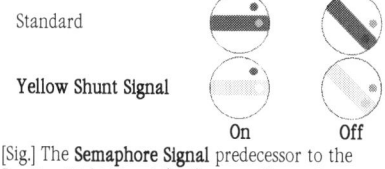

Standard

Yellow Shunt Signal

On   Off

[Sig.] The **Semaphore Signal** predecessor to the **Position Light Signal** (**PLS**), generally used to control Shunting Movements.

Semaphore Distant Signal

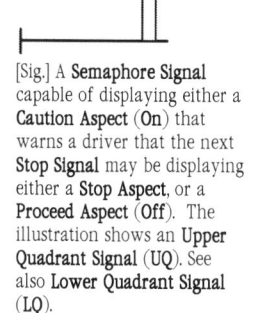

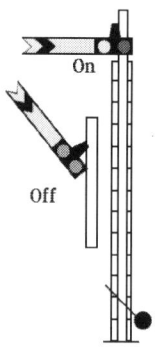

On

Off

[Sig.] A **Semaphore Signal** capable of displaying either a **Caution Aspect** (**On**) that warns a driver that the next **Stop Signal** may be displaying either a **Stop Aspect**, or a **Proceed Aspect** (**Off**). The illustration shows an **Upper Quadrant Signal** (**UQ**). See also **Lower Quadrant Signal** (**LQ**).

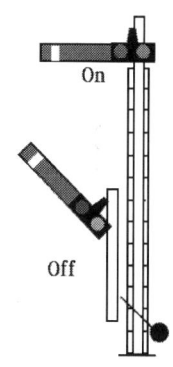

Semaphore Signal
[Sig.] Mechanical **Signals** generally consisting of moveable **Arms**, the shape, disposition and attitude of which (e.g. raised or lowered) all carry meaning. Most Semaphore Signals are operated by wires from a **Lever Frame**, but some are electrical where the distance from the **Signal Box** is great. There are as many patterns as there were **Railway Companies**, but **British Railways** (**BR**) standardised on the **Upper Quadrant Signal** (**UQ**) type. See also **Lower Quadrant Signal** (**LQ**). There are two main shapes of Arm:
a) The **Semaphore Stop Signal** Arm, which can show either a **Proceed Aspect** or **Stop Aspect**. This is a rectangular Arm coloured **Red** with a vertical white stripe at its outer end. It shows a Stop Aspect when the Arm is horizontal and a Proceed Aspect when the Arm is raised at 45° (Upper Quadrant) or lowered by 45° (Lower Quadrant).
b) The **Semaphore Distant Signal** Arm, which can show either a Proceed Aspect or **Caution Aspect**. This is a rectangular Arm with a fishtailed end, coloured **Yellow** with a black chevron stripe at its outer end. It shows a Caution Aspect when the Arm is horizontal and a Proceed Aspect when the Arm is raised at 45° (Upper Quadrant) or lowered by 45° (Lower Quadrant).
See also **Semaphore Disc Signal**.

Semaphore Signalling
A **Signalling** arrangement which uses the position of special **Arms** to convey **Movement Authorities** to **Train** drivers. **Colour Light Signalling** is a development of this system.

Semaphore Stop Signal

On

Off

[Sig.] A **Semaphore Signal** capable of displaying either a **Stop Aspect** (**On**) or a **Proceed Aspect** (**Off**). The illustration shows an **Upper Quadrant Signal** (**UQ**). See also Lower Quadrant Signal (**LQ**).

Semi
[Sig. Col.] Contraction of **Semi-automatic Signal**.

Semi-automated Train Operation (STO)
A system where **Trains** are partially controlled by drivers on board, in that they operate the stopping of the trains, door closure and driver-to-passenger communications but not the normal driving of the Trains between **Stations**.

Semi-automatic Signal
[Sig.] A **Signal** that normally works as an **Automatic Signal**, but can also be a **Controlled Signal**, operated by a **Signal Box** (**SB**) or **Ground Frame** (**GF**).

SEMI
AE
123

ELLIS' BRITISH RAILWAY ENGINEERING ENCYCLOPÆDIA

Semi-fast
Semi-fast Passenger Train
Semi-fast Train
[Ops.] A **Train** that calls at only a reduced number of **Stations** on a **Route**, rather than at **All Stations** or no Stations. See also **Express**.

Semi-open Coach
[TRS] A **Passenger Coach** with both **Compartments** and open plan seating.

Semi-outside Double Slip Diamond
A **Double Slip Diamond** in which the **Slip Switch** **Switch Toes** are outside the **Common Crossings** (making it an **Outside Double Slip Diamond**) but the **Slip Rails** pass either side of the **Obtuse Crossings**. See also **Inside Double Slip Diamond**.

Semi-outside Single Slip Diamond
A **Single Slip Diamond** in which the **Slip Switch** **Switch Toes** are outside the **Common Crossings** (making it an **Outside Single Slip Diamond**) but the **Slip Rails** pass either side of the **Obtuse Crossing**. See also **Inside Single Slip Diamond**.

Semi-permanently Coupled
[TRS] Two or more **Rail Vehicles** designed to operate normally as a fixed **Formation** but which can be **Uncoupled** and re-coupled to form new Formations.

Semi-supported Joint

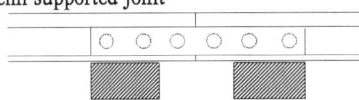

[PW] A **Fishplated Rail Joint** between **Running Rails** where the supporting **Sleepers** are partially or wholly inside the limits of the **Fishplates**. See also **Supported Joint**, **Suspended Joint**.

Semi-welded Crossing
See **Part Welded Crossing**, **Electro-slag Welded Vee**.

SEML
South East Main Line.

SEMMMS
(*semms*) South East Manchester Multi-modal Study.

Senior Person in Charge of Possession (SPICOP)
See **Person in Charge of Possession (PICOP)**.

Sensitive Edge
[LUL] A pressure-sensitive rubber extrusion fitted to the edge of the sliding doors to reduce the risk of persons becoming trapped as the doors close.

Sensitive Edge Brake Relays
[LUL] **Relays** that de-energise when the **Sensitive Edge** system is activated, resulting in an **Emergency Brake Application**.

Sensitive Relay
[Sig.] Generally a **Neutral Relay** with a high coil resistance and low power consumption. It may be used to give accurate timings in conjunction with a capacitor / resistor unit.

Sentinel
[NR] Operated by the **National Competency Control Agency (NCCA)**, Sentinel is the brandname for the competency control system based on photographic identity cards. The cards give details of medical fitness and railway related competencies, including:
- AOD:HS
- AOD:LXA
- AOD:PO
- Authorised Person (AP)
- Controller of Site Safety (COSS)
- Engineering Supervisor (ES)
- Handsignaller (HS)
- Individual Working Alone (IWA)
- Lookout (LKT, LO)
- Nominated Person (NP)
- Personal Track Safety (PTS)
- Person In Charge of Possession (PICOP)
- Protection Controller (PC)
- Points Operator (PO)
- Rail Incident Officer (RIO)
- Senior Person In Charge of Possession (SPICOP)
- Signaller
- Track Welder (TW)

The Sentinel website should be consulted for a complete list..

Sentinel Card
[NR Col] The photographic identity card issued by the **Sentinel** scheme. See **National Competency Control Agency (NCCA)**.

Sentinel Number
[NR Col] A unique number allocated to any person registered on the **Sentinel** system. **National Competency Control Agency (NCCA)**.

Separated Green Zone
[NR Obs.] The former term for a **Safe System of Work (SSoW)** based on a **Site Warden Warning**. The term **Green Zone** is also obsolete.

SEPEX
[TRS] A contraction of separate excitement; normally referring to **Traction Motors** where the armature and field coils of the electric motor are fed with independently controlled currents.

Sequential Locking
[Sig.] An arrangement of the **Interlocking** of a **Signalling System** that only permits the operation of the controls in a specific order. This is a non-**Reciprocal Locking** arrangement.

Sequential Track Circuits
[Sig.] A means of **Signalling** a **Single Line** accessible from one end only. The **Line** is divided into three or more **Track Circuits (TC)** which must be **Occupied** and **Cleared** in the correct order before the **Interlocking** will acknowledge that the Line is **Clear** for the passage of another **Train**.

SER
Signalling Equipment Room.

Serco
(Tradename) A service company carrying out **Maintenance** and data collection work, as well as being a partner in the **Merseyrail** franchise.

Series Bonding
[Sig.] An arrangement of the **Bonding** of a **Track Circuit** (**TC**) such that the failure of any one **Bond** causes the Track Circuit to become **De-energised** and show **Occupied**. See also **Parallel Bonding**.

Series I Design Range
Series II Design Range
[NR] A new set of standard **Overhead Line Equipment** (**OLE**) designs incorporating best practice from British and European Railways. Series I allows for 25kV AC **Traction Power** at **Permissible Speeds** (**PS**) up to 125mph and Series II for speeds up to 100mph. It can be configured as a classic **Booster Transformer** (**BT**) or **Autotransformer** (**AT**) system. The **Contact Wire** (**CW**) is a solid 107mm² silver-copper wire tensioned at 11kN, suspended from a 19/2.1 stranded bronze II **Catenary Wire**, also tensioned at 11kN, by flexible current-carrying **Droppers**. The nominal **System Height** is 1300mm. An **Aerial Earth** connection is standard. The Contact and Catenary are automatically tensioned using independent **Tensorex C+** □ **Spring Tensioners**. This range also sees the introduction of an **Omnia** aluminium **Cantilever Arm** in place of the more traditional galvanised steel tube arrangement.

Serious Injuries
Physical injuries that are listed in Regulation 2(4) of the **Railways (Accident Investigation and Reporting) Regulations 2005**.

Serpell Report
[Hist.] The colloquial name for a report produced in 1982 by a committee chaired by Sir David Serpell KCB CMG OBE at the request of the Secretary of State for Transport, which proposed reshaping and generally reducing the **National Railway Network** (**NRN**). The most memorable option was option A, which reduced **The Network** from 10,370 **Route Miles** down to 1,630 Miles. The aim was to reduce operating costs and maximise revenue by concentrating on the most profitable **Lines**. The report was abandoned after a massive outcry. Sir David had previously worked with Dr **Beeching**.

Service
[Ops.] A **Passenger Train** or **Freight Train** making a scheduled journey.

Service Brake
[TRS] A brake that is designed to stop a **Rail Vehicle** when it is moving.

Service Braking
a) [TRS] The normal application of the brakes on a **Train** producing a comfortable deceleration, typically 7% to 9**% of g**. This is a less severe deceleration than that produced under **Emergency Braking**
b) [LUL] The position of the **Controller** used during normal, non-emergency, stopping of a Train.

Service Braking Distance
[Sig.] The distance required to decelerate from one speed to a lower speed under **Service Braking** conditions using the **Service Brake**. This distance is used to determine the positioning of **Warning Indicators** (**WI**) for changes in **Permissible Speed** (**PS**) and **Enhanced Permissible Speed** (**EPS**). It is also used to determine the **Signal Spacing**.

Service Controller
[LUL] Formerly called the **Line Controller**, on **London Underground Limited** (**LUL**) the person in the control centre who is responsible for overseeing the operation of a **Line**.

Service Operator
[LUL] A member of staff controlling and supervising the movement of **Trains** over a section of **Route**, within a **Line** under the direction of the **Service Controller**.

Service Perturbation
[NR Ops.] A disruption to the **Timetable** (**TT**) that is considered beyond an acceptable deviation from the Timetable; e.g. **Trains** are re-ordered, diverted, terminated short of destination (see **PINE**) or cancelled (see **CAPE**).

Service Rail
See **Plant Rail**.

Service Tunnel
[Civ.] A **Tunnel** used to gain access to **Running Tunnels** and the underground plant and equipment.

Service Tunnel Transport System (STTS)
[CT] The transport system in place in the **Service Tunnel** using specialised guided road vehicles which can operate as conventional road vehicles on suitable surfaces.

Serviceable
a) See **Serviceable Rail**, **Serviceable Sleeper**
b) [NR] **Slope Condition Rating** for an **Earthwork** such as an **Embankment**, **Cutting** or natural slope; the lowest-risk categorisation; the others are **Marginal** and **Poor**.

Serviceable Rail
[PW] **Rail** that has carried **Railway Vehicles**, and is of reduced or worn dimensions, but is otherwise suitable for re-use in the **Track**, albeit at a lower **Track Category** or status.

Serviceable Sleeper
[PW] A **Sleeper** that has previously been laid in the **Track**, but is suitable for re-use on other **Lines**, albeit at a lower **Track Category** or status.

SET
a) (Tradename) South Eastern **Trains** (Holdings) Ltd, a **Train Operating Company** (**TOC**)
b) [IÉ] **Signalling**, Electrical and Telecommunications.

ELLIS' BRITISH RAILWAY ENGINEERING ENCYCLOPÆDIA

Set
a) See **Set of Points**, **Set of Switches**
b) [PW] A bend induced in a **Rail**, generally in **Switch and Crossing Rails**, which ensures that the **Rail Web** remains central to the machined Rail through an assembly
c) [Sig.] To place a **Signal**, **Route** or **Points** to the desired **Aspect** or position. See also **Clear** clause a), **Normal**, **Reverse**, **Pull Off** clause a), **Put Back**.
d) [Sig.] See **Latch**
e) [Ops.] A group of vehicles normally marshalled together. So, a **Locomotive**, **Coaches** and a **Driving Van Trailer** (**DVT**) which spend all their time together are a **Set**, as are the vehicles of an **Multiple Unit** (**MU**) □ **Train**
f) [Hist.] On a **Rope-worked Railway** a number of **Wagons** coupled together to run as a unit on a rope-worked or gravity-worked **Railway**. Also **Run**.

Set Against
[Sig.] Describing a **Signal** displaying a **Stop Aspect** or **Trailing Points** □ **Set** for the other **Route**.

Set Back
[Ops.] To move a **Train** backwards a short distance. See also **Propel**.

Set Down Only
[Ops.] A **Booked Call** or **Station Stop** provided so that **Passengers** may **Alight** only. It is used as a means of discouraging overcrowding. The opposite is **Pick-up Only**.

Set of Points
Alternative term for a **Set of Switches**, favoured by the **Operating** and **Signalling** □ **Disciplines**.

Set of Switches
[PW] Assemblies for both sides of a **Switch** comprising a pair of **Switch Half Sets** together with **Soleplates**, **Stretcher Bar** brackets and Stretcher Bars. Also **Full Set of Switches**. This term is preferred by the **Permanent Way** □ **Discipline**, but referred to by the **Operating** and **Signalling** functions as a **Set of Points**.

Set Rider
[Hist.] On a **Rope-Worked Railway** a person appointed to ride on a **Set** whose duties would include releasing the haulage rope when the Set reached a pre-determined point known as the **Mark**.

Set Speed
[Sig.] The speed above which a **Train** would have its brakes automatically applied by the intervention of a **Train Protection and Warning System** (**TPWS**) installation. See **Overspeed Sensor System** (**OSS**), **Train Stop Sensor** (**TSS**).

SETA
[Sig.] **S**ignalling **E**quipment **T**echnical **A**gent.

SETTOL
[NR] **S**easonal **T**reatment **O**n**l**ine, a database that is used to manage the **National Seasonal Infrastructure Treatment Plan**.

SEU
See **S**ignalling **E**quivalent **U**nit.

Seven Day Railway (7DR)
[NR] An aspiration to reduce the impact of **Engineering Works** such that the **Train Operating Companies** (**TOC**) and **Freight Operating Companies** (**FOC**) can operate a full service every day of the week.

SEWCML
[Hist.] Structures Engineer **W**est **C**oast **M**ain **L**ine.

SEZ
See **S**ignal **E**xclusion **Z**one.

SF
Shunting **F**rame, See **Ground Frame** (**GF**).

SFAIRP
So **F**ar **a**s **i**s **R**easonably **P**racticable. See also **ALARP**, **GAMAB**.

SFD
[Sig.] **S**ignalling **F**acilities **D**iagram.

SFN
See **S**trategic **F**reight **N**etwork.

SFNSG
Strategic **F**reight **N**etwork Steering Group.

SFO
a) **S**tation **F**acility **O**perator
b) **S**tation **F**acility **O**wner
c) **S**enior **F**ire **O**fficer.

SFS
Strategic **F**reight **S**ite.

SFT
See **S**tress **F**ree **T**emperature.

SG
a) See **Switch Letters**. See also **SGV**, **SGVs**, **SGVS**.
b) **S**pheroidal **G**raphite (cast iron)

SGE
(Tradename) **S**iemens and **G**eneral **E**lectric **Railway** □ **Signal** Co Ltd., a manufacturer of **Signalling Equipment**.

SGI
a) **S**pheroidal **G**raphite **C**ast **I**ron
b) See **S**ignaller's **G**eneral **I**nstructions.

SGR
Stage **G**ate **R**eview.

SGRC
[Sig.] **S**ignal **G**roup **R**eplacement **C**ontrol, the **IECC** equivalent of a **Group Replacement Switch**.

SGT
See **Structure Gauging Train**. Also **S**erco **G**auging □ **Train**

SGV
[PW] Vertical □ Flat Bottom (FB) □ Full Depth Switches. The SG describes the length and **Switch Radius**.

SGVs
[PW] Denotes Vertical □ 113A □ Flat Bottom (FB) □ Shallow Depth Switches, length SG.

SGVS
[PW] Denotes Vertical □ CEN56E1 □ Flat Bottom (FB) □ Shallow Depth Switches, length SG.

SH
See **Steam Heating**.

Shatter Cracks
[PW] A type of **Rail Defect** that normally appears deep in the **Rail Head** during or shortly after manufacture. They are caused by elevated Hydrogen levels in the **Rail Steel** during production.

SHA
Safety **H**azard **A**nalysis.

Shackle
[Col.] See **Screw Coupling**.

Shadow Strategic Rail Authority (sSRA)
See **Strategic Rail Authority (SRA)**.

Shadowing
[PW] A problem inherent in **Ultrasonic Rail Flaw Detection** where a small **Rail Flaw** near the surface of the **Rail** can mask a much larger Flaw deeper within the Rail.

Shaft
[Civ.] The vertical construction linking a **Tunnel** to the surface above. Originally used for the movement of materials during construction and to allow the tunnelers to gain access to the works, these openings are normally retained for ventilation purposes. See also **Eye**, **Garland**.

Shallow Concrete Sleeper
Shallow Depth Concrete Sleeper
[PW] A **Concrete Sleeper** with a construction depth less than that of a normal **Concrete Sleeper**. A Shallow Sleeper will typically have a **Rail Seat Depth** of 165mm, whereas a normal Concrete Sleeper will measure 200mm at this point. Such Sleepers are normally prefixed **E**, as in **EF** and **EG**. See also **Class of Sleeper**.

Shallow Depth Switch
[PW] A **Switch** assembly in which the **Switch Rail** is produced from an asymmetrical **Rail Section** of shallower depth than that used for the **Stock Rail**, allowing the switch rail to pass over the un-machined foot of the Stock Rail when the Switch is in the closed position. Also **Thick Web Switch**.

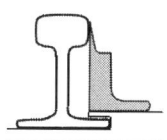

Shark (ZUA, ZUB, ZUP, ZUV, ZUW)
[NR] A 20 ton **Brake Van** fitted with retractable **Ballast Ploughs** front and rear. See **Wagon Names**.

Sharp Angle Crossing
[PW] A **Crossing** with a large angle between the two **Running Rails**, or small **N Value**. Also **Wide Angle Crossing**.

Sharp Curve
[PW] A **Curve** with a small Radius (**R**). The opposite is a **Flat Curve**.

SHC
SHC Clip
SHC Fastening
See **Spring Hook Clip**.

SHDSL
[Tel.] **S**ymmetric **H**igh-speed **D**igital **S**ubscriber **L**ine.

Shed
a) Widely used term for a **Traction Maintenance Depot (TMD)** or the buildings within which such work is carried out
b) [Elec.] The disk-shaped fins forming part of an **Overhead Line Equipment (OLE)** □ **Insulator**
c) [Col.] Nickname for the Canadian-built **Class** 66 **Diesel Locomotive**, inspired by the roof shape and the corrugated body sides.
d) [Col.] A **Multiple Unit (MU)** with faults
See also **Train Shed**.

Shed Apron
An area of (concrete) hard standing forming a **Level Crossing** across the end of a **Shed**. See also **Apron**.

Shed Plug
The device used to connect the **Traction Supply** to a **Train** which would normally use **Conductor Rails**, while it is in a **Depot** (which do not normally have Conductor Rails inside the **Maintenance** sheds).

Shed Receptacle
[TRS] The socket provided on a **Motor** □ **Car** into which the **Shed Plug** is plugged.

Shed Road
In a **Depot**, a **Line** which continues into a **Shed**.

Shed Switch
[TRS] A three-position switch provided on **Trains** which use **Conductor Rails** which, when turned to:
• SHED allows 630V Train equipment to be powered from the **Overhead Trolley Leads** but isolates the **Shoegear**
• OFF isolates all 630V train equipment on the Train
• TRACK allows 630V Train equipment to be powered from the Conductor Rails.

Shed Test Magnet
[Sig.] An **Automatic Warning System (AWS)** □ **Permanent Magnet** fixed to the **Track** at the exit from a **Traction Maintenance Depot (TMD)**, used to test and verify that the AWS equipment on the passing **Traction Units** is functioning correctly. See also **Permanent AWS Magnet**, **Permanent AWS Inductor**, **Permanent Inductor**, **Permanent Magnet**.

Sheerness-on-Sea Accident
At 18:57 on the 26th February 1971 a ten-**Car** □ **Electric Multiple Unit (EMU)** entered Sheerness-on-Sea **Station**, made no attempt to brake, ran through a short **Sand Drag** and collided with the **Buffer Stop**, coming to a stand nearly 30 metres across the **Concourse**. One person on the Concourse died and 13 were injured. The cause was determined to be the driver "blacking out" as the **Train** entered the Station, based on evidence of a previous head injury and subsequent similar episodes. **TPWS Mini** would have prevented this **Accident**.

Shelf Relay
[Sig.] A **Signalling** □ **Relay** designed to be installed on a shelf (rather than plugging it into a rack). Such devices consist of a glass container the size of a goldfish bowl with terminal posts mounted on an insulating board across the top.

433

Shell Track
[PW Obs.] Inverted bowl-shaped single **Rail** "pots", originally cast iron and later of sheet steel, devised by **Hugh Greaves** during the 1840s, British patent number 742 in 1852. They were developed further by Griffith, Livesey and MacLellan through to the 1880s. Spacing bars were used to maintain the Gauge. See also **Pot Sleepers**.

Shelling
[PW] A type of shallow **Rail Defect** found at the **Rail End**, in which a flake of the **Running Surface** breaks away.

Shells
See **Fishplate Insulations**. Also **Liners**.

Sherardizing
A surface treatment in which a heated iron or steel part is exposed to Zinc dust, creating an Iron / Zinc alloy. After minor post-treatment a uniform and hardwearing surface finish is achieved. Named for its inventor Sherard Cowper-Coles, this treatment is often applied to **Rail Clips** fitted in **Tunnels**.

SHERPA
Systematic Human Error Reduction and Prediction Approach

Sheth
[Hist.] A transom or a vertical side member of wood or metal forming part of the framing of early forms of both **Passenger** and **Freight Vehicles**.

Shields Junction Accident
At 22:12 on 30th August 1973 an **Electric Multiple Unit** (**EMU**) running at 65mph ran into the back of a slow moving **Diesel Multiple Unit** (**DMU**). Fire broke out and The EMU driver and four **Passengers** in the EMU **Leading Vehicle** died, with 51 others injured. The probable cause was determined to be that the EMU driver had suffered a heart attack but had cancelled the **Automatic Warning System** (**AWS**) at three **Signals** and not released the **Driver's Safety Device** (**DSD**). This **Accident** would have been prevented by **Train Protection and Warning System** (**TPWS**).

Shift
a) [PW] The offset introduced between a **Circular Curve** and a straight when they are connected by a **Transition Curve**. See **Straight to Curve Transition, Transition Shift**
b) The period of time a person works. See **Back Shift, Front Shift**.

Shims
a) See **Fishplate Shims, Key Liner**
b) See **Baseplate Shims**
c) [TRS] Packings to a maximum value of 30mm (2 by 15mm) used to compensate for **Frame Twist** in a **Wagon**.

Shingle
[LUL] Occasional alternative term for **Ballast**.

Shipper-owned Container (SOC)
A freight **Container** that is owned by the party requiring the goods to be carried.

Shoe
See **Current Collection Shoe**.

Shoe Box
[Col.] Nickname given to **Class** 73 **Electro-diesel Locomotives** due to their size and shape.

Shoegear
[TRS] Equipment carried by a **Train** and used for current collection on **Third Rail** systems. Shoegear comprises a cast iron **Shoe** that is usually mounted on an insulating beam attached to the side of the **Bogies**, close to **Rail Level**. It is sometimes equipped with devices to enable it to be retracted if required to isolate the vehicle or on-board systems which it supplies. See also **Cinderella, Current Collection Shoe**.

Shooting
Shooting a Speed
[Obs.] To use **Railway Fog Signals** or **Detonators** on the **Rails** to provide advanced warning of an **Emergency Speed Restriction** (**ESR**). Shooting has now been replaced by the use of **Emergency Indicators** and **Permanent AWS Inductors**.

Shop Fitted Joint
Shop Made Joint
[PW] An **Insulated Rail Joint** (**IRJ**) assembled and tested in a factory. Typically these are 30, 36, 45 or 60 feet long (9144, 10980, 13725 or 18288mm) The alternative is a **Site Fitted Joint, Site Made Joint**.

Shop Weld
[PW] A **Flash Butt Weld** (**FBW**) made either in a **Depot** or factory.

Shore
That part of the **Railway** universe that is not a moving **Train**.

Shore Supply
[TRS] A fixed electrical supply used to run the **Electric Train Heating** (**ETH**), lighting, charge batteries and run air conditioning on **Passenger Coaches** without needing a **Locomotive**. Used in **Depots** and **Sidings** where **Maintenance** and **Stabling** are carried out. See also **Hotel Power**.

Short Base Versine Error
[PW] A lateral misalignment of the **Running Rail** over a distance of less than 5 metres.

Short Circuit
The (generally) unwanted condition when the two poles of an electrical supply are connected together.

Short Circuit Bond
[Sig.] A **Bond** placed beyond the **Insulated Rail Joints** (**IRJ**) of the final **Track Circuit** (**TC**) on a **Line**, to detect failure of both Insulated Rail Joints. This is the only Bond required on a **Line** that is both a **Non-electrified Line** and a **Non-Track Circuited Line**.

Short Circuiting Bar
A heavy L-shaped metal bar which is hooked over the **Running Rail** and dropped onto the **Conductor Rail** in order to either maintain the Conductor Rail in a discharged state (**Dead**) when taking a **DC Isolation** or to discharge the **Traction Current** in an emergency. To prevent the user suffering severe burns, a wooden **Paddle** is used to drop it onto the Running Rail.

Short Circuiting Device (SCD)
A piece of equipment used specifically for connecting the **Conductor Rail** and **Traction Return Rail** together to prevent the Conductor Rail becoming energised during a **Possession**. See **Fixed Short Circuiting Device, Key Strap, Machine Mounted Short Circuiting Device, Short Circuiting Bar, Short Circuiting Strap.**

Short Circuiting Strap
A flexible **Short Circuiting Device (SCD)**.

Short Earth
A **Local Earth** shorter than 1.5 metres, for use at **Designated Earthing Points (DEP)**. They have a **Pole Applied Clamp** at both ends and are generally coloured orange. See also **Long Earth**.

Short End
a) [PW] To reduce the length of a **Sleeper** at one end in order to avoid an obstruction such as a **Catch Pit** in the **Sixfoot**.

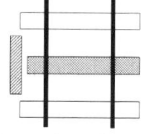

b) Describing the end of a **Rail Crane** where the superstructure is closest to the **Buffer Beam**. The opposite is **Long End**. See also **Over End**.

Short Rail
[PW]
a) [NR] Any **Rail** that is shorter than 60' (18.288m) long. See also **Standard Short Rail**
b) [LUL] Any continuous Rail less than 36.6m (120') in length.

Short Rail Joint
[LUL] A **Fishplated Rail Joint** located between two **Short Rails**.

Short Range Signal
[Sig.] A **Colour Light Signal** deliberately designed to be readable only at a short distance, generally to avoid confusion with other **Signals** on adjacent and faster **Lines**. See also **Spread Lens**.

Short Sleeper Beam
[PW] A spreader beam equipped with four, seven or eight sets of special hooks, allowing a **Rail Crane** or **Road Rail Excavator** to lift four, seven or eight **Sleepers** at once. See also **Crane Beam, Janglers, Sleeper Beam**.

Short Term Planning - Electronic Data Interface (STP EDI)
[NR Ops.] A file format proposed for the transfer of **Short Term Planning (STP)** □ **Train** schedule details from **Train Operating Company (TOC)** □ **Train Planning** systems to Network Rail's **(NR)** □ **Integrated Train Planning System (ITPS)**.

Short Term Planning (STP)
[NR] The process covering one-off bids by **Train Operating Companies (TOC)** for **Train Paths**. See also **Spot Bids**.

Short Wavelength Corrugations
[PW] **Rail Corrugations** with a wavelength of between 25mm and 500mm. At typical **Permissible Speeds (PS)**, this equates to frequency of between 50Hz and 2kHz. This variety of Rail Corrugation is largely caused by resonance within the **Track Structure**. See also **Long Wavelength Corrugations, Roaring Rails**.

Short Wheelbase
[TRS] Describing a **Rail Vehicle** with a **Wheelbase** of less than 8 metres (approximately 26 feet 2 $^3/_4$ inches). See also **Long Wheelbase**.

Short Working
[Ops. Col.] The condition when a **Train** is terminated short of its intended destination. See also **Pine**.

Shortt, William Hamilton
(1881 - 1971) award winning horologist and Engineer on the London and South-western Railway (**L&SWR**) from 1906 to 1946. From 1908 to 1910 he was Secretary to a sub-committee of the **Railway Engineer's Association (REA)** dealing the speed of trains round curves, and presented papers to the Institute of Civil Engineers (**ICE**) on the subject. It appears likely that this work encouraged **Emile Hallade**. He went on to design the most accurate pendulum clock ever built.

Shortts No. 2
[Hist.] A graphical method of plotting and adjusting **Versines** to calculate design **Slues** for realignment of the **Track**. See also **Hallade, Versine Diagram**.

Shots
See **Railway Fog Signal**. Also **Bangers, Crackers, Detonators, Dets, Foggies**.

Shoulder Ballast
[PW] The **Ballast** placed on or just outside the **Sleeper Ends** to improve the **Lateral Resistance (LR)** of the **Track**. See also **Ballast Shoulder**.

Shoulder Hump
See **Ballast Shoulder Surcharge**.

Shoulder Peak
[Ops.] The hour before and after the morning and evening peak.

Shoulder Peak Services
[Ops.] **Trains** running in the hour before and after the morning and evening peak.

Shovel
[PW] The common name of the standard hand tool used for manual excavation of **Ballast**. Also (colloquially) **Spade**. See also **Bar, Duff Jack, Keying Hammer**.

Shovel Packing
[PW] Introducing **Ballast** into **Voids** beneath **Sleepers** and **Bearers** and then consolidating it using a **Shovel**. See also **Measured Shovel Packing (MSP), Ballast Packing**.

Shrewsbury Accident
At 02:08 on 15th October 1907, a **Passenger Train** attempted to negotiate the 200metre radius 10mph curve at the north end of Shrewsbury **Station** at a speed estimated as in excess of 60mph and **Derailed** by overturning. 18 died, 30 seriously injured and 31 with minor injuries. No adequate explanation was determined for the driver's failure, other than to note that he had been disciplined for inattention in the past and may have been asleep.

Shrimp (YNP)
[NR] A flat **Wagon** used for transporting **Panels** and **Rails**. See **Wagon Names**.

SHRT
South Hampshire **Rapid Transit**.

Shunt
a) [Ops.] The act of moving **Rail Vehicles** within a defined locality for the purpose of constructing, splitting and **Marshalling** □ **Trains** or positioning Rail Vehicles for work activities. Also **Shunting**.
b) [Sig.] A temporary electrical connection made for the purpose of testing the integrity or sensitivity of a circuit. See also **Drop Shunt**, **Prevent Shunt**
c) [Sig.] To operate a **Track Circuit** (**TC**).

Shunt Limit
[Sig.] A **Lineside Sign** marking the **Limit of Shunt** (**LOS**).

Shunt Move
Shunt Movement
[Ops.] A **Train Movement** made under the authority of a **Position Light Signal** (**PLS**), for the purpose of assembling or dividing a **Train** or moving a Train between **Lines**.

Shunt Neck

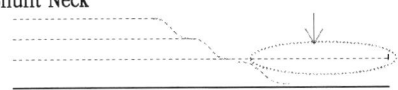

A **Track** leading to the **King Points** area of a **Fan** of **Sidings** that permits a **Shunting Locomotive** to work without the need to be on a **Running Line**. Also **Shunt Spur**.

Shunt Route
[Sig.] A **Route** required for **Shunting** purposes. The **Line** concerned may or may not be **Clear**. The **Movement Authority** for such a Route is normally given by a **Shunt Signal**. See also **Route Class**.

Shunt Signal
[Sig.] A Signal provided to control **Shunting** operations, namely low speed, short distance Movements. See **Dolly**, **Ground Disc**, **Ground Position Light Signal** (**GPLS**), **Position Light Signal** (**PLS**), **Semaphore Disc Signal**, **Shunt-ahead Signal**, **Subsidiary Signal**.

Shunt Spur
See **Shunt Neck**.

Shunt Token
[Sig.] A type of **Electronic Token** used for **Shunt Movements** in **Radio Electronic Token Block** (**RETB**) areas.

Shunt-ahead Signal
[Sig.] A variety of **Subsidiary Signal** which controls **Shunt Movements** □ Beyond a Main **Signal**. See also **Draw Ahead**.

Shunter
[Ops.] A person whose duties are directing and controlling **Shunting**, including **Coupling** and Uncoupling □ **Rail Vehicles** and operating **Hand Points** in **Sidings**.

Shunter's Assurance
[Ops.] A method of operation of a **Depot** or **Yard** in which the person in charge of the Depot or Yard tells the **Signaller** that the Signaller may allow a **Train** to enter. See also **Shunter's Plunger**, **Shunter's Release**.

Shunter's Plunger
Shunters Release
[Sig.] A method of operation of a **Depot** or **Yard** in which the person in charge of the Depot or Yard Operates a **Plunger** when it is safe for a **Train** to enter. In turn, this action normally **Releases** a **Slot** on the **Entry Signal**. See also **Shunter's Assurance**.

Shunting
See **Shunt** clause a). See also **Fly Shunting**, **Gravity Shunting**, **Hump Shunting**, **Loose Shunting**.

Shunting Frame
[Sig.] A **Lever Frame** or other control system that is **Released** by a **Signal Box** (**SB**) for the purpose of making local **Shunt Movements**.

Shunting Gong
[Sig. Obs.] A **Gong** used by a **Signaller** to alert a **Shunter** that they can bring the **Train** to rest and **Set Back**, where **Semaphore Signals** would be invisible. Now rare, an example of their use was in Bangor **Tunnel**.

Shunting Locomotive
[TRS] A **Locomotive** optimised for **Shunting** □ **Trains** and therefore typically small, low geared and with good all round visibility from the driving **Cab**. Modern examples include the virtually universal 350 horse power **Class** 08 **Diesel Electric Locomotive**, wheel arrangement 'C' (see **Diesel and Electric Locomotive Notation**). Also **Jockey**, **Pilot**, **Station Pilot**.

Shunting Move
Shunting Movement
See **Shunt Move**.

Shunting Pole
[Ops.] A wooden pole fitted with a hook on one end, that allows a **Shunter** to couple and uncouple **Rail Vehicles** with **Three Link Couplings** and **Instanter Couplings** without needing to go between them.

Shunting Signal
See **Shunt Signal**.

Shut Down
To close down a **Locomotive** when it is no longer to be used – usually involving switching off any engines, ensuring that the parking brake is applied, and all keys are removed before locking the Locomotive **Cab**(s).

Shut In
[Col.] Describing a **Train** or **Rail Vehicle** placed clear of and protected from a **Running Line**, e.g. Shut In a **Siding**.

Shuttle
[CT] A type of **Train** operated by **Eurotunnel** to carry road vehicles between Folkestone and Calais through the **Channel Tunnel**.

SHWW
(*schwuh*) Sandbach Wilmslow (project).

SI
a) See **Speed Indicator**
b) See **Section Insulator**
c) See **Signalling Instruction**
d) See **Standard Indicator**
e) See **Stencil Indicator**
f) Site Investigation
g) Site Instruction
h) [NR] Sponsor's Instruction.

SIC
a) [Elec.] Single Insulator Cantilever, a support and Registration cantilever using only a single large Insulator. Commonly used in **GEFF** and **Series 1** □ **Overhead Line Equipment (OLE)** systems
b) System Interface Committee.

SICA
(*seeka*) [NR Sig.] **Signalling** □ **Infrastructure** Condition Assessment.

SICA LX
(*seeka-el-ex*) [NR Sig.] **Signalling** □ **Infrastructure** Condition Assessment for **Level Crossings (LC, LX)**.

SICAT
(*seeka-tee*) [NR Sig.] **Signalling** □ **Infrastructure** Condition Assessment for **Telecommunications**.

Sick and Tired
[Col.] An insulting alternative for the **Signal and Telecommunications (S&T)** □ **Discipline**.

SID
[LUL] **Signalling** Interface Display.

Side
Term used to describe the location of features adjacent to the **Railway** in terms of their position relative to the **Down Line** or **Up Line**. Something located on the same side of the Railway as the Down Line would therefore be described as being on the **Down Side**, e.g. Down Side **Carriage Sidings**.

Side Arms
[NR] Alternative term for **Side Rollers**.

Side Bearer
[TRS] A component located on the side frame of a **Bogie** (one per side) which provides vertical support to the **Wagon** □ **Frame** whilst allowing the Bogie to rotate. On some Bogie designs the vertical support provided is only significant when the vehicle body rolls.

Side Bearer Block
[TRS] The support material that is located on the side frame of the **Bogies** of certain **Wagons** and which supports the weight of the Wagon body.

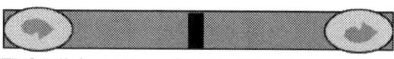

Side Buffers
[TRS] Full description of the traditional arrangement of **Buffers**, i.e. one each side symmetrical about the **Coupling Hook**. See also **Automatic Coupling**.

Side Contact
Side Contact Conductor Rail
[Elec.] An arrangement of a **Conductor Rail** where the **Current Collection Shoe (Shoe)** bears sideways on the **Conductor Rail**, rather than the more common arrangement of vertically downwards, called **Top Contact**.

Side Cutting Gauge
[PW] A device which measures the amount of **Sidecutting (Sidewear)** present on a **Rail**. It does so by measuring relative to the **Rail Web**, ignoring the **Outside Edge (OE)** completely, and so produces a different reading from the **Sidewear Gauge**.

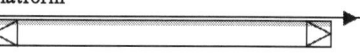

Side Platform
A **Platform** that serves a **Line** on one side only. This type of Platform must be at least 2.5 metres wide. See also **Bay Platform, Island Platform**.

Side Rail Loader
A general term for a **Wagon** equipped with a pair or trio of small cranes used for the loading and unloading of **Standard Rails**. Colloquial names include **Arneke, Elk, Stumec, Trident**. See also **Sleeper Delivery Train (SDT), The Slinger**.

Side Rollers
[PW] Temporary lateral supports with vertical rollers used to restrain a **Free Rail** during **Stressing**. There are many types, each designed to fit onto the **Housing** of a particular **Rail Fastening**. Also **Side Arms**. See also Bottom Roller.

Side Swipe
A collision between two **Trains** where one impacts the side of another. See also **Head On**.

Side Wall
a) [PW] The vertical faces of the outside of the **Box Section** of a **Cast Crossing**
b) [Civ.] The part of a **Tunnel** wall between ground level and the **Springing**.

Side Wear
See **Sidewear**.

Sidecutting
[PW] An alternative term for **Sidewear**.

Sidelight
[Sig.] A small aperture on the side of a **Colour Light Signal** which indicates to a very close observer (such as a technician) the **Aspect** of the **Signal**. See also **Pig's Ears**.

Sidetip
Sidetip Excavator
A tracked or wheeled loading shovel that is capable of rotating its bucket vertically about one end. This is advantageous as it avoids unnecessary maneouvering when loading excavated material into vehicles placed alongside a narrow excavation, i.e. a typical **Railway** □ **Reballasting** site.

Sidewear
[PW] A progressive removal of **Rail** metal generally afflicting the **High Rail** on **Curves**, due to the high lateral forces produced when a **Train** negotiates a Curve with insufficient **Cant (C)** or high **Cant Deficiency (D)**. Eventually the **Rail Head** assumes a profile complimentary to the passing **Wheelsets**, increasing the likelihood that Wheelsets will **Climb the Rail**. Sidewear is measured using a **Sidewear Gauge** (or a **Sidecutting Gauge**). Also referred to as **Sidecutting**.

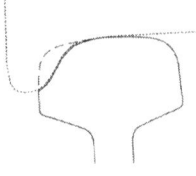

Sidewear Gauge
[PW] A measuring device used to determine quantitatively the amount of **Sidewear** present on a **Rail**. There are two types available:
a) The older variety reads down to zero, at which point the **Sidewear Scar** will be coincident with the bottom of the **Running Face** of the Rail
b) The same quantity is measured in reverse by the newer **Sidecutting Gauge**, but this device ignores any Sidewear present on the **Outside Edge (OE)** of the Rail being measured.

Sidewear Scar
[PW] The imprint left on the **Rail** where metal has been removed by passing **Wheel Flanges**.

Sidewear Total
[PW] The **Sidewear** readings for both **Running Edge (RE)** and **Outside Edge (OE)** of the same **Rail** added together.

Sidewinder
[PW Obs.] An early type of **Elastic Rail Fastening** used on early **Concrete Sleepers**. Examples are extremely rare in the UK.

Siding
A low speed **Track**, off the **Main Line**, not fitted with **Signals** and used for marshalling, **Stabling**, storing, loading and unloading **Rail Vehicles**. They are separate from but often connected to a **Running Line** at one end only, at which position a **Signal** to control the exit may be located. The other end of a **Terminal** Siding is normally provided with a **Buffer Stop**. The collective term is a **Group, Fan** or **Raft**. A Siding connected to a Running Line at both ends is often termed a **Through Siding**. The archaic usage was *sideling*, possibly related to *sideline*.

Siding Overrun
Describing a **Train** running off the end of a dead end **Siding**, generally through and over the **Buffer Stop** provided.

Siding Switch
[Elec.] An electrical switch mounted on an **Overhead Line Structure** that allows the **Overhead Line Equipment (OLE)** for a **Group of Sidings** to be connected and disconnected from another **Electrical Section**.

SIDS
[LUL] Station Area Identification Signs.

Siemens, Dr. Ernst Werner von
(1816-1892) born in Lenthe, Prussia. An electrical engineer, he improved telegraph equipment, pioneered undersea cables and built the world's first practical **Electric Railway** at Berlin in 1879. He founded what is now Siemens AG.

Sierra
The **Phonetic Alphabet** word representing **S**.

SIFE
Slough International Freight Exchange.

SIFER
Salon International de l'Industrie Ferroviaire; an international trade show for **Railway** suppliers, held in France.

SIG
Signalling Innovation Group.

SIGAS
[LUL] Stop Identification Geographic Along the Route.

Sighting
[Sig.]
a) The act of determining an appropriate location for a **Signal**. See **Signal Sighting**.
b) The observation of a **Signal** by a driver.

Sighting Board
a) [PW] A T-shaped wooden gauge, used in threes for laying **Track Drains** and for **Track Maintenance**. See also **Boning Rods**. Known to the general construction industry as **Profile Boards**.
b) [Sig.] A board, painted white, placed behind the **Arm** of a **Semaphore Signal** to improve its readability. See also **Back Board**.

Sighting Distance
a) [RB] The distance from the site of work at which **Trains** must be seen in order to give adequate **Warning Time** to those on site when working on an **Open Line**. On **Lines** with a high **Permissible Speed (PS)** it may be necessary to use **Distant Lookouts**, a **Lookout Operated Warning System (LOWS)** or **PeeWee** to achieve this distance
b) [Sig.] The distance from which a **Signal** can be reliably observed and the **Aspect** and **Indicators** read reliably. See **Sighting Point**
c) [Sig.] The distance at which a **Train** should be visible to a **Footpath Crossing (FP)** user where no other warnings are provided.

Sighting Hole
[Sig.] A small (around 6mm, $1/4$" diameter) hole drilled in the casing of a **Colour Light Signal** □ **Head** parallel to the beam(s) of the **Signal Lamps**. This hole is used to align the **Signal** correctly at the **Sighting Point**.

Sighting Point
[Sig.] The first point a driver can reliably observe an **Indicator**, **Lineside Sign** or **Signal** with **Aspect** and Indicators. See **Sighting Distance**, **Sighting Time**. This is normally deemed to be at the **Automatic Warning System Magnet** (**AWS Magnet**).

Sighting Time
[Sig.] The time a driver has to read and process information from an **Indicator**, **Lineside Sign** or **Signal** with **Aspect** and Indicators. This time is therefore the length of time taken to travel from the **Sighting Point** to the item being observed. This must equal or exceed the **Reading Time**.

Sign the Road
[Ops.] When drivers have completed their **Route Knowledge**, they are then permitted to Sign the Road and drive that **Route** unsupervised.

Signal
[Sig.] A device used to display **Movement Authorities** to **Train** drivers, e.g. **Stop**, **Proceed** and **Caution**. There are four distinct types:
a) **Semaphore Signals**, which convey their instructions by differently positioned **Arms**, commonly supplemented by coloured lights at night
b) **Colour Light Signals**, which convey their instructions using similar principles to traffic lights (except that **Railway** Colour Light Signals sometimes have two **Yellows** and are arranged with the **Red** light nearest the driver's eye level, typically the bottom). Other varieties of Colour Light Signal include **Fibre Optic Signals**, **LED Signals**, **Optic Diode** and **Searchlight Signals**
c) **Position Light Signals** (**PLS**), which convey instructions by changing arrangements of white and coloured lights
d) **Handsignals**.

Signal and Telecommunications (S&T)
[BR now Col.] The function within **British Railways** (**BR**) responsible for the design, installation and maintenance of **Signalling Equipment** and **Telecommunications** systems. See also **Sick and Tired**. Also **Signalling and Telecommunications**.

Signal Aspect Sequence
See **Aspect Sequence**.

Signal Assessment Tool / Detailed Assessment (SAT/DA)
[NR] A two stage risk-based model used to measure the relative risk of a **Signal Passed at Danger** (**SPAD**) at a particular **Signal** and attach a measure to the severity of the outcome of such a SPAD. The first (**SAT**) part models an average Signal based on **Timetable** data. Any high scoring Signals (for instance scores higher than 100) are then taken forward to the second (**DA**) part where specific factors are added to the model and mitigation measures identified. The object is to ensure that the proposed Signal has an overall SPAD risk that is **As Low As Reasonably Practicable** (**ALARP**). See also **Signal Over-run Risk Assessment** (**SORA**).

Signal Box (SB)
[Sig.] A building which houses one or more **Signallers**, equipment used for the control of **Points** and **Signals**, and communication with other Signal Boxes. The term did not enter common usage until the late 19th century when it replaced the earlier term **Signal Cabin**. Until the term Signal Box entered more widespread usage it was used to identify the usually small structure housing the **Levers**, etc., for a **Gated Level Crossing** and the associated **Signals**. The lowest level of technology used is **Mechanical Signalling**, such as **Rodding** and **Wires**, directly working the Points and **Semaphore Signals** purely by human effort. Mechanical Signal Boxes have been replaced by **Power Signal Boxes** (**PSB**) on busy and **High Speed Lines**. These control the Points and Signals by means of electrical circuits, and often the associated **Interlocking** is located some miles from the Signal Box (a **Remote Interlocking**). The state of the art is full computer control, where the Signaller interacts with the **Signalling System** using a VDU, keyboard and pointing device. Also **Control Point**, **Signal Box** (**SB**). See also **Integrated Electronic Control Centre** (**IECC**), **Network Management Centre** (**NMC**).

Signal Box Boundary
[Sig.] The edge of the area controlled by a **Signal Box** (**SB**). This may or may not also be an **Interlocking Boundary**.

Signal Box Diagram
[Sig.] A **Track** plan of the area controlled by a **Signal Box** (**SB**), provided to assist the **Signaller**. It normally shows **Track Names**, **Signal Numbers**, **Point Numbers** and **Platforms**. See also **Illuminated Diagram**, **Non-Illuminated Diagram**.

Signal Box Diagram Colours

Down Direction □	Green
Running Lines	Brown
Up Direction Running Lines	Blue
	Yellow
Non-track Circuited Lines	Black
Signal Box	Red
Frame or Panel	Black line
Signaller	Black dot
Semaphore Stop Signals	Red : the white bar is not shown.
Semaphore Distant Signals	Yellow: the black chevron is not shown.
Level Crossings	
Platforms	Orange
Significant buildings	
Colour Light Stop Signals	Red
Colour Light Distant Signals	Yellow
Signals controlled by others	Open white

439

Signal Box Etiquette
[Col.] The **Operating Floor** of a **Signal Box** (**SB**) is often a busy place, with each **Signaller** meticulously guiding the fates of many experienced drivers and the lives of many thousands of **Passengers**. Therefore, always:
- Pre-arrange your visit and only visit for a good reason
- Remember that the Signaller may have many very good reasons to ignore you
- Be sure to enter your details in the visitor's book or **Train Register** as directed
- Be alert and never distract the Signaller, particularly with camera flashes or mobile telephone calls
- Remember this is the Signaller's office – be prepared to wipe your feet, feed the **Cat** and make the **Tea**, if asked.

Signal Box Notes
[Sig.] A list of the key features of a **Signal Box** or **Signalling Control Centre**, including any **Functions** that are not clear from the **Signalling Plan** or **Scheme Plan**.

Signal Box Panel
[Sig.] The control **Panel** within a **Power Signal Box** (**PSB**) containing the pushbuttons, selectors and electrical switches required by the **Signaller** in order to operate the **Signalling System** in a particular area. This Panel may also contain the related **Indicators** and **Train Describer Berths**, or they may be housed in a separate **Illuminated Diagram**. Types of panel include **Entrance / Exit** (**NX**), **Individual Function Switch** (**IFS**) and **One Control Switch** (**OCS**).

Signal Box Simplifier
[Ops.] A document which provides a simple guide for the **Signaller** as to which **Train** should be sent to which **Route** or **Platform**. It is produced from the **Working Timetable** (**WTT**).

Signal Box Special Instruction
[NR Sig.] Instructions that may exist in a specific **Signal Box** which are only applicable to that location and are supplementary to the **Rule Book**. They generally deal with situations peculiar to that Signal Box, such as quarry blasting.

Signal Bridge
[Sig.] An alternative term for a **Signal Gantry**.

Signal Cabin
[Sig. Hist.] Early name for what would now be called a **Signal Box**.

Signal Element
[Sig.] A generic term describing any one of the following:
- A single **Aspect** of a **Main Signal** (a Double Yellow **Aspect** counts as one element)
- A **Position Light Junction Indicator** (**PLJI**)
- The display of an **Alphanumeric Route Indicator** (**ARI**)
- A **Semaphore Arm** or **Semaphore Disc Signal**
- An Aspect in a **Position Light Signal** (**PLS**)

The number of Signal Elements a **Signal** has is used as part of the calculation of the **Minimum Reading Time** (**MRT**) required for the Signal.

Signal Exclusion Zone (SEZ)
[Sig.] The length of **Track** around a **Signal** in which it is not permitted to place **Speed Indicators** (**SI**). This is currently defined as a point 50 **Yards** □ On the Approach to the **Automatic Warning System Magnet** (**AWS Magnet**) to 100 Yards **Beyond** the Signal. If no AWS Magnet is present, then the Zone is 100 Yards On the Approach to the Signal to 100 Yards Beyond the Signal.

Signal Gantry

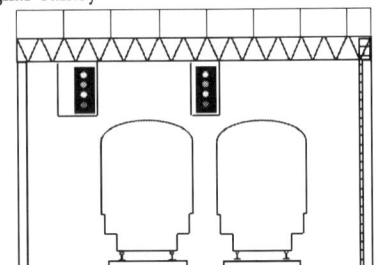

[Sig.] A portal frame or **Cantilever** structure supporting one or more **Gantry Signals**, used where there is insufficient space between the **Tracks** for Straight Post Signals.

Signal Head
[Sig.] The section of a **Colour Light Signal** that contains the lamps and lenses required to display the **Aspects**.

Signal Headway
See **Technical Headway**. See also **Headway**, **Planning Headway**.

Signal Identification Plate
[Sig.] The plate affixed to a **Signal** bearing the **Signal Number**. See **Signs Related to Signals**.

Signal Lamp
a) [Sig.] A lamp mounted behind the **Spectacle Glass** of a **Semaphore Signal** and arranged to shine towards oncoming **Trains**, allowing drivers to observe the **Signal Aspect** during the hours of darkness. The same lamp provides the **Back Light**. Formerly oil lamps, most such devices are now electric

b) [Sig.] The filament lamp used in a **Colour Light Signal**, **Position Light Signal** (**PLS**) or **Searchlight Signal**

c) See **Bardic Lamp**.

Signal Memory
[Sig.] Within a **Solid State Interlocking** (**SSI**), 384 bytes of RAM used to store, amongst other things, an **Approach Locking** timer and an **Aspect** code for 128 **Signals**. It is used to decide which Aspect to display, for sequencing the **Distant Signals**, and for deciding when the Signal can be turned on and the forward Route(s) □ **Released**.

ELLIS' BRITISH RAILWAY ENGINEERING ENCYCLOPÆDIA

Signal Number
[Sig.] A unique identifier given to each **Signal** that permits both driver and **Signaller** to agree which Signal is which. In **Absolute Block** (**AB**) areas, where there are often long gaps between Signals, all the Signals controlled by a single **Signal Box** are given a simple number, often beginning with 1. In **Track Circuit Block** (**TCB**) areas, where the Signals tend to be regularly spaced and closer together, they are given a prefix relating to the **Controlling Signal Box**. Former practice was to number the first Signal on the **Down Line** as number 1, and work in the **Down Direction** irrespective of which **Line** the signals were on. Modern practice is to number the Down Line in even numbers in ascending order in the Down Direction, and the **Up Line** in odd numbers descending in the Up Direction. Signals that are **Repeater Signals** (**R**) or **Co-Acting Signals** (**CA**) share the same number as the main Signal, but with the suffix R or CA added. It is common practice in large **Re-signalling Schemes** to leave groups of un-used numbers to allow for future developments.

Signal Off Indicator
[Sig.] An alternative term for an **Off Indicator**.

Signal Overlap (O/L)
[Sig.] The distance beyond a **Signal** that is proved **Clear** prior to the signal **On the Approach to** it being **Cleared**. The standard Overlap was 200 **Yards** (183m) but shorter distances are permitted and longer distances may be required under certain circumstances.

⊢◯⊖ A   ⊢◯⊖ B
....
◄─────────►

Signal A will not display a **Proceed Aspect** unless the line between A and B is un-occupied (Clear), and the Overlap **Beyond** B is also un-occupied (Clear). See also **Safe Over-run Distance** (**SOD**).

Signal Over-run
[Ops.] A failure of a **Train** to correctly obey the instructions given by any **Signal**. This includes **Shunt Signals** as well as **Main Aspects**. See also **Signal Passed At Danger** (**SPAD**), **Safe Over-run Distance** (**SOD**).

Signal Over-run Risk Assessment (SORA)
(*sore-ah*) [Sig.] Fore-runner of the **Signal Assessment Tool / Detailed Assessment** (**SAT/DA**), a structured method of quantifying the risk of a **Signal Passed at Danger** (**SPAD**) based on layout, **Timetable** and other relevant factors.

Signal Passed At Danger (SPAD)
[NR Ops.] A **Train** failing to stop correctly at a **Signal** displaying a **Stop Aspect**. Thus a failure of **Signalling System** and driver to adequately maintain a safe distance between Trains. There are many reasons why such an event may occur, and they were previously categorised according to the cause, see **SPAD Category**. This grading system has been replaced by the **SPAD Severity** ranking, which measures the outcome. Mitigations may include **Banner Repeater Signals**, **Countdown Markers**, **Defensive Driving** techniques, **SPAD Indicators** and **Trap Points**. Light Rail (**LR**) uses the term **Signal Passed at Stop** (**SPAS**).

Signal Passed at Stop (SPAS)
[LR] An event where a driver fails to bring a **Tram** to rest before passing a **Signal** displaying a **Stop Aspect**. Heavy Rail (**HR**) uses the term **Signal Passed at Danger** (**SPAD**).

Signal Post (SP)
[Sig.] The vertical column that supports a **Signal Head**.

Signal Post Replacement Key
[Sig.] The key used to operate a **Signal Post Replacement Switch**. See **Key a Signal to Danger**.

Signal Post Replacement Switch
[Sig.] An electrical switch located on or near an **Automatic** or **Semi-automatic** □ **Colour Light Signal** that allows a member of staff with an appropriate **Signal Post Replacement Key** to **Key a Signal to Danger**.

Signal Post Telephone (SPT)
[Tel.] A telephone located on or near a **Signal** that allows a driver or other member of staff to communicate only with the **Controlling Signal Box**.

▨▨ ▨▨⑤

The decals applied to such telephones are shown above. The example with the numeral indicates that a driver of a **Train** detained at the Signal should wait five minutes before contacting the **Signaller**, rather than the normal two minutes. See also **Rule 55, Zero Plated**.

Signal Profile
[Sig.] The physical arrangement of the various **Signal Elements**, such as **Alphanumeric Route Indicators** (**ARI**), **Arms**, **Aspects**, **Junction Indicators** (**JI**) and **Position Light Signals** (**PLS**) that comprise one **Signal** from the point of view of a driver. Also **Form**.

Signal Protection
[RB, Ops.] Placing **Signals** at **Danger** to stop **Trains** entering an area where other Trains, people or objects may be on the **Track** or where there is no Track at all.

Signal Rail
[Sig.] An alternative for **Insulated Rail**. Also **Signalling Rail**.

441

Signal Repeater
[Sig.] An **Indicator** that replicates the **Aspect** displayed by a **Signal** in a **Signal Box** of by means of a **Needle Indicator**, a **Light Repeater** or **On/Off Indicator**. See also **Banner Repeater**, **Banner Repeating Signal**.

Signal Reversion
[Sig., Ops.] The situation where a **Signal** changes to show a more restrictive **Aspect** after a driver has passed the Signal **On the Approach to** it, thus shortening the available safe **Deceleration Distance** (**DD**). See **Signal Passed at Danger** (**SPAD**), category B.

Signal Section
[Sig.] In a **Track Circuit Block** (**TCB**) area, that portion of **Line** between two consecutive **Main Signals**, irrespective of where they are controlled from.

Signal Sighting
[Sig.] The act of ensuring that a **Signal** can be accurately observed by a driver in sufficient time to allow the **Aspect** and **Indicators** to be interpreted and acted upon before reaching the Signal. This exercise is carried out by a **Signal Sighting Committee** (**SSC**). See also **Minimum Reading Time** (**MRT**), **Sighting Time**.

Signal Sighting Committee (SSC)
[Sig.] A working party convened to ensure that **Signals**, **Indicators** and some **Lineside Signs** are located in positions which allow them to be accurately observed by a driver travelling at speed. There is always a **Signal Sighting Committee Chairman**, and representatives of the **Signalling**, **Civil Engineering** (**CE**) and **Electrification** ▫ **Disciplines** as required, as well as someone with relevant experience of driving **Trains**. A **Signal Sighting Form** (**SSF**) is produced to record the recommendations of the committee.

Signal Sighting Committee Chairman
[Sig.] The nominal head of a **Signal Sighting Committee** (**SSC**), it is their job to ensure that an agreement is reached for each **Signal**, **Indicator** and **Lineside Sign** considered. Following a period of formal training, Signal Sighting Committee Chairmen are approved by each **Network Rail** (**NR**) ▫ **Territory** in which they operate. It is normal for a Chairman to have a **Signalling** background.

Signal Sighting Form (SSF)
[Sig.] A pro-forma document showing the dimensions, location, position, **Signal Profile** and other information relevant to **Signals** and some other **Indicators**. The details are agreed by the **Signal Sighting Committee** (**SSC**) but the form may be produced by the designer.

Signal Sighting Survey
[Sig.] A preliminary investigation undertaken to verify the practicality of locating **Signals** in their proposed locations, in terms of construction and general visibility. Such a **Survey** would normally be undertaken early in the design process.

Signal Spacing
Two Aspect Signals:

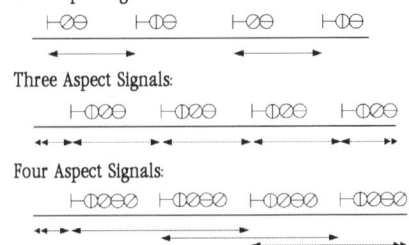

Three Aspect Signals:

Four Aspect Signals:

[Sig.] The spacing between successive **Main Signals** is determined by the **Permissible Speed** (**PS**), **Gradient** and rate of deceleration of **Trains**. These factors produce a **Deceleration Distance** (**DD**) which determines the distance between the **First Caution** (the first point the driver is aware that they may have to stop) and the relevant **Stop Aspect**. See also $^2/_3$ / $^1/_3$ **Rule**.

Signal Standback
Signal Standback Allowance
The distance provided within a design which allows a driver to bring their **Train** to a stand **On The Approach to** a **Signal** and easily observe the **Aspect**. This distance is normally 15 to 25 metres. See also **Professional Driving**..

Signal Stick
The "freezing" of a **Signal** at a **Stop Aspect** after the passage of a **Train**, to prevent it from showing a **Proceed Aspect** until the **Route** is cancelled and **Set** again.

Signal Wire
[Sig.] Seven-strand galvanised steel **Wire**, (6 x 1.40mm plus 1 x 1.50mm) used to connect a **Semaphore Signal** to its **Controlling Signal Box** or **Lever Frame** in **Mechanical Signalling**. The system is arranged so that tension in the **Wire** pulls the **Signal** to its **Least Restrictive Aspect**, and a large balance weight at the Signal returns the **Arm** to its **Most Restrictive Aspect** when this tension is released or the **Wire** breaks, making the system largely **Fail Safe**. These Wires are supported along their length on posts carrying small pulleys.

Signal Wire Adjuster
Signal Wire Tensioner
[Sig.] A device used in **Mechanical Signalling** to adjust the length of **Signal Wires**. This is necessary on long runs as changes in temperature can cause large variations in Wire length.

Signal(wo)man
[Hist.] A politically correct but clumsy attempt to remove gender distinctions from the title of **Signalman**. Now superseded by the term **Signaller**.

Signalbox (SB)
See **Signal Box** (**SB**).

Signalled
[Sig.] Being equipped with **Signals** or some form of **Signalling System**. The opposite is **Un-signalled**.

Signalled Direction
[Sig.] The direction in which **Trains** move along a **Track** under **Main Aspects**. See also **Normal Direction**.

Signalled Route
[Sig.] A **Route** through a **Junction** for which a **Main Aspect**, **Route Indication** or **Position Light Signal** (**PLS**) is available. There may be many more ways of moving through a **Junction** than there are **Signalled Routes**, normally because the remainder offer no advantage. See also **Preferred Route**.

Signaller
The current term for a person engaged in operating a **Signal Box** or the operational supervision of a **Signalling System**. See also **Bobby**, **Signal(wo)man**, **Signalman**.

Signaller's Area
[Sig.] The area of **Railway** controlled or supervised by one **Signaller**, as defined by boundaries between **Signal Box Panels** or **Signaller's Workstations**.

Signaller's Control Device
[Sig.] The item a **Signaller** uses to issue commands to the **Signalling System**; this could a button, **Lever**, switch or trackball.

Signaller's Display Subsystem (SDS)
[Sig.] The system used by the **Signaller** to interface with an **Integrated Electronic Control Centre** (**IECC**). See also **DIS**, **Signaller's Workstation**.

Signaller's General Instructions (SGI)
[NR] The document setting out the procedures to be followed by **Signallers**. It is also a **Railway Group Standard** (**RGS**), GO/RT 3062.

Signaller's Panel
[Sig.] An alternative for **Signal Box Panel**.

Signaller's Route List
[Sig.] A document giving all the **Point Ends** and **Releases** between the **Entrance Signal** and **Exit Signal** of a **Route** and the positions to which they must be **Set**. A Route List exists for every **Route** in a **Signaller's Area**. They are used when **Power Operated Points** are Set manually during disconnections.

Signaller's Workstation
[Sig.] A development of the **Signal Box Panel**, the **Signaller** is provided with a display of the **Signal Box Diagram** on a VDU and a trackball to operate the **Signalling Functions**. Its main advantages are that it can easily be changed, and provision of **Automatic Route Setting** (**ARS**) is simple. Signalling Workstations are found in the newer **Integrated Electronic Control Centres** (**IECC**). Also **Signalling Workstation**.

Signalling
[Sig.] A collective term for all things to do with **Signals** and the remote display of **Movement Authorities** to drivers.

Signalling and Telecommunications
See **Signal** and **Telecommunications** (**S&T**).

Signalling Centre (SC)
[Sig.] A term used to describe more modern **Signal Boxes** (**SB**) housing **Electronic Signalling Control Systems** (**SCS**). Also **Signalling Control Centre** (**SCC**). See also **Integrated Electronic Control Centre** (**IECC**).

Signalling Circuit Diagram
[Sig.] A circuit diagram showing the electrical power and data interconnections between the various components in a **Signalling System**. The symbols and mnemonics used are highly stylised. Also **Wiring Diagram**.

Signalling Control Centre (SCC)
[Sig.]
a) The control centre for all the **Signalling Systems** associated with **ERTMS** including the **signallers** who operate the equipment to manage the **Train** service.
b) See **Signalling Centre** (**SC**).

Signalling Control System (SCS)
[Sig.] The means by which the requests made by the **Signaller** are converted into **Movement Authorities** and **Train Movement** data is processed. The current systems are:
- Mechanical **Signalling**, and manual systems such as **Absolute Block** (**AB**)
- **Track Circuit Block** (**TCB**) controlled by electromechanical systems such as **Relay Interlocking** (**RI**)
- Microprocessor based **Interlocking** systems such as **Solid State Interlocking** (**SSI**)
- Computer-based systems such **Computer Based Interlocking** (**CBI**).

Signalling Controls
[Sig.] Intermediary **Signalling Functions** which control, **Release** or are Released by other Signalling Functions. The relationship between all these is laid out in a **Control Table**.

Signalling Diagram
[NPT] The common but non-preferred alternative for a **Signal Box Diagram** or **Signalling Plan**.

Signalling Engineer
[Sig.] A person involved in the design, manufacture, installation, **Testing** or **Maintenance** of **Signals** and **Signalling Equipment**.

ELLIS' BRITISH RAILWAY ENGINEERING ENCYCLOPÆDIA

Signalling Equipment
[Sig.] Collective term for the fixed equipment specifically used for the purpose of safely controlling the passage of **Trains**. This includes Automatic Warning Systems (AWS), Axle Counters, Banner Repeating Signals, Block Bells, Block Instruments, Cable Troughs, Close Doors Indicators (CDI), Colour Light Signals, Compensators, Driver's White Lights (DWL), Distant Boards, Ground Frames (GF), Ground Position Light Signals (GPLS), Ground Switch Panels (GSP), Integrated Electronic Control Centres (IECC), Interlocking equipment, Junction Indicators (JI), Lamp Repeaters, Level Crossing Barriers, Levers, Location Cases, Off Indicators, Point Machines, Point Detectors, Point Rodding, Position Light Signals (PLS), Power Signal Boxes (PSB), REB, Relay Rooms, Relays, Radio Electronic Token Block (RETB) equipment, Right Away Indicators (RAI), Searchlight Signals, Semaphore Signals, Signal Box Diagrams, Signal Boxes (SB), Signal Box Panels, Signal Post Telephones (SPT), Signal Wires, Signalling Power Supplies (SPS), Technician's Terminal, Train Describers (TD), Train Protection and Warning Systems (TPWS), Track Circuit Interrupters (TCI), Track Circuits (TC), Treadles, Warning Indicators (WI), Whistle Boards.

Signalling Equivalent Unit (SEU)
[NR Sig.] A means of rapidly costing and measuring outputs for **Signalling** works; an equivalent unit is a single **Trackside** output function controlled by the **Interlocking**, including every **Signal**, each controlled **Point End**, **Plungers** and any other attribute that requires a particular **Control Function** and each **Ground Frame** (GF). Partial renewals are allocated partial values (50 per cent for external equipment, 45 per cent for an Interlocking, two per cent for a control centre and 3 per cent for control equipment). The SEUs recorded do not cover minor works and only include individual schemes with an anticipated forecast cost greater than £5 million, with the exception of stand-alone **Level Crossing** projects where one SEU is recorded for renewal of the control circuitry interface.

Signalling Facilities Diagram
[Sig.] A plan, produced at an early stage in the development of a project, showing operating requirements and infrastructure features, including the **Track Layout**, **Stations**, **Level Crossings**, etc. It is used as a basis for producing the **Scheme Plan**.

Signalling Function
[Sig.]
a) A discrete component of a **Signalling System**, listed on **Control Tables** with a unique identity and the circuitry or mechanism by which that component is controlled or **Proved**. Such components include **Level Crossing Barriers**, **Points**, **Releases**, **Signals** and **Track Circuits** (TC). All identities are unique within a **Signaller's Area**, to avoid confusion
b) A collective term describing all those engaged in **Signalling** activities, including designers, **Installers**, **Testers**, **Maintainers** and **Signallers**. See also **Discipline**.

Signalling Maintenance Assistant (SMA)
[BR Sig.] The local manager directly responsible for managing teams of **Signal** engineering staff.

Signalling Maintenance Specification (SMS)
[Sig.] Documents mandating the **Maintenance** which should be carried out to **Signalling Equipment**.

Signalling Migration
[NR Sig.] The 35-year programme to transfer control of all **Signalling** in England, Wales and Scotland into 14 **Rail Operating Centres** (ROC).

Signalling Plan
[Sig.] A plan drawn to a scale longitudinally but to a convention laterally, that describes an existing **Signalling System** by means of standard **Signalling Symbols** and a standard **Colouring Convention**. See also **Signalling Scheme Plan**. Also **Signalling Diagram**.

Signalling Plan Correlation
Signalling Plan Survey
[Sig.] A Survey undertaken, generally with a measuring wheel, to verify that a **Signalling Plan** accurately reflects the equipment present on the ground. This is normally undertaken very early in the design lifecycle, prior to any significant design work being undertaken. See also **Correlation**.

Signalling Power Supply
[EP] The dedicated (typically single-phase 650V AC or three-phase 400V AC) power supply used exclusively for the **Signalling System**. See also **Principal Supply Point** (PSP).

Signalling Principles Tester
[Sig.] A **Signalling Engineer** professionally qualified to undertake testing activities which are independent of the design; and provide suitable and sufficient evidence to confirm that the operational, technical, and safety principles demanded by the designated authorities have been validated.

Signalling Rail
[Sig.] An alternative for **Insulated Rail**. Also **Signal Rail**.

Signalling Scheme
[Sig.] A proposed alteration or group of alterations to a **Signalling System**. Also **Resignalling Scheme**. See also **Outline Project Specification** (OPS), **Remodelling**, **Signalling Scheme Plan** (SSP).

Signalling Scheme Plan (SSP)
[Sig.] A plan drawn to a scale longitudinally but to a convention laterally, that describes the proposed alterations to an existing **Signalling System** by means of standard **Signalling Symbols** and a standard **Colouring Convention**. See also **Signalling Plan**.

Signalling Solutions Ltd. (SSL)
(Tradename) [Sig.] A company formed in 2007 by combining the **Signalling** resources and products of Alstom Transport Information Solutions UK and Balfour Beatty Rail Projects (BBRP), based in Radlett, Hertfordshire.

Signalling Supply Point (SSP)
[EP] An electrical installation supplying power to the **Signalling System**. Such installations are generally provided with an alternative means of supply should the primary supply fail. This may include alternative connections to the local **Distribution Network Operator** (DNO), a **Traction Derived Supply** or a stand-by generator. See also **Principal Supply Point** (PSP).

Signalling Symbols
[Sig.] Standard symbols used on **Signalling Scheme Plans** and **Signalling Plans** to denote **Signalling Equipment**. (See the **Symbols** section at the beginning of the book for common symbols in use on plans).

Signalling System
[Sig.]
a) A series of electrical, electronic, electro-mechanical and mechanical units brought together to form a system which controls the safe movement of **Trains**.
b) The integrated **Train Control System**, including **Signalling Equipment**, **Telecommunications** equipment, warning systems such as **TOWS** and **Train** related data transmission equipment.

Signalling Workstation
a) See **Signaller's Workstation**
b) See **Signaller's Display System** (SDS)

Signalman
[Obs.] Former title of the post of **Signaller**, i.e. a person employed to supervise and operate a **Signalling System**. See also Bobby, Signal(wo)man.

Signals Railway Track Explosive
The new Euro-normalised name for a **Railway Fog Signal**. See also **Bangers, Crackers, Detonator, Dets, Shots**.

Signing a Route
See **Sign the Road**.

Signing Back
a) [Sig.] The final activity carried out by a **Tester in Charge** (TIC), the point at which they sign the **Testing Certificate** and allow **Trains** to run.
b) The final activity carried out by an **Engineering Supervisor** (ES), **Person in Charge of Possession** (PICOP) or **Senior Person in Charge of Possession** (SPICOP), when they relinquish control of the part of the **Railway** previously under their control. Also **Handing Back**, Handing Back the Road.

Signing on Point (SOP)
The building at which **Traincrew** (drivers, **Guards**) report for duty and receive details of their day's duties and any special instructions that apply to them.

Signing Out
[Sig.] The taking out of use of a large amount of **Signalling Equipment** at once (often a one or more whole **Interlockings**) in order to carry out major works. See **Signalling Scheme, Signing Back**.

Signing Out a Route
[Sig.] The temporary removal of a **Route** from an **Interlocking**, generally by the **Maintenance** technician.

Signing the Book
[Col.]
a) The action of a **Locomotive** □ **Fireman** or **Second Man** in carrying out **Rule 55** on the instructions of the driver and signing the **Train Register**
b) The action of signing the Train Register or the visitors book when visiting a **Signal Box**.

Signing the Route
See **Sign the Road**.

Signs Related to Automatic Warning System (AWS)
[NR]

AWS Gap  — End of AWS Gap

Commencement of AWS Special Working  — End of AWS Special Working

AWS Cancelling Indicator

Signs related to Cab Signalling
[CT]

Warning of commencement of Cab Signalling  — Commencement of Cab Signalling

Termination of Cab Signalling  — Cab Signalling Fixed Block Marker

Non-franchisable □ Block Section □ Ahead  — Cab Signalling Shunt Marker

ELLIS' BRITISH RAILWAY ENGINEERING ENCYCLOPÆDIA

Signs Related to Cab Signalling (cont)
[NR]

AE 123
ETCS ▫ Block Marker ID plate

ETCS Block Marker

P
Passable ETCS Block Marker

RETB Countdown markers

Signs related to Electrification
[NR]

Neutral Section Warning Indicator [CTRL]

Neutral Section

Designated Earth Point

Lower **Pantograph**

Raise Pantograph

Warning of **Traction System** Changeover

Changeover to 750V DC **Conductor Rail** (750 BR)

Changeover to 25kV AC **OLE** (Eurotunnel) (25000 ET)

Limit of Electrification

Open Circuit Breaker

Close Circuit Breaker

Signs Related to Enhanced Permissible Speed
[NR]

Enhanced Permissible Speed

EPS 125
Warning Indicator

EPS 125
Commencement Indicator

Signs related to Level Crossings
[NR]

Advance Warning Board

W
Whistle Board

X 40
Speed restriction for **ABCL** and **AOCL**

10 W
Speed restriction for Open Crossing

X
Sighting Board for **ETCS** Signalling

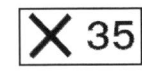

X 35
Wrong Direction speed restriction for **Automatic** Level Crossing

Signs related to Lineside Safety
[NR]

Warning / Limited clearance

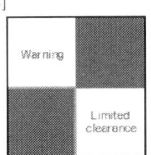

Limited Clearance

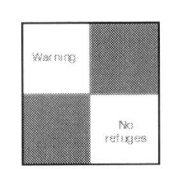

Warning / No refuges

No Refuges

446

ELLIS' BRITISH RAILWAY ENGINEERING ENCYCLOPÆDIA

Signs related to Operations
[NR]

Kilometre Post (lower figure is 100m interval)

Car Stop

Marker for Spring Catch Points

Low Adhesion Warning

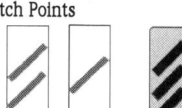

Countdown Markers

Sandite Markers Warning-Start-Stop

Rear Clear (for Class shown)

Mid-platform **Train** □ **Berth** Marker

Signs related to Permissible Speed
[NR]

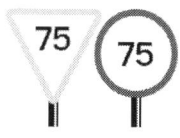

Warning Indicator and **Commencement Indicator**

Standard Differential Warning Indicator and **Commencement Indicator**

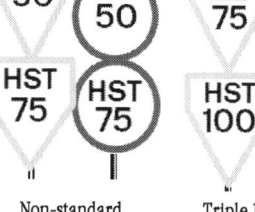

Non-standard Differential Warning Indicator and **Commencement Indicator**

Triple Differential Warning Indicator and **Commencement Indicator**

Signs related to Radio
[NR]

RETB Channel

NRN Channel

CSR Channel

Start of **GSM-R**

End of GSM-R

CSR **Signal** □ **Alias Plate**

GSM-R Signal Alias Plate

Start of **IVRS**

End of IVRS

Signs Related to Signal Post Telephones
[NR]

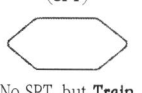

Signal Post Telephone (**SPT**)

SPT

No SPT, but **Train Detection** present

Limited Clearance SPT

447

ELLIS' BRITISH RAILWAY ENGINEERING ENCYCLOPÆDIA

Signs Related to Signals
[NR]

Auto Signal

Semi-automatic Signal

Distant Signal

Intermediate Block Home Signal

Controlled Signal □ (Non-Passable)

Distant Board

Signal reminder

Signal Countdown Marker

SPAD Indicator

Signs related to Telephones
[NR]

Telephone to **ECR**

Telephone to ECR, for public use

General telephone

Telephone to **Signaller** (not an **SPT**)

Signs related to the Channel Tunnel Rail Link (CTRL)

Rule Book Change Sign, □ Network Rail to CTRL

Signs related to TSRs and ESRs
[NR]

Warning Indicator

Commencement

Termination

Spate

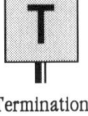

Temporary **AWS** Cancellation

SIGTAN
[NR] **S**ignalling **E**quipment **T**echnical **A**dvice **N**otice.

SIGWEN
[NR] **S**ignalling **E**quipment **W**orkshop **E**ngineering **N**otice.

SIIMS
Site **I**nvestigation and **I**nstru**m**entation **S**ystem.

SIL
a) **S**afety **I**ntegrity **L**evel
b) **SPAD** **I**nhibit **L**ong
c) **S**ingle **I**n **L**ine.

Silent Death
[Col.] Generic nickname for **Electric Multiple Units** (**EMU**), after their quiet approach.

Silver Bullets
[Col.] Nickname for the 90 ton **Bogie** china clay slurry **Tank Wagon**, **CARKND** TEA.

Silver Command
See **Gold / Silver / Bronze Command**.

448

Silver Migration
[Sig.] The unwanted transportation of metallic silver over and through insulation. In **Railway** □ **Signalling**, it is most commonly found on **Relay** plugboards and bases. Starting on the surface, in time it penetrates into the insulating material. The resulting path can conduct electricity and is able to create connections between adjacent contacts. For silver migration to take place the following conditions must be in place:
- Silver or silver plated contacts
- Moisture
- An insulating material which can absorb moisture such as black phenolic Relay bases
- A standing voltage across the insulation.

The most common place for this migration to occur is on the black phenolic Relay plugboard, and so modern plugboards are made of a material that resists moisture penetration and is coloured blue to indicate its type. Tin-plated Relay spades are also used instead of the original silver plated type.

Silver Spots
[PW] An historic name for the high spots along the **Rail Head** of a **Rail** displaying **Rail Corrugation**.

Silverlink
(Tradename) [Hist.] A former **Train Operating Company** (**TOC**), now **London Overground** (former Metro services) and **London Midland** (former County services).

SIM
[Sig.] Simulator Subsystem, part of the IECC system Signalling Interface Module.

SIMBIDS
(*simm-bids*) See **Simplified Bi-Directional Signalling**.

SIMBIDS Crossover
A **Crossover** installed in conjunction with **SIMBIDS**.

Similar Flexure Turnout
[PW] A **Turnout** in which the **Curve** of the diverging **Track** is of the same **Hand** as the **Main Line**. Also **Off the Inside**. The opposite is a **Contraflexure Turnout**.

SIMIS-W
(Tradename) [Sig.] An **Interlocking** system manufactured by Siemens.

Simple Catenary
[Elec.] An **Overhead Line Equipment** (**OLE**) □ **Catenary** which consists of two **Wires**, a **Catenary Wire** and a **Contact Wire** (**CW**). See also **Compound Catenary**.

Simple Feeding System

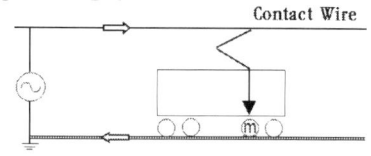

[Elec.] The simplest arrangement of electrical equipment for the supply of **Traction Current** in an **Overhead Line Equipment** (**OLE**) system. The Traction Current is fed to the Contact Wire (**CW**) where it is collected by the **Pantograph**, passed through the **Traction Motors** and returned via the wheels to **Traction Return Rail** and **Earth**. This system has the disadvantage that over long distances the supply voltage will decrease dramatically due to resistive losses in the Contact Wire.

Simplified Bi-Directional Signalling (SIMBIDS)
[Sig.] A **Signalling System** that allows **Wrong Direction Working** at reduced speed or capacity to be implemented and controlled, without the need for a **Pilotman**. Such arrangements are normally only used during **Possessions** or other times of disruption.

Simplified Direct Reporting (SDR)
[Sig.] A system of manual reporting of **Train Running Times** to TRUST. This system replaced Electronic Train Recording (ETR).

Simplified Double Junction

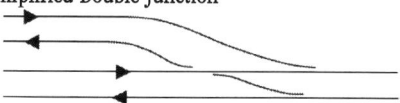

A **Switch and Crossing Layout** (**S&C Layout**) in which the **Double Junction** arrangement is achieved using two **Single Leads** (**Turnouts**) and one **Crossover**, removing the need for a **Diamond Crossing**. Also **Crossover-based Double Junction**.

Simplifier
See **Signal Box Simplifier**.

SIMU
(Tradename) [Hist.] Southern **Infrastructure Maintenance Unit** (IMU).

SIN
a) See **Special Instruction Notice**
b) Substance Identification Number
c) Site Instruction Notice.

SINAC
Special Inspection Notice Action Complete.

SINC
Site of Importance for Nature Conservation.

SINCS
Signalling Incident Management System.

Sine Curve
See **Sinusoidal Transition**.

Single Aspect
Single Aspect Signal
[Sig.] A Colour Light Signal capable of displaying only one Aspect, generally Yellow (Y) (Caution Aspect) or Red (R) (Stop Aspect). The latter is also sometimes termed a Fixed Red.

Single Bank
Single Banker
Single Bank Tamper
[PW] A Tamping and Lining Machine (Tamper) equipped with one pair of Tamping Tines, allowing it to Tamp one Sleeper at a time. All Switch and Crossing Tampers (S&C Tampers) have this arrangement. Other arrangements include Double Bank Tamper, Continuous Action Tamper (CAT), Triple Bank Tamper.

Single Bore Tunnel
a) In Railway usage, a narrow Tunnel built to carry one single Track only
b) Elsewhere, a Tunnel with only one Bore. In this case the number of Tracks is generally described, e.g. Double Track Single Bore.
See also Twin Bore Tunnel.

Single Car
Single Car Unit
[TRS] A special case of a Multiple Unit Train (MU Train) composed of a single vehicle. Also Railcar.

Single Compound
a) See Single Slip Diamond
b) See also Double Compound, Double Slip Diamond
c) The technical definition of a Compound □ Locomotive, unnecessary as all such Locomotives were Single Compound machines.

Single Cut
[Sig.] The provision of controls in only the Feed or Return side of a circuit, used only where there is no risk of False Feeds or faults to Earth.

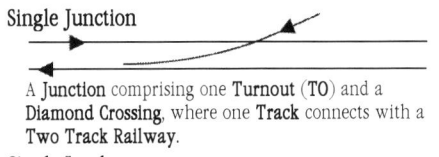

Single Junction

A Junction comprising one Turnout (TO) and a Diamond Crossing, where one Track connects with a Two Track Railway.

Single Lead
An alternative for Turnout (TO, T/O).

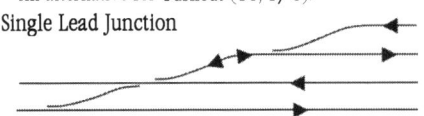

Single Lead Junction

An alternative Junction Layout to a Double Junction; the joining Line is first reduced to a Single Line, and then this is connected to the Main Line using a Single Lead or Turnout (TO) followed by a Crossover. The point of the exercise is to remove Diamond Crossings from the Main Line, and to reduce the resulting number of Point Ends left in the Main Line to a minimum. This layout is unsuitable for heavily trafficked Junctions, as the short length of Single Line removes the facility for Parallel Movements.

Single Line
a) The Track over which Trains run during Single Line Working (SLW)
b) A Line with a single Track on which Trains normally run in both directions, see Up & Down
c) A description of a machine which can work wholly within the confines of the Standard Loading Gauge of one Track, for example a Single Line Gantry (SLG), Single Line Spoil Handling System (SLSHS).

Single Line Diagram (SLD)
A Track Diagram that represents each Track as one line. They are drawn to scale longitudinally, but not in any other direction. See also Isolation Diagram, Quail Map, Signalling Plan.

Single Line Gantry (SLG)
[PW] A wheeled portal frame crane which runs on Plant Rails laid clear of the Sleeper Ends. They are used in pairs to remove or lay Track Panels and, in conjunction with a Sleeper Beam, to remove or lay new Sleepers. As the name implies, they are self-contained within a Single Line, allowing Traffic to run on the adjacent Line if required.

Single Line of Way
[Arch.] Alternative term for a Single Track Railway.

Single Line Section
a) Part of a Line on which Trains normally work in both directions, within which only one Train is permitted at any one time. This typically occurs between Passing Loops
b) [Ops.] That part of a Route that is being temporarily operated as a Single Line during Single Line Working (SLW). See also Pilotman.

Single Line Spoil Handling System (SLSHS)
[PW] A Train consisting of a number of Spoil Wagons equipped with a top conveyor system to allow the vehicles to be loaded from one end, and a discharge conveyor at the bottom to allow them to be unloaded individually if required. Also known as the Starfer after the company who made it, it is intended for use with the High Output Ballast Cleaner (HOBC).

Single Line Working (SLW)
[Ops.] The temporary use of one Track for traffic working in both directions. See also Pilot Working, Pilotman.

Single Links
[TRS] In a Wagon suspension, a loop of steel interposed between the Eye Bolt and Leaf Spring to provide a degree of freedom to the assembly.

Single Manned
[Hist.] Describing a Traction Unit having only a driver and no Second Man.

Single Option Development (SOD)
[NR] A stage of scheme development where one option, the Preferred Option, has been selected and this is being developed to a higher level of feasibility prior to Detailed Design. See also Governance for Railway Investment Projects (GRIP).

Single Pipe Air Brake

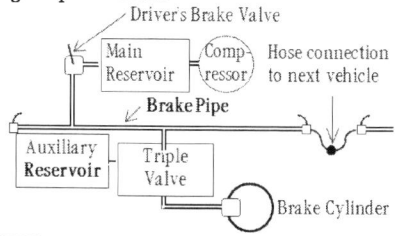

[TRS] An Automatic Brake that uses compressed air within a single pipe. During "Release", pressure in the Brake Pipe rises and air enters the Triple Valve which opens a path between the Brake Pipe and the Auxiliary Reservoir, and the Brake Cylinder and an exhaust port. The air escapes and a spring pushes the piston back releasing the brakes. The Auxiliary Reservoir is also replenished ready for another application. During "Application", air pressure in the Brake Pipe drops and is detected by the Triple Valve which closes the connection between the Brake Cylinder and the exhaust and opens a path from Auxiliary Reservoir to Brake Cylinder. The Auxiliary Reservoir fills the Brake Cylinder, applying the brakes against the spring. To partially apply the brakes, the driver moves the brake valve to "**Lap**" while air is escaping during an Application. The Triple Valve sees the Auxiliary Reservoir pressure falling while the Brake Pipe pressure stays constant. The valve stops half-way between Application and Release and the Brake Cylinder pressure is held constant. See also **Two Pipe Air Brake**.

Single Rail
See **Common Rail (CR)**.

Single Rail Bonding
See **Common Rail Bonding**.

Single Rail Track Circuit
See **Common Rail Track Circuit**.

Single Slip
A contracted form of **Single Slip Diamond**.

Single Slip Diamond

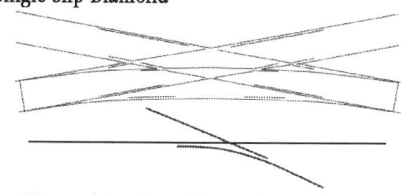

A **Diamond Crossing** with two **Slip Switches** to provide an additional directional facility. Also **Slip, Single Slip, Single Compound, Diamond with Single Slip**.

Single Slip Switch Diamond
A **Switch Diamond (SD)** with two **Slip Switches** to provide an additional directional facility. See also **Single Slip Diamond**.

Single Tongue Catch Point

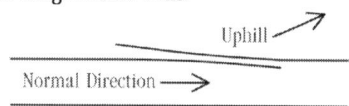

An assembly of one **Switch Half Set** fitted in the **Trailing** direction and held open by a spring. A passing **Train** will close the **Switch** as it passes by in the **Right Direction**, but will be **Derailed** if it attempts to pass in the **Wrong Direction**. This is an **Unworked Catch Point**. On **Main Lines** a **Point Machine** may be provided to close the Switch as a Train approaches correctly. This is a **Worked Catch Point**. They are used to **Derail** vehicles which are **Running Away** on a **Running Line**. See also **Double Tongue Catch Point, Catch Point (CP)**.

Single Tongue Trap (STT)
Single Tongue Trap Point
An assembly of one **Switch Half Set** similar to a **Single Tongue Catch Point**, except that a **Trap Point** is always **Worked**. They are intended to **Derail** vehicles attempting to make **Unauthorised Movements** and therefore protect other **Trains**. See also **Double Tongue Trap (DTT), Double Tongue Trap Point**.

Single Track
A **Route** with one **Track**.

Single Track Cantilever (STC)

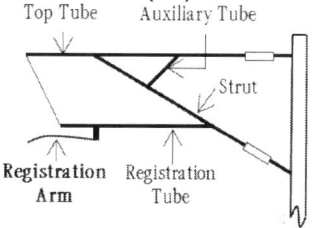

[Elec.] An **Overhead Line Structure** that provides support for the **Catenary** on a single **Track** by means of the **Cantilever** principle. See also **Twin Track Cantilever (TTC)**.

Single Way
[Hist.] A **Tramway** comprising **Wood Sleepers** and wooden **Rails**, the latter formed from single depth scantlings typically 4" (100mm) square.

Single Yellow (Y)
[Sig.] An **Aspect** displayed by a **Colour Light Signal**, consisting of a single **Yellow** light. This indicates to the approaching driver that the next **Main Signal** will be showing a Stop Aspect. See **Caution Aspect**. See also **Double Yellow (YY)**.

Singling
[Col.] The act of removing all but one **Track** of a **Multiple Track Railway**. See also **Dequadrification**.

SINMON
Special Inspection Notice Monitor.

Sinusoidal Transition
[PW] A **Transition Curve** giving a flatter, more gradual entry and exit than the normal **Cubic Parabola**, but with a more rapid rate of change over the middle third of the **Transition**. This geometry is not in widespread use.

SIO
Senior **I**nvestigating **O**fficer.

SIP
See **S**trike **i**n **P**oint.

Siphon
Siphon Culvert
[Civ.] A U-shaped pipe carrying a stream under a **Cutting**. The water flows in at the top at one side and the imbalance of pressures forces water out of the other end. They are prone to silting up and springing spectacular leaks.

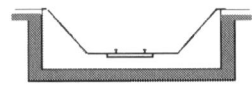

SIPS
[NR] Standard **I**nfrastructure **P**erformance **S**ystem, the Civil Engineering equivalent of the **PALADIN** Data **E**xtract **a**nd **R**ecording **S**ystem (**PEARS**).

SIS
a) **S**taff **I**nformation **S**ystem
b) **SPAD I**nhibit **S**hort.

SISA
Supporting **I**nfrastructure **S**afety **A**ssessment.

SISS
a) **S**tation **I**nformation and **S**urveillance **S**ystems
b) [NPT] **S**tation **I**nformation and **S**ecurity **S**ystems

SIT
a) See **S**leeper **I**ntegrity **T**ester
b) **S**afety **I**mprovement **T**eam.

Site Access Cabin
[NR] A cabin at the site entrance occupied by a **Site Access Controller** (**SAC**).

Site Access Control
Site Access Controller (SAC)
[NR] A means of controlling access to a site, checking the validity of **PTS** cards and disseminating safety information, and the title of the person who carries this duty out. This post is not the same as a **Controller of Site Safety** (**COSS**).

Site Access Register
[NR] A record maintained by a **Site Access Controller** (**SAC**) of, and signed by, all those who enter and leave the site. Signing the register is an acknowledgement that the Site Access Controller's briefing has been given and understood.

Site Clear Message
[LUL] A message passed from the **Protection Master** to the **Track Access Controller** stating that it is safe for **Trains** to run and all staff are clear of the **Line Clear** area.

Site Fitted Joint
[PW] An **Insulated Rail Joint** (**IRJ**) assembled and tested on site. The alternative is a **Shop Fitted Joint**, **Shop Made Joint**, **Site Made Joint**.

Site Lookout
Where one or more **Advance Lookouts** are provided, the person actually giving the warning to the working party is the **Site Lookout**.

Site Made Joint
See **Site Fitted Joint**.

Site of Work
The physical location of **Work** activity undertaken by a **Work Group**. This is not the same as a **Work Site**.

Site Person in Charge (SPC)
[LUL] The person in overall control of the **Work Site** in **Engineering Hours** and in a specified area and a **Possession**. Equivalent to an **Engineering Supervisor** (**ES**) on **Network Rail** (**NR**).

Site Warden (SW)
[NR] A person appointed by a **Controller of Site Safety** (**COSS**) to warn all staff to stay in the safe area where no fence is provided, i.e. more than 2 metres for the nearest line open to **Movements**.

Site Warden Warning
[NR] A method of protecting staff **Working □ On or Near the Line**, by providing one or more **Site Wardens** (**SW**) to alert members of staff who have moved too close to the **Track**. This term replaces **Separated Green Zone**.

SITS
Security **I**ncident **T**racking **S**ystem.

SIU
Station **I**nterface **U**nit See also **Station Information and Security Systems** (**SISS**).

SIVS
a) **S**taff **I**nformation **VDU S**ystem
b) **S**taff **I**nformation **VDU S**tepping
c) **S**tation **I**nformation **VDU S**tepping
d) **S**tation **I**nspector **V**iewing **S**ystem.

Six Bells
[Col.] The **Bell Code** for **Obstruction Danger**.

Six Foot
See **Sixfoot**.

Six Hole
Six Hole Joint
[PW Col.] A **Fishplate** fitted with six **Fishbolt Holes**, or a **Fishplated Rail Joint** made with this type of Fishplate. Normally found as **Insulated Fishplates** in **Main Lines**.

Sixfoot

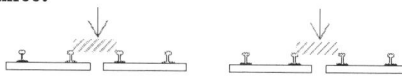

a) The standard minimum interval between two adjacent **Tracks** on a **Railway**, as measured between **Outside Edges** (**OE**). Surprisingly for Track related dimensions, it is actually six feet (1830mm) between **Outside Edges** (**OE**)
b) [Col.] Term used for the space between two adjacent **Tracks**, irrespective of the distance involved. See also **Tenfoot**, **Wideway**, **Widespace**
c) [PW] The operation of using an adjacent **Track** as a reference for **Alignment**, as in **Sixfooting**. Also **Six Foot**.

Sixfoot Back Drive
[Sig.] A **Back Drive** (**Supplementary Drive**) located in the **Sixfoot** adjacent to a **Set of Switches**.

Sixfoot Drain
A **Track Drain** laid in the **Sixfoot**. Also **6 Foot Drain**.

Sixfooting
[PW] Setting out one **Track** from another by placing it so that the **Outside Edges** (**OE**) are 6' (1830mm) apart. This is often done on **Relaying** sites to obtain a quick and consistent **Alignment** close to the actual dimension, leaving the **Tamper** to do the rest.

Sixty Foot
[PW Col.] The length of a **Standard Rail**, also used as a measure of distance along the **Railway**. There are 88 Sixty Foots in one **Mile**. See also **Length**, **Rail Length**. The metric equivalent is 18.288m.

SK
[TRS] An acronym representing a **Corridor □ Standard Class □ Coach**.

Skako
(Tradename) A manufacturer of access, concrete and materials handling equipment, based in Denmark. Manufacturer of some **Auto Ballaster □ Wagons**, See **Octopus** (**YDA**).

Skate
a) [NR] A **Wagon** (**CARKND □ YDA**) used for the transportation of skips as part of the **Skip Train**. Each Wagon carries seven skips. See **Wagon Names**
b) See **Rail Skate**.

Skateboard
[Col.] Term used for **Class** 153 **Diesel Multiple Unit** (**DMU**) due to them being one coach on wheels.

Skew
Describing something crossing a **Railway** at an angle other than 90°, e.g. a Skew **Bridge** or **Skew Level Crossing**.

Skew Back
[Col.] The wedge shaped stone or concrete block placed on top of an **Abutment** or **Pier**, which in turn provides a foundation for the **Arch Ring**. Also **Springing**.

Skew Level Crossing

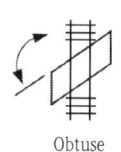

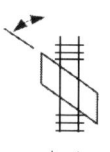

Obtuse   Acute

A **Level Crossing** (**LC**, **LX**) where the angle measured in an anti-clockwise direction from the road to the **Railway** is more (an obtuse skew) or less (an acute skew) than a right angle.

Skim Dig
[PW] An excavation that removes only a shallow layer (typically 75mm) of **Ballast** from beneath the **Sleepers**.

Skip
[Col.] Nickname given to **Class** 67 **Diesel Locomotive** because of their shape.

Skip Train
[BR Obs.] An early attempt at producing a **Spoil Train** that could be loaded from one end. This allowed **Reballasting** work on **Single Lines** to take place, often making some previously impractical **Relaying Items** financially viable. The Skip Train used flat **Wagons**, a number of normal builder's skips to store the **Spoil** with a small mobile gantry and a conveyor being provided to load the end skip. When full this skip would be changed by the gantry for another, empty skip. A fine machine, but it was relatively slow. Its more modern counterpart is the **Single Line Spoil Handling System** (**SLSHS**).

Skipper
[TRS] Name given to the **Class** 140 **Pacers**, used in the South West of England.

Skip-stopping
[Ops.] A stopping pattern where a **Train** does not call at all **Stations**. Also **Semi-fast**.

Skirted Fishplate
[PW] A **Fishplate** of increased depth that provides additional strength at **Fishplated Rail Joints** between **Bull Head Rails** (**BH**). Also **Deep Skirted Fishplate**.

Skl 12
Skl 14
Skl 15
(Tradename) [PW] Types of **Rail Clip** manufactured by **Vossloh**.

SKM
(Tradename) Sinclair Knight Merz, an Australian firm of Consulting Engineers and now part of **Jacobs** whose headquarters is in Pasadena, California, USA.

Skull Hook Clip (SHC)
[PW Col.] Nickname for a **Spring Hook Clip**, after Jack Skull, **Permanent Way Engineer** (**PWE**) of the **Western Region** (**WR**) of British Rail (**BR**) at the time of its introduction.

SkV
(Tradename) [PW Hist.] The first of the SkV series of **Alumino-thermic Welding** processes, which was not approved for widespread use in the UK. After trials it was developed into the **SkV-F**.

SkV-E
(Tradename) [PW] A development of the **SkV-F** □ **Alumino-thermic Welding** process, designed to eliminate **Black Holes**. Produced by **Thermit Welding**.

SkV-F
(Tradename) [PW] A type of **Alumino-thermic Weld**, widely used in the UK. See also **SkV-E**. Produced by **Thermit Welding**.

SkV-L50
(Tradename) [PW] A version of the standard **SkV-F** □ **Alumino-thermic Weld**, capable of welding a 50mm gap. Also referred to as a **Wide Gap Weld**. Produced by **Thermit Welding**.

SkV-L80
(Tradename) [PW] A version of the standard **SkV-F** □ **Alumino-thermic Weld**, capable of welding an 80mm gap. This allows defective standard **SkV-F** welds to be removed and the **Rails** re-welded without using any extra Rail. Also referred to as a **Wide Gap Weld**. Produced by **Thermit Welding**.

SL
a) See **Slow Line**
b) See **Surface Length**
c) [TRS] An acronym representing a **Eurostar** □ **Sleeping Car**
d) Separate Lead (*separate led*), a type of construction used in High Voltage (**HV**) cables where each core has a separate sheathing of lead.

SL&DHA
Signalling Logic and Geographical Data Hazard Assessment.

SLA
Service Level Agreement.

Slab Track
[PW] **Track** without **Ballast** or **Sleepers**, continuously supported by a continuous reinforced concrete slab. Also **PACT Track, Paved Track**. See also **Street Running Track**.

Slack
[Col.]
a) A **Track Fault** consisting of a depression in the vertical alignment (**Top**). See also **Swag**.
b) A common term for an **Emergency Speed Restriction (ESR)** or **Temporary Speed Restriction (TSR)**.

Slack Adjusters
[TRS] A component of a brake system that automatically takes up any slack in the **Brake Rigging** caused by the wearing of the **Brake Blocks** or pads and therefore maintains constant braking effort as such wear occurs.

Slag
[Hist.] Blast furnace slag, used as a cheap alternative to **Ballast**.

Slam Door Stock
[TRS] Describing **Passenger Carrying Vehicles** with doors that require shutting by hand, See also **Plug Doors, Power Operated Doors**.

Slam Doors
[TRS] Side hinged **Car Doors** on **Passenger Coaches**, operated by the **Passengers** themselves. See also **Central Door Locking (CDL), Plug Doors, Power Operated Doors**.

Slattern
A **Railway** □ **Telegraph Code** meaning "Cannot agree to your proposal".

Slave Arrestor(s)
Additional brake unit(s) added **Beyond a Friction Retarder Buffer Stop** to assist with stopping heavy **Trains**.

Slave Rail
[PW] A short length of **Plain Rail**, often **Scrap Rail**, used for the positioning and lifting of **Switch and Crossing (S&C)** □ **Bearers**, prior to the installation of the **Switch and Crossing Units (S&C Units)**. See also **Plant Rail, Service Rail**.

SLC
a) [Sig.] Single **Location Case**
b) (Tradename) [PW] Super **Lining Control**, a system fitted to some **Plasser and Theurer** 06 type **Tamping** machines to allow them to align the **Track** as well.

SLC Platform
Single **Location Case Platform**.

SLCC
Safety Leadership and Culture Change.

SLD
See **Single Line Diagram**.

SLE
[TRS] An acronym representing a **Sleeping Car** - either **Passenger Class**.

SLED
[TRS] An acronym representing a **Sleeping Car** - either **Passenger Class** with disabled facilities.

Sleeper
a) [PW] A beam made of wood, pre-stressed reinforced concrete or steel placed at regular intervals at right angles to and under the **Rails**. Their purpose is to support the Rails and to ensure that the correct **Gauge** is maintained between the Rails. **Wood Sleepers** come in two varieties, **Softwood Sleepers** and **Hardwood Sleepers**, and a **Baseplate** or **Chair** is often used provide additional support to the Rails and prevent their longitudinal rotation. **Concrete Sleepers** and **Steel Sleepers** often have **Housings** for **Rail Fastenings** built into them
b) [Col.] contraction of **Sleeping Car Train**.

Sleeper Beam
[PW] A spreader beam equipped with a number of lifting chains and specialised hooks used to lift more than one **Sleeper** at a time. **Short Sleeper Beams** are used with **Road Rail Excavators** and generally have four, seven or eight pairs of hooks. **Crane Beams** are designed to lift half a **Length** of Sleepers, and therefore have 12, 13 or 14 pairs of hooks at appropriate **Sleeper Spacings**. **TRM Beams** can deal with a whole Length, and so have 24, 26 or 28 pairs of hooks at appropriate Sleeper Spacings. See also **Janglers**.

Sleeper Blocks
[PW Hist.] (Generally) stone blocks used to support the **Rails** and used in pairs, one under each Rail. Management of **Track Gauge** was either not provided (to allow horses free passage along the **Fourfoot**) or achieved using **Tie Bars**.

Sleeper Bonker
[PW Col.] the **Sleeper Integrity Tester** (**SIT**).

Sleeper Bottom (SB)
[PW] A colloquial alternative name for the **Soffit** (underside) of a **Sleeper**. See also Below Sleeper Bottom (BSB), Bearer Bottom (BB).

Sleeper Crossing
A **Level Crossing** (LC, LX) surface constructed using **Wood Sleepers**. Often found in **Sidings**, their use at crossing points used by the public has diminished as the requirements for skid resistance and easy removal for **Mechanised Maintenance** have become more onerous.

Sleeper Delivery Train (SDT)
(Tradename) [PW] Proper name for **The Slinger**, A **Train** of specially adapted **Salmon** □ **Wagons** (**CARKND** □ **YFA**) used for loading, transporting and off-loading **Continuous Welded Rail** (**CWR**) and **Steel Sleepers**. Each Wagon has two small **Propped Cantilever** cranes mounted along one side, controlled from a central point. **Sleepers** are handled using a special lightweight **Sleeper Beam**, allowing 100 **Yards** of **Track** to be laid at a standard 1970mm **Sixfoot** simultaneously. Pioneered by **Jarvis** Ltd.

Sleeper Dogs
See **Timber Dogs**.

Sleeper Ends
[PW]
a) That part of a **Sleeper** that is not in the **Fourfoot** of the **Track** supported by said Sleeper
b) The vertical faces at the extremities of a **Sleeper**.

Sleeper Gall
[PW] Attrition of the **Rail Seat** of a **Concrete Sleeper** caused by disintegration of the **Rail Pad** and no action being taken to replace it.

Sleeper Integrity Tester (SIT)
[PW] A device that assesses the state of **Wood Sleepers** whilst in situ in the **Track**. It taps a **Sleeper** and listens to the result, earning it the nickname of the **Bonker** or **Sleeper Bonker**. Sleepers score between 1 (good) and 6 (scrap). Used to identify Sleepers for **Patch Resleepering** or treatment with **Borate Rods**.

Sleeper Nips
See **Timber Dogs**.

Sleeper Pad
See **Chair Pad**.

Sleeper Slide
[PW] A method of **Reballasting** very short (less than 10 **Yard**, 9 metre) lengths of **Track**. First, two or three **Sleepers** are removed from one end and the space excavated and re-filled using a small excavator or similar. The next Sleeper is then slid along the Track into the space and the operation repeated as necessary. The Sleepers removed at the start of the work are then inserted into the remaining space at the end of the Reballasting, spaced and **Clipped Up** and all Sleepers **Packed**. The **Ballast Profile** is restored, with additional **Ballast** provided as required.

Sleeper Soffit
[PW]
a) For all purposes relating to a monolithic **Wood Sleeper** or **Concrete Sleeper**, the horizontal lower face of the **Sleeper**
b) For measurement purposes on a **Steel Sleeper**, the lower edges of the central section.

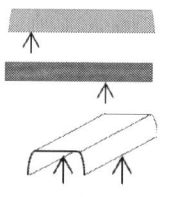

Sleeper Spacing
[PW]
a) Common parlance when describing the spacing between **Sleepers** is to quote the number of Sleepers in a 60 foot (18.288m) **Length**. Normal values are 24, 26 and 28, with 30 being an exceptional case used on **High Cant Deficiency Curves** (**HCD Curves**). These frequencies equate to approximately 760, 705, 650 and 610mm (approximately 30, 28, 26 and 24 inch) centres for Sleepers laid under **Continuous Welded Rail** (**CWR**) □ **Track**. Sleepers under **Jointed Track** were laid with those nearest the **Fishplated Rail Joints** closer together in an attempt to increase the mechanical strength of the Rail Joint
b) The action of regularising or changing the spacing of Sleepers. See also **Respacing**.

Sleeper Squaring
[PW] The action of returning **Sleepers** to a position where their longitudinal axis is normal to the centre line of the **Track**. On **Curves** with high **Cant Deficiency** (**D**) values the low end of Sleepers are prone to "walking" towards oncoming **Trains**, reducing the **Gauge**.

Sleeper Tongs
See **Timber Dogs**.

Sleeper Zero
The **Sleeper** nearest to the **Point of Derailment** (**POD**). Adjacent Sleepers are then numbered in a negative sequence **On the Approach** to the POD, and in a positive sequence **Beyond** it.

Sleepered Lead

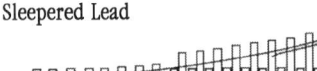

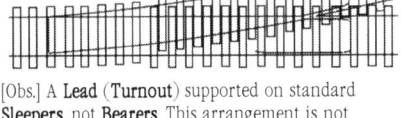

[Obs.] A **Lead** (**Turnout**) supported on standard **Sleepers**, not **Bearers**. This arrangement is not current practice because of the lack of lateral ties to retain the **Turnout Route** in the correct relationship to the **Main Line**

Sleeping Car
[TRS] A **Passenger Coach** divided into a number of private compartments, each with sleeping facilities. Used on long distance, overnight, **Express Passenger Trains** which are colloquially called **Sleepers**.

Sleeping Car Train
[Ops.] A **Train** composed of **Sleeping Cars**. Colloquially shortened to **Sleeper**.

Sleeping Dog
Sleeping Dog Crossing
[Col.] A **Footpath Crossing** (**FP**) that has fallen into disuse and been fenced off but is still legally a right of way. The term stems from "Let sleeping dogs lie", as to attempt to formally close the Crossing may draw attention to it.

Sleeping Policeman
[Col.] name for an **Emergency Indicator** (**EI**), after their slowing effect on passing **Train** drivers. Also **Dalek**, **Metal Mickey**.

Sleet Brush
[TRS] A brush mounted on the **Shoebeam**, used for clearing **Snow** and ice from the **Conductor Rail**.

Sleet Train
[LUL] See **De-icing Train**.

Sleeves
a) See **Fishbolt Insulations**
b) [Elec.] Devices fitted to a **Hook Switch** to prevent their accidental operation. See **Orange Sleeve**, **White Sleeve**.

SLEP
[TRS] An acronym representing a **Sleeping Car** - either **Class** - with pantry.

Slew
Slewing
Relating to the rotation of the superstructure of a crane or excavator. See also **Slue**, **Slueing**, **Sluing**.

SLF
[TRS] An acronym representing a **First Class** □ **Sleeping Car**.

SLG
See **Single Line Gantry**.

SLHA
Signalling **L**ayout **H**azard **A**nalysis.

Slide Baseplate
[PW] A **Baseplate** for a **Flat Bottom Switch** having a horizontal flat surface upon which the **Switch Rail** can be moved laterally.

Slide Baseplate Distance Block
[PW] A metal spacer fitted at **Slide Baseplates**, retained in place by the **Stock Rail Bolt**, to provide lateral support to the **Switch Rail** in the area between the end of the **Switch Planing** and the **Switch Heel** when that **Switch Half Set** is closed.

Slide Baseplate Jaw
[PW] The vertical portion of a **Slide Baseplate**, to which is bolted the **Slide Baseplate Jaw Block**, **Stock Rail** and **Slide Baseplate Distance Block** (if required).

Slide Baseplate Jaw Block
[PW] A cast metal block fitted between a **Slide Baseplate Jaw** and the relevant **Stock Rail** and is secured by a **Stock Rail Bolt**.

Slide Chair
[PW] A **Chair** for a **Bull Head Switch** having a horizontal flat surface upon which the **Switch Rail** can be moved laterally.

Slide Chair Distance Block
[PW] A metal spacer fitted at **Slide Chairs**, retained in place by the **Stock Rail Bolt**, to provide lateral support to the **Switch Rail** in the area between the end of the **Switch Planing** and the **Switch Heel** when that **Switch Half Set** is closed.

Slide Table
[PW] The horizontal, flat portion of a **Slide Chair** or **Slide Baseplate** upon which the **Switch Rail** slides.

Slide-and-Plug Door
See **Sliding Plug Door**.

Sliding Buffer Stop
An alternative term for a **Friction Retarder Buffer Stop**.

Sliding Plug Door
A type of **Powered Door** system in which, during opening, the **Door Leaf** initially moves out and clear of the **Carbody** before sliding open. Also **Slide-and-plug Door**.

Slim Jims
[Col.] Modified **Class** 33 **Locomotives**, built specially for the Hastings **Line**. Named after their narrow dimensions, a requirement on this less-than-generously constructed **Route**.

Slinger
[Col.]
a) A common contraction of **Crane Slinger**. See also **Crane Controller**
b) (Tradename) See **Sleeper Delivery Train** (**SDT**).

Slip
a) See **Double Slip Diamond**, **Single Slip Diamond**
b) [Civ. Col.] Contraction of **Bank Slip**, see also **Slip Circle**, **Slip Plane**
c) See **Slip Road**
d) See **Slip Switch**
e) See **Slip Coach**.

Slip Circle
[Civ.] A common form of **Slip Plane** in which the plane is curved about a horizontal axis, leading to the **Slip** being a **Rotational Failure**.

Slip Coach
[Obs.] A popular method of improving **Train** performance during the late 19th and early 20th century, particularly of those **Trains** leaving the capital. It involved detaching the last **Coach** (or **Coaches**) whilst still on the move, at speed. Carried out at a predetermined point, the **Coaches** concerned could be brought to rest at the appropriate **Station** without delaying the **Train**. Some services Slipped many **Coaches** at different locations on their journey. The last such operation occurred in 1960.

Slip Connection
A connection which permits movements to be made from one line to another at a **Diamond Crossing**. Also **Slip Road**. See also **Double Slip Diamond**, **Single Slip Diamond**.

Slip Coupling
a) [TRS Obs.] A special **Coupling** fitted to **Slip Coaches** which allowed the **Guard** to release it remotely
b) [Hist.] A coupling used to attach a **Set** to the haulage rope of a **Rope-worked Incline**. Designed to permit disconnection of the **Set** from the haulage rope by a **Bankhead Man** rather than by a **Set Rider**.

Slip Plane
[Civ.] The boundary along which the material involved in a **Bank Slip** or **Landslip** separates from the rest of the **Earthwork**. See also **Slip Circle**.

Slip Road
The additional **Track** or **Tracks** in a **Double Slip Diamond** or **Single Slip Diamond**. Also **Slip Connection**.

Slip Switch
A **Switch** used to permit **Trains** to change **Tracks** in a **Diamond Crossing**. See **Double Slip Diamond**, **Single Slip Diamond**.

Slipper
a) [PW] A polymer insert fitted to **Slipper Baseplates** to reduce friction, see **Slipper Insert**
b) A metal device placed behind a vehicle wheel to prevent the vehicle rolling away. See also **Scotch**.

Slipper Baseplate
[PW] A **Slide Baseplate** fitted with a low friction polymer (**UHMWPE**) slide insert (**Slipper**) to reduce the effort needed to operate the **Switches**. It is not necessary to lubricate this type of **Baseplate**; in fact lubrication shortens the life of the polymer **Slipper Insert** as it encourages grit to stick to the polymer surface, making it wear away faster.

Slipper Insert
See **Slipper** clause a).

Slipper Run
[LUL] Device fitted to the **Timbers** in a **Switch and Crossing Layout** (**S&C Layout**) to ensure that low **Negative Shoes** are safely carried over the **Running Rails**.

Slipper Support
[PW] A cast metal bracket designed to support a **Slipper Insert** over the **Rail Foot** of the **Stock Rail** in a **Shallow Depth Switch** fitted with **Slipper Baseplates**.

Slipping Structures
[Elec. Col.] A term used to describe **Overhead Line Equipment** (**OLE**) **Structures** whose foundations are moving, typically away from the track by rotation about their lower ends.

SLK
[TRS] An acronym representing a **Composite** □ **Sleeping Car**.

SLL
South London Line.

SLO
See **Site Lookout**.

SLOA
(Tradename) **S**team **L**ocomotive **O**perators **A**ssociation.

SLOE
Single **L**ist **o**f **E**nhancements.

Slope
[Civ.] Generally, a contraction of **Cutting** Slope or **Embankment** Slope, meaning the inclined sides of such constructions.

Slope Failure
[Civ.] A **Bank Slip**, landslip, rock fall or other unintentional downward movement of material in a **Cutting** or **Embankment**, generally leading to a need for emergency action.

Slope of Formation
See **Crossfall**.

Slope Stability Hazard Index (SSHI)
[NR Civ.] A standardised method for assessing the condition of **Earthworks** with respect to their potential instability. It determines the risk of failure against five potential failure modes, namely **Rotational Failure**, translational failure, **Earth Flow**, **Washout**, and animal burrowing.

SLOR
See **S**econd **L**ine **o**f **R**esponse.

Slot

Slotting
[Sig.] A **Control** which requires two **Signal Boxes** to co-operate to **Release** a **Signal** or **Points**.

Slotted Joint Points
[Sig.] Alternative for **Trailable Points**.

Slotted Semaphore Signal
[Sig.] A **Semaphore Signal** arranged so that the **Arm** disappears into a slot in the post when the **Signal** is **Off**. This is a poor arrangement, as demonstrated by the **Abbots Ripon Accident**. This type is no longer in use.

Slough
(*sluff*) [Arch.] A collapse or slide of soil or rock into a hole or depression.

Slow (S)
See **Slow Line** (**SL**).

Slow Acting Relay
[Sig.] A **Relay** with a deliberately long **Operation Time** and **Release Time**.

457

Slow Line (SL)
A **Track** of lesser importance than a **Fast Line** but which runs alongside a Fast Line. A **Slow Line** may not be slower than the **Fast Line**. Also **Relief Line, Secondary Line, Local Line**. Typically shortened to **Slow** (**S**), for instance **Down Slow** (**DS**).

Slow to Operate Relay
[Sig.] A **Relay** with a deliberately long **Operation Time** that is significantly longer than the **Release Time**.

Slow to Release Relay
[Sig.] A **Relay** with a deliberately long **Release Time** that is significantly longer than the **Operation Time**.

SLR
Selsey **Light Railway**.

SLS
[TRS] An acronym representing a **Second Class □ Sleeping Car**.

SLSC
[TRS] An acronym representing a **Sleeping Car Support Coach**.

SLSHS
(*slush*) See **Single Line Spoil Handling System**.

SLTC
Station **l**ong **t**erm **c**harge.

SLU
a) See **Standard Length Unit**
b) **S**afety **L**egislation **U**pdate
c) [LUL] **S**tation **L**ast **U**sed.

Slue
Slueing
[PW] The correct terms for making lateral adjustments to the position of the **Track**. Doing so to meet some form of design **Alignment** is referred to as **Lining**. The incorrect terms are **Slew** and **Slewing** which refers to the rotation of the superstructure of a crane or excavator.

Slue Convention
[PW] A local consensus on which direction is indicated by a positive **Slue**. There are two main views:
a) That a positive Slue is outwards on a **Curve**; this is the convention used in **Hallade**. For **Straight Track**, "outwards" generally refers to the Hand of the preceding curve
b) That a positive Slue is to the right when viewed looking towards the higher chainage
Because of this dichotomy, the application of positive and negative Slues should be clearly stated on all design outputs. **Track** to be Slued is generally coloured blue on **Horizontal Geometry** drawings.

Slug
[Col.] Nickname for the **Class** 37/9 **Diesel Locomotive** as they were slow to build up power and accelerate.

Sluing
[PW] A variant spelling of **Slueing**.

Slurried Ballast
[PW] **Ballast** that has become contaminated by concrete dust, silt, and soil suspended in water. See also **Slurry, Slurry Bed, Slurry Spot, Wet Bed, Wet Spot**.

Slurry
[PW] A liquid formed by the mixing of surface water and toilet discharge with clay, concrete dust and soil under the pumping action of passing **Trains**. See also **Slurried Ballast**.

Slurry Bed
Slurry Spot
[PW] A **Bed** containing **Slurried Ballast**. More commonly called a **Wet Bed** or **Wet Spot**.

SLW
See **Single Line Working**.

SL*xx*
Signal Lamp, e.g. SL32, SL33, SL35.

SM
a) **S**upervisory **M**anager
b) **S**ite **M**anager.

SM(T)
Section **M**anager (**T**rack).

SMA
a) **S**ignalling □ **M**aintenance **A**ssistant
b) **S**tatistical **M**ultiplexer **A**ppreciation
c) **S**trathclyde **M**anning **A**greement
d) **S**ingle **M**anning **A**greement.

Small Part Steel (SPS)
[Elec.] The assortment of bolts, brackets, clamps, tubes, etc. that are used in the assembly of an **Overhead Line Electrification** (**OLE**) system.

Smallman Clip
[Hist.] A clip, which did not self-tension, used to attach a vehicle to an **Under-rope Haulage** wire rope. Also **Star Clip**.

Smalls
[PW Col.] A collective term for the small components used in the construction of the **Track**, such as **Chairscrews, Rail Clips, Coachscrews, End Posts, Fastenings, Fishbolts, Fishplates, Rail Foot Insulators**, nuts, **Nylons, Pads** and washers.

SMART
(*smart*) [NR] **S**ignal **M**onitoring **a**nd **R**eporting to **TRUST**, a system which collects and forwards information automatically on actual **Train □ Running**.

Smartlock
(Tradename) [Sig.] An **Interlocking** system produced by **Alstom**.

SME
a) **S**ignal □ **M**aintenance **E**ngineer
b) **S**tructures **M**aintenance **E**ngineer
c) [NR] **S**tructures **M**anagement **E**ngineer.

SMFD
Systems **M**anagement **F**ramework **D**esign.

SMG
a) [NR] Systems Management Group
b) Science Museum Group. See also **Railway Heritage Designation Advisory Board**.

SMGS
Soglashenije o Meshdunarodnom Shelesnodoroshnom Grusowom Soobstschenii, an Eastern European convention concerning the international carriage of **Goods** by **Rail**.

SMIS
(*smiss*) See **Safety Management Information System**.

Smoke Board
Smoke Plate
[Civ.] A plate attached to the underside of an **Overbridge** (**OB**) to protect the **Structure** from blasts of smoke and steam produced by passing **Steam Locomotives**.

Smokebox
[TRS] On a **Steam Locomotive**, an enclosure at the front of the **Boiler** into which combustion gases from the **Firebox** are drawn, together with ash and char carried by the gases, through the **Boiler Tubes**. See also **Blastpipe**, **Blower Rings**.

Smooth Lining
[PW] An automated system fitted to **Tampers**, capable of re-aligning a length of **Track** by averaging out the **Alignment** errors, rather than by reference to a **Design Alignment**. Also **Four Point Lining**, **Maintenance Lining**.

SMOS
(*smozz*) [Elec.] Structure Mounted Outdoor Switchgear. See **Earthing Switch**, **Feeder Switch**, **Motorised Switch**, **Section Switch**, **Siding Switch**.

SMOWS
Safe Method of Work Statement. See also **Method Statement**, **Work Package Plan** (**WPP**).

SMP
Standard **Maintenance** Procedure.

SMPS
Soglashenijeo Meshdunarodnom Passagierskom Soobstschenii, an Eastern European convention concerning the international carriage of **Passengers** by **Rail**.

SMR
Snowdon Mountain **Railway**.

SMS
a) Safety Management Systems
b) Signal □ **Maintenance** Standard
c) Signal Maintenance Specification
d) Site Management Statement

SMSE
Senior **Maintenance** Support Engineer.

SMT
a) Signalling □ Maintenance □ Testing
b) See **Southern Measurement Train**.

SMTH
[NR] **Signalling** □ **Maintenance** □ **Testing** Handbook.

SMVT
Secondary Means of Vertical Transportation.

SmW
(Tradename) [PW] Schnellschweissenverfahren mit Wulst. A variety of **Alumino-thermic Weld**. Now superseded by the **SkV-F Weld** and other similar processes.

SMWI
[NR] **Signalling** □ **Maintenance** **Work** Instructions.

SN
a) See **Special Notice**
b) The **ATOC** code for **Southern**

Snakegrid
(Tradename) A mathematical transformation process which provides a coordinate grid system with a unity scale factor along a trend line that follows the project in plan and height, allowing long infrastructure projects to be designed on a single coherent coordinate system. Developed and marketed by the UCL Department of Civil, Environmental and Geomatic Engineering.

Snap-through Buckle
[Civ.] A phenomenon which can occur in shallow **Arches** when high loading causes a sudden reversal of curvature over all or part of the structure.

SNCB
Societe National des Chemins de Fer Belges, the Belgian national **Railway** organisation.

SNCF
Societe National des Chemins de Fer Francais, the French national **Railway Authority**.

SNCI
Site of Nature Conservation Importance.

SNEP
Single National European Rail □ **Traffic** Management System (**ERTMS**) Programme, Now the **National ERTMS Programme** (**NEP**).

Snifting Valve
[TRS] An anti-vacuum valve fitted to a **Steam Locomotive** which admits air to the **Superheater Tubes** and hence to the cylinders (or direct to the cylinders on non-Superheated Locomotives) when the Locomotive is **Coasting**, and therefore not requiring steam. Not universally fitted and often later removed as the air temperatures produced by later **Superheaters** interfered with cylinder lubrication.

Snipe Cut
[PW] The removal of metal from the **Stock Rail** side of the **Switch Rail** at the **Heel of Planing**, intended to improve the **Free Wheel Clearance** (**FWC**) at this location.

Snow
a) Crystalline aqueous precipitation, produced by rapid freezing of damp air currents, often requiring the deployment of a **Snowman**, **Snow Blowers** or **Snow Ploughs**.
b) [PW Col.] The metal powder produced when a wheel **Sidewears** a **Rail**, from its white appearance prior to rusting.

Snow Blower
a) A large powered fan and **Snow Plough** combination that removes very deep **Snow** from the **Line** and blows it clear of the **Track**. Some are **Self-propelled** and others require a **Locomotive** to **Propel** them
b) [Civ.] A timber structure used on exposed **Single Lines** (typically in Scotland) at locations where drifting **Snow** has previously been a problem. A pair of inclined structures are placed on opposite sides of the Line, arranged so that any crosswind accelerates before it crosses the Track, reducing the quantity of Snow it drops there:

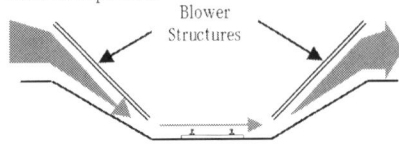

Blower Structures

Snow Fence
A fence, typically consisting of chestnut palings or **Scrap** □ **Sleepers** planted vertically on end, placed at a location where drifting **Snow** has previously been a problem. The fence is placed well back from the **Track** and is intended to slow the wind, causing it to deposit the Snow clear of the **Railway**.

Snow Hut
[Prob. Obs.] The **Lineside** shelter a **Snowman** uses as part of his duties.

Snow Plough
[TRS] A large V-shaped plough mounted on a dedicated **Rail Vehicle** and propelled by a **Locomotive** at a brisk pace. They are useful for clearing average quantities of **Snow**, but deep drifts require a **Snow Blower**. See also **Miniature Snow Plough**.

Snow Shed
[Civ.] A heavy roof provided over the **Line** at locations where **Snow** may accumulate, from avalanches or drifting.

Snow, Wrong Kind of
See **Wrong Kind of Snow**. See also **Snow** clause a).

Snowman
[Hist.] An employee despatched to a **Junction** during heavy **Snow** falls to keep the **Flangeways** and **Switches** clear. This system is now rarely employed, as all new **Switches** in **Running Lines** are fitted with **Electric Points Heating** which maintains the **Switch Rail** / **Stock Rail** at +3°C, reducing the build-up, and subsequent compaction between the **Switch Rail** and **Stock Rail**, of Snow.

SNR
[Sig.] **Signal** □ **Normal** □ **Relay**.

SNRN
South **N**ottinghamshire **Rail** **N**etwork.

Snubbing Device
A diode or relay fitted to the electric motor of a **Point Machine** to protect the control equipment from reverse currents generated during the motor's operation.

SNWPT
(*snow-pot*) [NR] **S**ignalling **N**ew **W**orks **P**roject **T**eam. An in-house design and scheme development organisation. Became **Signalling & Telecommunications** Programme Engineering (**STPE**) in a 2003 reorganisation.

SNX
See **Swing Nose Crossing**.

SO
a) **S**aturdays **O**nly
b) [TRS] An acronym representing a **Standard Class** □ **Open Coach**.

SOAP
Stereo **O**blique **A**erial **P**hotography.

SOC
a) **S**tation **O**perating **C**ompany
b) See **Shipper-owner Container**.

SOCO
(*socko*) **S**cene(s) **o**f **C**rime **O**fficer.

SOD
a) See **Single Option Development**
b) See **Safe Overrun Distance**.

SODA
Single **O**ption **D**evelopment **A**uthority.

SoFA
Statement **o**f **F**unds **A**vailable.

Soffit
a) [Civ.] An alternative for the **Crown** of an **Arch**
b) The top of a pipe
c) [Civ.] The underside of a **Bridge Deck**
d) [PW] The underside of a **Sleeper** or **Bearer**. Also **Invert**.

Soffit Erosion
The wearing away of material from the underside of a **Sleeper**. See also **Sleeper Soffit**.

Soffit Pad
[PW] A resilient material bonded to the **Soffit** (underside) of a **Sleeper** to reduce ground borne vibrations.

Soft Spot
[PW]
a) A soft metal insert let into holes in the **Legs** of **Cast Crossings** adjacent to the **Fishplate** positions, which can then be drilled on site to accept **Bondwires**
b) Describing an area in which the strength of the underlying **Formation** is low.

Soft Tilt Off
[NR Sig.] The point at which the authority to **Tilt** is withdrawn by the **Tilt Authorisation and Speed Supervision System** (**TASS**) and the **Tilting Train** commences its return to **Tilt Neutral**. Should the **Train** fail to return to Tilt Neutral (due to a failure of the system) then the Train will automatically brake to a stand. For this reason there is a full **Braking Distance** (**BD**) between the Soft Tilt Off location and the commencement of the **Tilt Prohibited Zone** (**TPZ**).

Softwood Sleeper
[PW] A variety of **Wood Sleeper** produced from Douglas Fir (*Pseudotsuga menziesii*) and pressure treated with a preservative. Such **Sleepers** are generally used on low speed **Lines** carrying low **Maximum Axle Loads** e.g. **Sidings**. See also **Hardwood Sleeper**.

Soham Explosion
On 2nd June 1944, as his ammunition **Train** was pulling into Soham **Station** in Cambridgeshire, driver Benjamin Gimbert saw the **Wagon** next to the **Locomotive** on fire. He drew **Fireman** James Nightall's attention to the fire and stopped the Train. By now the whole of the Wagon was in flames. Realising the danger, Gimbert instructed Nightall to uncouple the Wagon immediately behind the blazing Wagon. This done, Gimbert pulled the Locomotive and burning Wagon forward. As they approached the **Signal Box**, Gimbert shouted to the **Signaller** to stop a **Mail Train** which was almost due. Simultaneously, the bombs in the blazing Wagon exploded. A 7m deep crater was blown in the **Track** and 600 buildings were damaged. Fireman Nightall was killed instantly, and the Signaller later died of his injuries. Despite being next to the explosion, Gimbert survived. Both Gimbert and Nightall were awarded the George Cross for their bravery.

SOI
See **Special Operating Instruction**.

Soil Slope Hazard Index (SSHI)
[NR] A score reflecting the potential for a soil slope to fail and cause harm..

Solari
a) (Tradename) Contraction of Solari di Udine, a manufacturer of information display systems. based in Udine, Italy
b) [Col.] Generic term for the large **Departure Boards** found in the **Concourses** of larger **Stations**.

Sole (ZCA, ZCO)
[NR] A drop side **Open Wagon** used for the transportation of **Ballast** and **Sleepers**. See **Wagon Names**.

Solebar
[TRS] The longitudinal structural members forming the spine of a **Rail Vehicle**, located below the **Carbody**. The Solebar is supported by the **Bogies** or other **Running Gear**.

Soleplate
[PW] A metal plate fitted on the **Switch Toe Timber** beneath the **Chairs** or **Baseplates** of **Bullhead** (BH) and **Flat Bottom** (FB) □ **Switch and Crossing Layouts** (S&C Layouts) on **Timber Bearers** and **113A Vertical** on **Concrete Bearers** to provide additional **Gauge** restraint by means of stops welded to the plate. Soleplates are available to suit all standard **Switches**, fitted with insulations and extensions for **Point Machine** fixing.

Solid State Interlocking (SSI)
[Sig.] A microprocessor-based **Signalling System** using two-out-of-three voting to perform the **Train Detection**, **Interlocking** and control functions.

Soling
[Hist.] Use of broken stone with sizes up to 9" (225mm) laid by hand directly onto the **Formation** as a means of reducing the loss of **Ballast** due to shrinkage and absorption. See also **Pitching**.

Solum
[Scot.] A term for the **Formation**.

Somersault Signal
[Sig.] A variety of **Semaphore Signal** □ **Arm** that is pivoted half way along the Arm. This removes the possibility of accumulations of **Snow** and ice holding the Arm in the wrong position, as happened in the **Abbots Ripon Accident**. Also **Balanced Semaphore Arm**. See also **Slotted Semaphore Signal**.

Sonneville System
(Tradename) [PW] A Low Vibration Track (**LVT**) system pioneered by Roger Sonneville. It consists of a **Slab Track** construction, into which are set two parallel rows of rubber-booted blocks. Each block supports a **Rail**, restrained by a **Rail Fastening**. The system reduces ground-borne vibration.

Sonning Cutting Accident
Shortly after 06:40 on 24th December 1841 a Train consisting of a **Locomotive** "Heela", two **Third Class** □ **Coaches** and 18 **Freight** □ **Wagons** ran into a **Slip** in Sonning **Cutting**, causing the **Passenger** vehicles to be crushed by the **Wagons**. The report observed that the 24" (610mm) high sides on the Passenger vehicles allowed the Passengers to be flung out of the Coaches, worsen the severity of the outcome. Eight died and 17 were injured.

SOP
a) See **Strike Out Point**
b) See **Signing on Point**
c) Standard Operating Procedure
d) Setting Out Point.

SOR
[LUL] Station Operations Room.

SORA
(*sore-ah*) See **Signal Over-run Risk Assessment**.

SORAT
Signal Overrun Risk Assessment Tool, See **Signal Over-run Risk Assessment (SORA)**.

Sorbite
Finely dispersed iron carbide within normal iron, produced either by the quenching of **Austenite** or by tempering **Martensite**. In steel, this structure is associated with good strength and toughness. See also **Sandberg Process**.

Sorting Sidings
Sidings used to permit the formation of vehicles into **Trains** and to re-distribute vehicles between Trains. Also **Marshalling Sidings**.

SOS
a) Single Option Selection
b) Secretary of State (for Transport)

SOT
a) [PW] Speed-Off Tamp. See **Follow up Tamp** (FUT)
b) Stoke-on-Trent.

SOTF
Switch **o**n **t**o **F**ault; a protection function intended to immediately trip a **Circuit Breaker** (**CB**) if it is closed onto a circuit that already has a fault.

Source Record
[Sig.] The version of the **Signalling** design records that does not have certification on it (a "**Clean Copy**") that is copied to make the **Production Copies**. Source Records are normally negatives or CAD files. See also **Master Record**. See also **National Records Group** (**NRG**).

South Central
(Tradename) [Hist.] A former **Train Operating Company** (**TOC**).

South West Trains
(Tradename) A **Train Operating Company** (**TOC**) which operates trains from London Waterloo to Woking, Basingstoke, Southampton, Portsmouth, Exeter, Reading, Bournemouth and Weymouth.

Southall Accident
On the 19th September 1997 a **High Speed Train** (**HST**) passed one or more **Signals** showing a **Stop Aspect** and collided with an aggregate **Train** that was being crossed in front of the HST. The **Automatic Train Protection** (**ATP**) and **Automatic Warning System** (**AWS**) equipment on the **Passenger Train** were both defective. Seven **Passengers** lost their lives in the crash and ensuing fuel fire. See also **Ladbroke Grove**, **Uff-Cullen Inquiry**.

Southeastern Trains (SET)
(Tradename) A **Train Operating Company** (**TOC**) which operates all the services in the south east London suburbs, the whole of Kent and part of Sussex, which are primarily commuter services to/from central London

Southern
(Tradename) A **Train Operating Company** (**TOC**) which operates predominantly commuter services between London, Surrey and Sussex, services to Gatwick, Milton Keynes and Brighton, and South Coast services.

Southern Measurement Train (SMT)
[NR] The sister train to the **New Measurement Train** (**NMT**) based in the Southern **Territory**. It is a Eurailscout UFM160 unit capable of recording at 100mph.

Southern Railway (SR)
[Hist.] One of the **Big Four** □ **Railway Companies** following **Grouping**.

Southern Region (SR)
[BR, NR] The geographical division of **British Railways** responsible for southern England, and then a similar organisation in **Network Rail** (**NR**).

SOVRN
See **S**uicides and **O**pen **V**erdicts on the **R**ailway **N**etwork Project.

SOWC
[Sig.] **S**hows **O**ccupied **W**hen **C**lear, a common **Track Circuit** (**TC**) fault. See also **Right Side Failure** (**RSF**), **SCWO**.

SoWoS
(*soe-woss*) (Tradename) [PW Hist.] An **Alumino-thermic Welding** process for **Low Carbon Austenitic Manganese Steel** (**LCAMS**) □ **Rail**.

SOYSPAD
(*soy-spad*) See **S**tarting **O**ff **Y**ellow **S**ignal **P**assed **a**t **D**anger.

SP
a) [NR] On a sign forming part of a **Non-standard Differential Speed Restriction**, it indicates that this value apples only to **Sprinter** (**Class** 15x) **Diesel Multiple Units** (**DMU**) and other similar types of **Train** (such as Class 16x, 17x), where authorised
b) See **Signal Post**
c) **S**ingle **P**hase.

SPA
a) **S**cheme **P**erformance **A**ssessment
b) **S**pecial **P**rotection **A**rea.

Space
[Sig.] On a **Lever Frame**, the gap left when a **Lever** is removed and the function is no longer in use.

Spacer Block
See **Heel Block**.

Spacia
(Tradename) A company specialising in the development and rental of unused space in buildings and **Structures** (e.g. **Viaduct** □ **Arches**) forming part of **Operational Land**.

Spacing
[PW]
a) See **Sleeper Spacing**
b) See **Respacing**.

SPAD
(*spad*) See **S**ignal **P**assed **a**t **D**anger.

SPAD Alarm
[Sig.] An audible and visual alarm in a **Signal Box** to alert the **Signaller**, arising from a **Train** passing a **Signal** at **Danger**. See **Signal Passed at Danger**.

SPAD Category
Signal **P**assed **a**t **D**anger Category.
a) [NR Sig. Hist.] SPADs were previously categorised according to the cause:
Category A - any SPAD that occurs at a correctly displayed **Stop Aspect** due to driver error and time was available to stop at the **Signal**
Category B - any SPAD which occurs when a Stop Aspect is displayed as a result of failed **Signalling** equipment or **Signal Reversion**, which the driver may or may not have time to react to correctly
Category C - any SPAD which occurs because the Signal was made to display a **Stop Aspect** in an emergency, and insufficient time was available to bring the Train to a stop at the Signal
Category D - when an unattended Train or vehicles, without a **Traction Unit** attached, **Run Away**. If the vehicles **Run Away** as a result of an improperly controlled **Propelling** operation, then this is a Category 'A' SPAD.
This grading system has been replaced by the **SPAD Severity Ranking**, which measures the outcome.
b) [LUL Sig.] **London Underground** still use the A-D

ranking given above, with the A category further split into A1 to A4 according to how much blame is attached to the driver (1 being all of it, 4 being very little).

SPAD I
[Sig.] **Signal Passed At Danger** Indicator, see **SPAD Indicator**.

SPAD Indicator
(*spad indicator*) [Sig.] A **Signal**, placed **Beyond** a critical **Main Signal**, which is only **Lit** when the associated Signal is **Passed At Danger** (**SPAD**). It displays only a **Red Aspect** and has a blue and white striped **Backboard** to differentiate it from other Signals in the same area.

SPAD Latch
(*spad latch*) [Sig.] A **Control** applied to certain other **Signals** protecting a **Junction**, which **Replaces** them to **Danger** in the event that a **Train** passes a particular Signal showing a **Stop Aspect**. This action helps to reduce the likelihood that a **Signal Passed at Danger** (**SPAD**) will result in a collision.

SPAD Severity
SPAD Severity Category
SPAD Severity Ranking
[NR] A risk ranking for the outcome of a **SPAD**:
- Category 1 - an **Overrun** of less than 25 **Yards**, Train remains within **Signal Overlap**, no damage, injuries or **Fatalities**
- Category 2 - an Overrun of between 26 and 200 Yards, Train remains within Signal Overlap, no damage, injuries or Fatalities
- Category 3 - Overrun greater than 200 Yards or Train exceeds Signal Overlap, no damage, injuries or Fatalities
- Category 4 - Overrun resulting only in damage to **Track** and no injuries or Fatalities
- Category 5 - Overrun resulting in **Derailment** and no injuries or Fatalities
- Category 6 - Overrun resulting in a collision and no injuries or Fatalities
- Category 7 - Overrun resulting in injuries but no Fatalities
- Category 8 - Overrun resulting in Fatalities.

This system replaced the previous **SPAD Category** system, which recorded the cause.

Spade
[Col.] An alternative name for a **Shovel**.

Spade Ended Steel Sleeper
[PW] A type of **Steel Sleeper** where the ends of the trough section have been flattened and bent downwards to present a large surface area to the **Ballast**. This form is a development of the **Crimp Ended Steel Sleeper** and represents the current standard.

SPADMIS
(*spad-miss*) **S**ignal **P**assed **a**t **D**anger **M**anagement **I**nformation **S**ystem.

SPADRAM
(*spad-ram*) [NR] **S**ignal **P**assed **a**t **D**anger **R**eduction **A**nd **M**itigation Group.

SPADWEB
[NR] A web-based SPAD forum, now replaced by **OPSWEB** (http://www.opsweb.co.uk/).

Spalling
a) [PW] The breaking out of the surface of a **Rail** in flakes due to the propagation of shallow sub-surface cracks
b) [Civ.] The separation of pieces of concrete from a concrete structure as a result of the concrete deteriorating due to weathering, temperatures or pressure.

Span
[Civ.] A subdivision of a **Bridge Deck**, being that part between an **Abutment** and an adjacent **Pier**, between two adjacent Piers or between the two Abutments.

Spandrel
Spandrel Wall
[Civ.] The approximately triangular wall which occupies the space above the **Arch** or Arches of an **Arch Bridge**.

Span-wire
[LR] A type of Overhead Line Equipment (**OLE**) support structure where the **Contact Wire** (**CW**) is suspended via a **Delta Suspension** and **Registration Arm** from a single transverse wire which is attached at either end to buildings or structures.

SPARCS
Stored **P**rogramme **A**utomatic **R**emote **C**ontrol **S**ystem.

Spare Lever (S)
[Sig.] In a **Lever Frame**, a Lever which is not used for the operation of any **Signalling Equipment**. The opposite is a **Working Lever**. See also **Lever Worked To Maintain Locking**.

SPARK
An interactive world wide web based tool (http://www.sparkrail.org/) provided for the **Rail Industry** by **RSSB** to share information and help drive innovation. SPARK is now being developed in partnership with UIC and the **IRRB**.

Sparkler
[Col.]
a) [PW] Nickname for the igniter used in **Alumino-Thermic Welding**
b) An **Electric Train** using **Conductor Rails**.

Sparky
[Col.]
a) [PW] Nickname for a **Mobile Flash Butt Welder** (**MFBW**)
b) Nickname for any **Electric Locomotive**.

SPAS
[LR] See **Signal Passed At Stop**.

Spate
Spated
(*spayte, spay-ted*) {possibly Speed Previously Advised Terminated Early}. A **Temporary Speed Restriction** (**TSR**) where the **Warning Indicator** (**WI**), **Speed Reminder Signs**, **Speed Indicator** (**SI**) and **Termination Board** (**T Board**) have been erected, but the restriction does not apply, either because it was not imposed or is no longer required. The boards must be erected and removed as published in the **Weekly Operating Notice** (**WON**), but the actual restriction does not have to be shown. A Spated **Commencement** indication is a diagonal black band on a yellow background, see **Spate Indicator**.

Spate Indicator
[NR] A **Lineside Sign** consisting of a diagonal black band on a yellow background which indicates the start of a **Temporary Speed Restriction** (**TSR**) that has not been imposed or has been removed early. See **Spated**.

SPC
a) **Station** Pedestrian Crossing
b) [LUL] See **Site Person in Charge**.

SPC-G
An acronym denoting a **Station** Pedestrian Crossing (a **Footpath Crossing** at a **Station**) equipped with unlocked **Gates** on both sides of the **Track**.

SPC-GL
An acronym denoting a **Station** Pedestrian Crossing (a **Footpath Crossing** at a **Station**) equipped with **Gates** on both sides of the **Track** that are locked by the **Signaller** or **Crossing Keeper** prior to the approach of **Trains**.

SPC-GMSL
An acronym denoting a **Station** Pedestrian Crossing (a **Footpath Crossing** at a **Station**) equipped with unlocked **Gates** and **Miniature Stop Lights** (**MSL**) on both sides of the **Track**.

SPC-MSL
An acronym denoting an un-gated **Station** Pedestrian Crossing (a **Footpath Crossing** at a **Station**) equipped with **Miniature Stop Lights** (**MSL**).

SPC-Open
An acronym denoting a **Station** Pedestrian Crossing (a **Footpath Crossing** at a **Station**) with no **Gates** or **Miniature Stop Lights** (**MSL**).

SPD
Sustained Planned Disruption.

Special
[Col.] Contraction of **Special Train**.

Special Crossing Reminder Appliance
[Sig.] A device which has to be removed from a **Signal** switch for the Signal protecting a **Level Crossing** (**LC, LX**) before the switch can be operated.

Special Earthworks Examination
[NR Civ.] An out of course examination of an **Earthwork** undertaken where there is concern regarding its stability or following a failure.

Special Instruction Notice (SIN)
[NR Sig.] A document issued mandating a particular requirement for installation, **Commissioning** or **Maintenance** of a particular piece of **Signalling Equipment**. They are included in the suite of Network Rail Company Standards (**NRCS**).

Special Notice (SN)
See **Special Traffic Notice** (**STN**).

Special Operating Instruction (SOI)
[NIR] An instruction prepared to cover operation of a special vehicle, **Train** or other event which is issued for a specific occasion or series of events.

Special Running Notice
[IÉ] A weekly **Operating Publication** which gives details of all the planned variations from the **Working Timetable** (**WTT**).

Special Signal Sighting Committee (SSSC)
[Sig.] A **Signal Sighting Committee** (**SSC**) convened to review, discuss and make recommendations on the sighting of one or more **Signals** or **Indicators**, normally following an **Accident** or incident.

Special Speed Restriction Board (SSRB)
[NR Sig.] A **Lineside Sign** showing a St Andrew's cross, previously placed On the Approach to certain types of **Open Level Crossings** (**OC**). It gives the maximum **Permissible Speed** (**PS**) over the **Level Crossing** (**LC, LX**) concerned. They were sometimes preceded by an **Advance Warning Board** (**AWB**). Now superseded, see **Signs Related to Level Crossings**.

Special Traffic Notice (STN)
[NR Ops.] A weekly **Operating Publication** that gives details of all the planned variations from the **Working Timetable** (**WTT**). Also **Special Notice** (**SN**).

Special Train
[Ops.] A **Train** not shown in the **Working Timetable** (**WTT**) and Running under a **Special Traffic Notice** (**STN**). Commonly contracted to **Special**.

Specials
[Sig.] Within a **Solid State Interlocking** (**SSI**), these are directives in the **Geographic Data Language** that instruct the **Control Interpreter** to take pre-configured shortcuts when processing frequently occurring constructs.

Spectacle Glass
[Sig.] The **Red** (**R**), **Yellow** (**Y**) or **Green** (**G**) glass or plastic insert used in a **Semaphore Signal** to colour the light emitted by the **Signal Lamp**, and thus indicate the **Signal Aspect** to the driver during the hours of darkness.

Speed
[Col.] Contraction of **Temporary Speed Restriction** (**TSR**), as in "having to put a Speed on". See also **Slack**.

Speed Board
[Col.] Nickname for a **Speed Indicator** (**SI**).

Speed Code
[CT] A code transmitted to **Trains** by the Transmission Voie Machine (**TVM**) ▫ **Signalling System** indicating the maximum speed at which they are permitted to travel.

Speed Constraints Chart
Speed Constraints Diagram
A chart of speed verses **Mileage**, populated with constraints such as:
* Existing **Permissible Speeds** (**PS**)
* **Deceleration Distances** (**DD**) and **Signal Sighting** data for **Signals**,
* **Track Construction**, **Track Geometry** and **Track Quality** constraints, see also **Third Way**
* **Bridge** strength capabilities and **Route Availability** (**RA**) limitations
* **Station** locations
* **Overhead Line Equipment** (**OLE**) limitations, see **Wire Gradient**
* Substandard **Structure Clearances**

These charts are then used to identify potential improvements in **Permissible Speed** and to catalogue a scope of works. See **Journey Time Improvement** (**JTI**).

Speed Control After Tripping (SCAT)
[LUL] A system which ensures that a **Train** can only proceed at a slow speed for a defined period of time after **Tripping** past a **Signal** showing a **Stop Aspect**.

Speed Indicator (SI)
[NR] A **Lineside Sign** that marks the **Commencement** of a **Speed Restriction**, or displays the **Permissible Speed** (**PS**) or **Enhanced Permissible Speed** (**EPS**). See also **Permanent Speed Restriction** (**PSR**), **Temporary Speed Restriction** (**TSR**) and **Emergency Speed Restriction** (**ESR**). The colloquial alternative is **Speed Board**.

Temporary	Cut Out	Reflectorised

Speed of Divergence
The maximum permitted speed on a **Diverging Route**. See also **Turnout Speed**.

Speed Profile
a) A table showing changes in **Permissible Speed** (**PS**), **Enhanced Permissible Speed** (**EPS**) or both, together with the **Mileage** of each change
b) A graph representing the above.

Speed Restriction
Any imposed reduction of **Permissible Speed** (**PS**) or **Enhanced Permissible Speed** (**EPS**). There are three main types:
a) **Permanent Speed Restrictions** (**PSR**), imposed as a result of geometrical constraints
b) **Temporary Speed Restrictions** (**TSR**), imposed to protect **Trains** from poor **Track**, poor **Bridges** from **Trains** and staff from **Trains**
c) **Emergency Speed Restrictions** (**ESR**), to deal with the unplanned and unforeseen.
See also **Linespeed**.

Speed Set
[TRS] A system which can be engaged by the **Train** driver once a certain speed is reached and which will maintain that speed automatically by varying the **Traction Power** applied. It is analogous to 'cruise control' in a car.

Speed Supervision
[Sig.] Generically, any system which restricts over-speeding. See **Tilt and Speed Supervision System** (**TASS**) and **Train Protection and Warning System** (**TPWS**).

Speno
a) (Tradename) A manufacturer of **Railway** equipment. And the colloquial name for the **Rail Grinding Train** owned and operated by Speno.
b) A **Railway** ▫ **Telegraph Code** meaning "See special notice ... hence today".

Spent Ballast
[PW] **Ballast** that has been removed from under the **Track** because it is no longer able to adequately permit free drainage of rainwater or support the **Track**, due to small size or contamination. Also **Spoil**.

SPI
a) Sequence Position Indicator
b) Safety Performance Indicators.

SPICOP
[NR] Senior Person In Charge of Possession.

Spider
a) See **Impedance Bond**
b) See **Spider Plate**
c) [Col. prob. Obs.] The large four-legged handles used to tip **Mermaid** (**ZJV**) **Wagons**.

Spider Plate
a) [NR] A metal plate, often housed in metal box coloured red, used to form a common connection point for many **Bonds** in one place in a **Traction Current Return** system.
b) [LUL] Two busbars within a metal cabinet, provided where an electrical connection is made between the **Network Rail** (**NR**) Spider Plate and **London Underground** (**LU**) ▫ **Infrastructure**. The cabinet also contains equipment to monitor the current flow and voltage between the two systems.

Spigot
a) The non-socketed end of a pipe.
b) [TRS] A peg, in some cases retractable, used to retain **Containers** laterally on a **Wagon** deck. See also **Twistlock**, **Twistlock Fastening**.

Spike
[PW] Wrought iron parallel-sided fastenings, without screw threads, used to fasten **Chairs** for either **Double Headed Rails** (DH) or **Bull Head Rails** (BH) to **Wood Sleepers** during the mid to late years of the 19th century. Originally used in conjunction with Trenails and, later, **Chairscrews**. See **Trenail and Spike Fastening**. See also BR1 Spike, Dog Spike, Elastic Spike, Macbeth Spike

Spike Extractor
A tool specially designed to assist in the removal of **Spike Fastenings** such as **BR1 Spikes** and **Elastic Spikes**.

Spike Fastening
See BR1 Spike, Dog Spike, Elastic Spike, Macbeth Spike.

Spike Lock
[PW possibly Obs.] A metal liner used to maintain the tension and thus the **Toe Load** of **Elastic Spikes** in worn holes.

Spiking
[PW] A belt-and-braces method of securing a **Switch Half Set**, supported on **Timbers**, closed. It involves securing a **Fishplate** against the **Closed Switch** using two **Chairscrews** screwed into a **Bearer** near the **Switch Toe**. See also **Scotch**.

Spinnaker
(Tradename) A **Rail** □ **Container Terminal** operating system produced by Tideworks of Seattle, USA. It provides and enforces loading criteria to **Wagons** ensuring Container weights, heights en route, widths, **Dangerous Goods** barrier distances and load compatibility are maintained. The system provides an interface to **TOPS** for validation prior to Train dispatch detailing all the Wagon and Container positions along with Dangerous Goods information.

SPIR
Significant Performance Incident Review.

Splay
[PW]
a) An alternative for **Flare**
b) As a suffix to a description of a **Common Crossing**, a Common Crossing having a **Flare** in both **Wing Rails** at the **Crossing Heel** ends of the Wing Rails. This is the more normal variety. This type of Crossing is also called a **Flare**. See also **Parallel Wing** (PW), **Double Parallel Wing** (DPW).

Splice
[PW] The machined portion of the **Common Crossing Point Rail** and **Common Crossing Splice Rail** where the two **Rails** are fastened together to form a **Crossing Vee**.

Splice Rail
See Common Crossing Splice Rail.

Splice Rail Nose
[PW] The machined end of the **Head** of a **Common Crossing Splice Rail**.

Splice to Heel Check
[PW] A **Check Rail** tapered to fit into a **Switch Heel**.

Splicing
[PW] The action of joining two shorter **Switch and Crossing** (S&C) □ **Bearers** together end to end to make one long Bearer using a **Fishplate** secured with **Chairscrews** onto the upper surface of both Bearers. Banned for **Timber Bearers**, Modular S&C uses the method as standard with **Concrete Bearers**.

Split
[Ops.] To deliberately divide a **Train**.

Split Detection
[Sig.] An arrangement where separate **Switch Detection** is provided for each **Set of Switches** or **Point End** in a **Switch and Crossing Unit** (S&C Unit) with multiple **Switches** or **Point Ends**. This permits easy diagnosis of faults as the status of each detector is displayed separately. See also **Out of Correspondence**.

Split Switch
a) [PW] A type of **Switch** where the **Stock Rail Set** is divided equally between the **Stock Rails** of both Switch **Half Sets**. Also **Split Turnout, Symmetrical Switch, Y Turnout**.
b) [Ops.] A powered **Set of Switches** (Set of Points) that has been damaged by a **Train** □ **Running** through them in the **Trailing** direction when they were not correctly set. This generally results in a **Crippled Switch** Rail, bent **Stretcher Bars** and occasionally a **Derailed** Train
c) [Ops.] A Set of Switches that has been damaged by a Train Running through them in the **Facing** direction when the Switches were not fully **Thrown**, see **Splitting the Points**

Split Timbered

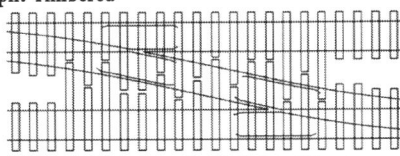

[PW] Describing a complex **Switch and Crossing Layout** (S&C Layout) where the **Bearers** or **Timbers** are discontinuous along their length to allow the use of shorter and more manageable pieces. See also **Break the Timbering**.

Split Turnout
A **Turnout** (**Single Lead**) where the **Main Line** and Turnout Route are the same Radius (**R**) and opposite Hand. Also **Y Turnout**.

Splitting Banner Repeater
Splitting Banner Repeater Signal
[NPT] See **Splitting Banner Repeating Signal**.

Splitting Banner Repeating Signal
[Sig.] A pair of **Banner Repeating Signals** provided On the Approach to a Junction **Signal** in order to reduce **Signal Sighting** problems by giving the driver advance notice of the presence of a **Stop Aspect**. One Banner Repeating Signal reproduces the **Main Route**, the other the **Diverging Route**.

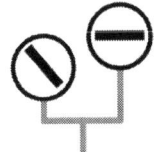

Splitting Distant Signals
Splitting Distants
[Sig.]
a) Two **Colour Light Signals** located adjacent to each other, giving the driver information about the state of the **Junction** □ Beyond the next **Signal**.
b) Two **Semaphore Distant Signals** located adjacent to each other, giving the driver information about the state of the Junction Beyond the next **Stop Signal**.

Splitting the Points
A situation where the left hand wheels go one way and the right hand wheels go the other at a **Set of Facing Points**:
a) As a result of poor **Maintenance** or mechanical failure
b) As a result making the **Movement** before the switches were fully **Thrown**.

SPM
Senior Project Manager.

SPMT
Self-propelled Modular Transporter.

Spoil
Material of no immediate use arising from construction or **Reballasting** works, including **Spent Ballast**.

Spoil Bank
See **Spoil Heap**.

Spoil Heap
A mound of generally unusable material produced during the construction or subsequent **Maintenance** of the **Railway**. Also **Spoil Bank**.

Spoil Tip
A designated location to which **Spoil Wagons** are taken for unloading.

Spoil Train
A **Train** of suitable **Engineering Vehicles** provided expressly for the purpose of conveying away **Spoil**. See also **Spoil Wagon**.

Spoil Wagon
A **Rail Vehicle** specifically constructed or adapted to transport excavated material. Varieties include ex-revenue **Mineral Wagons** with welded up doors to bespoke **Big Box** vehicles.

Spoon
[Col.] Nickname given to the **Class** 47 **Diesel Locomotive** due to the sound of their **Horn**.

Spoon Points
[PW Arch.] A means by which **Rail Vehicles** could access a **Siding** without the need for either **Switches** or a **Common Crossing** to be installed in the **Main Line**. The Spoon Point had a pair of independent **Turnout Rails** arranged so that they could be lifted onto the Rails of the Main Line, each having ramped ends at the **Switch Toe** end and one with a cut-out section at the **Crossing** position to allow the Rail to sit on top of the Main Line **Running Rails** See also **Non-intrusive Crossing System (NICS)**.

Spooner's Rail Joint
[PW Arch.] A four-hole **Rail Joint** for **Bull Head Rail** fitted with **Fishplates** each of which embrace the **Rail Web** and half of the **Rail Foot**. Devised by C E Spooner (1818 - 1889) and used on, among others, the Festiniog **Railway**.

SPORTIS
(*spor-tiss*) [BR] Super Portable Ticket Issuing System, a "luggable" device capable of managing the issuing of and payment for **Tickets** on the move, including processing credit and debit card transactions. It is a development of the **PORTIS** device. See also **APTIS**.

Spot Bid
[NR Ops.] A request for one or more **Train Paths** made by a **Train Operating Company (TOC)** after the **Timetable (TT)** is agreed.

Spot Moulds
[PW Col.] See **Step Moulds**.

Spot Resleepering
[PW] Replacing only those **Sleepers** which have decayed badly and were incapable of supporting the **Chairs** or **Baseplates**, especially at **Rail Joints**. See also 1 in x Resleepering, Patch Resleepering.

SPOTIS
Simplified Passenger Operated Ticket Issuing System.

Spotted Dick
[PW Col.] Alternative name for the Colour Coded Quality (**CCQ**) chart depicting **Track Quality** bands by **Eighth of a Mile**.

SPP
Sustained Poor Performance.

Sprag
[Col.] A stout stick placed through the spokes or holes of a **Wagon** wheel to ensure the vehicle does not roll away. The practice and thus the term is no longer in common use in this sense, but is used as a colloquial description of applying the brakes on or otherwise immobilising a **Rail Vehicle**.

Sprague, Frank Julian
(1857-1934) American pioneer of **Electric Traction** and designer of the first **Multiple Unit** control mechanism.

Spread Lens
[Sig.] A lens for use in a **Colour Light Signal** with a wide angle beam pattern rather than the near parallel beam of a normal lens. They are used to allow better **Sighting** when there are many different **Routes** converging at the **Signal**, or where a short range is required to reduce confusion with other Signals. See **Short Range Signal**.

Spreader Bar
[PW] A plate attached to the **Running Rail**, forming part of a **Rail Lubricator** assembly. Its purpose is to distribute the grease along the **Running Face** to be picked up by the passing **Wheel Flanges**.

SPRG
[Sig.] Signal Post □ Replacement Group.

Spring Buckle
[TRS] A retaining strap which wraps round the leaves of a **Leaf Spring** at the centre point.

Spring Clip
[PW]
a) A **Rail Fastening** made in the form of a shaped metal device secured to an ST **Baseplate** by an inverted T-headed bolt located into an integral socket in the casting.
b) [Col.] The collective term for any Rail Fastening system that relies on the spring action to perform its function.

Spring Crossing
See **Flexible Wing Crossing**.

Spring Hook Clip (SHC)
[PW Obs.] A type of self-tensioning **Rail Fastening** for **Flat Bottom Rail** (**FB**) consisting of a flat steel plate hooked in to two hoops cast into a **Concrete Sleeper**. The original rectangular SC3 clips date from 1958; the V-shaped type from 1964. Also known colloquially as a **Skull Hook Clip**, after one of the system's early champions, Jack Skull.

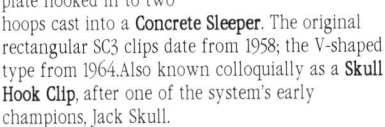

Spring Plank
[TRS] The transverse member in older **Bogie** designs, which was suspended from the **Bogie Side Frames** and carried the **Secondary Suspension**, in turn supporting the vehicle body. See **Swing Motion Bogie**.

Spring Points
Spring Switch
See **Train Operated Switch** (**TOS**).

Spring Tensioner
[Elec.] A device which uses a large spring and cam to auto-tension **Catenary Wires** and **Contact Wires** (**CW**) in an **Overhead Line Electrification** (**OLE**) system, providing the same tension across a wide temperature range. One such is the **Tensorex C** (Tradename).

Spring Wing Crossing
See **Flexible Wing Crossing**.

Springing
[Civ.] The junction between the inclined brickwork of the **Arch Ring** and the vertical brickwork of an **Abutment** or **Pier**. See also **Skew Back**.

Sprinter
The brand name of the **Class** 150 **Diesel Multiple Unit** (**DMU**). See also **Express Sprinter**, **Super Sprinter**.

SPS
a) See **Small Part Steel**
b) See **Signalling Power Supply**. See also **Principal Supply Point** (**PSP**).
c) Standby **Power Supply**.

SPT
a) See **Signal Post Telephone**
b) Standard **Pattern Timetable**
c) Strathclyde **Passenger Transport**. Also SPTA, SPTE.

SPTA
Strathclyde **Passenger Transport Authority** (**PTA**).

SPTE
Strathclyde **Passenger Transport Executive** (**PTE**).

SPU
Strategic Planning Unit.

Spuller
[PW Col.] A combined spanner and **Panpuller** for Pandrol **Rail Fastenings**, used by **Patrollers**.

Spur
a) Contraction of **Shunt Spur**, see **Shunt Neck**
b) [Sig.] In a **Track Circuit** (**TC**), a length of **Running Rail** that is electrically common to a **Series Bonded** □ **Rail**, but is not in series with it.

SPV
Special Purpose Vehicle. A private sector entity set up to fund a **Railway** □ **Infrastructure** enhancement project.

SPW
[NR] Under the **Bridge Condition Marking Index** (**BCMI**) handbook, shorthand for **Spandrel Wall**.

SPWEE
Safety Procedures for Working on Electrical Equipment.

Squadron Tamping
[NR] A method of improving the rate at which **Reballasted** □ **Track** is returned to **Design Level** and **Design Line**. Rather than have one **Tamping and Lining Machine** (**Tamper**), one **Ballast Regulator** (**Regulator**) and one **Dynamic Track Stabiliser** (**DTS**) making up to three passes through the site, up to three of each type of machine is run through once. A typical formation might thus be Tamper – Regulator – DTS – Tamper – Regulator – DTS – Tamper – Regulator. This method is only economic when on very long sites and where time is especially constrained. See also **Yellow Cavalry**.

Square
[PW]
a) At right angles to the centre line of the **Track**
b) A large tee square used to accurately position **Fishplated Rail Joints** and **Welds** (**W**) opposite Each other on **Curved Track**
c) Describing two related features on opposite **Rails** of the same **Track** but located at exactly the same position longitudinally.

Square Crossing
[PW]
a) A description of a **Common Crossing** where the intersecting **Tracks** do so at 90°, or nearly 90°
b) A term used to describe a **Switch and Crossing Layout** (**S&C Layout**) containing **Crossings** where the angle of intersection of the **Gauge Lines** is 90°, or nearly 90°.

Square Span
[Civ.] A **Bridge** that crosses the **Railway** at or very close to an angle of 90° to the centreline of the **Track**.

Square Wheel
[Col.] A **Rail Wheel** with one or more **Wheel Flats**.

Squaring
[PW]
a) Setting or re-setting **Sleepers** or **Bearers** to their correct orientation of right angles to the **Track Centre Line**. Sleepers have a tendancy to "walk" towards traffic about their high end on **Curves** as a result of the action of passing **Trains**. Also **Sleeper Squaring**
b) Using a large tee square to set out the positions of **Fishplated Rail Joints** in **Jointed Track** on Curves. See also **Short Rail**
c) Marking out the proposed positions of items such as Fishplated Rail Joints, **Switch Toes** and **Welds (W)** to ensure that they are at the same position longitudinally, see **Squaring Off**

Squaring Off
[PW] The process of ensuring that two features (normally **Fishplated Rail Joints**, **Switch Toes** and **Welds**) are directly opposite each other in the two **Rails** of the same **Track**. It is achieved either by using a **Square**, or by a simple application of Pythagoras' theorem. In the diagram A and B are the two joints. The dimensions in the table give the relevant pairs of measurements to ensure that A and B are Square to each other.

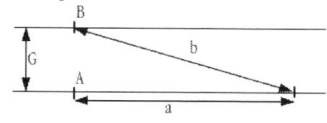

G, Gauge (mm)	a	b
4' - 8 3/8" (1432)	7' - 1" (2159)	8' - 6" (2591)
	11' - 7" (2531)	12' - 6" (2310)
	12' - 10" (3912)	13' - 8" (4166)
4' - 8 1/2" (1435)	10' - 7" (3226)	11' - 7" (2531)

Squat
[PW] A **Rail Defect** and form of **Rolling Contact Fatigue (RCF)** usually occurring as a result of a local **Track Defect**. Often accompanied by deformation of the **Running Surface** and **Shadowing**.

Squid (ZDA)
[NR] A 32 ton capacity **Open Wagon** used for the transportation of materials. See **Wagon Names**.

SR
a) [Sig.] **Slot** □ **Repeater**, an indication in the **Signal Box (SB)** of the status of a Slot
b) [Sig.] **Shunter's** □ **Release**
c) [Sig.] On a **Signalling Circuit Diagram**, denotes a wire coloured silver
d) [Sig.] Single **Rail**, see **Single Rail Track Circuit**, **Single Rail Bonding**
e) See **Staff Responsible Mode**.
f) Scotrail
g) See **Southern Railway**
h) See **Southern Region**
i) The **ATOC** code for **First Scotrail**

SR&EE
[NR] Senior **Renewals** and **Enhancement Engineer**.

SRA
See **Strategic Rail Authority**.

SRAWS
[Sig. Hist.]
a) **Signal** Repeating **Automatic Warning System (AWS)**
b) **Southern Region** Automatic Warning System, an improved version of AWS developed by the Southern Region of **British Railways (BR)**. It was capable of indicating all four **Main Aspects** of a **Colour Light Signal** to the driver, compared with the normal two. It was never widely adopted.

SRB
a) [Sig.] **Signal** Reminder Board
b) Short Rest Break.

SRCL
[Sig.] Short Range **Colour Light Signal**.

SRCT
a) Service Recovery Commencement Time
b) Southern **Region** □ **Control**.

SRE/PW
SRE/PW Drawings
[PW Hist.] Standard **Railway** Equipment, **Permanent Way**. Standard drawings for Bull Head (BH) □ **Track** components. Developed around 1927.

SRFI
Strategic **Rail** □ **Freight** Interchange.

SRG
Safety Review Group.

SRI
a) **Standard Route Indicator**. See also **Theatre Route Indicator**
b) [Hist.] **Signalling** Restructuring Initiative, an agreement which required **Signallers** to operate computer equipment not directly part of their signalling duties, and thus to operate **Electronic Train Reporting (ETR)** equipment.
c) **SPAD** Remove Inhibits.

SRM
See **Safety Risk Model**.

SRNTP
[NR] Southern **Region** New **Trains** Programme. A programme to replace **Mark 1 Rolling Stock** and strengthen **Traction Power Supplies**.

SRP
a) **Station** Regeneration Programme
b) System Review Panel
c) Safety Review Panel.

SRPSU
[NR] Southern **Region** Power Supply Upgrade.

SRRT
a) **SPAD** Risk Ranking Tool
b) Safety Risk Ranking Tool.

SRS
a) [NR] Strategic Route Section
b) Safety Responsibility Statement
c) System Requirements Specification
d) (Tradename) Swedish **Rail** Systems, a Swedish manufacturer of specialist **Railway** plant, particularly **Panel Lifting Equipment** and **Road Rail Vehicles**.

SRT
See **S**ectional **R**unning **T**ime.

SS
Strategic **S**ourcing.

SSA
a) See **S**elf-**s**upporting **A**nchor
b) [NR] **S**tation **S**pecific **A**nnexe.

SSAA
Static **Sandite** **A**uto-**a**pplicator, fixed Sandite dispensers operated by passing **Trains**.

SSADS
Signalling **S**chemes **A**sset **D**ata **S**tore, a database of the evolving signalling schemes.

SSC
See **S**ignal **S**ighting **C**ommittee.

SSCI
[Civ.] **S**oil **S**lope **C**onsequence **I**ndex.

SSD
a) [Sig.] **S**ubsystem for **SPAD** **D**etection, part of the IECC system
b) **S**olid **S**tate **D**isk.

SSDC
Signalling **S**ystems **D**irect **C**urrent.

SSF
a) See **S**ignal **S**ighting **F**orm
b) **S**tationary **S**peed **F**eature.

SSFTA
Subsystem **F**ault **T**ree **A**nalysis.

SSG
a) **S**afety **S**trategy **G**roup
b) **S**tandards **S**teering **G**roup
c) **S**tandards **S**trategy **G**roup, a body which provides a strategic overview of the development of UK **Railway** standards and their eventual alignment with **Technical Standards for Interoperability** (**TSI**) and Euro Norms (**EN**).

SSHA
Subsystem **H**azard **A**nalysis.

SSHI
See **S**oil **S**lope **H**azard **I**ndex.

SSI
See **S**olid **S**tate **I**nterlocking.

SSIC
[Sig.] **S**olid **S**tate **I**nterlocking **C**ontroller.

SSICA
[NR Sig.] **S**econdary **S**ignalling □ **I**nfrastructure **C**ondition **A**ssessment. See also **PSICA**, **SICA**.

SSIDES
[Sig.] **S**olid **S**tate **I**nterlocking **D**esign.

SSIDWS
[Sig.] **S**olid **S**tate **I**nterlocking **D**esign **W**ork**s**tations.

SsiFT
[Sig.] **S**ignal **S**ighting **F**orm **T**ool.

SSIHA
[Sig.] **S**ubsystem **I**nterface **H**azard **A**nalysis.

SSISIM
[Sig.] **S**olid **S**tate **I**nterlocking **S**imulator.

SSL
a) See **S**ignalling **S**olutions **L**imited
b) See **S**ub-**s**urface **L**ines
c) [TRS] **S**hort **S**wing **L**ink **B**ogie.

SSM
Station **S**tewardship **M**easure.

SSMS
Site **S**pecific **M**ethod **S**tatement.

SSO
[Ops.] **S**pecial **S**top **O**rder. An instruction to a driver requiring them to stop at a specified location or make a **Station Stop** not normally in the **Timetable**.

SsoW
See **S**afe **S**ystem **o**f **W**ork.

SSOWP
Safe **S**ystem **o**f **W**ork **P**lanner.

SSOWPS
See **S**afe **S**ystem **o**f **W**ork **P**lanning **S**ystem.

SSP
a) See **S**ignalling **S**upply **P**oint
b) See **S**ignalling **S**cheme **P**lan
c) **S**tatic **S**peed **P**rofile
d) **S**tandard **S**ignalling **P**rinciple.

SspaM
(*spam*) [NR] **S**trategic **S**ignal **S**pacing **M**odel.

SSR
a) See **S**teel **S**leeper **R**elaying
b) **S**trategic **S**ub-**R**oute.

sSRA
[Hist.] **S**hadow **S**trategic **R**ail **A**uthority, the title given to the **Strategic Rail Authority** (**SRA**) in the interim whilst the relevant legislation was ratified by parliament. When it gained its powers, the 'shadow' and the leading 's' were dropped. The SRA has now been absorbed into the Department for Transport (**DfT**) and the **Office of the Rail Regulator** (**ORR**), this latter organisation in turn replaced by the **Office of Rail Regulation** (**ORR**).

SSRB
See **S**pecial **S**peed **R**estriction **B**oard.

SSRS
a) **S**ub-**s**urface **R**ailway **S**tation.
b) **S**ub-**s**ystem **R**equirements **S**pecification.

SSSC
See **S**pecial **S**ignal **S**ighting **C**ommittee.

SSSI
Site of **S**pecial **S**cientific **I**nterest.

SSTD
[Sig.] **S**olid **S**tate **T**rain **D**escriber (**TD**).

SSTIS
Small **S**tation □ **T**icket **I**ssuing **S**ystem.

SSV
a) **S**ystem **S**afety **V**alidation
b) **S**taff **S**ervice **V**ehicle.

SSWT
Stagecoach **S**outh **W**estern **T**rains. See **South Western Trains**.

ST
Stop and Telephone.

St. Andrew's Cross
A warning sign provided on the highway at **Open Level Crossings** (OC). See **Special Speed Restriction Boards** (SSRB).

St. George's Cross
See **Advance Warning Board** (AWB).

Stabled

Stabling
The temporary storage (parking) of **On Track Machines** (OTM), **Rail Vehicles** and **Trains** whilst they are not in use, typically overnight, or until needed next. The vehicles are placed out of service, made inaccessible to the public and usually have all systems on them switched off.

Stabling Light
[LUL] A red light placed on the end of a **Train** to mark the Train's position when **Stabled**.

Stabling Point
A generic term for any facility used for **Stabling** purposes.

Stabling Sidings
Sidings predominantly used for **Stabling** purposes.

STABS
[BR Hist.] **S**ignalling and **T**elecommunications **A**rea **B**udget **S**ystem.

Staff
See **Train Staff**. See also **Token**.

Staff and Ticket Working
[Sig.] A variation on **Staff Working** where a driver not taking the **Train Staff** (or **Token**) through the **Section** takes a written **Ticket** completed by the **Signaller** as authority to proceed. This method may be applied when two or more **Trains** must follow each other in the same direction. Only the Signaller in possession of the Train Staff may issue Tickets. Before the direction of traffic can be reversed the Staff must be transported to the other end of the Section by the last Train.

Staff Instrument
[Sig.] A device used to automatically control the issuing and return of **Train Staffs**.

Staff Responsible Mode (SR)
[Sig.] Under the **European Rail Traffic Management System** (ERTMS), an operational mode that allows a driver to move a **Train** under their own responsibility in an ERTMS equipped area, but only:
a) When the **Signalling System** is unable to issue a **Movement Authority** (MA).
b) When authorised by the **Signaller** to use the override function on the **Driver Machine Interface** (DMI) unit in the **Driving Cab**.
c) When a Train is "awakening" at a location which is invalid or unknown to the system.

Staff Working
[Sig.] A method of operating a **Railway** where the **Movement Authority** is given in the form of a special **Train Staff**. A driver may not enter the **Section** unless they are in possession of the Train Staff. See also **Staff and Ticket Working**.

Stage
A discrete task or step within a larger scheme, generally representing a change to the **Signalling** or **Operational Layout**. See **Stageworks**, **Staging**.

Stage Plans
See **Stageworks Plan**.

Stagework Joint
[Sig.] An **Insulated Rail Joint** (IRJ) provided for the duration of a temporary situation during **Stageworks**.

Stageworks
a) A method of implementing major changes in small steps, each step being a complete task. Often these tasks are carried out at weekends in **Possessions**, with **Trains** □ **Running** relatively normally during the weeks between.
b) A task that requires alterations to the **Signalling** or **Operational Layout**, see **Stage**.

Stageworks Plan
[Sig.] A **Signalling Scheme Plan** (SSP) detailing the alterations to be carried out within one **Stage**.

Stagger
a) The amount by which two related items on opposite **Rails** are offset along the **Track**, e.g. **Fishplated Rail Joints**, **Knuckles** (KN), **Switch Toes**, **Welds**. Also **Lead**.
b) [PW] The difference in levels between the two **Low Rails** of adjacent **Tracks**. See also **Plane of the Rails**
c) [PW] The difference in levels between the **Planes of the Rails** of adjacent **Tracks**, see **Track Stagger**
d) [Elec.] The offset of the **Contact Wire** (CW) from the **Track Centre Line** at a **Registration Point** in an **Overhead Line Electrification** (OLE) system. Such Staggers are normally alternated on **Straight Track** (**Tangent Track**) to avoid wearing a notch into the **Carbons** of the **Pantographs**. On **Curves** the Stagger tends to be always to the outside of the curve, with the **Mid-span Offsets** (MSO) arranged to be on the inside throughout
e) [Sig.] The phase or polarity difference between one **Track Circuit** (TC) and the next.

471

Stagger Change

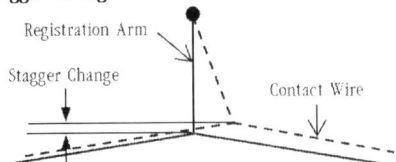

[Elec.] The amount by which the designed **Stagger** of a **Contact Wire** (**CW**) changes at a **Registration Point** as a result of thermal expansion and contraction in the Contact Wire. As the Contact Wire moves longitudinally, it pulls the **Registration Arms** round, changing their effective length.

Stagger of Knuckles

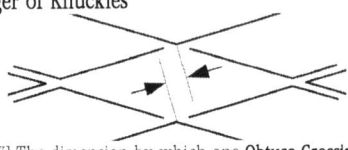

[PW] The dimension by which one **Obtuse Crossing** leads another in order to maintain the correct **Gauge** on both **Routes** through a **Diamond Crossing**.

Staggered Joint

[PW] A pair of **Fishplated Rail Joints**, in opposite **Rails** of the same **Track** and nearly but not quite opposite each other.

Staggered Platforms

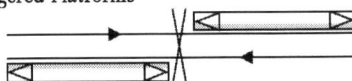

An arrangement of **Station** □ **Platforms** where the Platforms are not placed opposite each other, but are often on opposite sides of a **Level Crossing** (**LC**, **LX**). By placing the Platform **Beyond** the Level Crossing, a **Train** will come to a stand clear of the highway, allowing the **Gates** or **Barriers** to be opened to road traffic sooner.

Staging

The process by which a major **Remodelling** or **Resignalling** project is broken down into smaller items of work, generally to ensure maximum continuity of service in the process. Each **Stage** may have its own **Signalling Scheme Plan** (**SSP**), known as a **Stageworks Plan**. The preparation of a **Staging Book** also allows the various parties to check that all the contracted works are included and no abortive work is planned. A large scheme may have hundreds of distinct Stages.

Staging Book

A document containing individual explanations of the **Stages** of a staged project. The presentation is normally in the form of a series of coloured diagrams showing the work in each **Stage**, one per page, with notes on times, plant, **Engineering Trains** and work content. See **Staging**.

Staging Joint

See **Stagework Joint**.

Stainless Steel Deposit

[LUL] Alternative term for **Track Circuit Continuity Welding**. Also **Eutectic Strip**, **Rumble Strip**, **Zigzag Welding**, **Zigzagging**.

Staircase of Speeds

See **Cascade**.

Staith

An alternative term for a **Coal Drop**.

Stakeholders

Collective term for all those with a commercial, engineering, financial or regulatory interest in a project. Typically this will include the client, **Depot Facility Operators** (**DFO**), **Freight Operating Companies** (**FOC**), Her Majesty's Railway Inspectorate (**HMRI**), Station Facility Owner (**SFO**), Station Operating Companies (**SOC**), Department for Transport (**DfT**), **Territory** □ **Asset Stewards** and **Train Operating Companies** (**TOC**).

STAMP

a) [NR] Structures Asset Management Plan
b) [NR] Signalling Tools and Methods Programme.

Stanchion

a) [Elec.] A colloquial alternative for the upright part(s) of any **Overhead Line Structure**
b) [TRS] A removable vertical bar on the side, end or in the centre of certain flat **Wagons** to assist in preventing the load sliding off. See also **Bolster**.

Standage

The amount of space a facility such as a **Loop** or **Platform** has to accommodate **Trains**. See also **Standard Length Unit** (**SLU**).

Standard

a) See **Railway Group Standard** (**RGS**)
b) See **Network Rail Company Standard** (**NRCS**)
c) See **Standard Class**.

Standard Alphanumeric Route Indicator (SARI)

A full-size **Alphanumeric Route Indicator** (**ARI**), see also **Miniature Alphanumeric Route Indicator** (**MARI**). Previously called a **Theatre Route Indicator** and **Multi-lamp Route Indicator** (**MLRI**), both terms are now obsolete. See also **Fibre Optic Route Indicator** (**FORI**).

Standard Class

The modern name for **Second Class**, the minimum comfort mode of **Passenger** travel available by **Train** with the possible exception of standing up, see **Passengers in Excess of Capacity** (**PIXC**).

Standard Deviation (SD)

The statistical measure used for quantitative analysis of **Track Recording** data, normally calculated per **Eighth of a Mile**. See **High Speed Track Recording Coach** (**HSTRC**) for a description of the measurements taken.

Standard Differential Speed Restriction
[NR] A Permanent Speed Restriction (PSR) with two values. The top figure (normally the lower value) applies to Freight Trains, e.g. Classes 4, 6, 7 and 8, and the bottom (normally the higher value) applies to Passenger Trains. There are three main reasons for the imposition of this type of restriction:
a) A Bridge with poor strength, where the reduced speed is governed by the strength of the structure. See Route Availability Value (RA Value)
b) A High Cant Deficiency Curve (HCD Curve), where the reduced speed is governed by the upper limit of Cant Deficiency (D) for Freight Vehicles
c) The Signalling System does not provide sufficient Braking Distance (BD) or Deceleration Distance (DD) for Freight Trains
See also Non-standard Differential Speed Restriction. Referred to as "top over bottom", in the example shown this would be "50 over 75". Also Differential Speed Restriction (DSR).

Standard Differential Warning Indicator
[NR] A Lineside Sign provided to give drivers advance notice of a Standard Differential Speed Restriction. The top figure (normally the lowest value) applies to Freight Trains, e.g. Classes 4, 6. 7 and 8, and the bottom (normally the highest value) applies to Passenger Trains. The Warning Indicator (WI) must show the same information as the related Speed Indicator (SI).

Standard Gauge
[PW] The Gauge of the Track as determined by the Railway Regulation (Gauge) Act 1846. Prior to the introduction of Flat Bottom (FB) □ Continuous Welded Rail (CWR) it was 1435mm, (4' - 8 $^1/_2$"). It then changed to 1432mm, (4'- 8 $^3/_8$") and has now reverted back to 1435mm (1438mm in track laid with CEN60 rails) between Running Edges (RE). See also Cape Gauge, Narrow Gauge, Broad Gauge.

Standard Gauge Railway
A Railway whose Running Rails are spaced at the Standard Gauge of 4' - 8 $^1/_2$" (1435mm). See also Narrow Gauge Railway, Broad Gauge Railway.

Standard Gauge Track
Track laid to the Standard Gauge determined by the Railway Regulation (Gauge) Act 1846.

Standard Indicator (SI)
[Sig.] An Alphanumeric Route Indicator (ARI) meeting the requirements of Performance Category 2 for Readability. See also Miniature Indicator (MI).

Standard Length Unit (SLU)
A common unit of measurement for Train length, one SLU being 21 feet (6405mm). See also Extra Length Unit (ELU).

Standard Loading Gauge
See Standard Vehicle Gauge.

Standard Quota Assessment
[NR] A tool developed by the National Safety Improvement Team that describes the factors known to contribute to Signaller workload and helps create a profile as to how much multi-tasking the Signaller is managing.

Standard Rail

Standard Rail Length
[PW] The longest length of Rail that can be loaded onto Rail Vehicles at the manufacturers' premises and transported to site. Historically this was 18.288m (60 feet), but is now 36.576m (120 feet). Also Length, Rail Length.

Standard Route Indicator (SRI)
See Theatre Route Indicator, see also Standard Indicator (SI).

Standard Short Rail
[PW] A Rail whose length is less than a Standard Rail but is otherwise specified, e.g. 59' - 9" (18.212m), 59' - 6" (18.136m). These rails are used to reduce the Stagger of the Fishplated Rail Joints on Jointed Track on Curves, as the inside Rail is shorter.

Standard Weld
[PW Col.] An unofficial term used to describe the Thermit □ SkV-F □ Weld, whose welding gap is 22 to 24mm.

Standards
a) See Railway Group Standards (RGS)
b) See Network Rail Company Standards (NRCS).

Standback
See Signal Standback.

Standing Off
Describing a Switch Rail that is not quite fully closed up to its associated Stock Rail. This may be because:
- It has not been manufactured correctly
- It has been badly handled during delivery and / or installation
- Accumulations of foreign matter such as Ballast, coal dust, leaves, grease or Snow has become trapped in the opening
- Poor Maintenance has allowed excessive play in the Switch Operating Mechanism
- The Switch Tip has become deformed and is holding the rest of the Switch Rail away
- The Switch Rail or Stock Rail has Lipping
- The Switch Rail is Crippled

STANOX
[NR] Station identification numbers used in TOPS. These codes can also refer to non-Station locations such as Sidings and Junctions. STANOX codes are grouped by geographical area - the first two digits specify the area in which the location exists; e.g. 30xxx covers Blackpool, Preston, Euxton, Balshaw Lane and Lostock Jn.

Stansted Express
(Tradename) A Train Operating Company (TOC).

Staplehurst Accident
On 9th June 1865 a Gang of men were changing Rails between Trains on the small Beult Viaduct near Staplehurst. Their Protection of the Line was inadequate and a Boat Train ran into the Work Site, killing 10 Passengers and injuring 49. Amongst those narrowly escaping injury was the author Charles Dickens.

STAR
Signalling and Telecommunications Asset Register.

Star Clip
[Hist.] A clip, which did not self-tension, used to attach a vehicle to an Under-rope Haulage wire rope. Also Smallman Clip.

Star Crack
[PW] A Fatigue Crack in a Rail originating at and propagating radially away from a Fishbolt Hole. The incidence of these cracks can be lessened by Cold Expanding of Bolt Holes (CX) and identified by increased inspection using Ultrasonic Rail Flaw Detection (URFD).

Star Track
[NR] A Permanent Way design apprenticeship scheme.

Starfer
(Tradename) A manufacturer of Railway plant based in Italy. Also a colloquial name for the Single Line Spoil Handling System (SLSHS), which they built.

Starfish (ZCO)
[NR] A drop side Open Wagon used for the transportation of Ballast and Sleepers. See Wagon Names.

StARlink
St Andrews Rail Link Campaign.

Starter

Starter Signal
[Sig. Col.] Term for a Section Signal. Also Starting Signal.

Starting Against Signal Signal Passed at Danger (SASSPAD)

Starting Against Signal SPAD
[Ops.] A sub-classification of Signal Passed at Danger (SPAD) where the driver moves off from rest despite the presence of a Stop Aspect. This type of SPAD most frequently occurs in Stations, where the Buzzer Signal from the Guard or Conductor becomes mistakenly associated with moving off. Such an error is also known as Ding Ding and Away.

Starting Off Yellow Signal Passed at Danger (SOYSPAD)

Starting Off Yellow SPAD
[Ops.] A sub-classification of Signal Passed at Danger (SPAD) where the driver moves off from rest through a Yellow Aspect (Caution Aspect) and runs through the next Signal showing a Red Aspect (Stop Aspect).

Starting Signal
[Sig.]
a) In Absolute Block, a Stop Signal □ Beyond, and worked from, a Signal Box. If no Advanced Starting Signal is provided, it is the Section Signal.
b) See also Platform Starter, Platform Starting Signal.

Static
Not moving, not under load. The opposite in this sense is Dynamic.

Static Analysis
a) An analysis undertaken on an object or system that is at rest.
b) In terms of Pedestrian Flow, an analysis of capacity against relevant standards undertaken using simple calculations.

Static Brake Test
[TRS] A test conducted on the braking system of a stationary Train, after the Train has been formed and prior to it leaving that location.

Static Crosslevel
[PW] The difference in vertical level between the two Running Rails when there is no Train present on the Track. See also Dynamic Crosslevel.

Static Envelope
[TRS] The sectional outline of a Rail Vehicle when it is at rest, unladen, on straight and level Track, with no allowances of any kind added. See also Kinematic Envelope (KE), Swept Path, Thrown Envelope.

Static Gauge
a) See Static Track Gauge
b) See Static Gauging.

Static Gauging
[PW] A method of producing an approximate Kinematic Envelope (KE) by adding an allowance to the Static Envelope in defined areas. C1 is an example of this approach. This means that a vehicle with the appropriate Static Envelope should be Clear on any Route designed to accommodate the appropriate approximate Kinematic Envelope, as the allowances do not depend on the characteristics of the vehicle itself. This method errs very much on the side of caution, and it has been superseded by Kinematic Gauging in the drive for ever larger Vehicle Gauges.

Static Level
[PW] The level of a Rail of a Track when not under load from Trains. See also Dynamic Level.

Static Load Gauge
[PW] An alternative term for Static Envelope.

Static Offset
[Elec.] A Mid-span Offset (MSO) measured under windless conditions.

Static Track Gauge
[PW] The Gauge of the Track, measured when no Trains are present. See also Dynamic Track Gauge.

Static Twist
[PW] **Twist** measured when no **Trains** are present. The opposite and more useful measure is **Dynamic Twist**.

Static Vehicle Gauge
[Hist.] The profile of a **Rail Vehicle** at rest, taken at right angles to the longitudinal axis of the vehicle. See also **C1, C1A, C2, C3**.

Station
A specially constructed structure solely intended to facilitate the **Boarding** and **Alighting** of **Passengers**. The minimum provision is therefore just a **Platform**; however a Station this small would generally be called a **Halt**. Typically, stations also have access to the public highway and some form of shelter. Historically, some Stations dealt solely with loose **Goods** traffic, and these were known as **Goods Stations**.

Station Adoption Scheme
[NR] A scheme under which the community takes an active part in the management and or maintenance of their local **Station**. There are two main models (with frequent overlaps):
- 'Adopt a Station' schemes run by **Train Operating Companies** (**TOC**), where Station 'monitors' report problems to the TOC on a regular basis
- **Friends of Stations** - where groups undertake a wide variety of activities, ranging from providing comments to Station enhancements such as gardens and planters, cycle racks through to art work and signage.

Station Box
a) [Civ.] On a **Railway** built below ground, this is the large, typically reinforced concrete, hollow box-like structure which houses a **Station**.
b) [Sig.] A **Signal Box** located at a **Station**, one of the terms sometimes used to differentiate between the many Signal Boxes found at complex **Junction Layouts** in the days of **Mechanical Signalling**.

Station Category
A ranking arrangement for **Stations** on the **National Railway Network** (**NRN**):

No.		Description	Usage
A	25	National hub	>2m
B	66	Regional interchange	>2m
C1	275	Important feeder (city)	0.5-2m
C2		Important feeder (other)	
D	302	Medium staffed	0.25-0.5m
E	675	Small staffed	<250k
F1	1,192	Small unstaffed (basic)	<250k
F2		Small unstaffed (low usage)	<100k

Station Change
[NR] The formal procedure by which **Network Rail** agrees alterations to **Station** facilities with the operator and users of that **Station**. See also **Network Change**.

Station Concourse
The circulation area of a **Station**, generally forming a link between the **Platforms**, **Booking Hall** and main entrance. Major **Terminal Stations** tend to have large, spacious concourses.

Station Envelope
[LUL] The area from the **Hindwall** to the **Headwall** of the same **Station** including space enclosed by the operational boundary and any structure that forms part of, or is integral to the Station complex and is directly accessed from the Station. Where the platforms at a Station are staggered, the station area will be taken at right angles from each Headwall and Hindwall to a centre line

Station Grounds
[LUL] The **Track** at **Stations**, between **Tunnel Headwalls** in Tube Line sections and between the ends of **Platforms** elsewhere.

Station Limits
a) [NR] The section of **Line** between the **Home Signal** and the **Section Signal** for the same Line controlled by the same **Signal Box** (**SB**). It is the area where **Shunting** may safely take place. The term does not apply on Lines signalled by **Track Circuit Block** (**TCB**), only **Absolute Block** (**AB**). Station Limits exist in such circumstances whether there is a **Station** at the location or not
b) [LUL] The section of Line that includes the Station **Platform** and the length of a **Train** either side of it.

Station Pilot
[Col.] An alternative term for a **Shunting Locomotive** normally used in a **Station**.

Station Stop
[Ops.] Describing the action of bringing a **Train** to a stand at a **Station** in order that **Passengers** may **Alight** or **Board**. See also **Booked Call, Calling, Pick Up Only, Platform Work, Set Down Only**.

Station Throat
Describing the division of **Running Lines** into the **Platform Lines** at one or both ends of a **Station**. These sites are usually constricted, producing complex **Junction** arrangements. See also **Pinch Point**.

Station Train Radio
[LUL] A radio system with limited range used by **Station** staff.

Station Working
[Hist.] Special instructions pertaining to the **Working** of **Trains** at larger **Stations** which included the use of **Permissive Working** and **Calling-on Signals**.

Station-related Level Crossing
A **Level Crossing** (**LC, LX**) which forms a means for accompanied or non-accompanied **Passengers** (or members of public) to cross between **Platforms** or to access the Platform from the road (or car park) or vice versa. Such a Crossing may be of any type, but staff-only Crossings are excluded, see **Barrow Crossing**.

Statutory Hydraulic Boiler Test
[TRS] A pressure test carried out at around 130% of normal working pressure prior to first use, following repairs and at regular intervals thereafter.

STC
See **Single Track Cantilever**.

ELLIS' BRITISH RAILWAY ENGINEERING ENCYCLOPÆDIA

Steady State Maintenance
The policy of carrying out just sufficient work to keep a system in the same overall condition it was when the policy began. See also **Maintenance Holiday**, **Reactive Maintenance**, **RT1A**.

Steam Brake
[TRS] The **Service Brake** on a **Steam Locomotive**, operated by steam from the boiler acting on a piston which applies brake blocks to the wheel treads via rodding. On ex-**GWR** ▫ **Passenger** ▫ **Locomotives** the Steam Brake is controlled via the driver's **Vacuum Brake** control valve.

Steam Heat
Steam Heating
[TRS] A heating system for **Passenger Coaches** that used steam generated by the **Locomotive**. Whilst steam was plentiful during the era of the **Steam Locomotive**, the new **Diesel Locomotives** and **Electric Locomotives** were fitted with a boiler to provide the steam supply. Steam Heating has been replaced on modern Trains by **Electric Train Heating** (ETH), running off generators or transformers in the Locomotive.

Steam Locomotive
[TRS] A **Locomotive** that uses steam to provide the **Tractive Effort**. The steam is generated by heating water in a boiler using coal, oil, wood or peat. The water and fuel is carried either on the Locomotive or in a dedicated **Tender** permanently coupled to the Locomotive. See also **Fireless Locomotive**, **Steam Turbine Locomotive**.

Steam Traction
[TRS] A **Motive Power Unit** or **Traction Unit** which utlises steam as its source of power.

Steam Turbine Locomotive
[TRS Hist.] A **Locomotive** utilising steam to power a steam turbine. This turbine drove the driving wheels through a reduction gearbox.

Steel Key
[PW] A **Key** manufactured from spring steel intended for use in **Bull Head** (BH) ▫ **Chairs** as a replacement for the traditional **Wood Key**. See also **Panlock Key**.

Steel Relay
[PW] An item of work including **Complete Renewal** of the **Track** with **Steel Sleepers** (and new **Rail**, but not necessarily including **Reballasting**). See **Steel Sleeper Relaying** (SSR).

Steel Sleeper
[PW] A **Sleeper** manufactured, currently, from a C-shaped rolled steel section. The **Sleeper Ends** are turned down to provide **Lateral Resistance** (LR) and **Housings** for **Rail Fastenings** added to complete the product. Types include **Crimp Ended Steel Sleeper**, **Spade Ended Steel Sleeper**, **W400**, **W600**. Also **Tin Sleeper**.

Steel Sleeper Evolution
Steel Sleepers are not a recent invention; by the late 1920s there were at least six different types of steel sleeper for **Bullhead Rail** (BH) in use;
a) Francis Webb's, in which the 'chair' components of the **Sleeper** were fabricated from sheet steel and attached to the Sleeper by means of rivets
b) Rafarel's patent, a two-piece cast iron **Chair**, one side of which hooked into the upper surface of the Sleeper, the other side being secured by, presumably, a bolt
c) Sandberg's patent in which the **Chair Jaws** were pressed upward from underneath the Sleeper
d) Harvey's patent in which each Chair was secured to the Sleeper by a projection pressed upward at one end of the Chairs plus two clips spot-welded to the Sleeper at the other
e) Guest Keen and Nettlefold's (GKN's) patent in which the two Chairs were cast onto the upper surface of the Sleeper
f) Unit; a one piece casting of Sleeper and Chairs.

Steel Sleeper Relaying (SSR)
[PW] The wholesale replacement of the existing **Sleepers** with new **Steel Sleepers** on a particular **Track**. The use of Steel Sleepers also generally indicates that the existing **Ballast** will be **Scarified** and re-used, although new **Continuous Welded Rail** (**CWR**) is normally included in the scope of works. The absence of **Re-ballasting** means that this type of work is relatively fast and outputs of the order of 400 metres (440 **Yards**) per shift can be obtained.

Steelwork Only
[PW] A **Switch and Crossing Layout** (S&C Layout) provided by a manufacturer where only the **Switches**, **Crossings**, **Check Rails** and **Closure Rails** are supplied.

Steeple Coping
[Civ.] A **Parapet Coping** with an isosceles section, fitted to **Parapets** over **High Speed Lines** fitted with **Overhead Line Electrification** and intended to prevent climbing of the **Parapet Wall**.

STEF
Signalling & Telecommunications (S&T) Engineering Forum.

STELLA
Support the East Lancashire Line Association.

Stencil Indicator (SI)
[Sig. Obs.] A variety of **Alphanumeric Route Indicator** (ARI) that utilises a backlit stencil and frosted screen to display the characters. As they are of low luminous intensity, they are generally used for slow speed **Routes** such as **Shunt Routes**. Formally a **Miniature Alphanumeric Route Indicator** (MARI), true Stencil Indicators are no longer fitted new.

Stent Sleepers
[PW Obs.] Reinforced, neither pre-stressed nor post-tensioned, **Concrete Sleepers** developed to compensate for the shortage of **Wood Sleepers** during the second world war. The tendency for the **Sleepers** to crack soon after installation prompted the development of pre-stressed Sleepers in 1942.

ELLIS' BRITISH RAILWAY ENGINEERING ENCYCLOPÆDIA

Step Gauge
See **Stepped Gauge**.

Step Moulds
[PW] Sand moulds used in an **SkV** type **Aluminothermic Welding Process**, designed to accommodate various amounts of differential **Headwear** or **Rail Wear** between the two **Rails** being joined. The colloquial term **Spot Moulds** comes from the marking system used to identify the amount of wear each one is designed to accommodate: one spot is up to 3mm, two spots is up to 6mm and three spots indicates that the mould will deal with up to 9mm difference in wear.

Step Plate Junction
[Civ.] An instantaneous change in the diameter of a **Tunnel**. The **Headwalls** and **Hindwalls** of **Tube Stations** are examples.

Step Rail
[Obs.] A very early type of **Embedded Rail** briefly used in early **Tramways**. The vertical step presented a serious hazard to other highway users and was rapidly replaced by the **Grooved Rail**.

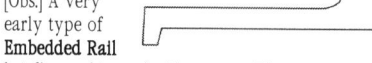

Step *x*
Step *x* Braking
See **Braking Steps**.

Stephenson Gauge
[Col.] Alternative term for **Standard Gauge**, 4' - 8 $^{1}/_{2}$" (1435mm).

Stephenson, George
(1781-1848) born in Wylam, Northumberland. A self-educated son of a colliery fireman, George rose to be Enginewright at Killingworth Colliery. Hearing of the work done by **Hedley** and **Hackworth** at Wylam Colliery, Stephenson convinced his manager to allow him to develop a **Steam Locomotive**. The 'Blucher' was the first truly successful **Locomotive** to use **Adhesion** alone. After building the Stockton and Darlington, his company's Locomotive 'Rocket' won the **Rainhill Trials** and Stephenson went onto build the Liverpool & Manchester, Manchester & Leeds, Birmingham & Derby, Normanton & York and Sheffield & Rotherham **Railways**. He is erroneously named "The father of Railways", when in fact much development work was done prior to his involvement. It would instead be fair to describe him as a principal developer of Railways.

Stephenson, Robert
(1803-1859) son of **George Stephenson**. Joining his father in the family **Steam Locomotive** business, Robert went on to be appointed chief engineer of the **London** & Birmingham **Railway**, as well as designing **Bridges** and Railways all over the world.

Stepped Fishplate
[PW] Alternative name for a **Lift Fishplate**. Also **Jump Fishplate**.

Stepped Gauge
A measuring device with one straight edge and a series of steps cut into the other, each one creating a known dimension to the long straight edge. Typical increments are single millimetres (for use with **Sidewear Gauges**) and $^{1}/_{4}$" (5-6mm) for use with **Crosslevel Gauges**. Also **Chicken Ladder**.

Stepped Weld
[PW] A **Weld** made between **Rails** of the same **Rail Section**, but of different depths. This occurs where old Rail meets new Rail. See **Step Moulds**. A Weld made between dissimilar Rail Sections is called a **Composite Weld**.

Stepping
[Sig.] The process by which a **Train Reporting Number** is moved from one **Berth** to the next in a **Train Describer** (**TD**) system. See **Train Describer Stepping**.

Stepping Distance
The distance between the outer edge of a **Platform** and the nearest edge of the step or floor of a **Passenger Vehicle**. The **Railway Group Standards** (**RGS**) state that the distances between the **Platform Edge** and the floor or step should not exceed 250mm vertically, 275mm horizontally, and 350mm on the diagonal. This in turn places constraints on the curvature of Platforms; see **Centre Throw**, **End Throw**. Compliance with the Stepping Distance requirements can be incompatible with **Structure Clearances** for certain types of **Train**.

STEPS
(*steps*)
a) A **Track Access** charging system for **Freight** which generates rates for **Freight** services
b) (Tradename) A computer application produced by Mott MacDonald Limited for modelling **Passenger Flow** and behaviour in **Stations** and other public places. See also **Fruin**, **Legion**.

Stevens Rail
[Col. Hist.] Alternative term for **Flat Bottom Rail** (**FB**) coined after Col. Robert L. Stevens, president of the Camden and Amboy Railroad, commissioned **Rails** of this pattern from mills at Dowlais in the UK. The Rails were delivered to the US in May 1831. See also **Vignoles Rail**.

Stewardship
The management of an asset by designating lead responsibility to an individual.

477

Stewarton Accident
At 06:12 on 27th January 2009 the last six **Tank Wagons** □ **Derailed** as a 10 **Wagon** □ **Train** crossed a metal **Underbridge** south of Stewarton, Ayrshire The **Bridge** collapsed and the Derailed Wagons overturned. A large quantity of diesel oil and kerosene leaked from four of the Derailed Wagons. The collapse was discovered to be a result of un-noticed corrosion of and later failure of the east and centre **Main Girders**, and incorrect assumptions made during previous **Structure Assessments**.

STEX
Stansted Express.

Stick
a) [Sig.] A term sometimes used to describe a **Signalling Function** that stores the status of **Points** or **Signals**, often until instructed to forget, See also **Signal Stick**. Also **Latch**, see **SPAD Latch**.
b) See **Stick and Bubble**
c) [Sig. Col.] term for a **Signal**, particularly on LUL □ **Lines**.

Stick and Bubble
[Col.] A primitive **Crosslevel** constructed using a plank of wood approximately 2 to 2.5m (6' - 6" to 8') long and a spirit level, used during **Reballasting** works to provide an approximate depth guide to excavator drivers. The board is placed on the nearest **Rail** of the adjacent **Track** and levelled. The appropriate depth is then measured below the other end, adjusted according to the design levels. See **Differences, L, Relatives**. They have been partially superseded by the use of **Laser Levelling** equipment, but remain as the back-up system in times of poor visibility and / or equipment failure. Also **Board and Bubble**.

Stiff
[PW Col.] Describing a section of **Track** that has a **Rail Level** higher than that intended by the designer. Also **High**. The opposite is **Low**. See also **Knob, Slack, Swag**.

Stillage
[PW]
a) A short length of **Serviceable** □ **Track** or a purpose designed framework placed at the side of the Track and used to deliver, store and collect items of specialised engineering plant such as **Jacker Packers** and **Permaquip Trolleys**
b) Historically a prepared level area used for the assembly of **Plain Line** □ **Track Panels**. This was often itself a Track Panel, as these make an ideal surface on which to assemble further Track Panels.

Stingray (YGA, YGB)
[NR] A **Seacow** (**YGA, YGB**) fitted with a generator, allowing it to power the lights fitted to some Seacow and **Sealion** (YGN) □ **Ballast Hopper** □ **Wagons**. See **Wagon Names**.

Stirrup Frame
Stirrup Signal Frame
[Sig. Obs.] A very early (c. 1840) type of **Frame** where the Semaphore Signals were actuated by the **Signaller** depressing a stirrup-shaped pedal to which the **Signal Wire** was connected.

Stitch Wire
[Elec.] A V-shaped **Conductor** suspended from the **Catenary Wire** at **Registration Points**, which in turn supports the **Contact Wire** (**CW**) or **Intermediate Catenary Wire** in earlier equipment.

STK
STkm
Single **Track** kilometres

STM
a) Specific Transmission Module
b) Special Transmission Module
c) Single Track Miles.

STN
See **Special Traffic Notice**.

STO
a) See **Semi-automated Train Operation**
b) Semi-automatic Train Operation
c) Senior Technical Officer, a **British Railways** (BR) grade. See also **Draughtsman**.

Stoat
[Col.] A person whose singular focus on a particular hobby (e.g. **Railways**) often leads to other peripheral activities (e.g. bathing, laundry, shaving, etc.) being severely neglected or abandoned altogether.

Stoat's Nest Accident
At 16:30 on 29th January 1910 a **Passenger Train** □ **Derailed** at speed as it passed through Stoat's Nest **Station** (later renamed Coulsden) on the London, Brighton and South Coast **Railway** (**LB&SCR**). Five **Passengers** on the **Train** and two on the **Platform** were killed, and 65 were injured, eight seriously. The cause was determined to be one wheel shifting outward on its axle, causing it to ride up the **Running Face** of the **Rail** at a **Junction**.

Stock
Collective term for all **Rail Vehicles**, often prefixed with a term identifying a sub-grouping. These may include **Departmental**, diesel, electric, engineering, **Freight, InterCity, Multiple Unit**, and **Passenger**. Also **Rolling Stock**.

Stock and Crew Change
[LUL] The exchange of **Traincrew** and **Rolling Stock** between two **Services** such that each set of Rolling Stock assumes the identity of the other Service.

Stock Book
A publication containing lists of **Rail Vehicle** identification numbers.

Stock Rail
[PW] The fixed **Rail** in a **Switch Half Set**. The other Rail is the **Switch Rail**. Also **Back Rail**.

Stock Rail Bolt
[PW] The bolt which secures the **Stock Rail** to a **Slide Baseplate** or **Slide Chair**. See also **Slide Baseplate Distance Block, Slide Baseplate Jaw Block, Slide Chair, Slide Chair Distance Block**.

Stock Rail Front
[PW] The full and correct term for the **Fronts** of a standard **Set of Switches**, being the length of **Stock Rail** that projects beyond the **Switch Toe**.

Stock Rail Set
[PW] The lateral angle through which a **Stock Rail Front** is turned to produce the **Turnout** side **Stock Rail**. It is this that determines the **Hand** of a **Switch**.

Stone
[Col.] A description of **Ballast**.

Stone Block Sleeper
[PW Hist.] A stone block, typically of granite, measuring approximately 450mm x 450mm x 300mm deep (18" x 18" x 12") and used to support the frequent **Rail Joints** found on early **Plateways** and **Railways**. Each **Rail** is supported independently with no **Gauge Retention** facility. Whilst this allowed horses to walk easily in the **Fourfoot**, the system fell out of favour with the introduction of heavier **Locomotives** and subsequent increases in speeds.

Stone Faiveley
(Tradename) [Elec.] A manufacturer of **Pantographs**.

Stone Guard
[TRS] A five-piece fibreglass plate, retrofitted with plastic plates on the leading edge, installed under the **Bogies** to enhance the protection of the **Tilt System** on **Class** 221 **Voyager** □ **Trains** from flying **Ballast**

Stoneblower
[PW Col.] Common (and descriptive) term for a **Pneumatic Ballast Injection Machine**, an **On Track Machine (OTM)** that automatically lifts and aligns the **Track** before carrying out the **Stoneblowing (Pneumatic Ballast Injection (PBI))** process. Similar in concept to an **Automatic Tamping and Lining Machine (Tamper)**.

Stoneblowing
[PW Col.] A development of **Measured Shovel Packing (MSP)**, in which the **Track** is raised to the desired position and chippings are blown into the space produced under the **Sleepers**. This process has the major advantage that the existing **Ballast Pyramid** is not disturbed, resulting in far better results than can be achieved by any other method. Stoneblowing has been mechanised and automated in the form of the **Stoneblower** (formally, a **Pneumatic Ballast Injection Machine**). The technical term for the process is **Pneumatic Ballast Injection (PBI)**.

Stop
See **Stop Aspect**.

Stop and Caution
[Ops.] The action of stopping a **Train** and relaying specific instructions to the driver regarding potential obstructions, or a requirement to examine the **Line**.

Stop and Proceed
[Ops.] A **Degraded Mode** of **Train** operation where, under certain failure conditions, a **Train** detained at an **Automatic Signal** is permitted by the **Signaller** to pass the **Signal** at **Danger** at low speed, ready to stop at the next **Signal**. See also **Talking Past**

Stop Aspect
[Sig.]
a) A **Colour Light Signal** displaying a **Red** light (or no light at all)
b) A **Semaphore Stop Signal** with its **Arm** horizontal.

Stop Block
[Col.] An alternative term for a **Buffer Stop**. Sometimes contracted to **Block**.

Stop Board
Stop Indicator
A **Lineside Sign** instructing a driver to stop. The sign often carries additional instructions such as "... and await instructions" or "... and telephone". See also **SAI**, **ST**.

Stop Loop
[LR] A **Track** based receiver that detects a manually initiated signal from a **Tram** and initiates a **Signalling System** sequence.

Stop Order
[ops.] A formal written instruction issued to a driver, requiring them to stop their **Train** at a specific location, typically to allow **Engineering Staff** to **Alight**.

Stop Over Distant

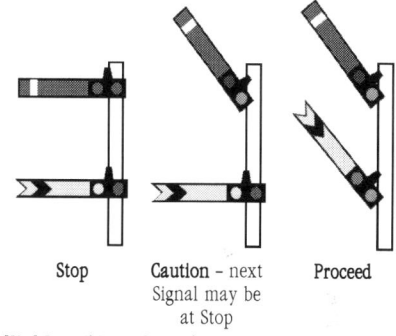

| Stop | Caution – next Signal may be at Stop | Proceed |

[Sig.] Describing a **Semaphore Signal** which has a **Stop Signal** mounted above a **Distant Signal** (typically controlled by the next **Signal Box**) on the same post. A mechanical arrangement called **Slotting** prevents a **Red** Stop Signal from being displayed above a green Distant Signal.

Stop Signal
[Sig.] A **Signal** capable of showing a **Stop Aspect**. Thus also applied to any Signal actually showing a Stop Aspect at that time.

Stopping Train
[Ops.] A **Passenger Train** timetabled to stop at every **Station** along a **Route**. Also **All Stations**, **Local Passenger Train**, **Parliamentary Train**, **Parly**. See also **Express Train**, **Semi-fast Train**.

Stops
[Col.] Contraction of **Buffer Stops**, as in "On the Stops".

STOPS
Signalling and Telecommunications Out-turn Processing System.

ELLIS' BRITISH RAILWAY ENGINEERING ENCYCLOPÆDIA

Storage Sidings
Sidings used for the long term Stabling of Rail Vehicles awaiting their next potential use. Also Stabling Sidings.

STORM
Support the Oldham, Rochdale and Manchester Rail Lines.

Stott Report
Following the accident at the Automatic Open Crossing Remotely Monitored (AOCR) at Lockington on 26th July 1986, the Department of Transport commissioned a review of Automatic Open Level Crossings. It appointed Professor P F Stott to carry out an independent review of their safety. In his report (Automatic Open Level Crossings, a Review of Safety, Report by Professor P F Stott CBE FEng; HMSO, ISBN 0-11-550831-7) Stott concluded that in collisions, road fatality rates appeared to be directly related to Train speed and Rail fatality rates were one-sixth of the road rate, based on the figures for the previous ten years. The report concluded that pedestrian fatalities at Automatic Open Crossings were not a significant problem, with none killed in the preceding ten years. The report recommended that the conditions for Automatic Open Crossings should be such that the predicted fatality rate for each Crossing should be less than one in a hundred years, similar to the rate at Automatic Half Barrier (AHB) Crossings. This was to be achieved by placing limits on the Permissible Speed (PS) dependent on the road and Rail traffic levels (the Traffic Moment), modified to take account of the effect of the non-linear relationship between accident probability and road traffic levels (known as the Effective Traffic Moment). The higher the Effective Traffic Moment, the lower the Permissible Speed (PS) over the Crossing. 80% of then-current AOCR failed to meet the criteria. The majority were fitted with Half Barriers and became Automatic Barrier Crossings Locally Monitored (AHCL) types.

Stovepipe
[Elec.] A vertical tubular structural member used in Overhead Line Electrification (OLE) □ Portal Structures.

Stow Position
[LUL] The position of the Traction/Brake Controller (TBC) in which it is placed fully inside the arm of the Train Operator's seat.

Stowell's Diamond
[Sig.] A Swinger used in non-Catch Handle Locking □ Lever Frames.

Stowmarket Control
[Sig.] An arrangement where a Strike In is provided 125m away from a Manually Controlled Barrier (MCB) Level Crossing where the Protecting Signal is closer than 50m, so that a Train can approach the Signal and start the Level Crossing Sequence but the Barriers do not fall until the Signaller activates them. This stops road traffic but means that the Signaller can stop the Level Crossing Sequence if he confirms that the Train has stopped at the Protecting Signal. A Timed Release may be provided where the Signaller cannot do this by observation.

STP
See Short Term Planning.

STP EDI
See Short Term Planning – Electronic Data Interface.

STPE
Signalling and Telecommunications Programme Engineering, the successor to SNWPT since the 2003 reorganisation.

STPR
Strategic Transport Programme Review.

STR
Special Train Reminder.

Str.
Shorthand for Straight Track.

Straddle Switches
Straddle Trap Points
Straddle Traps
See Wide to Gauge Trap Points. See also Trap Points.

Straight Air Brake
[TRS] A brake system which acts only on the Locomotive wheels and not on the rest of the Train at all. Also Direct Brake.

Straight Cut Switch
[PW]
a) A Switch assembly in which a Joggled (stepped) Stock Rail accommodates the Rail Head of the Switch Rail. Also Joggled Switch.
b) A Switch assembly in which the Rail Foot of both the Switch Rail and Stock Rail are both cut vertically to allow the Switch Rail to close up to the Stock Rail.
See also Chamfered Switch, Inset Switch, Undercut Switch.

Straight Fishplate
[PW] A Fishplate used to join two Rails of identical Rail Sections and identical Rail Depths together.

Straight Planed
Straight Planed Switch

A Switch that contains straight planed Switch Rails: that is, the Running Edge (RE) of the Switch Rail is straight throughout the length of the Head Planing, seen in plan. See also Curved Planed Switch.

Straight Post Signal
[Sig.] Describing a **Signal** mounted on a single straight vertical post. See also **Gantry Signal**, **Offset Signal**.

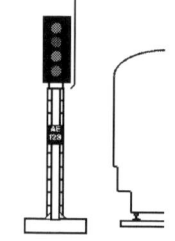

Straight Road
[Col.] A term for the **Route** through a **Junction** when all the **Points** are **Normal**. This is not necessarily the straightest **Track Alignment**.

Straight to Curve Transition
[PW] A **Curve** of uniformly varying Radius (**R**) connecting a straight (infinite Radius) to a **Circular Curve** or vice versa. In the illustration, R is the Curve Radius, L is the length of the **Transition Curve** and S is the **Transition Shift**.

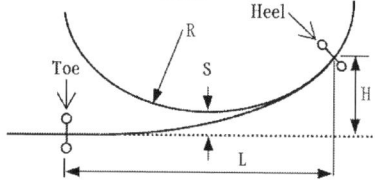

H is 4S for a **Cubic Parabola** and 6S for a **Bloss Spiral**. See also **Transition Length**, **Curve to Curve Transition**.

Straight Track
Track laid in a straight line, or as near to as straight line as to be treated as such. Also referred to as **Tangent Track**. For Track design purposes, a **Curve** with a Radius (**R**) of greater than 112.5km is considered Straight.

Straight-Ahead Route
The non-diverging (and usually the fastest) **Route** from a **Junction Signal**.

Straight-ahead Route
[Sig.] The non-**Diverging Route** and typically the fastest **Route** from a **Junction Signal**. See also **Turnout Route**.

STRAIT
(*strate*) [PW] Straightening of **Rail** □ **Welds** by Automated Iteration Techniques; a converted **Tamper** used for **Rail Joint Straightening** work.

Strap Out
Strapping Out
[Sig.] Describing the activity of temporarily connecting together terminals in the wiring of a **Signalling System** in order to bypass a **Signalling Function**, typically **Points Detection** or a **Track Circuit (TC)**. See also **Frig**, **Minimum Works Alteration (MWA)**.

Strap Rails
[PW] The two short lengths of **Rail** laid in the **Fourfoot** of **Adjustment Switches** and secured to the four **Bearers** with **Chairscrews**. Their purpose is to maintain the correct Bearer spacing as the Rails move longitudinally, but they also provide additional vertical stiffness at the overlap of the Rails, avoiding a potential point of weakness.

Strapman
Strapmen
[LUL] Term used to describe the staff responsible for applying **Short Circuiting Straps**.

Strategic Freight Network (SFN)
As part of its high level strategy to address the growing demands on the network for moving **Passengers** and **Freight**, the **DfT**'s July 2007 White Paper 'Delivering a sustainable **Railway**' proposed the development of a Strategic Freight Network in England and Wales. The SFN's objectives are :
- Allowing longer and heavier trains
- Providing efficient operating characteristics on **Freight Routes**
- 7-day and 24-hour capability on Freight Routes
- Provision of **W12** □ **Loading Gauge**
- Provision of a **UIC GB+** (or 'European') **Gauge** freight link to the rest of the UK network
- New Freight capacity
- **Electrification** of Freight Routes
- Strategic **Rail Freight** interchanges and terminals
- A strategic Freight capacity initiative

Strategic Materials
Materials which are of importance to the **Railway** industry and must not be disposed of. Generally this description applies to obsolescent **Signalling Equipment**. See **Strategic Spares**.

Strategic Rail Authority (SRA)
[Hist.] The Strategic Rail Authority came into being on the 1st February 2001 following the passage of the Transport Act 2000. Prior to this date it operated under the title **Shadow Strategic Rail Authority (sSRA)**. In January 2002 it published its master plan, setting out the strategic priorities for the **National Railway Network (NRN)** over the next 10 years. The SRA was tasked with delivery of this plan, in particular the key targets of 50% growth in passenger traffic, 80% growth in freight moved and a reduction in London area overcrowding. As well as providing a direction for the NRN, the SRA had responsibility for consumer protection, the development of **Freight**, **Freight Grants**, and for guiding investment projects aimed at improving and expanding network capacity. It was also responsible for managing franchises for **Passenger** services. Latterly, the SRA was disbanded, with safety matters moving to the **Office of Rail Regulation (ORR)** plus a new body called **Rail Safety and Standards Board (RSSB)** (now just called RSSB), and money matters coming under control of the Department for Transport (**DfT**).

Strategic Spares
Redundant equipment, normally **Signalling Equipment**, which is recovered and retained for refurbishment and re-use elsewhere. See also **Strategic Materials**.

Stray Current
[Elec.] That fraction of the **Traction Current** that is not collected by the **Traction Current Return** system and instead leaks to the nearest grounded conductor nearby. This can cause electrochemical corrosion of the grounded conductor, unwelcome if this is a gas pipe. A combination of insulating materials and collection mats are used to control the problem.

STRC
a) Scottish **Track Renewals Company** (TRC)
b) Southern **Track Renewals** Company.

Street Running Track
Street Track
A form of **Track Construction** specifically designed for integration into highway carriageways. Such systems typically utilise a **Grooved Rail**, some form of elastomeric embedment and a substructure compatible with road pavement systems. Particular issues include skid resistance, surface water drainage and **Stray Current** precautions on systems with **DC Electrification**.

Strengthened
[PW] A prefix added to descriptions of **Switch and Crossing Layouts** (**S&C Layouts**) (e.g. Strengthened Switch Diamond) to indicate that they are reinforced for welding into **Continuously Welded Rail** (**CWR**). Such strengthening includes the addition of **Back Rails**, **Stress Transfer Blocks**, etc.

Stress Condition
[PW] The description of the value of the **Stress Free Temperature** (**SFT**) of a length of **Continuous Welded Rail** (**CWR**), as in correctly **Stressed Rail**, **Overstressed Rail** or **Understressed Rail**. It also includes the actual SFT of the **Rail**, as in "**Stress Free** at 31°C".

Stress Free
[PW] Describing a **Rail** that is in a neutral state, neither in tension nor compression. See also **Natural Stressing**.

Stress Free Temperature (SFT)
[PW] The **Rail Temperature** at which there are no compressive or tensile forces in a section of **Continuous Welded Rail** (**CWR**). In the UK in the open air this is 24°- 27°C. See **Natural Stressing**, **Restressing** and **Stressing**.

Stress Graded
[Elec.] A term referring to the bend applied to electrical components that are live at 25kV and positioned close to earthed equipment, such as **Bridge Arms**. The radius reduces the likelihood of electrical arcing across the smaller air gap.

Stress Naturally
See **Natural Stressing**.

Stress Restoration
[PW] The operation of **Stressing** a **Continuous Welded Rail** (**CWR**) to restore the **Stress Free Temperature** (**SFT**) that existed before work took place. It is generally only used where the physical length and duration of the works is short, such as replacing failed **Insulated Rail Joints** (**IRJ**) or removing **Defective Rails**.

Stress Transfer Block
[PW] A **Heel Anchor Block** which is used to transfer **Thermal Stresses** between **Switch Rail** and **Stock Rail** in **Switch and Crossing Layouts** (**S&C Layouts**) used in **Continuous Welded Rail**. RT60 designs do not have Stress Transfer Blocks as standard on **Switches** longer than B.

Stress Transition Length
[PW] The length of **Track** at the end of a section of **Continuous Welded Rail** (**CWR**) adjacent to **Adjustment Switches** throughout which the stress may vary from that of the adjoining **Track** to that of the **Stressed Rail**.

Stressed
Stressed Rail
[PW] A length of **Continuous Welded Rail** (**CWR**) (excluding any **Stress Transition Lengths**) that has been tensioned to, or the **Fastening Down** was carried out at, a temperature of between 24 and 27°C (75 to 80°F) and **Welded**, or joined with **Tight Joint Fishplates**. Stressed Rail should only be cut using a gas torch to avoid the danger of the **Rail** catching and shattering the blade of a Disc Saw. Whilst also used to describe CWR that has been Fastened Down at lower or higher temperatures, these should more correctly be called **Understressed Rail** and **Overstressed Rail** respectively. See also **Blue Item**, **Red Item**.

Stressing
[PW] The act of tensioning **Continuous Welded Rail** (**CWR**) so as to ensure it is free of stress at a particular (higher) **Rail Temperature**. This temperature is known as the **Stress Free Temperature** (**SFT**) and is normally 24 to 27°C (75 to 80°F). The method of tensioning normally used is by **Rail Tensors**, though other methods such as **Natural Stressing** and **Rail Warmers** exist. The terms Destressing, Restressing and Stressing are used interchangeably, but Destressing is not a preferred term.

Stressing Certificate
[PW] The certificate completed and signed by the person responsible for the **Stressing** work, detailing the location, **Line**, **Mileages**, **Pull Length**, **Rail Temperature**, **Calculated Extension**, **Actual Extension**, **Pull Force**, pressure gauge readings, etc.

Stressing Diagram
Stressing Plan
[PW] A scale drawing showing which **Rails** are to be **Stressed** between which limits and in which order.

Stressing Naturally
See **Natural Stressing**.

Stressing Point Weld
[PW] The **Weld** made at the point in the **Rail** where the stress is applied. See also **Closing Weld**.

Stretcher
Stretcher Bar
[PW, Sig.] A bar that links the two **Switch Rails** in a **Set of Switches** (**Set of Points**) and maintains their correct relationship, e.g. one is open when the other is closed. Long **Switches** can have as many as six, and the minimum is normally two, to guard against failure. The Stretcher Bar nearest the **Switch Toe** is the **Front Stretcher Bar** or **First Stretcher Bar**. On **Power Operated Switches** there will be two First Stretcher Bars, one (the **First Signalling Stretcher Bar**) relates to the **Switch Detection** and the other (the **First Permanent Way Stretcher Bar**) being the one actually holding the Switch Rails in the correct relationship. Stretcher Bars are normally attached to the Switch Rails by means of bolted brackets. See **Lambrigg Accident**, **Potters Bar Accident**.

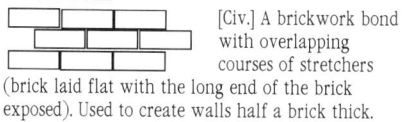

Stretcher Bond
[Civ.] A brickwork bond with overlapping courses of stretchers (brick laid flat with the long end of the brick exposed). Used to create walls half a brick thick.

Strike In
Strike In Point (SIP)
[Sig.]
a) The location on the Approach to an **Automatic Level Crossing** at which an **Approaching Train** triggers the operating sequence of the **Level Crossing** (**LC, LX**)
b) The location on the Approach to a **Manual Level Crossing** at which an Approaching Train triggers the operating sequence for the **Crossing Operator** or **Signaller**
c) The location at which any automated warning system that is triggered by an Approaching Train, e.g. **Automatic Track Warning Systems** (**ATWS**), **Train Operated Warning Systems** (**TOWS**) is activated.

Strike Out
Strike Out Point (SOP)
[Sig.]
a) The point at which the rear end of a **Train** triggers the cycle to raise the **Barriers**, silence the **Audible Warning** and extinguish the warning lights as required at an **Automatic Level Crossing**
b) The location at which any automated warning system that is triggered by an approaching **Train**, e.g. **Automatic Track Warning Systems** (**ATWS**), **Train Operated Warning Systems** (**TOWS**) is de-activated.

String
a) [PW] Two or more **Rails** welded together to make a 300, 600 or 720 foot (91m, 183m or 219.6m) length of Rail, generally used to describe **Long Welded Rails** (**LWR**) on a **Long Welded Rail Train** (**LWRT**)
b) [PW] The low-tech surveying equipment used in **Hallade Surveys** and for setting out **Switch & Crossing Layouts** (**S&C Layouts**), see **White Line**
c) [PW] (verb) To survey using the **Hallade** method
d) [Ops.] Many **Wagons** coupled together. See also **Raft**, **Rake**
e) [PW] A representation of a continuous feature (such as a **Rail**) in the **BRT**, **InRail**, **MOSS**, or **MXRail** design packages.

String Course
[Civ.] A thin projecting layer of brickwork or stone running horizontally around a building or **Structure**.

String Line
[Elec.] Describing a means of determining the **Mid-span Offset** (**MSO**) due to a **Curve**, measured over the length of a **Span**. See also **Hallade**, **Versine**.

Stringers
[Civ.] Structural members running the length of a **Bridge Deck** and used to provide structural support of the **Deck**.

Strip Heater
See **Electric Strip Heater**.

Strip Pad
[PW] Long lengths of **Rail Pad** material for use on **Slab Track**, or for cutting to size on site for use on **Universal Baseplates** in S&C Layouts.

Stroke Post
See **Wire Assister**.

STRU
[Hist.]
a) Scottish **Track Renewal Unit** (**TRU**)
b) Southern **Track Renewal Unit**.

Structure
a) [Elec.] An alternative for an **Overhead Line Structure**
b) Any construction such as a **Bridge**, **Tunnel** or **Retaining Wall**, but excluding **Embankment** and **Cutting** slopes, which are **Earthworks**.

Structure Assessment
[Civ.] The determination of the safe load carrying capacity of a structure, particularly a **Bridge**, that takes into account its physical condition and location. The term includes site inspection with site measurements and the carrying out of any calculations and checks. Also **Bridge Assessment**.

Structure Assessment Code (of Practice)
[Civ.] A document that describes what is required in a calculation for a **Structure Assessment** and gives guidance on how the calculations are to be performed.

Structure Bond
[Elec.] A **Bond** connecting a **Structure** to the **Traction Return Rail** for safety purposes.

Structure Clearance
[PW] The calculated clearance between a **Lineside** ◻ **Structure** and a **Vehicle Swept Envelope**, taking account of appropriate **Track Tolerances** and the accuracy of the survey measurements.

Structure Gauge
[PW]
a) The set of *minimum* dimensions relative to the **Track** to which any **Structure** must conform. See also **Electrification Clearances**, **Kinematic Envelope** (**KE**), **Loading Gauge**
b) [Obs.] A large wooden template in the shape of the sectional profile of a **Train**, which is placed upright on the **Rails** under the **Structure** and clearance measurements taken between it and the Structure. See **Laser Sweep Survey**, **Structure Gauging**, **Structure Gauging Train** (**SGT**).

Structure Gauging
See **Gauging Survey**.

Structure Gauging Train (SGT)
[NR]
a) [Obs.] A vehicle-based **Gauging** system using a precise plane of white light and video capture systems to measure the position of **Lineside** ◻ **Structures**. The **Train** also includes forward facing video cameras, but since the Gauging system must run at night, these rely on floodlights for illumination.
b) See *Structure Gauging Train 2* (SGT2)

Structure Gauging Train 2 (SGT2)
[NR] A **Train** consisting of a former **Mark** 2d First Open (**FO**) **Passenger Coach** 977986 with a modified **Coupling** system at one end; this is attached to a former Mark 2f Trailer Standard Open (**TSO**) 977985, which is fitted with laser-based angle and distance scanning equipment at one end.

STS
a) Single **Track** Simulation
b) Safety Test Specification.

ST-SES
Single **Track** Subway Environmental Simulation Programme.

STT
See **Single Tongue Trap**.

STTS
See **Service Tunnel Transport System**.

Stub Axle
[TRS] A short axle which does not extend for the full width of a vehicle. Common on **Low-Floor Trams**, they allow a single-level interior for improved access.

Stub End
[Elec.] A section of **Conductor Rail** that is connected to the electrical supply at one end only.

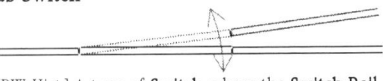

Stub Switch
[PW Hist.] A type of **Switch** where the **Switch Rail** remains fixed at the **Toe** and the **Heel** of the Switch Rail moves between **Turnout** and **Main Line** positions to facilitate the **Switch** action. Not a common sight. See also **Flexible Switch**, **Loose Heel Switch**.

Stumec
(Tradename) A manufacturer of **Railway** plant, including the small cranes used on **Side Rail Loader** ◻ **Wagons**

Stumec Wagon (YFA, YFB, YFO, YBA, YBB, YBO, YBP, YBQ, YMA, YMO)
[NR] A **Salmon** or **Sturgeon** ◻ **Wagon** fitted with two small cranes, used to load **Rails**. A typical **Stumec** vehicle has a capacity of 50 tons but cannot actually carry this many **Standard Rails**. There are two variants: the basic type and a **Covered Stumec** for use under **Live** ◻ **Overhead Line Equipment** (**OLE**). See **Side Rail Loader**, **Wagon Names**. See also **Elk**, **Trident**.

Sturgeon (YBA, YBB, YBO, YBP, YBQ)
[NR] A 51 ton capacity **Wagon** used for the transportation of **Rails** and **Sleepers**. See **Wagon Names**.

SU
[TRS] An acronym representing a **Sandite Unit** Vehicle.

SUB
Shorthand for **Suburban Line**.

Sub-formation
The name given by non-**Railway** specialists to the **Formation**.

Sub-ganger
[Hist.] Under **British Rail** (**BR**) and its predecessors, the title of the second-in-command in a **Gang**. See also **Ganger**.

Subgrade
Specifically, the prepared upper surface of the ground or fill material on which the **Railway** is then built. Sometimes used as alternative to **Formation**. Also **Solum**.

Subitisation
The ability to enumerate a small quantity (seven or less) of similar items without counting. This is one of the mechanisms by which drivers identify which **Signal** applies to them on a large **Gantry** with many Signals.

Submarine
[Col.] Alternative term for a **Cutwater**. See also **Boat**.

Sub-overlap
[Sig.] Within a **Solid State Interlocking** (**SSI**), a Sub-overlap is allocated for each path through an **Overlap Track Circuit** that is part of an **Overlap**. Sub-overlaps may be **Locked** or **Free**.

Sub-route
a) A short length of smaller **Cable Trough** laid to provide a path to a particular **Signalling** installation, often from a junction with the main **Cable Route**
b) [Sig.] Within a **Solid State Interlocking** (**SSI**), one Sub-route is allocated to each path through a **Track Circuit** (**TC**) that lies on a **Route** (so one Sub-route may be part of several Routes). Sub-routes may be **Locked** or **Free**.

Sub-route Release Data
[Sig.] Within a **Solid State Interlocking** (**SSI**), a data file which specifies the conditions under which **Sub-routes** can be **Released**. Usually, the first Sub-route on a **Route** □ **Requires** the Route **Unset**, and the first **Track Circuit** (**TC**) □ **Clear**; subsequent Sub-routes are "chained", requiring the previous Sub-route(s) **Free** and the relevant Track Circuit Clear.

Sub-section
Sub Section
Subsection
[Elec.]
a) Part of an **Overhead Line Electrification** (**OLE**) □ **Electrical Section** that can be Isolated from all other parts of the system using a **Section Switch**
b) A **Conductor Rail** that can be Isolated by the opening of **Hook Switches**
See also **Section**.

Subsidiary Route Indicator (SRI)
See **Miniature Route Indicator** (**MRI**).

Subsidiary Signal
[Sig.] An additional **Semaphore Signal** controlling **Shunt Movements** and other **Permissive Movements**. It is always positioned below the **Semaphore Arm** with which it is associated.

Subsidiary Timetable Change
[NR] The intermediate **Timetable Change** which occurs in May.

Substandard Protection
[NR, Col.] An unofficial term used to describe those situations in a **Possession** or **Accident** where it is not possible to place the **Protection** at 400 metres or more from the designated **Points** or **Signal**.

Substation
A building or compound containing electrical equipment such as **Rectifiers**, switchgear and transformers used for the following purposes:
• Provision of **Traction Supply Current** to a **Conductor Rail System** or **Overhead Line Electrification** (**OLE**)
• Reduction and rectification of a high voltage supply from a **Regional Electricity Company** (**REC**).

Sub-station Gap
[Elec.] A gap in the **Conductor Rails** located between two abutting **Electrical Sections**.

Substructure
a) That part of a **Structure** that is below the ground level
b) The supporting structure under the **Track**, such as the **Ballast** and **Formation**.

Sub-surface Line
a) A **Line** or **Track** that is constructed below ground level.
b) [LUL] A Line built using the **Cut and Cover** method, the other "below ground" Lines being **Tube Lines** or **Deep Tube Lines**. The Sub-surface Lines are:
• Metropolitan & Circle and East London Lines
• Paddington (H&C) to Praed Street Junction
• Finchley Road and Notting Hill Gate to Minories Junction and Aldgate East Junction
• Whitechapel (**ELL**) to Surrey Quays.
• The District Line
• Ravenscourt Park **Substation** to Hammersmith (including the Piccadilly Line Tracks)
• West Kensington **Tunnel Mouth** to Whitechapel Junction and Campbell Road Substation (east of Bow Road)
• The Tunnel Mouth west of Fulham Broadway to Notting Hill Gate
• High Street Kensington to Gloucester Road.

Sub-surface Station
A **Station** whose **Platforms** are enclosed or underground as defined in clause 3 of the Fire Precautions (Sub-surface Railway Stations) Regulations 1989 (which are now replaced by the Fire Precautions (Sub-surface Railway Stations) Regulations 2009). In summary, a Station to which members of the public have access and of which more than 50% of any one **Platform** is within a tunnel or under a building. See **Kings Cross Accident**.

Subterranean Fire
An underground fire, but excluding fires in **Structures** such as basements, cellars and **Sub-surface Stations**. Subterranean Fires can be started and fed in many ways including gas build up in old mine workings, buried layers of decomposing household waste, **Lineside** fires that have ignited the roots of vegetation and contents of rabbit warrens, former **Spoil Tips** and **Locomotive Depot** ash tips.

Suburban Line
A **Line** normally carrying **Trains** serving a suburban area. See also **Rural Line**.

Subway
A pedestrian walkway passing under a **Railway**, although the term is also applied to similar provisions used by electric vehicles moving mail or supplies between **Platforms** in **Stations**.

SuDS
Sustainable Drainage Solutions.

Sugar
[Obs.] The obsolescent **Phonetic Alphabet** word representing S. Replaced by **Sierra**.

Suicide Pit
See **Platform Safety Pit**. Also **Jumper Pit**.

Suicides and Open Verdicts on the Railway Network Project (SOVRN)
A project started in 1999 aimed at finding ways of reducing the occurrence and the impact of suicides on the **Railway**.

Suit
[Col.] Derogatory term for a manager employed by the **Railway** who has no practical Railway experience of any kind whatsoever.

Sultan
A **Railway** □ **Telegraph Code** meaning "Train conveying load must travel on ... line as follows:- " and applied to **Out of Gauge Loads**.

Summit
a) The highest point on a **Route**
b) An alternative term for a **Convex Vertical Curve** or **Hog Curve**.

Sun
Common shorthand for Sunday.

Sun Locking
[Col.] An alternative term for carrying out **Stressing** operations in spring and summer, using the sun to produce the required heat to create expansion of the **Rail**. Also **Natural Stressing**.

Sunflower
[Col.] The colloquial name for the **Automatic Warning System** (**AWS**) visual indicator, which displays a set of yellow spokes when the system is activated.

SuO
Sundays Only.

Super Red
[NR PW] A length of **Track** (usually an **Eighth of a Mile**) over which the **Track Quality** (**TQ**) is worse than **Very Poor**, in that the **Standard Deviation** (**SD**) values for **Top** and **Line** are outside the maximum values for the **Permissible Speed** (**PS**) or **Enhanced Permissible Speed** (**EPS**).

Super Sprinter
The brandname of the **Class** 153, 155 and 156 **Diesel Multiple Units** (**DMU**). See also **Express Sprinter**, **Sprinter**.

Super Tench (FJA)
A **Container Flat** fitted with door-sided "modules" for use in **Engineering Work**.

Super Voyager
The brandname of the **Class** 221 **Tilting Train**, a **Diesel Electric Multiple Unit** (**DEMU**) operated by Virgin Trains (**VT**).

Supercapacitor
See **Electric Double-Layer Capacitor** (**EDLC**)

Superelevation
[PW] An alternative for **Cant** (**C, E**).

Superheater
Superheater Tubes
[TRS] In a **Steam Locomotive**, the apparatus where **Superheating** takes place; typically composed of pipes placed within additional **Boiler Tubes**. See **Snifting Valve**.

Superheating
[TRS] In a **Steam Locomotive**, the heating of steam above the boiling point of water (by up to 400°C, though 200°C is more typical) in separate **Superheater Tubes**, thereby increasing the energy contained in the steam and the power produced by a **Locomotive** so fitted. See also **Dryness Fraction**.

Superloc.
(*super-loke*) [Sig.] An alternative term for a small **Relocatable Equipment Building** (**REB**).

Superstructure
a) [TRS] The parts of a **Rail Vehicle** above the **Solebar**
b) The movable upper parts of a crane or excavator
c) [Civ.] That portion of a **Bridge** above the **Piers** and **Abutments**.

Supervised
[Ops.] Describing a **Level Crossing** (**LC, LX**) where the **Signaller** can visually observe the Level Crossing, either directly or by **CCTV**. See also **Monitored**.

Supervising Point
[Sig.] For a **Level Crossing** (**LC, LX**), the location from which the Crossing is monitored and or operated. This is typically a **Signal Box** (**SB**).

Supervisor Visual Track Inspection
[PW] See **Supervisor's Plain Line Inspection**.

Supervisor's Plain Line Inspection
[PW] A regular inspection of the **Track**, carried out by a supervisor in order to determine the actions necessary to respond to reports of basic visual track inspections carried out by **Patrollers**, review trends in conditions and check that basic inspections, **Maintenance** and **Renewal** work are effective. Also **Supervisor Visual Track Inspection**.

Supplementary Conductor
[Elec.] A **Wire** running in parallel with the **Catenary** and regularly connected to it, which is intended to reduce the impedance losses in an **Overhead Line Electrification** (**OLE**) system.

Supplementary Detector
[Sig.] A second set of **Detection** equipment fitted to a long **Set of Switches**, generally at the locations of the **Supplementary Drives**.

Supplementary Drive
[Sig.] An arrangement of **Rodding** and **Cranks**, hydraulics or **Torsion Drives** that transfers some of the motion of the **Switch Toes** to one or more points further down the **Switch**, nearer the **Switch Heel**. This system compensates for the flexibility of long **Switch Rails**. Also called a **Back Drive**. See also **Backdrive**, **High Performance Switch System** (**HPSS**), **Hydrive**.

Supplementary Operating Notice
[Ops.] A document containing amendments to work published in the **Weekly Operating Notice** (**WON**).

Supplementary Ventilation System (SVS)
An additional ventilation system brought into use in the **Channel Tunnel** when it has become necessary to stop **Trains** for any significant period of time.

Supported Joint

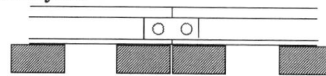

[PW, Hist.] A **Fishplated Rail Joint** supported by **Sleepers** placed directly beneath the **Rail Ends**. See also **Semi-supported Joint**, **Suspended Joint**.

Supported Monorail

A **Monorail** in which the **Passenger** cabin is located above the **Rail**. The opposite is a **Suspended Monorail**.

Suppression

[Sig.] Positive inhibition of the action of an **Automatic Warning System Magnet** (**AWS Magnet**) or **Train Protection and Warning System Loop** (**TPWS**) during a **Train** movement to which the AWS or TPWS indication would not apply.

Surelock

(Tradename) [Sig.] A **Point Machine** manufactured by **Invensys Rail**.

Surface Concrete Troughing (SCT)

[Civ.] A series of lidded concrete **Cable Troughs**, usually laid in the **Cess**, comprising a **Cable Route**. See also **C/1/x**.

Surface Length (SL)

[PW] The total length of a crack, measured on the surface of a **Rail Head**.

Surface Line

[LUL] A term used on **London Underground Lines** to differentiate above-ground **Lines** from the **Sub-surface Lines**. See also **Deep Tube Line**, **Tube Line**.

Surface Route

[NR] Generic term for a **Cable Route** built at ground level.

Surface Stock

[LUL] **Rolling Stock**, which has a **Vehicle Gauge** such that it cannot operate through **Tube Tunnels**.

Surfing

[Col.] The suicidal game played by delinquent juveniles, entailing riding on the outside of **Trains** (and trying not to get killed by **Signals**, **Overhead Line Structures**, other **Trains**, **Bridges**, etc.).

Surveys

a) Generally, see **Point Cloud**, **Topographical Survey**
b) For **Overhead Line Equipment** (**OLE**), see **Height and Stagger Survey**
c) Of and for **Signalling**, see **Cable Route Survey**, **Signal Sighting Survey**, **Signalling Plan Survey**,
d) Surveys of structures, see **Gauging Survey**, also **Structure Gauging**
e) Track specific, see **Hallade Survey**, **Switch and Crossing Survey**, **Theodolite Straight**, **Track Drainage Survey**,

Survival Space

[TRS] The spaces on a **Train** normally occupied by **Passengers** or **Traincrew**, see **Loss of Survival Space**.

Suspended Joint

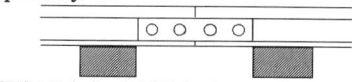

[PW] A **Fishplated Rail Joint** between **Running Rails** where the supporting **Sleepers** are wholly outside the limits of the **Fishplates**. See also **Semi-supported Joint**, **Supported Joint**, **Suspended Joint**.

Suspended Monorail

A **Monorail** in which the **Passenger** cabin is located below the **Rail**. The opposite is a **Supported Monorail**.

Suspension Packings

[TRS] Discs, shims or other material inserted in a suspension to adjust the height of the **Wagon** at that point. See also **Cone Packings**.

Sustrans

(Tradename) An organisation primarily concerned with the creation of cycle paths throughout the UK, many of which use former **Railway** □ **Formations**. Their name is a contraction of "sustainable transport".

SVC

$\underline{S}$tatic $\underline{V}$olt Ampere Reactive ($\underline{V}$AR) $\underline{C}$ompensator.

SVI

[NR] $\underline{S}$ponsor's $\underline{V}$ariation $\underline{I}$nstruction, now called a **Remit Variation Instruction** (**RVI**). Also **Requirements Change Request** (**R-CR**).

SVP

$\underline{S}$afety $\underline{V}$erification $\underline{P}$lan.

SVR

The $\underline{S}$evern $\underline{V}$alley **Railway**.

SVS

See **Supplementary Ventilation System**.

SW

The **ATOC** code for **South West Trains**.

SWA

$\underline{S}$pecial $\underline{W}$orking $\underline{A}$rrangements.

Swag

[PW Col.] A **Track Fault**. A depression in the longitudinal profile (**Top**) of the **Track**. Also **Slack**. See also **Low**.

Swamping

[Sig.] The effect by which bright sunlight reduces the contrast between a **Signal Aspect** and its surroundings, sometimes to the point of rendering the **Signal** unreadable. See also **Phantom Aspect**.

Swan Neck

[PW] The location within a **Non-adjustable Stretcher Bar** where the two sections join, normally including an insulating material. See also **Swan Neck Insulation**.

Swan Neck Insulation

[PW] A piece of non-conducting material fitted between the long and short sections of a **Non-adjustable Stretcher Bar** assembly to provide electrical isolation between the two **Switch Rails**.

Swap Body
A demountable road vehicle body that can be transferred directly to a suitable **Rail Vehicle**. They are constructed to European-standard dimensions.

Swap Body Vehicles
[TRS] **Rail Vehicles** that are designed to carry the trailers of road based lorries.

SWARMMS
South West Area Multi-modal Study.

SWAT
Southampton – West Midlands Action Team.

Sway
a) A mode of movement of a **Rail Vehicle** travelling at speed, describing the lateral and rotational movement of the **Carbody** as a result of changes in **Cant Deficiency** (D). See also **Centre Throw**, **End Throw**, **Tilt**, **Yaw**
b) [Elec.] The lateral allowances added to the normal position of a **Pantograph**, see **Pantograph Sway**. Also **Pansway**.

SWEAR
[NR] South Willesden Euston Area Resignalling.

Sweating the Asset
[Col.] A modern term describing the process of getting as much use as possible out of a facility whist at the same time carrying out as little **Maintenance** as possible. The older term is **Maintenance Holiday**.

Sweep
a) [Elec.] The total lateral movement of the **Contact Wire** (**CW**) across the **Pantograph** between any two **Registration Points**
b) [Sig.] The curved bars, used in pairs, which guide a **Lever** in a **Lever Frame**. They often provide an engagement for the **Catch Handle** mechanism.
c) [DLR] Using a moving **Train** to check that the **Line** □ **Ahead** is **Clear** of obstructions. A **Passenger Service Agent** will be at the **Lead Emergency Driving Position** observing. This operation is carried out prior to commencement of the day's **Passenger** service.

Sweep Ratio
[Elec.] The total lateral movement of the **Contact Wire** (**CW**) relative to the **Pantograph** within one **Span** divided by the **Span Length**. The sweep ratio is a minimum of 2mm and a maximum of 25mm per metre See also **Stagger**..

SWELTRAC
South West London Transport Conference.

Swept Envelope (SE)
The **Kinematic Envelope** (**KE**) of a **Rail Vehicle** enlarged by the effects of **Track Geometry**, including **Centre Throw**, **End Throw** and **Cant** (**C**, **E**) effects. See also **Swept Path**, **Thrown Envelope**.

Swept Path
The plan area occupied by a **Rail Vehicle** as it moves along the **Track**. The width of the Swept Path at any point is the same as the width of the **Swept Envelope**.

SWGPA
(*swag-pah*) [NR] **S**ignalling **W**orks **G**eographical **P**artnership **A**greement.

SWIFT
a) (*swift*) Structured 'What If?' Technique, a process for assessing level of safety risk
b) South Wales Integrated Fast Transit.

SWIM
(*swim*) [RT, NR] Sandbach to Wilmslow Including Macclesfield, a **Resignalling Scheme**. See **SHWW**.

SWIMCo
(*swim-coe*) [Hist.] South West Infrastructure □ Maintenance Company, now part of Amec **Rail**.

SWIMU
(*swim-you*) [Hist.] South Western Infrastructure Maintenance Unit (IMU).

Swing Bridge
[Civ.] A type of **Movable Bridge**; an **Underbridge** (**UB**) built such that one or more **Spans** can rotate in plan to provide an unobstructed opening for the passage of (generally) ships. See also **Bascule Bridge**, **Lift Bridge**.

Swing Motion Bogie
[TRS] A type of **Bogie** where the **Spring Plank** is suspended on rods from the **Bogie Frame**, allowing the **Bogie** to move freely laterally relative to the **Bogie Bolster**.

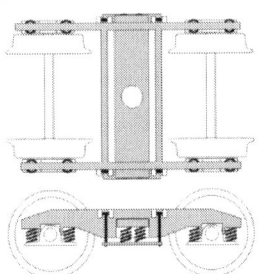

Swing Nose
[PW]
a) A contraction of **Swing Nose Crossing** (**SNX**)
b) The movable **Crossing Vee** section of a Swing Nose Crossing.

Swing Nose Crossing (SNX)

[PW] A **Common Crossing** in which the **Crossing Vee** (light grey) can be moved laterally to close up to each **Wing Rail** (dark grey) in turn. A sliding joint is provided in one of the **Legs** of the Crossing Vee to allow the necessary movement. This type of Crossing provides continuous support to the vehicle wheels as they pass. They are used in **Switch and Crossing Layouts** (**S&C Layouts**) that would otherwise have very large **N Values**, very **Flat Angles**. Since there is no gap between the **Crossing Nose** (**XN**) and Wing Rail as wheels pass, **Check Rails** are not required with this type of **Crossing**. There are currently no approved designs of Swing Nose Crossing for use on **Network Rail** □ **Infrastructure**.

Swinger

a) [Col.] An **Unbraked** □ **Rail Vehicle** attached to the rear of a **Fully Fitted** □ **Train**. See also **Unfitted Tail**

b) [Sig.] An additional device fitted to a **Tappet** in a **Mechanical Interlocking** using **Catch Handle Locking**, to allow or prevent relative movement between two related **Dogs** according to the position of the Tappet, in turn achieving a **Conditional Locking** arrangement. See also **Stowell's Diamond**.

Swinging Overlap

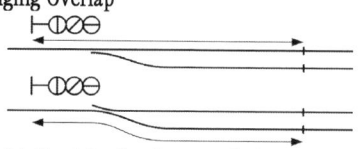

[Sig.] A **Signal Overlap** that extends through a **Set of Facing Points (Facing Switches)** □ **Beyond** the **Signal**, the **Track Circuits (TC)** forming the Signal Overlap being chosen according to the position of the Points. Usually associated with **Time Of Operation Locking** and **Conditional Locking** requirements.

SWISS

[RT, NR] (*swiss*) South Western Investment in Signalling Strategy.

Switch

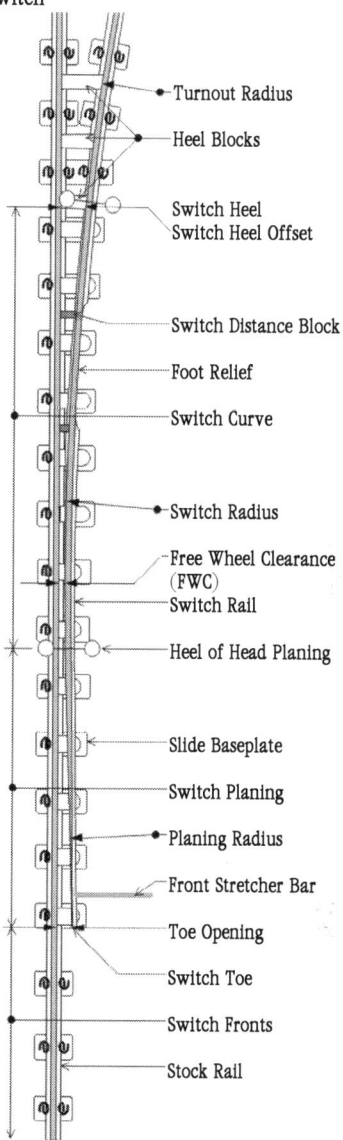

- Turnout Radius
- Heel Blocks
- Switch Heel
- Switch Heel Offset
- Switch Distance Block
- Foot Relief
- Switch Curve
- Switch Radius
- Free Wheel Clearance (FWC)
- Switch Rail
- Heel of Head Planing
- Slide Baseplate
- Switch Planing
- Planing Radius
- Front Stretcher Bar
- Toe Opening
- Switch Toe
- Switch Fronts
- Stock Rail

[PW] An assembly of two movable **Switch Rails**, two fixed **Stock Rails** and other components (**Baseplates**, bolts, **Distance Blocks**, **Soleplates**, **Stress Transfer Blocks** and **Stretcher Bars**) used to divert vehicles from one **Track** to another. One Switch Rail and one Stock Rail together make a **Switch Half Set**. Also **Chamfered Switch, Curved Planed Switch, Flexible Switch, Full Depth Switch, Inset Switch, Joggled Switch, Loose Heel Switch, Set of Switches, Shallow Depth Switch, Slip Switch, Straight Cut Switch, Straight Planed Switch, Stub Switch, Tangential Switch, Two Levelled Switch, Undercut Switch**. See also **Adjustment Switch, Point and Crossing (P&C), Switch and Crossing (S&C), Points**.

Switch Anchor
[PW] A steel strap assembly that holds a **Switch Rail** in position longitudinally relative to a **Stock Rail** at the **Switch Heel** in some designs of **Switches**. See also **Distance Blocks**, **Heel Blocks**.

Switch and Crossing (S&C)
Switches and Crossings
[PW] Track consisting of **Switches and Crossings** forming connections between **Lines**. Also **Connections**, **Heavy Work**, **Fittings**, **Point and Crossing (P&C)**. See also **Catch Points**, **Crossover**, **Diamond**, **Double Junction**, **Double Slip Diamond**, **Junction**, **Ladder**, **Lead**, **Scissors**, **Single Slip Diamond**, **Square Crossing**, **Switch Diamond**, **Tandem**, **Three Throw**, **Trap Points**, **Turnout**.

Switch and Crossing Layout (S&C Layout)
[PW] Two or more **Switch and Crossing Units (S&C Units)** grouped together and sharing some **Bearers** or **Rails**. Examples would include **Double Junctions**, **Junctions** and **Ladders**.

Switch and Crossing Manufacturer's Drawing
[PW] A detailed engineering drawing giving every component, part number and dimension required to fabricate a **Switch and Crossing Layout (S&C Layout)**. When prepared on paper they are typically produced at a scale of 1:50.

Switch and Crossing Rail (S&C Rail)
[PW] A **Rail** that forms part of a **Switch and Crossing Layout (S&C Layout)**. Such **Rails** are often curved, machined and specially drilled.

Switch and Crossing Survey (S&C Survey)
[PW] A Survey undertaken with a tape measure, **Track Gauge** and **Rail Callipers** to record at least the following for an **S&C Unit** or **S&C Layout**:
- Abutting S&C Units,
- Alignment,
- Ballast Condition,
- **Baseplate** type, condition and security (including **Chairscrews**, fixing screws and **Ferrules** as applicable),
- **Bearer** type and condition
- **Block** and bolt provision and security,
- **Chair** type, condition and security,
- **Check Rail** length and wear,
- Clearances,
- **Crossing Angle** and type,
- **Crossing Leg** lengths,
- Crosslevel,
- **Fastening** type(s),
- **Fishplate** condition, type and security,
- **Flangeway Gap** dimensions,
- [NR] **Free Wheel Clearance** (FWC),
- **Gauge** readings,
- Kicking Straps,
- Layout type (e.g. **Turnout**, **Crossover**, **Facing**, **Trailing**, **Left Hand**, **Right Hand**, etc.)
- Lead Lengths,
- Locations of **Insulated Rail Joints** (IRJ),
- Presence of **Rail Head** defects and mechanical damage anywhere on the Rails,
- **Rail Section**, lengths and **Rail Depths**,
- **Sidewear** or **Sidecutting** readings,
- Slide Table wear of **Slide Baseplates** or **Slide Chairs**,
- **Soleplate** provision and security (if fitted),
- **Stretcher Bar** provision, type, condition and security,
- Switch Type,
- Toe Opening,
- Track Intervals.

Switch and Crossing Tamper (S&C Tamper)
[PW] A **Tamping and Lining Machine (Tamper)** specially built to allow it to lift and tamp **Switch and Crossing Layouts (S&C Layouts)**. Typical modifications include adjustable lifting clamps, **Tamping Tines** which can be shifted laterally and swung in and out, enhanced **Slewing** capabilities, and on some machines, extended lifting arms capable of raising the extreme ends of **Long Bearers** or **Long Timbers** during the **Tamping Cycle**.

Switch and Crossing Unit (S&C Unit)
[PW]
a) Any major **Switch and Crossing (S&C)** component such as a **Crossing** or **Switch Half Set**
b) An assembly of Switch and Crossing components that is in itself complete e.g. a **Crossover**, a **Diamond Crossing**, a **Scissors Crossover**, a **Switch Diamond (SD)** or a **Single Lead**.

Switch Blade
[NPT] See **Switch Rail**.

Switch Clamp
[PW] A device used to render a **Switch** inoperable by clamping the **Switch Rail** and **Stock Rail** together. Such devices are generally fitted with an arrangement to allow them to be padlocked in place. Also **Clip**, **Switch Clip**.

Switch Climb
Switch Climbing Derailment
A fault condition in which the **Wheel Flange** of **Rail Wheel** runs up the end of the **Switch Rail** on the **Closed Switch** side, and the resulting derailment after either the Rail Wheel crosses the **Stock Rail** or drops into the gap between the Switch Rail and the Stock Rail.

Switch Clip
See **Switch Clamp**.

Switch Detection
[Sig.] The electrical switches, operated by the movement of the **Switch Rails** and **Stretcher Bars**, that confirm the position of the **Switches** back to the **Signalling System**. See also **Normal**, **Out of Correspondence**, **Reverse**, **Split Detection**. An alternative term is **Point Detection**.

Switch Diamond

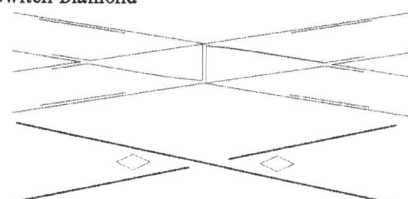

A **Diamond Crossing**, without **Check Rails**, in which the **Obtuse Point Rails** move, thus becoming (in pairs with similar **Rails** in the opposite **Obtuse Crossing**) **Switch Rails**.

Switch Distance Blocks
[PW] A block attached to the **Stock Rail** on the **Switch Toe** side of the **Switch Heel** to support the **Switch Rail** when that side is closed.

Switch Drive
[Sig.] The term for the mechanism that moves the **Switch Rail** relative to the **Stock Rail**. Also **Point Operating Equipment** (POE), **Switch Operating Mechanism**. See also **Back Drive**, **Supplementary Drive**.

Switch Entry Angle
[PW] The angle between the tangent to the **Planing Radius** at the **Switch Toe**, and the **Running Edge** (RE) of the **Stock Rail**.

Switch Fronts
[PW] The length of **Stock Rail** in advance of the **Switch Toe**. The length varies according to the Rail Section used:

Type	Imperial	Metric
BH □ Inclined	5' - 5"	1651mm
109 Inclined	5' - 5"	1651mm
110A Inclined	5' - 5"	1651mm
113A Inclined	5' - 5"	1651mm
113A Vertical	-	3070mm
113A Shallow Depth	-	3070mm
RT60	-	2670mm
NR60	-	2745mm

Also **Fronts**.

Switch Half Set
[PW] The assembly for one side of a **Switch** comprising a **Stock Rail**, a **Switch Rail**, **Chairs** or **Baseplates**, **Slide Chairs** or **Baseplates**, **Stress Transfer Blocks**, **Heel Blocks** or **Switch Anchors**, plus all appropriate bolts, nuts, washers and **Rail Clips** or **Keys**. Also **Half Set**, **Half Set of Switches**.

Switch Heater
Switch Heating
See **Points Heating**.

Switch Heel
[PW]
a) The point at which the **Switch Radius** and **Turnout Radius** meet tangentially
b) The end of the **Movable Length** of the **Switch Rail** furthest from the **Switch Toe**
c) The point at which the **Switch Rail** of a **Loose Heel Switch** pivots.
Often shortened to **Heel**.

Switch Heel Angle
[PW] The angle subtended at the **Stock Rail** by the tangent to the **Switch Heel**.

Switch Heel Offset
[PW] The normal offset from **Stock Rail** to **Switch Rail** □ **Running Edges** (RE) at the **Switch Heel**.

Switch Lead
(*switch leed*) [PW] The distance between the **Mathematical Switch Toe** position and the **Crossing Nose** of a **Turnout**, measured along the **Running Edge** (RE) of the straightest **Switch Rail**. Note that:
- For modern **Shallow Depth Switches** (113A / UIC54B) the Mathematical Switch Toe position is 165mm on the **Crossing** side of the actual **Switch Toes**
- For **NR60** and **RT60** designs the Mathematical Switch Toe position is 75mm on the Crossing side of the actual Switch Toes
- For all other **Switches** the Switch Toe and Mathematical Switch Toe are co-incident.

See also **Toe to Nose**.

Switch Letters
[PW] The letter used to describe the angle of divergence, from a straight Main Line, of a **Switch**. A is the sharpest angle of divergence, typically having the lowest **Turnout Speed**. The highest letter depends on the **Switch Type**:
- **Bullhead** Switches go up to F
- 109, 110A and 113A Inclined Switches go up to F in Straight Planed and G in Curved Planed (there is also an SG in Curved Planed)
- 113A Vertical Switches go up to H (there is also an SG)
- NR60 and RT60 Switches start at C and go up to H (there is also an SG).
- NR56V – TBA

Switch Lever
See **Hand Lever**.

Switch Motor
[Sig.] An electric, pneumatic or hydraulic motor used to operate **Switches** remotely. See **Point Machine**. Also **Point Motor**.

Switch Nomenclature Plate
A plate fixed to or next to an electrical switch describing the function of said switch. Also **Switch Plate**.

Switch Opening
See **Toe Opening**.

Switch Operating Mechanism
The assembly of **Stretcher Bars**, **Supplementary Drives**, **Rodding**, **Point Motors** and other actuating gear that is employed to control the movement of a set of **Switches**. Also collectively the **Switch Drive**. See **High Performance Switch Actuator** (HPSA), **High Performance Switch System** (HPSS), **Hydrive**, **HW** *xxxx*, **In-Bearer Clamplock** (IBCL).

Switch Panel
a) [PW] A **Track Panel** consisting of two **Switch Half Sets** and associated **Bearers**, from **Switch Fronts** to **Switch Heel** □ **Joint** or **Weld** (**W**).
b) [Sig. Col.] Alternative for an **Ground Switch Panel** (GSP), **Independent Function Switch** (IFS) □ **Signal Box Panel**, **OCS Panel** or part of an **Entrance / Exit Panel** (**NX, NX Panel**) where the **Illuminated Diagram** is separate.

Switch Planing
[PW] The machined portion of the **Rail Head** of the **Switch Rail** and the corresponding area of the head of the **Stock Rail** against which the Switch Rail closes. See **Chamfered**, **Curved Planed**, **Straight Cut**, **Straight Planed**, **Undercut**.

Switch Plate
A plate fixed to or next to an electrical switch describing the identity and function of the switch. Also **Switch Nomenclature Plate**. See also **Lever Plate**.

Switch Radius
[PW] The Radius (**R**) of the **Curve** from the tangent point at the end of the **Switch Planing** to the tangent point at the **Switch Heel**.

Switch Rail
[PW] The movable machined **Rail Section** that registers with the **Stock Rail** and forms part of a **Switch** assembly. Also **Switch Blade**, **Tongue Rail**. See also **Flexible Switch**, **Loose Heel Switch**, **Stub Switch**.

Switch Rail Extension Piece
[PW] A bracket fitted to the **Switch Toe** giving a means of connection for the **Point Machine** □ **Detector Rods**.

Switch Rail Set
[PW] The lateral angle through which a **Switch Rail** is turned to centralise the **Rail Web** throughout the **Planing** of the **Switch Rail**.

Switch Rail Vertical Set
[PW] The vertical angle at the **Heel** of the **Switch Planing** through which the **Switch Rail** of a **Two Levelled Switch** is turned to enable a difference in level between **Switch Rail** and **Stock Rail** to be created.

Switch Rollers
[PW] Rollers placed at specified intervals along the **Movable Length** of a **Switch Rail**, whose function is to lift the moving Switch Rail clear of the **Slide Tables**, thus reducing the effort required to **Reverse** the **Switches**. The rollers are arranged so that the **Closed Switch** is allowed to sit back down onto the Slide Table, increasing the support given to the Switch Rail. See **Austroroll**, **Schwihag**.

Switch Securing Block
[PW] A device used to render a switch inoperable by clamping the **Switch** and **Stock Rails** together. This achieved by fitting it into slots provided in the **Switch Toe** □ **Slide Baseplate**. Such devices are provided with an arrangement that allows them to be padlocked in place. Only useable on special Slide Baseplates used under **Flat Bottom** (FB) □ **Shallow Depth Switches**. Also known as a **Doughnut**, after its shape in plan.

Switch Slide Chairs
See **Slide Chairs**.

Switch Timber
[PW] A wood **Bearer** that supports the **Rails** in the **Switch** area of a **Switch and Crossing Layout** (S&C Layout).

Switch Tip
[PW] The top corner of the **Switch Rail** at the **Switch Toe**.

Switch Toe
[PW] The end of a **Switch Rail** that is first traversed by a **Rail Vehicle** negotiating a **Switch** in a **Facing** direction. Sometimes referred to as the **Switch Tip**.

Switch Toe Bearers
Switch Toe Timbers

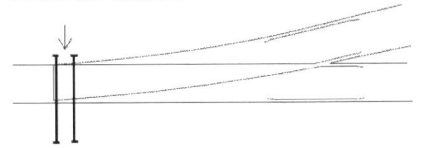

[PW] The two **Bearers** or **Timbers** located under the **Switch Toe**. These are often extended to support **Point Machines**. See also **Extended Bearers**, **Extended Timbers**.

Switch Type

[PW] Description of a **Set of Switches**, including the following:
- **Hand** of the Switches of the more important **Line** (left, right or **Split**)
- Which half of a **Half Set of Switches**, if applicable; e.g **Left Hand** Half Set
- **Main Line** Radius
- Cut, as in **Straightcut, Chamfered, Undercut** if required
- **Switch Planing** characteristics, as in **Curved Planed**, **Straight Planed** if required
- **Inclination** of the **Running Rails**, as in **Inclined** or **Vertical**
- Base **Rail Section** and **Rail Weight** for the Running Rails
- **Full Depth Switches** or **Shallow Depth Switches**,
- **Stock Rail** length,
- **Switch Letter**,
- **Switch Rail** length,
- **Fronts** length,
- **Strengthening** or **Creep Monitors**,
- Drilling for brackets,
- **Slide Chair** or **Baseplate** type.

Thus a typical description might be: "Straight Main Line, Right Hand □ Half Set of Left Hand Switches, standard Un-drilled □ Fronts, Vertical, E, Shallow Depth □ 113A Strengthened Switches with UHMWPE □ Slipper Baseplates".

Switched Out

[Sig.] Describing a **Signal Box** (**SB**) that has been temporarily disconnected from the operation of its **Control Area** by operation of the **King Lever** and **Block Switch**. This allows the Box to be closed. This is often done overnight on **Lines** when traffic is sparse and the long **Block Sections** created do not affect capacity.

Switchglide

(Tradename) [PW] A system of leaf springs with a low friction upper surface designed to lift the **Switch Rail** clear of the **Slide Table** whilst the **Switch** is open. Manufactured by **Portec Rail**.

Switching Station

[Elec.]
a) A generic term for any installation of **Overhead Line Equipment** (**OLE**) switchgear used for the remote switching of the power supply to the OLE. See also **Feeder Stations** (**FS**), **Track Sectioning Cabins** (**TSC**) and **Track Sectioning Locations** (**TSL**)
b) A building or compound containing electrical equipment used to connect high voltage supplies from the supply authority to **Substations** on **Lines** using **Conductor Rails**.

Switchlock

(Tradename) [PW] A proprietary device used to operate and secure manually operated **Switches**. Also **Clawlock, Pawlock**.

SWL

a) See **Safe Work Leader**
b) Safe Working Load.

SWML

[NR] South West Main Line, from London Waterloo via Southampton to Portsmouth.

SWON

[NR] A system that collates the input to the **Weekly Operating Notices** (**WON**). Previously **WONView**.

SWOT

a) Safe Working of Trains
b) Strengths, Weaknesses, Opportunities and Threats.

SWP

Safe Working Pressure.

SWS

a) [BR] Section **Works** Supervisor
b) Shorthand for **Switches**
c) South West **Sidings**

SWT

a) (Tradename) South West Trains, A **Train Operating Company** (**TOC**)
b) Signal Works □ Testing.

SWTH

[NR] Signal Works □ Testing Handbook. Also Works Testing.

SWW

(Tradename) South Wales & West, a **Train Operating Company** (**TOC**).

SX

Saturdays excepted, i.e. Saturday is the only day it doesn't happen.

Sykes

[Sig. Hist.] Common shorthand for WR **Sykes** & Co., a former manufacturer of **Signalling Equipment**.

Sykes Electro-mechanical Warning System

[Sig. Obs.] An early type of **Automatic Warning System** (**AWS**) which relied on electrical current from a **Track**-mounted ramp actuating a bell to indicate **Clear** and the opening of a valve in the **Train Pipe** to atmosphere via a siren for **Caution**

Sykes, William Robert

(1840-1917) born in London. **Signal** engineer and designer of the integrated **Lock and Block** (**Interlocking** and **Absolute Block** (**AB**)) system, patented in 1875 and first applied on the London Chatham & Dover **Railway** (**LC&DR**) in 1878. Founded his own **Signalling** company in 1889, WR Sykes & Co.

Symmetrical Switch

[PW] An alternative term for a **Split Switch**, one where the **Main Line** and **Turnout** have equal radii of opposite **Hand**.

Sympathy Possession

[Ops.] A **Possession** published to avoid conflicts and confusion arising from another Possession. An example of this would be where a **Main Line** is **Blocked**; then a **Branch Line** that has a **Junction** within that Main Line Possession would be shown Blocked in sympathy to avoid confusion.

Synchronous Motor
A type of **Traction Motor** arranged with the field coils mounted on the drive shaft and the armature coils on the housing, the opposite of normal practice. This is a single phase machine controlled by an **Inverter**. Much less common than the **Asynchronous Motor**.

Syphon
[Col.] Nickname given to **Class** 37 **Diesel Locomotives** based on their sound. Also **Growler**, **Tractor**.

SYPTE
South Yorkshire Passenger Transport Executive (**PTE**).

System Height
[Elec.] The total height of an **Overhead Line Equipment** □ **Catenary** system, i.e. the distance between the **Contact Wire** (**CW**) and the **Catenary Wire** at an **Overhead Line Structure** which is a **Registration Point**. Also **Encumbrance**.

SZ
[RT, NR]
a) Southern Zone
b) Scotland Zone.

T

T
a) In an abbreviated **Track Name** it denotes **Through**, as in **Through Line**
b) See **Termination Indicator**
c) [TRS] An acronym representing a **Trailer** □ **Coach**
d) [PW] An abbreviation for **Toe**, see **Switch Toe**
e) [NR] As the first letter of a **Wagon** □ **CARKND**, it means the vehicle is a tanker
f) [Sig.] On a **Signalling Circuit Diagram**:
 • As one of the leading letters of an **Equipment Code**, it means **Track Circuit (TC)**
 • As the last letter of an **Equipment Code**, it means transformer
g) [Sig.] Abbreviation found on drawings of **Signal Box Diagrams**, denoting the total number of **Levers**
h) The letter represented by **Tango** in the **Phonetic Alphabet**
i) Shorthand for **Tuesday**
j) [NR Ops.] In **Possession** planning, the date of the **Planning Week** concerned, so **T-14** is 14 weeks prior to the start of the relevant Planning Week
k) [NR] Under the **Bridge Condition Marking Index (BCMI)** handbook, shorthand for timber.

t
[Sig.] On a **Signalling Circuit Diagram** as the last letter of an **Equipment Code**, it means terminal.

T Board
a) [NR] A **Termination** □ **Board**, see **Termination Indicator**
b) [LUL] A sign showing that the **Headwall** telephone and / or **Tunnel Telephone** in a **Traction Current** section might be out of order.

T Spanner
See **Box Spanner**.

T&C
a) See **Testing and Commissioning**
b) Terms and Conditions.

T&H
The Tottenham & Hampstead (Barking to Gospel Oak Junction) Line.

T&L
See **Tamping and Lining**.

T&RS
Traction and Rolling Stock.

T&RSMD
Traction and Rolling Stock □ Maintenance □ Depot.

T&V
See **Trespass and Vandalism** (TP&V).

T&WA
See **Transport and Works Act** (TWA).

T/O
See **Turnout**. Also **TO**.

T12

T12 Protection
[NR Obs.] Former **Rule Book** section covering protection of personnel carrying out activities on the **Line** that do not affect the **Safety Of The Line**. See the new term **Line Blockage**.

T-12
[NR] The requirement for **Network Rail (NR)** to provide **Timetable (TT)** information on **Engineering Work** 12 weeks in advance of the works. See also **Informed Traveller**.

T-14
[NR] The first **Planning Meeting** for a particular **Possession** date, held nominally 14 weeks prior to the **Possession** date. At this meeting the number, extent and times of the Possessions are agreed, along with the nomination of the **Possession Manager**. See **T-6**. See also **T-8**.

T2
[NR Obs.] The former **Rule Book** section covering protection of **Engineering Work** or a **Hand Trolley** on a **Line** not under **Possession** and where no **Engineering Trains** will be involved. See the new term **Line Blockage**.

T2000
Thameslink 2000, a **Train Operating Company (TOC)**.

T22
[NR] The list giving the 22 most **SPAD**ded **Signals** in the UK.

T3
[NR] The rules applying to **Possessions** of **Running Lines**, also known as **Absolute Possession**. A Possession of the Line must be taken if:
 • **Engineering Work** on a **Running Line** will need the complete stoppage of all normal **Train Movements** on that **Line**, and
 • **Engineering Train** movements need to be made in connection with the **Work** or **On-track Plant (OTP)** will be used.
Under these arrangements the times and extents are agreed in advance, but **The Engineer** decides when the Possession is given up, not the **Signaller**. For further guidance consult the current Rule Book (GE/RT8000).

T3a
[NR Obs.] Formerly, a **Possession** taken in a **Siding**.

T4
a) [NR, Obs.] Previously, a protection arrangement used to ensure that **Trains** were not hit by **Ballast Cleaners**, **Cranes**, excavators and other plant working on adjacent **Lines**. This system has now effectively been replaced by the **Line Blockage**
b) [NR Obs.] A **Possession** taken in a **Siding**, which have to have their own protection methods owing to the absence of **Signalling**. This used to be called **T3a**. For further guidance consult the current Rule Book (GE/RT8000).

495

T4 Trailer
T5 Trailer
(Tradename) Types of low flat trailers with **Rail Wheels**, intended to be used with **Road Rail Excavators**.

T-6
[NR] A **Planning Meeting** held nominally six weeks prior to the **Possession** date, and the last opportunity to book a **Work Site** without making special arrangements. See **T-14**.

T-8
[NR Obs.] Formerly, a **Planning Meeting** held nominally eight weeks prior to the **Possession** date. Superseded by the **T-14** and **T-6** meetings.

TA
a) See **Tilt Active**
b) **Train Arrived**.

TAA
See **Track Access Agreement**.

TAB
[LUL] **T**urns **a**nd **B**ifurcations.

Table Incline
[Hist.] An incline provided with a wheeled horizontal table of sufficient size to carry one or more **Rail Vehicles**, a practice developed and used in some North Wales slate quarries.

Table of Signal Routes
[Sig.] A comprehensive list of **Signal Routes** shown on or accompanying a **Scheme Plan** or **Signalling Plan**.

Tablet
[Sig.] A type of **Token** used in **Electric Token Block** (**ETB**).

TABS
[NR] **T**rack **A**ccess **B**illing **S**ystem.

TAC
a) [NR] **T**rack **A**ssessment **C**oach
b) **T**elecoms **A**ppreciation **C**ourse
c) See **Track Access Controller**.

Tache Ovale
[PW] Literally translating as "kidney-shaped crack", this describes a **Rail Defect** in the form of a **Fatigue Crack** propagating laterally from an internal defect in a **Rail**. They are normally detected using ultrasound. See **Ultrasonic Rail Flaw Detector** (**URFD**).

Tackling Chain
[Hist.] A system used to attach a **Wagon** to the haulage rope on straight sections of the Cromford and High Peak **Railway**. It comprised a chain passing from the rear **Coupling** of the vehicle, under the rear axle, over the front axle and hooked onto the front **Drawbar Hook**. At the rear of the vehicle two chains of lighter, tapered, construction, one end of each attached to the tackling chain, were plaited around the haulage rope in opposite directions and secured by leather thongs.

TAD
(*tad*) See **T**hrough **A**lignment **D**esign.

TADS
[Tel.]
a) [NR] **T**elecommunications **A**sset **D**atabase **S**ystem
b) **T**ransmission **A**llocation **D**ata **S**ystem.

TAG
a) **T**rack **A**ccess **G**rant
b) [LUL] **T**ouch **and G**o.

Tail
a) [Elec.] A **Wire** connecting an **Equalising Plate** to a **Balance Weight Anchor** (**BWA**) or a **Fixed Anchor** (**FA**) in an **Overhead Line Electrification** (**OLE**) system.
b) [Sig., EP, Tel.] See **Tail Cable**, **Track Tail**.

Tail Cable
a) [Sig.] A heavy duty insulated **Conductor** linking **Signalling Equipment** located on or close to the **Track** (such as **Automatic Warning System** (**AWS**) **Magnets**, **Point Machines**, **Track Circuits** (**TC**) and **Treadles**) with **Disconnection Boxes** and **Locations**.
b) [EP, Tel.] An insulated **Conductor** linking **Points** Heating equipment and telephones with **Disconnection Boxes** and **Locations**.
Such cables are designed to resist the attentions of the **Permanent Way** (**PW**) staff who, at times, have scant regard for the integrity of electrical systems.

Tail Lamp
[Ops.] The **Red** light carried at the rear of a **Train**, which serves to assure staff that the entire **Train** has passed complete and no parts have become detached. On some **Southern Region** services operated by **Multiple Units** an illuminated red roller blind was used instead. See also **Tail-lamping**.

Tail Rope
[Hist.] On a **Rope-Worked Railway** a rope attached to the rear of a **Set** which would be used to haul a return Set vehicles if, for example the, **Track Gradient** and/or weather conditions prevented the vehicles descending under gravity alone.

Tail-lamping
[Ops. Col.] A means of **Signalling** ▫ **Trains** which utilises the observation and reporting of passing **Tail Lamps** as a means of ensuring that Trains have passed complete. Normally only used as a temporary measure.

TAIM
[TRS] **T**ubular **A**xle **I**nduction **M**otor.

Taith
(Tradename) The public transport organisation jointly representing the six county authorities in North Wales. It deals with public transport developments and improvements across the whole of North Wales.

Taken at Half-price
[Sig. Col.] A colloquial term meaning **Acceptance** of a **Train** into an **Occupied Section** on a **Line** where **Permissive Block** is permitted.

Taken at the Bells
[Sig. Col.] Acceptance of a **Train** under the **Warning Arrangement** □ (**Block Regulation** 5). Also **Under the Hammer**.

Talking Past
[Sig. Col.] The action of instructing a driver to pass a **Signal** displaying a **Stop Aspect**, normally as a result of a localised failure of **Signalling Equipment** such as a **Track Circuit** (**TC**). Also **Stop and Caution**.

TAMANS
[NR Tel] Telecommunications Asset Management and Networking Service, see **Network Rail Telecommunications** (**NRT**).

TAMAR
(*tay-mar*) [NR] **TPWS** Asset Maintenance and Recording, a database used to record and manage data related to **Train Protection and Warning System** (**TPWS**) installations.

Tamp, Regulate and DTS
[PW] A compound term describing the use of a **Tamping and Lining Machine** (**Tamper**), **Ballast Regulator** (**Regulator**) and a **Dynamic Track Stabiliser** (**DTS**) together to implement (generally) **Design Levels** and **Design Alignment**. This activity typically takes place following a **Track Renewal** or **Reballasting** operation.

Tamper
[PW] An **On Track Machine** (**OTM**) that can (generally) **Lift** and **Slue** the **Track** and simultaneously consolidate the **Ballast** under the **Sleepers**. Most machines employ some system to smooth out and average **Track Faults**, and apply predetermined **Lifts** and **Slues** to the **Track**. The most advanced add some degree of computing power to further increase the effective measurement baseline (thus averaging the errors all the better), the pinnacle being **GPS** guided machines and those capable of reading positional data from datums at the **Lineside**. The machines' full title is more properly **Tamping and Lining Machine**. See also **ALC**, **Automatic Track Alignment** (**ATA**), **Automatic Track and Top Alignment** (**ATTA**), **Continuous Action Tamper** (**CAT**), **Double Bank Tamper**, **GVA**, **Plain Line Tamper**, **Running Edge Face Of Steel** (**REFOS**), **SLC**, **Tamping Cycle**, **Track Machine Guidance** (**TMG**), **Single Bank Tamper**, **Switch and Crossing Tamper** (**S&C Tamper**).

Tamper Siding
A **Siding** used for the **Stabling**, fuelling and **Maintenance** of **On Track Machines** (**OTMs**) such as **Tampers**.

Tamping
[PW] The operation of **Lifting** the **Track** and simultaneously consolidating the **Ballast** beneath the **Sleepers**. This operation has largely been mechanised. See **Tamper**. See also **Measured Shovel Packing** (**MSP**), **Pneumatic Ballast Injection** (**PBI**, **Stoneblowing**).

Tamping and Lining (T&L)
[PW] The operation of **Lifting** and re-aligning the **Track** and consolidating the **Ballast** beneath the **Sleepers**. This operation has largely been mechanised. See **Tamper**. See also **Pneumatic Ballast Injection** (**PBI**, **Stoneblowing**), **Tamping**.

Tamping and Lining Machine
[PW] The infrequently used full title for a **Tamper**. See also **Continuous Action Tamper** (**CAT**). Also **Tamping Machine**.

Tamping Bank
[PW] The assembly of hydraulically operated tines and an asynchronous vibration system that is used to consolidate **Ballast** as part of the **Tamping Cycle** of a **Tamper**. Such **Banks** are arranged on a vertical slide to allow their deployment (dropping) and removal (raising). There is generally one Bank for each **Rail**, each capable of **Tamping** one **Sleeper** (**Single Bank Tamper**), two Sleepers (**Double Bank Tamper**) or three Sleepers (**Triple Bank Tamper**) in one operation. See also **Continuous Action Tamper** (**CAT**).

Tamping Cycle
[PW] The mechanised **Tamping** operation, including **Lifting** and **Lining** the **Track**, dropping the **Tamping Banks** into the **Ballast**, squeezing the **Tamping Tines** together, removing the Banks from the Ballast, releasing the Track and repeating the cycle if required. See also **Double Tamping**.

Tamping Machine
See **Tamper**. Also **Tamping and Lining Machine**.

Tamping Tine
[PW] The spade-ended tool used to consolidate the **Ballast** under a **Sleeper**, used in conjunction with either a **Kango Hammer** or **Tamping and Lining Machine** (**Tamper**).

TAN
[NR] **Track Access** Notice, the means of publishing short term additions and alterations to the **Train Plan**.

Tanalisation
(Tradename) Treating **Timber** against fungal and insect attack using a solution of Copper, Chromium and Arsenic salts. A trademark of Hicksons Ltd.

Tandem
a) See **Tandem Lift**
b) See **Tandem Turnout**
c) See **Tandem Working**.

Tandem Lift
The simultaneous use of two independent machines to lift a single, generally large, load.

497

Tandem Turnout

[PW] Two **Turnouts** combined, in which the **Toes** of the second **Turnout** are adjacent to the **Switch Heel** of the first. Also **Follow-on Leads**, **Double Turnout**, **Pannier Turnout**, See also **Three Throw**.

Tandem Working

[Ops.] Describing two **Locomotives** hauling one **Train**, both from the **Leading End**, the Locomotives being driven independently by a driver each. In modern times this arrangement is unusual, a more normal system being **Multiple Working**, where one driver controls two interconnected Locomotives.

Tangent Point

The intersection between a **Curve** and a tangent of that Curve. See also **Tangent Track**.

Tangent Track

[Elec.] A geometrical description of **Straight Track**, sometimes used by **Overhead Line Electrification** (**OLE**) engineers.

Tangential Crossover

[Elec.] Used on **High Speed** ▫ **Overhead Line Equipment** (**OLE**) systems instead of a crossing contact arrangement. The wires diverge or converge but do not actually cross until they are **Out Of Running**.

Tangential Switch

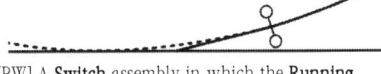

[PW] A **Switch** assembly in which the **Running Edges** (**RE**) of the projected **Switch Radius** and **Stock Rail** are tangential to each other in the closed position. See also **Intersecting Switch**,. **Non-intersecting Switch**

Tango

The **Phonetic Alphabet** word representing **T**.

Tango Coat

[LUL Col.] Orange high-visibility coat.

Tank Container

A special type of freight **Container** designed for the carriage of gases, liquids and solid substances

Tank Engine

[TRS] A **Steam Locomotive** fitted with an integral water tank and, generally, an integral coal bunker. The alternative is a **Tender Engine**.

Tank Wagon

[TRS] A **Wagon** permanently fitted with a tank for the transport of liquids or powders or a **Wagon** which has such a tank integral to it. See also **Class of Tank Wagon**.

TAP

a) **T**rack **A**ccess **P**oint
b) [LUL] **T**ouch **a**nd **P**ass
c) (Tradename) **T**rack **A**ccess **P**roductions, of Leighton Buzzard, supplier of in-cab video, training materials and **Track Diagrams**.

Tap Changer

[TRS] A **Camshaft** operated set of electrical switches, used on an **AC Electric Locomotive** to select from the different voltage values (known as **Taps**) available on the main transformer, and thus control the **Traction Motors**. Now generally superseded by **Thyristor** control.

TAPAS

a) [NR] **T**rain **A**utomatic **P**erformance **A**nalysis **S**ystem. A remote condition-based **Maintenance** system which exploits data produced routinely by **Trains**
b) [LUL] **T**imetables **A**vailable for **P**osting **a**t **S**tops.

Tapper Key

[Sig.] A momentary-action electrical switch used to send **Bell Codes** under the **Absolute Block** (**AB**) system. Also **Bell Tapper**, Morse Key.

Tappet

[Sig.] The flat metal bar linked to a **Lever** in a **Lever Frame**. The Tappet runs in a **Race**, is moved by the Lever and has notches (also called **Ports**) which interface with the **Dogs** or **Nibs** attached to the **Locking Slides** to perform the **Interlocking** ▫ Function.

Tappet Frame

[Sig.] A **Lever Frame** which utilises **Tappets**. See also **Tumbler Frame**.

Tappet Locking

[Sig.] The more common arrangement of **Mechanical Locking**, where each **Tappet** fits in a **Race** which is a vertical slot milled across the **Locking Tray**. The Locking Tray is a cast iron plate which has horizontal dividing strips called ribs which guide the **Locking Slides**. The **Dogs** or **Nibs** on these engage in the Tappets to perform the **Interlocking** ▫ Function. See also **Tumbler Locking**.

Tapping Pin

[PW] A sacrificial metal pin with a large flat head. It is used to seal the hole in the **Thimble** at the bottom of the **Crucible** while the **Thermit Weld** heating process takes place. When the reaction is complete the **Tapping Pin**, previously protected from the reacting Thermit mixture by a layer of ground-up **Slag**, is pushed up by the **Track Welder** (**TW**), releasing the molten metal into the moulds. See also **Self-tapping Thimble**.

Taps

Intermediate voltage connections on the secondary winding of a **Transformer**.

TAR

a) **T**rain **A**rrival **R**elay
b) **T**elecommunications **A**pparatus **R**oom. Also **TER**

TARDIS
(*tar-dis*) [NR] TOPS Ancillary Retrospective Data Information Service.

Tare
See Tare Weight.

Tare Deflated
[PW] One of the standard Gauging scenarios, this assumes that the Rail Vehicle is not loaded and any air bags in the Secondary Suspension system are deflated.

Tare Weight
[TRS] The weight of a Rail Vehicle capable of carrying a load when it is not carrying any load; i.e. its unladen weight. See also Gross Laden Weight (GLW).

Target
a) [Unk.] A device that indicates the position of a Set of Points to the driver
b) [Col.] A description of a regular Engineering Trip Train
c) [LUL] A pre-worded warning board
d) [Sig.] A device used by a Signal Sighting Committee (SSC) to indicate the proposed position of the Stop Aspect during Signal Sighting activities.

TARQUIN
(*tar-kwin*) (Tradename) [PW] Track and Ride Quality Investigation, a method of identifying Track requiring Reballasting or Formation Treatment, developed by Mott MacDonald Ltd., which makes use of Track Recording Coach (TRC) data, Ground Penetrating Radar (GPR) data, topological observation, drift geology and existing Track Drainage provision. The output is a risk value which can then be used to specify further investigation work. See also Trackbed Investigation (TBI).

TAS
Telecoms Asset Store.

TASC
Track and Service Car.

Task Briefing (TB)
[NR] A single page document issued to members of a Work Group, containing only the health, safety and welfare information relevant to that task. See also Work Package Plan (WPP).

TASR
Track Asset Systems Replacement.

TASS
(*tass*) See Tilt Authorisation and Speed Supervision System.

TASS Balise
See Tilt Authorisation and Speed Supervision System Balise.

TAT
Technical Assurance Testing.

ELLIS' BRITISH RAILWAY ENGINEERING ENCYCLOPÆDIA

Tattenhall Junction Accident
At 18:08 on 2nd July 1971 a Schools Excursion Train Derailed under an Overbridge at approximately 70 mph. The last three Coaches left the Track, killing two children, six Passengers were seriously injured and another 20 slightly injured. The cause was determined to be a Track Buckle caused by Rail Creep in Jointed Track, exacerbated by Elastic Spike Rail Fastenings, recent Lifting and Packing, and ineffective planning and management.

Tattersall, A.E.
One of the great Signalling Engineers, he worked on the Lancashire and Yorkshire (L&YR), Metropolitan, Great Northern (GNR) and in 1936 the London North Eastern (LNER) Railways, pioneering the use of Relays and Switch Panels.

TAV
[TRS] An acronym representing a Trailer Auxiliary Equipment Van.

TAWS
Train Activated Warning System. See Train Operated Warning System (TOWS). Also Automatic Track Warning System (ATWS).

Tay Bridge Accident
At around 19:15 on the night of 28th December 1879, the central 'high girders' of the recently opened Tay Bridge collapsed in a force 11 storm, taking with it a Train of six Coaches and 75 Passengers and Traincrew. Designed by Thomas Bouch, the Bridge was inadequately designed for the wind loadings found at the location, poorly constructed and inadequately maintained. This accident remains the greatest loss of life in a single structural collapse in the UK.

TB
a) See Tokenless Block.
b) See Task Briefing. See also Work Package Plan (WPP).

TB(SC)
[Sig.] Scottish Tokenless Block.

TBC
[TRS]
a) An acronym representing a Trailer □ Brake □ Composite Coach
b) See Traction Brake Controller.

TBCK
[TRS] An acronym representing a Trailer □ Brake □ Composite Coach with Kitchen.

TBE
[NR Hist.] Territory Building Engineer.

TBEWG
[NR Hist.] Territory Building Engineers Working Group.

TBF
[TRS] An acronym representing a Trailer □ Brake □ First Class □ Coach.

TBI
See Trackbed Investigation.

499

ELLIS' BRITISH RAILWAY ENGINEERING ENCYCLOPÆDIA

TBL
(Tradename) [Sig.] A type of **Automatic Train Protection** (**ATP**) fitted on the **Great Western Main Line** (**GWML**). Manufactured by ACEC Transport. See also **BR-ATP, SELCAB**.

TBM
a) Temporary Bench Mark
b) See **Tunnel Boring Machine**.

TBR
Time Break Recall.

TBS
See **Transmission Based Signalling**.

TBSK
[TRS] An acronym representing a **Trailer □ Brake □ Standard Class □ Coach** with Kitchen.

TBSO
[TRS] An acronym representing a **Trailer □ Brake □ Standard Class □ Open Coach**.

TBTC
TBTCS
See **Transmission Based Train Control** System. See also **Communications-Based Train Control** (**CBTC**).

TBW
See **Temporary Block Working.**.

TC
a) See **Track Circuit**.
b) See **Trip Cock**.
c) [TRS] An acronym representing a **Trailer □ Composite Coach**.

TC1
[NR] The reference number of the certificate signed by the **Tester in Charge** (**TIC**) on completion of the **Testing** of a new or modified **Signalling System**.

TCA
a) See **Track Circuit Actuator**
b) Track Circuit Assister.

TCAID
(*tee-cee-ade*) See **Track Circuit Actuator Interference Detector**.

TCB
a) See **Track Circuit Block**
b) **Trackside** Connection Box
c) [LUL] Ticket Collector's Box.

TCBR
Track Circuit □ Block Regulations.

TCC
Track Circuit Clip. See **Track Circuit Operating Clip** (**TCOC**).

TCCM
See **Train Coupling Compatibility Matrix**.

TCCOS
See **Traction Control Cut-Out Switch**.

TCCS
Train Control Command System.

TCE
[NR Hist.] Territory □ Civil Engineer.

TCF
[Sig.] Track Circuit Failure.

TCI
a) See **Track Circuit Interrupter**
b) (Tradename) Transportation Consultants International, now part of **AEA Technology** □ Rail (in turn now **DeltaRail**).

TCIC
Trip Cock Isolating Cock.

TCIS
Trip Cock Isolating Switch.

TCK
[TRS] An acronym representing a **Trailer □ Composite Coach** with Kitchen.

TCL
a) [PW] Track Centre Line, see **Centreline Design**
b) (Tradename) Tramtrack Croydon Ltd.

TCM
a) See **Track Chargeman**
b) Time Cycle **Maintenance**, an alternative term for **Cyclic Maintenance**
c) **Traincrew** Manager.

TCMS
[Sig.] Train Control Management System.

TCN
Train Communications Network.

TCOC
See **Track Circuit Operating Clips**.

T-COD
(*tee-kod*) See **Track Circuit Operating Device**.

TCPS
[TRS] Trip Cock Pressure Switch.

TCR
Transmission Control Relay.

TCRC
Trip Cock Resetting Cord.

TCS
a) See **Train Control System**
b) See **Tilt Control System**
c) **Traffic** Control System
d) Trip Circuit Supervision
e) **Traincrew** Supervisor.

TCSD
[TRS] An acronym representing a **Trailer □ Conductor □ Standard Class □ Coach** with disabled facilities (**HST**).

TCSDC
[Sig.] **Train Control System** (**TCS**) Development Contract (undertakes development of Train Control Systems and separation of **Control Centre** works).

TCS-F
[Sig.] **Train Control System** (**TCS**), Fixed Block implementation.

TCS-M
[Sig.] **T**rain **C**ontrol **S**ystem (TCS), **M**oving Block implementation.

TCSU
Traffic **C**ontrol **S**ignals **U**nit.

TCT
[LUL] **T**unnel **C**leaning **T**rain.

TD
See **T**rain **D**escriber.

TD Berth
See **T**rain **D**escriber Berth. Also Berth.

TD Stepping
See **T**rain **D**escriber Stepping.

TDA
TRUST **D**elay **A**ttribution.

TDB
Track **D**isconnection **B**ox.

TD-D
[Sig.] **T**rain **D**escriber (TD) **D**ata training course.

TDM
a) See **T**rack **D**esign **M**anual
b) See **T**ime **D**ivision **M**ultiplex.

TDMA
Time **D**ivision **M**ultiple **A**ccess.

TDN
See **T**rain **D**escription.

TDR
See **T**rain **D**ata **R**ecorder.

TDS
[Sig.] **T**esting **D**isplay **S**ubsystem, a subsystem within the IECC system.

TD-T
[Sig.] **T**rain **D**escriber (TD) **T**ransmission training course.

Tea
The lifeblood of the former **British Railways** (BR), without copious quantities of which the **National Railway Network** (NRN) would have ground to a halt. Today's **Contractor** is more likely to drink coffee, owing to the increased levels of stress encountered post-**Privatisation**.

TEB
Telephone **E**nquiry **B**ureau.

TEC
[LUL] **T**unnel **E**mergency **C**ommunication system. Also **Tunnel Telephone**.

Technical Assessment
The process of determining the condition of an asset by applying criteria to relevant data.

Technical Headway
[Sig.] The calculated minimum time interval between **Trains** that a **Signalling System** will permit to run entirely under **Proceed Aspects**. Where this Headway on a **Route** varies, it is the longest minimum interval that is used. See also **Planning Headway**.

Technical Running Time (TRT)
The theoretical time (normally expressed in seconds) that a particular **Train** takes between two defined points under normal operation. This figure is used as the basis for determining a **Sectional Running Time** (SRT).

Technical Staff
Persons engaged in the survey, design and implementation of those designs on the **Railway**. Also **Draughtsman**, PTO, STO, TO.

Technical Standards for Interoperability (TSI)
European legislation which mandates certain (minimum) common standards across the European Union, allowing "Inter-operation" without the need for territory specific modifications to vehicles.

Technical Workscope
[NR] A contract document which describes all project specific information and details the technical specification, implementation standards and assurance requirements for a project.

Technician's Console
Technician's Terminal
[Sig.] The Technician's Console allows close monitoring of the **Internal States** of several **Solid State Interlockings** (SSI) at a **Signal Control Centre**, and the online diagnosis of faults in the **Signalling Equipment**, etc. The Technician's Console also allows one to impose (temporary) restrictions on the behaviour of the Interlocking, by removing the **Signaller's** ability to **Set** certain **Routes** (**Route Bars**), move certain **Points** or **Clear** certain **Signals**. Also **Maintainer's Terminal**.

Tectona Grandis
Teak. See **Key**.

TED
[LUL] **T**raction **E**arth **D**etector.

TEDE
[NR] **T**erritory □ **E**arthworks and **D**rainage **E**ngineer.

TEE
Trans **E**urope **E**xpress.

Tee Piece
See **End Post**.

Tee-feed
[Elec.] An arrangement whereby one **Feeder Station** (FS) supplies the **Overhead Line Equipment** (OLE) in both directions along a **Route**.

Tee-headed Bolt
[PW] A bolt having a 'T' shaped head that locks into a suitable recess cast into a metal **Baseplate** or **Concrete Sleeper** to prevent rotation of the bolt during either tightening or loosening operations.

TEF
See **Track Engineering Form**.

TEFC
[LUL] Totally Enclosed Fan Cooled.

TEH
[Tel.] Trackside Equipment Housing.

Telecoms.

Telecommunications
The **Engineering Discipline** or **Function** responsible for the provision of telephone and data transmission facilities on the **Railway**. See **Thales**.

Telegraph Codes
Prior to the widespread use of telephones, Telex and fax machines, messages were sent around the **Railway** system by electric telegraph. For efficiency, common messages could be sent using short code words. Whilst electric telegraphs are rare nowadays, some of the Codes are still used, on occasion; see **Ack**, **Ajax**, **Amber**, **Arno**, **Arrow**, **Blocsid**, **Blox**, **Cabbage**, **Cape**, **Chik**, **Conflict**, **Cuckoo**, **Currant**, **Cyrus**, **Debris**, **Dedimus**, **Derwent**, **Earwig**, **Eider**, **Exlo**, **Fabric**, **Falcon**, **Fungus**, **Furno**, **Gobi**, **Hazard**, **Holly**, **Lacer**, **Longlo**, **Moselle**, **Nile**, **Oglo**, **Ohio**, **Oppos**, **Pine**, **Reed**, **Reliance**, **Sap**, **Savo**, **Slattern**, **Speno**, **Sultan**, **Walnut**, **Weser**, **Willow**, **Worgan**. See also **Wagon Names**.

Telephone Concentrator
[Tel.] A device used to collect many telephone circuits together onto one terminal, avoiding the need to provide a separate telephone instrument for each circuit. Generally used in **Signal Boxes** as the focal point of the relevant **Point Zone Telephones** (**PZT**) and **Signal Post Telephones** (**SPT**).

Telephone Protected Level Crossing (TLC)
A variety of **Level Crossing** (**LC**, **LX**) where the user is obliged to telephone the **Signaller** to make arrangements to cross. The Signaller does not monitor the Level Crossing.

Telescoping
[TRS] The outcome of a collision involving older **Rolling Stock**, where each successive vehicle is forced into the next in the manner of closing up like a telescope. This type of failure has been designed out of modern Coaches, using more rigid monocoques, better couplings and devices that ensure that the ends of the Coaches remain in line.

Tell Tale
a) [PW] A reference mark made before and during **Stressing** operations and prior to the creation of a **Rail Weld** to ensure that the person in charge of Stressing operations can monitor accurately the movement of the **Rails**. Tell Tales generally take the form of a chalk or pencil mark made both on the Rail and the **Sleeper**, the **Rail Fastenings** having been removed first. See also **Inner Tell Tales** (**ITT**), **Outer Tell Tales** (**OTT**)
b) [Sig.] A **Wire** or electrical switch (**Plunger**) which, when broken or operated alerts the **Signaller** to the need to **Replace** one or more **Signals** to **Danger** to avert an accident. The wire version is also called a **Trip Wire**.

TEM
Tender Evaluation Model.

Temporary
In any other field, Temporary would mean non-permanent or of short duration. On the **Railway**, it can mean anything but this, as Temporary arrangements often turn into permanent ones. This is particularly true of Temporary **Signal Boxes** (**SB**) and occasionally true of **Temporary Speed Restrictions** (**TSR**). In this latter case see **Historic TSR**.

Temporary Approach Control
[Sig.] **Approach Control** applied when abnormal arrangements require it, such as during **Engineering Work**.

Temporary Block Working (TBW)
[Sig.] A temporary **Absolute Block** □ **Signalling** arrangement, normally imposed during major **Engineering Works** or in times of accident or severe disruption, but not on **Single Lines** (see **Single Line Working** (**SLW**)).

Temporary Bond
A **Bond** applied across a gap in a **Rail** or between two Rails for one of the following reasons:
- [Elec.] To provide a **Traction Current Return** around a break in the **Track**, such as **Work Site** or **Broken Rail**
- [PW] To ensure that dangerous potentials do not develop in lengths of **Continuous Welded Rail** (**CWR**) laid in the **Cess** adjacent to **Electrified Lines**
- [Sig.] To provide electrical continuity in a **Track Circuit** (**TC**) during **Stageworks**.

Temporary Level Crossing
A **Level Crossing** (**LC**, **LX**) provided for a short duration, normally in connection with **Engineering Work**.

Temporary Magnet
[Col.] Term for a **Portable Automatic Warning System Magnet** (**Portable AWS Magnet**).

Temporary Non-compliance (TNC)
[NR] An exemption from some part of a **Railway Group Standard** (**RGS**) or **Network Rail Company Standard** (**NRCS**) for a specific length of time. This need can arise during **Stageworks** or because a new procedure, process or product has not been incorporated in to the Standard yet, but will be under the next revision. A permanent **Non-compliance** is a **Derogation**.

Temporary Panel
a) See **Temporary Track** clause b)
b) [Sig.] A **Signaller's Panel** provided as temporary measure.

Temporary Speed Restriction (TSR)
[NR] A **Speed Restriction** imposed for a short time, generally as a result of **Engineering Work**, to guarantee safe passage of **Trains**. Such a restriction is published in advance in the **Weekly Operating Notice** (**WON**).

Temporary Track
[PW]
a) Lightweight sectional **Track** used in conjunction with **Panel Lifting Units** such as **Fassetta**, **PAL**, **PLUM** and **PUM** to transport large items of **Permanent Way** (**PW**), particularly **Switch and Crossing Layouts** (**S&C Layouts**) longitudinally over newly laid **Ballast**
b) **Track Panels** made up from **Serviceable** components and used to fill gaps created during **Renewals** or **Remodelling** activity, following which the Temporary Track is removed. Also **Temporary Panels**.

Temporary Way
[Hist.] The rough **Track** laid by the **Contractor** when constructing a **Railway**. Upon completion of the main works this **Tramway** was used to deliver the final **Rails** and **Sleepers**, in turn forming the **Permanent Way** (**PW**).

Temporary Works
Work which is carried out to facilitate other elements of a project. Whilst by their nature they are have a limited life, Temporary Works are subject to the same design rules as permanent solutions.

TEMPRO
Trip End Model Presentation Program.

TEN
(ten) See **Trans European Network**. See also **Trans European Network Route** (**TENS Route**).

Tench (YPA)
[NR] A low-floor 51 ton capacity flat **Wagon** with low height doors, used for transporting **Rails** and **Sleepers**. See **Wagon Names**.

Tender
[TRS] A dedicated vehicle attached to a **Steam Locomotive** that carries the water and fuel. A **Locomotive** with a Tender is a **Tender Engine**.

Tender Engine
[TRS] A **Steam Locomotive** which has a dedicated vehicle attached to it for the purpose of carrying the water and fuel. The alternative is a **Tank Engine**.

Tender First
[Ops.] Describing a **Steam Locomotive** □ Running backwards (**Tenders** are semi-permanently **Coupled** to the back of Steam Locomotives).

Tenfoot
Ten Foot

a) The wide interval that must be provided when there are three or more **Tracks** on a **Route**, e.g., a **Four Track Railway**, having a **Down Slow**, **Up Slow**, **Down Fast** and **Up Fast** will typically have a **Sixfoot** between each **Slow** and **Fast** pair, and a **Tenfoot** between the two pairs of Tracks
b) [Col.] Description of any interval with a dimension greater than a Sixfoot. See also **Widespace**, **Wideway**.
Also 10 Foot. See also **Track Interval**.

Tenfoot Drain
[PW] A **Track Drain** laid in the **Tenfoot**.

TENS
(tenns) Trans European Network Strategy. See **Trans European Network Route** (**TENS Route**).

TENS Route
(tenns root) See **Trans European Network Route**.

Tension Length (TL)
[Elec.] A length of **Overhead Line Equipment** (**OLE**) □ **Catenary** that is tensioned from one **Balance Weight Anchor** (**BWA**) position. On long open stretches there are normally two Tension Lengths in one **Wire Run**, separated by a **Mid-point Anchor** (**MPA**) and having a BWA at each outermost end.

Tensorex C+
(Tradename) [Elec.] A type of **Spring Tensioner** manufactured by Pfisterer Srl of Milan, used in **GEFF**, **Series 1** and **Series 2** □ **Overhead Line Equipment** (**OLE**)

Tensors
See **Rail Tensors**.

TEP
a) See **Token Exchange Point**.
b) **Train** Equipment Panel.

TEPE
(tea-pea) [NR Hist.] Territory □ **Electrification and Plant Engineer**, previously the Zone Electrification and Plant Engineer (**ZEPE**).

TER
a) See **Time Element Relay**
b) **Telecommunications** Equipment Room
c) **Traction** Electricity Rules.
d) Trans-European North-South **Railway** Project
e) Trans European **Railway Network**.

TERF
TERFF
Trans-European **Rail** □ **Freight** Freeways.
TERFN
Trans European **Rail** □ **Freight** Network.
Terminal End
[Elec.] A location where the entire **Overhead Line Electrification** (**OLE**) system comes to a dead end, both physically and electrically. See also **Fixed Anchor**.
Terminal Line
A **Running Line** ending at a **Buffer Stop** or similar arrangement.
Terminal Platform
An alternative term for a **Bay Platform**.
Terminal Single Line
A dead-end **Single Line** which ends at a **Buffer Stop**, **Stop Board** or, very rarely, a **Signal**.
Terminal Station
A **Station** which only has **Bay Platforms**, i.e. it is a dead end. Also **Terminus Station**.
Terminating Train
[Ops.] A **Train** that is completing its journey at the next **Station** as shown in the **Timetable** (**TT**) and proceeding no further. The same **Rail Vehicles** may later form part or all of another Train, for instance a **Return Working**.
Termination Board (T Board)
See **Termination Indicator**.
Termination Indicator
[NR] A temporary **Lineside Sign** consisting of a black T on a yellow background marking the end of a **Temporary Speed Restriction** (**TSR**) or **Emergency Speed Restriction** (**ESR**). Also **Termination Board**, **T Board**.
Terminus
Terminus Station
A point at which a geographical **Route** ends. Specifically applied to **Passenger Stations** located at the ends of **Routes**. The plural is Terminii. See also **Terminal Station**.
TERN
(Tradename) [Sig.] **Token** Exchange using **R**andom **N**umbers, a simplified **Signalling System** based on the exchange of numeric Tokens.
Terram
(Tradename)
a) A manufacturer of various types of **Geotextile**
b) [Col.] The name of a non-woven permeable material widely used under the **Ballast** as a separator layer to reduce the upward migration of the **Formation**.
Territory
[NR Hist.] The **Network Rail** regional organisation, loosely equivalent in coverage to their predecessors, the **Regions** and, broadly, the **Zones**.

TES
See **T**rain **E**ntering **S**ection.
TESCO
(*tesco*) [Hist.] **T**echnical **E**ngineering **S**ervice **Co**mpany. A transitional organisation during **Privatisation** which provided engineering services associated with **Traction and Rolling Stock** (**T&RS**) maintenance.
TESG
Traction **E**lectricity **S**teering **G**roup.
TESS
Trackside **E**nergy **S**torage **S**ystems.
Test Logs
[Sig.] Queries produced by **Testers** during the **Testing** phase of a **Signalling Scheme**. These individually numbered documents must be responded to by the designer or installer and corrected or the variation justified to the **Tester In Charge** (**TIC**) before the Signalling Scheme can be brought into use at **Commissioning**. A single large **Resignalling Scheme** generates hundreds of Test Logs, ranging from small details such as the provision of arrows on **Speed Signs** to major principles such as **Permissive Working**.
Test Magnet
See **Shed Test Magnet**.
Test Panel
a) [Sig.] A control desk or **Panel** provided at the site of an **Interlocking** for testing and maintenance purposes. The function may be performed by a **Local Panel**
b) A small section of some construction or process produced to test a proposed method, competence or to satisfy a contractual requirement for quality assurance..
Test Service Car
Rail Vehicles used to provide realistic service behaviour for testing purposes and to act as **Translator Vehicles**.
Test Site A (TSA)
Test Site B (TSB)
[NR Hist.] Sites identified and prepared for testing of Class 390 Pendolino trains as part of the **West Coast Main Route Modernisation** (**WCRM**) project. Test Site A was located between Carnforth and Carlisle, and Test Site B between Rugby and Stafford.

ELLIS' BRITISH RAILWAY ENGINEERING ENCYCLOPÆDIA

Test Train
a) Any **Train** run for the sole purpose of collecting data, such as **Wire Height**, **Track Geometry** or **Rail Defects**. See IRIS, MENTOR, New Measurement Train (NMT), Track Recording Vehicle (TRV), Ultrasonic Test Unit (UTU).
b) A **Train** run within a recently **Resignalled** area to verify that all the **Signals** operate correctly, that all works are satisfactorily completed and, in the case of major alterations carried out over many weeks, to clean the rust off the **Rails**.
c) An otherwise normal **Train** run under special conditions, typically to verify the performance of new **Rolling Stock**. The special conditions may include a formal **Possession** of the **Line**, the barring of staff from the **Track** and speeds up to 10% over the maximum normally permitted.

Tester
[Sig.] A **Signalling** technician engaged in checking newly installed **Signalling Equipment** against the design documents and ensuring that the relevant current, resistance and voltage requirements are met.

Tester in Charge (TIC)
[Sig.] The **Signalling** engineer responsible for the correct **Testing and Commissioning** (T&C) of a new or altered **Signalling System**.

Testing
[Sig.] The operation carried out on a newly installed **Signalling System** awaiting **Commissioning**. The design is compared to the relevant standards and the installed system is compared to the design by the **Testers** and any differences recorded. These differences are highlighted on **Test Logs** to the designer by the **Tester in Charge** (TIC) and the system will not be commissioned unless all these Test Logs are satisfactorily resolved. See also **Closure List**, **Testing Plan**, **Testing Strategy**, **Through Testing**.

Testing and Commissioning (T&C)
[Sig.] Collective term for the activities carried out by **Signalling Engineers** immediately prior to the activation of a new or modified **Signalling System**. See also **Commissioning**, **Test Logs**, **Tester**, **Tester in Charge** (TIC), **Testing**, **Testing Certificate**, **Testing Plan**, **Testing Strategy**, **Wheels Free Period**.

Testing Certificate
[Sig.] The final document in the **Testing** process. Signed by the **Tester in Charge** (TIC), it confirms that the **Signalling System** is fully functional and all issues have been addressed.

Testing Copies
[Sig.] The **Testing Copies** of **Signalling Scheme Plans** (SSP), **Signal Sighting Forms** (SSF) and **Wiring Diagrams** made on pink paper for use by the **Testers** and **Tester in Charge** (TIC). The different colour is used to ensure that these copies are not confused with other documents. They are therefore also known as **Testing Pinks**. See also **Pink Copies**, **Pinks**.

Testing Pinks
[Sig. Col.] Common name for **Testing Copies**, after their normal colour.

Testing Plan
Testing Strategy
[Sig.] A document identifying in the order in which the parts of a modified **Signalling System** will be **Tested**, by whom, when and to which standards and design documents. See also **Testing Copies**.

TET
[LUL] Tunnel Emergency Telephone, see **Tunnel Telephone System** (TTS).

TETRA
(*tet-rah*) Terrestrial Trunked Radio, a means of linking dissimilar and incompatible radio communication systems.

TETS
See **Train Entering Terminal Station**.

TEU
Twenty-foot Equivalent Unit; a size description of shipping **Containers**.

TEW
TEW Engineering
(*chew*) (Tradename) [Sig.] A manufacturer of **Signal Box Panels**.

TF
a) See **Tilt Failed**. See also **Hard Over Tilt Failed** (HOTF)
b) [TRS] An acronym representing a **Trailer □ First Class □ Coach**.

TF25
[TRS] A type of **Low Track Force □ Bogie** developed by Powell Duffryn Rail, based on the **LTF25**.

TFC
a) See **Tilt for Comfort**
b) Telecommunications Fault Control
c) Track Facility Charge.

TFH
[TRS] An acronym representing a **Trailer □ First Class □ Coach** with **Handbrake**.

TfL
See **Transport for London**.

TFM
See **Trackside Functional Module**.

TFS
Traction □ Feeder Station (FS).

TGA
See **Traction Gel Applicator**.

TGCS
(Tradename) [PW] **Track Geometry** Control System, a system first fitted to **Plasser and Theurer □ Tampers** and used to control the **Lifting** and **Lining** process.

505

TGCS+
(Tradename) [PW] Track Geometry Control System plus, a system fitted to Matisa ▫ Tampers and used to control the Lifting and Lining process.

TGERI
[PW] Track Geometry Enhanced Reporting and Integration.

TGM
[LR] Transport Gateway Metro, a Light Rapid Transit (LRT) service proposed for the Woolwich Rail ▫ Tunnel in London.

TGP8 Gauge
[NR PW] A go/no-go device fitted with a specific P8 Wheel Profile, used to visualise the contact between a Rail Wheel and the Rail. The aim is to confirm that contact is made above a marker on the gauge (the 60° marker line).

TGP8 Track Gauge
[NR PW] A device for measuring the distance between the Rails, incorporating a TGP8 Gauge.

TGR
[PW]
a) [NR] Track Geometry Reports, a portal-based data delivery system
b) Track Geometry Reporting.

TGS
[TRS] An acronym representing a Trailer ▫ Guard ▫ Standard Class ▫ Coach (HST).

TGV
Train à Grande Vitesse, the French high speed Train.

Th
Common shorthand for Thursday.

Thales
(*tallus*) (Tradename) The previous Telecommunications provider on the National Railway Network (NRN). See Network Rail Telecommunications (NRT). See also BRT.

Thames Trains (TT)
A Train Operating Company (TOC).

Thameslink
(Tradename)
a) Brandname of the Route from Bedford to Brighton via Luton, Farringdon, London Bridge and Gatwick Airport
b) A former Train Operating Company (TOC), now First Capital Connect.

Thameslink 2000 (TL2000, TL2K)
[NR] The project under which the existing cross-London ▫ Thameslink ▫ Route was modernised.

Thameslink Programme
[NR] The project to further improve Thameslink, with new, longer Trains running at a higher frequency, improvements to Blackfriars, Farringdon and many other stations, and better interchange. The project is due for completion in 2018.

Theatre Route Indicator
[Sig. Obs.] An obsolete term for an Alphanumeric Route Indicator (ARI). See also Multi-lamp Route Indicator (MLRI), which is obsolete as well.

Theodolite Straight
[PW] A means of setting out a Straight using a theodolite to create a baseline and a levelling staff or tape measure to take offset measurements to the Track, for conversion into Slues. The theodolite baseline is established between calculated offsets from the Heel of each Transition Curve, using:

$$O = \frac{L^2}{6R}$$

Where:
O is the required offset
L is the Transition Length
R is the Radius of the relevant Curve.

Thermal Stress
Thermal Stresses
[PW] The compressive and tensile forces produced in a Rail or Layout by changes in temperature. Such tensile forces can exceed 600kN (60 Tonnes) in Continuous Welded Rail (CWR).

Thermit
[PW]
a) (Tradename) Common contraction of Thermit Welding (GB) Ltd., based in Rainham, Essex
b) See Thermit Weld
c) [Col.] Term used to describe any Alumino-thermic Weld.

Thermit Weld
(Tradename) [PW] A proprietary type of Alumino-thermic Welding process produced by Thermit Welding (GB) Ltd. Thermit is a registered trademark of Th. Goldschmidt AG. Also the adopted colloquial term for any such Weld. See also SkV, SkV-E, SkV-F, SkV-F L50, SkV-F L80, TWS.

Thermite
The name given to the metal produced by the Alumino-thermic Welding process.

Thick Based Baseplate
[PW] A Baseplate having an increased Rail Seat depth.

Thick Based Chair
[PW Hist.] A Chair having an increased Rail Seat depth.

Thick Web Switch
[PW]
a) [Obs.] A design of Shallow Depth Switches designed by Thomas Ward of Sandiacre and produced by Balfour Beatty. It was not adopted by British Rail (BR)
b) [NPT] See Shallow Depth Switches.

Thimble
[PW]
a) See **Rail Thimble**
b) The small tapered tube placed at the bottom of the **Crucible** used in the **Alumino-thermic Weld** process. Its purpose is to ensure that the **Tapping Pin** is seated on a perfectly flat surface. The Thimble is changed for every Weld. See also **Self-tapping Thimble**
c) A sleeve fitted to BJB □ **Rail Fastenings** to improve their **Toe Load**.

Third Class
[Obs.] A currently obsolete level of **Passenger** comfort. In the early days of **Railway** travel Third Class Passengers got a solid wooden bench with no padding, no heating, no glass in the windows and often no roof.

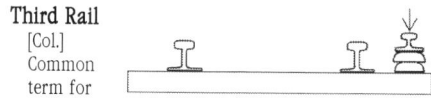

Third Rail
[Col.] Common term for a single **Conductor Rail** positioned on the **Sleeper Ends** outside the **Fourfoot**. Also **DC Rail, Hot Rail, Juice Rail, Positive Conductor Rail, Positive Rail, Pozzy Rail.**

Third Rail Electrification
[Col.] A general term used to cover the type of **Electrification** that involves the supply of DC **Traction Current** to **Trains** by means of a **Conductor Rail** laid along one side of the **Track**, known as the **Third Rail**.

Third Rail Insulator
See **Conductor Rail Insulator**.

Third Rail Tamper
[PW] A **Tamping and Lining Machine** (**Tamper**) that has been modified to allow it to **Tamp** a **Track** fitted with **Conductor Rails**. This modification typically takes the form of the removal of all the outermost **Tamping Tines**, as they would otherwise foul the Conductor Rail. and the fitting of slightly larger Tines in the remaining outer positions in the **Tamping Bank**(s). See also **Plain Line Tamper**.

Third Way
Third Way Analysis
[NR PW] A method of determining the speed capability of a section of **Track** and the work required to support higher speeds. It uses data collected by **Track Recording** vehicles such as the **New Measurement Train** (**NMT**) together with data from **GEOGIS** and **TiCLeD**. See also **Speed Constraints Diagram**.

Thirsk Accident
On 31st July 1967 at Thirsk a **Freight Train** composed of CemFlo cement **Tank Wagons** became **Derailed** and was then struck by an **Express Passenger Train** travelling at approximately 50mph. The initial Derailment was determined to have been caused by the poor ride qualities of these **Wagons** causing them to **Hunt** and in this case leave the **Track**. Seven died and 45 were injured.

Thomas Hughes Rail
[PW Obs.] Used in some welsh mine **Railways**, these Rails are iron bars with turned-down ends which could be inserted into holes in either slate **Sleepers** or purpose-made cast iron sills.

Three Armed Bandit
[PW Col. Obs.] Alternative name for an early type of **Track Relaying Machine** (**TRM**) which had three jibs. This arrangment of machine is now obsolete.

Three Aspect Signal
[Sig.] A **Colour Light Signal** capable of displaying three **Aspects**. These are typically **Red** (a Stop Aspect), **Yellow** (a Caution Aspect) and **Green** (a Proceed Aspect). See also **Three Aspect Signalling**.

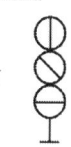

Three Aspect Signalling
[Sig.] An arrangement of **Colour Light Signals** which normally provides only **Red Aspects, Yellow Aspects** and **Green Aspects**. This can be achieved using only **Two Aspect Signals, Three Aspect Signals**, or a mixture of both:

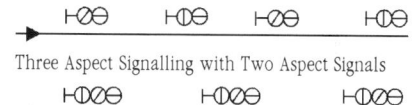

Three Aspect Signalling with Two Aspect Signals

Three Aspect Signalling with Three Aspect Signals

Three Aspect to Four Aspect Transition
[Sig.] The point at which **Three Aspect Signalling** changes to **Four Aspect Signalling**. There are three normal methods of achieving this:

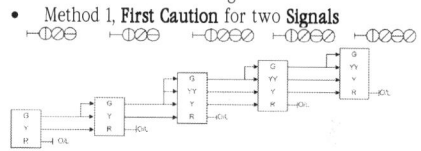

- Method 1, **First Caution** for two **Signals**

- Method 2, **Distant Signal**, see also **Wiltshire Distant**

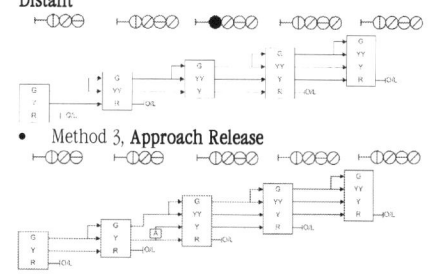

- Method 3, **Approach Release**

Three Link Coupling
[TRS] A **Coupling** consisting of a chain of three large identical links with no length adjustment available. See also **Instanter Coupling**.

Three Point Lining
[PW] A **Lining** system fitted to **Tampers** that allows design **Versines** to be applied to the **Track**.

Three Throw

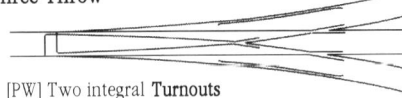

[PW] Two integral **Turnouts** in which the **Toes** of the two Turnouts are staggered over two adjacent **Timbers**. This provides two alternative routes from the **Main Line** at one location. See also **Tandem Turnout**.

Three-Piece Bogie

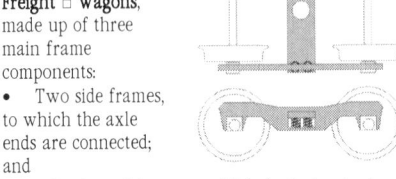

[TRS] A **Bogie**, used on Freight □ **Wagons**, made up of three main frame components:
- Two side frames, to which the axle ends are connected; and
- A horizontal beam on which the body pivots. The beam is supported off the side frames by suspension springs.

Three-state Banner Repeating Signal

[Sig.] A **Banner Repeating Signal** capable of displaying three indications:
- A horizontal black bar on a white background, meaning the **Signal** □ **Beyond** is displaying a **Stop Aspect** (Red)
- A diagonal black bar on a white background, meaning the **Signal Beyond** is displaying a **Caution Aspect**
- A diagonal black bar on a **Green** background, meaning the **Signal Beyond** is displaying a **Proceed Aspect** (Green)

Throat

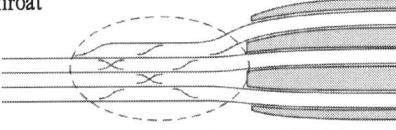

a) The area of **Switch and Crossing** (**S&C**) located between the small number of **Lines** approaching a facility and a facility with many Lines, such as a **Station** or **Yard**. See also **Station Throat**
b) [PW] The **Flangeway** space immediately in front of a **Crossing Nose**.

Thrombosis

[Col. Hist.] Nickname for a **Traffic Apprentice**, e.g. a bloody wandering **Clot** in the system.

Through

a) An item with an entrance or exit at both ends, e.g. **Through Platform**, **Through Siding**, **Through Station**
b) A **Bridge Deck** with both **Floor Beams** and overhead bracing, see **Full Through**. See also **Half Through**
c) Passing under or over many **Tracks**, see **Through Bearers**, **Through Connection**, **Through Timbers**.
d) Passing through many areas, see **Through Alignment Design** (TAD), **Through Service**, **Through Testing**, **Through Ticketing**
e) Bypassing items or objects, see **Through Line**, **Through Piped**.

Through Air Brake

See **Automatic Brake**.

Through Alignment

[PW] An **Alignment** design which considers a large section of the **Main Line** of a **Route** (or possibly a whole **Route**) as one homogenous whole, rather than a series of short sections. This term is commonly used when describing the proper practice when designing **Switch and Crossing Layouts** (**S&C Layouts**). Also **Through Alignment Design** (TAD).

Through Alignment Design (TAD)

[NR PW] A **Track Alignment** design that covers a whole **Route**, encompassing many smaller sites of work. Also referred to as a **Detailed Through Alignment Design** (DTAD).

Through Bearers

[PW] **Switch and Crossing** (**S&C**) □ **Bearers** that support **Rails** on more than one **Track**. Also **Long Bearers**, **Through Timbers**.

Through Carriage

[Ops.] A **Passenger Carriage** which forms part of two or more **Trains** as part of its normal journey. This arrangement is often found on European **Railways** where some carriages are conveyed across many countries by many **Railway Companies** in order to reach their destination. The intention is to avoid the **Passengers** having to **Alight** from and **Board** many different Trains.

Through Connection

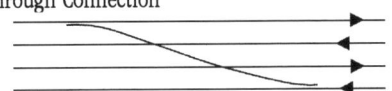

A variety of **Crossover** where the two connected **Tracks** have other Tracks between them. The intervening Tracks are crossed by means of **Diamond Crossings**.

Through Line

a) A **Track** provided to allow **Traffic** to pass through a **Station** without running over a **Line** adjacent to a **Platform**
b) A Line that passes through a facility, to distinguish it from **Bay Lines**, **Sidings** and **Terminal Lines**.

Through Piped
[TRS] Describes a **Rail Vehicle** that is equipped with suitable connections and pipework to carry **Air Brakes**, **Vacuum Brakes** or both through the vehicle from one end to the other, but these systems do not activate the vehicle's brakes at all. See also **Air Piped**, **Blow**, **Blow Through**, **Dual Piped**, **Vacuum Piped**.

Through Platform
A **Platform** which is not a **Bay Platform**, on which **Trains** can approach and leave in the same direction.

Through Routes
[Sig.] An alternative for **Override**.

Through Service
[Ops.] A **Train** which connects two disparate points, travelling via a location where it is more common for Trains to terminate.

Through Siding
A **Siding** that is connected to a **Running Line** at both ends.

Through Station
A **Station** that has some or a majority of, **Through Platforms**, where **Trains** pass through without having to **Reverse** or change direction.

Through Testing
[Sig.] A phase of **Testing** a **Signalling System** carried out after each individual circuit has been Tested, where each **Function** is Tested from as close to the **Signal Box Panel** to as close to the **Track** as possible. This verifies that all the interconnections are correctly made.

Through Ticketing
The ability to purchase a **Ticket** in one transaction for a journey using the services of more than one **Train Operating Company** (**TOC**).

Through Timbers (TT)
[PW] Wood **Switch and Crossing** (**S&C**) □ **Bearers** that support the **Rails** of more than one **Track**. Also **Long Timbers**, **Tied Timbers**.

Throughbolt
[PW] A bolt used to secure **Chairs** or **Baseplates** to **Sleepers** or **Bearers**, the bolt head being located in a recess on the underside of the **Sleeper** or in a special washer plate to prevent rotation of the bolt.

Throw
a) The lateral displacement of the ends and centre of a long **Rail Vehicle** negotiating a **Curve**, see **End Throw**, **Centre Throw**
b) [Col.] To **Reverse** a **Set of Points** or **Set of Switches**
c) The amount by which a **Set of Switches** moves when being moved from Normal to Reverse or vice versa.

Throw Back
[Sig. Col.] To rapidly **Replace** a **Lever** in times of emergency, such as trying to stop a **Train**.

Throw Bar
[Sig.] That part of a **Switch Operating Mechanism** which transfers the drive from the **Point Machine** to the **Switches**.

Thrown
a) [Col.] Of a **Set of Points** or **Set of Switches**, having been moved from Normal to Reverse or vice versa
b) Of a **Circuit Breaker** (**CB**) or electrical switch, to be opened or closed
c) Describing a **Vehicle Profile** that has allowances for **Centre Throw** and **End Throw** added.

Thrown Envelope
The **Static Envelope** with allowances added for **Centre Throw**, **End Throw** and **Vertical Throw**, but not **Dynamic** effects such as suspension movement. See also **Kinematic Envelope** (**KE**), **Swept Envelope** (**SE**), **Swept Path**.

THU
Ticket **H**andling **U**nit

Thunderbirding
[Ops. Col.] A regular arrangement where an **Electric Train** is hauled, **Pan Down**, by a **Diesel Locomotive** as part of a **Timetabled** service over a Non-electrified Line. See **Thunderbirds**. Also **Diesel Hauling**.

Thunderbirds
a) [Col.] Term originally used to describe **Diesel Locomotives** held in reserve to rescue stranded **Trains** on the then recently **Electrified** □ **East Coast Main Line** (**ECML**)
b) [Col.] Any **Locomotive** providing such a service
c) The group of **Virgin Trains** (**VT**) rescue Locomotives that all have names related to the Thunderbirds TV series - *FAB!*

Thyristor
A type of diode with a controlling gate which allows current to pass through it when the gate is energised. The gate is closed by the current being applied to the Thyristor in the reverse direction. Thyristors (also referred to colloquially as **Choppers**) are used for traction power control in place of **DC Resistance Control** systems. A Gate Turn Off Thyristor (**GTO**) is a development in which the current is turned off by applying a pulse of current to the gate.

TI
a) **T**raction **I**nterface
b) **T**raffic **I**nspection
c) [BR] **T**raffic **I**nspector
d) [BR] **T**icket **I**nspector. Also Travelling Ticket Inspector (**TTI**).

TI21
(Tradename) [Sig.] A type of audio frequency **Jointless Track Circuit** (**JTC**) manufactured by Adtranz.

TIC
a) See **Tester In Charge**
b) See **Track Inspection Coach**
c) Technical Investigation Centre
d) Travel Information Centre.

TIC2
[NR] The planned replacement for the **Track Inspection Coach** (**TIC**).

TICA
a) Telecommunications ◻ Infrastructure Condition Assessment
b) **Track** Infrastructure Condition Assessment.

Ticket
a) A small receipt that entitles a **Passenger** to travel on a **Train** subject to certain restrictions such as **Route**, origin, destination, date, time and class of accommodation. It does not guarantee that a Passenger will be conveyed on a particular Train, will have a seat, or can travel at whim. See also **Conditions of Carriage**
b) A document issued to a driver authorising them to enter the **Section** ◻ **Beyond**, a system normally only used during times of disruption or failure
c) [Sig.] An authorised sub-division of the **Staff** or **Token** for a **Single Line Section**.
d) [Col.] term for a certificate of competence, e.g. "I've got a **Lookout** Ticket".

Ticket Line
Generic term for the line in a **Station** dividing the **Paid Area** from the **Unpaid Area**. This may include provision of **Faregates** or manual **Ticket** checks. Also **Gateline**.

Ticket Working
[Sig.] A (generally) temporary method of **Signalling** ◻ **Trains** through a **Section** using written **Tickets** to manage the system.

TiCLeD
[NR] Tight Clearance Database.

TID
[NR]
a) See **Track Identity**
b) **Track** Identity Diagram
c) Train Identification, See **Head Code**, **Train Reporting Number**.

Tie
[US] Term for **Sleeper**.

TIE
Transport Initiative Edinburgh. See also **EARL**.

Tie Bar
Tie Rod
See **Gauge Tie Bar**.

Tie Ropes
[Elec.] Metal or synthetic ropes which provide vertical support for the **Cantilever** on a **Bracket Arm** and which attach to the **OLE Mast** (**OLE Pole**).

Tied Anchor
[Elec.] An **Anchor Structure** which has a **Back Tie** and separate **Anchor**. The alternative is a **Self-supporting Anchor** (**SSA**).

Tied Point
[PW] A location on a **Track** where no lateral deviation from design is permitted or possible. This is generally due to presence of a **Bridge**, **Junction**, **Level Crossing** (**LC**, **LX**) or **Platform**.

Tied Timber (TT)
[PW] An alternative term for a **Through Timber**, but also used as an alternative to **Through Bearer**. Particularly used when describing the location at which the geometrical design of one **Track** becomes linked with that of another. See also **Metre Opening**.

Tie-rods
[PW] Steel rods positioned to maintain the lateral spacing of **Longitudinal Timbers**. See also **Transom**.

TIF
Transport Innovation Fund.

Tight Gauge
[PW] **Track Gauge** that is less than the correct value, often due to poor manufacture or assembly of **Switch and Crossing Units** (**S&C Units**) or **Sleepers** no longer being **Square**.

Tight Joint
[PW]
a) A **Fishplated Rail Joint** between two **Rails** that is designed to be assembled without an **Expansion Gap** between the **Rail Ends**. Abbreviated to **TJ**
b) A **Fishplated Rail Joint** in which the installed expansion gap has fully closed up.

Tight Joint Fishplate
[PW] A **Fishplate** used in a **Tight Joint** (**TJ**).

Tight Plated Joint
Tight Rail Joint
See **Tight Joint** (**TJ**)

TIIS
Train Infrastructure Interface Specification.

Tilt
[TRS] Describing the feature fitted to the suspension systems of some **Trains** that allows them to rotate relative to their **Bogies** along a longitudinal axis. This rotation is analogous to the **Cant** (**C**, **E**) applied to the **Track** and allows Trains so fitted to exceed the maximum speed (**Permissible Speed** (**PS**)) imposed on conventional non-**Tilting Trains**. See **Active Tilt**, **Enhanced Permissible Speed** (**EPS**), **Passive Tilt**, **Rate of Rotation of Carbody**, **Soft Tilt Off**, **Tilt Neutral**, **Tilt Passive**, **Tilt Prohibited Zone** (**TPZ**).

Tilt Actuators
[TRS] Hydraulic or electric rams mounted between a **Bogie** and the **Carbody** of a **Tilting Train** that create a difference in roll angle between the **Bogie Bolster** and the vehicle Carbody. The Actuators are controlled by the **Tilt Control System**.

ELLIS' BRITISH RAILWAY ENGINEERING ENCYCLOPÆDIA

Tilt Authorisation and Speed Supervision System (TASS)
[NR Sig.] A system of passive **Track** mounted **Balises** and **Train** mounted detectors that issues the following authorities:
- Authority for a **Tilting Train** to **Tilt** over a particular section of Track (called a **Tilt Authority**)
- Authority for a Train to disregard **Train Protection and Warning System** (**TPWS**) □ **Trigger Loops** and run at **Enhanced Permissible Speed** (**EPS**) over a particular section of Track (called an EPS Authority)
- Authorities are issued for a specified distance from each Balise, the authority is deemed to have lapsed when that distance is reached. The system also manages the speed of the Train by intervening if the driver is exceeding the maximum **Safe Speed** by as little as 3%.

Tilt Authorisation and Speed Supervision System Balise (TASS Balise)
[NR Sig.] A passive data transmitter which provides location, speed **EPS Authority** and **Tilt Authority** messages to relevant passing **Trains**. They are activated by a radio signal transmitted by the Train itself.

Tilt Authority
[NR Sig.] The data message transmitted to a **Tilting Train** by **Lineside** equipment such as **Balises** that indicates that **Tilt** is permitted as far as the next transmitter or over a fixed interval. This arrangement is only required when **Tilt Prohibited Areas** exist along a **Route**, since if no restrictions exist the Train may Tilt at any point. See also **Tilt Authorisation and Speed Supervision System (TASS)**.

Tilt Control System (TCS)
[TRS] A system fitted to a **Tilting Train** which, depending on the input from sensors, control servo valves or amplifiers, drive the **Tilt Actuators** hydraulically or electrically to provide the **Tilt** function. The control system also has an interface to the driver and the **Tilt Authorisation and Speed System** (**TASS**) that enables the Tilt to operate in active mode (**Tilt Active**) or locks it out of use as inactive (**Tilt Locked**).

Tilt Failed (TF)
[TRS, Ops.] Describing a **Tilting Train** whose **Tilting** mechanism has failed. For the purposes of **Gauging** it is normally assumed that the system then assumes the worst possible position, which is typically tilted to one extreme or the other. See also **Hard Over Tilt Failed (HOTF)**, **Tilt Passive**.

Tilt for Comfort (TFC)
[TRS] The use of the **Tilt** mechanism on a **Tilting Train** to Tilt on **Curves**, even though this is not mandated by the **Track Geometry**. The object of the exercise is to reduce or negate the effects of **Cant Deficiency** (**D**) at **Permissible Speed** (**PS**).

Tilt Inhibit
[NR Sig.] A message passed to a **Tilting Train** by a **Tilt Authorisation and Speed Supervision System Balise** (**TASS Balise**) which instructs the **Train** to return to **Tilt Neutral** (i.e. stop **Tilting**). See **Tilt Prohibited Zone** (**TPZ**).

Tilt Locked
[TRS] Describing a **Tilting Train** whose **Tilting** mechanism has been locked in the upright position and isolated.

Tilt Neutral
[TRS] Describing a **Tilting Train** not **Tilted**, i.e. upright.

Tilt Passive
[TRS] Describing a **Tilting Train** whose **Tilting** mechanism is functioning correctly but is intentionally not tilting the **Train**. See also **Tilt Failed** (**TF**).

Tilt Prohibited Zone (TPZ)
[NR] A length of **Track** where the conditions do not permit a **Tilting Train** to **Tilt** safely. This is normally due to substandard **Passing Clearances** or **Structure Clearances**. See **Tilt Inhibit**.

Tilt System
[TRS] All the components required to allow a **Tilting Train** to **Tilt** its **Carbody** relative to the **Plane of the Rails**, typically on **Curves**. The main components comprise: the power source to provide the energy for the Tilt action, the **Tilt Actuators** and pendulum links; the **Tilt Control System** including all sensors, computers, programs, interfaces and monitoring; and a means of transmitting the power to the actuators, typically hydraulic.

Tilting Train
[TRS] A **Train** that is capable of rotating (**Tilting**) itself relative to its **Bogies** along a line parallel to its longitudinal axis. This allows it to reduce the level of **Cant Deficiency** (**D**) experienced by its occupants and cargo and commercially more relevant, to run at an increased speed (the **Enhanced Permissible Speed** (**EPS**)) relative to more conventional, non-Tilting Trains by doing so. There are two main methods of achieving this **Tilt**:
- **Active Tilt**, where sensors at the **Leading End** instruct hydraulic actuators to rotate the Train. This allows the Train to take most advantage of the opportunities available. The **Advanced Passenger Train** (**APT**), **Class** 390 **Pendolino** and Class 221 **Super Voyager** are **Active Tilting Trains**.
- **Passive Tilt**, where the plan rotation of the **Bogie** frame relative to the frame of the vehicle causes the Train body to roll appropriately. This system is highly reactive and cannot take full advantage of all situations, since the Radius to roll relationship is fixed. Some **Freight Vehicles** have Passive Tilt capabilities.

See also **Hard Over Tilt Failed (HOTF)**, Rate of Rotation of Carbody, Tilt Actuators, Tilt Failed (TF), Tilt Inhibit, Tilt Neutral, Tilt Passive, Tilt Prohibited Zone (TPZ), Tilt Control System, Tilt System.

511

TIM
a) **Ticket** **I**ssuing **M**achine
b) [LUL] **T**rack **I**nfrastructure **M**anager.

TIMARR
Track **I**nspection **Maintenance** and **Renewal** **R**eview.

Timber Bearers
[PW] Collective term for the wood **Bearers** used under **Switch and Crossing Layouts** (**S&C Layouts**). Such Timbers are generally made of a hardwood chosen for its longevity, such as **Jarrah** or **Karri**. See **Hardwood Sleeper**. Often contracted to **Timbers**.

Timber Dogs
[PW] A pair of metal bars hinged together at their middles, with comfortable handles at one end and sharp inward facing hooks at the other. When the device is placed around a **Sleeper**, **Bearer** or other timber section and the handles lifted, the hooks dig in allowing the timber to be lifted. They are normally used in at least pairs. Also **Dogs**, **Nips**, **Sleeper Dogs**, **Sleeper Nips**, **Timber Nips**.

Timber Ends
[PW] That part of a **Timber** that extends beyond the outermost **Rails** of a **Switch and Crossing Layout** (**S&C Layout**).

Timber Nips
See **Timber Dogs**.

Timber Rake
[PW] An alternative term for **Bearer Rake**.

Timber Track
[PW] **Track** laid with **Wood Sleepers**.

Timber Wind
[PW] (*timber wined*) An alternative term for **Bearer Wind**.

Timbering
[PW] The arrangement of **Timbers** (**Bearers**) under a **Switch and Crossing Layout** (**S&C Layout**). See also **Break the Timbering**, **Metre Opening**, **Splicing**, **Switch Toe Bearers**, **Switch Toe Timbers**, **Through Bearers**, **Through Timbers**.

Timbers
See **Timber Bearers**.

Time Division Multiplex (TDM)
A system for transmitting data from many sources over a single cable. Each item of source data is examined in turn and encoded for transmission. Since the system only transmits one source at a time, it is unsuitable for data where timing is critical. Its main use on the **Railway** is linking **Remote Interlockings** back to the **Controlling Signal Box**, and between **Locomotives** and **Driving Van Trailers** (**DVT**).

Time Element Relay (TER)
[Sig.] A **Relay** whose contacts do not **Operate** or **Release** until a pre-determined time has passed. They are used where the operation of a **Signalling Function** must be delayed to ensure safe functioning of the **Signalling System**. Also **Timer**

Time Interval Working
[Sig. Obs.] A very ineffective system that relies on trying to maintain a suitable time interval between successive **Trains**. The second Train is allowed to set off from a specific location, such as a **Station**, after the correct prescribed time has elapsed since the previous Train left. The system has the serious flaw that it does not guarantee physical separation between Trains, and was abandoned in favour of **Block Sections** and **Fixed Signals** in the mid-1800s. See **Clayton Tunnel Accident**.

Time of Operation Locking
[Sig.] A means of preventing a **Signal** or other device from being operated while another piece of equipment is changing state. This is typically the **Locking** of **Facing Points** immediately **Beyond** an **Exit Signal**, when a **Train** is approaching the Signal. It is generally the time required to open the **Detection** contacts, unlock, move and **Lock** the **Points**, and close the Detection contacts.

Time Out
[Sig.] The operation of **Signalling Equipment** after a pre-determined time following the **Occupation** of a **Track Circuit** (**TC**) by a **Train**. See also **Timing Off**.

Time Release
A **Control** applied to prevent a **Signalling Function** such as a **Signal** or **Points** being operated until a specified time has elapsed since some other operation or activation.

Timed At
[Ops.] Describing the maximum speed used to calculate the **Technical Running Time** (**TRT**) to be used as the basis of a **Sectional Running Time** (**SRT**) in a **Timetable** (**TT**).

Timed Release
[Sig.] See **Time Release**.

Timed to a Stand
[Sig.] A method of determining that a **Train** has come to rest by waiting from the point in time at which the Train occupies only the **Berth Track Circuit** at a **Signal** showing a **Stop Aspect** until the Train cannot possibly still be moving. The end of this period can then trigger other events. Also **Timed Off**. See also **Time Element Relay** (**TER**).

Timer
[Sig. Col.] See **Time Element Relay**.

Timetable (TT)
[Ops.] The document which sets out which points a **Train** runs between and at what times. There are two main types:
- The **Passenger Timetable**, which is the simple condensed document which shows only **Passenger Trains** and the stopping points and times. The master version is the **Great Britain Passenger Railway Timetable** (GBPTT)
- The **Working Timetable** (**WTT**), which lists all Trains and all relevant points with times. There are two versions, one for **Freight Trains** and one for **Passenger Trains** (including **Empty Coaching Stock** (**ECS**) Trains).

Timetable Change
[NR Ops.] The bi-annual re-issue of the **Working Timetable** (**WTT**) and **Great Britain Passenger Railway Timetable** (**GBPRT**). Under EU Directive 2001/14/EC (amended by 2002/844/EC) all European Timetables change at **Midnight** (in this case 23:59) on the second Saturday in December and at Midnight on the second Saturday in June. The UK **Railway Industry** chooses to ignore the latter date and uses Midnight (23:59) on the third Saturday in May:

Timetable Year	Primary Timetable Change	Subsidiary Timetable Change
2015/16	12 Dec 2015	14 May 2016
2016/17	10 Dec 2016	20 May 2017
2017/18	09 Dec 2017	19 May 2018
2018/19	08 Dec 2018	18 May 2019
2019/20	07 Dec 2019	16 May 2020
2020/21	12 Dec 2020	15 May 2021
2021/22	11 Dec 2021	14 May 2022
2022/23	10 Dec 2022	20 May 2023
2023/24	09 Dec 2023	18 May 2024
2024/25	07 Dec 2024	17 May 2025
2025/26	13 Dec 2025	16 May 2026
2026/27	12 Dec 2026	15 May 2027
2027/28	11 Dec 2027	20 May 2028
2028/29	09 Dec 2028	19 May 2029
2029/30	08 Dec 2029	18 May 2030
2030/31	07 Dec 2030	17 May 2031

TIMI
(*timm-e*) [NR] **Telecommunications** □ **Maintenance Instruction**.

Timing Load (TL)
[Ops.] The **Gross Trailing Weight** (**GTW**) assumed for each **Train** when calculating **Train Running Times**.

Timing Off
[Sig.] See **Timed to a Stand**.

Timing Point
[Ops.] Any physical location where Train timings are planned or measured, such as **Station** or **TIPLOC**.

Tin Sleeper
[PW Col.] A term for a **Steel Sleeper**.

Tines
See **Tamping Tines**.

TIOS
[NR] **Tilt Inhibit** and **Overspeed**.

TIP
See **Train Infrastructure Performance**.

Tip
a) See **Ballast Tip**
b) See **Tipping Out**.

TIPLOC
(*tip-lock*) [NR Ops.] **Timing Point Location**, a point on the **Railway** where **TRUST** timings are taken.

TIPP
Train Information Positioning Points.

Tipping Out
[PW] The action of removing a **Rail** from **Chairs** and **Baseplates** using **Bars**.

TIPS
(*tipps*) [BR Obs.] **Telecommunications Installation and Procurement Service**.

TIR
Transports Internationaux Routiers.

TIS
a) See **Train in Section**
b) **Traction Interlock Switch**
c) **Train Information System**
d) See **Track Isolating Switch**
e) **Ticket Issuing System**.

TISE
Track Inspector (**Special Examiner**).

TISP
[Sig.] **Train In Section** □ **Proving**, a function within a **Solid State Interlocking** (**SSI**).

TIT
See **Track Inspection Train**.

TIU
Train Interface Unit.

TIV
See **Track Inspection Vehicle**.

TIW
Ticket Issuing Window.

TJ
See **Tight Joint**.

TJ*x*
TJF*x*
[PW] Types of **Tight Joint Fishplate**. The number denotes the quantity of **Fishbolt Holes**, normally two or four. The additional F shows that the **Fishplate** is flat, i.e of a thinner cross section than a normal TJ Fishplate and without any longitudinal ribs, for use in restricted clearance areas such as between the **Legs** of **Cast Crossings**.

TL
a) See **Transition Length**
b) See **Through Line**
c) See **Timing Load**
d) See **Train Line**
e) See **Tandem Lift**.

ELLIS' BRITISH RAILWAY ENGINEERING ENCYCLOPÆDIA

TL2000
TL2K
See **Thameslink 2000**.

TLA
An acronym meaning a Three Letter Acronym, the commonest length of acronym in normal use. See also **ETLA**, **VETLA**.

TLC
a) See **Telephone Protected Level Crossing**
b) Time Location Chart
c) Tender Loving Care, a euphemism for subjecting **Mechanical Signalling** equipment, **Trains** and **Track** to heavy blows with a hammer.

TLIC
Train Line Isolating Cock.

TLV
[Hist.] **Track Loading Vehicle**.

TM
a) **Train Manager**
b) **Tripcock Manual**

TMD
a) See **Traction Maintenance Depot**. Also TMD(D), TMD(E).
b) **Train Mass Detector**.

TMD(D)
Traction Maintenance Depot (**Diesel**). Also **Diesel Maintenance Depot** (**DMD**).

TMD(E)
Traction Maintenance Depot (**Electric**). Also **Electric Maintenance Depot** (**EMD**).

TME
a) **Track** ▫ **Maintenance Engineer**
b) **Telecommunications** ▫ **Maintenance Engineer**.

TMG
See **Track Machine Guidance**.

TML
See **Trans-manche Link**.

TMM
Travel Midland Metro.

TMO
Train Man Operated. A variety of **Level Crossing** (**LC**, **LX**). See **Traincrew Operated**. Also TMO(B).

TMO(B)
Train Man Operated Level Crossing (**Barriers**), a variety of **Traincrew Operated** ▫ **Level Crossing** which specifically has **Barriers** rather than **Gates**.

TMP
Traffic Management Plan.

TMR
[Sig.] Triple Modular Redundancy. See **Central Interlocking Processors**.

TMS
a) See **Train Management System**
b) **Traffic Management System**.

TMST
Trans-manche Super **Train**, See **Eurostar**.

TMZ
See **Tri-metallic Zone**.

TNC
See **Temporary Non-compliance**.

TN-C
[EP] Type of electrical supply where a combined Neutral and Protective Earth (**PE**) is provided.

TN-C-S
[EP] Type of electrical supply where a separate Protective Earth (**PE**) is provided as well as a Neutral connection, but the Neutral is not fully separate; the Neutral and PE are typically connected at a point somewhere between substation and consumer.

TNM
Train Network Management.

TNP
Translation and Network Processor.

TN-S
[EP] Type of electrical supply. Where a separate Protective Earth (**PE**) is provided as well as a Neutral connection all the way from the point of supply.

TnT
See **Top and Tail**, Top and Tail Working.

TO
a) Technical Officer, originally a **British Railways** (**BR**) grade. See also **Draughtsman**
b) See **Turnout**. Also T/O
c) **Ticket Office**.

TOC
a) (*tock*) See **Train Operating Company**
b) Test on Completion.

TOC on Self
[NR] Describing **Train Minute Delays** caused by a failure attributable to the **same Train Operating Company** (**TOC**).

TOD
[TRS] An acronym representing a **Tourist** ▫ **Standard Class** ▫ **Open Coach** with access and facilities for the disabled traveller.

Toe
a) [PW] The movable end of a **Switch Rail**. Also **Switch Toe**
b) [Civ.] The bottom of a **Cutting** or **Embankment** slope. Also **Foot**. The opposite is **Crest**
c) [PW] That part of a **Rail Fastening** that bears on the **Rail Foot Insulator**
d) [PW] The outermost part of the **Rail Foot** of a **Flat Bottom Rail** (**FB**)
e) [PW] The point at which a **Transition Curve** has its maximum Radius (**R**).

TOE
[TRS] An acronym representing a **Tourist** ▫ **Standard Class** End **Open Coach**.

514

Toe Load
[PW]
a) The actual loading produced on the **Rail Foot** by a **Rail Fastening**
b) The design load on the Rail Foot that should be produced by a correctly fitted Rail Fastening (typically 2kN to 14kN for each one).

Toe Opening
[PW] A specified distance, between the **Gauge Face** of a **Stock Rail** and the **Back Edge** of an open **Switch Rail**, measured over the **Clamp Lock** of **Clamp Lock Switches**, and otherwise at the **Switch Tip** for **Switches** operated by other means. Also **Switch Opening**.

Toe Timbers
See **Switch Toe Timbers**.

Toe to Nose
Toe to Nose Dimension
[PW] The distance between the **Switch Toe** and **Crossing Nose** of a **Turnout** or **Lead**, measured along the **Main Line**.

Toe to Toe

Switches installed so that in a **Unidirectional Line**, one **Switch Toe** is **Facing** and one is **Trailing**. Also **Follow on Leads**, **Follow-ons**. See also **Back to Back**.

Toe to Toe Dimension
[PW] The dimension between **Switch Toes** arranged **Toe to Toe**.

TOES
Train **O**peration and **E**nergy **S**imulator.

TOHD
[NR] **T**otal **O**perations Processing System (**TOPS**) **H**elp **D**esk.

TOIM
[NR, Hist.] **T**erritory □ **O**perations **I**nterface **M**anager.

Token
[Sig.] A device (often a metal **Tablet**) carried by a driver as authority to enter a **Section** of **Line** controlled by the **Electric Token Block** (**ETB**) system. The system is arranged so that once a Token is issued to one driver no other token can be issued for that Section of Line. This system is **Interlocked** with the **Signals** to prevent unauthorised **Train** movements. A modern variation of this principle of operation is **Radio Electronic Token Block** (**RETB**).

Token Catcher
[Sig. Col.] More correctly called token exchange equipment, comprising a **Locomotive**-mounted plus (usually) a ground mounted installation which permitted the collection and giving-up of a **Single Line Section** □ **Token** while the **Train** was running at up to 60mph..

ELLIS' BRITISH RAILWAY ENGINEERING ENCYCLOPÆDIA

Token Control Point
[Sig.] A location other than a **Signal Box** where physical **Tokens** are distributed or returned. See also **Token Exchange Point**.

Token Exchange
[Sig.] The process by which a driver either hands or transmits a **Token** to a **Signaller** or vice versa.

Token Exchange Point (TEP)
[NR Sig.] A location at which drivers relinquish and acquire electronic tokens in a **Radio Electronic Token Block** (**RETB**) area.

Token Instrument
[Sig.] The self-contained apparatus designed and used to control the correct issue and return of **Tokens**. See also **Auxiliary Token Instrument**.

Token Section
[Sig.] A portion of **Line** to which only one particular **Token** applies. See also **Signal Section**.

Token Transfer Magazine
[Sig.] A device which permits the secure bulk transfer of **Tokens** between **Token Instruments** having to issue them and return them. This need would arise if there was a regular imbalance between the **Up Direction** and **Down Direction** movements, leading to a build-up of **Tokens** at one end.

Tokenless Block
[Sig.] A variety of **Electric Token Block** (**ETB**) in which the **Token** only exists in terms of electrical signals. Generally used on **Single Lines**, the acceptance of a **Train** □ **Locks** the **Block Instruments** until that Train is proved to have left the **Section** by means of a **Track Circuit** (**TC**) or **Treadle** at the other end of the Section.

TOL
a) [Sig.] See **Train on Line**
b) (Tradename) First **T**ram **O**perations **L**td.

Tolerable Risk
A term used to indicate the point of maximum tolerability that society is prepared to live with. Risks above this level must be reduced or the activity/project abandoned.

Tollerton Control
[NR Sig.] A time delay introduced into the operation of **Track Circuits** (**TC**) at the boundary between **Route Relay Interlocking** (**RRI**) and **Solid State Interlocking** (**SSI**) areas or where similar timing issues exist, to eliminate spurious premature **Releases** caused by the different reaction times of the two systems.

TOLO
Train **O**perator **L**iaison **O**fficer.

TOM
a) **T**icket **O**ffice **M**achine
b) **T**rain **O**perations **M**anager.

Tommy
[Obs.] The obsolescent **Phonetic Alphabet** word representing T. Replaced by **Tango**.

515

Tommy Dodd
[Sig. Col.] Alternative name for a **Ground Signal** or **Shunt Signal**. Also **Dolly, Dummy, Dodd, Ground Disc Signal, Ground Position Light Signal** (GPLS).

TOMS
Train **O**peration **M**anagement **S**ystem.

TOMSC
Train **O**peration and **M**anagement **S**tandards **C**ommittee.

Tongue
[TRS] The part of the **Wedgelock** □ **Autocoupler** which forms the mechanical draw bar between two **Coupled** Autocouplers.

Tongue Lipping
[PW] An advanced state of **Lipping** where the displaced metal has formed flexible flaps down the **Gauge Face** of the **Rail**.

Tongue Rail
[NPT] See **Switch Rail**.

Tons per Yard
[PW] A rule of thumb used to determine the quantity of new **Ballast** required following particular types of work:
- 1-1.5 for **Ballast Cleaning** (**Returning**)
- 2.5 for **Ballast Cleaning** (**Excavating**)
- 3 for **Traxcavating**
- 3.5 for **Formation Renewal**

Additional allowances (typically 0.5) are made for high **Cant** values and new **Track Drains**.

Tool Van
[TRS] A **Van** used solely for the transportation of tools and equipment, normally as part of a **Recovery Train** or **Wiring Train**.

TOOS
Taken **O**ut **o**f **S**ervice.

Top
[PW] Describing the vertical alignment of a **Track** over a short distance. Over long lengths it is called the **Longitudinal Section**.

TOp
See **Train Operator**, clause b).

TOP
See **Train Operated Points**.

Top and Tail
Top and Tail Working
[Ops.] To have a **Locomotive** at both ends of a **Train**, to remove the need to **Propel** or **Run Round**. Usually employed during disruption or as part of **Engineering Work**.

Top Ballast

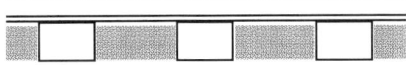

[PW] **Ballast** above the underside of the **Sleepers**, **Bearers** or **Timbers**. See also **Ballast Shoulder**. See **Boxing In Ballast, Crib Ballast**.

Top Chord
[Civ.] The topmost longitudinal structural member of a **Truss**.

Top Contact
Top Contact Conductor Rail
The most common arrangement of **Conductor Rail**, where the **Current Collection Shoe** (**Shoe**) bears vertically downwards on the top of the Conductor Rail. Other arrangements are **Bottom Contact** and **Side Contact**. When not stated, Top Contact is implied in the UK.

Top Endless Haulage
[Hist.]. A development of the **Ginney Line** which utilises an endless rope running over the tops of the vehicles, which are secured to the rope either by a clamping device or a lashing chain. The top haulage system obviated the need for the provision of sheaves or rollers at **Track** level as the vehicles were spaced sufficiently closely along the haulage rope to minimise the risk of the rope dragging along the **Ballast**. Also known as **Over-rope Haulage**. See also **Hambone Clip**.

Top of Ramp (TOR)
The point at which a **Platform Ramp** meets the **Platform Surface**, and thus the limit of the full height **Platform**. The related term is **Bottom of Ramp** (**BOR**).

Top Planing
[PW]

a) The longitudinal profile of the **Running Surface** of the **Crossing Nose** (**XN**) area of a **Crossing Vee** or **Obtuse Crossing Point Rail**, from the Crossing Nose towards the **Crossing Heel**, formed by machining. Its purpose is to reduce the effects of passing wheel tyres impacting on the Crossing Nose
b) The longitudinal profile of the **Running Surface** of a **Switch Rail**
Also **Topping**.

Top Shift
[Col. Nth.] Alternative term for a night shift.

TOPE
[NR] **T**erritory □ **O**utside **P**arty **E**ngineer.

Tope (ZCV, ZDV)
[NR] A 21 ton capacity **Spoil Wagon**, converted in BR days from **Revenue** □ **Hopper Wagons** by simply welding up the doors. See **Wagon Names**.

Topographical Survey
A measured Survey carried out using a theodolite to measure angles, distance measuring equipment and Global Positioning Systems (GPS) to relate features of interest to some form of co-ordinate system, typically the UK Ordnance Survey (OS) grid. Normally used for **Track** and **Civil Engineering** projects, features can be measured to accuracies of ±5mm or better. Typical features collected might include:
- Adjustment Switches,

- Automatic Warning System (AWS) Magnets,
- Bridge Abutments and Bridge Piers,
- Cable Routes,
- Catchpits,
- CCTV and Driver Only Operation (DOO) equipment,
- Check Rails,
- Conductor Rails,
- Crossing Noses and Switch Toes,
- Edges of Earthworks,
- Fences,
- Guard Rails
- Insulated Rail Joints (IRJ),
- Level Crossings (LC, LX),
- Location Cases,
- Mileposts and Kilometre Posts,
- Obtuse Crossing Knuckles
- Overhead Line Equipment Structures (OLE Structures),
- Parapets,
- Platform Furniture,
- Platforms,
- Point Heating Equipment,
- Rail Lubricators,
- Running Edges,
- Signs and Signals,
- Track Geometry marks
- Train Protection and Warning System (TPWS) equipment,
- Trees,
- Under Track Crossings (UTX)
- Walkways,
- Welds and Rail Joints.

This kind of Survey is often carried out in conjunction with a Drainage Survey, Gauging Survey and Height and Stagger Survey. See also Snakegrid.

Topping
[PW] An alternative for Top Planing.

TOPS
(*tops*) [NR] Total Operations Processing System, a mainframe based computer system originally developed by the Southern Pacific Railroad in the USA and introduced on the British Rail (BR) network in 1975. It is used to track Rail Vehicles. It deals with destination, load, location and Maintenance information for all vehicles on the Network. Vehicle data is entered for every movement, allowing virtually real time updates, see Automatic Train Reporting (ATR), TRUST. See also BOTTOMS.

TOR
See Top of Ramp.

ToRFM
Top of Rail Friction Modifier.

Torque Arm
[TRS] A transmission element that prevents movement of a Cardan Shaft and allows generated torque to be transmitted between the engine and the wheels.

Torque Tightened
A bolted fastening assembly that has been tightened to a predetermined load by means of a torque wrench.

TORR
See Train Operated Route Release.

Torsional Back Drive
See Torsional Supplementary Drive.

Torsional Stiffness
[TRS] Applied to a Rail Vehicle, the resistance the vehicle structure has to twisting along its length. High Torsional Stiffness can exacerbate a non-Bogie two-axle Vehicle's sensitivity to Twist Faults.

Torsional Supplementary Drive
A variety of Supplementary Drive that utilises a rotating shaft to transfer the motion along the Switches, rather than the traditional arrangement of cranks and Rodding. This system is often associated with the High Performance Switch System (HPSS). This arrangement is sensitive to errors in the alignment of the Bearers to which it is attached.

TORUS
Transport Operations Rapid Update System.

Total Load

Total Loading
[PW] Describing the action of setting a Ballast Cleaner to discard all the excavated material and return none to the Track. Also called Excavating. The opposite is Riddling or Screening.

Total Obscuration
[Sig.] An Obscuration which affects all part of the Signal Element. See also Partial Obscuration.

Total Operations Processing System (TOPS)
[NR] A mainframe-based computer system used to track Rail Vehicles. Always referred to by its acronym, see TOPS.

Total Tonnage Capability
A proposed Infrastructure capability parameter that will provide an assessment of the additional Equivalent Million Gross Tonnes Per Annum (EMGTPA) that can be accommodated on an identified section of a Route.

Toton Signal
[NR] An alternative term for a Loading / Unloading Indicator. See also Creep Signal.

Tottenham North Junction Accident
At 05:18 on 4th October 1929 a Goods Train apparently passed a Signal at Danger on the Down ▫ Branch Line and ran onto the Down Main Line in front of an Express Passenger Train, which collided with it at 40 mph. The Goods Train had been detained at the Signal for some time, awaiting the passage of the Express, and the Goods driver claimed that the Signal had Cleared for him (it had not). Nine were injured. This accident would have been prevented by Trap Points.

TOU
a) See **Train Operating Unit**
b) **T**ime and **O**dometer **U**nit.

Tourist
[TRS] A seating arrangement in a **Passenger Coach** where seats are grouped around tables rather than in rows without tables.

Towing Bar
a) See **Emergency Recovery Adaptor**
b) [Hist.] An implement which allowed the **Guard** of **Passenger Vehicles** on a **Rope-worked Railway** to pick up the haulage rope from the guide rollers and attach it to the appropriate end vehicle, in use on systems which permitted **Trains** of **Passenger**-carrying vehicles to form their own **Sets** and follow closely behind Sets of coal-carrying vehicles.

TOWS
(*toze* or *tau-z*) [NR] See **T**rain **O**perated **W**arning **S**ystem.

TP
a) See **Tangent Point**
b) See **Tilt Prohibited**
c) The **ATOC** code for **First Transpennine Express**

TP Hut
See **T**rack **P**aralleling **Hut** (TPH).

TP&SN
Three **P**hase and **S**witched **N**eutral.

TP&V
See **T**respass and **V**andalism.

TPAV
[LUL] **T**unnel and **P**ublic **A**rea **V**entilation.

TPC
a) **T**rain **P**erformance **C**alculator
b) **T**rackside **P**rocessing **C**entre.

TPE
See **First TransPennine Express**.

TPEG
Train **P**rotection **E**xecutive **G**roup.

TPH
a) See **Trains per Hour**. Also **tph**
b) **T**rack **P**aralleling **H**ut. Also **TP Hut**.

tph
See **Trains per Hour**. Also **TPH**.

T-piece
[Col.] An alternative name for an insulating **End Post** in an **Insulated Rail Joint** (**IRJ**) assembly.

TPL
Third **P**arty **L**ogistics.

TPMS
Track **P**osition **M**onitoring **S**ystem.

TPO
a) See **T**ravelling **P**ost **O**ffice
b) **T**ree **P**reservation **O**rder.

TPPP
Transport **P**olicies and **P**rogramme **P**ackage, Government funding made available to support integrated transport development proposals.

TPR
a) [Sig.] **T**rack □ **R**epeating □ **R**elay
b) See **T**rain **P**lanning **R**ules.

TPS
a) **T**raction **P**ower **S**upply
b) **T**rack **P**aralleling **S**ite
c) [LUL] **T**otal **P**urchased **S**ervices

TPT
Train **P**ositioning and **T**racking.

TPWS
See **T**rain **P**rotection and **W**arning **S**ystem. Also **TPWS+**, **TPWS-A**, **TPWS-E**, **TPWS Mini**.

TPWS Indicator
See **T**rain **P**rotection and **W**arning **S**ystem Indicator.

TPWS Loop
See **T**rain **P**rotection and **W**arning **S**ystem Loop.

TPWS OS
TPWS Outer Signal)
[NR Sig.] Where **TPWS+** would not give the desired protection, **TPWS OS** may be fitted. With TPWS OS, no **OSS+** is provided, but the **Signal** □ on the **Approach** is fitted with **TPWS**. When the **Junction Signal** is showing a **Stop Aspect** and no **Forward Route** is **Set**, the Signal on the Approach will be also be held at **Red** until the **Train** has passed its **Over Speed Sensor** (**OSS**). This arrangement is also known as **Conditional Double Reds** (**CDRs**).

TPWS+
[NR Sig.] **T**rain **P**rotection and **W**arning **S**ystem (**TPWS**) Plus, which has additional **Over Speed Sensor** (**OSS**) loops to increase the effectiveness of the system at approach speeds higher than 75mph (120kph).

TPWS-A
[NR Sig.] **T**rain **P**rotection and **W**arning **S**ystem (**TPWS**), basic model.

TPWS-E
[NR Sig.] **T**rain **P**rotection and **W**arning **S**ystem (**TPWS**) with Eurobalise.

TPWSSA
(Tradename) **T**rain **P**rotection and **W**arning **S**ystem (**TPWS**) **S**ystem **A**uthority (Ltd).

TPZ
See **Tilt Prohibited Zone**.

TQ
a) See **Track Quality**
b) **T**echnical **Q**uery
c) [Sig.] On a **Signalling Circuit Diagram**, denotes a wire coloured turquoise.

TQM
[PW]
a) **Track Quality** Manager, see also **Track Quality Supervisor** (**TQS**), **Tamper Supervisor**
b) An analysis tool included in the **Trackmaster** software suite.

TQN
Technical Query Notification.

TQS
See **Track Quality Supervisor**.

TQSUM
Track Quality Summary.

TR
See **Track Relay**.

TRA
a) Time Recording Assistant
b) **Train** □ **Running Away**.

TRA Alarm
See **Train Running Away Alarm**.

Trac Gopher
[PW] A small **On-track Machine** (**OTM**) which is capable of removing the **Ballast** from under the **Track** it is located on and placing it in **Spoil Wagons** on an adjacent Track. Its main advantage is that it carry this operation out with access to only one side of the Track concerned (the **Cutter Bar** does not encompass the Track), but this is offset by its relatively slow output and lack of **Screening** facilities.

Trac Rail Transposer
(Tradename) [PW] A machine used to move single **Rails** within a **Work Site**. It is self-powered and travels on its own pair of Caterpillar tracks. The Rails are carried near to the ground and directly below the vehicle, between the caterpillar tracks. Manufactured by McCulloch Rail in Ballantrae, Scotland.

TRACA
[NR] **Track** Condition Assessment.

TRACE
(Tradename) Transport Radio Asset Control Equipment: a Racal system for monitoring the locations of public transport vehicles to provide input to **TORUS**.

Track
a) An assembly of metal **Rails** supported by concrete, **Timber** or **Steel Sleepers**, **Bearers**, or **Longitudinal Timbers** and held in place by specialised **Baseplates**, **Chairs** and or **Fastenings**, placed in **Ballast** or other form of support, used for the passage of vehicles fitted with special **Rail Wheels**. Also **Line**, **Road**, **Way**.
b) A Track is one **Line** amongst others.

ELLIS' BRITISH RAILWAY ENGINEERING ENCYCLOPÆDIA

Track Access
[NR]
a) Time spent working **On or About the Line**, thus a collective term for **Possessions** and **Line Blockages**
b) The use of Network Rail's (**NR**) □ **Lines** for **Running** □ **Trains**.

Track Access Agreement (TAA)
[NR] The agreement by which the terms of a **Train Operating Company's** (**TOC**), **Freight Operating Company's** (**FOC**) or other **Train** operator's use of Network Rail (**NR**) □ **Lines** is formalised.

Track Access Charges
[NR] The fee paid by a **Train Operating Company** (**TOC**), **Freight Operating Company** (**FOC**) or other **Train Operator** to **Network Rail** (**NR**) for the use of the **Track**, **Signalling** and Electric Traction Supply (if applicable) during the running of a particular **Train**. The fee is determined by reference to many factors, including maximum speed of the Train, **Timing Load** (**TL**), type of **Traction** employed, type of **Line**, etc. See also **Train Minute Delay**.

Track Access Controller (TAC)
[LUL] The post with responsibility for granting authorities to **Protection Masters** to access the **Track** during **Engineering Hours** by means of reference numbers and agreed call-back times, and for managing the return of the **Line** to **Traffic**.

Track Alignment
[PW] The plan geometry and position of the **Track**. See also **Alignment**, **Horizontal Alignment**, Track Geometry.

Track Ballast
[PW] Crushed stone, nominally 48mm in size and of a prescribed angularity, used to support **Sleepers**, **Timbers** or **Bearers** both vertically and laterally. The stone used is generally Granite or Quartzite, but hard Limestone has also been employed. Not to be confused with the traditional construction grade of ballast, which is largely ungraded. Also **Bottom Ballast**, **Boxing-in Ballast**, **Shoulder Ballast**, **Slag**, **Stone**, **Top Ballast**, **Tunnel Ballast**. See also **Shingle**. Commonly contracted to **Ballast**.

Track Bed
See **Trackbed**.

Track Bobbing
See **Track Circuit Bob**.

Track Bond
An electrical cable connecting two pieces of **Rail**. See also **Bond**.

Track Brakes
[TRS] A braking system which acts directly on the **Rail** rather than the **Rail Wheels**. Contemporary systems use electromagnets as in **Magnetic Track Brakes** (**MTB**), but some heritage systems employ mechanical friction pads.

519

ELLIS' BRITISH RAILWAY ENGINEERING ENCYCLOPÆDIA

Track Buckle
[PW] Most commonly, a sudden, short and un-designed lateral bend in the **Track** caused by a lack of **Lateral Resistance** (**LR**), poor **Track Maintenance** and (generally) high **Rail Temperatures**. Sometimes abbreviated to **Buckle**. A Buckle can also occur vertically in **Lightweight Track**. They have the potential to **Derail** a **Train**.

Track Cable
[Sig.] A **Tail Cable** for a **Track Circuit** (**TC**) that connects directly to the **Rail**. Also **Track Tail**.

Track Cant
See **Cant**.

Track Category
a) [BR Obs.] Prior to 1988, a 4 x 4 matrix of **Permissible Speed** (**PS**) vs. **Annual Tonnage**, producing 16 categories ranging from A1 (high speed / high tonnage) to D4 (low speed / low tonnage).
b) [BR Obs.] Between 1988 and 1994, an enhanced 36 category matrix which included a measure for **Axle Load**. This produced categories of the form *SSSATT*, where *SSS* is the upper bound of five speed bands, *A* is the Axle Load code and *TT* is the upper bound of five tonnage bands:

Speed		Axle Load		Annual Tons	
0-20*	20*	Sprinter	S	<1	01
0-35	35	< 20t	N	1-3	03
36-75	75	> 20t	H	3-7	07
76-105	105			7-15	15
106-125	125			15-30	30

* The 20 speed band was applied to **Freight Only Lines**
c) [BR, RT, NR] A measure of the robustness of the construction of a **Track**, which now ranges from 6 (little used and at a low Permissible Speed) to 1A (high speed and / or very high annual tonnage). These classifications were derived from the previous **Track Construction** standards in force up to 1993 and a translation of work carried out by the UIC on **Equivalent Million Gross Tonnes per Annum** (**EMGTPA**) measures. The required Track Category is determined from the **Enhanced Permissible Speed** (**EPS**) or **Permissible Speed** (**PS**), and the EMGTPA figure for the Track concerned, which is used in turn to determine the Track Construction required.

Track Centre
Track Centre Line
[PW] A line drawn parallel to and equidistant from the two **Running Edges** (**RE**) of a **Track**. It is used in the design of the **Track Geometry**.

Track Chargeman (TCM)
[BR PW Obs.] The grade within the former **British Railways** (**BR**) organisation that applied to those who were placed in charge of a **Permanent Way** (**PW**) □ **Gang**. They were previously titled **Gangers**. The subordinate grades were Leading Trackman and Trackman. The next direct promotional step up was to become an Assistant **Permanent Way Section Supervisor** (**APWSS**) or **Relaying** Supervisor.

Track Circuit (TC)
[Sig.] An electrical or electronic device used to detect the *absence* of a **Train** on a defined section of **Track** using the **Running Rails** in an electric circuit. In its basic form, a source of electrical current is connected between the Running Rails at one end of the section to be detected. At the other end a **Relay** coil (or equivalent) is connected between the **Rails**.

When there is no **Rail Vehicle** present, the current source energises the Relay coil and the section is proved **Clear**. When a **Rail Vehicle** enters the section, the action of wheels and axles is to short the Relay out, causing it **Drop Away** (**DA**) and create an open circuit. It can be seen that should the current source fail, the system reverts to a **Fail-Safe** □ **Danger** condition. However, many modern Rail Vehicles are of insufficient weight to reliably short the Rails, and other measures such as **Track Circuit Assisters** (**TCA**) have to be employed. Some vehicles are incapable of activating any circuit and are dealt with under special arrangements. Older technology used **AC** or **DC** feeds and **Insulated Rail Joints** (**IRJ**) to divide the track into sections, newer technology dispenses with the need for IRJs by using **Audio Frequency Track Circuits**, see **Virtual Joint**. See also **Axle Counter**.

Track Circuit Actuator (TCA)
[Sig. NPT] Equipment fitted to certain **Trains** to improve their ability to operate **Track Circuits** (**TC**). See **Track Circuit Assister** (**TCA**).

Track Circuit Actuator Interference Detector (TCAID)
[Sig. NPT] Additional equipment working in conjunction with a **Track Circuit** (**TC**) to detect the presence of a working **Track Circuit Actuator** (**TCA**). See **Track Circuit Assister Interference Detector** (**TCAID**).

Track Circuit Assister (TCA)
[Sig.] Equipment fitted to certain **Trains** to improve their ability to operate **Track Circuits** (**TC**). A 165kHz signal is generated between the wheels, assisting in the breaking down of the insulation at the **Wheel / Rail Interface** caused by leaves, rust, etc. The non-preferred term is **Track Circuit Actuator** (**TCA**).

Track Circuit Assister Interference Detector (TCAID)
[Sig.] Additional equipment working in conjunction with a **Track Circuit** (**TC**) to detect the presence of a working **Track Circuit Assister** (**TCA**). It detects the presence of a 165kHz signal in the **Rail** and makes the Track Circuit show occupied. The non-preferred term is **Track Circuit Actuator Interference Detector** (**TCAID**).

520

Track Circuit Block (TCB)
Track Circuit Block Principles
[Sig.] A **Signalling System** where the **Line** ▫ **Beyond** each **Signal** is automatically **Proved** ▫ **Clear** to the end of the **Overlap** Beyond the next Signal using Track Circuits (TC) or another means of automatic Train absence detection, such as Axle Counters.

Track Circuit Bob
[Sig.]
a) The momentary **Clearing** of a **Track Circuit** (**TC**) that is in fact **Occupied**.
b) [NPT] The apparent momentary Occupation of a Track Circuit which is in fact **Clear**.
Also **Track Bobbing**.

Track Circuit Bond
[Sig.] A **Bond** fitted to the **Rails** to ensure the continuity of a **Track Circuit** (**TC**) at a **Fishplated Rail Joint** or other discontinuity.

Track Circuit Continuity Welding

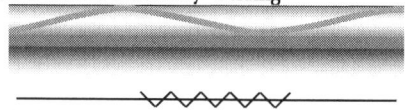

[Sig.] A stainless steel strip applied to the **Rail Head** by arc welding. Its purpose is to improve **Rail Wheel** to **Rail** contact in little used or heavily contaminated areas, such as the **Buffer Stop** ends of **Bay Lines**, **Shunt Necks**, etc. It is applied in a zigzag formation to prevent it being wound up onto passing Wheels, and so it is also known as a **Stainless Steel Deposit**, **Rumble Strip**, **Zigzagging**, **Zigzag Welding**. Also **Eutectic Strip**.

Track Circuit Indicator
[Sig.] A lamp or electromechanical device that indicates the status of a particular **Track Circuit** (**TC**), i.e. whether it is **Clear** or **Occupied**.

Track Circuit Interrupter (TCI)
[Sig.] A mechanical device that disconnects a **Track Circuit** (**TC**) should a **Train** pass over it. They are used in locations where the presence of a Train may be temporary, but is in any case a fault condition, e.g. a Train taking the **Route** into a **Sand Drag**.

Track Circuit Memory
[Sig.] Within a **Solid State Interlocking** (**SSI**), 512 bytes of RAM which are allocated to store the status of 256 **Track Circuits** (**TC**). Each record includes an eight-bit timer to record how long the Track Circuit has been in the current state. The **Geographic Data** can test the timer along with the status flags, which are often used for **Automatic Signals** which revert to **Green** after a suitable interval since the last **Train** went through.

Track Circuit Minimum Length
[Sig.] The minimum length of a **Track Circuit**, which has to be greater than the longest **wheelbase** of the Rail Vehicles to be detected. **Axle Counters** also require a minimum length of **Track Section** for **Train Detection**.

ELLIS' BRITISH RAILWAY ENGINEERING ENCYCLOPÆDIA

Track Circuit Operating Clip
A pair of spring clips connected by a **Wire**, used to short out **Track Circuits** (**TC**) by connection across the **Rails** in times of emergency.

Track Circuit Operating Device (T-COD)
[NR] A more robust and reliable form of **Track Circuit Operating Clip**, it is used to operate **Track Circuits** (**TC**) when taking a **Possession**.

Track Circuit Rail
[Sig.] The **Rail** used by the **Signal Engineer** for **Track Circuit** (**TC**) purposes at locations where **Single Rail Track Circuits** are in use. Also **Insulated Rail**, **Signal Rail**.

Track Circuit Tails
[Sig.] Cables which make the final link between the **Signalling System** and the **Track** for **Track Circuit** (**TC**) purposes. Also **Tail Cable**, **Track Tail**.

Track Construction
[PW] The term for a description of the types of components used in a particular piece of **Track**. It will include:
- Ballast Depth
- Sleeper Material
- Sleeper Spacing
- New Sleepers **Serviceable** Sleepers
- Rail Fastening System
- Jointed Track or CWR
- Rail Section
- Grade of Rail Steel
- New Rail or Serviceable Rail

The Track Construction governs the maximum speed of **Trains** and the **Equivalent Million Gross Tonnes per Annum** (**EMGTPA**) which may be carried over the Track under consideration. See also **Track Category**.

Track Design Handbook
Track Design Manual (TDM)
[BR, RT, NR] Formerly **British Railways** (**BR**) ▫ **Civil Engineering Handbook** No. 49, now **Network Rail Company Standard** (**NRCS**) NR/L2/TRK/2049, retitled the Track Design Handbook. It contains all the relevant information for the design of **Track Geometry** and **Track Layouts**, both for **Plain Line** and **Switch and Crossing Layouts** (**S&C Layouts**).

Track Drain
[PW] A **Drain** intended, designed and constructed to carry surface water away from the **Track**. Track Drains are **Collector Drains**, and are normally laid where they will not be disturbed by **Automatic Ballast Cleaners** (**ABC**).

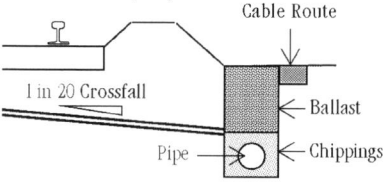

See also **Cess Drain**, **Channel Drain**, **Sixfoot Drain**, **Tenfoot Drain**.

521

Track Drainage Survey
[PW] A **Survey** which records the following information for a **Track Drain**:
- **Catchpit** locations and construction
- Pipe, channel and ditch sizes
- **Cross Drains**
- **Invert** levels for the pipes
- Direction of flow (if any)
- Locations of **Outfalls**.

Track End
[Sig.] An alternative term for a **Track Cable**. Also **Track Circuit Tail**, **Track Tail**.

Track Engineering Forms (TEF*xxxx*)
[NR PW] A suite of standard forms used to record everything from the outcome of a "**Plain Line** ▫ **Wheelburns** and **Squats** Assessment" (TEF3001) to (currently) "Implementation Approval to Use OmniVision® to Deliver **Basic Track Inspection** (TEF3229).

Track Fault
[PW] Any variation in the position of the **Track** from the designed position. Varieties include **Alignment Variations**, **Crosslevel Errors**, **Gauge Variations**, **Slack**, **Swag**, **Twist**, **Wet Beds**. See also **Bump**, **Rough Ride**.

Track Fixity
[NR PW] An expression of the security of the lateral position of the **Track**. Possible descriptions are **Low Track Fixity** (normal **Ballasted Track**), **Medium Track Fixity** (Track that has received **Ballast Gluing** or similar) and **High Track Fixity** (**Slab Track** and other **Directly Fastened Track** arrangements). This measure affects some of the **Gauging Tolerances** used in **Structure Gauging**.

Track Forces
[PW] The forces imposed on the **Track** by passing **Trains**. These include:
- Vertical (including impact forces)
- Horizontal (on **Curves**)
- Longitudinal (from braking)
- Rotational (where lateral loading at the **Rail Head** causes **Rail Rotation** about its outer edge).

Track Gauge
[PW]
a) The distance between the **Running Edges** (RE) of related **Running Rails**, measured between two points just below the crown of the **Rail** (14mm on NR, 13mm on LUL). See also **Gauge**, **Standard Gauge**.
b) A device for measuring Track Gauge, often fitted with devices for measuring **Cant** (**C**, **E**), **Crosslevel** and **Flangeway** dimensions as well. Also known as a **Cant Stick**, **Crosslevel**.

Track Geometry
[PW]
a) The horizontal and vertical Alignment of the **Track**, including **Cant** (**C**, **E**) **and Cant Deficiency** (**D**). See also **Circular Curve**, **Long Section**, **Straight Track**, **Top**, **Transition Curve**, **Vertical Curve**
b) See also **Track Quality** (**TQ**).

Track Geometry Recording
[PW] The automated measurement and storage of **Track Geometry** information for use later in analysis. See also **EM SAT**, **High Speed Track Recording Coach** (**HSTRC**), **New Measurement Train** (**NMT**), **Southern Measurement Train** (**SMT**), **Track Recording Unit** (**TRU**).

Track Geometry Recording Train
[PW] A specially equipped **Train** that automatically measures and stores track **Geometry Information** for the **Lines** over which it runs. See **New Measurement Train** (**NMT**), **Southern Measurement Train** (**SMT**), **Track Recording Unit** (**TRU**).

Track Geometry Trace
[PW] A graphical output from a **Track Geometry Recording** system that shows the features of the **Track** that have been recorded, such as its **Cant** (**C**, **E**), **Horizontal Geometry** and **Vertical Alignment**.

Track Gradient
The **Gradient** of the **Track**.

Track Identity (TID)
[NR] A four digit number of the form DN*XX*, where:
D denotes the **Normal Direction**:
1 Up
2 Down
3 Bi-Directional
4 A Merry Go Round Loop (MGR Loop)

N is the **Track Name**:
1 **Main** or **Fast**
2 **Relief**, **Slow** or **Through**
3 **Goods**
4 **Single Line**
5 **Loop**
6 A **Terminal Track** or **Bay Line**
7 A **Crossover**
8 **Other**
9 A **Siding**

XX is most commonly 00, but where two **Lines** at the same location would otherwise have the same number, then the second one becomes 01. The convention is applied looking in the Down direction and the Line most to the left would be 00 and the next to the right would be 01. So, 1200 may be the Up Slow, and 1201 might be the Up Through, being on the right of the Up Slow. Further, the third digit may also be used to indicate a **Group of Sidings**, where there are many Groups, e.g. 2910 is the leftmost group, 2920 is the next to the right. The final digit then indicates the siding number within that Group (if it is used at all). This system is widely used in computerised records and in the **GEOGIS** database.

Track Inspection Coach (TIC)
[NR] A backup **Track Geometry Recording** vehicle (999508) which began life as an **Inspection Saloon** in 1962. It is due to be replaced in 2012 by **TIC2** (977974).

Track Inspection Train (TIT)
Track Inspection Vehicle (TIV)
[PW] A means of carrying out a visual survey and limited geometrical assessment of the **Track**. See **Whitewash**.

Track Interval
a) The general term for the space between two parallel **Lines** or **Tracks** or pairs of Lines or Tracks.

Sixfoot   Tenfoot   Sixfoot

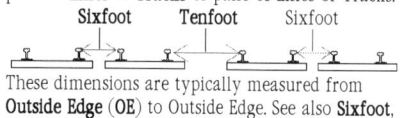

These dimensions are typically measured from **Outside Edge** (**OE**) to Outside Edge. See also **Sixfoot**, **Tenfoot**, **Widespace**, **Wideway**.
b) The actual dimension between adjacent Tracks, measured from **Running Edge** (**RE**) to Running Edge. For a Sixfoot on **Network Rail** □ **Lines** this is 1970mm.

Track Irregularity
[PW] A feature of the **Track Geometry**, the magnitude of which exceeds permitted thresholds specified in the standards. See **L1**, **L2**, **Level 1 Exceedence**, **Level 2 Exceedence**.

Track Isolating Switch (TIS)
[Elec.] An electrical switch located in a cabinet at the **Lineside**, used to electrically separate **Electrical Sub-sections**.

Track Jumping
[Sig.] An effect that occurs when a fast moving **Train** passes over a very short **Track Circuit** (**TC**) or **Spur** of a longer Track Circuit, not giving the **Track Relay** time to de-energise. See also **Joint Hopping**.

Track Layout
The arrangement of **Tracks** (**Lines**) at a particular location on a **Route**. This can include:
- Number of Tracks, see **Double Track**, **Four Track Railway**, **Multi-track Railway**, **Single Line**, **Two Track Railway**
- How those **Lines** are arranged relative to each other.

Track Level
a) [PW] An alternative to **Rail Level**, the vertical position of the **Track** at any given point
b) A general description of being at a similar level to the **Track**. See also **Formation Level**, **Platform Level**.

Track Locking
[Sig.] The **Locking** of **Points**, **Swing Nose Crossings** (**SNX**) etc. when a **Train** is present, to prevent them moving under the Train.

Track Machine Guidance (TMG)
[NR PW] A system used to provide a spatial reference system for **Tamping and Lining Machines** (**Tampers**), consisting of frequent permanent reflective reference points located along the **Track** and an automated total station theodolite installed on the Tamper. The Tamper is programmed with angle and distance data from every point on the **Design Alignment** to at least two of the fixed references, allowing it to return the Track to its correct **Alignment** with a high degree of repeat accuracy.

Track Maintenance
[PW] Activities relating to the day to day upkeep of the **Track**, such as **Tamping**, **Ultrasonic Rail Flaw Detection** (**URFD**), **Weld Repair** and digging out **Wet Spots**. See **Permanent Way Maintenance** (**PWM**)

Track Maintenance Engineer (TME)
[NR PW] The **Network Rail** manager responsible for the **Safety Of The Line**, delivery of **Track Maintenance**, and the line management of the **Track Section Managers** (**TSM**), within a defined area.

Track Miles
The total length of all **Running Lines** between two geographical points.

Track Names
To differentiate between different **Tracks** at a particular location, they are named according to direction and general function. Directions are **Down**, **Up**, and **Up and Down**, **Bi-directional**. Function descriptions include:
- **Arrival** or **Departure** - A **Track** on which **Trains** enter or leave a facility
- **Avoiding** - A Track provided for the sole purpose of avoiding a bottleneck or constriction, which may offer limited **Routes** compared with the main Tracks
- **Backing Out** - peculiar to **Terminal Stations**, to allow arrived Trains to be **Propelled** out to **Carriage Sidings**
- **Bay** - A Terminal Line provided with a Platform at a Station
- **Branch** - indicating that the Track forms part of a **Branch Line**
- **Carriage** - A Track provided for the transfer of **Coaches**, generally between a **Depot** and a Station. This may also include qualifiers for the Coaches themselves, such as **Empty Carriage**
- **Chord** or **Curve** - A Track connecting two other Routes together
- **Company name** - A Track named after the company that built it, e.g. Maryport & Carlisle, Waterloo & City
- **Compass points** - e.g. East, South
- **Cripple** - A Track used for storing vehicles unfit to run, generally of **Siding** status
- **DC** - describing Tracks used solely by **Trains** using **Conductor Rail Electrification** (or Tracks historically used in this manner)
- **Electric** - A Track equipped with an **Electric Traction Supply**, sometimes used to describe a Track

with Conductor Rail Electrification in an area generally fitted with **Overhead Line Equipment** (**OLE**)
- Elevation – E.g. **High Level**, **Low Level**
- **Empty Stock** – A track used only by **Passenger Trains** not conveying **Passengers**
- **Engine** – A Track provided for the transfer of **Locomotives**, generally between a **Motive Power Depot** (**MPD**) and a Station
- Facility – A Track used because it allows access to a particular item of plant or equipment, e.g. **Carriage Washer**, **Fuelling Line**, **Wheel Lathe**. These are normally of Siding status
- **Fast** – Normally the most important Track, but not necessarily the highest speed
- **Goods** – A Track normally only used by **Freight Trains**
- Historic names – Some Track Names defy explanation, sometimes relating to features long since demolished and forgotten. Preston has two, the Derby Siding and the Bakehouse Siding. There are many Klondike Sidings, sometimes a legacy of mining traffic (and sometimes not...)
- **Independent** – A Track that misses out a major facility, such as a Station
- **Interchange** – A Track provided to allow Trains to pass from one system to another, often only used by Empty Stock
- **Loop** – A length of Track provided to allow slower Trains to stand **Clear** and allow faster Trains to pass
- **Local** – A Track normally used only by **Commuter Trains** or **Stopping Trains**
- **Main** – A common alternative for Fast, particularly where there are only two Tracks
- **Number** – As in Number 2 Relief Line
- **Passenger** – describing a Track normally only used by Passenger Trains, as in Passenger Loop
- Place names – Describing the source or destination of the majority of Trains using it, e.g. Airport, Dock, Potteries, West London, etc.
- **Platform** – A Track adjacent to a Platform
- **Relief** – An alternative for Slow [WR]
- **Reversible** – An alternative for Bi-directional.
- Service name – descriptions of the service using the Track, such as **Motorail**, Suburban or City
- Siding
- **Slow** – Generally the second line in importance after Fast, unless the second line has a particular function
- **Through** – Often describing a Track at a Station that has no platform face, or a Siding joined to a **Running Line** at both ends (as in Through Siding)
- Vehicle type – A Track named after the specific vehicle using it, e.g. Restaurant Car, **Tamper**; generally of Siding status

A Track may have many of these names together, particularly where there are many Tracks at one location. Examples of such compound names include Down Liverpool Independent, Up Low Level Goods. See also **Track Identity** (**TID**).

Track Noise
Noise generated by the passage of **Trains**, generally arising from the interaction between the **Rails** and Rail Wheels.

Track Panel
[PW] A length of **Track** assembled and transportable as a unit, i.e. two **Rails** together with the designed number of **Sleepers** and **Rail Fastenings**. The typical length for such a Panel is 60' (18.288m). See also **Switch Panel** clause a).

Track Paralleling Hut (TPH, TP Hut)
[Elec.] A building containing electrical switchgear used to electrically connect many **Electrical Sections** of **Conductor Rail**.

Track Patrols
[PW] Visual inspections carried out on foot, covering the **Track** and including a superficial inspection of other **Lineside** items such as fencing and **Track Drains** carried out by a trained member of staff (**Patroller**) on a regular basis. The frequency of these visits depends on the **Equivalent Million Gross Tonnes Per Annum** (**EMGTPA**), **Enhanced Permissible Speed** (**EPS**), **Permissible Speed** (**PS**) and **Track Construction**.

Track Quality (TQ)
[PW] An assessment of processed **Track Geometry Recording** data against predetermined guidelines and the categorisation of each **Eighth of a Mile** section into bands of **Good**, **Satisfactory**, **Poor**, **Very Poor**, or **Super Red**. The categorisation is relative to speed. See also **Ride Quality**.

Track Quality Band
[PW] A predetermined range of acceptable **Track Geometry** measurements for a **Track** with a band of **Maximum Speeds**, against which actual measurements are compared to deduce the **Track Quality** (**TQ**). The measurement used is the **Standard Deviation** (**SD**).

Track Recording
[PW] The activity of gathering quantitative data about the **Track Geometry** of a **Track** on a **Route**. This is normally carried out by means of a specially equipped vehicle. Typically the data recorded is:
- Alignment
- Cant (C or E)
- Radius I
- Track Gauge
- Top
- Twist

See **High Speed Track Recording Coach** (**HSTRC**), **NEPTUNE**, **New Measurement Train** (**NMT**), **Southern Measurement Train** (**SMT**), **Track Recording Coach** (**TRC**), **Track Recording Trolley**, **Track Recording Unit** (**TRU**), **Track Recording Vehicle** (**TRV**).

Track Recording Coach (TRC)
[NR] Formerly known as the **High Speed Track Recording Coach** (**HSTRC**), this vehicle (999550) briefly formed part of the **New Measurement Train** (**NMT**) until it was replaced by the new **Production Vehicle** (**PV**). It is now generally used in the south east, coupled to the **Electrification Measurement Vehicle** (**EMV**).

Track Recording Coach (TRC)
[PW]
a) Generally, a **Passenger Coach** built or converted to be used as a means of gathering Track Geometry data
b) [NR] A converted **Mark** II Passenger Coach equipped with **Track** measurement equipment and data recording equipment. It is normally run as the middle vehicle of a five **Coach** □ **Train**. Utilising **Automatic Warning System** (**AWS**) **Magnets** as locatable features, it records **Alignment**, **Crosslevel**, **Curvature**, Radius (**R**), **Top**, **Track Gauge** and **Twist**. The data is processed and filtered into 220 **Yard** (approximately 200m) sections known as **Eighths** (8 x 220 Yards is one **Mile**) and for each category various presentations are possible, including the **Manhattan Skyline**. The data is used to determine **Track Maintenance** strategies. Previously called the **High Speed Track Recording Coach** (**HSTRC**). See also **New Measurement Train** (**NMT**).

Track Recording Trolley
[PW] A small, low speed (and often un-powered) trolley equipped for recording basic **Track Geometry** data such as **Cant**, **Track Gauge**, **Line**, **Top** and **Twist**. See **Matisa Track Recording Trolley** (**MTRT**), **NEPTUNE**.

Track Recording Unit (TRU)
[NR PW] A former **Class** 150 **Diesel Multiple Unit** (**DMU**) (950001) converted to carry **Track Geometry Recording**, **Omnicom** recording, **Radio Electronic Token Block** (**RETB**) coverage testing and **Ground Penetrating Radar** (**GPR**) equipment.

Track Recording Vehicle (TRV)
[PW]
a) Generic term for any vehicle used solely for **Track Recording**
b) [LUL] A 1973 **Tube** car converted and equipped to measure **Track Geometry**.

Track Relay (TR)
[Sig.] A **Relay** whose coil forms part of a **Track Circuit** (**TC**). It is this Relay that is de-energised by the presence of **Train**.

Track Relaying
[PW] An alternative for **Renewal of Way** (**ROW**). Also **Track Renewal**.

Track Relaying Machine (TRM)
[PW] A self-propelled twin jib **Rail Crane** used to remove and lay **Track Panels** and transport **Sleepers** using a **Sleeper Beam**.

Track Relaying Train (TRT)
[PW] A **Train** capable of un-clipping, removing the **Rails** and **Sleepers** from under itself, grading the **Ballast**, placing new Sleepers and new Rail and **Clipping Up** all as one operation. Production rates of one Sleeper every six seconds (around 350 metres per hour) are typical.

Track Renewal
[PW] An alternative for **Renewal of Way** (**ROW**)
A term used to describe all activities that are not day to day **Track Maintenance** activities.
Also **Track Relaying**.

Track Renewal Company (TRC)
Track Renewal Contractor
A company specialising in **Track Renewal**. Most of the UK examples were formed from the **Track Renewal Units** (**TRU**) after **Privatisation**.

Track Renewal Item
See **Relaying Item**.

Track Renewals Unit (TRU)
[Hist.] A transitional trading arrangement during the **Privatisation** process, consisting of the **Track Renewals** functions of the various **British Railways Infrastructure Services** (**BRIS**) Units. Most were bought by major construction companies. They were:
- Central Track Renewals Unit (**CTRU**)
- Eastern Track Renewals Unit (**ETRU**)
- Northern Track Renewals Unit (**NTRU**)
- Scottish Track Renewals Unit (**STRU**)
- South Eastern Track Renewals Unit (**SETRU**)
- South Western Track Renewals Unit (**SWTRU**)
- Western Track Renewals Unit (**WTRU**).

Track Section
a) [PW] An area of Railway defined for **Track Maintenance** purposes
b) [Sig.] A length of **Track** with fixed boundaries between which the **Train Detection System** provides information about its **Clear** or **Occupied** status.

Track Section Manager (TSM)
[NR PW] The local **Network Rail** manager directly responsible for managing teams of **Track Maintenance** staff.

Track Sectioning Cabin (TSC)
[Elec.] A building containing electrical switchgear used to connect together two or more **Electrical Sections**.

Track Sectioning Location (TSL)
[Elec.] An outdoor compound containing electrical switchgear used to connect together two or more **Electrical Sections**.

Track Sharing
a) The use of common **Infrastructure** by both **Light Rail** and **Heavy Rail** vehicles, a rare occurrence in the UK
b) The use of the same **Railway Corridor** by both **Light Rail** and **Heavy Rail** systems, more common in the UK.

Track Slab
[PW] A continuous concrete pavement providing support and lateral restraint to the **Rails** in a **Slab Track** system. See also **Hedgehog Sleeper**, **Paved Concrete Track** (**PACT**), **Paved Track**.

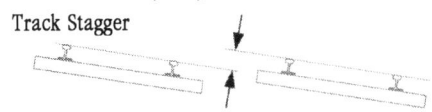

Track Stagger

[PW] The offset between the **Plane of the Rails** of two adjacent **Tracks**, measured at whichever **Sixfoot** □ **Rail** gives the smallest value. The perfect arrangement is for both **Tracks** to be in the same plane at all times, but this is not always possible, particularly at high values of **Cant** (**C, E**). Previous guidance suggests that the dimension should not exceed 50mm.

Track Structure
[PW] Describing the **Formation**, **Ballast**, **Sleepers**, Rail **Fastenings** and **Rails** as a single structural unit.

Track Substructure
[PW] The **Ballast**, **Formation**, and any **Geotextile**, **Sand Blanket**, etc.

Track Superelevation Recorder
[PW Obs.] A small **Hand Trolley** drawn by two men and fitted with a pivoted, weighted pointer which moved over a scale to indicate the **Crosslevel**.

Track Support
[PW] The **Ballast**, incorporating any filter or **Geotextile** layer laid on the formation to support the **Track**.

Track Support Zone

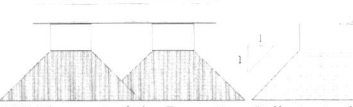

[PW] That part of the **Formation, Ballast**, etc. that directly supports the **Track**. It is normally deemed to include the volume contained within a line drawn at 45° from the edges of the **Sleeper**, but this angle depends on the strength of the underlying formation. See also **Ballast Pyramid**.

Track Tail
[Sig.] A heavy duty single core cable forming the final link between the **Rails** and the **Signalling System** in a **Track Circuit** (**TC**). Also **Track Circuit Tail**. See also **Dirty End**.

Track Tolerances
[PW] The amounts by which the **Track** can be permitted be in error relative to the design. The main categories are:
- **Alignment**, normally given as ±10mm absolute position and ±2mm change between successive **Versines** on a 10m Chord
- **Cant**, often specified as ±2mm
- **Gauge**, generally ±2mm
- **Top**, normally given as ±10mm absolute position and ±2mm change between successive Versines on a 10m Chord
- **Twist**, normally 1 in 400 at worst.

Installation and **Maintenance** tolerances are different for **Ballasted Track**, maintenance being greater.

Track Tools
[PW] The suite of specialist implements and devices intended to assist the **Track Worker** in their efforts. These include:
- Ballast Basket
- Ballast Fork
- Box Spanner (or Screw Dolly)
- Crosslevel Gauge
- Disc Saw
- Ferrule Cup
- Fishbolt Spanner
- Heel Bar
- Impact Wrench (or Bance Wrench)
- Keying Hammer
- Panpuller
- Pansetter
- Point Bar
- Rail Drill (or Rotabroach)
- Rail Saw
- Rail Skate
- Rail Turning Bar
- Ratchet Jack (or Duff Jack)
- Running-on Spanner
- Shovel (sometimes called a Spade)
- Sighting Boards
- Spike Extractor
- Stepped Gauge (or Chicken Ladder)
- Torque Wrench
- Trolley (or Bogie)

Track Trolley
See **Hand Trolley**.

Track Trolley Operator
[LUL] A person trained and certificated to take charge and use **Electric Track Trolleys** and trailers.

Track Twist
See **Twist Fault**.

Track Type
[NR PW] A standard designation denoting whether **Track** is of **Jointed** (**Jtd.**) or **Continuously Welded Rail** (**CWR**) construction.

Track Typical Section

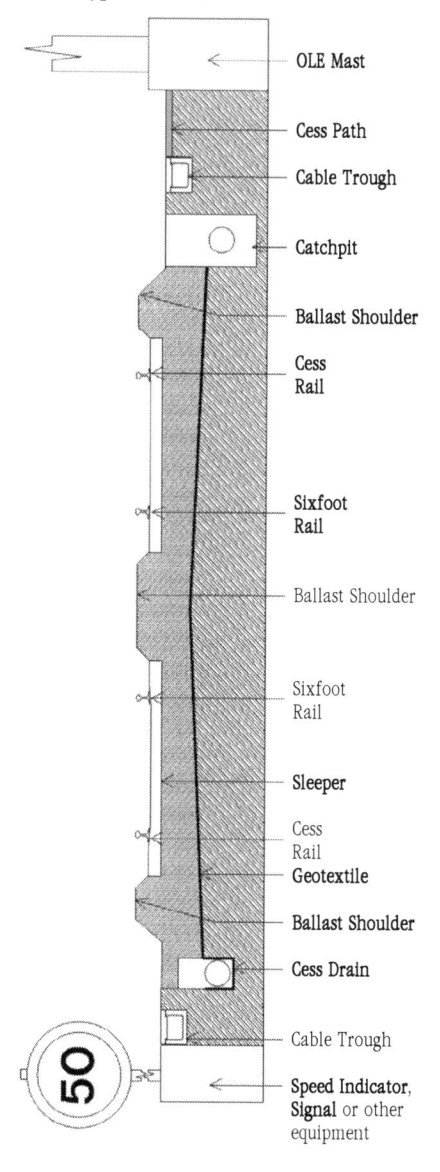

- OLE Mast
- Cess Path
- Cable Trough
- Catchpit
- Ballast Shoulder
- Cess Rail
- Sixfoot Rail
- Ballast Shoulder
- Sixfoot Rail
- Sleeper
- Cess Rail
- Geotextile
- Ballast Shoulder
- Cess Drain
- Cable Trough
- Speed Indicator, Signal or other equipment

ELLIS' BRITISH RAILWAY ENGINEERING ENCYCLOPÆDIA

Track Visitor Permit (TVP)
[NR] A document issued by the **National Competency Control Agency** (**NCCA, Sentinel**). Each TVP has a unique reference number and can only be used for:
- Specialist **Work** in **Fenced**, **Safegaurded** or **Site Warden Warning** protected areas
- **Walking** in all other areas.

One TVP can be used at up to four different locations within a 24 hour period provided these locations are printed on the TVP. All TVPs have a limited validity in terms of dates, times and location(s). TVP holders need to wear personal protective equipment as required for staff who are required to go **On or Near the Line**. Since TVP holders are likely to have no Railway knowledge, the **Controller of Site Safety** (**COSS**) must accompany the TVP holder at all times for the duration of the visit. The TVP must be destroyed when no longer required.

Track Welder (TW)
[PW] A person whose specific duties include the making of **Alumino-thermic Welds**, although they are often trained in **Electric Arc Welding** for use in the **Weld Repair** of **Crossings** and **Rails**.

Track Width
The space occupied by one **Track**, normally used in terms of excavations and is thus around 3.2m (10' - 5").

Track Worker
[NR] for the purpose of the Rule Book (**RB**), those staff who go on to the **Operational Railway** but not including:
- Train drivers
- Guards
- Shunters
- Signallers
- Crossing Keepers
- Those who act as a **Designated Person** (**DP**).

See also **Trackworker**.

Track, Evolution of
The earliest recorded use of a **Track** structure most nearly resembling a current form in use in the UK is in 1604, possibly as a direct development of **Mine Railways** then extant in either the Harz mountains from at least the early 16th century. and/or from the Tirol from the 12th century. These constructions should not be confused with **Rutways** either resulting from wear caused by vehicle wheels or from grooves cut manually into the bedrock (See also **Trackway**) The earliest recorded Track (In the UK) used wooden rails, either one per side or two on top of each other on each side, laid on transverse logs (**Sleepers**). Later, these wooden rails were fitted with iron capping strips to increase their life. This reduced the life of the wooden **Wagon** wheels, so in the 1730s iron wheels were developed. These in turn wore the capped wooden rails out faster, so iron rails were introduced in the 1760s.
Around this time the **Plateway** began to become popular, beginning to fall out of favour by 1830.
In 1789 William Jessop used **Edge Rails** and vehicles with flanged wheels. Early **Rails** were cast in short lengths (of the order of a yard (915mm) see **Fishbelly Rail**) and in 1820 John Birkinshaw was granted a patent for an improved process for rolling wrought iron Rails up to 18' (5.49m) long. These Rails were typically supported in **Chairs** at 3' (915mm) spacing, the Chairs being secured by spikes to **Wood Sleepers** or stone blocks.
Until **George Stephenson** selected 4' - 8$\frac{1}{2}$" (1435mm) as his **Gauge** of choice and imposed it in the UK, there was much variation.

Trackbed
a) The surface of the **Ballast** on which the **Bearers**, **Sleepers** or **Timbers** are laid
b) The area of Ballast occupied by **Track** (applied to **Lines** where the Track has been removed, leaving the Ballast)
c) An area formerly occupied by Track from which all **Rails**, Sleepers and Ballast have been removed, to leave only the **Earthworks** and **Bridges**.

Trackbed Investigation (TBI)
[NR] An analytical model used to identify areas of poor **Formation** and to predict Formation lifespan. The model uses many sources of data, including:
- **Track Quality Data** collected by **the New Measurement Train** (NMT)
- **Ground Penetrating Radar** (GPR)
- Ground Investigation
- Geology
- Topography
- **Permissible Speed** (PS)
- **Equivalent Million Gross Tonnes per Annum** (EMGTPA)
- Track Construction.

See also **TARQUIN**.

Track-Ex
[NR PW] A computerised tool for predicting the risk of **Rolling Contact Fatigue** (**RCF**) based on recorded data, proposed **Track Geometry** and idealised vehicle behaviours.

Trackform
[PW] An alternative term for the type of construction used in building a **Track**, similar in usage to **Track Construction**.

TrackLab
A **Track Recording Vehicle** (**TRV**), previously known as **Laboratory 5** see **TRIM**.

Trackmaps
(Tradename) The current publisher of the industry-standard **Quail Maps**, based in Bradford-on-Avon, Wiltshire.

Trackmaster
(Tradename) [PW] A computer based system which displays **Track Recording Vehicle** (**TRV**) data, allows auditing of this data, the planning of **Track Maintenance** work and forecasting of **Ballast** life. Produced by **AEA Technology** (now **DeltaRail**).

Trackside
An alternative term for **On or Near the Line**. See also **Cess**, **Dirty End**, **Fourfoot**, **Ten Foot**.

Trackside Functional Module (TFM)
[Sig.] Electronic devices which provide an interface between the **Control Interlocking Processor** in a **Solid State Interlocking** (**SSI**) and the **Trackside** □ **Signalling Equipment**. Two types of module are provided:
- **Signal Modules** to drive **Aspects** on **Signal** and detect **Lamp Proving** inputs, etc.,
- **Points Modules** to drive **Points** and report their Detection.

Both types of module can report **Track Circuit** inputs. Both Signal Modules and Points Modules have identical interfaces to the **Baseband Data Highway**, and are configured to respond to a **Command Telegram** with an immediate **Data Telegram**.

Tracksys
(Tradename) [PW] A **Track Geometry** processing system, produced by **DeltaRail** and used on the **New Measurement Train** (**NMT**).

Tracktools
[NR] A spreadsheet-based application for determining individual site **Renewal** strategy.

Track-to-train Radio
[CT] A radio system enabling the **Railway Control Centre** (**RCC**) to speak to all **Train** drivers either individually or generally, and drivers to speak to the RCC.

Trackway
[Hist.] a very early form of **Track** which used grooves cut into the bedrock or into stone blocks (to form a kind of **Plateway** structure) to guide normal cart wheels. The earliest recognised example is across the Isthmus of Corinth, called the Diolkos, dating from around 600 BC. See **Track, Evolution of**.

Trackwork
a) An alternative collective term equivalent to **Permanent Way** (PW)
b) (Tradename) A company specialising in **Track**, based in Doncaster.

Trackworker
See **Track Worker**.

Traction
[TRS] Collective term for all **Locomotives** and **Multiple Units** (MU) See also **Diesel Traction**, **Electric Traction**, **Steam Traction**, **Traction Unit**.

Traction Bleed Resistors
[LUL] A resistor network connected between each pole of the **Traction Supply** system and **Earth** which ensures that the positive pole to earth voltage is two thirds of the applied voltage and the negative pole to earth voltage is one third of the applied voltage.

Traction Bond
[Elec.] A **Bond** specifically provided to carry **Traction Return Current** around a discontinuity in the **Rail**, though it may also carry **Track Circuit** (TC) current. See also **Yellow Bond**.

Traction Brake Controller (TBC)
[TRS] Common on modern **Locomotives**, **Traction Units** and **Trams**, a single handle which is pushed forward to accelerate and pulled back to decelerate the vehicle.

Traction Control Cut-out Switch (TCCOS)
[TRS] An electrical switch providing electrical isolation of the **Traction** control equipment on a **Rail Vehicle**.

Traction Current
[Elec.]
a) The flow of electrical energy from the **Feeder Station** (FS), through the **Overhead Line Equipment** (OLE) and back through the **Traction Return Rail**
b) The flow of electrical energy from the Feeder Station, through the **Conductor Rails** and back through the Traction Return Rail
c) [LUL] The flow of electrical energy from the Feeder Station, through the **Positive Conductor Rails** and back through the **Negative Conductor Rail**.

Traction Current Plunger
[LUL] A switch used to initiate disconnection of the **Traction Current** in an emergency.

Traction Current Rail
[Elec.] Alternative for **Conductor Rail**. Also **Current Rail**.

Traction Current Return
[Elec.] The complete return path for the **Traction Supply Current** back to the **Feeder Station** (FS).

Traction Current Return Rails
See **Traction Return Rail**.

Traction Current Section
[Elec.] An alternative term for an **Electrical Section**.

Traction Gel
Non-proprietary term for products such as **Sandite**.

Traction Gel Applicator (TGA)
A **Lineside** installation consisting of a hopper containing 75 litres of **Traction Gel**, which is dispensed on to the **Rail Head** via an applicator. The application is triggered by a **Train** sensor on the **Approach To** the unit.

Traction Inspector
[Ops.] A person whose job it is to examine, train and supervise drivers of **Trains**.

Traction Maintenance Depot (TMD)
A facility at which **Traction Units** are inspected, maintained, overhauled and rebuilt.

Traction Motor
[TRS] The electric motor used as the means of turning the **Powered Axles** on a **Rail Vehicle** using **Electric Traction** or **Diesel Electric Traction**. The use of electric motors in this way, particularly on a high power **Diesel Electric Locomotive**, simplifies the transmission system, as a direct mechanical drive to many axles would be cumbersome.

Traction Power
[Elec.] Generic term for the electricity provided for the **Traction Units** operating on an **Electrified Railway**. The term is used to distinguish this use from others, such as domestic power, **Signalling** power, etc.

Traction Rail
[Elec.] The **Rail** used for **Traction Return Current**. See **Common Rail**.

Traction Return Circuit
[Elec.] The electrical path taken by the **Traction Return Current** from the **Traction Unit** (such as an **Electric Multiple Unit** (EMU) or **Electric Locomotive**) back to the **Feeder Station** (FS) via:
• The **Traction Return Rail**, Return Conductor (RC) and **Booster Transformer** (BT) in a Booster Transformer system
• The Traction Return Rail, **Autotransformer** (AT) and **Negative Feeder** in an Autotransformer system
• The Traction Return Rail in **Third Rail** ▫ **Conductor Rail** system
• The **Fourth Rail** in a four **Rail** Conductor Rail system.

Traction Return Current
[Elec.] The **Traction Current** returning to the **Feeder Station** (FS).

Traction Return Rail
[Elec.] The **Rail** of a **Track** used as the **Return** side of the **Traction Current** circuit on an **Electrified Railway**.

Traction Supply
[Elec.] The supply of electricity used to power the **Conductor Rail** or **Overhead Line Equipment** (**OLE**).

Traction Supply Current
[Elec.] The **Traction Current** supplied by a **Feeder Station** (**FS**). See also **Grid Feeder**.

Traction Unit
[TRS] Any vehicle capable of moving itself and other **Rail Vehicles** under its own power on **Rails**. See also **Locomotive**, **Multiple Unit Train**, **Road Rail Vehicle**.

Traction/Brake Controller
See **Traction Brake Controller** (**TBC**).

Traction-derived Supply
An AC supply obtained by stepping down the voltage of the **Traction Supply** using a **Transformer**. Typically, the 25kV AC **Overhead Line Electrification** (**OLE**) supply is stepped down to 650V AC for use as an alternative **Signalling Power Supply**.

Tractive Effort
[TRS] The longitudinal force produced by a **Traction Unit**. Also **Drawbar Pull**.

Tractor
[Col.] Nickname given to **Class** 37 **Diesel Locomotive** based on their sound. Also **Growler**, **Syphon**.

Traffic
[Ops.]
a) A common term for the flow of **Trains** on a **Railway**
b) [Hist.] The department that managed the day to day operation of Trains. See **Railway Operations**.

Traffic Circular
[LUL] A weekly publication by **London Underground Limited** (**LUL**) that provides details of **Train** service and other operating information, including changes to the **Timetable**.

Traffic Hours
[LUL] The time between the end of one period of **Engineering Hours** and the beginning of the subsequent period of Engineering Hours.

Traffic Moment
The number of road vehicles using a **Level Crossing** (**LC**, **LX**) multiplied by the number of **Trains** passing in a given period. See also **Effective Traffic Moment**.

Traffic Regulating Rules
[Ops.] Rules applied by **Signallers**, or programmed in the **Automatic Route System** (**ARS**), when deciding on priorities between **Trains** at **Junctions**.

TRAIL
Transportation Reliability, Availability and Integrated Logistics.

Trail
See **Trailed**, **Trailed Through**.

Trailable Points
Trailable Switch
Trailable Turnout
[Sig.]
a) See **Train Operated Switch**
b) A **Set of Points** (**Switches**) fitted with a special **Point Machine** or **One Way Lever** so that a **Movement** in the **Trailing Direction** with the Points Set in the opposite position does not cause damage to the Points (Switches) **Point Operating Equipment** (**POE**) or **Point Machine**. Also **Slotted Joint Points**.

Trailed
Trailed Through
A **Movement** through a **Set of Points** in the **Trailing Direction**, when the **Switches** were not **Set** for the Movement. Unless the Points are designed for this, damage will result as the **Wheelsets** attempt to force open the **Closed Switch**.

Trailer
a) Describing a **Set of Points** arranged in the **Trailing** direction. The opposite is a **Facer**
b) [TRS] Any vehicle in a **Multiple Unit Train** that does not have any **Powered Axles**
c) The additional single axle trolley attached to the back of some **On Track Machines** (**OTM**).

Trailer Coaching Stock
[TRS] All **Passenger** and **Non-Passenger Coaching Stock** (**NPCS**) that does not have its own source of **Traction**, including vehicles with a driving position but excluding those **Trailer** vehicles that form part of **Multiple Unit Trains**.

Trailing
Aligned away from **Trains** approaching in the **Normal Direction**, so the direction of traffic over **Points** (**Switches**) where the Train passes the **Switch Heel** before the Switch Toe. The opposite is **Facing**. See **Trailing Crossing**, **Trailing Crossover**, **Trailing Junction**, **Trailing Points**, **Trailing Switch**. See also **Trailing End**, **Trailing Weight**.

Trailing Crossing
A **Crossing** installed such that **Traffic** normally travels from the **Crossing Heel** to the **Wing Rail Fronts**: the **Crossing Nose** points away from oncoming **Trains**. The opposite is a **Facing Crossing**.

Trailing Crossover
A **Crossover** where the **Switches** are installed in the **Trailing** direction in the more important **Track**. Also **Trailer**. The opposite is a **Facing Crossover**.

Trailing End
[Ops.] The rear end of a **Train** or **Traction Unit** in the direction of travel. The opposite is the **Leading End**.

Trailing Junction

Down →

In **GEOGIS** terms, a **Junction** between two **Routes** where the Routes converge in the **Down Direction** of the Route leaving the Junction. Alternatives include **Facing Junction**, **End-on Junction**.

Trailing Movement
A **Train** movement made through a **Crossover** or **Turnout** in the **Trailing** direction, i.e., moving from **Crossing** to **Switch Toe**.

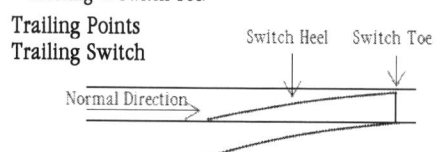

Trailing Points
Trailing Switch

Switch Heel   Switch Toe

Normal Direction

A **Set of Points** (**Set of Switches**) where two **Routes** converge in the Normal Direction of **Traffic**, e.g. traffic normally travels from **Switch Heel** to **Switch Toe**. Also **Trailer**. The opposite is **Facing Points**, **Facing Switch**.

Trailing Weight
[Ops.] The weight of a **Train** excluding the **Locomotive**(s).

TRAIN
Tele-**Rail** **A**utomated **I**nformation **N**etwork.

Train
[Ops.] One or more **Rail Vehicles**, coupled together as applicable, including some form of **Traction Unit**. A **Locomotive** on its own is a **Light Locomotive**. Any large number of similar vehicles coupled together is referred to as a **Rake** or **String**. Many similar purpose vehicles (particularly **Coaching Stock**) that are generally always marshalled together are a **Set**. Therefore, a **Multiple Unit Train** (including one or two powered vehicles) is a **Train**, whereas two **Hopper Wagons** coupled together is not (see **Rake** or **String**).

Train Accident Risk
The risk from an accident that has been caused by a **Train** (e.g. **Derailment** of the Train).

Train Anchor
A device used to anchor a **Train** or **Rail Vehicle** to the **Running Rail**. Also (confusingly) called a **Rail Anchor**.

Train Approaching Berth
[Sig.] The **Train Describer Berth** located at the extreme end of a **Signaller's Area** that allows the **Signaller** to anticipate the arrival of the **Trains** from another **Signal Box** (**SB**) and ensure that the appropriate **Route** is clear.

Train Arrangements
The document describing the **Consist**, departure times, arrival times and any intermediate **Shunting** activities required for an **Engineer's Train**. Also referred to as **Train Minutes**.

Train Arrestor
Any device designed to decelerate a slow moving **Train** to minimise damage to the **Train** or injury to staff and **Passengers** should it overrun the correct stopping position at a terminal location. This includes **Fixed Buffer Stops**, **Sand Drags**, **Sliding Buffer Stops**.

Train Brake
[TRS] A term used to differentiate the **Automatic Brakes** fitted throughout a **Train** from the brake system fitted to the **Locomotive**. See **Straight Air Brake**.

Train Continuity
[TRS] Fitted to some **Trains**, an electrical circuit which is energised only once certain conditions relating to the safety of the Train and its systems are satisfied. Should this circuit be interrupted by a change in the status of one of these systems then this circuit will de-energise and an **Emergency Brake** application will result. See also **Brake Wire**.

Train Control System (TCS)
[Sig.]
a) Generally, any arrangement imposed for the sole purpose of enforcing adequate physical separation between **Trains**. This definition therefore includes all **Block Section** based **Signalling Systems**, such as **Absolute Block** (**AB**), **Electric Token Block** (**ETB**), **Radio Electronic Token Block** (**RETB**) and **Track Circuit Block** (**TCB**), but not **Time Interval Working**
b) Specifically, in the case of the **European Train Control System** (**ETCS**) for example, a system which directly links the **Signalling System** to the propulsion and braking systems of the Train.

Train Coupling Compatibility Matrix (TCCM)
[Ops.] A **Network Rail** (**NR**) in-house application used within **Control Centres** to determine the optimum **Rescue Train** for a particular **Failed Train**.

Train Crew
See **Traincrew**.

Train Data Recorder (TDR)
[LUL] The equipment on a **Train** which records parameters such as speed, distance run and the positions of the driver's controls. Also **On Train Data Recorder** (**OTDR**), **On Train Monitoring Recorder** (**OTMR**).

Train Describer (TD)
[Sig.] A computerised system that tracks **Trains** along a **Route** and allows a **Signaller** to see what is where. It displays **Train Reporting Numbers** and moves them from one **Train Describer Berth** to the next as the Train **Occupies** and **Clears** □ **Track Circuits** (**TC**) or **Block Sections**. Such systems are automated, the display using Track Circuit occupation and clearing to update Train positions. See also **Automatic Train Reporting** (**ATR**).

Train Describer Berth (Berth, TD Berth)
[Sig.] Describing a small subsection of the **Railway**, each of which can be occupied by one **Train**. Each **Berth** displays the relevant **Train Reporting Number**. As the Train moves, the relevant Train Reporting Number is moved along its path from Berth to Berth.

531

Train Describer Stepping (TD Stepping)
[Sig.] The action of moving a **Train Reporting Number** from one **Train Describer Berth** to the next **Berth**, using a **Train Describer** (TD). This operation is triggered by the Train concerned moving from one Signal Section to the next, and does not take place in the event of a **Signal Passed at Danger** (**SPAD**).

Train Description (TDN)
[Ops.] An alternative for **Train Reporting Number**. Formerly called a **Head Code**.

Train Detection
Train Detection System
[Sig.] Generic term for any system that proves one of the following:
- The presence or absence of **Trains** and **Rail Vehicles** on a particular section of **Line**
- That such a Train has reached, is passing or has passed a specific position.

Where required, a Train Detection system may additionally detect the direction in which a Train is travelling. See **Axle Counter**, **Track Circuit**, **Treadle**.

Train Document
[NR Ops.] A series of sheets printed from the **TOPS** (**Total Operations Processing System**) giving information including a **Train's Reporting Number**; departure time; origin; destination points; maximum load; **Brake Force** and type, tonnage; **Route Availability** (**RA**); length limit and maximum speed. TOPS automatically checks whether the Train **Formation** conforms to prescribed criteria and standards when it produces the Train Document.

Train Entering Section (TES)
[Sig.] The **Bell Code** (two beats) given by one **Signal Box** (**SB**) to the next Signal Box **Beyond** to alert the second **Signaller** that the **Train** is actually on its way. This system is needed as the exchange of Bell Codes offering and accepting the Train concerned may have been some time earlier.

Train Examiner
[Ops.] A person employed at a **Depot** to check that **Trains** due to depart:
- Are correctly **Coupled**,
- Have their loads correctly secured,
- Have all straps, stanchions, doors, etc. stowed and secured,
- Have brake systems that are intact, connected and operative
- Have wheels that are free to rotate and that the brakes do not drag.

Train Formation
[Ops.] Describing a normally **Self-propelled** □ **On Track Machine** (**OTMs**) □ **Running** as part of a **Train**, including when **Coupled** to other OTM.

Train Guide
[NR Ops. Hist.] A person who was authorised to act on behalf of the **PICOP** or **Engineering Supervisor** (**ES**). The role was abolished in 1998 as a result of the recommendations from the Glynde incident.

Train ID
See **Train Reporting Number**.

Train in Section (TIS)
[Sig.] Term used to describe the presence of a **Train**, **On-Track Machine** (**OTM**) or **Traction Unit** in a **Signalling Section**.

Train Infrastructure Performance (TIP)
A basic **Train Performance** and **Timetable Modelling** system developed by **Network Rail** and based on Microsoft® Excel™.

Train Length
[Ops.] A somewhat flexible unit of length, generally used in context to mean the longest (or shortest) **Train** that will use a **Line** or facility.

Train Line (TL)
[TRS] An alternative term for a **Train Pipe**. Also **Main Line**.

Train Lines
[TRS] Electrical wires which carry control signals along the length of a **Train**.

Train Man Operated (TMO)
See **Traincrew Operated**.

Train Management System (TMS)
[TRS] An on-**Train** computer system which monitors and records fault and other event conditions associated with the Train's electrical and electronic systems.

Train Manager
[Ops.] A modern post encompassing the customer care elements of a **Guard's** duties, but excluding the **Ticket** collecting part.

Train Mile
[Ops.] A measure of the quantity of **Traffic**. One Train Mile is one **Mile** travelled by one **Train**; so 10 Trains travelling 200 Miles each is 2000 Train Miles.

Train Minute Delay
[NR Ops.] The sum of the number of minutes of delays encountered by all affected **Trains** (e.g. 20 trains delayed for three minutes each is 60 Train Minutes). This is used to estimate the financial value of penalties for failure and **Possession Overruns**.

Train Minutes
a) See **Train Arrangements**
b) A contraction of **Train Minute Delay**.

Train Movement
[Ops., Sig.] The movement of one or more **Rail Vehicles** coupled together from one point to another. See also **Authorised Movement**, **Facing Movement**, **Propelling Movement**, **Running Movement**, **Set Back Movement**, **Shunt Movement**, **Trailing Movement**, **Unauthorised Movement**, **Wrong Direction Movement**.

Train on Line (TOL)
[Sig.] The state of a **Block Section** when there is a **Train** or other obstruction between the **Section Signal** and the **Clearing Point**. See also **Line Clear** (**LC**), **Line Blocked** (**LB**).

Train Operated Points (TOP)
[PW, Sig.] An alternative for a **Train Operated Switch (TOS)**.

Train Operated Route Release (TORR)
[Sig.] A feature fitted to **Signalling Systems** that automatically **Clears** a previously **Set** □ **Route** after the passage of the **Train**, without intervention by the **Signaller**.

Train Operated Switch
[PW Sig.] A **Switch** that is automatically returned to its original, **Normal** position by means of a spring after a **Trailing** movement of a vehicle. Also **Spring Points, One Way Switch, Spring Switch, Trailable Switch, Hydro-Pneumatic Switch, Gas Bag Points**.

Train Operated Warning System (TOWS)
A permanently installed version of **PeeWee** in which the audible warning is triggered automatically by the **Occupation** of certain **Signal Sections** □ on the **Approach to** the installation. The warning time is usually pre-set to a minimum of 45 seconds. The system is nearly always referred to by its initials TOWS. Formerly, the acronym was FATCOWS.

Train Operating Company (TOC)
[NR] A company either owning a franchise to operate **Passenger Trains** or operating **Passenger Trains** under an **Open Access** arrangement.

Train Operating Unit (TOU)
[Hist.] The term for the transitional **Freight** organisations during **Privatisation**, namely **Freightliner (FL), Loadhaul, Mainline, Rail Express Systems (RES)** and **Transrail**, now called Train Operating Companies (**TOC**). See also **DB Schenker Rail (UK) Ltd**.

Train Operator
a) [RT, NR] An organisation holding a **Railway Safety Case (RSC)** and operating a regular service for the direct benefit of others. There are two main types, **Freight Operating Companies (FOC)** and **Train Operating Companies (TOC)**. Whilst many other organisations, such as **Renewals** □ **Contractors**, have a Railway Safety Case and can thus run **Trains**, their Trains are often **On-track Machines (OTMs)** and are not for the direct benefit of others. Contracted to **Operator**
b) [LUL] On **London Underground Limited (LUL)**, the person responsible for the safe operation of a **Train**, "driving" the train, opening and closing the exterior doors and occupying a seat in the **Leading Cab**. Abbreviated to **TOp**.

Train OPO Equipment - In-Cab
[LUL] Video monitors located within the **Driving Cab** to provide the **Train Operator** with a clear image of the **Platform Train Interface (PTI)** in order that doors may be closed safely and to enable the Train Operator to monitor the Train's exit from the **Station**, together with the associated CCTV cameras and other equipment installed on the **Platforms** themselves.

Train OPO Equipment - Platform
[LUL] Mirrors and monitors located adjacent to the **Driving Cab** door which provide the **Train Operator** with a clear image of **Platform Train Interface (PTI)** in order that Train doors may be closed safely.

Train Path
[Ops.] An allocation in the **Timetable (TT)** for a **Train** of a particular variety, but not necessarily a physical Train. There are many more Train Paths than there are Trains.

Train Performance
[TRS] The physical characteristics of a particular **Train**, namely:
- **Tractive Effort**
- Acceleration rate
- Maximum speed
- Braking rate.

Train Performance Model
[Ops.] A simulation of the physical characteristics of a particular **Train** in terms of **Tractive Effort**, air resistance, rolling resistance, etc. and used to determine **Sectional Running Times (SRT)** and **Attainable Speeds**. See also **Railsys, TIP, Vision**.

Train Pipe
[TRS]
a) A pressurised air main running the length of a **Train** equipped with **Air Brakes**. This pipe is kept permanently under pressure, the actual brake control being achieved by varying the pressure in the **Brake Pipe**. Also **Main Line, Train Line**.
b) In a Train fitted with continuous **Vacuum Brakes**, the pipe which runs the length of the Train connecting all the vehicles and is used for charging the vacuum cylinders on the vehicles and controlling application and **Release** of the brakes.

Train Plan
a) [NR Ops.] Part of the Integrated Operational **Railway** Planning System (**IORPS**), used for developing **Train Paths**, loaded into the Train Service Database (**TSDB**)
b) A document listing the **Engineering Trains** required for a project.

Train Planning
[Ops.] The activity of arranging a **Timetable (TT)**.

Train Planning Rules (TPR)
[NR Ops.] The new name for the **Rules of the Plan (ROP, ROTP)**, the guidelines applying to bids for **Train Paths** submitted by **Train Operators** and the rules applicable to **Timetables**.

Train Preparation
[Ops.] The activities carried out by a **Train Preparer**.

ELLIS' BRITISH RAILWAY ENGINEERING ENCYCLOPÆDIA

Train Preparer
[Ops.] A person appointed by a **Train Operator** and passed competent to carry out **Train Preparation** before departure. Duties include checking the **Train** for compliance with the **Train Document** and physically checking all Vehicles to ensure that they are properly **Coupled** (including **Brake Pipe** and electrical connections); the necessary lamps are provided on the **Train**; all vehicles appear safe to travel and all **Handbrakes** are released.

Train Protection and Warning System (TPWS)
[NR Sig.] An automatic **Trackside** and on-**train** system which enforces limits on the speeds of **Trains** that pass so as to avoid collisions. Consisting of **Track** mounted **Train Protection and Warning System Loops** and a Train mounted detector, the system is capable of both preventing a Train from passing a **Stop Signal** and from exceeding the **Permissible Speed (PS)** at a **Signal** (i.e. retarding a Train sufficiently at a **Caution Aspect** to ensure that it can safely stop at the next **Stop Aspect**). Despite the title it has no warning function. See **Overspeed Sensor System (OSS)**, **Train Stop System (TSS)**.

Train Protection and Warning System Indicator (TPWS Indicator)
[NR Sig.] In **No-Signaller Token Remote (NSTR)** and **Radio Electronic Token Block (RETB)** areas **Stop Boards** are provided in place of **Worked □ Signals**. These may be fitted with **TPWS**, which is controlled by the issuing of **Tokens**. In this situation, the signaller receives no indication in the event of a TPWS failure but **Lineside Indicators** are provided locally so that the driver can confirm that the TPWS is operating correctly. They consist of a blue light which indicates the following:
- Steady - **TPWS** Set
- Flashing - TPWS disarmed
- No indication - TPWS Failed.

TPWS Indicators are also provided at **Points Indicators** and **Level Crossing Indicators** for similar reasons.

Train Protection and Warning System Loop (TPWS Loop)
[NR Sig.] A system of transmitter loops laid in the **Fourfoot**. Laid in pairs, the first (the **Arming Loop**) arms the system and the second (the **Trigger Loop**) triggers it. If the time between these events is less than 0.974s, the **Train** mounted system will automatically bring the Train to a stand as quickly as possible. See **Overspeed Sensor System (OSS)**, **Set Speed**, **Train Stop Sensor (TSS)**.

Train Ready To Start (TRTS)
a) See **Train Ready To Start Indicator (TRTS Indicator)**
b) See **Train Ready To Start Plunger (TRTS Plunger)**

Train Ready To Start Indicator (TRTS Indicator)
[Sig.] An **Indicator** in the **Signal Box**, to indicate to the **Signaller** to **Clear** the **Platform Starting Signal**.

Train Ready To Start Plunger (TRTS Plunger)
[Sig.] An electrical switch (referred to by **Signalling Engineers** as a **Plunger**) provided on a **Platform** to allow the Platform staff to indicate to the **Signaller** that the **Train** is ready to depart. The Signaller has an **Indicator** in the **Signal Box (SB)** that illuminates to show that the Plunger has been operated. This system is provided at busy **Stations** to increase **Junction** efficiency, as a **Route** out of the Platform is only provided when the **Train** is ready, not from when it is booked to leave. See also **Train Ready To Start Indicator (TRTS Indicator)**.

Train Register
Train Register Book
[Sig.] The book in which a **Signaller** records movements of **Trains**, visitors and completion of other regular duties. They are also used to record details of disconnections, **Possessions** and other irregularities. In larger **Signal Boxes (SB)** operating **Track Circuit Block (TCB)** such as **Power Signal Boxes (PSB)** and **Integrated Electronic Control Centres (IECC)**, this function is achieved by a combination of electronic data, video and voice recordings. See also **Occurrence Book**.

Train Reporting Number
[NR Ops.] An identifier of the format $@xx:
$ is a number giving the **Class** of the **Train**
@ is a letter describing its destination **Region**, City or purpose:

A	
B	London
C	
E	Eastern Region
G	Birmingham
I	**Channel Tunnel**
L	Anglia
M	London Midland
O	Southern
S	Scotland
V	Western
X	Royal Train / **Out of Gauge (OOG)**
Z	Special, **Engineering**.

xx is a unique number for that day
Formerly known as **Head Codes**. Also SCHLID, **Train Description**, **Train ID**.

Train Running Away Alarm (TRA Alarm)
[Sig.] A warning to the **Signaller**, activated by anything passing a relevant **Main Signal** at **Danger**, which places or maintains all Main **Signals** protecting the area to Red unless the Signaller presses the **TRA** acknowledge button. Also **Spad Alarm**, see also **Spad Latch**.

Train Running Times
[Sig.] The time allowed for each **Class of Train** and **Timing Load** between strategic points such as **Stations** and **Junctions** on a **Route**. It is from these times that the **Timetable (TT)** is constructed.

Train Service Information (TSI)
[NR Ops.] A database of **Train** schedules formatted for use by the Train operations systems. It is updated daily with information from the **Train Service Database** (**TSDB**) provided via the **Common Interface File** (**CIF**). TSI holds all the Train schedules to be used by **TRUST** and related systems and passes them forward to TRUST. TSI is a batch processing system with a user interface provided by the **Train Service Information Access System** (**TSIA**).

Train Service Information Access System (TSIA)
[NR Ops.] A system which provides both on-line enquiries of train schedules and the ability to make **Very Short Term Plan** (**VSTP**) changes. Schedules are sourced from **Train Service Information** (**TSI**), **Short Term Planning** (**STP**) and **Long Term Planning** (**LTP**).

Train Shed
a) A large building used for the storage and **Maintenance** of **Locomotives** or **Trains**
b) The roofed part of a large **Station** that contains the **Platforms**, often a separate structure from the **Booking Hall** or **Station Concourse**.

Train Signalling Block Regulations
Train Signalling Regulations
[Sig.] The instructions used by **Signallers** which detail the rules relating to each different method of **Signalling**.

Train Spotter
A person whose hobby is noting passing **Rail Vehicle** numbers and ticking them off in a guide or reference book. Of particular interest to the hardened spotter are infrequently seen Rail Vehicles, unusual **Formations** of Rail Vehicles and the ticking off of every vehicle number in a **Class**. There are many sub-specialisms, including those who spot **On Track Machines** (**OTMs**), for example. See also **Anorak, Gricer, Stoat, Veg**.

Train Staff
a) [Sig.] Literally a wood or metal staff used on **One Train Working by Train Staff** □ **Lines** to ensure that only one **Train** is on a **Line** at any one time (since a driver may only proceed when in possession of the Train Staff). The keys for the **Release** arrangements are often attached to the Staff to ensure complete safety, as the **Connection** to the Line cannot then be unlocked without the Train Staff itself. Sometimes shortened to **Staff**
b) [Col.] Alternative for **Traincrew**.

Train Stop
A device that ensures compliance with a **Signal** displaying a **Stop Aspect** by automatically applying the brakes should the driver attempt to pass the relevant Signal. See also **Trip Cock, Train Stop Sensor** (**TSS**). Also **Trainstop**.

Train Stop Override
Train Stop Override Push Button
[NR] A button which prevents the **Train Protection and Warning System** (**TPWS**) □ **Train Stop Sensor** (**TSS**) from functioning for 60 seconds, which allows a train to pass a TPWS **Fitted** □ **Signal** at **Danger**.

Train Stop Sensor (TSS)
[NR] A type of **Train Protection and Warning System** (**TPWS**) installation consisting of an **Arming Loop** and a **Trigger Loop** adjacent to each other in the **Fourfoot**, giving a **Set Speed** of zero. Above this speed the brakes will automatically be applied. These **Loops** are normally located at a **Signal** capable of showing a **Stop Aspect** and are activated when a **Stop Aspect** is shown. See also **Overspeed Sensor System** (**OSS**).

Train Wheel Detector
[Sig.] Generic term for any device designed to detect the passage of a **Train** wheel. See **Axle Counter, FREDDY, Treadle**. Also forms part of **Hot Axle Box Detector** (**HABD**) and **Wheel Impact Load Detector** (**WILD**) installations.

Train xxx
[LUL] The unique identity of a particular **Train** in the **Timetable** (**TT**) indicated by the three digit number. The identity indicates the starting time, route and destination of the Train.

Traincrew
[Ops.] Collective term for the **Conductor**, driver, **Driver's Assistant, Guard** and **Train Manager** of a **Train**.

Traincrew Operated (TMO)
Traincrew Operated Crossing (TMO)
Describes a type of **Level Crossing** (**LC, LX**) where the **Train** driver or **Guard** operates the **Barriers** or **Gates**. This arrangement is used where the density of traffic on both the **Railway** and highway is very light indeed. Abbreviated to **TMO**, for **Train Man Operated**.

Traincrew Operated Barriers (TMO(B))
Describes a type of **Traincrew Operated** (**TMO**) □ **Level Crossing** (**LC, LX**) with **Barriers** operated by the **Train** driver or **Guard**.

Trainload Coal
[BR Hist.] An internal **BR** unit which specialised in the transportation of coal. See **Black Diamonds**.

Trainman
[BR Hist.] A member of **Traincrew** not qualified to drive a **Train** but who carried out other operational duties. This grade was created by **British Rail** (**BR**) in 1988 by amalgamating the roles of **Guard** and **Second Man**.

ELLIS' BRITISH RAILWAY ENGINEERING ENCYCLOPÆDIA

Trains Entering Terminal Stations (TETS)
[LUL] A bank of resistors, together with auxiliary control equipment, which reduce the voltage of a section of **Conductor Rail** at the entrance to a **Terminal Station** as a **Train** approaches the **Platforms**. See also **Moorgate Accident**, **Moorgate Control**.

Trains per Hour (TPH, tph)
[Ops.] A measure of the density of traffic passing a particular point, normally in one direction only. See also **Headway**.

Trainstop
See **Train Stop**.

Tram
[LR] Common term for a **Light Rail Vehicle (LRV)**, a self-propelled **Passenger** carrying **Rail Vehicle** intended for use on **Light Railways**. Normally powered by **Electric Traction**, such vehicles typically have enhanced braking capabilities and a smaller **Minimum Radius** than other Rail Vehicles.

Tram Phase
[LR] The section of the cycle of the traffic signals at a **Level Crossing (LC, LX)** where the right of way is with the **Tram**.

Tram Ready To Start
[LR] A system by which a **Tram** driver can initiate the **Tram Phase** of a highway **Signalling System**.

Tram Road
[LR] A **Railway** with one or more **Tracks**, not running along a public road, but having the running surface of the **Rails** at ground level.

TRAMM
(*tram*) (Tradename) See **General Purpose Track Repair And Maintenance Machine**.

Tram-train
The operation of **Light Rail Vehicles (LRV)** on **Heavy Rail (HR)** ▢ **Lines**.

Tramway
[LR] A **Railway** with one or more **Tracks** running along a public road and having the **Running Surface** of the **Rails** at the same level as the road surface to permit the free passage of road traffic. See also **Light Railway**.

Tramway OLE
Tramway Overhead Line Equipment
[LR Elec.] A type of **Overhead Line Equipment (OHLE)** which uses only a single **Contact Wire (CW)** which is unsupported between **Registrations**. It is used in low speed areas. Also **Trolley Wire**.

Trans European Network (TEN)
Trans European Network Strategy (TENS)
The system of key **Railway** ▢ **Routes** linking the extreme ends of the European Union. See **Trans European Network Strategy Route (TENS Route)**.

Trans European Network Strategy Route (TENS Route)
A **Main Line** included in the **Trans European Network (TEN)** Strategy. In the UK, the high speed Routes are:
* The **West Coast Main Line (WCML)** from London to Manchester, Liverpool, and Scotland.
* The **East Coast Main Line (ECML)** from London to Edinburgh
* The Channel Tunnel Rail Link (CTRL)
* The **Great Western Main Line (GWML)** from London to Bristol and Cardiff
* The Routes from Cork to Londonderry via Belfast, Dublin and Limerick

There are other Routes included as **Conventional Routes** (i.e. low speed) - this definition covers all other "inter-city" lines and some strategic branches.

Transboardment Bridge
[Ops.] A lightweight folding platform that allows **Passengers** to be transferred from a **Failed Train** to another **Train** drawn up alongside.

Transfesa
(Tradename) An owner and operator of **Freight Vehicles**, as well as co-ordinated road and **Rail Freight** operations.

Transformer
(Generally) a pair of coils wound on the same ferromagnetic core. The ratio of the number of turns in the input (primary) coil and the output (secondary) coil determines the output voltage relative to the input voltage. The secondary can have multiple output connections along its length, called **Taps**, each of which provides a different output voltage. Transformers are relatively heavy and normally used to convert high voltages into lower voltages. See also **Autotransformer (AT)**, **Booster Transformer (BT)**.

Transhipping
Transferring **Goods** from one **Freight Vehicle** to another, historically because of either a **Change Of Gauge** or because through working of one **Railway Company's** vehicles was not permitted over another company's **Tracks**.

Transhipping Shed
A form of **Goods Shed** within which the **Transhipping** of Goods took place.

Transit
Movement of **On-track Machines (OTM)** between locations where they are required to work or **Stable**.

Transition
a) See **Transition Beam**
b) See **Transition Panel**
c) See **Transition Rail**
d) See **Transition Section**
e) A colloquial contraction of **Transition Curve**
f) Any managed change between two different situations.

Transition Beam
See **Interface Slab**. Also **Transition Slab**.

Transition Curve (Trans.)
[PW]
a) A **Curve** with a uniformly varying Radius (**R**) from **Straight** to **Curve**, or vice versa. See **Straight to Curve Transition**
b) A Curve with a uniformly varying Radius from one Radius to another, see **Curve to Curve Transition**. See also **Compound Curve** See also **Cant Transition**.

Transition Heel
[PW] The point where a **Transition Curve** has its minimum Radius (**R**).

Transition Length (TL)
[PW] The length of a **Transition Curve** is determined by either the **Rate of Change of Cant** (**RgE**) or the **Rate of Change of Cant Deficiency** (**RgD**), whichever is the greater, the speed of **Trains**, the change in **Cant** (**C, E**) and **Cant Deficiency** (**D**) through the Transition Curve and, in the case of a **Tilting Train**, the **Rate of Rotation of Carbody**. The shortest possible Transition Curve is one in which the change of Cant and Cant Deficiency is the same. See also **Virtual Transition**.

Transition Migration
[PW] The tendency of **Transition Curves** to "wander" longitudinally under repeated passes of **Tampers** carrying out **Maintenance Lining**, particularly when the Transition is always tamped in the same direction. The easy solution is to alternate the direction in which the tampers work, the harder one is to always carry out **Design Tamping**.

Transition Panel
[PW] A **Track Panel** made up with **Transition Rails**, providing a change of **Rail Section**.

Transition Rail
[PW] A **Rail** with a **Transition Section** contained within it.

Transition Section
[PW] A specially forged **Rail** that changes **Rail Section** along its length. It is used to connect widely different Rail Sections where a **Fishplated Rail Joint** would be unacceptable, and no applicable **Composite Weld** is available. Typical Transition Sections are:
- CEN60E1 or CEN60E2 to 113A
- HUSH Rail to 113A
- Forth Bridge Rail to 113A.

Transition Shift
[PW] The offset applied to a **Curve** when providing a **Transition Curve** between it and another curve or a straight. See **Straight to Curve Transition** for full details.

Transition Slab
See **Interface Slab**. Also **Transition Beam**.

Transition Step
[PW] An alternative term for the **Versine Rise**, the difference between the **Versine** values of successive **Half Chords** in a **Transition Curve**. See **Hallade**.

Transitioned Crossover
[PW] A **Crossover** made up of two **Transitioned Turnouts**.

Transitioned Lead

Transitioned Turnout
[PW] A **Turnout** which has a **Transition Curve** between the **Turnout Curve** and the straight through the **Crossing**. This arrangement typically permits a higher speed than a **Circular Turnout** with the same **Switches**.

Translator Vehicle
[TRS] A **Rail Vehicle** designed to provide an interface between two incompatible Rail Vehicles, often **Passenger Coaches**. Typically they will deal with differences between **Brake Types**, **Couplings**, electrical connectors, etc. Also **Barrier Vehicle**.

Trans-manche Link (TML)
(Tradename) [Hist.] The company that constructed the **Channel Tunnel**.

Transmission Based Signalling (TBS)
[Sig.] A **Signalling System** in which the driver is authorised to proceed by means of radio transmissions to **Indicators** in the **Driving Cab** rather than by observing **Fixed Signals**. See **In-cab Signalling**, **Radio Electronic Token Block** (**RETB**).

Transmission Based Train Control (TBTC)
a) [Sig.] A continuous **Automatic Train Control** (**ATC**) system utilizing high-resolution train location determination, independent of **Track Circuits** (**TC**); continuous, high-capacity, bidirectional **Train-to-Wayside** data communications; and train borne and Wayside processors capable of supporting various **Grades of Automation** (**GoA**):
- GoA 1 is effectively a manual mode of operation
- GoA 2 is Semi-automated Train Operation (STO)
- GoA 3 is Driverless Train Operation (DTO)
- GoA 4 is Unattended Train Operation (UTO)

Most systems provide **Automatic Train Protection** (**ATP**) functions, as well as optional **Automatic Train Operation** (**ATO**) and **Automatic Train Supervision** (**ATS**) functions. Also **Communications-Based Train Control** (**CBTC**).
b) [LUL] The system being introduced on the Jubilee Line, see also **Little Red Cable, the**

Transom
[PW] A timber section fixed between **Longitudinal Timbers** which, together with transom bolts, maintain the **Track Gauge**.

Transponder
[Sig.] A **Trackside** device that passes information to passing **Trains**. See **Advanced Passenger Train Transponder** (**APT Transponder**). See also **Tilt Authorisation and Speed Supervision System Balise** (**TASS Balise**).

Transport Act 1947
[Hist.] An Act making provision for the **Nationalisation** of the **National Railway Network** (**NRN**).

Transport Act 1962
[Hist.] The Act which abolished the **British Transport Commission** (BTC) and transferred control of the **Railways** to the **British Railways Board** (BRB).

Transport and Works Act (TWA)
This 1992 Act repealed the **Light Railways Act 1896**, the **Tramways** Act 1870 and replaced the Private Bill procedure. From this date the Secretary of State for Transport issued Orders for new works, following a public enquiry.

Transport for Greater Manchester (TfGM)
The new name for **Greater Manchester Passenger Transport Executive** (GMPTE), the organisation responsible for providing **Light Rail** □ **Metrolink** services, subsidised bus services and traffic signals in the Greater Manchester area.

Transport for London (TfL)
Transport for London was created in 2000 as the integrated body responsible for the Capital's transport system. The primary role of TfL, part of the Greater London Authority, is to implement the Mayor of London's transport strategy and manage transport services. TfL is responsible for London's buses, the **Underground**, the **Docklands Light Railway** (DLR) and the management of Croydon Tramlink and London river services, Victoria coach station, London's transport museum, a 580km network of main roads, all of London's 4,600 sets of traffic lights, the central London congestion charging scheme and regulation of the city's taxis and private hire vehicles.

Transportable Token Unit (TTU)
[NR Sig.] A portable **Cab Display Unit** (CDU) for **Radio Electronic Token Block** (RETB) for use on **Road Rail Vehicles**, **On Track Plant** (OTP) or on the Lineside.

Transposing
[PW] Extending the useful life of the **Rails** in a **Track**, particularly on a **Curve**, by swapping the two Rails on the same **Sleepers**. The term is also used when one Rail is moved across, but the other is replaced.

Transposition Bond
a) [Elec.] A **Bond** fitted to connect two sections of the **Traction Return Rail** together where it changes from one **Rail** of a **Track** to the other
b) [Sig.] A Bond fitted to connect two sections of a **Track Circuit Rail** together where it changes from one Rail of a Track to the other.
See also **Yellow Bond**.

Transposition Joints
[PW, Elec., Sig.] A pair of **Insulated Rail Joints** (IRJ), one in each **Running Rail** of a **Track**, provided to allow a **Track Circuit** (TC) and or **Traction Return Rails** to swap from one **Rail** to the other.

Transrail
(Tradename) [Hist.] A **Freight Operating Unit** (FOU) set up under **Privatisation**, and then bought and merged with the others (**Loadhaul** and **Mainline**) plus the postal carrier **Rail Express Systems** (RES) to form **English Welsh and Scottish Railways** (EWS). See also DB Schenker Rail (UK) Ltd., Freight Operating Company (FOC).

Transverse Profile
[PW]
a) The convex **Rail Head Profile** running across the **Rail Head** from **Gauge Corner** to **Field Side**. Typical profiles include ATL, ATH and HR1
b) The profile of a section taken through a **Cast Crossing**.

Trap Points
[PW, Sig.] An assembly of either one or a pair of **Switch Half Sets** of Facing □ **Worked Switches** intended to **Derail** □ **Rail Vehicles** in the event of their **Unauthorised Movement**. Often employed to protect against **Conflicting Movements** onto **Running Lines** or on the exits from **Sidings**. Also **Traps**. Trap Points consisting of one **Switch Half Set** are termed **Single Tongue Trap Points** (STT), and those with two are **Double Tongue Trap Points** (DTT) **Wide to Gauge Trap Points** or **Straddle Switches**. Also known as **Safety Points**. See also **Catch Points**.

Trap Road

A short length of **Track** extending beyond the exit of a **Loop** or **Siding**, intended to provide a **Signal Overlap** (O/L) to allow a driver to stop safely having incorrectly passed the **Loop Exit Signal** at **Danger**. They typically end in **Buffer Stops**, **Sand Drags** or nothing at all.

Trapping Arrangements
Trapping Protection
[Sig.] A general term encompassing all mechanical measures design to intercept **Un-Authorised Movements**. Such measures include **Interlaced Retarder Trap Points**, **Sand Drags**, **Trap Points**.

Traps
[Col.] Alternative term for a set of **Trap Points**.

TRATIM
(Tradename) [Ops.] A system for generating **Train** timings, produced by **AEA Technology** (now DeltaRail).

Travel Mode
a) The method of movement of an **On Track Machine** (**OTM**), item of plant, **Road Railer** (**RR**) or **Rail Vehicle** used to move between sites of work, where there is a choice. See **Rail Mode, Road Mode, Self-propelled** and **Train Formation**
b) Describing a **Ballast Cleaner, Ballast Regulator, Dynamic Track Stabiliser** (**DTS**), **Rail Crane** or **Tamper** that has had its various booms, conveyors, trolleys, jibs, **Tamping Banks**, etc. stowed and secured ready for travel to another site.

Travelling Post Office (TPO)
a) [Hist.] A **Van** equipped to deal with the receipt, franking and sorting of mail
b) [Hist.] A **Train** conveying such vehicles.

Traverser
A moveable deck, typically around 22m (72 feet) long, with **Rails** fixed to its upper surface. The deck moves laterally on further Rails, allowing single **Rail Vehicles** to be transferred between **Tracks**; typically found in **Maintenance Depots**. See also **Sector Plate, Turntable**.

Trax
[PW Col.] A contraction of **Traxcavate**, now universally meaning to **Excavate** with tracked excavators. (A **Traxcavator** was a specific type of tracked loading shovel used on **Reballasting** sites).

Traxcavate
[PW Col.] The long version of **Trax**.

Traxcavator
a) (Tradename) [Hist.] A type of tracked loading shovel either fitted with a left-hand **Sidetip** or 4-in-1 or forward-tipping bucket. The word "Traxcavator" comes from combining Tractor and Excavator, originally manufactured by the Trackson Company of Milwaukee, Wisconsin, which was in turn bought by Caterpillar in 1952
b) [PW Col.] Common name for any tracked excavator, See **Trax, Traxcavate**. See also **Drott**.

TRB
a) **Train** Recording Book
b) See **Train Register Book**.
c) [TRS] An acronym representing a **Trailer** Buffet Unclassified.

TRC
a) See **Track Recording Coach**
b) See **Track Renewal Company, Track Renewal Contractor**
c) Tough Rubber Cover
d) Train Running Controller.

TRE
a) [NR] **Track** Recording Engineer
b) (Tradename) Total Route Evaluation, a system developed by **URS**

Tread
[TRS] The part of a **Rail Wheel** that runs on the top of the rail. See **Wheel Profile**.

Tread Brake
[TRS] An arrangement in which a brake block bears on the tyre of the wheel. See also **Clasp Brake, Disc Brake**.

Tread Chamfer
[TRS] The approximately 45° chamfer applied to the outer edge of the **Outer Tread** of a **Rail Wheel**. See **Wheel Profile**.

Tread Corner
[TRS] An alternative term for **Tread Chamfer**.

Tread Datum
[TRS] The point at which the **Inner Tread** meets the **Outer Tread**, 70mm from the **Flange Back**. See **Wheel Profile**.

Treadle
[Sig.] An electrical switch mounted on the **Rail** with an actuating lever which is operated by the **Wheel Flanges** of passing **Rail Vehicles**. They are used particularly to activate **Automatic Level Crossings**.

TRED
Third Rail Earthing Device.

Trenail and Spike
Trenail and Spike Fastening
[PW Obs.] A fixing for **Chairs** for **Bullhead** (**BH**) **Rail Sections** in which one or more of the securing holes cast in the Chair were fitted with a hollow oak dowel (the Tre(e)-nail) into which a steel spike was driven to secure the assembly.

Trenching
[NR PW] The action of excavating the **Ballast Shoulders** in advance of a **Track Relaying Train** (**TRT**). This is done in order that the **Train** has space into which it can push the surplus **Ballast** generated as part of its operation.

Trepanning
a) Using a circumferential cutter to remove an annulus of material
b) [PW] The method used in the **Rotabroach** □ **Rail Drill**. Trepanning is considerably quicker than drilling a full hole with a twist drill, as only 25% of the material is actually removed by the cutter, the rest falling out as a solid plug.

Trespass and Vandalism (TP&V)
One of the major safety risks on modern **Railways**. See also **Q Trains**.

Trespass Guard
See **Cattle-cum-Trespass Guard**.

Trevithick, Francis
(1812-1877) Son of **Richard Trevithick**, became resident engineer and **Locomotive** Superintendent on the Grand Junction Railway (**GJR**), transferred to Crewe Locomotive Works in 1843 where he employed a young **Francis William Webb**.

Trevithick, Richard
(1771-1833) born in Illogan, Cornwall. An innovative engineer and pioneer of high-pressure steam applications, he created a prototype **Steam Locomotive** in 1796 and a fully functional Steam Locomotive running on **Rails** in 1804. Trevithick produced a **Locomotive** for the Wylam Colliery, and the more famous 'Catch Me Who Can' that ran in Euston Square in the summer of 1808. Regarded by his peers (including **George Stephenson**) as the cornerstone of early Locomotive development, he died virtually penniless.

TRFB
[TRS] An acronym representing a **Trailer** Restaurant Buffet **First Class** □ **Coach** (**HST**).

TRFM
[TRS] An acronym representing a **Trailer** Restaurant First Class □ Modular Coach (HST).

TRGM
[PW] **Track Geometry**, a standard form of data file.

Trial Hole
A shallow excavation carried out to examine the ground conditions beneath the **Track** or to determine the extent of a buried feature such as a **Bridge Abutment** or **Bridge Pier**. In the former case such holes are rarely dug to more than 450mm (18 inches) **Below Sleeper Bottom** (**BSB**).

Triangle
A layout of three **Tracks** which in plan form the three sides of a triangle. It is possible to reverse a complete **Train** by using such a layout if space is available.

Tribometer
A device that can measure the adhesion between a **Rail Wheel** and **Rail**. See also **Mu** (μ).

TRIBUTE
(*trib-yute*) [NR] A Personal Computer based **Ticket** issuing designed to replace the **All Purpose Ticket Issuing System** (**APTIS**). Formerly New Generation Ticketing (**NGT**).

Tri-compo
Tri-composite Coach
[TRS Hist.] A **Passenger Coach** with segregated areas for First Class, Second Class and Third Class □ Passengers.

TRID
[NR] Track Identifier; see **Track Identity** (**TID**).

Trident
[Prob. Obs.] A one-off **Side Rail Loader** having three cranes, allowing it to handle shorter **Rails** than the two **Side Rail Loader**-fitted vehicles **Arneke** and **Stumec**. See **Wagon Names**.

Trigger
[Sig.] An alternative for **Catch Handle**.

Trigger Loop
[NR Sig.] The second **Track** mounted transmitter a **Train** encounters as part of a **Train Protection and Warning System** (**TPWS**) installation. This Loop activates the protection system if the timer fitted to the Train is still running following an **Arming Loop**. See **Overspeed Sensor System** (**OSS**), **Train Stop Sensor** (**TSS**).

TRIM
[PW] **Track** Inertial Measurement, see **Tracklab**.

TRIME
[Elec., TRS] Third Rail In-service Monitoring Equipment, a joint University of Birmingham, Southern, **Network Rail** (**NR**) and **RSSB** programme aimed at improving the interaction of **Conductor Rails** and **Current Collection Shoes**.

Tri-metallic Zone (TMZ)
[PW] The short section at each corner of a **Cast Austenitic-manganese Steel Crossing** (**Cast AMS Crossing**) where a piece of stainless steel is introduced to allow the **Crossing Legs** to be flash welded to the **AMS** casting. Also **Sandwich Weld**.

TRIMS
[Hist.] Total **Railtrack** Incident Monitoring System, the potential replacement for Fault Reporting and Monitoring & Equipment System (**FRAME**).

Trip
a) [Ops.] A regular **Train** movement for conveying **Rail Vehicles** between two local points on **The Network**, calling as required, to detach and attach other Rail Vehicles. See **Tripping**. See also **Engineering Trip Train**, **Target**
b) The automatic opening of a **Circuit Breaker** (**CB**) when a fault occurs in the circuit it is protecting
c) [Ops.] The activation of a **Tripcock**.

Trip Cock
See **Tripcock**.

Trip Timbers
[LUL] Longer than standard length **Sleepers** intended to support a **Train Stop**.

Trip Wire
[Sig.] A wire, stretched on poles parallel to the **Railway**, located at points where the possibility of exists of aircraft overrunning the ends of runways at airports. The Trip Wire is arranged so that if it is impacted or broken the **Signalling System** will Revert to **Stop Aspects** and the **Traction Supply Current** (if any) will be disconnected to protect **Trains** and the accident site. Similar arrangements are also used in **Cuttings** to detect falls of rock. Also **Tell Tale**.

ELLIS' BRITISH RAILWAY ENGINEERING ENCYCLOPÆDIA

Tripcock
[TRS] A brake valve mounted on the outside of a vehicle **Bogie** close to **Track Level**. The valve has a protruding arm that can be activated by the raised arm of a mechanical **Train Stop**. This Train Stop is raised when the associated **Signal** is showing a **Stop Aspect**, so that if the driver attempts to incorrectly pass the Signal the brakes will be applied automatically.

Triple Bank
Triple Bank Tamper
[PW] A **Tamper** that is capable of Tamping three **Sleepers** simultaneously. See also **Double Bank**, **Double Bank Tamper**.

Triple Differential Speed Restriction
[NR] A **Permanent Speed Restriction** (**PSR**) with three values. The upper part of the Sign shows the lowest two speed values in conventional **Differential Speed Restriction** format. The bottom and largest speed value is reserved for particular types of **Train** as shown on the **Speed Indicator** (**SI**). For further information see **Non-standard Differential Speed Restriction**.

Triple Differential Warning Indicator
[NR] A **Warning Indicator** (**WI**) provided to indicate to a driver that a **Triple Differential Speed Restriction** is ahead. See also **Differential Warning Indicator**, **Non-standard Differential Warning Indicator**.

Triple Intersection
[PW] A part of a **Scissors Crossover** where two **Common Crossings** and **One Obtuse Crossing** form one unit. See also **Saddle Crossing**.

Triple Valve
[TRS] The valve which controls the operation of the **Air Brake** on a vehicle, so called because it originally comprised three valves. The triple valve contains a slide valve which detects changes in the **Brake Pipe** pressure and arranges the connections inside the valve accordingly:
- When the Brake Pipe has a high pressure, it recharges the **Auxiliary Reservoir** and opens the brake cylinder exhaust, releasing the brake
- At low pressure, it closes the brake cylinder exhaust and allows the Auxiliary Reservoir air to feed into the brake cylinder, applying the brake
- At intermediate pressure, it holds the air pressures in the Auxiliary Reservoir and brake cylinder at the current level, maintaining the current brake effort.

Triple Voltage
[TRS] Describing a **Traction Unit** that can be supplied by three types of **Electrification** system, typically 25kV AC **Overhead Line Equipment** (**OLE**), 750V DC **Conductor Rails** and direct current Overhead Line Equipment. Such a Traction Unit is the **Class** 373 Eurostar.

Tripped
[Ops.] The condition when the front **Tripcock** on a **Train** applies the **Brakes**, normally after passing a **Signal** displaying a **Stop Aspect**. See also **Back Tripped**.

Tripping
[Ops.]
a) A term describing the short-distance movement of **Freight**. See **Trip**
b) A suitably equipped **Train** attempting to pass a **Signal** at showing a **Stop Aspect** and activating the **Tripcock**
c) Of a Circuit Breaker (CB), opening the main contacts in response to a fault condition.

TRIS
<u>T</u>eleconferencing **<u>R</u>ailways** <u>I</u>nformation <u>S</u>ystem.

TRM
See **Track Relaying Machine**.

TRM Beam
[PW] **<u>T</u>rack <u>R</u>elaying <u>M</u>achine** <u>B</u>eam, a Sleeper Beam designed to be lifted using a **Track Relaying Machine** (**TRM**). Most TRM Beams have attachment points allowing the handling of 24, 26 or 28 **Sleepers** at the correct **Sleeper Spacing**. See also **Janglers**.

TROC
(*trock*) [NR]
a) **<u>T</u>rain** □ **<u>R</u>unning** □ **<u>O</u>perations** □ **<u>C</u>ontrol**
b) **<u>T</u>rack <u>R</u>enewal <u>O</u>perations <u>C</u>ontrol**.

Trolley
[Col.] Common contraction of **Hand Trolley**. Also **Bogie**, **Gibbon**.

Trolley Jumper
Cables suspended from a trolley running on twin busbars carrying the **Traction Supply** along the entire length of a **Shed Road** and terminating in a **Shed Plug**..

Trolley Wire
[Elec.] An arrangement of **Overhead Line Equipment** (**OLE**) consisting only of a single **Contact Wire** (**CW**). It is generally only suitable for low speed operation, normally **Sidings**. Named after its use on **Tram** and trolley bus systems. Also **Tramway OLE**, **Tramway Overhead Line Equipment**.

Troop Train
[Ops.] A **Train** carrying troops on military business.

TroTred
(Tradename) An injection moulded modular **Surface Cable Trough** (**SCT**) incorporating a anti-slip walkway on the lid, allowing the **Cable Route** and **Cess Path** to be combined. Manufactured by Trojan Services of Chichester.

ELLIS' BRITISH RAILWAY ENGINEERING ENCYCLOPÆDIA

Troughing
[Col.] Contraction of Cable Trough.

Troughs
See Water Troughs.

Trout (ZFO)
[NR] A 24 ton Ballast Hopper □ Wagon with both centre and side discharge chutes. See Wagon Names.

TRS
a) Temporary Restriction of Speed. See Temporary Speed Restriction (TSR)
b) See Train Ready To Start (TRTS)
c) Train Reporting System.

TRSB
[TRS] An acronym representing a Trailer Restaurant Buffet Standard □ Coach (HST).

TRSM
Transitional Risk Sharing Mechanism.

TRSMD
Traction and Rolling Stock □ Maintenance Depot.

TRT
a) See Track Relaying Train
b) See Technical Running Time
c) [NR] Track Recording Train, see New Measurement Train (NMT).

TRTS
See Train Ready To Start.

TRTS Indicator
See Train Ready To Start Indicator.

TRTS Plunger
See Train Ready To Start Plunger.

TRU
a) See Track Recording Unit
b) See Track Renewals Unit.

TRUB
[TRS] An acronym representing a Trailer Buffet Unclassified Coach (HST).

Truck
a) [NPT] An alternative for Wagon, rarely used by those inside the Railway Industry
b) [TRS] An alternative for Bogie, see also Pony Truck.

TRUK
[TRS] An acronym representing a Trailer Restaurant Unclassified Kitchen Coach (HST).

Trunking
A term describing the long-distance movement of Freight.

Truss

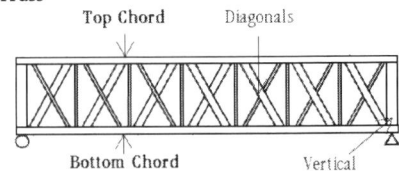

[Civ.] A structure supporting a Bridge Deck, formed from individual structural members in tension and compression. The illustration shows a Howe Truss.

TRUST
(*trust*) [NR] Train □ Running System using TOPS, a computer system that processes reports of Train Running and compares it with the Timetables (TT). The results of this processing are used to generate delay attribution claims. Normally referred to by its initials.

TRUST-DA
(*trust-dee-ay*) [NR] Train □ Running System on TOPS Delay Attribution, The system which records the duration and cause of delays identified by TRUST.

TRV
See Track Recording Vehicle.

TRW
Training Workstation.

TS
[TRS] An acronym representing a Trailer □ Standard Class □ Coach.

TS&I
Technical Services and Innovation.

TSA

TSB
See Test Site A, Test Site B.

TSBR
Train to Signal Box Radio.

TSC
a) See Track Sectioning Cabin
b) Train Service Code
c) [NIR] Track Safety Co-ordinator.

TSCB
Traction Supply □ Circuit Breaker.

TSD
a) [TRS] An acronym representing a Trailer □ Standard Class □ Coach with disabled toilet
b) [NR] Train Systems Delivery, part of the West Coast Route Modernisation (WCRM) project.

TSDB
a) Train System Data Base
b) Train Service Database.

TSE
[NR] Territory □ Signalling Engineer, previously called the Zone Signalling Engineer (ZSE).

TSG
[NR] Tactical Safety Group.

TSH
[TRS] An acronym representing a **Trailer** □ **Standard Class** □ **Handbrake** □ **Coach**.

TSI
a) See **Technical Standard for Interoperability**
b) See **Train Service Information**.

TSIA
See **Train Service Information Access System**.

TSL
See **Track Sectioning Location**.

TSLG
Technical **S**trategy **L**eadership **G**roup

TSM
a) [NR] **Track** □ **Section** **M**anager
b) **Train** **S**topping **M**arker

TSMS
(Tradename) **T**otal **S**upplier **M**anagement **S**ystem, a Balfour Beatty / Achilles service.

TSO
[TRS]
a) An acronym representing a **Tourist** □ **Standard Class** □ **Open** □ **Coach**
b) An acronym representing a **Trailer** Standard Class Open Coach.

TSOB
[TRS] An acronym representing a **Tourist** □ **Standard** □ **Open** □ **Coach** with Buffet.

TSOT
[TRS] An acronym representing a **Tourist** □ **Standard** □ **Open Coach** (Trolley/Buffet).

TSPA
T-SPA
(*tea-spar*) (Tradename) [PW] **T**rack **S**trategic **P**lanning **A**pplication, a decision-support tool developed by Serco.

TSR
See **Temporary Speed Restriction**.

TSR Board
See **Commencement Indicator**.

TSRB
[TRS] An acronym representing a **Trailer** □ **Standard Class** Restaurant Buffet **Coach**.

TSRGD
The **T**raffic **S**igns **R**egulations and **G**eneral **D**irections 2002, the law that sets out the design and conditions of use of official traffic signs that can be lawfully placed on or near roads in England, Scotland, Wales, and the Isle of Man. This includes signs used on the highway in association with **Light Rail** (**LR**) systems.

TSS
a) [Sig.] See **Train Stop Sensor**. Part of the **Train Protection and Warning System** (**TPWS**)
b) **T**rack **S**ectioning **S**ite.

TSSA
(*tessa*) (Tradename) **T**ransport **S**alaried **S**taffs' Association, a trade union representing clerical and technical staff on the **Railway**. Originally called the Railway Clerks Association.

TSSC
[NR] **T**icketing and **S**ettlement **S**cheme **C**ouncil. The governing body of Rail Settlement Plan (**RSP**).

TSSG
[NR] **T**rack **S**afety **S**trategy **G**roup.

TSSU
Time **S**lot **S**haring **U**nit.

TSW
[TRS] An acronym representing a **Trailer** □ **Standard Class** □ **Coach** with Wheelchair accommodation.

TT
a) See **Timetable**
b) See **Tied Timber**
c) See **Through Timber**
d) See **Thames Trains**.

TTC
See **Twin Track Cantilever**.

TTCCTV
Track to **T**rain **C**losed **C**ircuit **Tele**vision.

TTD
Track / **T**rain **D**ynamics, see also **Wheel / Rail Interface**.

TTDB
[NR] **T**ime**t**able **D**ata**b**ase. A facility which allows the public to view Timetable information remotely through the Internet or VDUs at **Stations**.

TTE
[NR] **T**erritory □ **T**rack **E**ngineer.

TTI
Travelling **T**icket **I**nspector.

TTP
Time**t**able **P**rocessor.

TTR
Track to **T**rain **R**adio.

TTRA
Time**t**able **R**obustness **A**nalysis.

TTS
See **Tunnel Telephone System**.

TTW
Travel **t**o **W**ork.

TT-*x*
[NR] Denoting an event happening x weeks prior to the issue of a **Timetable** (**TT**).

Tube Line
[LUL] Term used to differentiate underground **Tracks** in **Bored Tunnels** or **Cut and Cover** (**Sub-surface Lines**) from those above ground (**Surface Lines**) on London Underground Lines. The Tube Line sections are:
a) The Bakerloo Line,
- Queen's Park Network Rail (NR) boundary to

543

London Road Tunnel Mouth and the end of the Line south of Elephant & Castle,
b) The Central Line,
- White City Depot tunnel mouths and White City Tunnel Mouths to Leyton substation,
- West of Leytonstone Tunnel Mouth to east of Newbury Park tunnel mouth,
c) The Jubilee Line,
- Finchley Road to the end of the Line south of Charing Cross and Canning Town Tunnel Mouth,
d) The Northern Line,
- Hendon Tunnel,
- Golders Green Tunnel Mouth and East Finchley Tunnel Mouth via Bank and via Charing Cross to Morden,
e) The Piccadilly Line,
- Hounslow West to Heathrow,
- Barons Court to Bounds Green Tunnel Mouth,
- Southgate Tunnel,
f) The Victoria Line,
- The end of the Line north of Walthamstow Central to the end of the Line south of Brixton,
- Northumberland Park Tunnel Mouth to Seven Sisters,
g) The Waterloo and City line,
- Bank to Waterloo.
See also **Deep Tube Line**.

Tube Lines Limited
[LUL Hist.] One of two **Infrastructure** companies (see also **Metronet Rail Limited**) in a Public-Private Partnership [PPP] with **London Underground**. Initially known as Infraco JNP it was responsible for the **Maintenance**, renewal, and upgrade of the Infrastructure on three London Underground **Lines**, namely the Jubilee, Northern and Piccadilly on a 30-year contract. The company was founded in 2002 by a consortium of Amey plc, Bechtel and Jarvis plc. In 2005, Jarvis sold its stake to fellow shareholder Amey for £147 million. In May 2010 Transport for London (TfL) announced it was to buy the remaining shareholders out after a funding shortfall.

Tube Stock
[LUL] **Trains** specifically designed to run on the **Tube Lines**, particularly the narrow underground **Tunnels** of **London Underground Limited**. See also **Balanced Stock**.

Tubeplate
[TRS] The plates at the front and rear of a **Boiler**, which seal the Boiler and hold the **Boiler Tubes** in place.

TUCA
<u>T</u>unnelling and <u>U</u>nderground <u>C</u>onstruction <u>A</u>cademy.

Tug
[Col.] Nickname for the **Class** 60 **Diesel Locomotive**.

TUM
<u>T</u>echnical <u>U</u>ser <u>M</u>anual.

Tumbler Frame
[Sig.] A **Lever Frame** that achieves the **Interlocking** functions by means of **Tumblers** rather than Tappets. See also **Tappet Frame**.

Tumbler Locking
[Sig.] An arrangement of **Mechanical Locking** where two "tumblers", one each side of each **Lever** (although only one is necessary for **Distant Signals**) rotate as the Catch Handle is operated. This in turn drives the **Locking Bars** located behind the Levers along the length of the **Frame** to lock other Levers that would otherwise Set □ **Conflicting Moves**. The (now) more common arrangement is **Tappet Locking**.

Tuned Zone
[Sig.] In an installation of **Audio Frequency Track Circuits**, the area between two adjacent **Track Circuit areas**.

Tunna, Norman, GC
(29th April 1908 – 4th Dec. 1970) On 26th September 1940, when the German Air Force carried out a large bombing raid on the Morpeth dock area of Birkenhead, Merseyside, Norman Tunna discovered two incendiary bombs burning in a sheeted **Open Wagon** loaded with 250lb bombs. Disregarding his own safety, Tunna removed the sheet and extinguished the incendiary bombs. He then removed these from the Wagon. He was awarded the George Cross for his actions.

Tunnel
[Civ.] A means of gaining passage past obstructions such as mountains and wide rivers, or through densely populated conurbations. Constructed by one of four common methods:
- **Bored Tunnel**, using a cutting shield and occasional explosive blasting, the resultant 'bore' is then lined with concrete or steel to prevent collapse
- 'Cut and Cover', where the ground is excavated from above, the Tunnel built and then the space above backfilled. This method is only suitable for near-surface tunnels
- 'Cover and Cut', where the walls of the Tunnel are constructed by piling down from the surface. The Tunnel roof is then built across the tops of the piles just below ground level. Following backfilling above, the spoil or dumpling is then removed from inside the Tunnel
- **Immersed Tube**, where the tunnel is constructed in sections, sunk to the bottom and pieced together. The water is then pumped out

On **Network Rail** (**NR**), a **Bridge** becomes a Tunnel (primarily for inspection purposes) when the distance between the **Portals** is greater than 50 metres (55 **Yards**).

Tunnel Air Lines
[LUL] Pipes located on the side of **Tunnels** that are used to carry compressed air to **Trackside** equipment.

Tunnel Ballast
[Hist.] **Ballast** produced to a 28mm specification instead of the normal 48mm. The widespread introduction of **Tamping and Lining Machines** (**Tampers**) meant that the greater control this reduced grading gave for manual work was no longer required.

Tunnel Boring Machine (TBM)
[Civ.] A machine which uses a large rotating cutting head to excavate a **Tunnel**. See also **Tunnel Shield**.

Tunnel Controls
[Sig.] An application of **First Train Moving Away**, which ensures that the following **Train** can enter a **Tunnel** with reasonable expectation that it will not be stopped at a **Signal** within the Tunnel.

Tunnel Gauge
A wooden template with fingered projections used to measure the **Tunnel** profile.

Tunnel Gong
[Sig. Hist.] A metal gong located in a **Tunnel**, allowing the **Signaller** to send appropriate messages, using a coded number of beats, to drivers.

Tunnel Lights
[LUL] Lights that are provided in the **Running Tunnels** throughout the **Deep Tube** system which illuminate whenever the **Traction Current** is **Discharged**.

Tunnel Lining
[Civ.] The structural layer applied to the inside of a **Tunnel** to support the remaining material. There are many types:
- Tunnels made through rock typically have no lining, or only small panels of brickwork where required
- Older Tunnels in soft ground often have brick **Linings**
- More modern Tunnels have sprayed or segmental pre-cast concrete (**PCC**) Linings
- Many **Tube Lines** have segmental cast iron Linings.

Tunnel Mouth
[Civ.] The opening at one end of a **Tunnel**, also **Tunnel Portal**.

Tunnel Portal
[Civ.] The structure at one end of a **Tunnel**, also **Tunnel Mouth**.

Tunnel Rail
[NR] A **Rail Section** designed for use in **Tunnels**: these were the 97 $^1/_2$ Pound □ **Bull Head** and 113 Pound □ **Flat Bottom** Rail Sections. See also **Tunnel Section Conductor Rail**.

Tunnel Ring
[Civ.] In a **Tunnel** constructed of segments, one complete band of segments.

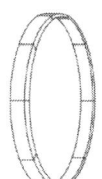

Tunnel Ring Axis
[Civ.] The line through the **Tunnel Ring** centre perpendicular to the **Tunnel Ring Centre Line**.

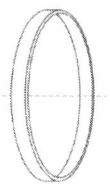

Tunnel Ring Centre-line
[Civ.] The line which passes through the centres of both the **Tunnel Ring** and the **Key**.

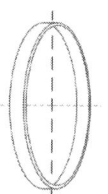

Tunnel Section Conductor Rail
[LUL] A rectangular **Conductor Rail** used on the **Deep Tube Lines**.

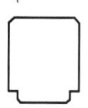

Tunnel Shaft
[Civ.] A vertical opening between a **Tunnel** and ground level above, often originally provided for construction purposes and retained for ventilation. Also **Shaft**, **Ventilation Shaft**.

Tunnel Shield
[Civ.] A machine which simultaneously supports the cutting face and allows its excavation. Pioneered by Marc Isambard Brunel (father of Isambard Kingdom **Brunel**), Peter Barlow and later James Henry **Greathead**, it works by pushing against the **Tunnel Lining** behind itself. See also **Tunnel Boring Machine** (**TBM**).

Tunnel Signal
[NR Sig.]
a) A **Signal** located within a **Tunnel**
b) A Signal which if it were to display a **Stop Aspect**, the next **Train** to stop at the Signal would stop wholly or partly in a Tunnel.

Tunnel Telephone
Tunnel Telephone System (TTS)
[LUL Tel.] An emergency communications system fitted to the **Tube Lines** of **London Underground Limited**. In addition to fixed telephones, the system consists of two bare **Wires** spaced about 4 $^1/_2$ inches (115mm) apart on the **Tunnel Wall** and at the same level as the driver's window. Shorting them together will switch the **Traction Current** off, and attaching a telephone handset allows communication with the **Line Controller**. Also Emergency Traction Current Discharge System (**ETCDS**), Tunnel Emergency Telephone (**TET**).

Tunny (ZCO, ZCV)
[NR] A dropside **Wagon** used for the transportation of **Ballast** and **Sleepers**. See **Wagon Names**.

TUPE
(*chew-pea*) Transfer of Undertakings (Protection of Employment) Regulations 1981. The mechanism by which the staff of the outgoing Contractor are transferred to the new Contractor when the work remains the same.

Turbostar
(Tradename) The brandname of the Class 170 and 171 Diesel Mechanical Multiple Units (DMMU).

Turbot (YCV, YCW)
[NR] A 34 ton capacity dropside Open Wagon used for the transportation of Ballast and Spoil. See Wagon Names. See also Heron (YCV).

Turn Back
[Ops.] A Train that is timetabled to travel to a destination, Reverse and return

Turn Back Siding

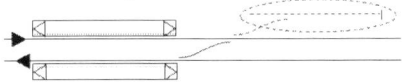

A Siding provided at a Through Station for the purpose of allowing the Traincrew of a Multiple Unit Train to change ends without occupying a Platform during a Turn Back.

Turn In
[Ops. Col.] To divert a Train to the Slow Lines, Relief Lines or Goods lines from the Main Line or Fast Line. See also Turn Out.

Turn Out
[Ops. Col.] To divert a Train onto the Main Line or Fast Line from a slower Line. See also Turn In.

Turn Your Back on Passing Trains
There are many reasons for turning one's back on a passing Train (having made sure one is in a Place of Safety first):
- To avoid Arc Eye from Trains using Conductor Rails
- To avoid a face full of sewage discharged from Trains using Live Discharge Toilets
- To reduce the risk from dust and stones falling from and being swept along by the Train.

Turnout (TO, T/O)

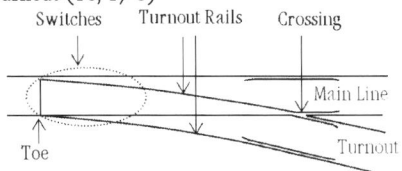

a) [PW] A Junction that comprises a Switch, an acute Common Crossing and appropriate Closure Rails. Also Half Lead, Lead, Single Lead, Connection, Points

b) [Sig.] A contraction of Turnout Route.

Turnout Curve
[PW] The Curve from the Tangent Point (TP) at the Switch Heel to the Intersection of Gauge Lines (IP) of a Common Crossing. See also Turnout Radius.

Turnout Opening
[PW] The distance between the adjacent Rails of the Main Line and Turnout Route in a Turnout at any given distance from the Crossing.

Turnout Radius
[PW] The Radius (R) of the Curve from the Tangent Point (TP) at the Switch Heel to the Intersection of Gauge Lines (IP) of a Common Crossing.

Turnout Route
[PW] The slowest, most Curved or least important path through a Switch and Crossing Layout (S&C Layout), Switch and Crossing Unit (S&C Unit), or from a Junction Signal.

Turnout Speed
a) [Sig.] The maximum speed permitted through the Turnout Route of Facing Points when they are Set for the Diverging Route
b) [PW] The designed maximum speed on the Turnout Route of a Single Lead. This speed may be higher than that which is actually permitted. See also Crossover Speed.

Turnover Locomotive
[Ops.] A Locomotive which waits at a Terminal Station to take an incoming Train away in the opposite direction where there are no facilities to Run Round the Train. The incoming Locomotive then becomes the new Turnover Locomotive.

Turnrail
[Arch.] An historic name for a Turntable, especially one installed in a Plateway or early Railway, to either turn Rail Vehicles or to permit abrupt changes of direction of travel.

Turntable
a) A large movable platform pivoted about its centre with Rails set in its upper surface, allowing Locomotives to be turned end for end or transferred between Tracks set out radially from the Turntable. See also Roundhouse, Sector Plate.
b) A hydraulically operated frame mounted centrally beneath some small On Track Machines (OTM) which, when extended, allows the machine to be rotated through either 180° or 90° and moved onto a Stillage or road transporter.

Turntable Bolt
A Bolt which engages with an appropriate aperture adjacent to the selected departure Track to prevent the Turntable making an unintended Movement.

Turret Beacon
See Laser Beacon.

TV
[NR]
a) The Trent Valley Route between Rugby and Stafford
b) Trent Valley, as in Lichfield TV.

TVC
[TRS] Tilt Authorisation and Speed Supervision System (TASS) Vital Computer.

TVIC
[TRS] Triple Valve Isolating Cock.

TVM
a) [CT] Transmission Voie Machine, Track to Train transmission
b) Ticket Vending Machine.

TVM Signalling
[CT] The Signalling System used in the Channel Tunnel which indicates to the driver the maximum permitted speed at any moment and overrides the driver's actions should it be exceeded.

TVP
See Track Visitor Permit.

TVR
Traction Voltage Recorder.

TVSC
Thames Valley Signalling Centre.

TW
a) See Track Welder
b) The ATOC code for Nexus (Tyne & Wear Metro).

TWA
See Transport and Works Act.

TWE
[NR] Track Welding Engineer.

Tweedy
[Sig. Hist.] Common shorthand for J Tweedy & Co., a former manufacturer of Signalling Equipment.

TWI
The Welding Insitute.

Twin Block Sleeper

[PW] Originally patented by Dudley Hepburn Stent in 1923, a Sleeper consisting of two reinforced concrete blocks connected by a steel tie rod. Use in the UK is generally confined to Light Rail (LR). See also Monoblock Sleeper.

Twin Boom Anchor Portal
[Elec.] An Overhead Line Equipment (OLE) Structure used to anchor the Catenary Wire and Contact Wire (CW) directly above the Track, even in Multi-track areas. This eliminates the need for Headspans or other arrangements which take the wires to an anchor in the Cess. Commonly used on GEFF equipment.

Twin Bore Tunnel
A Tunnel which consists of two related Bores. See also Single Bore Tunnel.

Twin Contact
[Elec.] An arrangement of the Overhead Line Equipment (OLE) found in vertically restricted areas (normally beneath Overbridges (OB)) where there are two parallel Contact Wires (CW) arranged horizontally and no Catenary Wires. See also Contenary.

Twin Jib Crane
See Track Relaying Machine (TRM).

Twin Relay
[Sig.] A unit that contains two electrically and mechanically independent Relays. See Left Hand Relay, Right Hand Relay.

Twin Track
Describing a Route with two Tracks, also Double Track.

Twin Track Cantilever (TTC)
[Elec.]

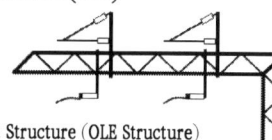

An Overhead Line Equipment Structure (OLE Structure) with a single upright which supports the Catenary for two Tracks by means of the cantilever principle.

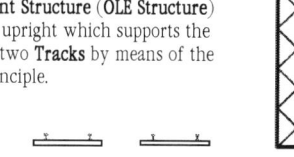

Twin Tracking
a) The act of adding a second Track to a Single Track □ Railway to make it Double Track. See also Doubling
b) Occasionally, the removal of one or more Tracks to leave two. See also Dequadrification.

TWINS
Track Wheel Interaction Noise Software.

Twist
[PW]
a) The point at which a Twist Rail twists
b) A Track Fault. See Twist Fault. Also Track Twist.

Twist Fault
[PW] A rapid change in Cant (C, E) or Crosslevel. Twist calculated by measuring the Crosslevel at two points a short distance (5m, 15 feet or 3m, 9 feet) apart, and then expressing the difference as a 1 in x □ Gradient over the interval. Values of Twist of 1 in 100 or worse cause Derailments. Cant Transitions are in effect Twist Faults, but are designed to have x greater than 400.

Twist Rail
Symbol:

Plan view:

[PW] A length of Rail having a Twist built into it to change the Inclination of the Rail from (generally) 1 in 20 (Inclined) to (generally) Vertical or vice versa. The Twist occurs with the Running Edge (RE) as the point of rotation, and can be located by finding the small steps in the edges of the Rail Foot. Because the Twist is towards one end of the Rail, Twist Rails are Handed.

Twistlock
Twistlock Fastening
[TRS] A device fitted to **Container Vehicles** and used to retain the **Containers** in place in transit. A vertical pin, onto which the Container fits, has a rotating upper part. Hole and pin are oval, so rotation of the pin locks the Container in place. See also **Spigot**.

TWO
Transport and **W**orks **O**rder, See **Transport and Works Act** (**TWA**). See also **Nationally Significant Infrastructure Projects** (**NSIP**).

Two Aspect Signal

Distant Signal   Stop Signal

[Sig.] A **Colour Light Signal** capable of displaying two **Aspects**. These are normally **Yellow** / **Green** (a **Distant Signal**) or **Red** / **Green** (a **Stop Signal**).

Two Aspect Signalling
[Sig.] An arrangement of **Colour Light Signals** which normally uses **Signals** displaying **Red** and **Green** □ **Aspects** (**Stop Signals**).

Two Level Baseplate
[PW] A **Baseplate** for **Flat Bottom** (**FB**) □ **Two Level Switches** having the **Rail Seats** for **Stock Rail** and **Switch Rail** at two different levels to give differential **Cants** (**C, E**). See also **Thick Based Baseplate**.

Two Level Chair
[PW] A **Chair** for use in **Bull Head** (**BH**) □ **Two Level Switches**, having the two **Rail Seats** for **Stock Rail** and **Switch Rail** at different levels to give differential **Cants** (**C, E**). See also **Thick Based Chair**.

Two Levelled Switch
[PW] A **Switch** assembly having a vertical **Set** imparted at the **Heel of The Switch Planing** in one of the Half Sets, fitted into **Two Level Chairs** or **Two Level Baseplates** to permit **Cant** (**C, E**) to be built up or decreased on the **Turnout** between the **Planing Heel** and the **Switch Heel**.

Two Levelled Switch and Crossing Layout
[PW] A **Switch and Crossing Layout** (**S&C Layout**) utilising **Two Level Baseplates**, **Two Level Chairs** and **Two Levelled Switches** to provide different design **Cant** (**C, E**) values on the **Main Line** and **Turnout** in a **Junction**.

Two Pipe Air Brake
[TRS] An **Air Brake** system that has a **Brake Pipe** and a **Main Reservoir Pipe** which is used to rapidly charge the **Auxiliary Reservoir** on each vehicle. This overcomes a problem with a simple Air Brake in that it is possible to use air in the Auxiliary Reservoir more quickly than the Brake Pipe can recharge it. The **Main Reservoir Pipe**. runs the length of the **Train**, fed from the compressor and **Main Reservoir**. A one-way valve allows air from the Main Reservoir Pipe to top up the Auxiliary Reservoir but prevents a loss of air from the Auxiliary Reservoir if the Main Reservoir pressure is lost. All Two Pipe systems use **Distributors** rather than **Triple Valves**.

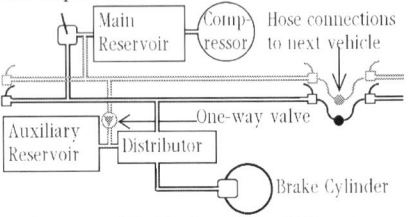

See **Passenger** / **Freight Changeover**, **Pulling the String**

Two Track Line
Two Track Railway
Describing a **Railway** with two **Tracks**. See also **Double Track**.

Two Way Lever
A **Hand Lever** that can operate a **Switch** in both directions. See also **One Way Lever**.

TWPTA
Tyne and **W**ear **P**assenger **T**ransport **A**uthority (**PTA**).

TWPTE
Tyne and **W**ear **P**assenger **T**ransport **E**xecutive (**PTE**).

TWS
(Tradename) **T**hermit **W**elding **S**ervices, a division of **Thermit Welding** (**GB**) Ltd.

Tx
[Sig.] On a **Signalling Circuit Diagram**:
- As the leading letters of an **Equipment Code**, it means transmitting
- As the last letters of an Equipment Code, it means transmitter.

T-*x*
[NR] Denoting an event happening *x* weeks prior to a particular event, typically a **Possession**.

Tyer
[Sig. Hist.] Common shorthand for Tyer & Co., a former manufacturer of **Signalling Equipment**.

Tyer, Edward
(1830-1912). British **Signalling** pioneer who developed the **Absolute Block** (**AB**) □ **Signalling** and **Tablet** exchange systems.

Type Approval
[NR] An approval given to a product when it has been demonstrated that the product conforms to all the necessary requirements and standards. Products may not be used on the **National Railway Network** until they are type approved, except under controlled trials for agreed periods.

Tyre
[TRS] The nominally horizontal part of a **Rail Wheel**, that which contacts the **Rail Crown**. Also **Tread**.

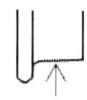

Tyre Turning
The machining of the **Tyre** of a **Rail Wheel** to remove imperfections built up through wear in service and to restore the original **Wheel Profile**. See also **Wheel Lathe**.

U

U
a) In an abbreviated **Track Name**, it denotes **Up**. Examples include Up **Goods Loop** (UGL), Up Line (UL), Up Main (UM), Up **Passenger Loop** (UPL), Up Relief (UR), Up Slow (US)
b) [Sig.] On a **Signalling Circuit Diagram**:
- As one of the leading letters of an **Equipment Code**, it means **Route**.
- As the last letter of an Equipment Code, it means unit
c) The letter represented by **Uniform** in the **Phonetic Alphabet**
d) [NR Civ.] Under the **Bridge Condition Marking Index** (**BCMI**) handbook, shorthand for unknown material

U/S
[Col.] Shorthand for **Unserviceable**.

U14
[NR PW] An **Ultrasonic Rail Flaw Detection** (**URFD**) procedure which uses a vertical probe and a probe inclined at 70° to vertical to examine the **Rail**. The probes can be offset towards either the **Gauge Side** or **Field Side** of the Rail.

U15
[NR PW] An **Ultrasonic Rail Flaw Detection** (**URFD**) procedure developed for use with the Sperry Roller Search Unit (**RSU**).

U3
[NR PW] An **Ultrasonic Rail Flaw Detection** (**URFD**) procedure which uses a vertical probe and a probe inclined at 70° to vertical to examine the centre of the **Rail**.

U5
[NR PW] A manual **Ultrasonic Rail Flaw Detection** (**URFD**) procedure using a vertical probe and a probe inclined at 70° to vertical to examine individual defects in the **Rail Head**.

UAL
Up □ Avoiding □ Line.

UAT
a) Universal Asset Types
b) Ultrasonic Axle Testing
c) Universal Access Toilet.

UB
a) See **Underbridge**. See also **Underline Bridge**
b) Universal Beam.

UBS
Uninterruptible Power Supply (**UPS**) Bypass Switch.

UC
Universal Column.

UD
See **Un-drilled**.

UEEIV
Union Europäischer Eisenbahn Ingenieur Verbände, the Union of European **Railway** Engineer Associations.

UEL
Up □ Electric □ Line.

UF
See Up Fast.

Uff-Cullen Inquiry
A joint inquiry, following the **Southall Accident** and **Ladbroke Grove Accident**, into **Train** Protection Systems.

UFL
Up □ Fast □ Line.

UFN
Until Further Notice.

UGL
Up □ Goods Loop.

UGMS
See Unattended Geometry Measurement System.

UHMWPE
Ultra-High Molecular Weight Poly-Ethylene, a polymer material used to make **Slippers** for **Slipper Baseplates**.

UIC
a) See Union Internationale des Chemins de Fer,
[TRS] Unit Isolating Cock.

UIC 33
[PW] A 33 **Kilogramme per Metre** □ **Rail Section** used for **Check Rails**. Now designated CEN33C1.

UIC 54B
[PW] An asymmetrical 54 **Kilogramme per Metre** □ **Rail Section** used to build **Shallow Depth Switches**. Now designated CEN54E1A1.

UIC 56
[PW] A 56 **Kilogramme per Metre** □ Flat Bottom (FB) □ **Rail Section** equivalent to 113A. Now designated CEN56E1.

UIC 60
[PW] A 60 **Kilogramme per Metre** □ **Rail Section** that was used on heavily trafficked lines on the **National Railway Network** (NRN). See CEN60E1, CEN60E2. See also RT60.

UIC 60B
[PW] A 60 **Kilogramme per Metre** □ **Rail Section** used for the early designs of **Thick Web Switches**. Now designated UIC60E1A1.

ELLIS' BRITISH RAILWAY ENGINEERING ENCYCLOPÆDIA

UIC Classification
[TRS] An alternative to **Whyte's Notation**, this system is more versatile, making fewer assumptions about **Locomotive** layout. It is composed as follows:
- Upper-case letters, designating a number of consecutive **Driving Axles**, starting at A for a single axle, B for two, etc.
- Numbers, designating consecutive non-driving axles, starting with 1 for a single axle
- Lower-case "o", which indicates that the preceding Driving Axles are powered separately, e.g. by individual Traction Motors
- An apostrophe, indicating that the preceding group of axles is mounted on a separate bogie. This indication is not always used
- A plus sign "+", indicating that the Locomotive or Multiple Unit consists of permanently coupled and mechanically separated individual vehicles
- Brackets can be used to group letters and numbers describing the same bogie. For example, (A1A) indicates a three axle bogie with the outer two axles driven
- Garratt Locomotives are indicated by bracketing or placing plus signs between all individual units

The designation can also have additional suffixes, denoting other features of the Locomotive:
- h: **Superheated** steam
- n: Saturated steam
- v: **Compound**
- Turb: Turbine
- t: Tank locomotive

For a **Steam Locomotive**, these can be followed by a number, indicating the number of cylinders.
Some examples of arrangements common in the UK are shown below.

(Driven Axles are shown thus:: (●))

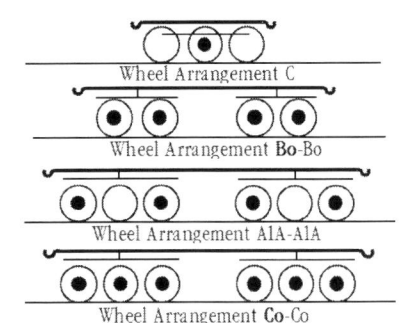

Wheel Arrangement C

Wheel Arrangement Bo-Bo

Wheel Arrangement A1A-A1A

Wheel Arrangement Co-Co

UIC GA
UIC GA Profile
[TRS] The successor to **PPI** or **Berne Gauge** (being slightly taller) and strictly speaking a target profile, as it does not include all the normal allowances for **Sway** etc. All the **UIC** profiles are 3290mm wide; this one is 4320mm high.

UIC GB
UIC GB Profile
[TRS] Strictly speaking a target vehicle profile, as it does not include all the normal allowances for **Sway** etc. All the **UIC** profiles are 3290mm wide; this one is 4320mm high. It differs from **UIC GA** in having a flatter top (e.g. more square).

UIC GB+
UIC GB+ Profile
[TRS] Strictly speaking a target vehicle profile, as it does not include all the normal allowances for **Sway** etc. All the **UIC** profiles are 3290mm wide; this one is 4320mm high. It differs from **UIC GB** in having an even flatter top (e.g. it is nearly square).

UIC GB2
UIC GB2 Profile
[TRS] The new name for the **UIC GB+** profile.

UIC GC
UIC GC Profile
[TRS] Strictly speaking a target vehicle profile, as it does not include all the normal allowances for **Sway** etc. All the **UIC** Profiles are 3290mm wide; this one is 4650mm high. It differs from the other UIC Profiles in being nearly square.

UIC Sprung Bearer
[TRS] A standard sprung vehicle **Side Bearer** that relies on steel springs to support the vehicle body on the **Bogie** side frame.

UK ERTMS
[Sig.] The UK implementation of the **European Rail Traffic Management System** (**ERTMS**), including the **European Train Control System** (**ETCS**), Global System for Mobile Communications – Railway (**GSM-R**), UK practices and management systems such as Harmonisation of European Rules for Operating ERTMS (**HEROE**) and the European Rail Traffic Management Layer (**ETML**).

UK1 Gauge
[NR] The **Vehicle Gauge** specified in the **Technical Standards for Interoperability** (**TSI**) on **High Speed Lines** (**HSL**). It does not cover the **Class** 373 **Eurostar**. The adopted version is Issue 2. UK1 was defined as an alternative to the European **GB** reference profile generally mandated in the TSI, in consideration of the Gauge required by an **Interoperable Train** operating on the three principal **Main Lines** in Great Britain. This defines the UK special case. It was developed from the largest sized vehicle that could pass along these principal routes without consideration of **Diversionary Routes** or Depots, it is operationally unworkable.

UK1 OLE
UK1 Overhead Line Equipment
[NR Elec.] Overhead Line Equipment installed to the standards required by the **Technical Standards for Interoperability** (**TSI**) on **High Speed Lines** (**HSL**), namely speeds up to and including 125mph (200kph) and the **UK1 Gauge**.

UK2 Gauge
[NR] Also known as **W14 Gauge**, this profile is intended to represent a range of **Intermodal** vehicles on a range of **Wagons**. It consists of a rectangle 3940mm high by 2680mm wide. This **Gauge** is not currently in use.

UKRIA
United Kingdom Rail Industry Awards.

UKRITT
(Tradename) United Kingdom Rail Industry Training Trust

UKSTT
(Tradename) UK Society for Trenchless Technology.

UKTram
(Tradename) [LR] Representative body for **Light Rail** in the UK supporting operators, promoters, manufacturers, contractors and consultants covering not just **Tramways** but also **Ultra Light Rail** and **Personal Rapid Transit** (PRT) modes.

ULR
See **Ultra Light Rail**.

Ultra Light Rail (ULR)
[LR] **Tramway**-style operations that use lightweight and often self-powered **Rail Vehicles**. An example of this kind of vehicle is the **Parry People Mover** (PPM).

Ultrasonic Rail Flaw Detection (URFD)
[PW] A method of detecting and assessing the size of **Rail Defects** (**Rail Flaws**) by means of ultrasound. See also URFDO.

Ultrasonic Rail Flaw Detector Operator (URFDO)
[PW] A person trained in the operation of the ultrasonic equipment used in the detection of **Rail Flaws**. See also **Ultrasonic Rail Flaw Detector** (URFD).

Ultrasonic Test Unit (UTU)
[NR PW] A **Multiple Unit Train** equipped with **Ultrasonic Rail Flaw Detection** equipment. It is capable of scanning both **Rails** at speeds up to 40mph with reliable results, although detailed analysis of each **Rail Flaw** still requires manual methods.

Ultrasonic Testing Team
[PW] A team trained in the operation of **Ultrasonic Rail Flaw Detection** (URFD) equipment used in the detection of **Rail Flaws**.

UM
Standard abbreviation for **Up Main**.

Unattended Geometry Measurement System (UGMS)
[PW] A **Track Geometry** measurement and recording system fitted to some **Passenger** □ **Rolling Stock**. It collects and records:
- Location
- Speed
- Top
- Alignment
- Gauge
- Crosslevel
- Curvature

This data is automatically downloaded at fixed locations such as **Maintenance Depots** or **Major Stations** whenever the **Train** calls.

Unattended Train Operation (UTO)
A transport system in which guided vehicles run fully automatically without any operating staff on board.

Unauthorised Movement
a) [Sig. Ops.] A **Train** or **Locomotive** □ **Movement** that has not been instructed by the **Signaller**, and for which the Signaller has not **Set a Route**. Such movements can be accidental (a vehicle rolling away down a hill, a **Runaway**) or due to driver error (**Ding Ding and Away**, or a **SPAD**)
b) [Ops.] An otherwise legal **Shunting Movement** made without the authority of the **Shunter**, **Engineering Supervisor** (**ES**) or nominated competent person.

Unbraked
[TRS] Describing a **Rail Vehicle** with no **Automatic Brake** of any kind, though the vehicle may be equipped with a **Handbrake**. Also **Unfitted**. See O, P, Q, R. The opposite is **Braked**.

Uncle
[Obs.] The obsolescent **Phonetic Alphabet** word representing U. Replaced by **Uniform**.

Unclipping
[PW]
a) The activity of removing **Rail Clips** and thus **Unfastening** the **Rail**
b) [Col.] Universal term for **Unfastening**, irrespective of the **Rail Fastening** system, Rail Clips or not.

Uncouple
[Ops.] To separate two connected **Rail Vehicles**.

Uncoupling
a) The action of separating two connected **Rail Vehicles**
b) [LUL] A vehicle fitted with the ability to easily **Uncouple** and **Couple Up** (not all vehicles on LUL have this facility).

Under Road Crossing (URX)
A **Ducted Cable Route** laid under the highway and parallel to the **Track**, carrying the **Signalling** and **Telecommunications** (collectively **S&T**) or **Electrical and Plant** (**E&P**) cables which normally run alongside the Track.

ELLIS' BRITISH RAILWAY ENGINEERING ENCYCLOPÆDIA

Under Roller
[PW] A small roller placed laterally under a **Rail** being **Stressed** in order to reduce the friction of the Rail on the **Sleeper**. Under Rollers are generally placed every 14 Sleepers. See also **Side Rollers**.

Under the Hammer
[Sig. Col.] A term meaning the **Acceptance** of a **Train** under the **Warning Arrangement** □ (**Block Regulation** 5, **Bell Code** 3-5-5). It relates to the hammer-shaped **Subsidiary Signals** used by the former Midland **Railway** (**MR**).

Under the Hill
[Col.] Term for being in a **Tunnel**, originally applied to the **Single Bore Tunnels** at Woodhead and latterly to many others.

Under the Wires
[Col.] Describing an activity taking place on a **Line** fitted with **Overhead Line Electrification** (**OLE**) equipment. See also **On the DC**.

Under Track Crossing (UTX)
A **Ducted Cable Route** carrying **Signalling** and **Telecommunications** (collectively **S&T**) or **Electrification and Plant** (**E&P**) cables under the **Track**.

Under Traffic
Normally describes operations carried out whilst **Trains** are still **Running**.

Underbolt
[Sig.] control of a **Lever** by one worked from another **Signalbox**, usually in connection with **Distant Signals**. To show the state of the **Control**, **Indicators** were generally provided. See also **Bolt**, **Slot**. Alternatively referred to as an **Overbolt**.

Underbridge (UB)
[Civ.] A **Bridge** that allows passage under the **Railway**. The opposite is **Overbridge** (**OB**). See also **Underline Bridge**.

Undercut Switch
[PW] A **Switch** assembly in which the **Switch Rail** is machined to recess under the **Rail Head** of the **Stock Rail**.

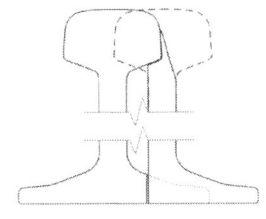

Underframe
[TRS] The structural assembly underneath the floor of a **Rail Vehicle** which supports the weight of the Vehicle and its load and resists longitudinal forces.

Underframe Wear Plate
[TRS] The flat sheet of steel located on the **Underframe** of some **Wagons**, above the **Side Bearing Block**, that acts as a rubbing surface.

Underground Railway
A **Railway** with a majority of its **Track** constructed in underground **Tunnels**.

Underground Station
a) A **Station** located on an **Underground Railway**. See also **Sub-surface Station**
b) A **Station** located on the Glasgow, Liverpool or London underground systems, often irrespective of whether they are below the ground or not.

Underline Bridge (UB)
[Civ.] An alternative term for an **Underbridge** (**UB**) used to avoid confusion, since Highway Engineers would alternatively claim that this type of **Bridge** is an **Overbridge** (**OB**). The opposite is an **Overline Bridge** (**OB**). See also **Intersection Bridge**.

Undershot Curve
[PW] A **Curve** of too sharp a **Radius**, that has to have a short length of a greater **Radius** introduced into it in order for it to meet a **Straight** correctly. See also **Overshot Curve**.

Understressed Rail
[PW] **Continuous Welded Rail** (**CWR**) that has a **Stress Free Temperature** (**SFT**) lower than 23°C (70°F), i.e. it displays a higher than normal compressive stress at high temperatures and a lower than normal tensile stress at low temperatures. This may lead to the **Rail** concerned being prone to suffering a **Track Buckle**. See also **Blue Item**. The opposite is **Overstressed Rail**, **Red Item**.

UNDM
[LUL] A code denoting an **Uncoupling** □ **Non-driving** □ **Motor** □ **Car**.

Undrilled (UD)
[PW] Describing a **Rail** not having **Fishbolt Holes** drilled in it. Also **Plain Rail**. See also **Back Hole Drilled**, **Drilled Both Ends** (**DBE**), **Drilled One End** (**DOE**).

Unfastening
[PW] The action of undoing the **Rail Clips**, **Keys** or other **Rail Fastenings** from the **Rail** so as to release it and allow the Rail to be moved, removed or **Stressed**. Also **Unclipping**.

Unfitted
Unfitted Vehicle
[TRS] A **Rail Vehicle** having no **Automatic Brake** facilities of any kind. Also **Unbraked**. See **O**.

Unfitted Tail
[Ops. Col.] A term for vehicles without **Automatic Brakes** marshalled at the rear of a **Train**. Also **Swinger**.

Unfitted Train
[Ops.] A **Train** that has no **Automatic Brake** of any kind. See also **Loose Coupled**.

Uni-directional Line
A **Line** or **Track** on which **Trains** only ever **Run** in one direction only.

UNIFE
Union des Industries Ferroviaires Européennes; the Union of European **Railway** Industries, formed by the amalgamation of the AICMR (Association Internationale des Constructeurs de Matériel Roulant), AFEDEF (Association des Fabricants Européens d'Equipements Ferroviaires) and CELTE (Constructeurs Européens des Locomotives Thermiques et Electriques)

Uniform
The **Phonetic Alphabet** word representing **U**.

Union Internationale des Chemins de Fer (UIC)
An international organisation formed in 1922 comprising a union of various **Railway** companies and administrations. It agrees and publishes common standards and practices.

Un-insulated Knuckle
[Elec.] An **Overhead Line Equipment** (**OLE**) □ **Knuckle** arranged so that the two **Wire Runs** do not cross, but are electrically connected together at all times. See also **Insulated Knuckle**.

Un-insulated Overlap
[Elec.] An **Overlap Span** that is arranged so that the two **Tension Lengths** are permanently connected together electrically.

UNISIG
(Tradename) [Sig.] A trade association comprising **Signalling Equipment** manufacturers. Its members are **Alstom**, Ansaldo Signal, AŽD Praha, **Bombardier**, **CAF**, **Siemens** and Thales.

Unit
[Col.] A common contraction of **Multiple Unit Train**.

Unit Loads
Freight which is moved and handled in a consolidated / unitised form, for instance in **Containers**.

Unit Train
[Ops.] An alternative term to **Block Train**.

Unit Weight
[PW] The basis on which all **Rails** are described and differentiated. See **Kilograms per Metre**, **Pounds per Yard**. See also **Rail Section**, **Rail Weight**.

Universal Baseplate
[PW] A **Baseplate** with a horizontal **Rail Seat** which can be used to support both **Switches** and **Crossings**.

Universal Tamper
[PW] A **Tamping and Lining Machine** (**Tamper**) designed and built to **Tamp** both **Plain Line** (**PL**) and **Switch and Crossing Layouts** (**S&C Layouts**) with equal ease. Most Tampers are either **Plain Line** Tampers only, or are **Switch and Crossing Tampers** (**S&C Tampers**) which can **Tamp Plain Line**, albeit slowly.

Unpaid Area
The areas of a **Station** which can be accessed by the general public and which is separated from the **Paid Area** by **Faregates** or **Ticket** checks.

Unprotected Wrong Side Failure (UWSF)
[Sig.] A failure of one part of a **Signalling System** that is not protected by any other part of the Signalling System, i.e. the system does not **Fail Safe**. Also known as a High Risk Failure.

Unreadable
[Sig.] A **Signal** or an **Element** of a Signal which is not considered to be **Readable**. A Signal or Element may become Unreadable in specific circumstances, for example at a particular distance from the Signal, or in certain ambient lighting conditions.

Unsafe Track Condition
[PW] A **Track** irregularity or **Track Fault** of such magnitude that it requires immediate action.

Unset
[Sig.] An alternative for not **Set**. See also **Latch**.

Un-signalled Line
[Sig.] A **Line** that has no **Signalling** of any description. Most **Sidings** are therefore Un-signalled Lines.

Unsolicited Brake Application
An application of the **Train** □ **Brakes** which is not initiated by the driver or **Traincrew**.

Un-sprung Mass
[TRS] The mass of the axles, axle boxes, springs and anything else that is not isolated from the **Track** by springs. This may include **Traction Motors** if they are **Axle Hung**.

Unstrengthened
Unstrengthened Switches
[PW] **Switches** which have not been designed to transfer the thermal stresses arising from **Continuously Welded Rail** (**CWR**) between the **Switch Rails** and **Stock Rails**. See also **Strengthened**, **Strengthened Switches**.

Unstressed Continuous Welded Rail
Unstressed CWR
[PW] **Continuous Welded Rail** (**CWR**) that has been installed and not **Stressed**, or has been cut and re-joined but not Stressed. See also **Blue Item**, **Red Item**.

Unworked
[Sig.] A **Catch Point** (**CP**), Set of Points, Set of Switches or a Trap Point not under the control of a **Signaller**.

Unworked Catch Points
[Sig.] A **Catch Point** (**CP**) that is not controlled by a **Signaller**, meaning that it cannot be closed by a Signaller for a **Movement** in the **Wrong Direction**.

Unworked Points
Unworked Switches
[Sig.] A **Set of Points** or **Set of Switches** not under the control of a **Signaller** or of a **Ground Frame** (**GF**). See also **Train Operated Switch** (**TOS**).

Up (U)
In a direction towards **London**, the capital, the original **Railway Company's** headquarters or the lowest mileage. The choice of which direction is Up is littered with exceptions to convention. Also **Uphill**, **Up Along**. The opposite direction is **Down** (**D**).

Up Along
[Col.] Another term for in the **Up Direction**. The opposite is **Down Along**.

Up and Down
Traditionally denotes a **Single Line** that is **Bi-directional** in normal use. This should be contrasted with **Down and Up**, which denotes two separate **Lines**, one in the **Down Direction** and one in the **Up Direction**.

Up Direction
Moving in a direction towards **London**, the capital, the original **Railway Company's** headquarters or the lowest **Mileage**. This term is often used when describing **Train Movements** made in the opposite direction to the **Normal Direction**. The opposite is **Down Direction**.

Up Fast (UF)
The name generally given to the nominally more important of the two **Up Lines** (**UL**) in a **Four Track Railway**. It may or may not be faster (i.e. have a higher **Permissible Speed** (**PS**)) than the other Up Line, normally called the **Up Relief** (**UR**) or **Up Slow** (**US**). The opposite is **Down Fast** (**DF**).

Up Line (UL)
A **Track** on which the **Normal Direction** of **Trains** is in the **Up Direction**, i.e. towards **London**, the capital, the original **Railway Company's** headquarters or lowest **Mileage**. The opposite is **Down Line** (**DL**).

Up Main (UM)
The common term for the **Up Line** (**UL**) when there are only two **Tracks** with opposite **Normal Directions**. The other is thus the **Down Main** (**DM**).

Up on Stilts
Up on Stools
See **Ballast Stools**.

Up Relief (UR)
[WR] An alternative term for the **Up Slow** (**US**), the name generally given to the nominally less important of the two **Up Lines** (**UL**) in a **Four Track Railway**. It may or may not be slower (i.e. have a lower **Permissible Speed** (**PS**)) than the other Up Line, normally called the **Up Fast** (**UF**). The opposite is **Down Relief** (**DR**).

Up Side
Being located on the same side of the **Railway** as the **Up Line** (**UL**). The opposite is **Down Side**.

Up Slow (US)
The name generally given to the nominally less important of the two **Up Lines** in a **Four Track Railway**. It may or may not be slower (i.e. have a lower **Permissible Speed** (**PS**)) than the other Up Line, normally called the **Up Fast** (**UF**). An alternative term is **Up Relief** (**UR**). The opposite is **Down Slow** (**DS**).

Uphill
a) In a direction up the **Local Gradient**
b) [Col.] Another term for the **Up Direction**.

UPL
Up □ **Passenger Loop**. The opposite is **Down Passenger Loop** (**DPL**).

Uplift
[Elec.] The vertical movement of a **Contact Wire** (**CW**) caused the passage of a **Pantograph** beneath it.

Uplift Dropper
[Elec.] A **Dropper** used at locations where the **Overhead Line Equipment** (**OLE**) has a low Encumberance. See also **Loop Dropper**.

Upper Fillet
[PW] The curved portion of a **Rail Section** between the **Upper Fishing Surface** and the **Rail Web**.

Upper Fishing Surface
[PW] The contact surface between the underside of the **Rail Head** and the upper surface of a **Fishplate**.

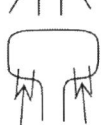

Upper Quadrant
Upper Quadrant Signal (UQ)
[Sig.] A **Semaphore Signal** that is in the **Clear** position when the **Arm** is 45° above horizontal. See also **Lower Quadrant Signal** (**LQ**).

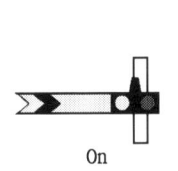

On   Off

UPS
Uninterruptible Power Supply.

UPSU
Uninterruptable Power Supply Unit

UPWSF
See **Unprotected Wrong Side Failure**.

Urchin (ZCA)
[NR] An **Open Wagon** used for the transportation of **Ballast** and **Spoil**. See **Wagon Names**.

URFD
See **Ultrasonic Rail Flaw Detection**.

URFDO
(*urf-doh*) See **Ultrasonic Rail Flaw Detector Operator**.

Urgent Safety Advice (USA)
Guidance issued by the **Rail Accident Investigation Branch** (**RAIB**) to the **Rail Industry** and the safety authority which deals with matters of immediate concern. The aim is to prevent another accident being caused by the particular deficiencies that have been found in the early stages of the investigation. There will be reason to suppose that these deficiencies are not a one-off and could happen elsewhere.

URL
Up □ Relief □ Line.

Urmston Accident
Just before 18:20 on 11th December 1958, between Urmston and Trafford Park, a tracked crane involved in placing concrete in connection with construction of a new **Overbridge** became unstable and toppled across the **Track**. An **Express Train** collided with the jib of the crane and partially **Derailed**. This Train was then struck by a second Train. One **Passenger** died (after climbing out of the first Train and being struck by the second). The arrangements for protecting the **Safety of the Line** were found to be wholly inadequate.

URPS
Un-remunerative **Passenger** Services.

URS
(Tradename) Formerly United Research Services, an international **Infrastructure** consultancy. The company acquired Scott Wilson Group in 2010. URS head office is in San Francisco, USA.

URX
See Under Road Crossing.

US
a) See Up Slow
b) Shorthand for Unserviceable.

US&S
(Tradename) Union Switch & **Signal**, a manufacturer of **Signalling Equipment**.

USA
See Urgent Safety Advice.

Usable Length
[Ops.] The part of a **Platform** that can be used by **Passengers** for egress from and access to **Trains**, measured along the **Platform Edge**. See also **Operational Length**.

User Worked
User Worked Crossing (UWC)
A **Level Crossing** (**LC**, **LX**) where the **Barriers** or **Gates** are operated by the user. There is generally no indication of the approach of **Trains**, but a telephone will be provided for contacting the **Signaller**. Some are fitted with **Red/Green** (**R/G**) □ **Miniature Stop Lights** (**MSL**). See also **Accommodation Crossing**.

User Worked Gate Crossing (UWG)
A **User Worked Crossing** (**UWC**) which has **Gates** that are operated by the user.

USI
[Sig.] Universal Signalling Interface.

USL
Up Slow □ Line.

USSR
Un-supervised Service Rate.

UST
[PW] Ultrasonic Testing. See Ultrasonic Rail Flaw Detection (URFD).

UT
a) [PW] Ultrasonic Testing. **See Ultrasonic Rail Flaw Detection** (**URFD**)
b) Up □ Through Line.

UTO
See Unattended Train Operation. See also Automatic Train Operation (ATO).

UTU
See Ultrasonic Test Unit.

UTU2
[NR] An **Ultrasonic Test Unit** (**UTU**) equipped with the Sperry Roller Search Unit (**RSU**).

UTV
Utility Towing Vehicle.

UTX
See Under Track Crossing.

U-Type Bridge

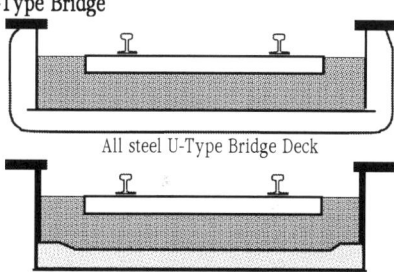

All steel U-Type Bridge Deck

Composite U-type Bridge Deck

[NR Civ.] A variety of **Bridge Deck** utilising the Vierendeel principle. Two variations exist, one with an all steel deck and the other with a **Composite Deck**.

UWC
See User Worked Crossing.

UWCt
User Worked Crossing with telephone

UWG
See User Worked Gate Crossing.

UWR
[PW] Unstressed Welded Rail. See Unstressed Continuous Welded Rail.

UWSF
See Unprotected Wrong Side Failure.

UWTF
Unprotected Wrong side Telecommunications Failure.

UXO
Unexploded Ordnance

… Ellis' British Railway Engineering Encyclopædia

V

V

a) [NR] As the last letter in a **Wagon** □ **CARKND**, this denotes that the Wagon has **Vacuum Brakes**
b) As a prefix or suffix on a **Baseplate** (e.g. **VASP, Pan V**) it indicates the component holds the **Running Rail** vertically, not **Inclined**. See also **Vertical**
c) See **Versine**
d) See **Equilibrium Speed** (V_e), **Maximum Speed** (V_m)
e) See **Crossing Vee**
f) See **Junction Vee**
g) [NR] As the first letter of a Wagon CARKND, it means that the vehicle is a **Van**
h) [Sig.] On a **Signalling Circuit Diagram**:
• As one of the leading letters of an **Equipment Code**, it means **Trainstop** (including **Train Protection and Warning System** (**TPWS**))
• As the last letter of an Equipment Code, it means Trainstop (including TPWS)
i) The letter represented by **Victor** in the **Phonetic Alphabet**
j) [LUL] The **Victoria Line**.

V&V
Verification and **V**alidation.

V/Comm SIC
Vehicle / **C**ommunications **S**ystem **I**nterface **C**ommittee.

V/S SIC
Vehicle / **S**tructures System **I**nterface **C**ommittee.

V/T SIC
Vehicle / **T**rack System **I**nterface **C**ommittee.

V/TC SIC
Vehicle / **T**rain **C**ontrol **S**ystem **I**nterface **C**ommittee.

V/TS SIC
Vehicle / **T**raction **S**upply **S**ystem **I**nterface **C**ommittee.

V/V SIC
Vehicle / **V**ehicle **S**ystem **I**nterface **C**ommittee.

VAB
See **V**ehicle **A**cceptance **B**ody.

Vacuum Brake (VB)
Vacuum Braked
[TRS] Describes a **Rail Vehicle** equipped with an **Automatic Brake**, normally maintained in the off position by a vacuum. See **V, W, X**.

Vacuum Circuit Breaker (VCB)
A type of **Circuit Breaker** (**CB**) where a vacuum is used to extinguish the arc which occurs as the two contacts of the Circuit Breaker are moved apart.

Vacuum Piped
[TRS] Describes a **Rail Vehicle** equipped with pipes carrying **Vacuum Brake** through the vehicle, but not operating the vehicle brakes (if any). See **B, P, R**.

VAE
(Tradename) A division of **V**oestalpine AG, specialising in **Railway** engineering.

Validation
The activity that determines that a system meets its specified requirements in all respects. It involves consideration of whether the specification of the system sufficiently and accurately represents the needs of the intended user.

Value of Preventing a Fatality (VOPF, VPF)
A financial value used in assessing the total economic value of a project. According to the **DfT** it is currently £1,763,000.

VAMPIRE
(*vam-pire*) (Tradename) **V**ehicle Dyn**a**mic **M**odelling **P**ackage **i**n a **R**ailway **E**nvironment. A dynamic modelling system for **Rail Vehicles** which allows a virtual model of any Rail Vehicle to be run over real measured **Track Geometry**. Produced by **Delta Rail** (formerly **AEA Technology**).

Van
[TRS] An enclosed **Rail Vehicle**, with rigid sides, used solely for the transportation of **Freight**, **Goods**, post or parcels traffic. Often prefixed with the nominal purpose of the vehicle, such as Parcels Van, Tool Van. See **V**.

Vane Relay
[Sig.] A **Relay** used in 50Hz **AC Track Circuits**, where immunity from DC. **Traction Current** interference is required. Comprised of a thin aluminium vane which is pivoted on a spindle and able to rotate, torque to rotate the vane to the energised position is provided by the interaction of two coils whose AC magnetic fields (ΦL & ΦC) induce eddy currents in the vane. The local coil (TQ) is permanently connected to a 110V AC supply whilst the control coil (TR) receives its energy from the track circuit itself (1V to 3V AC, depending on type). The local coil (TQ) induces continuous eddy currents in the vane, but no mechanical torque results if the control coil remains de-energised; the counterbalance action of the vane ensures that the relay remains on its backstop.

VAPE Screws
(Tradename) [PW] **Chairscrews** used for securing **Baseplates** and gauge restraining/spacer blocks in RT60 **Switch and Crossing** (**S&C**) and **NR60** S&C to **Concrete Bearers**.

VASP Baseplate
(Tradename) [PW] A **Vertical Baseplate** for direct fixing to concrete **Bridge Decks**, **Slab Track** etc., fitted with eccentric bushes to permit fine lateral adjustment to be made to the position of the baseplate. It is the **Vertical** version of the **ASP Baseplate**.

VATT
[Hist.] **V**irgin **A**ctive **T**ilting **T**rain. See **Pendolino**.

VB
See **V**acuum **B**rake.

VC
See **Vertical Curve**.

VCA
Video **C**ontent **A**nalysis.

VCB
See **Vacuum Circuit Breaker**.

VCC
(Tradename) [Hist.] **V**irgin **C**ross **C**ountry, a **Train Operating Company** (**TOC**). Also **VXC**. See **Virgin Trains** (**VT**).

VCM
Vinyl **C**hloride **M**onomer, 1-Chloroethene (C_2H_3Cl).

VDM
[PW] **V**ehicle **D**amage **M**atrix, a Radius vs **Cant** table produced for a specific **Rail Vehicle** and used by the **Track-Ex** tool.

VDP
(Tradename) [PW] **V**ertical **D**esign **P**ackage, a software program produced by **Laser Rail** (now part of **Balfour Beatty Rail**) and designed to assist with the design of **Longitudinal Sections**.

V_e
[PW] The **Equilibrium Speed** for a **Curve**, normally in kilometres per hour (kph).

VE
Value **E**ngineering, making design and specification decisions purely on the basis of perceived value; not engineering at all. See also **VM**.

Vecom
(Tradename) A proprietary system used to detect the presence of a **Tram** at specific locations on a network, operate **Points** and make demands to Road Traffic Signals (**RTS**). Manufactured by Peek Traffic Solutions of the Netherlands.

Vee
a) See **Crossing Vee**
b) See **Junction Vee**.

Vee Rail
[PW] The forged and machined **Rail** forming one half of an **Electro-slag Welded Crossing Vee**.

Veg
(*vedge*) [Col.] Alternative for **Train Spotter** (they take root at the side of the **Line**).

Vegetation Management
The process of ensuring that trees and shrubs adjacent to the **Track** do not encroach onto the Track, become dangerously unstable or create **Abnormal Rail Head Conditions** by shedding leaves onto the **Rail Head**. See also **De-vegging**, **Leaf Fall Season**.

Vehicle Acceptance Body (VAB)
[NR] A body accredited by **RSSB** (formerly the **Railway Safety and Standards Board**) to exclusively undertake **Engineering Acceptance** for **Rail Vehicles**. In summary, their function is to ensure that new or modified Rail Vehicles do not present a hazard. Under the **Railways and Other Guided Transport Systems (Safety) Regulations 2006** (ROGS, ROGTS), a **Competent Person** may undertake this work, although all VABs are deemed to be Competent Persons.

Vehicle Approvals Certification
The process by which a **Vehicle Acceptance Body** (**VAB**), accredited by **RSSB**, assesses the compliance of **Rail Vehicles** and related maintenance procedures with **Rail Industry** standards and issues **Certificates of Engineering Acceptance** (**CEA**).

Vehicle Gauges
[NR] Generically, the maximum cross sectional profile of any given **Rail Vehicle**. However, there are two main sub-types of Vehicle Gauge:
a) **Static Vehicle Gauge**, which is the cross sectional profile of the vehicle at rest. Generally, an allowance is then added all round to allow for dynamic effects. See **C1, C2, C3**
b) **Kinematic Envelope** (**KE**) or **Kinematic Vehicle Gauge**, which is the cross sectional profile of the vehicle under all possible fault and failure modes plus widening due to **Sway**, See **SB1c**, **UIC GA**, **UIC GB**, **UIC GB+**, **UIC GB2**, **UIC GC**, **UK1**, **UK2**, **W6**, **W6A**, **W6A Exception**, **W7**, **W8**, **W9**, **W10**, **W10w**, **W11**, **W12**, **W14 W18**. See also **Crush Laden**, **Hard Over Tilt Failed** (**HOTF**), **Tare Deflated**.
Kinematic Vehicle Gauges are the current norm, as they allow the previously cautious clearance allowances to be reduced as a result of greater confidence in the service profile of the vehicle.

Vehicle Inspection and Brake Test (VIBT)
[TRS] A periodic maintenance activity undertaken to ensure that a **Rail Vehicle** is in a serviceable condition and its brakes are functional.

Vehicle Overhang
[TRS] The distance between the front axle centre and foremost part of a **Rail Vehicle**. See **Clearance Point** (**CP**), **Fouling Point** (**FP**).

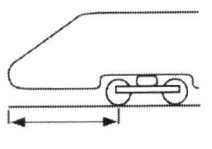

Vehicle Recognition System (VRS)
[LR] A system used to send information from **Light Rail Vehicles** (**Trams**) to both the control point and the **Street Running** signal system. The VRS equipment generates a modulated carrier signal which is picked up by a cable loop, buried in the road surface or mounted on the sleepers of **Segregated Track**. At the start of each journey the driver enters a route code into the vehicle's VRS control panel. This sets up the description of the Tram on the diagram at Control and, if required, calls for the **Points** to change on Street Running sections. The "(Tram) ready to start" request is also sent by the VRS.

Vehicle Type Codes (CARKND)
[NR] The three letter **Wagon** codes used by **Total Operations Processing System** (**TOPS**) to identify the different types of **Rail Vehicle**. The first letter describes the type of vehicle, and the last letter describes the type of brakes fitted to the vehicle, see **Brake Types**. See also **AARKND**.

Vehicular Scour
[Civ. Col.] Damage caused to the **Soffits** and **Intradoses** of **Bridges** by overly tall road vehicles.

VEID
See **V**isual **E**lectronic **I**nformation **D**isplay.

Ventilation Shaft
See **Tunnel Shaft**.

VeRA
Verification of **R**oute **A**vailability database

VERSE Testing
(*verse testing*) [PW] A method of determining the **Stress Condition** of a **Rail** by measuring the force required to deflect the Rail vertically over a known **Chord**. Developed by **AEA Technology** (now **DeltaRail**).

Versine (v)
[PW] The distance from the circumference of a circle to the mid-point of a **Chord** of that circle.

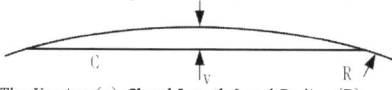

The Versine (v), **Chord Length** l and Radius (**R**) are related by the equation:

$$R = \frac{C^2}{8v}$$

Where R, C, and v are all in the same units, normally millimetres. This is the underlying geometrical principle of the **Hallade** method of **Curve Re-alignment**.

Versine Rise
[PW] The numerical difference between successive **Versine** values in a **Transition Curve**. Also **Transition Step**. See **Hallade**.

Vertical (V)
[PW Col.] A common contraction of **Vertical Design**, **Vertical Plain Line** and **Vertical Rail**. It is so contracted because the majority of **Running Rails** are **Inclined** at **1 in** 20 towards each other.

Vertical Baseplate
[PW] A **Baseplate** designed to hold the **Running Rail** vertically rather than **Inclined** at 1 in 20. The reference codes for most Vertical Baseplates contain the letter **V**.

Vertical Circulation
Collective term for any structure or device provided to allow **Passengers** to move between different levels, particularly in a **Station**. Examples might include escalators, lifts or stairs provided between the **Platform Level** and the **Concourse** in an **Underground Station**.

ELLIS' BRITISH RAILWAY ENGINEERING ENCYCLOPÆDIA

Vertical Concrete Sleeper
[PW] A **Concrete Sleeper** designed to hold the **Running Rails** vertical by means of horizontal **Rail Seats**, rather than the normal arrangement of **Inclined** at 1 in 20.

Vertical Curve (VC)
[PW] A vertical **Transition Curve** introduced to reduce the vertical acceleration of **Trains** passing from one **Gradient** to another. Standard design rules lay down that any gradient change of greater than 0.15% requires the introduction of a Vertical Curve. The form of Transition Curve used on the **National Railway Network** (**NRN**) is the square parabola, of the form $y=ax^2$, although pure circular curves are used elsewhere. Vertical Curves may be **Convex Vertical Curves**, otherwise known as **Hog Curves**, and **Concave Vertical Curves**, otherwise known as **Sag Curves**.

Vertical Curve Offset
[PW] The **Offsets** from a straight **Gradient** to a **Vertical Curve** (**VC**), used to actually construct the Vertical Curve using a **Laser Beacon**.

Vertical Design
Vertical Design S&C
Vertical Design Switch and Crossing
[NR PW] A standard suite of **Switch and Crossing** (**S&C**) designs in which the vertical axes of all the **Rails** are at right angles to the longitudinal axis of the **Bearers** or **Timbers**. The other arrangement is **Inclined Switch and Crossing**. Vertical S&C was called **113A Vertical**, now **CEN56 Vertical** (**NR56V**), and the Inclined types are **Bullhead Inclined** (**BHI**), **Flat Bottom Inclined** (**FBI**) which used **109 Pound** and **110A Rail**, and **RT60** and **NR60**. See also **NR60V**.

Vertical Door Stanchion
[TRS] The vertical structural part of a **Door Portal**.

Vertical Plain Line
[PW] **Plain Line** (i.e. not **Switches and Crossings** (**S&C**)) constructed with **Vertical Rails** by means of **Vertical Baseplates** or **Vertical Concrete Sleepers**.

Vertical Rail
[PW] A **Rail** whose vertical axis is at right angles to the longitudinal axis of the **Bearers**, **Sleepers** or **Timbers**.

Vertical Ride
The amount of vertical movement that a **Rail Vehicle**, load or person would be subjected to during a journey.

Vertical S&C
See **Vertical Design Switch and Crossing**.

Vertical Switch
[PW] A **Switch** in which the vertical axes of the **Stock Rails** are at right angles to the longitudinal axis of the **Bearers** or **Timbers**. The other arrangement is an **Inclined Switch**. All Flatbottom **Switch Rails** are **Vertical** throughout the movable length (whether the Stock Rail Vertical is or not).

561

ELLIS' BRITISH RAILWAY ENGINEERING ENCYCLOPÆDIA

Vertical Tappet Lever Frame
[Sig.] A variety of **Lever Frame** where the **Tappets** are arranged vertically below the **Levers**, rather than horizontally on a **Locking Shelf** behind the **Levers**.

Vertical Throw

A rare situation where the long **Wheelbase** of a **Passenger Coach** traversing a long **Sag** □ **Vertical Curve** (**VC**) with a small Radius (**R**) causes the **Coach** to strike the **Soffit** of the structure above, in most known cases in a **Tunnel**.

Verticals
[Civ.] Structural members connecting the **Top Chord** and **Bottom Chord** of a **Truss**. Usually they are at right angles to each of the Chords.

Very Poor
[NR] A length of **Track** (usually an **Eighth of a Mile**) over which the **Track Quality** (**TQ**) is worse than **Poor**, in that more than the **Standard Deviation** (**SD**) values for **Top** and **Line** are outside the 100% values for the **Permissible Speed** (**PS**) or **Enhanced Permissible Speed** (**EPS**).

Vestibule
[TRS] The entrance area in the vicinity of a **Passenger Door**.

VETLA
Very Extended Three Letter Acronym. See also ETLA, TLA.

VF
Voice Frequency.

VHLC
[Sig.] **Vital Harmon Logic Controller**, a variety of **Solid State Interlocking** (**SSI**).

Viaduct
[NR Civ.] A **Bridge** structure with five or more **Spans**.

Viaduct Inspection Unit (VIU)
A specialised access platform mounted on a specially built **Rail Vehicle**. It is capable of providing a safe working platform immediately under the **Arch** □ **Soffits** of the **Viaduct** or **Bridge** it is standing on. Nicknamed the **Guzunder**.

VIBT
See **Vehicle Inspection and Brake Test**.

VICOS
(*viy-kos*) (Tradename) Vehicle and Infrastructure Control and Operating System, a network control and management system produced by Siemens Transportation.

Victor
The **Phonetic Alphabet** word representing **V**.

VID
Visual Information Display.

Vignoles Rail
[PW Col.] A pioneering type of **Flat Bottom Rail** (**FB**) promoted by **Charles Blacker Vignoles** from 1836 onwards. Evidence suggests that the **Rail Section** was devised by Robert L Stevens in the early 1830s and first rolled at Dowlais for export to the USA.

Vignoles, Charles Blacker
(1793-1875) An experienced surveyor, Vignoles joined **George Stephenson** on the Liverpool & Manchester, but was removed by George Stephenson as the two did not get on. He went on to build the St. Helens & Runcorn Gap **Railway**, the Dublin & Kingstown Railway, the Sheffield, Ashton-Under-Lyne and Manchester Railway (which included the Woodhead **Tunnel**) and the Midland Counties Railway. His later and most impressive work was done in Europe.

VIM
Vehicle Dynamic Modelling Package in a **Railway** Environment (**VAMPIRE**) Interaction Manager.

VIP
[PW] Vertical Intersection Point.

Virgin Trains (VT)
(Tradename) A **Train Operating Company** (**TOC**) which operates services between Glasgow, North West England, North Wales, the West Midlands and London, and also between Birmingham and Glasgow / Edinburgh.

VIRR
Vehicle Incursion Risk Ranking.

Virtual Headwall
[LUL] Where no **Headwall** exists at a **Station** because there is no **Tunnel**, the **Virtual Headwall** will be considered to be at the top of the **Platform Ramp** (**TOR**) or steps at the end of the **Platform**.

Virtual Joint
[Sig. Col.] A boundary between two **Jointless Track Circuits**, where no **Insulated Rail Joint** (**IRJ**) is provided. So named because the position of the boundary is marked on the **Signalling Plan** as if it were an IRJ for clarity, but no IRJ is provided on the ground.

Virtual Jointed
[PW Col.] **Track** laid with **Continuously Welded Rail** (**CWR**) which is displaying regular dips corresponding to the historic location of **Fishplated Rail Joints**. See also **Ballast Memory**, **Scarifying**.

Virtual Quarry (VQ)
An area of land adjacent to a **Siding** used to stockpile large quantities of **Ballast**. They allow the re-loading of **Ballast Trains** at locations that have no actual quarries. Ballast is delivered in considerable bulk at regular and convenient times, allowing substantial savings. See also **Virtual Tip**.

Virtual Tip
An area of land adjacent to a **Siding** used to stockpile **Spoil** from **Re-ballasting** works, allowing the **Spoil Trains** to be returned to service quickly in areas where no normal **Tip** exists. This system also permits the processing of the Spoil before it leaves **Railway** property, allowing any re-usable element to be salvaged before the remainder is disposed of. See also **Virtual Quarry** (**VQ**).

Virtual Transition
[PW] The effect of an instantaneous change in horizontal Radius (**R**). The effective length of the **Transition Curve** is therefore the **Wheelbase** (**WB**) of the passing vehicles, which is taken to be 12.2m (40 feet). Therefore any real Transition Curve of length less than 12.2m (40 feet) can also be considered a Virtual Transition.

Visibility
[Sig.] Of a **Signal** or **Element**, the quality of the driver's approach view of the Signal as determined by measurable, physical factors such as:
- relative **Intensity**
- colour contrast
- colour accuracy
- susceptibility to high levels of incident light
- spatial positioning of the Signal
- alignment and beam width; degree of obscuration
- time to view
- distance to the next Signal.

VISION
(*vision*) (Trademane) [Ops.] Visualisation and Interactive Simulation of Infrastructure and Operations on Rail Networks, a computer model produced by **AEA Technology** (now **DeltaRail**) that is capable of analysing **Timetables** against actual **Track Layouts** and **Junctions**, as well as investigating the effect of poor timekeeping, **Signal** failures, etc.

Visual Electronic Information Display (VEID)
A piece of equipment that automatically delivers pre-recorded visual messages at pre-programmed intervals so that customers receive relevant information at the appropriate time and place.

Visual Examination
Visual Examination of Structures
[NR Civ.] An examination to identify changes in the condition of a **Structure** carried out from a safe observation location, without using special access equipment but using permanent access ladders and walkways, binoculars and hand held lighting where necessary.

Vital
[Sig. Obs.] Alternative term for **Safety Related**. The opposite (also obsolete) term is **Non-vital**.

Vital Rail
(Trademark) An **Infrastructure** □ **Contractor** based in Manchester.

VIU
See **Viaduct Inspection Unit**.

ELLIS' BRITISH RAILWAY ENGINEERING ENCYCLOPÆDIA

V-Laser
[BR Obs.] A system developed by **British Rail Research** (**BRR**) in the 1980s which used a laser range finding device to control the level of the blade of a **Laser Dozer**. The system was overtaken by the use of **Laser Beacons**.

VLCV
[TRS] Variable Load Control Valve.

VLD
Voltage Limiting Device.

VLV
[TRS] Variable Load Valve.

VM
Value Management, ensuring that a project delivers best value against agreed criteria. See also **VE**.

V_m
[PW] The **Maximum Speed** for a **Curve**, normally given in Kilometres per hour (kph).

VME
VME Bus
Versa Module Europa, a standard electronic connection system which supports the use of plug-in Eurocards.

VMFL
[TRS] Vehicle Mounted **Flange Lubricator**.

VMI
[TRS] Vehicle Maintenance Instruction.

VMOI
[TRS] Vehicle Maintenance and Overhaul Instruction.

VMS
(Trademark) Variable Message Signs, based in Hebburn, Tyne and Wear.

VMT
Vehicle Miles Travelled.

VMx
[NR] Standard **Value Management** events within the **Governance for Railway Projects** (**GRIP**) Process:
VM Description
1 Project Definition workshop is used to confirm the remit of a project during the Output Definition stage of a project. **FAST** diagrams are often used at this stage to understand the functions of a project
2 Option Selection workshop is used to filter out and select options during GRIP stages 2-3 (option selection) to filter and analyse the options to aid single option decision making and eliminate any unnecessary cost
3 Value Engineering which is used at GRIP Stage 3 (single option selection) to identify where savings can be made and eliminate any unnecessary cost
4 Lessons Learned is used to identify successes and problems from the project, this study is commonly carried out at the end of a project

ELLIS' BRITISH RAILWAY ENGINEERING ENCYCLOPÆDIA

VNCAB
[NR TRS] **V**ehicle and **N**etwork **C**hange **A**pprovals **B**oard.

VOBC
[TRS]
a) **V**ehicle **O**n-**b**oard **C**omputer
b) **V**ehicle **O**n-**b**oard **C**ontrol.

VOG
Vale **o**f **G**lamorgan.

VOI
[TRS] **V**ehicle **O**verhaul **I**nstruction.

Void Meter
[PW] A device that measures the vertical deflection of the **Track** under passing **Trains**, and hence the size of the **Voids** under the **Sleepers** or **Bearers**. This information can then be used to determine the **Dynamic Crosslevel**, **Dynamic Level** and **Dynamic Twist**.

Voided Sleepers
[PW] A **Track Fault** caused by gaps in the **Ballast** under the **Sleepers**, reducing the vertical support provided to the Sleepers. See **Voiding**.

Voiding

Voids
[PW] A **Track Fault** consisting of spaces under **Sleepers** or **Bearers** in the **Packing Area**, often caused by inadequate packing or differential settlement between Sleepers. Tell-tale signs include rounded pale **Ballast** on top of the **Sleeper Ends** and pronounced vertical deflection of the **Track** under passing **Trains**. It is Voiding that is responsible for **Track Faults**, such as **Twist Faults**, that only appear when the Track is loaded.

Volts-free Contacts
[Sig.] **Relay** contacts that are provided for switching external inputs. Also **Potential-free Contacts**.

VOPF
See **V**alue **o**f **P**reventing a **F**atality.

Vortok Coil
(Tradename) [PW] A proprietary type of **Maintenance Coil**.

Vossloh
(Tradename) A manufacturer of equipment for **Rail Vehicles**, **Rail Fastenings** and **Switch and Crossing** (**S&C**) components based in Wedohl, Germany.

Vossloh SN
(Tradename) [PW] A type of adjustable **Lateral Resistance** improvement device, now approved in place of the standard **Lateral Resistance End Plate** (**LREP**).

Voussoir
[Civ.] A wedge-shaped element, typically a stone, used in building an **Arch**.

Voyager
(Tradename) The brandname of the **Class** 220 **Diesel Electric Multiple Unit** (**DEMU**).

VPF
See **V**alue of **P**reventing a **F**atality.

VPI
a) [Sig.] **V**ital **P**rocessor **I**nterlocking
b) **V**apour **P**hase **I**nhibitor.

VPM
Value **p**er **M**inute.

VQ
See **V**irtual **Q**uarry.

VRAC
[NR] **V**ehicle and **R**oute **A**cceptance **C**ontract.

VRDI
[Tel.] **V**oice **R**adio **D**ialling **I**nterface.

VRG
(Tradename) **V**irgin **R**ail **G**roup. See also **Virgin Trains** (**VT**), **Virgin West Coast** (**VWC**), **Virgin Cross Country** (**VXC**).

VRS
See **V**ehicle **R**ecognition **S**ystem.

VS
[TRS] **V**igilance **S**ystem. This system works in conjunction with the **Driver's Safety Device** (**DSD**). If any one of the main controls has not been operated for one minute, the system assumes that the driver is incapacitated, and the warning sounds. The driver has seven seconds to reset the DSD; otherwise a **Full Service Braking** or **Emergency Braking** application will be initiated. See **Driver's Safety Device** (**DSD**).

VSDAC
[Sig.] **V**ital **S**ignal **D**river (**AC**).

V-shaped Crack
[PW] A type of **Rolling Contact Fatigue** (**RCF**) crack which shows a clear branch normally approximately perpendicular to the original crack. This is often accompanied by a deformation of the **Running Surface** and **Shadowing**.

VSOE
(Tradename) **V**enice **S**implon-**O**rient-**E**xpress.

VSRP
[NR] **V**ehicle **S**ystem **R**eview **P**anel.

VSTP
[NR Ops.] **V**ery **S**hort **T**erm **P**lan.

VT
a) The **ATOC** code for **Virgin Trains**
b) [Sig.] On a **Signalling Circuit Diagram**, denotes a wire coloured **v**iole**t** or purple
c) **V**oltage **T**ransformer.

VTAC
[NR] **V**ariable **T**rack **A**ccess **C**harges.

VTISM
a) **V**ehicle / **T**rack **I**nteraction **S**trategic **M**odel
b) **V**ehicle / **T**rack **I**nterface **S**trategic **M**odel.

VTS
Voltage Transformer Supervision. Monitoring of a voltage transformer's output directly and operation of any protective device on this output.

VTT
Virtual Test **Track**.

VUC
[NR] Variable Usage Charge.

VUPM
Vehicle Users in Pedestrian Mode.

VV&I
Verification, Validation and Integration.

V-value
[PW] The correction factor sometimes applied at the end of a **Transition** during **Tamping and Lining**.

VVVF
Variable Voltage Variable Frequency.

VWC
(Tradename) Virgin West Coast, see **Virgin Trains** (**VT**).

VXC
(Tradename) Virgin Cross Country, see **Virgin Trains** (**VT**).

W

W
a) [NR] As the last letter in a **Wagon** □ CARKND, this denotes that the Wagon has **Vacuum Brakes** and **Through Piping** for **Air Brakes** which does not operate the vehicle brakes. Also known as Vacuum Brake, **Air Piped**
b) Shorthand for **Weld**
c) See **W**histle Board
d) [Sig.] On a **Signalling Circuit Diagram**:
- As one of the leading letters of an **Equipment Code**, it means **Points**
- As the last letter of an Equipment Code, it means Points operating apparatus
e) Abbreviation found on drawings of **Signal Box Diagrams**, denoting **Working Levers**.
f) The letter represented by **W**hisky in the Phonetic Alphabet
g) Shorthand for **W**ednesday
h) As the last letter of an acronym representing a **Footpath Crossing** it means the **Crossing** has **W**icket Gates.

W&B
(Tradename) [Hist.] **W**ales and **B**orders, a **Train Operating Company** (**TOC**), now Arriva Trains Wales (**ATW**).

W/B
Shorthand for **W**est**b**ound.

W/S
Shorthand for **W**ork**s**tation.

W10
[NR] A **Swept Envelope** suite for **Container Vehicles** carrying standard 9' - 6" **Containers**. It is nominally a 4075mm high by 2500mm wide rectangle.

W10w
[NR] The 2600mm ('wide') variant of the **W10** □ **Swept Envelope** suite.

W11
W11 Gauge
[NR]
a) A standard **Vehicle Gauge** for **Container Vehicles** carrying either 9' - 6" high by 2550mm wide or 9' high by 2600mm wide **Containers** on 980mm deck height **Spigot Fastening** FSA Vehicles or 1000mm deck height **Twistlock Fastening** KFA Vehicles. This Gauge will allow the passage of a significant proportion of the anticipated **W12** □ **Traffic** without requiring most of the expensive **Gauge Clearance** work to be undertaken
b) The Vehicle Gauge now called **W18, W18 Gauge**.

W12
[NR] A composite **Swept Envelope** representing a range of **Container Vehicles** under load. It is nominally a rectangle 4000mm high and 3000mm wide.

W14
a) (Tradename) A **Rail Fastening** system manufactured by **Vossloh**. See also **Skl 14**
b) See **UK2 Gauge**. Also **W14 Gauge**.

W14 Gauge
[NR] See **UK2 Gauge**.

W18
W18 Gauge
[RT] The UK designation for the developed **UIC GC Profile**, which is nominally a rectangle 4650mm high and 3000mm wide. This is currently the largest European Vehicle Gauge. Previously called **W11, W11 Gauge**.

W5 Gauge
[Hist.] The first "W gauge", for **Freight** Vehicles, introduced in 1951.

W6
W6 Gauge
[NR] A standard **Vehicle Gauge**, applying to the majority of **Freight Vehicles** and **Locomotives** in the UK. It is nominally 3965mm high **Above Rail Level** (**ARL**) and 2820mm wide with a curved top.

W600
A **Steel Sleeper** designed for use in **Lines** carrying high **Axle Loads** and high levels of **Traffic**.

W6A
W6A Gauge
[NR] The title of the standard **Vehicle Gauge** for **Container Vehicles** carrying standard 8' **Containers**. See **W7**.

W6A Exception
W6A Exception Gauge
[NR] The former name for the **W8** □ **Vehicle Gauge**.

W6A SPL
[NR] A special category applied to **Lines** whose **Track Alignment** or **Structures** impose restrictions on the overall length and **Bogie Centres** the of **W6A** vehicles that can be allowed to run on it.

W7
W7 Gauge
[NR] The newer title for the former **W6A** □ **Vehicle Gauge** for **Container Vehicles** carrying standard 8' containers. It is nominally similar to **W6** with the addition of a 3620mm high by 2500mm wide rectangle overlaid on it.

W8
W8 Gauge
[NR] A standard **Vehicle Gauge** for **Container Vehicles** carrying standard 8'- 6" **Containers**. It is nominally similar to **W6A** with the addition of a 3770mm high by 2500mm wide rectangle overlaid on it. Previously called **W6A Exception**.

W9
W9 Gauge
[NR] Formerly known as **SB1c**, this is the standard UK **Vehicle Gauge** for **Swap Body Vehicles**. It is nominally similar to **W6A** with the addition of a 3715mm high by 2525mm wide rectangle overlaid on it.

W9 Plus
W9 Plus Gauge
Based on **W9**, this **Vehicle Gauge** includes a small additional area to allow slightly larger S coded **Containers** to be accommodated, e.g. S32 loads on **Wagons** with a 945mm deck height and S45 loads on Wagons with an 825mm deck height.

WA
a) [Elec.] Welded Angle, a type of construction used for **Overhead Line Equipment Structures** (**OLE Structures**)
b) [RT] West Anglia Line, from Liverpool Street to Cambridge and **Branch Lines**.

WABCO
(*wabb-coe*) (Tradename) Westinghouse **Air Brake Company**.

WABTEC
(*wabb-tek*) (Tradename) The Westinghouse Air Brake Technologies Corporation, an international manufacturer of **Rolling Stock** equipment, based (in the UK) in Doncaster.

WAC
Waste Acceptance Criteria.

WACC
Weighted Average Cost of Capital.

Wacker Pack
a) Three vibrating plate compactors (**Wacker Plates**) connected by a frame, allowing one operator to evenly consolidate the **Ballast** over the width of one **Sleeper** in one pass
b) To use Wacker Plates to consolidate newly laid Ballast.

Wacker Plate
(Tradename) A heavy duty vibrating plate compactor produced by Wacker, the weapon of choice when consolidating **Track Ballast**. See also **Wacker Pack**.

WAD
(Tradename) WA Developments Ltd., now part of Stobart **Rail**.

WAG
Wide Aisle Gate.

WAGE
[NR] West Anglia Great Eastern.

Wages Grades
[BR] Under **British Rail** the group of staff that included **Trackmen**, etc. See also **Conciliation Grades, Conciliation Staff, P&T Staff**.

WAgeX
[Col.] The nickname given to the **Locomotive Hauled** service operated by Arriva Trains Wales (**ATW**), due to its funding by the Welsh Assembly Government.

WAGN
(*wag-unn*) (Tradename) See **West Anglia Great Northern**, A **Train Operating Company** (**TOC**).

Wagon
Generic term for all but the most specialised and distinctive **Freight Vehicles**.

Wagon Names
[NR] A technique first used to reduce telegraph traffic, virtually all current **Engineering Vehicles** have a name. Generally aquatic (though a few are birds, mammals, mythical creatures and tradenames) these names are widely used when writing **Train Arrangements**. Some of the names include: **Barbel, Bass, Bream, Brill, Carp, Catfish, Chub, Clam, Coalfish, Cockle, Cod, Conger, Crab, Dace, Dogfish, Dolphin, Eel, Egret, Falcon, Gannet, Gane, Grampus, Gudgeon, Gunnel, Haddock, Hake, Halibut, Heron, Herring, Lamprey, Limpet, Ling, Lobster, Minnow, Mackerel, Manta, Marlin, Merdog, Mermaid, Mullet, Octopus, Osprey, Otter, Oyster, Parr, Perch, Pike, Pilchard, Piranha, Plaice, Pollock, Porpoise, Prawn, Puffin, Roach, Rudd, Salmon, Sea Urchin, Seacow, Seahare, Seahorse, Seal, Sealion, Shark, Shrimp, Skako, Skate, Sole, Squid, Starfer, Starfish, Stingray, Stumec, Sturgeon, Super Tench, Tench, Tope, Trident, Trout, Tunny, Turbot, Urchin, Walrus, Whale, Whelk, Whiting, Winkle** and **Zander**. See also **Fishkind**.

Wagon Number
The unique identification number given to each and every **Wagon** on the **Railway** system. These numbers are collected by a specialised sub-species of **Train Spotter**.

Wagonway
Waggonway
[Hist.] Typically, a pre-Industrial Revolution **Railway** which used horses to haul **Wagons** along specialised wood **Track**.

WAIF
[NR] Work Arising Identification Form, for **Ellipse**.

WAIMU
[Hist.] West Anglia **Infrastructure Maintenance Unit** (**IMU**).

Waist
[TRS] The point on a section through a **Rail Vehicle** at which the Vehicle has maximum width. This is typically located between the **Solebar** and window level. See **Rail Vehicle Section**.

Walking
[RB] Making your way on foot from point A to point B without carrying out any other activity. Additional activities, such as inspection, mean you are **Working**.

Walnut
A **Railway** □ **Telegraph Code** meaning "Make all necessary arrangements as far as you are concerned".

Walrus (YGV)
[NR] A 40 ton capacity **Ballast Hopper** with both centre and side chutes. See **Wagon Names**.

Walton Junction Accident
At around 11:40 on the 29th June 1867, an incorrectly routed **Express Passenger Train** ran into the rear of a stationary coal **Train** at Walton **Junction**, just south of later Warrington Bank Quay **Station**. The cause of the **Accident** was concluded to be the inattention of the **Signaller**. However, the **Signals** and **Points** at the Junction were not **Interlocked** and there were no **Facing Point Locks (FPL)**, arrangements which would have prevented this Accident. Five died instantly, three died shortly thereafter of injuries received and 70 were injured. A fatal Accident with similar causes occurred at the same location on 1st January 1862. See also **Lock, Block and Brake**.

WAR
<u>W</u>ork <u>A</u>s <u>R</u>equired. See **Train Arrangements**.

WARA
<u>W</u>ork <u>A</u>ctivity <u>R</u>isk <u>A</u>ssessment

WARC
[NR] <u>W</u>est <u>A</u>nglia <u>R</u>oute <u>C</u>ontroller.

Ward Coupler
[LUL Obs.] A mechanical coupler found on some **Engineers Vehicles**.

WARE
(Tradename) <u>W</u>oolwich <u>A</u>rsenal <u>R</u>ail <u>E</u>nterprises; the company that owns and operates the **Docklands Light Railway (DLR)** □ **Lines** from King George V to Woolwich Arsenal.

WARM
[RT] <u>W</u>est <u>A</u>nglia <u>R</u>oute <u>M</u>odernisation.

Warn On
[SR Sig. Col.] A term meaning to offer a **Train** to the **Signal Box** □ **Beyond** using the **Block Bell**.

Warning Arrangement
[Sig.] The **Acceptance** of a **Train** under Block Regulation 5, Section □ **Clear**, but Station or Junction □ Blocked, Bell Code 3-5-5. See also **Under the Hammer**.

Warning Board
[NR] A temporary **Lineside Sign** placed at the **Deceleration Distance (DD)** from the commencement of an **Emergency Speed Restriction (ESR)** or **Temporary Speed Restriction (TSR)**, giving the driver time to decelerate safely. The sign consists of the restriction in miles per hour, with two white lights placed in a horizontal line below. A retro-reflective version is available, which has the dual advantages of not requiring batteries and not requiring anyone to remember to change the aforesaid batteries. See also **Nuneaton Accident**.

Warning Distance
The minimum distance at which it is necessary to **Give a Warning** which gives everyone in the **Workgroup** time to reach a **Position Of Safety** at least ten seconds before the **Train** arrives.

Warning Indicator (WI)
a) A **Lineside Sign** placed at the appropriate braking distance from its associated **Speed Indicator (SI)**, giving a driver sufficient time to decelerate to the reduced **Permissible Speed (PS)** concerned. Reductions of ⅓ or more from above 50mph require that the Warning Indicator is provided with an **Automatic Warning System Permanent Magnet (AWS Permanent Magnet)** placed appropriately (normally 200 **Yards**, 183m) **On the Approach** to the sign. This combination of Sign and Magnet is colloquially referred to as a **Morpeth Board**. Previously called an **Advance Warning Indicator (AWI)**

b) [Col.] See **Warning Board**.

Warning Route
[Sig.] A **Route** □ **Set** □ **Beyond** a **Signal** when the full Signal Overlap **(OL)** is not **Clear** Beyond the next Signal. The **Entrance Signal** is **Approach Controlled**.

Warning Signal
[Sig. Hist.] A **Semaphore Signal** bearing the letter W, or revealing one when the **Signal** is **Cleared**, to indicate to a driver that the **Train** has been accepted under the **Warning Arrangement** by the Signal Box □ Ahead.

Warning Time
a) [RB] The amount of time a particular group working on an **Open Line** require to stop work, make the site safe and move to a **Position of Safety (POS)** when warned of the approach of a **Train**

b) [Sig.] At a **Level Crossing (LC, LX)** the shortest possible time taken for **Trains** to travel over the **Sighting Distance** or, where **Whistle Boards** are provided, the shortest time between the sound being heard at the Crossing and the Train arriving at the Crossing. In calculations of Warning Time the highest **Attainable Speed** should be used.

WARP
[NR]
a) **W**atford **A**rea **Resignalling P**roject.
b) **W**est **C**oast **M**ain **L**ine (**WCML**) **A**ccelerated **R**eliability **P**roject.

Warships
[Col.] name for **Class** 42 and Class 43 **Diesel Locomotives**.

Washdrop
[PW Col.] Coloured paint dropped by a **Track Inspection Vehicle** (**TIV**). See **Whitewash**.

Washing the Hands, Importance of
When working on the **Track**, one should be aware of the presence of sewage, dust from brake pads and **Rat** urine on the **Ballast**, **Rails** and **Sleepers**. See **Leptospiral Jaundice**, **Live Discharge Toilets** and **Weil's Disease**.

Washout
a) [Civ.] A failure condition in which a **Bridge**, the **Formation**, an **Embankment** or occasionally the whole **Railway** is removed by fast flowing water or localised flooding
b) [TRS] The process of removing the relevant plugs and doors in a **Boiler**, and washing the accumulated mud, sludge and scale out with water jets.

Washout and Earthflow Risk Mapping (WERM)
A computerised process for identifying parts of the **Railway** at particular risk due to concentrated flows of water from neighbouring land.

Watchman
A person employed specifically to observe the condition of an element of **Infrastructure** and report or take other specified action in the event of undesirable event.

Water Catchment Tray
[Civ.] A **Structure** used to catch water entering a **Tunnel** from the surrounding ground and channel it into the Tunnel drainage system

Water Troughs
[Obs.] Consisting of long shallow troughs filled with water and laid between the **Rails** centrally in the **Fourfoot**, this system allowed **Steam Locomotives** fitted with a special scoop to collect water whilst moving at speed. Since the **Locomotives** had to carry less water, they could carry more coal, increasing their range. Water Troughs can only be placed on level sections of **Track**.

Waterproofing
[Civ.] An impermeable layer, often overlaid with a protective rubber mat, laid under the **Ballast** and used to prevent water penetrating and damaging the structure of the **Bridge Deck** beneath.

Watford Accident
On the 8th August 1996 a **Commuter Train** passed a **Signal** showing a **Stop Aspect** despite a full brake application. Upon coming to rest it was struck by an **Empty Coaching Stock** (**ECS**) □ **Train** which had been correctly signalled through a **Crossover** □ **Beyond** the Signal. The Commuter Train driver remained adamant that he had received no warning of the Stop Aspect and was acquitted of manslaughter. The situation was exacerbated by a short **Signal Overlap** and confusion regarding the presence of many changes in **Permissible Speed** (**PS**) □ **On The Approach to** the Signal. One person died and 69 received significant injuries.

WAV
See **W**et **A**ttrition **V**alue.

WaveTrain LCWS
(Tradename) A system for detecting approaching trains at level crossings by detecting sound waves through rails and activating warning indicators. Manufactured by **WaveTrain Systems AS** of Norway.

WaveTrain MTDS
(Tradename) A mobile system to detect **Approaching Trains** at **Maintenance** □ **Worksites** by detecting sound waves from **Trains** through the **Rails** and activating warning indicators. Manufactured by **WaveTrain Systems AS** of Norway.

WaveTrain Systems AS
(Tradename) Based in Lysaker, Norway, manufacturer of warning systems for **Trackworkers** and **Level Crossings**. See **WaveTrain LCWS**, **WaveTrain MTDS**

Way
[Col.] The **Track**. Also used as a nickname for the **Permanent Way**, as in "**Works** and Way", meaning **Bridges** and Track.

Waybeam
a) An alternative term for **Longitudinal Timber**
b) [Civ.] A structural member of a **Bridge Deck** that runs parallel to and directly below the **Rails**. This in turn generally supports **Longitudinal Timbers**, though the normal **Cross Sleepered Track** can be found
c) [Civ.] A temporary longitudinal load-bearing member which directly supports the **Track**, typically during **Bridge** works.

Wayside
Alternative term for **Lineside** when describing fixed equipment. Also **Shore**.

WBS
a) [Sig.] Common shorthand for **W**estinghouse **B**rake & (**S**axby) **S**ignal Co., a manufacturer of **Signalling Equipment**. See **Westinghouse Rail Systems Ltd.** (**WRSL**)
b) [NR] **W**ork **B**reakdown **S**tructure.

ELLIS' BRITISH RAILWAY ENGINEERING ENCYCLOPÆDIA

WC&ER
[Hist.] The **Pre-grouping** Whitehaven, Cleator and Egremont **Railway**, a London and North Western Railway (**LNWR**) and Furness Railway (**FR**) joint enterprise.

WCAS
[RT] West Coast Asset Store, see **West Coast Route Modernisation** (**WCRM**).

WCE
[RT] West Coast Engineering, see **West Coast Route Modernisation** (**WCRM**).

WCML
See **West Coast Main Line**.

WCPSU
[NR] West Coast Power Supply Upgrade.

WCRC
(Tradename) The West Coast **Railway** Company, a **Charter Train** operator, based at Carnforth in Lancashire.

WCRM
See **West Coast Route Modernisation**.

WCRR
World Congress on **Railway** Research.

WCRTCC
WCTCC
[NR] West Coast (**Rail**) Traffic Control Centre.

WDM
a) See **Wrong Direction Movement**
b) Wavelength-Division Multiplexing

WDM Protector
[NR] **Wrong Direction Movement** Protector. A person who is appointed to stop any **Train** from entering a section of **Line** on which a Wrong Direction Move is underway.

Wear Resisting Rail
[PW]
a) A **Rail** manufactured in accordance with Tables 1 and 2 of British Standard Specification 11: 1985 'Wear-resisting grades A&B' or UIC 860-0 'Wear-resisting grades A&B'. Also **WR**. See also **Grade A, Grade A Rail, Grade B, Grade B Rail**.
b) A Rail with a hardness exceeding 260 Brinell at the **Rail Crown**.

Weave
[Ops.] A description of the arrangements for a **Possession** on a **Four Track Railway** where **Trains** running on one pair of **Lines** are diverted onto the other pair during the Possession. This arrangement also generally carries the title of pair of Lines onto which Trains are diverted, e.g. **Slow Line** Weave. See also **Double Weave Junction**.

Web
See **Rail Web**.

Webb, Francis William
(1836 - 1906) Apprenticed to **Francis Trevithick** at Crewe **Locomotive** Works in 1851 and rose to become Chief Mechanical Engineer (CME) of the London North Western Railway (**LNWR**) from 1871 to 1903. He was Vice President of the Institution of Civil Engineers (**ICE**) and the Institution of Mechanical Engineers (**IMechE**).

WED
Weekend Day (shift).

Wedge
[LUL] The mechanical part of the **Wedgelock Autocoupler** □ **Automatic Coupling** which locks the adjacent tongues when **Coupled**.

Wedgelock
Wedgelock Autocoupler
[LUL] The standard **Automatic Coupling** used by **London Underground Limited**.

WEEB
[TRS] Winter Emergency Equipment Box, a box fitted within a vehicle on some **Class** 377/6 **Multiple Units** (**MU**).

Weedkilling Train
An **Engineer's Train** equipped with a chemical spray system to combat weeds on the **Track**.

Week Numbers
[NR] The first week in the planning and financial calendar is week one, which starts at 00:01 on the last Saturday before April 1st. Every six or seven years there are 53 weeks:

Year	Week One Start	Weeks in year
2012/13	31st March 2012	52
2013/14	30th March 2013	52
2014/15	29th March 2014	52
2015/16	28th March 2015	52
2016/17	26th March 2016	52
2017/18	25th March 2017	52
2018/19	31st March 2018	53
2019/20	30th March 2019	52
2020/21	28th March 2020	52
2021/22	27th March 2021	52
2022/23	26th March 2022	52
2023/24	25th March 2023	52
2024/25	30th March 2024	53
2025/26	29th March 2025	52
2026/27	28th March 2026	52

Weekly Circular
[IÉ Ops.] The Irish Railways equivalent of the **Weekly Operating Notice** (**WON**).

ELLIS' BRITISH RAILWAY ENGINEERING ENCYCLOPÆDIA

Weekly Operating Notice (WON)
a) [NR] A document published by **Network Rail** on a **Region** by Region basis, providing information about **Engineering Work**, **Speed Restrictions**, alterations to **The Network** and other relevant information to **Train** drivers. See also **Section A**, **Section B**, **Section C**, **Section D**
b) [NIR] On **Northern Ireland Railways**, a publication issued weekly which lists **Temporary Speed Restrictions** (**TSR**), details of **Special Trains** and **Timetables** (**TT**), Engineering Works, party travel bookings, additional **Operating Instructions**, and modifications to the **Rule Book Appendix**.

Weep Hole
Weep Pipe
[Civ.] A hole or pipe provided at or near ground level to allow water to escape from behind a **Retaining Wall** or **Bridge Abutment**.

WEF
[Ops.] With effect from, generally found in **Operating Notices**.

Weil's Disease
See **Leptospiral Jaundice**.

Weld (W)
[PW]
a) A **Rail Weld** made by the **Alumino-thermic Weld** process. See also **Delachaux**, **PLA 68**, **SkV**, **SkV-E**, **SkV-F**, **SkV-L50**, **SkV-L80**, **SmW**, **SoWoS**
b) A **Rail Weld** made in a **Depot** by means of the **Flash Butt Weld** (**FBW**) process. See also **Shop Weld**
c) A **Rail Weld** made by another process, such as an **Electron Beam Weld**, **Gas Pressure Weld**.

Weld Collar
[PW] The thickened portion of the **Rail Foot**, **Rail Web** and **Rail Head** produced as part of the **Alumino-thermic Weld** process.

Weld Portion
[PW] The measured quantity of component materials that is required for each **Alumino-thermic Weld**.

Weld Repair
[PW] The repair of cracks, damage and wear to **Crossings** and **Rails** using either:
• An **Electric Arc Welding** process, where the area concerned is cut back to sound metal using an angle grinder, with **Dye Penetrant Inspection** (**DPI**) and **Magnetic Particle Inspection** (**MPI**) being used to ensure that all necessary suspect metal is removed. The weld material is then built up in layers and the finished repair ground to its final profile
• A special form of **Alumino-thermic Weld** process, currently limited to **Plain Rails**.

Weld Shear
[PW] A portable device used to remove the majority of the excess weld material from a newly made **Alumino-thermic Weld**. There are two main types:
• Single Shears, which are generally manually operated and used for Standard Welds
• Double Shears, which cut from both sides simultaneously. These are normally petrol powered and are used on **PLA 68**, **SkV-L50** and **SkV-L80** □ Wide Gap Welds.

Weld Upset
[PW] **Weld** material left standing proud of the **Rail Head** on completion of the main **Alumino-thermic Weld** process, normally removed by grinding.

Weld Zone
[PW] The area of parent **Rail** adjacent to a **Weld** that will be affected metallurgically by the **Weld** process. This will include the **Heat Affected Zone** (**HAZ**).

Welded Crossing
A **Crossing** in which all the **Rail** components are welded together.

Welded Joint
[PW] Alternative for **Rail Weld** or **Weld (W)**, see **Alumino-thermic Weld**, **Electric Arc Weld**, **Electron Beam Weld**, **Flash Butt Weld** (**FBW**), **Gas Pressure Weld**, **Phillips Weld**, **Thermit Weld**.

Welded Rod (WR)
[Elec.] A type of fabrication used for **Overhead Line Structures**.

Welded Vee
[PW] A type of **Crossing** construction in which **Point Rail** and **Splice Rail** are welded together, machined to shape and the **Wing Rails** bolted on. See also **Electro-slag Welded Vee**.

Welding Gap
[PW] The distance between prepared **Rail Ends** required by a particular welding process, measured immediately before welding commences. The gap specified for the **Thermit Welding** □ **SkV-F** □ **Alumino-thermic Weld** process is 22 - 24mm, but this can be up to 80mm for other processes.

Well Wagon

[TRS] A **Wagon** built with a lower centre section to allow either tall loads to be carried or for easy access by vehicles.

Weltrol (YVP)
[NR] A low floor **Well Wagon** used for the transportation of excavating plant.

Welwyn Control
[Sig.] A **Control** applied in **Absolute Block** (**AB**) areas preventing the **Signaller** from accepting a second **Train** until the first has **Occupied** and **Cleared** the **Berth Track Circuit** for the **Home Signal**. Adopted and named after the **Accident** that took place at Welwyn on 17th June 1935, where the **Signaller** forgot about a Train he had already brought to a stand and allowed another to run into the rear of it. 14 died See also **Home Normal Control**, **Interlinking**.

WEN
a) (*wen*) Weekly Engineering Notice. See **Weekly Operating Notice** (**WON**)
b) Weekend Night (shift).

WERM
See **W**ashout and **E**arthflow **R**isk **M**apping.

Weser
A **Railway** □ **Telegraph Code** meaning "Say what arrangements have been made".

Wessex Trains
(Tradename)A **Train Operating Company** (**TOC**).

West Anglia Great Northern (WAGN)
(Tradename)A **Train Operating Company** (**TOC**).

West Coast Main Line (WCML)
[NR] The **Route** from **London** Euston to Glasgow via Rugby, Crewe, Preston and Carlisle, running up the West side of Britain. The main branches to Birmingham, Liverpool and Manchester, and the loops via Northampton and Stoke-on-Trent are also included.

West Coast Route Modernisation (WCRM)
[RT, NR] The multi-billion pound project to upgrade and enhance the **West Coast Main Line** (**WCML**), including provision for **Tilting Trains** running at **Enhanced Permissible Speeds** (**EPS**), the intention being to dramatically reduce journey times. **Virgin Trains** (**VT**) undertook to supply Tilting Trains capable of attaining 140mph (225kph), later delivered to time and named **Pendolino**. When originally conceived, the scheme was intended to deliver the following:
- Phase 0 - Period of interim and full **Running** of **Tilting Trains** at existing **Permissible Speeds** (**PS**)
- Phase 1 - Period of full running on the WCML up to speeds of 125mph (200kph) between 2002 & 2005
- Phase 2 - Full service after April 2005 up to speeds of 140mph (225kph).

Phase 2 (also known as **PUG2**) was abandoned in 2002, and a reduced-scope Phase 1 (also known as **PUG1**) was only partially commissioned in 2006.

West Ealing Accident
At 17:37 on 19th December 1973 an **Express Passenger Train** became derailed at 70mph at Longfield Avenue **Junction** when an open **Battery** box door on the **Locomotive** struck the **Point Machine** of a **Set** of **Facing Points**, allowing the **Trailing End** □ **Bogie** and part of the **Train** to take the slower **Turnout Route**. It transpired that the pear shaped **Drop Catches** were secured out of the way and the carriage locks were both left unlocked, all following **Maintenance** work the previous night. 10 **Passengers** died in the **Accident**.

West Yorkshire Combined Authority (WYCA)
Formed on 1st April 2014 when the West Yorkshire Integrated Transport Authority (**WYITA**) and the West Yorkshire Passenger Transport Executive (**WYPTE**) were dissolved.

Westbound
The opposite of **Eastbound**, as in travelling towards the west.

WESTCAD
(*west-cad*) (Tradename) [Sig.] **W**estinghouse **C**ontrol **a**nd **D**isplay system, a **Signalling Control System** (**SCS**).

Westcode

Westcode Brake
(Tradename) [TRS] A proprietary 'energise-to-release' braking system produced by the **Westinghouse** Brake and Signal Company. It is in use on many **Diesel Multiple Unit** (**DMU**) and **Electric Multiple Unit** (**EMU**) □ **Trains** in the UK. Failure of the electricity supply or a deliberate interruption by interlocks causes the brake to be fully applied. Normal **Service Brake** pressures are applied in a number of discrete steps.

Western Region (WR)
a) [BR WR] The regional division covering the **Great Western Main Line** (**GWML**), south Wales and the West Country
b) [NR WR] The regional division covering a similar area

Western Region Barrier Unit
[BR Sig.] A type of **Barrier Pedestal** that was originally designed and manufactured by and for the **Western Region** (**WR**) of **British Rail** (**BR**).

Western Region Box Girder Bridge

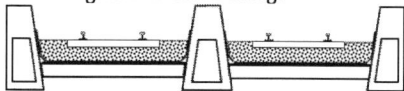

[NR Civ.] Originally developed by the **Western Region** (**WR**) of **British Railways** (**BR**), this form of **Bridge Deck** is now quite widespread. It consists of hollow box-section longitudinal members with a transversely ribbed floor. **Spans** of 15m are possible.

Westinghouse
See **Westinghouse Rail Systems Ltd.** (**WRSL**).

ELLIS' BRITISH RAILWAY ENGINEERING ENCYCLOPÆDIA

Westinghouse Rail Systems Ltd. (WRSL)
(Tradename) A manufacturer of, amongst other things **Signalling Equipment**, based in Chippenham. Part of the **Invensys Rail** Group. Often contracted to **Westinghouse**. See also **Saxby and Farmer**.

Westinghouse Stock
[LUL] **Trains** equipped with an **Automatic Air Brake** as the **Emergency Brake** and the **Service Brake** on Non-passenger Carrying Vehicles.

Westinghouse, George
(6th October 1846 – 12th March 1914). American, inventor of the Westinghouse **Air Brake** □ **Automatic Brake** system and the **Pantograph**, and an early champion of the widespread use of Alternating Current.

WESTRACE
(*west-race*) (Tradename) **W**estinghouse **R**adio **A**dvanced **C**ontrol **E**quipment.

Wet Attrition Value (WAV)
[PW] A measure of the wear resistance, and thus longevity, of **Ballast**.

Wet Bed
[PW] An alternative for **Wet Spot**. Also **Slurry Bed**, **Slurry Spot**.

Wet Bedders
[Col.] A derogatory collective **Nickname** for **Permanent Way (PW)** staff.

Wet Machine Room
[LUL] An escalator or lift machine room that is prone to or at risk of flooding or with floor-laden surface moisture.

Wet Spot
[PW] An area of **Ballast** contaminated with **Slurry**. Such Wet Spots spread under the action of passing traffic and can cause **Twist Faults** in extreme cases. Also called **Slurry Bed**, **Slurry Spot**, **Wet Bed**.

Wet Weld
[PW Col.] An **Alumino-thermic Weld** made in wet weather. The presence of precipitation increases the chances of steam bubbles and other defects in the **Rail Weld**, and so Wet Welds are classed as **Defective Welds**.

WF
See **Wheels Free**.

WG
As the last letter of an acronym representing a **Footpath Crossing** it means the **Crossing** has **W**icket **G**ates. Also **W**.

WH
[Sig.] On a **Signalling Circuit Diagram**, denotes the colour white.

Whale (YBA, YHA)
[NR] A 51 ton capacity **Ballast Hopper** with both centre and side chutes. See **Wagon Names**.

Wheel / Rail Interface
Collective term for the mechanical contact between a **Rail Wheel** and **Running Rail** and all related issues.

Wheel Backs
[TRS] The inside surfaces of a pair of **Rail Wheels**. See also **Back to Back Dimension**.

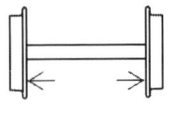

Wheel Burn
See **Wheelburn**.

Wheel Flange
[TRS] The extended portion of a **Rail Vehicle's** wheel that contacts the **Rail Head** and thus provides the **Wheelset** with directional guidance.

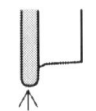

Wheel Flange Lubricator
See **Flange Lubricator**.

Wheel Flange Thickness
See **Flange Thickness**.

Wheel Flat
[TRS] A flat area worn into the tyre of a **Rail Wheel** by prolonged braking or a failure of the brakes to release. A wheel with one or more Flats is a **Square Wheel**. Also **Flat**.

Wheel Impact Load Detector (WILD)
A generic term for a **Rail** mounted strain gauge and **Axle Counter** system which record the load produced by each **Rail Wheel**. Excessively high values can indicate overloaded vehicles or **Wheel Flats**. Any such wheel detected normally results in the **Train** being stopped for inspection. See **Wheelchex**.

Wheel Lathe
[TRS] Found at **Depots** where **Locomotives**, **Multiple Unit Trains** and other **Rolling Stock** are maintained, this machine re-instates the correct **Tyre** and **Flange** profile on a **Rail Wheel** whilst the wheel is still attached to its parent vehicle. See also **Tyre Turning**.

Wheel Profile
[TRS] The shape of a section of a **Rail Wheel** taken through the axis of rotation. Typically this is a conical section with a **Flange** on the side of the greatest diameter.

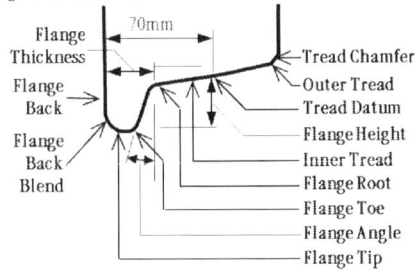

Flange Thickness — 70mm — Tread Chamfer
Flange Back — Outer Tread
— Tread Datum
Flange Back — Flange Height
Blend — Inner Tread
— Flange Root
— Flange Toe
— Flange Angle
— Flange Tip

Wheel Shunt
[TRS] An electrical connection between the hub and **Tyre** of a **Resilient Wheel**, provided to allow the **Traction Current** to return to the **Running Rails** and to allow the **Wheelset** to activate **Track Circuits** (**TC**).

Wheel Skate
[Ops.] A wheeled device reminiscent of a skateboard, used to lift a damaged **Rail Wheel** clear of the **Rail**, in turn allowing the Rail Vehicle to be moved (slowly) to a place of repair.

Wheel Slide
[TRS] The condition where the rotational speed of the wheel is lower than that corresponding to the actual linear speed of the **Train**.

Wheel Slide Prevention (WSP)
[TRS] A control system fitted to modern **Rolling Stock** that prevents the wheels locking up during times of reduced **Adhesion**. They work by automatically releasing and re-applying the brake on sliding **Wheelsets** in order to find and make use of the maximum level of Adhesion available. It is analogous to anti-lock braking on a motor car.

Wheel Slip
[TRS] The condition where the rotational speed of the wheel is greater than that corresponding to the actual linear speed of the **Train**. See also **Creep**.

Wheel Slip Prevention (WSP)
[TRS] A control system fitted to modern **Locomotives** and **Multiple Unit Trains** that prevents the driving wheels spinning out of control during times of reduced **Adhesion**. It is analogous to traction control on a motor car.

Wheel Slow-up
[TRS] The condition when a **Rail Wheel** rotates slower than speed dictated by the **Rail Vehicle**. It often deteriorates rapidly into **Wheel Slide**.

Wheel Timber
a) [PW SR] An alternative term for a **Longitudinal Timber**
b) A capping strip fixed to the upper surface of a Longitudinal Timber.

Wheel Transfer Area
[PW] A localised area of the **Wing Rails** and **Crossing Vee** or **Obtuse Point Rail** over which vehicle wheels transfer contact from one to the other, or vice versa.

Wheel Unloading
[TRS] Describing the worst-case effect of **Cant Deficiency** (**D**), load distribution, suspension travel, **Torsional Stiffness** and **Twist**, which can be the reduction of the force applied by one or more **Rail Wheels** to very low or even small negative values. This can lead to **Derailments**, see **Flange Climb**.

Wheelbase
Bogie Wheelbase
Inner Wheelbase
Bogie Centres
Outer Wheelbase

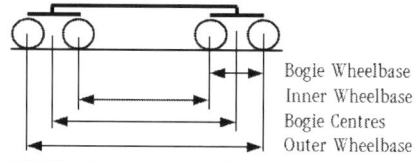

[TRS] The distance between the outermost points of contact of any wheel on the Rail for a given vehicle. See **Bogie Wheelbase**, **Inner Wheelbase** (**IWB**), **Outer Wheelbase** (**OWB**). See also **Bogie Centres**.

Wheelburn
[PW] A **Rail Defect** found on the **Running Surface** of the **Rail**. They are caused by the excess rotation of a **Driving Wheel** that has ceased to grip the Rail properly. Wheelburns are a potential source of more severe cracking and **Broken Rails**.

Wheelchex
(Tradename) A type of **Wheel Impact Load Detector** (**WILD**) system manufactured by **Delta Rail** (Formerly **AEA Technology**). Both **Rails** on a section of straight and **Level Track** are instrumented and measure the load imparted by a moving wheel. A large variation in the load imparted by a single wheel indicates the presence of a **Wheel Flat** or an out-of-round wheel.

Wheels Free (WF)
Wheels Free Period
Describing a period of time when a **Track** has no **Hand Trolleys**, **On Track Machines** (**OTM**), **Rail Vehicles**, **Road Rail Plant**, **Trains**, or other wheeled vehicles on it. This state is required for the final testing of **Track Circuits** (**TC**) and is normally put in place at the end of a **Possession** where Track Circuits have been disconnected.

Wheelset
[TRS] Two **Rail Wheels** mounted on their joining axle.

Wheelset Back-to-back Spacing
See **Back To Back Dimension**, clause a).

Wheelskate
See **Wheel Skate**.

Whelk (YNO)
[NR] A 58 ton capacity **Open Wagon** used for materials.

Whisky
The **Phonetic Alphabet** word representing **W**.

Whistle Board
A white circular sign with a grey edge and black **W** in the centre that indicates to a driver that they must sound the horn or whistle. This is often used to provide a warning to users of **Accommodation Crossings**, **Footpath Crossings** and **Occupation Crossings**.

ELLIS' BRITISH RAILWAY ENGINEERING ENCYCLOPÆDIA

White Circle
[TRS] A symbol applied to **Traction Units**, in this case **Class** 126 □ **First Generation Diesel Multiple Unit** (**DMU**), denoting which **Multiple Working** control system with which they are fitted. Only Traction Units bearing the same symbol can be connected safely. See **Blue Square**, **Blue Star**, **Green Circle**, **Orange Star**, **Red Circle**, **Red Diamond**, **Red Triangle**, **White Circle**, **White Diamond**, **Yellow Diamond**, **Yellow Triangle**

White Diamond
[TRS] A symbol applied to **Traction Units**, in this case **Class** 22, 41, 42 and 43 Locomotives, denoting which **Multiple Working** control system they are fitted with. Only Traction Units bearing the same symbol can be connected safely. See **Blue Star**, **Red Circle**, **Orange Square**, **Yellow Triangle** and **Red Diamond**.

White Gates
Gates provided at a **Level Crossing** (LC, LX) over a public road. See also **Black Gates**.

White Lights
[Sig.] One or two simple white lamps (often domestic in origin) provided at **Barrow Crossings** and other staff-only **Level Crossings** (LC, LX) to provide a basic **Fail Safe** level of reassurance to those using the Level Crossing. They are normally lit, indicating a safe condition, but extinguished by the presence of a **Train** on a selected group of **Track Circuits** (TC).

White Line
[PW] A straight line painted along the length of a new **Switch and Crossing Layout** (**S&C Layout**) by the manufacturer prior to shipping, which allows its speedy reconstruction on site. Such lines are generally aligned with some other site feature, such as another **Track** and lateral offsets to one or more **Running Edges** (RE) of the **Track**(s) being relaid. Used in conjunction with **Laths**.

White Pages
[NR] The part of the **Working Manual For Rail Staff** intended for those engaged in **Freight Train** operations, which sets out the mandatory tasks to ensure safe operation.

White Period
[Ops, Col.] A period during which no **Trains** are **Timetabled** to run on any **Line** on a **Route**, producing a blank, white space in the **Working Timetable** (WTT). Also **No Train Period** (NTP), **Out of Traffic Hours** (OOTH).

White Route Locking
[LUL Sig.] Authorising a **Train** to proceed on the reassurance provided the **Signaller's Panel** that the **Route** has been **Set** and **Locked**.

White Sleeve
[Elec.] A **Sleeve** fitted to a normally open **Hook Switch** that has been closed to prevent it from being opened accidentally.

Whitewash
Whitewash Coach
Whitewash Run
[PW Col.] Complementing the various geometry recording vehicles such as the **New Measurement Train** (NMT), **Track Recording Coach** (TRC) and **Track Recording Unit** (TRU) there are a number of **Track Inspection Vehicles** (TIV) equipped to detect the more extreme **Track Faults**. These vehicles do not produce detailed data and statistics, but rely on placing a coloured paint mark in the **Fourfoot** at each fault. These paint marks are green for **Level One Exceedances** and red for **Level Two Exceedances**. Because the vehicle is generally moving at speed, the paint is deposited at a known but variable point beyond the trigger, requiring the **Maintainer** to know the speed of the vehicle when it dropped the paint. The term Whitewash stems from the original paint used in the system. Also **Washdrop**.

Whiting (ZVV)
[NR] A **Wagon** used for the transportation of **Signalling** materials. See **Wagon Names**.

WHL
West Highland **Line**.

Whyte's Notation
[TRS] A means of describing the wheel arrangement of **Steam Locomotives** first described by F.M. Whyte. The basic from uses three numbers separated by hyphens. The first digit is the number of non-powered wheels on the leading **Bogie** or **Pony Truck** (if any), the second the number of coupled **Driving Wheels** and the third the number of non-powered wheels on the trailing Bogie or Pony Truck (if any). Where there are no wheels meeting the description a zero is used. All wheels on both **Rails** are counted. Certain types of Steam Locomotive such as **Garratt Locomotives** do not follow this simple pattern, so there are variations Examples (**Leading End** on the left):

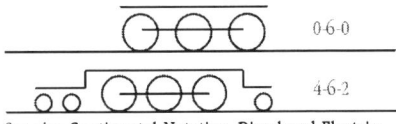

0-6-0

4-6-2

See also **Continental Notation**, **Diesel and Electric Locomotive Notation**.

WI
See **Warning Indicator**.

WIC
[TRS] Whistle Isolating **Cock**.

Wick Trimmers
[Col.] A collective **Nickname** for **Signalling** staff. See also **Sick and Tired**.

Wicket
Wicket Gate
A pedestrian-operated outward-opening (from the point of view of the **Railway**) gate found at some **Level Crossings** (**LC**, **LX**) such as **Footpath Crossings** (**FP**) or adjacent to **Gated Crossings**. They typically self-close under the action of gravity, a spring or both, always have latches, and they may also be Locked by the **Signalling System**. See **Elsenham Accident**.

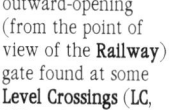

Wicket Gate Lever
[Sig.] A **Lever** which locks the **Wicket Gate(s)** at a **Controlled Level Crossing**.

Wide Angle Crossing
[PW] An **Acute Crossing** with a small **N Value**, or large angle at the **Intersection of Gauge Lines** (**IP**). Also **Sharp Angle Crossing**. The opposite is a **Flat Angle Crossing**.

Wide Gap Weld
[PW] A colloquial term for an **Alumino-thermic Weld** with a specified **Welding Gap** greater than 24mm. Also **PLA 68**, **SkV-L50** (50mm gap), **SkV-L80** (80mm gap).

Wide Gauge
[PW] **Track Gauge** that is wider than normal due to wear of the **Rails** or because of poor assembly or deterioration of components. The opposite is **Tight Gauge**.

Wide to Gauge (WTG)
[PW] Describing an unintentional situation where the measured **Track Gauge** is greater than the normal value. For the intentional situation see **Gauge Widening**.

Wide to Gauge Trap Points

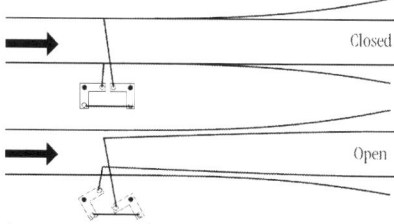

An arrangement of **Trap Points** for use in congested areas. They are **Double Tongue Trap Points** (**DTT**), but the **Stock Rails** curve in opposite directions. When closed the **Switches** permit free passage, but when open any **Train Movement** falls into the gap and continues in a straight line, eventually becoming wedged each side of the **Switch Rails**. There are two ways in which these can be applied:
- As conventional **Trap Points**
- As a **Point End** forming part of two **Crossovers**, where each Switch Rail is operated by a separate **Point Machine**.

Also **Straddle Switches**, **Straddle Trap Points**, **Straddle Traps**.

ELLIS' BRITISH RAILWAY ENGINEERING ENCYCLOPÆDIA

WIDEM
Wheelset **I**ntegrated **De**sign and **M**aintenance

Widespace
See **Wideway**.

Wideway
An **Interval** between **Tracks** that is wider than a **Tenfoot** (10', 3050mm). Also **Widespace**.

Wig-wag
Wig-wag Lights
[Col.] The paired flashing red lights provided at **Level Crossings** (**LC**, **LX**) to warn highway users that the Level Crossing is closing or is closed to road traffic.

WILD
See **W**heel **I**mpact **L**oad **D**etector.

WILH
Walk-**i**n **L**ocation **H**ut. See also **REB**, **Superloc**.

William
[Obs.] The obsolescent **Phonetic Alphabet** word representing **W**. Replaced by **Whisky**.

Williams
Common shorthand for **Henry Williams** Ltd.

Willow
A **Railway** □ **Telegraph Code** meaning "I will make all necessary arrangements".

Wiltshire Distant
[Sig.] An additional **Four Aspect Signal** provided as a method of transition from **Three Aspect Signalling** to **Four Aspect Signalling**.

WIMU
[Hist.] **W**estern **I**nfrastructure **M**aintenance **U**nit (**IMU**).

Wind
(*whined*) The change in **Bearer Rake** or **Timber Rake** in a **Switch and Crossing Layout** (**S&C Layout**).

Wing
a) See **Wing Rail**
b) See **Winging**.

Wing Front
[PW] The **Wing Rail** from the **Blunt Nose** to the Wing Front **Rail Joint**.

Wing Rail
[PW]

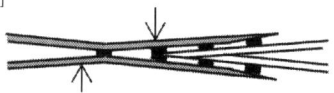

a) The short lengths of angled **Rail** fastened one to each side of the **Crossing Vee** in a **Common Crossing** assembly, extending in front and **Flared** to the rear of the **Crossing Nose**. Shortened to **Wing**

b) An angled length of Rail that, together with the **Obtuse Point Rails**, supports the **Wheelsets** passing over an **Obtuse Crossing**.

577

Wing Rail Front
[PW] The portion of the **Wing Rail** extending from the **Crossing Nose** to the **Front Joint**. Also **Wing Front**.

Wing Wall
[Civ.] A wall adjacent to **Bridge** □ **Abutments** which act as **Retaining Walls**.

Winging
[Col.] Turning a **Rail** end for end. Also **Rail Turning**.

Winkle (ZVV)
[NR] A **Wagon** used for the transportation of **Signalling** materials. See **Wagon Names**.

WIP
WESTRACE **I**nterface **P**rocessor.

Wire
a) [Col.] Term for a telegram, now used to describe the amendments to **Operating Publications**, typically **E Notices**, issued by Fax and Email systems.
b) See **Wires**.

Wire Adjuster
[Sig.] A mechanical linkage in a **Signal Box** for adjusting the tension of a **Signal Wire** in accordance with the prevailing external temperature.

Wire Assister
[Sig.] A weighted lever incorporated into a long run of **Signal Wire** to act as a counterweight to the self-weight of the wire. This would facilitate a 'clean' pull of the **Semaphore Signal Arm** to the **Off** position.

Wire Count
[Sig.] A checking procedure used in the installation or modification of **Signalling Systems**, whereby an independent person verifies the actual number of wires connected to each terminal against the number stated in the design.

Wire Deg.
Wire Degradation
[Sig.] A condition affecting certain types of wiring used in **Signalling Systems**, particularly **Free Wired Interlockings**. Wires consisting of steel strands insulated with natural rubber or early flexible polymers are prone to stiffening and cracking when aged, creating a risk of breakage during alterations. If this situation is widespread within an **Interlocking**, a moratorium on alterations may be imposed. Colloquially contracted to **Wire Deg.**

Wire Gradient
[Elec.] The gradient of the **Overhead Line Equipment** (**OLE**) □ **Contact Wire** (**CW**) relative to the **Track** beneath. As a guide, this gradient should be no steeper than **1 in** (5 times the maximum speed). For example, at 100 mph, the Wire Gradient should be flatter than 1 in 500.

Wire Height
[Elec.] The height of the **Overhead Line Equipment** (**OLE**) □ **Contact Wire** (**CW**) relative to the **Plane of the Rails**. See also **Height**, **Height and Stagger**.

Wire Run
[Elec.] A single continuous length **of Overhead Line Equipment** (**OLE**) □ **Catenary** running between **Anchors**. Also known as a **Tension Length** (**TL**). See also **Balance Weight Anchor** (**BWA**), **Mid-point Anchor** (**MPA**), **Spring Tensioner**.

Wires
a) [PW] Thin slivers of steel picked up by a **Rail** in the rolling mill and incorporated into the surface of the Rail. Such Rails are **Blemished Rails**
b) See **Lining Chord**, **Lining Wire**
c) Thin electrical **Conductors**, and therefore the **Overhead Line Equipment** (**OLE**)
d) [NR Col.] A nickname for the concept of **Overhead Line Equipment** (**OLE**), as in "working Under the Wires"
e) [Col.] Formerly, messages despatched by telegraph, now used as a nickname for the replacements sent by Fax and Email systems, see **Wire**.

Wiring Diagrams
See **Signalling Circuit Diagram**.

Wiring Train
[Elec.] A Train of **Engineering Vehicles** specially adapted for the installation and **Maintenance** of **Overhead Line Equipment** (**OLE**). See also **Drum Carrier**, **Tool Van**.

Witham Accident
On the 1st of September 1905 an **Express Passenger Train** was **Derailed** on a Diamond Crossing at Witham, killing 11 and injuring 71, some of whom perished in the ensuing fire (caused by gas lighting). Whilst not fully proven, it appears that three **Permanent Way** staff had removed some **Keys** from the **Crossing** and were attempting to replace them when the **Train** arrived.

Witness Mark
A physical mark such as that made on a **Rail** by a **Derailed** wheel.

WLAM
<u>W</u>hole <u>L</u>ife <u>A</u>sset <u>M</u>anagement.

WLCC
<u>W</u>hole <u>L</u>ife <u>C</u>ycle <u>C</u>ost.

WLL
[NR] <u>W</u>est <u>L</u>ondon □ <u>L</u>ine.

WLRM
<u>W</u>hole <u>L</u>ife <u>R</u>ail <u>M</u>odel.

WMAMMS
<u>W</u>est <u>M</u>idlands <u>A</u>rea <u>M</u>ulti-<u>m</u>odal <u>S</u>tudy.

WMCU
<u>W</u>eather <u>M</u>onitoring <u>C</u>ontrol <u>U</u>nit.

WMP
<u>W</u>aste <u>M</u>anagement <u>P</u>lan.

WMPBG
[TRS] <u>W</u>heelset □ <u>M</u>aintenance <u>B</u>est <u>P</u>ractice <u>G</u>roup.

WMPTA
West Midlands Passenger Transport Authority (PTA).

WMPTE
(*wump-tee*, but only informally) West Midlands Passenger Transport Executive (PTE).

WMSCC
[NR] West Midlands Signalling Control Centre, aka Saltley.

WON
(*wonn*) See Weekly Operating Notice.

WONview
See SWON.

Wood Key
[PW] A Key for Bull Head Rails (BH), made from wood, normally Oak (*Quercus robur*), historically Teak (*Tectona grandis*).

Wood Sleepers
[PW] Sleepers made from wood, normally from one of two sources:
a) Softwood Sleepers are produced from Douglas Fir (*Pseudotsuga menziesii*) and pressure treated with preservative. Such Sleepers are generally used on low speed Lines carrying low Axle Weights e.g. Sidings
b) Hardwood Sleepers are produced from Jarrah (*Eucalyptus marginata*), or Karri (*Eucalyptus diversicolor*) and related species. They require no special treatment. These Sleepers are often found in Main Lines as they have much greater strength than Softwood Sleepers and have good resistance to fungal decay.

Wood Spoilers
[BR Col.] Derogatory collective Nickname for Civil Engineers, particularly those engaged on Bridge works.

Woodentops
[BR Col.] Derogatory collective Nickname for Train drivers.

Worgan
A Railway □ Telegraph Code meaning "Following work will not now be carried out. Cancel all arrangements". See also CAPE.

Work
See Working.

Work Arising Identification Form (WAIF)
[NR] A form used to generate a new work order or to update or modify a work order already recorded on the Ellipse system.

Work Group
See Workgroup.

Work Package Plan (WPP)
[NR] The replacement for the Method Statement on Network Rail (NR) works. Projects are divided into work packages, each of which has a WPP detailing, limits, times, risks, tasks, etc. WPPs are briefed down to site using Task Briefings (TB).

Work Site
See Worksite.

Work Site Book
[NR] A document used to link Items of Work and Work Sites to the existing Possessions, which have been inputted into PPS since the T-14 meeting.

Worked
[Ops.] A Signal, Set of Switches or Set of Points under the control of a Signal Box (SB). The opposite is Unworked.

Worked Catch Point
a) A Catch Point (CP) that can operated from a Signal Box (SB), thus allowing Trains to run in the Wrong Direction, typically on a Single Line.
b) A Catch Point on a High Speed Line, one which is closed by a Point Machine prior to the passage of an Authorised Movement.

Worked Points
Worked Switches
[Sig.] A Switch or Set of Points under the control of a Signal Box (SB).

Workgroup
[NR] Staff within a Work Site whose safety is managed by a Controller of Site Safety (COSS).

Working
[NR] Any activity that is not Walking. Therefore Patrolling is Work, whereas making your way to a Signal Box (SB) is Walking.

Working Drive
[PW] The low-speed Traction System or gear used by an On Track Machine (OTM) when actually operating. See also Self-propelled. See also Travel Mode.

Working Lever (W)
[Sig.] In a Lever Frame, a Lever which is used for the operation of Signalling Equipment The opposite is a Spare Lever (S).

Working Manual for Rail Staff
An Operating Publication detailing how various loads should be dealt with and classified, from Dangerous Goods to Rail Cranes to Panels of Track. The various sections are colour coded for ease; Dangerous Goods appears on the Pink Pages, Rail Cranes on the Buff Pages.

Working Range
[PW] The range of Rail Temperatures over which correctly Stressed, consolidated and Ballasted □ Continuous Welded Rail (CWR) laid on Concrete Sleepers can be expected to function without suffering Buckling or tensile failure. In the UK this range is deemed to be -14°C to +53°C.

Working Reference Manual
[LUL] The London Underground Limited □ Operations □ Rule Book

Working Temperature Limits
[NR] The limits of **Rail Temperature** between which it is permitted to carry out works that affect the stability of the **Track**, particularly **Continuous Welded Rail** (**CWR**). These limits are normally -9°C and +32°C.

Working Timetable (WTT)
[Ops.] The version of the timetable for use by drivers and **Signallers**, giving full details of all **Trains**, including **Empty Coaching Stock** (**ECS**) movements and **Light Locomotives** (**Light Engines**) to the nearest $^1/_2$ minute (30 seconds).

Working, A
[Ops.] A planned **Train Movement** from one place to another, as in "To Work a **Train**". See also **Out of Turn Working**.

Works Inspection
[PW] An inspection of a new **Built up and Timbered** □ **Switch and Crossing Layout** (**S&C Layout**) by the client at the manufacturer's premises before the **Layout** is transported to site. The **Signalling** equivalent of this is a **Factory Acceptance Test** (**FAT**).

Works Scheduler
A person responsible for planning **Work** activities.

Works Testing
[Sig.] The processes governing the testing of completely new **Signalling Systems** and existing systems where the design has been changed. See **SWTH**.

Works, The
[BR] The organisation within the **British Railways** (**BR**) □ **Civil Engineer's** (**CE**) organisation responsible for the upkeep of **Bridges**, **Retaining Walls** and the like. In modern times they have now become **The Civils**.

Worksite
[NR] The area within a **Possession** that is managed by an **Engineering Supervisor** (**ES**). A Work Site is delimited by **Marker Boards** when Engineering Trains are present. It may contain many work groups, each controlled by a **Controller of Site Safety** (**COSS**).

Worksite Marker Board
See **Marker Board**.

Workstation
See **Signaller's Workstation**.

Worn Rails
[PW] **Rails** that have been worn away by passing **Rail Wheels** and are therefore no longer the original **Rail Section**. See also **Head Wear**, **Sidecutting**, **Sidewear**, **Rail Gall**.

WOSS
Workshop Overhaul Standard Specification.

WPA
Weeks per Annum.

WPP
See **Work Package Plan**.

WR
a) Wear Resistant, see **Wear Resisting Rail**
b) See **Western Region**
c) See **Welded Rod**
d) The **ATOC** code for West Coast Railway Co.

WRD
Wagon Repair Depot.

Wrexham & Shropshire (W&S)
(Tradename) An **Open Access Operator** which ran services between Wrexham, Shrewsbury, Birmingham and London Marylebone. It ceased operating on 28 January 2011.

Wriggle Diagram
[Civ.] A diagram indicating the deviation of a new **Tunnel** from the designed **Alignment** and level.

WRISA
Wheel Rail Interface System Authority Ltd.

WRM
Wheel / Rail Mechanisms, see **Rail / Wheel Interface**.

Wrong
[Sig. Col.] Term used for the position of a **Semaphore Signal** when it is between 5 and 30 degrees below horizontal and indicating that there is a fault with the **Signal** and the **Train** should stop and advise the **Signaller**.

Wrong Direction
In a direction opposite to the **Normal Direction** on the **Line** concerned. Also **Wrong Road**, **Bang Road**. The opposite is **Right Direction**, see also **Right Road**.

Wrong Direction Controls
[Sig.] A **Control** added to an **Automatic Level Crossing** (**LC**, **LX**) that allows it to respond correctly to **Wrong Direction Movements**. Abbreviated by adding the suffix **-X** to the description of the **Level Crossing**.

Wrong Direction Movement (WDM)
A **Rail Vehicle** or **Train Movement** made in the **Wrong Direction**, i.e. a direction opposite to that which **Trains** normally run on the **Line** concerned, not controlled by **Signals**. Also **Bang Road**, **Wrong Road**, **Wrong Road Movement**.

Wrong Direction Movement Protector
[LUL] A member of **Operating** staff appointed by the **Wrong Direction Movement** (**WDM**) Person In Charge to prevent a **Train** entering the area of the Wrong Direction Movement, using a **Flag** or Handlamp.

Wrong Direction Working
a) The running of **Trains** on a **Line** in the direction not fitted with **Fixed Signals** for such **Train Movements**
b) On Lines equipped with appropriate Fixed Signals, it is the running of Trains in the opposite direction to the **Normal Direction of Trains**.

Wrong Kind of Snow
[BR] The now infamous misquote, by the Tabloid newspapers, of a statement made on the 11th February 1991 by Terry Worral, then Director of Operations for British Rail, to explain the failure of **Electric Locomotives** in the recent **Snow** conditions. His actual words were: "We are having particular problems with the type of snow". Typical Snow falling in the UK consists of large sticky flakes, which are not easily blown about once they have settled. During the winter in question, the Snow was, unusually, light and powdery. Passing **Trains** disturbed this, and the powerful **Motor Blowers** sucked it into the **Traction Motors**. The hot motors then melted the Snow and the resulting water shorted the motors out.

Wrong Road
[Col] An alternative to **Wrong Direction**. Also **Bang Road**.

Wrong Road Movement
An alternative to **Wrong Direction Movement**.

Wrong Side Failure (WSF)
A failure that causes a piece of equipment to cease functioning in such a way as to cause danger to the **Safety Of The Line**. See **Protected Wrong Side Failure (PWSF)**. Unprotected Wrong Side Failure (**UWSF**).

Wrong Stick
[LUL] A term describing a **Train** being given the wrong **Route** at a **Junction**. When a driver sees a **Signal** showing the wrong **Route**, they should stop at the Signal and advise the **Signaller**. See also **Stick**.

WRSL
See **W**estinghouse **R**ail **S**ystems **L**td.

WRSSTD
[BR] **W**estern **R**egion **S**olid **S**tate **T**rain **D**escriber.

WSA
(Tradename) **W** **S** **A**tkins, an engineering consultancy based in Epsom, Surrey.

WSC
[NR] **W**eather **S**trategy **C**o-ordinator.

WSF
See **W**rong **S**ide **F**ailure.

WSL
(Tradename) **W**estinghouse □ **S**ignals **L**td.

WSMR
(Tradename) [Hist.] The former **W**rexham, **S**hropshire & **M**arylebone **R**ailway, an **Open Access Operator**. It ran services between Wrexham and London (Marylebone).

WSO
Work**s**tation **O**perator.

WSOSI
Wider **S**ources **O**f **S**afety **I**nformation.

WSP
a) See **W**heel **S**lide **P**revention
b) See **W**heel **S**lip **P**revention.

WSPER
(Tradename) A simulator operated by **Delta Rail** (formerly **AEA Technology**) which is used to test and optimise the performance of **Wheel Slide Prevention** / **Wheel Slip Prevention** (**WSP**) systems.

WST
Work **S**ite **T**idy.

WSTCF
[Sig.] **W**rong **S**ide **T**rack **C**ircuit **F**ailure. See **Wrong Side Failure (WSF)**.

WTD
Working **T**ime **D**irective.

WTF
Wrong Side **T**elecommunications **F**ailure; see **Wrong Side Failure (WSF)**.

WTG
a) See **W**ide **t**o **G**auge
b) See **G**auge **W**idening
c) See **W**ide **t**o **G**auge Trap Points.

WTOPS
Western **T**rain **O**perated **P**oints **S**cheme.

WTP
Willingness **t**o **P**ay.

WTT
See **W**orking **T**imetable.

WW
(Tradename) [Hist.] **W**ales and **W**est, a **Train Operating Company** (**TOC**) which became part of Wales and Borders (**W&B**), now Arriva Trains Wales (**ATW**).

WWL
[NR Civ.] Under the **Bridge Condition Marking Index** (**BCMI**) handbook, shorthand for **Wing Wall**.

W*xxx*
[PW] Varieties of **Steel Sleeper**, e.g. W400, W600.

WYCA
See **W**est **Y**orkshire **C**ombined **A**uthority.

WYG
(Tradename) **W**hite **Y**oung **G**reen, an engineering consultancy based in Leeds.

WYITA
West **Y**orkshire **I**ntegrated **T**ransport Authority, now part of West Yorkshire Combined Authority (**WYCA**).

WYPTA
West **Y**orkshire **P**assenger **T**ransport **A**uthority (**PTA**).

WYPTE
West **Y**orkshire **P**assenger **T**ransport **E**xecutive (**PTE**).

X

X

a) [NR] As the last letter in a **Wagon** □ **CARKND**, this denotes that the Wagon has both **Vacuum Brakes** and **Air Brakes**. Also called **Dual Braked** or **Dual Fitted**
b) [NR] As the last letter of a **Train** description, it means that the **Train** is a special excursion, e.g. **Footex**, a football special or **Gricex**, an enthusiasts' special. See also **-ex**
c) As a suffix to a **Level Crossing** (**LC**, **LX**) description, it indicates that the Level Crossing is fitted with **Wrong Direction Controls**
d) [Ops.] As the last letter of a **Timetable** (**TT**) description, it indicates that the Train does not run on the days of the week preceding the X, e.g. MX means not on Mondays
e) As a prefix it replaces the word "cross", as in **X Drain**, **Xing**, **X Level**, **Xover**
f) [NR] Shorthand for the **Platform Offset** at any given point. See also **Y**
g) [Sig] On a **Signalling Circuit Diagram**:
- As a bracketed suffix, it denotes an external power supply
- As one of the leading letters of an **Equipment Code**, it means **Annunciator**, **Level Crossing** or **Wrong Direction**.
- As the last letter of an Equipment Code, it means Annunciator
h) The letter represented by **X-ray** in the **Phonetic Alphabet**.

X Drain
Shorthand for **Cross Drain**.

X Level
Shorthand for **Cross Level**.

X Signal
[LUL] An **Automatic Signal** which must be treated as a **Semi-Automatic Signal**, e.g. it is a **Non-passable Signal**.

XC
The **ATOC** code for **Cross Country**, see also **VXC**.

X-factor
[TRS] The numerical value derived from a function of the **Carbody** □ **Yaw** torque, **Wheelbase** and **Axle Loads**. These values are determined by testing and measurement. Under normal circumstances the X-factor must not exceed a value of 0.1

x-foot
Generic term for the area between the **Running Rails**, where x is the nominal **Track Gauge**, e.g. two-foot, **Fourfoot**, **Fivefoot**.

XGE
[NR Civ.] Under the **Bridge Condition Marking Index** (**BCMI**) handbook, shorthand for transverse girder or beam end

XGI
[NR Civ.] Under the **Bridge Condition Marking Index** (**BCMI**) handbook, shorthand for transverse girder or beam inner.

Xing
[PW] Shorthand for **Crossing**.

XiTrack
(*ziy-track*) (Tradename) [PW] A **Ballast Gluing** process. Used to reinforce and stabilise the **Ballast** layer using a sprayed two-part polymer. The polymer penetrates the Ballast and sets to form a resilient, continuous, flexible layer which provides increased horizontal and vertical track stability. The properties of the resulting layer can be designed to suit. XiTrack Ltd. Was formed by 2Ei Ltd and Dow Hyperlast and is based in Derbyshire.

XLPE
Cross Linked Polyethylene.

Xmas
[Obs.] The obsolescent **Phonetic Alphabet** word representing **X**. Replaced by **X-ray**.

XN
[PW] Shorthand for **Crossing Nose**. See also **Fine Point** (**FP**).

Xover
Shorthand for **Crossover**.

XR
Shorthand for **Crossrail**.

X-ray
The **Phonetic Alphabet** word representing **X**.

XTP
[LUL] Cross-Track Projection, a method of displaying advertisements on the far wall of **London Underground Limited** (**LUL**) □ **Tube** □ **Stations**.

XYZIRGB
X, Y, Z (coordinates) Intensity, Red, Green, Blue (colour); a data storage format for Light Direction and Ranging (**LiDAR**) scans.

Y

Y
a) [Sig] An abbreviation for a **Single Yellow Aspect** on a **Colour Light Signal**. See also **Yellow**
b) [NR] As the first letter of a **Wagon** □ CARKND it indicates that the vehicle is an **Engineering Vehicle** with two **Bogies**
c) [NR] Shorthand for the **Platform Height** at any given point. See also **X**
d) [Sig] On a **Signalling Circuit Diagram**:
- As one of the leading letters of an **Equipment Code**, it means **Slotting** or disengaging
- As the last letter of an Equipment Code, it means Slotting or disengaging apparatus

e) The letter represented by **Yankee** in the **Phonetic Alphabet**
f) In equations, the letter normally used to represent lateral wheel forces. See also **Q**.
g) **Common Interface File Operating Characteristics Code** for Runs to Terminals/Yards as required.

Y Drain
A 'Y' shaped drainage channel cut into a **Cutting** or **Embankment** side and filled with broken stone, used to drain and stabilise the slope concerned.

Y Turnout
See **Split Turnout**.

Y&S
[Sig. Hist.] Common shorthand for Yardley & Smith, a former manufacturer of **Signalling Equipment**.

YAA
[NR] The **CARKND** representing a **Brill** □ **Wagon**.

Yankee
The **Phonetic Alphabet** word representing **Y**.

YAO
[NR] The CARKND representing a **Dolphin** □ **Wagon**.

Yard
a) An imperial unit equivalent to 914.4mm, 36 inches or $^1/_{1760}$ of a **Mile**. See **Mileage**
b) An area occupied by one or more **Groups** of **Sidings**. See **Marshalling Yard, Goods Yard**.

Yaw
[TRS]
a) A mode of movement of a **Rail Vehicle** that is travelling at speed, characterised by the ends of the vehicle moving repetitively from side to side in opposite directions.
b) The limited rotation of a **Bogie** about the vertical axis.
See **Yaw Damper**. See also **Centre Throw, End Throw, Sway**.

Yaw Damper
[TRS] A shock absorber fitted to certain types of **Bogies** to control their rotation in plan at high speeds. Often found on Bogies used in **Multiple Unit Trains**, **Yaw Dampers** and their associated brackets are located adjacent to **Platform Gauge** and can cause **Gauging** problems. Sometimes shortened to **Damper**. See also **Yaw**.

YB2
[NR] Yellow Book Issue 2.

YBA
[NR] The CARKND representing a **Sturgeon** □ **Wagon** with **Air Brakes** or a **Whale** Wagon.

YBB
[NR] The CARKND representing an **Air Braked**, □ **Vacuum Piped** □ **Sturgeon** □ **Wagon**.

YBO
[NR] The CARKND representing an **Unfitted** □ **Sturgeon** □ **Wagon**.

YBP
[NR] The CARKND representing an **Unbraked**, □ **Vacuum Piped** □ **Sturgeon** □ **Wagon**.

YBQ
[NR] The CARKND representing an **Unbraked**, □ **Air Piped** □ **Sturgeon** □ **Wagon**.

YCA
[NR] The CARKND representing a **Halibut** □ **Wagon**.

YCO
[NR] The CARKND representing a **Pilchard** □ **Wagon**.

YCV
[NR]
a) The CARKND representing a **Heron** □ **Wagon**
b) The CARKND representing a **Turbot** Wagon with **Vacuum Brakes**.

YCW
[NR] The CARKND representing a **Vacuum Braked**, □ **Air Piped** □ **Turbot** □ **Wagon**.

YDA
[NR] The CARKND representing an **Octopus** □ **Wagon** or a **Skate** Wagon.

YE
On a **Signalling Circuit Diagram**, denotes a wire coloured yellow. See also **Yellow (Y)**.

YEA
[NR] The CARKND representing a **Perch** □ **Wagon**.

YEA
[NR] The CARKND representing a **Porpoise** □ **Wagon**.

Yellow
a) [Sig.] The correct description of the **Caution Aspect** of a **Colour Light Signal**. See also **Single Yellow (Y), Double Yellow (YY)**
b) [Obs.] The obsolescent **Phonetic Alphabet** word representing **Y**. Replaced by **Yankee**.

Yellow Aspect
[Sig.] Alternative for a **Caution Aspect**, see also **Single Yellow Aspect**.

585

Yellow Bond
[Sig., Elec.]] A **Bond** that is required for both **Track Circuit** (**TC**) integrity and **Traction Return Current** purposes which must not be removed without permission from both the **Signalling** and **Electrification** disciplines.

Yellow Book
[NR] Full title Engineering Safety Management, A **Railway** publication first issued by **Railtrack** to provide guidance to staff involved in making changes to the Railway. See also **YB2**.

Yellow Cavalry
[PW Col.] A collective nickname for **On Track Machines** (**OTM**) used for **Mechanised Maintenance**, such as **Automatic Ballast Cleaners** (**ABC**), **Ballast Regulators**, **Dynamic Track Stabilisers** (**DTS**), **Stoneblowers** and **Tamping and Lining Machines** (**Tampers**).

Yellow Diamond
[TRS] A symbol applied to **Traction Units**, in this case **Derby Lightweight** □ **First Generation Diesel Multiple Unit** (**DMU**) with mechanical transmission, denoting which **Multiple Working** control system with which they are fitted. Only Traction Units bearing the same symbol can be connected safely. See **Blue Square**, **Blue Star**, **Green Circle**, **Orange Star**, **Red Circle**, **Red Diamond**, **Red Triangle**, **White Circle**, **White Diamond**, **Yellow Diamond**, **Yellow Triangle**

Yellow Peril
a) [NR Col.] A document issued in conjunction with a **Section C Notice** explaining the changes to a **Track Layout** or **Signalling System** associated with a large and or complex scheme in more detail.
b) [Col.] **Anorak** term for **On Track Machines** (**OTM**).

Yellow Shunt Signal
[Sig.]
a) A variety of **Shunt Signal** that only applies to the **Route** for which the **Signal** can be **Cleared**. Other **Movements** may pass it without it being Cleared
b) A **Ground Position Light Signal** (**GPLS**) using **Yellow** lights.

Yellow Triangle
[TRS] A symbol applied to **Traction Units**, in this case **Class** 35 **Locomotives**, denoting which **Multiple Working** control system they are fitted with. Only Traction Units bearing the same symbol can be connected safely. See **Blue Star**, **Red Circle**, **Orange Square**, **White Diamond** and **Red Diamond**.

Yellow Vest
[NR Col.] Nickname for the high visibility and latterly partially retro-reflective orange tabards and waistcoats that have been a mandatory minimum item of protective clothing when **On or About the Line** since 1972. First introduced in 1966, they were never actually yellow. Also **Diddy Vest**, **Mini Vest**, **Hi-vis. Vest**, **Hi-vis. Jacket**.

YFA
[NR] The **CARKND** representing a **Side Rail Loader** based on a **Salmon** □ **Wagon** with **Air Brakes**, an Air Braked **Sturgeon** Wagon converted into a Side Rail Loader, or a **Sleeper Delivery Train** Wagon.

YFB
[NR] The **CARKND** representing a **Side Rail Loader** based on a **Salmon** □ **Wagon**; **Air Braked**, □ **Vacuum Piped**.

YFO
[NR] The **CARKND** representing a **Side Rail Loader** based on an **Unfitted** □ **Salmon** □ **Wagon**, or an Unfitted **Sturgeon** Wagon converted into a Side Rail Loader.

YGA
[NR] The **CARKND** representing a **Seacow** □ **Wagon** or a **Stingray** Wagon with **Air Brakes**.

YGB
[NR] The **CARKND** representing an **Air Braked**, □ **Vacuum Piped** □ **Seacow** □ **Wagon** or Stingray Wagon.

YGH
[NR] The CARKND representing a **Sealion** □ **Wagon**.

YGV
[NR] The **CARKND** representing a **Walrus** □ **Wagon**.

YHA
[NR] The **CARKND** representing a **Whale** □ **Wagon**.

Ying
[Col.] Nickname given to **Class** 66 and 67 **Diesel Locomotives** for the sound of their turbocharger.

YJA
[NR] The CARKND representing the **Generator Wagon** for the **Track Relaying Train** (**TRT**).

YKA
[NR] The **CARKND** representing a **Manta, Marlin** or **Osprey** □ **Wagon**.

YLA
[NR] The **CARKND** representing a **Mullet** □ **Wagon**.

YLO
[NR] The **CARKND** representing an **Unfitted** □ **Gane** □ **Wagon**.

YLP
[NR] The **CARKND** representing an **Unbraked**, □ **Vacuum Piped** □ **Gane** □ **Wagon**.

YMA
[NR] The **CARKND** representing an **Eel** □ **Wagon**, **Parr** Wagon or **Salmon** Wagon with **Air Brakes**.

YMB
[NR] The **CARKND** representing an **Air Braked**, □ **Vacuum Piped** □ **Salmon** □ **Wagon**.

YMO
[NR] The **CARKND** representing an **Unfitted** □ **Salmon** □ **Wagon**.

YMP
[NR] The **CARKND** representing an **Unbraked**, □ **Vacuum Piped** □ **Salmon** □ **Wagon**.

YNO
[NR] The **CARKND** representing a **Prawn** □ **Wagon**.

YNP
[NR] The **CARKND** representing a **Shrimp** □ **Wagon**.

Yobbex
[Col.] Enthusiast's nickname for special football services. Also **Footex**.

Yodalarm
(Tradename) A common type of **Audible Warning** device used at **Level Crossings** (**LC**, **LX**). Manufactured by Clifford and Snell of London.

YOM
Year of Manufacture.

YPA
[NR] The **CARKND** representing a **Tench** □ **Wagon**.

YQA
[NR] The **CARKND** representing a **Parr** □ **Wagon** designed to carry **Sleepers**.

YRA
[NR] The **CARKND** representing a **Rail Beam** carrier **Wagon**, converted from a **Perch** (**YEA**) **Wagon**.

YSA
[NR] The **CARKND** representing a **Bogie** support vehicle, used with the **High Output Ballast Cleaner** (**HOBC**) and **Track Relaying Train** (**TRT**).

YVP
[NR] The **CARKND** representing a **Weltrol** □ **Wagon**.

YVQ
[NR] The **CARKND** representing a **Conger** □ **Wagon**, **Air Pipe** only.

YWA
[NR] The **CARKND** representing a **Salmon** □ **Wagon** with 60mph **Bogies** and **Air Brakes**.

YXA
[NR] The **CARKND** representing:
a) A **Conger** □ **Wagon** with **Air Brakes**
b) An **Otter** Wagon
c) A **Generator Wagon** for the **Sleeper Delivery Train**
d) A **Track Relaying Train** (**TRT**) □ **Sleeper** delivery Wagon.

Y*xx*
[TRS] Standardised **Bogie** designs. Y25 and Y32 are common in the UK. The range runs up to Y266, which is fitted to some **TGV** trains.

YY
[Sig.] An abbreviation for a **Double Yellow Aspect** on a **Colour Light Signal**.

Z

Z
a) [NR] As the first character of a **Wagon** □ **CARKND** it indicates that the vehicle is an **Engineering Vehicle** with two single axles
b) [Sig.] On a **Signalling Circuit Diagram** as any of the letters of an **Equipment Code**, it means special and the meaning is explained on the Diagram
c) The letter represented by **Zulu** in the **Phonetic Alphabet**
d) **Common Interface File Operating Characteristics Code** for "May convey traffic to **SB1C Gauge**. Not to be diverted from booked route without authority".

Z000
[NR] Colloquially known as the "zoo" template, a Primavera Project Planning (**P3**) programme template used by **Network Rail** (**NR**) for all projects.

ZAA
[NR] The **CARKND** representing a **Pike** □ **Wagon**.

Zander (ZKV)
[NR] An **Open Wagon** used for the transportation of **Ballast**. See **Wagon Names**.

ZAV
[NR] The **CARKND** representing a **Cod** □ **Wagon**.

ZBA
[NR]
a) The **CARKND** representing a **Carp** □ **Wagon**
b) The **CARKND** representing a **Hake** Wagon or **Rudd** Wagon.

ZBO
[NR] The **CARKND** representing an **Unfitted** □ **Grampus** □ **Wagon** or a **Lamprey** Wagon.

ZBP
[NR] The **CARKND** representing an **Unbraked**, □ **Vacuum Piped** □ **Grampus** □ **Wagon**.

ZBQ
[NR] The **CARKND** representing an **Unbraked**, □ **Air Piped** □ **Grampus** □ **Wagon**.

ZBV
[NR] The **CARKND** representing a **Grampus** □ **Wagon** with **Vacuum Brakes**.

ZBW
[NR] The **CARKND** representing a **Vacuum Braked** □ **Air Piped** □ **Grampus** □ **Wagon**.

ZCA
[NR] The **CARKND** representing a **Pollock** □ **Wagon**, □ **Seahare** Wagon, **Sea Horse** Wagon, **Sea Urchin** Wagon, **Sole** Wagon or an **Urchin** Wagon.

ZCO
[NR] The **CARKND** representing a **Haddock** □ **Wagon**, **Ling** Wagon, **Sole** Wagon, **Starfish** Wagon or an **Unfitted** □ **Tunny** Wagon.

ZCV
[NR] The **CARKND** representing a **Clam** □ **Wagon**, **Crab** Wagon, **Dace** Wagon, **Plaice** Wagon, **Tope** Wagon or a **Vacuum Braked** □ **Tunny** Wagon.

ZCX
[NR] The **CARKND** representing a **Chub** □ **Wagon**.

ZDA
[NR] The **CARKND** representing a **Bass** □ **Wagon**, **Roach** Wagon or **Squid** Wagon.

ZDV
[NR] The **CARKND** representing a **Tope** □ **Wagon**.

ZEA
[NR] The **CARKND** representing a **Bream** □ **Wagon** with **Air Brakes**.

ZEB
[NR] The **CARKND** representing an **Air Braked**, □ **Vacuum Piped** □ **Bream** □ **Wagon**.

Zebra
[NR] The obsolescent **Phonetic Alphabet** word representing Z. Replaced by **Zulu**.

Zed Dropper
[Elec.] An angled **Dropper** used at a **Mid-point Anchor**. This acts as a restraint to the **Contact Wire** (**CW**) in the event of an incident.

ZEPE
(*zeppy*) [RT Hist.] **Z**one □ **E**lectrification and **P**lant **E**ngineer.

Zero Plate
[Col.] A **Sign** indicating that the driver must contact the **Signaller** immediately upon being detained at the **Signal**. See also **Rule 55**, **Signal Post Telephone** (**SPT**).

ZEV
[NR] The **CARKND** representing a **Catfish** □ **Wagon**.

ZEX
[NR] The **CARKND** representing a **Dual Braked** □ **Bream** □ **Wagon**.

ZFA
[NR] The **CARKND** representing a **Gunnell** □ **Wagon**.

ZFO
[NR] The **CARKND** representing a **Trout** □ **Wagon**.

ZFV
[NR] The **CARKND** representing a **Dogfish** □ **Wagon** with **Vacuum Brakes** or a **Merdog** Wagon.

ZFW
[NR] The **CARKND** representing a **Vacuum Braked**, □ **Air Piped** □ **Dogfish** □ **Wagon**.

ZGA
[NR] The **CARKND** representing a **Seal** □ **Wagon**.

ZHD
See **Z**one **H**azard **D**irectory.

ZHLS
Zero **H**alogen **L**ow **S**moke, a type of insulation used in electrical wiring. See also **LSOH**.

ZHV
[NR] The **CARKND** representing a **Mineral** □ **Wagon**.

Zigzag Welding
Zigzagging
See **Track Circuit Continuity Welding**. Also Eutectic Strip, Rumble Strip.

ZJV
[NR] The **CARKND** representing a **Mermaid** □ **Wagon**.

ZKL 3000 RC
(Tradename) A remotely-controlled **Track Circuit** operating device which can be installed in the **Track** at a **Protecting Signal** for up to three months.

ZKV
[NR] The **CARKND** representing a **Zander** □ **Wagon**.

ZLR
(Tradename) Zero Longitudinal Restraint. Produced by **Pandrol**, a **Rail Fastening** which is designed to prevent **Track Forces** being transmitted to **Bridge** and other structures. The system uses a PR633 clip and an intermediate cast plate between the **Rail Foot** and the **Toe** of the **Clip**. This arrangement allows the **Rail** to move longitudinally while holding the Rail vertically and laterally in place and preventing **Rail Rotation**.

ZLV
[NR] The **CARKND** representing a **Herring** □ **Wagon**.

ZMV
[NR] The **CARKND** representing a **Mackerel** □ **Wagon**.

Zone
a) See **Railtrack Zones** (**RTZ**). See also **Network Rail** (**NR**), **Regions**, **Territories**.
b) See **Green Zone**, **Red Zone**
c) See **Platform Zones**.

Zone Hazard Directory (ZHD)
See **Hazard Directory**, **National Hazard Directory**

ZSE
[RT Obs.] **Zone** □ **Signalling** Engineer.

ZTE
[RT Obs.] **Zone** □ **Telecommunications Engineer**.

Z-type Bridge

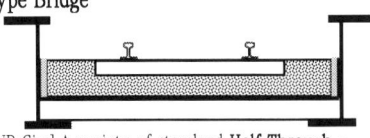

[NR Civ.] A variety of standard **Half Through** □ **Ballasted Deck** □ **Bridge** consisting of two Z shaped asymmetric main girders supporting a composite joists-in-concrete deck.

ZUA
[NR] The **CARKND** representing a **Bass** □ **Wagon**.

ZUB
[NR] The **CARKND** representing an **Air Braked**, □ **Vacuum Piped** □ **Shark** □ **Wagon**.

Zulu
a) **Phonetic Alphabet** word representing **Z**.
b) Shorthand for Greenwich Mean Time (**GMT**)
c) A special **Train**.

ZUP
The **CARKND** representing an **Unfitted** □ **Shark** □ **Wagon**.

ZUV
[NR] The **CARKND** representing a **Shark** □ **Wagon** with **Vacuum Brakes**.

ZUW
[NR] The **CARKND** representing a **Vacuum** Braked, □ **Air Piped** □ **Shark** □ **Wagon**.

ZVV
[NR] The **CARKND** representing a **Lobster** □ **Wagon** or a **Winkle** Wagon.

ZXQ
[NR] The **CARKND** representing the scanning vehicle of the **Structure Gauging Train** (**SGT**)

ZZ
[LUL] **Zig Zag**.

Length and Distance

Imperial	Subdivision	Metric	Application
One Mile	8000 Links	1.60934km	Geographical position
	5280 Feet	1609.344m	
	1760 Yards		
	80 Chains		
	88 Lengths		
Quarter Mile	2000 Links	402.336m	Geographical position
	1320 Feet		
	440 Yards		
	20 Chains		
	22 Lengths		
Eighth of a Mile	1000 Links	201.168m	Geographical position in **Track Quality** assessment
	660 Feet		
	220 Yards		
	10 Chains		
	11 Lengths		
Metric Only		200.000m	Maximum **Radius** requiring a continuous **Check Rail**
200 Yards	600 Feet	182.880m	Older standard (**CWR**) **Rail** length, Standard **Signal Overlap**.
Metric Only		30.000m	Metric **Hallade** □ **Chord Length**
96' - 6"		29.413m	Imperial Hallade Chord Length
One Chain	100 Links	20.1168m	Surveying
	66 Feet		**Speed Restriction** position
	22 Yards		
One Length	60 Feet	18.288m	Standard **Rail Length**
	20 Yards		
Metric Only		15.000m	Metric Hallade **Half Chord** (**HC**)
48' - 3"		14.707m	Imperial Hallade Half Chord
10 Yards	30 Feet	9144mm	Standard **Half Rail**
7 Yards	21 Feet	6401mm	**Standard Length Unit** (**SLU**)
16'		4880mm	**Clearance Point** (**CP**) to **Fouling Point** (**FP**) dimension
10'		3048mm	Standard minimum **Track Interval** between pairs of **Tracks**, the **Tenfoot**
9'	3 Yards	2743mm	Minimum safe distance from **Live** 25kV **Overhead Line Equipment** (OLE) (Quoted as 2.75m in safety publications)
Metric Only		1970mm	Standard minimum Track Interval, **Running Edge** (**RE**) to RE.
6'		1829mm	Standard minimum Track Interval, **Outside Edge** (**OE**) to OE, the **Sixfoot**.
4' - 8⁵/₈"		1438mm	**Track Gauge** for **Track** with CEN60 **Rails**
4' - 8¹/₂"		1435mm	Original and standard **Track Gauge**, The **Fourfoot**
4' - 8³/₈"		1432mm	Previous standard Track Gauge, the Fourfoot
Metric Only		1000mm	Limit of **Timbering** across **Turnout Opening**, the **Metre Opening**
One Yard	3'	914.4mm	Standard height of **Platform** □ **Above Rail Level** (**ARL**)
Metric Only		760mm	Minimum dimension RE to **Platform Edge**, **Eurostar** □ **Routes**
2' - 4³/₄"		730mm	Minimum dimension RE to Platform Edge, non-Eurostar Routes
One Foot	12"	305mm	Typical **Ballast Depth**
1 Link	7.92"	201.16mm	Subdivision of a Chain.
Metric Only		150mm	Maximum standard **Cant Value**

Further Reading

The following is a list of the classic railway books on my bookshelf. Sadly, not all are easily available, so best of luck!

Coleman, Terry, The Railway Navvies, Pimlico, 2000, ISBN 0712667075 (reprint)

Davies, Hunter, George Stephenson: The Remarkable Life of the Founder of the Railways, Hamlyn, 1980,
ISBN 0600200426

Head, Sir Francis B., Stokers and Pokers, David & Charles, 1968, ISBN 0715343270

Hidden, A, Investigation into the Clapham Junction Railway Accident, Department of Transport, Report Cm820, Her Majesty's Stationery Office, London, 1989, ISBN 0101082029

Prebble, John, The High Girders, Penguin Books, 1979, ISBN 0140045902

Robbins, Harold, The Railway Age, Mandolin, 1998, ISBN 1901341097 (reprint)

Rolt, LTC, Red For Danger, Macmillan, 1986, ISBN 0330291890

Rolt, LTC & Buchanan, Angus, Isambard Kingdom Brunel, Penguin Books, 1990, ISBN 0140117520

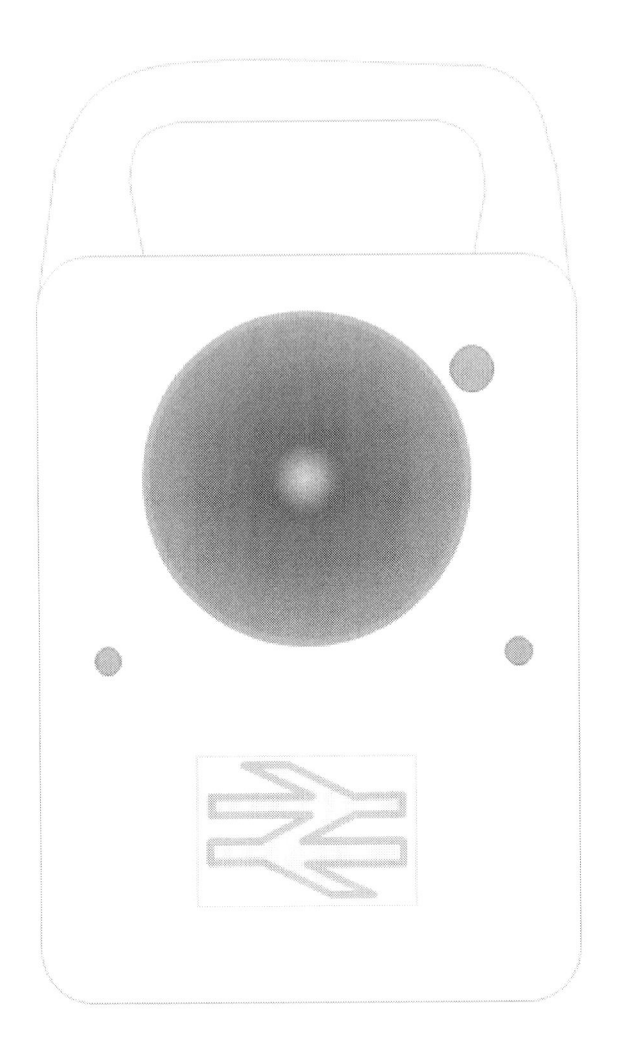

ELLIS' BRITISH RAILWAY ENGINEERING ENCYCLOPÆDIA

594

Printed in Great Britain
by Amazon